Commonly Used Commands

This is a list of commonly used console-based commands for Linux and other Unix-like operating systems. Each command has a short description and bare syntax. Nearly all programs in this list support much more complex command-line usage and options, so you should consult the appropriate man page for details. The list is organized by usage and/or purpose, but many commands will have overlapping roles on your system.

Note that Fedora Core includes thousands of other clients for use with your console or graphical desktop.

FILE UTILITIES

bzip2 Compress, uncompress input.
Syntax: **bzip2** [opts] [filenames]

cat Concatenate input. Syntax: **cat** [opts] [file]

cdrdao Write audio CD.
Syntax: **cdrdao** [opts] [device] [speed] [toc file]

cdrecord Burn data CD.
Syntax: **cdrecord** [opts] [device] [speed] [image]

chmod Set file read, write, and execution permissions.
Syntax: **chmod** [opts] [mode] [file]

chgrp Change file or directory group ownership.
Syntax: **chgrp** [opts] [group] [file]

convert Translate graphic file.
Syntax: **convert** [opts] [file1] [file2]

cp Copy a file. Syntax: **cp** [opts] [source] [destination]

cpio Copy, create, extract file archives.
Syntax: **cpio** [opts] [archive] [filelist]

chown Change ownership of file.
Syntax: **chown** [opts] [username] [file]

dd Convert and copy files. Syntax: **dd** [opts] [infile] [outfile]

df Show free disk space of mounted filesystems.
Syntax: **df** [opts] [file]

diff Generate file or directory difference list.
Syntax: **diff** [opts] [from] [to]

du Show disk usage of designated directory.
Syntax: **du** [opts] [path]

dump Back up a file system. Syntax: **dump** [opts] [files]

eject Eject removable media.
Syntax: **eject** [opts] [device/mount point]

fdisk Edit a device's partitions. Syntax: **fdisk** [opts] [device]

file Determine file type. Syntax: **file** [opts] [file]

find Return file system query. Syntax: **find** [opts] [path]

fgrep, egrep Search files named for lines matching given pattern. Syntax: **grep** [opts] [pattern] [file]

gpg Encrypt, decrypt files.
Syntax: **gpg** [file] [opts] [command]

gzip Compress, uncompress input. Syntax: **gzip** [opts] [file]

import Take screenshot of local or remote desktop.
Syntax: **import** [opts] [display] [file]

ln Create a symbolic link to file or directory.
Syntax: **ln** [opts] [target] [name]

locate Display all matching filenames on filesystem.
Syntax: **locate** [opts] [file]

ls List directory contents. Syntax: **ls** [opts] [path]

lsof List open files on the system. Syntax: **lsof** [opts] [file]

mkdir Create directory. Syntax: **mkdir** [opts] [dir]

FILE UTILITIES (CONTINUED)

mount Make a local or remote filesystem available locally.
Syntax: **mount** [opts] [device] [dir]

mv Rename a file or directory.
Syntax: **mv** [opts] [file] [destination]

parted Edit a device's partitions.
Syntax: **parted** [opts] [device]

restore Restore a file system. Syntax: **restore** [opts] [dump]

rm Remove named files or directories. Syntax: **rm** [opts] [file]

rmdir Remove directory. Syntax: **rmdir** [opts] [dir]

tar Create, list, or extract compressed or uncompressed archive. Syntax: **tar** [opts] [file1] [file2]

touch Create file or update timestamp.
Syntax: **touch** [opts] [file]

tree Display directory tree. Syntax: **tree** [opts] [path]

umount Remove a mounted device from filesystem.
Syntax: **umount** [opts] [dir]

zip, unzip Create or uncompress an archive.
Syntax: **zip** [opts]

INTERNET UTILITIES

curl Retrieve files via FTP, HTTP. Syntax: **curl** [opts] [URL]

dig Query domain name. Syntax: **dig** [domain] [opts]

elinks Text-based Web browser. Syntax: **elinks** [opts] [URL]

fetchmail Retrieve mail from remote server.
Syntax: **fetchmail** [opts] [mailserver]

ftp File Transfer Protocol client. Syntax: **ftp** [opts] [ftpserver]

mail Compose, read, send mail. Syntax: **mail** [opts] [user]

ncftp Remote FTP client. Syntax: **ncftp** [opts] [URL]

slrn Read Usenet news. Syntax: **slrn** [opts]

traceroute Display route to remote host.
Syntax: **traceroute** [opts] [host]

wget Retrieve files via FTP, HTTP. Syntax: **wget** [opts] [URL]

wvdial PPP connection utility. Syntax: **wvdial** [opts]

NETWORK UTILITIES

hostname Show or set the hostname of the computer.
Syntax: **hostname** [opts] [hostname]

ifconfig Configure a networking interface.
Syntax: **ifconfig** [interface] [opts] [address]

iwconfig Configure a wireless interface.
Syntax: **iwconfig** [interface] [opts]

nc Read, write files across a network. Syntax: **nc** [opts] [host]

netstat Print network information. Syntax: **netstat** [opts]

ping Measure packet round-trip between two hosts.
Syntax: **ping** [opts] [host]

scp Secure copy command.
Syntax: **scp** [opts] [user@host:file1] [user@host:file2]

Commonly Used Commands (continued)

NETWORK UTILITIES (CONTINUED)

sftp Secure FTP client. Syntax: **sftp** [opts] [host]

ssh Secure shell client. Syntax: **ssh** [opts] [host]

wall Send message to all users. Syntax: **wall** [opt] [message]

SYSTEM UTILITIES

apropos Display related manual page titles.
Syntax: **apropos** [opts] [keyword]

apt-get Install, remove, update software package.
Syntax: **apt-get** [command] [package]

at Execute command at specified time.
Syntax: **at** [opts] [time]

cal Display current or designated calendar.
Syntax: **cal** [opts] [month] [year]

cd Change directory; used for navigating.
Syntax: **cd** [opts] [path]

chkconfig Edit specified runlevel services.
Syntax: **chkconfig** [level] [service] [action]

crontab Execute command at regularly scheduled time.
Syntax: **crontab** [opts] [file]

date Display (or set) the current date and time.
Syntax: **date** [opts] [MMDDHHMMYY]

dmesg Display kernel messages. Syntax: **dmesg**

echo Print argument to output. Syntax: **echo** [opts] [string]

exit Exit out of current shell; logout. Syntax: **exit** [status]

free Display free memory, swap usage and other system info.
Syntax: **free** [opts]

hwclock Set system and/or hardware clock.
Syntax: **hwclock** [opts]

info Display GNU info page about command.
Syntax: **info** [opts] [name]

kill Stop or control a running process using a process ID.
Syntax: **kill** [opts] [PID]

man Display manual pages. Syntax: **man** [opts] [name]

mc Run a visual shell. Syntax: **mc** [opts]

minicom Console dialup client. Syntax: **minicom** [opts]

ps Show processes. Syntax: **ps** [opts]

pwd Print current working directory. Syntax: **pwd** [opts]

rpm Red Hat Package manager. Syntax: **rpm** [opts] [package]

screen Manage multiple console sessions.
Syntax: **screen** [opts] [command]

shutdown Reboot or shutdown the workstation/server.
Syntax: **shutdown** [opts] [time]

startx Start an X session from console.
Syntax: **startx** [opts]

uptime Display how long system has been running.
Syntax: **uptime** [opt]

w Show current system uptime, users logged in.
Syntax: **w** [opts] [user]

watch Execute given command every 2 seconds.
Syntax: **watch** [opts] [command]

whatis Display man page header for command.
Syntax: **whatis** [opts] [name]

SYSTEM UTILITIES (CONTINUED)

whereis Display location of command and man page.
Syntax: **whereis** [opts] [name]

which Show path of command. Syntax: **which** [opts] [name]

TEXT UTILITIES

aspell Check input spelling. Syntax: **aspell** [opts] [file]

dos2unix Convert DOS text files to UNIX format.
Syntax: **dos2unix** [opts] [infile] [outfile]

ed Edit lines of text. Syntax: **ed** [opts] [file]

emacs The GNU emacs editor. Syntax: **emacs** [opts] [file]

enscript Convert text file to PostScript document.
Syntax: **enscript** [opts] [file]

head Print a portion of the beginning of input.
Syntax: **head** [opts] [file]

less Display input one screenful at a time.
Syntax: **less** [opts] [file]

look Look up word in system dictionary.
Syntax: **look** [opts] [string] [file]

lp Print input to a local or remote printer.
Syntax: **lp** [opts] [printer] [file]

lpq Display the print queue. Syntax: **lpq** [opts] [queue]

lrpm Remove [stop] a print job.
Syntax: **lrpm** [opts] [job number]

more Page like less. Syntax: **more** [opts] [file]

nano Console-based text editor. Syntax: **nano** [opts] [file]

sed Edit stream of text. Syntax: **sed** [opts] [pattern] [file]

sort Sort input. Syntax: **sort** [opts] [in] [out]

tail Print a portion of the end of input.
Syntax: **tail** [opts] [file]

uniq Strip input of adjacent duplicate lines.
Syntax: **uniq** [opts] [file]

wc Count input's words, lines, and characters.
Syntax: **wc** [opts] [file]

vi Visual text editor. Syntax: **vi** [opts] [file]

USER ADMINISTRATION

adduser Create a new user for the system.
Syntax: **adduser** [opts] [user]

chfn Edit user information. Syntax: **chfn** [opts] [user]

chsh Change login shell. Syntax: **chsh** [opts] [username]

edquota Edit user disk quotas. Syntax: **equota** [opts] [user]

last Display list of last logged in users.
Syntax: **last** [opts] [tty]

passwd Change password. Syntax: **passwd** [opts] [user]

su Log in or perform action as other user.
Syntax: **su** [opts] [user]

sudo Allow root operations by specified users.
Syntax: **sudo** [opts] [command]

useradd Create new user. Syntax: **useradd** [opts] [user]

userdel Delete user. Syntax: **userdel** [opts] [user]

who Display logged in users. Syntax: **who** [opts] [file]

whoami Display your info. Syntax: **whoami** [opts]

Red Hat® Linux
Fedora™ 3
UNLEASHED

Bill Ball
Hoyt Duff

800 East 96th Street, Indianapolis, Indiana 46240

Red Hat Linux Fedora 3 Unleashed

International Standard Book Number: 0-672-32708-2

Library of Congress Catalog Card Number: 2004093740

Printed in the United States of America

First Printing: December 2004

07   06   05   4   3   2

Trademarks

Warning and Disclaimer

Bulk Sales

Sams Publishing offers excellent discounts on this book when ordered in quantity for bulk purchases or special sales. For more information, please contact

U.S. Corporate and Government Sales
1-800-382-3419
corpsales@pearsontechgroup.com

For sales outside the United States, please contact

International Sales
international@pearsoned.com

Acquisitions Editor
Shelley Johnston

Development Editor
Damon Jordan

Managing Editor
Charlotte Clapp

Project Editor
Andy Beaster

Indexer
Becky Hornyak

Proofreader
Wendy Ott

Technical Editors
Jason Byars
Dee-Ann LeBlanc
Chris Newman
Dave Taylor
Christopher Young

Publishing Coordinator
Vanessa Evans

Multimedia Developer
Dan Scherf

Designer
Gary Adair

Page Layout
Juli Cook

Contents at a Glance

Introduction 1

Part I   Installation and Configuration

    1   Introducing Fedora 13

    2   Preparing to Install Fedora 27

    3   Installing Fedora 53

    4   Post-Installation Issues 81

    5   First Steps with Fedora 117

    6   The X Window System 159

Part II   System Administration and Managing Services

    7   Managing Services 189

    8   Managing Software and System Resources 207

    9   Managing Users 237

   10   Managing the File System 263

   11   Backing Up, Restoring, and Recovery 311

Part III   System Services Administration

   12   Printing with Fedora 349

   13   Network Connectivity 375

   14   Managing DNS 433

   15   Internet Connectivity 481

   16   Apache Web Server Management 501

   17   Administering Database Services 549

   18   Secure File Transfer Protocol (FTP) Service 579

   19   Handling Electronic Mail 627

   20   News and Other Collaborative Communication . . 663

   21   C/C++ Programming Tools for Fedora 693

   22   Shell Scripting 715

   23   Using Perl 757

24 Kernel and Module Management 785

25 Productivity Applications 811

26 Multimedia Applications 835

Part IV **Appendix**

A Fedora Internet Resources 873

Index 885

Table of Contents

Introduction   **1**

What Is Linux?..2
    What Is Fedora Core? 2
    Roots of Red Hat and Fedora......................................3
    Licensing...4
Why Use Linux?...5
Who This Book Is For 7
What This Book Contains 7
Conventions Used in This Book 9

Part I   **Installation and Configuration**

1   **Introducing Fedora**   **13**

What Is Fedora Core?..15
    Inside Fedora Core...15
    Features of the Fedora Install....................................18
    Fedora File System Features......................................19
Fedora for Business...20
Fedora in Your Home...22
Getting the Most from Fedora and Linux Documentation.......................22
Fedora Developers and Documentation..24
Reference...25

2   **Preparing to Install Fedora**   **27**

Planning Your Fedora Deployment...28
    Business Considerations 28
    System Considerations 29
    User Considerations..30
    A Predeployment Planning Checklist...............................30
    Planning the Installation..31
Hardware Requirements 32
    Meeting the Minimum Fedora Core Hardware Requirements 32
    Using Legacy Hardware 33
    Planning for Hard Drive Storage for Your Fedora
        Installation Class...34

Checking Hardware Compatibility 35
Preparing for Potential Hardware Problems 37
Preparing and Using a Hardware Inventory 40
Preparing for the Install Process 43
Preparing to Install from a CD-ROM 44
Partitioning Before and During Installation 45
Choosing a Partitioning Scheme 47
Hosting Parts of the Linux Filesystem on Separate Partitions 47
Using Red Hat's kickstart Installation Method 48
Reference 51

3   Installing Fedora   53

Before You Begin the Installation 53
Research Your Hardware Specifications 53
Choose an Installation Type 54
Choose Software Installation Options 54
Planning Partition Strategies 55
The Boot Loader 56
Choosing How to Install Fedora 57
Installing from CD-ROM 58
Installing Using a Network 58
Step-by-Step Installation 60
Starting the Install 60
Partitioning Your Drive 66
Choosing, Configuring, and Installing the Boot Loader 69
Network Configuration 70
Firewall and Security Configuration 71
Setting the Time Zone 72
Creating a Root Password and User Accounts 73
Software Selection and Installation 74
Create a Bootdisk 75
Finishing the Install 77
Login and Shutdown 78
Reference 79

4   Post-Installation Issues   81

Troubleshooting Post-Installation Configuration Problems 81
Your Hardware and kudzu 82

Pointer and Keyboard Configuration 84
    Configuring Keyboards with Linux 84
    Configuring Pointing Devices in Fedora 88
Configuring Display Graphics 93
Configuring Sound Devices 95
Detecting and Configuring a Modem 96
    Configuring a Serial-Port Modem 96
    Configuring a Fax Modem 99
    Configuring minicom for Modem Use 100
    Configuring Controllerless Modems for Laptops 100
Configuring Power Management in Fedora 101
Resetting the Date and Time 103
    Using the date Command 104
    Using the hwclock Command 104
    Using the system-config-date Client 104
Managing PCMCIA 106
    Using PCMCIA 106
    Controlling PCMCIA Service 108
Configuring and Using CD, DVD, and CD-RW Drives 108
    Checking Drive Assignment 108
    Initializing IEEE 1394 CD Drives 110
Reference 114

5   First Steps with Fedora   117

Working with the Linux File System 118
    Viewing the Linux File System 119
    Use Essential Commands from the /bin and /sbin Directories 121
    Store the Booted Kernel and View Stored Devices in the
        /boot and /dev Directories 122
    Use and Edit Files in the /etc Directory 123
    Protect the Contents of User Directories—/home 126
    Use the Contents of the /proc Directory to Interact
        with the Kernel 126
    Work with Shared Data in the /usr Directory 127
    Temporary File Storage in the /tmp Directory 128
    Access Variable Data Files in the /var Directory 128
Logging In to and Working with Linux 128
    Text-based Console Login 128
    Working with Virtual Consoles 129

Using Simple Keyboard and Mouse Techniques in
a Linux Console Session 130
Logging Out 132
Logging In and Out from a Remote Computer 132
Changing Your User Information 134
Reading Documentation 135
Using man Pages 136
Finding and Reading Software Packages Documentation 136
Using the Shell 137
Using Environment Variables 139
Navigating and Searching with the Shell 142
Managing Files with the Shell 142
Compressing and Decompressing Files Through the Shell 143
Using the Text Editors 144
Working with vi 146
Working with emacs 147
Working with Permissions 148
Assigning Permissions 149
Directory Permissions 150
Understanding Set User ID (SUID) and Set Group ID (SGID)
Permissions 152
Working As root 153
Creating Users 155
Deleting Users 156
Shutting Down the System 156
Rebooting the System 157
Reference 158

6   The X Window System   159
Basic X Concepts 160
Using X11R6 161
Elements of the xorg.conf File 162
Configuring X 167
Starting X 171
Using a Display Manager 171
Starting X from the Console by Using startx 174
Selecting and Using X Window Managers 175
Using Red Hat's switchdesk 176
The Tab Window Manager 178

The Motif Window Manager 179
The sawfish Window Manager 179
The Metacity Window Manager (metacity) 181
The GNOME and KDE Desktop Environments 182
GNOME: The GNU Network Object Model Environment 182
KDE: The K Desktop Environment 184
Reference 186

Part II   System Administration and Managing Services

7   Managing Services   **189**

Understanding the Fedora Core Linux Boot Process 190
Beginning the Boot Loading Process 190
Loading the Linux Kernel 191
System Services and Runlevels 192
Runlevel Definitions 192
Booting into the Default Runlevel 194
Booting to a Non-Default Runlevel with GRUB 196
Understanding init Scripts and the Final Stage of Initialization ...197
Running Services Through xinetd 198
Controlling Services at Boot with Administrative Tools 199
Using the chkconfig Text-Based Command-Line Tool 199
Using the GUI-based Service Configuration Tool 202
Starting and Stopping Services Manually 202
Changing Runlevels 203
Using Service Management to Troubleshoot Problems in
  Fedora Core Linux 204
Reference 206

8   Managing Software and System Resources   **207**

Using RPM for Software Management 207
Command-Line and Graphical RPM Clients 209
Using rpm on the Command Line 211
Package Organization with RPM 214
Extracting a Single File from an RPM File 214
Graphical Package Management 215
Using Red Hat Network and Alternatives for Software Management ...217
APT 218
YUM 219

Compiling Software from Source..221
    Building RPMS from `src.rpm` Files.................................221
    Working with Source RPM Files......................................222
    Compile from Source Tarballs.......................................224
System Monitoring Tools...226
    Console-based Monitoring...226
    Using the `kill` Command to Control Processes......................228
    Using Priority Scheduling and Control..............................229
    Displaying Free and Used Memory with `free`.......................231
    Disk Quotas..232
    Graphical Process and System Management Tools......................232
    KDE Process and System Monitoring Tools............................234
Reference...235

9   Managing Users   237

User Accounts...237
    User IDs and Group IDs...239
    File Permissions...239
Managing Groups...240
    Group Management Tools...242
Managing Users..243
    User Management Tools..244
    Adding New Users...245
    Monitoring User Activity on the System.............................247
Managing Passwords..247
    System Password Policy...248
    The Password File..248
    Shadow Passwords...249
    Managing Password Security for Users...............................251
    Changing Passwords in a Batch......................................252
Granting System Administrator Privileges to Regular Users...............252
    Temporarily Changing User Identity with the `su` Command...........252
    Granting Root Privileges on Occasion—The `sudo` Command............254
    Control Via Restricted Shells......................................257
The User Login Process..257
Disk Quotas...259
    Implementing Quotas..259
    Manually Configuring Quotas..260
Reference...261

10 Managing the File System   **263**

The Fedora Core Linux File
   System Basics 263
      Physical Structure of the File System on the Disk 265
      File System Partitions 266
      Network and Disk File Systems 267
      Viewing Your System's File Systems 268
   Working with the ext3 File System 269
      Understanding the ext3 File System Structure 269
      Journaling Options in ext3 270
      Verifying File Integrity in ext3 File Systems with the fsck Utility .271
   Other File Systems Available to Fedora Core Linux 272
      The Reiser File System 272
      JFS and XFS File Systems 273
      DOS File Systems 273
      CD-ROM File Systems 274
   Creating a File System 274
      The Disk As a Storage Device 275
      Creating the Partition Table 275
      Creating the File System on the Partitioned Disk 279
      Creating a DOS File System with mkdosfs 282
   Mounting File Systems 282
      The mount Command 283
      The umount Command 284
      Mounting Automatically with /etc/fstab 284
      GUI Tools to Mount File Systems 286
   Relocating a File System 288
      Installing the New Drive 288
      Creating the Partition Table and Formatting the Disk 290
      Mounting the New Partition and Populating It with the
         Relocated Files 290
   Logical Volume Management 291
   File System Manipulation 291
      Creating a File System for Testing 292
      Using dumpe2fs 294
      Mounting a Partition As Read-Only on a Running System 296
      Converting an Existing ext2 File System to ext3 296
      Examine an initrd Image File 298
      Examine a Floppy Image File 299

Disk Tuning 299
  Using the BIOS and Kernel to Tune the Disk Drives 299
  The hdparm Command 300
File System Tuning 301
  The mke2fs Command 302
  The tune2fs Command 302
  The e2fsck Command 302
  The badblocks Command 303
  The noatime Option for the mount Command 303
Managing Files for Character Devices, Block Devices, and
  Special Devices 303
  Naming Conventions Used for Block and Character Devices 305
  Using mknod to Create Devices 305
Reference 307

11   Backing Up, Restoring, and Recovery   311

Choosing a Backup Strategy 311
  Why Data Loss Occurs 312
  Assessing Your Backup Needs and Resources 313
  Evaluating Backup Strategies 315
  Making the Choice 318
Choosing Backup Hardware and Media 318
  Removable Storage Media 318
  Network Storage 320
  Tape Drive Backup 320
Using Backup Software 321
  tar 321
  Backing Up Files with cpio 323
  The GNOME File Roller 325
  The KDE Archiving Tools (KDE ark and kdat) 326
  Using the dd Command for Archiving 327
  Using the Amanda Backup Application 328
  Alternative Backup Software 329
Copying Files 330
  Copying Files Using tar 330
  Compressing, Encrypting, and Sending tar Streams 331
  Copying Files Using cp 331
  Copying Files Using cpio 332
  Copying Files Using mc 332

Copying Files Using scp 333
Copying Files Using rsync 335
Undeleting Files 337
Using the ext2fs Undeletion Process 337
Reformatting with the -S Option When Experiencing
Unrecoverable File System Errors 338
Undeleting Files Using mc 338
System Rescue 339
The Fedora Core Rescue Disk 340
Backing Up and Restoring the Master Boot Record 340
Manually Restoring the Partition Table 341
Booting the System from the Rescue CD 342
Booting the System from a Generic Boot Floppy 342
Using a GRUB Boot Floppy 342
Using the Recovery Facility from the Installation Disk 343
Reference 345

Part III   System Services Administration

12   Printing with Fedora   349

Overview of Fedora Printing 350
Configuring and Managing Print Services 351
GUI-based Printer Configuration Quickstart 352
Console-based Printer Configuration Quickstart 353
Managing Printing Services 353
Creating and Configuring Local Printers 356
Creating the Print Queue 356
Editing Printer Settings 359
Creating Network Printers 361
Enabling Network Printing on a LAN 361
Session Message Block Printing 363
Network-Attached Printer Configuration and Printing 364
Console Print Control 366
Console-based Printer Configuration 366
Using Basic Print Commands 367
Manage Print Jobs 367
Using the Common UNIX Printing System 369
Creating a CUPS Printer Entry 369

Avoiding Printer-Support Problems 373
    All-in-One (Print/Fax/Scan) Devices 373
    Using USB and Legacy Printers 373
Reference 374

13   Network Connectivity   **375**

Networking with TCP/IP 375
    TCP/IP Addressing 376
    Using IP Masquerading in Fedora 378
    Ports 379
Network Organization 380
    Subnetting 380
    Subnet Masks 380
    Broadcast, Unicast, and Multicast Addressing 381
Hardware Devices for Networking 381
    Network Interface Cards 382
    Network Cable 384
    Hubs 385
    Routers and Bridges 385
    Initializing New Network Hardware 386
Using Network Configuration Tools 388
    Command-Line Network Interface Configuration 389
    Network Configuration Files 393
    Using Graphical Configuration Tools 396
Dynamic Host Configuration Protocol 399
    How DHCP Works 399
    Activating DHCP at Installation and Boot Time 400
    DHCP Software Installation and Configuration 401
    Using DHCP to Configure Network Hosts 402
    Other Uses for DHCP 405
Using the Network File System 405
    Installing and Starting or Stopping NFS 405
    NFS Server Configuration 406
    NFS Client Configuration 408
Putting Samba to Work 408
    Manually Configuring Samba with `/etc/samba/smb.conf` 410
    Setting Global Samba Behavior with the `[global]` Section 411
    Testing Samba with the `testparm` Command 413
    Starting the `smbd` Daemon 413

Mounting Samba Shares 414

Configuring Samba Using SWAT 415

Wireless Networking 419

Support for Wireless Networking in Fedora 419

Cellular Networking 421

Advantages of Wireless Networking 421

Choosing from Among Available Wireless Protocols 422

Securing a Wireless Network 423

Securing Your Network 423

Using `lokkit` and `system-config-securitylevel` for Firewalling .. 424

Passwords and Physical Security 426

Securing TCP/IP 427

Configuring and Using Tripwire 427

Devices 428

Securing DHCP 429

Securing NFS 429

Making Samba Secure 429

Keeping Up-to-Date on Linux Security Issues 429

Using Patches/Upgrades to Keep Your Network Secure 430

Reference 430

General 430

DHCP 431

Wireless 431

Security 431

Books 431

14   Managing DNS   **433**

Configuring DNS for Clients 434

Understanding the `/etc/host.conf` File 435

Understanding the `/etc/nsswitch.conf` File 435

Understanding the `/etc/hosts` File 436

Understanding the `/etc/resolv.conf` File 437

Understanding the Changes Made by DHCP 437

Essential DNS Concepts 438

How Nameservers Store DNS Structure Information 439

How DNS Provides Name Service Information to Users 439

Name Resolution in Practice 440

Reverse Resolution 444

What Did the Resolver Learn? 447

Using DNS Tools 448

    dig 448

    host 449

    nslookup 450

    whois 450

Configuring a Local Caching Nameserver 452

Your Own Domain Name and Third-Party DNS 453

Providing DNS for a Real Domain with BIND 454

    rndc.conf 456

    named.conf 457

    Logging 462

    Resolver Configuration 463

    Running the named Nameserver Daemon 464

Providing DNS for a Real Domain 464

    Forward Zone 465

    Reverse Zone 467

    Registering the Domain 468

Troubleshooting DNS 468

    Delegation Problems 469

    Reverse Lookup Problems 469

    Maintaining Accurate Serial Numbers 470

    Troubleshooting Problems in Zone Files 470

    Tools for Troubleshooting 471

    Using Fedora Core's BIND Configuration Tool 471

Managing DNS Security 472

    UNIX Security Considerations 473

    DNS Security Considerations 474

    Using DNS Security Extensions 477

    Using Split DNS 478

Reference 479

15 Internet Connectivity   **481**

Common Configuration Information 482

Laying the Foundation: The localhost Interface 483

    Checking for the Availability of the Loopback Interface 483

    Configuring the Loopback Interface Manually 484

Configuring Dial-up Internet Access 485

    Configuring a Dial-up Connection Manually 486

    Using the Fedora Core Internet Configuration Wizard 488

Configuring Digital Subscriber Line Access 491

Understanding Point-to-Point Protocol over Ethernet 492

Configuring a PPPOE Connection Manually 492

Troubleshooting Connection Problems 494

Configuring a Dial-in PPP Server 494

Reference 498

16   Apache Web Server Management   501

About the Apache Web Server 501

Installing the Apache Server 503

Installing from the RPM 503

Building the Source Yourself 505

Starting and Stopping Apache 508

Starting the Apache Server Manually 508

Using /etc/rc.d/init.d/httpd 510

Controlling Apache with Red Hat's service Command 511

Controlling Apache with Red Hat's chkconfig Command 511

Controlling Apache with Red Hat's system-config-services

Client 512

Runtime Server Configuration Settings 513

Runtime Configuration Directives 514

Editing httpd.conf 514

Apache Multi-Processing Modules 517

Using .htaccess Configuration Files 518

File System Authentication and Access Control 520

Restricting Access with allow and deny 520

Authentication 521

Final Words on Access Control 524

Apache Modules 524

mod_access 525

mod_alias 525

mod_asis 525

mod_auth 526

mod_auth_anon 526

mod_auth_dbm 526

mod_auth_digest 526

mod_autoindex 527

mod_cgi 527

mod_dir and mod_env 527

        mod_expires 527
        mod_headers 527
        mod_imap 528
        mod_include 528
        mod_info and mod_log_config 528
        mod_mime and mod_mime_magic 528
        mod_negotiation 528
        mod_proxy 528
        mod_rewrite 529
        mod_setenvif 529
        mod_speling 529
        mod_status 529
        mod_ssl 529
        mod_unique_id 529
        mod_userdir 530
        mod_usertrack 530
        mod_vhost_alias 530
    Virtual Hosting 530
        Address-based Virtual Hosts 530
        Name-based Virtual Hosts 531
    Logging 532
    Dynamic Content 534
        CGI 534
        SSI 536
        Basic SSI Directives 536
        Flow Control 540
    Graphic Interface Configuration of Apache 541
        Configuring Virtual Host Properties 542
        Configuring the Server 543
        Configuring Apache for Peak Performance 544
    Other Web Servers for Use with Fedora 544
        thttpd 544
        Sun ONE Web Server 545
        Stronghold 545
        Zope 545
        Zeus Web Server 546
        TWiki 546
    Reference 546

17 Administering Database Services   549

A Brief Review of Database Basics 550
    How Relational Databases Work 551
    Understanding SQL Basics 553
    Creating Tables 554
    Inserting Data into Tables 555
    Retrieving Data from a Database 556
Choosing a Database: MySQL Versus PostgreSQL 558
    Speed 559
    Data Locking 559
    ACID Compliance in Transaction Processing to Protect
        Data Integrity 560
    SQL Subqueries 561
    Procedural Languages and Triggers 562
    Available Applications 562
Installing and Configuring MySQL 562
    Initializing the Data Directory in MySQL 564
    Setting a Password for the MySQL Root User 564
    Creating a Database in MySQL 565
    Granting and Revoking Privileges in MySQL 565
Installing and Configuring PostgreSQL 567
    Initializing the Data Directory in PostgreSQL 567
    Creating a Database in PostgreSQL 569
    Creating Database Users in PostgreSQL 570
    Deleting Database Users in PostgreSQL 570
    Granting and Revoking Privileges in PostgreSQL 571
Database Clients 571
    SSH Access to a Database 572
    Local GUI Client Access to a Database 573
    Web Access to a Database 573
    The MySQL Command-Line Client 575
    The PostgreSQL Command-Line Client 576
    Graphical Clients 577
Reference 577

18 Secure File Transfer Protocol Service   579

Using FTP Clients 579
    Using `sftp` for Secure File Transfers 580
    The FTP Client Interface 581

Using the Text-based FTP Client Interface 581
Using Graphical FTP Clients 589
FTP Servers 592
Choosing an Authenticated or Anonymous Server 593
Fedora FTP Server Packages 593
Other FTP Servers 593
Installing FTP Software 594
The FTP User 595
xinetd Configuration for wu-ftpd 597
Configuring xinetd for the wu-ftp Server 598
Starting the Very Secure FTP Server (vsftpd) Package 599
Configuring the Very Secure FTP Server 599
Controlling Anonymous Access 600
Other vsftpd Server Configuration Files 600
Configuring the Wu-FTPd Server 602
Using Commands in the ftpaccess File to Configure
  wu-ftpd 603
Configure Access Control 604
Configure User Information 607
Configure System Logging 611
Configure Permission Control 612
Configure Commands Directed Toward the cdpath 614
Structure of the shutdown File 615
Configure FTP Server File-Conversion Actions 615
Strip Prefix 616
Strip Postfix 616
Add-On Prefix 616
Add-On Postfix 617
External Command 617
Types 617
Options 617
Description 618
An Example of Conversions in Action 618
Using Commands in the ftphosts File to Allow or Deny FTP Server
  Connection 618
Server Administration 619
Display Information About Connected Users 619
Count the Number of Connections 621
Use /usr/sbin/ftpshut to Schedule FTP Server Downtime 621
Use /var/log/xferlog to View a Log of Server Transactions 623
Reference 625

19   Handling Electronic Mail   627

How Email Is Sent and Received 628

The Mail Transport Agent 629

    Choosing an MTA 631

    The Mail Delivery Agent 632

    The Mail User Agent 632

Choosing a Mail Client (MUA) 633

    The mail Application 633

    Mutt 635

    Evolution 637

    Balsa 639

    KMail 639

    Mozilla Mail 640

    Other Mail Clients 640

Attachments—Sending Binary Files As Text 643

    BinHex 643

    yenc 643

    uuencode and uudecode 644

Basic Sendmail Configuration and Operation 645

    Configuring Masquerading 647

    Using Smart Hosts 647

    Setting Message Delivery Intervals 647

    Building the sendmail.cf File 648

    Mail Relaying 649

    Forwarding Email with Aliases 649

    Rejecting Email from Specified Sites 650

Using Fetchmail to Retrieve Mail 651

    Installing Fetchmail 651

    Configuring Fetchmail 652

Choosing a Mail Delivery Agent (MDA) 655

    Procmail 656

    Spamassassin 656

    Squirrelmail 656

    Virus Scanners 657

    Special Mail Delivery Agents 657

Mail Daemons 657

Alternatives to Microsoft Exchange Server 658

    Microsoft Exchange Server/Outlook Client 659

    CommuniGate Pro 659

    Samsung Contact (Formerly Known As HP OpenMail) 659

Bynari 659
SuSE OpenExchange 659
Kroupware 659
OpenGroupware (Formerly SKYRiX 4.1) 660
phpgroupware 660
PHProjekt 660
IMP/Horde 660
Conclusion 660
Reference 661
Web Resources 661
Books 662

20   News and Other Collaborative Communication   663
An Overview of Network News 664
Newsgroups 664
Selecting a Newsreader 665
The slrn News Client 665
The Pan News Client 666
The KNode News Client 667
The Mozilla News Client 669
Collaborating with TWiki 670
Internet Relay Chat 672
Internet Messaging with GAIM 674
Video Conferencing with GnomeMeeting 674
Mail List Configuration and Management with Mailman 676
Configuring a Local News Server 679
Types of News Servers 679
The INN Package and Configuration Files 681
Installing the INN Package 683
Configuring the innd Package 683
Reference 691

21   C/C++ Programming Tools for Fedora   693
Programming in C with Linux 694
Programming in C++ 695
Getting Started with Linux C/C++ Programming 696
The Process of Programming 697
Elements of the C/C++ Language 698

Using the C Programming Project Management Tools Provided
with Fedora Core Linux 699
    Building Programs with make 699
    Using the autoconf Utility to Configure Code 701
    Managing Software Projects with RCS and CVS 702
    Making Libraries with ar 705
    Debugging Tools 705
Using the GNU C Compiler 707
A Simple C Program 708
Graphical Development Tools 709
    Using the KDevelop Client 709
    Trolltech's QT Designer 710
    The Glade Client for Developing in GNOME 711
Additional Resources 713
Reference 714

22 Shell Scripting   **715**

The Shells Included with This Book 716
The Shell Command Line 716
    Shell Pattern-Matching Support 718
    Redirecting Input and Output 719
    Piping Data 720
    Background Processing 720
The Basics of Writing, Creating, and Executing a Shell Script 721
Creating and Executing a Simple Shell Program
with bash 722
    Running the New Shell Program 722
    Storing Shell Scripts for Systemwide Access 724
    Interpreting Shell Scripts Through Specific Shells 724
Using Variables in Shell Scripts 725
    Assigning a Value to a Variable 726
    Accessing Variable Values 727
Positional Parameters 727
    A Simple Example of a Positional Parameter 727
    Using Positional Parameters to Access and Retrieve Variables
    from the Command Line 728
    Using a Simple Script to Automate Tasks 729
Built-in Variables 731

Special Characters..732
    Use Double Quotes to Resolve Variables in Strings with
      Embedded Spaces..733
    Using Single Quotes to Maintain Unexpanded Variables............733
    Using the Backslash As an Escape Character............................734
    Using the Backtick to Replace a String with Output................735
Comparison of Expressions..735
    Comparison of Expressions in pdksh and bash.......................735
    Comparing Expressions with tcsh..740
Iteration Statements...745
    The for Statement..745
    The while Statement...746
    The until Statement...748
    The repeat Statement (tcsh)..749
    The select Statement (pdksh)...749
    The shift Statement...750
Conditional Statements...750
    The if Statement...750
    The case Statement..752
The break and exit Statements...754
Using Functions in Shell Scripts...754
Reference..756

23   Using Perl   757

Using Perl with Linux...758
    Perl Versions...759
    A Simple Perl Program...759
Perl Variables and Data Structures..761
    Perl Variable Types..761
    Special Variables..762
Operators...763
    Comparison Operators...763
    Compound Operators..764
    Arithmetic Operators...764
    Other Operators...764
    Special String Constants..765
Conditional Statements: if/else and unless...................................766
    if..766
    unless..767

Looping 767
    `for` 768
    `foreach` 768
    `while` 769
    `until` 769
    `last` and `next` 769
    `do ... while` and `do ... until` 770
Regular Expressions 770
Access to the Shell 771
Switches 772
Modules and CPAN 775
Code Examples 776
    Sending Mail 776
    Purging Logs 778
    Posting to Usenet 779
    One-Liners 780
    Command-line Processing 781
Reference 781
    Books 781
    Usenet 782
    WWW 782
    Other 783

24 Kernel and Module Management   **785**

The Linux Kernel 786
    The Linux Source Tree 786
    Types of Kernels 789
Managing Modules 790
When to Recompile 792
Kernel Versions 793
Obtaining the Kernel Sources 794
Patching the Kernel 795
Compiling the Kernel 797
Choosing a Configuration Interface 799
    Using `xconfig` to Configure the Kernel 801
    Creating an Initial RAM Disk Image 805
When Something Goes Wrong 806
    Errors During Compile 806
    Runtime Errors, Boot Loader Problems, and Kernel Oops 807

Kernel Tuning with `sysctl` 808
Reference 809

25 Productivity Applications   **811**

Office Suites for Fedora Core Linux 811
  Working with OpenOffice.org 812
  Working with GNOME Office 817
  Working with KOffice 820
PDA Connectivity 823
  Command-Line PDA Software for Fedora Core Linux 823
  GUI PDA Client Software 824
Scanner Applications for Fedora Core Linux 825
Web Design Tools 827
Fax Client Software 828
Other Office and Productivity Tools Included with
  Fedora Core Linux 830
Productivity Applications Written for Microsoft Windows 832
Reference 832

26 Multimedia Applications   **835**

Burning CDs and DVDs in Fedora Core Linux 836
  Creating CDs from the Command Line 837
  Creating DVDs from the Command Line 839
  Creating CDs with Fedora Core Linux Graphical Clients 841
Sound and Music 843
  Sound Cards 844
  Recording Sound 844
  Sound Formats 845
  Music Players 847
  Streaming Audio 848
Viewing TV and Video 848
  TV and Video Hardware 848
  Video Formats 851
  Viewing Video in Linux 852
  Viewing Television with Linux 853
  Personal Video Recorders 853
  DVD and Video Players 854
Using Still Cameras with Fedora Core Linux 855
  Webcams 855
  Handheld Digital Cameras 856

Using Scanners in Fedora Core Linux 857
Graphics Manipulation 859
    The GNU Image Manipulation Program 859
    Working with Graphics Formats 860
    Capturing Screen Images 863
Linux Gaming 864
    Installing nVidia Video Drivers 865
    Installing Unreal Tournament 2003 865
    Installing Wolfenstein—Enemy Territory 865
Reference 869

Part IV   Appendix

A   Fedora Internet Resources   873

Web Sites and Search Engines 874
    Web Search Tips 874
    Google Is Your Friend 875
    Red Hat Package Listings 875
    Certification 876
    Commercial Support 876
    Documentation 877
    Linux Guides 877
    The Fedora Project 878
    Red Hat Linux 878
    Mini-CD Linux Distributions 878
    Floppy-Based Linux Distributions 879
    Various Intel-Based Linux Distributions 879
    PowerPC-Based Linux Distributions 880
    Linux on Laptops and PDAs 880
    The X Window System 880
Usenet Newsgroups 881
Mailing Lists 883
    Fedora Project Mailing Lists 883
    Red Hat Mailing Lists 884
Internet Relay Chat 884

Index   885

Lead Authors

Bill Ball is the best-selling author of nearly 20 books about Linux, including several editions of *Red Hat Linux Unleashed*, Que Publishing's *Using Linux*, and Sams Publishing's *SuSE Linux Unleashed*. He is a technical writer, editor, and magazine journalist, and has been using computers for nearly 30 years. He first edited books for Que in 1986, and wrote one of the first best-selling Linux books, *Teach Yourself Linux in 24 Hours*, in 1997. He has authored articles and reviews in *Linux Journal*, developed technical online content for business Web sites, and has developed and released open-source software for the Mac OS and Palm OS platforms. He has been a fan of Linux and XFree86 since 1994 and uses the software on Intel-based PCs, Apple PowerMacs, and MIPS platforms. Bill is an active member of the Northern Virginia Linux Users Group (NOVALUG); teaches Linux courses at Stratford University in Falls Church, Virginia; and lives in the Shirlington area of Arlington, Virginia. He can be contacted through `http://www.tux.org/~bball`.

Hoyt Duff feels that a good word to describe his life experience is "former"—former senior vice president and senior commercial loan officer for a bank, former community college instructor, former restaurateur, and former special education teacher. He currently meets the needs of his inner ADD child by spending the summer months tending to his family business, a sport fishing pier (the longest on the East Coast), and playing cocktail piano on weekends. Hoyt even finds time to write about Linux as a columnist and regular contributor of reviews and tutorial for Linux Format magazine. Active in the TideWater UNIX Users Group (`www.twuug.org`), Hoyt enjoys the regular Linux installfests the most and will attempt to install Linux on anything that moves.

His computer experiences began with writing college course Fortran programs on an IBM 360/65, Pascal programming on the original IBM PC, and then taking a detour hacking 6502 assembler on a Commodore VIC20. Discovering Linux through an article in Boot magazine, he eventually got his first commercial writing assignment for its sister publication, MaximumLinux magazine. The philosophy that drives his life is "Fix it until it breaks," which is why he enjoys Linux so much. Hoyt can be contacted at `hoyt@maximumhoyt.com`.

Contributing Author

Chris Newman is a consultant programmer specializing in the development of custom Web-based database applications to a loyal international client base. A graduate of Keele University, Chris lives in Stoke-on-Trent, England, where he runs Lightwood Consultancy Ltd., the company he founded in 1999 to further his interest in Internet technology. Lightwood operates Web hosting services under the DataSnake brand and is proud to be one of the first hosting companies to offer and support SQLite as a standard feature on all accounts.

More information on Lightwood Consultancy Ltd. can be found at `http://www.lightwood.net`, and Chris can be contacted at `chris@lightwood.net`.

Dedication

First and foremost, to Cathy, my XYL, for her understanding and love. To Hoyt, KB4OQ, my coauthor, for his help and hospitality. And to Frank, AA4ZS, my Elmer, for his technical advice in a new lifelong pursuit—Bill, KG4ZQZ

To my wife of 29 years, Bobbie Lou, whose love, support, and understanding have made me a better person; to my daughters, Jeni and Megan, who have helped keep me that way, and to my Mom, Lisa, who has no idea what it is I write about but loves me anyway—Hoyt Duff

Acknowledgments

Bill Ball

To all my readers: Thank you for the numerous comments, criticisms, and critiques from all over the world—I cherish your thoughts. Thanks to my previous acquisitions editor, Katie Mohr, and my new acquisitions editor, Shelley Johnston, for helping make this book one of the best guides to Linux on the market. I wish Katie all the best in her new job, and hope that Shelley can put up with her new charge without losing her mind. Thanks also to fellow author Hoyt Duff for his contributions, advice, and help while writing this book. Thanks to Dave Taylor, DeeAnne LeBlanc, and Chris Newman for their technical expertise and to Lorna Gentry for applying expert development edits to this book's drafts. No acknowledgment in a Linux book would be complete without a big nod to the thousands of programmers around the world who freely share their knowledge, time, and talent in producing quality software such as Linux, XFree86, The GNU Project, and the many software packages created for or ported to Linux. Kind words are also due to friends and comrades-in-arms in the Northern Virginia Linux Users Group (NOVALUG), especially founder Greg Pryzby. NOVALUG has been and continues to be a communal source of inspiration for ideas, hardware hacks, and software fixes. Acknowledgment must be given to Richard M. Stallman for the GNU GPL and to Linus B. Torvalds for sharing Linux with the world. Finally, grateful thanks are extended to Virginia Beach, VA's Lynnhaven Pier for access to voracious bluefish, and to the best bartender in the world, Lorenzo Castrejon, and his wife, Consuelo, a fantastic gourmet cook at Las Palmas, the finest Mexican restaurant in Virginia Beach, Virginia.

Hoyt Duff

Until I participated in writing this book, I had no idea the amount of work that goes on behind the scenes by the many editors involved. The popular notion is that editors are mean people intent on destroying the authors' creation. That makes for good cocktail party chatter, but the reality is far from that stereotype. The editors associated with this book are delightful, professional folks who obviously enjoy what they do; I've learned a great deal about writing from them. Thank you Shelley, Lorna, Elizabeth, Rhonda, and all the staff at Sams Publishing.

Special thanks to coauthor Bill Ball, whose affable manner and smooth talk once again persuaded me to tackle this tough project along with him. His support has helped me through the rough spots. He's a pretty good fisherman as well.

The Red Hat folks, the beta testers, and all the software authors and open-source contributors who have helped make Linux the phenomenon that is has become are due my thanks and appreciation as well. Their accomplishments are legion. Without them, I might be writing Windows books.

Special thanks goes to Chris Newman for his contribution to this edition of *Red Hat Fedora Unleashed*. Without his hard work and fast and furious turnaround it never would have happened.

We Want to Hear from You!

As the reader of this book, you are our most important critic and commentator. We value your opinion and want to know what we're doing right, what we could do better, what areas you'd like to see us publish in, and any other words of wisdom you're willing to pass our way.

You can email or write me directly to let me know what you did or didn't like about this book—as well as what we can do to make our books stronger.

Please note that I cannot help you with technical problems related to the topic of this book, and that due to the high volume of mail I receive, I might not be able to reply to every message.

When you write, please be sure to include this book's title and authors as well as your name and phone or email address. I will carefully review your comments and share them with the authors and editors who worked on the book.

Email: opensource@samspublishing.com

Mail: Mark Taber
          Associate Publisher
          Sams Publishing
          800 East 96th Street
          Indianapolis, IN 46240 USA

Reader Services

For more information about this book or others from Sams Publishing, visit our Web site at www.samspublishing.com. Type the ISBN (excluding hyphens) or the title of the book in the Search box to find the book you're looking for.

Introduction

Welcome to *Red Hat Fedora 3 Unleashed*! This book covers the free Linux distribution named Fedora Core and includes a fully functional and complete operating system produced by the Fedora Project, sponsored by Red Hat, Inc.

If you're familiar with Red Hat Linux, you've made the right choice in choosing Fedora Core—you'll feel right at home after you install this cutting-edge operating system. Many of the familiar software tools, utilities, and applications you previously enjoyed while using Red Hat's free Linux distributions are included with Fedora Core, along with a number of improvements and new software packages.

If you're new to Linux and to Sams Publishing Unleashed books about Linux, congratulations—you've picked one of the best books on the market about Fedora Core. Get ready for an exciting, safe, and productive journey as you read this book and install the included software.

This book provides information to match the latest developments found in Fedora, and as always, includes a free copy of the latest distribution on DVD and CD-ROM. Linux, the kernel of a free operating system, is no longer the new kid on the block as it has been available for more than 10 years now. Linux forms the core of a stable, mature, and secure operating system. From embedded devices (such as PDAs) to laptops, desktops to servers, and mainframes to new Itanium CPUs, Linux continues to be in the vanguard and a major force in the free software marketplace.

Make no mistake: While Linux has been deployed in many corporate and enterprise-level environments, it is also steadily advancing toward use on millions of desktops. Thousands of open-source programmers around the world improve, test, and update the Linux kernel and Linux-related software packages. Their efforts have contributed much to the success of Linux for many different types of users. Fedora Core incorporates many of these software packages, along with the latest stable version of the Linux kernel. This means that you put Fedora to work right away.

This book contains everything you need to plan, install, configure, maintain, administer, rebuild, and use Fedora. You can use this software at school, at home, or in the workplace. You can also make as many copies of Fedora as you want and freely give away those copies to anyone interested in using Linux.

After an introduction to Red Hat, Inc., and the Fedora Core project, you'll see to how to set up and plan for an install. You'll then get step-by-step directions on how to install Fedora in a variety of ways. Following directions on configuration, you'll be introduced to basic system administration, followed by instructions on advanced administration techniques and concepts. A section on programming, productivity, and multimedia rounds out the host of skills you'll acquire and learn when you use this book. Keep in mind however, that this book assumes you have at least some experience with using a computer operating system.

What Is Linux?

Linux is the core, or kernel, of a free operating system first developed and released to the world by Linus Benedict Torvalds in 1991. Torvalds, then a graduate student at the University of Helsinki, Finland, is now a Fellow at the Open Source Development Lab (http://www.osdl.org). He is an engineer, and had previously worked for the CPU design and fabrication company, Transmeta, Inc. Fortuitously for all Linux users, Torvalds chose to distribute Linux under a free software license named the GNU General Public License (GPL).

> **NOTE**
>
> To learn more about Linus and how Linux grew from a hobby to a major movement in the software industry, read *Just for Fun*, by Linus Torvalds and David Diamond (HarperCollins, 2001).

The GNU GPL is the brainchild of Richard M. Stallman, the founder of the Free Software Foundation. Stallman, the famous author of the emacs editing environment and gcc compiler system, crafted the GPL to ensure that covered software would always be free and available in source code form. The GPL is the guiding document for Linux and its ownership, distribution, and copyright. Torvalds holds the rights to the Linux trademark, but thanks to a combination of his generosity, the Internet, thousands of programmers around the world, GNU software, and the GNU GPL, Linux will remain forever free and unencumbered by licensing or royalty issues. See the later section "Licensing" to learn more about the GNU GPL and other software licenses.

Linux, pronounced "lih-nucks," is free software. Combining the Linux kernel with GNU software tools—drivers, utilities, user interfaces, and other software such as The X.Org Foundation's X11R6 7.0 X Window System—creates a Linux distribution. There are many different Linux distributions from different vendors, but many are derived from or closely mimic Red Hat, Inc.'s distribution of Linux, Red Hat Linux.

> **NOTE**
>
> After you install Fedora, you can use the play command to hear how Linus pronounces "Linux." Use the command, along with a directory and file specification, known as a pathname, like this:
>
> ```
> $ play /usr/share/sndconfig/sample.au
> ```

What Is Fedora Core?

Fedora Core, or more simply, Fedora, is an operating system based on the Linux kernel, created, improved, and distributed by the Fedora Project at http://fedora.redhat.com.

The Fedora Project, sponsored by Red Hat, Inc., is an open source project supported by a worldwide community of software developers. Although Fedora is not supported by Red Hat, Inc., it incorporates improvements made to the Linux kernel and helps contribute to Red Hat, Inc.'s commercial Linux distributions and software. At the same time, Fedora also benefits from improvements made by Red Hat software engineers to Red Hat's products. Despite this symbiotic relationship however, Fedora Core is a free operating system, built entirely from free software, and is guided by a process open to all free software developers.

Roots of Red Hat and Fedora

In 1994, Marc Ewing and Bob Young combined forces to create Red Hat (named after a Cornell University lacrosse team hat) in order to develop, release, and market an easily installed, easily managed, and easy-to-use Linux distribution. Five years later, Durham, N.C.–based Red Hat, Inc. would have one of the most successful initial public offerings (IPOs) on the stock market. In 2001, Red Hat introduced a line of products aimed at the corporate and enterprise markets, and created versions of its Red Hat Linux distributions and associated software in a product line known as Red Hat Enterprise Linux. Additional software, services, and distributions were added to the product over the next several years, such as the Advanced Server (with support for seven different CPU architectures), ES for small- to mid-range enterprise use, and WorkStation (WS) releases.

Following the release of Red Hat Linux 9 in mid-2003, Red Hat, Inc. announced that it was discontinuing the sale of consumer-based Linux distributions. Previously, the distributions had been available in boxed sets with manuals on store shelves or in CD-ROM image format for free download over the Internet. Red Hat, Inc. then created the Fedora Project and formally opened its new home on October 22, 2003.

> **NOTE**
>
> Shortly after discontinuing the free and boxed consumer distributions, Red Hat, Inc. announced a new Linux distribution named Red Hat Linux Professional Workstation. The distribution includes eight CD-ROMs of software and source code, along with installation, administration, reference, and safety (security) manuals, a Java development kit, 30 days of install support, and one year of updates via the customer-exclusive Red Hat Network. The distribution is based on Red Hat's Enterprise Linux WS release, and is slated to retail for $95. For more information, browse to http://www.redhat.com/software/workstation/.

Today, the company, based in Raleigh, N.C., has grown from a handful of employees to more than 600 in 22 locations around the world.

Red Hat, Inc. was one of the first companies to adopt, promote, and use open source as a business model for supporting development, technical service, support, and sales of free software to the computer industry. Its business practices have spawned a shift in paradigm of proprietary attitudes prevalent in the monopolistic software industry, and the company is a role model and business leader in the open source movement. You learn more about Red Hat, Inc. and Fedora Core in Chapter 1, "Introducing Fedora."

CAUTION

The Fedora Core CD-ROM and DVD distribution included with this book is not supported by Red Hat, Inc. If you want technical support when using a Red Hat release, purchase a copy from Red Hat, Inc. at

`http://www.redhat.com`

You can also call to order. In the U.S., call

1-888-REDHAT1 (1-888-733-4281)

Elsewhere in the world, call

+1-919-754-3700

Red Hat is a trademark of Red Hat, Inc. Linux is a trademark owned by Linus Torvalds.

Do NOT contact Red Hat, Inc. for any type of support when using or attempting to install the software included with this book. Although every effort has been made to ensure that information in this book matches the included software, you should instead contact Sams Publishing for any problems related to the CD-ROMs contained in this book:

`http://www.samspublishing.com/software/`

Only users who purchase the "official" Red Hat Linux products from Red Hat, Inc., are entitled to support from Red Hat.

If you purchase an official Red Hat Linux distribution from Red Hat, Inc., you may find commercial software included on the distribution's CD-ROMs or DVD. These software packages are often included as an enticement to purchase more feature-laden or corporate versions, but you should carefully read any accompanying licensing agreements and be careful to not make unauthorized copies.

Licensing

Software licensing is an important issue for all computer users, and can entail moral, legal, and financial considerations. Many consumers think that purchasing a copy of a commercial or proprietary operating system, productivity application, utility, or game conveys ownership, but this not is true. In the majority of cases, the End User License Agreement, or EULA, included with a commercial software package, will state that you have only paid for the right to use the software according to specific terms. This generally means that you may not examine, make copies, share, resell, or transfer ownership of the software package. More onerous software licenses enforce terms that preclude you from distributing or publishing comparative performance reviews of the software. Even more insidious licensing schemes (and supporting legislation, especially in the United States), contain provisions allowing onsite auditing of the software's use!

This is not the case with the software included with this book. Although you cannot resell copies of this book's CD-ROMs labeled as "Red Hat Linux" (Red Hat is a trademark of Red Hat, Inc.), you are entirely free to make copies, share them with friends, and install the software on as many computers as you want—we encourage you to purchase additional copies of this book to give them as gifts, however. Make sure to read the file named README on the first CD-ROM included with this book for important information regarding the included software and disk contents. Look under the /usr/share/apps/LICENSES directory after you install Fedora to find a copy of the GNU GPL (along with copies of other software licenses). You'll see that the GPL provides unrestricted freedom to use, duplicate, share, study, modify, improve, and even sell software.

You can put your copy of Fedora to work right away in your home or at your place of business without having to worry about software licensing, per-seat workstation or client licenses, software auditing, royalty payments, or any other types of payments to third parties. However, you should be aware that although much of the software included with Fedora is licensed under the GPL, some packages on this book's CD-ROMs are licensed under other terms. There is a variety of related software licenses, and many software packages fall under a broad definition known as open source. Some of these include the Artistic License, the BSD License, the Mozilla Public License, and the Q Public License.

For additional information about the various GNU software licenses, browse to http:// www.gnu.org. For a definition of open source and licensing guidelines, along with links to the terms of nearly three dozen different open-source licenses, browse to http://www. opensource.org/.

Why Use Linux?

Millions of savvy computer users have been putting Linux to work for more than 10 years now. Over the last year, many individuals, small office/home office (SOHO) users, businesses, corporations, colleges, nonprofits, and local, state, and federal agencies in a number of countries have incorporated Linux with great success. And today, Linux is being incorporated into many IS/IT environments as part of improvements in efficiency, security, and cost savings. Using Linux is a good idea for a number of reasons. These reasons include

- Linux provides an excellent return on investment, or ROI. There is little or no cost on a "per-seat" basis. Unlike commercial operating systems, Linux has no royalty or licensing fees, and a single Linux distribution on CD-ROM can form the basis of an enterprisewide software distribution, replete with applications and productivity software. Custom corporate CD-ROMs can be easily crafted to provide specific installs on enterprisewide hardware. This feature alone can save hundreds of thousands, if not millions of dollars in Information Service/Information Technology costs—all without the threat of a software audit from the commercial software monopoly, or the need for licensing accounting and controls of base operating system installations.

- Linux can be put to work on the desktop. Linux, in conjunction with its supporting graphical networking protocol and interface, the X Window System, has worked well as a consumer UNIX-like desktop operating system since the mid-1990s. The fact

that UNIX is ready for the consumer desktop is now confirmed with the introduction, adoption, and rapid maturation of Apple Computer's BSD UNIX-based Mac
OS X—supported, according to Apple, by more than 3,000 OS X-specific programs,
known as native applications. This book's CD-ROMs contain more than 1,300 software packages, including Internet connection utilities, games, a choice of three
different office suites, thousands of fonts, and hundreds of graphics applications.

- Linux can be put to work as a server platform. Linux is fast, secure, stable, scalable,
  and robust. Latest versions of the Linux kernel easily support multiple-processor
  computers (optimized for eight CPUs), large amounts of system memory (up to 64GB
  RAM), individual file sizes in excess of hundreds of gigabytes, a choice of modern
  journaling file systems, hundreds of process monitoring and control utilities, and the
  (theoretical) capability to simultaneously support more than four billion users. IBM,
  Oracle, and other major database vendors all have versions of their enterprise software available for Linux.

- Linux has a low entry and deployment cost barrier. Maintenance costs can also be
  reduced as Linux works well on a variety of PCs, including legacy hardware, such as
  some Intel-based 486 and early Pentium CPUs. Although best program performance
  will be realized with newer hardware, as clients may be recompiled and optimized
  for Pentium-class CPUs, base installs can even be performed on lower-end computers
  or embedded devices with only 8MB of RAM. This feature provides for a much wider
  user base, extends the life of older working hardware, and can help save money for
  home, small business, and even corporate users.

- Linux appeals to a wide hardware and software industry audience. Versions of Linux
  exist for nearly every CPU. Embedded systems developers now turn to Linux when
  crafting custom solutions using ARM, MIPS, and other low-power processors. Linux
  is the first full operating system available for Intel's new Itanium CPU, and ports
  have been available for HP/Compaq's Alpha and Sun Microsystem's SPARC CPUs for
  some time. PowerPC users regularly use the PPC port of Linux on IBM and Apple
  hardware.

- Linux provides a royalty free development platform for cross-platform development.
  Because of the open source development model and availability of free, high-quality
  development tools, Linux provides a low-cost entry point to budding developers and
  tech industry startups.

- Big-player support in the computer hardware industry from such titans as IBM now
  lends credibility to Linux as a viable platform. IBM has enabled Linux on the
  company's entire line of computers, from low-end laptops through "Big Iron" mainframes. New corporate customers are lining up and using Linux as part of enterprise-
  level computing solutions.

Look forward to even more support as usage spreads worldwide throughout all levels of business in search of lower costs, better performance, and stable and secure implementations.

Who This Book Is For

This book is for anyone searching for guidance on using Fedora Core, which is for Intel-based PC platforms. Although the contents are aimed at intermediate to advanced users, even new users with a bit of computer savvy will benefit from the advice, tips, tricks, traps, and techniques presented in each chapter. Pointers to more detailed or related information are also provided at the end of each chapter.

Fedora's installer program, named Anaconda, makes the job of installing Linux as easy as possible. However, if you're new to Linux, you might need to learn some new computer skills, such as how to research your computer's hardware, how to partition a hard drive, and occasionally, how to use a command line. This book will help you learn these skills and show you how to learn more about your computer, Linux, and the software included with Fedora. System administrators with experience using other operating systems will be able to use the information presented in this book to install, set up, and run common Linux software services, such as the Network File System (NFS), a File Transfer Protocol (FTP) server, and a Web server (using Apache).

What This Book Contains

Red Hat Fedora 3 Unleashed is organized into five parts, covering installation and configuration, system administration, system services administration, programming and productivity, and a reference section. A complete set of the Fedora Core CD-ROMs is included, so you'll have everything you need to get started. This book starts by covering the initial and essential tasks required to get Fedora installed and running on a target system.

If you're new to Linux, and more specifically, Fedora, first read the chapters under Part I, "Installation and Configuration." You'll get valuable information on

- An overview of Fedora and Linux and their roles in various computing environments

- Planning for an installation by examining hardware requirements and the need for organizing how the system is installed

- Detailed steps that take you by the hand on different types of installations

- Critical advice on key configuration steps to fully install and configure Linux to work with your system's subsystems or peripherals, such as pointers, keyboards, modems, USB devices, power management, and—for laptop users—PCMCIA devices

- Initial steps needed by new users transitioning from other computing environments

- Configuration and use of the X Window System, the graphical interface for Linux

Part II, "System Administration and Managing Services," is aimed at users familiar with Linux, but targets information specific to the Fedora distribution. Using the information in this part's five chapters, intermediate users will find out how to

- Control and track down problems during the boot process.

- Manage software, processes, and other system resources.

- Manage users and groups.

- Work with a new journaling file system and craft remote file system mounting strategies.

- Ensure high-availability and reduce data loss through proper choice of backup media and strategies.

More advanced users integrating Fedora Core with the Internet and networking will want to read Part III, "System Services Administration." These chapters provide critical information related to

- Establishing local and remote printing services

- Connecting a Fedora system to a network using a variety of hardware, such as serial, Ethernet, and wireless connections

- Managing a domain name server

- Connecting to the Internet, firewalling for security, and offering Internet connection services to remote users

- Managing a Web server

- Crafting database systems and managing databases

- Providing secure FTP service

- Handling electronic mail

- Providing Network News service

Part IV, "Programming and Productivity," expands on the capabilities provided by every Fedora system by covering

- Basic development tools used for native Linux program and cross-platform development.

- Using Perl scripts for a variety of administrative tasks.

- Crafting new Linux kernels and managing kernel modules.

- Productivity applications included with, and available for Fedora, including various office suites, scheduling, graphics and scanner manipulation clients, and personal digital assistant (PDA) connectivity.

- Multimedia applications, including how to use various audio and video clients included with Linux, and an exploration of the Linux gaming experience.

- Using Linux to emulate other operating systems, or offering Linux services to other operating systems.

Part V, "Appendix," provides a list of Internet resources, such as top Linux Web sites, Usenet news groups, links to different Linux distributions, and other information, such as how to search for Linux-specific information.

Conventions Used in This Book

A lot of documentation is included with every Linux distribution, and Fedora Core is certainly no exception. Although the intent of *Red Hat Fedora 3 Unleashed* is to be as complete as possible, it is impossible to cover every option of every command included in the distribution. However, this book offers numerous tables of various options, commands, or keystrokes to help condense, organize, and present information about a variety of subjects.

This edition is also packed full of screenshots to illustrate nearly all Fedora- and Red Hat–specific graphical utilities—especially those related to system administration, or configuration and administration of various system and network services.

To help you better understand code listing examples and sample command lines, several formatting techniques are used to show input and ownership. For example, if the command or code listing example shows typed input, the input is formatted in boldface like this:

```
$ ls
```

If typed input is required, as in response to a prompt, the example typed input also is in boldface, like so:

```
Delete files? [Y/n] y
```

All statements, variables, and text that should appear on your display use the same bold-face formatting. Additionally, command lines that require root or superuser access are prefaced with a pound sign like this:

```
# printtool &
```

Command-line examples that can be run by any user are prefaced with a dollar sign ($), like so:

```
$ ls
```

The following elements provide you with useful little tidbits of information that relate to the discussion of the text.

> **NOTE**
>
> Notes will give you additional information that you might want to make note of as you are working, augment a discussion with ancillary details, or help point you to an article, whitepaper, or other online reference for more information about a specific topic.

> **TIP**
>
> A tip can contain special insight or a time-saving technique, as well as information about items of particular interest to you that you might not find elsewhere.

> **CAUTION**
>
> A caution will warn you about pitfalls or problems before you run a command, edit a configuration file, and choose a setting when administering your system.

> **Sidebars Can Be Goldmines**
>
> Just because it's in a sidebar doesn't mean that you won't find something new. Be sure to watch for these elements that bring in outside content that is an aside to go along with the discussion in the text. You'll read about other technologies, Linux-based hardware, or special procedures to make your system more robust and efficient.

Other formatting techniques used to increase readability include the use of italics for placeholders in computer command syntax. Computer terms or concepts also are italicized upon first introduction in text.

Finally, you should know that all text, sample code, and screenshots in Red Hat Linux and Fedora Unleashed were developed using Fedora and open-source tools.

Read on to start learning about and using the latest version of Fedora Core. Experienced users will want to consider the new information presented in this edition when planning or considering upgrades. New users, or users new to Fedora, will benefit from the details presented in this book.

PART I

Installation and Configuration

IN THIS PART

CHAPTER 1	Introducing Fedora	13
CHAPTER 2	Preparing to Install Fedora	27
CHAPTER 3	Installing Fedora	53
CHAPTER 4	Post-Installation Issues	81
CHAPTER 5	First Steps with Fedora	117
CHAPTER 6	The X Window System	159

CHAPTER **1**

Introducing Fedora

IN THIS CHAPTER

- What Is Fedora Core?
- Fedora for Business
- Fedora in Your Home
- Getting the Most from Fedora and Linux Documentation
- Fedora Developers and Documentation
- Reference

Welcome to *Red Hat Fedora 3 Unleashed!* Fedora Core is a new, unique Linux distribution and the first product of The Fedora Project, an open-source, community-driven project sponsored by Red Hat, Inc. Fedora Core, or more simply, Fedora, is a base Linux distribution available free over the Internet from http://fedora.redhat.com.

Fedora represents an evolution in the business direction of its sponsor, Red Hat, Inc. For nearly 10 years, Red Hat provided copies of its commercial Linux distribution, Red Hat Linux, free over the Internet. All that changed in October 2003 when Red Hat discontinued the sale and free distribution of its consumer-oriented Red Hat Linux.

As the company has since its inception, Red Hat, Inc. then released all of its work on the freely licensed software in the former consumer distribution. The work, which was to be a new version of Red Hat Linux, was then moved to a new Web site and subsequently was reborn as Fedora Core. Red Hat, Inc. now focuses its efforts on enterprise and corporate Linux-based products and services, but again, continues to make source code available for all of its products that are under an open-source license.

Red Hat's Enterprise Linux is a series of software products aimed for corporate and enterprise migration, deployment, and use. Although all Linux distributions could be considered the same underneath, as all use the Linux kernel, Red Hat, Inc. takes special pains to create, test, sell, and support commercial Linux distributions optimized for deployment on multiple hardware and CPU architectures. These high-performance enhancements include hardware-tweaked Linux kernels, fail-over and load-balancing clustering, and integrated Java support—essential for mission-critical applications and production environments.

About Red Hat, Inc.

Red Hat, Inc., is one of the world's foremost open-source development houses, and returns nearly all of its development efforts back to the Linux development community.

The company has been involved in many different open-source and GNU GPL projects, such as the Apache Web server, the glibc software libraries, the GNU Network Object Model Environment (GNOME), various GNU software tools and packages, the Linux kernel and device drivers, the PostgreSQL database system, and the Red Hat Package Manager (RPM).

Red Hat also supports many other projects by providing FTP service and Web hosting and is one of the few companies actively promoting and using the open-source business development model. This means that although many of its products are free, revenue streams are derived from spin-off and related technologies and services. These pursuits include embedded development (the open-source eCos operating system), training and certification programs such as the Red Hat Certified Engineer (RHCE) track, commercial software development, fee- and subscription-based support, consulting, and advanced software products, such as an advanced e-commerce platform, secure Web server, credit card verification system (CCVS), and the Red Hat Database.

One possible reason for the success of Linux could be "Best hack wins." In other words, software that works well, fills a critical need, is readily available in source form, and is distributed under a free software license (such as the GNU GPL) will quickly spread and see extensive use. The growth in popularity and widespread adoption of Linux around the world is a testament to quality, licensing, and need for Linux.

UNIX enjoyed a similar rapid-fire adoption after it was distributed in the early 1970s and fulfilled user needs on a number of fronts. However, its licensing was restrictive, caused much grief in some open-source communities (such as education), and continues to spawn problems to this day.

Here's the bottom line: You're holding nearly $1 billion worth of software in your hands. That's one estimate of what it would cost to develop as complete an operating system, graphical interface, and related software to equal the operating system included with this book.

It wasn't long ago that any new major project involving use of Linux by big business, government (on any level), or academia would have been big news. Today Linux is increasingly turned to by IS/IT strategists for computing solutions. Linux and related open-source software rules the Internet. Linux is the host platform of choice for traditional server operations. It is poised to take over the desktop, occupying the number-two spot behind a monolithic software entity.

NOTE

The list of Linux projects, efforts, and partnerships reads like a Who's Who of the software industry: Amazon, Ameritrade, Borland, Computer Associates, Dell, Hewlett-Packard/Compaq, IBM, Oracle, and SAP are just some of the enterprise-level players using Linux. Linux is also a key ingredient and shares an ever-increasing portion of server hardware sales from all large vendors, such as IBM, Hewlett-Packard/Compaq, and Dell.

What Is Fedora Core?

Fedora is the natural successor to Red Hat Linux and incorporates many of the features and software tools included with previous Red Hat Linux distributions. Red Hat Linux spawned many imitators in the Linux world in the past decade, and many of these imitators have gone on to create credible products and distributions.

As you learn in this chapter, Fedora is one of the most up-to-date Linux distributions available on the Internet. Here, you see why Fedora can be a good choice for a variety of computing environments and how, when combined with advances provided by the latest Linux kernel, can provide multitiered support for the academic, home, small business, and even corporate user.

Inside Fedora Core

A complete copy of the Fedora Core distribution requires eight CD-ROMs, but only the first four are necessary for a full install of the operating system. Half of the distribution consists of source code for all included software. There are more than 1,450 separate software packages in Fedora Core. This distribution comprises the Linux kernel, installation utilities, thousands of pages of documentation, several thousand fonts, a comprehensive graphical networking interface, and several thousand individual commands and clients.

Fedora incorporates a number of changes and adds new features compared to the last version of Red Hat Linux. This new distribution provides a base or "core" framework operating system and desktop comprised entirely of free software. Fedora includes the Bluecurve desktop theme and has an improved consistency in the two major graphical desktops available for use: the GNU Network Object Model Environment (GNOME) and the K Desktop Environment (KDE).

You can expect an extensive amount of Linux software to be supported by Fedora, and it is expected to eventually have a quite extensive library of contributed software packages outside of the Fedora Core release. This means that your first three Fedora Core CD-ROMs are just the beginning of a large collection of Linux software!

> **NOTE**
>
> Read more about GNOME and KDE in Chapter 6, "The X Window System."

Fedora provides the latest version of the X Window System, and its server, X11R6 7.0, which sports improved and integral font handling. The Linux desktop has never looked better, and you'll notice the difference when you browse the Web, use one of a dozen or so word processors and text editors included with Fedora, or view text at the command line in a terminal window.

If you're a veteran Red Hat user, you'll feel at home with Fedora, as it includes Red Hat's comprehensive suite of graphical administrative programs. The tools, shown in Table 1.1, combine and expand on the capabilities of standard Linux system utilities, and are intended for use by the root operator (known as the *superuser*) to administer a Fedora system. The software takes the place of (and in some cases upgrades and augments) many of the legacy command-line based tools traditionally used on a UNIX system. You'll see how to use these tools throughout this book.

TABLE 1.1   Red Hat Software Tools Included with Fedora Core Graphical Administration Tools

Name	Description
neat	Creates, edits, manages network devices
system-config-authentication	Manages user information and authentication protocol
system-config-bind	Configures domain name service
system-config-boot	Manages boot loading
system-config-date	Sets date, time zone
system-config-display	Configures X to work with your PC hardware
system-config-httpd	Apache Web server administration
system-config-keyboard	Configures keyboard type
system-config-kickstart	Creates automated install script
system-config-language	Sets system language
system-config-mouse	Configures mouse type, features
system-config-netboot	Configures network booting
system-config-network	Manages system network devices, settings
system-config-nfs	Configures network file system
system-config-packages	Manages system software
system-config-printer	Creates, edits, manages printers
system-config-proc	Manages kernel settings, processes
system-config-rootpassword	Sets, changes root password
system-config-samba	Manages a session message block (SMB) server
system-config-securitylevel	Configures firewall service
system-config-services	Starts, stops, restarts, or sets boot services
system-config-soundcard	Configures Fedora for sound
system-config-time	Sets system date, time zone
system-config-users	Manages system users
system-switch-mail	Toggles use of sendmail or postfix email services

Fedora includes Internet programs such as Mozilla, the open-source Web browser, along with productivity applications such as Ximian's Evolution, a mail, contact, and calendaring client, and OpenOffice.org, a Microsoft-compatible open-source office suite. You'll find all these, and many more applications on this book's CD-ROMs.

Other major features are the inclusion of the latest GNU gcc compiler system, supporting C/C++ language program development. You'll also get the newest major version of the Apache Web server, and the Common Unix Printing System (CUPS), which supports more than 1,000 different printers.

Fedora Core, as the next generation of Red Hat Linux 9, is slated for upgrades two to three times per year, according to the Fedora Project. In reality, however, work never ceases on the distribution because open-source developers, along with Red Hat engineers, will cross-pollinate Red Hat's Enterprise Linux and Fedora with software package upgrades, security updates, and bug fixes. Fedora's free, online upgrade system will be available via the Internet.

Red Hat, Inc., uses a 12- to 18-month release cycle for Enterprise Linux. This cycle is required to provide third-party application developers time to test, deploy, and market products. In the past, Red Hat has used a 6-month release schedule for the consumer version of Red Hat Linux, with a 3–4 month beta cycle for development and testing. Fedora Core will have a similar schedule, as the Fedora Project has stated it intends to "produce time-based releases of Fedora Core about 2–3 times a year."

As a Fedora user, you'll be able to quickly and easily obtain the latest software for your system at any time using a variety of commands and software management tools:

apt-get—The APT command-line software package tool from The Debian Project, used to upgrade, install, check, or remove software

system-config-packages—Red Hat's graphical package manager, used to install or remove applications (see Table 1.1)

rpm—The Red Hat Package Manager, which uses a database of installed packages to manage software on your system

up2date—Red Hat's Red Hat network update manager

yum—The Yellowdog Updater Modified, an automated software package manager based on RPM technology that resolves RPM dependencies

---

Distribution Version and Kernel Numbering Schema

There is a specific numbering system for Linux kernels, kernel development, and Fedora's kernel versions. Note that these numbers bear no relation to the version number of your Fedora Linux distribution. Fedora distribution version numbers are assigned by the Fedora Project, whereas most of the Linux kernel version numbers are assigned by Linus Torvalds and his legion of kernel developers.

To see the date your Linux kernel was compiled, use the uname command with its -v command-line option. To see the version of your Linux kernel, use the -r option. The numbers, such as 2.6.7-1, represent the major version (2), minor version (6), and patch level (7). The final number, (1), is the developer patch level and is assigned by the Fedora Project.

Even minor numbers are considered "stable" and *generally* fit for use in production environments, while odd minor numbers (such as a Linux 2.7 source tree) represent versions of the Linux kernel under development and testing. You will only find stable versions of the Linux kernel included with this book. You can choose to download and install a beta (test) version of the kernel, but this is not recommended for a system destined for everyday use. Most often, beta kernels are installed to provide support and testing of new hardware or operating system features.

Features of the Fedora Install

Installing Fedora can be accomplished in a number of ways. Many new users choose to simply boot from the first CD-ROM. The Fedora installer, named Anaconda (because it is written in the Python programming language), provides a default graphical interface for the installation process. The installer may be used to perform various initial actions before proceeding to an install, such as

- **Testing the CD-ROM media**—Useful for testing the integrity of your copies of the Fedora CD-ROMs. If you download .iso images of the Fedora CDs, you can also use an MD5SUM client to compare the prepublished checksums for the media against your .iso files.

- **Testing your PC's memory**—Useful for ensuring that your PC is in good form with functioning memory. Linux will use every available byte of RAM, and you want to make sure that you don't run into problems after the operating system is installed.

- **Updating the installer before the install**—In some cases, it might be necessary to use the latest version of the installer to work around a bug or problematic hardware, and this option can be used for a new version of the installer even though it is not on CD-ROM.

- **Rescuing the system**—In instances where a bootloader configuration has failed, or for some reason that system will not boot, the installer can be used to boot to a rescue mode; the existing file system can then be mounted and data can then be rescued or the system reconfigured to resolve the problem.

- **Specifying hardware "workarounds"**—Various options at the installer command line can be used to get around problematic or unsupported hardware posing an obstacle to your install.

- **Specifying an install method**—Fedora Core can be installed from a hard drive partition or over a network using FTP, NFS, HTTP or virtual networking.

See Chapter 3, "Installing Fedora," for specific details about various installer options. After the initial install and several screens to set install options, you can then choose a class of installation, such as

- **Custom**—This option is used to install your own selection of software packages, which can be useful to trim unwanted software from your new Fedora system.

- **Upgrade**—Use this option to upgrade an existing Red Hat system with the new Fedora desktop and software packages.

- **Server**—Select this option to create a Web, File Transfer Protocol (FTP), Network File System (NFS), or other server.

- **Personal Desktop**—Choose this install to use the new Fedora desktop and to create an Internet or multimedia workstation.

- **Workstation**—Choose this class to install development software, such as the GCC compiler suite and other programming tools to create a development system.

Fedora's installation process also allows you to install Linux in a variety of ways, using a text-based or graphical interface. See Chapter 3 to see how to install using CD-ROM, a hard drive, or a network. See Chapter 2, "Preparing to Install Fedora," for some important considerations to help you prepare to install Fedora.

Fedora File System Features

Fedora also uses the ext3 file system, developed by Dr. Stephen C. Tweedie and used by Red Hat's Enterprise Linux products. ext3 supports a form of low-level storage data handling known as *journaling*, previously only available under very expensive computer platforms. Journaling is accomplished using a variety of techniques, but the end result aims to ensure that data remains intact on the disk despite a system crash, power outage, or other mishap.

However, because Fedora is designed to be flexible and accommodating of all new Linux technologies, you can use other file systems for your workstation or server. This includes IBM JFS, a journaled file system designed for servers and used on many enterprise-level platforms. If you want to take advantage of fast restarts and enjoy good performance and reliability, JFS can be used as an alternative to ext3. However, ext3 offers benefits such as quick switching between legacy ext2 file systems and widespread use in the Linux community.

> **NOTE**
>
> More information about IBM's JFS file system for Linux can be found at
> http://oss.software.ibm.com/jfs/.

> **NOTE**
>
> Read a presentation by Red Hat's Dr. Stephen Tweedie, the creator of ext3, titled, "EXT3, Journaling File system" at http://olstrans.sourceforge.net/release/
> OLS2000-ext3/OLS2000-ext3.html for more details. You can also read how ext3 is used with the 2.4-series Linux kernel by browsing to Andrew Morton's page at http://
> www.zip.com.au/~akpm/linux/ext3/index.html.

Other journaling file systems should be supported by Fedora (such as reiserfs) and will have similar features.

Fedora also supports the creation of large RAID arrays, both via software using one or more storage devices and using hardware with specific device controllers. You can also use Logical Volume Management, or LVM, a sophisticated file system handling feature that allows parts of the file system (directory layout) to span one or more portions of separate physical storage media. This feature also allows resizing of the resulting partitions if system resource requirements change after initial configuration, and while the pertinent file systems are unmounted or mounted.

Other benefits of using Fedora are the inclusion digital signature verification of RPM packages (for enhanced security), RPM package dependency resolution suggestion (to more easily fix dependency diagnosis), and the `privoxy` server (to help filter out unwanted Web page pop-ups, and so on).

Fedora for Business

Linux has matured over the last 10 years, and features considered essential for use in enterprise-level environments, such as CPU architecture support, file systems, and memory handling, have been added and improved. The addition of virtual memory (the capability to swap portions of RAM to disk) was one of the first necessary ingredients, along with a copyright-free implementation of the TCP/IP stack (mainly due to BSD UNIX being tied up in legal entanglements at the time). Other features quickly followed, such as support for a variety of network protocols.

Fedora includes a Linux kernel that has the capability to use multiple processors. This allows you to use Fedora in more advanced computing environments with greater demands on CPU power. This kernel will support at least eight CPUs, but in reality, small business servers usually only use dual-CPU workstations or servers. However, Fedora has the capability to run Linux on more powerful hardware.

Fedora will automatically support your multiple-CPU Intel-based motherboard, and you'll be able to take advantage of the benefits of Symetric Multi-Processors (SMP) for software development and other operations.

The Linux kernels included with Fedora can use system RAM sizes up to 64GB, allow individual file sizes in excess of 2GB, and can host the demands of—theoretically, billions—of users.

Businesses that depend on large-scale, high-volume, and high-availability systems can now turn to Red Hat's Enterprise Linux products for stable, robust, scalable, and inexpensive solutions for various platform hosting. Storage in the terabyte range, no lengthy file system checks, and no downtime are just a few of the minimum requirements in such environments.

However, Fedora can be used in many of these environments by customers with widely disparate computing needs. Some of the applications for Fedora include desktop support, small file, print, or mail servers, intranet Web servers, and security firewalls deployed at strategic points inside and outside of company LANs.

Commercial Red Hat customers will benefit from Red Hat, Inc.'s engineering and support teams, as Red Hat works closely with many computer industry leaders, such as HP, Fujitsu

Limited, and IBM. This makes Red Hat Enterprise Linux work very well on a wide range of computers such as laptops, mid-range Intel Xeon and Itanium platforms, and some of the most powerful enterprise-class servers in the world.

Red Hat also develops platform and development tools for other CPUs, such as the Xstormy16 CPU from Sanyo, NEC's VR5500 MIPS, Motorola's 128-bit AltiVec and Book E PowerPC e500, SuperH, Inc.'s SuperH SH-5, and Intel's Xscale-based chips.

Red Hat Linux in Government

Red Hat Linux has a presence in many different government entities at different levels across the world. For example, the New Jersey State Police uses a Red Hat–based Oracle system, whereas India's Centre for Development of Advanced Computing uses Red Hat Linux in its high-performance computing lab.

Use of Linux is expanding rapidly in the U.S. federal sector. Red Hat Linux is on the General Services Administration Schedule, and the U.S. National Security Agency has offered a series of kernel patches to assist in building secure versions of Linux. Other agencies and departments, such as the U.S. Air Force, U.S. Marine Corps, Federal Aviation Administration, NASA, Departments of Defense, Agriculture, and Energy also use Linux-enabled platform solutions from IBM and Hewlett-Packard/Compaq.

Small business owners can earn great rewards by stepping off the software licensing and upgrade treadmill and adopting a Linux-based solution. Using Fedora not only avoids the need for licensing accounting and the threat of software audits, but also provides viable alternatives to many different types of commercial productivity software.

Using Fedora in a small business setting makes a lot of sense for additional reasons, such as not having to invest in cutting-edge hardware in order to set up a productive shop. Fedora easily supports older, or *legacy*, hardware; and savings are compounded over time by avoiding unnecessary hardware upgrades.

Additional savings will be realized, as software and upgrades are free. New versions of applications can be downloaded and installed at little or no cost, and office suite software is free.

Fedora is easy to install and network, and it "plays well with others," meaning that it will work well in a mixed-computing situation with other operating systems.

A simple Fedora server can be put to work as an initial partial solution, or made to mimic file, mail, or print servers of other operating systems. Clerical help will quickly adapt to using familiar Internet and productivity tools, while your business gets the additional benefits of stability, security, and a virus-free computing platform.

By carefully allocating monies spent on server hardware, a productive and efficient multiuser system can be built for much less than the cost of comparable commercial software. Combine these benefits with support for laptops, PDAs, and remote access, and you'll find that Fedora supports the creation and use of an inexpensive, yet efficient work environment.

Fedora in Your Home

Fedora's Personal Desktop install will copy a special set of preselected software packages onto your hard drive that is suitable for Small Office Home Office, or SOHO, users. This option provides a wealth of productivity tools for document management, printing, communication, and personal productivity.

The Personal Desktop installation requires nearly 2GB of hard drive space, but should easily fit onto smaller hard drives in older Pentium-class PCs. The install also contains administrative tools, additional authoring and publishing clients, a variety of editors, a GNOME-based X11 desktop, support for sound, graphics editing programs, and graphical and text-based Internet tools. You can customize the selection to include or sidestep installation of unwanted software. See Chapter 3 for details.

Connecting to the Internet is a snap, and Fedora supports modem dialup and other broadband connections, such as cable modems or Digital Subscriber Lines (DSL). See Chapter 15, "Internet Connectivity," for more information. When you do connect, you can do so in relative confidence, as firewall protection from malicious intruders and other attackers can be thwarted by running the `lokkit` or `system-config-securitylevel` clients. See Chapter 13, "Network Connectivity," to see how to set up a network.

If you have a digital camera, run the `gphoto2` client to download, organize, and manage your digital images. You can then fine-tune your pictures by editing them using one of the finest digital image editors in the world: The Gimp. See Chapter 26, "Multimedia Applications," for details on editing graphics.

Fedora can be used for a variety of purposes, and every user has different needs. Some of them might be esoteric. For example, I use Fedora to: program and manage thousands of frequencies on various radio scanners and amateur radio transceivers, run a high-frequency shortwave radio via a graphical interface on the desktop, host wireless (802.11b) printing for several workstations, manage digital recording of favorite TV episodes, provide secure remote access via a firewall, and listen to favorite music playlists via a server.

Getting the Most from Fedora and Linux Documentation

Nearly all commercial Linux distributions include shrink-wrapped manuals and documentation covering installation and configuration. You won't find official documentation included on the CD-ROMs provided with this book. However, you can read or get copies of assorted manuals or topic discussions online through `http://fedora.redhat.com/projects/docs/`. There you'll find the Fedora Project's links to various documentation projects.

You can also turn to Red Hat's official manuals and guides, particularly for Red Hat Linux 9, for interim information about Red Hat tools (such as those listed in Table 1.1) at `http://www.redhat.com/docs/manuals/linux/RHL-9-Manual/`. Note that the names that began with `redhat-config` in Red Hat Linux 9 now begin with `system-config` in Fedora Core.

Documentation for Fedora (and many Linux software packages) is distributed and available in a variety of formats.

Some guides are available in Portable Document Format (PDF) and can be read using Adobe's Acrobat Reader for Linux or the `xpdf` client. Guides are also available as bundled HTML files for reading with a Web browser such as `links`, KDE's `konqueror`, GNOME's `galleon`, or Mozilla. Along with these guides, Red Hat, Inc. provides various tips, Frequently Asked Questions (FAQs), and HOWTO documents.

You'll find traditional Linux software package documentation, such as manual pages, under the `/usr/share/man` directory, with documentation for each installed software package under `/usr/share/doc`.

Linux manual pages are compressed text files containing succinct information about how to use a program. Each manual page generally provides a short summary of a command's use, a synopsis of command-line options, an explanation of the command's purpose, potential caveats or bugs, the name of the author, and a list of related configuration files and programs.

For example, you can learn how to read manual pages by using the `man` command to display its manual page like so:

```
$ man man
```

After you press Enter, you'll see a page of text appear on the screen or in your window on the desktop. You can then scroll through the information using your keyboard's cursor keys, read, and then press the q key to quit reading. More information about using the command line will be found in Chapter 5, "First Steps with Fedora."

Many of the software packages also include separate documents known as HOWTOs that contain information regarding specific subjects or software.

If the HOWTO documents are simple text files in compressed form (with filenames ending in `.gz`), you can easily read the document by using the `zless` command, which is a text *pager* that allows you to scroll back and forth through documents (use the `less` command to read plain text files). You can start the command by using `less`, followed by the complete directory specification and name of the file, or *pathname*, like this:

```
$ less /usr/share/doc/httpd-2.0.50/README
```

To read a compressed version of this file, use the `zless` command in the same way:

```
$ zless /usr/share/doc/attr-2.4.1/CHANGES.gz
```

After you press Enter, you can scroll through the document using your cursor keys. Press the q key to quit.

If the HOWTO document is in HTML format, you can simply read the information using a Web browser, such as mozilla, or if reading from a console using the links or lynx text-only Web browsers, like this:

```
$ links /usr/share/doc/stunnel-4.0.5/stunnel.html
```

The links browser offers drop-down menus, accessed by clicking at the top of the screen. You can also press the q key to quit.

If the documentation is in PostScript format (with filenames ending in .ps), you can use the gv client to read or view the document like this:

```
$ gv /usr/share/doc/iproute-2.4.7/ip-crefs.ps
```

Finally, if you want to read a document in Portable Document Format (with a filename ending in .pdf), use the xpdf client like this:

```
$ xpdf /usr/share/doc/xfig/xfig-howto.pdf
```

> **NOTE**
>
> This book was developed and written using a complete install of all the software included with Fedora. You can use the CD-ROMs included with this book for your install or download your own copy, available as ISO9660 images (with filenames ending in .iso), and burn it onto 700MB CDRs.
>
> Along with the full distribution, you'll get the complete source code to the Linux kernel and source for all software in the distribution—more than 21 million lines of C and nearly 5 million lines of C++ code. Browse to http://fedora.redhat.com/download/ to get started.

Fedora Developers and Documentation

If you are interested in helping with the Fedora Project, you can assist in the effort by testing beta releases, writing documentation, and contributing software for the core or contributed software repositories. You should have some experience in installing Linux distributions, a desire to help with translation of documentation into different languages, or be able to use various software project management systems, such as CVS.

Reporting problems with Fedora Core during development is also part of the process! Bug reports are welcome and can be submitted according to guidelines outlined in Tammy Fox's and Havoc Pennington's Fedora Project Developer's Guide, found at http://fedora. redhat.com/participate/developers-guide/.

Writing documentation for Fedora requires a bit of discipline and experience with open-source document publishing tools. You can read more about the process by browsing to `http://fedora.redhat.com/participate/documentation-guide/`.

Mailing lists are also available as an outlet or forum for discussions about Fedora. The lists are categorized. For example, general users of Fedora Core can discuss issues on the *fedora-list* mailing list. Beta testers communicate via the *fedora-test-list,* developers via the *fedora-devel-list,* and documentation contributors via the *fedora-docs-list.* Mailing lists can be subscribed to by sending mail to `name_of_the_list-request@redhat.com`.

Reference

Each chapter in this book includes a "Reference" section listing links to additional or related information covered in the text. You can use these links to learn more about Fedora, Linux, and related technologies. You can also use the "Reference" section material to build custom sets of bookmarks to use while browsing or researching for more information about Linux:

`http://www-1.ibm.com/linux/`—Information from IBM regarding its efforts and offerings of Linux hardware, software, and services.

`http://www.dwheeler.com/sloc`—David A. Wheeler's amazing whitepaper covering the current state of GNU/Linux, its size, worth, components, and market penetration.

`http://fedora.redhat.com`—Home page for the Fedora Project, sponsored by Red Hat, Inc., and your starting point for learning more about Fedora.

`http://www.redhat.com/solutions/info/casestudies/`—A listing of government and corporate Red Hat, Inc. customers.

`http://fedora.redhat.com/docs/`—Web page with links to current Fedora documentation and release notes.

`http://www.tldp.org`—The definitive starting point for the latest updates to generic Linux FAQs, guides, and HOWTO documents.

`http://www.ciac.org/ciac/`—The U.S. Dept. of Energy's Computer Incident Advisory Web site, with details of security problems and fixes pertaining not only to Red Hat Linux, but many other operating systems. This site is useful for federal software contractors, developers, and system administrators.

`http://www.justlinux.com/`—One site to which new Linux users can browse to learn more about Linux.

CHAPTER **2**

Preparing to Install Fedora

IN THIS CHAPTER

- Planning Your Fedora Deployment
- Hardware Requirements
- Preparing for the Install Process
- Partitioning Before and During Installation
- Using Red Hat's `kickstart` Installation Method
- Reference

Proper preparation and planning before installation can pay big dividends later on. If you are deploying Linux using Fedora Core, you'll need to decide how you want to put it to use.

Installing Linux for the first time can seem daunting to inexperienced users or system administrators, but this chapter shows you how easy the installation can be if you make some simple preinstallation plans and decisions. Disk partitioning can be one of the most unfamiliar parts of the installation process, but it's an essential step toward configuring a multiplatform system. As you learn in this chapter, disk partitioning also is a manageable process when you take the time to plan ahead.

In this chapter, you learn how to prepare for an effective, efficient Fedora Core installation. The chapter begins with a checklist of considerations that can help you to plan how you will use Linux after installation, so you can plan for making the right choices during the installation itself. This chapter also outlines some of the basic hardware requirements for using Linux (with some specifics for the Fedora Core release on this book's CD-ROMs), and it highlights some potential hardware problems you can plan for—and avoid. The chapter also walks you through a general overview of the installation process, and it offers in-depth planning advice for partitioning your hard disk to support different configurations.

As you are about to learn, Fedora is a flexible Linux distribution that can adapt to a variety of hardware configurations and can be installed in a number of ways.

Planning Your Fedora Deployment

Before planning the specific steps of an installation, you need to make decisions about the type of deployment you want to undertake. Computing needs dictate the type of hardware and software solutions required for a successful deployment, but before making the plunge, some hard questions need to have been asked and answered, such as, "How will you use Fedora?" You learn more about these issues in the sections that follow. These sections also include a table you can use as a predeployment planning checklist and some final advice for planning the installation.

Business Considerations

Choosing an operating system for use in your business is an important decision. Migration to or adoption of a new hardware or software platform can have immediate and long-term effects on your organization. There is no magic formula to use in the decision-making process when contemplating a move, and freelance consultants, small business owners, medium-sized business, corporations, and other large business organizations will have different computing resources, objectives, and needs. For many businesses, computers are a critical and sometimes central component of business operations.

> **NOTE**
>
> Browse to Red Hat's Migration Center at http://www.redhat.com/solutions/migration/ to read success stories, market analyses, and technical reports on using Red Hat's Enterprise Linux products for business.

Fortunately, Linux is flexible enough to provide a full or partial migration and supports all of the major computing services required in today's business operations. Some of the more traditional services include electronic mail, file servers, network services (including firewalls), printing, Web hosting (Internet- and intranet-based), and database servers. If you desire commercial support, Red Hat, Inc. can provide one, more, or all of these services. Linux can also be put to work in stages to ease migration issues such as training or support.

Some of the ideas, issues, and concerns surrounding the Linux deployment are listed in Table 2.1. One consideration is the context of how Fedora will be put to work. In other words, how will the new operating system fit in with your existing hardware and software needs? Another consideration is the level of consensus in management and user willingness to change to or adopt a new software environment. However, this issue can be sidestepped by making the transition as invisible as possible to users, such as when Linux-based Web, file, or printing services replace existing servers.

The transition cost is another issue to consider. Fedora offers flexibility and reliability, but transitioning to a new platform can have unforeseen costs. Linux detractors sometimes point to added total cost of ownership (TCO) factors, such as support and training, and argue that these issues add significantly to the cost of a Linux migration. Although there might be some additional support costs, again, training might not be an issue, especially if Linux is invisibly deployed. Hidden charges might be offset by the low cost in licensing, deployment, scaling, maintenance, resource requirements, and support of legacy hardware.

You should know what you're going to do with Linux before you install it. In other words, what is the objective of your migration? If Fedora will be used as a replacement platform for network services, what services will be replaced? What types of applications will need support if Fedora is deployed as a new desktop for administrative users?

Some research might be required beforehand, and you might want to compare software performance of desired services against your existing infrastructure, using a time lined prototype install or deployment. Such testing is not a special requirement unique to a Linux migration, but a normal part of a careful consideration process before investing time and effort—which will represent your major costs because Linux and its major software are free.

System Considerations

Fedora is a perfect solution for many computing needs. However, choosing an operating system platform mandates consideration of a number of issues. Some of these issues are listed in Table 2.1. For example, how you choose to use Fedora will affect your choice of computer hardware, might affect your network configuration, and could dictate software policy issues (such as access, security, and allowable protocols).

Linux-based operating systems can be used to provide many different services. For example, one server might be boot management for a thin-client network in which workstations boot to a desktop by drawing a kernel and remotely mounted filesystems over a network. This mechanism is not supported out of the box, so some effort can be expended if such a system is required. Other services more easily implemented (literally in an hour or less) could be centralized server environments for file serving, Web hosting for a company intranet, or bridging of networks and routing services.

Linux supports nearly every network protocol, which enables it to be used to good effect even in mixed operating system environments. The security features of the Linux kernel and companion security software also make Linux a good choice when security is a top priority. Although no operating system or software package is perfect, the benefit of open source of the kernel and other software for Linux allows peer review of pertinent code and rapid implementation of any necessary fixes. Even with the secure features of Linux, some effort will have to be made in designing and implementing gateways, firewalls, or secure network routers.

Fedora can serve as a development platform for applications, e-commerce sites, new operating systems, foreign hardware systems, or design of new network devices using Linux as an embedded operating system. Setting up workstations, required servers, source code control systems, and industrial security will require additional effort.

Hardware compatibility can be an issue to consider when setting up a Linux server or building a Linux-based network. Fortunately, enlightened computer equipment manufacturers are beginning to realize that Linux-based operating systems (like other open-source operating systems such as BSD) are increasingly popular, support open standards, and offer technologies that can help rapid introduction of products into the market (through third-party developer communities).

Fedora Core can help ease system administration issues during migration. The latest suite of Red Hat's configuration utilities provide intuitive and easy to use graphical interfaces for system administration of many common services, such as networking, printing, and Windows-based file sharing. Fedora can also be used to support legacy application environments, such as DOS, if required.

User Considerations

Humans are creatures of habit. So it can be hard to transition a workforce, customer base, or other community to a new environment. The Fedora desktop, however, provides a friendly and familiar interface with menus and icons that new users can readily learn and put to work.

Part of the migration process can involve addressing user concerns, especially if Linux will take over the desktop. Fedora can be deployed in stages to make the migration process a bit easier, but the issue of user training will need to be addressed early on. This is especially true if users will be required to develop new skills or be aware of any caveats when using Linux (such as deleting all files in one's home directory). Although Fedora can be configured to provide a "turn-key" desktop in which only several graphical applications (such as a Web browser, organizer, or word processor) can be used, some users will want and need to learn more about Linux.

You can turn to formal Linux training from commercial vendors. System administrators can get training directly from Red Hat (go to `http://www.redhat.com/training`). For other issues concerning Linux in larger computing environments, browse to Linas Vepstas's Linux Enterprise Computing pages at `http://linas.org/linux/`.

A Predeployment Planning Checklist

Table 2.1 provides a minimal checklist you can use to help plan a deployment.

TABLE 2.1   Deploying Fedora

Consideration	Description
Applicability	How is Fedora going to be used?
Boot Management	Will remote booting be required?
Connectivity	Will the system be an intranet? Bandwidth requirements? Wireless? Mobile?
Context	How does this install fit in with academic, business, or corporate needs?
Consensus	Are managers and potential users onboard with the project?

TABLE 2.1   Continued

Consideration	Description
Comparison	Is this install part of platform comparison or benchmarking?
Development Platform	Will development tools be used?
Embedded Device	Is it an embedded device project?
Hardware	Are there any special hardware or device interfacing requirements?
Finance	How much is in the budget? Will cost comparison be required?
Marketing	Will a product or service be offered as a result?
Networking	What type of networking will be required?
Objective	Is there a specific objective of the install?
Power Management	Any special power or energy requirements?
Prototype Project	Is this a prototype or test install?
Public Relations	Does the public need to know?
Quality of Service	Is high availability or data integrity an issue?
Roadmap	What other steps might precede or follow the install?
Reporting	Are follow-up reports required?
Security	What level or type of security will be required?
Server	Is this a server installation?
Site Considerations	Does the location provide needed temperature and security, or does it even matter?
Software	Are any special device drivers needed for success?
Storage	Are there size or integrity needs? Has a backup plan been devised?
Timeline	Are there time constraints or deadlines to the install?
Training	Will special training be required for users or administrators?
Users	How many and what type of users are expected?
Workstation	Is this a workstation or personal desktop install? Is the workstation portable?

Don't forget to address follow-up issues on your migration roadmap. You should pay attention to how satisfied or how well new users, especially those new to Linux, are adapting if a new desktop is used. However, if Fedora is deployed in a mixed environment, many users might not even know (or need to know) that Linux is being used!

Planning the Installation

There are many factors in favor of using Fedora Core as a computing solution. The current distribution can fill many different roles on various tiers and hardware platforms because its preconfigured installation scripts are a tailored fit for development, workstation, e-commerce, server, and mobile platforms—only the required software will be installed.

Addressing concerns beforehand can help quell any worries or fears felt by new users. Some key factors for a successful installation include

- **Preparation**—Thoroughly discuss the migration or deployment, along with benefits, such as greater stability and availability of service.

- **Preconfiguration**—If possible, give users a voice in software choices or categories and poll for comments regarding concerns.

- **Correct installation**—Ensure that the installed systems are working properly, including access permissions, password systems, or other user-related issues and interaction with the deployment.

- **The right hardware to do the job**—Make sure that users have the hardware they need for their work, and that computers match the tasks required. For example, developers will have workstation requirements vastly different from administrative personnel.

Hardware Requirements

Fedora can be installed on and will run on a wide variety of Intel-based hardware. This does not include pre-Pentium legacy platforms, but many older PCs, workstations, rack-mounted systems, and multiprocessor servers are supported. Small, medium-sized, and even large-scale deployments of specially tuned Linux distributions are available through a number of companies such as IBM, which offers hardware, software, and service solutions (with more than 200 software solutions for clustering applications alone).

TIP

It is always a good idea to explore your hardware options extensively before jumping onboard with a specific vendor. You can buy computer hardware with a Linux distribution preinstalled. At the time of this writing, Dell Computers offered Linux systems (such as desktop PCs and notebooks) through `http://www.dell.com/redhat/`. IBM also offers Linux on its product line, and more information can be found through `http://www.ibm.com/linux/`. To find HP and preinstalled Linux systems, browse to `http://www.hp.com/linux/`. You can also buy low-cost desktop PCs with Linux through Wal-Mart's online store at `http://www.walmart.com` (click to select the electronics department).

In the first section of this chapter, you learned to consider how Linux can be used in your environment and how you can prepare for its installation and deployment. These considerations also play a role in determining the types of hardware you need in your installation. But the type of deployment you choose also determines the hardware required for a successful deployment of Linux—and post-deployment satisfaction. The range of Linux hardware requirements and compatible hardware types is quite wide, especially when you consider that Linux can be used with mainframe computers as well as embedded devices.

Meeting the Minimum Fedora Core Hardware Requirements

The Fedora Project publishes general minimum hardware requirements for installing and using its base distribution in a file named RELEASE NOTES on the first CD-ROM, or available at `http://fedora.redhat.com/docs/release-notes/`. For the current release, your PC should at least have a 200MHz Pentium CPU, 750MB hard drive space, and 64MB RAM for using (and installing) Fedora without a graphical interface. For obvious reasons, a faster CPU, larger capacity hard drive, and more RAM are desired. Servers and development workstations require more storage and RAM.

Using Legacy Hardware

If you have an older PC based on an Intel 486 CPU with only 32MB RAM and a 500MB hard drive (which can be hard to find nowadays), you can install other Linux distributions such as Debian from The Debian Project at http://www.debian.org.

> **CAUTION**
>
> One caveat is that if you prepare a hard drive with Linux in a PC with one CPU, such as a Pentium, and then install the drive in a PC with a 486 CPU, you should either make sure that a 486-based Linux kernel is installed, or perform a post-install of an appropriate kernel after moving the hard drive.

Installing Fedora on legacy hardware will be easier if you choose to use more recent Pentium-class PCs, but even older Pentium PCs can be used and purchased at a fraction of their original cost. Such PCs can easily handle many mundane but useful tasks. Some of the tasks suitable for older hardware include

- Acting as a firewall, router, or gateway
- Audio jukebox and music file storage server
- Handling electronic mail
- Hosting a remote printer and providing remote printing services
- Network font server
- Providing FTP server access
- Remote logging capture
- Secondary network-attached backup server
- Serving as an Intranet (internal LAN) Web server
- Unattended dial-up gateway, voice mailbox, or fax machine
- Use as a "thin client" workstation for basic desktop tasks

Older PCs can handle any task that does not require a CPU with a lot of horsepower. To get the most out of your hardware, don't install any more software than required (a good idea in any case, especially if you're building a server). To get a little performance boost, add as much RAM as economically and practically feasible. If you can't, cut down on memory usage by turning off unwanted or unneeded services. You can also recompile a custom Linux kernel to save a bit more memory and increase performance (see Chapter 24, "Kernel and Module Management").

> **NOTE**
>
> Fedora does not include XFree86 3.3.6. This version might be important because older, legacy video cards are no longer supported in the newer X11R6 7.0 distribution. You can download version 3.3.6 from The XFree86 Project, Inc. through `http://ftp.xfree86.org/pub/XFree86/3.3.6/binaries/`. Make sure to choose the appropriate version for your operating system!

Planning for Hard Drive Storage for Your Fedora Installation Class

Making room for Fedora requires you to decide on how to use existing hard drive space. You might decide to replace existing hard drives entirely, for example, or you might decide to use only one operating system on your computer, making partitioning unnecessary. A full install from this book's CD-ROMs will require at least 7GB hard drive space just for the software, so if you plan to install everything, a 10GB hard drive could be ideal for a workstation. Note that depending on how you plan to use Linux, a smaller capacity disk can be used, or a disk capacity many times the size of your system will be required.

> **NOTE**
>
> The following recommended installations and minimal storage requirements are based on a full install of the freely available version of Fedora Core distributed on the Internet. The copy of Fedora included with this book is the same, but you may find many additional software packages available from third-party Fedora contributors. Installing additional software will impact your storage requirements.

The Fedora installer offers a choice of installation types or *classes*, and each has its own hard drive storage requirements:

- **Workstation**—You'll need a minimum of 3GB hard drive storage, but much more if you choose to install everything. This installation is intended for developers and other users who want to use the entire spectrum of Linux software offered by the distribution.

- **Personal Desktop**—This is a new installation class for SOHO (small office/home office) users that installs a basic graphical desktop, along with requisite office and Internet productivity software; you'll need around 2.3GB of storage if you don't customize the default software selections.

- **Server**—You need at least 1.1GB of storage for the operating system and server software, but you also must take into consideration other storage requirements. For example, if you plan to run a Web site with a lot of graphics or serve other files, you might need to add storage to your system or accommodate remotely mounted storage locally.

- **Custom**—This installation supports a minimal install requiring a little over 600MB; however, you can also choose to install all the software in the distribution; in which case, you'll need 7GB or more of storage, along with several hundred megabytes of free space for temporary files.

The storage requirements for each of these classes can be revised somewhat, depending on the X desktop environment you choose (such as KDE or GNOME). Choosing the Custom install will let you choose specific software packages from the group package categories. Here are some software packages you might want to consider passing up in the installation process for a minimalist system:

- X Window System
- GNOME Desktop Environment
- KDE Desktop Environment
- Graphical Internet
- Office/Productivity
- Documentation
- Sound and Video
- Graphics
- All development software or libraries

Checking Hardware Compatibility

Fedora software for Intel-based PCs is compiled for the minimum x86 platform supported by the Linux kernel.

> **NOTE**
>
> The compatibility information in this chapter relates to Fedora Core. Other distributions might have different storage and CPU requirements.

Specific issues regarding Linux hardware compatibility can be researched online at a number of sites. Red Hat, Inc. offers a hardware compatibility database at `http://hardware.redhat.com/hcl/`. You can select hardware class, manufacturer, the version of Red Hat Linux, platform, and status of support.

Other sites, such as the Linux-USB device overview at `http://www.qbik.ch/usb/devices/`, offer an interactive browsing of supported devices, and printer compatibility can be researched at LinuxPrinting.org at `http://linuxprinting.org/`. Some hardware categories to consider in your research include

- Controller cards—Such as SCSI, IDE, Firewire

- CPUs—Intel, AMD, and others

- Input devices—Keyboards

- Modems—External, PCMCIA, PCI, and controllerless workarounds

- Network cards—ISA, PCI, USB, and others

- Pointing devices—Mice, tablets, and possibly touchscreens

- Printers—Various printer models

- RAM—Issues regarding types of system memory

- Sound cards—Issues regarding support

- Specific motherboard models—Compatibility or other issues

- Specific PCs, servers, and laptop models—Compatibility reports

- Storage devices—Removables, fixed, and others

- Video cards—Console issues (X compatibility depends on version of X11R6 or vendor-based X distribution used)

If you have a particular laptop or PC model, you should also check with its manufacturer for Linux support issues. Some enlightened manufacturers now offer a Linux operating system preinstalled, or have an in-house Linux hardware certification program. Laptop users will definitely want to browse to Linux on Laptops at `http://linux-laptop.net/`.

If you cannot find compatibility answers in various online databases, continue your research by reading the Linux Hardware HOWTO at `http://www.tldp.org/HOWTO/Hardware-HOWTO/`.

At that address, you'll find loads of general information and links to additional sources of information. Keep in mind that when PC hardware is unsupported under Linux, it is generally because the manufacturer cannot or will not release technical specifications or because no one has taken the time and effort to develop a driver. If you hit a roadblock with a particular piece of hardware, check the hardware manufacturer's support Web pages, or Google.com's Linux pages at `http://www.google.com/linux`. You can then type in a specific search request and hopefully find answers to how to make the hardware work with Linux. This is also a good way to research answers to questions about software issues.

Preparing for Potential Hardware Problems

Fedora Core will work "out-of-the-box" with nearly every Intel-based Pentium PC mother-board and laptop. Drivers for thousands of different types of hardware peripherals are included. But you can sometimes run into problems if Linux doesn't recognize a hardware item, if Fedora doesn't correctly initialize the hardware, or if an initialized item is incorrectly configured. For these reasons, some hardware items are prone to creating problems during an install. In the sections that follow, you learn some important pointers for avoiding these problems or resolving those that do occur.

Controllerless Modems

As you read earlier, most Linux hardware-related installation problems stem from a lack of technical specifications from the manufacturer, thwarting efforts of open-source developers to create a driver. In the recent past, one hardware item that triggered both types of difficulties was the controllerless modem, also colloquially known as a WinModem. The good news is that modem chipset manufacturers have been more forthcoming with driver details. Some original equipment manufacturers, such as IBM, have made a concerted effort to provide Linux support. Support for the ACP Mwave modem, used in ThinkPad 600/Es and 770s, is included in the Linux kernel. Drivers have been developed for many of the controllerless modem chipsets that formally didn't work with Linux.

If a driver isn't available for your controllerless modem, you have a few options. You can download the driver's source code and build the driver yourself. Alternatively, you can download a binary-only software package and install the driver.

Some controllerless modems might also need to be initialized and configured using a separate utility program. The modem, if supported, should work normally after installing and configuring the driver.

You can research Linux support for controllerless modems by browsing to
`http://www.linmodems.org/`.

Universal Serial Bus Devices

Fedora supports hundreds of different universal serial bus, or USB 1.1, devices. USB is a design specification and a protocol used to enable a host computer to talk to attached peripherals. Because of lack of manufacturer and device ID information or lack of technical specifications regarding certain chipsets, some devices might not work with Fedora. USB 1.1 devices are designed to support data transfer speeds between 1.5 and 12Mbps.

Common USB devices include cameras, keyboards, mice, modems, network interfaces, printers, scanners, storage devices, video (such as webcams), and hubs (to chain additional devices). Some problematic USB devices (at the time of this writing) include

- **Wireless**—Many 802.11b wireless USB network adapters, with the exception of those using Atmel chipsets

- **Scanners**—Many Canon, Visioneer, and Hewlett-Packard USB scanners

- **Webcams**—Selected Logitech and Creative Labs webcams

Although some enlightened manufacturers are aware of opportunities in the Linux marketplace, most still do not support Linux. It pays to determine Linux support before you buy any USB device; again, research Linux USB support and its current state of development by browsing to http://www.qbik.ch/usb/devices/.

The newer USB 2.0 specification enables devices (such as hard and CD drives) to use speeds up to 480Mbps. Fedora supports USB 2.0 with the ehci-hcd kernel module. This driver, in development since early 2001, enables the use of many forms of newer USB 2.0 devices as long as you have a supported USB controller. Check out the current state of Linux USB 2.0 support by browsing to http://www.linux-usb.org/usb2.html.

Motherboard-based Hardware

Small form factor PCs, thin-clients, notebooks, and embedded devices are part of a growing trend in the PC industry. Manufacturers are cramming more functionality into fewer chips in order to simplify design and lower power requirements. Today, many computers come with built-in video graphics, audio chipsets, and network interfaces, along with a host of peripheral support.

Common modern (1996–onward) PC motherboard form factors are designed according to industry-assigned specifications (usually from Intel) and are ATX (12 × 9.6 inches); MicroATX (9.6 × 9.6 inches); and FlexATX (9 × 7.5 inches). One of the newest and even smaller motherboard forms is from VIA Technologies, Inc.—the mini-ITX (approximately 6.5 × 6.5 inches), which has an embedded CPU. CPUs commonly used in all these motherboards will vary, and have different socketing requirements based on chipset pins: Socket 478 for K7-type CPUs (from AMD); Socket 370 for Pentium IIIs and Celerons from Intel, or C3s from VIA; and Socket 478 for Intel's Pentium 4s (early versions of which used a 423-pin socket). Older socket types are Socket A, Socket 7 (and Super 7), Slot 1, and Slot 2.

Fortunately, nearly all controllers, bridges, and other chipsets are supported by Linux. Although flaky or unsupported built-in hardware can (usually) be sidestepped by installing a comparable PCI card component, cutting-edge notebook users are at the most risk for compatibility problems because internal components are not user-replaceable. Potential pitfalls can be avoided through careful research (vote with your money for Linux-compatible hardware), or by choosing PC motherboards with a minimum of built-in features, and then using PCI (Peripheral Component Interconnect) or AGP (Accelerated Graphics Port) cards known to work.

CPU, Symmetric Multiprocessing, and Memory Problems

Fedora supports all Intel-based Pentium CPUs. Code is included in the Linux kernel to recognize the CPU type when booting, and to then implement any required fixes to overcome architecture bugs (such as the now-infamous divide-by-zero error). After you install Fedora Core, you can also rebuild the Linux kernel to specifically support and take advantage of the host PC's CPU. You might not realize extreme improvements in computational speed, but you'll be assured that Linux is crafted for your CPU's architecture, which can help stability and reliability. Details about rebuilding the Linux kernel are in Chapter 24. Some of the Intel-based CPUs with specific supporting code for Linux include those from Advanced Micro Devices, Transmeta, and VIA Technologies.

Fedora's Linux kernel also should automatically recognize and use the amount of installed RAM. The Linux kernel should also recognize and map out any memory holes in system memory (perhaps used for video graphics).

If you are installing Fedora on a working, stable PC, you should not have any problems related to the system's memory. If you're putting together a new system, you need to avoid combining or configuring the system in ways that will interfere with its ability to process data. Some issues to be aware of are

- Do not expect similar CPU performance across product lines from different manufacturers, such as AMD or VIA. Some CPU models offer better floating point or integer math operations, which are important for a number of CPU-intensive tasks (such as graphics, audio, and video rendering or conversion). If you need better performance, try to find a faster CPU compatible with your motherboard, or switch to a CPU with better floating point unit (FPU) performance.

- Overclocking can cause problems with overheating, memory access, and other hardware performance, and it isn't a good idea for any Linux system. Overclocking is a popular geek pastime and a great way to get a bit of performance boost out of slower CPUs by altering voltage settings and/or clock timings via the BIOS. You can try to push your CPU to higher speeds, but this approach is not recommended if your aim is system stability. The Linux kernel will report the recognized CPU speed upon booting (which you can view using the dmesg command).

- Along the same lines, CPU and motherboard overheating will cause problems. Proper attachment of the CPU's heatsink using a quality thermal paste (never use thermal tape), along with one or more fans providing adequate airflow will lessen the chance of hardware damage and system failure.

- You can run into problems if you switch the type of CPU installed in your computer, and especially if your PC's BIOS does not automatically recognize or configure for newly installed mainboard hardware and components. In some instances, a system reinstall is warranted, but BIOS issues should be resolved first.

- Not all CPUs support symmetric multiprocessing (SMP). Fedora readily supports use of two or more CPUs, and during installation will automatically install an appropriate Linux kernel. You can avoid problems by reading the Linux SMP HOWTO (available through http://www.tldp.org). Note that some CPUs, such as the current crop of VIA C3s, may not be used for SMP. Also, SMP motherboards require that all CPUs be identical. This means that you'll need two identical CPUs in order to take advantage of SMP.

- Faulty or bad memory will cause Linux kernel panics or Signal 11 errors (segmentation faults) causing a system crash or a program to abort execution. Linux is quite sensitive to faulty hardware, but will run with great stability in a correctly configured system with good hardware. Problems can arise from incorrect BIOS settings, especially if video memory must occupy and use a portion of system RAM. Always install quality (and appropriate) memory in your PC to avoid problems.

Preparing and Using a Hardware Inventory

Buying a turnkey Linux solution is one way to avoid hardware problems, and many vendors are standing by, ready to prescribe solutions. However, managing deployments aimed at using existing hardware requires some information collection.

If you are a small business or individual user, you are well-advised to prepare detailed checklists of existing hardware before attempting a migration to Linux. Not only will you benefit from the collected information, but you might also be able to sidestep or anticipate problems before, during, or after installation. Problems are most likely to occur with newer hardware, cutting-edge hardware such as new motherboard chipsets and video cards, or extraneous hardware such as operating system–specific scanners, printers, or wireless devices.

Table 2.2 provides a comprehensive checklist you can use to take inventory of target hardware, such as the computer and any peripherals. Veteran Linux users can take the collected information to build custom systems by adding known hardware or substituting cheaper but equivalent hardware.

TABLE 2.2   System and Peripheral Inventory Checklist

Item	Errata
Audio Devices	Microphone:
	Line out:
	Line in:
BIOS	Type:
	Revision:
	ACPI:
	APM:
CD-ROM Drive	Brand:
	Type:
CD-RW Drive	Brand:
	Type:
	CDR Write Speed:
	CD Re-Write Speed:
	CD-ROM Read Speed:
DVD Drive	Brand:
	Type:

TABLE 2.2   Continued

Item	Errata
DVD+/-RW Drive	Brand:
	Type:
Digital Camera	Brand:
	Model:
	Interface:
CPU	Brand:
	Socket Type:
	Speed:
Firewire (IEEE 1394)	Chipset:
	Device(s):
IrDA Port	Device number:
	Port IRQ:
Keyboard	Brand:
	Type:
Laptop	Brand:
	Model:
	Hibernation partition:
Legacy Ports	Parallel type:
	Parallel IRQ:
	RS-232 number(s):
	RS-232 IRQ(s):
Mice	Brand:
	Type:
Modem	Brand:
	Type:
Motherboard	Brand:
	Type:
	Chipset:
Monitor(s)	Brand:
	Model:
	Horizontal freq:
	Vertical freq:
	Max. Resolution:
Network Card	Wireless:
	Brand:
	Type:
	Speed:
PCI Bus	Version:
	Model:
	Type:

TABLE 2.2   Continued

Item	Errata
PCMCIA	Controller:
	Cardbus:
	Brand:
	Type:
Printer(s)	Brand:
	Model:
System RAM	Amount:
	Type:
	Speed:
S-Video Port	X Support:
Scanner	Brand:
	Model:
	Interface type:
Sound Card	Chipset:
	Type:
	I/O Addr:
	IRQ:
	DMA:
	MPU Addr:
Storage Device(s)	Removable:
	Size:
	Brand:
	Model:
	Controller(s):
	Rotational Speed:
Storage Device	Type:
Controller Tablet	Brand:
	Model:
	Interface:
Universal Serial Bus	Controller:
	BIOS MPS Setting:
	BIOS Plug-n-Play Setting:
	Device(s):
Video Device(s)	Brand:
	Model:
	Xinerama:
	Chipset:
	VRAM:

Use the checklist in Table 2.2 as a general guideline for recording your computer's hardware and other capabilities. You can get quite a bit of information through hardware manuals or other documentation included with your PC, video, sound, or network interface card. Don't worry if you can't fill out the entire checklist; Fedora will most likely recognize and automatically configure your PC's hardware during installation. Much of this information can be displayed by the dmesg command after booting. However, some of these details, such as your video card's graphics chipset and installed video RAM, can come in handy if you need to perform troubleshooting. You can also use the list as a post-installation check-off sheet to see how well Fedora works with your system.

Preparing for the Install Process

The basic steps in installing Fedora are to plan, install, and configure. You'll need to decide on how to boot to an install and how much room to devote to Linux. Then perform the install (a sample step-by-step installation is in Chapter 3, "Installing Fedora") and afterward, configure your system to host new users and specific software services. Much of the initial work will be done during the install process because the installer, Anaconda, will walk you through partitioning, configuring the desktop, and configuration of any recognized network adapter.

There are many different ways to install Fedora Core, and selecting an installation method might depend on the equipment on hand, existing bandwidth, or equipment limitations.

Here are some of the most commonly used installation methods:

- **CD-ROM**—Using a compatible CD-ROM drive attached to the computer (laptop users with an external CD-ROM drive will need PCMCIA support from a driver disk image included under the first CD-ROM's images directory).

- **DOS**—By using LOADLIN, you can boot to a Linux install by pointing LOADLIN to use a Fedora installation kernel and ramdisk. Run the DOS batch file, autoboot.bat, found under the dosutils directory on the first Fedora CD-ROM.

- **Network file system (NFS)**—You can install Fedora from a remotely mounted hard drive containing the Fedora Core software. To do this installation, you need to have an installed and supported network interface card, along with a boot floppy with network support. (You learn how to make boot floppies later in this section of the chapter.)

- **File Transfer Protocol (FTP)**—As with an NFS install, installation via FTP requires that the Fedora software be available on a public FTP server. You also need an installed and supported network interface card, along with a boot floppy with network support.

- **Hypertext Transport Protocol (HTTP)**—As with the FTP and NFS installs, installation via HTTP requires that the Fedora software be available on an accessible Web site. You also need an installed and supported network interface card, along with a boot floppy with network support.

- **Installation via the Internet**—If you have the bandwidth, it may also be possible to install Fedora via the Internet; however, this method might not be as reliable as using a local area network (LAN) because of availability and current use of Fedora Project or other servers on mirror sites.

- A **hard drive partition**—By copying the .iso images to a hard drive partition, you can then boot to an install.

- **Preinstalled media**—It is also possible to install Linux on another hard drive and then transfer the hard drive to your computer. This is handy, especially if your site uses removable hard drives or other media.

> **NOTE**
>
> More esoteric installations may be possible. Some Linux distributions support booting to an install via an Iomega Zip drive, via the Parallel Port Internet Protocol (PLIP), and even a null-modem cable supporting the Serial Line Internet Protocol (SLIP) or Point-to-Point Protocol (PPP). Browse to http://www.tldp.org and read Gilles Lamiral's PLIP Install HOWTO to see how to install Red Hat 7.0 using your PC's parallel port. Once installed, you can then try to upgrade to Fedora.

After booting and choosing to use either a graphical or text-based install interface, the installation procedure is nearly the same for each type of install. Chapter 3 walks you through a typical CD-ROM–based installation.

Preparing to Install from a CD-ROM

Installing Fedora can be as simple as inserting the first CD-ROM into your computer's CD drive and rebooting the computer. But if you choose this method, you should first make sure that your system's BIOS is set to boot from CD-ROM.

Entering the BIOS to make this change is usually accomplished by depressing a particular key immediately after turning on the computer, such as Del or F2. After entering the BIOS, navigate to the BIOS Boot menu, perhaps such as that shown in Figure 2.1.

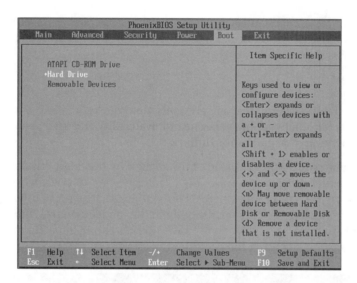

FIGURE 2.1   To boot to an install using your Fedora Core CD-ROM, set your BIOS to have your computer boot using its CD drive.

Partitioning Before and During Installation

Partitioning your hard drive for Linux can be done before or during installation.

If you plan to prepare your partitions before installing Linux, you'll need to use commercial partitioning software. Some of the popular commercial software you can use to create Linux partitions are PowerQuest's PartitionMagic or VCOM Products' Partition Commander. Alternatively, it may be possible to prepare partitions before installing Fedora by using the free FIPS.EXE command.

If you want to partition a hard drive using an existing Linux system, you can attach the hard drive to a spare IDE channel, and then use the Linux fdisk or GNU parted partitioning utilities. Both utilities offer a way to interactively partition and prepare storage media. Linux recognizes IDE hard drives using a device name such as /dev/hda (for the master device on IDE channel 0), /dev/hdb (for the slave device on IDE channel 0), /dev/hdc (for the master device on IDE channel 1), and /dev/hdd (for the slave device on IDE channel 1).

If a new hard drive is properly attached to your PC and you then boot Linux, you can see if the kernel recognizes the device by viewing the output of the dmesg command. You can then use fdisk with the device name to begin partitioning like so:

```
# fdisk /dev/hdb
```

Note that you'll need root permission, and in this example, the new drive is attached as a slave on IDE channel 0. Do not change partitioning on your root device, or you'll wreck your system! The `fdisk` command is interactive, and you can press **m** to get help when using the utility. You can use `parted` in much the same way if you specify the `i`, or interactive option on the command line like so:

```
# parted -i /dev/hdb
```

To get help when using `parted` interactively, press **?** or type **help** followed a command keyword. The `parted` command has other helpful features, such as the ability to copy a filesystem directly from one partition to another.

Finally, you can prepare partitions ahead of installation by booting your system using a live Linux distribution (such as the LNX Bootable Business Card, available at `http://www.lnx-bbc.org/`) and then using a native Linux utility such as `fdisk` to partition your drive. For details on using the `fdisk` partitioning utility and alternative software tools to partition your hard drive, see the section "How to Access and Manipulate the Partition Table" in Chapter 10, "Managing the Filesystem."

TIP

You can use the first Fedora CD-ROM to perform other tasks aside from installing Linux. The CD-ROM features a rescue mode and can also be used to partition and prepare a hard drive for Linux. See Chapter 3.

NOTE

It is possible to create a dual-boot configuration, which allows the choice of booting Fedora and another operating system, such as Windows XP. To configure your system for dual-booting, you must first install Windows and then install Linux. Note that many Windows system-restore CD-ROMs will wipe out all data on your hard drive, including Linux. During installation of Fedora, you install the GRUB Linux bootloader in the primary drive's Master Boot Record, or MBR. When properly configured, GRUB allows your system to reboot to Windows or Linux. See Chapter 24 for information on using GRUB, or browse to `http://www.gnu.org/software/grub/manual/` to read the GRUB manual.

CAUTION

Before you begin partitioning your drive, get your safety nets in order. First, back up all critical data! Any changes to your system's hard drive or operating system put your existing data at risk. To prevent the loss of time and resources that inevitably follow data loss, do full backups before you make any changes to your system. Create a bootdisk during the install (you'll be asked before the install finishes), so you'll be able to at least boot Linux if something goes wrong. See Chapter 11, "Backing Up, Restoring, and Recovery," for information on backups with Linux.

Choosing a Partitioning Scheme

Like deployment and installation of Linux, partitioning your hard drive to accept Fedora requires some forethought, especially if the target computer is going to be used other than as a home PC on which to learn Linux.

If Linux is to be the only resident operating system, you can have the installer automatically create and use a partition scheme according to the type of installation you select during the install. If you plan to have a dual-boot system in which you can boot Linux or another operating system, you'll need to manually partition your hard drive before and possibly during the install.

The simplest and most basic partitioning scheme for a Linux system requires a Linux native root partition and a swap partition. On a single-drive system with 10GB storage and 128MB RAM, the scheme might look like this:

```
Hard Drive Partition     Mount Point      Size
/dev/hda1                /                9.74GB
/dev/hda2                swap             256MB
```

On a system running Windows, the scheme might look like this:

```
Hard Drive Partition     Mount Point      Size
/dev/hda1                /mnt/dos         2GB
/dev/hda2                /                7.74GB
/dev/hda3                swap             256MB
```

> **CAUTION**
>
> Notebook users should be careful when partitioning. Many notebooks use a special partition equal to the size of install RAM in order to perform suspend-to-disk or other hibernation operations. Always examine your computer's initial partitioning scheme if configuring a dual-boot system, and leave the special partition alone! One way around this problem is to use a software suspend approach as outlined at http://swsusp.sourceforge.net/.

Hosting Parts of the Linux Filesystem on Separate Partitions

Your specific partitioning scheme will depend on how Fedora will be used. On a system being designed for expansion, greater capacity, or the capability to host additional software or users, you can use separate partitions to host various parts of the Linux file system. Some candidates for these separate partitions include

- /home—Users will store hundreds upon hundreds of megabytes of data under their directories. This is important data, perhaps even more so than the system itself. Using a separate partition (on a different volume) to store this user data helps make the data easier to find, and it segregates user and system data. You'll have to decide ahead of time how much storage to allocate to users. For a single workstation, you should reserve several gigabytes of storage.

- /opt—As the home directory for additional software packages, this directory can have its own partition or remote filesystem. Fedora does not populate this directory, but it might be used by other software packages you install later on. One gigabyte of storage should be adequate, depending on applications to be installed.

- /tmp—This directory can be used as temporary storage by users, especially if disk quotas are enforced; as such, it could be placed on its own partition. This directory can be as small as 100MB.

- /usr—This directory holds nearly all the software on a Fedora system and can become quite large if additional software is added, especially on a workstation configuration. Using a separate partition can make sense. A full install will require at least 6GB for this directory or more if additional software is added.

- /var—Placing this directory (or perhaps some of its subdirectories) on a separate partition can be a good idea, especially because security logs, mail, and print spooling take place under this tree. You should reserve at least one gigabyte of storage for /var, especially if using Fedora as a print server (as spooled documents will reside under /var/spool).

> **TIP**
>
> As a general rule, it is a good idea to segregate user and system data. Although a Linux system can be quickly restored, user data has a much greater value and can be much more difficult to replace. Segregating data can make the job of backing up and restoring much easier.

Using Red Hat's kickstart Installation Method

Automating the installation process can save system administrators a lot of time and effort during an initial deployment, upgrade, or maintenance cycle by managing multiple computers at one time. Fedora offers a highly automated installation technique called kickstart, developed by Red Hat, Inc., which can be used for unattended installation of Linux.

Red Hat's kickstart installation uses a single configuration file with a special, extensive syntax on a server, boot floppy, or other medium to install Fedora via CD-ROM, a hard drive partition, or a network connection. Using kickstart is easy and involves passing a kernel argument to the Fedora Linux boot kernel. The various arguments tell the boot kernel to look for a configuration file on floppy, a designated server, via a network, specific file, or CD-ROM.

You can use kickstart to install Fedora on one or more computers at the same time. First, set up a Web or FTP server with Fedora's installation files. For directions, see the section "Installing Using a Network" in Chapter 3. Next, create a network boot floppy using the techniques described in this chapter's "Creating a Boot and Auxiliary Driver Disk" section. Follow the directions given here (choosing an FTP install) and then copy the custom kickstart file to the network boot floppy. You can then use this floppy (and copies) to boot one or more PCs to a network install using your FTP server.

To begin the automated installation process, you create the configuration file that will be used by kickstart as an installation profile. You can configure the complex configuration file with Red Hat's Kickstart Configurator. To start the configuration, click the Kickstart item from the System Tools menu on the desktop, or run the system-config-kickstart or ksconfig command, like so:

```
# /usr/sbin/ksconfig
```

After you press Enter, you see the Kickstart Configurator dialog box, as shown in Figure 2.2.

Click to select various options, and then enter the specifics desired for the target system. Start by selecting the default system language, type of keyboard, mouse, and so on. Of course, automated installations work best when installing to similar equipment. When finished, press Ctrl+S, or use the Save file item from the File menu. The configuration will be saved with the name ks.cfg. When you use the kickstart installation method, the kickstart file will be read by computers booting to the install. The kickstart language covers nearly every aspect of an install with the exception of sound card, printer, or modem setup.

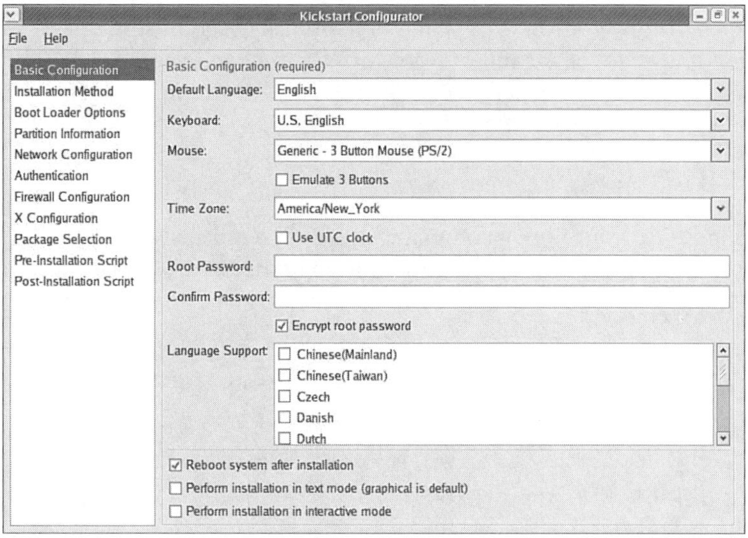

FIGURE 2.2   Red Hat's kickstart configuration tool, ksconfig, can be used to quickly and easily create installation profiles for use in automated installations.

For example, a portion of a `kickstart` file generated for an install might look like

```
#Generated by Kickstart Configurator

#System language
lang en_US

#Language modules to install
langsupport en_US

#System keyboard
keyboard us

#System mouse
mouse genericps/2

#System timezone
timezone --utc America/New_York

#Root password
rootpw --iscrypted $1$/n3yjyDV$AWoBZgRQq/lAxyRhX1JSM1
...
```

Note that not all the output of a sample `ks.cfg` is shown. However, you can see that this file will feed `kickstart` directions for an install, including an encrypted root password to be installed on the target system.

The next step is to copy your new `ks.cfg` to a boot disk created using one of the boot floppy images (found under the images directory on the first Fedora CD-ROM). You can do this with Linux by using the `mount` and `cp` commands. For example, take your boot disk, insert it into your PC, and then use the `mount` command (as root) like so:

```
# mount /mnt floppy
```

If Fedora has mounted your floppy automatically, you'll receive an error message such as `/dev/fd0 already mounted`. You can then simply copy the `ks.cfg` file to your floppy like so:

```
# cp ks.cfg /mnt/floppy
```

You can verify the contents of the floppy using the `ls` command like this:

```
# ls /mnt/floppy
boot.msg        general.msg      initrd.img       ks.cfg          ldlinux.sys
options.msg     param.msg        rescue.msg       snake.msg       splash.lss
syslinux.cfg    syslinux.png     vmlinuz
```

Then unmount the floppy using the `umount` command like so:

```
# umount /mnt/floppy
```

Remove the disk. It is now ready for use. When you use the disk to boot a PC, after booting, tell the install boot image that you'd like to perform a `kickstart` install like this:

```
linux ks=floppy
```

The installer will then use the specifications you outlined in the Kickstart Configurator and saved in `ks.cfg` to install Fedora.

Reference

The following is a list of references you can use to learn a bit more about partitioning, installation tools, and installing Fedora Core and Linux variants on a variety of hardware. You'll also find information about installation on hardware employed for embedded and mainframe solutions.

`http://www.redhat.com/solutions/migration/`—Red Hat's helpful Migration Center, with news, views, white papers, and other tips and research on migrating to a Linux solution.

`http://www.yale.edu/pclt/BOOT/DEFAULT.HTM`—A basic primer to partitioning that is operating system nonspecific.

`http://www-1.ibm.com/linux/`—Home page for Linux at IBM, with links to products, services, and downloads.

`http://www-124.ibm.com/developerworks/opensource/linux390/`—Home page for IBM S/390 Linux solutions.

`http://www.dell.com/linux/`—Dell Computer's Linux information pages.

`http://hardware.redhat.com/hcl/`—Entry point to Red Hat's hardware compatibility database.

`http://www.linux1394.org/`—Home page for the Linux Firewire Project, with information regarding the status of drivers and devices for this port.

`http://www.linux-usb.org`—Home page for the Linux USB Project, with lists of supported devices and links to drivers.

`http://elks.sourceforge.net/`—Home page for Linux for x286 and below CPUs, ELKS Linux.

`http://www.lnx-bbc.org`—Home page for the Bootable Business Card, a 50MB compressed Linux distribution that offers hundreds of networking clients, a live X session, Web browsing, PDA backup, wireless networking, rescue sessions, and file recovery.

`http://www.coyotelinux.com`—Home page for several compact Linux distributions offering firewalling and VPN services; the floppy-based distribution works quite well on older PCs and does not require a hard drive.

`http://www.freesco.org/`—Home page for a floppy-based Linux router solution that works on 386 PCs, requires only 6MB RAM, and provides bridging, firewalling, IP masquerading, DNS, DHCP, Web, telnet, print, time, and remote access functions.

`http://www.bitwizard.nl/sig11/`—A detailed overview of some root causes of Linux Signal 11 errors.

`http://www.gnu.org/software/parted/parted.html#introduction`—Home page for the GNU parted utility.

`http://www.linux.org/vendors/systems.html`—One place to check for a vendor near you selling Linux preinstalled on a PC, laptop, server, or hard drive.

CHAPTER **3**

Installing Fedora

IN THIS CHAPTER

- Before You Begin the Installation
- Choosing How to Install Fedora
- Step-by-Step Installation
- Login and Shutdown
- Reference

In this chapter, you learn how to do a basic installation of Fedora Core. You'll see how to boot and then install Fedora using the CD-ROMs included with this book. The chapter first shows how to prepare and research your install, choose a strategy on how Fedora will use your computer's hard drive, decide how to boot Fedora, and then how to complete the Fedora Core installation. You'll get a step-by-step walk-through of a sample installation, and then you learn how to log in to Fedora and shut down or reboot the system.

Before You Begin the Installation

Part of the process of installing Fedora Core (or any operating system for that matter) is to first research how well the new operating system will fit into an existing hardware environment, or if new hardware will be required to host the operating system. The following sections provide some basic points to consider when installing Fedora and augment the checklists and ideas presented in Chapter 2, "Preparing to Install Fedora."

You start by researching and documenting your hardware. This information can prove helpful later on during the installation.

Research Your Hardware Specifications

You should first have a basic understanding of your system's hardware, such as the type of mouse, keyboard, or monitor, the amount of installed system memory, and the size of the hard drive. You need to know the storage capacity of your hard drive in order to choose a partitioning scheme, for example. Knowing the difference between a PS/2 and USB mouse will ensure proper pointer configuration. Such information will help make the installation fast, efficient, and as trouble-free as possible.

Use the checklist shown in Table 2.2 in Chapter 2 to inventory or at least record some basic features of your system. Some items you'll need to know include the amount of installed memory, size of your hard drive, type of mouse, capabilities of the display monitor (such as maximum resolution), and number of installed network interfaces (if any).

Choose an Installation Type

You should also know what type of installation you plan to do beforehand (such as a workstation, server, firewall, gateway, router, development system, and so on). The type of install, or rather, the purpose of your intended install will dictate the type and amount of software installed (and also influence hard drive storage requirements).

For convenience, the Fedora installer offers a personal desktop, workstation, and server installation. Each type will install a set of preselected software libraries and applications. Use the custom installation option to select individual software packages and fine-tune your software selection. See Chapter 2 for details and hardware requirements for these installs.

> **NOTE**
>
> Although you can support nearly any operation (such as a development workstation or server) by installing all the software included with this book's CD-ROMs, this approach generally isn't a good idea unless you're testing new hardware or learning how to use Linux at home. The reason for this is that installing extraneous software not relevant to support-specific operations, especially in a business or production environment, can introduce security risks. For example, it would be unwise to have compilers and software development tools installed on an e-commerce Web server because successful intruders can simply upload and build malicious software with relative ease.

Choose Software Installation Options

Most new users with standalone Linux workstations will install all the software included with Fedora and depend on Red Hat's RPM technology (using up2date) or Fedora's support of yum to sort out and handle software dependencies (see Chapter 8, "Managing Software and System Resources," for more details about using these programs). Although Fedora is very stable and robust (read, doesn't crash), crafting an efficient, stable, and working system can sometimes require consideration about the type of software to use given your existing hardware. For example, don't expect to run a fully loaded multimedia workstation if you plan to use Fedora Core on an early Pentium-based PC. However, that same PC can easily support email, print, or FTP server operations and even perform light duty as an intranet documentation Web server.

Planning Partition Strategies

Part of planning a custom system involves implementing a partitioning strategy based on how you plan to use Fedora and, as previously mentioned, the capabilities of your existing hardware. For example, if you plan to host thousands of graphic images or audio files, how much storage will you need? If you plan to back up this collection, will you use a tape drive, burn copies of directories onto optical media, transfer files across a network, or will you simply copy the files to another hard drive?

If you are planning an installation for a corporate or enterprise-level environment, you must also consider future expansion or evolution of the system. You will want to craft a flexible system that can evolve with your business and its system needs.

Knowing how software is allocated on your hard drive for Linux involves knowing how Fedora organizes its *file system*, or layout of directories on storage media. This knowledge will help you make the most out of hard drive space; and in some instances, such as planning to have user directories mounted via NFS or other means, can help head off data loss, increase security, and accommodate future needs. Create a great system, and you'll be the hero of information services.

To plan the best partitioning scheme, research and know the answers to these questions:

- How much disk space does your system require?

- Do you expect your disk space needs to grow significantly in the future?

- Will the system boot just Fedora, or do you need a dual-boot system?

- How much data will require backup, and what backup system will work best? (See Chapter 11, "Backing Up, Restoring, and Recovery," for more information on backing up your system.)

CD-ROM Installation Jump Start

To install Fedora Core from the CDs included with this book, you must have at least a Pentium-class CPU, 800MB hard drive, and 64MB RAM. You'll need at least 128MB to install using Fedora's graphical installer. A 10GB hard drive can easily host the entire distribution, leaving about 3GB free for other data.

To begin the installation, set your PC's BIOS to boot from CD-ROM. Next, insert the first CD-ROM and boot your computer. Press Enter at the first screen and follow through the subsequent dialogs to install.

Remember or write down your system's root password. Also, even if you thoroughly test configuration of a graphical desktop during installation, you can choose to have Fedora boot to a text-based login (see the section "Step-by-Step Installation" later on). You can then start a graphical session after you finish the install, reboot, and log in. You can always set Fedora to boot to a graphical login later (see Chapter 6, "The X Window System," to see how).

If you have a floppy drive, create a boot disk during the install (see the "Step-by-Step Installation" section in this chapter). Finally, finish the install, remove the CD-ROM from your computer, and reboot. Then log in and enjoy Fedora!

The Boot Loader

You will need to decide how to boot your system. For example, you can boot Fedora from a hard drive or floppy disk using the default boot loader, the Grand Unified Boot Loader (known as GRUB), use a commercial boot loader (as discussed in Chapter 2), or choose to not use a boot loader at all. Not using a boot loader can make booting Fedora difficult, but not impossible. For example, you can use another operating system such as DOS to jump-start to a Fedora session.

A boot loader is most often installed in the master boot record (MBR) of an IDE hard drive, but can also be installed in the root Linux partition, or on a floppy disk. The boot loader can be used to pass essential kernel arguments to the Linux kernel for use during the boot process. Some arguments might include special disk geometry settings or specifying additional network interfaces. Fedora's boot loader, GRUB, supports special operations, such as booting from read-only memory (ROM) or flashed memory chips containing boot-loading code. Using a bootloader from a floppy disk will work with many PCs, but you should be aware that not all PC hardware BIOS supports booting via universal serial bus (USB) removable media or from a floppy disk. In fact, many PCs no longer include a floppy disk drive!

The GRUB loader works with all BSD UNIX variants and many proprietary operating systems. This utility also supports menuing, command lines, installed RAM detection, and diskless and remote network booting. GRUB also offers password protection.

> **NOTE**
>
> Red Hat's `mkbootdisk` command can be used to create floppy and CD-ROM boot media while using Linux. To do so, use the Linux kernel release number (returned by using the `uname -r` command) and a specified device. For example, to create a boot floppy, use the command like this:
>
> ```
> # mkbootdisk --device /dev/fd0 `uname -r`
> ```
>
> To create a CD-ROM boot image (which must then be burned onto a CDR or CDRW blank), use the command with its `-iso` option like this:
>
> ```
> # mkbootdisk --iso --device boot_cd.img `uname -r`
> ```

Fedora can also be booted from a DOS session using the LOADLIN program, a DOS PATH to the Linux kernel, and the location of Linux kernel, such as

```
LOADLIN c:\KERNEL\VMLINUZ root=/dev/hda2 ro
```

In this example, the kernel named VMLINUZ is loaded, and the second primary partition of the first IDE hard drive is specified at the root (/) partition of a Linux system.

> **NOTE**
>
> If you find that LOADLIN fails to boot Linux and complains about a large kernel size, you can either try using make bzimage to build a smaller kernel or rebuild a kernel that relies less on built-in features and more on loadable modules. See Chapter 24, "Kernel and Module Management," for more information.

When choosing a commercial boot loader, weigh its capabilities and options. A good boot loader will support multiple operating systems, the ability to boot different Linux kernels (in order to change the characteristics of a system or easily accommodate new hardware), password protection, custom boot displays, and sane defaults, such as requiring verification before overwriting existing configurations and accommodating other recognized filesystems or previously installed boot code.

If you run into trouble after installing Fedora Core, make sure to read the documentation for your boot loader to acquire any diagnostic information. Most boot loaders will report on any problems, and the solution might be commonly fixed. Your best (and least expensive) bet is to use GRUB because it is the default boot loader for Fedora Core.

Choosing How to Install Fedora

Fedora can be installed in a variety of ways using different techniques and hardware.

Most users will install Fedora by booting to the installation directly from a CD-ROM. Other options include

- Booting to an installation using a floppy diskette.

- Booting to an installation using Fedora's mini CD-ROM.

- Using a hard drive partition to hold the installation software.

- Booting from a DOS command line.

- Booting via a virtual network session. (See the file Release Notes included on the first Fedora Core CD-ROM for details.)

- Booting to an installation and installing software over a network using FTP or HTTP protocols.

- Booting to an installation and installing software from an NFS-mounted hard drive.

How you choose to install (and use) Fedora depends on your system's hardware, networking capabilities, corporate information service policy, or personal preference. The following sections describe the issues surrounding each of these types of installation.

Installing from CD-ROM

Most PCs' BIOS support booting directly from a CD-ROM drive, and offer the capability to set a specific order of devices (such as floppy, hard drive, CD-ROM, or USB) to search for bootable software. Turn on your PC, set your PC's BIOS if required (usually accessed by pressing an F or Del key after powering on), then insert Fedora Core's first CD-ROM, and boot to install Fedora.

To use this installation method, your computer must support booting from CD-ROM, and the CD-ROM drive must be recognizable by the Linux kernel. You can verify this by checking your BIOS and then booting your PC.

Older PCs with some CD-ROM drives might prove problematic when you desire to boot to an install using optical media. The good news is that this should no longer be a problem with most post-1995 personal computers. However, you can consult Table 3.1, which lists a driver disk image that can be used to support older drives.

The file boot.iso listed in Table 3.1 is a 4.5MB CD-ROM image found under the images directory on the first Fedora Core CD-ROM. The image can be burned onto a CDR, mini CDR, or business-card-sized CDR and supports booting to a network install. This is a convenient way to boot to a network install on a PC with a bootable CD-ROM drive, but no installed floppy drive, or when you don't want to use multiple floppies during an install requiring driver diskettes.

You burn the image onto optical media using the cdrecord command. For example, copy the file to your hard drive, insert a blank CDR into your CDRW drive, and then use a command line like so:

```
# cdrecord -v speed=4 dev=0,0,0 -data -eject boot.iso
```

This example will create a bootable CD-ROM, and then eject the new CD-ROM after writing the image. The speed (4 in this example) depends on the capabilities of your CD writing device. The device numbers are those returned by running cdrecord with its scanbus option, like so:

```
# cdrecord -scanbus
```

Installing Using a Network

Fedora can be installed using a local network (or even over the Internet if you have broadband access). You will need access to a Web, FTP, or NFS server hosting the installation packages. To boot to a network install, use a network boot floppy, a bootable CD-ROM created using the boot.iso boot image, or the first Fedora Core CD-ROM included with this book. Boot your PC with the boot floppy or, if you use CD-ROM, type **linux askmethod** at the boot prompt. Follow the prompts, and you'll then be asked to choose the type of network installation.

> **TIP**
>
> Just press Enter at the boot prompt if you boot to a network install using a CDR created with the boot.iso image. You'll boot a graphical network install.

To install using FTP, select the network IP address assignment for your target PC, such as DHCP, or manually enter an IP address along with optional gateway IP address and name-server addresses. You'll then be asked for the FTP site name. You can enter the name or IP address of a remote FTP server hosting the Fedora Core release. The name of the remote directory will depend on where the Fedora install files are located on the remote server.

Installing Fedora using the File Transfer Protocol (FTP) will require access to an FTP server (see Chapter 18, "Secure File Transfer Protocol [FTP] Service," to see how to set up a server and use FTP). You'll need to know the hostname or IP address of the server, along with the path (directory) holding the Fedora Core software. One way to prepare a server to host installs is to

1. Create a directory named Fedora under the FTP server's pub directory. The directory will usually be /var/ftp/pub on a Linux server.

2. Create a directory named base and a directory named RPMS underneath the Fedora directory.

3. Copy or download all RPM packages included with Fedora Core into the pub/Fedora/RPMS directory.

4. Copy all original base files (comps.rpm, comps.xml, hdlist, hdlist2, hdstg2.img, netstg2.img, stage2.img, TRANS.TBL) from the first CD-ROM's base directory into the pub/Fedora/base directory.

Using this approach, enter **pub** when asked for the name of the remote directory holding the Fedora Core install software.

Installing Fedora Core using a remotely mounted network file system (NFS) is similar to a hard drive installation, but requires access to an NFS server. You'll need access permission, a permitted IP address or hostname for your computer, the hostname or IP address of the NFS server, and the path to the Fedora Core software. See Chapter 13, "Network Connectivity," for more information about NFS and network addressing.

To install Fedora using HTTP, you will need the hostname or IP address of the remote Web server, along with the directory containing Fedora's software. See Chapter 16, "Apache Web Server Management," to see how to set up a Web server.

> **NOTE**
>
> See Chapter 18 for details on how to configure the vsftpd FTP server. Chapter 16 provides information on how to set up and configure Apache for Web service. See Chapter 13 for Samba settings. Note that you can have your server perform all three duties.

Step-by-Step Installation

This section provides a basic step-by-step installation of Fedora Core from CD-ROM. There are many different ways to proceed with an install, and the installer can provide a graphical or text-based interface in a variety of modes.

This example installation prepares a computer for general duties as a server, perhaps to host a File Transfer Protocol (FTP) site, a Web server using Apache, or session message block (SMB) services using Samba.

Before you begin, you should ensure that your computer is not connected to the Internet. Although you can use the installer to set up network protection during the install, it is best to check your system settings after any install and before opening up any public services (see the section "Firewall and Security Configuration" later in this chapter).

> **TIP**
>
> If you're installing to a system that has an older display monitor, it's a good idea to have your monitor's manual handy during the installation. If the install doesn't detect your monitor settings, you might need to specify the monitor's vertical and horizontal frequencies. This doesn't happen often, but if it does, you'll be prepared.

> **NOTE**
>
> Fedora Core's graphical installation dialogs are convenient and easy to use. However, you can use a text-based installation, which works with any PC. Simply specify linux text at the install boot prompt. Use the graphical install outlined here as a starting point for learning more about installing Fedora.

Starting the Install

To get started, insert the first Fedora Core CD-ROM and reboot your computer. You'll first see a boot screen that offers a variety of options for booting (see Figure 3.1). Options may be passed to the Linux install kernel by typing special keywords at the boot prompt. Note that the install kernel is different from the kernel that will be installed on your system during installation!

The basic options most often used are

- <ENTER>—Starts the install using a graphical interface. The graphical interface supports a mouse and offers check boxes and text fields for choosing software, configuring options, and entering information.

- linux text—Starts the install using a graphical text interface.

To install using a text-based interface (used for our example), type linux text and press Enter; otherwise, just press Enter to start the install.

Several function keys can be used at this first boot screen to cycle through four help screens providing additional install information. Use these function keys at the boot prompt to jump to different screens describing alternative installation options and modes:

- Pressing F1 returns to the initial boot screen.

- Pressing F2 details some boot options.

- Pressing F3 gives general installation information (described next in this chapter).

- Pressing F4 describes how to pass kernel video arguments, useful for configuring video hardware to support a graphical install at a specific resolution (such as 800-by-600 pixels).

- Pressing F5 describes Fedora Core's rescue mode.

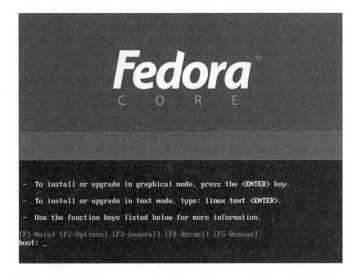

FIGURE 3.1   Select an installation option in this first Fedora Core boot screen.

Some of the options you can use at the boot prompt include

- `linux noprobe`—Disables probing of the system's hardware.

- `linux mediacheck`—Verifies the integrity of one or more install CD-ROMs.

- `linux rescue`—Boots to single-user mode with a root operator prompt, disabling X, multitasking, and networking; this option can be used if you need to reconfigure your boot loader or to rescue data from your system.

- `linux dd`—Uses a driver disk (a floppy image) and possibly one or more kernel arguments (such as `linux mem=512M expert`) to enable certain types of hardware, such as networking cards.

- `linux askmethod`—Prompts for the type of install to perform, such as over a network.

- `linux updates`—Starts an installation update.

- `memtest86`—Starts a cyclical, intensive series of memory tests of your PC's RAM.

- `linux nofb`—Starts a graphical installation, but does not use a framebuffer (helpful with problematic or unsupported video).

- `linux resolution=width x height`—Installs using a graphical display of *width*-by-*height* pixels (such as `resolution=800x600`), which can help match older or less capable display monitors and video cards.

The F4 screen lists options that can be used at the boot prompt to set a specific resolution for the installation. For example, this is done by typing `linux resolution=` at the boot prompt, along with an option such as `"800x600"`. Other options, such as optional arguments for kernel modules (in order to properly configure or initialize hardware) may be passed to the install kernel if you use the `noprobe` option.

> **TIP**
>
> The installer will start automatically in 60 seconds. Press the spacebar, reboot, or turn off your PC if you need to halt the install.

After you press Enter, the installer's kernel loads, and you're asked (in a text-based screen) if you would like to perform a media check of your CD-ROM, as shown in Figure 3.2.

This check can take quite some time (depending on the speed of your CD drive), but can ensure the integrity of the CD-ROM's contents, as an `md5sum` value is embedded on each CD-ROM. This check can help foil installation of malicious software from CD-ROMs with tampered contents. The check can also be helpful to make sure that the CD-ROM you are using will work on your PC and in your CD drive. To perform the check, choose OK; otherwise, use the Tab key to navigate to the Skip button and press Enter to choose it.

After checking your CD-ROM or skipping the check, the display will clear. The Fedora installer, Anaconda, will load, and you are presented with a graphical welcome screen as show in Figure 3.3. The installer should recognize your PC's graphics hardware and mouse. You can then click on the Release Notes button to get detailed information about Fedora Core, along with tips on hardware requirements and how to perform various installs.

If your pointing device (mouse) is not recognized, you can press Alt+R to "press" the Release Notes button. Similarly, you can click Alt+H to hide text shown on the left side of the screen, but you should take a minute to read the frame's contents.

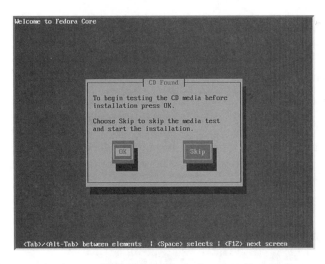

FIGURE 3.2   You can check your CD-ROM media before installing Fedora.

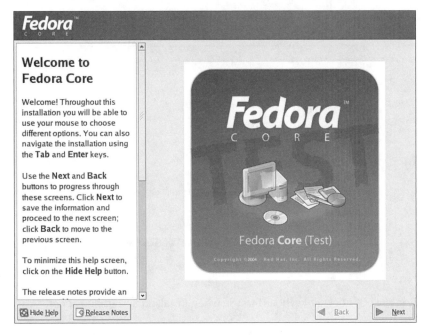

FIGURE 3.3   Read Help or Release Notes before installing Fedora.

Click Next (or press Alt+N) to continue, and the installer asks you to select one of 31 different languages for the installation, as shown in Figure 3.4.

You can navigate the installer's dialogs (during a text-based or graphical install) using the Tab key. You can scroll through lists using your cursor keys. Note that you can now "step backward" through the install by using a Back button. Select a language and click the Next button.

FIGURE 3.4   Select a language to use when installing Fedora.

You'll then be asked to select a keyboard for the install, as shown in Figure 3.5.

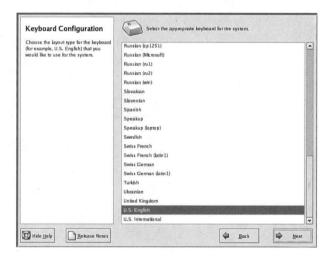

FIGURE 3.5   Select a default keyboard to use when installing and using Fedora.

Scroll to the appropriate keyboard option. You use this option to configure the install to support one of 53 different language keyboards. Click Next after making your selection.

If your PC's monitor was not detected, you might be asked to select your model from 132 different manufacturers. In rare instances, you might have to specify your monitor's exact horizontal and vertical frequencies. This can happen with older displays.

If an existing Linux install is detected, you'll be asked if you want to upgrade and reinstall; otherwise, you're then asked to select a type of installation, as shown in Figure 3.6.

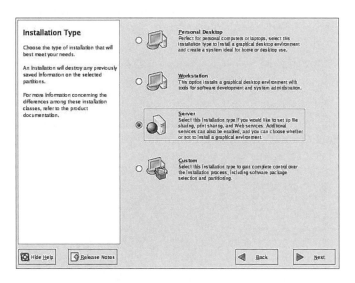

FIGURE 3.6   Select a type of installation.

Select a type of installation suitable for your intended use—we'll use a Server install for our example. As we mentioned earlier, you can use the Custom install instead to tailor the amount, type, and specific packages to be installed. This can be helpful in order to prune unnecessary software from your system and might save some time later on. After you select the installation type, click Next to continue. You'll then see a screen that offers a choice of partitioning schemes and tools.

NOTE

Fedora's installer also supports the ability to monitor background and install processes running during an installation. You can watch the progress of an install and hardware information reported by the Linux install kernel by navigating to a different console display or *virtual* console by simultaneously pressing the Ctrl, Alt, and appropriate Fn key (such as F1–F5).

Use this approach to watch for kernel messages, monitor hardware detection, gain access to a single-user shell, and view the progress of the installer script.

When using a graphical installer, press Ctrl+Alt+F4 (then Alt+F2 or Alt+F3) to navigate to the various screens. Press Alt+F7 to jump back to the installer. When performing a text-based installation, use Alt+F2 (then Alt+F3 or Alt+F4). Use Alt+F1 to jump back to a text-based install.

Partitioning Your Drive

You learned how to choose and plan a partitioning scheme in "Planning Partition Strategies," earlier in this chapter, based on the more specific partitioning information offered in Chapter 2. The Disk Partitioning Setup screen, shown in Figure 3.7, offers two options for disk partitioning. Here is what the options do:

- Using the Automatically Partition button conveniently partitions your hard drive according to the type of installation you selected and configures the partitions for use with Linux.

- Choosing the Manually Partition with Disk Druid button launches a graphical partition editor that enables the creation of custom partition schemes.

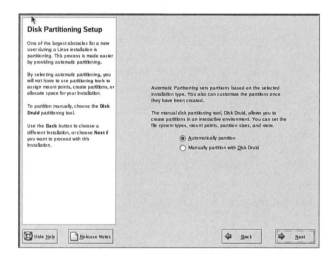

FIGURE 3.7   Select a partitioning scheme or tool.

> **NOTE**
>
> See the section "Partitioning Before and During Installation" in Chapter 2. Chapter 10, "Managing the File System," contains information on using another partitioning utility, the text-based Linux `fdisk` command.

For this example, select Manually Partition with Disk Druid button and click Next. If you are using a new hard drive that hasn't previously been partitioned, you'll be asked if you would like to create new partitions on the drive. Click the Yes button to initialize the drive. If you are using a hard drive that has been previously partitioned or formatted and the partitions are recognized, Disk Druid will present the partitions in its partition dialog. Figure 3.8 shows the graphical interface presented for a 6GB hard drive that hasn't been partitioned.

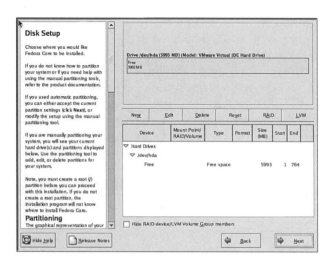

FIGURE 3.8   You can use Disk Druid to partition your drive before installing Fedora.

To use Disk Druid, select any listed free space, and then click the New button (or press Alt+W) to create a new partition. Alternatively,

- To get help, see the help frame on the left.
- To create free space, scroll to an existing partition and use the Delete button to delete the partition.

After you choose the New button, you see a screen as shown in Figure 3.9.

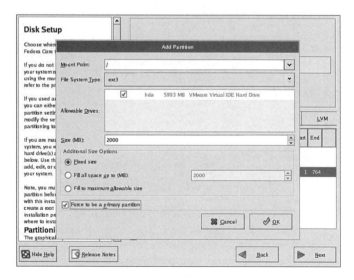

FIGURE 3.9   Set partition information about a selected or new partition on a hard drive.

You use the Add Partition dialog to assign a mount point (such as /boot or /), assign a filesystem (such as ext2, ext3, RAID, swap, or vfat) by using the drop-down menu set at ext3 by default, and assign the size of the partition. Remember that, at a minimum, your system should have a root (/) and swap partition. The ext3 filesystem is the best choice for your Linux partitions because it is the default and specifically supported by Fedora, but you can also use ext2 (and convert to ext3 later on—see Chapter 10). The size of the partition can be fixed by entering a number (in megabytes), or if you select the Fill All Available Space field, you will use all remaining free space (but not yet, as you need to create a partition for swap). Click OK to save the new partition information.

> **TIP**
>
> You can perform diagnostic checks on your storage media after installing Fedora by using various Linux software tools, as shown in Chapter 10.

Remember: Linux requires at least a root (/) and swap partition. The swap partition should be at least twice as large as the amount of installed memory (or more) in order to assure system performance if you run a lot of programs or host many users. After you create an initial partition for the root filesystem, repeat the steps to create a new partition, but select swap as the filesystem type using the drop-down menu. Figure 3.10 shows a simple, completed partitioning scheme with a separate /home partition on a server using a 6GB hard drive.

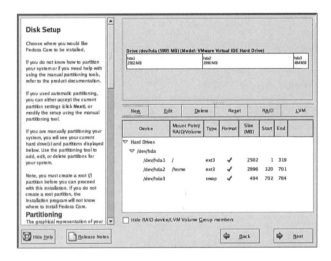

FIGURE 3.10   Review your partitioning scheme for your hard drive.

Take a moment to review your partitioning scheme. If you are not satisfied with the partitioning, you can make changes by selecting a partition and then using the Edit button to change the partition's information (such as mount point or type of filesystem). Use the

Delete button to delete the partition entry and to free up partition space. You can then use the New button again to create partitions in the space that is now free. When satisfied, click Next to continue the install.

Choosing, Configuring, and Installing the Boot Loader

After you accept the partitioning scheme, a screen appears asking you to select a boot loader for booting Fedora (see Figure 3.11). This screen also enables you to choose not to use a boot loader (when booting from floppy, a commercial boot utility, a DOS partition, or over a network), and the ability to boot other operating systems if you have configured a dual-boot system. Review "Choosing a Boot Loader," shown previously in this chapter, for more information on making this choice.

> **TIP**
>
> Fedora will work well with other operating systems, but the reverse is not always true. If you need specialized help with configuring a dual-boot system, check various HOWTOs at http://www.tldp.org for hints and tips.

Select the GRUB boot loader. GRUB is typically installed in the MBR of the first IDE hard drive in a PC. However, the boot loader can also be installed in the first sector of the Linux boot partition, or even not installed on the hard drive. (In which case, you'll need to create a boot floppy during the install; see "Create a Boot Disk," later in this chapter.) Note that you can also backtrack through the install process to change any settings.

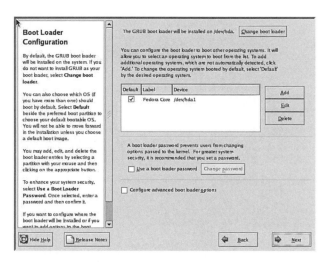

FIGURE 3.11   Select whether you want to use a boot loader and configure other boot options.

Note that you can assign a password for the boot loader. If you choose to use this option, you will need to enter a password at the GRUB boot screen (see the section "Login and Shutdown" at the end of this chapter for information on graphical logins). Carefully note the password! It does not have to be the same password used to log in, but if you pass-word protect booting through your computer's BIOS and use a boot loader password here, you will subsequently need to enter three passwords (BIOS, boot loader, and login) in order to access Linux. Type in a password of at least eight characters twice (once on each line); then click OK or Cancel to exit the dialog.

If you click the Configure Advanced Boot Loader Options button, you're asked for argu-ments to pass to the Linux kernel before booting. Kernel arguments are used to enable or disable various features of Linux at boot time. If you install the source to the Linux kernel, you'll find documentation about the more than 200 different kernel arguments in the file `kernel-parameters.txt` under the `/usr/src/linux/Documentation` directory.

Click Next to set your boot loader configuration. You'll then proceed to network interface configuration, as shown in Figure 3.12.

Network Configuration

If you have an installed network adapter, you are asked for network configuration details, as shown in Figure 3.12. Fedora can be set to automatically configure networking upon booting. Note that you can also configure networking following installation using Red Hat's `system-config-network` graphical network administration tool (see Chapter 13 for details about using these tools).

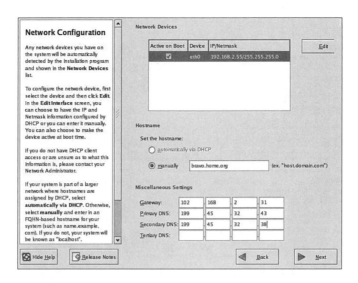

FIGURE 3.12   Select or enter networking configuration information.

> **NOTE**
>
> If the Linux kernel finds more than one network interface installed on your computer, you might be asked to configure a second Ethernet device. This might be the case, for example, if you are installing Fedora Core on a computer that will serve as a gateway or firewall. If you configure more than one Ethernet device, the device named `eth0` will be the first active interface when you start Fedora.

You can choose to have your interface information automatically set using DHCP. Otherwise, especially if you are configuring a DHCP server, manually enter an IP address, hostname, or gateway address (such as for a router), along with DNS information if you click the Edit button listed by the interface (such as `eth0` in the example).

After making your selection, click Next to continue. You'll be asked to select a firewall configuration.

Firewall and Security Configuration

Figure 3.13 shows the Fedora Core installer Firewall Configuration dialog, which offers an opportunity to set default security policies for the new server. Protecting your system using a firewall is especially important if your server is connected to a network (although it is best to first install Linux, set security policies, and then connect to a network). These settings in this installation screen determine how remote computers or users will be able to access your server. You can change these policies after finishing the install and logging in.

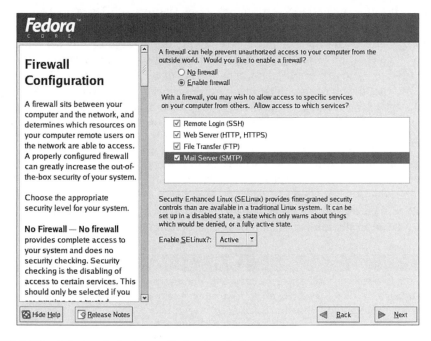

FIGURE 3.13   Select a desired security level and allowed services.

If you have a general idea of how you want to protect your computer, use the dialog shown in Figure 3.14 to turn on firewalling.

Choosing the No Firewall setting isn't recommended; use this setting only if Fedora will be used as a non-networked workstation.

> **NOTE**
>
> Note that you can also manually configure security settings after installation using the text-based `lokkit` command, `system-config-securitylevel` client, or graphical `gnome-lokkit` client. See Chapter 13 for details on how to protect your system using these clients and various security level settings.

Click any allowable services, as shown in Figure 3.14. For some servers, HTTP, FTP, and Simple Mail Transport Protocol (SMTP) requests are acceptable and reasonable. *Do not select or use the Telnet service, which is used to allow remote network logins.* For security reasons, the Secure SHell (SSH) service is a much better choice (see Chapter 5, "First Steps with Fedora," on how to use the `ssh` client).

Click Next to install the firewall security settings. You'll then be asked to select additional language support on your server. Again click Next when finished.

Setting the Time Zone

You're next shown a Time Zone Selection dialog (see Figure 3.14). There are two "clocks," or times, when using a PC: the hardware clock, maintained by hardware in the computer and a backup battery; and the system time, set upon booting and used by the Linux kernel. It is important to keep the two times accurate and in synchronization because automated system administration might need to take place at critical times. Many computer installations use computers with hardware clocks set to GMT, which stands for Greenwich Mean Time. (The more modern designation is *UTC* or *Coordinated Universal Time.*) The Linux system time is then set relative to this time and the default time zone, such as Eastern Standard Time, which is –5 hours of UTC.

Setting the computer's hardware clock to UTC (GMT) has the advantage of allowing the Linux system time to be easily set relative to the geographic position of the computer and resident time zone (such as a Linux laptop user who would like to create files or send electronic mail with correct time stamps, and who has traveled from New York to Tokyo). See Chapter 4, "Post-Installation Issues," for details on setting the date and time for Linux.

> **TIP**
>
> Read the manual page for the `hwclock` command to learn how to keep a running Linux system synchronized with a PC's hardware clock. See Chapter 4 for more details on using the `hwclock` command and Linux time-related software.

Choose your time configuration, and then click Next.

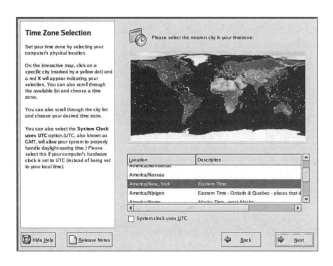

FIGURE 3.14   Select your time zone.

Creating a Root Password and User Accounts

You're next asked to enter a root operator password, as shown in Figure 3.15. Type in a password, press Tab or Enter, and then type it again to make sure that it is verified. The password, which is case sensitive, should be at least eight characters (or more) and consist of letters and numbers. Note that the password isn't echoed back to the display. Your root password is important because you will need it to perform any system administration or user management with Fedora.

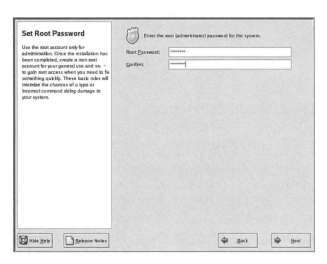

FIGURE 3.15   Type in, and don't forget, your root password.

CAUTION

Don't forget your system's BIOS, boot loader, or root passwords! Some equipment, such as note-book computers, might require factory replacement of motherboard components if the owner forgets the BIOS password. The BIOS settings on most desktop PCs can usually be reset via a jumper or removal and insertion of the motherboard battery. If you forget your boot loader pass-word, use a bootdisk (perhaps created during installation as shown later on in this chapter) or boot to a rescue mode using your first Fedora Core CD-ROM and reset the root password using the passwd command.

When finished, click Next to continue on to software package selection for your new server.

NOTE

You can only create a root account during a Fedora Core install. You will have to create user accounts later on after booting, using command-line programs (such as adduser) or the graphi-cal system-config-users client. Create an account for yourself and any additional users. Usernames traditionally consist of the first letter of a person's first name and the last name. For example, Cathy Taulbee would have a username of *ctaulbee*. Don't forget to enter a password for any new user! If you create a user without a creating a password, the new user will not be able to log in.

You should create at least one user for your server besides the root operator. This is for security purposes and to avoid logging in as root, either through the keyboard at the server or remotely over the network. The default shell and home directory settings should remain set at the defaults, which are the Bourne Again SHell (bash) and the /home directory.

NOTE

See Chapter 5 for how to become the root user or run root commands as a regular user. See Chapter 9, "Managing Users," for details on managing users.

Software Selection and Installation

The Package Group Selection dialog shown in Figure 3.16 displays the installer's suggested software for your class of installation (a server in our example).

If you choose to install a personal desktop, workstation, or other installation type, the software packages appropriate for that installation will be automatically selected for you. Each package (actually a Group) provides many different individual software packages (refer to "Choosing Software Installation Options," earlier in the chapter).

Scroll through the list of package groups, and then click a software package check box to select or deselect software to be installed. Note that the entire size (drive space require-ments) of the installed software will be dynamically reflected by your choices.

Click the Next button when finished to start installing Linux and the Fedora Core software.

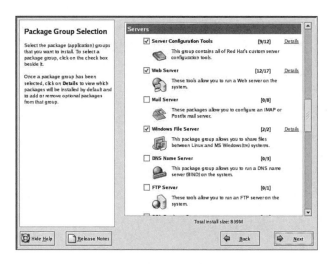

FIGURE 3.16   Select software package groups for installation.

The installer will then perform a quick dependency check and present a dialog informing you that a log of the install will be saved under the /root directory in the file named install.log. Press the Enter key to begin the installation of the software on your system. Be certain that you're ready when you confirm the process, as you cannot step back from this point on!

The installer will then format and prepare your new Linux partitions.

Next, the installer will prepare for the install by gathering a list of the RPM files and will start placing the software on the newly formatted partitions. This process can take anywhere from several minutes to two or more hours, depending on your PC and the amount of software you have chosen to be installed. The installer reports on the name of the current package being installed and the remaining time, as shown in Figure 3.17.

If you are installing over a network, go take a break because the install will proceed unattended through the software installation. If you are using this book's CD-ROMs, you might be prompted to remove the first CD-ROM and insert another. You might also be asked to repeat this operation using the third CD-ROM at some point.

Create a Bootdisk

When the software installation finishes, the installer will perform some temporary file cleanup, install the boot loader, and then ask if you'd like to create a boot diskette for possible use later on, as shown in Figure 3.18.

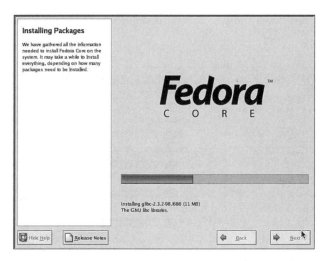

FIGURE 3.17   The Fedora installer formats your drive, and then installs selected software package groups.

You can create this boot disk now, or, as mentioned earlier, you can use Red Hat's `mkbootdisk` command later on while using Fedora. Select Yes or No. Having a boot disk can be handy, especially if an error was made during the install and the boot loader fails to boot Linux.

If you choose to create a boot disk, you'll need to have a blank disk on hand. Select Yes, insert a blank disk when prompted, create the boot disk, and continue the install.

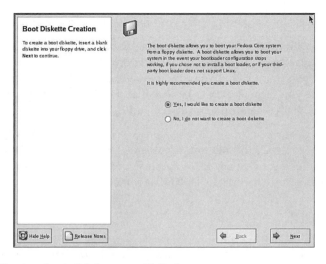

FIGURE 3.18   Create a boot disk for use with Fedora.

> **TIP**
>
> If you chose the X Window System, you can skip X configuration during the install and configure X after installation. This might be a better approach if the install fails to accurately probe your hardware or cannot configure X during the install, but you still desire to have X software installed. See Chapter 6 for details on configuring X to work with your PC's graphics card.

Finishing the Install

You're done! Press the Exit button, and the installer will eject any inserted CD-ROM and reboot. The GRUB boot loader will present a boot prompt as shown in Figure 3.19.

If you have set a GRUB password, press the p key, type your password, and press Enter. If you do nothing for 10 seconds or press Enter, either boot loader will boot Linux.

> **NOTE**
>
> After installation, you can edit the file /boot/grub/grub.conf and change the timeout= setting to change the boot time to a value other than 10 seconds.

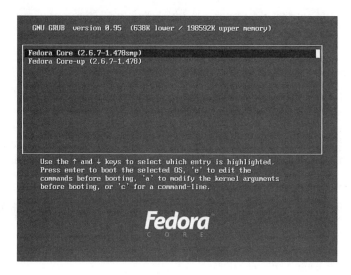

FIGURE 3.19   Boot Fedora with GRUB by pressing the Enter key or waiting 10 seconds.

Login and Shutdown

After rebooting your PC, you'll be able to log in to a Linux session. If you didn't choose to use X11 software during the installation, you'll log in at a text-based login prompt. If you configured X and enabled a graphical login, the screen will clear after your system boots, and you'll be presented with a graphical login screen, as shown previously in Figure 3.19.

To log in at the text-based prompt, type your username and press Enter. You'll then be prompted for your password. After you press Enter, you'll be at the Linux command line. If you use a graphical login, you can use the shutdown or reboot menus in the screen's dialog to shut down or reboot your system. To immediately shut down your system from the command line of a text-based session, use the su command and its -c option to run the shutdown command. In addition, use the -h or halt option and the keyword now, or the numeral 0, like this:

```
$ su - c "/sbin/shutdown -h now"
```

You can also use

```
$ su -c "/sbin/shutdown -h 0"
```

You can also use the shutdown command to immediately reboot your computer like this:

```
$ su -c "/sbin/shutdown -r now"
```

Or, you can use

```
$ su -c "/sbin/shutdown -r 0"
```

For new users, installing Fedora is just the beginning of a new and highly rewarding journey on the path to learning Linux. See Chapter 5 for additional information about using Linux commands. For Fedora system administrators, the task ahead is to fine-tune the installation and to customize the server or user environment.

Related Fedora and Linux Commands

You might use the following commands while installing Fedora:

dd—Convert and copy data

fdisk—The Linux disk partitioning utility

grub—The GNU boot loader for Linux and other operating systems

LOADLIN—A Linux boot loader for DOS

mkbootdisk—Red Hat's Linux boot disk creation utility

RAWRITE—A disk image utility for DOS

Reference

`http://fedora.redhat.com`—The place to start when looking for news, information, and documentation about installing, configuring, and using Fedora.

`http://www.powerquest.com/partitionmagic/`—Powerquest's PartitionMagic utility includes BootMagic, which can be used to support booting of Linux or, regrettably, other less-capable operating systems, such as Windows XP.

`http://www.v-com.com/product/sc7_ind.html`—V Communications, Inc.'s System Commander, a commercial 4.2MB download that can be used to support booting of any operating system capable of running on today's PCs. An intelligent partitioning utility, Partition Commander, is included.

`http://www.nwc.com/columnists/1101colron.html`—How to use Intel's Pre-execution Environment (PXE) protocol to remote boot workstations.

`http://www.gnu.org/software/grub/`—Home page for the GRUB boot loader.

`http://elserv.ffm.fgan.de/~lermen/HOME.html`—Home of the `LOADLIN` Linux loader.

`http://www.ibiblio.org/pub/Linux/docs/HOWTO/other-formats/html_single/`
`BootPrompt-HOWTO.html`—Link for obtaining BootPrompt-HOWTO, a guide to using the boot prompt for passing kernel arguments.

`http://www.tldp.org/HOWTO/Installation-HOWTO/index.html`—Link for obtaining Linux Installation-HOWTO, a guide to installing Linux by Eric S. Raymond.

## CHAPTER 4

Post-Installation Issues

IN THIS CHAPTER

- Troubleshooting Post-Installation Configuration Problems

- Your Hardware and kudzu

- Pointer and Keyboard Configuration

- Configuring Display Graphics

- Configuring Sound Devices

- Detecting and Configuring a Modem

- Configuring Power Management in Fedora

- Resetting the Date and Time

- Managing PCMCIA

- Configuring and Using CD, DVD, and CD-RW Drives

- Reference

As Chapter 3, "Installing Fedora," demonstrated, installing Fedora is an easy task in most situations. The installation process includes hardware probing, in which the installer surveys your system's hardware and then configures system settings accordingly. This process ensures that when the system boots, nearly all hardware is recognized and ready to operate.

If you're a system administrator (which you are even if you use Linux on a standalone workstation), however, you can expect to perform some post-installation configuration of your system. This chapter starts with some general advice on troubleshooting, and then offers some insight on how Fedora is set up to track your system's hardware. You'll then see how to start and use the command line or the desktop to display and diagnose the Linux kernel's output regarding several common PC hardware components. You'll also see several graphical configuration clients in action.

Troubleshooting Post-Installation Configuration Problems

As Linux continues to be developed, it has become increasingly fault-tolerant, meaning that if errors are encountered during the boot process, the errors won't cause a complete kernel or boot failure. Often, your computer might appear to be running fine, even though some device or process isn't working correctly. The sources of such problems might include modules that didn't load, services that didn't start, or devices that are being used at suboptimum levels (such as hard drive transfer speeds).

You'll find clues to many problems in dmesg output, or in the /var/log/messages file, a simple text file containing constantly updated kernel and system information that you can view in any editor. Take a moment to review this file or dmesg output after installing or configuring new hardware; you'll see that they show the progress of booting and starting services on your system.

The messages are generated by the kernel, other software run by /etc/rc.d/rc.sysinit, and Fedora's runlevel scripts. You might find what appear to be errors at first glance, but some errors are not really problems (for example, if a piece of hardware is configured but not present on your system).

When troubleshooting error messages, remember that "Google is your friend." Simply copy part or all of the error message and paste the information into a search field at http://www.google.com/linux/ and at http://marc.theaimsgroup.com/. You might find links to pages with information to help you solve your problem. You likely aren't the first person to encounter the problem. Reading the manual page for modprobe.conf and having perused /usr/src/linux-2.6/Documentation/devices.txt (and other files) will go a long way in helping you troubleshoot any problems.

Remember to only solve one problem at a time and always make a backup copy of any system file before you modify it. Don't use the common extension .bak because files with that extension can sometimes be overwritten. Here is a good method of copying the file:

```
# cp filename filename.original
```

And when restoring from that backup, don't rename the file, just copy it, like so:

```
# cp filename.original filename
```

(When these tips have saved you countless hours of frustration, thank us by purchasing copies of this book as gifts for your friends.)

Your Hardware and kudzu

When you add or replace hardware, for example, you'll need to configure the operating system to recognize and boot with the new components working properly. If you have enabled the kudzu service, Fedora will automatically detect new hardware upon rebooting; kudzu then enables you to remove configuration information about missing hardware and configure the new device. If you don't use kudzu, however, you might need to perform configuration manually without the support of automated hardware detection and configuration.

> **NOTE**
>
> The kudzu service maintains a database of your system's hardware information under the /etc/sysconfig directory in a file named hwconf. This service can be started, stopped, or restarted (like other operating system services) from the command line by using a script under the /etc/rc.d/init.d directory (named kudzu). You can add options or enable various features of kudzu, such as timeouts, by editing the KUDZU_ARGS= entry in the kudzu script (see the kudzu man page for the options). You can also use the command-line based service command or

the graphical system-config-services client to control kudzu. See Chapter 7, "Managing Services," for more information on using these commands.

You can perform many post-installation tasks without rebooting or downtime. With proper planning, you also can create a server or workstation configuration that allows "hot-swapping" of system storage and other components, eliminating the need for downtime. In this chapter, you learn how to configure various universal serial bus (USB) and FireWire (IEEE-1394) devices in addition to keyboards, modems, and notebook PCMCIA services.

Information about your system's installed hardware is contained in a number of files under the Fedora directory system. Aside from one or two *symbolic links*, or shortcut-type files created under the /dev directory for the convenience of system utilities, nearly all these hardware settings are in text files under the /etc directory. The contents of these files are used by various software services to manage your system's hardware, save changes to your hardware, ensure that settings are saved between reboots, and to properly configure your system upon booting. A number of these files are used by the /etc/rc.d/ rc.sysinit script when Linux starts. For example, some of these files include

/etc/sysconfig/hwconf—Lists the currently configured system hardware (used by kudzu)

/etc/sysconfig/apmd—Lists system power-management settings (used by the apmd deamon)

/etc/sysconfig/clock—Contains time zone, clock, and hardware clock settings (used by the hwclock command)

/etc/sysconfig/harddisks—System hard drive tuning parameters (using options available with the hdparm command)

/etc/sysconfig/irda—Provides configuration data concerning Infrared Data Association (IrDA) hardware

/etc/sysconfig/keyboard—Lists current keyboard mapping (and provides language settings)

/etc/sysconfig/mouse—Details the current system pointing device (such as whether or not a PS2 or USB mouse is used)

/etc/modprobe.conf—Defines device names, kernel hardware support modules to load, and any optional parameters (see Chapter 24, "Kernel and Module Management," for more information about Linux kernel modules)

/etc/pcmcia—A directory containing a Personal Computer Memory Card International Association (PCMCIA) hardware database and device settings (see the section "Managing PCMCIA" later in this chapter)

You'll find additional information about the files in /etc/sysconfig in the file named sysconfig.txt under the /usr/share/doc/initscripts directory.

> **CAUTION**
>
> Don't edit kudzu's text-file database of installed hardware; these files are updated dynamically by kudzu. If you have trouble with a device, however, you can check the information in these files when troubleshooting to see if the device is properly recognized and its definition matches the actual hardware.

Pointer and Keyboard Configuration

Fedora includes graphical tools that can quickly and easily change existing mouse and keyboard configuration settings. You also can use these tools to add support for a new keyboard or mouse on your system. These tools include

- mouseconfig—A dialog-based graphical mouse configuration tool for text-only consoles

- system-config-mouse—A graphical mouse configuration tool for the Red Hat desktop

- system-config-keyboard—A graphical keyboard configuration tool for the Fedora desktop or to configure a keyboard using a text console

The following sections explain how to use these tools to configure keyboards and pointing devices in Fedora.

Configuring Keyboards with Linux

> **NOTE**
>
> Linux supports many different types of keyboards. Up to the last few years, most keyboards used the PS/2 protocol (originally developed by IBM) and attached to a PC with a 6-pin mini-connector. Today, however, nearly all computers use USB connectors for user input devices. Although many of today's PCs (and notebooks) continue to provide PS/2 ports, most manufacturers are now introducing "legacy free" computers without direct PS/2 support.

You can make a number of keyboard configuration choices in Fedora. You can choose a keyboard language that supplies the keyboard letters, diacritical marks, and layout appropriate for the language you'll be keyboarding in during your console or graphical sessions. Other configuration options include changing the keyboard's translation table to remap the order of keys on your keyboard, swapping specific keys (such as Caps Lock and Ctrl), or changing the delay period between the press of the key and the appearance of the character onscreen. (This configuration can help you synch the character entry to your typing speed.)

You can make keyboard configuration changes through text-based (console) keyboard commands or by using the graphical user interface.

If you don't use X, use Red Hat's `system-config-keyboard` command to change your keyboard type and language. This command can be used without an active X session (or if you are using X, from inside a terminal window) like this:

```
# system-config-keyboard
```

After you press Enter, you'll see the Configure Keyboard dialog, as shown in Figure 4.1.

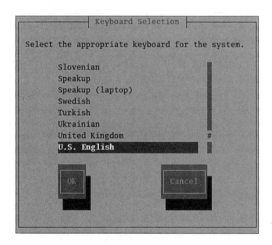

FIGURE 4.1   The `system-config-keyboard` command can be used to choose a keyboard map (language) for Fedora.

This dialog enables you to choose a new keyboard type.

Scroll through the list to highlight a desired keyboard type, and then use the Tab key to highlight the OK button and press Enter. The listings represent entries under the `/lib/kbd/keymaps/i386` directory, which are used to associate your keyboard's layout and keys with a language. The keyboard configuration is stored in the file `/etc/sysconfig/keyboard`, which might look like this:

```
KEYBOARDTYPE="pc"
KEYTABLE="us"
```

If you're using the Fedora desktop during an X session, you can use the graphical interface to select a keyboard language. To open the keyboard configuration dialog box, click the desktop panel System Settings Keyboard menu item, or use the `system-config-keyboard` client at the command line of a terminal window, like so:

```
$ system-config-keyboard
```

After you press Enter, you'll be prompted for the root password. Enter the password and click OK. You'll then see the Keyboard dialog box shown in Figure 4.2. This dialog box is similar to that displayed by system-config-keyboard.

FIGURE 4.2   The system-config-keyboard client is used during an X session to choose the language you will be keyboarding in during your desktop sessions.

Scroll through the list of languages, highlight a language, and then click OK to save your change.

Table 4.1 lists text-based and graphical commands you can use to manipulate or get information about your keyboard.

TABLE 4.1   Linux and X Keyboard-Related Commands

dumpkeys	Displays keyboard translation tables
kbd_mode	Modifies current keyboard mode
kbdrate	Changes keypress delay, repeats
loadkeys	Loads new keyboard table
showkey	Prints character, keycode, and other keystroke information
setleds	Displays, changes keyboard light-emitting diode (LED) settings
xkbcomp	Shows, sets keyboard character translations for X
xkbprint	Displays or saves X keyboard mappings
xset	Modifies keyboard settings for X
xmodmap	Changes key mappings for X

The X11 keyboard and other clients can be used to input a keyboard description into a running X server, show current keyboard character translations, change a keyboard map, and set other keyboard (and pointer) preferences. X11 settings are generally contained in a system's xorg.conf file (see Chapter 6, "The X Window System," for more information).

As a trivial example, the following short shell script (see Chapter 22, "Shell Scripting," for more information on how to use shell scripts) can be used to blink the keyboard Caps Lock LED on and off each second (press Ctrl+C to stop the blinking) while using the console:

```
#!/bin/sh
while :
  do
    setleds -L +caps ; sleep 1 ; setleds -L -caps ; sleep 1;
done
```

Perhaps a more useful example is to switch the Caps Lock and Ctrl keys on your keyboard. Some users might find keyboarding sessions a bit more comfortable if the locations are swapped. There are a number of ways to swap the keys. For your console-based sessions, use the loadkeys command to read in a file containing reverse key values for the keys:

```
keymaps 0-15
keycode 58 = Control
keycode 29 = Caps_Lock
```

You can then immediately swap the keys by using loadkeys to read in the file (perhaps named swapkeys) like so:

```
# loadkeys <swapkeys
```

The same swapping can be used for your Red Hat desktop by editing your /etc/X11/xorg.conf file's keyboard InputDevice section and adding

```
Option      "XkbOptions"  "ctrl:swapcaps"
```

Yet another way to get the same results is to create a file named .Xmodmap in your home directory that contains

```
remove Lock = Caps_Lock
remove Control = Control_L
keysym Control_L = Caps_Lock
keysym Caps_Lock = Control_L
add Lock = Caps_Lock
add Control = Control_L
```

Or you can save the settings in a file (such as mykeyswap) and use the xmodmap client to directly read in the new keys like so:

```
$ xmodmap mykeyswap
```

Note that this will only work if you use the xterm or rxvt terminal clients. See Chapter 6 for more information about the Red Hat desktop.

4

> **TIP**
>
> The `system-config-keyboard` command will present its graphical interface if launched from the command line during a graphical desktop session (that is, while using the X Window System). However, you can force `system-config-keyboard` to use its text-based console interface by including the `--text` option on the command line like this:
>
> `# system-config-keyboard --text`
>
> This technique can also be used with the `system-config-mouse` client discussed next and the `sndconfig` command discussed later in this chapter. Using a console-based interface with one of these commands can be handy if you do not want the client to launch over a network after you have connected from a remote host.

Configuring Pointing Devices in Fedora

This section introduces pointer device configuration for Red Hat. You'll see how to use the `mouseconfig` command to configure a mouse from a text-based console, or the graphical `system-config-mouse` client for configuring a mouse for your desktop.

> **NOTE**
>
> Many pointing devices, such as the IBM Trackpoint (found in several versions of IBM non-notebook keyboards) work fine with Fedora. However, if you use a trackball, joystick, or other devices such as the Synaptics TouchPad, the Cirque GlidePoint, and wireless or infrared (IrDA) pointers, you might need to experiment with different configuration settings or use a driver provided (hopefully) by the manufacturer.
>
> Linux PC tablet users will have good reason to rejoice with the release of the Linux 2.6–series kernel. The new kernel will feature built-in touchscreen support and other improvements to make life easier when using Linux on a tablet PC. Compaq Tablet TC1000 users can browse to `http://linux-tablet-pc.dhs.org/` for links to various drivers and supporting software. Some manufacturers provide direct links to Linux drivers or support reports. For example, Toshiba 3501 Tablet PC users can browse to `http://linux.toshiba-dme.co.jp/linux/eng/pc/ptg3501_report.htm` for additional information.
>
> Fedora does include some support for joystick use through the `jsattach`, `jscal`, and `jstest` commands (installed from the `joystick*.rpm` package). You can use these commands to support, calibrate, and test certain joystick makes and models.

The Fedora installer generally recognizes and correctly configures a computer's pointing device, but if you install a new pointing device, you'll need to reconfigure the system for its use.

When using a PS/2 pointing device, a file named `/dev/mouse` will point to `/dev/psaux`; when using a USB pointing device, `/dev/mouse` will point to `/dev/input/mice`. A serial mouse will have `/dev/mouse` point to a specific serial port, perhaps `/dev/ttyS0`. The `/dev/mouse` file is a symbolic link, used for the convenience of many Linux applications.

It is much more convenient for a program to look for /dev/mouse instead of /dev/input/mice, /dev/psaux, or /dev/ttyS0.

USB service (most likely initially configured by the installer) is started during the boot process by an entry in the system's module configuration file, /etc/modprobe.conf:

```
alias usb-controller usb-uhci
```

In this example, the PC platform uses a universal host controller interface (UHCI), and the uhci.o kernel module will be loaded from the /lib/modules/2.6-X/kernel/drivers/usb directory when Linux boots. Another USB controller commonly in use is the open host controller interface (OHCI), requiring loading of the ohci.o module to enable USB service.

If your pointing device does not work, you can use the dmesg command to see if Linux has recognized the device during the boot process. This can provide some diagnostic information because Linux or the driver (perhaps a module) usually outputs diagnostic information:

```
...
usb-uhci.c: USB UHCI at I/O 0xd800, IRQ 15
usb-uhci.c: Detected 2 ports
usb.c: new USB bus registered, assigned bus number 2
hub.c: USB hub found
hub.c: 2 ports detected
usb-uhci.c: v1.275:USB Universal Host Controller Interface driver
hub.c: USB new device connect on bus1/1, assigned device number 2
usb.c: USB device 2 (vend/prod 0x1241/0x1122) is not claimed by any \
active driver.
usb.c: registered new driver hiddev
usb.c: registered new driver hid
input0: USB HID v1.00 Mouse [1241:1122] on usb1:2.0
hid-core.c: v1.8 Andreas Gal, Vojtech Pavlik <vojtech@suse.cz>
hid-core.c: USB HID support drivers
mice: PS/2 mouse device common for all mice
...
```

In this example (your output might look different), the kernel has recognized a generic USB mouse. USB support is initially enabled by the usbcore.o kernel module. In this example, the USB controller interface is initialized and configured by loading the usb-uhci.o kernel module, and then additional modules, such as input.o and hid.o, will be loaded to support a mouse (and/or keyboard) USB device.

You can see what modules have been loaded by using the output of the lsmod command. Note that you might see different memory size values, depending on your computer and module version:

```
# lsmod
...
mousedev        4288  1
hid            18720  0 (unused)
input           3744  0 [mousedev hid]
usb-uhci       21636  0 (unused)
usbcore        59072  1 [hid usb-uhci]
```

As you can see, USB device support, especially for pointing devices, involves proper loading of a chain of modules rather than a single driver.

> **TIP**
>
> Upon booting or connection, every USB device reports a pair of numbers representing a vendor and associated product (model). Problems can arise if the vendor and product ID are not recognized by a pertinent Linux kernel module. If a device is not properly recognized, it might not work with Linux. It is sometimes possible to rebuild a USB kernel module and include your device's vendor and product ID in order to get the device to work. For example, if you have installed the Linux kernel source, the file named scanner.h under the /usr/src/linux-2.6/ drivers/usb directory contains many popular USB scanner vendor and product IDs that are used by the kernel's scanner.o kernel module. See Chapter 24 for more information about rebuilding the Linux kernel and kernel modules. For a list of the latest USB devices supported with Linux, browse to http://www.qbik.ch/usb/devices/.

After Linux has recognized your hardware, you can use the mouseconfig command to configure a new pointer. Start the command like this:

```
# mouseconfig
```

> **TIP**
>
> If Linux recognizes a two-button pointer, the mouseconfig command automatically selects three-button emulation. (A simultaneous depress of both buttons will send a middle-button click.)
>
> Using a three-button mouse is essential for copy and paste operations—either at a text console or during X sessions. The left mouse button is most often used for clicking and selection, whereas the right mouse button is generally used for configuration or property display. The middle button is used for scrolling and pasting text or graphics.

After you press Enter, the Configure Mouse dialog appears, as shown in Figure 4.3.

Scroll through the list of pointers. Tab to select the OK button and press Enter when finished.

If you're using X, use the desktop panel System Settings Mouse menu item, or the system-config-mouse client at the command line of a terminal window, like so:

```
$ system-config-mouse
```

After you press Enter, you'll be prompted for the root password. Type the password and then click the OK button; a graphical interface similar to mouseconfig's Configure Mouse dialog appears. Scroll through the listings, select an entry corresponding to your pointer, and then click the OK button.

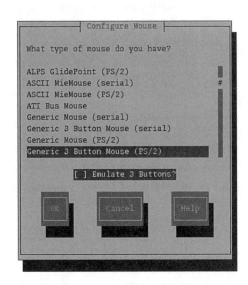

FIGURE 4.3 The mouseconfig command can be used to configure a new pointing device.

Pointer configuration entries are stored in the file /etc/sysconfig/mouse, and can be examined like this:

```
# cat /etc/sysconfig/mouse
MOUSETYPE="ps/2"
XMOUSETYPE="PS/2"
FULLNAME="Generic Mouse (USB)"
XEMU3=yes
DEVICE=/dev/mouse
```

In this example, a two-button USB pointer emulates a PS/2 pointing device.

The corresponding entry contained in the /etc/X11/xorg.conf, used by X.org for the Red Hat desktop looks like

```
Section "InputDevice"
    Identifier   "Mouse0"
    # Modified by mouseconfig
    Driver      "mouse"
```

```
    Option      "Device"         "/dev/mouse"
    Option      "Protocol"       "PS/2"
    Option      "Emulate3Buttons"    "yes"
    #Option     "ZAxisMapping"       "4 5"
EndSection
```

This entry enables the use of a USB pointing device during X sessions. See Chapter 6 to learn about X.

The ZAxisMapping entry (disabled in the preceding example) enables scrolling with a mouse that has a combination scroll-wheel and middle button. Many other types of input devices can be used with Linux and X.org. For information about using a mouse with X.org, read the file README.mouse under the /usr/X11R6/lib/X11/doc directory.

Mouse support for copy and paste operations during a Linux console session is provided by the General Purpose Mouse driver (gpm). gpm is a *daemon*, or software that runs in memory as a background process while you use Linux. If you make the appropriate configuration choices, the /etc/rc.d/init.d/gpm script starts the gpm daemon when Fedora boots. If you're not using X, you can configure Linux to start gpm when booting by using the ntsysv command from the console. Run the ntsysv command as root, like this:

```
# ntsysv
```

After you press Enter, you'll see the Services dialog box, as shown in Figure 4.4.

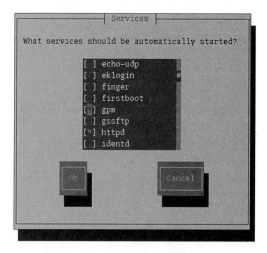

FIGURE 4.4   Use the ntsysv command to produce the Services dialog, in which you can select the gpm driver to start at boot time.

Scroll through the list of services using the Up or Down cursor keys to highlight the gpm service. Press the spacebar to toggle use of the service on (an asterisk will appear between the brackets) or off (no asterisk). Then tap the Tab key to highlight the OK button and press Enter to save your changes. The changes will take effect the next time you boot Red Hat.

> **NOTE**
>
> You can use the `chkconfig` command or the `system-config-services` client to configure Linux to run the `gpm` daemon when you're working in console mode (but not during X Window System sessions). Use the `chkconfig` command like this:
>
> ```
> # chkconfig --level 3 gpm on
> # chkconfig --level 5 gpm off
> ```
>
> See Chapter 7 to see how to configure when services run under Fedora.

Configuring Display Graphics

When you add or change the graphics devices used in your system after the initial installation, you must configure those devices. Adding or changing the display for your system can be as simple as swapping out the monitor or replacing a display adapter. For Intel-based PCs, this can mean switching from the use of the motherboard's built-in display adapter (if available)—by inserting a graphics card in the Accelerated Graphics Port (AGP) or Peripheral Component Interface (PCI) slot—or perhaps adding a second display adapter to support the use of multiple display monitors for X sessions.

Although a display monitor can be easily disconnected or reattached to a running system, insertion or removal of a graphics display adapter will require downtime—the bane of academic, enterprise, corporate, or small-business operations.

> **Linux and KVM**
>
> Keyboard, video, and mouse (KVM) hardware provides the capability to quickly switch display and control between banks of individual computers using a single monitor, keyboard, and pointer. This provides efficient organization, diagnostics and use of computers in larger installations, and allows a single operator to perform system administration tasks without physically moving to each computer.
>
> Using KVM can bring other cost savings. Eliminating the need for some monitors reduces the amount of storage required for the system and the amount of energy used to run and cool the system.
>
> Linux system administrators should be careful to research any hardware compatibility issues before implementing KVM. Many switches work regardless of the operating system and application used; however, take time to research what keyboard and pointer devices you'll need to use (such as whether serial I/O, PS/2, or USB devices might be required). Some KVM switches come with some form of an embedded operating system (even Linux) that provides hardware emulation; these switches will have power requirements.

Other issues to consider include cable construction, compatibility, and distance limitations, hardware or software switch configuration (such as providing push-button or key-combination switching), security, and scalability.

If you use X and want to control the graphical desktops of remote hosts on your network, use the Xvnc server and vnciewer clients. You can also try the x2x and X2vnc clients. Although not included with Red Hat, you can find these clients at http://ftp.digital.com/pub/Digital/ SRC/x2x/ and http://www.hubbe.net/~hubbe/x2vnc.html.

Smaller Linux–based operations can avoid the use of KVM switching hardware by instead leveraging the graphical networking features of X11, multiple terminal sessions, and virtual desktops. Text-based virtual consoles can also be used on servers or workstations that do not use X11 to manage multiple computers or to receive logging messages from various services (such as email or Web servers and the kernel). See Chapter 5, "First Steps with Fedora," to learn more about using virtual consoles. If you are limited to a single remote session window, use the screen command, a text-based window manager that enables a single terminal session to manage several shells. For additional information on using virtual consoles, see http://www.tldp.org/ HOWTO/Keyboard-and-Console-HOWTO.html.

Your Fedora desktop is provided by the X Window System, a client and server software package that is configured to use your computer's video card, monitor, keyboard, and mouse. If you use the graphical desktop and kudzu (discussed earlier in this chapter) and change your graphics card, monitor, keyboard, or mouse, you might be asked to remove existing hardware configuration and reconfigure the new equipment the next time you boot.

The details about configuring X.org for Linux are covered in Chapter 6, but the basic utility used to configure a new xorg.conf file is system-config-display, Red Hat's graphical X configuration tool. You can also use Xorg -configure, which can generate an xorg.conf file by probing installed hardware.

NOTE

Connecting and using an external monitor with a notebook can be convenient, especially if the external monitor provides a larger desktop than the notebook's built-in display. However, configuring an external display for a notebook can sometimes be a problem when using X11. The notebook's graphics chipset must be supported by an X.org driver module, and the module must enable switching or concurrent use of an external monitor. Fortunately, many notebook chipsets are supported, and some notebook manufacturers provide support information for configuring external displays. For example, if your notebook has a Neomagic chipset, use the internDisp and externDisp options in the notebook's xorg.conf to enable use of an external display. Keep in mind that although Red Hat, Inc. encourages and supports X.org development efforts, The X.Org Foundation LLC controls X.org development and X graphics support. See Chapter 6 for more information about Linux and X11.

Fortunately, creating a working xorg.conf file (found in the directory /etc/X11) is usually easily accomplished when installing Fedora. If a new video card or monitor is put in use before installation, it will most likely work because X.org supports many families and types of graphics chipsets. Although newer graphics chipsets might cause some display compatibility problems, it is usually possible to configure a basic working display using existing software. The X.Org Foundation and contributing developers do a great job of providing software that works with nearly every product on the market.

If you are experiencing X11 configuration problems during installation, skip the configuration. Boot Fedora, and then look for a document under the `/usr/X11R6/lib/X11/doc` directory with information about your computer's graphics card. Various README files with specifics about a particular chipset are included with X.org. You can also check the X.Org Foundation Web site (see the "Reference" section at the end of this chapter) for any errata, changes, updates, or new releases.

> **TIP**
>
> Before running any X configuration tool, be sure to make a copy or back up any working `xorg.conf` configuration file.

Configuring Sound Devices

Most workstation users want to have a configured sound card working with Linux. Sound support is generally configured when Linux first boots (or during the install process if the sound card is recognized). Fedora Core uses the Advanced Linux Sound Architecture (ALSA) to enable sound support on your workstation.

To use sound, you should then use ALSA's `alsamixer` command to unmute your sound card's channels and save the settings using the `alsactl` command:

```
# alsactl store 0
```

The state of your sound card will be saved in the file `/etc/asound.state`. These settings, such as channel volumes, can be retrieved later by using the `restore` option instead of `store`.

> **NOTE**
>
> You'll find complete documentation about the Linux kernel's sound support in various text files under the `/usr/src/linux-2.6/Documentation/sound/alsa` directory if you install the source code to Linux.

Configuration problems can arise, especially if your sound card's manufacturer won't or can't release specifications to help open-source developers create working drivers. If your sound card is not recognized, or is recognized but won't work, and using ALSA fails, you can turn to commercial sound drivers from 4Front Technologies. These relatively inexpensive drivers support more than 350 sound systems and are installed, configured, and controlled using shell scripts. Browse to `http://www.opensound.com` for more information.

Fedora also includes a Red Hat graphical sound card configuration client that can be used during an X session. Start the `system-config-soundcard` client by clicking your desktop panel's System Settings Sound card Detection menu or item, or by using the command at a terminal window like so:

```
$ system-config-soundcard
```

After you press Enter, you'll be prompted for the root password. Enter the password and click OK. The `system-config-soundcard` will try to automatically detect and configure your sound card. You'll then see a dialog you can use to test your sound card settings, as shown in Figure 4.5. Click on the Play test sound button to listen to a sample sound.

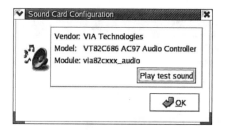

FIGURE 4.5   The `system-config-soundcard` client is used during an X session to configure a sound card for Fedora.

Detecting and Configuring a Modem

More than seven million users in the United States now connect to the Internet with cable or DSL service, but for many users a modem is the standard way to connect with an Internet service provider (ISP) using the Point-to-Point Protocol (PPP). Other common tasks for modems include sending and receiving faxes. If you add or change your modem after the initial installation, you will need to configure Fedora to use the new modem to perform all these tasks.

Fedora includes several tools you can use to configure and use an internal or external modem in your notebook or PC. Chapter 15, "Internet Connectivity," contains the details about configuring Fedora to connect to the Internet using a modem. This section covers how to configure and use modems using serial ports (using a standard formerly known as RS232, but now termed EIA232) or USB.

Configuring a Serial-Port Modem

Linux uses `/dev/ttySX`, `/dev/ttyUSBX`, or `/dev/usb/ttyUSBX` for serial ports, where X can range from 0 to 15. Many additional ports can be added to a system using multiport cards or chained USB devices. A PC's integral serial ports are generally recognized at boot time. To see a list of recognized ports for your system, pipe the `dmesg` command output through the `fgrep` command like so:

```
# dmesg | grep tty
ttyS00 at 0x03f8 (irq = 4) is a 16550A
ttyS01 at 0x02f8 (irq = 3) is a 16550A
```

In this example, the grep command reports that two serial ports have been recognized in the dmesg output. Note that the device matching ttyS00 is /dev/ttyS0, despite the kernel output. The PC's external modem can be attached (most likely using a male DB9 adapter) to either port. Under Linux, nearly all modem-dependent software clients look for a symbolic link named /dev/modem that points to the desired device. This link is not created by default, but as root, you can create this device manually using the ln command like this:

```
# ln -s /dev/ttyS0 /dev/modem
```

In this example, /dev/modem will point to the first serial port.

You can also use the graphical X client neat to configure a modem after the initial installation. Internet connection software such as Red Hat's system-config-network client (shown in Figure 4.6) will try to probe the system for an available modem. If a modem isn't found, you can manually enter modem data.

KDE provides the kppp client (shown in Figure 4.7) that can also be used to look for and set up a modem when you set up a new Point-to-Point Protocol (PPP) connection. Click the Query Modem button in kppp's dialog to search for an installed modem.

Fedora includes command-line–based diagnostic and serial-port configuration tools for the system administrator. For example, to get more information about a specific port, you can use the statserial command, along with a designated device like this:

```
# statserial /dev/ttyS0
Device: /dev/ttyS0
```

Signal Name	Pin (25)	Pin (9)	Direction (computer)	Status	Full Name
-----	---	---	---------	------	-----
FG	1	-	-	-	Frame Ground
TxD	2	3	out	-	Transmit Data
RxD	3	2	in	-	Receive Data
RTS	4	7	out	1	Request To Send
CTS	5	8	in	0	Clear To Send
DSR	6	6	in	0	Data Set Ready
GND	7	5	-	-	Signal Ground
DCD	8	1	in	0	Data Carrier Detect
DTR	20	4	out	1	Data Terminal Ready
RI	22	9	in	0	Ring Indicator

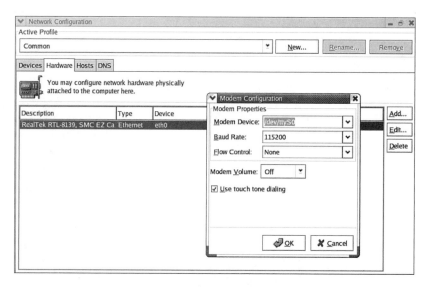

FIGURE 4.6 Red Hat's `system-config-network` client will probe for an available modem.

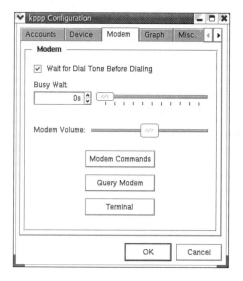

FIGURE 4.7 KDE's kppp client can be used to find and configure an available modem.

The sample output is a display of the associated device's port signals. Another tool is the `setserial` command that can be used to display port statistics and reconfigure a serial port's system interrupt or speed. This can be handy when using some serial devices, such as a cellular phone that requires specific serial-port characteristics. To get information about a specific port, use `setserial`, along with the device name like this:

```
# setserial -a /dev/ttyS0
/dev/ttyS0, Line 0, UART: 16550A, Port: 0x03f8, IRQ: 4
    Baud_base: 115200, close_delay: 50, divisor: 0
    closing_wait: 3000
    Flags: spd_normal skip_test
```

In this example, the characteristics of /dev/ttyS0 are displayed. The setserial command can also be used to configure or fine-tune a port's characteristics using 32 different command-line options and values.

One option for using a legacy serial device such as a modem on a PC that doesn't have a serial port but supports USB is to use a USB-to-serial converter. These devices provide a serial-port dongle and plug in to a USB hub or port. You can see the output and designated serial port by looking at the output of the dmesg command:

```
usb.c: registered new driver serial
usbserial.c: USB Serial support registered for Generic
usbserial.c: USB Serial Driver core v1.4
usbserial.c: USB Serial support registered for Keyspan PDA
usbserial.c: Keyspan PDA converter detected
usbserial.c: Keyspan PDA converter now attached to ttyUSB0 \
(or usb/tts/0 for devfs)
usbserial.c: USB Serial support registered for Keyspan PDA - (prerenumeration)
usbserial.c: USB Serial support registered for Xircom PGS - (prerenumeration)
usbserial.c: USB Serial support registered for Entregra PGS - (prerenumeration)
keyspan_pda.c: USB Keyspan PDA Converter driver v1.1
```

Configuring a Fax Modem

Linux should recognize and configure a designated serial port (such as /dev/ttyUSBX in the example) when the device is plugged in. Fedora also comes with a number of fax utilities that can be used to configure a system to send or receive phone faxes. One of the easier to configure fax utilities is the fax command. As root, you can configure the software by editing a few entries in the /usr/bin/fax shell script:

```
DEV=modem
FROM="1 555 555-1212"
NAME="Company Name"
```

The most important entry is DEV=, which won't need to be changed as long as /dev/modem points to an active fax-capable modem. You can also edit /usr/bin/fax to customize other entries, such as the fax viewing command. Use the test command-line option to check the settings like this:

```
# fax test
```

Sending a fax using the fax command is straightforward:

```
# fax send 5551212 document.txt
```

Configuring `minicom` for Modem Use

Use the `minicom` or `xminicom` script (used for launching `minicom` in a terminal window during an X session) for dial-up connections and terminal sessions to remote Linux systems. To configure this terminal program for use with an attached modem, start the client as root with its `-s` or setup option like this:

```
# minicom -s
```

After you press Enter, you'll see a setup dialog box. Select Serial-Port Configuration and press Enter. You'll then see a Configuration Settings dialog box as shown in Figure 4.8 that you can use to configure the program to work with an attached modem.

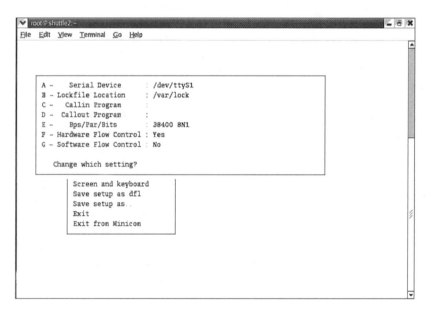

FIGURE 4.8   Use minicom's setup dialog to configure the program to work with an attached modem.

Configuring Controllerless Modems for Laptops

Other issues regarding modems focus on Linux notebook users with laptops using *controllerless* modems. These modems use proprietary software to emulate a hardware modem. Despite the release of binary-only drivers to enable use of some of these modems, these devices remain the bane of Linux notebook and some desktop users.

You might find some support for Lucent (but not Lucent AMR), Motorola SM56-type, the IBM Mwave, and Conexant HSF (not HCF) controllers. At the time of this writing, there was no support for any 3COM or U.S. Robotics controllerless modems. For links to drivers and more information, browse to the Linux Winmodem Web page at `http://www.linmodems.org`.

Configuring Power Management in Fedora

Advanced Power Management (APM) enables workstations and servers to automatically turn off when instructed to shut down. Most often used by Linux mobile users, APM can help extend battery sessions through the use of intelligent storage-cell circuitry, CPU "throttling" (similar to, but not the same as safety thermal throttling incorporated by Intel in Pentium III and IV CPUs), and control of displays and hard drives.

Most PCs support APM via the BIOS and hardware. APM support is configured, enabled, and then incorporated in the Linux kernel.

APM information is constantly updated in the file /proc/apm, which can look like this:

```
# cat /proc/apm
1.14 1.2 0x03 0x01 0x03 0x09 100% 10800 sec
```

This example provides information such as battery charge, along with time and percentage of time remaining. From left to right in the example is the driver version, BIOS version, status, AC status, battery status, battery state, remaining battery life, and number of seconds of life remaining. Some X11 clients, such as the asapm, xapmload, or GKrellM clients, parse this file and display icons or graphical power LEDs to present the information in an easier to digest form. These clients can be especially helpful for notebook users.

APM is supported by all kernels included with Fedora. However, problematic hardware or APM misconfiguration can cause kernel panics with some hardware, resulting in the inability to boot Linux. When this happens, you must reconfigure APM, and then build and install a new Linux kernel. (See Chapter 24 for more information.)

Basic Linux kernel APM configuration options include

- CONFIG_APM—Whether or not to configure APM support
- CONFIG_APM_IGNORE_USER_SUSPEND—Ignores keyboard suspend instruction
- CONFIG_APM_DO_ENABLE—Enables APM at boot
- CONFIG_APM_CPU_IDLE—Idle CPU when not used
- CONFIG_APM_DISPLAY_BLANK—Enables monitor or LCD panel blanking
- CONFIG_APM_RTC_IS_GMT—Determines clock setting
- CONFIG_APM_ALLOW_INTS—Allows interrupts during APM use (such as serial-port activity)
- CONFIG_APM_REAL_MODE_POWER_OFF—Enables powering down

Fedora includes several APM-related commands—such as apm that prints APM information and apmsleep, used to suspend and then awake notebook hardware at a specific time. Linux notebook users can use the apm command like this:

```
$ apm -v
APM BIOS 1.2 (kernel driver 1.16)
AC on-line, battery status high: 95%
```

Other power management incorporated in the kernel includes control of Peripheral Control Interface (PCI) devices and Display Power Management Signaling (DPMS) for enabled monitors, which can help energy costs by placing devices in a low-power state after a preset time. Screensaving, as most astute Linux system administrators and users know, is no longer necessary to protect displays from image "burn-in." And password protection enabled by the screensaver only provides a modicum of physical security.

Hardware health monitoring is supported by the lm_sensors software package, which acquired some notoriety when early versions allegedly caused IBM ThinkPad notebooks to suffer permanent damage. However, system administrators managing desktop PCs can benefit from using applications, such as the sensors command that takes advantage of the hardware monitoring features of the lm_sensors libraries.

You can customize the output of the sensors command by editing (as root) the file /etc/sensors.conf, but the default settings should work for your computer. To enable sensor reading, use the sensors-detect command to determine what kernel modules to load to enable sensor output:# /usr/sbin/sensors-detect. This program will help you determine which I2C/SMBus modules you need to load to use lm_sensors most effectively. You need to have i2c and lm_sensors installed before running this program. Also, you need to be `root', or at least have access to the /dev/i2c-* files, for most things. If you have patched your kernel and have some drivers built in, you can safely answer NO if asked to load some modules. In this case, things may seem a bit confusing, but they will still work.

It is generally safe and recommended to accept the default answers to all questions, unless you know what you're doing.

We can start with probing for (PCI) I2C or SMBus adapters. You do not need any special privileges for this.

```
Do you want to probe now? (YES/no):
```

Type YES and press Enter to begin the probe (*do not* if you have an IBM ThinkPad notebook; see http://www2.lm-sensors.nu/~lm78/cvs/browse.cgi/lm_sensors2/README.thinkpad for more information). The command will then begin a series of probes of your PC's motherboard and report on found hardware. After you answer the prompts, the program will display one or more recommended command lines (and perhaps a new entry to /etc/modprobe.conf) to enable sensor reporting. For example,

```
modprobe i2c-isa
modprobe via686a
```

You can then use the `sensors` command's `-f` option to view various component temperatures in Fahrenheit, like this:

```
$ sensors -f
via686a-isa-6000
Adapter: ISA adapter
Algorithm: ISA algorithm
2.0V:   +1.36 V (min = +1.79 V, max = +2.18 V)
2.5V:   +2.49 V (min = +2.24 V, max = +2.74 V)
I/O:    +3.28 V (min = +2.95 V, max = +3.62 V)
+5V:    +5.02 V (min = +4.47 V, max = +5.49 V)
+12V:   +11.62 V (min = +10.79 V, max = +13.18 V)
Case Fan: 2700 RPM (min = 48214 RPM, div = 2)
CPU Fan: 3497 RPM (min = 67500 RPM, div = 2)
SYS Temp: +98.8°F (limit = +295°F, hysteresis = -95°F)
CPU Temp: +98.8°F (limit = +295°F, hysteresis = -95°F)
SBr Temp: +79.3°F (limit = -74°F, hysteresis = -95°F)
```

Monitoring your system's hardware can be critically important, especially if you over clock the Central Processing Unit (CPU) in order to gain performance.

Resetting the Date and Time

The Fedora installer will query you during installation for default time zone settings, and whether or not your computer's hardware clock is set to Greenwich Mean Time (GMT)—more properly known as *UTC*, or Coordinated Universal Time.

Linux provides a system date and time; your computer hardware provides a hardware clock-based time. In many cases, it is possible for the two times to drift apart. Linux system time is based on the number of seconds elapsed since Jan. 1, 1970. Your computer's hardware time depends on the type of clock chips installed on your PC's motherboard, and many motherboard chipsets are notoriously subject to drift.

Keeping accurate time is not only important on a single workstation, but also critically important in a network environment. Backups, scheduled downtimes, and other network-wide actions need to be accurately coordinated.

Fedora provides several date and time utilities you can use at the command line or during an X session, including these:

> `date`—Used to display, set, or adjust the system date and time from the command line
>
> `hwclock`—A root command to display, set, adjust, and synchronize hardware and system clocks
>
> `system-config-date`—Red Hat's graphical date, time, and network time configuration tool

Using the `date` Command

Use the `date` command to display or set your Linux system time. This command requires you to use a specific sequence of numbers to represent the desired date and time. To see your Linux system's idea of the current date and time, use the `date` command like this:

```
# date
Wed Sep 10 14:17:01 EDT 2003
```

To adjust your system's time (say, to September 23, 2003 at 8 a.m.), use a command line, with the month, day, hour, minute, and year, like so:

```
# date 092308002003
Tue Sep 23 08:00:00 EDT 2003
```

Using the `hwclock` Command

Use the `hwclock` command to display or set your Linux system time, display or set your PC's hardware clock, or to synchronize the system and hardware times. To see your hardware date and time, use `hwclock` with its `--show` option like so:

```
# hwclock --show
Wed 10 Sep 2003 02:17:53 PM EDT  -0.193809 seconds
```

Use `hwclock` with its `--set` and `--date` options to manually set the hardware clock like so:

```
# hwclock --set --date "09/23/03 08:00:00"
# hwclock --show
Tue 23 Sep 2003 08:00:08 AM EDT -0.151718 seconds
```

In these examples, the hardware clock has been set using `hwclock`, which is then used again to verify the new hardware date and time. You can also `hwclock` to set the Linux system date and time using your hardware clock's values with the Linux system date and time.

For example, to set the system time from your PC's hardware clock, use the `--hctosys` option like so:

```
# hwclock --hctosys
```

To set your hardware clock using the system time, use the `--systohc` option like so:

```
# hwclock --systohc
```

Using the `system-config-date` Client

Red Hat's graphical X tool named `system-config-date` can be used to set your system date and time. Start the client by clicking the desktop menu's System Settings Date & Time menu item, or from the command line of an X11 terminal window like this:

```
$ system-config-date &
```

After you press Enter, you'll be asked to enter the root password. Type in the root password and click the OK button. You'll then see a window, as shown in Figure 4.9.

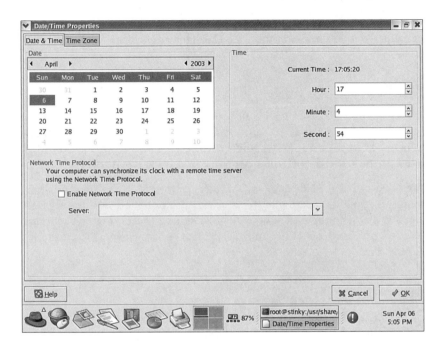

FIGURE 4.9   Use Red Hat's `system-config-date` client to set your system date and time.

Set the date and time by using the calendar and time fields. You can also have your workstation obtain updated date and time information via the network by entering a remote time server hostname in the Network Time Protocol field. This will require that the `ntpd` time daemon be properly configured and running.

> **NOTE**
>
> HTML documentation for using the `ntpd` daemon is in `/usr/share/doc/ntp*/ntpd.htm` (if `ntpd` is installed on your system).

Click on the Time Zone tab to change or verify your system's time zone. The current system time zone is designated by a file named `localtime` in the `/etc` directory, and is a copy of the pertinent time zone database file under the `/usr/share/zoneinfo` directory. For example,

```
$ ls -l /etc/localtime
-rw-r--r--   1 root     root          1267 Apr  1 16:39 /etc/localtime
 $ ls -l /usr/share/zoneinfo/America/New_York
-rw-r--r--   5 root     root          1267 Mar 13 18:00
/usr/share/zoneinfo/_America/New_York
```

This file will change if you make a time zone change using system-config-date.

Managing PCMCIA

Mobile Linux users take advantage of notebook PCMCIA slots to add 70-pin, credit-card-sized devices to support Ethernet LAN connectivity, wireless operations, FireWire devices, Compact Flash hard drives, external storage devices, serial ports, and modems. Many different types of PCMCIA cards and Compact Flash form-factor cards in a PCMCIA caddy are supported by the Linux kernel and David Hinds' Card Services software.

Power is provided to PCMCIA devices and adapters directly through the card slot, although some external hardware might require an additional power source. PCMCIA support is enabled and configured at boot time according to the /etc/sysconfig/pcmcia file and /etc/rc.d/init.d/pcmcia startup script. The /etc/sysconfig/pcmcia file might look something like

```
PCMCIA=yes
PCIC=yenta_socket
PCIC_OPTS=
CORE_OPTS=
```

Previous incarnations of Linux distros from Red Hat, Inc., and PCMCIA used specific controller information in this file. With the newer Linux kernels however, support is provided by kernel modules or direct Linux kernel support.

Using PCMCIA

The PCMCIA Card Services software provides diagnostic information by one or more high or low beeps upon card insertion. One high and one low beep indicate that a card is recognized, but failed to be configured. A single beep indicates that the card was only recognized. Two high beeps indicate that a card was recognized and configured.

For example, if you use a compact flash storage device and insert it into your notebook while using Fedora, you should hear two high beeps. You can then check to see what device has been assigned to the card by using the dmesg command:

```
$ dmesg
...
hde: SunDisk SDCFB-8, ATA DISK drive
ide2 at 0x100-0x107,0x10e on irq 3
```

```
ide-floppy driver 0.99.newide
hde: 15680 sectors (8 MB) w/1KiB Cache, CHS=245/2/32
 hde: hde1
 ...
```

Not all the output is shown here (and yours may look different), but this example shows that the card has been recognized and configured as the /dev/hde device (with a single partition, /dev/hde1). You can then use the device as any other storage medium (see Chapter 10, "Managing the File System," for more information on using hard drives with Linux).

Other devices can be similarly recognized and configured. For example, if you have a combination Ethernet and modem PCMCIA card and insert it into your notebook, you should hear two sets of high beeps (to indicate successful recognition and configuration of the network interface and modem). The Linux kernel will report the interface and device information:

```
$ dmesg
...
eth0: NE2000 (DL10019 rev 05): io 0x300, irq 3, hw_addr 00:E0:98:06:84:C5
ttyS04 at port 0x0af8 (irq = 3) is a 16450
 ..
```

Here, the network interface has been recognized as eth0 (see Chapter 13, "Network Connectivity," to see how to connect to a network). The modem is configured to use /dev/ttyS04.

Again, troubleshooting problems with PCMCIA cards can be difficult, especially with the explosion in popularity and type of 802.11b wireless networking cards. Such troubleshooting is likely to require downloading, building, and installing new drivers.

Fortunately, however, nearly all serial, modem, and Compact Flash storage cards are easily recognized and configured. Many Ethernet cards are also supported. To check on the current support status for many cards, read the file SUPPORTED.CARDS. You'll find a copy under the /usr/share/doc/kernel-pcmcia-cs-3.X.XX/ directory (where X.XX is the version of the package) if you install the pcmcia-cs RPM package.

> **NOTE**
>
> If you have trouble configuring and using a PCMCIA card, browse to the Linux PCMCIA home page at http://pcmcia-cs.sourceforge.net/. Click the SUPPORTED.CARDS link to see if your card is supported. Click the known problems link to see if other users with the same card are having problems, or if the card is not fully supported. If a new version of the PCMCIA kernel drivers are available and changes have been made to your card's drivers (or if a new driver has been developed), download and install the newer software. See Chapter 24 for information on installing the new PCMCIA modules, or follow the directions included with the PCMCIA software.

Controlling PCMCIA Service

Although PCMCIA cards can be inserted or removed while using Red Hat, be careful when using these cards. For example, do not remove a network card while connected to a remote computer. Don't pull a Compact Flash card or other storage media card (such as an IBM microdrive) while the card's file system is mounted and in use—you could corrupt the media's file system and experience loss of data.

You can control a PCMCIA device from the command line, and insert and remove the card without physically removing and then inserting the card. Use the `cardctl` command to control PCMCIA service to one or more card slots on your notebook or desktop PC with a PCMCIA adapter. The `cardctl` command is used to get and print information about an inserted card, suspend or resume power to a card, reset a card, perform a software insertion or removal, or to configure a card according to a particular, predefined "scheme" (such as using a network in the office or at home). The format of the command is `cardctl` `command slot_number` (such as 0 or 1).

For example, if you have inserted a compact flash card, eject the card (after unmounting its file system) using the `cardctl` command and its `eject` option, along with the card's slot number like this:

```
# cardctl eject 0
```

This can save power when running a notebook. When the card is again needed, you can subsequently "insert" the card like so:

```
# cardctl insert 0
```

Configuring and Using CD, DVD, and CD-RW Drives

Linux provides support for using a variety of CD and DVD devices and media. This section shows how to determine what device has been assigned to your CD drive and how to get additional drive information if the drive supports recording on optical media.

AT Attachment Packet Interface, or ATAPI IDE-based CD drives, are recognized during installation and work through the `ide-cd` kernel module. A symbolic link named `/dev/cdrom` will be created and will point to your CD's device (perhaps `/dev/hdb` or `/dev/hdc`). You can use many different types of CD drives with Linux, and you can easily replace, add, or upgrade your system to use a new drive. Part of a successful configuration involves the proper installation of the hardware and being able to determine the drive's device when using Linux.

Checking Drive Assignment

Linux recognizes CD and DVD drives upon booting if they're attached to your computer's motherboard with proper cabling and if they're assigned as either a master or slave on an

IDE channel. Look through your kernel boot message for the drive device assignment, such as

```
hdd: DVDROM 10X, ATAPI CD/DVD-ROM drive
```

If you have a DVD-capable drive, you generally should also have a symbolic link named /dev/dvd that points to your drive's device because many DVD clients, such as xine or vlc, will look for /dev/dvd by default. If you have a CD-RW drive, the Fedora installer will insert a kernel argument into your boot loader's configuration file that specifies use of the ide-scsi kernel. For example,

```
append="hdb=ide-scsi"
```

A similar entry in the grub boot loader's /etc/grub.conf file would look like this:

```
kernel boot/vmlinuz-6.5-1.358 ro root=/dev/hda2 hdb=ide-scsi
```

The first CD-RW drive will be assigned to the device /dev/scd0 (although it might still be initially recognized while booting as an IDE device), with subsequent drives assigned to /dev/scd1, and so on. In order to initialize your drive for use, the following modules should be loaded:

```
Module       Size Used by  Not tainted
sg          30244  0 (autoclean)
sr_mod      15192  0 (autoclean)
cdrom       27872  0 (autoclean) [sr_mod]
ide-scsi     8128  0
scsi_mod    96572  2 [sr_mod ide-scsi]
```

Look for kernel message output regarding the device such as this:

```
Attached scsi CD-ROM sr0 at scsi0, channel 0, id 0, lun 0
sr0: scsi3-mmc drive: 0x/32x writer cd/rw xa/form2 cdda tray
Uniform CD-ROM driver Revision: 3.12
```

Your ATAPI-based CD-RW drive will then work as a SCSI device under emulation, and the symbolic link /dev/cdrom should point to /dev/scd0. You can also use the cdrecord command (included with Red Hat's multimedia software packages) to acquire SCSI device information about your drive for later use during burning operation like this:

```
# cdrecord -scanbus
Cdrecord 1.10 (i686-pc-linux-gnu) Copyright (C) 1995-2001 Jörg Schilling
Linux sg driver version: 3.1.22
Using libscg version 'schily-0.5'
scsibus0:
    0,0,0   0) 'HL-DT-ST' 'RW/DVD GCC-4120B' '2.01' Removable CD-ROM
```

```
0,1,0    1) *
0,2,0    2) *
0,3,0    3) *
0,4,0    4) *
0,5,0    5) *
0,6,0    6) *
0,7,0    7) *
```

The pertinent information—0,0,0 in the example (SCSI bus, device ID, and Logical Unit Number, or lun)—can then be used during a burn operation like this:

```
# cdrecord -v speed=8 dev=0,0,0 -data -eject file_name.img
```

In this example, a CD-ROM data image named file_name.img is created on a CD-R or CD-RW media at a speed of 8, and the new disk will be ejected after the write operation has completed. See "Burning CDs in Fedora Core Linux" in Chapter 26, "Multimedia Applications," for other ways to create CD-ROMs.

> **NOTE**
>
> Fedora also includes the dvdrecord, dvd+rw-format, and growisofs commands, which can be used with DVD-R and DVD-RW drives.

Initializing IEEE 1394 CD Drives

This section provides some basic information you can use if you attach an IEEE 1394 CD drive to your system. These drives use a high-speed serial interface, better known as FireWire, which supports data transfers more than 30 times faster than the first version of USB (at speeds up to 400Mbps), although USB 2.0 devices are a bit faster.

Linux has supported IEEE 1394 since the advent of the 2.4-series kernel, and now works with many different devices, such as video cameras, VCRs, hard drives, scanners, PCMCIA cards, and CD, DVD, or CD-RW drives. The Red Hat Linux installer should recognize most IEEE 1394 interface hardware; if so, you will be able to use the device with Linux. One Linux IEEE 1394 component, the video1394 kernel module, currently supports more than 120 different digital video cameras. General support exists for many different hard drives and DVD or CD-RW drives.

If you install an IEEE 1394 interface after Fedora has been installed, you can initialize support for your device, such as a CD-RW drive, by loading the ieee1394 and ohci1394 kernel modules like this:

```
# insmod ieee1394
# insmod ohci1394
```

Next, look for relevant device information from the Linux kernel using the dmesg command:

```
ohci1394: $Revision: 1.80 $ Ben Collins <bcollins@debian.org>
PCI: Found IRQ 10 for device 00:0b.0
PCI: Sharing IRQ 10 with 00:07.5
ohci1394_0: OHCI-1394 1.0 (PCI): IRQ=[10] MMIO=[ee000000-ee000800] \
 Max Packet=[2048]
ieee1394: Device added: node 2:1023, GUID 00d0010500007d8e
ieee1394: sbp2: Driver forced to serialize I/O (serialize_io = 1)
ieee1394: sbp2: Node 2:1023: Max speed [S400] - Max payload [2048]
scsi1 : IEEE-1394 SBP-2 protocol driver
 Vendor: TEAC    Model: CD-W28E      Rev: 1.1A
 Type:   CD-ROM                ANSI SCSI revision: 02
```

In this example, the IEEE 1394 drivers have recognized a CD-RW drive (which will be assigned to /dev/scd1 because another CD-RW is also present on the system). You might also find that the sbp2 kernel module has loaded:

```
Module        Size Used by  Not tainted
sbp2          14400  0
ohci1394      15872  0 (unused)
ieee1394      25768  0 [sbp2 ohci1394]
```

> **NOTE**
>
> Fedora's installer should recognize any IEEE 1394 hardware in your PC during installation. Depending on your computer's hardware, you might find an entry in /etc/modprobe.conf such as alias ieee1394-controller ohci1394.

Again, use the cdrecord command and its –scanbus option to obtain information needed to use the drive under SCSI emulation:

```
# cdrecord -scanbus
Cdrecord 1.10 (i686-pc-linux-gnu) Copyright (C) 1995-2001 Jörg Schilling
Linux sg driver version: 3.1.22
Using libscg version 'schily-0.5'
scsibus0:
    0,0,0   0) 'HL-DT-ST' 'RW/DVD GCC-4120B' '2.01' Removable CD-ROM
    0,1,0   1) *
    0,2,0   2) *
    0,3,0   3) *
    0,4,0   4) *
    0,5,0   5) *
    0,6,0   6) *
```

4

```
    0,7,0   7) *
scsibus1:
    1,0,0  100) 'TEAC   ' 'CD-W28E        ' '1.1A' Removable CD-ROM
    1,1,0  101) *
    1,2,0  102) *
    1,3,0  103) *
    1,4,0  104) *
    1,5,0  105) *
    1,6,0  106) *
    1,7,0  107) *
```

The pertinent information for the IEEE 1394 drive—1,0,0 in the example (a drive attached to SCSI bus 1, assigned device 0 and a lun of 0)—can then be used during a read operation like this:

```
# export CDDA_DEVICE=1,0,0
# cdda2wav -B
Type: ROM, Vendor 'TEAC   ' Model 'CD-W28E        ' Revision '1.1A' MMC+CDDA
724992 bytes buffer memory requested, 4 buffers, 75 sectors
#Cdda2wav version 1.10_linux_2.4.17-0.13smp_i686_i686 real time sched. \
soundcard support
AUDIOtrack pre-emphasis copy-permitted tracktype channels
    1- 8      no       no    audio  2
Table of Contents: total tracks:8, (total time 52:12.72)
 1.( 5:25.67), 2.( 9:06.65), 3.( 5:50.68), 4.( 5:35.57), 5.( 7:28.35)
 6.( 6:34.60), 7.( 6:07.15), 8.( 6:01.05),

Table of Contents: starting sectors
 1.(     0), 2.(  24442), 3.(  65457), 4.(  91775), 5.( 116957)
 6.( 150592), 7.( 180202), 8.( 207742), lead-out( 234822)
CDINDEX discid: SBRXDC1u_.D2S6U1MWq7ksIYOUE-
CDDB discid: 0x5e0c3a08
CD-Text: not detected
CD-Extra: not detected
samplefile size will be 552301388 bytes.
recording 3130.09600 seconds stereo with 16 bits @ 44100.0 Hz ->'audio'...
percent_done:
100% track 1 successfully recorded
100% track 2 successfully recorded
...
```

In this example, an environment variable named CDDA_DEVICE with the drive's SCSI information is created, and the cdda2wav command is used to extract the entire contents of an audio CD into .wav file format, with each track saved in a separate file. Other utilities might only need to know the name of the device, such as /dev/scd1, like this:

```
# cdparanoia -d /dev/scd1 -B
cdparanoia III release 9.8 (March 23, 2001)
(C) 2001 Monty <monty@xiph.org> and Xiphophorus

Report bugs to paranoia@xiph.org
http://www.xiph.org/paranoia/

    Couldn't disable kernel command translation layer
Ripping from sector     0 (track 1 [0:00.00])
    to sector 234821 (track 8 [6:01.04])

outputting to track01.cdda.wav
...
```

> **NOTE**
>
> Fedora also includes the cdrdao command, which can create "Disk-At-Once" (DAO) audio and data CD-ROMs. Other types of CD recording supported by Linux drivers and various CD drives include "Track-At-Once" and "Session-At-Once," which turn the drive's laser on and off during various stages of the recording process.

In this example, the CD-RW device name is used, and again, all tracks from an audio CD will be extracted and saved as .wav audio files. Other graphical clients, such as xine, grip, and xcdroast, are included with Red Hat Linux and can be used to create or copy audio and data CDs. See Chapter 26 for more details on burning CDs.

> **Related Fedora and Linux Commands**
>
> You'll use these commands when performing post-installation configuration tasks:
>
> apm—Views or uses power management settings and commands
>
> cardctl—Controls PCMCIA slots and services
>
> cdda2wav—Extracts audio files from audio CDs
>
> cdparanoia—Extracts audio files from audio CDs
>
> cdrecord—Gets SCSI device information and burns CD-ROMs
>
> chkconfig—Controls services at each Linux runlevel
>
> dmesg—Views information reported by the Linux kernel
>
> insmod—Loads a kernel module into memory
>
> internet-druid—Red Hat's graphical X client (also run as system-config-network) used to detect and configure a modem when configuring a dialup Internet connection
>
> kppp—KDE's X PPP connection utility can detect and use a modem
>
> lsmod—Views loaded kernel modules

> `mouseconfig`—Configures a pointing device for Linux
>
> `ntsysv`—Controls services started when booting Linux
>
> `system-config-date`—Red Hat's graphical date and time client
>
> `system-config-display`—Red Hat's graphical X configuration client
>
> `system-config-soundcard`—Red Hat's graphical sound card configuration tool
>
> `system-config-keyboard`—Red Hat's graphical keyboard map configuration tool
>
> `system-config-mouse`—Red Hat's graphical pointer configuration tool
>
> `sensors`—Gets the system's power, fan speed, and CPU temperatures
>
> `setserial`—Configures a serial port from the command line
>
> `sndconfig`—Configures a sound card for Fedora from the console

Reference

The *Linux Keyboard and Console HOWTO*—Andries Brouwer's tome on keyboard and console issues; includes many troubleshooting tips.

`http://www.avocent.com/Cybex/PublicW2.nsf/gwMain?OpenFrameset`—Product details for a KVM switch running Linux.

`http://www.luv.asn.au/overheads/virtualconsoles.html`—Using virtual consoles with Linux.

`http://www.synaptics.com/products/touchpad.cfm`—Information about TouchPad pointing devices.

`http://www.compass.com/synaptics/`—Site for a Linux TouchPad driver.

`http://www.x.org/`—The X.Org Foundation, home of X11R6 7.0.

`http://www.alsa-project.org`—Home page for the Advanced Linux Sound Architecture project, an alternative set of sound drivers for Linux.

`http://www.opensound.com`—Commercial sound drivers for Linux.

`/usr/src/linux-2.6/Documentation/power/pci.txt`—Patrick Mochel's document regarding PCI power-management routes for Linux kernel and PCI hardware support programmers.

`http://www.tldp.org/pub/Linux/docs/HOWTO/Modem-HOWTO`—One of the newest HOWTOs on using modems with Linux.

`http://www.tldp.org/pub/Linux/docs/HOWTO/Serial-HOWTO`—David S. Lawyer's Serial HOWTO, with additional information about Linux and serial port use.

`http://www2.lm-sensors.nu/~lm78/cvs/lm_sensors2/doc/FAQ`—Information regarding the `lm-sensors` software for Linux.

`http://pcmcia-cs.sourceforge.net/`—Source for the latest PCMCIA drivers for Linux.

`http://www.camiresearch.com/Data_Com_Basics/RS232_standard.html`—A description and tutorial on the EIA232 (formerly RS232) standard.

`http://www.qbik.ch/usb/devices/`—The place to check for compatibility of USB devices for Linux.

`http://www.linmodems.org`—This site provides links to several drivers for controllerless modem use under Linux.

`http://www.linux1394.org/`—Home page for the Linux IEEE 1394 project with new information, links to updated drivers, and lists of compatible chipsets and devices.

`http://www.faqchest.com/`—The FAQchest, a searchable archive of FAQ's HOWTO's and mailing lists; an alternative to `http://marc.theaimsgroup.com/`.

`http://groups.google.com/`—Search Usenet group through Google; another alternative to `http://marc.theaimsgroup.com/`.

`http://www.fokus.gmd.de/research/cc/glone/employees/joerg.schilling/private/_cdrecord.html`—Home page for the `cdrecord` command and related utilities.

`http://arstechnica.com/guide/building/bios/bios-1.html`—An excellent discussion of BIOS options at ArsTechnica.

`http://www.linuxnetmag.com/en/issue5/m5devs1.html`—A brief article on how to make use of the information found in devices.txt.

CHAPTER 5

First Steps with Fedora

IN THIS CHAPTER

• Working with the Linux File System

• Logging In to and Working with Linux

• Changing Your User Information

• Reading Documentation

• Using the Shell

• Using the Text Editors

• Working with Permissions

• Working As root

• Reference

Fedora Core Linux offers a wonderful graphical interface for the desktop (see Chapter 6, "The X Window System"), along with many capable graphical administration tools. However, there are times when you can't manage or use Linux effectively if you don't know how to use text-based programs at the command line. In some situations and with some software packages, the command line offers the only means of interacting with a running system or reconfiguring server software.

In this chapter, you learn the basics of how to use Linux and how to accomplish many routine tasks at the command line. These basic operations include how to read text files or other Linux documentation, list directories, or move, copy, and rename files. New Linux system administrators will get an introduction to using the command line to create new users, manage file permissions, and to properly reboot or shut down a Linux system.

Some of the basic command-line skills covered in this chapter include

- **Performing routine tasks**—Logging in and out, using the text console, changing passwords, listing and navigating directories.

- **Basic file management**—Creating, renaming, or deleting files and directories.

- **Basic user management**—Creating or deleting users from the command line.

- **Basic system management**—Shutting down or rebooting, reading manual pages or other documentation, and using text-based tools to edit system configuration files.

Read this chapter if you're migrating to Linux from another platform; the information here is valuable for individual users or system administrators who are new to Linux and learning to use the command line for the first time.

TIP

When you've learned how to use the command line with Linux, you'll be comfortable using a UNIX command line. This chapter, then, can help provide the foundation information you need to work with other UNIX-like operating systems, such as FreeBSD.

NOTE

There are two types of users on a Linux system: normal users (see the section "Basic Linux User Skills") and the root operator, also known as the *superuser.* At big computing installations, one or more system administrators might have root access or superuser power on the system (perhaps for one-time only tasks). Normal users may rarely, if ever, interact with the root operator.

However, if you use Linux on your PC or notebook as a standalone workstation, you will be both a user and the root operator. Under Linux, root access is required to perform nearly all system and hardware configuration. This might be one of the primary reasons that some new users hold the view that using Linux requires a steep learning curve. Red Hat, Inc. and other Linux developers have put a lot of effort into making system administration easier for new users by developing improved graphical administration utilities. Because of the way Linux is designed, however, you must become comfortable working with the command line and doing some root-level work, especially if using Linux on a standalone PC. The benefits of learning how to use the command line and work as the superuser far outweigh the disadvantages of allowing your operating system to make important system, file, and user decisions for you. You are in charge of your operating system, not the other way around!

Working with the Linux File System

Fedora uses a *file system*, or layout of hierarchical directories similar to that used by other UNIX variants (such as Mac OS X). Nearly all Linux distributions use a similar directory structure, and Linux distribution vendors have generally agreed on the naming and location of critical Linux files and directories.

NOTE

The effort to build a consensus regarding the Linux directory structure began in 1993 with the File system Hierarchy Standard (FHS), a draft proposal that addressed not only Linux issues, but also for other operating systems, such as BSD. Red Hat, Inc. has stated that it is committed to stay compliant with the FHS, which specifies the location and names of files and directories. Fedora uses the current 2.2 standard. The latest 2.3 draft proposal offers a glimpse into the future and possible changes to the standard—perhaps such as the addition of a /srv directory for data used by system services (such as FTP or Web pages) and a /media directory for removeable storage devices (while still retaining /mnt as a temporary mount point). For more about FHS, see the link in the "Reference" section at the end of this chapter.

The universal layout of directories and file locations for Linux is extremely helpful for individual developers or companies creating distributions, packaging applications, and crafting system administration utilities. For example, knowing that the useradd command is always found under the /usr/sbin directory can simplify the creation of administrative shell scripts designed to be used by system administrators. This information can also help you if you use other UNIX-like operating systems or other Linux distributions and need to troubleshoot software installation, or plan the addition of major software packages onto your Fedora system.

To gain the full benefits of this universal layout, you must know how Linux-based operating systems are organized, what the contents are of files and directories on your system, and where files and software should be installed. Understanding the Linux file system is part of learning how to administer and use Linux. As the root operator, you should know the name and proper location of all files (aside from user data) not only to ensure a smoothly running system, but also especially for security reasons.

Viewing the Linux File System

Look at the layout of the Fedora Core Linux system by using the list directory contents command, ls, like this:

```
$ ls /
bin   dev   home    lib         misc  opt   root  tftpboot  usr
boot  etc   initrd  lost+found  mnt   proc  sbin  tmp       var
```

NOTE

This section provides an overview of the Fedora Core file system. You might find fewer or more directories than discussed here in your own system. When some software packages are installed, they create new directories. Updating software packages might also remove or change the name of some directories. See Chapter 8, "Managing Software and System Resources," for more information on installing, upgrading, or removing software from your Linux system.

To get a more detailed picture, use the tree command to show the root or base directory layout, along with associated subdirectories, like this (note that your system's /usr/src directory might be somewhat different, depending on the version of Fedora you have installed or if you have updated Fedora with a new kernel, and that not all subdirectories are listed):

```
$ tree -dx /
/
|-- bin
|-- boot
|-- dev
|-- etc
|    |-- X11
|    |-- cron.d
|    |-- ppp
|    |-- rc.d
|    |-- ssh
|    `-- sysconfig
|-- home
|    `-- bball
|-- lib
|    `-- modules
|-- lost+found
|-- misc
|-- mnt
|    |-- cdrom
|    `-- floppy
|-- opt
|-- proc
|-- root
|-- sbin
|-- tftpboot
|-- tmp
|-- usr
|    |-- X11R6
|    |    |-- bin
|    |    |-- include
|    |    |-- lib
|    |-- bin
|    |-- doc
|    |-- include
|    |-- lib
|    |-- local
|    |-- sbin
|    |-- share
|    |-- src
|    |    |-- linux-2.6 -> linux-2.6.7-1.478
|    |    |-- linux-2.6.7-1.478
|    |    `-- redhat
```

```
|   |    `-- sys
|
|
`-- var
    |-- ftp
    |-- log
    `-- spool
```

This example (pruned from more than 10,000 directories) shows the higher-level directories and corresponds to the directories and descriptions in Table 5.1.

TABLE 5.1   Basic Linux Directories

Name	Description
/	The root directory
/bin	Essential commands
/boot	Boot loader files, Linux kernel
/dev	Device files
/etc	System configuration files
/home	User home directories
/initrd	Initial RAM disk boot support (used during boot time)
/lib	Shared libraries, kernel modules
/lost+found	Directory for recovered files (if found after a file system check)
/mnt	Usual mount point for local, remote file systems
/opt	Add-on software packages
/proc	Kernel information, process control
/root	Superuser (root home)
/sbin	System commands (mostly root only)
/sys	Real-time information on devices used by the kernel
/tftpboot	Network boot support
/tmp	Temporary files
/usr	Secondary software file hierarchy
/var	Variable data (such as logs); spooled files

Some of the important directories in Table 5.1, such as those containing user and root commands or system configuration files, are discussed in the following sections. You'll use and edit files under these directories when you use Fedora.

Use Essential Commands from the /bin and /sbin Directories

The /bin directory (about 55MB if you do a full install) contains essential commands used by the system when running and booting Linux. In general, only the root operator uses the commands in the /sbin directory. Many (though not all) of these commands are *statically* linked; such commands do not depend on software libraries residing under the /lib or /usr/lib directories. Nearly all the other applications on your system are *dynamically* linked—meaning that they require external software libraries (also known as *shared libraries*) in order to run.

TIP

Because the system contains dynamically linked applications, you might sometimes get "dependency errors" when installing or upgrading software packages; in those situations, a supporting library (or application) might not be present. See Chapter 8 for more information on working with dynamically linked applications and other methods of avoiding such problems.

Store the Booted Kernel and View Stored Devices in the /boot and /dev Directories

The /boot directory contains a compressed version of the Linux kernel (loaded at boot time), along with other files that describe the kernel or provide information for booting Linux. When you rebuild or install a new kernel, the kernel and related files are placed in this directory (see Chapter 24, "Kernel and Module Management," for more information on rebuilding or installing a kernel).

Linux device files are contained under the /dev directory. Note that under Linux, nearly everything on your system is a file. This means that (with the exception of network interfaces; see note that follows list) regular files; directories; hard drive partitions; serial, printer, or USB ports; and video and sound devices all are files!

The /dev directory contains more than 7,500 files representing devices that may or may not be in use on your system. Some of the most commonly used devices in this directory include

- IDE (Integrated Drive Electronics) hard drives, such as /dev/hda and /dev/hdb.

- CD-ROM drives; some of which are IDE, whereas others are CD-RW (CD read/write) drives emulated as SCSI (Small Computer Systems Interface) devices such as /dev/scd0.

- Serial ports, such as /dev/ttyS0 for COM1, /dev/ttyS1 for COM2, and so on.

- Pointing devices, including /dev/psaux and others.

- Printers, such as /dev/lp0.

NOTE

Network interfaces (such as eth0 or ppp0) are not represented by Linux device files, but are created in memory when activated. See Chapter 13, "Network Connectivity," for more information.

Use and Edit Files in the /etc Directory

More than 20MB of system configuration files and directories reside under the /etc directory if you install all the software included with this book. Some major software packages, such as Apache, OpenSSH, and xinetd, have directories of configuration files under /etc. Other important system-related configuration files in /etc are

- fstab—The system file system table is a text file listing each hard drive, CD-ROM, floppy, or other storage device attached to your PC. The table indexes each device's partition information with a place in your Linux file system (directory layout) and lists other options for each device when used with Linux (see Chapter 10, "Managing the File System"). Nearly all entries in fstab can be manipulated by root using the mount command.

- inittab—The system initialization table defines the default runlevel, also known as *run-control* level or *system state*. Changes to this file can determine whether your system boots to a graphical or text login, as well as whether dial-up remote access is enabled. (You learn about default runlevels in the section "System Services and Runlevels" located in Chapter 7, "Managing Services." See the section "Starting X" located in Chapter 6 to learn more about changing inittab to boot to a graphical interface. Chapter 15, "Internet Connectivity," in the section "Configuring a Dial-In PPP Server" discusses editing inittab to enable dial-up remote access).

- modprobe.conf—This configuration file contains directions and options used when loading kernel modules to enable various types of hardware, such as sound, USB, networking, and so on (discussed in the section "Building and Installing Modules" in Chapter 24). The contents of this file are used during boot time, and the file can be manually edited or automatically updated by Red Hat's kudzu hardware management server (if enabled, as you learn later in this section).

- passwd—The list of users for the system, along with user account information. The contents of this file can be changed by various programs, such as useradd or chsh.

- printcap—The system's printer capabilities database (discussed in the section "Overview of Fedora Linux Printing" in Chapter 12, "Printing with Fedora").

- shells—A list of approved shells (command-line interfaces).

One of the most important directories under /etc for Fedora is sysconfig. This directory contains network activation scripts and hardware- and software-related information:

```
$ tree -afx /etc/sysconfig
/etc/sysconfig
¦-- /etc/sysconfig/amd
¦-- /etc/sysconfig/apm-scripts
¦    `-- /etc/sysconfig/apm-scripts/apmscript
¦-- /etc/sysconfig/apmd
```

5

```
...
¦-- /etc/sysconfig/clock
¦-- /etc/sysconfig/console
¦-- /etc/sysconfig/dhcpd
¦-- /etc/sysconfig/dhcrelay
¦-- /etc/sysconfig/gpm
¦-- /etc/sysconfig/grub
¦-- /etc/sysconfig/harddisks
¦-- /etc/sysconfig/hwconf

...
¦-- /etc/sysconfig/init
¦-- /etc/sysconfig/irda
¦-- /etc/sysconfig/keyboard
¦-- /etc/sysconfig/kudzu
¦-- /etc/sysconfig/mouse
¦-- /etc/sysconfig/named
¦-- /etc/sysconfig/netdump

...
¦-- /etc/sysconfig/network
¦-- /etc/sysconfig/network-scripts
¦    ¦-- /etc/sysconfig/network-scripts/ifcfg-eth0
...
¦    ¦-- /etc/sysconfig/network-scripts/ifup-wireless
¦    ¦-- /etc/sysconfig/network-scripts/init.ipv6-global
¦    ¦-- /etc/sysconfig/network-scripts/network-functions
¦    `-- /etc/sysconfig/network-scripts/network-functions-ipv6
¦-- /etc/sysconfig/networking
¦    ¦-- /etc/sysconfig/networking/devices
¦    ¦-- /etc/sysconfig/networking/ifcfg-lo
...
¦    `-- /etc/sysconfig/networking/profiles
¦         `-- /etc/sysconfig/networking/profiles/default
¦-- /etc/sysconfig/ntpd
¦-- /etc/sysconfig/pcmcia

...
¦-- /etc/sysconfig/redhat-config-users
¦-- /etc/sysconfig/redhat-logviewer
¦-- /etc/sysconfig/rhn
¦    ¦-- /etc/sysconfig/rhn/rhnsd
¦    ¦-- /etc/sysconfig/rhn/up2date
¦    `-- /etc/sysconfig/rhn/up2date-keyring.gpg
¦-- /etc/sysconfig/samba
¦-- /etc/sysconfig/sendmail
¦-- /etc/sysconfig/spamassassin
```

```
¦-- /etc/sysconfig/squid
¦-- /etc/sysconfig/syslog
...
¦-- /etc/sysconfig/ups
¦-- /etc/sysconfig/vncservers
¦-- /etc/sysconfig/xinetd
`-- /etc/sysconfig/yppasswdd
```

For brevity, not all directories and files are discussed here or listed in the example. /etc/sysconfig contains many different hardware and software settings critical to the operation of your Fedora system. Knowing the location and contents of these files can be helpful if you need to troubleshoot new hardware configurations.

The settings in various files under /etc/sysconfig (such as keyboard, mouse, sound, and so on) are usually created automatically by a related Red Hat or Fedora graphical or console-based configuration utility.

These contents might dynamically change if you use the kudzu hardware configuration service. The kudzu service also prompts you at boot time to remove, configure, or ignore a related setting if kudzu detects new or different hardware (such as a new USB keyboard, network card, or monitor). kudzu creates a file called hwconf that contains a hardware profile of your PC's current state. Note that if kudzu is not enabled or running, you can use device-specific configuration utilities such as redhat-config-keyboard, or you can manually edit configuration files.

Information about the type of pointing device attached to the PC, for example, is contained in the file /etc/sysconfig/mouse:

```
MOUSETYPE="ps/2"
XMOUSETYPE="PS/2"
FULLNAME="Generic 3 Button Mouse (PS/2)"
XEMU3=no
```

If a different mouse, say a three-button USB device, is attached to the computer, you can edit this information to reflect the hardware change:

```
MOUSETYPE="ps/2"
XMOUSETYPE="IMPS/2"
FULLNAME="Generic 3 Button Mouse (USB)"
XEMU3=no
```

CAUTION

If you're new to Linux, the redhat-config-mouse client is the best tool to use to configure a new mouse. You should only manually edit system hardware configuration files used by graphical management clients as a last resort.

Protect the Contents of User Directories—/home

The most important data on a Linux system reside in user's directories, found under the /home directory. Segregating the system and user data can be helpful in preventing data loss and making the process of backing up easier. For example, having user data reside on a separate file system or mounted from a remote computer on the network might help shield users from data loss in the event of a system hardware failure.

Use the Contents of the /proc Directory to Interact with the Kernel

The content of the /proc directory is created from memory and only exists while Linux is running. This directory contains special "files" that either extract information from or send information to the kernel. Many Linux utilities extract information from dynamically created directories and files under this directory, also known as a *virtual file system*. For example, the free command obtains its information from a file named meminfo:

```
$ free
              total      used      free    shared    buffers     cached
Mem:         223260    157800     65460         0      55400      58872
-/+ buffers/cache:      43528    179732
Swap:        491392       400    490992
```

This information constantly changes as the system is used. You can get the same information by using the cat command to see the contents of the meminfo file:

```
$ cat /proc/meminfo
            total:      used:      free:   shared:  buffers:    cached:
Mem:   228618240 161673216  66945024         0 56750080   60694528
Swap: 503185408    409600 502775808
MemTotal:       223260 kB
MemFree:         65376 kB
MemShared:           0 kB
Buffers:         55420 kB
Cached:          58872 kB
SwapCached:        400 kB
Active:         100328 kB
Inact_dirty:     25044 kB
Inact_clean:     19012 kB
Inact_target:    28876 kB
HighTotal:           0 kB
HighFree:            0 kB
LowTotal:       223260 kB
LowFree:         65376 kB
SwapTotal:      491392 kB
SwapFree:       490992 kB
Committed_AS:    51424 kB
```

The /proc directory can also be used to dynamically alter the behavior of a running Linux kernel by "echoing" numerical values to specific files under the /proc/sys directory. For example, to "turn on" kernel protection against one type of Denial Of Service (DOS) attack known as *SYN flooding*, use the echo command to send the number 1 (one) to the following /proc path:

```
# echo 1 >/proc/sys/net/ipv4/tcp_syncookies
```

> **NOTE**
>
> The Linux kernel has a number of built-in protections, but good system administration security policies and a secure firewall protecting your gateway, router, or Internet-connected system are the best protection you can use. See the section "Securing Your Network" in Chapter 13 for an overview of firewalling and examples of how to implement Red Hat's network security tools included with Fedora.

Other ways to use the /proc directory include

- Getting CPU information, such as the family, type, and speed from /proc/cpuinfo.

- Viewing important networking information under /proc/net, such as active interfaces in action under /proc/net/dev, routing information in /proc/net/route, and network statistics in /proc/net/netstat.

- Retrieving file system information (see /usr/src/linux-2.6/Documentation/file systems/proc.txt for more information).

- Reporting media mount point information via USB; for example, the Linux kernel will report what device to use to access files (such as /dev/sda) if a USB camera or hard drive is detected on the system. You can use the dmesg command to see this information or find information about these devices under the Device File System directory /proc/devfs (see the Linux Devfs FAQ in the file /usr/src/linux-2.6/Documentation/file systems/devfs/README if the source code for the Linux kernel is installed). The file /usr/src/linux-2.6/Documentation/usb/proc_usb_info.txt contains general information about USB and the /proc directory, as well as what to expect in files under this directory. Note that devfs might be supported, but will generally be superseded in the upcoming 2.6 kernel by /proc/udev, as a way of managing hot-plug devices on your system.

- Getting the kernel version in /proc/version, performance information such as uptime in /proc/uptime, or other statistics such as CPU load, swap file usage, and processes in /proc/stat.

Work with Shared Data in the /usr Directory

The /usr directory (nearly 5GB in size if you do a full install) contains software applications, libraries, and other types of shared data for use by anyone on the system. Many

Linux system administrators give /usr its own partition. A number of subdirectories under /usr contain the X Window System (/usr/X11R6), manual pages (/usr/share/man), software package shared files (/usr/share/name_of_package, such as /usr/share/emacs), additional application or software package documentation (/usr/share/doc), and an entire subdirectory tree of locally built and installed software, /usr/local.

Temporary File Storage in the /tmp Directory

As its name implies, the /tmp directory is used for temporary file storage; as you use Linux, various programs create files in this directory. The /tmp directory is cleaned of stale files each day by the tmpwatch command. (A stale file is any file not used after 10 days.) Fedora is configured by default to use tmpwatch to check /tmp each day by settings in your system's scheduling table, /etc/crontab.

Access Variable Data Files in the /var Directory

The /var directory contains subdirectories used by various system services for spooling and logging. Many of these variable data files, such as print spooler queues, are temporary, whereas others, such as system and kernel logs, are renamed and rotated in use. Incoming electronic mail is usually directed to files under /var/spool/mail.

Linux also uses /var for other important system services. These include the top-most File Transfer Protocol (FTP) directory under /var/ftp (see Chapter 18, "Secure File Transfer Protocol (FTP) Service"), and the Apache Web server's initial home page directory for the system, /var/www/html. (See Chapter 16, "Apache Web Server Management," for more information on using Apache).

Logging In to and Working with Linux

You can access and use a Linux system in a number of ways. One way is at the console with a monitor, keyboard, and mouse attached to the PC. Another way might be via a serial console, either by dial-up via a modem or a PC running a terminal emulator and connected to the Linux PC via a null modem cable. You can also connect to your system through a wired or wireless network using the telnet or ssh commands. The information in this section shows you how to access and use the Linux system using physical and remote text-based logins.

> **NOTE**
>
> This chapter focuses on text-based logins and use of Linux. Graphical logins and using a graphical desktop are described in the section "Starting X" in Chapter 6.

Text-based Console Login

If you sit down at your PC and log in to a Linux system that has not been booted to a graphical login, you see a prompt similar to this one:

```
Fedora Core release 2 (Tettnang)
Kernel 2.6.7-1.478.nptl on an i686

login:
```

Your prompt might vary, depending on the version of Fedora Core you're using. In any event, at this prompt, type in your username and press Enter. When you are prompted for your password, type it in and press Enter.

> **NOTE**
> Note that your password is not echoed back to you, which is a good idea.

Working with Virtual Consoles

After logging in, you will be using an interactive command prompt known as a *shell* in the Linux text-based or *console* mode.

While you're sitting at your command prompt, you can also use one or more *virtual* consoles or terminals. Virtual consoles allow you to log in to Linux multiple times. (Each login is called a *session*.) This can be useful if you are not using a graphical desktop, but want to use several interactive programs, such as a text editor and Web browser, at the same time. To do so, after you log in, run a program and then jump to another login prompt, log in, and start another session. Linux supports 63 virtual consoles, but only the first 6 are configured for use. (You can use 7 if you don't run X11.) Here's how to use virtual Linux consoles:

1. Log in. You'll be using the first virtual console, or vt1 by default.
2. Press F2. You should then see another login prompt. Log in again, and you are then using vt2, the second Linux console.
3. Press Alt+F1 to jump back to vt1.
4. Press Alt+F2 to jump back to vt2.

You can jump back and forth between sessions by using the Alt key plus the F key number of the desired session, such as F3, F4, F5, or F6.

One caveat when using virtual consoles is that there is a default limit on the available number (usually six) if an active X Window session is occupying vt7. To jump to a virtual console from an X session, press Ctrl+Alt+F2; you'll be at vt2. You can then jump back to your X session from the text-console by pressing Alt+F7 (to go to vt7, in use by X). You should also be careful to save any work in progress before you exit each session and to log out of each session when finished. If you do not, you could leave an open login and shell prompt available at the keyboard to anyone who walks by!

> **NOTE**
>
> In addition to virtual console keystrokes, the Linux console might also recognize the three-fingered salute (or Vulcan neck pinch), Ctrl+Alt+Del. This behavior (and the number of virtual terminals) can be controlled by the system administrator by editing the system's *initialization table,* `/etc/inittab`. See the Keyboard and Console HOWTO at `http://www.tldp.org/` for more details.

Using Simple Keyboard and Mouse Techniques in a Linux Console Session

Working with Linux in a console-based session usually involves entering commands from the keyboard. However, you can also use simple mouse controls as well. Linux keyboard combinations and mouse support help provide virtual console navigation, start special system actions (such as rebooting or shutting down), provide shortcuts to save typing, and can aid in reading files or viewing program output.

For example, you can scroll the contents of your screen from the console by pressing Shift+PageUp or Shift+PageDown, and can copy and paste text using your mouse buttons. This section shows you how to access default or custom menus at the text console, which can be helpful to get system information or to launch new programs.

If you use a mouse with Linux (and you most likely do), you can use your pointing device for copy and paste operations. This support is provided by gpm, the general purpose mouse server. The gpm server must be enabled or started while booting Linux (for more details, see the section "Controlling Services at Boot Using Administrative Tools" in Chapter 7). To copy a section of text, click and drag text with the left mouse button (button 1) held down. To paste text, click an insertion point, and then press the middle mouse button (button 2).

Button assignment, like all mouse controls during text console use, is managed by command-line options given to gpm when it is started. For example, if you look at the gpm startup script named gpm under the `/etc/rc.d/init.d/` directory, you'll see that it uses the file named gpm under the `/etc/sysconfig` directory to hold options:

```
# Additional options for gpm (e.g. acceleration), device
OPTIONS=""
DEVICE="/dev/mouse"
```

You can add options, detailed in the gpm manual page to change how your mouse works, enable or disable features, or assign special commands to a specific mouse button click. For example, to change your button order from 123 (left, middle, and right) to 321, edit the `/etc/sysconfig/gpm` file as root and change the OPTIONS entry like so:

```
OPTIONS="-B 321"
```

After saving your changes, restart gpm like so:

```
# /etc/rc.d/init.d/gpm restart
```

Your mouse buttons will now be reversed!

To aid users with a two-button mouse, Linux supports three-button *emulation*; emulation lets users simultaneously press the right and left mouse buttons to simulate a press of the middle button. You can enable this feature during installation or by using the mouseconfig command. See the section "Configuring Pointing Devices in Linux" in Chapter 4, "Post-Installation Issues," to see how to use mouseconfig.

The gpm server also provides the ability to reboot or shut down the system with the mouse. Depending on the combination of mouse buttons you press, you have several reboot or shutdown options. Begin by holding down either the left or right mouse button and triple-clicking the opposite button; depending on which mouse button you press next, one of these actions occurs:

- Pressing the left button causes an immediate reboot using the init command.

- Pressing the middle button reboots the system using the shutdown command.

- Pressing the right button causes the system to shut down immediately with the shutdown command.

You can also create custom menus that will pop up at a text-based Linux console by editing the file /etc/gpm-root.conf (as root) and starting the gpm-root command. When you run gpm-root without making changes to its configuration file, by default a system status dialog (with the date, time, CPU load, free memory, and swap file usage) will appear if you hold down the Ctrl key and press the middle mouse button.

You can change your keyboard layouts by using the loadkeys command. To use a different font for the console, try the setfont command. Fedora Core Linux comes with nearly 150 different console fonts, which are found under the /lib/kbd/consolefonts directory. See the section "Configuring Keyboards with Linux" in Chapter 4 to see how to use these commands.

> **NOTE**
>
> A text-based, dial-up login, also known as a *shell* account, looks much the same as a text-based login at a PC running Linux. Details about setting up Linux to answer the phone and provide a login prompt via a modem are in Chapter 15. Using dial-up access has some limitations, such as the inability to use virtual consoles. From a shell account, however, you can start programs in the background (using the ampersand, &), run programs after logging out with the nohup command, or use the screen command to simulate virtual terminals (an approach that works much like using virtual consoles). For more information on different shells included with Linux, see Chapter 22, "Shell Scripting."

Logging Out

Use the exit or logout commands to exit your session. Type the command and press Enter. You'll then be returned to the login prompt. If you use virtual consoles, remember to exit each console before leaving your PC. (Otherwise, someone could easily sit down and use your account.)

Logging In and Out from a Remote Computer

Although you can happily log in on your computer, an act known as a *local* log in, you can also log in to your computer via a network connection from a remote computer. Linux-based operating systems provide a number of remote access commands you can use to log in to other computers on your local area network (LAN), wide area network (WAN), or the Internet. Note that not only must you have an account on the remote computer, but also the remote computer must be configured to support remote logins—otherwise, you won't be able to log in.

> **NOTE**
>
> See Chapter 13 to see how to set up network interfaces with Linux to support remote network logins and Chapter 7 to see how to start remote access services (such as sshd).

The best and most secure way (barring future exploits) to log in to a remote Linux computer is to use the ssh or Secure Shell client. Your login and session are encrypted while you work on the remote computer. The ssh client features many different command-line options, but can be simply used with the name of the remote computer, like this:

```
[winky@shuttle winky]$ ssh shuttle2
The authenticity of host 'shuttle2 (192.168.2.70)' can't be established.
RSA key fingerprint is 45:93:1c:aa:02:32:8d:eb:c6:71:ce:26:97:17:5f:0b.
Are you sure you want to continue connecting (yes/no)? yes
```

The first time you connect with a remote computer using ssh, Linux displays the remote computer's encrypted identity key and asks you to verify the connection. After you type **yes** and press Enter, you're warned that the remote computer's identity (key) has been entered in a file named known_hosts under the .ssh directory in your home directory. You're also prompted to enter your password:

```
Warning: Permanently added 'shuttle2,192.168.2.70' (RSA) \
to the list of known hosts.
winky@shuttle2's password:
/usr/X11R6/bin/xauth:  creating new authority file /home/winky/.Xauthority
[winky@shuttle2 winky]$
```

After entering your password, you can then work on the remote computer. Again, everything you enter on the keyboard in communication with the remote computer is encrypted. Use the `exit` or `logout` commands to exit your session and return to the shell on your computer.

CAUTION

The next remote access command, `telnet`, is shown as an example because it is included with most Linux distributions, but you shouldn't use it: `telnet` transmits your username and password in clear text across the network, posing a huge security risk for your system. Also, note that this service must be explicitly turned on and allowed on the remote computer (by editing the file named `telnet` under the `/etc/xinetd.d` directory and then restarting `xinetd`; see the section "Starting and Stopping Services Manually" in Chapter 7 for more information on starting or restarting a system service).

The `telnet` command can be used, along with the name of a remote host or Internet Protocol (IP) address, to log in to a remote computer. For example, to log in to the host named `shuttle2` from the host named `shuttle`,

```
[winky@shuttle winky]$ telnet shuttle2
```

After you press Enter, you'll see some information presented by the remote computer, and you will then be prompted for your username on the remote system:

```
Trying 192.168.2.70...
Connected to shuttle2.home.org (192.168.2.70).
Escape character is '^]'.

Linux 2.6.7-1.478 (shuttle2.home.org) (15:43 on Friday, 30 August 2002)

login: winky
```

After you type your username (`winky` in this example), press Enter, and you'll be prompted for your password on the remote system:

```
Password:
Last login: Fri Aug 30 15:42:26 from 192.168.2.68
[winky@shuttle2 winky]$
```

After you type your password and press Enter (your password is not echoed back), you'll be informed of the last time you logged in, and you can then work on the remote computer. Use the `exit` or `logout` commands to exit your session and return to the shell on your computer.

Although it is possible to use `telnet` to log in to a remote computer over a wired and wireless network, such use is not recommended, especially via the Internet. When you type your username and then press Enter and type your password, your username and password are transmitted without encryption over the network. Transmitting usernames and passwords over a network without encryption is a bad idea for obvious reasons. However, if you have a physically secure internal network not connected to the Internet, have firewall policies in place, and don't use wireless networking, there is nothing wrong with using telnet. In fact, the encryption overhead of using ssh can reduce network transmission rates in some cases.

> **NOTE**
>
> It is possible to securely use telnet over an encrypted Virtual Private Network (VPN), but that is beyond the scope of this chapter and book. Besides, why bother when you can use ssh?

Changing Your User Information

Linux users are assigned a name, known as a *username*, by the root operator. One method of assigning usernames is to use one's first initial and last name in lowercase; for example, Beth Smith would have a username of *bsmith*. Each user must also have a password, which is used with the username either at a graphical or text-based login.

> **NOTE**
>
> Older versions of Linux operating systems limited the length of usernames to 8 characters. The current version of Fedora limits usernames to 32 characters. Good passwords should be a minimum of 8 characters long and contain upper- and lowercase letters, along with numbers. Random passwords for users can be generated using the mkpasswd command (which is included with the expect software package). For example, to automatically generate a 10-character password with three numbers and three digits, use mkpasswd -l 10 -d 3 -C 3. Good passwords are not birthdays, anniversaries, your pet's name, the name of your significant other, or the model of your first car!

You cannot change your username, but you can change your user information, such as address, phone, and so on. You make these changes using the chfn or *change finger information* command. This command will modify the contents of your entry in the system password file /etc/passwd, which is used by the finger command to display information about a system's user. For example, type **chfn** at the command line and press Enter:

```
$ chfn
Changing finger information for pjovanovich.
Password:
Name []: Pete Jovanovich
Office []: Suite 120 N. Arlington Blvd.
Office Phone []: 202 555-1212
Home Phone []: 202 555-1212
Finger information changed.
```

You're led through a series of prompts to enter new or updated information. Note that the chfn command will not let you use any commas when entering information. You can verify this information in a couple ways, for example, by looking at the contents of /etc/passwd:

```
$ grep pjovanovich /etc/passwd
pjovanovich:x:501:501:Pete Jovanovich,Suite 120 N. Arlington Blvd.,\
202 555-1212,202 555-1212:/home/pjovanovich:/bin/bash
```

You also can verify the updated user information by using the finger command:

```
$ finger pjovanovich
Login: pjovanovich                      Name: Pete Jovanovich
Directory: /home/pjovanovich             Shell: /bin/bash
Office: Suite 120 N. Arlington Blvd.    Office Phone: 202 555-1212
Home Phone: 202 555-1212
Never logged in.
No mail.
No Plan.
```

Reading Documentation

Although you learn the basics of using Fedora in this book, you need time and practice to master and troubleshoot more complex aspects of the Linux operating system and your distribution. As with any operating system, you can expect to encounter some problems or perplexing questions as you continue to work with Linux. The first place to turn for help with these issues is the documentation included with your system; if you can't find the information you need there, check Fedora's Web site.

> **NOTE**
>
> Checking Fedora's Web site for security updates and bug fixes is a good idea. Browse to http://fedora.redhat.com/download/.

Linux, like UNIX, is a self-documenting system, with manual pages accessible through the man command. Linux offers many other helpful commands for accessing its documentation. You can use the apropos command—for example, with a keyword such as partition—to find commands related to partitioning, like this:

```
$ apropos partition
GNU Parted [parted]   (8)  - a partition manipulation program
fdisk                 (8)  - Partition table manipulator for Linux
jfs_mkfs              (8)  - create a JFS formatted partition
jfs_mkfs [mkfs]       (8)  - create a JFS formatted partition
lvmdiskscan          (8)  - scan for all disks / multiple devices / partitions
➥ available
```

```
mpartition          (1)  - partition an MSDOS hard disk
partprobe           (8)  - inform the OS of partition table changes
pvcreate            (8)  - initialize a disk or partition for use by LVM
sfdisk              (8)  - Partition table manipulator for Linux
```

To find a command and its documentation, you can use the whereis command. For example, if you are looking for the fdisk command, you can do this:

```
$ whereis fdisk
fdisk: /sbin/fdisk /usr/share/man/man8/fdisk.8.gz
```

Using man Pages

To learn more about a command or program, use the man command, followed by the name of the command. Manual pages for Linux and X Window commands are within the /usr/share/man, /usr/local/share/man, and /usr/X11R6/man directories; so, for example, to read the rm command's man page, use the man command like this:

```
$ man rm
```

After you press Enter, the less command (a Linux command known as a pager) displays the manual page. The less command is a text browser you can use to scroll forward and backward (even sideways) through the document to learn more about the command. Type the letter **h** to get help, use the forward slash to enter a search string, or press **q** to quit.

> **NOTE**
>
> Although nearly all the hundreds of GNU Project commands included with Linux each have a manual page, detailed information about using a GNU command must be read using the info command. For example, to learn even more about bash (which has a rather extensive manual page), use the info command like this:
>
> ```
> $ info bash
> ```
>
> Press the N and P keys to navigate through the document, or scroll down to a menu item on the screen and press Enter to read about a specific feature. Press Q to quit reading.

Finding and Reading Software Packages Documentation

Documentation for various software packages is included in the /usr/share/doc directory; that directory is stored in another directory that's labeled with the associated package's name. You can find other Linux documentation, known as HOWTOs and Frequently Asked Questions (FAQs), online by browsing to http://www.tldp.org. HOWTO documents contain specific information related to a particular subject, such as printing, setting up a network, programming a serial port, or using a CD-ROM drive with Linux. These documents can be read by using your Web browser. Of course, one of the best online tools you can use is a good search engine, such as Google.

You can read document formats such as text with `less` or another pager or text reader. For example, to read a copy of the GNU General Public License (GPL), a file named `GPL_V2` under the `/usr/share/apps/LICENSES` directory, use `less` like this:

```
$ less /usr/share/apps/LICENSES/GPL_V2
```

After you press Enter, you can scroll back and forth through the file. Press Q to quit reading. If a document is in compressed form (ending in `.gz`), use the `zless` pager, which will decompress a document first:

```
$ zless /usr/share/man/es/man1/README.gz
```

Most users read document formats such as HTML using a Web browser in a graphical desktop. Fedora includes at least two versatile text-based Web browsers, however, accessed with the `lynx` and `links` commands. To browse an HTML file on your system without using X11, use either command, along with the path to the file. For example, to read an HTML version of the GNU GPL with `links`, use the command like this:

```
$ links /usr/share/doc/HTML/en/common/gpl-license.html
```

After you press Enter, use your Up and Down cursor keys to scroll back and forth through the file. Press Q, Enter to quit reading. If you have configured a mouse, click the left button near the top of the screen, and `links` will display its menus.

Using the Shell

The shell is an interactive command prompt with many different features:

- Input and output redirection
- Background processing
- Job control
- History editing
- Built-in help
- Command-line completion
- Command-line editing

The shell interprets keyboard commands and is generally used to launch other commands or programs using the shell's interpreter language known as *shell scripts*.

> **NOTE**
>
> Shell scripts are discussed in Chapter 22.

The shell you use is assigned by the last field in your entry in the system's `/etc/passwd` file. This example, for a hapless user named `winky`, shows that the login shell is `bash`:

```
winky:x:502:502::/home/winky:/bin/bash
```

The default shell for most Linux distributions, including Fedora, is the GNU `bash` or Bourne Again SHell, but other shells, such as `tcsh`, `ksh`, and `zsh` are available for use. You can use a different shell by typing its name at the command line. Alternatively, the root operator might assign a user to another shell when creating that user account (see "Working As `root`," later in this chapter).

> **CAUTION**
>
> If you're interested in trying a different shell with Linux, you can change your login shell using the `chsh` command, but make sure that the shell is actually installed on your system. For example, to change your default shell to `tcsh`, first use the `which` command to verify that it is installed:
>
> ```
> $ which tcsh
> /bin/tcsh
> ```
>
> This example shows that the `tcsh` shell is installed under the `/bin` directory. The `tcsh` shell should also be listed in your system's list of approved shells, `/etc/shells`. Check to make sure that it is listed:
>
> ```
> $ grep tcsh /etc/shells
> /bin/tcsh
> ```
>
> You can also use the `chsh` command's `-l` option to list valid system shells in order to verify that using `tcsh` is allowed. Because `tcsh` is installed and listed in `/etc/shells`, you can then change your shell using the `chsh` command:
>
> ```
> $ chsh
> Changing shell for winky.
> Password:
> New shell [/bin/bash]: /bin/ksh
> chsh: "/bin/ksh" does not exist.
> ```
>
> Note that the `chsh` command will report an error if you enter the name of a shell not installed on your system.
>
> ```
> $ chsh -s /bin/tcsh
> Changing shell for winky.
> Password:
> Shell changed.
> ```

If you now take a look at your /etc/passwd entry, you'll see /bin/tcsh as your default shell. The next time you log in, you'll use tcsh.

Using Environment Variables

A number of in-memory variables are assigned and loaded by default when the user logs in. These variables are known as shell *environment variables*, which can be used by various commands to get information about your environment, such as the type of system you are running, your home directory, and the shell in use. Environment variables are used by Linux operating systems to help tailor the computing environment of your system, and include helpful specifications and setup, such as default locations of executable files and software libraries. If you begin writing shell scripts, you might use environment variables in your scripts. Until then, you only need to be aware of what environment variables are and do.

The following list includes a number of environment variables, along with descriptions of how the shell uses them:

- PWD—To provide the name of the current working directory, used by the pwd command (such as /home/winky/foo)

- USER—To declare the user's name, such as winky

- LANG—To set language defaults, such as English

- SHELL—To declare the name and location of the current shell, such as /bin/bash

- PATH—To set the default location of executable files, such as /bin, /usr/bin, and so on

- LD_LIBRARY_PATH—To declare the location of important software libraries (because most, but not all, Linux commands use shared resources)

- TERM—To set the type of terminal in use, such as vt100, which can be important when using screen-oriented programs, such as text editors

- MACHINE—To declare system type, system architecture, and so on

> **NOTE**
>
> Each shell can have its own feature set and language syntax, as well as a unique set of default environment variables. See Chapter 22 for more information about using the different shells included with Fedora.

At the command line, you can use the env or printenv commands to display these environment variables, like so:

```
$ env
PWD=/home/bball
HOSTNAME=thinkpad.home.org
USER=bball
MACHTYPE=i386-redhat-linux-gnu
MAIL=/var/spool/mail/bball
BASH_ENV=/home/bball/.bashrc
LANG=en_US
DISPLAY=titanium:0
LOGNAME=bball
SHLVL=1
PATH=/usr/kerberos/bin:/usr/local/bin:/bin:/usr/bin: \
/usr/X11R6/bin:/home/bball/bin
SHELL=/bin/bash
HOSTTYPE=i386
OSTYPE=linux-gnu
HISTSIZE=1000
TERM=xterm
HOME=/home/bball
```

This abbreviated list shows a few common variables. These variables are set by configuration or *resource* files contained in the /etc, /etc/skel, or user /home directory. You can find default settings for bash, for example, in /etc/profile, /etc/bashrc, the .bashrc, or .bash_profile files installed in your home directory. Read the man page for bash for details about using these configuration files.

One of the most important environment variables is $PATH, which defines the location of executable files. For example, if as a regular user, you try to use a command that is not located in your $PATH, such as the ifconfig command, you'll see something like this:

```
$ ifconfig
-bash: ifconfig: command not found
```

However, you might know that ifconfig is definitely installed on your system, and you can verify this using the whereis command like so:

```
$ whereis ifconfig
ifconfig: /sbin/ifconfig /usr/share/man/man8/ifconfig.8.gz
```

You can also run the command by typing its full *pathname*, or complete directory specification like this:

```
$ /sbin/ifconfig
```

As you can see in this example, the ifconfig command is indeed installed. What happened is that by default, the /sbin directory is not in your $PATH. One of the reasons for this is that commands under the /sbin directory are normally intended to only be run by root. You can add /sbin to your $PATH by editing the file .bash_profile in your home directory (if you use the bash shell by default, like most Linux users). Look for the following line:

```
PATH=$PATH:$HOME/bin
```

You can then edit this file, perhaps using the vi editor (discussed in this chapter), to add the /sbin directory like so:

```
PATH=$PATH:/sbin:$HOME/bin
```

Save the file. The next time you log in, the /sbin directory will be in your $PATH. One way to use this change right away is to read in the new settings in .bash_profile by using the bash shell's source command like so:

```
$ source .bash_profile
```

You'll now be able to run ifconfig without the need to explicitly type its full pathname.

Some Linux commands also use environment variables, for example, to acquire configuration information (such as a communications program looking for a variable such as BAUD_RATE, which might denote a default modem speed).

To experiment with the environment variables, you can modify the PS1 variable to manipulate the appearance of your shell prompt. If you are working with bash, you can use its built-in export command to change the shell prompt. For example, if your default shell prompt looks like

```
[winky@shuttle2 ~]$
```

You can change its appearance by using the PS1 variable like this:

```
$  PS1='$OSTYPE r00lz ->'
```

After you press Enter, you'll see

```
linux-gnu r00lz ->
```

> **NOTE**
>
> See the bash manual page for other variables you can use for prompt settings.

Navigating and Searching with the Shell

Use the cd command (built into the shell) to navigate through the Fedora Linux file system. This command is generally used with a specific directory location, or *pathname* like this:

```
$ cd /usr/X11R6/lib/X11/doc
```

Under Fedora, the cd command can also be used with several shortcuts. For example, to quickly move up to the *parent* (higher-level) directory, use the cd command like this:

```
$ cd ..
```

To return to one's home directory from anywhere in the Linux file system, use the cd command like this:

```
$ cd
```

You can also use the $HOME shell environment variable to accomplish the same thing. Type this command and press Enter to return to your home directory:

```
$ cd $HOME
```

You can accomplish the same thing by using the tilde (~) like this:

```
$ cd ~
```

Linux also includes a number of GNU commands you can use to search the file system. These include

- whereis command—Returns the location of the command and its man page.
- whatis command—Returns a one-line synopsis from the command's man page.
- locate file—Returns locations of all matching file(s); an extremely fast method of searching your system, as locate searches a database containing an index of all files on your system; however, this database (about 4MB in size and named slocate.db under the /var/lib/slocate directory) is built daily at 4:20 a.m. by default, and will not contain pathnames to files created during the workday or in the evening.
- apropos subject—Returns a list of commands related to subject.

Managing Files with the Shell

Managing files in your home directory involves using one or more easily remembered commands. If you have any familiarity with the now ancient DOS, you'll recognize some of these commands (though their names are different from those you remember). Basic file management operations include paging (reading), moving, renaming, copying, searching, and deleting files and directories. These commands include

- `cat` filename—Outputs contents of filename to display

- `less` filename—Allows scrolling while reading contents of filename

- `mv` file1 file2—Renames file1 to file2

- `mv` file dir—Moves file to specified directory

- `cp` file1 file2—Copies file1 and creates file2

- `rm` file—Deletes file

- `rmdir` dir—Deletes directory (if empty)

- `grep` string file(s)—Searches through files(s) and displays lines containing matching string

Note that each of these commands can be used with pattern-matching strings known as wildcards or *expressions*. For example, to delete all files in the current directory beginning with the letters abc, you can use an expression beginning with the first three letters of the desired filenames. An asterisk (*) is then appended to match all these files. Use a command line with the `rm` command like this:

```
$ rm abc*
```

Linux shells recognize many types of filenaming wildcards, but this is different from the capabilities of Linux commands supporting the use of more complex expressions. You learn more about using wildcards in Chapter 22.

> **NOTE**
>
> Learn more about using expressions by reading the `ex` or `grep` manual pages.

Compressing and Decompressing Files Through the Shell

Another file management operation is compression and decompression of files, or the creation, listing, and expansion of file and directory archives. Linux distros usually include several compression utilities that you can use to create, compress, expand, or list the contents of compressed files and archives. These commands include

- `bunzip2`—Expands a compressed file

- `bzip2`—Compresses or expands files and directories

- `gunzip`—Expands a compressed file

- `gzip`—Compresses or expands files and directories

- `shar` file—Creates a shell archive of files

- `tar`—Creates, expands, or lists the contents of compressed or uncompressed file or directory archives known as *tape archives* or "tarballs"

- `unshar`—Reassembles files from the shell archive

- `uudecode file.uu`—Decodes an uuencoded text file to its binary form

- `uuencode file`—Encodes a binary file to text file format for transmission via email

> **NOTE**
>
> The `rpm` command can also be used to manage archived data, but is generally used for software development and management. See Chapter 8 for more information on using RPM.

Most of these commands are fairly easy to use. The `tar` command, however, has a somewhat complex (though capable) set of command-line options and syntax. Even so, you can quickly learn to use `tar` by remembering a few simple invocations on the command line. For example, to create a compressed archive of a directory, use `tar`'s `czf` options like this:

```
$ tar czf dirname.tgz dirname
```

The result will be a compressed archive (a file ending in `.tgz`) of the specified directory (and all files and directories under it). Add the letter v to the preceding options to view the list of files being added during compression and archiving. To list the contents of the compressed archive, substitute the c option with the letter t, like this:

```
$ tar tzf archive
```

Of course, if many files are in the archive, a better invocation (in order to easily read or scroll through the output) is

```
$ tar tzf archive ¦ less
```

To expand the contents of a compressed archive, use `tar`'s `xzf` options, like so:

```
$ tar xzf archive
```

`tar` decompresses the specified archive and extracts the contents in the current directory.

Using the Text Editors

Linux distributions include a number of applications known as *text editors* that you can use to create text files or edit system configuration files. Text editors are similar to word processing programs, but generally have fewer features, only work with text files, and might or might not support spell checking or formatting. The text editors range in features and ease of use, but are found on nearly every Linux distribution. The number of editors installed on your system depends on what software packages you've installed on the system.

Some of the console-based text editors are

- ed—A simple line editor without cursor support

- emacs—The comprehensive GNU emacs editing environment, which is much more than an editor; see the section "Working with emacs" later

- jed—A programmer's text editor with features such as colorized highlighting of text to help syntax checking and editing of programs

- joe—Joe's Own Editor, a text editor, which can be used to emulate other editors

- mcedit—A DOS-like text editor for UNIX-like systems

- nano—A simple text editor similar to the pico text editor included with the pine email program

- sed—A stream editor usually used in shell scripts (discussed in Chapter 22)

- vim—An improved, compatible version of the vi text editor (which we'll call vi in the rest of this chapter because it has a symbolic link named vi and a symbolically linked manual page)

Note that not all text editors described here are *screen-oriented*; editors such as ed and sed work on a line-by-line basis, or a stream of text, and do not support movement of a cursor on the screen. Some of the text editors for the X Window System, which provide a graphical interface, such as menu bars, buttons, scrollbars and so on, are

- gedit—A GUI text editor for GNOME

- kate—A simple KDE text editor

- kedit—A simple KDE text editor

- nedit—A programming text editor

- kwrite—A simple KDE text editor

A good reason to learn how to use a text-based editor, such as vi, is that system maintenance and recovery operations generally never take place during X Window sessions (negating the use of a GUI editor). Many larger, more complex and capable editors will not work when Linux is booted to its single-user or maintenance mode. (See Chapter 7 for more information about how Fedora Core boots.)

Another reason to learn how to use a text-based editor under the Linux console mode is that you'll be able to edit text files through dial-up or network shell sessions because many servers do not host graphical desktops.

Working with `vi`

The editor found on nearly every UNIX and Linux system is, without a doubt, the `vi` editor, originally written by Bill Joy. This simple to use but incredibly capable editor features a somewhat cryptic command set, but you can put it to use with only a few commands. Although older, more experienced UNIX and Linux users continue to use `vi` extensively during computing sessions, many newer users might prefer learning an easier to use text editor such as `pico` or GNU `nano`. Die-hard GNU fans and programmers definitely use `emacs`.

That said, learning how to use `vi` is a good idea. You might need to someday edit files on a Linux system with a minimal install, or a remote server without a more extensive offering of installed text editors. Chances are better than good that `vi` will be available.

You can start an editing session by using the `vi` command like this:

```
$ vi file.txt
```

The `vi` command works by using an insert, or editing mode, and a viewing (or command) mode.

When you first start editing, you'll be in the viewing mode. You can use your cursor or other navigation keys (as shown later) to scroll through the text. To start editing, tap the `i` key to insert text, or the `a` key to append text. When finished, use the Esc key to toggle out of the insert or append modes and into the viewing (or command) mode. To enter a command, type a colon (`:`), followed by the command, such as `w` to write the file, and press Enter.

Although `vi` supports many complex editing operations and numerous commands, you can accomplish work by using a few basic commands. These basic `vi` commands are

- Cursor movement—`h`, `j`, `k`, `l` (left, down, up, and right)
- Delete character—`x`
- Delete line—`dd`
- Mode toggle—`ESC`, `Insert` (or `i`)
- Quit—`:q`
- Quit without saving—`:q!`
- Run a shell command—`:sh` (use `'exit'` to return)
- Save file—`:w`
- Text search—`/`

> **NOTE**
>
> Use the `vimtutor` command to quickly learn how to use vi's keyboard commands. The tutorial takes less than 30 minutes, and it teaches new users how to start or stop the editor; navigate files; insert and delete text; and perform search, replace, and insert operations.

Working with `emacs`

Richard M. Stallman's GNU `emacs` editor, like `vi`, is included with Linux and nearly every other Linux distribution. Unlike other UNIX and Linux text editors, `emacs` is much more than a simple text editor—it is an editing environment and can be used to compile and build programs; act as an electronic diary, appointment book, and calendar; compose and send electronic mail; read Usenet news; and even play games. The reason for this capability is the `emacs` contains a built-in language interpreter that uses the Elisp (`emacs` LISP) programming language.

The GNU version of this editor requires more than 30MB of hard drive space. However, there are versions with less resource requirements, and at least one other text editor included with Linux, named `joe`, can be used as a `emacs` clone (albeit with fewer features).

You can start an `emacs` editing session like this:

```
$ emacs file.txt
```

> **TIP**
>
> If you start `emacs` when using X11, the editor will launch in its own floating window. To force `emacs` to display inside a terminal window instead of its own window (which can be useful if the window is a login at a remote computer), use the `-nw` command-line option like this: **emacs -nw file.txt.**

The `emacs` editor uses an extensive set of keystroke and named commands, but you can work with it using a basic command subset. Many of these basic commands require you to hold down the Ctrl key, or to first press a *meta* key (generally mapped to the Alt key). The basic commands are listed in Table 5.2.

TABLE 5.2   Emacs Editing Commands

Action	Command
Abort	Ctrl+g
Cursor left	Ctrl+b
Cursor down	Ctrl+n
Cursor right	Ctrl+f
Cursor up	Ctrl+p
Delete character	Ctrl+d

TABLE 5.2   Continued

Action	Command
Delete line	Ctrl+k
Go to start of line	Ctrl+a
Go to end of line	Ctrl+e
Help	Ctrl+h
Quit	Ctrl+x, Ctrl+c
Save As	Ctrl+x, Ctrl+w
Save file	Ctrl+x, Ctrl+s
Search backward	Ctrl+r
Search forward	Ctrl+s
Start tutorial	Ctrl+h, t
Undo	Ctrl+x, u

TIP

One of the best reasons to learn how to use emacs is that you can use nearly all the same keystrokes to edit commands on the bash shell command line. Another reason is that like vi, emacs is universally available on nearly every UNIX and Linux system, including Apple's Mac OS X.

Working with Permissions

Under Linux (and UNIX), everything in the file system, including directories and devices, is a file. And every file on your system has an accompanying set of permissions based on ownership. These permissions form the basis for security under Linux, and designate each file's read, write, and execute permission for you, members of your group, and all others on the system.

You can examine the default permissions for a file you create by using the umask command, or as a practical example, by using the touch command and then the ls command's long-format listing like this:

```
$ touch file
$ ls -l file
-rw-rw-r--   1 bball    bball            0 Jul 23 12:28 file
```

In this example, the touch command is used to quickly create a file. The ls command then reports on the file, displaying information (from left to right) in the first field of output (such as -rw-rw-r-- previously)

- **The first character of the field is the type of file created**—Common indicators of the type of file are a leading letter in the output. A blank (in the preceding example, which is represented by a dash) designates a plain file, d designates a directory, c designates a character device (such as /dev/ttyS0), and b is used for a block device (such as /dev/hda).

- **Permissions**—Read, write, and execute permissions for the owner, group, and all others on the system. (You learn more about these permissions later in this section.)

- **Number of links to the file**—The number one (1) designates that there is only one file, whereas any other number indicates that there might be one or more hard-linked files. Links are created with the ln command. A hard-linked file is an exact copy of the file, but it might be located elsewhere on the system. Symbolic links of directories can also be created, but only the root operator can create a hard link of a directory.

- **The owner**—The account that created or owns the file; you can change this designation by using the chown command.

- **The group**—The group of users who are allowed to access the file; you can change this designation by using the chgrp command.

- **File size and creation/modification date**—The last two elements indicate the size of the file in bytes and the date the file was created or last modified.

Assigning Permissions

Under Linux, permissions are grouped by owner, group, and others, with read, write, and execute permission assigned to each, like so:

```
Owner     Group     Others
rwx       rwx       rxw
```

Permissions can be indicated by mnemonic or octal characters. Mnemonic characters are

- r indicates permission for an owner, member of the owner's group, or others to open and read the file.

- w indicates permission for an owner, member of the owner's group, or others to open and write to the file.

- x indicates permission for an owner, member of the owner's group, or others to execute the file (or read a directory)

In the previous example for the file named file, the owner, bball, has read and write permission, as does any member of the group named bball. All other users may only read the file. Also note that default permissions for files created by the root operator will be different! This is because of umask settings assigned by the shell.

Many users prefer to represent permissions using numeric codes, based on octal (base-8) values. Here's what these values mean:

- 4 indicates read permission.

- 2 indicates write permission.

- 1 indicates execute permission.

In octal notation, the previous example file has a permission setting of 664 (read+write or 4+2, read+write or 4+2, read-only or 4). Although you can use either form of permissions notation, octal is easy to use quickly after you visualize and understand how permissions are numbered.

> **NOTE**
>
> In Linux, you can create groups to assign a number of users access to common directories and files, based on permissions. You might assign everyone in accounting to a group named accounting, for example, and allow that group access to accounts payable files while disallowing access by other departments. Defined groups are maintained by the root operator, but you can use the newgrp command to temporarily join other groups in order to access files (as long as the root operator has added you to the other groups). You can also allow or deny access to your files by other groups by modifying the group permissions of your files.

Directory Permissions

Directories are also files under Linux. For example, again use the ls command to show permissions like this:

```
$ mkdir foo
$ ls -ld foo
drwxrwxr-x   2 bball    bball        4096 Jul 23 12:37 foo
```

In this example, the mkdir command is used to create a directory. The ls command and its -ld option is used to show the permissions and other information about the directory (not its contents). Here you can see that the directory has permission values of 775 (read+write+execute or 4+2+1, read+write+execute or 4+2+1, and read+execute or 4+1).

This shows that the owner and group members can read and write to the directory and, because of execute permission, also list the directory's contents. All other users can only list the directory contents. (Directories require execute permission in order for anyone to be able to view their contents.)

You should also notice that the ls command's output shows a leading d in the permissions field. This letter specifies that this file is a directory; normal files will have a blank field in place. Other files, such as those specifying a block or character device, will have a different letter (see the section "Managing Files for Character Devices, Block Devices, and Special Devices" in Chapter 10 for more information about block devices).

For example, if you examine the device file for a Linux serial port, you'll see

```
$ ls -l /dev/ttyS0
crw-rw----   1 root      uucp       4,  64 Mar 23 23:38 /dev/ttyS0
```

Here, /dev/ttyS0 is a character device (such as a serial communications port and designated by a c) owned by root and available to anyone in the uucp group. The device has permissions of 660 (read+write, read+write, no permission).

On the other hand, if you examine the device file for an IDE hard drive, you'll see

```
$ ls -l /dev/hda
brw-rw----   1 root      disk       3,   0 Mar 23 23:37 /dev/hda
```

In this example, b designates a block device (a device that transfers and caches data in blocks) with similar permissions. Other device entries you will run across on your Linux system include symbolic links, designated by s.

You can use the chmod command to alter a file's permissions. This command uses various forms of command syntax, including octal or a mnemonic form (such as u, g, o, or a and rwx, and so on) to specify a desired change. The chmod command can be used to add, remove, or modify file or directory permissions in order to protect, hide, or open up access to a file by other users (except for root, who can access any file or directory on a Linux system).

The mnemonic forms of chmod's options (when used with a plus character, +, to add, or a minus sign, -, to take away) designate the following:

   u—Adds or removes user (owner) read, write, or execute permission

   g—Adds or removes group read, write, or execute permission

   o—Adds or removes read, write, or execute permission for others not in a file's group

   a—Adds or removes read, write, or execute permission for all users

   r—Adds or removes read permission

   w—Adds or removes write permission

   x—Adds or removes execution permission

For example, if you create a file, such as a readme.txt, the file will have default permissions (set by the umask setting in /etc/bashrc) of

```
-rw-rw-r--   1 bball     bball         12 Oct  2 16:48 readme.txt
```

As you can see, you and members of your group can read and write the file. Anyone else can only read the file (and only if it is outside of your home directory, which will have read, write, and execute permission set only for you, the owner). You can remove all write permission for anyone by using chmod, the minus sign, and aw like so:

```
$ chmod -aw readme.txt
$ ls -l readme.txt
-r--r--r--    1 bball    bball          12 Oct  2 16:48 readme.txt
```

Now, no one will be able to write to the file (except you, if the file is in your home or /tmp directory because of directory permissions). To restore read and write permission for only you as the owner, use the plus sign and the u and rw options like so:

```
$ chmod u+rw readme.txt
$ ls -l readme.txt
-rw-------    1 bball    bball          12 Oct  2 16:48 readme.txt
```

You can also use the octal form of the chmod command, for example, to modify a file's permissions so that only you, the owner, can read and write a file. Use the chmod command and a file permission of 600, like this:

```
$ chmod 600 readme.txt
```

If you take away execution permission for a directory, files might be hidden inside and may not be listed or accessed by anyone else (except the root operator, of course, who has access to any file on your system). By using various combinations of permission settings, you can quickly and easily set up a more secure environment, even as a normal user in your home directory.

Understanding Set User ID (SUID) and Set Group ID (SGID) Permissions

Another type of permission available for use under Linux is set user ID, known as *suid*, and set group ID (*sgid*) permissions. These settings, when used in a program, enable any user running that program to have program owner or group owner permissions for that program. These settings enable the program to be run effectively by anyone, without requiring that each user's permissions be altered to include specific permissions for that program.

One commonly used program with suid permissions is the passwd command:

```
$ ls -l /usr/bin/passwd
-r-s--x--x    1 root     root        13536 Jul 12  2000 /usr/bin/passwd
```

This setting allows normal users to execute the command (as root) in order to make changes to a root-only accessible file, /etc/passwd.

You also can assign similar permission using the chfn command. This command allows users to update or change finger information in /etc/passwd. You accomplish this permission modification by using a leading 4 (or the mnemonic s) in front of the three octal values.

> **NOTE**
>
> Other files that might have suid or guid permissions include at, rcp, rlogin, rsh, chage, chsh, ssh, crontab, sudo, sendmail, ping, mount, and several UNIX-to-UNIX Copy (UUCP) utilities. Many programs (such as games) might also have this type of permission in order to access a sound device.

Files or programs that have suid or guid permissions can sometimes present security holes because they bypass normal permissions. This problem is especially compounded if the permission extends to an executable binary (a command) with an inherent security flaw because it could lead to any system user or intruder gaining root access. In past exploits, this typically happened when a user fed a vulnerable command with unexpected input (such as a long pathname or option); the command would bomb out, and the user would be presented a root prompt. Although Linux developers are constantly on the lookout for poor programming practices, new exploits are found all the time, and can crop up unexpectedly, especially in newer software packages that haven't had the benefit of peer developer review.

Savvy Linux system administrators will keep the number of suid or guid files present on a system to a minimum. The find command can be used to display all such files on your system:

```
# find / -type f -perm +6000 -exec ls -l {} \;
```

> **NOTE**
>
> The find command is quite helpful and can be used for many purposes, such as before or during backup operations. See the section "Using Backup Software" in Chapter 11, "Backing Up, Restoring, and Recovery."

Note that the programs don't necessarily have to be removed from your system. If your users really don't need to use the program, you can remove execute permission of the program for anyone. You will have to decide, as the root operator, whether your users are allowed to, for example, mount and unmount CD-ROMs or other media on your system. Although Linux-based operating systems can be set up to accommodate ease of use and convenience, allowing programs such as mount to be suid might not be the best security policy. Other candidates for suid permission change could include the chsh, at, or chage commands.

Working As root

The root, or superuser account is a special account and user on UNIX and Linux systems. Superuser permissions are required in part because of the restrictive file permissions assigned to important system configuration files. You will need root permission in order to edit these files or to access or modify certain devices (such as hard drives). When logged in as root, you have total control over your system, which can be dangerous.

When you work in root, you have the ability to destroy a running system with a simple invocation of the rm command like this:

```
# rm -fr /
```

This command line will not only delete locate files and directories, but also could wipe out file systems on other partitions and even remote computers. This alone is reason enough to take precautions when using root access.

The only time you should run Linux as the superuser is when booting to runlevel 1, or system maintenance mode, to configure the file system, for example, or to repair or maintain the system. Logging in and using Linux as the root operator isn't a good idea because it defeats the entire concept of file permissions.

Knowing how to run commands as root without logging in as root can help avoid serious missteps when configuring your system. Linux comes with a command named su that allows you to run one or more commands as root and then quickly return you to normal user status. For example, if you'd like to edit your system's file system table (a simple text file that describes local or remote storage devices, their type, and location), you can use the su command like this:

```
$ su -c "nano -w /etc/fstab"
Password:
```

After you press Enter, you'll be prompted for a password that gives you access to root. This extra step can also help you "think before you leap" into the command. Enter the root password, and you'll then be editing /etc/fstab using the nano editor with line wrapping disabled.

CAUTION

Before editing any important system or software service configuration file, make a backup copy. Then make sure to launch your text editor with line wrapping disabled. If you edit a configuration file without disabling line wrapping, you could insert spurious carriage returns and line feeds into its contents, causing the configured service to fail when restarting. By convention, nearly all configuration files are formatted for 80-character text width, but this isn't always the case. By default, the vi and emacs editors don't use line wrap.

You can use sudo to assign specific users permission to perform specific tasks (similar to BSD UNIX and its "wheel" group of users). The sudo command works by first examining the file named sudoers under the /etc directory; you modify this file with the visudo command. See the section "Granting Root Privileges on Occasion—The sudo Command" in Chapter 9, "Managing Users," for details on how to configure and use sudo.

Creating Users

When a Linux system administrator creates a user, an entry in /etc/passwd for the user is created. The system also creates a directory, labeled with the user's username, in the /home directory. For example, if you create a user named *bsmith*, the user's home directory is /home/bsmith.

> **NOTE**
>
> In this chapter, you learn how to manage users from the command line. See Chapter 9 for more information on user administration with Fedora using graphical administration utilities, such as the redhat-config-users client.

Use the useradd command, along with a user's name to quickly create a user:

```
# useradd winky
```

After creating the user, you must also create the user's initial password with the passwd command:

```
# passwd winky
Changing password for user winky.
New password:
Retype new password:
passwd: all authentication tokens updated successfully.
```

Enter the new password twice. If you do not create an initial password for a new user, the user won't be able to log in.

You can view useradd's default new user settings by using the command and its -D option like this:

```
# useradd -D
GROUP=100
HOME=/home
INACTIVE=-1
EXPIRE=
SHELL=/bin/bash
SKEL=/etc/skel
```

These options display the default group ID, home directory, account and password policy (active forever with no password expiration), the default shell, and the directory containing defaults for the shell.

The useradd command has many different command-line options. The command can be used to set policies and dates for the new user's password, assign a login shell, assign group membership, and other aspects of a user's account.

Deleting Users

Use the userdel command to delete users from your system. This command will remove a user's entry in the system's /etc/passwd file. You should also user the command's -r option to remove all the user's files and directories (such as the user's mail spool file under /var/spool/mail):

```
# userdel -r winky
```

If you do not use the -r option, you will have to manually delete the user's directory under /home, along with the user's /var/spool/mail queue.

Shutting Down the System

Use the shutdown command to shut down your system. The shutdown command has a number of different command-line options (such as shutting down at a predetermined time), but the fastest way to cleanly shut down Linux is to use the -h or halt option, followed by the word now or the numeral zero (0), like this:

```
# shutdown -h now
```

or

```
# shutdown -h 0
```

To incorporate a timed shutdown and a pertinent message to all active users, use shutdown's time and message options, like so:

```
# shutdown -h 18:30 "System is going down for maintenance this evening"
```

This example will shut down your system and provide a warning to all active users 15 minutes before the shutdown (or reboot). Shutting down a running server can be considered drastic, especially if there are active users or exchanges of important data occurring (such as a backup in progress). One good approach is to warn users ahead of time. This can be done by editing the system Message of the Day (MOTD) motd file, which displays a message to users after login. To create your custom MOTD, use a text editor and change the contents of /etc/motd. You can also make downtimes part of a regular schedule, perhaps to coincide with security audits, software updates, or hardware maintenance.

You should shut down Fedora only for a few very specific reasons:

- You are not using the computer and want to conserve electrical power.
- You need to perform system maintenance that requires any or all system services to be stopped.
- You want to replace integral hardware.

> **TIP**
>
> Do not shut down your computer if you suspect that one or more intruders has infiltrated your system; instead, disconnect the machine from any or all networks and make a backup copy of your hard drives. You might want to also keep the machine running to examine the contents of memory and to examine system logs. See Chapter 13 and the section "Securing Your Network" on how to protect and monitor a network-connected system.

Rebooting the System

You should also use the `shutdown` command to reboot your system. The fastest way to cleanly reboot Linux is to use the `-r` option, and the word `now` or the numeral zero (0):

```
# shutdown -r now
```

or

```
# shutdown -r 0
```

Rebooting or shutting down can both have dire consequences if performed at the wrong time (such as during backups or critical file transfers, which arouse the ire of your system's users). However, Linux-based operating systems are designed to properly stop active system services in an orderly fashion. Other commands you can use to shut down and reboot Linux are the `halt` and `reboot` commands, but the `shutdown` command is more flexible.

> **Related Fedora and Linux Commands**
>
> The following programs and built-in shell commands are commonly used when working at the command line. These commands are organized by category to help you understand the command's purpose. If you need to find full information for using the command, you can find that information under the command's man page.
>
> Managing users and groups—chage, chfn, chsh, edquota, gpasswd, groupadd, groupdel, groupmod, groups, mkpasswd, newgrp, newusers, passwd, umask, useradd, userdel, usermod
>
> Managing files and file systems—cat, cd, chattr, chmod, chown, compress, cp, dd, fdisk, find, gzip, ln, mkdir, mksfs, mount, mv, rm, rmdir, rpm, sort, swapon, swapoff, tar, touch, umount, uncompress, uniq, unzip, zip
>
> Managing running programs—bg, fg, kill, killall, nice, ps, pstree, renice, top, watch
>
> Getting information—apropos, cal, cat, cmp, date, diff, df, dir, dmesg, du, env, file, free, grep, head, info, last, less, locate, ls, lsattr, man, more, pinfo, ps, pwd, stat, strings, tac, tail, top, uname, uptime, uptime, vdir, vmstat, w, wc, whatis, whereis, which, who, whoami
>
> Console text editors—ed, jed, joe, mcedit, nano, red, sed, vim
>
> Console Internet and network commands—bing, elm, ftp, host, hostname, ifconfig, links, lynx, mail, mutt, ncftp, netconfig, netstat, pine, ping, pump, rdate, route, scp, sftp, ssh, tcpdump, traceroute, whois, wire-test

5

Reference

The migration to a new computer operating system doesn't have to be painful to management and users. Providing easy-to-understand directions, some background information, and pre-configuration of an installed system can help the transition.

This section lists some additional points of reference with background information on the standards and commands discussed in this chapter. Browse these links to learn more about some of the concepts discussed in this chapter and to expand your knowledge of your new Linux community.

`http://www.winntmag.com/Articles/Index.cfm?ArticleID=7420`—An article by a Windows NT user who, when experimenting with Linux, blithely confesses to rebooting the system after not knowing how to read a text file at the Linux console.

`http://standards.ieee.org/regauth/posix/`—IEEE's POSIX information page.

`http://www.itworld.com/Comp/2362/lw-01-government/#sidebar`—Discussion of Linux and POSIX compliance.

`http://www.pathname.com/fhs/`—Home page for the Linux FHS, Linux File system Hierarchy Standard.

`http://www.tldp.org`—Browse the HOWTO section to find and read The Linux Keyboard and Console HOWTO—Andries Brouwer's somewhat dated but eminently useful guide to using the Linux keyboard and console.

`http://www.gnu.org/software/emacs/emacs.html`—Home page for the FSF's GNU `emacs` editing environment; you'll find additional documentation and links to the source code for the latest version here.

`http://www.vim.org/`—Home page for the `vim` (`vi` clone) editor included with Linux distros. Check here for updates, bug fixes, and news about this editor.

`http://www.courtesan.com/sudo/`—Home page for the `sudo` command. Check here for the latest updates, security features, and bug fixes.

CHAPTER **6**

The X Window System

IN THIS CHAPTER

- Basic X Concepts
- Using X11R6
- Starting X
- Selecting and Using X Window Managers
- The GNOME and KDE Desktop Environments
- Reference

The X Window System, also known as X11R6, X11, and simply X, provides the graphical networking interface for your Fedora desktop. X started as a consortium-based project at the Massachusetts Institute of Technology in the early 1980s, and over the years it has gone through several major revisions. X is managed in open-source form by an organization named X.org.

X uses a client/server model. *Clients* are simply X programs written to take advantage of the network communication and graphics drawing protocols available in supporting software libraries. The X server communicates with clients and manages many different aspects of a local or remote desktop session. The X server used with Fedora is X11R6 7.0, an open-source version of the X Window System provided by The X.Org Foundation.

Today there are X.Org distributions for many different platforms besides Intel-based PCs. The open-source version of X from The X.Org Foundation included with Fedora is a merger of the previous releases of X11R6 and XFree86, the version of X Windows shipped with earlier versions of Fedora Core and Red Hat Linux.

This chapter shows you how to work with the version of X11 included with Fedora. After a brief overview of X and X.org, you'll learn how to configure X to work with Linux on your computer, useful if you install a new video card or attach a new LCD panel. You'll learn how to start X and select and use X window managers—the X clients that draw and manage window displays, decorations, and onscreen icons. You'll also get an introduction to Fedora's graphical desktop environment.

The Red Hat and Fedora Core Desktop

Red Hat, Inc. initially caused quite a stir among veteran Linux users because of the decision to introduce consistency in the menus, dialogs, and client look and feel of GNOME and the K Desktop Environment (KDE), starting with Red Hat Linux 8.0. This action, part of the natural evolution of Red Hat's product line, provides a basic framework for the Red Hat desktop as a base Linux product in future commercial product lines. The new desktop is evolving, and enables Red Hat, Inc. to more easily integrate advanced products, such as enterprise-level Web, database, application, or development server software.

Bluecurve, the new Red Hat desktop theme, is also used with Red Hat Linux 9 and now Fedora. While considered heresy by some die-hard users on both sides of the GNOME and KDE camps, the new theme consistency actually helps novice Red Hat and Fedora users easily migrate from other operating systems by enabling them to learn a single set of controls and preferences while working in the new graphical interface.

The truth is that Fedora offers you the choice of whether to use the Red Hat desktop or another theme. You are entirely free to use a different desktop and to configure GNOME or KDE to look entirely different from the default graphical desktop. Fedora also includes alternative and legacy window managers, such as the Motif Window Manager mwm, and the twm window manager (which are discussed later in this chapter).

Basic X Concepts

The underlying engine of X11 is the X protocol, which provides a system of managing displays on local and remote desktops. The protocol uses a client/server model that allows an abstraction of the drawing of client windows and other decorations locally and over a network. An X server draws client windows, dialog boxes, and buttons that are specific to the local hardware and in response to client requests. The client, however, doesn't have to be specific to the local hardware. This means that system administrators can set up a network with a large server and clients and enable users to view and use those clients on workstations with totally different CPUs and graphics displays.

NOTE

As an example of X's support for remote client use, much of the original text of this chapter was written using the Sun Microsystems StarOffice office suite, but the keyboard and display used for writing were attached to an Apple G4 Cube running PPC Linux and a PowerPC version of XFree86; StarOffice was launched from an Intel-based PC running Red Hat Linux. Subsequent revisions were made on an IBM 390X laptop running Red Hat 9, using the open-source OpenOffice.org office suite via a wireless network connection and launched from a shoebox-sized computer running Red Hat 8.0. Final versions were done via a remote 802.11b X11 connection using Fedora Core, and launching StarOffice from a dual-CPU SMP server running Red Hat 7.3.

X11's form of distributed processing means that Fedora, along with X11R6, can be used as a stable, cost-efficient desktop PC platform for using clients launched from a more powerful server, minicomputer, or mainframe. The X model provides a way to continue to use legacy PCs when more powerful systems are put in place, and it can help centralize the job of system management.

X is popular with UNIX and Linux users, system administrators, and network engineers for a number of reasons. X is extremely portable and works with nearly every hardware-based graphics system on the market. This allows X to be deployed and used with high-end workstations and diminutive embedded devices. X also provides portable and multiplatform programming standards that truly allow write-once, cross-platform development.

Another attractive feature of X is its networking capabilities, which easily allow management of thousands of workstations, deployment of thin-client desktops, remote launching of applications, and standardization of installations—all working over a variety of media, such as Ethernet and wireless network connections. Although early releases of X supported only a handful of display architectures, subsequent versions have enabled the use of compressed fonts, *shaped* (that is, nonrectangular) windows, and a graphical login manager, known as a *display manager* (see the section "Using a Display Manager," later in this chapter). X also provides a mechanism for customizing how X clients appear: It allows you to edit text files that contain window or button appearance settings. These settings, known as *resources*, are available for nearly every X11 client.

Many small office/home office (SOHO) environments and computer hobbyists run Linux and X locally on nonnetworked PCs. But small business, academic, corporate, and enterprise-class environments can also reap the benefits of adopting and using X and Fedora for network computing. By using X, administrative staff, users, and in-house developers can enjoy custom or standardized desktops, and applications can be stored in and launched from a single location. This can make the job of system and software maintenance a lot easier.

Using X11R6

X11R6 7.0 is the X server that is used with Fedora. The base X.Org distribution consists of 30 RPM packages (almost 120MB), which contain the server, along with support and development libraries, fonts, various clients, and documentation. An additional 1,000 or more X clients, fonts, and documentation are also included with Fedora.

> **NOTE**
>
> A full installation of X and related X11R6 files can consume more—usually much more—than 170MB of hard drive space. This is because additional clients, configuration files, and graphics (such as icons) are under the /usr/bin and /usr/share directory trees. You can pare excessive disk requirements by judiciously choosing which X-related packages (such as games) to not install on workstations. However, with the increased capacity of most desktop PC hard drives today, the size requirements are rarely a problem, except in configuring thin-client desktops or embedded systems.

The /usr/X11R6 directory and its subdirectories contain the majority of XFree86's software. Some important subdirectories are

- /usr/X11R6/bin—This is the location of the X server and various X clients. (Note that not all X clients require active X sessions.)

- /usr/X11R6/include—This is the path to the files necessary for developing X clients and graphics such as icons.

- /usr/X11R6/lib—This directory contains required software libraries to support the X server and clients.

- /usr/X11R6/lib/X11—This directory contains fonts, default client resources, system resources, documentation, and other files that are used during X sessions and for various X clients. You'll also find a symbolic link to this directory, named X11, under the /usr/lib directory.

- /usr/X11R6/lib/modules—This path to drivers and the X server modules used by the X server enables use of various graphics cards.

- /usr/X11R6/man—This directory contains directories of manual pages for X11 programming and clients.

The main components required for an active local X session will be installed on your system if you choose to use a graphical desktop. These components are the X server, miscellaneous fonts, a *terminal client* (that is, a program that provides access to a shell prompt), and a client known as a *window manager*. Window managers, which are discussed later in this chapter (see the section "Selecting and Using X Window Managers"), administer onscreen displays, including overlapping and tiling windows, command buttons, title bars, and other onscreen decorations and features.

Elements of the xorg.conf File

The single most important file required to launch X on a desktop is the xorg.conf configuration file. This text file can be created during installation or modified post-installation by using the system-config-display client (see "Configuring X," later in this chapter). xorg.conf is located under the /etc/X11 directory and contains file locations, hardware descriptions, and specifications needed by the xorg server in order to work with the computer's graphics card and display monitor.

You'll be better equipped to troubleshoot configuration problems and add or remove features of the X session if you understand the contents of the xorg.conf file. The components, or sections, of xorg.conf specify the X session, or *server layout*, along with paths for files used by the server, server options, optional support modules to load, descriptions of the mouse and keyboard, graphics device, monitor, screen layout, and video modes to use. Of the 12 sections of an xorg.conf file, these are the essential components:

- ServerLayout—Defines the display, defines one or more screen layouts, and names input devices.

- Files—Defines the location of colors, fonts, or port number of the font server.

- Module—Tells the X server what graphics display support code modules to load.

- InputDevice—Defines the input devices, such as the keyboard and mouse; multiple devices can be used.

- Monitor—Defines the capabilities of any attached display; multiple monitors can be used.

- Device—Defines one or more graphics cards and specifies what optional (if any) features to enable or disable.

- Screen—Defines one or more resolutions, color depths, perhaps a default color depth, and other settings.

The following sections provide short descriptions of these elements; the xorg.conf manual page contains full documentation of all the options and other keywords you can use to customize your desktop settings.

The ServerLayout Section

As noted previously, the ServerLayout section of the xorg.conf file defines the display and screen layouts, and it names the input devices. A typical ServerLayout section from an automatically configured xorg.conf file might look like this:

```
Section "ServerLayout"
        Identifier      "Default Layout"
        Screen       0  "Screen0" 0 0
        InputDevice     "Mouse0" "CorePointer"
        InputDevice     "Keyboard0" "CoreKeyboard"
        InputDevice     "DevInputMice" "AlwaysCore"
EndSection
```

In this example, a single display is used (the numbers designate position of a screen), and two default input devices, Mouse0 and Keyboard0, are used for the session.

The Files Section

The Files section of the xorg.conf file might look like this:

```
Section "Files"
    RgbPath     "/usr/X11R6/lib/X11/rgb"
    FontPath    "unix/:7100"
EndSection
```

This section lists available session colors (by name, in the text file `rgb.txt`) and the port number to the X font server. The font server, `xfs`, is started at boot time and doesn't require an active X session. If a font server isn't used, the `FontPath` entry could instead list each font directory under the `/usr/X11R6/lib/X11/fonts` directory, as in this example:

```
FontPath "/usr/X11R6/lib/X11/fonts/100dpi"
FontPath "/usr/X11R6/lib/X11/fonts/misc"
FontPath "/usr/X11R6/lib/X11/fonts/75dpi"
FontPath "/usr/X11R6/lib/X11/fonts/PEX"
FontPath "/usr/X11R6/lib/X11/fonts/Speedo"
...
```

These directories contain the default compressed fonts that are available for use during the X session. The font server is configured by using the file named `config` under the `/etc/X11/fs` directory. This file contains a listing, or catalog, of fonts for use by the font server. By adding an `alternate-server` entry in this file and restarting the font server, you can specify remote font servers for use during X sessions. This can help centralize font support and reduce local storage requirements (even though only 25MB is required for the almost 5,000 fonts installed with Red Hat Linux and X).

The `Module` Section

The `Module` section of the `xorg.conf` file specifies loadable modules or drivers to load for the X session. This section might look like this:

```
Section "Module"
        Load   "GLcore"
        Load   "dbe"
        Load   "extmod"
        Load   "fbdevhw"
        Load   "pex5"
        Load   "glx"
        Load   "pex5"
        Load   "record"
        Load   "xie"
EndSection
```

These modules can range from special video card support to font rasterizers. The modules are located in subdirectories under the `/usr/X11R6/lib/modules` directory.

The `InputDevice` Section

The `InputDevice` section configures a specific device, such as a keyboard or mouse, as in this example:

```
Section "InputDevice"
        Identifier "Keyboard0"
```

```
        Driver        "keyboard"
        Option   "XkbRules"        "xfree86"
        Option   "XkbModel"        "pc105"
        Option   "XkbLayout"       "us"
EndSection
Section "InputDevice"
        Identifier   "Mouse0"
        Driver       "mouse"
        Option       "Protocol" "PS/2"
        Option       "Device" "/dev/psaux"
        Option       "ZAxisMapping" "4 5"
        Option       "Emulate3Buttons" "no"
EndSection
```

You can configure multiple devices, and there might be multiple InputDevice sections.
The preceding example specifies a basic keyboard and a three-button PS/2 mouse (actually,
a ThinkPad TrackPoint pointer). An InputDevice section that specifies use of a USB device
could be used at the same time (to enable mousing with PS/2 and USB pointers) and
might look like this:

```
Section "InputDevice"
        Identifier   "Mouse0"
        Driver       "mouse"
        Option       "Device" "/dev/mouse"
        Option       "Protocol" "IMPS/2"
        Option       "Emulate3Buttons" "off"
        Option       "ZAxisMapping" "4 5"
EndSection
```

> **NOTE**
>
> If you change your computer's pointing device, you should then run Fedora's
> system-config-mouse client, which automatically updates your system's xorg.conf file.

The Monitor Section

The Monitor section configures the designated display device as declared in the
ServerLayout section, as shown in this example:

```
Section "Monitor"
        Identifier   "Monitor0"
        VendorName   "Monitor Vendor"
        ModelName    "Monitor Model"
        HorizSync    31.5-48.5
```

```
        VertRefresh 50-70
        Option "dpms"
EndSection
```

Note that the X server automatically determines the best video timings according to the horizontal and vertical sync and refresh values in this section. If required, old-style mode-line entries (used by distributions and servers prior to XFree86 4.0) might still be used. If the monitor is automatically detected when you configure X (see the section "Configuring X," later in this chapter), its definition and capabilities are inserted in your xorg.conf file from the MonitorsDB database. This database contains more than 600 monitors and is located in the /usr/share/hwdata directory.

The Device Section

The Device section provides details about the video graphics chipset used by the computer, as in this example:

```
Section "Device"
        Identifier  "Videocard0"
        Driver      "savage"
        VendorName  "Videocard vendor"
        BoardName   "S3 Savage4 Pro+"
        VideoRam    8192
EndSection
```

This example identifies an installed video card as using an S3 Savage graphics chipset. The Driver entry tells the Xorg server to load the savage_drv.o module from the /usr/X11R6/lib/modules/drivers directory. Available video RAM (which is 8MB in this example) is specified in the VideoRam entry. Different chipsets have different options. For example, here's the entry for a NeoMagic video chipset:

```
Section "Device"
        Identifier  "NeoMagic (laptop/notebook)"
        Driver      "neomagic"
        VendorName  "NeoMagic (laptop/notebook)"
        BoardName   "NeoMagic (laptop/notebook)"
    Option      "externDisp"
    Option      "internDisp"
EndSection
```

In this example, the Device section specifies the driver for the graphics card (neomagic_drv.o) and enables two chipset options (externDisp and internDisp) to allow display on the laptop's LCD screen and an attached monitor.

The XFree86 server supports hundreds of different video chipsets. If you configure X11 but subsequently change the installed video card, you need to edit the existing Device section or generate a new xorg.conf file, using one of the X configuration tools discussed in this chapter, to reflect the new card's capabilities. You can find details about options for some chipsets in a companion manual page or in a README file under the `/usr/X11R6/lib/` `_X11/doc` directory. You should look at these sources for hints about optimizations and troubleshooting.

The `Screen` Section

The `Screen` section ties together the information from the previous sections (using the `Screen0`, `Device`, and `Monitor Identifier` entries). It can also specify one or more color depths and resolutions for the session. Here's an example:

```
Section "Screen"
        Identifier "Screen0"
        Device     "Videocard0"
        Monitor    "Monitor0"
        DefaultDepth    16
        SubSection "Display"
                Depth     16
                Modes     "1024x768" "800x600" "640x480"
        EndSubSection
EndSection
```

In this example a color depth of thousands of colors and a resolution of 1024×768 is the default, with optional resolutions of 800×600 and 640×480. Multiple `Display` subsection entries with different color depths and resolutions (with settings such as `Depth 24` for millions of colors) can be used if supported by the graphics card and monitor combination. You can also use a `DefaultDepth` entry (which is `16`, or thousands of colors, in the example), along with a specific color depth to standardize display depths in installations.

You can also specify a desktop resolution larger than that supported by the hardware in your monitor or notebook display. This setting is known as a *virtual* resolution in the `Display` subsection. This allows, for example, an 800×600 display to pan (that is, slide around inside) a virtual window of 1024×768.

> **NOTE**
>
> If your monitor and graphics card support multiple resolutions and the settings are properly configured, you can use the key combination of Ctrl+Alt+Keypad+ or Ctrl+Alt+Keypad- to change resolutions on-the-fly during your X session.

Configuring X

Although the Fedora Core installer can be used to configure X during installation, problems can arise if the PC's video card is not recognized. If you are unable to configure X during installation (see Chapter 3, "Installing Fedora"), do not specify booting to a graphical configuration and skip the X configuration portion of the installation. Note that some installs, such as for servers, don't require that X be configured for use in order to support active X sessions but might require installation of X and related software to support remote users and clients.

You can use the following configuration tools, among others, to create a working `xorg.conf` file:

- `system-config-display`—This is Red Hat's graphical configuration tool, which launches an X session to create an `xorg.conf` file.

- `xorg`—The X server itself can create a skeletal working configuration.

The following sections discuss how to use each of these software tools to create a working `xorg.conf` file.

Configuring X with the `system-config-display` Client

You can use the `system-config-display` client to create or update an `xorg.conf` file. You can start by clicking the Display menu item from the desktop panel's System Settings menu if you are already running X, but you can also begin, as root, by starting the client from the command line during a console session, like this:

```
# system-config-display
```

The screen clears, and `system-config-display` attempts to start an X session. If you start this client during an X session, its main window appears, as shown in Figure 6.1.

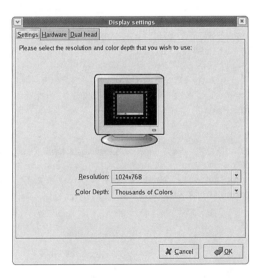

FIGURE 6.1   The `system-config-display` client provides a graphical configuration interface for creating or updating a system's xorg.conf file. Here you see the Display Settings main screen, offering resolution and color-depth settings.

The Display Settings main screen is a dialog showing the current monitor and video card settings (if configured). You can change the resolution (horizontal and vertical pixels) and color depth (number of supported colors) by clicking one or the other of the drop-down menus. Click the OK or Cancel button to save or cancel any change.

If you click the Hardware tab, other configuration options become available as shown in Figure 6.2.

FIGURE 6.2   `system-config-display`'s Hardware settings are used to configure a monitor and video card (and multihead video card) for X11R6.

Click the Configure button in the Monitor Type area of the Hardware tab dialog to change your Monitor settings, as shown in Figure 6.3. You can use this dialog to configure a different monitor or to change current monitor settings.

First, scroll through the list of monitor brands (from the `MonitorDB` database), and then click the small triangle to the left of the name of the manufacturer or type. You'll then see a list of model names. Click to select one, and when you are finished, click the OK button to use the new settings or click the Cancel button to abort changes.

To configure a video card, you can click the Video Card area's Configure button in the Hardware tab dialog. The Video Card dialog appears, as shown in Figure 6.4.

You can scroll through the list of video cards. You can click one to select it and when you are finished, click the OK button to finalize your selection.

If your video card supports the use of two or more monitors, you can use the Dual head tab to configure multiple monitor support. `Xorg` supports multiple displays using a feature named Xinerama. This feature enables multiple monitors to appear as a single display, and each display can be located in any quadrant of a screen's layout.

FIGURE 6.3   You can scroll to select a new monitor to use for your X sessions.

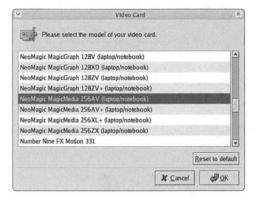

FIGURE 6.4   Use the Hardware tab's Video Card Configure button to choose a new video card for your X sessions.

In order to use Xinerama for your desktop sessions, you must start the Xorg server with its +xinerama option. Your xorg.conf file must also have proper settings, and each display must be capable of supporting identical color depth (usually 16bpp or thousands of colors). Details about using Xinerama with Xorg can be found in the Xorg man page and in the Xinerama HOWTO at http://www.tldp.org/HOWTO/Xinerama-HOWTO/.

When you have finished your changes to your X server settings, click the OK button. You'll then see a dialog advising that you'll need to log out and then log back (or exit your X session and restart X) in order to use the new settings.

The new settings will be stored in a new xorg.conf file under the /etc/X11 directory. If you find that the new settings do not work, you can simply copy the backup xorg.conf file named `xorg.conf.backup` to `xorg-conf` in the same directory to revert to your original settings.

Using `xorg` to Configure X

You can create the `xorg.conf` file manually by typing one from scratch using a text editor, but you can also create one automatically by using the Xorg server or configuration utilities (as discussed in the previous sections). As the `root` operator, you can use the following on the server to create a test configuration file:

```
# Xorg -configure
```

After you press Enter, a file named `xorg.conf .new` is created in `root`'s home directory, the `/root` directory. You can then use this file for a test session, like this:

```
# Xorg -xf86config /root/xorg.conf.new
```

Starting X

You can start X sessions in a variety of ways. The Fedora Core installer will set up the system initialization table `/etc/inittab` to have Linux boot directly to an X session using a *display manager* (that is, an X client that provides a graphical login). After you log in, you'll use a local session (running on your computer) or, if the system is properly configured, an X session running on a remote computer on the network. Logging in via a display manager requires you to enter a username and password. You can also start X sessions from the command line. The following sections describe these two methods.

Using a Display Manager

An X display manager presents a graphical login that requires a username and password to be entered before access is granted to the X desktop. It also allows you to choose a different desktop for your X session. Whether or not an X display manager is presented after you boot Linux is controlled by a *runlevel*—a system state entry in `/etc/inittab`. The following runlevels are defined in the file:

```
# 0 - halt (Do NOT set initdefault to this)
# 1 - Single user mode
# 2 - Multiuser, without NFS (The same as 3, if you do not have networking)
# 3 - Full multiuser mode
# 4 - unused
# 5 - X11
# 6 - reboot (Do NOT set initdefault to this)
```

Runlevel 5 is used for multiuser mode with a graphical X login via a display manager; booting to runlevel 3 provides a console, or text-based, login. The `initdefault` setting in the `/etc/inittab` file determines the default runlevel:

```
id:5:initdefault:
```

In this example, Linux boots and then ends up running X.

The default display manager might also be specified in /etc/inittab, like this:

```
x:5:respawn:/usr/bin/xdm -nodaemon
```

However, Fedora uses a shell script named prefdm, found under the /etc/X11 directory, to set the display manager:

```
x:5:respawn:/etc/X11/prefdm -nodaemon
```

According to this script, the display manager is based on the file named desktop under the /etc/sysconfig directory. The words GNOME, KDE, and XDM following a DESKTOP= entry determine what display manager is used for login. The following sections describe how to configure the three most commonly used display managers: gdm, kdm, and xdm).

Configuring gdm

The gdm display manager is part of the GNOME library and client distribution included with Fedora and provides a graphical login when a system boots directly to X. Its login (which is actually displayed by the gdmlogin client) hosts pop-up menus of window managers, languages, and system options for shutting down (halting) or rebooting the workstation. Although you can edit (as root) gdm.conf under the /etc/X11/gdm directory to configure gdm, a much better way to configure GNOME's display manager is to use the gdmsetup client.

You can use the gdmsetup client, shown in Figure 6.5, to configure many aspects and features of the login display. You launch this client from the GNOME desktop panel's System Settings Login Screen menu item, or from the command line, like this:

```
# gdmsetup &
```

After you press Enter, you see the GDM Setup window, as shown in Figure 6.5.

You can specify settings for security, remote network logins, the X server, and session and session chooser setup by clicking on the tabs in the GDM Setup dialog.

Configuring kdm

The kdm client, which is part of the KDE X desktop suite, offers a graphical login similar to gdm. You configure kdm by running the KDE Control Center client kcontrol, as the root operator, by clicking the Control Center menu item from the KDE kicker or desktop panel menu. You can also start KDE Control Center by using the kcontrol client at the command line like so:

```
$ kcontrol &
```

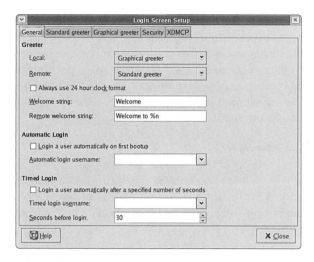

FIGURE 6.5   You use `gdmsetup` to configure the `gdmlogin` screen when using `gdm` as a display manager.

In the Index tab of the left pane of the KDE Control Center window, you click the System Administration menu item to open its contents, and then you click the Login Manager menu item. The right pane of the Control Center window displays the tabs and configuration options for the `kdm` Login Manager, as shown in Figure 6.6.

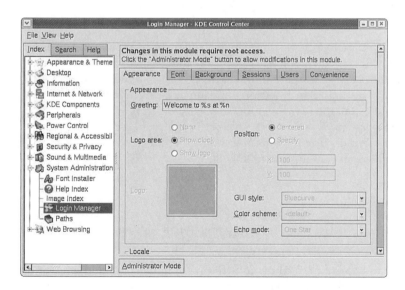

FIGURE 6.6   You configure `kdm` by choosing tabs and settings in the Control Center dialog box.

In order to make any changes to the KDE display manager while logged in as a regular user, you must first click the Administrator Mode button, and then enter the root operator password. You can click on a tab in the Control Center dialog to set configuration options. Options in these tabs allow you to control the login display, prompts, user icons, session management, and configuration of system options (for shutting down or rebooting). After you have made your configuration choices in each tab, click the Apply button to apply the changes immediately; otherwise, the changes are applied when the X server restarts.

Using the xdm Display Manager

The xdm display manager is part of the Xorg distribution and offers a bare-bones login for using X. Although it is possible to configure xdm by editing various files under the /etc/X11/xdm directory, GNOME and KDE offer a greater variety of options in display manager settings. The default xdm login screen's display is handled by the xsetroot client, which is included with Xorg, and Owen Taylor's xsri client, as specified in the file Xsetup_0 in the xdm directory under /etc/X11. The xsri client may be used to set the background color of the login display's desktop and to place an image in the initial display.

Starting X from the Console by Using startx

If you have Fedora set to boot to runlevel 3, a text-based console login, you can start an X session from the command line. You use the startx command (which is actually a shell script) to do so. You launch the X server and an X session by using startx, like this:

```
$ startx
```

startx first looks in your home directory for a file named .xinitrc. This file can contain settings that will launch an alternative desktop and X clients for your X session. The default system .xinitrc is found in the /etc/X11/xinit directory, but a local file can be used instead to customize an X session and launch default clients. For example, you can download and install the mlvwm window manager, which is available from http://www2u.biglobe.ne.jp/~y-miyata/mlvwm.html in the /usr/local/bin directory. You can then use the mlvwm desktop for your X session along the xterm terminal client by creating an .xinitrc file that contains the following:

```
xterm &
exec /usr/X11R6/bin/mlvwm
```

Using a custom .xinitrc is not necessary if you're using Fedora's desktop, which runs X and either a GNOME-aware window manager or KDE as a desktop environment.

You can also use the startx command with one or more command-line options. These options are passed to the X server before it launches an X session. For example, you can use startx to specify a color depth for an X session by using the -depth option, followed by a number such as 8, 16, 24, or 32 for 256, thousands, or millions of colors (as defined in the X configuration file and if supported). Using different color depths can be useful during development, for testing how X clients look on different displays, or to conserve use of video memory, such as when trying to get the highest resolution (increased color depth can sometimes affect the maximum resolution of older video cards).

For example, to start a session with thousands of colors, you use the `startx` command like this:

```
$ startx -- -depth 16
```

Another option that can be passed is a specific dots-per-inch (dpi) resolution that is to be used for the X session. For example, to use 100 dpi, you use the `-dpi` option followed by 100, like this:

```
$ startx -- -dpi 100
```

You can also use `startx` to launch multiple X sessions. This feature is due to Linux support for *virtual consoles*, or multiple text-based displays. To start the first X session, you use the `startx` command followed by a *display number*, or an X server instance (the first is 0, using screen 0) and a number that represents a virtual console. The default console used for X is number 7, so you can start the session like this:

```
$ startx -- :0 vt7
```

After X starts and the window manager appears, you press Ctrl+Alt+F2 and then log in again at the prompt. Next, you start another X session like this, specifying a different display number and virtual console:

```
$ startx -- :1 vt8
```

Another X session starts. To jump to the first X session, you press Ctrl+Alt+F7. You use Ctrl+Alt+F8 to return to the second session. If you exit the current session and go to another text-based login or shell, you use Alt+F7 or Alt+F8 to jump to the desired session.

Using `startx` is a flexible way to launch X sessions, but multiple sessions can be confusing, especially to new users, and are a horrific resource drain on a system that does not have enough CPU horsepower and memory. A better approach is to use multiple workspaces, also known as *virtual desktops*, as discussed in the following section.

Selecting and Using X Window Managers

A window manager is launched immediately after the X server starts. The window manager handles the drawing and display of graphical session windows and their onscreen controls and features. Without a window manager, X client windows cannot be moved about the screen, resized, minimized or maximized, and so on.

Many different window managers are available for Linux, providing a number of choices for how the desktop appears and functions. This wealth of desktop choices appeals to many people who use Linux and X.

A window manager provides an X display and customized desktop by handling window decoration, movement, placement, and resizing operations. A window manager can also handle icons, and it can support icon-docking and other window operations such as tiling and overlays. Another important window manager task is *focus policy*—how and when a window becomes active. A window can become active when the pointer is over it, for example, or it might require a mouse click for activation.

A window manger might also provide menuing on the root desktop or after a button is clicked in a client's window title bar. Some window managers support the use of special keyboard keys to move the pointer and emulate mouse button clicks. Another feature is the capability to provide multiple workspaces, or a *virtual desktop*, which isn't the same as the virtual screen; whereas a virtual screen is a desktop that is larger than the display, a virtual desktop offers two, four, or eight additional complete workspaces.

Some window managers support advanced features, such as drag and drop of icons that represent files or system devices. This allows the user to easily copy, print, delete, link, or move files—even over a network or the Internet.

> **NOTE**
>
> Many different window managers are available for Linux. You don't have to use Fedora's default selection of window managers. This is part of the freedom of using Linux and a testament to the flexibility of the X architecture. You can download, install, and run nearly any other window manager for X without problems. One of the best places to find links and information to other window managers is Matt Chapman's Window Managers for X page, at `http://xwinman.org/`. Many of these window managers can be downloaded and installed by using RPM, apt, or yum, or built and installed from source.

The following sections describe how to select a default desktop, switch to a different desktop, and configure different window managers for X.

Using Red Hat's `switchdesk`

You can use Red Hat's `switchdesk` client to change the default window manager or desktop environment such as GNOME or KDE. A *desktop environment* includes a window manager and a suite of related clients, such as productivity or utility applications. Most desktop environments also include the ability to save a session *state* (such as running applications, the applications' window size and positions, and so on), using a feature known as *session management*.

You can also use the `switchdesk` utility when running X or at a text-based console, along with a keyword (such as `GNOME` or `KDE`), to set the default X desktop before launching X.

For example, to specify that you want to use the KDE desktop environment as the default, you use switchdesk like this:

```
$ switchdesk KDE
Red Hat Linux switchdesk 3.9
Copyright (C) 1999-2001 Red Hat, Inc
Redistributable under the terms of the GNU General Public License
Desktop now set up to run KDE.
For system defaults, remove /home/bball/.Xclients
```

This example shows that the default X session will now use KDE. Settings are saved in the file named .Xclients in the home directory. You can launch switchdesk during an X session by clicking the Desktop Switching Tool menu item from the System Settings More System Setting menu or from the command line of an X11 terminal like this:

```
$ switchdesk &
```

After you press Enter, you get a graphical dialog offering a choice of window managers for X sessions (depending on the window managers that are installed on the system), as shown in Figure 6.7.

FIGURE 6.7   You use switchdesk to set the default window manager for X sessions.

Choosing a window manager is a matter of preference, necessity, or policy. You might prefer to use one of the older window managers—such as the Tab Window Manager (twm) or the Motif Window Manager (mwm)—on legacy PCs because they have fewer system resource requirements (that is, they require less hard drive space, CPU horsepower, and system memory). Newer desktop environments require 64MB or even more memory for good performance. The following sections describe some of the most popular window managers and their uses.

The Tab Window Manager

The Tab Window Manager (twm), which is included with Xorg and also sometimes known as Tom's Window Manager, is a legacy client that provides modest but essential features in a small (less than 1MB) memory footprint. It supports window decorations, menus, icons, and other features, but it does not support virtual desktops, session management, and other features, such as drag and drop.

The twm is used as a fallback, or *failsafe*, window manager for Fedora as it requires much less video and system memory. It is included with the Xorg software distribution and will be used as your window manager after you log in or start X in the event the system or your default window manager settings are lost or unusable. The twm resource file, system.twmrc, is located under the /etc/X11/twm directory. You can configure this file to provide a default desktop with a custom application menu if you save your settings to a file named .twmrc in your home directory. The format of this configuration file is documented in the twm man page.

A sample twm desktop is shown in Figure 6.8, displaying the xosview, xclock, xcalc, and xterm clients. The default desktop color can be changed using the xsetroot client. You access the desktop menu in twm by left-clicking in a blank area of the main window, known as the root display.

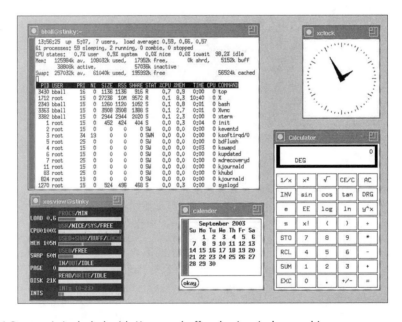

FIGURE 6.8   twm is included with Xorg and offers basic window and icon management.

The Motif Window Manager

mwm, the Motif Window Manager, is included with Fedora to provide a legacy X desktop. It is a clone window manager that closely mimics the original mwm window manager that was part of the OSF/Motif distribution from The Open Software Foundation. The mwm window manager is part of a Motif 1.2–compatible set of programming libraries and development files named LessTif.

mwm can even use the same configuration files as the OSF/Motif version. mwm's default resource file is located in /etc/X11/ system.mwmrc. You can edit this file to provide custom settings when it is located in your home directory and is named .mwmrc.

A sample mwm desktop is shown in Figure 6.9. Note that the Motif Window Manager offers more sophisticated window decorations (controls such as borders and title bar items) than the twm window manager.

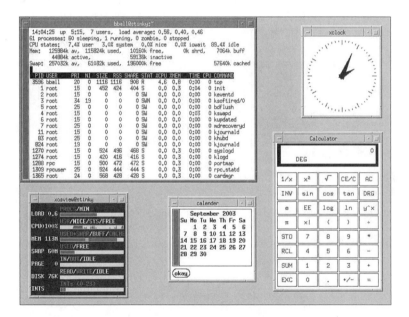

FIGURE 6.9 The Motif Window Manager provides a simple desktop for Red Hat Linux.

The sawfish Window Manager

The sawfish window manager is a GNOME-aware window manager (meaning that it can take advantage of some of the special features of GNOME). This window manager has a host of features, and it includes separate graphical clients, such as sawfish-ui, which is used to set focus policy, and other options. The sawfish systemwide defaults appear in a series of files and directories under the /usr/share/sawfish directory.

sawfish is not offered as a choice when you're using switchdesk, but you can use it for your next X session by using this simple .xinitrc file in your home directory (note that sawfish must be installed):

```
xsetroot -solid lightblue
gnome-terminal &
gnome-panel &
sawfish
```

This .xinitrc file sets your X session to start with the xsetroot client to set the desktop background to a light blue color, and then launches a terminal window and a desktop panel with sawfish as the window manger. Start your X session by using the startx command. (Delete the .xinitrc file to go back to using your switchdesk defaults.)

You access the sawfish menus by pressing and holding down the middle mouse button (button 2) in a blank area of the root display. The sample sawfish desktop created by the example .xinitrc is shown in Figure 6.10.

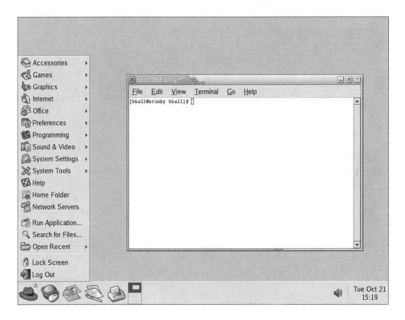

FIGURE 6.10   The sawfish window manager supports GNOME libraries.

The sawfish window manager also supports *themes*, or sets of related settings that can change the appearance of the desktop. Different themes can sometimes be used to improve viewing and readability of the desktop, such as when using a PC in a room with very bright or very dim lighting. These settings are installed under the /usr/share/ sawfish/1.2/themes directory.

> **NOTE**
>
> You can create an .xinitrc file that specifies metacity instead of sawfish to run the metacity window manager, which is used by default with GNOME. The metacity window manager is a no-frills client, but it can use different themes.

The Metacity Window Manager (metacity)

The metacity window manager is used for the GNOME desktop, but can be used as a standalone window manager. This can be helpful if you want to have a desktop that mimics the default Fedora desktop on a legacy computer with restricted system resources (such as an older laptop or PC with a slower Pentium CPU and limited RAM).

Configure a simple .xinitrc file in your home directory (similar to that for twm or mwm) that looks like this:

```
xsetroot -solid lightblue
gnome-terminal &
gnome-panel &
sawfish
```

After you start an X session, you can then start various clients. A sample metacity desktop is shown in Figure 6.11.

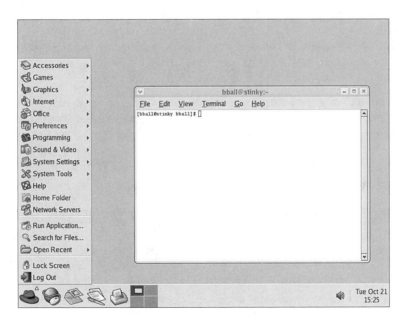

FIGURE 6.11   The metacity window manager can be used by itself for your X sessions.

> **Metacity Themes**
>
> You can design your own themes (color, shape, and window decoration schemes) for the
> `metacity` window manager. Browse to `http://developer.gnome.org/doc/tutorials/`
> `metacity/metacity-themes.html` for more details. To change the desktop theme while using
> GNOME, click the Theme menu item from the desktop panel's Preferences menu. (You learn
> more about using the Theme Preferences settings in "GNOME: The GNU Network Object Model
> Environment," later in this chapter.)

The GNOME and KDE Desktop Environments

A desktop environment for X provides one or more window managers and a suite of
clients that conform to a standard graphical interface based on a common set of software
libraries. When they are used to develop associated clients, these libraries provide graphical consistency for the client windows, menus, buttons, and other onscreen components,
along with some common keyboard controls and client dialogs. The following sections
briefly discuss the two desktop environments that are included with Fedora Core: GNOME
and KDE.

GNOME: The GNU Network Object Model Environment

The GNOME project, which was started in 1997, is the brainchild of programmer whiz
Miguel de Icaza. GNOME provides a complete set of software libraries and clients. GNOME
depends on a window manager that is GNOME aware. This means that in order to provide
a graphical desktop with GNOME elements, the window manager needs to be written to
recognize and use GNOME. Some compliant window managers that are GNOME-aware
include Havoc Pennington's `metacity` (the default GNOME window manager),
Enlightenment, Window Maker, IceWM, and `sawfish`.

Fedora uses GNOME's user-friendly suite of clients to provide a consistent and user-
friendly desktop. GNOME is a staple feature of Red Hat's commercial Linux distributions
and Fedora because Red Hat, Inc. actively supports its development. GNOME clients are
found under the `/usr/bin` directory, and GNOME configuration files are stored under the
`/etc/gnome` and `/usr/share/gnome` directories, with user settings stored in the home directory under `.gnome`.

> **Ximian GNOME for Red Hat**
>
> In 1999, Miguel de Icaza and Nat Friedman, the original GNOME developers, created a company
> and a product now known as Ximian. Ximian is a polished GNOME environment that offers not
> only an updated suite of GNOME clients, but also groupware software that provides integrated
> mail, calendar, addressing, and instant messaging services.
>
> In August 2003, Ximian was acquired by Novell, Inc. The Ximian GNOME distribution, now
> named Ximian Desktop 2, isn't included with Red Hat's Linux distros or Fedora, but you may be
> able to install it via CD-ROM or, if you have broadband access, in about an hour or less over the

Internet. Versions are available for many different Linux distributions (even those on non-Intel platforms).

To get started, you can go to Novell's Ximian Desktop Web site at `http://www.novell.com/products/desktop/download.html`. You first use `wget` to quickly download a graphical installer, which is then used to select a download site, selected files, and the base Ximian distribution. The download and installation are done as an automatic process, and Ximian replaces your default GNOME software with its own GNOME distribution. After installation, you can quickly install updates and bug fixes by using an update icon on the Ximian desktop.

A representative GNOME desktop, running the `gconftool-2` client used for setting themes, is shown in Figure 6.12.

FIGURE 6.12 Fedora's GNOME desktop uses the `metacity` window manager and offers a selection of GNOME (and KDE) themes.

You can configure your desktop in various ways and by using different menu items under the Preferences menu. For a comprehensive icon view of preference items, click the Control Center menu item from the desktop panel's Preferences menu. A graphical shell named Nautilus then launches. Nautilus was originally developed by Eazel (which ceased operations shortly before summer 2001). The Nautilus shell is used for the Fedora desktop as a file browser and desktop utility.

The Nautilus main window, shown in Figure 6.13, shows Preference icons. You can then click any icon (such as Background or Screensaver) and its dialog to change your desktop's appearance, focus behavior, window behavior, placement, sound, and workspace settings.

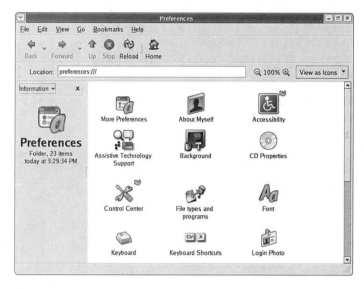

FIGURE 6.13   You can customize your Fedora desktop by using Preference settings that are available in the Nautilus graphical shell.

KDE: The K Desktop Environment

KDE, which is included with Fedora, has been available for Linux, Xorg, and XFree86 since 1996. KDE is a graphical desktop environment that offers a huge suite of clients, including a free office suite named KOffice. KDE clients are located under the /usr/bin directory, and nearly all clients have a name that begins with k.

The directory .kde in your home directory contains custom settings and session information. You can use KDE's Control Center, as shown in Figure 6.14, to customize desktop settings. You can launch this client by clicking the Control Center menu item from KDE's desktop menu (hosted by the panel along the bottom of your desktop, known as the *kicker*) or from the command line, like so:

```
$ kcontrol &
```

FIGURE 6.14   You can use the KDE Control Center to manage nearly every aspect of KDE desktop sessions.

Related Red Hat, Fedora, and Linux Commands

You can use these commands to create and configure the X Window System in Fedora Core Linux:

Xorg—The X server that is provided with the X Window System distribution from The X.Org Foundation

mouseconfig—Red Hat's text-based GUI pointing-device–configuration program

kcontrol—The KDE Control Center client

system-config-display—Red Hat's graphical X11R6 configuration tool

system-config-mouse—Fedora's graphical mouse configuration tool

gdmsetup—The GNOME display manager configuration client

startx—A shell script that is used to start one or more X sessions from the shell command line

xsri—A display manager root desktop decoration client

Reference

`http://www.x.org`—Curators of the X Window System.

`http://www.x.org/Downloads_mirror.html`—Want to download the source to the latest revision of X? Start at this list of mirror sites.

`http://www.xfree86.org`—Home of The XFree86 Project, Inc., which has provided a graphical interface for Linux for nearly 10 years.

`http://www.kde.org`—The place to get started when learning about KDE and the latest developments.

`http://www.gnome.org`—The launch point for more information about GNOME, links to new clients, and GNOME development projects.

`http://people.redhat.com/~hp/metacity/`—Havoc Pennington's `metacity` download page, where you can get the latest full-source version of this window manager.

`http://sawmill.sourceforge.net`—The home page for the `sawmill` window manager.

`http://www.windowmaker.org`—The source for the latest version of Window Maker.

`http://www.icewm.org`—IceWM's home page.

`http://www.lesstif.org`—The home page of the LessTif project, which aims to provide GNU GPL versions of OSF/Motif-compatible software libraries.

`http://scwm.sourceforge.net`—The home page of a lightweight, yet virtual desktop-enabled, window manager.

`http://www.fvwm.org`—The home page for FVWM2, where you can download the latest version.

`http://www.novell.com/products/desktop/`—The place to get started with Ximian GNOME.

PART II

System Administration and Managing Services

IN THIS PART

CHAPTER 7	Managing Services	189
CHAPTER 8	Managing Software and System Resources	207
CHAPTER 9	Managing Users	237
CHAPTER 10	Managing the File System	263
CHAPTER 11	Backing Up, Restoring, and Recovery	311

CHAPTER **7**

Managing Services

IN THIS CHAPTER

- Understanding the Fedora Core Linux Boot Process
- System Services and Runlevels
- Running Services Through xinetd
- Controlling Services at Boot with Administrative Tools
- Starting and Stopping Services Manually
- Changing Runlevels
- Using Service Management to Troubleshoot Problems in Fedora Core Linux
- Reference

In this chapter, you learn about the process that Fedora Core Linux goes through when it boots. After you turn on the power switch, the boot process begins with the computer executing code stored in a chip called the BIOS; this process occurs no matter what operating system you have installed. The Linux boot process begins when the code known as the boot loader starts loading the Linux kernel and doesn't end until the login prompt appears.

This chapter also discusses how system states (known as runlevels) can control what system services are started upon bootup. These services are simply applications running in the background that provide some needed function to your system, such as getting information from your mouse and sending it to the display; or a service could monitor the partitions to see whether they have enough free space left on them. Services are typically loaded and run (also referred to as being started) during the boot process.

As a system administrator, you'll use the skills you learn in this chapter to control your system's services and manage runlevels on your computer. Understanding the management of the system services and states is essential to understanding how Linux works (especially in a multiuser environment) and will help untangle the mysteries of a few of your Fedora Core Linux system's configuration files.

You can manage nearly every aspect of your computer and how it behaves after booting via configuring and ordering boot scripts, as well as by using various system administration utilities included with Fedora Core Linux. In this chapter, you learn how to work with these boot scripts and system administration utilities. This chapter also offers advice for troubleshooting and fixing problems that might arise with software configuration or the introduction or removal of various types of hardware from your system.

Understanding the Fedora Core Linux Boot Process

Although the actual boot loading mechanism for Linux varies on different hardware platforms (such as the SPARC, Alpha, or PowerPC systems), Intel-based PCs running Fedora Core Linux most often use the same mechanism throughout product lines. This process is accomplished through a Basic Input Output System, or BIOS. The BIOS is an application stored in a chip on the motherboard that initializes the hardware on the motherboard (and often the hardware that's attached to the motherboard). The BIOS gets the system ready to load and run the software that we recognize as the operating system.

As a last step, the BIOS code looks for a special program known as the boot loader or boot code. The instructions in this little bit of code tell the BIOS where the Linux kernel is located, how it should be loaded into memory, and how it should be started.

Beginning the Boot Loading Process

If all goes well, the BIOS looks for a bootable volume (a floppy disk, CD-ROM disc, hard drive, RAM disk, or other media). The bootable volume contains a special hexadecimal value written to the volume by the boot loader application (likely either GRUB or LILO, although LILO is not provided with Fedora Core) when the boot loader code was first installed in the system's drives. The BIOS searches volumes in the order established by the BIOS settings (for example, the floppy first, followed by a CD-ROM, and then a hard drive) and then boots from the first bootable volume it finds. Modern BIOS's allow considerable flexibility in choosing the device used for booting the system.

NOTE

If the BIOS does detect a hardware problem, the boot process will fail and the BIOS will generate a few beeps from the system speaker. These "beep codes" indicate the nature of the problem the BIOS has encountered. The codes vary among manufacturers, and the diagnosis of problems occurring during this phase of the boot process is beyond the scope of this book and does not involve Linux. If you encounter a problem, you should consult the motherboard manual or contact the manufacturer of the motherboard.

Next, the BIOS looks on the bootable volume for boot code in the partition boot sector also known as the Master Boot Record (MBR) of the first hard disk. The MBR contains the boot loader code and the partition table—think of it as an index for a book, plus a few comments on how to start reading the book. (We cover the MBR in more detail in Chapter 10, "Managing the File System.") If the BIOS finds a boot loader, it loads the boot loader code into memory. At that point, the BIOS's job is completed, and it passes control of the system to the boot loader.

The boot loader locates the Linux kernel on the disk and loads it into memory. After that task is completed, the boot loader passes control of the system to the Linux kernel. You can see how one process builds on another in an approach that enables many different operating systems to work with the same hardware.

Fedora Core Linux can use a variety of boot loaders, including GRUB (the default for Fedora Core), LILO (a long-time standard but not available with Fedora Core), BootMagic (a commercial program), and others.

> **NOTE**
>
> Linux is very flexible and can be booted from multiple images on a CD-ROM, over a network using PXE or NetBoot, or on a headless server with the console display sent over a serial or network connection. Work is even underway to create a special Linux BIOS at http://www.linuxbios.org/ that will expedite the boot process because Linux does not need many of the services offered by the typical BIOS. This might be important to the future of Linux as Microsoft wants to integrate the BIOS into the MS Windows operating system.
>
> This kind of flexibility enables Linux to be used in a wide variety of ways, such as remote servers or diskless workstations, that are not generally seen in personal home use.

Loading the Linux Kernel

In a general sense, the kernel manages the system resources. As the user, you don't often interact with the kernel, but instead just the applications that you are using. UNIX refers to each application as a process, and the kernel assigns each process a number called a PID, or process ID. First, the Linux kernel loads and runs a process named init, which is also known as the "father of all processes" because it starts every subsequent process. The init process looks for a list of instructions in a file named /etc/rc.d/rc.sysinit. That script issues a number of commands that are only run once—each time the system is turned on.

> **NOTE**
>
> Details about the sequence of events that occur when the Linux kernel is loaded can be found in the file /usr/src/linux-2.6/init/main.c if you have installed the Linux kernel documentation.

This next step of the boot process begins with a message that the Linux kernel is loading, and a series of messages will be printed to the screen, giving you the status of each command in rc.sysinit script language. A failure should display an error message. The -quiet option may be passed to the kernel at boot time to suppress many of these messages.

Although it isn't intended that you modify the rc.sysinit script, knowledge of the contents of the file might aid you in diagnosing a problem if the boot process fails during this step. Look at /etc/rc.d/rc.sysinit, and you'll discover that it's just a text file filled with shell script language. (You can learn about scripting behavior in Chapter 22, "Shell Scripting.")

After the rc.sysinit script has been run, the basic system is configured and the kernel is in control of the system. If the boot process were halted at this point, the system would just sit idle and the screen would be blank. In order to make the system useful for users, we need to start the system services. Those services are some of the applications that allow us to interact with the system.

System Services and Runlevels

After finishing with rc.sysinit script during the bootloading process, the init command uses the Linux system initialization table found in /etc/inittab to boot Fedora Core Linux to a specific system state. The state of the system is commonly referred to as its runlevel.

Several different ways of starting and stopping system services exist, and Fedora Core uses a method derived from System V UNIX. The System V (pronounced "System Five") method uses runlevels and different combinations of services to define different states of operation. Runlevels determine which of the many available system services are started, as well as in which order they start. A special runlevel is used to stop the system, and a special runlevel is used for system maintenance. As you'll see, there are other runlevels for special purposes.

> **NOTE**
>
> The System V method makes extensive use of symbolic links, which are ways to reference a file in another location and make it appear as if it were in two or more places at once. The benefit is that you only need to edit one file to change them all. In addition, any reorganization to be done means that only links need to be changed, not the files themselves. You'll find more about symbolic links in Chapter 10, as well as later in this chapter.

You'll use runlevels to automatically manage the system services running on your computer. All these special files and scripts are set up during your installation of Fedora Core Linux, and they receive their initial values based on your choices during the installation—as described in Chapter 3, "Installing Fedora," and Chapter 4, "Post-Installation Issues." You can change and control them manually, as you learn later in this chapter using tools of varying sophistication.

Runlevel Definitions

The Fedora Core Linux runlevels are defined for the Fedora Core system in /etc/inittab.

Each runlevel tells the `init` command what services to start or stop. Although runlevels might all have custom definitions, Fedora Core Linux has adopted some standards for runlevels:

- **Runlevel 0**—Known as halt, this runlevel is used to shut down the system.

- **Runlevel 1**—This is a special runlevel, defined as single, which boots Fedora Core Linux to a root access shell prompt where only the root user may log in. It has networking, X, and multiuser access turned off. This is the maintenance or rescue mode. It allows the system administrator to perform work on the system, make backups, or repair configuration or other files.

- **Runlevel 2**—This runlevel is identical to runlevel 3, except that it does not start any networking services.

- **Runlevel 3**—This runlevel dictates that Fedora Core Linux be booted to a console, or text-based mode, with networking and multiuser access.

- **Runlevel 4**—This runlevel is undefined, and it can readily be configured to boot Fedora Core Linux to a custom system state.

- **Runlevel 5**—This runlevel boots Fedora Core Linux to a networking, multiuser state with an active X session. This is the most common runlevel for home users who want a graphical interface.

- **Runlevel 6**—This runlevel is used to reboot the system.

Runlevel 1 (also know as single-user mode or maintenance mode) is most commonly used to repair file systems and change the root password on a system when the password has been forgotten. Trespassers with physical access to the machine also can use Runlevel 1 to access your system.

Booting into the Default Runlevel

Entries in /etc/inittab use a field-based notation that determines the runlevel—when to execute the process, whether or not the process is executed when booting, whether or not to wait for the process to complete, and when to execute the process during booting. The default choices are adequate and only need be changed in unique circumstances that the average user is not likely to encounter.

The value of the default entry, or the initdefault line in /etc/inittab, determines the particular system state in which Fedora Core Linux will be when the login prompt is finally presented. For example,

```
id:5:initdefault:
```

In this example, Fedora Core Linux boots to runlevel 5, a network-enabled, multiuser mode with an active X session and a graphical login. The value 5 is forwarded to the script named rc under the /etc/rc.d directory. This script is used when booting or changing runlevels; it also acts as an interpreter when you boot Fedora Core Linux in "Interactive" mode by pressing **i** during the boot.

After /etc/rc.d/rc.sysinit has finished, init uses the corresponding /etc/inittab entry that matches the designated default runlevel. Using the previous example, the line in /etc/inittab would then be

```
l5:5:wait:/etc/rc.d/rc 5
```

Under the /etc/rc.d directory are a series of directories that correspond to each runlevel:

```
# ls /etc/rc.d
init.d  rc0.d  rc2.d  rc4.d  rc6.d     rc.sysinit
rc      rc1.d  rc3.d  rc5.d  rc.local
```

Assuming that the value is 5, the rc script then executes all the scripts under the /etc/rc.d/rc.5 directory and then launches the graphical login.

If Fedora Core Linux is booted to runlevel 5, for example, scripts beginning with the letter K followed by scripts beginning with the letter S under the /etc/rc.d/rc5.d directory are then executed:

```
# ls /etc/rc.d/rc5.d/
K01yum          K20bootparamd   K28amd      K45named      K61ldap
K74ypxfrd       S05kudzu        S24pcmcia   S85gpm        K05innd
K20iscsi        K30sendmail     K46radvd    K65identd     K84bgpd
S08ip6tables    S25netfs        S90crond    K05saslauthd  K20netdump-server
K34dhcrelay     K50netdump      K65kadmin   K84ospf6d     S08ipchains
S26apmd         S90FreeWnn      K10psacct   K20nfs        K34yppasswdd
K50snmpd        K65kprop        K84ospfd    S08iptables   S28autofs
```

S90xfs	K10radiusd	K20rstatd	K35atalk	K50snmptrapd
K65krb524	K84ripd	S10network	S40smartd	S92lisa
K12canna	K20rusersd	K35dhcpd	K50tux	K65krb5kdc
K84ripngd	S12syslog	S44acpid	S95anacron	K12mailman
K20rwalld	K35smb	K50vsftpd	K70aep1000	K85zebra
S13irqbalance	S55cups	S95atd	K12mysqld	K20rwhod
K35vncserver	K54dovecot	K70bcm5820	K90isicom	S13portmap
S55sshd	S97messagebus	K15httpd	K20spamassassin	K35winbind
K54pxe	K74ntpd	K91isdn	S14nfslock	S56rawdevices
S97rhnsd	K15postgresql	K24irda	K40mars-nwe	K55routed
K74ups	K95firstboot	S17keytable	S56xinetd	S99local
K16rarpd	K25squid	K45arpwatch	K61hpoj	K74ypserv
S00microcode_ctl	S20random	S84privoxy	S99mdmonitor	

These scripts are actually symbolic links to system service scripts under the /etc/rc.d/ init.d directory (yours might look different, depending on whether you are working with a workstation or server installation and the services or software packages installed on your system):

```
# ls /etc/rc.d/init.d/
```

acpid	bgpd	firstboot	ip6tables	keytable	mars-nwe	nfs
postgresql	ripd	smartd	vncserver	zebra	aep1000	bluetooth
FreeWnn	ipchains	killall	mdmonitor	nfslock	privoxy	
ripngd	smb	vsftpd	amd	bootparamd	functions	iptables
kprop	messagebus	nscd	psacct	routed	snmpd	wibind
anacron	canna	gkrellmd	irda	krb524	microcode_ctl	ntpd
pxe	rstatd	snmptrapd	xfs	apmd	cpqarrayd	gpm
irqbalance	krb5kdc	mysqld	ospf6d	radiusd	rusersd	
spamassassin	xinetd	arpwatch	crond	halt	iscsi	kudzu
named	ospfd	radvd	rwalld	squid	ypbind	
atalk	cups	hpoj	isdn	ldap	netdump	pand
random	rwhod	sshd	yppasswdd	atd	dhcpd	
httpd	isicom	lisa	netdump-server	pcmcia	rarpd	
saslauthd	syslog	ypserv	autofs	dhcrelay	identd	kadmin
lm_sensors	netfs	portmap	rawdevices	sendmail	tux	
ypxfrd	bcm5820	dovecot	innd	kdcrotate	mailman	
network	postfix	rhnsd	single	ups	yum	

The rc5.d links are prefaced with a letter and number, such as K15 or S10. The (K) or (S) in these prefixes indicate whether or not a particular service should be killed (K) or started (S) and pass a value of stop or start to the appropriate /etc/rc.d/init.d script. The number in the prefix executes the specific /etc/rc.d/init.d script in a particular order. The symlinks have numbers to delineate the order in which they are started. Nothing is sacred about a specific number, but some services need to be running before others are started. You wouldn't want your Fedora Core Linux system to attempt, for example, to mount a remote network file system (NFS) volume without first starting networking and NFS services.

After all the system services are started for our runlevel, `init` starts the graphical login (because we are in runlevel 5). The graphical login's definition appears toward the end of `/etc/inittab` and looks like this:

```
# Run xdm in runlevel 5

x:5:respawn:/etc/X11/prefdm -nodaemon
```

This example shows that the shell script named `prefdm` executes the proper X11 display manager when Fedora Core Linux is booted to runlevel 5.

Booting to a Non-Default Runlevel with GRUB

After you select a default runlevel, that runlevel will be selected every time you restart the system from a power-off state. There might come a time when you do not want to boot into that runlevel. You might want to enter the maintenance mode or start the system without an active X server and graphical login in order to modify or repair the X server or desktop manager. You'll need to follow several specific steps to boot to a non-default runlevel if you use the default boot loader for Fedora Core, GRUB.

> **NOTE**
>
> If you have enabled a GRUB password, you must first press **p**, type your password, and then press Enter before using this boot method.

The GRUB boot loader passes arguments, or commands, to the kernel at boot time. These arguments are used, among other things, to tell GRUB where the kernel is located and also to pass specific parameters to the kernel, such as how much memory is available or how special hardware should be configured.

To override the default runlevel, you can add an additional kernel argument to GRUB as follows:

At the graphical boot screen, press **e** (for edit), scroll down to select the kernel, and press **e** again.

Press the spacebar, type **single** or **1** (Fedora Core allows S and **s** as well), and press Enter.

Finally, press **b** to boot, and you'll boot into runlevel 1 instead of the default runlevel listed in `/etc/inittab`.

Fedora Core Linux includes several command-line and graphical system administration utilities you can use to start, stop, reorder, or restart various services in different runlevels.

These commands (discussed later in this chapter) work by renaming, removing, or creating symbolic links from /etc/rc.d/init.d to /etc/rc.d/rc.* as appropriate. Many administrators use these commands to change the symbolic links to the scripts under each /etc/rc.d/rc* directory rather than do it by hand.

The locations of symbolic links can also be confusing. Red Hat (and now Fedora Core) has traditionally kept them in one place, and the Linux Standards Base (LSB) requires that they now be located elsewhere. Because other scripts reference these files and it would be difficult to change them all, Fedora Core places symbolic links in the places specified by the LSB.

As you might surmise, symbolic links are very powerful tools in the system administrator's toolbox.

Understanding init Scripts and the Final Stage of Initialization

Each /etc/rc.d/init.d script, or init script, contains logic that determines what to do when receiving a start or stop value. The logic might be a simple switch statement for execution, as in this example:

```
case "$1" in
  start)
        start
        ;;
  stop)
        stop
        ;;
  restart)
        restart
        ;;
  reload)
        reload
        ;;
  status)
        rhstatus
        ;;
  condrestart)
        [ -f /var/lock/subsys/smb ] && restart || :
        ;;
  *)
        echo $"Usage: $0 {start|stop|restart|status|condrestart}"
        exit 1
esac
```

7

Although the scripts can be used to customize the way that the system runs from power-on, absent the replacement of the kernel, this script approach also means that the system does not have to be halted in total to start, stop, upgrade, or install new services.

Note that not all scripts will use this approach, and that other messages might be passed to the service script, such as restart, reload, or status. Also, not all scripts will respond to the same set of messages (with the exception of start and stop, which they all have to accept by convention) because each service might require special commands.

> **TIP**
>
> You can write your own `init` scripts using the existing scripts as examples. Example scripts can also be found in `/usr/share/doc/initscripts/sysvinitfiles`, along with a brief tutorial written by Red Hat and a brief explanation of all the options available to use in `init` scripts.

After all the system scripts have been run, your system is configured and all the necessary system services have been started. If you are using a runlevel other then 5, the final act of the `init` process is to launch the user shell—`bash`, `tcsh`, `zsh`, or any of the many command shells available. The shell launches and you see a login prompt on the screen.

Running Services Through `xinetd`

The `xinetd` daemon is a replacement for `inetd`, and is a daemon that listens for requests for services on certain ports and starts those services as required. It's called a super server because it controls other servers; its purpose is to conserve resources by not running services when not needed. The `xinetd` daemon is more secure than the older `inetd`, offers better logging facilities than `inetd`, and can redirect service requests to another machine. It does not require the root user to start any services.

The configuration file for `xinetd` is found at `/etc/xinetd.conf`, configuration files for individual services are located in `/etc/xinet.d/`; the particulars of its format are covered in the man page for `xinetd.conf`, which also provides an example file listing. Fedora Core provides the appropriate server RPM packages already configured to use `xinetd` if possible. If you are installing servers manually from source code, the included documentation will describe the appropriate `xinetd` configuration. Services run under `xinetd` cannot be started and stopped in the same manner as the services run from scripts in `/etc/rc.d/init.d`; you must restart the `xinetd` service itself and let it control those services.

Here is a sample listing of the `rsync` file `/etc/xinet.d/rsync`:

```
# default: off
# description: The rsync server is a good addition to an ftp server, as it \
#        allows crc checksumming etc.
service rsync
```

```
{
        disable = yes
        socket_type     = stream
        wait            = no
        user            = root
        server          = /usr/bin/rsync
        server_args     = --daemon
        log_on_failure  += USERID
}
```

The items are straightforward and will vary from service to service. Although you can edit this by hand, it can be configured via the command-line or graphical service configuration clients.

Controlling Services at Boot with Administrative Tools

As the master control file for system startup, /etc/inittab and its corresponding system of symbolic links control system services. You can manage /etc/inittab and its symbolic links using these graphical and non-graphical administrative tools:

- chkconfig—A small script that helps you configure system services.
- ntsysv—A graphical interface for the chkconfig configuration script.
- system-config-services—A full graphical services configuration client. This application is found in the System Services/Server settings menu as the Services menu item.

The following sections explain how to use all these administrative tools to configure and manage services in Fedora Core Linux.

Using the chkconfig Text-Based Command-Line Tool

Traditionally, the command-line tool chkconfig has been used to effect administration of the services and their associations in the different runlevels. chkconfig was a major improvement over the process of configuring the symbolic links by hand. It is an effective, text-based command-line tool that you can use to display, diagnose, or change the starting or stopping of system services (as available under /etc/rc.d/init.d) in each runlevel.

For example, to list all services that will be turned on in runlevel 5, you can pipe the output of chkconfig through the grep command like this:

```
# /sbin/chkconfig --list | grep '5:on' | sort
anacron         0:off   1:off   2:on    3:on    4:on    5:on    6:off
apmd            0:off   1:off   2:on    3:on    4:on    5:on    6:off
atd             0:off   1:off   2:off   3:on    4:on    5:on    6:off
autofs          0:off   1:off   2:off   3:on    4:on    5:on    6:off
```

```
canna            0:off   1:off   2:on    3:off   4:on    5:on    6:off
crond            0:off   1:off   2:on    3:on    4:on    5:on    6:off
```

Not all the output is shown here, but as you can see, chkconfig can display the value of off or on for each service and each runlevel. The sample output only shows those services that will be started in runlevel 5. The chkconfig command can be used to reassign start or stop values for each runlevel and each service. As an example, to alter the scripts to start power management (controlled by the apmd script under /etc/rc.d/init.d) when using Fedora Core Linux during runlevel 5, use chkconfig like this:

```
# chkconfig --level 5 apmd on
```

You can then verify this action by again grepping chkconfig's output like this:

```
# chkconfig --list | grep apmd
apmd             0:off   1:off   2:on    3:on    4:on    5:on    6:off
```

The chkconfig command does not start or stop a service; instead, it alters the scripts that start or stop a service, or it can report on the status of a service. Affecting only the current runlevel by default, other runlevels can be modified by using the –levels option. You would use the ntsysv or service commands or run the daemons directly in order to actually start or stop services (as described later in this chapter). All these tools have useful man pages to refresh your memory of all the available options.

ntsysv is a graphical interface you can use to access chkconfig and use a graphical interface. ntsysv is an ncurses-based interface, meaning that it offers crude, block graphics and elements you can tab through and select by pressing the spacebar (see Figure 7.1).

When you have the ntsysv application open, you can scroll through the list of services and toggle a service on or off by pressing the spacebar on the keyboard. When finished, use the Tab key to highlight the OK or Cancel button. Your changes will be saved and used the next time Fedora Core Linux is booted.

> **NOTE**
>
> ntsysv is simple to use and it's an excellent tool for a system without X, but it only works for the runlevel you are currently in. Use the --level option to modify other runlevels.

The Fedora Core tool setup is an ncurses-based menu for all the available ncurses-based command-line configuration tools (see Figure 7.2). It can be used to access ntsysv and all the other command-line configuration tools.

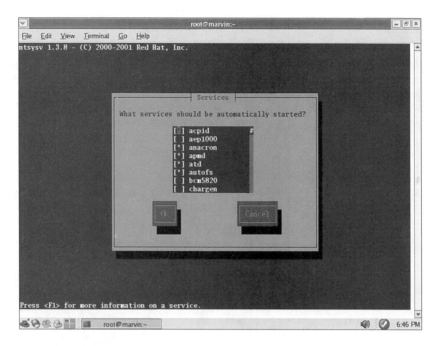

FIGURE 7.1 The ntsysv utility only manages which services are started in the current runlevel. Use the --level option to modify other runlevels.

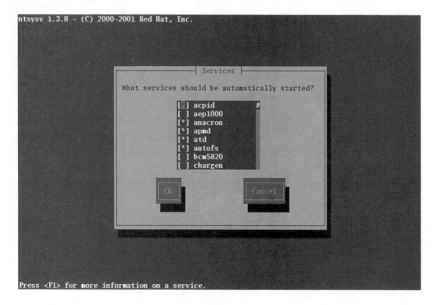

FIGURE 7.2 Use the setup command's System Services item to access the ntsysv command.

Using the GUI-based Service Configuration Tool

Fedora Core's developers have added GUIs to many text-only, command-line–based system administration tools as Linux has matured. These tools provide an easier-to-use interface and don't require memorization or lookup of command-line options. Fedora Core provides its own Service Configuration tool for the control and administration of services (see Figure 7.3). You can access the GUI menu selection from the System Settings/Server Settings menu, and then select Services. The command-line name of this tool is `system-config-services`.

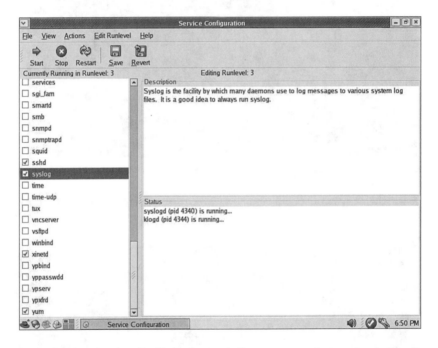

FIGURE 7.3   The new Service Configuration tool allows you to select runlevels to edit, displays all the available services, and provides an explanation of what the service does.

Starting and Stopping Services Manually

If you change a configuration file for a system service, it's usually necessary to stop and restart the service to make it read the new configuration. If you are reconfiguring the X server, it's often convenient to change from runlevel 5 to runlevel 3 to make testing easier and then switch back to runlevel 5 to re-enable the graphical login. If a service is improperly configured, it is easier to stop and restart it until you have it configured correctly than it is to reboot the entire machine.

There are several ways to manually start or stop services or to change runlevels while using Fedora Core Linux. The traditional way to manage a service (as root) is to call the service's **/etc/rc.d/init.d** name on the command line with an appropriate keyword, such as **start**, status, or **stop**. For example, to start the automated nightly update of the YUM RPM package database, call the **/etc/rc.d/init.d/yum** script like this:

```
# /etc/rc.d/init.d/yum start
Enabling nightly yum update:                              [  OK  ]
```

The script will execute the proper program(s) and report the status of it. Stopping services is equally easy, and in fact, you can also check the status of some services by using the status keyword like this:

```
# /etc/rc.d/init.d/yum status
Nightly yum update is enabled.
```

In this example, the yum script reports that the daemon is running. This information might be useful for other system management tasks.

A much easier way to manually start or stop a service is to use a script named service. Using service, you don't have to know the full pathname to the system service; you only need to know the name of the system service you want to manipulate. Using this approach, the previous YUM example looks like this:

```
# service yum start
Nightly yum update is enabled:                            [  OK  ]
```

Of course, the GUI tools mentioned before also have the functionality to start and stop specific services in your current runlevel. The tool you choose is a matter of personal preference; a good system administrator will be aware of them all.

Changing Runlevels

After making changes to system services and runlevels, you can use the telinit command to change runlevels on-the-fly on a running Fedora Core Linux system. Changing runlevels this way allows system administrators to alter selected parts of a running system in order to make changes to the services or to put changes into effect that have already been made (such as reassignment of network addresses for a networking interface).

For example, a system administrator can quickly change the system to maintenance or single-user mode by using the telinit command with its **S** option like this:

```
# telinit S
```

The telinit command uses the init command to change runlevels and shut down currently running services. The command then starts services for the specified runlevel, where in this example, the single-user runlevel is the same as runlevel 2. The init command can only be run from a console, not from an xterm running in an X session.

After booting to single-user mode, you can then return to multiuser mode without X, like this:

```
# telinit 3
```

If you have made changes to the system initialization table itself, /etc/inittab, use the telinit command's **q** command-line option to force init to re-examine the table.

> **TIP**
>
> Linux is full of shortcuts: If you exit the single-user shell by typing **exit** at the prompt, you'll go back to the default runlevel without worrying about using telinit.

Using Service Management to Troubleshoot Problems in Fedora Core Linux

Reordering or changing system services during a particular runlevel is rarely necessary when using Fedora Core Linux unless some disaster occurs. But system administrators should have a basic understanding of how Linux boots and how services are controlled in order to perform troubleshooting or to diagnose problems. By using additional utilities such as the **dmesg | less** command to read kernel output after booting or by examining system logging with **cat /var/log/messages | less**, it is possible to gain a bit more detail about what is going on when faced with troublesome drivers or service failure.

To better understand how to troubleshoot service problems in Fedora Core Linux, take a look at the diagnosis and resolution of a typical service-related issue.

In this example, X won't start: You don't see a desktop displayed, nor does the computer seem to respond to keyboard input. The X server might either be hung in a loop, repeatedly failing, or might exit to a shell prompt with or without an error message.

The X server only attempts to restart itself in runlevel 5, so to determine whether the X server is hung in a loop, try switching to runlevel 3.

> **TIP**
>
> If you're working on a multiuser system and might inadvertently interrupt the work of other users, ask them to save their current work; then change to a safer runlevel, such as single user mode.

Change to runlevel 3 by switching to another virtual console with Ctrl+Alt+F2, logging in as root, and running the command **telinit 3**. This switch to runlevel 3 will stop the X server from attempting to restart itself.

Now you can easily examine the error and attempt to fix it.

First, try to start the X server "naked" (without also launching the window manager). If you're successful, you'll get a gray screen with a large X in the middle. If so, kill X with the Ctrl+Alt+Backspace key combination, and look at your window manager configuration. (This configuration varies according to which window manager you have chosen.)

Let's assume that X won't run "naked." If we look at the log file for Xorg (it's clearly identified in the /var/log directory), we'll pay attention to any line that begins with (EE), the special error code. We can also examine the error log file, .xsessions-error, in our home directory if such a file exists.

If we find an error line, the cause of the error might or might not be apparent to us. The nice thing about the Linux community is that it is very unlikely that you are the first person to ever experience that error. Enter the error message (or better, a unique part of it) into http://www.google.com/linux and discover what others have had to say about the problem. You might need to adjust your search to yield usable results, but that level of detail is beyond the scope of this chapter. Make adjustments and retest as before until you achieve success.

Fix the X configuration and start X with **startx**. Repeat as necessary.

CAUTION

Before making any changes to any configuration file, always make a backup copy of the original, unmodified file. Our practice is to append the extension .original to the copy because that is a unique and unambiguous identifier.

If you need to restore the original configuration file, don't rename it, but copy it back to its original name.

When this advice has saved you valuable time and effort—and it will—you can express your appreciation by buying a copy of this book as a gift for a friend.

Relevant Fedora Core Linux Commands

Here are some of the commands you learned about in this chapter:

chkconfig—Fedora Core's text-only command-line runlevel configuration utility.

ntsysv—Fedora Core's text-based system services configuration tool for the command line.

setup—Actually a BASH script, it is a menu to all the individual ncurses-based configuration tools, including ntsysv.

system-config-services—Fedora Core's GUI runlevel configuration tool, named Configure Services.

telinit—Changes the current runlevel.

Reference

`http://www.linuxgazette.com/issue70/ghosh.html`—A Linux Gazette article on "Bootstrapping Linux," which includes much detail on the BIOS and MBR aspects of the boot process.

`http://www.lostcircuits.com/advice/bios2/1.shtml`—The LostCircuits BIOS guide; much detail on the meaning of all those BIOS settings.

`http://www.rojakpot.com/default.aspx?location=1`—The BIOS Optimization Guide; details on tweaking those BIOS settings to your heart's content.

`http://www-106.ibm.com/developerworks/linux/library/l-slack.html`—A link through IBM's Web site to an article on booting Slackware Linux, along with a sidebar about the history of System V versus BSD `init` scripts.

`/usr/src/linux/init/main.c`—The best place to learn about how Linux boots. Fascinating reading, really. Get it from the source!

`http://sunsite.dk/linux-newbie/`—Home page for the Linux Newbie Administrator Guide—A gentle introduction to Linux System Administration.

The GRUB Manual—The still yet-to-be-completed manual can be found at `http://www.gnu.org/software/grub/manual/`. On your Fedora Core system, **`info grub`** provides a plethora of information and a sample `grub.conf` file (`/boot/grub/menu.lst` is a symbolic link to `/boot/grub/grub.conf`; use either name) can be found in `/usr/doc/grub`.

"LILO User's Guide"—Werner Almesberger's definitive technical tome on the LInux LOader, or LILO, and how it works on Intel-based PCs. Look under the `/usr/share/doc/lilo*/doc` directory for the file `User_Guide.ps`, which can be viewed using the gv client. LILO has been dropped from Fedora Core; GRUB is now the default boot loader supported in the distribution.

"Managing Initscripts with Red Hat's chkconfig"—by Jimmy Ball, *Linux Journal*, April 2001; pp. 128–132.

"Grub, Glorious Grub"—Hoyt Duff, *Linux Format*, August 2001; pp. 58–61. A tutorial on the GRUB boot leader.

`http://www.redhat.com/docs/manuals/linux/RHL-9-Manual/custom-guide/s1-services-serviceconf.html`—Red Hat's guide to use the `system-config-service` client (then called `redhat-config-service`).

`http://www.linuxbase.org/spec/refspecs/LSB_1.0.0/gLSB/sysinit.html`—The Linux Standard Base description of system initialization; this is the standard.

## CHAPTER 8

Managing Software and System Resources

IN THIS CHAPTER

- Using RPM for Software Management
- Using Red Hat Network and Alternatives for Software Management
- Compiling Software from Source
- System Monitoring Tools
- Reference

This chapter introduces concepts, procedures, and software you can use to manage installed system resources on a Fedora Core Linux system. Managing the system resources—including software, storage, and memory—of your computer is important for a number of reasons. Good resource management promotes and supports efficient, productive sessions, a stable system, and satisfied users. Managing these resources involves installing, removing, upgrading, or rebuilding software packages—each a vital task that can contribute to your system's security.

As a Fedora Core Linux system administrator, you should also know how to maximize your system's resources by managing memory and storage for the most efficient system use. Properly managing your system resources ensures that you won't run out of room for new software, and you can expand the system to fit changing needs and new projects. In other words, system resource management is essential to providing the best possible computing experience for your users.

Fedora Core Linux provides a variety of tools for system resource management. The following sections introduce the RPM Package Manager (RPM), along with command-line and graphical software-management tools. You'll also learn about monitoring and managing memory and disk storage on your system.

Using RPM for Software Management

RPM was derived (in part) from early Linux package management software—named RPP, PMS, and PM—that was written in Perl. RPM was first used with Red Hat Linux 2.0 in late 1995, and then rewritten in C for the Red Hat Linux 3.0.3 (Picasso) release in 1996. Since then, the rpm command has been the prime feature of Red Hat's unique software management system, which is based on the concept of pristine sources, or the capability to use a single, initial archive of a program's source code to build packages for different systems and to track versions. With the release of Red Hat 8.0 (Psyche) in 2002, Red Hat offered a slightly updated graphical management interface for its venerable RPM application.

In addition to improving the package management of early software management scripts, RPM version 4.1 introduced software features designed to ease the task of building software for different platforms from a single set of source-code files. Changes can be tracked and kept outside a developer's initial source code and multiple packages can be built from scratch and installed at the same time—simultaneously, RPM also verifies installation dependencies. Additional features, such as a checksum and GNU Privacy Guard (GPG) signatures, enable binary software packages to be safely distributed without the fear of virus infection or the inclusion of Trojan code.

The rpm command uses the RPM system to install, remove (erase), upgrade, verify, and build software archives known as .rpm files. These archives, or packages, contain package identification (a signature), checksums (mathematically derived validation values), and an archive of the software, either in source or binary form. A .rpm package also contains quite a bit of additional information, such as a name, version, and basic description, and can include pre- and post-installation scripts used for software installation, erasure, or upgrading.

The RPM database installed on your computer keeps track of which versions of which packages are installed. RPM uses your system's /var/lib/rpm directory to store files (actually databases) containing information about the software installed on your system. You can use the ls command to view these files (you might see file sizes different from those shown here, depending on the amount of software you have installed):

```
$ ls -l /var/lib/rpm
total 53820
-rw-r--r--    1 rpm      rpm        5423104 Oct 14 19:53 Basenames
-rw-r--r--    1 rpm      rpm          12288 Oct 14 12:32 Conflictname
-rw-r--r--    1 root     root         16384 Oct 14 17:31 __db.001
-rw-r--r--    1 root     root       1318912 Oct 14 17:31 __db.002
-rw-r--r--    1 root     root        458752 Oct 14 17:31 __db.003
-rw-r--r--    1 rpm      rpm        1179648 Oct 14 19:53 Dirnames
-rw-r--r--    1 rpm      rpm        5521408 Oct 14 19:53 Filemd5s
-rw-r--r--    1 rpm      rpm          24576 Oct 14 19:53 Group
-rw-r--r--    1 rpm      rpm          20480 Oct 14 19:53 Installtid
-rw-r--r--    1 rpm      rpm          45056 Oct 14 19:53 Name
-rw-r--r--    1 rpm      rpm       41070592 Oct 14 19:53 Packages
-rw-r--r--    1 rpm      rpm         348160 Oct 14 19:53 Providename
-rw-r--r--    1 rpm      rpm          98304 Oct 14 19:53 Provideversion
-rw-r--r--    1 rpm      rpm          12288 Oct 14 19:53 Pubkeys
-rw-r--r--    1 rpm      rpm         237568 Oct 14 19:53 Requirename
```

```
-rw-r--r--   1 rpm      rpm       176128 Oct 14 19:53 Requireversion
-rw-r--r--   1 rpm      rpm        94208 Oct 14 19:53 Sha1header
-rw-r--r--   1 rpm      rpm        49152 Oct 14 19:53 Sigmd57
-rw-r--r--   1 rpm      rpm        12288 Oct 14 19:53 Triggername
```

The primary database of installed software is contained in the file named Packages. As you can see from the preceding example, this database can grow to 33MB (and perhaps larger) if you perform a full installation of Fedora Core Linux (more than 4GB of software). After you install Fedora Core Linux, rpm and related commands will use this directory during software management operations.

Command-Line and Graphical RPM Clients

As a Fedora Core Linux system administrator, you'll use the rpm command or the Fedora Core graphical clients to perform one of five basic tasks. These operations, which must be conducted by the root operator, include the following:

- Installing new software

- Erasing or removing outdated or unneeded packages

- Upgrading an installed software package

- Querying to get information about a software package

- Verifying the installation or integrity of a package installation

The rpm command has more than 60 different command-line options, but its administrative functions can be grouped according to the previous five types of action. Graphical RPM clients provide easy-to-use interfaces to these operations. As a system administrator, you'll have a choice between using a graphical interface and using rpm's various command-line options. The general format of an rpm command is

rpm *option packagename*

The basic options look like this:

- -i—Installs the selected package or packages.

- -e—Erases (removes) the selected package or packages.

- -U—Removes the currently installed package, and then installs software with the contents of the selected package or packages, leaving the existing configuration files.

- -q—Queries the system or selected package or packages.

- -V—Verifies installed or selected package or packages.

Two Handy Options

By appending vh to any option, you get

v	Some status feedback.
h	Hash marks as the work proceeds.

Many additional options can also be added to or used in conjunction with these options. These are summarized in the following table:

Option	Used To
rpm -i	Installs a package
Useful options to -i:	
--excludedocs	Doesn't install documentation to save space
--replacepkgs	Replaces the package with a new copy of itself
--force	The "big hammer"—Ignores all warnings and installs anyway
--noscripts	Doesn't execute any pre- or post-install scripts
--nodeps	Ignores any dependencies
--root *path*	Sets an alternative root to *path*
rpm -e	Erases (deletes) a package
Useful options to -e:	
--nodeps	Ignores any dependencies
rpm -U	Upgrades a package, removing the older one but keeping modified files, such as configurations
Useful options to -U:	
--oldpackage	Permits downgrading to an older version
Other options are the same as with rpm -I:	
rpm -q	Queries about package information
Useful options to -q:	
-p *file*	Displays all information about the package *file*.
-f *file*	What package owns the file *file*?
--whatprovides *x*	Determines what packages provide *x*.
--whatrequires *x*	Determines what packages require *x*.
-i	Summarizes the package information.
-l	Lists the files in package.
--scripts	Displays the contents of any install, uninstall, or verifies scripts.
--provides	Displays the capabilities package provides.
--requires	Displays the capabilities package requires.
rpm -V	Verifies packages against the RPM database

Useful options to -V:

-a	Verifies all installed packages
rpm -K	Uses GPG to verify a downloaded package

Useful options to -K:

--nosignature	If you lack public GPG encryption keys, do not have GPG installed, or are legally prohibited from using GPG, this still verifies the package using size and MD5 checksums.

Details on obtaining the Fedora Core public GPG encryption key and using it are at http://www.rpm.org/max-rpm/s1-rpm-checksig-using-rpm-k.html.

> **RPM Is for Programmers, Too!**
>
> Remember that RPM was created not only to provide an easy to use administrative tool, but also as a developer's tool for use in multiplatform source-code package management. Programmers using rpm for development and distribution will use its rpmbuild command, along with a myriad of additional command-line flags. RPM can be used to build binaries, execute programs, test installations, verify and sign packages, build source packages, track versions, and target builds for specific architectures. Details can be found at the RPM home page (listed in the "Reference" section at the end of this chapter).

Using rpm on the Command Line

Because the new graphical RPM client can only install and uninstall RPM packages (for now—more functionality is promised), you will still end up administering RPM packages from the command line. You can perform all the five basic rpm operations using the rpm command from the command line. This section gives you an introduction to performing those operations. It also provides examples of how to install, verify, query, remove, and upgrade a software package.

The most common rpm operation is software installation. Using rpm is an easy way to keep track of installed software, and it can be used to quickly remove undesired packages. Use the -i option, along with the full or partial name (using regular expressions) of a software package, to install software with rpm. For example, to install the unace archiving package, use the rpm command like this:

```
# rpm -ivh http://mirrors.zoreil.com/plf.zarb.org/mandrake/10.0/
i586/unace-2.2-2plf.i586.rpm
Retrieving http://mirrors.zoreil.com/plf.zarb.org/mandrake/10.0/
i586/unace-2.2-2plf.i586.rpm
warning: /var/tmp/rpm-xfer.48amVs: V3 DSA signature: NOKEY, key ID 8df56d05
Preparing...                ######################################### [100%]
   1:unace
######################################### [100%]
```

This example uses the v and h options, which provide a more verbose output and display of hash marks to show the progress of the installation. The example also demonstrates the capability of rpm to use HTTP or FTP servers to fetch files for installation. It also shows that rpm can use GPG keys to validate a file. (The key was not installed in our example.)

You can also use rpm to query its database after installing packages to verify an installation. Use the -V option, along with the name of a software package, to verify installation of your system. For example, to verify the unace archiving package, use the rpm command like this:

```
# rpm -V unace
```

> **NOTE**
>
> If everything is correct with your software installation, your system will display no response to rpm -V after you run the command; only problems are displayed.

As you can see from the following program output, you can get additional information about a package by adding additional verification options (such as two more v's) to the -V option. To get more information about an installed package, use one or more forms of the rpm query options. For example, to display concise information about an installed package, use the -q option, along with the i option and the installed package name, like this (note that your version will be different from that shown here):

```
# rpm -qi unace
Name        : unace               Relocations: (not relocateable)
Version     : 2.2                      Vendor: Penguin Liberation Front
Release     : 2plf                 Build Date: Sat 01
➥Mar 2003 12:13:48 PM EST
Install date: Tue 02 Sep 2003 03:46:28 PM EDT     Build Host:
➥baader.subversion.alt
Group       : Archiving/Compression   Source RPM: unace-2.2-2plf.src.rpm
Size        : 401368                 License: freeware
Packager    : Guillaume Rousse <guillomovitch@zarb.org>
URL         : http://www.winace.com
Summary     : Decompressor for .ace format archives
Description :
Unace is a utility to extract, view, and test the contents of an ACE archive.
```

This form of the rpm query provides quite a bit of information about the software package. (You can also query packages before installation by providing a pathname for them.)

If this package isn't up-to-date, you can easily and quickly upgrade the package by downloading a newer version and then using rpm's -U or upgrade option like this:

```
# rpm -Uvh unace-2.2-2plf.i586.rpm
Preparing...              ######################################### [100%]
   1:unace                 ######################################### [100%]
```

Note that it wasn't necessary to remove the currently installed software package—the U option removes the old version of the software (saving the old configuration files), and then automatically installs the new software.

You can also upgrade your system software by using the rpm command's -F or "freshen" option, which will fetch a designated package from a remote FTP or HTTP server. For example, to upgrade the fetchmail-conf package, use rpm like this:

```
# rpm -Fv ftp://ftp.tux.org/linux/redhat/updates/9/en/os/i386/\
initscripts-7.14-1.i386.rpm
Retrieving ftp://ftp.tux.org/linux/redhat/updates/9/en/os/i386/\
initscripts-7.14-1.i386.rpm
Preparing packages for installation...
initscripts-7.14-1
```

Use the -e option, along with the name of a software package, to remove or erase software from your system with rpm. For example, to remove the unace archiving package, use the rpm command like this:

```
# rpm -e unace
```

Note that if the operation succeeds, no messages will be displayed on your system. You can quickly search for the names of installed packages by piping the output of rpm -qa through the grep and sort commands (see Chapter 5, "First Steps with Fedora," for additional information on grep and sort); here's how to do that search:

```
# rpm -qa ¦ grep mail ¦ sort
fetchmail-6.2.0-7

mailcap-2.1.14-1.1
mailx-8.1.1-31.1
mozilla-mail-1.4.1-8
procmail-3.22-11
sendmail-8.12.10-1.1
sendmail-cf-8.12.10-1.1
```

This example returns a sorted list of all packages with names containing the word mail.

> **NOTE**
>
> Another essential feature of the rpm command is its --rebuilddb option. If your system's RPM database becomes corrupted, this is your first (and perhaps only) option for restoring software management services. We hope that you never have to use this option; help ensure that by always backing up your data!

Package Organization with RPM

Software packages on your Fedora Core Linux system are organized into various groups, as you see later in this chapter. Using a group organization helps Fedora Core keep software organized by category and provides for hierarchical listings of software when using graphical RPM clients. You never have to manipulate these groups, but understanding the concept of package organization can help you gain familiarity with the way Fedora Core Linux works.

Extracting a Single File from an RPM File

Occasionally, it is useful to extract a single file from an RPM package. You can do so using the command-line version of mc, the Midnight Commander. In Figure 8.1, the Midnight Commander is displaying the contents of the yum .rpm file. The Midnight Commander is a UNIX clone of the famous DOS Norton Commander, a file management utility. Using mc, just highlight the RPM file and press Enter; the contents of the RPM file will be displayed. In the listing, you can browse the file structure of the RPM file and use mc to copy files from it.

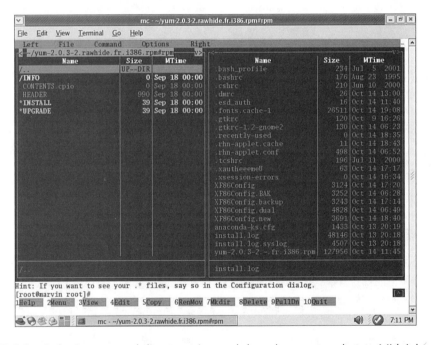

FIGURE 8.1   A classic two-panel directory view and drop-down menus betray Midnight Commander's DOS inspiration, but it's a full-featured Linux file manager.

You might want to know what a .rpm script will do before you install the application. You can use the F3 key in mc to view the script files. If you want to look at the scripts without using mc, use this command:

```
# rpm -q --scripts filename > scripts.txt
```

This command pipes the scripts into a file, where you can examine it with a text editor. You could also pipe it to the less pagination command to view the scripts on your display:

```
# rpm -q --scripts filename ¦ less
```

Graphical Package Management

The Fedora Core Linux graphical package management tool identified in the menu as Add/Remove Software is actually an application named system-config-packages. This application replaces kpackage, gnorpm, and xrpm—all of which are no longer provided. Add/_Remove Software allows you to select packages arranged in categories and install or remove them. With the addition of YUM to Fedora Core, you may now add your own packages to the Fedora Core graphical tools' database, improving its usefulness over earlier versions.

Launch the Fedora Core GUI package manager by clicking the Start button on your desktop, and then choose System Settings, Add/Remove Applications. The package management tool launches with the Add and Remove Software screen, shown in Figure 8.2.

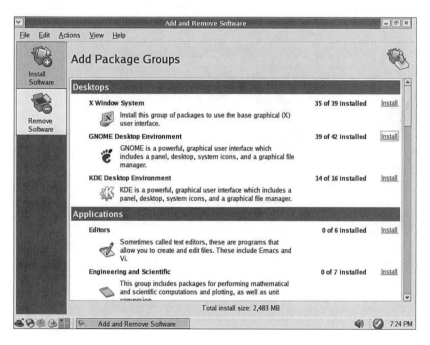

FIGURE 8.2   The initial screen of the package management tool will look familiar if you installed Fedora Core; it's the package selection screen used by the installation program.

The packages listed in the screen are organized into the groups Desktops, Applications, Servers, Development, and Systems groups. Graphical buttons on the left allow you to choose one of two modes: install or remove. To choose individual package groups for installation or removal, first click the appropriate graphical button. The numbers to the right of the package group name indicate the number of packages installed on your system and the total number of packages available in the group. In Figure 8.2, you can see that 39 of 42 possible GNOME packages have been installed.

> **TIP**
>
> The View menu choice allows you to toggle between the default group listing and a listing by individual packages—handy if you know the name of the package you seek. In Package View mode, check the box next to the package name to install or remove it; the package manager will always resolve any dependency issues.

Clicking on the Remove Software or Install Software buttons on the left of the Add Package Groups window brings up a window with a listing of packages associated with the related category. Figure 8.3 shows the details available for the KDE Desktop Environment package.

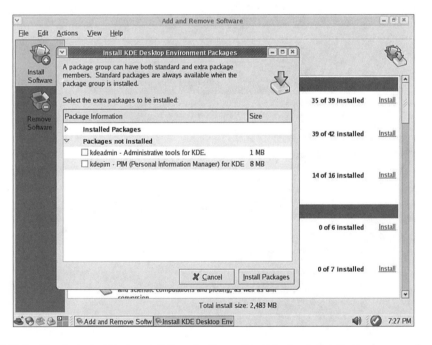

FIGURE 8.3   The Installed Packages listing (collapsed in this view) details the base packages installed when the main category is selected. Packages Not Installed are those that you have the option of installing.

Using Red Hat Network and Alternatives for Software Management

For the Red Hat 8 and 9 releases, the only command-line application for the management of system software provided by Red Hat was RPM; the only GUI tool for management was the Red Hat Packages graphical client (`system-config-packages`) now identified as Add/Remove Software. For the average person, RPM is hopelessly complicated; it includes extra complexity to allow it to be used as a general `.rpm` file-building and development tool, features not normally used by many people. The graphical software management client has been improved for Fedora Core to enable the use of local and remote YUM (that stands for YellowDog Updater modified, first used in the YellowDog [PPC] Linux distribution) repositories.

Not previously covered in this book is the Red Hat Network (`https://rhn.redhat.com`— see Figure 8.4). RHN hasn't been covered because it is not free to the users of this book (or to users of the freely-available FTP download version) and it is limited to managing only the software that is provided by Red Hat. Other alternatives are now available.

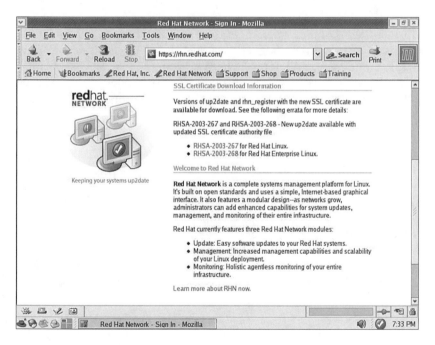

FIGURE 8.4 The Red Hat Network provides automated update subscription services. It only works with software provided by Red Hat and is designed for commercial users.

The RHN service is a client-server mechanism through which a user subscribes to a channel on the server (a repository of software for a specific release of Fedora Core). The local client (identified by a round icon at the right of the desktop panel) can manually or automatically connect to the Red Hat Network server, obtain a list of updates, errata, and security fixes and install them; one subscription is required for each client.

> **NOTE**
>
> If this client-server model appeals to you and you want to use it for your network, you can sign up for subscriptions or consider one of two Open Source Up2Date server alternatives: Current at `http://current.tigris.org/`, or NRH-up2date at `http://www.nrh-up2date.org/index.html`. These two projects are attempting to provide RHN-like services under your control so that you can use non-Red Hat and non-Fedora packages with the service.

Although there are several alternatives for `rpm/system-config-packages`, two of the most useful are APT and YUM. These package management applications go a long way toward solving dependency problems and easing the use of RPM to manage software. Both can install software from either local or remote repositories. Interestingly, the YUM application is now provided in Fedora, and `system-config-packages` has been modified to be used as a graphical front end for it.

The benefit to installing and using either of these two applications is that they allow you easy access to and installation of programs that Red Hat or Fedora Core can't or won't provide (such as multimedia and non-GPL licensed applications). Since the APT and YUM mirrors for Fedora all have current Fedora Core updates, it is not necessary for you to use up2date or RHN to keep your computer software current. The following sections discuss the APT and YUM applications in more detail.

APT

Originally developed for Debian Linux and modified to use with `rpm` packages by Connective Linux, APT and its GUI interface Synaptic are easy to install and use. There are two primary providers of APT packages and repositories; either provider is a good choice. However, because of version conflicts between packages, the two projects' files should not be used together. FreshRPMs at `http://www.freshrpms.net/` is one provider; the Fedora Project at `http://fedora.mplug.org/` is the other. The Fedora Project has now been integrated into the briefly-lived Red Hat Linux Project and renamed Fedora Core. We will use FreshRPMs as an example because they provide packages not available from Fedora Core.

Here's how you install and configure APT:

- Read the introduction to APT in the `/apt/` section of the `http://freshrpms.net` site.

- Install the FreshRPMS GPG key (you need to have `lynx` installed, or simply download and `gpg --import` the downloaded text file):

    ```
    # lynx -source http://freshrpms.net/packages/RPM-GPG-KEY.txt ¦ gpg --import
    ```

- Install the correct version of apt from FreshRpms.

  ```
  # rpm -ivh http://ftp.freshrpms.net/pub/freshrpms/fedora/linux/2/apt/
  apt-0.5.15cnc6-1.1.fc2.fr.i386.rpm
  ```

- Review the man page of apt. The most important commands are apt-get update and
  apt-get install *packagename*.

  ```
  # man apt
  ```

- The list of apt repositories is preconfigured in /etc/apt/sources/list, but the index
  of packages that is available needs to be updated with

  ```
  # apt-get update
  ```

- Once the update of the packages list is completed, we suggest that you install
  Synaptic, the GUI package manager shown in Figure 8.5.

  ```
  # apt-get install synaptic
  ```

- Launch synaptic from the command line, browse the available packages, and install
  what you like.

  ```
  # synaptic &
  ```

The Synaptic graphical interface is nicely laid out (see Figure 8.5). It allows you to view a
list of all available packages and any dependencies required for them. It also provides a
graphical interface to add new repositories.

YUM

Some developers believe that although APT is a good tool, using it for .rpm packages is a
hack. APT also is believed to be bloated with unnecessary code used for the Debian .deb
packages. A new tool, YUM, was developed using the Python language because the Fedora
Core installer, Anaconda, was written in Python and much of the code could be shared.
This decision is what has made YUM the choice for integration into the Fedora Core distribution. It works much the same as APT, but lacked a GUI tool. The Fedora developers have
integrated support for YUM into the graphical Red Hat/Fedora package management tool.
You can obtain YUM from the Fedora site as well as from FreshRPMs.net; the home page
of YUM is at http://linux.duke.edu/projects/yum/.

Here's how you install and configure YUM:

- Read the HOWTO and Users FAQ at the Fedora site http://fedora.mplug.org/.
- Install the Fedora GPG key:

  ```
  # lynx -source http://fedora.mplug.org/FEDORA-GPG-KEY ¦ gpg --import
  ```

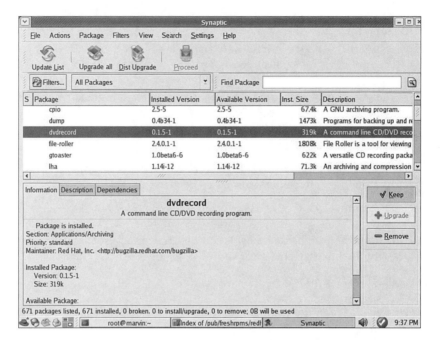

FIGURE 8.5   Synaptic is a graphical interface to the APT package management application making it incredibly easy to use.

- Install the correct version of YUM.

```
# rpm -ivh http://ftp.freshrpms.net/pub/freshrpms/fedora/linux/2/yum/
yum-2.0.7-3.1.fc.fr.noarch.rpm
```

- Review the man page for yum to familiarize yourself with all available options.

```
# man yum
```

Once YUM is installed, the following commands are useful (remember that the Fedora graphical client is available if you configure it to use YUM repositories):

yum list—A list of all packages available from the repository.

yum list installed—A list of all packages installed on your computer.

yum list updates—A list of all updates available for your computer.

yum install *packagename*—Installs *packagename*.

yum update—Run without a *packagename*, YUM will update all installed packages.

yum remove *packagename*—Removes a package and dependencies.

yum upgrade—Run without a package name, YUM will upgrade all packages and remove any obsoleted packages; yum update will not remove obsoleted packages.

You'll find either APT or YUM to be useful additions to Fedora Core. We suggest that you use the one from FreshRPMs.net if you want to install some of the multimedia applications described in Chapter 26, "Multimedia Applications."

Compiling Software from Source

Not all the software you might want to use is available in rpm packages or in the exact form that you desire. Many complicated programs have options that can only be selected at compile time and many smaller, special-purpose applications only exist as source code. Fedora Core provides all the tools necessary for you to compile source code into binary applications. First, we'll cover building from source rpm files, and then manipulating source rpm files and finally, building from source tarballs.

> **NOTE**
>
> For other software package formats, you can use the File Roller application (found in the Accessories menu) to easily display, browse, read, and extract contents of compressed files, including legacy archives such as tarballs or compressed tar archives (recognized by their .gz or .tgz extensions). Other compressed files, such as those created with the compress command (ending in .Z) or bzip2 files (ending in .bz2), are also supported by File Roller. The File Roller client will also convert compressed archives between gzip and bzip2 formats.

Building RPMS from src.rpm Files

A rule of thumb is that you never build rpms as the root user even though the directories are already set up at /usr/src/redhat as follows:

```
# tree /usr/src/redhat
/usr/src/redhat
¦-- BUILD
¦-- RPMS
¦    ¦-- athlon
¦    ¦-- i386
¦    ¦-- i486
¦    ¦-- i586
¦    ¦-- i686
¦    `-- noarch
¦-- SOURCES
¦-- SPECS
`-- SRPMS
```

Using the mkdir command, re-create this directory tree structure in your home directory; you can name the new directory redhat (or anything you like). You might even want to create a new user just to build rpms and source code. (You can compile without being root; you just can't install the software systemwide as a regular user.)

The configuration information for building rpms is kept in three places:

/usr/lib/rpm/*/macros—The systemwide defaults.

/etc/rpm/macros.*—Where systemwide changes are kept.

~/.rpmmacros—Where user-specific changes are kept.

Because we need to tell rpm that we will not be using the systemwide default build location for our user, we can

```
$ echo "%_topdir $HOME/redhat" > $HOME/.rpmmacros
```

> **TIP**
>
> Here, we use > instead of >> to blank the file in case there is already content in it. The >> construct appends information to a file.

To select a temporary directory

```
$ echo "%_tmppath $HOME/tmp" >> $HOME/.rpmmacros
```

To set any compiler optimization flags (here, we're using an Athlon processor as an example), we'll use

```
$ echo "-o3 -march=athlon" >> $HOME/.rpmmacros
```

To rebuild a src.rpm file as a regular user, you would use

```
$ rpmbuild --recompile packagename.src.rpm
```

After a successful build, you will find the binary file(s) in ~/redhat/RPMS/athlon.

You can install them as root with

```
# rpm -Uvh --replacepkgs --replacefiles packagename.rpm
```

If the build fails, the error message will point you to a solution (usually a dependency has not been satisfied). You'll find that a lot of the packages named with -devel will be needed before you compile from source code. Install the package for the missing dependency and retry the compile.

Working with Source RPM Files

You might want to modify a source package for your own uses such as adding documentation, changing default settings, or patching the source code itself. Fedora Core provides the source code to its distribution in the form of source RPM files. You can access the source code on disks 4 and 5 of the downloadable CD images or obtain them from the Fedora Core FTP site.

TIP

An important part of the RPM file is called the `.spec` file, a specification file. It tells RPM how to behave with the particular source files during compilation, installation, and erasure.

As an example, we'll use information that was found at `http://elektron.its.tudelft.nl/~rbos36/mdkfreetype2.html` (the page has now been removed by the author) to modify the freetype2 library provided with Fedora Core in order to enable the bytecode interpreter. The code for the interpreter has been disabled by default because of redistribution licensing concerns that don't affect individual use. Enabling the interpreter will result in improved rendering of the TrueType fonts. We used the file from Red Hat 7.3 as our example, but the source file from 10 should work as well.

Begin work by first installing the source RPM package with `rpm -i`. (Note that here we are building as root to follow the example from the Web page; you should typically build packages as a regular user.) In our example, obtain the `freetype-2.1.9-2.src.rpm` and install it with `rpm -i`. The source code files are placed in `/usr/src/redhat/SOURCES`.

Copy the source file (it's a compressed `tar` file) to `/tmp`, and then `cd` (change directories) there to unpack and modify it:

```
# cp freetype-2.1.9.tar.bz2 /tmp
# cd /tmp
```

Because it's a `.bz2` (BZip2 compressed) `tar` file, un-tar it with

```
# tar xjvf freetype-2.1.9.tar.bz2
```

and cd to the new directory:

```
# cd freetype-2.1.9
```

Using the text editor of your choice, edit the file `include/freetype/config/ftoption.h` and find the line

```
#undef TT_CONFIG_OPTION_BYTECODE_INTERPRETER
```

Change it to

```
#define TT_CONFIG_OPTION_BYTECODE_INTERPRETER
```

Save it and exit the text editor.

Next, re-create the compressed archive:

```
# cd /tmp
# tar cfj freetype-2.1.9.tar.bz2 ./freetype-2.1.9/
```

Put it back in your source directory:

8

```
# mv freetype-2.1.9.tar.bz2 /usr/src/SOURCES
```

Now edit the .spec file in /usr/src/redhat/SPECS to change the line beginning with Release to increment the number found there. (We are changing the version number by doing this, so it will not conflict with the version of the application we will be replacing.) Make any changes to the %description line to describe your changes if you desire, and save the file.

Build the binary RPM with

```
# rpmbuild -bb freetype.spec
```

During the build process, RPM will detect a patch and ask you about the patch; press y for "yes" to continue.

The new RPMs (actually four of them) are found in /usr/src/redhat/RPMS/i386. We only need the one named freetype-2.1.9; you can install it with rpm -Uvh. (This is why we changed the version number; if we had not, RPM would not upgrade to the "same" version. Had we not changed the version number, we could have forced the installation with the --replacepackages --replacefiles option.)

The font server needs to be restarted to use the new library, so we use the service command as shown in Chapter 7, "Managing Services."

```
# service xfs restart
```

Enjoy your new look—provided by better rendering of the fonts.

Compile from Source Tarballs

Compiling applications from source is not that difficult. Most source code is available as compressed source *tarballs*—that is, tar files that have been compressed using gzip or bzip. The compressed files will typically uncompress into a directory containing several files. It's always a good idea to compile source code as a regular user to limit any damage that broken or malicious code might inflict, so create a directory named source in your home directory.

From wherever you downloaded the source tarball, uncompress it into the ~/source directory using the -C option to tar:

```
$ tar zxvf packagename.tgz -C ~/source
```

```
$ tar zxvf packagename.tar.gz -C ~/source
```

```
$ tar jxvf packagename.bz -C ~/source
```

```
$ tar jxvf packagename.tar.bz2 -C ~/source
```

If you're not certain what file compression method was used, employ the `file` command to figure it out:

```
$ file packagename
```

Now, change directories to ~/source/*packagename* and look for a file named README, INSTALL, or a similar name. Print the file out if necessary because it will contain specific instructions on how to compile and install the software. Typically, the procedure to compile source code is

```
$ ./configure
```

which runs a script to check if all dependencies are met and the build environment is correct. Then,

```
$ make
```

to compile the software. And finally, as root:

```
# make install
```

If the compile fails, check the error messages for the reason and run

```
$ make clean
```

before you start again. You can also run

```
$ make uninstall
```

to remove the software if you don't like it.

An alternative to running `make install` is a program named CheckInstall, which will produce an `rpm` file for your installation. This method allows the RPM database to be aware of and keep track of all the files you are installing. See the following sidebar on CheckInstall for more information.

A Handy Software Installation Tool—CheckInstall

When you compile applications from source and install them, they won't show up in the RPM database and therefore can't be managed by RPM.

You can provide RPM management for these applications by using a program named CheckInstall. At its simplest, `checkinstall` is a drop-in substitute for the `make install` step in building from source code.

For example, when compiling from source code, you would traditionally use

```
# ./configure
# make
# make install
```

Using CheckInstall, the steps would look like this:

```
# ./configure
# make
# checkinstall
```

CheckInstall will create a binary `.rpm` package and install the application from it. This makes the new application part of the RPM database. The new `.rpm` file is left for you in `/usr/src/redhat/RPMS/i386`. The new application can later be uninstalled with `rpm -e`.

Some applications arrive in the form of a shell script wrapper. Using the shell script as the argument to CheckInstall will provide a `.rpm` file of the installed files and add them to your RPM database. Not all applications will install with CheckInstall. Read its accompanying documentation carefully.

CheckInstall can be downloaded from `http://asic-linux.com.mx/~izto/checkinstall/index.php`.

System Monitoring Tools

Monitoring your server or workstation is an important task, especially in a commercial or corporate environment. Whether you're working on critical application programming or conducting e-commerce on the Internet, you'll want to track your system's health signs while it's running. Good Fedora Core Linux system administrators are also quite vigilant about watching running processes on their systems, including resources such as CPU and disk, memory, network, and printer usage. Even though the task isn't strictly part of standard security operations, such as examining system logs and network traffic, monitoring resource usage can help you spot misuse and avoid developing problems, such as unwanted intruder connections to your network.

The next sections introduce just a few of the basic tools and approaches used to monitor a running Linux system. Some of the tools focus on in-memory processes, whereas others, such as file system reporting and network monitoring, have more comprehensive uses. You'll also see how to control some system processes using various command-line and graphical tools included with Fedora Core Linux.

Console-based Monitoring

Traditional UNIX systems have always included the ps or process display command. This command lists the running processes on the system and identifies who owns them and how much of the system resources are being used.

Because of the architecture of the Linux kernel and its memory management, Linux also provides much process reporting and control via the command line. This feature can be accessed manually through the /proc file system, a pseudo-file system used as a direct interface to the kernel. (You see how it's used in the upcoming discussion of the ps command.) The /proc file system is frequently used by application programmers who construct an interface for the raw information it provides. This file system is too complex to adequately deal with in the context of this chapter, but you can benefit from reading the `proc` man page and `/usr/src/linux-2.4/Documentation/filesystems/proc.txt` to examine the list and description of the scores of kernel values available. You then can write shell scripts (see Chapter 22, "Shell Scripting") to use those values as needed.

Processes can be controlled at the command line as well. Whenever a program or command is launched on your Fedora Core Linux system, the process started by the kernel is assigned an identification number, called a PID or Process ID. This number is (generally) displayed by the shell if the program is launched in the background, like this:

```
$ xosview &
[1] 11670
```

In this example, the `xosview` client has been launched in the background, and the (`bash`) shell reported a shell job number (`[1]` in this case). A job number or job control is a shell-specific feature that allows a different form of process control (such as sending or suspending programs to the background and retrieving background jobs to the foreground; see your shell's manual pages for more information if you are not using `bash`).

The second number displayed (`11670`, in this example) represents the process ID. You can get a quick list of your processes by using the `ps` command like this:

```
$ ps
  PID TTY          TIME CMD
  736 tty1     00:00:00 bash
  743 tty1     00:00:00 startx
  744 tty1     00:00:00 tee
  752 tty1     00:00:00 xinit
  756 tty1     00:00:09 kwm
  ...
11670 pts/4    00:00:00 xosview
11671 pts/4    00:00:00 ps
```

Note that not all output from the display is shown here. But as you can see, the output includes the process ID, abbreviated as PID, along with other information, such as the name of the running program. Like any UNIX command, many options are available; the `proc` man page has a full list. A most useful option is aux, which provides a friendly list of all the processes. You should also know that `ps` works not by polling memory, but through the interrogation of the Linux `/proc` or process file system. (`ps` is one of the interfaces mentioned at the beginning of this section.)

The `/proc` directory contains quite a few files—some of which include constantly updated hardware information (such as battery power levels, and so on). Linux administrators will often pipe the output of `ps` through a member of the `grep` family of commands in order to display information about a specific program, perhaps like this:

```
$ ps aux | grep xosview
USER       PID %CPU %MEM   VSZ  RSS TTY      STAT START    TIME COMMAND
```

```
bball          11670  0.3   1.1    2940  1412 pts/4
➥S    14:04         0:00   xosview
```

This example returns the owner (the user who launched the program) and the PID, along with other information, such as the percentage of CPU and memory usage, size of the command (code, data, and stack), time (or date) the command was launched, and name of the command. Processes can also be queried by PID like this:

```
$ ps 11670
  PID TTY    STAT   TIME COMMAND
11670 pts/4  S      0:00 xosview
```

You can use the PID to stop a running process by using the shell's built-in `kill` command. This command will ask the kernel to stop a running process and reclaim system memory. For example, to stop the `xosview` client in the example, use the `kill` command like this:

```
$ kill 11670
```

After you press Enter (or perhaps press Enter again), the shell might report

```
 [1]+  Terminated             xosview
```

Note that users can only `kill` their own processes, but `root` can kill them all. Controlling any other running process requires root permission, which should be used judiciously (especially when forcing a `kill` by using the -9 option); by inadvertently killing the wrong process through a typo in the command, you could bring down an active system.

Using the `kill` Command to Control Processes

The `kill` command is a basic UNIX system command. We can communicate with a running process by entering a command into its interface, such as when we type into a text editor. But some processes (usually system processes rather than application processes) run without such an interface, and we need a way to communicate with them as well, so we use a system of signals. The `kill` system accomplishes just that by sending a signal to a process, and we can use it to communicate with any process. The general format of the `kill` command is

```
# kill option PID
```

A number of signal options can be sent as words or numbers, but most are of interest only to programmers. The most common ones you will use are

```
# kill PID
```

This tells the process with that PID to stop. (You supply the actual PID.)

```
# kill -9 PID
```

This is the signal for `kill` (9 is the number of the SIGKILL signal); use this combination when the plain `kill` shown previously doesn't work.

```
# kill -SIGHUP PID
```

This is the signal to "hangup"—stop—and then clean up all associated processes as well. (Its number is -1.)

As you become proficient at process control and job control, you will learn the utility of a number of `kill` options. A full list of signal options can be found in the `man signal` page.

Using Priority Scheduling and Control

Every process cannot make use of the systems resources (CPU, memory, disk access, and so on) as it pleases. After all, the kernel's primary function is to manage the system resources equitably. It does this by assigning a priority to each process so that some processes get better access to system resources and some processes might have to wait longer until their turn arrives. Priority scheduling can be an important tool in managing a system support-ing critical applications or in a situation in which CPU and RAM usage must be reserved or allocated for a specific task. Two legacy applications included with Red Linux include the `nice` and `renice` commands. (`nice` is part of the GNU `sh-utils` package, whereas `renice` is inherited from BSD UNIX.)

The `nice` command is used with its `-n` option, along with an argument in the range of -20 to 19, in order from highest to lowest priority (the lower the number, the higher the priority). For example, to run the `xosview` client with a low priority, use the `nice` command like this:

```
$ nice -n 12 xosview &
```

The `nice` command is typically used for disk or CPU-intensive tasks that might be obtru-sive or cause system slowdown. The `renice` command can be used to reset the priority of running processes or control the priority and scheduling of all processes owned by a user. Regular users can only numerically increase process priorities (for example, make tasks less important) using this command, but the root operator can use the full `nice` range of scheduling (-20 to 19).

System administrators can also use the `time` command (here, `time` is used to measure the duration of elapsed time; the command that deals with civil and sidereal time is the `date` command) to get an idea about how long and how much of a system's resources will be required for a task (such as a shell script). This command is used with the name of another command (or script) as an argument like this:

```
# time -p find / -name core -print
/dev/core
/proc/sys/net/core
```

```
real 1.20
user 0.14
sys 0.71
```

Output of the command displays the time from start to finish, along with user and system time required. Other factors you can query include memory, CPU usage, and file system Input/Output (I/O) statistics. See the `time` command's manual page for more details.

Nearly all graphical process monitoring tools include some form of process control or management. Many of the early tools ported to Linux were clones of legacy UNIX utilities. One familiar monitoring (and control) program is `top`. Based on the `ps` command, the `top` command provides a text-based display, constantly updated console-based output showing the most CPU-intensive processes currently running. It can be started like this:

```
# top
```

After you press Enter, you'll see a display as shown in Figure 8.6. The `top` command has a few interactive commands: pressing `h` displays the help screen; pressing `k` prompts you to enter the `pid` of a process to kill; pressing `n` prompts you to enter the `pid` of a process to change its nice value. The `top` man page describes other commands and includes a detailed description of what all the columns of information `top` can display actually represent; have a look at top's well-written `man` page.

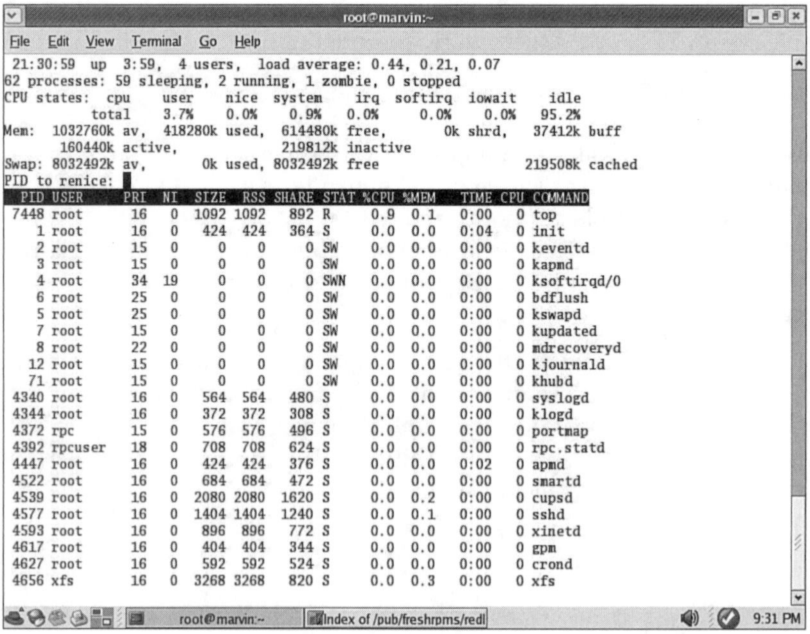

FIGURE 8.6   The `top` command can be used to monitor and control processes. Here, we are being prompted to re-nice a process.

The top command displays quite a bit of information about your system. Processes can be sorted by PID, age, CPU or memory usage, time, or user. This command also provides process management, and system administrators can use its k or r keypress commands to kill or reschedule running tasks.

The top command uses a fair amount of memory, so you might want to be judicious in its use and not leave it running all the time.

Displaying Free and Used Memory with free

Although top includes some memory information, the free utility will display the amount of free and used memory in the system in kilobytes (the -m switch displays in megabytes). On one system, the output looks like this:

```
# free
                    total      used       free     shared    buffers     cached
Mem                 255452     251132     4320     0         19688       77548
-/+ buffers/cache:  153896     101556
Swap:               136512     31528      104984
```

This output describes a machine with 256MB of RAM memory and a swap partition of 137MB. Note that some swap is being used although the machine is not heavily loaded. Linux is very good at memory management and "grabs" all the memory it can in anticipation of future work.

> **TIP**
>
> A useful trick is to employ the watch command; it will repeatedly rerun a command every 2 seconds by default. If you use
>
> ```
> #  watch free
> ```
>
> you'll see the output of the free command updated every two seconds.

Another useful system monitoring tool is vmstat (virtual memory statistics). This command reports on processes, memory, I/O, and CPU typically providing an average since the last reboot, or you can make it report usage for a current period of time by telling it the time interval in seconds and the number of iterations you desire, like

```
# vmstat 5 10
```

which will run vmstat every 5 seconds for 10 iterations.

Use the uptime command to see how long it has been since the last reboot and to get an idea of what the load average has been; higher numbers mean higher loads.

Disk Quotas

Disk quotas are a way to restrict the usage of disk space either by user or by groups. Although rarely—if ever—used on a local or standalone workstation, quotas are definitely a way of life at the enterprise level of computing. Usage limits on disk space not only conserve resources, but also provide a measure of operational safety by limiting the amount of disk space any user can consume.

Disk quotas are more fully covered in Chapter 9, "Managing Users."

Graphical Process and System Management Tools

The GNOME and KDE desktop environments offer a rich set of network and system monitoring tools. Graphical interface elements, such as menus and buttons, and graphical output, including metering and real-time load charts, make these tools easy to use. These clients, which require an active X session and in some cases (but not all) root permission, are included with Fedora Core Linux.

If you view the graphical tools locally while they are being run on a server, you must have X properly installed and configured on your local machine. Although some tools can be used to remotely monitor systems or locally mounted remote file systems, you'll need to properly configure pertinent X11 environment variables, such as $DISPLAY, in order to use the software or use the ssh client's -X option when connecting to the remote host.

Fedora Core Linux includes the xosview client, which provides load, CPU, memory and swap usage, disk I/O usage and activity, page swapping information, network activity, I/O activity, I/O rates, serial port status, and if APM is enabled, the battery level (such as for a laptop).

For example, to see most of these options, start the client like this:

```
# xosview -geometry 406x488 -font 8x16 +load +cpu +mem +swap \
 +page +disk +int +net &
```

After you press Enter, you'll see a display as shown in Figure 8.7.

The display can be customized for a variety of hardware and information, and the xosview client (like most well-behaved X clients) obeys geometry settings such as size, placement, or font. If you have similar monitoring requirements, but want to try a similar but different client from xosview, try xcpustate, which has features that enable it to monitor network CPU statistics foreign to Linux. Neither of these applications is installed with the base set of packages; you need to install them manually if you want to use them.

Some of the graphical system and process monitoring tools included with Fedora Core Linux include the following:

- vncviewer—AT&T's open source remote session manager (part of the Xvnc package), which can be used to view and run a remote desktop session locally. This software requires an active session, but it requires a background X session on the remote computer.

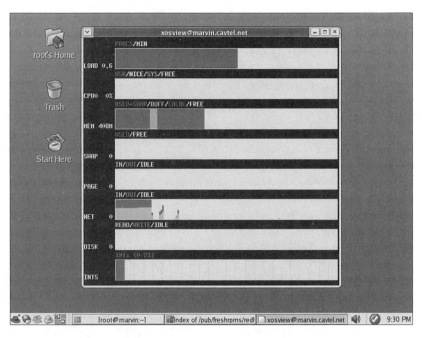

FIGURE 8.7   The `xosview` client displays basic system stats in a small window. You can choose from several options to determine what it will monitor for you.

- `nmapfe`—A GTK+ graphical front end to the `nmap` command. This client provides system administrators with the ability to scan networks to monitor the availability of hosts and services.

- `ethereal`—This graphical network protocol analyzer can be used to save or display packet data in real time and has intelligent filtering to recognize data signatures or patterns from a variety of hardware and data captures from third-party, data-capture programs, including compressed files. Some protocols include AppleTalk, Andrew File System (AFS), AOL's Instant Messenger, various Cisco protocols, and many more.

- `gnome-system-monitor`—Replacing `gtop`, this tool is a simple process monitor offering two views: a list view and a moving graph. It is accessed via the System Tool menu selection as the System Monitor item (see Figure 8.8).

The System Monitor menu item (shown in Figure 8.8) is found in the System Tools menu. It can be launched from the command line with

```
# gnome-system-monitor
```

From the Process Listing view (chosen via the tab in the upper left portion of the window), select a process and click on More Info at the bottom left of the screen to display details on that process at the bottom of the display. You can select from three views to filter the display, available in the drop-down View list: All Processes, My Processes (those you alone own), or Active Processes (All Processes that are active).

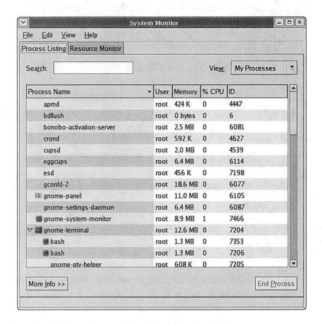

FIGURE 8.8   The Process Listing view of the System Monitor.

Choose Hidden Processes under the Edit command accessible from the top of the display to show any hidden processes (those that the kernel does not enable the normal monitoring tools to see). Select any process and kill it with End Process.

The processes can be re-niced by selecting Edit, Change Priority. The View selection from the menu bar also provides a memory map. In the Resource Monitor tab, you can view a moving graph representing CPU and memory usage (see Figure 8.9).

KDE Process and System Monitoring Tools

KDE provides several process and system monitoring clients. The KDE graphical clients are integrated into the desktop taskbar by right-clicking on the taskbar and following the menus.

These KDE monitoring clients include the following:

- kdf—A graphical interface to your system's file system table that displays free disk space and enables you to mount and unmount file systems using a pointing device.

- ksysguard—Another panel applet that provides CPU load and memory use information in animated graphs.

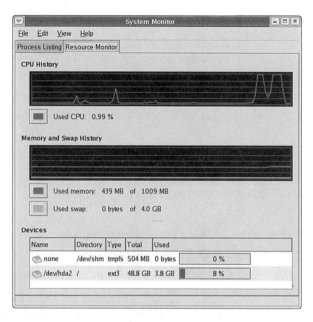

FIGURE 8.9   The Graph view of the System Monitor. It shows CPU usage, Memory/Swap usage, and disk usage. To get this view, select the Resource Monitor tab.

Relevant Fedora Core and Linux Commands

You'll use these commands while managing your Fedora Core Linux system resources and software packages:

system-config-packages—The Fedora Core GUI Package Manager.

nice—Runs a program at a specified priority.

rpm—The RPM Package Manager.

ps—Displays a list all running processes.

top—Displays and manages running processes.

rpmbuild—Builds RPM source and binary packages.

uptime—Tells the length of time since the last reboot and load average.

vmstat—Provides virtual memory statistics.

kill—Stops a process.

Reference

http://www.rpm.org—Home page for the Fedora Core Package Manager. This site provides essential links to the latest version of RPM software for Linux and X desktop environments, such as GNOME.

`http://www.rpm.org/max-rpm/`—Link to the start of an update to Ed Bailey's classic tome and RPM reference book, *Maximum RPM*.

`http://linux.tnc.edu.tw/techdoc/maximum-rpm/rpmbook/node15.html`—History of the Red Hat Package Manager.

`http://www.smoogespace.com/documents/behind_the_names.html`—A history of Red Hat Linux releases, and a good place to learn about the connection between the names of the releases.

`http://www.gnupg.org/`—Home page for GNU Privacy Guard, an unencumbered free replacement for Pretty Good Privacy.

`http://www.debian.org/doc/manuals/project-history/ch-detailed.en.html`—History of the Debian Linux package system.

`http://and.sourceforge.net/`—Home page of the and auto nice daemon, which can be used to prioritize and reschedule processes automatically.

`http://sourceforge.net/projects/schedutils/`—Home page for various projects offering scheduling utilities for real-time scheduling.

`http://freetype.sourceforge.net/patents.html`—A discussion of the FreeType bytecode interpreter patents.

`http://www.ethereal.com`—Home page for the Ethereal client.

`http://www.realvnc.com/`—The home page for the Virtual Network Computing remote desktop software, available for a variety of platforms, including Fedora Core Linux. This software has become so popular that it is now included with nearly every Linux distribution.

`http://www.nrh-up2date.org/index.html`—A replacement for Red Hat's Up2Date application.

CHAPTER **9**

Managing Users

IN THIS CHAPTER

- User Accounts
- Managing Groups
- Managing Users
- Managing Passwords
- Granting System Administrator Privileges to Regular Users
- The User Login Process
- Disk Quotas
- Reference

In this chapter, you learn how to perform the tasks necessary to manage users of your Fedora Core Linux system. The control of users is critical to the responsible management of the system resources. Allowing someone access to a computer is more than just permitting him to sit at a terminal and type. You need to know how to establish new user accounts and place them in groups, how to create new home directories for those users, and how to populate the directories with an initial set of files. Managing users also requires that you know how to establish user passwords and how to grant users file and directory permissions, so they can have access to files they need and are prohibited from accessing files they have no business using.

In this chapter, you learn how to accomplish all these tasks and others for managing user accounts. You'll learn about the different types of users and the responsibilities of the superuser (that's typically the administrator of all system administrators, also known as root) so that you'll have a better idea of what roles you will play as a system administrator. In addition, you'll learn how to delegate superuser power to others when it's appropriate.

User Accounts

Three kinds of users are at work in the typical Fedora Core Linux system environment: the superuser, the regular user, and the system user. All three have important roles and must work cooperatively to accomplish their tasks.

All users have accounts. Fedora Core uses the /etc/passwd file to hold user account information. Each user, regardless of type, will have a one-line entry of account information stored in the /etc/passwd text file. Each account entry contains a username (used for logging in), a password field containing an x (as passwords are actually contained in /etc/shadow), a

User ID (UID), and a Group ID (GID). The fifth field contains optional human ID information, such as real name, office location, phone number, and so on. The last two fields are the location of the user's home directory and the user's default login shell. See the section "The Password File" later in this chapter for more information.

Fedora Core uses the traditional form of UNIX file ownership and permissions. Each file (which includes directories and devices) can be assigned read, write, and/or execution permission to an owner, a member of a group, or anyone on the system. (This information can be viewed with the ls command, using -l for files or -ld for directories.) Fedora Core's file security is derived by combining ownerships and permissions. It's the superuser's responsibility to make sure that all users have proper filenames, UIDs, and GIDs and that sensitive system files are protected from improperly permissive write permission assignment.

The superuser is also known by the name root. Although many system administrators might exist on a large system, only one root user has (and grants) all privileges on the system. The root user is defined as having a User ID of zero and a Group ID of zero. (We'll discuss those IDs later in the chapter, but you can see how that ID is unique to root.)

The root user can use any program, manipulate any file, go anywhere in the file system, and do anything within the Fedora Core Linux system. For reasons of security, that kind of raw power should only be given to a single trusted individual.

It's often practical for that power to be delegated by the root user to other users. This delegation is referred to as an elevation of privileges, and these individuals are known as superusers because they enjoy the same powers that root enjoys. This approach is normally only used on large systems in which one person can't effectively act as the system administrator.

> **NOTE**
>
> On your Fedora Core system, when you log in as root, you are root or the superuser. In this chapter, the terms root, superuser, system administrator, and sysadmin are used interchangeably, although they need not all refer to a single person.

The regular user is a person who logs on to and uses the computer to accomplish some non-administrative task. Regular users don't participate in the management or administration of the computer on a global scale, but they may be permitted to manage their own personal settings and configurations—if the root user doesn't take that privilege away.

The superuser grants privileges to regular users by means of file and directory permissions. (Those are covered in Chapter 5, "First Steps with Fedora.") For example, if the superuser does not want you to change your settings in ~/.profile (the ~ is a shell shortcut representing your home directory; see Chapter 22, "Shell Scripting"), root can alter the permissions so that you may read from, but not write to, that file.

> **CAUTION**
>
> Because of the potential for making a catastrophic error as the superuser (using the command `rm -rf /*` is the canonical example), always use your system as a regular user and become root only temporarily to do sysadmin duties. While you are on a multiuser system, you should consider this advice an absolute rule; if `root` were to delete the wrong file or kill the wrong process, the results could be disastrous for the business. On your home system, you can do as you please and running as `root` makes many things easier, but less safe. In any setting, however, the risks of running as `root` are significant.

The system user is not a person, but a process running on the computer. The system user requires ownership of files and processes so that it can do its job in a secure manner. (Fedora Core calls these users logical users.) For example, the system user named apache owns the Web server (assuming that you are using Apache) and all the associated files. No one else (except root) may have access to those files in a way that Apache does not permit. Unlike regular users, system users do not have a home directory or password and cannot log in like a regular user.

You will find a list of all the users on a system in the /etc/passwd file. Fedora Core refers to these users as the standard users because they will be found on every Fedora Core computer as the default set of system (or logical) users provided during the initial installation. This "standard" set differs between Linux distributions.

User IDs and Group IDs

A computer is a number oriented machine. It identifies users and groups by numbers known as the User ID (UID) and Group ID (GID). The alphabetic names displayed on your screen are there exclusively for the convenience of the biological entities that so often annoy the computer.

As was already mentioned, the root user is UID 0. Numbers from 1 through 499 and 65,534 are the system, or logical, users. Regular users have UIDs beginning with 500; Fedora Core assigns them sequentially beginning with this number.

With only a few exceptions, the GID is the same as the UID. Those exceptions are system users who need to act with root permissions: sync, shutdown, halt, and operator.

Fedora Core creates a private GID for every UID of 500 and greater. The system administrator can add other users to a GID or create a totally new group and add users to it. Unlike Windows NT and some UNIX variants, a group cannot be a member of another group in Linux.

File Permissions

As you learned in Chapter 5, permissions are of three types: read, write, and execute (r, w, x). For any file or directory, permissions can be established in three categories: user, group, and `global`. In this section, we focus on group permissions, but here's a highlight of the commands used to change the `group`, `user`, or `access` permissions of a file or directory:

- `chgrp`—Changes the group ownership of a file or directory.
- `chown`—Changes the owner of a file or directory.
- `chmod`—Changes the access permissions of a file or directory.

These commands, which modify file ownerships and permissions, can be used to model organizational structure and permissions in the real world onto your Fedora Core system (see the next section, "Managing Groups"). For example, a Human Resources department can share health-benefit memos to all company employees by making the files readable (but not writable) by anyone in an accessible directory. On the other hand, programmers in the company's Research and Development section, while being able to access each other's source code files, would not have read or write access to HR pay-scale or personnel files (and certainly wouldn't want HR or Marketing poking around R&D).

These commands are used to manage group and file ownerships and permissions from the command line. Use the `chgrp` command to allow (or restrict) groups of users access to specific directories and files. The `chown` command can be used to set ownerships, but may only be used by `root`. Use the `chmod` command to set read and write permissions for files you own. Refer to Chapter 5 of this book or the man page of each command for details on these commands.

User Stereotypes

As is the case in many professions, exaggerated characterizations (stereotypes or caricatures) have emerged for users and system administrators. Many stereotypes contain elements of truth mixed with generous amounts of hyperbole and humor and serve to assist us in understanding the characteristics of and differences in the stereotyped subjects. The stereotypes of the "luser" and the "BOFH" (users and administrators, respectively) also serve as cautionary tales describing what behavior is acceptable and unacceptable in the computing community. Understanding these stereotypes allows you to better define the appropriate and inappropriate roles of system administrators, users, and others. The canonical reference to these terms is found in the alt.sysadmin.recovery FAQ found at `http://www.ctrl-c.liu.se/~ingvar/asr/overview.html`.

Managing Groups

Groups establish relationships among users in which they share a common set of permissions. An individual cannot read or write to a file owned by another user. But if users are in the same group, they may both read and write to files owned by the group while retaining the privacy and security of their own files.

Group permissions can be used to facilitate group work on a project involving common files and to control access to devices such as the modem and floppy drive. This approach also represents a secure method of limiting access to system resources to only those users who need them. As an example, the sysadmin could put the users hoyt, bill, lorna, liz, dee-ann, and shelley in a new group named unleashed. Those users could each create files intended for their group work and chgrp those files to unleashed. Now, everyone in the unleashed group—but no one else except root—can work with those files. The sysadmin would probably create a directory owned by that group so they could have an easily accessed place to store those files. The sysadmin could also add other users like rhonda and kitty to the group and remove existing users when their part of the work is done. The sysadmin could make the user shelley the group administrator so that shelley could decide how group membership should be changed.

Different UNIX operating systems implement the group concept in various ways. Fedora Core uses a scheme called UPG, the User Private Group, in which all users are assigned to a group with their own name by default. (The user's username and group name are identical.) All the groups are listed in /etc/group file.

Here is a partial list of a sample /etc/group file:

```
# cat /etc/group
root:x:0:root
bin:x:1:root,bin,daemon
daemon:x:2:root,bin,daemon
sys:x:3:root,bin,adm
adm:x:4:root,adm,daemon
tty:x:5:
disk:x:6:root
lp:x:7:daemon,lp
mem:x:8:
kmem:x:9:
wheel:x:10:root
mail:x:12:mail,postifx
news:x:13:news
wine:x:101:
pcap:x:77:
floppy:x:19:hoyt
popusers:x:45:
slipusers:x:46:
mailman:x:41:
mysql:x:27:
ldap:x:55:
pvm:x:24:
hoyt:x:500:
```

In this example, there are a number of groups, mostly for services (mail, mysql, and so on) and devices (floppy, disk, and so on). As previously mentioned, the system services groups enable those services to have ownership and control of their files. For example, adding postfix to the mail group, as shown previously, enables the postfix application to access mail's files in the manner that mail would decide for group access to its file. Adding a regular user to a device's group permits the regular user to use the device with permissions granted by the group owner. Adding user hoyt to the group floppy, for example, would allow hoyt to use the floppy drive device. You will learn how to add and remove users from groups in the next section.

Group Management Tools

Fedora Core provides several command-line tools for managing groups as well as graphical tools. Many experienced sysadmins prefer the command-line tools because they are quick and easy to use and they can be included in scripts if the sysadmin desires to script a repetitive task.

Here are the most commonly used group management command-line tools:

> groupadd—This command creates and adds a new group.
>
> groupdel—This command removes an existing group.
>
> groupmod—This command creates a group name or GIDs, but doesn't add or delete members from a group.
>
> gpasswd—This command creates a group password. Every group can have a group password and an administrator. Use the -A argument to assign a user as group administrator.
>
> useradd -G—The -G argument adds a user to a group during the initial user creation. (More arguments are used to create a user.)
>
> usermod -G—This command allows you to add a user to a group as long as the user is not logged in at the time.
>
> grpck—A command for checking the /etc/group file for typos.

As an example, there is a CD-RW device (/dev/scd0) on our computer that the sysadmin wants a regular user named shelley to have access to. To grant shelley that access, we would use these steps:

1. Add a new group with the groupadd command.

   ```
   # groupadd cdrw
   ```

2. Change the group ownership of the device to the new group with the chgrp command.

   ```
   # chgrp cdrw /dev/scd0
   ```

3. Add the approved user to the group with the usermod command.

   ```
   # usermod -G cdrw  shelley
   ```

4. Make user `shelley` the group administrator with the `gpasswd` command so that she can add new users to the group.

```
# gpasswd -A shelley
```

Now, the user `shelley` has permission to use the CD-RW drive, as would anyone else added to the group by the superuser or `shelley` because she is now also the group administrator and can add users to the group.

The sysadmin can also use the graphical interface that Fedora Core provides, as shown in Figure 9.1. It is accessed as the Users and Groups item from the System Settings menu item.

FIGURE 9.1   Just check the box to add a user to a group.

You'll note that the full set of group commands and options are not available from the graphical interface, limiting the usefulness of the GUI to a subset of the most frequently used commands. You learn more about using the Fedora Core User Manager GUI in the next section of this chapter.

Managing Users

We have mentioned users previously, but in this section we will examine how the sysadmin can manage the users. Users must be created, assigned a `UID`, provided a home directory, provided an initial set of files for their home directory, and assigned to groups so that they may use the system resources securely and efficiently. The system administrator might elect to restrict a user's access not only to files, but to the amount of disk space they use as well. (You learn more about that in the "Managing Disk Quotas" section in Chapter 8, "Managing Software and System Resources.")

User Management Tools

Fedora Core provides several command-line tools for managing users as well as graphical tools. Many experienced sysadmins prefer the command-line tools because they are quick and easy to use and they can be included in scripts if the sysadmin desires to script a repetitive task.

Here are the most commonly used commands used to manage users:

> useradd—This command is used to add a new user account to the system. Its options permit the sysadmin to specify the user's home directory and initial group or to create the user with the default home directory and group assignments.
>
> useradd -G—This command sets the system defaults for creating the users' home directory, account expiration date, default group, and command shell. See the specific options in man useradd. Used without any arguments, it displays the defaults for the system. The default set of files for a user are found in /etc/skel.

NOTE

The set of files initially used to populate a new user's home directory are kept in /etc/skel. This is very convenient for the system administrator because any special files, links, or directories that need to be universally applied can be placed in /etc/skel and will be duplicated automatically with appropriate permissions for each new user.

```
# ls -al /etc/skel
total 44
drwxr-xr-x    3 root     root         4096 Aug 29 09:11 .
drwxr-xr-x   86 root     root         8192 Aug 29 14:51 ..
-rw-r--r--    1 root     root           24 Aug  7 06:08 .bash_logout
-rw-r--r--    1 root     root          191 Aug  7 06:08 .bash_profile
-rw-r--r--    1 root     root          124 Aug  7 06:08 .bashrc
-rw-r--r--    1 root     root         5531 Aug  6 07:07 .canna
-rw-r--r--    1 root     root          854 Aug  9 17:21 .emacs
-rw-r--r--    1 root     root          120 Aug 16 12:49 .gtkrc
drwxr-xr-x    3 root     root         4096 Aug 12 05:26 .kde
```

Each line provides the file permissions, the number of files housed under that file or directory name, the file owner, the file group, the file size, the creation date, and the filename.

As you can see, root owns every file here, but the adduser command (a symbolic link to the actual command named useradd) copies everything in /etc/skel to the new home directory and resets file ownership and permissions to the new user.

Certain user files may exist that the system administrator doesn't want the user to change; the permissions for those files in /home/username can be reset so that the user can read them but can't write to them.

userdel—This command will completely remove a user's account (thereby eliminating that user's home directory and all files it contains).

passwd—This command updates the "authentication tokens" used by the password management system.

TIP

To lock a user out of his account, use the command

```
# passwd -l username
```

This prepends a ! to the user's encrypted password; the command to reverse the process uses the -u option. This is a more elegant and preferred solution to the problem than the traditional UNIX way of manually editing the file.

usermod—This command changes several user attributes. The most commonly used arguments are -s to change the shell and -u to change the UID. No changes can be made while the user is logged in or running a process.

chsh—This command changes the user's default shell. For Fedora Core Linux, the default shell is /bin/bash, known as the Bash, or Bourne Again Shell.

Adding New Users

The command-line approach to adding this user is actually quite simple and can be accomplished on a single line. In the example shown here, the sysadmin will use the useradd command to add the new user kevin. The command adduser (a variant found on some UNIX systems) is a symbolic link to useradd, so both commands work the same. In this example, we use the -p option to set the password the user requested; we use the -s to set his special shell, and the -u option to specify his UID. (If we created a user with the default settings, we would not need to use these options.) All we want to do can be accomplished on one line:

```
# useradd kevin -p guitarplayeR -s /bin/zsh -u 507
```

The sysadmin can also use the graphical interface that Fedora Core provides, as shown in Figure 9.2. It is accessed as the Users and Groups item from the System Settings menu item. Here, the sysadmin is adding a new user to the system where user kevin uses the zsh command shell.

These are the steps we used to add the same account as shown in the preceding command, but using the graphical User Manager interface:

1. Launch the Fedora Core User Manager graphical interface by clicking on the Users and Groups menu item found in the System Settings menu.

2. Click on the Add User button to bring up the Add User dialog window.

3. Fill in the form with the appropriate information as described in the first paragraph in this section.

4. Click on the drop-down Login Shell menu to select the zsh shell.

5. Check the Specify User ID box to permit access to the UID dialog.

6. Using the arrows found in the UID dialog, increment the UID to 549.

7. Click OK to save the settings.

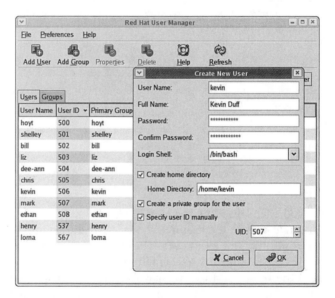

FIGURE 9.2   Adding a new user is simple. The GUI provides a more complete set of commands for user management than for group management.

Note that the user is being manually assigned the UID of 549 because that is his UID on another system machine that will be connected to this machine. Because the system only knows him as 549 and not as kevin, the two machines would not recognize kevin as the same user if two different UIDs were assigned.

> **NOTE**
>
> A Linux username can be any alphanumeric combination that does not begin with a special character reserved for shell script use (see Chapter 22 for disallowed characters, mostly punctuation characters). In Chapter 5, we told you that usernames are typically the user's first name plus the first initial of her last name. That's a common practice on larger systems with many users because it makes life simpler for the sysadmin, but is not a rule nor a requirement.

Monitoring User Activity on the System

Monitoring user activity is part of the sysadmin's duties and an essential task in tracking how system resources are being used. The w command will tell the sysadmin who is logged in, where he is logged in, and what he is doing. No one is able to hide from the superuser. The w command can be followed by a specific user's name to show only that user.

The ac command provides information about the total connect time of a user measured in hours. It accesses the /var/log/wtmp file for the source of its information.

> **TIP**
>
> Interestingly, a phenomenon known as "timewarp" can occur in which an entry in the wtmp files jumps back into the past and ac will show unusual amounts of time accounted for users. Although this can be attributed to some innocuous factors having to do with the system clock, it is worthy of investigation by the sysadmin since it can also be the result of a security breach.

The ac command is most useful in shell scripts to generate reports on operating system usage for management review.

The last command searches through the /var/log/wtmp file and will list all the users logged in and out since that file was first created. The user reboot exists so that you might know who has logged in since the last reboot. A companion to last is the command lastb, which shows all failed, or bad, logins. It's useful for determining if a legitimate user is having trouble or if a hacker is attempting access.

> **NOTE**
>
> The accounting system on your computer keeps track of usage user statistics and is kept in the current /var/log/wtmp file. That file is managed by the init and login processes. If you want to explore the depths of the accounting system, use the GNU info system: info accounting.

Managing Passwords

Passwords are an integral part of Linux security, and they are the most visible part to the user. In this section, you'll learn how to establish a minimal password policy for your system, where the passwords are stored, and how to manage passwords for your users.

System Password Policy

An effective password policy is a fundamental part of a good system administration plan. The policy should cover:

- Allowed and forbidden passwords

- The frequency of mandated password changes

- The retrieval or replacement of lost or forgotten passwords

- Password handling by users

The Password File

The password file is /etc/passwd, and it is the database file for all users on the system. The format of each line is as follows:

```
username:password:uid:gid:gecos:homedir:shell
```

The fields are self-explanatory except for the GECOS field. This field is for miscellaneous information about the user, such as the users' full name, his office location, office and home phone numbers, and possibly a brief text message. For security and privacy reasons, this field is little used nowadays, but the system administrator should be aware of its existence since the GECOS field is used by traditional UNIX programs such as finger and mail. For that reason, it is commonly referred to as the *finger information field*. The data in this field will be comma delimited; the GECOS field can be changed with the cgfn (change finger) command.

Note that a colon separates all fields in the /etc/passwd file. If no information is available for a field, that field is empty, but all the colons remain.

If an asterisk appears in the password field, that user won't be permitted to log on. Why does this feature exist? So a user can be easily disabled and (possibly) reinstated later without having to be created all over again. The system administrator manually edits this field, which is the traditional UNIX way of accomplishing this task. Fedora Core provides improved functionality with the passwd -1 command mentioned earlier.

Several services run as pseudo-users, usually with root permissions. These are the system, or logical, users mentioned previously. You wouldn't want these accounts available for general login for security reasons, so they are assigned /sbin/nologin as their shell, which prohibits any logins from those "users."

A partial list of /etc/passwd reveals

```
# cat /etc/passwd
root:x:0:0:root:/root:/bin/bash
bin:x:1:1:bin:/bin:/sbin/nologin
daemon:x:2:2:daemon:/sbin:/sbin/nologin
```

```
adm:x:3:4:adm:/var/adm:/sbin/nologin
lp:x:4:7:lp:/var/spool/lpd:/sbin/nologin
sync:x:5:0:sync:/sbin:/bin/sync
shutdown:x:6:0:shutdown:/sbin:/sbin/shutdown
halt:x:7:0:halt:/sbin:/sbin/halt
mail:x:8:12:mail:/var/spool/mail:/sbin/nologin
news:x:9:13:news:/var/spool/news:
uucp:x:10:14:uucp:/var/spool/uucp:/sbin/nologin
operator:x:11:0:operator:/root:/sbin/nologin
games:x:12:100:games:/usr/games:/sbin/nologin
gopher:x:13:30:gopher:/var/gopher:/sbin/nologin
ftp:x:14:50:FTP User:/var/ftp:/sbin/nologin
nobody:x:99:99:Nobody:/:/sbin/nologin
vcsa:x:69:69:virtual console memory owner:/dev:/sbin/nologin
mailnull:x:47:47::/var/spool/mqueue:/dev/null
ldap:x:55:55:LDAP User:/var/lib/ldap:/bin/false
postfix:x:89:89::/var/spool/postfix:/bin/true
pvm:x:24:24::/usr/share/pvm3:/bin/bash
hoyt:x:500:500::/home/hoyt:/bin/bash
```

Note that all the password fields don't show a password, but contain an x because they are *shadow passwords*, a useful security enhancement to Linux, discussed in the following section.

Shadow Passwords

It is considered a security risk to keep any password in /etc/passwd because anyone with read access can run a cracking program on the file and obtain the passwords with little trouble. To avoid this risk, *shadow passwords* are used so that only an x appears in the password field of /etc/passwd; the real passwords are kept in /etc/shadow, a file that can only be read by the sysadmin (and PAM, the Pluggable Authentication Modules authentication manager; see the "PAM Explained" sidebar for an explanation of PAM).

Special versions of the traditional password and login programs must be used to enable shadow passwords. Shadow passwords are automatically enabled during the installation phase of the operating system on Fedora Core systems.

Let's examine a partial listing of the shadow companion to /etc/passwd, the /etc/shadow file:

```
# cat /etc/shadow
root:$1$aBcw2?t3$uR6L63j2GdlNNu3aEc.a/.:11817:0:99999:7:::
bin:*:11817:0:99999:7:::
daemon:*:11817:0:99999:7:::
adm:*:11817:0:99999:7:::
```

```
lp:*:11817:0:99999:7:::
sync:*:11817:0:99999:7:::
shutdown:*:11817:0:99999:7:::
halt:*:11817:0:99999:7:::
mail:*:11817:0:99999:7:::
news:*:11817:0:99999:7:::
ldap:!!:11817:0:99999:7:::
postfix:!!:11817:0:99999:7:::
pvm:!!:11817:0:99999:7:::
hoyt:$1$2_TVY.iW$IMzyd/3W9lzW6tD2Qu9FS/:11818:0:99999:7
```

The fields are separated by colons and are, in order:

> The user's login name.
>
> The encrypted password for the user.
>
> The number of days since Jan 1, 1970 that the password was last changed. This date is know in UNIX circles as the "epoch." Just so you'll know, the billionth second since the epoch occurred was in September 2001; that was the UNIX version of Y2K; not much happened because of it.
>
> The number of days before the password can be changed (prevents changing a password and then changing it back to the old password right away—a dangerous security practice).
>
> The number of days after which the password must be changed. This can be set to force the change of a newly issued password known to the system administrator.
>
> The number of days before the password expiration that the user is warned it will expire.
>
> The number of days after the password expires that the account is disabled (for security).
>
> The number of days since Jan 1, 1970 that account has been disabled.
>
> The final field is a "reserved" field and is not currently allocated for any use.

Note that password expiration dates and warnings are disabled by default in Fedora Core. These features are not used on home systems and usually not used for small offices. It is the sysadmin's responsibility to establish and enforce password expiration policies.

The permissions on the /etc/shadow file should be set so that it isn't writable or readable by regular users: The permissions should be 600.

PAM Explained

Pluggable Authentication Modules (PAM) is a system of libraries that handle the tasks of authentication on your computer. It uses four management groups: account management, authentication management, password management, and session management. This allows the system administrator to choose how individual applications will authenticate users. Fedora Core has preinstalled and preconfigured all the necessary PAM files for you.

The configuration files in Fedora Core are found in /etc/pam.d. These files are named for the service they control, and the format is as follows:

```
type control module-path module-arguments
```

The `type` field is the management group that the rule corresponds to. The `control` field tells PAM what to do if authentication fails. The final two items deal with the PAM module used and any arguments it needs. Programs that use PAM typically come packaged with appropriate entries for the `/etc/pam.d` directory. To achieve greater security, the system administrator can modify the default entries. Misconfiguration can have unpredictable results, so back up the configuration files before you modify them. The defaults provided by Fedora Core are adequate for home and small office users.

As an example of a PAM configuration file with the formatted entries as described previously is shown next. Here are the contents of `/etc/pam.d/system-config-users`:

```
#%PAM-1.0
auth       sufficient    /lib/security/pam_rootok.so
auth       required      /lib/security/pam_stack.so service=system-auth
session    required      /lib/security/pam_permit.so
session    optional      /lib/security/pam_xauth.so
account    required      /lib/security/pam_permit.so
```

Amusingly, even the PAM documents state that you don't really need (or want) to know a lot about PAM to use it effectively.

You'll likely only need the PAM system administrator's guide. Look under the `/usr/share/doc/pam*` directory for additional documents in PostScript, text, and HTML formats.

If you configure your system to use LDAP or `kerberos` authentication during install and are unable to log on to the machine using the local root account, be aware that there is a known bug in the `/etc/pam.d/system-auth` file. As a temporary fix, change the line that reads

```
account required /lib/security/$ISA/pam_unix.so
```

to

```
account sufficient /lib/security/$ISA/pam_unix.so
```

The underlying problem appears to be a flaw in the way that PAM handles intervals for requests for authorization. This issue has existed since Red Hat 7.3 and does not appear to be fixed in Fedora Core.

Managing Password Security for Users

Selecting appropriate user passwords is always an exercise in trade-offs. A password such as *password* (don't laugh, it's been used too often before in the real world) is just too easy to guess by an intruder as are simple words or number combinations (a street address, for example). A security auditor for one of my former employers would take the cover sheet from the employees' personnel file (which contained the usual personal information of name, address, birth date, and so on) and would then attempt to log on to a terminal with passwords constructed from that information—and often succeeded in logging on.

On the other hand, a password such as 2a56u'"F($84u&#^Hiu44Ik%$([#EJD is sure to present great difficulty to an intruder (or an auditor). However, that password is so difficult to remember that it would be likely that the password owner would write that password down and tape it next to her keyboard. I worked for a business in which the safe combination was written on the ceiling tile over the safe; the manager couldn't remember it and was told he shouldn't keep it on a piece of paper in his wallet. This is but one of many examples of poor security in the field.

The sysadmin has control, with settings in the /etc/shadow file, over how often the password must be changed. The settings can be changed using a text editor, the change command, or a configuration tool such as Fedora Core's User Manager, as shown in Figure 9.1. Click on the Password Info tab under that particular user's Properties to set individual password policies.

Changing Passwords in a Batch

On a large system, there might be times when a large number of users and their passwords need some attention. The superuser can change passwords in a batch by using the chpasswd command, which accepts input as a name/password pair per line in the following form:

```
# chpasswd username:password
```

Passwords can be changed *en masse* by redirecting a list of name and password pairs to the command. An appropriate shell script can be constructed with the information gleaned from Chapter 22.

However, Fedora Core also provides the newusers command to add users in a batch from a text file. This command also allows a user to be added to a group, and a new directory can be added for the user as well.

Granting System Administrator Privileges to Regular Users

On occasion, it is necessary for regular users to run a command as if they were the root user. They usually don't need these powers, but they might on occasion—for example, to temporarily access certain devices or run a command for testing purposes.

There are two ways to run commands with root privileges: The first is useful if you are the superuser and the user; the second if you aren't the regular user (as on a large, multiuser network).

Temporarily Changing User Identity with the su Command

What if you are also root, but are logged on as a regular user because you're performing nonadministrative tasks and you need to do something that only the superuser can do? The su command is available for this purpose.

> **NOTE**
>
> A popular misconception is that the su command is short for *super user*; it just means *substitute user*. An important but often overlooked distinction is that between su and su -. In the former instance, you become that user but keep your own environmental variables (like paths). In the latter, you inherit the environment of that user. This is most noticeable when you use su to become the super user, root. Without appending the -, you do not inherit the path variable that includes /bin or /sbin, so you must always enter the full path to those commands when you just su to root.

Because almost all Linux file system security revolves around file permissions, it can be useful to occasionally become a different user with permission to access files belonging to other users or groups or to access special files (such as the communications port /dev/ttyS0 when using a modem or the sound device /dev/audio when playing a game). You can use the su command to temporarily switch to another user identity, and then switch back.

> **TIP**
>
> It's never a good idea to use an IRC (Internet Relay Chat) client as the root user, and you might not want to run it using your regular user account. Simply create a special new user just for IRC and su to that user in a terminal widow to launch your IRC client.

The su command spawns a new shell, changing both the UID and GID of the existing user and automatically changes the environmental variables associated with that user, known as inheriting the environment. See Chapter 5 for more information on environmental variables.

The syntax for the su command is

```
$ su option  username  arguments
```

The man page for su gives more details, but some highlights of the su command are

```
-c, --command COMMAND
   pass a single COMMAND to the shell with -c


-m, --preserve-environment
   do not reset environment variables


-l   a full login simulation for the substituted user,
the same as specifying the dash alone
```

You can invoke the su command in different ways that yield diverse results. By using su alone, you can become root, but you keep your regular user environment. This can be verified by using the printenv command before and after the change. Note that the working directory (you can execute pwd as a command line to print the current working directory) hasn't changed. By executing the following, you become root and inherit root's environment:

```
$ su -
```

By executing the following, you become that user and inherit the superuser's environment—a pretty handy tool. (Remember: Inheriting the environment comes from using the dash in the command; omit that, and you keep your "old" environment.) To become another user, specify a different user's name on the command line:

```
$ su - other_user
```

When leaving an identity to return to your usual user identity, the exit command. For example, while logged on as a regular user,

```
$ su - root
```

the system prompts for a password:

```
Password:
```

When the password is entered correctly, the root user's prompt appears:

```
#
```

To return to the regular user's identity, just type

```
# exit
```

This takes you to the regular user's prompt:

```
$
```

If you need to allow other users access to certain commands with root privileges, it is necessary to give them the root password so that they can use su—that definitely isn't a very secure solution. The next section describes a more flexible and secure method of allowing normal users to perform selected root tasks.

Granting Root Privileges on Occasion—The sudo Command

Often it is necessary to delegate some of the authority that root wields on a system. For a large system, this makes sense because no single individual will always be available to perform superuser functions. The problem is that UNIX permissions come with an "all or nothing" authority. Enter sudo, an application that permits the assignment of one, several, or all of the root-only system commands.

Once configured, using sudo is simple. An authorized user merely precedes the superuser-authority–needed command with the sudo command, like so

```
$ sudo command
```

After getting the user's password, sudo checks the /etc/sudoers file to see if that user is authorized to execute that particular command; if so, sudo generates a "ticket" for a specific length of time that authorizes the use of that command. The user is then prompted for his own password (to preserve accountability and provide some measure of security) and then the command is run as if root had issued it. During the life of the ticket, the command can be used again without a password prompt. If an unauthorized user attempts to execute a sudo command, a record of the unauthorized attempt is kept in the system log and a mail message is sent to the superuser.

Three man pages are associated with sudo: sudo, sudoers, and visudo. The first covers the command itself, the second the format of the /etc/sudoers file, and the third the use of the special editor for /etc/sudoers. You should use the special editing command because it will check the file for parse errors and lock the file to prevent others from editing it at the same time. The visudo command uses the vi editor, so you might need a quick review of the vi editing commands found in Chapter 5 in the section "Working with vi". You begin the editing by executing the visudo command with

```
# visudo
```

The default /etc/sudoers file looks like this:

```
# sudoers file.
#
# This file MUST be edited with the 'visudo' command as root.
#
# See the sudoers man page for the details on how to write a sudoers file.
#
# Host alias specification

# User alias specification

# Cmnd alias specification

# Defaults specification

# User privilege specification
root    ALL=(ALL) ALL

# Uncomment to allow people in group wheel to run all commands
# %wheel        ALL=(ALL)       ALL
```

```
# Same thing without a password
# %wheel        ALL=(ALL)       NOPASSWD: ALL


# Samples
# %users  ALL=/sbin/mount /cdrom,/sbin/umount /cdrom
# %users  localhost=/sbin/shutdown -h now
```

The basic format of a sudoers line in the file is

```
user host_computer=command
```

The user can be an individual user or a group (prepended by a % to identify the name as a group). The host_computer is normally ALL for all hosts on the network and localhost for the local machine, but the host computer can be referenced as a subnet or any specific host. The command in the sudoers line can be ALL, a list of specific commands, or a restriction on specific commands (formed by prepending a ! to the command). A number of options are available for use with the sudoers line, and aliases can be used to simplify the assignment of privileges. Again, the sudoers man page will give the details, but here are a few examples:

If we uncomment the line,

```
# %wheel        ALL=(ALL)       NOPASSWD: ALL
```

any user we add to the wheel group can execute any command without a password.

Suppose that we want to give user lorna permission across the network to be able to add users with the graphical interface. We would add the line

```
lorna ALL=/system-config-users
```

or perhaps grant permission only on her local computer:

```
lorna 192.168.1.87=/usr/bin/system-config-users
```

If we want to give the editor group systemwide permission with no password required to delete files,

```
%editors ALL=NOPASSWD: /bin/rm
```

If we want to give every user permission with no password required to mount the CD drive on the localhost,

```
ALL localhost=NOPASSWD:/sbin/mount /dev/scd0 /mnt/cdrom /sbin/umount /mnt/cdrom
```

It is also possible to use wildcards in the construction of the sudoers file. Aliases can be used as well to make it easier to define users and groups. Although the man page for sudoers contains some examples, http://www.komar.org/pres/sudo/toc.html provides illustrative notes and comments of sudo use at a large aerospace company. The sudo homepage at http://www.sudo.ws/ is also a useful resource for additional explanations and examples.

The following command presents users with a list of the commands they are entitled to use:

```
$ sudo -l
```

Control Via Restricted Shells

Using restricted shells is actually the opposite of granting additional privileges to users. There might be situations in which you want to restrict a user to a very specific subset of privileges permitted to other users. If you have a desire to severely restrict what a user can do (for reasons of security, distribution of a turnkey system, or custom system installation), you can provide him with a restricted shell. To run a restricted bash shell, you would use the -r option. It's easy to try yourself, just enter the following at your prompt:

```
$ bash -r
```

Then try to do something that you could do before as a regular user, such as listing the files in your home directory:

```
$ ls -a
```

You then see

```
bash: ls: No such file or directory
```

The cd command, redirection, using / in command names, and several other commands and options are also disabled in the restricted shell. (The man page for bash details specific restrictions; the appropriate information is at the very end of the very long man page.) Don't rely on a restricted shell as your only means of controlling user activity; although using restricted shells applies some tight restrictions, a very determined user might find a way to confound the restrictions. Always use appropriate permission and password controls as well.

The User Login Process

It's useful to know what happens during the process when a user attempts to log in—if for nothing else than troubleshooting for that one user in the accounting department who can't get logged on to run the payroll program and get the payroll checks printed on time. Understanding this process also involves understanding the purpose of the default user installation files that are found in /etc/skel. This section helps illuminate the login process for you.

The login process is used for entering, or "signing on" to a system and is summarized in steps as follows:

1. Login prompts for a username.

2. If the /etc/nologin file exists and the user isn't root, a warning message is issued and the login process is halted. The /etc/nologin file is typically used when the system will be shut down shortly and new logins should be restricted.

3. The /etc/usertty file is examined to see if any restrictions are specified for the user. As a security measure, root logons can be restricted to specific terminals and regular users can have the same restrictions placed on them as necessary.

4. The system prompts for a password; it is checked against the encrypted password kept in /etc/shadow. Unsuccessful attempts are logged via the syslog facility and can be reviewed with the lastd command.

5. The UID and the GID of the tty (terminal) being used are set.

6. The TERM environment, if it has been set, is preserved.

7. The HOME, PATH, SHELL, TERM, MAIL, and LOGNAME environment variables are set. (If the -p option is used, all preexisting environmental variables are preserved.)

8. The PATH defaults to /usr/local/bin:/bin:/usr/bin: for normal users and to /sbin:/bin:/usr/sbin:/usr/bin for root.

9. Normal greeting messages and mail checking are disabled if the file .hushlogin exists in the users' home directory; otherwise, those messages are displayed at the end of the logon process.

10. The user's command shell is started at this point, presenting the user with a command prompt. If no shell is specified for the user in /etc/passwd, /bin/sh is used by default. (Some UNIX operating systems will just log you back out.) If no home directory is specified in /etc/passwd, / is used.

When you log in as a regular user, the files that control your environment are found in your /home/username directory. These configuration files are normally hidden from view because their filename is preceded by a period (as in .bashrc—these are known as "dot files").

The name of the file indicates which program it is associated with. The files .bash_logout, .bash_profile, and .bashrc all determine how the bash shell is used by the user. (These files can, of course, be preset by the system administrator with the user given only read access, so the files can't be changed. Other shells have their own associated files.)

The .screenrc file determines the console screen environment, and the .Xdefaults file determines much the same thing for X11. For Fedora Core, the .dmrc file sources the file /etc/X11/dm/Sessions/Default.desktop, which sets the default desktop for the entire system. The .Xclients-default file is created by running the switchdesk command (the Desktop Switching Tool is the name of the GUI interface) to change the default desktop for that user. You would use this command if you occasionally launched X11 from the command line and desired to change your default desktop. Fedora Core sets the default as GNOME.

Other files might be present depending on the system and the system administrator. The point is that the environment of each user can be set globally through the use of files in /etc/skel and individually by allowing user modification of the files in their /home directory (or not, depending on the system administration policies).

The system logs all user logins, as well as all uses of su and sudo commands for the sysadmin's review. (The init, syslogd, and klogd applications create the logs.) Modern security monitoring programs (or simple scripts you create) can scan these files (such as /var/log/messages) for anomalies and signal possible security violations.

Disk Quotas

On large systems with many users, you need to control the amount of disk space a user has access to. Disk quotas are designed for this purpose. Quotas, managed per each partition, can be set for both individual users as well as groups; quotas for the group need not be as large as the aggregate quotas for the individuals in the groups.

When files are created, both a user and a group own them; ownership of the files is always part of the metadata about the files. This makes quotas based on both users and groups easy to manage.

> **NOTE**
>
> Disk quota management is never done on a home system and rarely, if ever, done on a small office system.

To manage disk quotas, you must have the quota package installed on your system; it is usually installed by default. Quota management with Fedora Core Linux is not enabled by default and has traditionally been enabled and configured manually by system administrators. Sysadmins use the family of quota commands, such as quotacheck to initialize the quota database files, edquota to set and edit user quotas, setquota to configure disk quotas, and quotaon or quotaoff to control the service. (Other utilities include warnquota for automatically sending mail to users over their disk space usage limit.)

Implementing Quotas

To reiterate, quotas might not be enabled by default, even if the quota software package is installed on your system. When quotas are installed and enabled, you can see which partitions have either user quotas, group quotas, or both by looking at the fourth field in the

/etc/fstab file. For example, one line in /etc/fstab shows that quotas are enabled for the /home partition:

```
/dev/hda5      /home    ext3        defaults,usrquota,grpquota 1 1
```

The root of the partition with quotas enabled will have the files quota.user or quota.group in them (or both files if both types of quotas are enabled), and the files will contain the actual quotas. The permissions of these files should be 600 so that users cannot read or write to them. (Otherwise, users would change them to allow ample space for their music files and Internet art collections.) In order to initialize disk quotas, the partitions must be remounted. This is easily accomplished with the following:

```
# mount -o ro,remount partition_to_be_remounted mount_point
```

The underlying console tools (complete with man pages) are

- quotaon, quotaoff—Toggles quotas on a partition.

- repquota—A summary status report on users and groups.

- quotacheck—Updates the status of quotas (compares new and old tables of disk usage); it is run after fsck.

- edquota—A very basic quota management command.

Manually Configuring Quotas

Manual configuration of quotas involves changing entries in your system's file system table, /etc/fstab, to add the usrquota mount option to the desired portion of your file system. As an example in a simple file system, quota management can be enabled like this:

```
LABEL=/              /                  ext3    defaults,usrquota        1 1
```

Group-level quotas can also be enabled by using the grpquota option. As the root operator, you must then create a file (using our example of creating user quotas) named quota.user in the designated portion of the file system, like so:

```
# touch /quota.user
```

You should then turn on the use of quotas using the quotaon command:

```
# quotaon -av
```

You can then edit user quotas with the edquota command to set hard and soft limits on file system use. The default system editor (vi unless you change your EDITOR environment variable) will be launched when editing a user's quota.

Any user can find out what their own quotas are with

```
$ quota -v
```

> **NOTE**
>
> There are no graphical tools supported by Fedora Core that can be used to configure disk quotas. A Quota mini HOWTO is maintained at `http://www.tldp.org/HOWTO/mini/Quota.html`.

Related Fedora Core Commands

You'll use these commands to manage user accounts in Fedora Core Linux:

`ac`—A user account-statistics command

`chage`—Sets or modifies user password expiration policies

`chfn`—Creates or modifies user finger information in `/etc/passwd`

`chgrp`—Modifies group memberships

`chmod`—Changes file permissions

`chown`—Changes file ownerships

`chpasswd`—Batch command to modify user passwords

`chsh`—Modifies a user's shell

`groups`—Displays existing group memberships

`logname`—Displays a user's login name

`newusers`—Batches user management command

`passwd`—Creates or modifies user passwords

`su`—Executes shell or command as another user

`sudo`—Manages selected user execution permissions

`system-config-users`—Fedora Core's graphical user management tool

`useradd`—Creates, modifies, or manages users

`userinfo`—Fedora Core's graphical `chfn` command

`usermod`—Edits a user's login profile

`userpasswd`—Fedora Core's graphical user password command

Reference

`http://www.ibiblio.org/pub/Linux/docs/HOWTO/other-formats/html_single/_User-Authentication-HOWTO.html`—The User-Authentication HOWTO describes how user and group information is stored and used for authentication.

`http://www.ibiblio.org/pub/Linux/docs/HOWTO/other-formats/html_single/Shadow-Password-HOWTO.html`—The Shadow-Password HOWTO delves into the murky depths of shadow passwords and even discusses why you might not want to use them.

http://www.ibiblio.org/pub/Linux/docs/HOWTO/other-formats/html_single/
_Security-HOWTO.html—A "must read" HOWTO, the Security HOWTO is a good overview
of security issues. Especially applicable to this chapter are sections on creating accounts,
file permissions, and password security.

http://www.secinf.net/unix_security/Linux_Administrators_Security_Guide/—A
general guide, the Linux System Administrator's Security Guide has interesting sections on
limiting and monitoring users.

http://www.ibiblio.org/pub/Linux/docs/HOWTO/other-formats/html_single/
Config-HOWTO.html—How can you customize some user-specific settings? The Config
HOWTO Software Configuration gives some advice.

http://www.ibiblio.org/pub/Linux/docs/HOWTO/other-formats/html_single/
Path.html—How can one know the true path? The Path HOWTO sheds light on this issue.
You need to understand paths if you want to guide the users to their data and applica-
tions.

http://www.courtesan.com/sudo/—The superuser do command is a powerful and elegant
way to delegate authority to regular users for specific commands.

http://www.kernel.org/pub/linux/libs/pam/index.html—The Pluggable Authentication
Modules are complex and highly useful applications that provide additional security and
logging for passwords. PAM is installed by default in Fedora Core. It isn't necessary to
understand the intricacies of PAM in order to use it effectively.

http://localhost/localdomain/—Your Fedora Core system contains man and info pages
on just about everything covered here. Use man -k to search on a keyword.

CHAPTER **10**

Managing the File System

IN THIS CHAPTER

- The Fedora Core Linux File System Basics
- Working with the ext3 File System
- Other File Systems Available to Fedora Core Linux
- Creating a File System
- Mounting File Systems
- Relocating a File System
- Logical Volume Management
- File System Manipulation
- Disk Tuning
- File System Tuning
- Managing Files for Character Devices, Block Devices, and Special Devices
- Reference

A Linux file system is more than just a format for your hard drive or floppy disk and more than just the disk itself or the formatting process. The file system is the structure and organization of data on a data storage device. In other words, it's how your data is organized and stored in files, disk drives, and removable media.

In this chapter, you learn about the structure of the disks themselves, the file systems that can be placed on them, and how to work with those file systems. You also learn some background and history about the file systems that Linux can use. This chapter also provides some basic information about the file system's default settings, as well as how you can adapt those settings to better match your system and its needs. At the end of the chapter, you learn how to build a test file system and use the loopback file system so that you can safely explore all the file system commands without risking any damage to your system.

Also covered are the use of the file system table, fstab, and instructions for formatting ext3, reiserfs, and DOS drives. This chapter also discusses the special files for character and block devices, as well as the device file system, devfs. The Resource section is full of sources with extensive information on file system-related topics.

The Fedora Core Linux File System Basics

The Fedora Core Linux file system, like all UNIX file systems, is used for storing not only data, but also metadata (infomation about the files, such as who the file owner is, what permissions are associated with the file, and other file attributes).

The Fedora Core Linux file system is much more complex than most people care to know about. Its features are patterned after features found on commercial UNIX systems, as well as those included in research or experimental file systems. In this section of the chapter, you learn what the Fedora Core Linux file system is, how it's structured, and how you work with it in the management of the Fedora Core Linux system—both as a user and a system administrator.

Fortunately, the native Linux file system is robust and works well with the default settings. Fedora Core has conveniently provided an easy-to-use setup tool for use during the installation, but here, you also learn how to manage file system settings manually.

Providing a great deal of flexibility, the file system support allows Linux users to access files on file systems used by other operating systems. A sampling of the Fedora Core kernel modules for supported file systems is as follows:

bfs—SCO Unixware Boot file system

coda—Carnegie Mellon University network file system

cramfs—Compressed ROM file system

ext3—Linux Extended File System 3 (adds journaling to ext2)

fat—Microsoft File Allocation Table file system: FAT 12 and FAT 16

freevxfs—Free version of the Veritas VxFS file system used by SCO: Unixware, Sun Solaris, HP-UX

hfs—Macintosh: Hierarchial file system

jfs—IBM's journaled file system

minix—Minix file system

msdos—Microsoft File Allocation Table -16

ncfps—Novell Corporation protocol file system

nfs—Network file system

ntfs—Windows NT, Windows 2000, Windows XP

reiserfs—Reiser file system

romfs—ROM file system

smbfs—File system based on the use of the Shared Message Block protocol used by Microsoft and Samba

sysv—System V Coherent file system: Xenix, System V, Coherent

udf—Universal Disk Format (DVD-ROM file system)

ufs—UNIX file system used on BSD, Sun, and Mac OS X

umsdos—MS-DOS file system with Linux permissions

vfat—Microsoft File Allocation Table file system known as FAT32

Support for ext3, ext2, NFS, and iso9660 file systems is compiled into the Linux kernel; all others are available as modules.

There isn't an exact correlation between the file system source code and the modules compiled for the default kernel. The kernel documentation for the file systems can be found at `/usr/src/linux-2.6/Documentation/file systems/`. The usage of some of these file system modules is mentioned in the man page for mount.

Physical Structure of the File System on the Disk

If you were to visualize the file system on the physical disk, it would resemble a series of boxes known as blocks. The first block on the disk is a special block that contains the boot sector; subsequent blocks contain the operating system, applications, and your data.

Each individual block is made up of smaller groups of data:

- A superblock (called by that name because it contains redundant information about the overall file system).

- Redundant file system descriptors—All the redundant information is useful for reliability and recovery from disasters and errors.

- A bitmap of the block.

- A bitmap of the inode table.

- Information from the inode table.

- The data blocks.

Inodes and File Attributes

The information that constitutes a file in the ext2/etx3 file system begins with the inode.

The inode contains the following description of the file: the file type, its access rights, its owners, several different timestamps, the file size, and pointers to data blocks that hold the file information. When you want to access a file, the kernel uses those pointers to calculate where the data resides physically on the disk.

File attributes are also stored in the inode. The chattr command enables the root operator to manipulate some special attributes of files on an ext2/3 file system. One of the most interesting uses of the chattr command is to make a file *immutable*, meaning that it can not be deleted, renamed, written to, or modified by anyone, even root (at least until the immutable attribute is un-set). To make a file immutable (the word means unalterable; not capable of change)

```
# chattr +i filename
```

and to change it back

```
# chattr -i filename
```

Another interesting flag is the s flag, which tells the system to zero out all the blocks used for that file when the file is deleted.

10

> To observe the existing attributes of a file, use
>
> # lsattr filename
>
> The chattr utility is part of the e2fsprogs package.
>
> The file attributes include file *permissions*. The traditional UNIX systems of permissions is controlled with chmod. Posix Access Control Lists extend this functionality.
>
> ACL supports permissions for users and groups beyond the traditional owner/group/world scheme. They enable finer-grained control of permissions for files. Implementing ACLs in Linux will be a major step toward making it useful for Enterprise computing.
>
> To learn more about Access Control Lists, visit the Posix ACLs for Linux Web site: http://acl.bestbits.at/.

How big are these blocks? The default size is 1,024 bytes, but the size can be made smaller or larger when the file system is first created. The optimum size is determined by the application of the particular machine. If you typically use very large files, a larger block size can speed up disk I/O operations at the expense of slower I/O for smaller files; the reverse is also true. For an individual system, it might require monitoring over time and benchmarking before an optimal value is determined. For most users, the defaults have been found satisfactory.

File System Partitions

File system partitions are ways to logically organize blocks of data on the physical drive media and are parts of the overall file system on your computer. No single universal partition format exists. In addition to the commonly used DOS partition format (used by Linux as well), Fedora Core also provides support for the following partition types:

- Acorn
- Alpha OS (compiled into the kernel)
- Amiga
- Atari
- Macintosh (compiled into the kernel)
- BSD (compiled into the kernel)
- Minix (compiled into the kernel)
- SunOS/Solaris (compiled into the kernel)
- Unixware slices (compiled into the kernel)
- SGI (compiled into the kernel)
- Windows Logical Disk Manager
- DEC Ultrix (now owned by Hewlett Packard)

> **NOTE**
>
> Other modules and support are likely available if you care to search the Internet for them; try searching on the keyword file systems on `http://freshmeat.net/` and `http://www.google.com/linux/`. As is always the case with Open Source operating systems, any skilled and enterprising soul can write his own file system modules.

Network and Disk File Systems

We can separate file systems into two broad categories: those that can be used over a network and local disk file systems. You are provided with all the applications necessary to work with both categories of file systems when using Fedora Core Linux.

Network file systems are physically stored somewhere other than your local computer but appear as if they are mounted on your local computer.

> **NOTE**
>
> Mounting is the UNIX method of attaching a file system (also referred to as a volume) to the file system tree at a mount point. Using the `mount` command is covered later in this chapter.

Some common network file system types are

- NFS—The Network File System was developed by Sun and is in common use. It has no built-in security because it was originally designed to run over friendly networks. Although considered problematic by some, it is easy to implement. It is typically used between UNIX peers. Fedora Core supports client and server installations of this file system.

- Coda—Similar to NFS, Coda offers support for disconnected operation and security caching (keeping a local copy of files in case the network connection is lost). Fedora Core only provides kernel compatibility with Coda; the actual client and server code is available from `http://www.coda.cs.cmu.edu/`.

- InterMezzo—Similar in features to Coda, InterMezzo is a GPL project. The server daemon can be obtained from `http://www.inter-mezzo.org/`.

- NCP—Used to mount Novelle Netware volumes, its use is more fully described in the Linux Network Administrators Guide at `http://www.tldp.org/LDP/nag2/x-087-2-ipx.ncpfs.client.html`.

- SMB—The network-focused Server Message Block protocol was developed by Microsoft. The Linux implementation is known as Samba and currently works quite well. It is typically used between Linux and Microsoft Windows peers. Netatalk is the Macintosh equivalent protocol.

Disk file systems are found on a physical device; they are the hard drive in your desktop or laptop computer. Some common disk file system types are

- FAT is a disk-oriented, table-based (a linked list) file system used by Microsoft. It has been regularly extended to add functionality. Microsoft's Enterprise-level file system is known as NTFS. (You learn more about this system in "DOS File Systems," later in this chapter.)

- ext2, ext3, and reiserfs are inode based. (You learn about reiserfs in "The Reiser File System," later in this chapter.)

The JFS (Journaled File System from International Business Machines) and XFS (from Silicon Graphics, Inc.) file systems are available for use with Fedora Core Linux, but primarily as migration aids for those migrating existing file systems to Linux.

A journaling file system adds a journal, or hidden file, to the data on the drive. Because of the way data is written to a disk, the kernel might be holding some of the data while it is deciding where to place it. If your computer were to suffer a failure, that cached data would be lost. A journaling file system keeps that data in a special place until the kernel decides to formally write it to the disk. If a system failure occurs, a special application (fsck) knows that the data was never formally written and will make certain that it is written in the correct place. This ensures that no data is lost. Journaling file systems are actually much more complex than this, but the mechanics of them are beyond the scope of this chapter. Journaling file systems such as ext3, reiserfs, JFS, and XFS are major improvements over older, non-journaling file systems.

Viewing Your System's File Systems

Your installation of Fedora Core Linux might have its own unique set of usable virtual file system modules. You can view the file systems that your system can access right now (and verify your kernel's support for these file systems) by using the following command:

```
# cat /proc/file systems
```

Your output will vary, depending on your system's hardware and kernel settings. The test system we used for this chapter presented this output:

```
nodev   rootfs
nodev   bdev
nodev   proc
nodev   sockfs
nodev   tmpfs
nodev   shm
nodev   pipefs
        ext2
nodev   ramfs
```

```
        iso9660
nodev  devpts
        ext3
nodev  usbdevfs
nodev  usbfs
        ReiserFS
        vfat
nodev  nfs
nodev  autofs
nodev  binfmt_misc
```

The entries not preceded by nodev aren't of interest to us because they don't tell us any information about the file system. On this machine, the ext2, ext3, vfat, reiserfs, and iso9660 file systems are supported. Modules for other file systems could be loaded if needed.

Working with the ext3 File System

Red Hat had invested heavily in the development of the ext3 file system and provides support for the ext3 file system as the journaling file system for its distribution. Red Hat (and now Fedora Core) does not provide that level of support for other file systems. Other distributions such as SuSE and Mandrake support the Reiser file system. (You learn about these in later sections of this chapter.)

The ext3 file system is an update to the ext2 file system, which has been one of the most popular Linux file systems for some time. You can choose to use the ext3 file system during a fresh install or automatically convert to an ext3 file system when you upgrade your present system to the current version of Fedora Core Linux. All the ext2 tools provided by Fedora Core have been upgraded to work with both ext2 and ext3. We mention the ext2 tools only because you will see the ext2 file system mentioned frequently; ext3, as supplied with Fedora Core Linux, is completely compatible with ext2.

Understanding the ext3 File System Structure

Fedora Core's rationale for choosing ext3 may be compelling. Although it provides availability, data integrity, and speed similar to other file system choices, ext3 has one unique advantage: It's an easy transition from ext2 to ext3, and the transition is forgiving of mistakes along the way. It is also potentially possible to recover a deleted file from an ext3 file system; such a recovery is not possible at all for a reiserfs file system.

> **NOTE**
>
> The downside to using ext3 seems to be performance related. A recent benchmarking evaluation (see http://fsbench.netnation.com/) of all Linux file systems placed ext3 at the bottom for general performance. What the study really demonstrates is that you must match the file system to the application for best all-around performance.

10

The `ext3` file system can accommodate files as large as 2TB, directories as large as 2TB, and a maximum filename length of 255 characters. (With special kernel patches, this limit can be increased to 1,024 characters if the standard length is insufficient for your use.) The `ext3` file system can allocate and use empty space in a very efficient manner.

The usage of space is so efficient that `ext3` file systems typically don't need defragmenting (rearranging the files to make them contiguous). The dynamic allocation of resources is also the source of one Achilles heel for the file system. When a file is deleted, its inode is erased and the data blocks associated with it are freed; they might very well be reallocated immediately, and the old data lost forever.

> **NOTE**
>
> A defragmentation program for the `ext2` file system does exist, but it is infrequently used, isn't typically included with standard Linux distributions such as Fedora Core Linux, and isn't recommended for general use. The `ext2/3` file system assigns blocks of space for files based on their parent directories; this spaces files out all over the physical disk, leaving room to keep files contiguous and reduce fragmentation. However, a file system full of files at 90% of its capacity can become badly fragmented.

Every file system varies in structure, depending on its efficiency, security, and even proprietary designs to deliberately limit cross-compatibility. The `ext3` file systems were designed to follow UNIX design concepts, particularly "everything is a file."

For example, a directory in the `ext3` file system is simply a file; that file contains the names of the files to be found in that directory, and the locations of those files. The list of names is linked so that space isn't wasted because of varying filename lengths.

Journaling Options in `ext3`

The `ext3` file system has several options that, depending on your needs, allow you to select how much information is journaled. According to Red Hat, the typical journal requires a second or so to be read and recovered. The time needed to recover from an improper shutdown of a journaled file system isn't dependent on the file system size, but the amount of data in the journal.

The default setting provided by Fedora Core is adequate for most needs. The optimal choice depends on so many factors (computer usage, hardware used, and testing and evaluation methods) that a meaningful discussion is beyond the scope of this chapter. You learn in this chapter what the choices are and how they differ, but whether a choice is right for you can only be determined on an individual basis.

Like all journaling file systems, the traditional file system check (`fsck`) isn't necessary on an `ext3` file system. Although only mildly annoying on a 20GB drive on your machine at home, imagine the seemingly endless hours that a `fsck` would take to run on a terabyte of data. This feature is shared in common with the other journaling file systems.

When choosing journaling options, you can trade off data integrity (keeping your data current and valid) for data transfer speed in your file system's operation; you can't have both because of the nature of the file system design. You can choose to expose some of your data to potential damage in the case of an improper shutdown in exchange for faster data handling; or, you can sacrifice some speed to keep the state of the file system consistent with the state of the operating system.

Three modes available as options to ext3 are as follows:

> writeback—Enables old data to stay in the file system, attaining the fastest speed possible. It doesn't schedule any data writes; it just enables the kernel's 30-second writeback code to flush the buffer.

> ordered—Keeps the data consistent, but with some sacrifice in speed (the default mode for Fedora Core).

> journal—Requires more disk space to journal more data. You might see slower performance because data is written twice, but there are some speed benefits if you are doing synchronous data writes as in database operations.

For most of us, the default selection represents a good trade-off. Fedora Core supports booting from an ext3 formatted root file system with the proper drivers loaded in the initrd image.

The mode is selected by using the appropriate mount option in /etc/fstab. For example, to set the file system mode to the fastest of the three modes, use data=writeback as the option. For more details, see man mount.

Verifying File Integrity in ext3 File Systems with the fsck Utility

The file system integrity is assured through the use of the fsck, or file system check, program—one of five commands in the library that are used to maintain and modify the ext3 file system.

When fsck is run, it performs a sequential analysis of the file system information available in the file system if it detects a directory that cannot be traced back to the root or an undeleted file with a zero link count. It places these directories and files in the /lost+found directory that is created on each physical partition by the file system formatting process. Some blocks are reserved for this and other uses of the superuser. It is possible to reduce this allocation to free additional space for regular users by special arguments to the formatting program mke2fs.

To run the fsck command, use the name of the file system as the argument. If you want to fsck the file system at /dev/hdc, for example, do this:

```
# fsck /dev/hdc
```

10

> **TIP**
>
> If you are logged on as a regular user and su to root using su, you will not inherit root's environment and path, meaning that the preceding command will not work without using the full path: /usr/sbin/fsck.
>
> Either type the full path each time, or become root with su -, which causes you to inherit root's environment and path; you have less to type.

The file system state is tracked in the ext3 file systems. A special field in the superblock tells the kernel that, after the file system is mounted read/write, it is marked as not clean; when it is properly unmounted, it is marked as clean. If a file system isn't unmounted properly, it could contain corrupt data because all the file data might not have been written to it. (This is what the journaling file systems such as ext3 strive to eliminate.) When the system is booted, this flag is checked and if it is not clean, the program fsck is run. (Actually, fsck is a wrapper program that runs the appropriate version of fsck for the file system in use: fsck.minix, fsck.ext2, fsck.ext3, fsck.reiserfs, fsck.msdos, and fsck.vfat.) If the kernel detects an inconsistency in the superblock field, the file system is marked erroneous, and the file system check is forced even if other indicators suggest that fsck doesn't need to be run.

By default, the system will run fsck on a file system after a periodic number of reboots, regardless of the status of the clean flag. This behavior is triggered by a mount counter kept in the superblock or after a predetermined amount of time has elapsed since the last reboot (information also kept in the superblock). These parameters can be adjusted through the tune2fs command; this command can also be used to modify how the kernel handles the erroneous flag and, interestingly, the number of blocks reserved for the superuser, also known as root. This latter option is useful on very large or very small disks to make more disk space available to the user.

Other File Systems Available to Fedora Core Linux

Although ext3 is certainly an acceptable root file system, there are other alternatives. No operating systems can support as many root file systems as can Linux. Every file system has its strengths and weaknesses. Some are better with small files, some are better with large files, some are better at writing data, and some are better at reading data. Unfortunately, there is no one perfect file system. The following sections discuss some of the other common file systems available for use with Fedora Core Linux.

The Reiser File System

The other popular journaling file system for Linux is the written-from-scratch Reiser file system, reiserfs. It is used primarily in the SuSE and Mandrake distributions, which support booting from a reiserfs root file system. reiserfs offers similar features to ext3, but there is no easy migration path from an already existing ext2 partition, as you learn to do in "Converting an Existing ext2 File System to ext3," later in this chapter. In the past, reiserfs didn't work well over NFS mounts, but recent versions of the nfsd daemon have fixed those problems. Fedora Core does offer reiserfs, but doesn't offer support for booting from it as the root partition file system, nor does it offer the choice to format non-root partitions as reiserfs during the installation process.

reiserfs is offered primarily for compatibility with existing reiserfs partitions you might want to access. Although the Reiser file system can be used as a root file system (meaning that Linux can be booted from a Reiser file system), Fedora Core has chosen not to support that option.

> **NOTE**
>
> The reiserfs file system has undergone a major update and release with Reiser4. The project, sponsored by The Defense Advanced Research Projects Agency (DARPA), aims to introduce improvements in a number of areas, such as maximum number of directories, files, links, sizes of individual files and size of the file system (nearly 18 terabytes). Other improvements include performance improvements and encryption. It is expected to be released early in 2004.

JFS and XFS File Systems

Two commercial UNIX file systems have been ported (rewritten) to allow them to be used in Linux. IBM has provided its Journaled File System (JFS) that is used with its commercial UNIX named AIX. Silicon Graphics, Inc. (SGI) has provided its XFS file system used by its commercial UNIX named IRIX. Because these file systems are generally suited for Enterprise systems rather than home or small office systems, it seems likely that they are offered in Fedora Core Linux to ease the transition of IRIX and AIX users to Linux by eliminating the need for these users to reformat their very large file systems.

Beginning with kernel 2.6, XFS is fully supported in the kernel.

DOS File Systems

The extent of DOS file system support in Linux is often surprising to newcomers, but the DOS file system proved to be a viable option in the early years of Linux. Because Microsoft has been the dominant operating system on Intel computers, Linux has always worked toward coexistence with DOS.

Microsoft DOS and the consumer-oriented Windows operating systems use a file system known as FAT (File Allocation Table). FAT32 is the typical system used today. The number following the FAT name indicates the size of the space for naming address pointers; the more space, the larger a section of contiguous space can be identified and accessed. FAT32 is the most recent version of FAT, and it's backward compatible with other versions of FAT. (Older versions aren't forward compatible.)

The Fedora Core Linux kernel can access all versions of FAT formatted partitions (including floppy disks) using the vfat kernel module.

10

CD-ROM File Systems

If you use CD-ROM or DVD-ROM media, you need to understand a little bit about the file system and how it works with Linux. To the average user, the file system of a CD-ROM looks just like a native Linux file system. It's not the native file system, but the features of the Virtual File System make it possible for it to appear that way. The CD-ROM file system standards continue to evolve to accommodate new technology.

iso9660

The file system typically used on a CD-ROM is known as `iso9660`, the name of the standard that defines the format. Each operating system translates the `iso9660` file system into the native file system of the operating system (with some restrictions). Several extensions have been created to address certain special needs. The Rock Ridge extension allows long filenames and UNIX-like symbolic links. The Joliet extension allows Unicode characters and long filenames, useful when dealing with non-English languages. El Torito CDs contain a bootable image and, with a suitable BIOS, can boot an operating system from the CD.

Universal Disk Format

The Universal Disk Format, or UDF, is the file system used on DVD discs. UDF has a number of built-in features such as allowing larger files, having improved file descriptors, and packet writing that the `iso9660` file system can't easily accommodate. The UDF format is the next step in compact disc technology.

Creating a File System

To create a file system on a disk that has never had a partition table on it or to change the partition table (called repartitioning the disk), you must first create the new partition table. In this section, you begin by learning about the basic structure and workings of the disk as a storage device. This information is fundamental to your understanding of the file system creation process. You then learn to create a partition table using the `fdisk` and `GNUparted` commands. As with all similar Linux commands, each has its own strengths and weaknesses and none is a perfect choice for all situations. In the end, the partition table you create will be the same no matter which command you use. You then learn to create the file system, using commands appropriate for the type of file system you want to create.

> **NOTE**
>
> The Microsoft version of `fdisk` creates both a partition table and the boot loader. In Linux, `fdisk` only creates the partition table. The boot loader is created later by LILO, GRUB, or another boot loader; no boot loader is necessary to create a file system and store data on a disk, just a partition table.
>
> In fact, IDE disks physically installed as something other than `/dev/hda` (such as `/dev/hdc`, the secondary master drive) won't have a boot loader written to them; the space where the boot

loader code normally resides will likely be blank. For SCSI disks, the drive designated in the BIOS as the bootable drive will have the boot loader written to it.

The Disk As a Storage Device

Because data storage devices are central to the file system, it's important to understand the workings of the most common data storage device—the hard disk drive. Although they work with a different medium, the basic storage functions of floppy disks and removable disk drives are similar to those of the hard disk.

Mechanically, the hard drive is a metal box that encloses disks, also known as platters, which have a magnetic coating on each side. Multiple disks are typically connected to the same spindle and rotated by motor. The read and write heads for each side of the disk are moved by a second motor to position them over the area of the disk where the data you are looking for is stored. Each platter is organized into cylinders (the default size is 512 bytes) and sectors, and each platter has a head. Each drive has some electronics on a controller card that, along with the disk controller card on the motherboard of the computer, are capable of placing the heads at the correct space to retrieve the data.

The three components, cylinders, heads, and sectors (CHS), are referred to as the drive geometry and are used to identify specific locations on the drive. The CHS information for the drive is detected by the system BIOS and passed on to the operating system.

The first sector of the disk is called the MBR, or Master Boot Record. It is the most important sector on the disk because it contains the boot loader code and the partition table (the table containing pointers to beginning and end of the logical partitions on the disk). The BIOS gets the system's hardware ready, and then executes the boot loader code. The boot loader code and the boot loader program load the kernel and turn over control of the system to the kernel. Then, Linux is on its way to providing us with one of the best operating system experiences in the world.

The MBR sector is 512 bytes long; the first 446 bytes contain the boot loader code. The next 64 bytes contain the partition table, and the final 2 bytes contain a special code (the hexadecimal values of 55 and AA, respectively) that identifies that sector as the MBR. More details about the MBR can be found Chapter 11, "Backing Up, Restoring, and Recovery."

Creating the Partition Table

Fedora Core provides several tools to create, examine, and modify the partition table.

Because not all the tools we review are likely to be installed on your system (or other system you might be working on for now), this chapter describes making a partition table using some command-line and graphical tools that Fedora Core Linux provides.

The partition table only has enough room for four partitions. When the format was first created, it must have been assumed that four would be plenty. Complex, modern systems with very large hard drives make multiple partitions desirable for any number of unique reasons. To get around this problem, one of the four partitions—typically, partition number four—can be used as an *extended* partition. In other words, in the partition table, it looks like a big partition taking up the rest of the disk. Actually, it's a link to a table that contains the offsets to as many as 63 partitions for IDE disks and 15 for SCSI disks. One extended partition is chained to the next one in this manner.

CAUTION

Fedora and Red Hat have modified their supplied version of `fdisk` to limit the number of IDE partitions to 15 to match the limit for SCSI disks. That's a problem if you already have more than 15 IDE partitions as their `fdisk` will simply delete without warning those partitions if you use it! If you use less than 15 partitions, there will be no problem. If this causes a problem for you, compile your own `fdisk` from pristine sources and file a bug report with Fedora/Red Hat.

NOTE

Zip disks are typically delivered with a single partition numbered 4. This has some arcane relevance to Apple computer users, but is of no importance to Linux users who are free to use any valid number they choose.

The `fdisk` Command

The Linux `fdisk` command edits the partition table.

You must be the superuser (`root`) before you can run the console tool `fdisk` (also said in Linux shorthand as "run `fdisk` as `root`"). Only hard drives (IDE and SCSI) can be accessed with `fdisk`, and you must use the device name as an argument. USB hard drives are accessed under SCSI emulation and are treated just as if they were SCSI devices. For example, to open `fdisk` and use it on the first IDE hard drive on the system, you would type this

```
# fdisk /dev/hda
```

and you would see something like this:

```
# fdisk /dev/hda
The number of cylinders for this disk is set to 4982. There is nothing wrong
➥with that, but this is larger than 1024, and in certain setups could
➥cause problems with software that runs at boot time:
1) software that runs at boot time (e.g., old versions of LILO)
2) booting and partitioning software from other OSes (e.g., DOS FDISK or the
   ➥OS/2 FDISK)
```

Pressing the `m` key displays the help screen as follows:

```
Command (m for help): m
Command action
   a   toggle a bootable flag
   b   edit bsd disklabel
   c   toggle the dos compatibility flag
   d   delete a partition
   l   list known partition types
   m   print this menu
   n   add a new partition
   o   create a new empty DOS partition table
   p   print the partition table
   q   quit without saving changes
   s   create a new empty Sun disklabel
   t   change a partition's system id
   u   change display/entry units
   v   verify the partition table
   w   write table to disk and exit
   x   extra functionality (experts only)
```

Pressing the p key will display the volume's partition information as follows (note that your drive information will be different):

```
Command (m for help): p

Disk /dev/hda: 255 heads, 63 sectors, 4982 cylinders
Units = cylinders of 16065 * 512 bytes

   Device Boot   Start    End    Blocks  Id System
/dev/hda1   *       1    383   3076416   b Win95 FAT32
/dev/hda2         384    387     32130  83 Linux
/dev/hda3         388   1025   5124735  83 Linux
/dev/hda4        1026   4982 31784602+  5 Extended
/dev/hda5        1026   1042    136521  82 Linux swap
/dev/hda6        1043   1552   4096543+ 83 Linux
/dev/hda7        1553   4102 20482843+ 83 Linux
/dev/hda8        4103   4500   3196903+ 83 Linux
/dev/hda9        4501   4982   3871633+ 83 Linux
```

Older versions of fdisk would default to /dev/hda. The author of fdisk decided that wasn't a good thing, so now you must always type the device name.

10

TIP

The fdisk command is only dangerous to explore if you write the changes to the partition table. Because you are specifically asked whether you want to do this, poke around to satisfy your curiosity and avoid pressing the w key when you're done; just use q to quit. Armed with this knowledge, don't feel too shy if you're curious about the partition table. But if you really don't want to take a chance on breaking anything, play it safe and use the -1 (that's the letter L, not the numeral 1) as in

```
# fdisk -l /dev/had
```

fdisk happily prints the contents of the partition table to the screen (often referred to as stdout, or standard output) and exits without placing you in the edit mode.

It's always a good idea to keep a hard copy of your edited partition table. You can redirect the output of fdisk -1 to a file

```
# fdisk -l device > mypartitiontable.txt
```

or send it to the printer with

```
# fdisk -l device | kprinter
```

In the first example, a redirector symbol (>) is used to redirect the listing from stdout to a file. In the second example, we used a pipe (¦) to send the output directly to the printer (assuming that you have one connected).

Now that you are running fdisk as root, you can create a partition table. We will assume that you have installed a brand-new drive as /dev/hdb (the Primary Slave IDE device) and want to partition the entire drive as a single partition. Launch fdisk with

```
# fdisk /dev/hdb
```

Use the n key to create a new partition, and fdisk will prompt you for the beginning cylinder:

```
First Cylinder (1-9729, default 1) :
```

Press the Enter key to accept the default of 1. Now, fdisk prompts

```
Using the default value of 1
Last Cylinder or +size or +sizeM or +sizeK (2-9729, default 9729) :
```

Here, you can give the size in cylinders, the size in kilobytes, the size in megabytes, or accept the default value (which is the last cylinder on the disk). Press the Enter key to accept the default.

```
Using default value of 9729
```

And we are back at the fdisk prompt:

```
Command (m for help) :
```

Enter the w command to write the new partition table to the disk, and fdisk will exit, returning you to the command prompt.

The parted Command

In the past, Red Hat used a partition editor during its installation process named Disk Druid; the underlying code for Disk Druid has been replaced by GNUparted (also known simply as parted, the name of the command itself). GNUparted is the GNU partition editor and a very powerful utility. You use parted to create, delete, move, resize, and copy ext2, ext3, and FAT32 partitions. Although GNUparted displays a GUI interface during the installation process, it really is a console utility. GNUparted can be used from the command line.

Creating the File System on the Partitioned Disk

After you have partitioned the disk for a specific file system, you can create the file system on it. In the DOS world, this two-part process is described by DOS as low-level formatting (creating the partitions and partition table) and formatting (creating the file system). In the UNIX world, the latter is known as creating a file system. In this section, you learn how to create a file system in Linux.

An unformatted disk storage device (a floppy disk, hard disk drive, or removable media) typically arrives to you with a low-level format, which has been done with a tool such as fdisk or superformat. Although the disk might have a boot block and partition information, it typically lacks the file structure needed for a file system.

> **NOTE**
>
> If you are preparing to create a file system on any device other than a floppy disk, examine it with fdisk or another utility of your choice and modify the partition table accordingly (following the instructions you saw in the preceding sections of this chapter).

To create the file system structure, you need to do what is sometimes referred to as a high-level format. For FAT file systems, this is accomplished by the format command. In Linux, you use the mke2fs -j command to create an ext3 file system.

> **NOTE**
>
> If you are creating a Reiser file system, use the mkreiserfs command. To create a DOS file system, use the mkdosfs command. Other commands for other file systems include
>
> mkfs.bfs—The SCO file system
>
> mkfs.ext2—The ext2 file system
>
> mkfs.minix—The minix file system
>
> mkfs.msdos—The MS-DOS file system
>
> mkfs.vfat—The FAT32 file system
>
> The special tools used to manipulate the FAT and MS-DOS file systems files are known as the Mtools.

10

Using `mke2fs` to Create the File System

The `mke2fs` command is used to create both the `ext2` and the `ext3` file systems. At its simplest, the command is used as

```
# mke2fs psrtition
```

such as

```
# mke2fs /dev/hdc4
```

Here are some of the most useful options for `mke2fs`:

-c—This option checks for bad blocks during file system creation.

-N—This option overrides the default number of inodes created. (The default number is usually a good choice, but you might need to use this option to allow additional usable disk space.)

-m—This option frees up some space on the disk, but you do so at your peril. By default, the system allocates 5% of the blocks to the superuser—to be used in file recovery during `fsck`. You can lower that allocation, but you might not leave enough blocks for `fsck` to recover enough files.

-L—This option gives the volume a label, which is useful if you need to be reminded what the file system is used for; it also provides some flexibility in identifying volumes in `/etc/fstab`.

-S—This option is a last-ditch effort for recovering a munged file system; it writes only the superblock and descriptors, leaving the information in the inodes unchanged. Always run `fsck` after using this option.

As you can see, `mke2fs` offers a few options to make more space available for the regular users. But that extra space always comes from the superuser's space for recovering damaged files. The default settings accommodate most users, so think carefully before using one of these options. Hard disks are getting less expensive all the time, so adding another might be a better solution.

Using `mkfs.ext3`

To make a new `ext3` file system, you use the `mke2fs` command with the `-j` or `-J` option, or call the command as `mkfs.ext3`. (There is no `mke3fs` command, but there should be to be consistent.) Use the `tune2fs` command on an existing `ext2` file system to add journaling. (You learn how to convert an existing `ext2` file system into an `ext3` file system later in this chapter. Here, x represents a partition:

```
# tune2fs /dev/hdx -j
```

Some arguments you can use with this command include

-j—This option adds an `ext3` journal to the new file system using the default values. Note that you must be using a kernel that has `ext3` support to actually make use of the journal.

-J *journal-options*—This option overrides the default ext3 journal parameters so that you can choose the options you desire. The following journal options are comma separated and can take an argument using the = sign:

size=journal-size—This option creates a journal of journal-size megabytes. With a minimum size of 1,024 blocks, it can't be more than 102,400 blocks. There must be enough free space in the file system to create a journal of that size.

device=external-journal—This option associates the file system with a journal not contained within the file system (one that must have already been created with the command mke2fs -O *journal_device journal_name*); in other words, the journal and the data files don't have to be on the same device.

> **NOTE**
>
> The latter two options in the arguments list are mutually exclusive.

To select the ext3 journaling mode, you must add the appropriate entry in /etc/fstab.

Because the ext3 file system is a new version of the ext2 file system with journaling added, it supports the same options as ext2, as well as the following additions:

noload—This option disables the ext3 file system's journal when mounting; it becomes an ext2 file system.

data=journal / data=ordered / data=writeback—This option specifies the journaling mode; "ordered" is the default. Metadata is always journaled.

journal—The slowest, but most secure mode because all the data is written to the journal before it is written to the regular file system.

ordered—This is the default mode in which all data is written to the main file system prior to its metadata being committed to the journal.

writeback—With this option, data can be written into the main file system after its metadata has been committed to the journal. This option enables old data to appear in files after a crash and journal recovery, but it is the fastest option.

Using mkreiserfs

The Reiser file system journals file data and handles smaller files more efficiently than the ext3 file system. Although it is suitable for use as the root file system, Fedora Core does not officially support its use in that way. You use the mkreiserfs command to create a Reiser file system. The default values for mkreiserfs work well. To create a Reiser file system, use

```
# mkreiserfs device
```

10

Creating a DOS File System with mkdosfs

It's possible to create DOS file systems without owning any Microsoft software using the mkdosfs command. To create a DOS file system in an image file (useful with some emulators such as Bochs), use the -C option. The -n option allows you to specify a volume label. To create a 1.4M DOS file system as an image file with the label dosfloppy, the sector size (-S) should be 512 and the block count should be 1440. Use the -v option to provide verbose output so that we can observe what happens.

```
# mkdosfs -n dosfloppy -v -C floppy.img -S 512 1440
```

> **TIP**
>
> To create a DOS file system on a floppy disk drive, use
>
> ```
> # fdformat device
> ```

A complete review of all the argument options and syntax for creating a DOS file system can be found in man mkdosfs. The new file system must be mounted (as described in the following section) and then formatted with the mformat command—one of the Mtools.

Mounting File Systems

File systems in UNIX are very flexible in that they need not be physically present on your computer; you can have network access to other file systems on other machines. The Linux file system structure (the Virtual File System we spoke of at the beginning of the chapter) makes it appear as if all the file systems, regardless of type and location, are local and mounted somewhere on the root file system. As the system administrator, you decide what file systems are to be made available and where they will be attached, or mounted, to the root file system. The standard arrangement of the file system tree is that installed by default by Fedora Core Linux. The source of that standard arrangement is found in the File System Hierarchy Standards. Although a detailed discussion of those standards is beyond the scope of this section, they can be examined at http://www.pathname. com/fhs/. In this section, you learn how to mount file systems to the root file system and add file systems to the system, and you learn the traditional mount points of commonly used file systems as well.

In Linux (and its UNIX cousins), all file systems—whether local, remote, images on a disk, or in memory—are mounted on a single point known as root (which isn't the same as the root operator, also known as the superuser). This mount point is written as a forward slash, /, which is read and pronounced "root." The resulting file directory hierarchy all starts from /. Once mounted, the physical location of the files is unimportant because they all appear to be local.

Even if the file systems are different (FAT, ext2, HPFS, ntfs, and so on), the Linux kernel modules and the VFS make them all appear as part of the directory tree as native files. Listing the file systems as native files obviates the need for any applications to be aware of the physical location of the file or the true nature of the native file system. As a result, programming these applications is simplified because the applications only have to work with what they think are local, native files.

Any file system can be mounted anywhere, but some places are more traditional than others. Removable media devices are traditionally mounted under the /mnt directory (for example, floppy drives on /mnt/floppy and CD-ROM drives on /mnt/cdrom). The /mnt directory is the traditional place to mount removable or remote file systems that are unrelated to the local system directories that branch from the root mountpoint.

The mount **Command**

File systems are mounted with the mount command and unmounted, curiously enough, with the umount command.

During the installation, you have the opportunity to decide where and how your partitions will be mounted. You indicate your choices, and Fedora Core automatically stores them in /etc/fstab, the File System Table, for you. The mount command looks at /etc/fstab and mounts the file system according to those set preferences. You learn more about the File System Table later in this section.

The syntax for mount is

```
mount -t type file system_to_be mounted mount_point
```

Here are the components of the mount command, and a brief explanation of each:

> type—Always preceded by the -t argument and followed by a space, and then the type of file system you are mounting. Typical file systems types are: ext2, ext3, vfat, iso9660, hpfs, hfs, ntfs, and others. For many file systems, mount can detect what type they are automatically, and the -t argument is superfluous (and is replaced with auto).

> file system_to_be mounted (as represented by the partition on which it resides)—This is the device name of the file system you want to mount, typically in the form of /dev/hdx, /dev/scx, or /dev/fdx.

> mount_point—The place in the directory tree where you want to mount the file system. Curiously, you can mount a file system over part of an existing file system. For example, if you have an existing directory at /foo with a single file named bar, and you mount a file system at /foo that includes a file named snafu, a listing of the directory /foo won't show the file bar, but only the file snafu. To show both files is a feature called *transparency*, which unfortunately isn't in the current Linux repertoire.

The only real restriction to "mount anything anywhere" is that the critical system files in /bin, /etc, /lib, /dev, /proc, and /tmp need to be accessed at bootup, which typically means that they need to be on the same physical disk. If they can't be accessed at bootup, Linux won't load and run.

10

Here are a few examples of using the `mount` command:

Mounting a floppy:

```
# mount -t vfat /dev/fd0 /mnt/floppy
```

Mounting a CD-ROM:

```
# mount -t iso9660 /dev/scd0 /mnt/cdrom
```

Mounting a Network File System (NFS) volume:

```
# mount -t nfs remote_host:/dir [options] mount_point
```

Numerous `mount` options exist. These options are used primarily in the `/etc/fstab` file. You can invoke a `mount` option by preceding it (or a comma-delimited string of options) with the `-o` switch. The `mount` options are listed in the `fstab` section of this chapter.

The `umount` Command

To unmount a file system, use the `umount` command with the following syntax:

```
umount mount_point
```

You can also unmount by device name:

```
umount device_name
```

> **CAUTION**
>
> Don't use `umount -a` to unmount everything that the system doesn't require to run (or isn't currently using). Unmounting *everything* is a particularly bad idea on a multiuser, networked system because your users will undoubtedly lose access to some or all their files. So, as any good sysadmin will tell you, don't do that.

Mounting Automatically with `/etc/fstab`

A special file, `/etc/fstab`, exists to provide the system with predetermined options and mountpoints so that the file systems can be automatically or manually mounted with minimal typing and without having to recall arcane Linux syntax.

The `/etc/fstab` file can only be written to by the superuser. The commands `fsck`, `mount`, and `umount` all read information from `/etc/fstab`. Each file system gets its own line with the information separated by tabs.

On each line of `fstab`, the first field indicates the block device or remote file system that will be mounted. The second field identifies the mount point on the local system where the file system will be mounted. The third field is the file system type, and the fourth field is a comma-delimited list of mount options. Options include

exec—If this option is specified, binaries can be executed from this file system.

noauto—This means that the -a option won't cause the file system to be mounted and it won't be mounted at bootup.

noexec—If this option is specified, binaries cannot be executed from this file system.

nosuid—This option does not permit set-user-identifier or set-group-identifier bits to take effect.

ro—This option mounts the file system as read-only.

rw—This option mounts the file system as read/write.

sync—Reading from and writing to the files are done synchronously.

user—This option allows a regular (not just root) user to mount the file system, but it includes the options noexec, nosuid, and nodev by default unless they are overridden by exec, dev, and suid.

For iso9660 file systems, the interesting option is unhide, which shows hidden and associated files.

The fstab man pages contain an in-depth description of fstab and its options.

The fifth field of /etc/fstab is used by dump (a traditional UNIX backup program) to determine whether the file system should be dumped (backed up); 1 is yes, and 0 is no. Default values are set for you during the initial installation. They are of concern only if you actually use dump; then you would set the value to 1 for the file systems you wanted to back up.

The sixth field is used by fsck to determine how fsck needs to interact the file system—0 means that fsck is never run on the file system (a FAT32 file system, for example); 1 means that fsck will be run on the drive at a predetermined time. 2 is recommended for non-root file systems so that fsck isn't run on them as frequently.

Here is a simple /etc/fstab file from a system with a RAID0 ext3 root partition and dual-booted with MS Windows.

```
LABEL=/12      /              ext3    defaults               1 1
none           /dev/pts       devpts  gid=5,mode=620         0 0
none           /proc          proc    defaults               0 0
none           /dev/shm       tmpfs   defaults               0 0
/dev/hda11     swap           swap    defaults               0 0
/dev/cdrom     /mnt/cdrom     iso9660 noauto,owner,kudzu,ro  0 0
/dev/fd0       /mnt/floppy    auto    noauto,owner,kudzu     0 0
/dev/hda1      /mnt/win_c     vfat    auto,quiet,exec        0 0
```

Notice the two entries marked with the kudzu option. This is the result of the actions of updfstab, which keeps fstab synchronized with the state of any removable devices on the system such as CD-ROMs, floppy drives, Zip and Jaz drives, LS-120 drives, and some digital cameras. The `quiet` option shown for the Windows partition will suppress error messages and is recommended if you use the Wine application.

> **NOTE**
>
> Device labels can be very useful. You can use the label in `/etc/fstab`, and if you have many devices, their labels might be easier for you to remember and track than would their device names. You can also shuffle around partitions without editing `fstab`, just by changing their labels. The `e2label` command is easier to remember than the analogous `tune2fs` command. (Because UNIX commands aren't really that easy to remember, we are given the `man` pages to refresh our memory.)
>
> The command `e2label` can display or change the label of a device. (You also can change a device label with `tune2fs -L`.) For example, to change the label of `/dev/hda4` to archives, use
>
> ```
> # e2label /dev/hda4 archives
> ```

As mentioned earlier, you record mounting preferences in `/etc/fstab` during installation. You only need to modify `/etc/fstab` if you make changes to your mounts or desire to change the default settings to address the specific needs of your system.

As long as the superuser understands the syntax and options of the `fstab` file, she can edit the file with any text editor.

GUI Tools to Mount File Systems

The `usermount` graphical file system management client is available for use with Fedora Core Linux. Although Fedora Core provides `usermount` as the default file system mounting tool, it is not as feature-rich as KDiskFree, which is installed when you select the KDE desktop during installation.

The K Desktop Environment (KDE) provides several disk- and file system-related utilities. You might find one or more available on your Fedora Core system if you select KDE for installation. Found in the Extras menu under System Tools, the KDiskFree menu item (it is `kdf` from a command line) displays all the file systems noted in the `/etc/fstab` file, presents information about them, and allows you to easily mount and unmount them (see Figure 10.1). KWikDisk enables mounts and unmounts from a panel applet.

> **TIP**
>
> KWikDisk is the KDE panel applet for KDiskFree. You would normally right-click on the KDE panel and add the applet to the panel. Fedora Core has omitted KWikDisk from the KDE applet menu, but still includes it with Fedora Core. Launch it from a command line, and it will appear on the KDE panel or on the GNOME desktop. Clicking on the KWikDisk panel icon launches an abbreviated version of KDiskFree:
>
> ```
> $ kwikdisk &
> ```

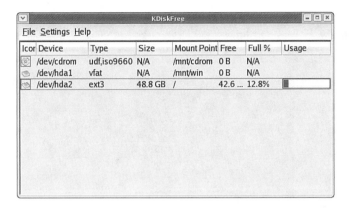

FIGURE 10.1   KDiskFree provides a graphical interface to tools used to configure custom mount options, as well as mount, or unmount disks.

The User Mount Tool, accessed from the System Tools menu as the Disk Management menu item, is a convenient way to mount and unmount file systems (see Figure 10.2). It also allows you to format floppy disks.

Floppy Formatter is a KDE tool to easily format a floppy in ext2 or FAT format. You can start it by choosing System Tools, Floppy Formatter. Floppy Formatter can format floppy disks in 3.5" and 5.25" high and low density formats (see Figure 10.3).

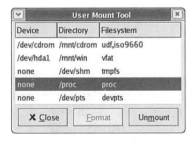

FIGURE 10.2   The User Mount Tool is the default Fedora Core disk management GUI tool. It can mount and unmount file systems, as well as the cdrom device.

Automounting with the Automount Daemon (amd) and autofs

The automount daemon will watch specified devices and will mount the devices when they are accessed and unmount them when there has been no activity. The configuration files are /etc/auto.master and /etc/auto.misc. The former file contains only comments; the latter contains examples and the sole entry used by Fedora Core to automount the CD-ROM drive. If you insert a CD, after a long pause, a file browser will appear on your desktop. Many people find this behavior annoying and prefer to disable automount.

10

Because `autofs` is started at boot time and controls the `automount` daemon, simply don't run `autofs`. Use the `checkconfig`, `ntsysv`, or GUI clients to edit the startup scripts for your runlevel (see Chapter 7, "Managing Services," for details).

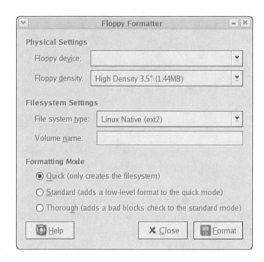

FIGURE 10.3   Point and click for floppy formatting makes it easy. A larger choice of formatting options (like a 1.7MB 3.5" floppy) would be nicer. The Floppy Formatter is found under the System Tools menu.

Relocating a File System

Many home users start with a single disk partition that mounts not only the root file system files, but also all the other files. Although this might work quite well for most home users, there might come a time when the physical disk becomes full. Adding another drive and moving part of the file system there isn't difficult, but it is the source of many questions from new Linux users. This section of the chapter explains how to do this kind of file system relocation.

In this example, we will install a new IDE hard drive to `/dev/hdb` (the primary slave drive), create a single partition on it, format it as an `ext3` file system, and move all of the user files located in `/home` to it. Once done, we will make it mount, by default, at the `/home` mountpoint by editing the `/etc/fstab` file.

Installing the New Drive

First, physically install the drive, making certain that the master/slave jumpers are set correctly to set the drive as a slave drive. Also be certain that the jumpers are set correctly on the existing master drive. (Some drives require a different jumper setting, depending on whether they are a single master drive or a master drive with a slave drive; others offer a "cable-select" option to automatically set the drive status.) Failing to ensure that the jumpers are set correctly is a common error made even by people who are familiar with computer hardware.

After you have installed the drive, it must be correctly detected by the BIOS. Many modern BIOSes have an autodetect feature, or you can manually enter the drive CHS information in the BIOS (found on the drive label or documentation).

NOTE

Linux can ignore the BIOS-provided CHS information and use information that you provide when loading the kernel, passing it as a kernel argument. Although this is a very powerful Linux option, it is now only used when working with obsolete BIOSes from more than three or four years ago and when you are attempting to use a hard drive that is larger than the BIOS was designed to address. In these cases, the CHS information helps the boot loader program know where the kernel is on the disk and helps the kernel understand how the data on the drive is organized, enabling Linux to make older hardware remain useful long after it has become obsolete. For more detailed information, you can look at the Large Disk HOWTO and the BootPrompt HOWTO if you have problems with drive geometry and the BIOS.

Most modern large drives use the LBA setting (Logical Block Addressing) to deal with the BIOS size limitations. If the drive isn't detected, check the power connection, the IDE cable connection (the red stripe usually goes next to the power connector, but always double-check), and the master/slave jumpers. If all these are fine, you might have a bad drive, or the two hard drives if made by different manufacturers) might not be playing nice with each other (especially if they were made by different manufacturers).

To check further, reset the jumper of the new drive to make it the master drive, disconnect the old drive, and plug in the new one in its place. If the new drive is now correctly detected, suspect some incompatibility between the drives. Always make cable changes to the drives with the power off, or you will damage the drive.

TIP

If you were to examine the partition table with a hexadecimal editor, you would find that with only 10 bits in which to store the partition's cylinder offset (an index to data on the disk); no disk can have any more than 1,024 cylinders.

One creative way to get around that limitation is to increase the number of heads so that the number of cylinders can remain small enough to fit the partition table. This scheme is known as Logical Block Addressing, or LBA. Modern BIOSes (post-1998 or so) support it, but older ones do not. But because Linux is capable of being told about the drive geometry at boot time, it isn't as big a problem to Linux users as it is to users of other operating systems. For more detailed information, you can look at the Large Disk HOWTO and the BootPrompt HOWTO if you have problems with large hard disks.

10

Creating the Partition Table and Formatting the Disk

Once installed and recognized by the BIOS, a partition table needs to be created. Use fdisk (or the program of your choice) to create a single partition on the drive, remembering to write the changes to the MBR before you exit the program (see "Creating the Partition Table," earlier in this chapter).

Formatting the drive is next. Because we are creating a new ext3 file system, we use the j option, as

```
# mke2fs -cj /dev/hdb1
```

Notice that we are checking the drive (using the -c option) for bad blocks as we format. Even though it adds considerable time to formatting the drive, an initial bad block check is always a good idea. The program will identify bad blocks and not use them; bad blocks would only corrupt our data if we didn't mark the file system to ignore them.

Mounting the New Partition and Populating It with the Relocated Files

For the example that follows, it is assumed that /home was a directory that was part of the partition mounted at /, not a separate partition to begin with.

Here, we create a temporary mount point and mount the new partition:

```
# mkdir /mnt/newpartition
# mount -t ext3 /dev/hdb1 /mnt/newpartition
```

It's now time to copy all the files from /home to /mnt/newpartition. It's important that we preserve the time and date stamps for the files and the permissions. We're copying entire directories and subdirectories, so we use one of our three basic copying methods (tar, cpio, or cp) that best accommodates this:

```
# cp -a /home/* /mnt/newpartition
```

We need to modify /etc/fstab so that our new ext3 partition will be mounted correctly:

```
/dev/hdb1    /home ext3  defaults    1 2
```

Here, we have chosen to use the default mount options for the ext3 partition. The defaults are identical to those for the ext2 file system, as well as additionally selecting the default data=ordered journaling mode.

Anytime we reboot, the new partition containing the copied files will automatically be mounted at /home. But before we do that, cd to /home and enter this:

```
# touch thisistheoldhomepartition
```

Now we can mount the new partition:

```
# umount /mnt/newpartition
```

```
# mount /dev/hdb1 /home
```

Note that if you do an

```
# ls -al /home
```

you will not see the `thisistheoldhomepartition` file we created with the `touch` command. So what happened to the old files? They are still there, but just hidden because we mounted a directory "over" them. When we are satisfied that all is well, we can unmount our newly created home partition and delete the files in the partition that contains the `thisistheoldhomepartition` file.

> **TIP**
>
> You can use the previously explained technique as a placeholder or warning for any temporarily mounted file system so that you don't mistakenly think that the file system is mounted when it isn't.

Logical Volume Management

The previous example showed you how to add a new drive to overcome a lack of disk space. What if this could be done without all the mounting and file copying? That's where Logical Volume Management (LVM) is useful. Using LVM, disk space from multiple drives can be pooled into a single logical volume.

As with any new technology, there is a steep learning curve involved in using LVM, not the least of which is its vocabulary. Within this vocabulary, partitions are known as physical volumes, or pv. We add pvs to a volume group that defines a logical volume on which we can create our file system.

On a heavily used system, the files being backed up can change during the backup, and the restored files might be in an unstable condition. LVM can also make snapshots of the logical volume that can then be mounted and backed up.

For more information on LVM under Linux, read the LVM HOWTO at `http://tldp.org/ HOWTO/LVM-HOWTO/` which explains the terminology as well as a guide to setting up and using LVM on a Linux system.

File System Manipulation

Different people have various learning styles. For those of you who prefer examples rather than lectures, here are a few practical examples in which you learn how to create a file

10

system within a file and mount it using the *loopback file system*—a special file system that allows us to accomplish this useful feat. You can use the file system you create to experiment with and practice almost all the commands found in this chapter with no fear of damaging your system.

Creating a File System for Testing

Because most of us don't have a spare computer or hard drive on which to experiment and practice, we can make one of our own by creating an image file containing the file system of our choice and using the loopback file system to mount it. That way, we don't run the risk of accidentally wreaking havoc on the system itself. Although you could also use a floppy drive for these same exercises, their small size limits your flexibility.

Step 1—Make a Blank Image File

Use the dd command to create a file with a block size of 1,024 bytes (a megabyte) and create a file that is 10MB in size. (You need to have enough free space on your hard drive to hold a file this big, so adjust the size accordingly.) We want 10,000 1KB (1,024-byte) blocks, so we select a count of 10000.

If we wanted a floppy-sized image, we would have selected a block size (bs) of 512 and a count of 2880 for a 1.4MB floppy or 5760 for a 2.88MB floppy. Here's how to do that:

```
# dd if=/dev/zero of=/tmp/fedoratest.img bs=1024 count=10000
```

We see the computer respond with the following:

```
10000+0 records in
10000+0 records out
```

If we check our new file command, we see this:

```
# file /tmp/fedoratest.img
/tmp/fedoratest.img: data
```

Step 2—Make a File System

Now we need to make the system think that the file is a block device instead of an ASCII file, so we use losetup, a utility that associates loop devices with regular files or block devices; we will be using the loopback device, /dev/loop0.

```
# losetup /dev/loop0 /tmp/fedoratest.img
```

Now we can format the file as an ext2 file system:

```
# mke2fs /dev/loop0
```

We see the computer respond as follows:

```
mke2fs 1.27 (8-Mar-2003)
File System label=
OS type: Linux
Block size=1024 (log=0)
Fragment size=1024 (log=0)
2512 inodes, 10000 blocks
500 blocks (5.00%) reserved for the super user
First data block=1
2 block groups
8192 blocks per group, 8192 fragments per group
1256 inodes per group
Superblock backups stored on blocks:
    8193

Writing inode tables: done
Writing superblocks and file system accounting information: done

This file system will be automatically checked every 21 mounts or 180 days, \
whichever comes first. Use tune2fs -c or -i to override.
```

Step 3—Mounting Our Test File System

After your test file system has been created, you can experiment with the different options for the formatting commands you will be using. It will be useful to make a mount point for our image file

```
# mkdir /mnt/image
```

and then mount it

```
# mount /dev/loop0 /mnt/image
```

We can do this now because we already have the loopback file system associated with the image file. Later on if we remount it, we must use the following format to use the loopback option:

```
# mount -o loop /tmp/fedoratest.img /mnt/image
```

After mounting the new file system, we can look at it and see that the /lost+found directory has been created on it and that the df command returns

```
# df -h /mnt/image
File System     Size Used Avail Use% Mounted on /dev/loop0      \
9.5M  13k 8.9M   1% /mnt/image
```

To unmount it, use this:

```
# umount /mnt/image
```

Make a backup of the image just in case we break the original:

```
# cp /tmp/fedoratest.img fedoratest.bak
```

After the test file system is created, you can create directories, copy files to it, delete files, attempt to recover them, and, in general, create controlled chaos on your computer while you are learning and practicing valuable skills. If you damage the file system on the image beyond repair, unmount it, delete it, and create a new one (or copy a new one from that backup).

Using dumpe2fs

You can use the program dumpe2fs to examine the structure of your ext3 file system.

The syntax for the command is

```
dumpe2fs [ -bfhixV ] [ -ob superblock ] [ -oB blocksize ] device
```

To examine our image file system using dumpe2fs, first unmount it, and then use this:

```
# dumpe2fs /tmp/fedoratest.img
```

```
dumpe2fs 1.27 (8-Mar-2003)
File System volume name:  <none>
Last mounted on:          <not available>
File System UUID:         03644acf-581c-410f-b4b6-10958992016e
File System magic number: 0xEF53
File System revision #:   1 (dynamic)
File System features:     filetype sparse_super
File System state:        not clean
Errors behavior:          Continue
File System OS type:      Linux
Inode count:              2512
Block count:              10000
Reserved block count:     500
Free blocks:              9664
Free inodes:              2501
First block:              1
Block size:               1024
Fragment size:            1024
Blocks per group:         8192
Fragments per group:      8192
```

```
Inodes per group:       1256
Inode blocks per group: 157
Last mount time:        Fri May 16 14:36:33 2003
Last write time:        Fri May 16 14:37:09 2003
Mount count:            2
Maximum mount count:    21
Last checked:           Fri May 16 14:35:39 2003
Check interval:         15552000 (6 months)
Next check after:       Wed Nov 12 13:35:39 2003
Reserved blocks uid:    0 (user root)
Reserved blocks gid:    0 (group root)
First inode:            11
Inode size:             128

Group 0: (Blocks 1-8192)
 Primary Superblock at 1, Group Descriptors at 2-2
 Block bitmap at 3 (+2), Inode bitmap at 4 (+3)
 Inode table at 5-161 (+4)
 8018 free blocks, 1245 free inodes, 2 directories
 Free blocks: 175-8192
 Free inodes: 12-1256
Group 1: (Blocks 8193-9999)
 Backup Superblock at 8193, Group Descriptors at 8194-8194
 Block bitmap at 8195 (+2), Inode bitmap at 8196 (+3)
 Inode table at 8197-8353 (+4)
 1646 free blocks, 1256 free inodes, 0 directories
 Free blocks: 8354-9999
 Free inodes: 1257-2512
```

A *lot* of information is in the metadata for the file: Every conceivable bit of information about the file system is displayed. Most of it is of use only to file system developers, not system administrators. Match up the information shown with the file system characteristics presented previously in this chapter to get a better picture of how it all fits together and what can be useful to you.

You can use the -b option to display a list of the blocks that are marked as "bad" and use the -f option to force dumpe2fs to ignore any problems it might have with file system flags it can't read.

You can use the next two options in recovering lost data. The stressed out and desperate system administrator (that's you) would be the "file system wizard" referred to.

>   -ob *superblock*—Use a specific alternate superblock when examining the file system. This option
>   isn't usually needed except by a file system wizard who is examining the remains of a very badly
>   corrupted file system.

10

-oB *blocksize*—Use blocks of "blocksize" bytes when examining the file system. This option isn't usually needed except by a file system wizard who is examining the remains of a very badly corrupted file system.

Another program, debugfs, can be used to manipulate a file system as well as repair and recover a damaged file system. Because it is such a powerful command, it doesn't run by default with the capability to write any changes to the file system; that functionality must be explicitly enabled when the command is run. By entering the help command at the debugfs prompt, a menu of command options is displayed; the q command exits the program.

Mounting a Partition As Read-Only on a Running System

Remember that to do almost any kind of file system manipulation (formatting, checking, and so on), you should unmount the file system; by doing so, you avoid having any writes made to the file system, which would corrupt it.

How do you remount partitions on a running system? For example, to remount the /home partition (assuming that it's on a separate physical partition from root) as read-only to run fsck on it and then remount it as read-write, use the remount option for mount:

```
# mount -o ro,remount /home
```

> **NOTE**
>
> Remounting won't work if a normal user is logged in because /home will be busy (in use).

Now we can run fsck on the partition. When done,

```
# mount -o rw,remount /home
```

puts it back in service.

If you reboot your system to mount the root file system read-only for maintenance (enter the maintenance mode, s, as described in Chapter 7.

```
# mount -o rw,remount /
```

will remount it read-write and you can continue on. That's easier than unmounting and remounting the device.

Converting an Existing ext2 File System to ext3

An existing ext2 file system is easily converted to ext3 to take advantage of the benefits of journaling. After you convert an existing file system, any other operating system—including BeOS, Windows (with the appropriate drivers), and other UNIX systems that have drivers to access ext2 partitions—can access ext3 partitions. To those operating systems (and their drivers), your converted file system still looks just like an ext2 file system.

To begin the conversion to ext3, you use the tune2fs utility to add the journal to an existing ext2 file system. In this example, you are changing /dev/hda2, an already formatted ext2 partition.

```
# tune2fs -j /dev/hda2
```

It doesn't matter if hda2 is mounted or unmounted at the time of the migration; if it is mounted, you will see a new file, .journal, in the directory.

Next, edit the line for /dev/hda2 in /etc/fstab and change the value from ext2 to ext3. It will be mounted as an ext3 file system the next time you reboot.

> **NOTE**
>
> If you have decided to convert your root file system to take advantage of the benefits of the ext3 file system, bear in mind that you cannot run tune2fs -j on it while it's unmounted because you can't unmount the root file system. Because the file system is mounted when you run tune2fs -j, the .journal file on it will be visible when you finish the migration.
>
> When compiling a new kernel, make certain to include ext3 file system support in your new kernel by selecting that choice in your kernel configuration (see Chapter 24, "Kernel and Module Management"). Also, note that you do not need to perform the actions described in the next section if you have just freshly installed Fedora Core Linux.

Making an Initial Ramdisk

You need to create an initrd image file to load the ext3 driver and mount the root partition as an ext3 partition. The initrd file is an initial ramdisk that contains a small kernel and enough of the Linux OS to load drivers so that the real kernel and the rest of the operating system can load.

> **NOTE**
>
> If you forget to create the initrd file, your system will still boot, but it will mount the root partition as ext2. That's very clever—none of the other journaling file systems are as forgiving.

To create the file, run the mkinitrd utility before you reboot.

```
# mkinitrd /boot/initrd-2.6.7-1.478.img 2.6-7-1.478
```

The first argument is the name of the initrd file that will be placed in the /boot directory. The name can be anything; the name shown here follows the usual naming convention; you can find a number of other naming options in the mkinitrd man page. The second argument after the mkinitrd command is the version of the kernel you want to use. The value you enter here doesn't have to be the version you are currently using, but it must match the version you use when you boot (and the kernel must support ext3).

After you run the utility, edit /etc/lilo.conf or /boot/grub.conf to change the initrd loaded at boot time. Add the following line to the appropriate LILO stanza:

```
initrd=/boot/initrd-2.6.7-1.478.img
```

> **NOTE**
>
> LILO is no longer used in Fedora, but you may have it on an older system upgraded to Fedora.

Using GRUB, add the same line beneath the kernel line in the section that references your kernel.

```
initrd (hd0,0)/boot/initrd-2.6.7-1.478.img
```

Examine an initrd Image File

The initrd.img file is automatically created during the installation process (if necessary) or with the mkinitrd command. You never need to examine it, but if you are curious about what's in the initrd.img file, just take a look: It's really just a gzipped ext2 file system. To examine it, first copy it to the /tmp directory and add the .gz suffix to it:

```
# cp /boot/initrd-2.6.7-1.478.img /tmp/initrd-2.6.7-1.478.img.gz
```

If your system doesn't have an initrd.img file in /boot, mount your boot floppy and see if it has one. Next, uncompress it as follows:

```
# gunzip /tmp/initrd-2.6.7-1.478.img.gz
```

Mount it as follows:

```
# mount -o loop /tmp/initrd-2.6.7-1.478.img /mnt/image
```

and browse the directory to your heart's content.

Not every system will have an initrd.img file. It's typically used to load device drivers for file systems (such as Reiser) or hardware (such as the Promise RAID IDE controller) that must be in place before the system can continue booting. Some floppy-based Linux distributions use initrd.img to load a minimal operating system that can then uncompress and load the working file system from the floppy.

You can also mount .iso images in the same way, but remember that they are always read-only because of the nature of the underlying iso9660 file system; you can write to the other images unless you explicitly mount them as read-only. If you want to read and write to the files in an iso file system, you must first copy the files to a device that is mounted read-write, make your changes, and then use mkisofs to create a new .iso image. This is a common "gotcha" for many users.

Examine a Floppy Image File

The floppy boot images on the installation CD have different configurations to address special situations, as explained in their accompanying documentation. If you find the need to modify one for your unique situation or if you are curious to know what's in any of the boot floppy images that are on the install CD, mount the image using the mount command as follows:

```
# mount -o loop /image /mnt/image
```

Disk Tuning

Many Linux users love to tinker under the hood to increase the performance of their computers, and Linux gives you some great tools to do just that. Whereas Mom used to tell me, "Don't fix what's not broken," Dad always said, "Fix it until it breaks." In this section, you learn about many of the commands used to tune, or "tweak," your file system.

Before you undertake any "under the hood" work with Linux, however, keep a few points in mind. First, perform a benchmark on your system before you begin. Linux doesn't offer a well-developed benchmarking application, but availability changes rapidly. You can search online for the most up-to-date information for benchmarking applications for Linux. If you are a system administrator, you might choose to create your own bench-marking tests. Second, tweak only one thing at a time so that you can tell what works, what doesn't work, and what breaks. Some of these tweaks might not work or might lock up your machine.

Always have a working boot floppy handy and remember that you are personally assum-ing all risks for attempting any of these tweaks.

Using the BIOS and Kernel to Tune the Disk Drives

One method of tuning involves adjusting the settings in your BIOS. Because the BIOS is not Linux and every BIOS seems different, always read your motherboard manual for better possible settings and make certain that all the drives are detected correctly by the BIOS. Change only one setting at a time.

Linux does provide a limited means to interact with BIOS settings during the boot process (mostly overriding them). In this section, you will learn about those commands.

Other options are in the following list, and are more fully outlined in the BOOTPROMPT HOWTO and the kernel documentation. These commands can be used to force the IDE controllers and drives to be optimally configured. Of course, YMMV (Your Mileage May Vary) because these don't work for everyone.

ide*x*=dma—This will force DMA support to be turned on for the primary IDE bus, where *x*=0, or the secondary bus, where *x*=1.

ide*x*=autotune—This command will attempt to tune the interface for optimal performance.

ide*x*=ata66—If you have ATA66 drives and controllers, this command will enable support for it.

hd*x*=ide-scsi—This command will enable SCSI emulation of an IDE drive. This is required for some CD-RW drives to work properly in write mode and it might provide some performance improvements for regular CD-R drives as well.

idebus=*xx*—This can be any number from 20 to 66; autodetection is attempted, but this can set it manually if dmesg says that it isn't autodetected correctly or if you have it set in the BIOS to a different value (overclocked). Most PCI controllers will be happy with 33.

pci=biosirq—Some motherboards might cause Linux to generate an error message saying that you should use this. Look in dmesg for it; if you don't see it, you don't need to use it.

These options can be entered into /etc/lilo.conf or /boot/grub/grub.conf in the same way as other options are appended.

> **NOTE**
>
> Red Hat 9 introduced a new GUI utility to access the tunable kernel parameters. Although not yet fully fleshed out in Fedora Core, the Kernel Tuning utility (system-config-proc) provides a graphical interface to the /proc file system. When fully completed, this will permit full access to every tunable kernel parameter and provide online help about the available choices as well. Such on-the-fly changes to the /proc file system can be done manually with the sysctrl command as described in Chapter 24.

The hdparm **Command**

The hdparm utility can be used by root to set and tune the settings for IDE hard drives. You would do this to tune the drives for optimal performance.

Once a kernel patch and associated support programs, the hdparm program is now included with Fedora Core. You should only experiment with the drives mounted read-only because some settings can damage some file systems when used improperly. The hdparm command also works with CD-ROM drives and some SCSI drives.

The general format of the command is this:

```
# hdparm command device
```

The man entry for hdparm is extensive and contains useful detailed information, but since the kernel configuration selected by Fedora Core already attempts to optimize the drives, it might be that little can be gained through tweaking. Because not all hardware combinations can be anticipated by Fedora Core or by Linux and performance gains are always useful, you're encouraged to try.

> **TIP**
>
> You can use the hdparm command to produce a disk transfer speed result with
>
> `# hdparm -tT device`
>
> Be aware, however, that although the resulting numbers appear quantitative, they are subject to several technical qualifications beyond the scope of what is discussed and explained in this chapter. Simply put, don't accept values generated by hdparm as absolute numbers, but only as a relative measure of performance.

Systemwide tweaks to hdparm are formally handled through the /etc/sysconfig/harddisks files, but this file's use is poorly documented and, therefore, of little use.

> **TIP**
>
> If you recall from Chapter 7, the system turns off DMA for any CD-RW drives detected via a shell script command in rc.sysinit. This might not be appropriate for your hardware. You can turn it back on simply by adding the line options ide-cd dma=1 to /etc/modules.conf.

File System Tuning

Never content to leave things alone, Linux provides several tools to adjust and customize the file system settings. The belief is that hardware manufacturers and distribution creators tend to select conservation settings that will work well all the time, leaving some of the potential of your system leashed—that's why you have chosen Fedora Core Linux Unleashed to help you.

The Linux file system designers have done an excellent job of selecting default values used for file system creation and the 2.6 version of the Linux kernel now contains new code for the IDE subsystem that significantly improves I/O (imput/output) transfer speeds over older versions, obviating much of the need for special tweaking of the file system and drive parameters if you use IDE disks. Although these values work well for most users, some server applications of Linux benefit from file system tuning. As always, observe and benchmark your changes.

> **Synchronizing the File System with sync**
>
> Because Linux uses buffers when writing to devices, the write won't occur until the buffer is full, until the kernel tells it to, or if you tell it to by using the sync command. Traditionally, the command is given twice, as in the following:
>
> `# sync ; sync`

It's really overkill to do it twice. Still, it can be helpful prior to the unmounting of certain types of media with slow write speeds (such as some USB hard drives or PCMCIA storage media), but only because it delays the user from attempting to remove the media too soon, not because two syncs are better than one.

The mke2fs Command

mke2fs -O sparse_super will create a file system with sparse superblocks, reducing the space allocated to root for file system repair. This isn't a performance enhancement per se, but it will free up additional space on a drive. This command only works on pre-2.2 kernels and is included here because a number of existing references don't make that distinction. With kernel version 2.2, the sparse superblock option has been moved to tune2fs, and this feature is turned "on" by default, so you will always create any new file systems with sparse superblocks.

mke2fs -b blocksize will set the block size. The block size chosen can also have an effect on the performance of the file system. A larger block size works better with large files and vice versa. There doesn't seem to be any hard and fast rule about this, and most advice is to accept the default block size of 1,024KB unless you want to spend some time running benchmarks.

The tune2fs Command

With tune2fs, you can adjust the tunable file system parameters on an ext2 or ext3 file system. A few performance-related items of note are as follows:

To disable file system checking, the -c 0 option sets the maximal mount count to zero.

The interval between forced checks can be adjusted with the -I option.

The -m option will set the reserved blocks percentage with a lower value, freeing more space at the expense of fsck having less space to write any recovered files.

Decrease the number of superblocks to save space with the -O sparse_super option. (Modern file systems use this by default.) Always run e2fsck after you change this value.

More space can be freed with the -r option that sets the number of reserved (for root) blocks.

Note that most of these uses of tune2fs free up space on the drive at the expense of the capability of fsck to recover data. Unless you really need the space and can deal with the consequences, just accept the defaults; large drives are now relatively inexpensive.

The e2fsck Command

This utility checks an ext2/ext3 file system. Some useful arguments taken from man e2fsck are as follows:

-c—Checks for bad blocks and then marks them as bad.

-f—Forces checking on a clean file system.

-v—Verbose mode.

The badblocks Command

Although not a performance tuning program per se, the utility badblocks checks a (preferably) unmounted partition for bad blocks. It is not recommended that you run this command by itself, but rather allow it to be called by fsck. It should only be used directly if you specify the block size accurately—don't guess or assume anything.

The options available for badblocks are detailed in the man page. They allow for very low-level manipulation of the file system that is useful for data recovery by file system experts or for file system hacking, but are beyond the scope of this chapter and the average user.

The noatime Option for the mount Command

noatime is an option for /etc/fstab. When noatime is used, the system doesn't update inode access times on the referenced file system, which results in faster access if the files are frequently accessed and you aren't concerned about the last access time information. This is useful for a file system containing Usenet News archives or mp3 files, for example.

Managing Files for Character Devices, Block Devices, and Special Devices

For UNIX and Linux, *everything* is a file. In this section, you learn about special types of files found in Linux that represent all the devices found on your system and handle all the input and output on your system. You also learn how to identify and create them.

If you have installed the kernel documentation, it will contain a text file named /usr/src/linux-2.6/Documentation/devices.txt, an excerpt of which reads

```
3 char  Pseudo-TTY slaves
     0 = /dev/ttyp0     First PTY slave
     1 = /dev/ttyp1     Second PTY slave
    ...
   255 = /dev/ttyef   256th PTY slave

  These are the old-style (BSD) PTY devices; Unix98
  devices are on major 136 and above.

 block  First MFM, RLL and IDE hard disk/CD-ROM interface
     0 = /dev/hda       Master: whole disk (or CD-ROM)
    64 = /dev/hdb       Slave: whole disk (or CD-ROM)
```

10

```
For partitions, add to the whole disk device number:
  0 = /dev/hd?       Whole disk
  1 = /dev/hd?1      First partition
  2 = /dev/hd?2      Second partition
  ...
 63 = /dev/hd?63  63rd partition
```

```
For Linux/i386, partitions 1-4 are the primary
partitions, and 5 and above are logical partitions.
Other versions of Linux use partitioning schemes
appropriate to their respective architectures.
```

The number 3 at the upper left of the preceding listing represents the *major number* that identifies a class of device. In this case, major 3 identifies both character devices (Pseudo-TTY slaves) and block devices (IDE drives). The columns of numbers that follow under the device types are called the *minor numbers*; any device can be identified uniquely by its major and minor number. Linux uses these numbers internally; you usually see the name of the device as it is listed in the /dev directory. The major/minor numbers do show up in kernel error messages from time to time, and understanding the numbers helps you debug the problem. As you'll see in the next section, the mknod command needs to be told those numbers in order to create a device. Take some time to browse the entire file because it contains some interesting information that provides answers to many frequently asked questions.

The /dev directory contains all the special files known as device files. The files are placed in /dev during the original installation, and you can also create device files to go there if you need them.

During the normal operation of Linux, you never need to bother with the files in /dev, but if you want to look at all the files in /dev, use this command:

```
# ls -l --sort=none /dev | less
```

The --sort=none argument keeps the devices mostly grouped by major numbers for your viewing convenience; redirecting the output of the command (known as piping) through the less command allows you to use the PageUp and PageDown keys to navigate the long list rather than have it scroll off the screen. There are too many devices to list here, but they will all be either *block* or *character* devices.

A character device is a file that handles data one character at a time and processes data sequentially. Examples include TTY (display console) devices, SCSI tape drives, the keyboard, audio devices, the Coda network file system, among others.

Block devices are files that have a beginning, an end, and a fixed size; data can be written and read from anywhere inside them in any order. Because a block device can be much larger than the data it contains, utilities such as tar and cpio work with the files' data rather than the size, so they can store and retrieve the data directly off the block device rather than require a formatted file on a block device. (You can see how those commands are used in Chapter 11.) This works especially well with tape devices because they are character devices rather than block devices and aren't formatted in the way that block devices are formatted.

Special devices are block or character devices established for a special purpose. Two special devices of interest are

- /dev/null—This is the null device, also called the "bit bucket." Any output written to it is discarded. It is useful to redirect messages to it when you don't want them displayed on the standard output or written to a file. For example,

  ```
  $ ls 2> /dev/null
  ```

  will display the file listing to the screen, but will not display any error messages even though the ls command might generate one; we redirected the standard error messages (2>) to /dev/null. Almost all commands generate messages to the standard output and standard error when run, and sometimes, as when running a script, it is useful to not see the messages.

- /dev/zero—This device has an inexhaustible supply of zeros; use all you want—it makes more. It's very useful for writing strings of zeros to a device or file, such as when preparing an image of a file system (perhaps to be copied onto compact flash or other media).

Naming Conventions Used for Block and Character Devices

The traditional naming system for block and character devices has been in use for a while. In /usr/src/linux-2.6/Documentation/devices.txt, the device name for the first partition of the first IDE disk would be /dev/hda1. If it were a SCSI disk, it would be /dev/sda1 (shown elsewhere in devices.txt file).

All device names are included in devices.txt, and all the devices that have been created on your system are listed in the /dev directory. That directory also can hold links; for example, /dev/cdrom can actually be a link back to the actual device that is your CD-ROM (perhaps /dev/hdc? or /dev/scd0?). /dev/mouse and /dev/modem are commonly used symbolic links in the /dev directory.

Using mknod to Create Devices

If you need a device file in /dev that's not already there for some reason, you can create the special file with the mknod command. You might have noticed that /dev lists devices that you don't have. That's because the device's listing must appear in /dev before the system can use the actual device; if you install the hardware at some point in the future, the system won't create the device files on-the-fly. So, if you're preparing to install a

10

device, and you check /dev but find that it doesn't contain the device's file, you can create the file with mknod.

Creating files with mknod is a straightforward process as long as you know what type of device you are creating the file for and what the device's major and minor numbers are.

The syntax of mknod is

```
# mknod [OPTION].. NAME TYPE [MAJOR MINOR]
```

The useful option -m allows you to set the mode at file creation instead of doing it separately with the chmod command.

You can obtain the values for NAME, TYPE, MAJOR, and MINOR from devices.txt, which even has a block of experimental numbers if you are inclined to experiment.

The Device File System—devfs

An alternative device file system known as the Device File System (devfs) will soon come into common use in Linux. It only has entries for devices that you have attached to your system, and the naming convention is different from the traditional system. It can be used in tandem with the traditional system. Although Fedora Core supports devfs in the kernel sources, it is not enabled by default because Red Hat does not yet believe it is stable for Enterprise use.

Naming conventions are different with devfs. For example, /dev/hda1 is named /dev/ide/hd/c0b0t0u0p1 and is a symbolic link to /dev/ide/host0/bus0/target0/lun0/part1.

The Device File System is similar to the /proc file system in that it is a virtual file system; the devices exist in memory and not as actual files on the drive.

Why use devfs? There are some limitations to the use of major and minor numbers (128 maximum are available), which is why H. Peter Anvin maintains devices.txt, and access to new device numbers is limited. The address space could be enlarged, but this creates some performance issues. It also gets around the requirement that the /dev directory be on the root file system, making read-only root file systems difficult to use. You can't share a root file system using NFS, and you can't embed it in a ROM file system. The workaround requires creating a ramdisk and copying the contents of /dev there.

Non-UNIX file systems can't be mounted as the root file system because they don't support the special characteristics of UNIX file systems. devfs can solve these types of problems and provide even more flexibility to Linux. FreeBSD, BeOS, Plan9, and QNX use devfs; so it's not a new concept, just new to Linux.

For additional details, read the Linux DEVFS FAQ at http://www.atnf.csiro.au/~rgooch/linux/docs/devfs.html.

Relevant Fedora Core and Linux Commands

You use these commands when managing file systems in Fedora Core Linux:

df—Shows free disk space

du—Displays disk usage

dump—An ext2 file system backup utility

dumpe2fs—Shows information about an ext2 file system

e2fsadm—Administers an LVM/ext2 file system

e2image—Creates an image file of ext2 file system data

fdisk—The standard Linux partition table editor

fsck—Checks or repairs a file system

lsraid—Displays information about Linux RAID devices

mformat—Formats a DOS floppy disk; part of the Mtools suite of tools

mkfs—Creates various file systems and acts as a wrapper for the actual programs that do the work

mkisofs—Creates a CD-ROM file system in iso960 format

mkreiserfs—Creates a Linux reiserfs file system

mkswap—Prepares a Linux swap device

mount—Mounts a supported file system

parted—The GNU partition editor and resizing utility

reiserfsck—Checks a Linux reiserfs file system

resize_reiserfs—Resizes a Linux reiserfs file system

smbmount—Mounts an smbfs file system

stat—Shows file or file system status

swapon—Displays swap usage or start using system swap device

swapoff—Turns off swap usage

sync—Flushes file system buffers

tune2fs—Changes file system parameters on ext2 file systems

umount—Unmounts a file systems

usermount—The Fedora Core graphical file system mounting and formatting tool

Reference

http://www.ibiblio.org/pub/Linux/docs/HOWTO/other-formats/html_single/ File Systems-HOWTO.html—In the File Systems HOWTO, you'll find extensive information on native Linux file systems, as well as more exotic file systems.

http://www.ibiblio.org/pub/Linux/docs/HOWTO/other-formats/html_single/ Partition.html—A great deal of detailed information is contained in the Linux Partition HOWTO on partitions and their requirements.

http://batleth.sapienti-sat.org/projects/FAQs/ext3-faq.html—The Linux ext3 FAQ is an unofficial FAQ with some useful info, especially for converting an ext3 partition back to ext2.

10

`http://www.ibiblio.org/pub/Linux/docs/HOWTO/other-formats/html_single/`
`Ext2fs-Undeletion.html`—You deleted a file on your ext2/3 partition? The Linux Ext2fs Undeletion mini HOWTO is there to help you out, as is Chapter 11 of this book.

`http://www.ibiblio.org/pub/Linux/docs/HOWTO/other-formats/html_single/`
`Ext2fs-Undeletion-Dir-Struct.html`—You deleted a directory on your ext2/3 partition? Read the Ext2fs Undeletion of Directory Structures HOWTO to see how to rescue your data.

`http://www.ibiblio.org/pub/Linux/docs/HOWTO/other-formats/html_single/`
`Loopback-Root-FS.html`—Here's the concept: Not only can we have a traditional file system, but also we can have a file system inside a large file located on some other file system. The Loopback Root File System HOWTO examines how this is done.

`http://www.ibiblio.org/pub/Linux/docs/HOWTO/other-formats/html_single/`
`Loopback-Encrypted-File System-HOWTO.html`—You can use the loopback device to mount an encrypted file system, for example /home, for security reasons.

`http://www.ibiblio.org/pub/Linux/docs/HOWTO/other-formats/html_single/`
`LVM-HOWTO.html`—Throw away those concepts that marry physical disks to finite-sized file systems; the Logical Volume Manager HOWTO explains how to overcome that kind of restrictive thinking.

`http://linux.org.mt/article/lvm`—A good overview and discussion of Logical Volume Managers.

`http://www.coda.cs.cmu.edu/`—The Coda network file system homepage.

`http://www.inter-mezzo.org/`—The InterMezzo network file system homepage.

`http://www.math.ualberta.ca/imaging/snfs/`—Secure NFS via an SSH Tunnel is a very interesting attempt to address a security shortcoming of NFS over a public network.

`http://www.ibiblio.org/pub/Linux/docs/HOWTO/other-formats/html_single/`
`UMSDOS-HOWTO.html`—If you are interested in using the umsdos file system, the UMSDOS HOWTO provides ample information to you.

`http://www.ibiblio.org/pub/Linux/docs/HOWTO/other-formats/html_single/`
`NFS-Root.html`—The NFS-Root mini HOWTO.

`http://www.ibiblio.org/pub/Linux/docs/HOWTO/other-formats/html_single/`
`NFS-Root-Client-mini-HOWTO.html`—Explains in detail how to set up and use NFS for exporting root file systems.

`http://www.ibiblio.org/pub/Linux/docs/HOWTO/other-formats/html_single/`
`Multi-Disk-HOWTO.html`—The Multi Disk System Tuning HOWTO contains explanations of the drive and controller hardware that are useful, as well as discussion of file systems. It offers an interesting section on optimizing multidisk setups.

http://www.ibiblio.org/pub/Linux/docs/HOWTO/other-formats/html_single/ Software-RAID-HOWTO.html—The Software-RAID HOWTO is an excellent tour de force of software RAID.

http://www.ibiblio.org/pub/Linux/docs/HOWTO/other-formats/html_single/ Tips-HOWTO.html—The Linux Tips HOWTO provides some useful tips that make it worth the time to read because it addresses some file system problems such as "Is there enough free space?" and "How do I move directories between file systems?"

http://www.ibiblio.org/pub/Linux/docs/HOWTO/other-formats/html_single/ Large-Disk-HOWTO.html—Still unsure about drive geometry, the limits to LILO and GRUB, and those very large disks? The Large Disk HOWTO goes into useful detail about that. It also tells you how to handle disks that use disk managers such as OnTrack and EZ_Drive.

http://www.ibiblio.org/pub/Linux/docs/HOWTO/other-formats/html_single/ BootPrompt-HOWTO.html—The BootPrompt HOWTO informs you of boot time arguments that can be passed to the kernel to deal with misbehaving hardware, configure non-PNP devices, and so on.

http://www.atnf.csiro.au/~rgooch/linux/docs/devfs.html—It's coming. It's a new technology to Linux, and you should start to learn about it from the Linux Devfs (Device File System) FAQ.

http://www.namesys.com/—Details about the improvements in reiserfs and the release of Reiser4 (see http://www.namesys.com/v4/v4.html).

http://www.linux-usb.org/USB-guide/x498.html—The USB Guide for mass storage and other USB devices. If you have a USB device and need to know if it's supported and how to access it, check here. (Tip: USB storage devices are emulated as SCSI devices.)

http://www.coker.com.au/bonnie++/—The homepage of bonnie, a disk benchmarking tool. It also contains a link to RAID benchmarking utilities and Postal, a benchmarking utility for SMTP servers.

CHAPTER **11**

Backing Up, Restoring, and Recovery

IN THIS CHAPTER

• Choosing a Backup Strategy

• Choosing Backup Hardware and Media

• Using Backup Software

• Copying Files

• Undeleting Files

• System Rescue

• Reference

This chapter examines the practice of safeguarding data through backups, restoring that same data if necessary, and recovering data in case of a catastrophic hardware or software failure. After reading this chapter, you'll have a full understanding of the reasons for sound backup practices. You can use the information in this chapter to make intelligent choices about which strategies are best for you. The chapter also shows you how to perform some types of data recovery and system restoration on your own and when to seek professional assistance.

Choosing a Backup Strategy

Backups are always trade-offs. Any backup will consume time, money, and effort on an ongoing basis; backups must be monitored, validated, indexed, stored, and new media continuously purchased. Sound expensive? The cost of not having backups is the loss of your critical data. Re-creating the data from scratch will cost time and money, and if the cost of doing it all again is greater than the cost associated with backing up, you should be performing backups. At the where-the-rubber-meets-the-road level, backups are nothing more than insurance against financial loss for you or your business.

Your first step in formulating and learning to use an effective backup strategy is to choose the strategy that's right for you. First, you must understand some of the most common (and not so common) causes of data loss so that you're better able to understand the threats your system faces. Then, you need to assess your own system, how it's used and by whom, your available hardware and software resources, and your budget constraints. The following sections look at each of these issues in detail, as well as offering some sample backup systems and discussing their use.

Why Data Loss Occurs

Files disappear for any number of reasons: They can be lost because the hardware fails and causes data loss; your attention might wander and you accidentally delete or overwrite a file. Some data loss occurs as a result of natural disasters and other circumstances beyond your control. A tornado, flood, or earthquake could strike, the water pipes could burst, or the building could catch on fire. Your data, as well as the hardware, would likely be destroyed in such a disaster. A disgruntled employee might destroy files or hardware in an attempt at retribution. And any equipment might fail, and it all will fail at some time—most likely when it is extremely important for it not to fail.

> **A CASE IN POINT**
>
> A recent Harris poll of Fortune 500 executives found that roughly two thirds of them had problems with their backups and disaster-recovery plans. How about you?

Data can also be lost because of malfunctions that corrupt the data as it attempts to write to the disk. Other applications, utilities, and drivers might be poorly written, buggy (the phrase most often heard is "still beta quality"), or might suffer some corruption and fail to correctly write that all-important data you have just created. If that happened, the contents of your data file would be indecipherable garbage of no use to anyone.

All of these accidents and disasters offer important reasons for having a good backup strategy; however, the most frequent cause of data loss is human error. Who among us hasn't overwritten a new file with an older version or unintentionally deleted a needed file? This applies not only to data files, but also to configuration files and binaries. While perusing the mail lists or the Usenet newsgroup postings, stories about deleting entire directories such as /home, /usr, or /lib seem all too common. Incorrectly changing a configuration file and not saving the original in case it has to be restored (which it does more often than not because the person reconfigured it incorrectly) is another common error.

> **TIP**
>
> To make a backup of a configuration file you are about to edit, use the cp command:
>
> ```
> $ cp filename filname.original
> ```
>
> And to restore it,
>
> ```
> $ cp filename.original filename
> ```
>
> Never edit or move the *.original file, or the original copy will be lost. If it is, you can extract the configuration files from an .rpm file to at least provide the out-of-the-box configuration; Chapter 8, "Managing Software and System Resources," explains how to do that.

Proper backups can help you recover from these problems with a minimum of hassle, but you have to put in the effort to keep backups current, verify their intactness, and practice restoring the data in different disaster scenarios.

Assessing Your Backup Needs and Resources

By now you have realized that some kind of plan is needed to safeguard your data, and, like most people, you are overwhelmed by the prospect. Entire books, as well as countless articles and whitepapers, have been written on the subject of backing up and restoring data. What makes the topic so complex is that each solution is truly individual.

Yet, the proper approach to making the decision is very straightforward. You start the process by asking

- What data must be safeguarded?

- How often does the data change?

The answers to these two questions determine how important the data is, determine the volume of the data, and determine the frequency of the backups. This in turn will determine the backup medium. Only then can the software be selected that will accommodate all these considerations. (You learn about choosing backup software, hardware, and media later in this chapter.)

Available resources are another important consideration when selecting a backup strategy. Backups require time, money, and personnel. Begin your planning activities by determining what limitations you face for all of these resources. Then, construct your plan to fit those limitations, or be prepared to justify the need for more resources with a careful assessment of both backup needs and costs.

> **TIP**
>
> If you aren't willing or capable of assessing your backup needs and choosing a backup solution, there exists a legion of consultants, hardware vendors, and software vendors who would love to assist you. The best way to choose one is to query other UNIX and Linux system administrators (located through user groups, discussion groups, or mail lists) who are willing to share their experiences and make recommendations. If you can't get a referral, ask the consultant for references and check them out.

Many people also fail to consider the element of time when formulating their plan. Some backup devices are faster than others, and some recovery methods are faster than others. You need to consider that when making choices.

It's a good idea to examine incidents of data loss in the past and decide if your chosen scheme will adequately address that loss. Finally, examine what effect a total disaster might have. In each case, ask yourself: What data am I protecting? How will it be safe?

How will it be restored, and how long will that take? The answers to all these questions should help you form your plan.

To formulate your backup plan, you need to determine the frequency of backups. The necessary frequency of backups should be determined by how quickly the important data on your system changes. On a home system, most files never change, a few change daily, and some change weekly. No elaborate strategy needs to be created to deal with that. A good strategy for home use is to back up (to any kind of removable media) critical data frequently and back up configuration and other files weekly.

At the enterprise level on a larger system with multiple users, a different approach is called for. Some critical data is changing constantly, and it could be expensive to re-create; this typically involves elaborate and expensive solutions. Most of us exist somewhere in between these extremes. Assess your system and its use to determine where you fall in this spectrum.

Backup schemes and hardware can be elaborate or simple, but they all require a workable plan and faithful follow-through. Even the best backup plan is useless if the process isn't carried out, data isn't verified, and data restoration isn't practiced on a regular basis. Whatever backup scheme you choose, be sure to incorporate in it these three principles:

- **Have a Plan**—Design a plan that is right for your needs and have equipment appropriate to the task. This involves assessing all the factors that affect the data you're backing up. We'll get into more detail later in the chapter.

- **Follow the Plan**—Faithfully complete each part of your backup strategy, and then verify the data stored in the backups. Backups with corrupt data are of no use to anyone. Even backup operations can go wrong.

- **Practice Your Skills**—Practice restoring data from your backup systems, so when the time comes, you're ready (and able) to benefit from the strength of your backup plan. (For restoring data, see the section "Using Backup Software.")

NOTE

If you are a system administrator serving other users (as opposed to being both the system administrator and the sole user), your insistence on following system policies and adhering to backup procedures might make you the object of cruel jokes or cause you to be shunned at the office holiday party. However, when you recover a file for those same people, you will become their best friend (for the moment, at least).

Sound Practices

You have to create your own best-backup plan, but here are some building blocks that go into the foundation of any sound backup program:

- Maintain more than one copy of critical data.
- Label the backups.

- Store the backups in a climate-controlled and secure area.
- Use secure, offsite storage of critical data.
- Establish a backup policy that makes sense and can be followed religiously.
- Routinely verify backups and practice restoring data from them.
- Routinely inspect backup media for defects and regularly replace them (after destroying the data on them if it is sensitive).

Evaluating Backup Strategies

Now that you're convinced you need backups, you need a strategy. It's difficult to be specific about an ideal strategy because each user or administrator's strategy will be highly individualized, but here are a few general examples:

- **Home User**—At home, the user has the Fedora Core installation CDs that take an hour or so to reinstall, so the time issue is not a major concern. The home user will want to back up any configuration files that have altered, keep an archive of any files that have been downloaded, and keep an archive of any data files created while using any applications. Unless the home user has a special project (such as writing this book) in which constant backups are useful, a weekly backup is adequate. The home user will likely use a floppy disk, CD-RW drive, or other removable media for backups.

- **Small Office**—Many small offices tend to use the same strategy as the Home User, but are more likely to back up critical data daily and use manually changed tape drives. If they have a tape drive with adequate storage, they will likely have a full system backup as well because restoring from the tape is quicker than reinstalling from the CDs. They also might be using CD-RW or DVD writers for backups. Although they will use scripts to automate backups, most of it is probably done by hand.

- **Small Enterprise**—Here is where backups begin to require higher-end equipment such as autoloading tape drives with fully automated backups. Commercial backup software usually makes an introduction at this level, but a skillful system administrator on a budget can use one of the basic applications discussed in this chapter. Backups are highly structured and supervised by a dedicated system administrator.

- **Large Enterprise**—These are the most likely settings for the use of expensive, proprietary, highly automated backup solutions. At this level, data means money, lost data means lost money, and delays in restoring data mean money lost as well. These system administrators know that backups are necessary insurance and plan accordingly.

Does all this mean that Enterprise-level backups are better than those done by a Home User? Not at all. The "little guy" with Fedora Core Linux can do just as well as the

Enterprise operation at the expense of investing more time in the process. By examining the higher-end strategies, we can apply useful concepts across the board.

> **NOTE**
>
> If you are a new sysadmin, you might be inheriting an existing backup strategy. Take some time to examine it and see if it meets the current needs of the organization. Think about what backup protection your organization really needs, and determine if the current strategy meets that need. If it doesn't, change the strategy. Consider whether the current policy is being practiced by the users, and, if not, why it is not.

> **Backup Levels**
>
> UNIX uses the concept of backup levels as a shorthand way of referring to how much data is backed up in relation to a previous backup. It works this way:
>
> A level 0 backup is a full backup. The next backup level would be 1.
>
> Backups at the other numbered levels will back up everything that has changed since the last backup at that level or a numerically higher level (the dump command, for example, offers 10 different backup levels). For example, a level 3 followed by a level 4 will generate an incremental backup from the full backup, whereas a level 4 followed by a level 3 will generate a differential backup between the two.

The following sections examine a few of the many strategies in use today. Many strategies are based on these sample schemes; one of them can serve as a foundation for the strategy you construct for your own system.

Simple Strategy

If you need to back up just a few configuration files and some small data files, copy them to a floppy disk, engage the write-protect tab, and keep it someplace safe. If you need just a bit more backup storage capacity, you can copy the important files to a Zip disk (100,250 and 750MB in size), CD-RW disk (up to 700MB in size), or DVD-R disk (up to 4.4GB for data).

In addition to configuration and data files, you should archive each user's home directory, as well as the entire /etc directory. Between the two, that backup would contain most of the important files for a small system. Then, you can easily restore this data from the backup media device you've chosen, after a complete reinstall of Fedora Core Linux, if necessary.

Experts believe that if you've more data than can fit on a floppy disk, you really need a formal backup strategy. Some of those are discussed in the following sections. We use a tape media backup as an example.

Full Backup on a Periodic Basis

This backup strategy involves a backup of the complete file system on a weekly, biweekly, or other periodic basis. The frequency of the backup depends on the amount of data being backed up, the frequency of changes to the data, and the cost of losing those changes.

This backup strategy isn't complicated to perform, and it can be accomplished with the swappable disk drives discussed later in the chapter. If you are connected to a network, it is possible to mirror the data on another machine (preferably offsite); the rsync tool is particularly well suited to this task. Recognize that this doesn't address the need for archives of the recent state of files; it only presents a snapshot of the system at the time the update is done.

Full Backups with Incremental Backups

This scheme involves performing a full backup of the entire system once a week, along with a daily incremental backup of only those files that have changed in the previous day, and it begins to resemble what a sysadmin of a medium to large system would traditionally use.

This backup scheme can be advanced in two ways. In one way, each incremental backup can be made with reference to the original full backup. In other words, a level 0 backup is followed by a series of level 1 backups. The benefit of this backup scheme is that a restoration requires only two tapes (the full backup and the most recent incremental backup). But because it references the full backup, each incremental backup might be large (and grow ever larger) on a heavily used system.

Alternatively, each incremental backup could reference the previous incremental backup. This would be a level 0 backup followed by a level 1, followed by a level 2, and so on. Incremental backups are quicker (less data each time), but require every tape to restore a full system. Again, it is a classic trade-off decision.

You might need to retrieve the version of a file from six days ago or a file that was deleted last week. Such requests from users are not uncommon or unreasonable, and you need to be prepared to meet their needs.

Modern commercial backup applications such as Amanda or BRU assist in organizing the process of managing complex backup schedules and tracking backup media. Doing it yourself using the classic dump or employing shell scripts to run the tar, pax, or cpio applications requires that the system administrator handle all the organization herself. For this reason, complex backup situations are typically handled with commercial software and specialized hardware that are packaged, sold, and supported by vendors.

Mirroring Data or RAID Arrays

Given adequate (and often expensive) hardware resources, you can always mirror the data somewhere else, essentially maintaining a real-time copy of your data on hand. This is often a cheap, workable solution if no large amounts of data are involved. The use of RAID arrays (in some of their incarnations—see Chapter 10, "Managing the File System," for more information on RAID) provides for a recovery if a disk fails.

Note that RAID arrays and mirroring systems will just as happily write corrupt data as valid data. Moreover, if a file is deleted, a RAID array won't save it. RAID arrays are best suited for protecting the current state of a running system, not for backup needs.

Making the Choice

Only you can decide what is best for your situation. After reading about the backup options in this book, put together some sample backup plans; run through a few likely scenarios and assess the effectiveness of your choice.

In addition to all the other information you've learned about backup strategies, here are a couple of good rules of thumb to remember when making your choice:

- If the backup strategy and policy is too complicated (and this holds true for most security issues), it will eventually be disregarded and fall into disuse.

- The best scheme is often a combination of strategies; use what works.

Choosing Backup Hardware and Media

Any device that can store data can be used to back it up, but that's like saying that anything with wheels can take you on a cross-country trip. Trying to fit a megabyte worth of data on a stack of 1.4MB floppy disks is an exercise in frustration, and using a $5,000 automated tape device to save a single copy of an email is a waste of resources.

Many people use what hardware they already have for their backup operations. Many consumer grade workstations have a floppy drive and possibly a CD-RW drive, but they typically don't have the abundant free disk space necessary for performing and storing multiple full backups.

In this section, you learn about some of the most common backup hardware available and how to evaluate its appropriateness for your backup needs. With large storage devices becoming increasingly affordable (160GB IDE drives can be had for around $100) and prices falling on DVD recorders, decisions about backup hardware for the small business and home users has become more interesting.

Removable Storage Media

At one time, every computer came with a floppy drive, but those drives are becoming less common and are no longer being provided as standard equipment with many new computers. Some sysadmins remove them because they can be used as a means of penetrating system security. (Remember that physical access to a machine means that it is insecure; a floppy drive provides a way to bypass the system administrator to load and run malicious programs.) Many modern laptops do not provide floppy drives except as an option.

Floppy drives are cheap and disposable solutions for making simple, quick backups of a few files by the user, but the media are easily damaged, lost, and accidentally overwritten. They also unexpectedly fail at times. Floppies now represent the low-rent district for data storage.

Zip Drives

You can use removable or portable drives as part of your backup strategy. Of all the removable hard drive manufacturers, Iomega seems to have acquired some staying power with its Zip (100, 250, and 750MB) drive. Although these drives have good support in Fedora Core Linux, in the past they have been plagued with mechanical problems that have rendered data irretrievable. Their reliability has improved, but shy away from any older drives. These drives have been ubiquitous and are common in the publishing industry. They are now less frequently encountered and are being supplanted by CD writers.

USB and Solid-State Drives

USB hard drives and solid-state "pen" drives are the new kids on the block with prices dropping over the last year or two; a 64MB "pen" drive costs slightly less than $30 and capacities up to 2GB are available for around $500. USB drives have a large capacity for their size. (Sandisks, also known as Compact Flash devices, are typically small, though sizes up to 1GB are available if you are wealthy enough to afford them.) Both USB hard drives and solid-state drives are highly portable. Support for these drives under Fedora Core Linux is very good, accommodating these drives by emulating them as SCSI drives. (The system sees them usually as /dev/scd1.) Watch for improved support and ever falling prices in the future. The newer USB 2.0 hard drives are significantly faster than the older USB 1.0 hard drives. A 100GB USB hard drive will cost about $150. The biggest benefits of USB drives are data transfer speed and portability.

FireWire Drives

FireWire (IEEE1394) hard drives are similar to USB drives; they just use a different interface to your computer. Many digital cameras and portable mp3 players use FireWire. Kernel support is available if you have this hardware; a 100GB FireWire drive will cost about $180, roughly twice IDE drive prices. Found mostly on the Mac, controller and drive hardware exists for the PC platform as well.

CD-RW and DVD+RW/-RW Drives

Compared to floppy drives and some removable drives, CD-RW drives and their cousins, DVD+RW/-RW drives, can store large amounts of data and are useful for a home or small business. Once very expensive, CD burners and media are relatively inexpensive today, although automated CD changing machines, necessary for automatically backing up large amounts of data, are still quite costly. A benefit of CD and DVD storage over tape devices is that the archived uncompressed file system can be mounted and its files accessed randomly just like a hard drive (you do this when you create a data CD, see Chapter 26, "Multimedia Applications"), making the recovery of individual files easier.

Each CD-RW disk can hold 650MB to 700MB of data (the media comes in both capacities at roughly the same cost); larger chunks of data can be split to fit on multiple disks. Some backup programs support this method of storage. Once burned and verified, the shelf life for the media is at least a decade or longer. Prices increase with writing speed, but a serviceable CD-RW drive can be purchased for less than $100.

DVD+RW/-RW is similar to CD-RW, but it is more expensive and can store up to 4.4GB of uncompressed data per disk. These drives are selling for less than $100. Writing to DVD drives requires special software, and, unfortunately, Linux development is somewhat behind the curve for DVD writing. Fedora Core does provide the latest software to write to DVD+RW drives. (DVD-RW support is still experimental.)

Network Storage

For network backup storage, remote arrays of hard drives provide one solution to data storage. With the declining cost of mass storage devices and the increasing need for larger storage space, network storage (NAS, or Network Attached Storage) is available and supported in Linux. These are cabinets full of hard drives and their associated controlling circuitry, as well as special software to manage all of it. These NAS systems are connected to the network and act as a huge (and expensive) mass storage device.

More modest and simple network storage can be done on a remote desktop-style machine that has adequate storage space (up to eight 160GB IDE drives is a lot of storage space, easily accomplished with off-the-shelf parts), but then that machine (and the local system administrator) has to deal with all the problems of backing up, preserving, and restoring its own data, doesn't it? Several hardware vendors offer such products in varying sizes.

Tape Drive Backup

Tape drives have been used in the computer industry from the beginning. Tape drive storage has been so prevalent in the industry that the `tar` command (the most commonly used command for archiving) is derived from the words Tape ARchive. Modern tape drives use tape cartridges that can hold 70GB of data (or more in compressed format). Capacities and durability of tapes vary from type to type and range from a few gigabytes to hundreds of gigabytes with commensurate increases in cost for the equipment and media. Autoloading tape-drive systems can accommodate archives that exceed the capacity of the file systems.

> **TIP**
>
> Older tape equipment is often available in the used equipment market and might be useful for smaller operations that have outgrown more limited backup device options.

Tape equipment is well supported in Linux and, when properly maintained, is extremely reliable. The tapes themselves are inexpensive, given their storage capacity and the ability to reuse them. Be aware, however, that tapes do deteriorate over time and, being mechanical, tape drives can and will fail.

> **CAUTION**
>
> Neglecting to clean, align, and maintain tape drives puts your data at risk. The tapes themselves are also susceptible to mechanical wear and degradation. Hardware maintenance is part of a good backup policy. Don't ever forget that it's a question of when—not if—hardware will fail.

Using Backup Software

Because there are thousands of unique situations requiring as many unique backup solutions, it comes as no surprise that Linux offers many backup tools. Fedora Core provides the classic command-line backup software tar, dump, and cpio. The following sections discuss each of those tools and examine how dd and cp commands can be used to copy files. (Those copies can be considered backups if you store them safely.) Fedora Core provides a graphical interface for tar named Kdat that exploits the KDE desktop's drag-and-drop functionality. Fedora Core Linux also provides a graphical archiving tool, File Roller, that can create and extract files from archives. Finally, Fedora Core provides support for the Amanda backup application—a sophisticated backup application that works well over network connections and can be configured to automatically back up all the computers on your network. Amanda works with drives as well as tapes. The book *Unix Backup and Recovery* by W. Curtis Preston includes a whole chapter on setting up and using Amanda, and this chapter is available online at http://www.backupcentral.com/amanda.html.

> **NOTE**
>
> The software in a backup system must support the hardware, and this relationship can determine which hardware or software choices you make. Many sysadmins choose a particular backup software not because they prefer it to other options, but because it supports the hardware they own.
>
> The price seems right for free backup tools, but consider the software's ease of use and automation when assessing costs. If you must spend several hours implementing, debugging, documenting, and otherwise dealing with overly elaborate automation scripts, the real costs go up.

tar

The tar tool, the bewhiskered old man of archiving utilities, is installed by default. It is an excellent application (these kinds of applications are also sometimes referred to as a tool, or a utility) for saving entire directories full of files. For example, here's the command used to back up the /etc directory:

```
# tar cvf etc.tar /etc
```

Here, the options use tar to create an archive, be verbose in the message output, and use the filename etc.tar as the archive name for the contents of the directory /etc.

> **NOTE**
>
> Historically, tar has been shunned because it could not back up device files; that is no longer true with GNUtar, the GNU version of tar that Fedora Core provides. GNUtar also handles gzip and bzip compression that UNIX tar could not. Don't listen to the old UNIX hackers who warn you away from tar.

Alternatively, if the output of `tar` is sent to the standard output and redirected to a file, the command appears as follows:

```
# tar cv /etc > etc.tar
```

and the result is the same.

All files in the `/etc` directory will be saved to a file named `etc.tar`. With an impressive array of options (see the `man` page), `tar` is quite flexible and powerful in combination with shell scripts. With the `-z` option, it can even create and restore `gzip` compressed archives while the `-j` option works with `bziped` files.

> **TIP**
>
> Do you have backup tapes made with MTF that you would like to extract a file from? The Microsoft Tape Format is used to back up Windows NT files and can be read with a Linux utility named `mtf`.
>
> This Linux program works with SCSI tape drives. Software compression and archives that span tapes are not yet supported. Download the source code from `http://www.layton-graphics.com/mtf/`.

Creating Full and Incremental Backups with `tar`

If you want to create a full backup,

```
# tar cjvf fullbackup.tar.bz2 /
```

will create a `bzip2` compressed tarball (the `j` option) of the entire system.

To perform an incremental backup, you must locate all the files that have been changed since the last backup. (For simplicity, assume that you do incremental backups on a daily basis.) To locate the files, use the `find` command:

```
# find / -newer name_of_last_backup_file ! -a -type f -print
```

When run alone, `find` will generate a list of files systemwide and print it to the screen. The `! -a -type` eliminates everything but regular files from the list; otherwise, the entire directory would be sent to `tar` even if the contents weren't all changed.

Pipe the output of our `find` command to `tar` as follows:

```
# find / -newer name_of_last_backup_file ! -type d -print |\
 tar czT - backup_file_name_or_device_name
```

Here, the `T -` option gets the filenames from a buffer (where the `-` is the shorthand name for the buffer).

> **NOTE**
>
> The `tar` command can back up to a raw device (one with no file system) as well as a formatted partition. For example,
>
> ```
> # tar cvzf /dev/hdd  /boot  /etc /home
> ```
>
> backs up those directories to device `/dev/hdd` (not `/dev/hda1`, but to the unformatted device itself).
>
> The `tar` command can also back up over multiple floppy disks:
>
> ```
> # tar czvMf /dev/fd0 /home
> ```
>
> will back up the contents of `/home` and spread the file out over multiple floppies, prompting you with this message:
>
> ```
> Prepare volume #2 for `/dev/fd0' and hit return:
> ```

Restoring Files from an Archive with `tar`

The xp option in `tar` will restore the files from a backup and preserve the file attributes as well, and `tar` will create any subdirectories it needs. Be careful when using this option because the backups might have been created with either relative or absolute paths. You should use the `tvf` option with `tar` to list the files in the archive before extracting them so that you'll know where they will be placed.

For example, to restore a `tar` archive compressed with `bzip2`,

```
# tar xjvf fedoratest.tar.bz2
```

To list the contents of a `tar` archive compressed with `bzip2`,

```
# tar tjvf fedoratest.tar.bz2
drwxrwxr-x hoyt/hoyt          0 2003-09-04 18:15:05 fedoratest/
-rw-rw-r-- hoyt/hoyt        163 2003-09-03 22:30:49
                            ➥fedoratest/fedora_screenshots.txt
-rw-rw-r-- hoyt/hoyt        840 2003-09-01 19:27:59
                            ➥fedoratest/fedora_guideline.txt
-rw-rw-r-- hoyt/hoyt       1485 2003-09-01 18:14:23 fedoratest/style-sheet.txt
-rw-rw-r-- hoyt/hoyt        931 2003-09-01 19:02:00 fedoratest/fedora_TOC.txt
```

Note that because the pathnames don't start with a backslash, they are relative pathnames and will install in you current working directory. If they were absolute pathnames, they would install exactly where the paths state.

Backing Up Files with `cpio`

The `cpio` tool (installed by default) is great for saving individual files scattered throughout a file system as opposed to all the files that are located in a single directory. You can generate a list of files and pipe them to `cpio`; those files then become part of the archive. Interestingly, RPM files (Red Hat Package Manager) are modified `cpio` files. The `rpm2cpio` command can be used to unpack (rather than install) RPM files if needed. (See Chapter 8 for more information on RPM files.)

Create a `cpio` Archive

To see how `cpio` works, you can create a list of files from the `/etc` directory and then use that list to create the `cpio` archive:

```
# find /etc -print > filelist
# cat filelist ¦ cpio -o > backup.cpio
```

To do it all on one line (UNIX people like to do that), try this:

```
# find /etc -print ¦ cpio -o > backup.cpio
```

Note that you can concatenate several file lists together and use `grep` to search for and remove files you don't want in the archive. (Using `cat` and `grep` are covered in Chapter 5, "First Steps with Fedora.") You can use these basic commands to build scripts (see Chapter 22, "Shell Scripting") that can perform complex and elaborate backups tailored to your particular needs; such is the power of the GNU tools provided with Linux. The `man` page for `cpio` lists an impressive array of options for backing up and restoring files.

> **NOTE**
>
> You can name your backups anything you want, but it's a good idea to follow the filename conventions of using the `.tar`, `.tgz`, `.cpio` extensions, for example. Also, include the current date and time in the filename—easily done when using shell scripts and `cron` to perform backups. (See Chapter 22 for examples of shell scripting.)

Restoring Files from an Archive with `cpio`

The `-im` option in `cpio` will restore the files from a backup and preserve the file attributes as well. Whereas `tar` will create any subdirectories it needs, the `-d` option needs to be explicitly added to `cpio` for the same result. Be careful because the backups might have been created with relative or absolute paths. You should use `-otv` with `cpio` to list the files in the archive before extracting them so that you'll know where they will be placed.

To restore a `cpio` archive,

```
# cpio -imd fedoratest.cpio
```

To list the contents of a cpio file,

```
# cpio -otv fedoratest.cpio
drwxrwxr-x hoyt/hoyt        0 2003-09-04 18:15:05 fedoratest/
-rw-rw-r-- hoyt/hoyt      163 2003-09-03 22:30:49
                          ➥fedoratest/fedora_screenshots.txt
```

```
-rw-rw-r-- hoyt/hoyt        840 2003-09-01 19:27:59
                            ➥fedoratest/fedora_guideline.txt
-rw-rw-r-- hoyt/hoyt       1485 2003-09-01 18:14:23 fedoratest/style-sheet.txt
-rw-rw-r-- hoyt/hoyt        931 2003-09-01 19:02:00 fedoratest/fedora_TOC.txt
```

Note that because the pathnames don't start with a backslash, they are relative pathnames and will install in your current working directory. If they were absolute pathnames, they would install exactly where the paths state.

> **NOTE**
>
> Two of the oldest and most primitive UNIX applications are the dump and restore commands. dump examines files on an ext2 and ext3 file system and determines which files need to be backed up. The backups can span multiple media and levels (dump levels determine the amount of data to be backed up). The dump archives are restored using the restore program. You can use restore across a network and use it to restore full and incremental backups. These bare-metal UNIX applications are feature-rich but awkward to use, even for some UNIX old-timers; for that reason, we don't cover their use in this chapter. Most users prefer the simpler GUI network backup utilities, such as those you learn about in "Alternative Backup Software," later in this chapter, or prefer to use tar.

The GNOME File Roller

The GNOME desktop file archiving graphical application File Roller (file-roller) will view, extract, and create archive files using tar, gzip, bzip, compress, zip, rar, lha, and several other compression formats. Note that File Roller is only a front-end to the command-line utilities that actually provide these compression formats; if they are not installed, File Roller cannot use that format.

> **CAUTION**
>
> File Roller will not complain if you select a compression format that is not supported by installed software until after you attempt to create the archive. Install any needed compression utilities first.

File Roller is well-integrated with the GNOME desktop environment to provide convenient drag-and-drop functionality with the Nautilus file manager. To create a new archive, select Archive, New to open the New Archive dialog box and navigate to the directory where you want the archive to be kept. Type your archive's name in the Selection: /root text box at the bottom of the New Archive dialog box. Use the Archive type drop-down menu to select a compression method. Now, drag the files that you want to be included from Nautilus into the empty space of the File Roller window, and the animated icons will show that files are being included in the new archive. When you're done, a list of files will be shown in the previously blank File Roller window (see Figure 11.1). To save the archive, simply select Archive, Close. Opening an archive is as easy as using the Archive, Open dialog to select the appropriate archive file.

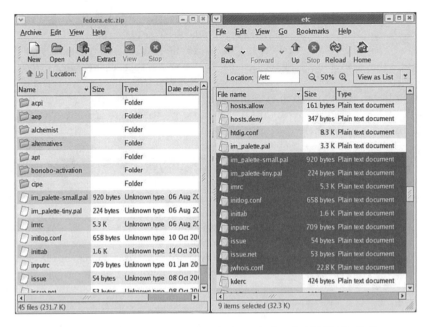

FIGURE 11.1   Drag and Drop files to build an archive with the GNOME File Roller.

The KDE Archiving Tools (KDE ark and kdat)

Fedora Core provides you with the KDE ark and kdat GUI tools for backups; they are installed only if you select the KDE desktop during installation. Archiving has traditionally been a function of the system administrator and not seen as a task for the individual user, so no elaborate GUI was believed necessary. Backing up has also been seen as a script driven, automated task in which a GUI is not as useful.

The KDE ark Archiving Tool

You launch ark by launching it from the command line. It is integrated with the KDE desktop (like File Roller is with GNOME), so it might be a better choice if you use KDE. This application provides a graphical interface to viewing, creating, adding to, and extracting from archived files as shown in Figure 11.2. Several configuration options are available with ark to ensure its compatibility with MS Windows. You can drag and drop from the KDE desktop or Konqueror file browser to add or extract files, or you can use the ark menus.

As long as the associated command-line programs are installed, ark can work with tar, gzip, bzip2, zip, and lha files (the latter four being compression methods used to save space by compaction of the archived files).

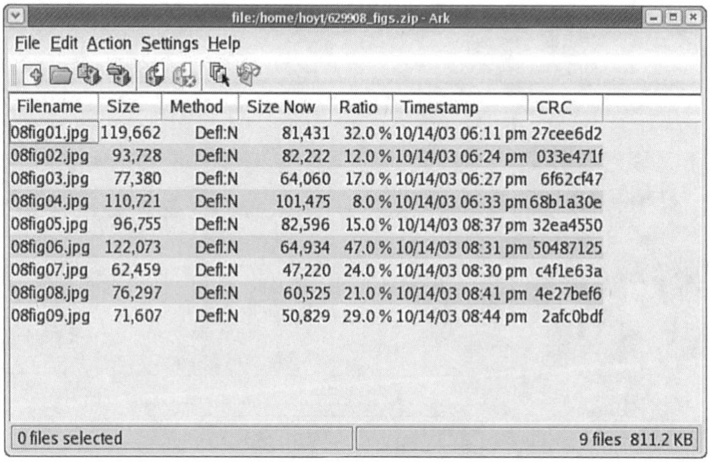

FIGURE 11.2   Here, the contents of a .zip file containing the screenshots used for Chapter 8 are displayed.

Existing archives are opened after launching the application itself. You can add files and directories to the archive or delete them from the archive, as shown in Figure 11.3. After opening the archive, you can extract all of its contents or individual files. You can also perform searches using patterns (all `*.jpg` files, for example) to select files.

Choosing New from the File menu creates new archives. You then type the name of the archive, providing the appropriate extension (`.tar`, `.gz`, and so on), and then proceed to add files and directories as you desire.

Using the dd Command for Archiving

Although the dd command isn't normally thought of as an archiving tool, it can be used to mirror a partition or entire disk, regardless of the information either contains. dd is useful for archiving copies of floppy disks while retaining the capability to restore the data to a floppy intact. For example,

```
# dd if=/dev/fd0 of=floppyimage1.img
```

Swapping the `if=` and `of=` values reverses the process. Although best known for copying images, dd can also be used to convert data, and it is especially useful when restoring older archives or moving data between big endian and little endian systems. Although such esoteric details are beyond the scope of this chapter, remember dd if you need to convert data from obsolete formats.

CAUTION

Don't confuse the `if=` and `of=` assignments; if you do, dd will be more than happy to overwrite your valid data with garbage. Use the carpenter's rule: "Measure twice—cut once."

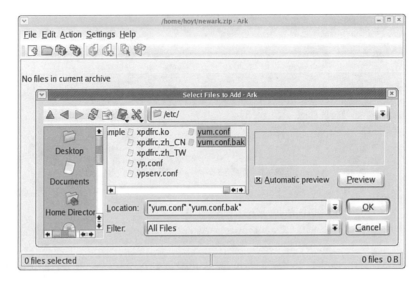

FIGURE 11.3   The opening view of ark presented as a simple GUI browser. Here, several files are being selected to add to the new archive.

Using the Amanda Backup Application

Provided with Fedora Core, Amanda is a powerful, network backup application created by the University of Maryland at College Park. Amanda is a robust backup and restore application best suited to unattended backups with an autoloading tape drive of adequate capacity. It benefits from good user support and documentation.

Amanda's features include compression and encryption. It is intended for use with high-capacity tape drives, floptical, CD-R, and CD-RW devices.

Amanda uses GNU tar and dump; it is intended for unattended, automated tape backups, and isn't well-suited for interactive or ad hoc backups. The support for tape devices in Amanda is robust, and file restoration is relatively simple. Although Amanda doesn't support older Macintosh clients, it will use Samba to back up Microsoft Windows clients, as well as any UNIX client that can use GNU tools (which includes Mac OS X). Because Amanda runs on top of standard GNU tools, file restoration can be made using those tools on a recovery disk even if the Amanda server isn't available. File compression can be done on either the client or server, thus lightening the computational load on less powerful machines that need backing up.

CAUTION

Amanda doesn't support dump images larger than a single tape and requires a new tape for each run. If you forget to change a tape, Amanda continues to attempt backups until you insert a new tape, but those backups won't capture the data as you intended them to. Don't use too small a tape or forget to change a tape, or you won't be happy with the results.

There is no GUI interface for Amanda. Configuration is done in the time-honored UNIX tradition of editing text configuration files located in /etc/amanda. The default installation in Fedora Core includes a sample cron file because it is expected that you will be using cron to run Amanda regularly. The client utilities are installed with the package am-utils; the Amanda server must be obtained from the Amanda Web site. As far as backup schemes are concerned, Amanda calculates an optimal scheme on-the-fly and schedules it accordingly. It can be forced to adhere to a traditional scheme, but other tools are possibly better suited for that job.

The man page for Amanda (the client is amdump) is well written and useful, explaining both the configuration of Amanda as well as detailing the several programs that actually make up Amanda. The configuration files found in /etc/amanda are well commented; they provide a number of examples to assist you in configuration.

The program's home page is http://www.amanda.org. There, you will find information on subscribing to the mail list, as well as links to Amanda-related projects and a FAQ.

Alternative Backup Software

The free download version of Fedora Core doesn't provide any other sophisticated backup applications. (The version targeted to businesses usually does.) Commercial and other freeware backup products do exist; BRU and Veritas are good examples of effective commercial backup products. Here are some useful free software backup tools that aren't installed with Fedora Core Linux:

- flexbackup—This backup tool is a large file of Perl scripts that makes dump and restore easier to use. flexbackup's command syntax can be accessed by using the command with the -help argument. It also can use afio, cpio, and tar to create and restore archives locally or over a network using rsh or ssh if security is a concern. Its home page is http://www.flexbackup.org/.

- afio—This tool creates cpio-formatted archives, but handles input data corruption better than cpio (which doesn't handle data input corruption very well at all). It supports multi-volume archives during interactive operation and can make compressed archives. If you feel the need to use cpio, you might want to check out afio at http://freshmeat.net/projects/afio/.

- cdbackup—Designed for the home or small office user, cdbackup will work with any backup and will restore software that can read from stdin, write to stdout, and can handle linear devices such as tape drives. It makes it easier to use CD-Rs as the storage medium. Similar applications are available elsewhere as well; the home page for this application is at http://www.muempf.de/index.html.

Many other alternative backup tools exist, but covering all of them is beyond the scope of this book. Two good places to look for free backup software are Freshmeat (http://www.freshmeat.net) and Google (http://www.google.com/linux).

Copying Files

Often, when you have only a few files that you need to protect from loss or corruption, it might make better sense to simply copy the individual files to another storage medium rather than to create an archive of them. You can use the tar, cp, rsync, or even the cpio commands to do this, as well as a handy file management tool known as mc. Using tar is the traditional choice because older versions of cp didn't handle symbolic links and permissions well at times, causing those attributes (characteristics of the file) to be lost; tar handled those file attributes in a better manner. cp has been improved to fix those problems, but tar is still more widely used. rsync has recently been added to Fedora Core and is an excellent choice for mirroring sets of files, especially when done over a network.

Many choices exist for using file copying as a backup technique, and your choice will depend on your priorities. If you're interested in the simplest method, choose cp -a. The tar alternative is the next best option. cpio is better suited to creating archives than it is to simply copying files. mc might offer the best combination of ease, power, and flexibility, but it cannot be counted on to be found on every system; you should find tar and cp everywhere. The following sections describe how to use each of these methods so that you can better determine which is best for your situation.

To illustrate how to use file copying as a backup technique, the examples here show how to copy (not archive) a directory tree. This tree includes symbolic links and files that have special file permissions we need to keep intact.

Copying Files Using tar

One choice for copying files into another location would be to use the tar command where you would create a tar file that would be piped to tar to be uncompressed in the new location. To accomplish this, first change to the source directory. Then, the entire command resembles

```
# tar cvf - files ¦ (cd target_directory ; tar xpf -)
```

where *files* are the filenames you want to include; use * to include the entire current directory.

Here's how the command shown works: You have already changed to the source directory and executed tar with the cvf - arguments that tell tar to

> c—Create an archive.
>
> v—Verbose; lists the files processed so we can see that it's working.
>
> f—The filename of the archive will be what follows. (In this case, it is -.)
>
> -—A buffer; a place to hold our data temporarily.

The following `tar` commands can be useful for creating file copies for backup purposes:

> l—Stay in the local file system (so you don't include remote volumes).
>
> `atime-preserve`—Don't change access times on files, even though you're accessing them now, to preserve the old access information for archival purposes.

The contents of the `tar` file (held for us temporarily in the buffer, which is named `-`) are then piped to the second expression, which will extract the files to the target directory. In shell programming (see Chapter 22), enclosing an expression in parentheses causes it to operate in a subshell and be executed first.

First we change to the target directory, and then

> x—Extract files from a `tar` archive.
>
> p—Preserve permissions.
>
> f—The filename will be `-`, the temporary buffer that holds the `tar`'ed files.

Compressing, Encrypting, and Sending `tar` Streams

The file copy techniques using the `tar` command in the previous section can also be used to quickly and securely copy a directory structure across a LAN or the Internet (using the ssh command). One way to make use of these techniques is to use the following command line to first compress the contents of a designated directory, and then decompress the compressed and encrypted archive stream into a designated directory on a remote host:

```
$ tar cvzf - data_folder | ssh remote_host `( cd ~/mybackup_dir; tar xvzf - )'
```

The `tar` command is used to create, list, and compress the files in the directory named data_folder. The output is piped through the ssh (secure shell) command and sent to the remote computer named *remote_host*. On the remote computer, the stream is then extracted and saved in the directory named */mybackup_dir*. You will be prompted for a password in order to send the stream.

Copying Files Using `cp`

To copy files, we could use the `cp` command. The general format of the command when used for simple copying is

```
$ cp -a source_directory target_directory
```

The `-a` argument is the same as giving `-dpR`, which would be

> -d—Dereferences symbolic links (never follows symbolic links) and copies the files that they point to instead of copying the links.

-p—Preserves all file attributes if possible. (File ownership might interfere.)

-R—Copies directories recursively.

The cp command can also be used to quickly replicate directories and retain permissions by using the -avR command-line options. Using these options preserves file and directory permissions, gives verbose output, and recursively copies and re-creates subdirectories. A log of the backup can also be created during the backup by redirecting the standard output like this:

cp -avR directory_to_backup destination_vol_or_dir **1>/root/backup_log.txt**

or

cp -avR fedora /test2 1>/root/backup_log.txt

This example makes an exact copy of the directory named /fedora on the volume named /test2, and saves a backup report named backup_log.txt under /root.

Copying Files Using cpio

You can use cpio instead of tar to make backup file copies, but remember that cpio really works with lists of files. So you must first create the list and feed it to cpio.

find source_directory **-print** ¦ **cpio -pudv** target_directory

Here, use the find command on the current directory with the -print option to generate a list of files in that directory. Then pipe that file list to cpio. When cpio gets the file list, it

-p—Runs in copy-pass mode. (We are not creating an archive file here.)

-u—Replaces all files without asking (unconditional).

-d—Creates directories if needed.

-v—Lists all files copied (verbose).

Copying Files Using mc

The Midnight Commander is a command-line file manager that is useful for copying, moving, and archiving files and directories. The Midnight Commander has a look and feel similar to the Norton Commander of DOS fame. By executing mc at a shell prompt, a dual-pane view of the files is displayed. It contains drop-down menu choices and function keys to manipulate files. It also uses its own virtual file system, enabling it to mount FTP directories and display the contents of tar files, gzipped tar files (.tar.gz or .tgz), bzip files, DEB files, and RPM files, as well as extract individual files from them. As if that weren't enough, mc contains a File Undelete virtual file system for ext2/3 partitions. By using cd to "change directories" to an FTP server's URL, you can transfer files using the FTP protocol. The default font chosen for Fedora Core makes the display of mc ugly when used in a tty console (as opposed to an xterm), but doesn't affect its performance.

Figure 11.4 shows a shot of the default dual-panel display. Pressing the F9 key drops down the menu, and pressing F1 displays the Help file. A "feature" in the default GNOME terminal intercepts the F10 key used to exit mc, so use F9 instead to access the menu item to quit, or simply click on the menu bar at the bottom with your mouse. The configuration files are well documented, and it would appear easy to extend the functionality of mc for your system if you understand shell scripting and regular expressions. It is an excellent choice for file management on servers not running X.

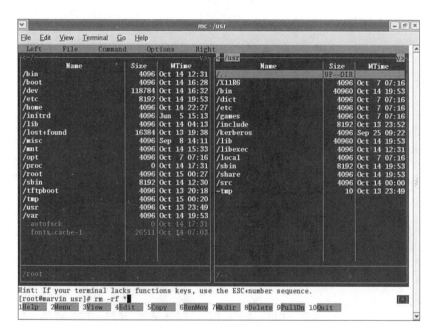

FIGURE 11.4   The Midnight Commander is a highly versatile file tool. If it does not display properly on your screen, launch it with the -a argument to force ASCII mode.

Copying Files Using scp

The traditional way to copy files from one computer to another is to use uucp, the UNIX-to-UNIX copy program, or to use one of the rtools, rcp. The rtools are insecure over a public network and are subject to several exploits. It is best not to use them at all because they have been supplanted by more secure tools based on the secure shell, ssh.

> **NOTE**
>
> The file transfer protocol known as FTP can be used to copy files from one computer to another, but this requires that an FTP server be running, and the server is subject to security problems of its own.
>
> See Chapter 18, "Secure File Transfer Protocol (FTP) Service," for more details on FTP.

The scp command uses ssh for file copying. Useful arguments for this command include

- -p—Preserves modification times, access times, and modes from the original file.

- -r—Recursively copies entire directories.

- -v—Verbose mode for debugging problems.

- -C—Enables file compression.

The syntax of an scp copy command is

```
scp [arguments] [source] [target]
```

For example, if we want to copy the file /home/hoyt/fedora.txt to ~/docs on our account on a remote host

```
$ scp -p /home/hoyt/fedora.txt hoyt@192.168.168.4:/home/hoyt/docs
```

After it prompts us for a password, we see

```
fedora.txt    100% ************************    0    00:00
```

This indicates that the transfer was completed. If we had subdirectories to transfer, we would have used the -r (recursive) argument.

Actually, it can be much easier than the example because scp assumes that all paths are relative to the home directory of the user unless the full path is given.

Taking this into consideration, our example becomes

```
$ scp -p fedora.txt hoyt@192.168.168.5:docs
```

And it can be made even easier. Creating a file named ~/.ssh/config with the following contents:

```
Host = titan
HostName = 192.168.168.5
User = hoyt
ForwardAgent = yes
```

```
ForwardX11 = yes

Compression = yes
```

allows us to simply use

```
$ scp -p fedora.txt titan:docs
```

> **NOTE**
>
> If you are comfortable with FTP, you might want to consider a cousin of scp: sftp. It provides
> the common FTP command set. If no sftp server is running on the remote host, simply use scp
> to copy the sftpserv binary to your remote home directory. (Often, ~/bin is in your path.) The
> FTP client gftp supports sftp and gives you a GUI client as well.

Copying Files Using rsync

rsync is a file transfer tool now included with Fedora Core. According to the rsync man
page, it is a "faster, flexible replacement for rcp, the traditional remote copy application."
We've already mentioned that rcp is not a secure method of transferring files.

A significant benefit of using rsync is that it speeds up file transfers by transferring only
the differences between the two sites across a network link. rsync can copy links, devices,
owners, groups, and permissions, and it can be told to exclude certain files. rsync can use
ssh (via the command line or setting the RSYNC_RSH variable) and does not require root
privileges. rsync has support for anonymous or authenticated rsync servers for use in
mirroring.

The man page is extremely well written and provides four excellent examples of how rsync
can be used to transfer files matching a pattern, can recursively transfer files, and can be
used locally (without a server).

The rsync command has some 62 options (not including short and long variants of the
same option). A few particularly useful options are

- -z—Uses gzip compression.

- -P—Keeps partial files and reports on the progress of the transfer.

- --bwlimit=KBPS—Sets a maximum bandwidth rsync might use.

- --exclude-from=FILE—All excluded files listed in a separate file; pattern matching is enabled.

- -x—Doesn't cross file system boundaries.

- -n—Dry run for testing.

- -l—Copies symlinks, not the files themselves.

- -L—Copies the file, not the symlink.

-r—Copies recursively.

-v—Verbose output.

The rsync utility can be run as a daemon to establish an rsync server, listening on TCP port 873 by default. The configuration of the server is handled by the contents of the /etc/rsyncd.conf file; the man page for rsyncd.conf provides the details. The daemon can be launched standalone or via xinetd to suit your needs.

The rsync Web site provides an examples page showing examples of

- Backup to a central server with a 7-day increment

- Backup to a spare disk

- Mirroring a CVS tree

- Automated backup at home over a modem

A time and bandwidth saving trick is to use rsync to only re-download that part of an ISO file that is incorrect, rather than downloading the entire 650MB–700MB of the file. First, you must locate an rsync server that is offering the .iso images you seek. Look at the Fedora Core mirrors at http://www.redhat.com/download/mirror.html and select one that offers "D", the identifier for .iso images.

An rsync server will provide *modules*, or directory trees as symbolic names. To determine if a server provides an rsync module, use the query:

```
rsync some.site.com::
```

If an rsync server is running on that site, you'll see a list of available rsync modules. If we try

```
$ rsync ftp-linux.cc.gatech.edu::

GEORGIA TECH SOFTWARE LIBRARY

Unauthorized use is prohibited.  Your access is being logged.

If you run a publicly accessible mirror, and are interested in
mirroring from us, please contact lxmirror@cc.gatech.edu.

- - - - - - - - - - - - - - - - - - - - - - - - - - - - - - - - - - - - - - - - - - - - - - - - - - - - - - - - - - - -



altlinux       mirror of ftp.altlinux.ru
arklinux       mirror of arklinux.org
asplinux       mirror of ftp.asp-linux.com
```

```
debian              mirror of ftp.debian.org
debian-cd           mirror of ftp.debian.org
mandrake            mirror of ftp.mandrake.com
redhat              mirror of ftp.redhat.com
<SNIP>
```

To use this rsync service, we would explore the *redhat* module to discover the file path to the .iso images using rsync -r and the module name to explore it recursively.

To use rsync to repair our defective .iso images, we point rsync at the "good" image and at our "bad" image like so:

```
# rsync -a -vvv --progress ftp-linux.cc.gatech.edu::\
redhat/linux/9/en/iso/i386/shrike-i386-disc1.iso\
 ~/downloads/shrike-i386-disc1.iso
```

rsync compares the two files and will download only the needed replacement parts for our local file much faster than downloading the entire image again.

Undeleting Files

Up to this point, we have discussed backing up data and restoring that data. In some situations, however, you need to restore data that has not been backed up because you just accidentally deleted it. File recovery (and system recovery, which you learn about in a later section) requires a high level of expertise to successfully complete. There are data recovery businesses that are good at data and system recovery, and they prosper because the task is so difficult. The information presented here, along with practice on your part, can assist you in attempting to do it yourself or enable you to recognize when a professional service is warranted.

Using the ext2fs Undeletion Process

On multiuser systems, when files are deleted, their inodes are made available immediately for use by the system. In that case, recovering that data intact is very unlikely, although not impossible. The first rule in undeleting a file is to stop all disk writes as soon as possible. If the system is heavily used, the old inode will likely be overwritten quite soon. The sooner you stop disk writes after deleting a file, the better chance you have of restoring at least some of the file.

After you have unmounted the file system containing the deleted files, you must attempt to methodically find the deleted parts of the file and reassemble them. Essentially, this involves examining the raw data on the disk using pattern matching to identify candidates for recovery, and then decoding the candidates' inode information to re-link the files if possible. It is a time-consuming process and should be reason enough to encourage you to back up the files in the first place. On a single-user system, the chances of recovery are better because fewer writes to the disk have occurred after the file deletion.

File recovery isn't something to be attempted without preparation and practice; both will improve your chances of recovering more of the data. The Ext2fs Undeletion mini-HOWTO (see the section "Reference" at the end of this chapter) has been written to detail the process. Again, file recovery *requires some practice* before you would be ready to use it in the real world.

> **TIP**
>
> If you want to experiment with learning to restore files, use the information in the "Examples" section of Chapter 10 to create a loopback file system to experiment with. Using that, you can safely delete and undelete files without taking a chance on damaging your system by inadvertently changing critical files or deleting directories.

Reformatting with the -S Option When Experiencing Unrecoverable File System Errors

In attempting to recover data from a damaged disk with file system errors that can't be fixed with fsck, you can run the mke2fs command with the -S option like this (for example, if you are having trouble with the ext2/3 partition on /dev/hda2):

```
# mke2fs -S /dev/hda2
```

The -S argument writes new superblock information, but doesn't write new inodes; this might make the missing data salvageable, or it might not depending on the damage. You must run e2fsck on the unmounted partition after using the mke2fs command in this manner.

Because a directory is a file as well, the same techniques for file recovery can be used to recover entire directories. The Ext2fs Undeletion of Directory Structures mini-HOWTO (see the section "Reference" at the end of this chapter) is written as a companion to the Ext2fs Undeletion mini-HOWTO—both of which should be on everyone's required reading list if you want to successfully undelete any files. The manual technique described in the HOWTOs is too long and complex to be covered in this book.

Undeleting Files Using mc

The Midnight Commander can make use of a virtual file system and includes a special undelete file system that can be used on ext2/3 partitions. The mc utility is just an interface to the ext2fs library, and the virtual file system handles for you the nitty-gritty details of the file system that the previous paragraph alluded to. As with any simplified solution to complex issues, mc must make some assumptions for you that might result in less data being recovered than if you use the manual method. For that reason, using mc for recovering deleted files is not a standard method.

To use the recovery file system, you must cd in one of the panels to the special filename formed by combining the prefix /#undel: with the partition name where your deleted file resides. For example, to attempt to recover a deleted file on /dev/hda2, do this:

```
# cd /#undel:hda2
```

Be patient because it will take quite a while for the deleted files to be displayed. You will see a list of inodes that you can examine with the text editor (using the F4 key); then use the F12 key to perform a Save As operation, renaming the file to something appropriate for your use. Repeat this process until you have renamed and saved all the files. Press the Shift+F10 key to exit when done. Note that you might be able to recover only pieces of files and might not be able to recover any at all.

> **NOTE**
>
> If you need to know what is on a drive or disk that can't be easily mounted (it could be a non-Linux format, or could contain un-formatted, raw data), use
>
> ```
> # dd if=/dev/hda1 count=1 bs=512 ¦ file -
> ```
>
> which produces output similar to the following:
>
> ```
> 1+0 records in
> 1+0 records out
> standard input:              x86 boot sector, \
> system MSWIN4.1, FAT (16 bit)
> ```
>
> To discover what an unknown floppy disk is, use this:
>
> ```
> # dd if=/dev/fd0 count=1 bs=512 ¦ file -
> ```
>
> which produces output similar to the following:
>
> ```
> 1+0 records in
> 1+0 records out
> standard input:              x86 boot sector, system )\
> _3oEIHC, FAT (12 bit)
> ```

System Rescue

There will come a time when you need to engage in system rescue efforts. This need arises when the system will not even start Linux so that you can recover any files. This problem is most frequently associated with the boot loader program or partition table (discussed in Chapter 8), but it could be that critical system files have been inadvertently deleted or corrupted. If you have been making backups properly, these kinds of system failures are easily, though not quickly, recoverable through a full restore. Still, valuable current data might not have been backed up since the last scheduled backup, and the backup archives are found to be corrupt, incomplete, or missing. A full restore also takes time you might not have. If the problem causing the system failure is simply a damaged boot loader, a damaged partition table, a missing library, or misconfiguration, a quick fix can get the system up and running and the data can then be easily retrieved.

In this section, we will first examine a way to back up and restore the boot loader itself or, having failed to do that, restore it by hand. Then we'll look at a few alternatives to booting the damaged system so that we can inspect it, fix it, or retrieve data from it.

The Fedora Core Rescue Disk

Fedora Core provides a rescue disk hidden in the first installation CD. To use it, insert the first installation CD and reboot the computer, booting from the CD just as you did when you installed Fedora originally. At the intro screen, press the F1 key to see all the available choices, but simply enter linux rescue at the LILO boot prompt to enter rescue mode like

```
boot: linux rescue
```

You'll learn more about the rescue mode later in this section, but feel free to explore it at any time. A graphical interface is not available, so you'll need to bone up on your command-line skills. If necessary, you can perform all the operations discussed in this section from rescue mode.

Backing Up and Restoring the Master Boot Record

The Master Boot Record (MBR) is the first 512 bytes of a hard disk. It contains the boot loader code in the first 446 bytes and the partition table in the next 64 bytes; the last 2 bytes identify that sector as the MBR. The MBR can become corrupted, so it makes sense to back it up.

This example uses the dd command as root to back up the entire MBR. If the boot loader code changes from the time you make this image and restore the old code, the system won't boot when you restore it all; it's easy enough to keep a boot floppy handy and then re-run LILO if that's what you are using.

To copy the entire MBR to a file, use this:

```
# dd if=/dev/hda of=/tmp/hdambr bs=512 count=1
```

To restore the entire MBR, use this:

```
# dd if=/tmp/hdambr of=/dev/hda bs=512 count=1
```

To restore only the partition table, skipping the boot loader code, use this:

```
# dd if=/tmp/hdambr of=/dev/hda bs=1 skip=446 count=66
```

Of course, it would be prudent to move the copy of the MBR to a floppy or other appropriate storage device. (The file is only 512 bytes in size.) You will need to be able to run dd on the system in order to restore it (which means that you will be using the Fedora Core rescue disk as described later, or any equivalent to it).

Manually Restoring the Partition Table

A different way of approaching the problem is to have a printed copy of the partition table that can then be used to restore the partition table by hand using the Fedora Core rescue disk and the fdisk program.

We can create a listing of the printout of the partition table with fdisk using the -l option (for list), as follows:

```
# fdisk /dev/hda -l > /tmp/hdaconfig.txt
```

or send the listing of the partition table to the printer:

```
# fdisk /dev/hda -l ¦ kprinter
```

We could also copy the file /tmp/hdaconfig.txt to the same backup floppy as the MBR for safekeeping.

Now that we have a hard copy of the partition table (as well as having saved the file itself somewhere), it is possible to restore the MBR by hand at some future date.

Use the Fedora Core Rescue Disk for this process. After booting into rescue mode, you will have the opportunity to use a menu to mount your system read/write, not to mount your system, or to mount any found Linux partitions as read-only. If you plan to make any changes, you will need to have any desired partitions mounted with write permission.

Once logged on (you are root by default), start fdisk on the first drive:

```
# fdisk /dev/had
```

Use the p command to display the partition information and compare it to the hard copy you have. If the entries are identical, you have a problem somewhere else; it's not the partition table.

If there is a problem, use the d command to delete all the listed partitions.

Now use the n command to create new partitions that will match the partition table from your hard copy. Make certain that the partition types (ext2, FAT, swap and so on) are the same. If you have a FAT partition at /dev/hda1, make certain that you set the bootable flag for it; otherwise, Windows or DOS won't boot.

If you find that you have made an error somewhere along the way, just use the q command to quit fdisk without saving any changes and start over. Without specifically telling fdisk to write to the partition table, no changes are actually made to it.

When the partition table information shown on your screen matches your printed version, write the changes to the disk with the w command; you will be automatically exited from `fdisk`. Restart `fdisk` to verify your handiwork, and then remove the rescue disk and reboot.

It helps to practice manually restoring the partition table on an old drive before you have to do it in an emergency situation.

Booting the System from the Rescue CD

For advanced Linux users, you can use the rescue CD to boot the system (rather than boot the rescue operating system on the CDROM) if the boot loader code on your computer is damaged or incorrect. To use the Rescue CD to boot your system from `/dev/hda1`, for example, first boot the CD and press the F1 key. At the LILO prompt, enter something similar to this example. Note that you are simply telling the boot loader what your root partition is.

```
boot: linux rescue root=/dev/hda1
```

Booting the System from a Generic Boot Floppy

If you failed to make a boot floppy or cannot locate the one you did make, any Linux boot floppy (a slightly older version or one borrowed from a friend) can be pressed into service as long as it has a reasonably similar kernel version. (The major and minor numbers match—for example, 2.6.5 would likely work with any 2.6 system, but not with a 2.4 system.) You would boot your system by manually specifying the root and boot partitions as described previously. Although you are almost guaranteed to get some error messages, you might at least be able to get a base system running enough to replace files and recover the system.

> **TIP**
>
> In both preceding cases, it is assumed that you don't need any special file system or device drivers to access the root partition. If you do, add the `initrd=` argument to the LILO line pointing to the appropriate `initrd` file on your system. If you don't know the exact name of the `initrd` file, you are out of luck with LILO, so learn to use a GRUB boot floppy as well.

Using a GRUB Boot Floppy

The Grand Unified Boot Loader (GRUB) can attempt to boot a system from a floppy without a viable custom-made boot floppy. The image for the floppy can be downloaded from `ftp://alpha.gnu.org/gnu/grub/grub-0.95-i386-pc.ext2fs` and copied to a floppy using `dd`. (`rawrite.exe` would be used on a Microsoft system.) Or, if you have a boot floppy from an existing system using GRUB, that one will work as well.

GRUB has its own command shell, file system drivers, and search function (much like command completion in the bash shell). It is possible to boot using the GRUB floppy, examine the drive partitions, and search for the kernel and `initrd` image as well, using them to boot the system. Worthy of a chapter all its own, the GRUB documentation is extensive: In addition to `info grub` (the `info` system is similar to the `man` system for documentation), the GRUB documents contain a tutorial worth reading. The flexibility and power of GRUB are what influenced Red Hat to make it the default boot loader for Fedora Core Linux. The GRUB boot loader is shown in Figure 11.5.

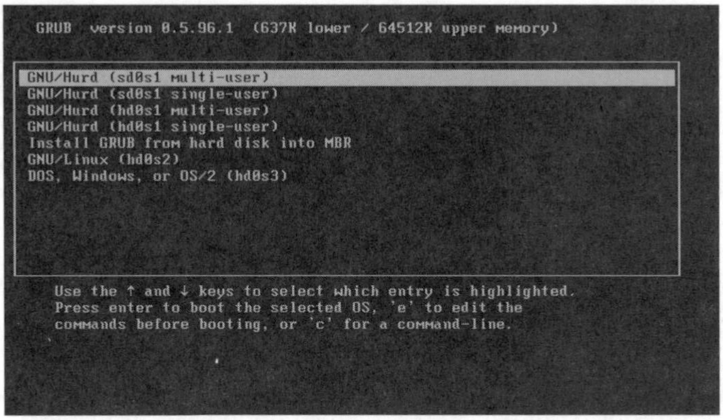

FIGURE 11.5   The GRUB boot loader gives you incredible flexibility in booting even unfamiliar systems.

Using the Recovery Facility from the Installation Disk

As in the previous example, use the `linux rescue` command at the LILO boot prompt (:) to launch the CD in rescue mode. Rescue mode runs a version of Fedora Core from the CD-ROM that is independent from your system. It permits you to mount your root partition for maintenance. This alternative is useful when your root partition is no longer bootable because something has gone wrong. Fedora Core is constantly improving the features of the Recovery Facility.

Upon beginning the rescue mode, you get your choice of language and keyboard layouts. You are given an opportunity to configure networking in rescue mode and are presented with a nice ncurses-based form to fill in the information. The application will attempt to find your existing partitions and will offer you a choice of mounting them read-write, read-only (always a wise choice the first time), or skip any mounting and drop to a command prompt. With multiple partitions, you must then indicate which is the root partition. That partition is then mounted at `/mnt/sysimage`. When you are finally presented with a command prompt, it is then possible to make your system the root file system with

```
# chroot /mnt/sysimage
```

To get back to the rescue file system, type **exit** at the prompt. To reboot, type **exit** at the rescue system's prompt.

The rescue function does offer support for software RAID arrays (RAID 0, 1, and 5), as well as IDE or SCSI partitions formatted as ext2/3. After asking for input if it is unsure how to proceed, you eventually arrive at a command shell as root; there is no login or password. Depending on your configuration, you might or might not see prompts for additional information. If you get lost or confused, you can always reboot. (It helps to practice the use of the rescue mode.)

In rescue mode, a number of command-line tools are available for you, but no GUI tools are provided. For networking, you have the ifconfig, route, rcp, rlogin, rsh, and ftp commands. For archiving (and restoring archives), cpio, uncpio, gzip, gunzip, dd, zcat, and md5sum commands are there. As for editors, vi is emulated by busybox and pico, jmacs and joe are provided by the joe editor. There are other useful system commands. A closer look at these commands reveals that they are all links to a program called busybox (home page at http://www.busybox.net/).

BusyBox provides a reasonably complete POSIX environment for any small or embedded system. The utilities in BusyBox generally have fewer options than their full-featured GNU cousins; however, the included options "provide the expected functionality and behave very much like their GNU counterparts." This means that you should test the rescue mode first to see if it can restore your data and see which options are available to you because the BusyBox version will behave slightly differently from the full GNU version. (Some options are missing; some options don't work quite the same—you need to know if this will affect you *before* you are in an emergency situation.)

There are a few useful tricks to know when using rescue mode. If your system is functional, you can use the chroot command to change the root file system from the CD to your system in this manner:

```
# chroot /mnt/sysimage
```

You'll find yourself at a new command prompt with all your old files in—hopefully—the right place. Your familiar tools—if intact—should be available to you. To exit the chrooted environment, use the exit command to return to the rescue system prompt. If you use the exit command again, the system will reboot.

The rescue environment provides a nice set of networking commands and network-enabled tools such as scp, sftp, and some of the rtools. It also provides rpm, which can fetch packages over a network connection. Installing them is tricky because you want them installed in the file system mounted at /mnt/sysimage, not at /. To accomplish that, use the --root argument to set an alternate path to root:

```
# rpm -ivh --root /mnt/sysimage ftp://location/package.rpm
```

Alternatives to the Fedora Core Rescue CD

The Fedora Core rescue CD might be inadequate for your system restoration needs; it might lack specific Ethernet device support, file system support, or the kind of full utility functionality that you require for a successful recovery operation. An alternative exists in the SuperRescue CD created by H. Peter Anvin.

Essentially, the SuperRescue CD is a reasonably full and robust Red Hat distribution (based on Red Hat 7.2 and the 2.4.20-rc1 kernel) that runs completely from a bootable CD. The best thing about the SuperRescue CD is that it comes with build scripts, so it is incredibly easy to add new software (that special driver or application) and create a new CD. The home page is at `http://freshmeat.net/projects/superrescue/`, but you can grab a copy directly at `http://www.kernel.org/pub/dist/superrescue/v2/`.

Relevant Fedora Core Commands

The following commands are useful in performing backup, recovery, and restore operations in Fedora Core Linux:

`amdump`—Amanda is a network-based backup system, consisting of 18 separate commands, for use with Linux.

`ark`—A KDE desktop GUI archiving utility.

`cp`—The copy command.

`scp`—The secure shell copy command.

`cpio`—A data archive utility.

`dd`—A data copy and conversion utility.

`gzip`—The GNU compression utility.

`tar`—The GNU tape archive utility.

Reference

`http://www.tldp.org/LDP/solrhe/Securing-Optimizing-Linux-RH-Edition-v1.3/whywhen.html`—A thorough discussion with examples of using `dump` and `restore` for backups.

`http://en.tldp.org/LDP/solrhe/Securing-Optimizing-Linux-RH-Edition-v1.3/chap29sec306.html`—Making automatic backups with `tar` using `cron`.

`http://kmself.home.netcom.com/Linux/FAQs/backups.html`—The Linux Backups mini FAQ contains some useful, although brief, comments on backup media, compression, encryption, and security.

`http://www.tldp.org/`—The Linux Documentation Project offers several useful HOWTO documents that discuss backups and disk recovery.

`http://www.ibiblio.org/pub/Linux/docs/HOWTO/other-formats/html_single/Ext2fs-Undeletion.html`—If you need to undelete a file from an ext2/3 file system, the Linux Ext2fs Undeletion mini HOWTO is the document for you. You will be more successful if you practice.

`http://www.ibiblio.org/pub/Linux/docs/HOWTO/other-formats/html_single/`
`Ext2fs-Undeletion-Dir-Struct.html`—The Ext2fs Undeletion of Directory Structures is a companion HOWTO to the Linux Ext2fs Undeletion mini HOWTO, helping you cope with an errant `rm -rf *`.

`http://www.ibiblio.org/pub/Linux/docs/HOWTO/other-formats/html_single/`
`Bootdisk-HOWTO.html#AEN1483`—Here's a list of LILO Boot error codes to help you debug a cranky system that won't boot.

`http://www.ibiblio.org/pub/Linux/docs/HOWTO/other-formats/html_single/`
`Ftape-HOWTO.html`—This is a HOWTO for the floppy tape device driver.

`http://www.linux-usb.org/USB-guide/x498.html`—The USB Guide for mass storage devices. If you have a USB device and need to know if it's supported, check here.

`http://www.ibiblio.org/pub/Linux/docs/HOWTO/other-formats/html_single/`
`LILO-crash-rescue-HOWTO.html`—This HOWTO describes how to use floppy-based recovery disks, but the general techniques are universal. The techniques covered include checking the integrity of the target file system. It's a little thin in content, but it is notable for its related URL links.

`http://www.backupcentral.com/amanda.html`—This is the Amanda chapter of *UNIX Backup and Recovery* (written by John R. Jackson and published by O'Reilly and Associates). The chapter is available online and covers every aspect of using Amanda. The site features a handy search tool for the chapter.

`http://twiki.org/cgi-bin/view/Wikilearn/RsyncingALargeFileBeginner`—Rsyncing a large file to "repair" a local ISO image that does not pass the md5sum check.

`http://www.lycoris.org/sections.php?op=viewarticle&artid=8`—Lycoris ISO rsync mini HOWTO. A step-by-step tutorial on using `rsync` to sync files.

`http://www.mikerubel.org/computers/rsync_snapshots/`—Automated snapshot-style backups using `rsync`.

`http://www.mondorescue.org/`—Mondo Rescue is a bare-metal backup/rescue tool independent of Fedora Core, using CD, DVD, tape, or NFS; it can produce bootable CDs to restore the system.

`http://www.ccp14.ac.uk/ccp14admin/linux-server/mondorescue/dvd_mondo.html`—A HOWTO for using MondoRescue to back up on a DVD.

`http://www.linuxorbit.com/modules.php?op=modload&name=Sections&file=index&req=`
`viewarticle&artid=222&page=1`—A HOWTO using split and mkisofs to manually back up large archives to CD.

PART III

System Services Administration

IN THIS PART

CHAPTER 12	Printing with Fedora	349
CHAPTER 13	Network Connectivity	375
CHAPTER 14	Managing DNS	433
CHAPTER 15	Internet Connectivity	481
CHAPTER 16	Apache Web Server Management	501
CHAPTER 17	Administering Database Services	549
CHAPTER 18	Secure File Transfer Protocol Service	579
CHAPTER 19	Handling Electronic Mail	627
CHAPTER 20	News and Other Collaborative Communication	663
CHAPTER 21	C/C++ Programming Tools for Fedora	693
CHAPTER 22	Shell Scripting	715
CHAPTER 23	Using Perl	757
CHAPTER 24	Kernel and Module Management	785
CHAPTER 25	Productivity Applications	811
CHAPTER 26	Multimedia Applications	835

## CHAPTER 12

Printing with Fedora

IN THIS CHAPTER

- Overview of Fedora Printing
- Configuring and Managing Print Services
- Creating and Configuring Local Printers
- Creating Network Printers
- Console Print Control
- Using the Common UNIX Printing System
- Avoiding Printer-Support Problems
- Reference

Fedora supports more than 600 printers from more than 40 manufacturers, and it is possible to mix and match printing hardware with newer computers. In this chapter, you learn about printing services offered in Fedora. You'll see that your Linux system can be put to work right away as a print server platform, for use by local or remote Linux, UNIX-like, or Windows workstations.

Here, you learn about the many different programs, files, and directories that are integral to supporting printing under Fedora. The chapter also shows you simple techniques for configuring new printers. You learn a variety of methods for making printers available for use quickly and easily, and you learn some important workarounds for connecting printer and system hardware with differing port configurations.

Fedora uses the Common UNIX Printing System (CUPS). Other printing systems, such as LPRng, can be used as the printing system, but you might not be able to use some of the graphical print management utilities included with Fedora. This chapter focuses on using CUPS, but a short section is devoted to setting up a remote Linux print server using LPRng for printing.

The Internet Printing Protocol

CUPS supports the Internet Printing Protocol (IPP) and offers a number of unique features, such as network printer directory (printer browsing) services, support for encryption, and support for PostScript Printer Description (.ppd) files.

According to the Internet Engineering Task Force (IETF), IPP grew out of a 1996 proposal by Novell to create a printing protocol for use over the Internet. Since then, the system has been developed and has matured into a stable print system for use on a variety of Linux and UNIX-like operating platforms.

Overview of Fedora Printing

Fedora's print filter system is the main engine that enables the printing of many types of documents. The heart of that engine is the GNU GPL version of Aladdin, Inc.'s Ghostscript interpreter, the gs client. The system administrator's printer configuration tool is the system-config-printer client.

> **NOTE**
>
> Fedora's print system can be used to print to local (attached) or remote (network) printers. If you use a local printer, it is represented by a printer device, such as /dev/lp0 or /dev/usb/lp0 (if you have a USB printer). Local and remote printers use print *queues* defined in your system's printer capabilities database, /etc/printcap. A document being printed is known as a print *job*, and you can view and control your list, or queue, of current print jobs in the spool directory, which is /var/spool/cups. Note that you may only control your print jobs; only the root operator can control print jobs of any user on the system.

To add a printer to your system, you use the system-config-printer client to create, configure, and save the printer's definition. The client saves the definition as an entry in your system's printer capabilities database, /etc/printcap. Each definition contains a text field with the name of the printer, its host, and name of the print queue. Printed documents will be spooled to the /var/spool/cups directory. A sample printcap definition might look like

```
# This file was automatically generated by cupsd(8) from the
# /etc/cups/printers.conf file.  All changes to this file
# will be lost.
lp¦lp:rm=stinky:rp=lp:¨
```

CUPS maintains its own database of defined printers under the /etc/cups directory in a file named printers.conf. For example, an associated printer defined in /etc/printcap previously might have the following entry in /etc/cups/printers.conf:

```
<DefaultPrinter lp>
Info Created by redhat-config-printer 0.6.x
DeviceURI parallel:/dev/lp0
Location HP 648 local printer
State Idle
Accepting Yes
JobSheets none none
QuotaPeriod 0
PageLimit 0
KLimit 0
</Printer>
```

This example shows the definition for the printer named `lp`, along with its associated device, description, state, and other information. The various possible fields and entries in this file are documented in the `printer.conf` man page.

CUPS uses a print server (daemon) named `cupsd`, also called a *scheduler* in the CUPS documentation. The server can be controlled, like other Fedora services, by the `service` command or `system-config-services client`. How the server works on a system is determined by settings in its configuration file, `cupsd.conf`, found under the `/etc/cups` directory. CUPS executables are found under the `/usr/lib/cups` directory.

The `cupsd.conf` man page documents more than 80 different settings for the server, which you can configure to match your system, network, or printing environment. Default CUPS-related files and directories are stored under the `/usr/share/cups` directory. Logging can be set to seven different levels, with information about access and errors stored in log files under the `/var/log/cups` directory.

Resource requirements can be tailored through other settings, such as `MaxCopies` to set the maximum number of copies of a print job by a user, `MaxJobs` to set a limit on the number of active print jobs, and `MaxJobsPerUser` to set a limit on the number of active jobs per user. The `RIPCache` setting (8MB by default) controls the amount of memory used for graphics cache during printing.

For example, if you want to limit printing to 20 copies of a document or page at a time and only 10 simultaneous print jobs per user, use settings such as

```
MaxCopies 20
MaxJobsPerUser 10
```

> **TIP**
>
> Don't forget to restart the CUPS server after making any changes to its configuration file. Changes are only activated when the service is restarted (when the daemon rereads its configuration file). See the section "GUI-Based Printer Configuration Quickstart" later on.

Because CUPS does not use the traditional Berkeley-style print spooling system, `lpd`, you can change the name of the printer capabilities database from the default `/etc/printcap`. Encryption can be used for printing, with secure access behavior determined by settings in `/etc/cups/client.conf`. Network access settings include port, connection, IP address, domains, and limits to the number and size of client requests.

Configuring and Managing Print Services

Your task as a system administrator (or root operator of your workstation) is to properly define local or remote printers and to ensure that printing services are enabled and running properly. Fortunately, Fedora includes Red Hat's graphical print service configuration tools that make this job easy. You should use the Red Hat tools to configure printing, as you learn in this section of the chapter. But first, take a moment to read through a quick overview of the configuration process.

CAUTION

Do not manually edit your /etc/printcap. Any changes will be lost when printing service is restarted or if your system is rebooted. If you need to create customized printer entries, save the entries in /etc/printcap.local and then restart print service.

You can configure printing services using either the command-line `system-config-printer-tui` program or the `system-config-printer-gui` graphical interface. Most of the detailed information in this chapter refers to the use of the GUI. The overview sections that follow, however, give you solid foundation in both configuration approaches. You learn the details of these processes in later sections of the chapter.

GUI-based Printer Configuration Quickstart

Configuring a printer for Fedora is easy but must be done using root permission. Make sure that the `cupsd` daemon is installed and running. If you elect to use printing support when you install Fedora, the daemon and related software will be installed. If you're not sure if `cupsd` is running, you can use the `service` command with the name of the service and the `status` keyword like so:

```
# service cups status
```

You will either see

```
cupsd is stopped
```

or if `cupsd` is running, an acknowledgement, along with its process ID, such as:

```
cupsd (pid 2923) is running...
```

If `cupsd` is installed but not running, start the daemon like so:

```
# /etc/rc.d/init.d/cups start
```

You can also start the daemon using the `service` command like so:

```
# service cups start
```

If you're using the desktop, select the Printing menu item from the System Settings menu. You will be asked to enter the root password. If not, you're using X as root, which is a bad idea. Log out, and then log back in as a regular user! After entering the root password, the printer configuration dialog appears.

You then simply follow the prompts to define your printer and add local or remote printing services. You should print a test page before saving your changes. Use the printer configuration client or the File menu's Print menu item from a GNOME or KDE client.

> **NOTE**
>
> The `system-config-printer` utility is an update to the now-legacy `printtool` client included with previous Red Hat Linux distributions. Although you might also find related tools (or symbolic links), such as `printtool`, `printconf-tui`, and `/usr/sbin/printconf-gui` installed on your system, you should use the `system-config-printer` client to manage printers under Fedora.

## 12

Console-based Printer Configuration Quickstart

Local or remote print services can also be configured locally or on a server without the X Window System. To do so, you use Red Hat's text-based `system-config-printer-tui` printer configuration utility. You need to run this command as root:

```
# system-config-printer-tui
```

The screen clears after you press Enter, and you'll see the command's main dialog. (You see this screen in the section titled "Console-based Print Commands," later in this chapter.)

> **NOTE**
>
> If you launch `system-config-printer` as root when not using X at a console, the `system-config-printer-tui` interface will be used.

You use the Tab key and spacebar to navigate the dialogs and expand lists of devices. You can create a new printer entry by highlighting the New button and pressing Enter. Use the Up or Down cursor keys to select and highlight an existing entry; then highlight the Edit button and press Enter to edit a previously defined printer.

You can then print documents from the command line using the `lpr` command, view any active jobs using the `lpq` command, and control the print queue by using the `lrpm` command.

Managing Printing Services

After defining a printer, you can use the command line to view and control your print jobs, or if root, all print jobs and printers on your system.

Table 12.1 contains a partial list of CUPS and related printing commands and drivers included with Fedora.

TABLE 12.1   Print-related Commands and Drivers

Name	Description
a2ps	Formats text files for PostScript printing
accept	Controls CUPS print job destinations
cancel	Cancels a CUPS print job
disable	Controls CUPS printers
dvi[lj,lj4l,lj2p,lj4]	Converts TeX DVI files to specific PCL format
enable	Controls CUPS printers
encscript	Converts text files to PostScript
escputil	Epson Stylus inkjet printer utility
grolbp	groff driver for Canon LBP-4 and LBP-8 laser printers
gs	The Ghostscript interpreter
gsbj[dj500, lp]	Ghostscript BubbleJet printer drivers
gsdj[dj500,lj,lp]	Ghostscript DeskJet printer drivers
lpadmin	CUPS command-line based printer utility
lp	Starts a CUPS print job
lpc	A Berkeley-subset CUPS printer control client
lpf	General printer filter
lprm	A Berkeley-compatible CUPS job queue utility
lpstat	Displays CUPS print jobs and printer status
mpage	PostScript text formatting utility
pbm[2ppa,page,to10x,toepson, toppa,toptx]	Portable bitmap conversion utilities
pr	Text formatting command
psmandup	Duplex printing utility for non-duplex printers
reject	Controls CUPS print job destinations
setup	Launches printer configuration tool
smbclient	SMB print spooler
smbprint	SMB print shell script
smbspool	SMB printer spooler
thinkjettopbm	Portable bitmap to ThinkJet printer conversion utility

Most Linux systems use PostScript as the default document format for printing. Fedora uses the gs command along with CUPS to manage local and remote print jobs and the type of data transferred during a print job. The gs command is used to translate the document stream into a format accepted by the destination printer (which most likely uses HPCL).

You can use the Ghostscript interpreter gs to display its built-in printer devices by using the gs interpreter with its --help command-line option like this:

```
# gs --help
```

Fedora includes graphical clients you can use to view many different types of documents. For example, to display PostScript documents (including compressed PostScript documents) or PostScript images, use the gv client. To display Portable Document Format (PDF) documents, you can use gv or the xpdf client.

The gs command outputs many lines of help text on command-line usage and then lists built-in printer and graphics devices. Another way to get this information is to start gs and then use the devicenames == command like this:

```
# gs
GNU Ghostscript 7.05 (2002-04-22)
Copyright (C) 2002 artofcode LLC, Benicia, CA.  All rights reserved.
This software comes with NO WARRANTY: see the file PUBLIC for details.
Loading NimbusRomNo9L-Regu font from /usr/share/fonts/default/Type1/
➥n021003l.pfb... \
2410668 1053956 1642520 347466 0 done.
Loading NimbusSanL-Regu font from /usr/share/fonts/default/Type1/n019003l.pfb...
 2785628 1379834 1662616 358654 0 done.
Using NimbusSansL-Regu font for NimbusSanL-Regu.
[/miff24 /psmono /alc8500 /lp2563 /pkmraw /stp /iwlq /pbm /md1xMono /epson /bjc600
➥/lbp310 \
/coslw2p /cdjcolor /bj10v /cdj1600 /djet500 /x11rg16x /atx23 /x11gray4 /st800
➥/jpeggray /necp6 \
/psgray /alc2000 /lp8000 /pksm /lxm3200 /jetp3852 /pbmraw /DJ630 /epsonc /bjc800
➥/lbp320 \
/coslwxl /cdjmono /bj10vh /cdj500 /laserjet /x11rg32x /atx24 /x11mono /stcolor
➥/pdfwrite /oce9050 \
/psrgb /cups /lq850 /pksmraw /lx5000 /la50 /pgm /DJ6xx /escp /faxg3 /lips2p /cp50
➥/cdj550 \
/mag16 /cdj670 /ljetplus /ljet4pjl /atx38 /bmpmono /sunhmono /pswrite /oki182 /bit
➥/cljet5 /lxm5700m \
/tiffcrle /lex7000 /la70 /pgmraw /DJ6xxP /fs600 /faxg32d /bjc880j /declj250 /pj
➥/mag256 /cdj850 /ljet2p\
 /lj4dithp /bmpa16 /bmpgray /t4693d2 /epswrite /okiibm /bitrgb /cljet5c /m8510
➥/tiffg3 /lex5700 /la75
...
```

Not all the devices are listed in this example.

At least two versions of Ghostscript are available for Linux. One version is named "AFPL Ghostscript," which went by the former name "Aladdin Ghostscript." This version is licensed under the Aladdin Free Public License, which disallows commercial distribution. The other version is called "GNU Ghostscript," which is distributed under the GNU General Public License. For details about the different versions or for answers to questions regarding licensing, see the Ghostscript home page at `http://www.cs.wisc.edu/~ghost/`.

Creating and Configuring Local Printers

Creating a local printer for your Fedora system can be accomplished in six easy steps. You must have root permission to use the `system-config-printer` client. The `cupsd` daemon should also be running before you begin (start the daemon manually as shown earlier in this chapter, or use the `ntsysv`, `chkconfig`, or `system-config-services` commands to ensure that `lpd` is started at boot time).

To launch `system-config-printer`, select the Printing menu item from the GNOME or KDE desktop panel's System Settings menu or use the command line of an X terminal window like this:

```
# system-config-printer &
```

Creating the Print Queue

The Red Hat Linux `system-config-printer` tool walks you through a process to create a new print queue, which effectively defines a new printer on your system. To begin configuration of a local (attached) printer, click the New toolbar button in `redhat-config-printer`'s main window. An Add a New Print Queue configuration dialog appears, as shown in Figure 12.1.

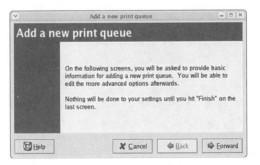

FIGURE 12.1   Click the New toolbar button to start the configuration of a new printer for your system; when the wizard's dialog appears, click the Forward button to begin.

Click the Forward button; the Queue Name dialog appears. Type a desired name for the new printer (such as lp), enter a short description, and then click the Forward button. The Queue type dialog appears, as shown in Figure 12.2. Click the queue type drop-down menu to select the type of printer you're adding. You can configure a local, or networked printer supported by the Common UNIX Printing System (CUPS), the `lpd` daemon on a remote server, a Session Message Block (SMB) server, Netware Core Protocol (Novell), or a JetDirect interface. To configure a printer attached to your computer, select the locally connected Queue type, click to select the printer device (which might be `/dev/lp0` or `/dev/usb/lp0`), and then click Forward. You can also use the Custom device button to enter a different port, such as `/dev/ttyS0`, for a serial printer.

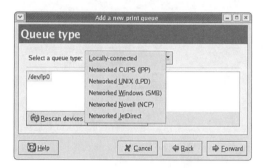

FIGURE 12.2   Click the drop-down menu to select a locally connected printer queue type.

The Printer model dialog shown in Figure 12.3 presents a drop-down menu you can use to choose the manufacturer of your printer, or you can simply choose a generic type of connected printer.

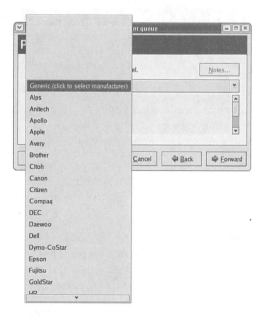

FIGURE 12.3   Click the drop-down menu to select your printer's manufacturer or printer type.

Note that you can configure a printer for Fedora even if it isn't attached to your computer. After you select your printer's manufacturer, a list of printers from that manufacturer (such as HP, as shown in Figure 12.4) will appear. Select your printer from the list, and then click the Forward button.

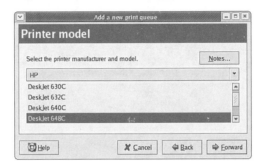

FIGURE 12.4   Select your printer from the list and click the Forward button to finish the configuration of a locally connected printer.

Don't worry if you don't see your printer listed in the selection; it is possible to select a related, though different, printer model and still be able to print to your printer. For example, many HP printers can be used by selecting the Deskjet 500 for monochrome or 500C model for color printing.

> **NOTE**
>
> You can also browse to http://www.linuxprinting.org/ to find out what drivers to use with your printer or to see a cross-referenced listing of printers supported by each driver. You might also find new and improved drivers for the latest printers on the market.

You can experiment to see which printer selection works best for your printer if its model is not listed. You might not be able to use all the features of your printer, but you will be able to set up printing service. Click Forward when you've made your choice.

The Finish and Create New Print Queue dialog shows you the printer type, printer device, and selected printer, so you can confirm that the information is correct (see Figure 12.5). If you need to change the options, click Back to return to previous dialogs. To create the new print queue, click Finish.

When the print queue has been created, you will be asked if you would like to print a test page. Click Yes to save your new printer setup and to print a test page. If you click No, a test page will not be printed, and you will need to delete the new printer entry or save or cancel your changes before you quit system-config-printer.

You can see the new printer defined in the system-config-printer main window as shown in Figure 12.6.

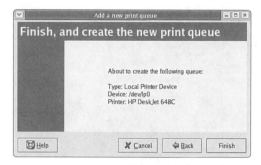

FIGURE 12.5   Double-check your settings before you commit to creating a new printer entry in /etc/printcap; when the settings are right, click Finish to create the new print queue.

FIGURE 12.6   New printer entries created in /etc/printcap will be displayed in system-config-printer's main window.

> **TIP**
>
> You can also configure multiple print queues for the same printer. Use this technique to test printing using different print drivers with the same printer. Create a new queue, give it a specific name, (such as testpcl3), and select a different printer. Finish the configuration and print a test page to compare the results against other entries to find the best output. You can also use this technique to define a monochrome or color printer entry for the same printer or to use different drivers for different types of media (such as regular or photo paper).

Editing Printer Settings

You also use the system-config-printer tool to edit the newly defined printers. To edit the printer settings, highlight the printer's listing in the Printer configuration dialog, and then click on the toolbar's Edit button. The Edit a Print Queue dialog appears, as shown in Figure 12.7.

The first tab in this dialog enables you to assign a new name for the printer.

In this example, the printer has the name lp. Other tabs in this dialog enable you to change the queue type or queue options (such as whether to print a banner page or set the image area of a page), to select or update the driver, or to choose available driver options for the printer (shown in Figure 12.8).

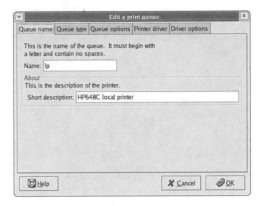

FIGURE 12.7   Edit a printer's settings by using tabs in `system-config-printer`'s Edit a Print Queue window.

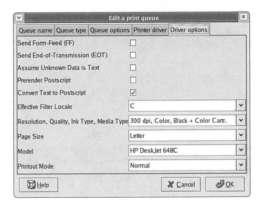

FIGURE 12.8   A printer's driver settings can be changed in the Driver Options tab of `system-config-printer`'s Edit a Print Queue window.

Click the Help button to read detailed information about the different options, which are used to force a page eject, support character rendering, and set a different resolution or a default page orientation. Printer/driver notes are available if you are selecting a different driver in the Printer Driver tab.

When you have finished editing your printer definition (or *queue*), click the OK button. Use the Apply command in the Action menu to save the definition and automatically restart the `cupsd` daemon. This step is extremely important; you need to update the printer settings and restart the `cupsd` daemon to force it to reread your new settings. Click Quit from the Action menu when finished.

Creating Network Printers

Setting up remote printing service involves configuring a print server and then creating a remote printer entry on one or more computers on your network. This section introduces a quick method of enabling printing from one Linux workstation to another Linux computer on a LAN. You also learn about Session Message Block printing using Samba and its utilities. Finally, this section discusses how to configure network-attached printers and use them to print single or multiple documents.

Enabling Network Printing on a LAN

To set up printing from one Linux workstation to another across a LAN, you need root permission and access to both computers, but the process is simple and easy to perform.

First, log in or ssh to the computer to which the printer is attached. This computer will be the printer server. Use the hostname or ifconfig commands to obtain the hostname or IP address and write down or note the name of the printer queue. If the system uses LPRng instead of CUPS, you'll need to edit the file named /etc/lpd.perms. Scroll to the end of the file and look for the remote permission entry:

```
# allow local job submissions only
REJECT SERVICE=X NOT SERVER
```

Remote printing is not enabled by default, so you must comment out the service reject line with a pound sign (#):

```
# allow local job submissions only
#REJECT SERVICE=X NOT SERVER
```

Save the file, and then restart the lpd daemon.

This will allow incoming print requests with the proper queue name (name of the local printer) from *any* remote host to be routed to the printer. After you have finished, log out and go to a remote computer on your LAN without an attached printer.

> **TIP**
>
> LPRng, like CUPS, can be configured to restrict Print services to single hosts, one or more specific local or remote users, all or part of a domain, or a LAN segment (by specifying an IP address range). An entry in /etc/lpd.perms, for example, to only allow print requests from hosts on 192.168.2.0, would look like this:
>
> ```
> ACCEPT SERVICE=X REMOTEIP=192.168.2.0/255.255.255.0
> ```
>
> The lpd.perms man page (included as part of the LPRng documentation) contains an index of keywords you can use to craft custom permissions. Don't forget to restart the lpd daemon after making any changes to /etc/lpd.perms (or /etc/lpd.conf).

If the computer with an attached printer is using Fedora and you want to set up the system for print serving, again use the system-config-printer client. You can create a new print queue, but the easiest approach is to edit settings for an existing queue and enable "sharing" of the printer.

To enable sharing, start the system-config-printer, and then click on the name of the printer to be shared over your network. Click Sharing from the Action menu, and you'll then see a dialog as shown in Figure 12.9.

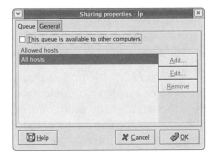

FIGURE 12.9   Sharing allows you to offer a locally attached printer as a remote printer on your network.

Click the check box in the dialog to allow sharing of the printer. By default, all remote hosts will be allowed access, but you can edit the settings to add, remove, or specify host access to your printer. Click the Edit button to specify access over a network interface (such as eth0, eth1, and so on), a range of IP addresses, or a specific host.

> **TIP**
>
> If you will share your CUPS-managed printer with other Linux hosts on a LAN using the Berkeley-type print spooling daemon, lpd, check the Enable LPD Protocol item under the Sharing dialog's General tab. Next, check that the file cups-lpd under the /etc/xinetd.d directory contains the setting disable = no and then restart xinetd. This will allow CUPS to run the cups-lpd server and accept remote print jobs sent by lpd from remote hosts. Don't forget to save your changes and restart CUPS!

When finished, click the OK button, and then use Quit from the Action menu to exit.

To create a printer queue to access a remote UNIX print server, use system-config-printer to create a printer, but select the Networked UNIX (LPD) type (refer to Figure 12.2). Click Forward, enter a printer name and description, and you'll be asked to enter the hostname (or IP address) of the remote computer with a printer, along with the printer's queue name, as shown in Figure 12.10.

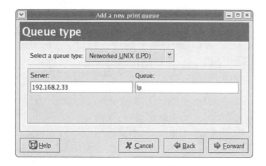

FIGURE 12.10   Enter the hostname or IP address of the remote computer with a printer, along with the remote printer's queue name.

> **NOTE**
>
> Browse to `http://www.faqs.org/rfcs/rfc1179.html` to read more about using the Strict RFC1179 Compliance option when configuring Fedora to be able to print to a remote UNIX printer. This 12-year-old Request For Comments (RFC) document describes printing protocols for the BSD line print spooling system. The option is used to allow your documents to print to remote servers using the older print system or software conforming to the standard.

Click the Forward button after entering this information; then continue to configure the new entry as if the remote printer were attached locally (use the same print driver setting as the remote printer). When finished, don't forget to save the changes!

You can also test the new remote printer by clicking the Tests menu item and using one of the test page items, such as the ASCII or PostScript test pages. The ASCII test page prints a short amount of text to test the spacing and page width; the PostScript test page prints a page of text with some information about your printer, a set of radial lines one degree apart, and a color wheel (if you use a color printer).

Session Message Block Printing

Printing to an SMB printer requires Samba, along with its utilities such as the `smbclient` and associated `smbprint` printing filter. You can use the Samba software included with Fedora to print to a shared printer on a Windows network or set up a printer attached to your system as an SMB printer. For details about using Samba, see Chapter 13, "Network Connectivity." This section describes how to create a local printer entry to be able to print to a remote shared printer using SMB.

Setting up an SMB or shared printer is usually accomplished under Windows operating systems through configuration settings using the Control Panel's Network device. After enabling print sharing, reboot the computer. In the My Computer, Printers folder, right-click the name/icon of the printer you want to share and select Sharing from the pop-up menu. Set the Shared As item; then enter a descriptive shared name, such as HP400, and a password.

You must enter a shared name and password in order to configure the printer when running Linux. You'll also need to know the printer's workgroup name, IP address, printer name, and have the username and password on hand. To find this information, choose Start, Settings, Printers; then right-click on the shared printer's listing in the Printers window and choose Properties from the pop-up window.

On your Fedora system, use `system-config-printer` to create a new local printer queue and assign it a name; then, however, select the Networked Windows (SMB) type in the Add a New Print Queue dialog. Click the drop-down list by the name of any active Samba server on your LAN (CELLO in example shown in Figure 12.11). SMB printers offered by the server will appear in the drop-down list, and can be selected for use, or you can click the Specify button and create your own entry. When you click Forward, you'll then be asked to enter a username and password for the remote share if passwords are required.

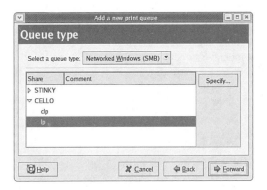

FIGURE 12.11   Create a shared remote printer using required information for Windows.

Click Forward, and then create a printer queue with characteristics that match the remote printer. (For example, if the remote printer is an HP 400 Deskjet, select the driver listed for that device in your configuration.)

Network-Attached Printer Configuration and Printing

Fedora supports other methods of remote printing, such as using a Novell Netware–based print queue or using a printer attached directly to your network with an HP JetDirect adapter. Some manufacturers even offer Linux-specific drivers and help. For example, HP/Compaq provides graphical printer configuration tools and software drivers for other Linux distributions at `http://h20000.www2.hp.com/bizsupport/TechSupport/Home.jsp`.

You can set up network-attached printing quickly and easily using a variety of devices. For example, NETGEAR's PS101 print server adapter works well with Linux. This tiny device (a self-hosted print server) is an adapter that directly attaches to a printer's Centronics port, eliminates the use of a parallel-port cable, and enables the use of the printer over a network. The PS101 offers a single 10Mbps Ethernet jack and, after initial configuration and assignment of a static IP address, can be used to print to any attached printer supported by Fedora.

A JetDirect- or UNIX-based configuration using `system-config-printer` can be used to allow you to print to the device from Fedora or other remote Linux hosts. To see any open ports or services on the device, use the `nmap` command with the print server adapter's IP address like this:

```
$ nmap 192.168.2.52
Starting nmap V. 2.54BETA22 ( www.insecure.org/nmap/ )
Interesting ports on  (192.168.2.52):
(The 1536 ports scanned but not shown below are in state: closed)
Port       State       Service
21/tcp     open        ftp
23/tcp     open        telnet
80/tcp     open        http
139/tcp    open        netbios-ssn
515/tcp    open        printer
9100/tcp   open        jetdirect
Nmap run completed -- 1 IP address (1 host up) scanned in 10 seconds
```

To configure printing, choose `system-config-printer`'s JetDirect option; then specify the device's IP address (192.168.2.52 in the example), and port 9100 (as shown previously—you're clued that this is the right port by the Service entry, which states `jetdirect` in the example). Alternatively, you can configure the device and attached printer as a UNIX-based print server, but you will need to use PS1 as the name of the remote printer queue. Note that the device hosts a built-in Web server (HTTP on port 80); you can administer the device by browsing to its IP address (such as `http://192.168.2.52` in the example). Other services, such as FTP and telnet, are supported but undocumented:

```
$ telnet 192.168.2.52
Trying 192.168.2.52...
Connected to 192.168.2.52 (192.168.2.52).
Escape character is '^]'.

Welcome to Print Server

PS>monitor
(P1)STATE: Idle
TYPE: Parallel
PRINTER STATUS: On-Line

PS>exit
Connection closed by foreign host.
```

> **TIP**
>
> Curiously, NetGear does not promote the PS101 as Linux-supported hardware even though it works. Other types of network-attached print devices include Bluetooth-enabled printers and 802.11b wireless Ethernet print servers such as Trendware's TEW-PS3, or HP/Compaq's parallel port-based WP 110, and the JetDirect 380x with USB. As always, research how well a product, such as printer or print server, works with Linux before purchasing!

Console Print Control

Older versions of Red Hat Linux used the 4.3BSD line-printer spooling system and its suite of text-based printing utilities. (Newer versions of these utilities, with the same names, are included with your Fedora CD-ROMs, but are part of the CUPS package; refer to Table 12.1.) The commands support the launching of print jobs in the background (as a background process), printing of multiple documents, the capability to specify specific local and networked printers, control of the printers, and management of the queued documents waiting in the printer's spool queue.

Console-based Printer Configuration

The `system-config-printer-tui` tool offers all the convenience and features of Red Hat's graphical printer configuration client without the need for a currently running X session. As you learned earlier, you run this command as root:

```
# system-config-printer-tui
```

After you press Enter, the command's main dialog appears, as shown in Figure 12.12. You use the Tab and spacebar keys to navigate among and choose controls in this dialog.

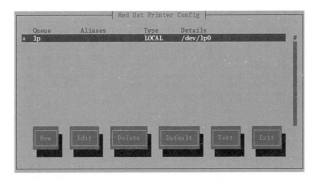

FIGURE 12.12   Use Red Hat's `system-config-printer-tui` printer configuration utility to create or edit printers during console-based Linux sessions.

Using Basic Print Commands

After configuring your printer, you can print from the desktop using any printer-capable graphical clients. If you don't use the desktop, but prefer to use or access your Fedora system using a text-based interface, you can enter a number of print commands from the command line, as well. The main CUPS commands used to print and control printing from the command line are as follows:

- lp—The line printer spooling command; used to print documents using a specific printer

- lpq—The line printer queue display command; used to view the existing list of documents waiting to be printed

- lpstat—Displays server and printer status information

- lprm—The line printer queue management command; used to remove print jobs from a printer's queue

- lpc—The line printer control program; used by the root operator to manage print spooling, the lpd daemon, and printer activity

These commands offer a subset of the features provided by CUPS, but can be used to start and control printers and print queues from the command line.

You print files (documents or images) using the lp command, along with a designated printer and filename. For example, to print the file mydoc.txt using the printer named lp, use the lp command and its -d command-line option and the printer's name, like this:

```
# lp -dlp mydoc.txt
```

Manage Print Jobs

You can also print multiple documents from the command line. For example, to print a number of files at once to the lp printer, use lpr like so:

```
# lp -dlp *.txt
```

This approach uses the wildcard capabilities of the shell to feed the lpr command all files in the current directory with a name ending in .txt for printing. Use the lpq command to view the printer's queue like so:

```
# lpq
lp is ready and printing
Rank    Owner   Job    File(s)                      Total Size
active  root    7      classes.conf                 3072 bytes
```

The lpq command reports on the job, owner, job number, file being printed, and size of job. The job *number* (7 in this example) is used by CUPS to keep track of documents printing or waiting to be printed. Each job will have a unique job number. To stop the print job in this example, use the lprm command, followed by the job number, like this:

```
# lprm 7
```

The lprm command removes the spooled files from the printer's queue and kills the job. Print job owners, such as regular users, can only remove spooled jobs that they own. As the root operator, you can kill any job.

Only the root operator can use the lpc command to administer printers and queues, as the command is primarily used for printer and queue control. You, as a regular user, cannot use it to rearrange the order of your print jobs, but you can get a display of the status of any system printer. Start lpc on the command line like this:

```
# /usr/sbin/lpc
```

The lpc command has built-in help, but only five commands: exit, help, quit, status, and ?. The status command will show the status of a specified printer or all printers:

```
# lpc
lpc> ?
Commands may be abbreviated.  Commands are:

exit    help    quit    status    ?
lpc> status
lp:
        printer is on device 'parallel' speed -1
        queuing is enabled
        printing is enabled
        no entries
        daemon present
netlp:
        printer is on device 'parallel' speed -1
        queuing is enabled
        printing is enabled
        no entries
        daemon present
lpc> quit
```

The preceding sample session shows a status report for two printers, lp and netlp. Another helpful command is lpstat, which you use like this with its -t option:

```
# lpstat -t
scheduler is running
system default destination: lp
```

```
device for lp: parallel:/dev/lp0
device for netlp: parallel:/dev/lp0
lp accepting requests since Jan 01 00:00
netlp accepting requests since Jan 01 00:00
printer lp is idle.  enabled since Jan 01 00:00
printer netlp is idle.  enabled since Jan 01 00:00!)
```

This command lists all status information about printer queues on the local system.

Using the Common UNIX Printing System

You can use CUPS to create printer queues, get print server information, and manage queues by launching a browser (such as mozilla) and browsing to http://localhost:631. CUPS provides a Web-based administration interface, as shown in Figure 12.13.

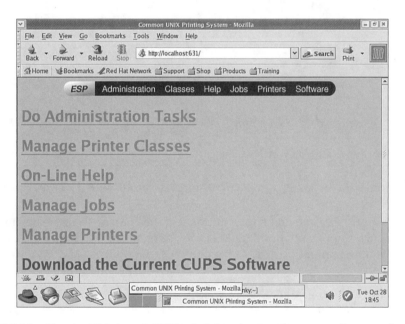

FIGURE 12.13   Use the Web-based CUPS administrative interface to configure and manage printing.

If you click on the Do Administration Tasks item in the browser page, you'll be asked to enter the root password, as shown in Figure 12.14.

Creating a CUPS Printer Entry

This section provides a short example of creating a Linux printer entry using CUPS' Web-based interface. Use the CUPS interface to create a printer and device queue type (such as local, remote, serial port, or Internet); then enter a device uniform resource identifier

(URI), such as `lpd://192.168.2.35/lp`, which represents the IP address of a remote UNIX print server, and the name of the remote print queue on the server. You will also need to specify the model or make of printer and its driver. A Printers page link allows you to print a test page, stop printing service, manage the local print queue, modify the printer entry, or add another printer.

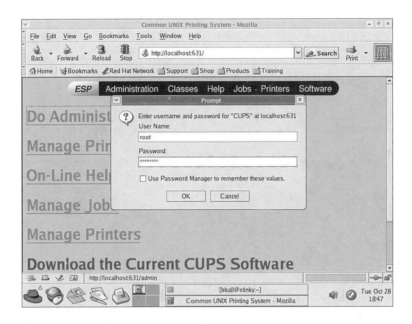

FIGURE 12.14   Enter the root password to perform printer administration with CUPS.

In the Admin page, click the Add Printer button and then enter a printer name in the Name: field (such as `lp`), a physical location of the printer in the Location: field, and a short note about the printer (such as its type) in the Description: field. Figure 12.15 shows an example entry for an HP648C.

Click the Continue button. You can then select the type of printer access (local, remote, serial port, or Internet) in the Device page as shown in Figure 12.16. For example, to configure printing to a local printer, choose Parallel Port #1, or for a remote printer, the LPD/LPR Host or Printer entry.

Again click Continue and select a printer make as requested in Figure 12.17.

After you click Continue, you will then select the driver. After creating the printer, you can then use the Printer page, as shown in Figure 12.18, to print a test page, stop printing service, manage the local print queue, modify the printer entry, or add another printer.

CUPS offers many additional features and once installed, configured, and running, provides transparent traditional UNIX printing support for Fedora.

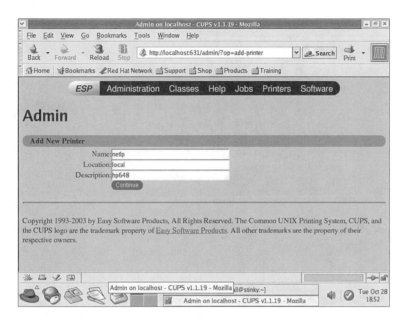

FIGURE 12.15   Use CUPS to create a new printer queue.

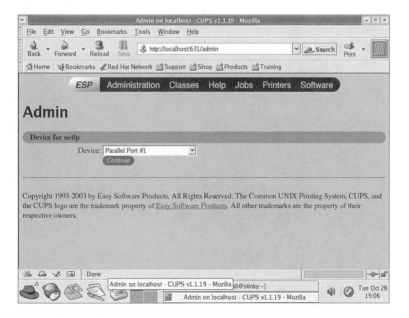

FIGURE 12.16   Select a printer device in the CUPS administrative page.

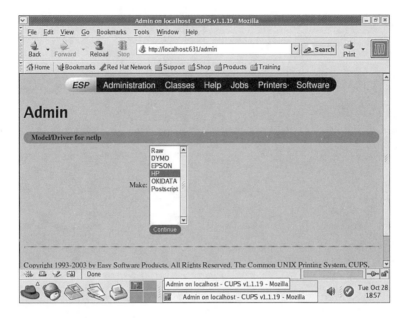

FIGURE 12.17   Select printer make when creating a new queue.

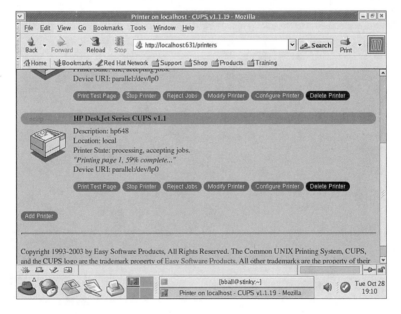

FIGURE 12.18   Manage printers easily using the CUPS Printer page.

> **NOTE**
>
> To learn more about CUPS and to get a basic overview of the system, browse to
> http://www.cups.org/.

Avoiding Printer-Support Problems

## 12

Troubleshooting printer problems can be frustrating, especially if you find that your brand new printer is not working properly with Linux. First, keep in mind that nearly all printers on the market today work with Linux. However, there are some vendors with higher batting averages in the game of supporting Linux. If you care to read a scorecard, browse to http://www.linuxprinting.org/vendors.html.

All-in-One (Print/Fax/Scan) Devices

Problematic printers, or printing devices that may or may not work with Fedora include multifunction, or all-in-one type printers that combine scanning, faxing, and printing services. You would be well-advised to research any planned purchase, and avoid any vendor unwilling to support Linux with drivers or development information.

One shining star in the field of Linux support for multifunction printers is HP support of the HP OfficeJet Linux driver project at http://hpoj.sourceforge.net/. Printing and scanning is supported on many models, with fax support in development.

Using USB and Legacy Printers

Other problems can arise because of a lack of a printer's USB vendor and device ID information—a problem shared by some USB scanners under Linux. For information regarding USB printer support, you can check with the Linux printing folks (at the URL in the start of this section) or with the Linux USB project at http://www.linux-usb.org.

Although many newer printers require universal serial bus (USB), excellent support still exists for legacy parallel-port (IEEE-1284) printers with Linux, enabling sites to continue to use older hardware. You can take advantage of Linux workarounds to set up printing even if the host computer does not have a traditional parallel printer port or if you want to use a newer USB printer on an older computer.

For example, to host a parallel port–based printer on a USB-only computer, attach the printer to the computer using an inexpensive USB-to-parallel converter. USB-to-parallel converters typically provide a Centronics connector; one end of that connector is plugged in to the older printer, whereas the other end is plugged in to a USB connector. The USB connector is then plugged in to your hub, desktop, or notebook USB port. On the other hand, you can use an add-on PCI card to add USB support for printing (and other devices) if the legacy computer does not have a built-in USB. Most PCI USB interface cards add at least two ports, and devices can be chained via a hub.

> **Related Fedora and Linux Commands**
>
> The following commands help you manage printing services:
>
> `accept`—Controls print job access to the CUPS server via the command line
>
> `cancel`—Cancels a print job from the command line
>
> `cancel`—Command-line control print queues
>
> `disable`—Controls printing from the command line
>
> `enable`—Command-line control CUPS printers
>
> `lp`—Command-line control of printers and print service
>
> `lpc`—Displays status of printers and print service at the console
>
> `lpq`—Views print queues (pending print jobs) at the console
>
> `lprm`—Removes print jobs from the print queue via the command line
>
> `lpstat`—Displays printer and server status
>
> `system-config-printer`—Red Hat's graphical printer onfiguration tool
>
> `system-config-printer-tui`—Red Hat text-dialog printer configuration tool

Reference

`http://www.linuxprinting.org/`—Browse here for specific drivers and information about USB and other types of printers.

`http://www.hp.com/wwsolutions/linux/products/printing_imaging/index.html`—Short, but definitive information from HP regarding printing product support under Linux.

`http://www.linuxdoc.org/HOWTO/Printing-HOWTO/`—Grant Taylor's Printing HOWTO, with information on using various print services under Linux.

`http://www.cups.org/`—A comprehensive repository of CUPS software, including versions for Red Hat Linux.

`http://www.pwg.org/ipp/`—Home page for the Internet Printing Protocol standards.

`http://www.linuxprinting.org/cups-doc.html`—Information about the Common UNIX Printing System (CUPS).

`http://www.cs.wisc.edu/~ghost/`—Home page for the Ghostscript interpreter.

`http://www.samba.org/`—Base entry point for getting more information about Samba and using the SMB protocol with Linux, UNIX, Mac OS, and other operating systems.

## CHAPTER 13

Network Connectivity

IN THIS CHAPTER

- Networking with TCP/IP
- Network Organization
- Hardware Devices for Networking
- Using Network Configuration Tools
- Dynamic Host Configuration Protocol
- Using the Network File System
- Putting Samba to Work
- Wireless Networking
- Securing Your Network
- Reference

One of Linux's strongest features is its networking capabilities. Linux can emulate or share files with almost every operating system. Linux can talk to Mac OS, Mac OS X, Netware, BSD, all flavors of UNIX, and even Windows (with the help of SAMBA). Linux servers can be easily and quickly deployed in heterogeneous networks and will run for weeks or even months without failures. It's that kind of flexibility and performance that can account for Linux's increased wired and wireless presence in the workplace and in homes.

This chapter introduces some basic concepts about networking with Linux and shows you how to configure, manage, and use *network interface cards (NICs)* and various network services with Fedora. You'll see how to use command-line programs to control networking on your system, as well as how to launch and use several of Red Hat's graphical network management clients. You'll need to perform many of these tasks using root permission, but you'll see how easily network management can be performed when using Linux. You'll also see how to protect your system on any network using Red Hat's graphical firewall configuration utility.

Networking with TCP/IP

The basic building block for any network based on UNIX hosts is the Transport Control Protocol/Internet Protocol (TCP/IP) suite of three protocols. The suite consists of the Internet Protocol (IP), Transport Control Protocol (TCP), and Universal Datagram Protocol (UDP). IP is the base protocol. The TCP/IP suite is *packet*-based, which means that data is broken into little chunks on the transmit end for transmission to the receiving end. Breaking data up into manageable packets allows for faster and more accurate transfers. In TCP/IP, all data travels via IP packets, which is why addresses are referred to as IP addresses. It is the lowest level of the suite.

TCP is a connection-based protocol. Before data is transmitted between two machines, a connection is established between them. When a connection is made, a stream of data is sent to the IP to be broken into the packets that are then transmitted. At the receiving end, the packets are put back in order and sent to the proper application port.

On the other hand, UDP is a connectionless protocol. Applications using this protocol just choose their destination and start sending. UDP is normally used for small amounts of data or on fast and reliable networks. If you're interested in the internals of TCP/IP, see the "Reference" section at the end of this chapter for places to look for more information.

Fedora and Networking

Chances are that your network card was configured during the installation of Fedora. You can however, use the `ifconfig` command at the shell prompt or Red Hat's graphical network configuration tools, such as `system-config-network`, to edit your system's network device information or to add or remove network devices on your system. Hundreds of networking commands and utilities are included with Fedora—far too many to cover in this chapter and more than enough for coverage in two or three volumes.

Nearly all Ethernet cards can be used with Linux, along with many PCMCIA wired and wireless network cards. The great news is that many USB wireless network devices also work just fine with Linux (and more will be supported with upcoming versions of the Linux kernel. Check the Linux USB Project at `http://www.linux-usb.org` for the latest developments or to verify support for your device).

After reading this chapter, you might want to learn more about other graphical network clients for use with Linux. The GNOME `ethereal` client, for example, can be used to monitor all traffic on your LAN or specific types of traffic. Another client, NmapFE, can be used to scan a specific host for open ports and other running services.

TCP/IP Addressing

To understand networking with Linux, you need to know the basics of TCP/IP addressing. Internet IP addresses (also known as public IP addresses) are different from those used internally on a Local Area Network, or LAN. Internet IP addresses are assigned (for the United States and some other hosts) by the American Registry for Internet Numbers, available at `http://www.arin.net/`. Entities that need an Internet address apply to this agency to be assigned an address. The agency assigns Internet service providers (ISPs) one or more blocks of IP addresses, which the ISPs can then assign to their subscribers.

You'll quickly recognize the current form of TCP/IP addressing, known as IPv4 (IP version 4). In this method, a TCP/IP address is expressed of a series of four decimal numbers—a 32-bit value expressed in a format known as dotted decimal format, such as `192.168.120.135`. Each set of numbers is known as an *octet* (eight ones and 0s, such as `10000000` to represent 128) and ranges from 0 to 255.

The first octet usually determines what *class* the network belongs to. There are three classes of networks. The classes are

Class A—Consists of networks with the first octet ranging from 1 to 126. There are only 126 Class A networks—each composed of up to 16,777,214 hosts. (If you're doing the math, there are potentially 16,777,216 addresses, but no host portion of an address can be all 0s or 255s.) The "10." network is reserved for local network use, and the "127." network is reserved for the *loopback* address of 127.0.0.1. Loopback addressing is used by TCP/IP to enable Linux network-related client and server programs to communicate on the same host. This address will not appear and is not accessible on your LAN.

> **NOTE**
>
> Notice that 0 isn't included in Class A. The 0 address is used for network-to-network broadcasts. Also, note that there are two other classes of networks, Class D and E. Class D networks are reserved for multicast addresses and not for use by network hosts. Class E addresses are deemed experimental, and thus are not open for public addressing.

Class B—Consists of networks defined by the first two octets with the first ranging from 128 to 191. The "128." network is also reserved for local network use. There are 16,382 Class B networks—each with 65,534 possible hosts.

Class C—Consists of a network defined by the first three octets with the first ranging from 192 to 223. The "192." network is another that is reserved for local network use. There are a possible 2,097,150 Class C networks of up to 254 hosts each.

No host portion of an IP address can be all 0s or 255s. These addresses are reserved for broadcast addresses. IP addresses with all 0s in the host portion are reserved for network-to-network broadcast addresses. IP addresses with all 255s in the host portion are reserved for local network broadcasts. Broadcast messages are not typically seen by users.

These classes are the standard, but a *netmask* also determines what class your network is in. The netmask determines what part of an IP address represents the network and what part represents the host. Common netmasks for the different classes are

Class A—255.0.0.0

Class B—255.255.0.0

Class C—255.255.255.0

Because of the allocation of IP addresses for Internet hosts, it is now impossible to get a Class A network. It is also nearly impossible to get a Class B network (all the addresses have been given out, but some companies are said to be willing to sell theirs), and Class C network availability is dropping rapidly with the current growth of Internet use worldwide. See the following sidebar.

Limits of Current IP Addressing

The current IPv4 address scheme is based on 32-bit numbering and limits the number of available IP addresses to about 4.1 billion. Many companies and organizations (particularly in the United States) were assigned very large blocks of IP addresses in the early stages of the growth of the Internet, which has left a shortage of "open" addresses. Even with careful allocation of Internet-connected host IP addresses and the use of *Network Address Translation* (to provide communication to and from machines behind an Internet-connected computer), the Internet might run out of available addresses.

To solve this problem, a newer scheme named IPv6 (IP version 6) is being implemented. It uses a much larger addressing solution based on 128-bit addresses, with enough room to include much more information about a specific host or device, such as Global Positioning Server (GPS) or serial numbering. Although the specific details about the entire contents of an IPv6 address have yet to be finalized, all Internet-related organizations appear to agree that something must be done to provide more addresses. According to Vint Cerf, one of the primary developers of the TCP/IP protocol, "There will be nearly 2.5 billion devices on the Internet by 2006, and by 2010 half the world's population will have access to the Internet."

You can get a good overview of the differences between IPv4 and IPv6, policies regarding IP address assignments, and the registration process of obtaining IP addresses by browsing to `http://www.arin.net/library/index.html`. Read the Linux IPv6 HOWTO by browsing to `http://tldp.org/HOWTO/Linux+IPv6-HOWTO/`.

Fedora supports the use of iIPv6 and includes a number of networking tools conforming to IPv6 addressing. Support for IPv6 can be configured by using settings and options in the file named `network` under the `/etc/sysconfig` directory, along with changes to related network configuration files, such as `/etc/hosts`. Many IPv6-based tools, such as `ipcalc6`, `ping6`, and `traceroute6`, are available for Fedora. See various files under the `/usr/share/doc/initscripts` directory for more information specific to setting up IPv6 addressing with Linux and Fedora.

Migration to IPv6 is slow in coming, however, because the majority of computer operating systems, software, hardware, firmware, and users are still in the IPv4 mindset. Supporting IPv6 will require rewrites to many networking utilities, portions of operating systems currently in use, and firmware in routing and firewall hardware.

Using IP Masquerading in Fedora

Three blocks of IP addresses are reserved for use on internal networks and hosts not directly connected to the Internet. The address ranges are `10.0,0,0` to `10.255.255.255`, or 1 Class A network; `172.16.0.0` to `172.31.255.255`, or 16 Class B networks; and `192.168.0.0` to `192.168.255.255`, or 256 Class C networks. Use these IP addresses when building a LAN for your business or home. Which class you choose can depend on the number of hosts on your network.

Internet access for your internal network can be provided by a PC running Fedora or other broadband or dial-up router. The host or device is connected to the Internet and is used as an Internet gateway to forward information to and from your LAN. The host should also be used as a *firewall* to protect your network from malicious data and users while functioning as an Internet gateway. A PC used in this fashion will typically have at least two network interfaces. One is connected to the Internet with the other connected to the computers on the LAN (via a hub or switch). Some broadband devices also incorporate four or more switching network interfaces. Data is then passed between the LAN and the Internet using *Network Address Translation*, or *NAT*, better known in Linux circles as *IP Masquerading*. See the section "Network Security" later in this chapter.

> **NOTE**
>
> Don't rely on a single point of protection for your LAN, especially if you use wireless networking, provide dial-in services, or allow mobile (laptop or PDA) users internal or external access to your network. Companies, institutions, and individuals relying on a "moat mentality" have often discovered to their dismay that such an approach to security is easily breached. Make sure that your network operation is accompanied by a security policy that stresses multiple levels of secure access, with protection built into every server and workstation—something easily accomplished when using Linux.

Ports

Most servers on your network have more than one task. For example, Web servers have to serve both standard and secure pages. You might also be running an FTP server on the same host. For this reason, applications are provided *ports* to use to make "direct" connections for specific software services. These ports help TCP/IP distinguish services so that data can get to the correct application. If you check the file /etc/services, you will see the common ports and their usage. For example, for FTP, HTTP, and Post Office Protocol (email retrieval server), you'll see

```
ftp        21/tcp
http       80/tcp      www www-http  # WorldWideWeb HTTP
pop3       110/tcp     pop-3         # POP version 3
```

The ports defined in /etc/services in this example are 21 for FTP, 80 for HTTP, and 110 for POP3. Other common port assignments are 25 for *Simple Mail Transport Protocol (SMTP)* and 22 for *Secure Shell (SSH)* remote login. Note that these ports are not set in stone, and you can set up your server to respond to different ports. For example, although port 22 is listed in /etc/services as a common default for SSH, the sshd server can be configured to listen on a different port by editing its configuration file /etc/ssh/sshd_config. The default setting (commented out with a pound sign) looks like this:

```
#Port 22
```

Edit the entry to use a different port, making sure to select an unused port number, such as

```
Port 2224
```

Save your changes, and then restart the sshd server. (See Chapter 7, "Managing Services," to see how to restart a service.) Remote users must now access the host through port 2224, which can be done using ssh's -p (port) option like so:

```
$ ssh -p 2224 remote_host_name_or_IP
```

Network Organization

Properly organizing your network addressing process grows more difficult as the size of your network grows. Setting up network addressing for a Class C network with fewer than 254 devices is simple. Setting up addressing for a large, worldwide company with a Class A network and many different users can be extremely complex. If your company has fewer than 254 *hosts* (meaning any device that requires an IP address, including computers, printers, routers, switches, and other devices) and all your workgroups can share information, a single Class C network will be sufficient.

Subnetting

Within Class A and B networks, there can be separate networks called *subnets*. Subnets are considered part of the host portion of an address for network class definitions. For example, in the 128. Class B network, you can have one computer with an address of 128.10.10.10 and another with an address of 128.10.200.20; these computers are on the same network (128.10.), but they have different subnets (128.10.10. and 128.10.200.). Because of this, communication between the two computers requires either a router or a switch (both are discussed later in the "Network Devices" section). Subnets can be helpful for separating workgroups within your company.

Often subnets can be used to separate workgroups that have no real need to interact with or to shield from other groups information passing among members of a specific workgroup. For example, if your company is large enough to have its own HR department and payroll section, you could put those departments' hosts on their own subnet and use your router configuration to limit the hosts that can connect to this subnet. This configuration prevents networked workers who aren't members of the designated departments from being able to view some of the confidential information the HR and payroll personnel work with.

Subnet use also enables your network to grow beyond 254 hosts and share IP addresses. With proper routing configuration, users might not even know they are on a different subnet from their co-workers. Another common use for subnetting is with networks that cover a wide geographic area. It isn't practical for a company with offices in Chicago and London to have both offices on the same subnet, so using a separate subnet for each office is the best solution.

Subnet Masks

Subnet masks are used by TCP/IP to show which part of an IP address is the network portion and which part is the host. Subnet masks are usually referred to as *netmasks*. For a pure Class A network, the netmask would be 255.0.0.0; for a Class B network, the netmask would be 255.255.0.0; and for a Class C network, the netmask would be 255.255.255.0. Netmasks can also be used to deviate from the standard classes.

By using customized netmasks, you can subnet your network to fit your needs. For example, your network has a single Class C address. You have a need to subnet your network. Although this isn't possible with a normal Class C subnet mask, you can change the mask to break your network into subnets. By changing the last octet to a number greater than 0, you can break the network into as many subnets as you need.

For more information on how to create customized subnet masks, see Day 6, "The Art of Subnet Masking," in *Sams Teach Yourself TCP/IP Network Administration in 21 Days*. This chapter goes into great detail on how to create custom netmasks and explains how to create an addressing cheat sheet for hosts on each subnet. You can also browse to the Linux Network Administrator's Guide and read about how to create subnets at `http://www.tldp.org/LDP/nag2/index.html`.

Broadcast, Unicast, and Multicast Addressing

Information can get to systems through three types of addresses: unicast, multicast, and broadcast. Each type of address is used according to the purpose of the information being sent, as explained here:

Broadcasting—Transmits information to all the hosts on a network or subnet. *Dynamic Host Configuration Protocol (DHCP)* uses broadcast messages when the DHCP client looks for a DHCP server to get its network settings, and *Reverse Address Resolution Protocol (RARP)* uses broadcast messages for hardware address to IP address resolution. Broadcast messages use .255 in all the host octets of the network IP address. (10.2.255.255 will broadcast to every host in your Class B network.)

Unicast—Sends information to one specific host. Unicast addresses are used for telnet, FTP, SSH, or any other information that needs to be shared in a one-to-one exchange of information. Although it is possible that any host on the subnet/network can see the information being passed, only one host is the intended recipient and will take action on the information being received.

Multicasting—Broadcasts information to groups of computers sharing an application, such as a video conferencing client or online gaming application. All the machines participating in the conference or game require the same information at precisely the same time to be effective.

Hardware Devices for Networking

As stated at the beginning of this chapter, networking is one of the strong points of the Linux operating system. This section covers the classes of devices used for basic networking. Note that this section talks about hardware devices, and not Linux networking devices, which are discussed in the section, "Using Network Configuration Tools."

Network Interface Cards

A computer must have a *NIC* to connect to a network. Currently, there are several topologies (ways of connecting computers) for network connections. These topologies range from the old and mostly outdated 10BASE-2 to the much newer and popular wireless Wi-Fi or 802.11 networking.

A Dual-Host No-NIC Network

The truly frugal can also "network" two Linux workstations using a null-modem or LPT cable and PPP, as shown in the PPP HOWTO at `http://tldp.org/HOWTO/PPP-HOWTO/direct.html`. Just connect two PCs running Linux together with a null-modem cable, and use the `pppd` daemon on each end. If one Linux host is connected to a network or has a dialup connection, that PC will become a gateway for the other host. You will need to use `pppd`'s `defaultroute` option on the serial-only host when connecting.

Each NIC has a unique address (the hardware address, known as Media Access Control, or MAC), which identifies that NIC. This address is six pairs of hexadecimal bits separated by colons (:). A MAC address looks similar to this: 00:60:08:8F:5A:D9. The hardware address is used by DHCP (see "DHCP" later in this chapter) to identify a specific host. It is also used by the *Address Resolution Protocol (ARP)* and *Reverse Address Resolution Protocol (RARP)* to map hosts to IP addresses.

This section covers some of the different types of NIC used to connect to your network.

Token Ring

Token ring networking was developed by IBM. As the name implies, the network is set up in a ring. A single "token" is passed from host to host, indicating the receiving host's "permission" to transmit data.

Token ring has a maximum transfer rate of 16Mbps (16 million bits per second). Unlike 10BASE-2 and 10BASE-5, token ring uses what is called *unshielded twisted pair (UTP)* cable. This cable looks a lot like the cable that connects your phone to the wall. Almost all token ring NICs are recognized by Linux.

10BASE-T

10BASE-T was the standard for a long time. A large number of networks still use it. 10BASE-T also uses UTP cable. Instead of being configured in a ring, 10BASE-T mostly uses a star architecture. In this architecture, the hosts all connect to a central location (usually a hub, which you learn about later in the section titled "Hubs"). All the data is sent to all hosts, but only the destination host takes action on individual packets. 10BASE-T has a transfer rate of 10Mbps.

10BASE-T has a maximum segment length of 100 meters. There are many manufacturers of 10BASE-T NICs, and most are recognized by Red Hat.

100BASE-T

100BASE-T is quickly becoming the most popular network. It has a speed of 100Mbps with the same ease of administration as 10BASE-T. For most networks, the step from 10BASE-T to 100BASE-T is as simple as replacing NICs and hubs. Most 100BASE-T NICs and hubs can also handle 10BASE-T and can automatically detect which is in use. This allows for a gradual network upgrade and usually doesn't require rewiring your whole network. Nearly every known 100BASE-T NIC and most generic NICs are compatible with Linux, thanks to Donald Becker of `http://www.scyld.com`. 100BASE-T requires category 5 unshielded twisted pair cabling.

Fiber Optic and Gigabit Ethernet

Fiber optic is more commonly used in newer and high-end installations because the cost of upgrading can be prohibitive for older sites.

Fiber optics were originally used on *Fiber Distributed Data Interface (FDDI)* networks, similar to token ring in structure except that there are two rings—one is primary, whereas the other is secondary. The primary ring is used exclusively, and the secondary sits idle until there is a break in the primary ring. At this point, the secondary ring takes over, keeping the network alive. FDDI has a speed of 100Mbps and has a maximum ring length of 62 miles. FDDI uses several tokens at the same time that, along with the faster speed of fiber optics, account for the drastic increase in network speed.

As stated, switching to a fiber optic network can be very costly. To make the upgrade, the whole network has to be rewired (as much as U.S. $150 per network connection), and all NICs must be replaced at the same time. Most FDDI NICs are recognized by Linux.

Gigabit Ethernet, capable of 1000Mbps, is now becoming more widespread in use with movement toward a 10 Gigabit standard. Fiber-related Gigabit is termed 1000BASE-X, whereas 1000BASE-T Gigabit Ethernet uses twisted-pair (see the section, "Unshielded Twisted Pair"). Red Hat supports 1000BASE-T and a number of Gigabit NICs.

Wireless Network Interfaces

Wireless has really taken off in the past year or two. Wireless networking, as the name states, doesn't require any network cables. Upgrading is as easy as replacing network cards and equipment, such as routers and switches. Wireless networking equipment can also work along with the traditional wired networking using existing equipment. Wireless technology is used mostly for users with either laptop or handheld computers, but desktop Peripheral Component Interface (PCI) adapters with wireless hardware are available.

It might not be practical to upgrade a desktop or large server to wireless just yet if the wiring is already in place. Wireless networking is still generally slower than a traditional wired network. However, this situation is changing with wider adoption of newer protocols, such as 802.11g (supporting the common 802.11b and faster but less popular 802.11a), along with the introduction of more compliant and inexpensive wireless NICs.

13

As of this writing, the price for wireless networking equipment is low enough that many home users are using wireless networking to eliminate the need to run cable throughout their houses. With each new version of Linux, more and more wireless NICs are compatible. (It's usually better to get brand name wireless NICs: You have a better chance of compatibility.) Check the `http://www.hpl.hp.com/personal/Jean_Tourrilhes/Linux/` Web page for more specific hardware compatibility information. More on wireless networking is discussed later in this chapter.

Network Cable

Currently, three types of network cable exist—coaxial, unshielded twisted pair (UTP), and fiber. Coaxial cable (rarely used today) looks a lot like the coaxial cable used to connect your television to the cable jack or antenna. UTP looks a lot like the cable that runs from your phone to the wall jack (the jacks are a bit wider). Fiber cable looks sort of like the RCA cables used on your stereo or like the cable used on your electrical appliances in your house (two separate segments connected together). The following sections discuss UTP and fiber network cable in more detail.

Unshielded Twisted Pair

Unshielded twisted pair (UTP) uses color-coded pairs of thin copper wire to transmit data. Six categories of UTP exist—each serving a different purpose:

Category 1 (Cat1)—Used for voice transmissions such as your phone. Only one pair is used per line—one wire to transmit and one to receive. An RJ-11 plug is used to connect the cable to your phone and the wall.

Category 2 (Cat2)—Used in early token ring networks. Has a transmission rate of 4Mbps (million bits per second) and has the slowest data transfer rate. An RJ-11 plug is also used for cable connections.

Category 3 (Cat3)—Used for 10BASE-T networks. It has a transmission rate of 10Mbps. Three pairs of cables are used to send and receive signals. RJ-11 or RJ-45 plugs can be used for Cat3 cables, usually deferring to the smaller RJ-11. RJ-45 plugs are similar in design to RJ-11, but are larger to handle up to four pairs of wire and are used more commonly on Cat5 cables.

Category 4 (Cat4)—Used in modern token ring networks. It has a transmission rate of 16Mbps and is less and less common as companies are switching to better alternatives. RJ-45 plugs are used for cable connections.

Category 5 (Cat5)—The fastest of the UTP categories with a transmission rate of up to 100Mbps. It is used in both 10BASE-T and 100BASE-T networks and uses four pairs of wire. Cat5 cable came out just as 10BASE-T networks were becoming popular and isn't much more expensive than Cat3 cable. As a result, most 10BASE-T networks use Cat5 UTP instead of Cat3. Cat5 cable uses RJ-45 plugs.

Category 6 (Cat6)—Also rated at 100Mbps, this cable is available in two forms: stranded for short runs (25-meter) and solid for up to 100-meter runs, but which should not be flexed.

Fiber Optic Cable

Fiber optic cable (fiber) is usually orange or red in color. The transmission rate is 100Mbps and has a maximum length of 62 miles. Fiber uses a two-pronged plug to connect to devices. A couple of advantages to fiber are that because it uses light instead of electricity to transmit its signal, it is free from the possibility of electromagnetic interference and is also more difficult to tap into and eavesdrop.

Hubs

Hubs are used to connect several hosts together on a star architecture network. Hubs can have any number of connections; the common sizes are 4, 8, 16, 24, and 48 connections (ports)—each port has a light that comes on when a network connection is made (link light). The use of hubs enables you to expand your network easily; you can just add new hubs when you need to add new connections. Each hub can connect to the other hubs on the network, typically, through a port on the hub called an *uplink* port. This enables two hubs, connected by their uplink ports, to act as one hub. Having a central location where all the hosts on your network can connect allows for easier troubleshooting of problems. If one host goes down, none of the other hosts are affected (depending on the purpose of the downed host). Because hubs aren't directly involved with the Linux operating system, compatibility isn't an issue.

> **TIP**
>
> Troubleshooting network connections can be a challenge, especially on large networks. If a user complains that he has lost his network connection, the hub is a good place to start. If the link light for the user's port is lit, chances are the problem is with the user's network configuration. If the link light isn't on, either the host's NIC is bad, the cable is not inserted properly, or the cable has gone bad for some reason.

Routers and Bridges

Routers and bridges are used to connect different networks to your network and to connect different subnets within your network. Routers and bridges both serve the same purpose of connecting networks and subnets, but they do so with different techniques. The information in the following sections will help you choose the connection method that best suits your needs.

Bridges

Bridges are used within a network to connect different subnets. A bridge will blindly relay all information from one subnet to another without any filtering and is often referred to as a *dumb gateway*. This can be helpful if one subnet in your network is becoming over-burdened and you need to lighten the load. A bridge isn't very good for connecting to the Internet, however, because it lacks filtering. You really don't want all traffic traveling the Internet to be able to get through to your network.

Routers

Routers can pass data from one network to another, and they allow for filtering of data. Routers are best suited to connect your network to an outside network, such as the Internet. If you have a Web server for an internal intranet that you don't want people to access from the Internet, for example, you can use a router's filter to block port 80 from your network. These filters can be used to block specific hosts from accessing the Internet as well. For these reasons, routers are also called *smart gateways*.

Routers range in complexity and price from a Cisco brand router that can cost thousands of dollars to other brands that can be less than $200.

Initializing New Network Hardware

All the initial network configuration and hardware initialization for Fedora is normally done during installation. At times, however, you will need to reconfigure networking on your system, such as when a host needs to be moved to a different subnet or a different network, or if you replace any of your computer's networking hardware.

Linux creates network interfaces in memory when the kernel recognizes that a NIC or other network device is attached to the system. These interfaces are unlike other Linux interfaces, such as serial communications ports, and will not have a corresponding device file in the /dev directory. Unless support for a particular NIC is built in to your kernel, Linux must be told to load a specific kernel module to support your NIC. More than 100 such modules are located in the /lib/modules/2.6.XX-XX/kernel/drivers/net directory (where XX-XX is your version of the kernel).

You can initialize a NIC in several ways when using Linux. When you first install Fedora, automatic hardware probing detects and configures your system to use any installed NICs. If you remove the original NIC and replace it with a different make and model, your system won't automatically detect and initialize the device unless you configure Fedora to use automatic hardware detection when booting. If you have enabled the kudzu hardware daemon, (see Chapter 7, "Managing Services," and Chapter 8, "Managing Software and System Resources"), it will detect the absence of the old NIC and the presence of the new NIC at boot time and prompt you for permission to change your system's NIC configuration information.

If you do not use automatic hardware detection and configuration, you can initialize network hardware by

- Manually editing the /etc/modprobe.conf file to prompt the system to recognize and support the new hardware upon reboot

- Write a script or insert commands into the /etc/rc.d/rc.local file to initialize the new hardware upon booting, taking care to avoid software service dependencies; in other words, not attempting remote connections or file system mounting until hardware is initialized and configured

- Manually load or unload the new device's kernel module with the `modprobe` command

The following sections explain the first and last of the preceding methods.

Editing the `/etc/modprobe.conf` File

You can manually edit the `/etc/modprobe.conf` file to add a module dependency entry (also known as a *directive*) to support a new NIC or other network device. This entry includes the device's name and its corresponding kernel module. After you add this entry, the Linux kernel recognizes your new networking hardware upon reboot. Fedora runs a module dependency check upon booting.

For example, if your system uses a RealTek NIC, you could use an entry like this:

```
alias eth0 8139too
```

The example entry tells the Linux kernel to load the `8139too.o` kernel module to support the `eth0` network device. On the other hand, if you have an Intel Ethernet Pro NIC installed, you would use an entry like this:

```
alias eth0 eepro100
```

Other parameters can be passed to a kernel module using one or more option entries, if need be, to properly configure your NIC. See the `modprobe.conf` manual page for more information on using entries. For more specifics regarding NIC kernel modules, examine the module's source code because no manual pages exist (a good opportunity for anyone willing to write the documentation).

> **TIP**
>
> Linux kernel and network tools can be used to diagnose problems or troubleshoot problematic NICs. However, if you browse to Don Becker's Linux Ethercard Status, Diagnostic and Setup Utilities page at `http://www.scyld.com/ethercard_diag.html`, you'll find more than two dozen hardware-specific utilities for a variety of PCI and legacy ISA Ethernet network cards. These tools can be extremely helpful if you run into trouble during NIC recognition or configuration.

Using `modprobe` to Manually Load Kernel Modules

You do not have to use an `/etc/modprobe.conf` entry to initialize kernel support for your new network device. As root, you can manually load or unload the device's kernel module using the `modprobe` command, along with the module's name. For example, use the following command line to enable the example RealTek NIC:

```
# modprobe 8139too
```

After you press Enter, you will see this device reported from the kernel's ring buffer messages, which can be displayed by the dmesg command. Here's a portion of that command's output:

```
$ dmesg
...
eth0: RealTek RTL8139 Fast Ethernet at 0xce8ee000, 00:30:1b:0b:07:0d, IRQ 11
eth0: Identified 8139 chip type 'RTL-8139C'
eth0: Setting half-duplex based on auto-negotiated partner ability 0000.
...
```

Note that at this point, an IP address or other settings have not been assigned to the device. Linux can use multiple Ethernet interfaces, and the first Ethernet device will be numbered eth0, the second eth1, and so on. Each different Ethernet device recognized by the kernel might have additional or different information reported, depending on its kernel module. For example,

```
$ dmesg
...
eepro100.c:v1.09j-t 9/29/99 Donald Becker http://cesdis.gsfc.nasa.gov/linux/drive
rs/eepro100.html
eepro100.c: $Revision: 1.36 $ 2000/11/17 Modified by Andrey V. Savochkin <saw@saw
.sw.com.sg> and others
PCI: Found IRQ 10 for device 00:0d.0
eth0: Intel Corporation 82557 [Ethernet Pro 100], 00:90:27:91:92:B5, IRQ 10.
  Board assembly 721383-007, Physical connectors present: RJ45
  Primary interface chip i82555 PHY #1.
  General self-test: passed.
  Serial sub-system self-test: passed.
  Internal registers self-test: passed.
  ROM checksum self-test: passed (0x04f4518b).
...
```

In this example, an Intel Ethernet Pro 100 NIC has been recognized. To disable support for a NIC, the kernel module can be unloaded, but usually only after the device is no longer in use. Read the next section to learn how to configure a NIC once it has been recognized by the Linux kernel and how to control its behavior.

Using Network Configuration Tools

If you add or replace networking hardware after your initial installation, you must configure the new hardware. You can do so using either the command line or the graphical configuration tools. To configure a network client host using the command line, you can use a combination of commands or edit specific files under the /etc/sysconfig directory.

To configure the hardware through a graphical interface, you can use Red Hat's graphical tool for X11 called `system-config-network` or the console-based `netconfig` command. This section introduces command-line and graphical software tools you can use to configure a network interface and network settings on your Red Hat system. You'll see how to control your NIC and manage how your system interacts with your network.

Using the command-line configuration tools can seem difficult if you're new to Linux. For anyone new to networking, the `system-config-network` graphical tool is the way to go. Both manual and graphical methods require root access to work. If you don't have root access, get it before trying any of these actions. You should not edit any scripts or settings files used by graphical network administration tools on your system. Your changes will be lost the next time the tool, such as `system-config-network`, is run! Either use a manual approach and write your own network setup script, or stick to using graphical configuration utilities.

> **NOTE**
>
> The network configuration process described in this section is for client hosts. You cannot perform server network configuration, such as domain name system (DNS) and DHCP during installation. (See Chapter 14, "Managing DNS," for more information on configuring DNS; see the "DHCP" section later in this chapter for more information on that item.)

Command-Line Network Interface Configuration

You can configure a network interface from the command line using the basic Linux networking utilities. You configure your network client hosts with the command line by using commands to change your current settings or by editing a number of system files. Two commands, `ifconfig` and `route`, are used for network configuration. The `netstat` command displays information about the network connections.

`/sbin/ifconfig`
`ifconfig` is used to configure your network interface. You can use it to

- Activate or deactivate your NIC or change your NIC's mode

- Change your machine's IP address, netmask, or broadcast address

- Create an IP alias to allow more than one IP address on your NIC

- Set a destination address for a point-to-point connection

You can change as many or as few of these options as you'd like with a single command. The basic structure for the command is as follows:

`/sbin/ifconfig [network device] options`

Table 13.1 shows a subset of `ifconfig` options and examples of their uses.

TABLE 13.1   `ifconfig` Options

Use	Option	Example
Create alias	`-[network device]` `10.10.10.10`	`ifconfig eth0:0_:[number]`
Change IP address		`ifconfig eth0 10.10.10.12`
Change the netmask	`netmask [netmask]`	`ifconfig eth0 netmask 255.255.255.0`
Change the broadcast	`broadcast [address]`	`ifconfig eth0 broadcast 10.10.10.255`
Take interface down	`down`	`ifconfig eth0 down`
Bring interface up	`up (add IP address)`	`ifconfig eth0 up (ifconfig eth0` `10.10.10.10)`
Set NIC promiscuous mode on [off]	`[-]promisc`	`ifconfig eth0 promisc [ifconfig eth0` `-promisc]`
Set multicasting mode on [off]	`[-]allmulti`	`ifconfig eth0_allmulti [ifconfig` `eth0 -allmulti]`
Enable [disable] point-to-point address 10.10.10.20	`[-]pointopoint` `[address]`	`ifconfig eth0_pointopoint [ifconfig` `eth0 pointopoint_10.10.10.20]`

The `ifconfig` man page shows other options that enable your machine to interface with a number of network types such as AppleTalk, Novell, IPv6, and others. Again, read the man page for details on these network types.

> **NOTE**
>
> Promiscuous mode causes the NIC to receive all packets on the network. It is often used to sniff a network. Multicasting mode enables the NIC to receive all multicast traffic on the network.

If no argument is given, `ifconfig` displays the status of active interfaces. For example, the output of `ifconfig`, without arguments and one active and configured NIC, looks similar to this:

/sbin/ifconfig

```
eth0    Link encap:Ethernet HWaddr 00:30:1B:0B:07:0D
        inet addr:192.168.2.70 Bcast:192.168.2.255 Mask:255.255.255.0
        UP BROADCAST RUNNING MULTICAST MTU:1500 Metric:1
        RX packets:127948 errors:0 dropped:0 overruns:0 frame:0
        TX packets:172675 errors:0 dropped:0 overruns:0 carrier:0
        collisions:7874 txqueuelen:100
        RX bytes:19098389 (18.2 Mb) TX bytes:73768657 (70.3 Mb)
        Interrupt:11 BASE- address:0x2000

lo      Link encap:Local Loopback
```

```
inet addr:127.0.0.1 Mask:255.0.0.0
UP LOOPBACK RUNNING MTU:16436 Metric:1
RX packets:215214 errors:0 dropped:0 overruns:0 frame:0
TX packets:215214 errors:0 dropped:0 overruns:0 carrier:0
collisions:0 txqueuelen:0
RX bytes:68739080 (65.5 Mb) TX bytes:68739080 (65.5 Mb)
```

The output is easily understood. The `inet` entry displays the IP address for the interface. `UP` signifies that the interface is ready for use, `BROADCAST` denotes that the interface is connected to a network that supports broadcast messaging (`ethernet`), `RUNNING` means that the interface is operating, and `LOOPBACK` shows which device (`lo`) is the loopback address. The *Maximum Transmission Unit (MTU)* on `eth0` is 1,500 bytes. This determines the size of the largest packet that can be transmitted over this interface (and is sometimes "tuned" to other values for performance enhancement). `Metric` is a number from 0 to 3 that relates to how much information from the interface is placed in the routing table. The lower the number, the smaller the amount of information.

The `ifconfig` command can be used to display information about or control a specific interface using commands as listed in Table 13.1. For example, to deactivate the first Ethernet device on a host, use the `ifconfig` command, the interface name, and the command `down` like so:

 # ifconfig eth0 down

You can also configure and activate the device by specifying a hostname or IP address and network information. For example, to configure and activate ("bring up") the `eth0` interface with a specific IP address, use the `ifconfig` command like this:

 # ifconfig eth0 192.168.2.35 netmask 255.255.255.0 up

If you have a host defined in your system's `/etc/hosts` file (see the section "Network Configuration Files" later in this chapter), you can configure and activate the interface according to the defined hostname like this:

 # ifconfig eth0 trusty.home.org up

Read the next section to see how to configure your system to work with your LAN.

/sbin/route

The second command used to configure your network is the `route` command. `route` is used to build the routing tables (in memory) implemented for routing packets as well as displaying the routing information. It is used after `ifconfig` has initialized the interface. `route` is normally used to set up static routes to other networks via the gateway or to other hosts. The command configuration is like this:

```
/sbin/route [options] [commands] [parameters]
```

To display the routing table, use the `route` command with no options. The display will look similar to this:

```
# /sbin/route
Kernel IP routing table
Destination     Gateway          Genmask          Flags Metric Ref Use Iface
149.112.50.64   *                255.255.255.192  U     0      0   0   eth0
208.59.243.0    *                255.255.255.0    U     0      0   0   eth0
127.0.0.0       *                255.0.0.0        U     0      0   0   lo
default         149.112.50.65    0.0.0.0          UG    0      0   0   eth0
```

In the first column, `Destination` is the IP address (or, if the host is in `/etc/hosts` or `/etc/networks`, the hostname) of the receiving host. The `default` entry is the default gateway for this machine. The `Gateway` column lists the gateway that the packets must go through to reach their destination. An asterisk (*) means that packets go directly to the host. `Genmask` is the netmask. The `Flags` column can have several possible entries. In our example, `U` verifies that the route is enabled and `G` specifies that `Destination` requires the use of a gateway. The `Metric` column displays the distance to the `Destination`. Some daemons use this to figure the easiest route to the `Destination`. The `Ref` column is used by some UNIX flavors to convey the references to the route. It isn't used by Linux. The `Use` column indicates the number of times this entry has been looked up. Finally, the `Iface` column is the name of the interface for the corresponding entry.

Using the `-n` option to the route command will give the same information substituting IP addresses for names and asterisks (*) and looks like this:

```
# /sbin/route -n
Kernel IP routing table
Destination     Gateway          Genmask          Flags Metric Ref Use Iface
149.112.50.64   0.0.0.0          255.255.255.192  U     0      0   0   eth0
208.59.243.0    0.0.0.0          255.255.255.0    U     0      0   0   eth0
127.0.0.0       0.0.0.0          255.0.0.0        U     0      0   0   lo
0.0.0.0         149.112.50.65    0.0.0.0          UG    0      0   0   eth0
```

The `route` command can add to the table using the `add` option. With the `add` option, you can specify a host (`-host`) or a network (`-net`) as the destination. If no option is used, the route command assumes that you are configuring the host issuing the command. The most common uses for the `route` command are to add the default gateway for a host, for a host that has lost its routing table, or if the gateway address has changed. For example, to add a gateway with a specific IP address, you could use the following:

```
# /sbin/route add default gw 149.112.50.65
```

Note that you could use a hostname instead of an IP address if desired. Another common use is to add the network to the routing table right after using the `ifconfig` command to configure the interface. Assuming that the 208.59.243.0 entry from the previous examples was missing, replace it using the following command:

```
# /sbin/route add -net 208.59.243.0 netmask 255.255.255.0 dev eth0
```

You also can use /sbin/route to configure a specific host for a direct (point-to-point) connection. For example, say that you have a home network of two computers. One of the computers has a modem through which it connects to your business network. You typically work at the other computer. You can use the route command to establish a connection through specific hosts using the following command:

```
# /sbin/route add -host 198.135.62.25 gw 149.112.50.65
```

The preceding example makes the computer with the modem the gateway for the computer you are using. This type of command line is useful if you have a gateway or firewall connected to the Internet. There are many additional uses for the route command, such as manipulating the default packet size. See the man page for those uses.

/bin/netstat

The netstat command is used to display the status of your network. It has several parameters that can display as much or as little information as you prefer. The services are listed by *sockets* (application-to-application connections between two computers). You can use netstat to display the information in Table 13.2.

TABLE 13.2   netstat Options

Option	Output
-g	Displays the multicast groups configured
-i	Displays the interfaces configured by ifconfig
-s	Lists a summary of activity for each protocol
-v	Gives verbose output, listing both active and inactive sockets
-c	Updates output every second (good for testing and troubleshooting)
-e	Gives verbose output for active connections only
-C	Displays information from the route cache and is good for looking at past connections

Several other options are available for this command, but they are used less often. As with the /sbin/route command, the man page can give you details about all options and parameters.

Network Configuration Files

As previously stated, seven network configuration files can be modified to make changes to basic network interaction of your system. The files are

/etc/hosts—A listing of addresses, hostnames, and aliases

/etc/services—Network service and port connections

`/etc/nsswitch.conf`—Linux network information service configuration

`/etc/resolv.conf`—Domain name service domain (search) settings

`/etc/host.conf`—Network information search order (by default, `/etc/hosts` and then DNS)

`/etc/sysconfig/network`—The hostname, IP address, boot activation control, and gateway settings (along with optional IPv6 settings)

`/etc/sysconfig/network-scripts/ifcfg-eth0`—Network settings for the `eth0` network device; see the file `sysconfig.txt` under the `/usr/share/doc/initscripts/` directory for details about optional settings

After the first six of these files are modified, the changes are active. As with most configuration files, comments can be added with a hash mark (#) preceding the comment. The last file (`/etc/sysconfig/network`) requires the networking daemons to be restarted before the file is used. All seven of these files have a man page written about them for more information.

Adding Hosts to `/etc/hosts`

The `/etc/hosts` file is a map of IP to hostnames. If you aren't using DNS or another naming service, and you are connected to a large network, this file can get quite large and can be a real headache to manage. A small `/etc/hosts` file can look something like this:

```
127.0.0.1      localhost.localdomain  localhost
128.112.50.69  myhost.mydomain.com    myhost
128.112.50.169 yourhost.mydomain.com  yourhost
```

The first entry is for the loopback entry. The second is for the name of the machine. The third is another machine on the network. If no naming service is in use on the network, the only host that myhost will recognize by name is yourhost. (IP addresses on the network can still be used.)

If your network is using a naming service, the last line isn't needed and can be deleted. However, if myhost connects to yourhost frequently, it might be good to leave the entry so that myhost doesn't need to consult the naming service each time. This can save time and reduce the strain on the network or the name service server. Edit this file if you need to change your hostname or IP address or if you aren't using a naming service and a host has been added to your network.

Service Settings in `/etc/services`

The `/etc/services` file maps port numbers to services. The first few lines look similar to this (the `/etc/services` file can be quite long, more than 500 lines):

```
# Each line describes one service, and is of the form:
#
# service-name port/protocol [aliases ...]   [# comment]
```

```
tcpmux      1/tcp                   # TCP port service multiplexer
tcpmux      1/udp                   # TCP port service multiplexer
rje         5/tcp                   # Remote Job Entry
rje         5/udp                   # Remote Job Entry
echo        7/tcp
echo        7/udp
discard     9/tcp       sink null
discard     9/udp       sink null
systat      11/tcp      users
```

Typically, there are two entries for each service because most services can use either TCP or UDP for their transmissions. Usually once /etc/services is initially configured, you will not need to change it.

Using /etc/nsswitch.conf After Changing Naming Services

This file was initially developed by Sun Microsystems to specify the order that services are accessed on the system. A number of services are listed in the /etc/nsswitch.conf file, but the most commonly modified entry is the hosts entry. A portion of the file can look like this:

```
passwd:    files
shadow:    files
group:     files

#hosts:    db files nisplus nis dns
hosts:     files dns
```

This tells services that they should consult standard UNIX/Linux files for passwd, shadow, and group (/etc/passwd, /etc/shadow, /etc/group, respectively) lookups. For host lookups, the system will check /etc/hosts and if there is no entry, it will check DNS. The commented hosts entry lists the possible values for hosts. Only edit this file if your naming service has changed.

Setting a Name Server with /etc/resolv.conf

/etc/resolv.conf is used by DNS, the Domain Name Service. (DNS is covered in detail in Chapter 14.) The following is an example of resolv.conf:

```
nameserver 192.172.3.8
nameserver 192.172.3.9
search mydomain.com
```

This sets the nameservers and the order of domains for DNS to use. The contents of this file will be set automatically if you use Dynamic Host Configuration Protocol, or DHCP (see the section "DHCP" later in this chapter).

Setting DNS Search Order with `/etc/host.conf`

The `/etc/host.conf` file lists the order in which your machine will search for hostname resolution. The following is the default `/etc/host.conf` file:

```
order hosts, bind
```

In this example, the host will check the `/etc/hosts` file first and then perform a DNS lookup. A couple more options control how the name service is used. The only reason to modify this file is if you use NIS for your name service or you want one of the optional services. The `nospoof` option can be a good option for system security. It will compare a standard DNS lookup to a reverse lookup (host-to-IP then IP-to-host) and fail if the two don't match. The drawback is that often when proxy services are used, the lookup will fail, so you will want to use this with caution.

Examining Host Network Settings in `/etc/sysconfig/network`

Changes to `/etc/sysconfig/network` won't take effect until you restart the networking daemons or reboot the system. If you use Red Hat's graphical configuration network tools (described in the next section), you should not edit this file. The file might look like this:

```
NETWORKING=yes
HOSTNAME=myhost
GATEWAY=192.112.50.99
```

A `GATEWAYDEV` setting is also available to associate a specific network device (such as `eth0` or `eth1` and so on). An additional optional entry to `/etc/sysconfig/network` is for NIS domain machines and would look like this:

```
NISDOMAIN=rebel
```

The `network` file previously supported a `FORWARD_IPV4` value, which determined whether the host forwarded IP packets (usually "yes" for routers). This setting is now saved in `/etc/sysctl.conf` as a `net.ipv4.ip_forward` setting, which can be modified if the forwarding changes are required. See the `sysctl.conf` man page for more information.

Using Graphical Configuration Tools

As mentioned earlier, if you're new to networking or still becoming proficient with the command line, the graphical configuration tool is your best method for configuring new hardware in Fedora. Like most graphical tools, `system-config-network` allows you to fill in the blanks; press the proper buttons, and the tool will modify the required files and issue the proper commands. Remember, you must be root to run `system-config-network`.

There are two ways to start `system-config-network`: from the command line of an X11 terminal window with the command `system-config-network`, using the panel's Run Application menu item, or by clicking the System Setting's Network menu item from a GNOME or KDE desktop panel menu. (In either case, you'll be prompted to enter the root password.)

Once started, `system-config-network` might ask if you'd like to create a new device. If you've installed Fedora on a computer with an existing network card, however, the screen shown in Figure 13.1 appears after you start `system-config-network`.

FIGURE 13.1   Use the initial `system-config-network` networking screen to begin configuring your network client host.

Click the DNS tab to configure your system's DNS settings, hostname, or DNS search path. Click the Hosts tab, and then either click the New or Edit button (after selecting a host) to create or edit an entry in your system's `/etc/hosts` file, for example, to add the IP addresses, hostnames, and aliases of hosts on your network see Figure 13.2 for an example of editing a host entry.

Click on the Devices tab, and then either click New or select an existing setting and click Edit to automatically or manually set up an Ethernet device. Figure 13.3 shows the Add New Device Type dialog box with all necessary information in place for a *static*, or fixed IP address assignment. Choose how your card will get its configuration, manually from Dynamic Host Configuration Protocol (see the next section) or from Bootp. Just fill in the blanks as needed.

> **NOTE**
>
> Bootp is the initial protocol that DHCP was built on, and it has mostly been replaced by DHCP.

When you have finished configuring your NIC or editing an IP address or assignment scheme for a NIC, save your changes using the File menu's Save menu item. Note that you can also use the Profile menu (as shown in Figure 13.1) to create different network configurations and IP address assignments for your installed NICs. This is handy if you want to create, for example, a different network setup for home or work on a laptop running Fedora.

FIGURE 13.2   Highlight an existing entry, and then click the Edit button to change /etc/hosts entries in the Hosts tab of the Network Configuration screen.

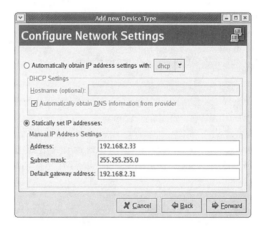

FIGURE 13.3   Configure an Ethernet device in the Configure Network Setting screen of the Add New Device Type dialog.

Dynamic Host Configuration Protocol

As the name implies, *Dynamic Host Configuration Protocol (DHCP)* configures hosts for connection to your network. DHCP allows a network administrator to configure all TCP/IP parameters for each host as he connects to the network after activation of a NIC. These parameters include automatically assigning an IP address to a NIC, setting name server entries in /etc/resolv.conf, and configuring default routing and gateway information for a host. This section first describes how to use DHCP to obtain an IP address assignment for your NIC, and then how to quickly set up and start a DHCP server using Fedora.

> **NOTE**
>
> You can learn more about DHCP by reading RFC2131 "Dynamic Host Configuration Protocol." Browse to http://www.ietf.org/rfc/rfc2131.txt.

How DHCP Works

DHCP provides persistent storage of network parameters by holding identifying information for each network client that might connect to the network. The three most common pairs of identifying information are

- **Network subnet/host address**—Used by hosts to connect to the network at will

- **Subnet/hostname**—Enables the specified host to connect to the subnet

- **Subnet/hardware address**—Enables a specific client to connect to the network after getting the hostname from DHCP

DHCP also allocates to clients temporary or permanent network (IP) addresses. Once a temporary assignment, known as a *lease*, has elapsed, the client can request to have the lease extended, or, if the address is no longer needed, the client can relinquish the address. For hosts that will be permanently connected to a network with adequate addresses available, DHCP allocates infinite leases.

DHCP offers your network some advantages. First, it shifts responsibility for assigning IP addresses from the network administrator (who can accidentally assign duplicate IP addresses) to the DHCP server. Second, DHCP makes better use of limited IP addresses. If a user is away from the office for whatever reason, the user's host can release its IP address for use by other hosts.

Like most things in life, DHCP is not perfect. Servers cannot be configured through DHCP alone because DNS doesn't know what addresses that DHCP assigns to a host. This means that DNS lookups aren't possible on machines configured through DHCP alone; therefore, services cannot be provided. However, DHCP can make assignments based on DNS entries when using subnet/hostname or subnet/hardware address identifiers.

Activating DHCP at Installation and Boot Time

During installation, you can instruct the Fedora installer to save DHCP settings for your NIC. After installation, you can also use the `system-config-network` client to edit the TCP/IP configuration information required to properly initialize and configure your NIC to connect your system to the local network and Internet. When you select a *dynamic*, or DHCP-assigned IP addressing scheme for your NIC, the broadcast address is set at 255.255.255.255 because `dhclient`, the DHCP client used for IP configuration, is initially unaware of where the DHCP server is located, so the request must travel every network until a server replies.

DHCP-specific information is simply saved as a `BOOTPROTO=dhcp` entry for your NIC under the `/etc/sysconfig/network` directory (in settings and scripts for a specific device, such as eth0).

Other settings specific to obtaining DHCP settings are saved in the file named `dhclient.conf` under the `/etc` directory and are documented in the `dhclient.conf` man page. More than 100 options are also documented in the `dhcp-options` man page.

However, using DHCP is not that complicated. If you want to use DHCP and know that there is a server on your network, you can quickly configure your NIC by using the `dhclient` like so:

```
# dhclient
Internet Software Consortium DHCP Client V3.0pl2
Copyright 1995-2001 Internet Software Consortium.
All rights reserved.
For info, please visit http://www.isc.org/products/DHCP

Listening on LPF/lo/
Sending on   LPF/lo/
Listening on LPF/eth0/00:a0:24:aa:f5:17
Sending on   LPF/eth0/00:a0:24:aa:f5:17
Sending on   Socket/fallback
DHCPREQUEST on eth0 to 255.255.255.255 port 67
DHCPACK from 192.168.2.254
```

```
save_previous /etc/yp.conf
save_previous /etc/resolv.conf
bound to 192.168.2.253 -- renewal in 9906 seconds.
```

In this example, the first Ethernet device, eth0, has been assigned an IP address of 192.168.2.253 from a DHCP server at 192.168.2.54. The renewal will take place in about two hours and 45 minutes.

> **NOTE**
>
> The file named dhcpd under the /etc/sysconfig directory can contain any optional command-line arguments, such as NIC lease times (the amount of time an interface has an assigned address). See the dhcpd manual page for options.

DHCP Software Installation and Configuration

Installation of the DHCP client and server might be easiest during the initial install of Fedora, but you can also use RPMs later on, or download and build the source code yourself. The RPMs are available on your Fedora CD-ROMs or from a mirror FTP site (see Chapter 8, "Managing Software and System Resources," for more information). This section describes configuring the dhclient and setting up and running the dhpcd daemon.

DHCP dhclient

As previously mentioned, DHCP use for an installed NIC is easily accomplished when installing Fedora on your host (read more about installation in Chapter 3, "Installing Fedora"), and during the network step of installation, you can choose to have DHCP initiated at boot time. If you choose to do this (and choose to install the DHCP client package), the DHCP client, dhclient, will send a broadcast message that the DHCP server will reply to with networking information for your host. That's it; you're done.

> **NOTE**
>
> Previous distributions of Red Hat Linux used the pump client instead of dhclient to configure NICs using DHCP.

If you choose to install from source, you will have to (as root) download and install the server packages that include dhclient. Unpack the source file, run ./configure from the root of the source directory, run make, and then run make install. This should put the DHCP client binaries where they will start at the correct time in the boot process.

You can however, fine-tune how dhclient works, and where and how it obtains or looks for DHCP information. You probably won't need to take this additional effort; but if you do, you can create and edit a file named dhclient.conf, and save it in the /etc directory with your settings. A few of the dhclient.conf options include

- `timeout time` ;—How long to wait before giving up trying (60 seconds default)

- `retry time` ;—How long to wait before retrying (5 minutes default)

- `select-timeout time` ;—How long to wait before selecting a DHCP offer (0 seconds default)

- `reboot time` ;—How long to wait before trying to get a previously set IP (10 seconds default)

- `renew date` ;—When to renew an IP lease, where *date* is in the form of `<weekday>` `<year>/<month>/<day>` `<hour>:<minute>:<second>`, such as `4 2004/1/1 22:01:01` for Thursday, January 4, 2004 at 10:01 p.m.

See the `dhclient.conf` man page for more information on additional settings.

DHCP Server

Again, the easiest way to install the DHCP server on your computer is to include the RPMs at install time or to use RPMs if you've installed your machine without installing the DHCP server RPMs. If you are so inclined, you can go to the Internet Software Consortium (ISC) Web site and download and build the source code yourself (`http://www.isc.org`).

If you decide to install from a source downloaded from the ISC Web site, the installation is very straightforward. Just unpack your `tar` file, run `./configure` from the root of the source directory, run `make`, and finally, if there are no errors, run `make install`. This will put all the files used by the DHCP daemon in the correct places. If you have the disk space, it's best to leave the source files in place until you are sure that DHCP is running correctly; otherwise, you can delete the source tree.

> **NOTE**
>
> For whichever installation method you choose, be sure that a file called `/etc/dhcpd.leases` is created. The file can be empty, but it does need to exist in order for `dhcpd` to start properly.

Using DHCP to Configure Network Hosts

Configuring your network with DHCP can look difficult, but is actually easy if your needs are simple. The server configuration can take a bit more work if your network is more complex and depending on how much you want DHCP to do.

DHCP Server Configuration

Configuring the server takes some thought and a little bit of work. Luckily, the work only involves editing a single configuration file, `/etc/dhcpd.conf`. To start the server at boot time, use the `service`, `ntsysv`, or `system-config-services` commands.

The /etc/dhcpd.conf file contains all the information needed to run dhcpd. Fedora includes a sample dhcpd.conf in /usr/share/doc/dhcp*/dhcpd.conf.sample. The DHCP server source files also contain a sample dhcpd.conf file.

The /etc/dhcpd.conf file can be looked at as a three-part file. The first part contains configurations for DHCP itself. The configurations include

- **Setting the domain name**—option domain-name "example.org".

- **Setting DNS servers**—option domain-name-servers ns1.example.org, ns2.example.org (IP addresses can be substituted.)

- **Setting the default and maximum lease times**—default-lease-time 3600 and max-lease-time 14400.

Other settings in the first part include whether the server is the primary (authoritative) server and what type of logging DHCP should use. These settings are considered default and can be overridden by the subnet and host portion of the configuration in more complex situations.

NOTE

The dhcpd.conf file requires semicolons (;) after each command statement. If your configuration file has errors or runs improperly, check for this.

The next part of the dhcpd.conf deals with the different subnets that your DHCP server serves; this section is quite straightforward. Each subnet is defined separately and can look like this:

```
subnet 10.5.5.0 netmask 255.255.255.224 {
 range 10.5.5.26 10.5.5.30;
 option domain-name-servers ns1.internal.example.org;
 option domain-name "internal.example.org";
 option routers 10.5.5.1;
 option broadcast-address 10.5.5.31;
 default-lease-time 600;
 max-lease-time 7200;
}
```

This defines the IP addressing for the 10.5.5.0 subnet. It defines the IP address ranging from 10.5.5.26 through 10.5.5.30 to be dynamically assigned to hosts that reside on that subnet. This example shows that any TCP/IP option can be set from the subnet portion of the configuration file. It shows which DNS server the subnet will connect to, which can be good for DNS server load balancing, or which can be used to limit the hosts that can be reached through DNS. It defines the domain name, so you can have more than one domain on your network. It can also change the default and maximum lease time.

If you want your server to ignore a specific subnet, the following entry can be used to accomplish this:

```
subnet 10.152.187.0 netmask 255.255.255.0 {
}
```

This defines no options for the 10.152.187.0 subnet; therefore, the DHCP server ignores it.

The last part of your dhcp.conf is for defining hosts. This can be good if you want a computer on your network to have a specific IP address or other information specific to that host. The key to completing the host section is to know the hardware address of the host. As you learned in "Hardware Devices for Networking," earlier in this chapter, the hardware address is used to differentiate the host for configuration. Your hardware address can be obtained by using the ifconfig command as described previously. The hardware address is on the eth0 line labeled "Hwaddr".

```
host fantasia {
   hardware ethernet 08:00:07:26:c0:a5;
   fixed-address fantasia.fugue.com;
}
```

This example takes the host with the hardware address 08:00:07:26:c0:a5 and does a DNS lookup to assign the IP address for fantasia.fugue.com to the host.

DHCP can also define and configure booting for diskless clients like this:

```
host passacaglia {
   hardware ethernet 0:0:c0:5d:bd:95;
   filename "vmunix.passacaglia";
   server-name "toccata.fugue.com";
}
```

The diskless host passacaglia will get its boot information from server toccata. fugue.com and use vmunix.passacaglia kernel. All other TCP/IP configuration can also be included.

> **CAUTION**
>
> Remember, only one DHCP server should exist on a local network to avoid problems. Your DHCP might not work correctly on a LAN with hosts running outdated legacy operating systems. Often Windows NT servers will have the Windows DHCP server installed by default. Because there is no configuration file for NT to sort through, that DHCP server will configure your host before the Linux server if both machines are on the same LAN. Check your NT servers for this situation and disable DHCP on the NT server; afterward, your other DHCP-enabled hosts should configure correctly. Also, check to make sure that are no conflicts if you use a cable or DSL modem, wireless access point (WAP), or other intelligent router on your LAN that can provide DHCP.

Other Uses for DHCP

A whole host of options can be used in dhcpd.conf: Entire books are dedicated to DHCP. The most comprehensive book is *The DHCP Handbook*, available at http://www. dhcp-handbook.com/. You can define NIS domains, configure NETBIOS, set subnet masks, and define time servers, or many other types of servers—to name a few of the DHCP options you can use. The preceding example will get your DHCP server and client up and running.

The DHCP server distribution contains an example of the dhcpd.conf file that you can use as a template for your network. The file shows a basic configuration that can get you started with explanations for the options used.

Using the Network File System

The network file system (NFS) was developed by Sun Microsystems as a way for computers to share files as if they were local to the remote machine. NFS is commonly used to share home directories between hosts within a network. This reduces the need to have a home directory on every computer and ensures that no matter which computer you log in to, your home directory will be consistent.

Another popular use for NFS is to share binary files between similar computers. If you have a new version of a package that you want all machines to have, you only have to do the upgrade on the NFS server, and all hosts running the same version of Fedora will have the same upgraded package.

Installing and Starting or Stopping NFS

NFS is installed by default on Fedora and consists of several programs that work together to provide the NFS server service. One is rpc.portmapper, which maps NFS requests to the correct daemon. Another is rpc.nfsd, which is the NFS daemon. A third one is rpc.mountd, which controls the mounts and unmounts of file systems.

To have NFS automatically started when Fedora boots, use command-line or graphical administrative utilities, such as chkconfig, ntsysv, or system-config-services. Make sure to have the portmap service started because it is used as part of the service. One way to manually start or stop NFS is by directly calling its service control script nfs like this:

```
# /etc/rc.d/init.d/nfs start
Starting NFS services:              [ OK ]
Starting NFS quotas:                [ OK ]
Starting NFS daemon:                [ OK ]
Starting NFS mountd:                [ OK ]
```

In this example, NFS has been started. Use the stop keyword instead to stop the service. This approach at controlling NFS is handy, especially after configuration changes have been made. You can also use the service command or the graphical system-config-services client in the same way. See the next section on how to configure NFS support on your Fedora system.

NFS Server Configuration

The NFS server can be configured by editing the /etc/exports file. This file is similar to the /etc/fstab file in that it is used to set the permissions for the file systems being exported. The entries look like this:

```
/file/system yourhost(options) *.yourdomain.com(options) 192.15.69.0/24(options)
```

This shows three common clients to share /file/system to. The first, yourhost, shares /file/system to just one host. The second, .yourdomain.com, uses the asterisk (*) as a wildcard to enable all hosts in yourdomain.com to access /file/system. The third share enables all hosts of the Class C network, 192.15.69.0, to access /file/share. For security, it is best not to use shares like the last two across the Internet because all data will be readable by any network the data passes by.

Some common options are shown in Table 13.3.

TABLE 13.3   /etc/fstab Options

Option	Purpose
rw	Gives read and write access
ro	Gives read-only access
async	Writes data when the server feels the need, not the client
sync	Writes data as it is received

The following is an example of an /etc/exports file:

```
# /etc/exports file for myhost.mydomain.com
/usr/local        yourhost(ro,show)
/home/jkennedy    *.yourdomain.com(rw,hide,sync)
```

This file *exports* (makes available) /usr/local to yourhost. The mount is read-only (which is good for a directory of binary files that don't get written to). It also allows users on yourhost to see the contents of file systems that might be mounted on /usr/local. The second export mounts /home/jkennedy to any host in yourdomain.com. It doesn't allow subsidiary file systems to be viewed, but you can read and write to the file system.

After you have finished with the /etc/exports file, the following command

```
# /usr/sbin/exportfs -r
```

will export all the file systems in the /etc/exports file to a list named xtab under the /var/lib/nfs directory, which is used as a guide for mounting when a remote computer asks for a directory to be exported. The -r option to the command reads the whole /etc/exports file and mounts all the entries. The exportfs command can also be used to export specific files temporarily. An example using exportfs to export a file system would be

```
/usr/sbin/exportfs -o async yourhost:/usr/tmp
```

This command will export /usr/tmp to yourhost with the async option.

Make sure to restart the NFS server after making any changes to /etc/exports. If you prefer, you can use Red Hat's system-config-nfs graphical client to set up NFS while using the X Window System. Start the client by clicking The System Settings menu, and then the NFS Server menu item from the Server Settings menu. You can also start the client from the command line of an X terminal window, like so:

```
$ system-config-nfs &
```

After you press Enter, you'll be prompted for the root password. Type in the password, click OK, and you'll see the main window. Click the Add button, and you'll see the Add NFS Share dialog box, as shown in Figure 13.4.

FIGURE 13.4   Red Hat's system-config-nfs client can be used to quickly set up local directories for export using NFS.

In the Directory text box, type in a name of a directory to be exported; in the Host(s) text box, type in a hostname or the IP address of a remote host that is to be allowed access to the directory. By default, a directory is exported as read-only, but you can choose read and write access by clicking either option in the Basic Permissions area of the dialog box. When finished, click the OK button, click the Apply button, and then use the File menu to quit.

NFS Client Configuration

To configure your host as an NFS client (to acquire remote files or directories), edit the /etc/fstab file as you would to mount any local file system. However, instead of using a device name to be mounted (such as /dev/hda1), enter the remote hostname and desired file system to be imported. For example, one entry might look like this:

```
# Device            Mount Point   Type  Options       Freq Pass
yourhost:/usr/local  /usr/local   nfs   nfsvers=3,ro  0    0
```

> **NOTE**
>
> If you use autofs on your system, you'll need to use proper autofs entries for your remote NFS mounts. See the section 5 man page for autofs.

The options column uses the same options as standard fstab file entries with some additional entries such as nfsvers=3, which specifies the third version of NFS. You can also use the mount command, as root, to quickly attach a remote directory to a local file system by using a remote host's name and exported directory. For example,

```
# mount -t nfs 192.168.2.67:/music /music
```

After you press Enter, the entire remote directory will appear on your file system. You can verify the imported file system using the df command like so:

```
# df
File system        1k-blocks     Used Available Use% Mounted on
/dev/hda2          18714368  9642600   8121124  55% /
/dev/hda1             46636    13247     30981  30% /boot
none                 120016        0    120016   0% /dev/shm
192.168.2.67:/music 36875376 20895920 14106280  60% /music
```

Make sure that the desired mount point exists before using the mount command. When finished using the directory (perhaps for copying backups), the umount command can be used to remove the remote file system. Note that if you specify the root directory (/) as a mount point, you won't be able to unmount the NFS directory until you reboot (because Linux will complain that the file system is in use).

Putting Samba to Work

Samba uses the session message block (SMB) protocol to enable the Windows operating system (or any operating system) to access Linux files. Using Samba, you can make your Fedora machine look just like a Windows computer to other Windows computers on your network. You do not need to install Windows on your PC.

Samba is a very complex program—so much so that the book *Samba Unleashed* (Sams Publishing, 2000, ISBN 0-672-31862-8) is more than 1,200 pages long. The Samba man page (when converted to text) for just the configuration file is 330KB and 7,013 lines long. Although Samba is complex, setting it up and using it doesn't have to be difficult. There are many options, and that can account for Samba's complexity. Depending on what you want, Samba's use can be as easy or as difficult as you'd like it to be.

Fortunately, Fedora includes the Samba Web Administration Tool, or SWAT, which can be used to configure Samba by using the Mozilla Web browser. SWAT provides an easy way to start and stop the Samba server, set up printing services, define remote access permissions, and create Samba usernames, passwords, and shared directories. This section delves into the basics of configuring Samba, and you should first read how to manually configure Samba to get an understanding of how the software works. At the end of this section, you'll see how to enable, start, and use SWAT to set up simple file sharing.

Like most of the software that comes with Fedora, Samba is licensed under the GPL and is free. It comes as both an RPM and as source code. In both cases, installation is very straightforward, and the software can be installed when you install Fedora or are using RPM software packages. The Samba RPMs should be on one of your Fedora install disks, or the latest version can be downloaded from the Internet, preferably from the Fedora Project (at `fedora.redhat.com`) or an authorized mirror site. See Chapter 8 for more information on using RPM packages.

Installing from source code can be a bit more time-consuming. If you don't want to install using Fedora's default locations, however, installing from the source code is a more configurable method. Just download the source from `http://www.samba.org` and unpack the files. Change into the source directory and as root, run the command `./configure` along with any changes from the defaults and then run `make`, `make test` (if you want), followed by `make install` to install Samba in the specified locations.

If you install Samba using your Fedora CD-ROMs, you can find a large amount of documentation in the directory tree starting at `/usr/share/doc/samba*/doc/` in several formats including PDF, HTML, and text, among others. Altogether, almost 3MB of documentation is included with the source code.

Once Samba is installed, you can either create the file `/etc/smb.conf` or use the `smb.conf` file supplied with Samba, which is located by default under the `/etc/samba` directory with Fedora. Nearly a dozen sample configuration files can be found under the `/usr/share/doc/samba*/examples` directory.

> **NOTE**
>
> Depending on your needs, `smb.conf` can be a simple file of less than 20 lines to a huge file spanning many pages of text. If your needs are complex, I would suggest picking up a copy of *Samba Unleashed* at your favorite bookstore.

Manually Configuring Samba with `/etc/samba/smb.conf`

The `/etc/samba/smb.conf` file is broken into sections. Each section is a description of the resource shared (share) and should be titled appropriately. There are three special sections:

- `[global]`—Establishes the global configuration settings (defined in detail in the `smb.conf` manual page and Samba documentation, found under the `/usr/share/doc/samba/docs` directory)

- `[homes]`—Shares users' home directories and specifies directory paths and permissions

- `[printers]`—Handles printing by defining shared printers and printer access

Each section in your `/etc/samba/smb.conf` configuration file should be named for the resource being shared. For example, if the resource `/usr/local/programs` is being shared, you could call the section `[programs]`. When Windows sees the share, it will be called by whatever you name the section (`programs` in this example). The easiest and fastest way to set up this share is with the following example from `smb.conf`:

```
[programs]
path = /usr/local/programs
writeable = true
```

This bit will share the `/usr/local/programs` directory with any valid user who asks for it and will make that directory writable. It is the most basic share because it sets no limits on the directory.

Here are some parameters you can set in the sections:

- Requiring a user to enter a password before accessing a shared directory

- Limiting the hosts allowed to access the shared directory

- Altering permissions users are allowed to have on the directory

- Limiting the time of day that the directory is accessible

The possibilities are almost endless. Any parameters set in the individual sections override the parameters set in the `[global]` section. The following section adds a few restrictions to the `[programs]` section.

```
[programs]
path = /usr/local/programs
writeable = true
valid users = jkennedy
browseable = yes
create mode = 0700
```

The `valid users` entry limits `userid` to just `jkennedy`. All other users can browse the directory because of the `browseable = yes` entry, but only `jkennedy` can write to the directory. Any files created by `jkennedy` in the directory will give `jkennedy` full permissions, but no one else will have access to the file. This is exactly the same as setting permissions with the `chmod` command. Again, there are numerous options, so you can be as creative as you want to when developing sections.

Setting Global Samba Behavior with the `[global]` Section

The `[global]` section set parameters establishes configuration settings for all of Samba. If a given parameter isn't specifically set in another section, Samba will use the default setting in the `[global]` section. The `[global]` section also sets the general security configuration for Samba. The `[global]` section is the only section that doesn't require the name in brackets.

Samba assumes that anything before the first bracketed section not labeled `[global]` is part of the global configuration. (Using bracketed headings in `/etc/samba/smb.conf` will make your configuration file more readable.) The following sections discuss common Samba settings to share directories and printers. You'll then see how to test your Samba configuration.

Sharing Home Directories Using the `[homes]` Section

The `[homes]` section shares out Fedora home directories for the users. The home directory is shared automatically when a user's Windows computer connects to the Linux server holding the home directory. The one problem with using the default configuration is that the user will see all the configuration files (such as `.profile` and others with a leading period in the filename) that he normally wouldn't see when logging on through Linux. One quick way to avoid this would be to include a path option in the `[homes]` section. To use this solution, each user who requires a Samba share of his home directory needs a separate "home directory" to act as his Windows home directory.

For example, this pseudo home directory could be a directory named `share` in each user's home directory on your Fedora system. You can specify the path option when using SWAT by using the `%u` option when specifying a path for the default `homes` shares (see the section "Configuring Samba Using SWAT" later in this chapter). The complete path setting would be

```
/home/%u/share
```

This setting specifies that the directory named `share` under each user's directory will be the shared Samba directory. The corresponding manual `smb.conf` setting to provide a separate "home directory" looks like this:

```
[homes]
        comment = Home Directories
        path = /home/%u/share
        valid users = %S
```

```
read only = No
create mask = 0664
directory mask = 0775
browseable = No
```

If you have a default [homes] section, the share shows up in the user's Network Neighborhood as the user's name. When the user connects, Samba scans the existing sections in smb.conf for a specific instance of the user's home directory. If there isn't one, Samba looks up the username in /etc/passwd. If the correct username and password have been given, the home directory listed in /etc/passwd is shared out at the user's home directory. Typically the [homes] section will look like this (the browseable = no entry will prevent other users from being able to browse your home directory and is a good security practice):

```
[homes]
browseable = no
writable = yes
```

This example shares out the home directory and makes it writable to the user. To specify a separate Windows home directory for each user, it would look like this:

```
[homes]
browseable = no
writable = yes
path = /path/to/windows/directories
```

Sharing Printers by Editing the [printers] Section

The [printers] section works much like the [homes] section but defines shared printers for use on your network. If the section exists, users will have access to any printer listed in your Fedora /etc/printcap file.

Like the [homes] section, when a print request is received, all the sections are scanned for the printer. If no share is found (with careful naming, there should not be unless you create a section for a specific printer), the /etc/printcap file is scanned for the printer name that is then used to send the print request.

For printing to work properly, printing services *must* be set up correctly on your Fedora computer. (See Chapter 12, "Printing with Fedora," for more information.) A typical [printers] section will look like the following:

```
[printers]
comment = Red Hat Printers
browseable = no
printable = yes
path = /var/spool/samba
```

The /var/spool/samba is a spool path set just for Samba printing.

Testing Samba with the `testparm` Command

Once you have created your /etc/smb.conf file, you can check it for correctness. This is done with the `testparm` command. This command will parse through your /etc/smb.conf file and check for any syntax errors. If none are found, it's a good bet that your configuration file will work correctly. It does not, however, guarantee that the services specified in the file will work. It is merely making sure that the file is correctly written.

As with all configuration files, if you are modifying an existing, working file, it is *always* prudent to copy the working file to a different location and modify that file. Then, you can check the file with the `testparm` utility. The command syntax is as follows:

```
# testparm /path/to/smb.conf.back-up
Load smb config files from smb.conf.back-up
Processing section "[homes]"
Processing section "[printers]"
Loaded services file OK.
```

This output shows that the Samba configuration file is correct, and, as long as all the services are running correctly on your Fedora machine, Samba should be working correctly. Now copy your old smb.conf file to a new location, put the new one in its place, and restart Samba with the command /etc/init.d/smb restart. Your new or modified Samba configuration should now be in place.

Starting the `smbd` Daemon

Now that your smb.conf file is correctly configured, you can start your Samba server daemon. This can be done with the /usr/sbin/smbd command, which (with no options) starts the Samba server with all the defaults. The most common option that you will change in this command is the location of the smb.conf file; you change this option if you don't want to use the default location /etc/smb/smb.conf. The -s option allows you to change the smb.conf file that Samba uses; this option is also useful for testing whether a new smb.conf file actually works. Another useful option is the -l option, which specifies the log file that Samba uses to store information.

To start, stop, or restart Samba from the command line, use the `service` command, the `system-config-services` client, or the /etc/rc.d/init.d/smb script with a proper keyword, such as `start`, like so:

 # /etc/rc.d/init.d/smb start

Using the `smbstatus` Command

The `smbstatus` command will report on the current status of your Samba connections. The syntax is

```
/usr/bin/smbstatus [options]
```

Some of the available options are shown in Table 13.4.

TABLE 13.4   `smbstatus` Options

Option	Result
`-b`	Brief output.
`-d`	Verbose output.
`-s /path/to/config`	Used if the configuration file used at startup is not the standard one.
`-u username`	Shows the status of a specific user's connection.
`-p`	Lists current smb processes. This can be useful in scripts.

Connecting with the `smbclient` Command

The `smbclient` command allows users on other Linux hosts to access your smb shares. You can't mount the share on your host, but you can use it in a way that's very similar to an FTP client. Several options can be used with the `smbclient` command. The most used will be `-I` followed by the IP address of the computer you are connecting to. The `smbclient` command does not require root access to run.

```
smbclient -I 10.10.10.20 -Uusername%password
```

This will give you the following prompt:

```
smb: <current directory on share>
```

From here, the commands are almost identical to the standard UNIX/Linux FTP commands. Note that you can omit a password on the `smbclient` command line. You will then be prompted to enter the Samba share password.

Mounting Samba Shares

There are two ways to mount Samba shares to your Linux host. Mounting a share is the same as mounting an available media partition or remote NFS directory except that the Samba share will be accessed using SMB. (See Chapter 10, "Managing the File System," to see how to mount partitions.) The first method uses the standard Linux mount command:

```
mount -t smbfs //10.10.10.20/homes /mount/point -o username=jkennedy,dmask=777,\
  fmask=777
```

> **NOTE**
>
> The hostname can be substituted for an IP address if your name service is running or the host is in your /etc/hosts file.

This command will mount `jkennedy`'s home directory on your host and will give all users full permissions to the mount. The permissions are equal to the permissions on the `chmod` command.

The second method produces the same results using the `smbmount` command as follows:

```
# smbmount //10.10.10.20/homes /mount/point -o username=jkennedy,dmask-777,\
  fmask=777
```

To unmount the share, use the standard

```
# umount /mount/point
```

These `mount` commands can also be used to mount true Windows client shares to your Fedora host. Using Samba, you can configure your server to provide any service that Windows can serve, and no one but you will ever know.

Configuring Samba Using SWAT

The Samba team of developers has made administering Samba a snap with the Samba Web Administration Tool, or SWAT. SWAT is a Web-based configuration and maintenance interface that gets as close to a point-and-click Samba environment as possible. This section provides a very simple example of how to use SWAT to set up SMB access to a user's home directory and how to share a directory.

You'll need to perform a few steps before you can start using SWAT. First, make sure that you have the Samba and the `samba-swat` RPM packages installed. You then enable SWAT access to your system by editing the file `/etc/xinetd.d/swat` by changing the following line:

```
disable = yes
```

Change the word `yes` to the word `no`, like so:

```
disable = no
```

Save the file, and then restart the `xinetd` daemon, using either the `system-config-services` client or the `xinetd` shell script under `/etc/rc.d/init.d` like so:

```
# /etc/rc.d/init.d/xinetd restart
```

Next, start an X session, launch the Mozilla Web browser, and browse to the `http://localhost:901` uniform resource locator (URL). You'll be presented a login prompt. Enter the root username and password, and then click the OK button. The screen will clear, and you'll see the main SWAT page, as shown in Figure 13.5.

TIP

You can also configure Samba using Red Hat's `system-config-samba` client. Launch the client from the command line of an X terminal window or select the System Settings, Samba Server menu item (as shown later in Figure 13.9).

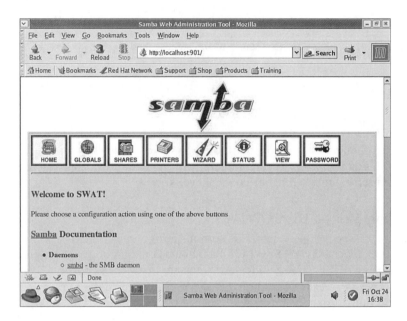

## 13

FIGURE 13.5   SWAT can be used to easily configure and administer Samba on your system.

First, click the GLOBALS icon in SWAT's main page. You'll see a page as shown in Figure 13.6. Many different options are in the window, but you can quickly set up access for hosts from your LAN by simply entering one or more IP addresses or a subnet address (such as 192.168.2.—note the trailing period, which allows access for all hosts; in this example, on the 192.168.2 subnet) in the Hosts Allow field under the Security Options section. If you need help on how to format the entry, click the Help link to the left of the field, and a new Web page will appear with the pertinent information.

When finished, click the Commit Changes button to save the global access settings. The next step is to create a Samba user and set the user's password. Click the PASSWORD icon on the main SWAT page (refer to Figure 13.5). The Server Password Management page opens, as shown in Figure 13.7. Type a new username in the User Name field; then a password in the New Password and Re-type New Password fields.

> **NOTE**
>
> You'll need to supply a username of an existing system user, but the password used for Samba access does not need to match the existing user's password.

When finished, click the Add New User button. SWAT will then create the username and password and will display "Added user username" (where username is the name you entered). The new Samba user should now be able to gain access to the home directory from any allowed host if the Samba (smb) server is running.

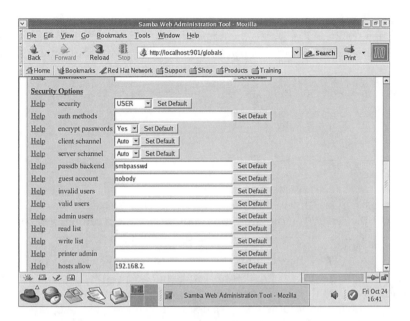

FIGURE 13.6   Configure Samba to allow access from specific hosts or subnets on your LAN.

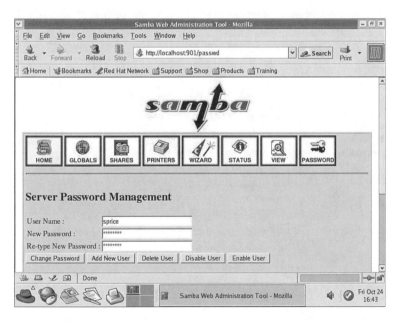

FIGURE 13.7   Enter a Samba username and password in the SWAT Password page.

For example, if you have set up Samba on a host named `shuttle2` that has a user named `sprice`, the user will be able to access the home directory on `shuttle2` from any remote host (if allowed by the GLOBALS settings), perhaps by using the `smbclient` command like so:

```
$ smbclient //shuttle2/sprice -U sprice
added interface ip=192.168.2.68 bcast=192.168.2.255 nmask=255.255.255.0
Password:
Domain=[MYGROUP] OS=[Unix] Server=[Samba 2.2.5]
smb: \> pwd
Current directory is \\shuttle2\sprice\
smb: \> quit
```

Click the Status icon (as shown in Figure 13.5 or 13.7) to view Samba's status, or to start, stop, or restart the server. You can use various buttons on the resulting Web page to control the server and view periodic or continuous status updates.

You can also use SWAT to share a Linux directory. First, click the Shares icon in the toolbar at the top of the main Samba page, as shown in Figure 13.5. Type in a share name in the Create Shares field, and then click the Create Shares button. The SWAT page will display the detailed configuration information, a dialog as shown in Figure 13.8, providing access to detailed configuration for the new Samba share.

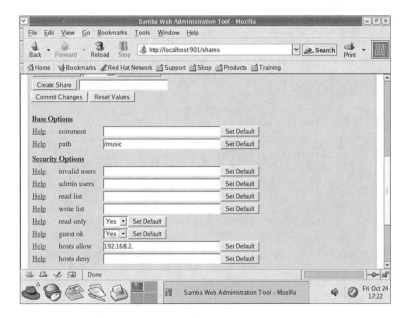

FIGURE 13.8   Use the SWAT Shares page to set up sharing of a portion of your Linux file system.

Type in the directory name (such as /music) you want to share in the Path field under BASE- options. Select No or Yes in the Read Only field under Security options to allow or deny read and write access. Select Yes in the Guest OK option to allow access from other users and specify a hostname, IP address, or subnet in the Hosts Allow field to allow access. Click the Commit Changes button when finished. Remote users can then access the shared volume. This is how a Linux server running Samba can easily mimic shared volumes in a mixed computing environment!

Alternatively, use the system-config-samba client (from the command line or the Server Settings Samba Server menu item on the System Settings menu). Figure 13.9 shows the properties of a shared directory named /music. Use the Add button to create new shares and the Properties button to edit the share's access options. Use the Preferences menu to edit your Samba server's general settings or to create and manage Samba users.

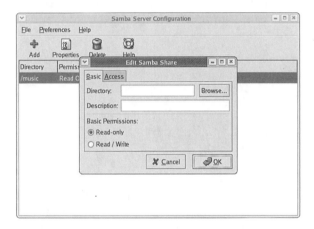

FIGURE 13.9   Configure a Samba share by editing the share defaults.

Wireless Networking

As stated earlier, Linux has had support for wireless networking since the first standards were developed in the early '90s. With computers getting smaller and smaller, the uses for wireless networking increased; meanwhile, the transmission speeds are increasing all the time. There are several different ways to create a wireless network. The following sections introduce you to several Linux commands you can use to initialize, configure, and manage wireless networking on your Fedora system.

Support for Wireless Networking in Fedora

The Linux kernel that ships with Fedora provides extensive support for wireless networking. Related wireless tools for configuring, managing, or displaying information about a wireless connection include

- `iwconfig`—Used to set the network name, encryption, transmission rate, and other features of a wireless network interface

- `iwlist`—Displays information about a wireless interface, such as rate, power level, or frequency used

- `iwpriv`—Used i to set optional features, such as roaming, of a wireless network interface

- `iwspy`—Shows wireless statistics of a number of nodes

Support will vary for different wireless devices—most likely in the form of a PCMCIA adapter—although some USB wireless devices now work with Linux. In general, Linux wireless device software (usually in the form of a kernel module) will support the creation of an Ethernet device that can be managed by traditional interface tools such as `ifconfig`—with wireless features of the device managed by the various wireless software tools.

For example, when a wireless networking device is first recognized and initialized for use, the driver will most likely report a new device:

```
wvlan_cs: WaveLAN/IEEE PCMCIA driver v1.0.6
wvlan_cs: (c) Andreas Neuhaus <andy@fasta.fh-dortmund.de>
wvlan_cs: index 0x01: Vcc 3.3, irq 3, io 0x0100-0x013f
wvlan_cs: Registered netdevice eth0
wvlan_cs: MAC address on eth0 is 00 05 5d f3 1d da
```

This output (from the `dmesg` command) shows that the `eth0` device has been reported. If DHCP is in use, the device should automatically join the nearest wireless subnet and will be automatically assigned an IP address. If not, the next step is to use a wireless tool such as `iwconfig` to set various parameters of the wireless device. The `iwconfig` command, along with the device name (`eth0` in this example), will show the status:

```
# iwconfig eth0
eth0    IEEE 802.11-DS ESSID:"GreyUFO" Nickname:"Prism I"
        Mode:Managed Frequency:2.412GHz Access Point: 00:02:2D:2E:FA:3C
        Bit Rate:2Mb/s  Tx-Power=15 dBm  Sensitivity:1/3
        RTS thr:off  Fragment thr:off
        Encryption key:off
        Power Management:off
        Link Quality:92/92 Signal level:-11 dBm Noise level:-102 dBm
        Rx invalid nwid:0 Rx invalid crypt:0 Rx invalid frag:0
        Tx excessive retries:0 Invalid misc:4  Missed beacon:0
```

This example shows a 2Mbps connection to a network named `GreyUFO`. To change a parameter, such as the transmission rate, use a command-line option with the `iwconfig` command like so:

```
# iwconfig eth0 rate 11M
```

Other options supported by the `iwconfig` command include `essid`, used to set the NIC to connect to a specific network by `named`; `mode`, used to enable the NIC to automatically retrieve settings from an access point or connect to another wireless host; or `freq`, to set a frequency to use for communication. Additional options include `channel`, `frag`, `enc` (for encryption), `power`, and `txpower`. Details and examples of these options are in the `iwconfig` manual page.

You can then use the `ifconfig` command or perhaps a graphical Red Hat tool to set the device networking parameters, and the interface will work as on a hardwired LAN. One handy output of the `iwconfig` command is the link quality output, which can be used in shell scripts or other graphical utilities for signal monitoring purposes (see Chapter 22, "Shell Scripting," for an example).

Cellular Networking

The ads are starting to crop up on TV: This cellular service will allow you to check your email anywhere your cellular phone can reach; that cellular company will provide news and other information via the Internet to your phone. Personal digital assistants have cellular add-ons or even built-in options.

For example, if your laptop has a cellular modem, you can use it to dial in to your network. This isn't truly wireless networking if the network dialed in to is wired, but it illustrates how far-reaching wireless networks can go. As long as your cellular service follows you, you can dial in to any network you have access to (be it home or office) from any location in the world to check your email and use it to send electronic files to your associates. And many newer cell phones can be used as a modem by attaching a cable from the phone to a serial or USB port on a laptop. As with most devices, the majority of brand-name PCMCIA cards will work with Linux. A lot of generic equipment (such as serial I/O cards) should work, but you are taking a chance if the card is not supported (see the section "Managing PCMCIA" in Chapter 4, "Post-Installation Issues").

Advantages of Wireless Networking

The advantage to wireless networking is the mobility and the potential range. If you have a large enough antenna network, your network can stretch many miles. This would be an expensive network, but one that would easily break out of the brick and mortar confines of the office.

Wireless networking would also be a great advantage to college campuses to eliminate the need to tear through walls to install cabling because more and more students expect to have a network connection in their dorm rooms. Wireless networking cards are becoming more reasonable in price and can easily be issued to each student as he requires them.

Home networkers can also benefit from wireless networking. For those who cannot do wired network modifications to their homes, wireless networking removes the unsightly wires running along baseboards and ceilings that are required to connect computers in different rooms. With a wireless home network, you aren't even confined to inside the house. Depending on the transmit power of your router, you can sit out in your backyard and watch clouds drifting by as you type away. Wireless routers are coming down in price with each passing day.

Choosing the right types of wireless devices is an important decision. The next sections discuss some of the basic differences between current protocols used for wireless networking.

Choosing from Among Available Wireless Protocols

The Institute of Electrical and Electronics Engineers (IEEE) started to look seriously at wireless networking in 1990. This is when the 802.11 Standard was first introduced by the Wireless Local Area Networks Standards Working Group. The group based the standard roughly around the architecture used in cellular phone networks. The wireless network is controlled by a base station, which can be just a transmitter attached to the network or, more commonly these days, a router.

Larger networks can use more than one base station. Networks with more than one base station are usually referred to as distribution systems. Use of a distribution system can be used to increase coverage area and support roaming of wireless hosts. You can also employ external omnidirectional antennas to increase coverage area, or if required, use point-to-point, or directional antennas to connect distant computers or networks. Right now, the least expensive wireless Linux networks are built using devices (such as access points or NICs) supporting 802.11b, although prices are rapidly dropping for faster 802.11g devices.

An early standard, 802.11a, offers greater transmission rates than 802.11b, and a number of 802.11a wireless NICs are available (some products provide up to 72Mbps, but will not work with 802.11b devices). Wireless networking devices based on 802.11g, which has the speed improvement of 802.11a and is compatible with 802.11b, are becoming more widely available. Other wireless protocols include Bluetooth, which provides up to 720Kbps data transfers. Bluetooth is intended for short-range device communications (such as for a printer) and only supports a typical range of 10 meters. (Under some circumstances, its range can extend to 100 meters.) Bluetooth is unlike IrDA, which requires line-of-sight (devices that are aimed at each other). Bluetooth use will conflict with 802.11 networks because it also uses the 2.4GHz band. You can find out more by browsing to http://www.bluetooth.com.

The 802.11 standard specifies that wireless devices use a frequency range of 2400MHz–2483.5MHz. This is the standard used in North America and Europe. In Japan however, wireless networks are limited to a frequency range of 2471MHz–2479MHz because of Japanese regulations. Within these ranges, each network is given up to 79 non-overlapping frequency channels to use. This reduces the chance of two closely located wireless networks using the same channel at the same time. It also allows for channel hopping, which can be used for security.

Securing a Wireless Network

Because wireless networking has some unique security issues, those issues deserve a separate discussion here. (General network security issues are discussed in "Securing Your Network," later in this chapter.)

Wireless networking, although convenient, can be very insecure by its very nature because transmitted data (even encrypted data) can be received by remote devices. Extra care must be used to protect the actual frequency used by your network. Great progress has been made in the past couple of years, but the possibility of a security breech is increased when the attacker is in the area and knows the frequency to listen on. It should also be noted that the encryption method used by more wireless NICs is weaker than other forms of encryption (such as SSH) and should not be considered as part of your security plan.

> **TIP**
>
> Always use OpenSSH-related tools, such as ssh or sftp, to conduct business on your wireless LAN. Passwords will not be transmitted as plain text, and your sessions will be encrypted. See Chapter 5, "First Steps with Fedora," to see how to connect to remote systems using ssh. See Chapter 18, "Secure File Transfer Protocol Service," to see how to use the sftp command.

The better the physical security is around your network, the more secure it will probably be (and this applies to wired networks as well). Keep wireless transmitters (routers, switches, and so on) as close to the center of your building as possible. Note or monitor the range of transmitted signals in order to determine if your network is open to mobile network sniffing—now a geek sport known as *war driving*. (Linux software is available at http://sourceforge.net/project/showfiles.php?group_id=57253.) An occasional walk around your building not only can give you a break from work, but it can also give you a chance to notice any people or equipment who should not be in the area.

Securing Your Network

The only way to make sure that your system is secure is to lock the system in a room and never even turn it on. This isn't very practical, but it's true.

As long as anyone has access to your system, whether physical or over a network, there is the threat that information stored on the network can be compromised. The more access given, the higher the threat. If your network is connected to the Internet, the threat of someone breaking into your computer is very real.

No home computer using a cable modem, regular modem, or DSL to access the Internet is safe. As DSL and cable modems become more common, the home computer has become a favorite target for skript kiddies to use as stepping stones to get to larger corporate networks or to set up your computer to take part in massive, coordinated attacks on remote networks. This not only means that the private information on your computer can be accessed at will, but also, if a skript kiddie uses your computer to launch a cyber attack or a virus, your computer can be taken as evidence.

If this information causes you concern, it should. Although there is no way to stop a serious cracker who is intent on getting into your computer or network, there are ways to make it harder for him and to warn you when he does. This section discusses some system weak points and highlights a few security tools included with Fedora that you can put to use right away.

Built-in Protection in the Kernel

A number of networking and low-level protective services are built into the Linux kernel. These services can be enabled, disabled, or displayed using the `sysctl` command, or by echoing a value (usually a `1` or a `0` to turn a service on or off) to a kernel process file under the `/proc` directory. One of the newest features is the Exec-shield kernel enhancement. This feature protects your system by randomizing the location of processes in virtual memory and disallowing execution of parts of memory after a program loads. See the Fedora Release Notes for more information.

Using `lokkit` and `system-config-securitylevel` for Firewalling

First and foremost, always use a hardware-based or software-based firewall on the computer connected to the Internet. Fedora includes a graphical firewall configuration client named `system-config-securitylevel`, along with a console-based firewall client named `lokkit`. Use these tools to implement selective or restrictive policies regarding access to your computer or LAN.

Start the `lokkit` command from a console or terminal window. You must run this command as root, or you will see an error message like this:

```
$ /usr/sbin/lokkit
ERROR - You must be root to run lokkit.
```

Use the su command to run `lokkit` like this:

```
$ su -c "/usr/sbin/lokkit"
```

After you press Enter, you'll see a dialog as shown in Figure 13.10. Use the Tab key to navigate to enable or disable firewalling. You can also customize your firewall settings to allow specific protocols access through a port and to designate an Ethernet interface for firewalling if multiple NICs are installed. Note that you can also use a graphical interface version of `lokkit` by running the `gnome-lokkit` client during an X session.

Using `system-config-securitylevel` is a fast and easy way to implement a simple packet-filtering ruleset with filtering rules used to accept or reject TCP and UDP packets flowing through your host's Ethernet or designated device, such as eth0 or ppp0. The rules are created on-the-fly and implemented immediately in memory using `iptables`.

Start `system-config-securitylevel` from the System Settings menu's Security level menu item. You'll be prompted for the root password and the client's window will then appear.

Figure 13.11 shows firewalling enabled for the eth0 Ethernet device, allowing incoming secure shell and HTTP requests.

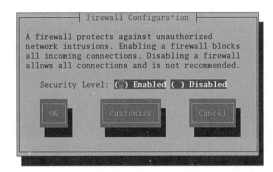

FIGURE 13.10   Red Hat's `lokkit` command quickly generates firewall rules in memory for Linux.

FIGURE 13.11   Red Hat's `system-config-securitylevel` client can also be used to quickly generate and implement standard or simple custom firewall rules for Linux.

Fedora and Firewalling

Fedora also supports the older, but still popular `ipchains` packet-filtering software, which can be used to construct effective firewalling rules on Linux firewalls, gateways, servers, and workstations. Linux also supports the more capable `iptables`, or NetFilter system, which offers additional controls and logging facilities used to build filtering *rulesets* or filtering instructions.

Unfortunately, Fedora does not include any command-line or graphical interface utilities you can use to build, save, and test complex `iptables` rulesets, usually implemented as shell scripts. You will need to do this if you want to control outgoing as well as incoming packets. However, you

> can write your own using a text editor such as vi. Many experienced Linux users will hand-tune rulesets for specific application in advanced network situations, such as development of routing rules.
>
> For a good overview and all the details about using `iptables` for a variety of gateway and firewall systems, read Robert L. Ziegler's excellent book, *Linux Firewalls, Second Edition,* available from New Riders. You can also browse to his site at `http://www.linux-firewall-tools.com/ linux/firewall/index.html`, which offers a graphical, Web-based firewall design and construction tool you can use to quickly build a custom `ipchains`-based ruleset file.

You can use Fedora to create a custom firewall, perhaps supporting IP masquerading (also known as NAT) by using either `ipchains` or `iptables`. You'll find two example scripts under the `/usr/share/doc/rp-pppoe/configs` directory, which are used when connecting to the Internet using a Digital Subscriber Line (DSL).

Passwords and Physical Security

The next step toward better security is to use secure passwords on your network and ensure that users use them as well, especially the root password. If the root password on just one machine is cracked, the whole network is in trouble. For somewhat more physical security, you can force the use of a password with the LILO or GRUB boot loaders, remove bootable devices such as floppy and CD-ROM drives, or configure a network-booting server for Fedora. This approach is not well supported or documented at the time of this writing; but you can read about one way to do this in Brieuc Jeunhomme's Network Boot and Exotic Root HOWTO, available at `http://www.tldp.org/HOWTO/Network-boot-HOWTO/`. You can also read more about GRUB and LILO in Chapter 24, "Kernel and Module Management."

Also, keep in mind that some studies show that as much as 90% of network break-ins are by current or former employees. If a person no longer requires access to your network, lock out access or, even better, remove the account immediately. A good security policy also dictates that any data associated with the account be first backed up and retained for a set period to ensure against loss of important data.

After making sure that your password use is secure, check your use of services. If you don't need a service, don't start it. Although NFS can be very helpful, it isn't overly secure. Just the concept of sharing a whole file system over a network is insecure. Some other potentially vulnerable services are Web services, telnet, FTP—especially anonymous ftp—finger, and remote services such as rlogin, rcp, and rwho.

Finally, be aware of physical security. If a potential attacker can get physical access to your system, getting full access becomes trivial. Keep all servers in a locked room, and ensure that only authorized personnel are given access to clients.

Securing TCP/IP

There isn't much you can do to change TCP/IP and make it more, or less, secure. It is the standard. Just be sure that no user can access parts of the network that he is not supposed to by using good subnetting practices. Use tools such as nmap to scan your network for potential weaknesses such as unused ports being open. Many network administrators (with permission, of course) will try to break into their business network from their home PC to test security, which isn't a bad idea.

Configuring and Using Tripwire

Tripwire is a security tool that will check the integrity of normal system binaries and report any changes to syslog or by email. Tripwire is a good tool for ensuring that your binaries have not been replaced by Trojan horse programs. Trojan horses are malicious programs inadvertently installed because of identical filenames to distributed (expected) programs, and they can wreak havoc on a breached system. Fedora does not include the free version of Tripwire, but it can be used to monitor your system. To set up Tripwire for the first time, go to http://www.tripwire.org, and then download and install an open source version of the software. After installation, run the twinstall.sh script (found under /etc/tripwire) as root like so:

```
# /etc/tripwire/twinstall.sh
----------------------------------------------
The Tripwire site and local passphrases are used to
sign a variety of files, such as the configuration,
policy, and database files.

Passphrases should be at least 8 characters in length
and contain both letters and numbers.

See the Tripwire manual for more information.


----------------------------------------------
Creating key files...

(When selecting a passphrase, keep in mind that good passphrases typically
have upper and lower case letters, digits and punctuation marks, and are
at least 8 characters in length.)

Enter the site keyfile passphrase:
```

You'll then need to enter a password of at least eight characters (perhaps best is a string of random madness, such as 5fwkc4ln) at least twice. The script will generate keys for your site (host) and then ask you to enter a password (twice) for local use. You'll then be asked to again enter the new site password. After following the prompts, the (rather extensive) default configuration and policy files (`tw.cfg` and `tw.pol`) will be encrypted. You should then back up and delete the original plain-text files installed by Fedora's RPM package.

To then initialize Tripwire, use its `--init` option like so:

```
# tripwire --init
Please enter your local passphrase:
Parsing policy file: /etc/tripwire/tw.pol
Generating the database...
*** Processing Unix File System ***
....
Wrote database file: /var/lib/tripwire/shuttle2.twd
The database was successfully generated.
```

Note that not all the output is shown here. After Tripwire has created its database (which is a snapshot of your file system), it will use this baseline along with the encrypted configuration and policy settings under the `/etc/tripwire` directory to monitor the status of your system. You should then start Tripwire in its integrity checking mode, using a desired option. (See the `tripwire` manual page for details.) For example, you can have Tripwire check your system and then generate a report at the command line, like so:

```
# tripwire -m c
```

No output is shown here, but a report will be displayed in this example. The output could be redirected to a file, but a report will be saved as `/var/lib/tripwire/report/` `hostname-YYYYMMDD-HHMMSS.twr` (in other words, using your host's name, the year, month, day, hour, minute, and seconds). This report can be read using the `twprint` utility, like so:

```
# twprint --print-report -r \
/var/lib/tripwire/report/shuttle2-20020919-181049.twr ¦ less
```

Other options, such as emailing the report, are supported by Tripwire, which should be run as a scheduled task by your system's scheduling table, `/etc/crontab` on off-hours. (It can be resource intensive on less powerful computers.) The Tripwire software package also includes a `twadmin` utility you can use to fine-tune or change settings or policies or to perform other administrative duties.

Devices

Do not ever advertise that you have set a NIC to promiscuous mode. Promiscuous mode (which can be set on an interface by using `ifconfig`'s `promisc` option) is good for monitoring traffic across the network and can often allow you to monitor the actions of someone who might have broken into your network. The `tcpdump` command will also set a designated interface to promiscuous mode while the program runs; unfortunately, the `ifconfig` command will not report this fact while `tcpdump` is running! Keep in mind that this is one way that a cracker will use to monitor your network to gain the ever-so-important root password.

> **NOTE**
>
> Browse to http://www.redhat.com/docs/manuals/ to read about how to detect unauthorized network intrusions or packet browsing (known as network *sniffing*). You can use the information to help protect your system. Scroll down the page and click the Security guide link.

And don't forget to use the right tool for the right job. Although a network bridge can be used to connect your network to the Internet, it wouldn't be a good idea. Bridges have almost become obsolete because they will forward any packet that comes their way. That isn't good when it is connected to the Internet. A router will allow you to filter which packets are relayed.

Securing DHCP

DHCP so far appears to be fairly secure on UNIX/Linux servers. Be sure that only root can modify the dhcpd.conf file, and you should have no DHCP-related security issues.

Securing NFS

As mentioned previously, even the concept of what NFS does is a potential security nightmare. If you use your favorite Internet search engine and search for "NFS exploits," you will be given many, many different listings. If you don't need NFS to share files across your network or to mount remote directories, be sure that it is disabled and not enabled to start at boot time (using the ntsysv or chkconfig commands).

Making Samba Secure

Samba is well-written. There aren't too many exploits (security flaws that can be used for malicious purposes). The biggest security holes are the ones created by improper configuration or incorrect file permissions on important files. Like DHCP, you need to protect your configuration file (/etc/smb.conf). Other precautions to take include making sure that you have the latest, most secure and stable version installed and using software packages included for Fedora. Be careful giving privileges with Samba, restrict anonymous access to your server, and you should be safe.

Keeping Up-to-Date on Linux Security Issues

A multitude of Web sites relate to security. One in particular hosts an excellent mailing list. The site is called Security Focus, and the mailing list is called BugTraq. BugTraq is well-known for its unbiased discussion of security flaws. Be warned: It receives a relatively large amount of traffic (20–100+ messages daily).

Often security holes are discussed on BugTraq before the software makers have even released the fix. The Security Focus site has other mailing lists and sections on its Web site dedicated to Linux in general and is an excellent resource.

Related Fedora and Linux Commands

You'll use these commands when managing network connectivity in your Fedora system:

dhclient—Automatically acquire, and then set IP info for a NIC

ethereal—GNOME graphical network scanner

gnome-lokkit—Red Hat's basic graphical firewalling tool for X

ifconfig—Displays and manages Linux networking devices

iwconfig—Displays and sets wireless network device parameters

lokkit—Red Hat's basic graphical firewalling tool

netconfig—Red Hat's console-based graphical network interface configuration tool

route—Displays and manages Linux kernel routing table

setup—Red Hat's console-based graphical management tool

ssh—The OpenSSH remote-login client and preferred replacement for telnet

system-config-nfs—Red Hat's graphical NFS configuration tool

system-config-network—Red Hat's graphical network and service management client for X

system-config-securitylevel—Red Hat's graphical firewall configuration utility

---

Using Patches/Upgrades to Keep Your Network Secure

One of the keys to security not mentioned previously is to keep up-to-date with at least the latest stable versions of your software. Each time a new version of a software package comes out, it corrects any known security holes found in the previous release. Also be sure to keep your operating systems patched to the latest patch level. Your network security is only as strong as the weakest host.

See Chapter 8 for details on how to use RPM to update Fedora with newer software packages. See Chapter 24 to see how to update your Linux kernel (even if you use RPM).

With effort, your system can be secure enough to keep most intruders out. Just keep your software up-to-date and keep yourself informed of potential security threats to your software, and you should be fine.

Reference

The following Web sites and books are great resources for more information on the topics covered in this chapter. Networking is complex. The more you take the time to learn, the easier setting up and maintaining your network will be.

General

http://fedora.redhat.com/docs—Links to additional documentation for Fedora.

http://www.ietf.org/rfc.html—Go here to search for, or get a list of, Request for Comments (RFC).

DHCP

`http://www.oth.net/dyndns.html`—For a list of Dynamic DSN service providers, go to this site.

`http://www.isc.org/products/DHCP/dhcpv3-README.html`—The DHCP README is available at this site.

Wireless

`http://www.ieee.org`—The Institute of Electrical and Electronics Engineers (IEEE) Web site.

`http://www.mozillaquest.com/Network_02/Wireless_Network_Technology_03_Story-01.html`—Wireless networking with Red Hat 7.2.

`http://crl.cs.uiuc.edu/doc/wireless_redhat.html`—Wireless networking using Red Hat Linux at the Computing Research Laboratory (CRL), the information technology support group for the Department of Computer Science at the University of Illinois at Urbana-Champaign.

`http://www.sorgonet.com/network/wirelessnoap/`—Building a wireless network without using an access point, using Red Hat 8.0.

Security

`http://www.redhat.com/docs/manuals/linux/RHL-9-Manual/custom-guide/s1-basic-firewall-gnomelokkit.html`—Red Hat's guide to basic firewall configuration. Newer documentation will appear at `http://fedora.redhat.com`.

`http://www.insecure.org/nmap/`—This site contains information on `nmap`.

`http://www.securityfocus.com/`—The Security Focus Web site.

`http://www.tripwire.org`—Information and download links for the open source version of Tripwire.

Books

Sams Teach Yourself TCP/IP Network Administration in 21 Days, Sams Publishing, ISBN: 0-672-31250-6

TCP/IP Network Administration, O'Reilly Publishing, ISBN: 1-56592-322-7

Practical Networking, Que Publishing, ISBN: 0-7897-2252-6

Samba Unleashed, Sams Publishing, ISBN: 0-672-31862-8

The DHCP Handbook, Sams Publishing, ISBN: 0-672-32327-3

CHAPTER 14

Managing DNS

IN THIS CHAPTER

- Configuring DNS for Clients
- Essential DNS Concepts
- Using DNS Tools
- Configuring a Local Caching Nameserver
- Your Own Domain Name and Third-Party DNS
- Providing DNS for a Real Domain with BIND
- Providing DNS for a Read Domain
- Troubleshooting DNS
- Managing DNS Security
- Reference

Computers on a network need to be found to be useful. We need to be able to identify each computer so we can connect to them and communicate with them. Each computer needs a unique address. Most of today's networks use the Internet Protocol (IP), so each computer on these networks has a unique IP address to identify it. An IP address is a very large 32-bit number, but we have a shortcut method of displaying that number called the "dotted quad" address. The dotted quad form of the address is made of four 8-bit numbers separated by dots. For example, a computer with the address 3232250992, has the dotted quad form 192.168.60.112. It's easier to use and remember the dotted quad form of an IP address. If we only ever connect to one or two computers, remembering one or two of these numeric addresses isn't too difficult. But if we want to regularly connect to a lot of computers, remembering a lot of numbers becomes quite difficult. To help our memories, we can use names instead of numbers. These names, hostnames like `fedora.redhat.com`, are easier to remember than numbers. What allows us to use names is DNS (the domain name system). DNS provides a translation system, translating the names to numbers and the numbers to names.

Hostnames are merely a convenience for users. Communication with other computers still requires IP addresses. Each hostname, therefore, must be translatable into a unique IP address. This translation process is called name resolution and is performed by software known as a resolver. All the DNS magic is accomplished through a client-server model. For the average user, local configuration involves the DNS client, which queries a remote DNS server to exchange information. The DNS servers are typically maintained by Internet service providers (ISPs) and large corporate networks, although anyone can configure and run a DNS server. All computers on networks need to have a properly configured DNS client.

This chapter introduces DNS concepts and practice using BIND (Berkeley Internet Name Domain), the de facto standard DNS software for UNIX. In this chapter, you learn some of the concepts that are basic to DNS and its functions, including how DNS structure information is stored, how DNS serves name information to users, and how name resolution actually works. You learn how to use BIND to configure nameservers and how to provide DNS for a domain. This chapter also teaches you some important techniques for keeping DNS functions secure, as well as some of the most important troubleshooting techniques for tracking down potential problems related to your DNS functions.

If you are not going to be a DNS administrator, much of the information in this chapter will be of no practical use to you. But the knowledge of DNS that you can gain in this chapter might help you understand DNS problems that occur—so you'll realize that it is not your computer that is broken!

You'll also see how, after you register a domain name, you can obtain third-party DNS service so that you don't have to maintain a DNS server. Also, the commonly used DNS-related tools are explained with a focus on how they can be used to troubleshoot domain name resolution problems that you're likely to encounter.

DNS is essential for many types of network operations, and especially so when providing connectivity to the outside world via the Internet. DNS was designed to make the assignment and translation of hostnames fast and reliable and to provide a consistent, portable namespace for network resources. Its database is maintained in a distributed fashion to accommodate its size and the need for frequent updates. Performance and bandwidth utilization are improved by the extensive use of local caches. Authority over portions of the database is delegated to people who are able and willing to maintain the database in a timely manner, so updates are no longer constrained by the schedules of a central authority.

DNS is a simple—but easily misconfigured—system. Hostname resolution errors might manifest themselves in ways that are far from obvious, long after the changes that caused the errors were made. Such naming errors can lead to unacceptable and embarrassing service disruptions.

An understanding of the concepts and processes involved in working with BIND will help to make sure that your experiences as a DNS manager are pleasant ones.

Configuring DNS for Clients

Later in the chapter, we will focus on setup and configuration in order to provide DNS. In this section, we will briefly examine the setup and configuration required for a computer to use DNS services. The important user setup and configuration processes for DNS will likely have been accomplished during the initial installation of Fedora Core. After the initial installation, further DNS configuration can be accomplished by one or more of these methods:

Using Dynamic Host Control Protocol (DHCP)—in which case, some system settings are updated by the `dhclient` command without intervention by a local or remote administrator or user

Using the `system-config-network` GUI configuration tool

Manually editing the system's `/etc/host.conf` configuration file to specify the methods and order of name resolution

Manually editing the system's `/etc/nsswitch.conf` configuration file to specify the methods and order of name resolution

Manually editing the system's `/etc/hosts` file which lists specific hostnames and IP addresses

Manually editing the system's `/etc/resolv.conf` configuration file to add nameserver, domain, or search definition entries

Successful DNS lookups depend on the system's networking being enabled and correctly configured. You can learn more about how to accomplish that in Chapter 15, "Internet Connectivity."

When an application needs to resolve a hostname, it calls system library functions to do the name resolution. If the GNU C library installed is version 2 or greater, then the `/etc/nsswitch.conf` configuration file is used. Older versions of the library use `/etc/host.conf`. Fedora uses the newer GNU C library, but `/etc/host.conf` is still provided for applications that have been statically linked with other libraries. The two files should be kept in sync.

Understanding the `/etc/host.conf` File

The file `/etc/host.conf`, known as the resolver configuration file, specifies which services to use for name resolution and what order they are to be used. This file has been superceded by `/etc/nsswitch.conf`, but is still provided for applications that use other libraries.

By default with Fedora Core, this file contains

```
order hosts,bind
```

The order shown here is to first consult `/etc/hosts` for a hostname. If the hostname is found in `/etc/hosts`, use the IP address specified there. If it is not found in `/etc/hosts`, then try and resolve the name using DNS (BIND).

One other option is available, although not set by default. This is `nis`, which is Sun's Network Information Service.

Understanding the `/etc/nsswitch.conf` File

The file `/etc/nsswitch.conf` is the System Databases and Name Service Switch configuration file. It contains methods for many types of lookups, but here we are concerned with

DNS resolution, so the line we are interested in is the `hosts` line. This line defines the methods to be used for resolving hostnames and the order in which to apply them. The methods used are

db—local database files (`*.db`)

files—use the local file /etc/hosts

dns—use BIND

nis—use Sun's NIS (Network Information Service)

nisplus—use Sun's NIS+

The default line with Fedora Core is

```
hosts: files dns
```

With this default, the same methods and order are specified as in the default `/etc/host.conf`. First, `/etc/hosts` is searched, and then DNS is used.

Another example would be

```
hosts: files dns nisplus nis
```

In this example, name searches that fail in `/etc/hosts` and with DNS will continue to the NIS services (`nisplus` and `nis`). NIS included with Fedora Core is the `ypserv` daemon.

When you are testing your configuration, you may want to halt name searching at a specific point. You can use the entry `[NOTFOUND=return]`. For example, to stop searching after looking in `/etc/hosts`, you would use the line

```
hosts: files [NOTFOUND=return] dns nisplus nis
```

Understanding the /etc/hosts File

The file `/etc/hosts` contains a table of local hosts (hostnames and IP addresses) used for local DNS-type lookups. The file is used if the keyword hosts is included in the order line of `/etc/host.conf`.

Using `/etc/hosts` to provide hostnames and hostname aliases can be effective when used on small networks. For example, a short `/etc/hosts` might look like this:

```
...
192.168.1.3    wind.maximumhoyt.com      wind webserver #always breaks
192.168.1.4    marvin.maximumhoyt.com     marvin mailserver
192.168.1.5    titan.maximumhoyt.com      titan cvshost
192.168.1.6    hp.maximumhoyt.com      hp
...
```

This example shows a short list of hosts. The format of the file is an IP address, a `hostname/domain name`, and aliases (such as `marvin` and `mailserver`). Using this approach, a system administrator would maintain and update a master hosts list, and then replicate the complete `/etc/hosts` file to every computer on the LAN. Users are then able to access other systems by simply using the hostname alias (such as `marvin`). The format of `/etc/hosts` is easy to understand and easy to maintain, and can be used in conjunction with DNS, and in conjunction with a Dynamic Host Configuration Protocol (DHCP) server on the same network.

Two disadvantages of using `/etc/hosts` become readily apparent on a large network: maintenance and replication. Maintaining huge lists of IP addresses, hostnames, and aliases—along with ensuring that changes are regularly updated to every host on the network—can be a challenge.

The `/etc/hosts` file can be edited with a text editor, or by using the `system-config-network` GUI configuration tool which can be launched from the Network menu item in the System Settings menu. The Hosts tab allows editing the file.

Understanding the `/etc/resolv.conf` File

The file `/etc/resolv.conf` specifies how DNS searches are made. The file contains a list of nameservers (DNS servers to connect to) and some options.

For example, a simple, but usable `/etc/resolv.conf` generally contains at least two name-server entries, specifying a primary and secondary nameserver. This example uses fictitious internal IP addresses:

```
nameserver 192.168.1.1
nameserver 192.168.1.2
search mydomain.com
```

The IP addresses listed in the `/etc/resolv.conf` file are usually assigned by an ISP and represent the remote nameservers. Other optional keywords, such as domain and search, are used to specify a local domain and search list for queries; the two terms are mutually exclusive, however (and we'll explain these terms shortly). If you have both, the last one listed will be used.

The information in `/etc/resolv.conf` can be configured from the `system-config-network` tool by launching the tool from the Network menu item in the System settings menu. The DNS tab allows you to enter or edit the DNS information, as shown in Figure 14.1.

Understanding the Changes Made by DHCP

If your system is set to use DHCP (Dynamic Host Control Protocol), when the DHCP connection is made any existing `/etc/resolv.conf` is saved as `resolv.conf.predhclient` and a new `/etc/resolv.conf` is created with the DNS information supplied by DHCP. When DHCP is released, the saved file is moved back as `/etc/resolv.conf`.

FIGURE 14.1   The GUI Network Configuration tool is one of Fedora Core's best designed GUI tools, permitting extensive network configuration.

Essential DNS Concepts

We begin with a look at the ideas behind DNS, prior to discussing the details of the software used to implement it. An understanding at this level is invaluable in avoiding the majority of problems administrators commonly experience with DNS, as well as in diagnosing and quickly solving the ones that do occur. The following overview omits several small details in the protocol because they aren't relevant to the everyday tasks of a DNS administrator. If you need more information about DNS, consult the DNS standards, especially RFC 1034. (The RFCs related to DNS are distributed with BIND. Fedora Core installs them in /usr/share/doc/bind-*/rfc/.)

The domain namespace is structured as a tree. Each domain is a node in the tree and has a name. For every node, there are *resource records (RRs)*—each of which stores a single fact about the domain. (Who owns it? What is its IP address?) Domains can have any number of children, or subdomains. The root of the tree is a domain named "." (similar to the "/" root directory in a file system.)

Each of the resource records belonging to a domain store a different type of information. For example,

- A (Address) records store the IP address associated with a name.

- NS (Nameserver) records name an authoritative nameserver for a domain.

- SOA (Start of Authority) records contain basic properties of the domain and the domain's zone.

- `PTR` (Pointer) records contain the real name of the host to which the IP belongs.

- `MX` (Mail Exchanger) records specify a mail server for the zone.

Each record type is discussed in detail later in this chapter.

Every node has a unique name that specifies its position in the tree, just as every file has a unique path that leads from the root directory to that file. That is, in the domain name, one starts with the root domain "`.`" and prepends to it each name in the path, using a dot to separate the names. The root domain has children named `com.`, `org.`, `net.`, `de.`, and so on. They, in turn, have children named `ibm.com.`, `wiw.org.`, and `gmx.de.`.

In general, a fully qualified domain name (FQDN) is one that contains the machine name, and the domain name, such as

`foo.example.com.`

is similar to the following path:

`/com/example/foo`

Contrary to the example, the trailing dot in an FQDN is often omitted. This reverse order is the source of confusion to many people who first examine DNS.

How Nameservers Store DNS Structure Information

Information about the structure of the tree, and its associated resource records, is stored by programs called nameservers. Every domain has an authoritative nameserver that holds a complete local copy of the data for the domain; the domain's administrators are responsible for maintaining the data. A nameserver can also cache information about parts of the tree for which the server has no authority. For administrative convenience, nameservers can delegate authority over certain subdomains to other, independently maintained, nameservers.

The authoritative nameserver for a zone knows about the nameservers to which authority over subdomains has been delegated. The authoritative nameserver might refer queries about the delegated zones to those nameservers. So, we can always find authoritative data for a domain by following the chain of delegations of authority from "`.`" (the root domain) until we reach an authoritative nameserver for the domain. This is what gives DNS its distributed tree structure.

How DNS Provides Name Service Information to Users

Users of DNS need not be aware of these details. To them, the namespace is just a single tree—any part of which they can request information about. The task of finding the requested RRs from the resource set for a domain is left to programs called *resolvers*. Resolvers are aware of the distributed structure of the database. They know how to contact the root nameservers (which are authoritative for the root domain) and how to follow the chain of delegations until they find an authoritative nameserver that can give them the information they are looking for.

At the risk of stretching the analogy too far, you can think of domains as directories in a file system and resource records as files in these directories. The delegation of authority over subdomains is similar to having an NFS file system mounted under a subdirectory: Requests for files under that directory would go to the NFS server, rather than this file system. The resolver's job is to start from the root directory and walk down the directory tree (following mount points) until it reaches the directory that contains the files they are interested in. (For efficiency, they can then cache the information they find for some time.) This is why things appear to be listed in "reverse" order. This process is examined in detail next.

In practice, there are several authoritative nameservers for a domain. One of them is the master (or primary) nameserver, where the domain's data is held. The others are known as slave (or secondary) nameservers, and they hold automatically updated copies of the master data. Both the master and the slaves serve the same information, so it doesn't matter which one a resolver asks. The distinction between master and slave is made purely for reasons of reliability—to ensure that the failure of a single nameserver doesn't result in the loss of authoritative data for the domain. As a bonus, this redundancy also distributes the network load between several hosts so that no one nameserver is overwhelmed with requests for authoritative information.

> **NOTE**
>
> As a DNS administrator, it is your responsibility to ensure that your nameservers provide sufficient redundancy for your zones. Your slaves should be far away from the master so that power failures, network outages, and other catastrophes don't affect your name service.

Despite these precautions, the load on DNS servers would be crushing without the extensive use of local caches. As mentioned before, nameservers are allowed to cache the results of queries and intermediate referrals for some time so that they can serve repeated requests for data without referring to the source each time. If they didn't do this, root nameservers (and the nameservers for other popular zones) would be contacted by clients all over the world for every name lookup, wasting a huge amount of resources.

Name Resolution in Practice

When a Web browser issues a request for an IP address, the request is sent to a local nameserver, which resolves the name, stores the result in its cache, and returns the IP address. To better understand this process, take a moment to see what happens behind the scenes when a Web browser issues a request for the IP address of www.ibm.com. This example mimics the actions of the resolver by using the incredibly useful dig utility to follow the chain of delegations between zones until you find the A record you are looking for.

(Because most nameservers would follow the delegations for you, this example uses the +norec dig parameter to turn off recursion. That is, if the nameserver doesn't know how to answer your query, it will not issue further queries on its own.)

> **NOTE**
>
> There are 13 root nameservers around the world. Several are located in the United States—Virginia, California, and Maryland. Others are located in London, Stockholm, and Tokyo. These root servers do not hold "master lists" of IP addresses and domain names, but simply hand off requests to other nameservers.
>
> After a recent DOS (Denial of Service) attack on the root servers, at least one of them now runs an alternative application to BIND.

Begin by randomly selecting one of the 13 root nameservers (ranging from a.root-servers.net to m.root-servers.net; we picked e), and ask what it knows about an A record for www.ibm.com:

```
$ dig @e.root-servers.net www.ibm.com A +norec

; <<>> DiG 9.1.3 <<>> @e.root-servers.net www.ibm.com A +norec
;; global options:  printcmd
;; Got answer:
;; ->>HEADER<<- opcode: QUERY, status: NOERROR, id: 52356
;; flags: qr; QUERY: 1, ANSWER: 0, AUTHORITY: 13, ADDITIONAL: 13

;; QUESTION SECTION:
;www.ibm.com.                   IN      A


;; AUTHORITY SECTION:
com.                    172800  IN      NS      A.GTLD-SERVERS.NET.
com.                    172800  IN      NS      G.GTLD-SERVERS.NET.
com.                    172800  IN      NS      H.GTLD-SERVERS.NET.
com.                    172800  IN      NS      C.GTLD-SERVERS.NET.
com.                    172800  IN      NS      I.GTLD-SERVERS.NET.
com.                    172800  IN      NS      B.GTLD-SERVERS.NET.
com.                    172800  IN      NS      D.GTLD-SERVERS.NET.
com.                    172800  IN      NS      L.GTLD-SERVERS.NET.
com.                    172800  IN      NS      F.GTLD-SERVERS.NET.
com.                    172800  IN      NS      J.GTLD-SERVERS.NET.
com.                    172800  IN      NS      K.GTLD-SERVERS.NET.
com.                    172800  IN      NS      E.GTLD-SERVERS.NET.
com.                    172800  IN      NS      M.GTLD-SERVERS.NET.
```

14

```
;; ADDITIONAL SECTION:
A.GTLD-SERVERS.NET.        172800   IN      A      192.5.6.30
G.GTLD-SERVERS.NET.        172800   IN      A      192.42.93.30
H.GTLD-SERVERS.NET.        172800   IN      A      192.54.112.30
C.GTLD-SERVERS.NET.        172800   IN      A      192.26.92.30
I.GTLD-SERVERS.NET.        172800   IN      A      192.36.144.133
B.GTLD-SERVERS.NET.        172800   IN      A      192.33.14.30
D.GTLD-SERVERS.NET.        172800   IN      A      192.31.80.30
L.GTLD-SERVERS.NET.        172800   IN      A      192.41.162.30
F.GTLD-SERVERS.NET.        172800   IN      A      192.35.51.30
J.GTLD-SERVERS.NET.        172800   IN      A      210.132.100.101
K.GTLD-SERVERS.NET.        172800   IN      A      213.177.194.5
E.GTLD-SERVERS.NET.        172800   IN      A      192.12.94.30
M.GTLD-SERVERS.NET.        172800   IN      A      202.153.114.101


;; Query time: 819 msec
;; SERVER: 192.203.230.10#53(e.root-servers.net)
;; WHEN: Wed Sep 26 10:05:08 2001
;; MSG SIZE  rcvd: 461
```

The QUERY: 1, ANSWER: 0 in the response means that e.root-servers.net didn't know the answer to your question. It does know the authoritative nameservers for the com TLD, and it refers your query to them in the AUTHORITY section. (Not too long ago, all the root-servers.net nameservers were themselves authoritative for the com TLD, but additional delegations were recently introduced.)

The resolver's next step would be to select one of these listed servers at random, to use the IP addresses mentioned in the ADDITIONAL section of the response to connect to the server, and to repeat the question. This is what we do now, having chosen i.gtld-servers.net:

```
$ dig @i.gtld-servers.net www.ibm.com A +norec
; <<>> DiG 9.1.3 <<>> @i.gtld-servers.net www.ibm.com A +norec
;; global options:  printcmd
;; Got answer:
;; ->>HEADER<<- opcode: QUERY, status: NOERROR, id: 61562
;; flags: qr; QUERY: 1, ANSWER: 0, AUTHORITY: 5, ADDITIONAL: 5

;; QUESTION SECTION:
;www.ibm.com.                    IN      A
```

```
;; AUTHORITY SECTION:
ibm.com.                    172800   IN      NS      INTERNET-SERVER.ZURICH.ibm.com.
ibm.com.                    172800   IN      NS      NS.WATSON.ibm.com.
ibm.com.                    172800   IN      NS      NS.ERS.ibm.com.
ibm.com.                    172800   IN      NS      NS.ALMADEN.ibm.com.
ibm.com.                    172800   IN      NS      NS.AUSTIN.ibm.com.


;; ADDITIONAL SECTION:
INTERNET-SERVER.ZURICH.ibm.com. 172800 IN A      195.212.119.252
NS.WATSON.ibm.com.          172800   IN      A       198.81.209.2
NS.ERS.ibm.com.             172800   IN      A       204.146.173.35
NS.ALMADEN.ibm.com.         172800   IN      A       198.4.83.35
NS.AUSTIN.ibm.com.          172800   IN      A       192.35.232.34


;; Query time: 8337 msec
;; SERVER: 192.36.144.133#53(i.gtld-servers.net)
;; WHEN: Wed Sep 26 10:06:46 2001
;; MSG SIZE  rcvd: 240
----------
```

We still have 0 ANSWERs, but we are clearly getting closer. The response lists the names and IP addresses of five authoritative nameservers for the ibm.com domain. (Notice the abnormally large query time. This tells us that our choice of i.gtld-servers.net was, for some reason, a poor one. Intelligent resolvers remember this fact, and would pick a different server in future. BIND only does this for the root servers, though.)

We choose NS.WATSON.ibm.com, and repeat our question:

```
----------
$ dig @NS.WATSON.ibm.com www.ibm.com A +norec

; <<>> DiG 9.1.3 <<>> @NS.WATSON.ibm.com www.ibm.com A +norec
;; global options:  printcmd
;; Got answer:
;; ->>HEADER<<- opcode: QUERY, status: NOERROR, id: 32287
;; flags: qr aa ra; QUERY: 1, ANSWER: 4, AUTHORITY: 5, ADDITIONAL: 5


;; QUESTION SECTION:
;www.ibm.com.                         IN      A


;; ANSWER SECTION:
www.ibm.com.                1800     IN      A       129.42.18.99
www.ibm.com.                1800     IN      A       129.42.19.99
www.ibm.com.                1800     IN      A       129.42.16.99
```

```
www.ibm.com.              1800    IN      A       129.42.17.99


;; AUTHORITY SECTION:
ibm.com.                  600     IN      NS      ns.watson.ibm.com.
ibm.com.                  600     IN      NS      ns.austin.ibm.com.
ibm.com.                  600     IN      NS      ns.almaden.ibm.com.
ibm.com.                  600     IN      NS      ns.ers.ibm.com.
ibm.com.                  600     IN      NS
Âinternet-server.zurich.ibm.com.


;; ADDITIONAL SECTION:
ns.watson.ibm.com.        600     IN      A       198.81.209.2
ns.austin.ibm.com.        86400   IN      A       192.35.232.34
ns.almaden.ibm.com.       86400   IN      A       198.4.83.35
ns.ers.ibm.com.           259200  IN      A       204.146.173.35
internet-server.zurich.ibm.com. 1800 IN A         195.212.119.252


;; Query time: 441 msec
;; SERVER: 198.81.209.2#53(NS.WATSON.ibm.com)
;; WHEN: Wed Sep 26 10:08:21 2001
;; MSG SIZE  rcvd: 304
```
- - - - - - - - - -

NS.WATSON.ibm.com knew the answer to our question, and for the first time, the response contains an ANSWER section that lists four A records for www.ibm.com. Most resolvers pick one at random and return it to the program that initiated the name resolution. This concludes our search.

Reverse Resolution

Given an IP address, it is often necessary to find the name associated with it (while writing Web server logs, for example). This process is known as reverse resolution or reverse lookup, and is accomplished with the help of an elegant subterfuge. IP addresses (similar to filenames) are "backward" from the DNS point of view. Because we can only associate RRs with DNS names, we must find a way to write an IP address, with its left-to-right hierarchy (129.42.18.99 belongs to 129.*), as a DNS name with a right-to-left hierarchy (ibm.com belongs to com).

We do this by reversing the order of the octets in the address, and then appending .in-addr.arpa (a domain used exclusively to support reverse lookups) to the result. For example, 129.42.18.99 would be written as 99.18.42.129.in-addr.arpa. PTR (Pointer) records associated with this special name would then tell us the real name of the host to which the IP belongs.

We can look for PTR records in the usual fashion—by following a chain of delegations from a root server. We examine this process briefly by resolving 203.200.109.66 (which is one of the dial-up IP addresses that an ISP assigns to its customers). We ask a root name-server 66.109.200.203.in-addr.arpa

```
----------
$ dig @a.root-servers.net 66.109.200.203.in-addr.arpa PTR +norec
; <<>> DiG 9.2.1 <<>> @a.root-servers.net 66.109.200.203.in-addr.arpa PTR +norec
;; global options:  printcmd
;; Got answer:
;; ->>HEADER<<- opcode: QUERY, status: NOERROR, id: 64298
;; flags: qr; QUERY: 1, ANSWER: 0, AUTHORITY: 5, ADDITIONAL: 1


;; QUESTION SECTION:
;66.109.200.203.in-addr.arpa.     IN       PTR


;; AUTHORITY SECTION:
203.in-addr.arpa.         86400    IN       NS       ns1.apnic.net.
203.in-addr.arpa.         86400    IN       NS       ns3.apnic.net.
203.in-addr.arpa.         86400    IN       NS       ns.ripe.net.
203.in-addr.arpa.         86400    IN       NS       rs2.arin.net.
203.in-addr.arpa.         86400    IN       NS       dns1.telstra.net.


;; ADDITIONAL SECTION:
ns.ripe.net.              172800   IN       A        193.0.0.193


;; Query time: 57 msec
;; SERVER: 198.41.0.4#53(a.root-servers.net)
;; WHEN: Wed Sep  4 21:15:24 2002
;; MSG SIZE  rcvd: 178
----------
```

Continuing with NS.TELSTRA.NET, we have

```
----------
$ dig @NS.TELSTRA.NET 66.109.200.203.in-addr.arpa PTR +norec

; <<>> DiG 9.2.1 <<>> @NS.TELSTRA.NET 66.109.200.203.in-addr.arpa PTR +norec
;; global options:  printcmd
;; Got answer:
;; ->>HEADER<<- opcode: QUERY, status: NOERROR, id: 12099
;; flags: qr ra; QUERY: 1, ANSWER: 0, AUTHORITY: 2, ADDITIONAL: 2


;; QUESTION SECTION:
```

14

```
;66.109.200.203.in-addr.arpa.    IN      PTR


;; AUTHORITY SECTION:
200.203.in-addr.arpa.    142315  IN      NS      dns.vsnl.net.in.
200.203.in-addr.arpa.    142315  IN      NS      ns3.vsnl.com.

;; ADDITIONAL SECTION:
dns.vsnl.net.in.         33557   IN      A       202.54.1.30
ns3.vsnl.com.            5370    IN      A       203.197.12.42

;; Query time: 293 msec
;; SERVER: 203.50.0.137#53(NS.TELSTRA.NET)
;; WHEN: Wed Sep  4 21:18:09 2002
;; MSG SIZE  rcvd: 132


- - - - - - - - - -
```

And then,

```
- - - - - - - - - -


$ dig @ns3.vsnl.com. 66.109.200.203.in-addr.arpa PTR +norec

; <<>> DiG 9.2.1 <<>> @ns3.vsnl.com. 66.109.200.203.in-addr.arpa PTR +norec
;; global options:  printcmd
;; Got answer:
;; ->>HEADER<<- opcode: QUERY, status: NXDOMAIN, id: 37848
;; flags: qr aa ra; QUERY: 1, ANSWER: 0, AUTHORITY: 1, ADDITIONAL: 0

;; QUESTION SECTION:
;66.109.200.203.in-addr.arpa.    IN      PTR

;; AUTHORITY SECTION:
200.203.in-addr.arpa.    86400   IN      SOA     dns.vsnl.net.in.
helpdesk.giasbm01.vsnl.net.in. 200001059 86400 7200 2592000 345600

;; Query time: 259 msec
;; SERVER: 203.197.12.42#53(ns3.vsnl.com.)
;; WHEN: Wed Sep  4 21:19:16 2002
;; MSG SIZE  rcvd: 114
- - - - - - - - - -
```

What happened here? In previous responses, the status has always been NOERROR, but this
one has a status of NXDOMAIN (Nonexistent Domain), and the flags section has the aa

(Authoritative Answer) flag. This means that the name we are looking for is known not to exist. In contrast, the response from the root nameservers didn't have the aa flag set, and said "We don't know about this name: Ask somebody else." The authoritative answer from `ns3.vsnl.com` says "I know that this name doesn't exist, and you might as well stop looking."

The administrators at `vsnl.net.in` clearly haven't bothered to set up `PTR` records for their dial-up IP address pool. If they had, the response would have looked like the ones we've seen before and would have included a `PTR` record. As it is, the response lists the `SOA` record for zone including the email address of the domain contact, `helpdesk@giasbm01.vsnl.net.in`, should we choose to complain about broken reverse resolution.

What Did the Resolver Learn?

Based on the work we've done up to this point, we have a list of names and addresses of the authoritative nameservers for the com TLD. In the future, if we are asked to resolve, say `www.samspublishing.com`, we can direct our query to `gtld-servers.net` from the start instead of wasting one query on a root server. However, the NS records have an expiry time (also known as Time To Live, or `TTL`, which you learn about in "The Zone File," later in this chapter) of `2D`, meaning that the information is only guaranteed as accurate for two days. This lag time for updates is why you will see announcements made that it might take a few days for DNS changes to propagate throughout the Internet.

Similarly, we know the authoritative nameservers for `ibm.com`, which are for use in queries involving `ibm.com` during the next two days. For instance, a Web browser might ask for the IP address of `commerce.ibm.com` when a user clicks on a link on the IBM Web page. We can save two queries by asking `NS.WATSON.ibm.com` again. Of course, we also have the four `A` records for `www.ibm.com` in our cache, and we can return one of them if the browser asks us to resolve the name again.

All this information (including that gleaned from the reverse resolution process) can be cached by your computer until expiry and used to speed up further queries.

You have also learned some things that a resolver cannot remember or use. You can guess from the names, for instance, that the DNS administrators at IBM have, as recommended, delegated their DNS service to servers that are distant both geographically and on the network. You can see that IBM runs four Web servers on the same network—perhaps to gracefully handle the load. We know that the DNS administrators at VSNL (a large ISP) aren't as conscientious as they could be because they have only two nameservers for their entire domain and don't have correct reverse mappings.

DNS is endlessly fascinating, and a few hours of playing with `dig` are well rewarded. By doing so, you can learn some interesting things about DNS and you gain familiarity with dig queries and responses that will prove very useful in debugging problems with your own DNS setup.

Using DNS Tools

There are a number of standard tools included with Fedora that allow you to work with DNS. These tools, found in the `bind-utils` and `whois` packages, have everyday uses that don't require DNS administrator skills. If you want to know what domain name belongs to an IP address, or vice versa, these are the tools to use to track down that information. Forward lookups are where you map a name to an IP address; reverse lookups are where you map an address to a name.

Here are the tools you will use:

- dig (Domain Information Groper)
- host
- nslookup
- whois

The following sections briefly describe these tools and provide examples of their use.

dig

A command-line utility, the Domain Information Groper will query DNS nameservers. By default, `dig` uses the nameservers listed in `/etc/resolv.conf` and will perform an NS (Nameserver) query. Reverse lookups are accomplished with the `-x` argument with a default A (Address) query.

Here is an example of a forward lookup with `dig`:

```
$ dig www.pearson.com

; <<>> DiG 9.2.2 <<>> www.pearson.com
;; global options:  printcmd
;; Got answer:
;; ->>HEADER<<- opcode: QUERY, status: NOERROR, id: 59962
;; flags: qr rd ra; QUERY: 1, ANSWER: 1, AUTHORITY: 3, ADDITIONAL: 2

;; QUESTION SECTION:
;www.pearson.com.               IN      A

;; ANSWER SECTION:
www.pearson.com.        86400   IN      A       165.193.130.83

;; AUTHORITY SECTION:
pearson.com.            86400   IN      NS      ns1-p.dns.pipex.net.
pearson.com.            86400   IN      NS      ns.pearson.com.
pearson.com.            86400   IN      NS      ns0-p.dns.pipex.net.
```

```
;; ADDITIONAL SECTION:
ns0-p.dns.pipex.net.    66542    IN      A       158.43.129.80
ns1-p.dns.pipex.net.    66542    IN      A       158.43.193.80

;; Query time: 294 msec
;; SERVER: 64.83.0.10#53(64.83.0.10)
;; WHEN: Mon Sep  1 16:42:00 2003
;; MSG SIZE  rcvd: 151
```

A reverse lookup with dig:

```
$ dig -x 165.193.130.83

; <<>> DiG 9.2.2 <<>> -x 165.193.130.83
;; global options:  printcmd
;; Got answer:
;; ->>HEADER<<- opcode: QUERY, status: NOERROR, id: 63402
;; flags: qr rd ra; QUERY: 1, ANSWER: 1, AUTHORITY: 2, ADDITIONAL: 0

;; QUESTION SECTION:
;83.130.193.165.in-addr.arpa.    IN      PTR

;; ANSWER SECTION:
83.130.193.165.in-addr.arpa. 43200 IN    PTR
prs-sun-106-nyeh-peshr-hme0-4.digisle.net.

;; AUTHORITY SECTION:
130.193.165.in-addr.arpa. 43200 IN       NS      ns.digisle.net.
130.193.165.in-addr.arpa. 43200 IN       NS      ns1.digisle.net.

;; Query time: 41 msec
;; SERVER: 64.83.0.10#53(64.83.0.10)
;; WHEN: Mon Sep  1 16:42:21 2003
;; MSG SIZE  rcvd: 135
```

host

A command-line utility, host performs forward and reverse lookups by querying DNS nameservers, much as does dig.

Here's an example of a forward lookup with host:

```
$ host www.pearson.com
www.pearson.com has address 165.193.130.83
```

Here's a reverse lookup with host:

```
$ host 165.193.130.83
83.130.193.165.in-addr.arpa domain name pointer
prs-sun-106-nyeh-peshr-hme0-4.digisle.net.
```

nslookup

A command-line utility, nslookup can be used in an interactive and non-interactive manner to query DNS nameservers. Note that nslookup is deprecated.

Here's an example of a forward lookup using nslookup:

```
$ nslookup www.pearson.com
Note:  nslookup is deprecated and may be removed from future releases.
Consider using the `dig' or `host' programs instead.  Run nslookup with
the `-sil[ent]' option to prevent this message from appearing.
Server:        64.83.0.10
Address:       64.83.0.10#53

Non-authoritative answer:
Name:   www.pearson.com
Address: 165.193.130.83
```

Here's a reverse lookup using nslookup:

```
$ nslookup 165.193.130.83
Note:  nslookup is deprecated and may be removed from future releases.
Consider using the `dig' or `host' programs instead.  Run nslookup with
the `-sil[ent]' option to prevent this message from appearing.
Server:        64.83.0.10
Address:       64.83.0.10#53

Non-authoritative answer:
83.130.193.165.in-addr.arpa     name = prs-sun-106-nyeh-peshr-hme0-4.digisle.net.

Authoritative answers can be found from:
130.193.165.in-addr.arpa        nameserver = ns.digisle.net.
130.193.165.in-addr.arpa        nameserver = ns1.digisle.net.
```

Note that using a reverse lookup does not tell you the Fully Qualified Domain name of the server using that IP address. To determine that, we need to use the whois client.

whois

A command-line utility from the whois package, whois queries the database at whois.networksolutions.com.

For an IP lookup

```
$ whois 165.193.130.83


OrgName:    Cable & Wireless
OrgID:      CWUS
Address:    3300 Regency Pkwy
City:       Cary
StateProv:  NC
PostalCode: 27511
Country:    US


NetRange:   165.193.0.0 - 165.193.255.255
CIDR:       165.193.0.0/16
NetName:    CWDI-BLK6
NetHandle:  NET-165-193-0-0-1
Parent:     NET-165-0-0-0-0
NetType:    Direct Allocation
NameServer: NS.DIGISLE.NET
NameServer: NS1.DIGISLE.NET
Comment:
RegDate:
Updated:    2002-08-23


TechHandle: ZC221-ARIN
TechName:   Cable & Wireless
TechPhone:  +1-919-465-4023
TechEmail:  ip@gnoc.cw.net


OrgAbuseHandle: SPAMC-ARIN
OrgAbuseName:   SPAM COMPLAINTS
OrgAbusePhone:  +1-800-977-4662
OrgAbuseEmail:  abuse@cw.com


OrgNOCHandle: NOC99-ARIN
OrgNOCName:   Network Operations Center
OrgNOCPhone:  +1-800-977-4662
OrgNOCEmail:  trouble@cw.net


OrgTechHandle: UIAA-ARIN
OrgTechName:   US IP Address Administration
OrgTechPhone:  +1-800-977-4662
OrgTechEmail:  ipadmin@clp.cw.net
```

```
OrgTechHandle: GIAA-ARIN
OrgTechName:   Global IP Address Administration
OrgTechPhone:  +1-919-465-4096
OrgTechEmail:  ip@gnoc.cw.net


# ARIN WHOIS database, last updated 2003-08-31 19:15
# Enter ? for additional hints on searching ARIN's WHOIS database.
```

And for a domain name lookup (which is not what whois is used for)

```
$ whois www.pearson.com

Whois Server Version 1.3


Domain names in the .com and .net domains can now be registered
with many different competing registrars. Go to http://www.internic.net
for detailed information.

No match for "WWW.PEARSON.COM".
```

Configuring a Local Caching Nameserver

A caching nameserver builds a local cache of resolved domain names and provides them to other hosts on your LAN. This speeds up DNS searches and saves bandwidth by reusing lookups for frequently accessed domains and is especially useful on a slow dial-up connection or when your ISP's own nameservers malfunction.

If you have BIND and BIND-utils installed on your computer, you can configure a caching nameserver by installing the caching-nameserver package. This sets up the configuration file /etc/named.conf, the /var/named directory, and the configuration files in /var/named (localhost.zone, named.ca, and named.local).

To start the caching nameserver, you can start the named service manually (see Chapter 8, "Managing Software and System Resources") or use the system-config-services GUI configuration tool. This can be started by choosing the Services menu option in the Server Settings menu, which is in the System Settings menu, and then selecting named and using the Start button.

To get your local computer to use the caching nameserver, reconfigure the file /etc/resolv.conf to comment out any references to your ISP's nameservers, and set the only nameserver to be the localhost (127.0.0.1). The /etc/resolv.conf for the caching-nameserver host is

```
#/etc/resolv.conf
#nameserver 83.64.1.10
#nameserver 83.64.0.10
nameserver 127.0.0.1
```

Other machines on your network should have the IP of the local caching-nameserver in their /etc/resolv.conf files. Assuming that the IP address for the computer running the caching nameserver is 192.168.1.5, then the /etc/resolv.conf files on the other machines on your network should be

```
#/etc/resolv.conf
#nameserver 83.64.1.10
#nameserver 83.64.0.10
nameserver 192.168.1.5
```

Ad Blocking with a Caching Nameserver

Another advantage of setting up a caching nameserver is that you can use it to block ads and objectionable sites by using bogus DNS zones to block specific domains. You do this by overriding the DNS lookup of the sites you want to block. Configuration is simple. First, determine the sites that you want to block. For example, you may want to block all access to doubleclick.net. Create an entry in /etc/named.conf like this

```
zone "doublelick.net" { type master; file "fakes"; };
```

Then create a new file /var/named/fakes. This should contain

```
$TTL 1D
@        IN      SOA     wind.maximumhoyt.com. hostmaster.maximumhoyt.com. (
                         2004081701 8H 2H 4W 1D)

@        IN      NS      wind.maximumhoyt.example.com.
@        IN      A       127.0.0.1
*        IN      A       127.0.0.1
```

where wind.maximumhoyt.com should be replaced by the hostname of the caching nameserver. This will point all DNS lookups of doubleclick.net to 127.0.0.1, where they will not be found. In order to make the change effective, you'll need to restart named so that the new configuration information is read. Chapter 8 describes several different ways of restarting the named service, here's one of them:

```
# kill -HUP 'pidof named'
```

Once named has been restarted, attempts to resolve all doubleclick.net addresses will fail, the ads will not be loaded and will not be displayed, and your browsing experience will be faster.

Your Own Domain Name and Third-Party DNS

It is possible to have your own domain name and provide third-party DNS service for it, meaning that you do not have to configure and administer a DNS nameserver for yourself. You can even have a mail address for your domain without having a mail server.

Here's a summary of the major tasks involved in providing a third-party DNS service to your own domain name:

- Register and pay for a unique domain name. Several companies now offer to register these names, so shop around for the most reasonable price and perform some Google background checks on the company before using them.

- Use a third-party DNS provider to provide DNS services. One popular provider is ZoneEdit (www.maximumhoyt.com uses ZoneEdit as well, although there are a number of other free-of-cost providers) and provides detailed steps to use the service. ZoneEdit also provides mail forwarding services, so mail addressed to you@your.own.domain is forwarded to your regular ISP mail account. ZoneEdit also allows you to use DynamicDNS, which enables you to run a server on a dynamically assigned IP (from a cable or dial-up provider), yet still have DNS servers locate you. ZoneEdit can also provide a startup Web page space for you or forward requests to an already established page with a long, complicated address.

- Return to your domain name registrar and tell it what nameservers will be authoritative for your domain.

Once you've completed the preceding tasks, it will take about three days for the information to propagate around the Internet.

Providing DNS for a Real Domain with BIND

BIND is the de facto standard DNS software suite for UNIX. It contains a nameserver daemon (named) that answers DNS queries, a resolver library that enables programs to make such queries, and some utility programs. BIND is maintained by the ISC (Internet Software Consortium) at the Web site http://www.isc.org/bind/.

Three major versions of BIND are in common use today: 4, 8, and 9. The use of BIND 4 is now *strongly* discouraged (because of numerous security vulnerabilities and other bugs), and won't be discussed here. BIND 8, with many new features and bug fixes, is now quite widely deployed. It is actively maintained, but still vulnerable to a variety of attacks; its use is *strongly* discouraged as well. Fedora Core now provides BIND 9.

> **NOTE**
>
> If you are upgrading from BIND 8 to BIND 9, make sure to read the file /usr/share/doc/bind-9.2.3/misc/migration for any issues regarding configuration files (which will cause BIND not to run) and use of existing shell scripts. An HTML version of the BIND 9 manual is the file Bv9ARM.html under the /usr/share/doc/bind-9.2.3/arm directory.

In this chapter, we discuss the use of BIND 9, which ships with Fedora Core. BIND 9 was rewritten from scratch in an attempt to make the code more robust and leave behind the problems inherent in the old code. It is compliant with new DNS standards and represents a substantial improvement in features, performance, and security.

The bind RPM package contains the named daemon and a wealth of BIND documentation. The bind-utils RPM package contains, among other things, the invaluable dig(1) utility. If you choose to compile BIND yourself, you can download the source distribution from the ISC's Web site and follow the build instructions therein.

> **NOTE**
>
> You will also find build instructions in the file README under the /usr/share/doc/bind-9.2.3 directory.

Once you install the RPMs, the following directories are of special interest because they contain the file used by BIND and contain the information shown in the listing.

```
. . . . . . . . . .

/etc/                        The rndc.conf, named.conf configuration files.
/usr/bin/                    dig, host, nslookup, nsupdate.
/usr/sbin/                   named, rndc, and various support programs.
/usr/share/doc/bind-9.2.3/   BIND documentation.
/usr/share/man/              Manual pages.
/var/named/*                 Zone files.

. . . . . . . . . .
```

If you install from source, the files will be in the locations you specified at configure time, with the default directories under /usr/local/.

The following example uses BIND to configure a nameserver, and then expand it as necessary to provide useful DNS service. To accomplish this, you must configure named (the nameserver daemon) and rndc components (a control utility that permits various interactions with a running instance of named). You also might need to configure the resolver software, as discussed later.

Three configuration files are used:

- rndc.key to specify the key used to authenticate between rndc and named
- rndc.conf to configure rndc
- named.conf to configure named

When rndc communicates with named, it uses cryptographic keys to digitally sign commands before sending them over the network to named. The configuration file, /etc/rndc.key, specifies the key used for the authentication.

The only authentication mechanism currently supported by named is the use of a secret key, encrypted with the HMAC-MD5 algorithm, and shared between rndc and named. The easiest way to generate a key is to use the dnssec-keygen utility. In the following example, you are asking the utility to generate a 128-bit HMAC-MD5 user key named rndc:

```
$ dnssec-keygen -a hmac-md5 -b 128 -n user rndc
Krndc.+157+14529
$ cat Krndc.+157+14529.private
Private-key-format: v1.2
Algorithm: 157 (HMAC_MD5)
Key: mKKd2FiHMFe1JqXl/z4cfw==
```

The utility creates two files with .key and .private extensions, respectively. The Key: line in the .private file tells us the secret that rndc and named need to share (mKKd2FiHMFe1JqXl/z4cfw==). When we have this, we can set up the rndc.key configuration file which is shared by both rndc.conf and named.conf.

```
key "rndc" {       algorithm          hmac-md5;      secret
"mKKd2FiHMFe1JqXl/z4cfw=="; };
- - - - - - - - - -
```

rndc.conf

rndc uses a TCP connection (on port 953) to communicate with named. The configuration file, /etc/rndc.conf by default, must specify a server to talk to, as well as include the corresponding key (which must be recognized by named) to use while talking to it.

```
- - - - - - - - - -
# Use the key named "rndc" when talking to the nameserver "localhost."
server localhost {
    key                "rndc";
};

# Defaults.
options {
    default-server     localhost;
    default-key        "rndc";
};

# Include the key to use
include "/etc/rndc.key;
- - - - - - - - - -
```

The file needs to have three sections:

- The server section defines a nameserver (`localhost`) and specifies a key (`rndc`) to be used while communicating with it.

- The options section sets up reasonable defaults (because the file might list multiple servers and keys).

- The key section includes the file we have already created, `/etc/rndc.key`.

Should you need it, the `rndc(8)` and `rndc.conf(5)` manual pages contain more information.

named.conf

You next must configure `named` itself. Its single configuration file (`/etc/named.conf`) has syntax very similar to `rndc.conf`; this section describes only the small subset of configuration directives essential to the configuration of a functional nameserver. For a more exhaustive reference, consult the BIND 9 ARM (Administrator Reference Manual); it is distributed with BIND, and Fedora Core installs it under `/usr/share/doc/bind-*/arm/`).

Only the options and named sections in the `named.conf` file are absolutely necessary. The options section must tell `named` where the zone files are kept, and `named` must know where to find the root zone ("`.`"). We also set up a controls section to enable suitably authenticated commands from `rndc` to be accepted. Because clients (notably `nslookup`) often depend on resolving the nameserver's IP, we set up the `0.0.127.in-addr.arpa` reverse zone as well.

We start with a configuration file similar to this:

```
----------options {     # This is where zone files are kept.    directory
        "/var/named"; };

# Allow rndc running on localhost to send us commands. controls {     inet
127.0.0.1         allow { localhost; }        keys { rndc; }; };""include
"/etc/rndc.key";

# Information about the root zone. zone "." {      type            hint;
file              "root.hints"; }; # Lots of software depends on being
able to resolve 127.0.0.1 zone "0.0.127.in-addr.arpa" {     type
            master;     file            "rev/127.0.0"; };
----------
```

The options section is where we specify the directory in which `named` should look for zone files (as named in other sections of the file). You learn about using other options in later examples in this chapter.

Next, we instruct `named` to accept commands from an authenticated `rndc`. We include the key file, `/etc/rndc.key`, and the controls section saying that `rndc` will be connecting from localhost and using the specified key. (You can specify more than one IP address in the allow list or use an access control list as described in the section "Security.")

The "." zone tells named about the root nameservers with names and addresses in the root.hints file. This information determines which root nameserver is initially consulted. (The decision is frequently revised based on the server's response time.) Although the hints file can be obtained via FTP, the recommended, network-friendly way to keep it synchronized is to use dig. We ask a root nameserver (it doesn't matter which one) for the NS records of "." and use the dig output directly:

```
# dig @j.root-servers.net. ns > /var/named/root.hints
# cat /var/named/root.hints
; <<>> DiG 8.2 <<>> @j.root-servers.net . ns
; (1 server found)
;; res options: init recurs defnam dnsrch
;; got answer:
;; ->>HEADER<<- opcode: QUERY, status: NOERROR, id: 6
;; flags: qr aa rd; QUERY: 1, ANSWER: 13, AUTHORITY: 0, ADDITIONAL: 13
;; QUERY SECTION:        ;; ., type = NS, class = IN

;; ANSWER SECTION:
.                6D IN NS        H.ROOT-SERVERS.NET.
.                6D IN NS        C.ROOT-SERVERS.NET.
.                6D IN NS        G.ROOT-SERVERS.NET.
.                6D IN NS        F.ROOT-SERVERS.NET.
.                6D IN NS        B.ROOT-SERVERS.NET.
.                6D IN NS        J.ROOT-SERVERS.NET.
.                6D IN NS        K.ROOT-SERVERS.NET.
.                6D IN NS        L.ROOT-SERVERS.NET.
.                6D IN NS        M.ROOT-SERVERS.NET.
.                6D IN NS        I.ROOT-SERVERS.NET.
.                6D IN NS        E.ROOT-SERVERS.NET.
.                6D IN NS        D.ROOT-SERVERS.NET.
.                6D IN NS        A.ROOT-SERVERS.NET.

;; ADDITIONAL SECTION:
H.ROOT-SERVERS.NET.      5w6d16h IN A    128.63.2.53
C.ROOT-SERVERS.NET.      5w6d16h IN A    192.33.4.12
G.ROOT-SERVERS.NET.      5w6d16h IN A    192.112.36.4
F.ROOT-SERVERS.NET.      5w6d16h IN A    192.5.5.241
B.ROOT-SERVERS.NET.      5w6d16h IN A    128.9.0.107
J.ROOT-SERVERS.NET.      5w6d16h IN A    198.41.0.10
K.ROOT-SERVERS.NET.      5w6d16h IN A    193.0.14.129
```

```
¦    L.ROOT-SERVERS.NET.        5w6d16h IN A    198.32.64.12
¦    M.ROOT-SERVERS.NET.        5w6d16h IN A    202.12.27.33
¦    I.ROOT-SERVERS.NET.        5w6d16h IN A    192.36.148.17
¦    E.ROOT-SERVERS.NET.        5w6d16h IN A    192.203.230.10
¦    D.ROOT-SERVERS.NET.        5w6d16h IN A    128.8.10.90
¦    A.ROOT-SERVERS.NET.        5w6d16h IN A    198.41.0.4
¦
¦
¦    ;; Total query time: 4489 msec
¦    ;; FROM: lustre to SERVER: j.root-servers.net  198.41.0.10
¦    ;; WHEN: Mon Sep 10 04:18:26 2001
¦    ;; MSG SIZE  sent: 17  rcvd: 436
- - - - - - - - - -
```

The Zone File

The zone `0.0.127.in-addr.arpa` section in `named.conf` says that we are a master name-server for that zone and that the zone data is in the file `127.0.0`. Before examining the first real zone file in detail, look at the general format of a resource record specification:

```
name        TTL     class   type    data
```

Here, `name` is the DNS name with which this record is associated. In a zone file, names ending with a "." are fully qualified, whereas others are relative to the name of the zone. In the zone `example.com`, `foo` refers to the fully-qualified name `foo.example.com`. The special name `@` is a short form for the name of the zone itself. If the name is omitted, the last specified name is used again.

The `TTL` (Time To Live) field is a number that specifies the time for which the record can be cached. This is explained in greater detail in the discussion of the `SOA` record in the next section. If it is omitted, the default `TTL` for the zone is assumed. `TTL` values are usually in seconds, but you can append an `m` for minutes, `h` for hours, or `d` for days.

BIND supports different record classes, but for all practical purposes, the only important class is `IN`, for Internet. If no class is explicitly specified, a default value of `IN` is assumed; to save a little typing, we don't mention the class in any of the zone files we write here.

The type field is mandatory and names the `RR` in use, such as `A`, `NS`, `MX`, or `SOA`. (We will only use a few of the existing `RR`s here. Consult the DNS standards for a complete list.) The data field (or fields) contains data specific to this type of record. The appropriate syntax will be introduced as we examine the use of each `RR` in turn.

Here is the zone file for the `0.0.127.in-addr.arpa` zone:

```
- - - - - - - - - -
¦    $TTL 2D
¦    @       SOA     localhost. hostmaster.example.com. (
¦                            2001090101  ; Serial
¦
```

```
¦                           24h          ; Refresh
¦                           2h           ; Retry
¦                           3600000      ; Expire (1000h)
¦                           1h)          ; Minimum TTL
¦              NS      localhost.
¦
1      PTR    localhost.
---------
```

The $TTL directive that should begin every zone file sets the default minimum time to live for the zone to two days. This is discussed further in the next section.

The Zone File's SOA Record

The second line in the zone file uses the special @ name that you saw earlier. Here, it stands for 0.0.127.in-addr.arpa, to which the SOA (Start of Authority) record belongs. The rest of the fields (continued until the closing parenthesis) contain SOA-specific data.

The first data field in the SOA record is the fully qualified name of the master nameserver for the domain. The second field is the email address of the contact person for the zone. It is written as a DNS name by replacing the @ sign with a "."; foo@example.com would be written as foo.example.com.. (Note the trailing ..)

Don't use an address such as a.b@example.com because it is written as a.b.example.com, and will later be misinterpreted as a@b.example.com.

> **TIP**
>
> It is important to ensure that mail to the contact email address specified in the SOA field is frequently read because it is used to report DNS setup problems and other potentially useful information.

The next several numeric fields specify various characteristics of this zone. These values must be correctly configured, and to do so, you must understand each field. As shown in the comments (note that zone file comments aren't the same syntax as named.conf comments), the fields are serial number, refresh interval, retry time, expire period, and minimum TTL.

Serial numbers are 32-bit quantities that can hold values between 0 and 4,294,967,295 ($2^{32}-1$). Every time the zone data is changed, the serial number must be incremented. This change serves as a signal to slaves that they need to transfer the contents of the zone again. It is conventional to assign serial numbers in the format YYYYMMDDnn; that is, the date of the change and a two-digit revision number (for example, 2001090101). For changes made on the same day, you increment only the revision. (This reasonably assumes that you don't make more than 99 changes to a zone in one day.) For changes on the next day, the date is changed and the revision number starts from 01 again.

The refresh interval specifies how often a slave server should check whether the master data has been updated. It has been set to 24 hours here, but if the zone changes often, the value should be lower. (Slaves can reload the zone much sooner if they and the master both support the DNS NOTIFY mechanism. Most DNS software does.) The retry time is relevant only when a slave fails to contact the master after the refresh time has elapsed. It specifies how long it should wait before trying again. (It is set to two hours here.)

If the slave is consistently unable to contact the master for the length of the expire period (usually because of some catastrophic failure), it discards the zone data it already has and stops answering queries for the zone. Thus, the expire period should be long enough to allow for the recovery of the master nameserver. It has repeatedly been shown that a value of one or two weeks is too short. One thousand hours (about six weeks) is accepted as a good default.

As you read earlier, every RR has a TTL, which specifies how long it can be cached before the origin of the data must be consulted again. If the RR definition doesn't specify a TTL explicitly, the default TTL (set by the $TTL directive) is used instead. This enables individual RRs to override the default TTL as required.

The SOA TTL, the last numeric field in the SOA record, is used to determine how long negative responses (NXDOMAIN) should be cached. (That is, if a query results in an NXDOMAIN response, that fact is cached for as long as indicated by the SOA TTL.) Older versions of BIND used the SOA minimum TTL to set the default TTL, but BIND 9 no longer does so. The default TTL of 2 days and SOA TTL of 1 hour is recommended for cache friendliness.

The values used previously are good defaults for zones that do not change often. You might have to adjust them a bit for zones with very different requirements; in which case, the Web site http://www.ripe.net/docs/ripe-203.html is recommended reading.

The Zone File's Other Records

The next two lines in the zone file create NS and PTR records. The NS record has no explicit name specified, so it uses the last one, which is the @ of the SOA record. Thus, the nameserver for 0.0.127.in-addr.arpa is defined to be localhost.

The PTR record has the name 1, which becomes 1.0.0.127.in-addr.arpa (which is how you write the address 127.0.0.1 as a DNS name). When qualified, the PTR record name 1 becomes localhost. (You will see some of the numerous other RR types when we later configure our nameserver to be authoritative for a real domain.)

TXT Records and SPF (Sender Policy Framework)

One record not already mentioned is the TXT record. This record is usually used for documentation purposes in DNS, but a recent proposal is using the TXT record to help in the fight against email address forgery, spam, and phishing attacks.

One problem with email and SMTP is that when email is being delivered, the sender can claim that the email is coming from trusted.bank.com, when it really is coming from smalltime. crook.com. When the recipient of the email gets the email, it looks like valid instructions from `trusted.bank.com`, but if they do trust the email and follow the instructions, their bank accounts can become vulnerable.

These situations can be controlled by using SPF.

Domains can publish the valid IP address of their email servers in specially formatted TXT records. A TXT record could look like this:

```
trusted.bank.com. IN TXT "v=spf1 ip4:37.21.50.80 -all"
```

This record specifies that only one IP address is allowed to send mail for `trusted.bank.com`.

Receiving email servers can then do one extra check with incoming email. When an email arrives, they know the IP address that the email is coming from. They also know that the sender claims to be coming from `trusted.bank.com`, for example. The receiving email server can look up the DNS TXT record for `trusted.bank.com`, extract the allowed IP addresses, and compare them to the IP address that the email really is coming from. If they match, that's an extremely good indication that the email really is coming from `trusted.bank.com`. If they don't match, then that's a very good indication that the email is bogus and should be deleted or investigated further.

The SPF system does rely on cooperation between senders and receivers. Senders must publish their TXT records in DNS, and receivers must check the records with incoming email.

If you want more details on SPF, visit the home page at `http://spf.pobox.com/`.

Logging

We now have all the elements of a minimal functioning DNS server, but before we experiment further, some extra logging will allow us to see exactly what named is doing. Log options are configured in a logging section in named.conf, and the various options are described in detail in the BIND 9 ARM.

All log messages go to one or more channels—each of which can write messages to the syslog, to an ordinary file, to stderr, or to null. (Log messages written to null are discarded.) Categories of messages exist, such as those generated while parsing configuration files, those caused by OS errors, and so on. Your logging statement must define some channels and associate them with the categories of messages that you want to see.

BIND logging is very flexible, but complicated, so we'll only examine a simple log configuration here.

The following addition to named.conf will set up a channel called custom, which writes time-stamped messages to a file and send messages in the listed categories to it.

```
logging {
    channel custom {
        file "/tmp/named.log";   # Where to send messages.
        print-time yes;          # Print timestamps?
```

```
┆           print-category yes;      # Print message category?
┆         };
┆
┆
┆         category config      { custom; };    # Configuration files
┆         category notify      { custom; };    # NOTIFY messages
┆         category dnssec      { custom; };    # TSIG messages
┆         category general     { custom; };    # Miscellaneous
┆         category security    { custom; };    # Security messages
┆         category xfer-out    { custom; };    # Zone transfers
┆         category lame-servers { custom; };
┆     };
┆
┆ - - - - - - - - - -
```

> **NOTE**
>
> Retaining and frequently examining your logs is especially important because syntax errors often cause BIND to reject a zone and not answer queries for it, causing your server to become lame (meaning that it is not authoritative for a zone for which it is supposed to be).

Resolver Configuration

The last step before running BIND is to set up the local resolver software. This involves configuring the /etc/hosts, /etc/resolv.conf, and /etc/nsswitch.conf files.

To avoid gratuitous network traffic, most UNIX resolvers still use a hosts-like text file named /etc/hosts to store the names and addresses of commonly used hosts. Each line in this file contains an IP address and a list of names for the host. Add entries to this file for any hosts you want to be able to resolve independently from DNS. If the entry is found in /etc/hosts, the resolver does not have to contact a DNS server to resolve the name, which reduces network traffic.

/etc/resolv.conf specifies the addresses of preferred nameservers and a list of domains relative to which unqualified names will be resolved. You specify a nameserver with a line of the form nameserver 1.2.3.4 (where 1.2.3.4 is the address of the nameserver). You can use multiple nameserver lines (usually up to three). You can use a search line to specify a list of domains to search for unqualified names.

A search line such as search example.com example.net would cause the resolver to attempt to resolve the unqualified name xyz, first as xyz.example.com, and, if that fails, as xyz.example.net. Don't use too many domains in the search list because it slows down resolution.

A hosts: files dns line in /etc/nsswitch.conf will cause the resolver to consult /etc/hosts before using the DNS during the course of a name lookup. This allows you to override the DNS by making temporary changes to /etc/hosts, which is especially useful during network testing. (Older resolvers might require an order hosts, bind line in the /etc/host.conf file instead.)

Running the named **Nameserver Daemon**

Finally! You can now start named with /etc/rc.d/init.d/named start. You should see messages similar to the ones that follow in the syslog (or according to the logging configuration you have set up). One way to do this is to monitor the log file with the tail command; that will scroll the changes in the file down the screen.

```
#  tail -f /var/log/messages
----------
October  9 23:48:33 titan named[2605]: starting BIND 9.2.3 -u named
October  9 23:48:33 titan named[2605]: using 1 CPU
October  9 23:48:33 titan named[2608]: loading configuration from '/etc/named.conf'
October  9 23:48:33 titan named[2608]: no IPv6 interfaces found
October  9 23:48:33 titan named[2608]: listening on IPv4 interface lo, 127.0.0.1#53
October  9 23:48:33 titan named: named startup succeeded
October  9 23:48:33 titan named[2608]: listening on IPv4 interface\
 eth0, 192.168.2.68#53
October  9 23:48:33 titan named[2608]: command channel listening on 127.0.0.1#953
October  9 23:48:33 titan named[2608]: zone 0.0.127.in-addr.arpa/IN: \
loaded serial 1997022700
October  9 23:48:33 titan named[2608]: zone localhost/IN: loaded serial 42
October  9 23:48:33 titan named[2608]: running
----------
```

You can use rndc to interact with this instance of named. Running rndc without arguments displays a list of available commands, including the ability to reload or refresh zones, dump statistics and the database to disk, toggle query logging, and stop the server. (Unfortunately, rndc does not yet implement all the commands that were supported by ndc—the control program shipped with earlier versions of BIND.)

You should now be able to resolve 1.0.0.127.in-addr.arpa locally (try dig @localhost 1.0.0.127.in-addr.arpa PTR +norec) and other names via recursive resolution. If you cannot accomplish this resolution, something is wrong, and you should read the "Troubleshooting DNS" section later to diagnose and correct your problem before proceeding further. Remember to read the logs!

Providing DNS for a Real Domain

You can expand the minimal nameserver configuration you just created into one that performs useful name service for a real domain. Suppose that your ISP has assigned to you the IP addresses in the 192.0.2.0/29 range (which has six usable addresses: 192.0.2.1-6) and that you want to serve authoritative data for the domain example.com. A friend has agreed to configure her nameserver (192.0.2.96) to be a slave for the domain, as well as a backup mail server. In return, she wants the foo.example.com subdomain delegated to her own nameservers.

Forward Zone

First, we must introduce the zone to named.conf:

```
zone "example.com" {
    type master;
    file "example.com";
};
```

and create the zone file

```
$TTL 2D
@       SOA     ns1.example.com. hostmaster.example.com. (
                        2001090101  ; Serial
                        24h         ; Refresh
                        2h          ; Retry
                        3600000     ; Expire (1000h)
                        1h)         ; Minimum TTL
        NS      ns1.example.com.
        NS      ns2.example.com.
        MX 5    mx1.example.com.
        MX 10   mx2.example.com.
        A       192.0.2.1


; Addresses
ns1     A       192.0.2.1           ; Nameservers
ns2     A       192.0.2.96
mx1     A       192.0.2.2           ; Mail servers
mx2     A       192.0.2.96
www     A       192.0.2.3           ; Web servers
  dev   A       192.0.2.4
work    A       192.0.2.5           ; Workstations
play    A       192.0.2.6


; Delegations
```

```
┆   foo     NS      dns1.foo.example.com.
┆   foo     NS      dns2.foo.example.com.
┆   dns1.foo A      192.0.2.96
┆   dns2.foo A      192.0.2.1
┆ ----------
```

The SOA record is similar to the one you saw before. (Note that the next five records all use the implicit name @, which is short for example.com.)

The two NS records define ns1.example.com (our own server, 192.0.2.1) and ns2.example.com (our friend's server, 192.0.2.96) as authoritative nameservers for example.com.

The MX (Mail Exchanger) records each specify a mail server for the zone. An MX RR takes two arguments: a priority number and the name of a host. In delivering mail addressed to example.com, the listed MXes are tried in increasing order of priority. In this case, mx1.example.com (our own machine, 192.0.2.2) has the lowest priority and is always tried first. If the attempt to deliver mail to mx1 fails (for whatever reason), the next listed MX, mx2.example.com (our friend's server), is tried.

The A record says that the address of example.com is 192.0.2.1, and the next few lines specify addresses for other hosts in the zone: our nameservers ns1 and ns2, mail servers mx1 and mx2, two Web servers, and two workstations.

Next, we add NS records to delegate authority over the foo.example.com domain to dns1 and dns2.foo.example.com. The A records for dns1 and dns2 are known as *glue* records, and they enable resolvers to find the address of the authoritative nameservers so that they can continue the query. (If we were using dig, the NS records for dns1 and dns2 would be listed in the AUTHORITY section of the response, whereas the ADDITIONAL section would contain their addresses.)

Notice that dns2.foo.example.com is 192.0.2.1, our own nameserver. We are acting as a slave for the foo.example.com zone and must configure named accordingly. We introduce the zone as a slave in named.conf and specify the address of the master nameserver:

```
┆ ----------
┆
┆   zone "foo.example.com" {
┆       type slave;
┆       file "foo.example.com";
┆       masters {
┆           192.0.2.96;
┆       };
┆   };
┆ ----------
```

Similarly, our friend must configure 192.0.2.96, which is a master for foo.example.com and a slave for example.com. (She must also configure her server to accept mail addressed to example.com. Usually, mx2 would just queue the mail until it could be delivered to mx1.)

Reverse Zone

Let us pretend that we live in a perfect world: Our highly competent ISP has successfully delegated authority of our reverse zone to us, and we must set up named to handle reverse resolution as well. This process is very similar to what you used to set up the reverse zone for 0.0.127.in-addr.arpa. Now, however, you must determine your zone's name.

DNS can only delegate authority at the "." in domain names; as a result, you can set up reverse zones for the whole of a class A, B, or C network because they are divided at octet boundaries in the IP address. This approach is clearly unsuitable for classless subnets such as ours because the divisions aren't at octet boundaries, but in the middle of an octet. In other words, our network can't be described as x.* (class A), x.y.* (class B), or x.y.z.* (class C). The latter comes closest, but includes several addresses (such as 192.0.2.22) that don't belong to our tiny 192.0.2.0/29 network. To set up a reverse zone for our network, we must resort to the use of classless delegation (described in RFC 2317).

The ISP, which is authoritative for the 2.0.192.in-addr.arpa zone, must either maintain your reverse zone for you or add the following records into its zone file:

```
          - - - - - - - - - -
          1          CNAME    1.1-6
          2          CNAME    2.1-6
          3          CNAME    3.1-6
          4          CNAME    4.1-6
          5          CNAME    5.1-6
          6          CNAME    6.1-6


          1-6        NS       192.0.2.1
          1-6        NS       192.0.2.96
          - - - - - - - - - -
```

The first CNAME record says that 1.2.0.192.in-addr.arpa is an alias for 1.1-6.2.0. 192._in-addr.arpa. (The others are similar. We don't have CNAME records for network and broadcast addresses 0 and 7 because they don't need to resolve.) Resolvers already know how to follow CNAME aliases while resolving names. When they ask about the 1-6 domain, they find the NS records defined previously and continue with their query by asking our nameserver about 1.1-6.2.0.192.in-addr.arpa.

So, we must set up a zone file for 1-6.2.0.192.in-addr.arpa. Apart from the peculiar name, this zone file is similar in every respect to the reverse zone we set up earlier, and should contain six PTR records (apart from the SOA and NS records). Note that we make

192.0.2.96 (ns2) a slave for the reverse zone as well, so the administrator must add a suitable zone statement to `named.conf` for it.

CAUTION

Be aware that in the real world you might have to wait for months for your ISP to get the reverse delegation right, and your reverse zone will remain broken until then.

Registering the Domain

You now have a working DNS setup, but external resolvers cannot see it because there is no chain of delegations from the root nameservers to yours. You need to create this chain by registering the domain; that is, by paying the appropriate registration fees to an authority known as a registrar, who then delegates authority over the chosen zone to your nameservers.

Nothing is magical about what a registrar does. It has authority over a certain portion of the DNS database (say, the `com`. TLD), and, for a fee, it delegates authority over a subdomain (`example.com`) to you. This delegation is accomplished by the same mechanisms that were explained earlier in our delegation of `foo.example.com`.

The site `http://www.iana.org/domain-names.htm` contains a list of all the TLDs and the corresponding registrars (of which there are now several). The procedure and fees for registering a domain vary wildly between them. Visit the Web site of the registrar in question and follow the procedures outlined there. After wading through the required amounts of red tape, your domain should be visible to the rest of the world.

Congratulations! Your job as a DNS administrator has just begun.

Troubleshooting DNS

Several sources offer good information about finding and fixing DNS errors. The DNSRD Tricks and Tips page at `http://www.dns.net/dnsrd/trick.html` and the comp.protocols. tcp-ip.domains FAQ (an HTML version is located at `http://www.intac.com/~cdp/cptd-faq/`) are good places to start. This section discusses some of the more common errors and their cures.

NOTE

RFC 1912, entitled "Common DNS Operational and Configuration Errors," discusses several of the most common DNS problems at length. It's available at `http://www.intac.com/~cdp/cptd-faq/`.

Delegation Problems

Your zone must be delegated to the nameservers authoritative for them, either by the root nameservers or the parents of the zone in question. Improper delegation can cause the name service for your domain to become dysfunctional, prevent some networks from using the name service, as well as numerous other problems. These problems typically occur only in the initial stages of setting up a domain when the delegations have not propagated widely yet.

If you experience such problems, you can use `dig` to follow delegation chains and find the point at which problems occur. Tools such as `dnswalk` might also be useful (see "Tools for Troubleshooting," later in this chapter).

Lame delegation is another common DNS delegation problem. *Lame delegation* occurs when a nameserver is listed as being authoritative for a zone, but in fact isn't authoritative (it has not been configured to be a master for the zone); the nameserver in a lame delegation is called a lame server. Unfortunately, lame delegations are very common on the Internet. They can be the temporary result of domains being moved or (especially in the case of reverse zones) more permanent configuration errors that are never detected because of a lack of attention to detail.

If your registrar's bills for your domain aren't promptly paid, the registrar might discontinue the delegation of authority for your zone. If this happens (and the whois record for your domain will usually mention this), the best thing to do is quickly pay the registrar and ask him to renew the delegation. It's better not to let it happen, though, because such changes can take a relatively long time to make and propagate.

Reverse Lookup Problems

Reverse lookup problems are often very hard to diagnose because they manifest themselves as failures in systems other than DNS. Many security sensitive services perform reverse lookups on the originating host for all incoming connections and deny the connection if the query fails.

Even if reverse resolution succeeds, many servers might reject connections from your host if your A and PTR records do not match. (That is, the PTR record for a particular IP address refers to a name, and the A record for that name refers to a different IP address.) They perform a double lookup to verify that the PTR and A records match to eliminate spoofing attacks. Maintain your reverse zones carefully at all times.

Delegation problems are a frequent source of woe. Unfortunately, many ISPs appear unable to understand, configure, or delegate reverse zones. In such cases, you often have little choice but to try and tell them what to do to fix the problem, and if they refuse to listen, find a new ISP (or live with broken DNS).

Another typical symptom of failing reverse lookups is an abnormally long delay on connection attempts. This happens when the server's query for a PTR record isn't answered and times out (often because of network problems or the nameserver being down). This can be baffling to diagnose, but you should suspect DNS problems whenever you hear questions such as "Hey! Why is my Web browser `telnet` taking so long to connect?"

Maintaining Accurate Serial Numbers

Accurate serial numbers are very important to the correct operation of slave servers. An increase in the serial number of a zone causes slaves to reload the zone and update their local cache.

A very common mistake that system administrators make is forgetting to increment the serial number after a change to the zone data. If you make this mistake, secondary name-servers won't reload the zone, and will continue to serve old data. If you suspect that the data on the master and slave servers are out of sync, you can use `dig` to view the SOA record for the zone on each server (`dig @master domain SOA` and `dig @slave domain SOA`) and compare the serial numbers in the responses.

Another common problem is setting the serial number to an incorrect value—either too small or too large. A too small serial number causes slaves to think that they possess a more up-to-date copy of the zone data, but this is easily corrected by increasing the serial number as necessary. A too large serial number is more problematic and requires more elaborate measures to repair.

Serial number comparisons are defined in such a way that if a serial number—when subtracted from another with no overflow correction—results in a positive number, the second number is newer than the first, and a zone transfer is required. (See RFC 1982 "Serial Number Arithmetic" for details.) You can exploit this property by temporarily setting the serial number to 2^{32} (4,294,967,296), waiting for all the slaves to reload the zone, and then setting it to the correct number.

Troubleshooting Problems in Zone Files

The most common error in zone data is to forget that names in a zone file are relative to the origin of the zone, not to the root. Writing `www.example.com` in the zone file for `example.com`, and expecting it to be fully qualified, causes names such as `www.example.com.example.com` to show up in the DNS. You should either write www, which is qualified to the correct `www.example.com`, or write `www.example.com.` (with the trailing period) to indicate that the name is fully qualified.

The SOA record should contain (as the first field) the domain name of the master server (not a CNAME) and a contact address (with the @ replaced by a ".") to report problems to. Mail sent to this address should be read frequently. The other fields should contain sensible values for your zone, and the serial number should be correctly incremented after each change.

As discussed earlier, A and PTR records should always match; that is, the A record pointed to by a PTR should point back to the address of the PTR record. Remember to quote the two arguments of HINFO records if they contain any whitespace. Avoid the use of CNAME records for MX, NS, and SOA records.

In general, after making changes to zone data, it is a good idea to reload named and examine the logs for any errors that cause named to complain or reject the zone. Even better, you could use one of the verification tools such as dnswalk, discussed briefly next.

Tools for Troubleshooting

BIND includes the always useful dig program, as well as named-checkconf (to check /etc/named.conf for syntax errors) and named-checkzone (to do the same for zone files). We also especially recommend dnswalk and nslint. dnswalk is a Perl script that scans the DNS setup of a given domain for problems. It should be used in conjunction with RFC 1912, which explains most of the problems it detects. nslint, like the analogous lint utility for C programs, searches for common BIND and zone file configuration errors.

By occasionally using these programs to troubleshoot DNS problems (especially after non-trivial zone changes) you go far toward keeping your DNS configuration healthy and trouble free.

Using Fedora Core's BIND Configuration Tool

Fedora Core Linux provides a dozen or more different graphical configuration tools system administrators can use to configure network (and system) services. One of these tools is system-config-bind, a deceptively simple BIND configuration tool that requires an active X session and must be run with root privileges.

You can launch this client by using the command system-config-bind from a terminal window or by selecting the Domain Name Service menu item from the Server Settings menu. It is automatically installed if you select the Fedora Core configuration tools.

> **NOTE**
>
> Using system-config-bind and then saving any changes will overwrite existing settings! If you prefer to manually edit your named configuration files, do not use system-config-bind. Always make a backup of the configuration files in any event—you'll be glad you did.

After you type the root password and press Enter, the client launches. You'll then see its main window, as shown in Figure 14.2.

system-config-bind can be used to add a forward master zone, a reverse master zone, MX records, or a slave zone. Click the Add Record button to select an entry for configuration, as shown in Figure 14.3.

Existing settings can be edited or deleted by first selecting and then clicking the Edit or Delete buttons in the system-config-bind dialog. When you have finished entering or editing your custom settings, select the Apply menu item from the File menu. Configuration files will be saved in /etc/named.conf and under the /var/named directory.

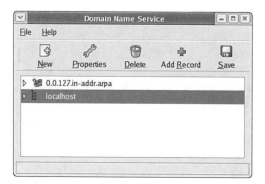

FIGURE 14.2   Fedora Core's `system-config-bind` utility can be used to create, modify, and save basic domain nameserver settings.

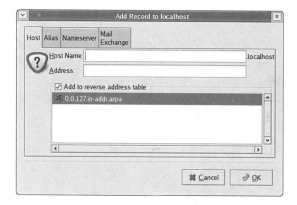

FIGURE 14.3   Use `system-config-bind` to add a new DNS record to your server or edit the existing settings.

Managing DNS Security

Security considerations are of vital importance to DNS administrators because DNS wasn't originally designed to be a very secure protocol and a number of successful attacks against BIND have been found over the years. The most important defense is to keep abreast of developments in security circles and act on them promptly.

DNS is especially vulnerable to attacks known as poisoning and spoofing. *Poisoning* refers to placing incorrect data into the DNS database, which then spreads to clients and caches across the world, potentially causing hundreds of thousands of people to unwittingly use the bad data. Although DNS poisoning can occur because of carelessness, it has serious implications when performed deliberately. What if someone set up a clone of a common Web site, redirected users to it by DNS poisoning, and then asked them for their credit card numbers? *Spoofing* is the practice of forging network packets, and making name-servers believe that they are receiving a valid answer to a query is one of the ways malicious poisoning can be performed.

BIND has often been criticized as being very insecure, and although recent versions are greatly improved in this regard, DNS administrators today must take several precautions to ensure that its use is adequately protected from attacks. Of course, it is important to always run the latest recommended version of BIND.

TIP

One of your strongest defenses against DNS security risks is to keep abreast of developments in security circles and act on them promptly. The BugTraq mailing list, hosted at `http://www. securityfocus.com/`, and the SANS Institute at `http://www.sans.org/` are good places to start.

UNIX Security Considerations

The most important step in securing any UNIX system is to configure the environment BIND runs in to use all the security mechanisms available to it through the operating system to its advantage. In short, this means that you should apply general security measures to your computer.

Run `named` with as few privileges as it needs to function. Don't run `named` as `root`. Even if an attacker manages to exploit a security hole in BIND, the effects of the break-in can be minimized if `named` is running as user `nobody` rather than as `root`. Of course, `named` needs to be started as `root` (because it needs to bind to port 53), but it can be instructed to switch to a given user and group with the `-u` and `-g` command-line options.

Starting `named` with a command such as `named -u nobody -g nogroup` is highly recommended. Remember, however, that if you run multiple services as `nobody`, you increase the risks of a compromise. In such a situation, it is best to create separate accounts for each service and use them for nothing else. Fedora Core runs `named` as the logical user `named`.

You can also use the `chroot` feature of UNIX to isolate `named` into its own part of the file system. If correctly configured, such a file system "jail" will restrict attackers—if they manage to break in—to a part of the file system that contains little of value. It is important to remember that a *chroot jail* isn't a panacea, and it doesn't eliminate the need for other defensive measures.

CAUTION

Programs that use `chroot` but don't take other precautions as well have been shown to be insecure. BIND does take such precautions. See the chroot-BIND HOWTO at `http://www.ibiblio. org/pub/Linux/docs/HOWTO/other-formats/html_single/Chroot-BIND-HOWTO.html`.

14

For a `chroot` environment to work properly, you need to set up a directory that contains everything BIND needs to run. It is recommended that you start with a working configuration of BIND, create a directory, say `/usr/local/bind`, and copy over the files it needs into subdirectories under that one. For instance, you will need to copy the binaries, some system libraries, the configuration files, and so on. Consult the BIND documentation for details about exactly which files you need.

When your `chroot` environment is set up, you can start `named` with the `-t /usr/local/bind` option (combined with the `-u` and `-g` options) to instruct it to `chroot` to the directory you have set up.

You might also want to check your logs and keep track of resource usage. `named` manages a cache of DNS data that can potentially grow very large; it will also happily hog CPU and bandwidth, making your server unusable. This is something that can be exploited by clever attackers, but you can configure BIND to set resource limits. Several such options in the `named.conf` file are available, including datasize, which limits the maximum size of the data segment (and thus the cache). One downside of this approach is that `named` might be killed by the kernel if it exceeds these limits, meaning that you have to run it in a loop that restarts it if it dies (or run it from `/etc/inittab`).

DNS Security Considerations

Several configuration options exist for `named` that can make it more resistant to various potential attacks. The most common ones are briefly described next.

For more detailed discussions of the syntax and use of these options, refer to the BIND 9 documentation.

> **TIP**
>
> The Security Level Configuration Tool (`system-config-securitylevel`) has been updated to make implementation of the firewall simpler. The new "on/off" choice (rather than "levels" as before) allows you to employ a firewall without requiring any special configuration for your DNS server.

Defining Access Control Lists

Specifying network and IP addresses multiple times in a configuration file is tedious and error prone. BIND allows you to define access control lists (ACLs), which are named collections of network and IP addresses. You use these collections to ease the task of assigning permissions.

Four predefined ACLs exist:

- any—Matches anything
- none—Matches nothing

- localhost—Matches all the network interfaces local to your nameserver

- localnets—Matches any network directly attached to a local interface

In addition, you can define your own lists in named.conf, containing as many network and IP addresses as you prefer, using the acl command as shown:

```
- - - - - - - - - -

acl trusted {
    192.0.2.0/29;        // Our own network is OK.
    localhost;           // And so is localhost.
    !192.0.2.33/29;      // But not this range.
};
- - - - - - - - - -
```

Here, you see that you can use a ! to negate members in an ACL. Once defined, you can use these ACLs in allow-query, allow-transfer, allow-recursion, and similar options, as discussed next.

Controlling Queries

As mentioned before, most nameservers will perform recursive resolution for any queries they receive unless specifically configured not to do so. (We suppressed this behavior by using dig +norec.) By repeatedly fetching data from a number of unknown and untrusted nameservers, recursion makes your installation vulnerable to DNS poisoning. (In other words, you get deliberately or inadvertently incorrect lists.) You can avoid this problem by explicitly denying recursion.

Recursive queries can be disabled by adding a recursion no statement to the options section of named.conf. It might still be desirable to allow recursive queries from some trusted hosts, however, and this can be accomplished by the use of an allow-recursion statement. This excerpt would configure named to disallow recursion for all but the listed hosts:

```
- - - - - - - - - -

options {
    ...

    recursion no;
    allow-recursion {
        192.0.2.0/29;
        localnets;        // Trust our local networks.
        localhost;        // And ourselves.
    };
};
- - - - - - - - - -
```

You can choose to be still more restrictive and allow only selected hosts to query your nameserver by using the `allow-query` statement (with syntax similar to `allow-recursion`, as described previously). Of course, this solution won't work if your server is authoritative for a zone. In that case, you will have to explicitly `allow-query { all; }` in the configuration section of each zone for which you want to serve authoritative data.

Controlling Zone Transfers

You also can use queries to enable only known slave servers to perform zone transfers from your server. Not only do zone transfers consume a lot of resources (they require a `named-xfer` process to be forked each time) and provide an avenue for denial of service attacks, but also there have been remote exploits via buffer overflows in `named-xfer` that allow attackers to gain root privileges on the compromised system. To prevent this, add sections such as the following to all your zone definitions:

```
- - - - - - - - - -

zone "example.com" {
    ...
    allow-transfer {
        192.0.2.96;        // Known slave.
        localhost;         // Often required for testing.
    };
};
- - - - - - - - - -
```

Alert named to Potential Problem Hosts

Despite all this, it might be necessary to single out a few troublesome hosts for special treatment. The server and black hole statements in `named.conf` can be used to tell `named` about known sources of poisoned information or attack attempts. For instance, if the host `203.122.154.1` is repeatedly trying to attack the server, the following addition to the options section of `named.conf` will cause our server to ignore traffic from that address. Of course, you can specify multiple addresses and networks in the black hole list.

```
- - - - - - - - - -

options {    ...
blackhole {        203.122.154.1;    };};
- - - - - - - - - -
```

For a known source of bad data, you can do something such as the following to cause your nameserver to simply stop asking the listed server any questions. This is different from adding a host to the black hole list. A server marked as bogus will never be sent queries, but it can still ask us questions. A black holed host is simply ignored altogether.

```
- - - - - - - - - -

server bogus.info.example.com {    bogus yes;};
- - - - - - - - - -
```

The AUS-CERT advisory AL-1999.004, which discusses denial of service attacks against DNS servers, also discusses various ways of restricting access to nameservers and is a highly recommended read. A copy is located at `ftp://ftp.auscert.org.au/pub/auscert/` `_advisory/AL-1999.004.dns_dos`. Among other things, it recommends the most restrictive configuration possible and the permanent black-holing of some addresses known to be popular sources of spoofed requests and answers. It is a good idea to add the following ACL to the black hole list of all your servers:

```
- - - - - - - - - -

/* These are known fake source addresses. */acl "bogon" {    0.0.0.0/8;    #
Null address    1.0.0.0/8;    # IANA reserved, popular fakes    2.0.0.0/8;
    192.0.2.0/24;  # Test address    224.0.0.0/3;   # Multicast addresses

    /* RFC 1918 addresses may be fake too. Don't list these if you
       use them internally. */    10.0.0.0/8;    172.16.0.0/12;
192.168.0.0/16;};
- - - - - - - - - -
```

Using DNS Security Extensions

DNSSEC, a set of security extensions to the DNS protocol, provides data integrity and authentication by using cryptographic digital signatures. It provides for the storage of public keys in the DNS and their use for verifying transactions. DNSSEC still isn't widely deployed, but BIND 9 does support it for inter-server transactions (zone transfers, NOTIFY, recursive queries, dynamic updates). It is worth configuring the TSIG (Transaction Signature) if your slaves also run BIND 9. We briefly discuss using TSIG for authenticated zone transfers here.

To begin, use dnssec-keygen, as we did with rndc, to generate a shared secret key. This key is stored on both the master and slave servers. As before, we extract the Key: data from the `.private` file. The following command creates a 512-bit host key named transfer:

```
- - - - - - - - - -

$ dnssec-keygen -a hmac-md5 -b 512 -n host transfer
- - - - - - - - - -
```

Next, we set up matching key statements in named.conf for both the master and slave servers (similar to the contents of the /etc/rndc.key file which we created earlier).

Remember not to transfer the secret key from one machine to the other over an insecure channel. Use ssh, sftp (secure FTP), or something similar. Remember also that the shared secrets shouldn't be stored in world readable files. The statements, identical on both machines, would look something similar to this:

```
- - - - - - - - - -
key transfer {
    algorithm "hmac-md5";
    secret "...";            # Key from .private file
};


- - - - - - - - - -
```

Finally, we set up a server statement on the master, to instruct it to use the key we just created when communicating with the slave, and enable authenticated zone transfers with the appropriate allow-transfer directives:

```
- - - - - - - - - -
server 192.0.2.96 {
    key { transfer; };
};


- - - - - - - - - -
```

The BIND 9 ARM contains more information on TSIG configuration and DNSSEC support in BIND.

Using Split DNS

BIND is often run on firewalls—both to act as a proxy for resolvers inside the network and to serve authoritative data for some zones. In such situations, many people prefer to avoid exposing more details of their private network configuration via DNS than is unavoidable (although there is some debate about whether this is actually useful). Those accessing your system from outside the firewall should only see information they are explicitly allowed access to, whereas internal hosts are allowed access to other data. This kind of setup is called split DNS.

Suppose you have a set of zones that you want to expose to the outside world and another set that you want to allow hosts on your network to see. You can accomplish this with a configuration such as the following:

```
- - - - - - - - - -
acl private {    localhost;    192.168.0.0/24;    # Define your internal
network suitably.};view private_zones {    match { private; };    recursion yes;
    # Recursive resolution for internal hosts.   zone internal.zone {
       # Zone statements;    };    # More internal zones.};view public_zones
```

```
{    match { any; }    recursion no;zne external.zone {       # Zone statements;
    };   # More external zones.};
----------
```

Further, you might want to configure internal hosts running named to forward all queries to the firewall and never try to resolve queries themselves. The forward only and forwarders options in named.conf do this. (forwarders specifies a list of IP addresses of the nameservers to forward queries to.)

The BIND 9 ARM discusses several details of running BIND in a secure split-DNS configuration.

Related Fedora Core and Linux Commands

You'll use the following commands to manage DNS in Fedora Core Linux:

dig—The domain information groper command, used to query remote DNS servers

host—A domain nameserver query utility

named—A domain nameserver included with Fedora Core Linux

system-config-bind—A GUI tool to configure DNS information

nsupdate—A Dynamic DNS update utility

rndc—The nameserver control utility included with BIND

Reference

http://www.dns.net/dnsrd/—The DNS Resources Database.

http://www.isc.org/products/BIND/—The ISC's BIND Web page.

http://archive.quadratic.net/docs/Bv9ARM.pdf—The BIND 9 Administrator Reference Manual.

The Concise Guide to DNS and BIND, by Nicolai Langfeldt (Que Publishing, 2000)—An in-depth discussion of both theoretical and operational aspects of DNS administration.

http://www.ibiblio.org/pub/Linux/docs/HOWTO/other-formats/html_single/Chroot-BIND-HOWTO.html—A guide to how chroot works with BIND 9.

http://langfeldt.net/DNS-HOWTO/—The home page of the DNS HOWTO for BIND versions 4,8, and 9.

http://www.ibiblio.org/pub/Linux/docs/HOWTO/other-formats/html_single/DNS-HOWTO.html#s3—Setting up a resolving, caching nameserver. Note that the file referenced as /var/named/root.hints is called /var/named/named.ca in Fedora Core.

http://spf.pobox.com/—The home page of SPF (Sender Policy Framework), a method of preventing email address forgery.

## CHAPTER 15

Internet Connectivity

IN THIS CHAPTER

- Common Configuration Information
- Laying the Foundation: The localhost Interface
- Configuring Dial-up Internet Access
- Configuring Digital Subscription Line Access
- Troubleshooting Connection Problems
- Configuring a Dial-in PPP Server
- Reference

Fedora Core Linux supports Internet connections and the use of Internet resources in many different ways. You'll find a wealth of Internet-related software included with this book's version of Fedora Core Linux, and you can download hundreds of additional free utilities from a variety of sources. To use them, you'll need to have a working Internet connection.

In this chapter, you'll learn how to set up an Internet connection in Fedora Core Linux using a modem and Point-to-Point Protocol (PPP) as well as other connection methods, including Digital Subscriber Line (DSL) and cable modem service. Just a few years ago, getting a dial-up connection working was difficult—hence, an entire chapter of this book was devoted to it. Nowadays, as long as you have a hardware modem, dial-up configuration is simple. The Red Hat engineers and the Linux community have made great progress in making connectivity easier.

Although many experienced Linux users continue to use manual scripts to establish their Internet connectivity, new users and experienced system administrators alike will find Fedora Core's graphical network configuration interface, the Internet Connection Wizard, much easier to use. You learn how to use the Internet Connection Wizard in this chapter, as well as how to quickly configure Fedora Core Linux to provide dial-in PPP support. The chapter also describes how to use Roaring Penguin's DSL utilities for managing connectivity through a cable modem connection.

> **Linux and America Online**
>
> The America Online service (AOL) is often cited as a reason that many more people don't use Linux. Why? Because AOL uses a proprietary protocol to connect and a proprietary user interface to access AOL content; no Linux interface is available (although

one has been rumored for a while). Simply put, if you wanted to use Linux, you were forced to choose some Internet connection other than AOL.

Not surprisingly, an enterprising group of people are working on a Linux dialer that will access a legitimate AOL account. It does not provide the unique AOL user interface nor access AOL email and suggests that you use AOL's Web-based email interface, but the Linux dialer does provide connectivity to the Internet via an AOL account.

The Penggy (formerly Pengaol) page at `http://www.peng.apinc.org/eng/` provides links to binary RPM packages as well as source tarballs and HOWTOs. This software is not sanctioned by AOL, but it might allow an AOL user to experiment with Linux.

Common Configuration Information

Although Fedora Core enables great flexibility in configuring Internet connections, that flexibility comes at the price of an increase in complexity. To configure Internet connectivity in Fedora Core Linux, you must know more about the details of the connection process than you can learn from the information typically provided by your Internet service provider (ISP). In this section of the chapter, you learn what to ask about and how to use the information.

Some ISPs are unaware of Linux or unwilling to support its use with their service. Fortunately, that attitude is rapidly changing, and the majority of ISPs offer services using standard protocols that are compatible with Linux, even if they (or their technical support people) aren't aware that their own ISPs are Linux friendly. You just need to press a little for the information you require.

If you are using a dial-up modem account (referred to in Linux as PPP for the Point-to-Point Protocol it uses), your ISP will provide your computer with a static or dynamic IP (Internet Protocol) address. A dynamic IP address changes each time you dial in, whereas a static IP address remains the same. The ISP also might automatically provide your computer with the names of the domain name service servers (DNS). You will need to know the telephone number that your computer will dial in to for making the connection; your ISP supplies that number, too. You'll also need a working modem and need to know the device name of the modem (usually `/dev/modem`).

> **NOTE**
>
> Most IP addresses are dynamically assigned by ISPs; they have a pool of addresses, and you get whatever address is available. From the ISP's viewpoint, a small number of addresses can serve a large number of people because not everyone will be online at the same time. For most Internet services, a dynamic IP works well because it's the ISP's job to route that information to you, and they sit in the middle—between you and the service you want to use. But a dynamic IP address changes, and if someone needs to find you at the same address (if you run a Web site or a file transfer site, for example), an IP that changes every time you log on won't work well. For that, you need a static IP. Because your ISP can't reuse that IP with its other customers, it will likely

charge you more for a static IP than a dynamic IP. The average consumer doesn't need the benefit of a static IP, so he is happy paying less for a dynamically assigned IP. Also, the DNS information can be provided automatically by the ISP by the Dynamic Host Configuration Protocol, or DHCP. This is discussed in depth in Chapter 13, "Network Connectivity."

If you are using DSL access or a cable modem, you might have a dynamic IP provided through DHCP, or you might be assigned a static IP. You might automatically be provided with the names of the DNS servers if you use DHCP, or you will need to manually set up DNS (in which case, you will need to know the IP addresses of the DNS servers).

In all cases, you will need to know your username, your password, and for the configuration of other services, the names of the mail servers and the news server. This information can be obtained from your ISP if you specifically ask for it.

> **NOTE**
>
> The information in this book will help you understand and avoid many connection issues, but you might experience connection problems. Keep the telephone number of the technical help service for your ISP on hand in case you aren't able to establish a connection. But be aware that few ISPs offer Linux support, and you might need to seek help from a Linux-savvy friend or a Linux user's group if your special circumstances can't be handled from the knowledge you gain from this book.

Laying the Foundation: The `localhost` Interface

Prior to connecting to the Internet or network, you must create a dummy or `localhost` interface. This interface, known as `lo` (the loopback interface), is used by the TCP/IP protocol to assign an IP address to your machine and is required for establishing a PPP interface. The `lo` interface is also used by many network-aware applications and is easy to set up.

Checking for the Availability of the Loopback Interface

Fedora Core normally takes care of setting up this interface during the installation. You can use the `ifconfig` command as `root` to see if it is already available. The command and its response will look similar to this if `lo` is available:

```
# /sbin/ifconfig
lo        Link encap:Local Loopback
          inet addr:127.0.0.1  Mask:255.0.0.0
          UP LOOPBACK RUNNING  MTU:16436  Metric:1
          RX packets:12 errors:0 dropped:0 overruns:0 frame:0
          TX packets:12 errors:0 dropped:0 overruns:0 carrier:0
          collisions:0 txqueuelen:0
          RX bytes:760 (760.0 b)  TX bytes:760 (760.0 b)
```

The sample output shows that the loopback interface is active and running, that it has been assigned the typical loopback IP address 127.0.0.1, that the broadcast mask of 255.0.0.0 is used, and that the interface hasn't had much traffic (RX = receive and TX = transmit). If you don't see something similar to the example, you'll need to configure the localhost interface by hand after reading the remainder of this section. Otherwise, you can skip to the next section.

Configuring the Loopback Interface Manually

The localhost interface's IP address is defined in a text file that can be used by Fedora Core Linux to store network IP address information. This file is called /etc/hosts and should exist on a system even if it's empty. The file provides IP addresses and associated hostnames to the Linux kernel and other network-related utilities. Prior to configuring network interfaces, you might find that the /etc/hosts file only contains a single line:

```
127.0.0.1        localhost.localdomain            localhost
```

This line defines the special localhost interface and assigns it an IP address of 127.0.0.1. You might hear or read about terms such as localhost, loopback, and dummy interface; all these terms refer to the use of the IP address 127.0.0.1. The term *loopback interface* indicates that to Linux networking drivers, it looks as though the machine is talking to a network that consists of only one machine; the kernel sends network traffic to and from itself on the same computer. *Dummy* interface indicates that the interface doesn't really exist as far as the outside world is concerned; it exists only for the local machine. You can read more about networking in Chapter 13.

Each networked Fedora Core Linux machine on a LAN will use this same IP address for its localhost. If for some reason a Fedora Core Linux computer does not have this interface, edit the /etc/hosts file to add the localhost entry, and then use the ifconfig and route commands as root to create the interface like this:

```
# /sbin/ifconfig lo 127.0.0.1
# /sbin/route add 127.0.0.1 lo
```

These commands will create the localhost interface in memory (all interfaces, such as eth0 or ppp0, are created in memory when using Linux), and then add the IP address 127.0.0.1 to an internal (in-memory) table so that the Linux kernel's networking code can keep track of routes to different addresses.

Use the ifconfig command as shown previously to test the interface.

You should now be able to use the ping to check that the interface is responding properly like this (using either localhost or its IP address):

```
# /bin/ping -c 3 localhost
PING localhost.localdomain (127.0.0.1) from 127.0.0.1 : 56(84) bytes of data.
```

```
64 bytes from localhost.localdomain (127.0.0.1): icmp_seq=0 ttl=255 time=212 \
usec
64 bytes from localhost.localdomain (127.0.0.1): icmp_seq=1 ttl=255 time=80 usec
64 bytes from localhost.localdomain (127.0.0.1): icmp_seq=2 ttl=255 time=50 usec

--- localhost.localdomain ping statistics ---
3 packets transmitted, 3 packets received, 0% packet loss
round-trip min/avg/max/mdev = 0.050/0.114/0.212/0.070 ms
```

The -c option is used to set the number of pings, and the command, if successful (as it was previously), will return information regarding the round-trip speed of sending a test packet to the specified host.

Configuring Dial-up Internet Access

Most ISPs provide dial-up connections supporting PPP because it is a fast and efficient protocol for using TCP/IP over serial lines. PPP is designed for two-way networking; TCP/IP provides the transport protocol for data. One hurdle faced by new Fedora Core Linux users is how to set up PPP and connect to the Internet. It isn't necessary to understand the details of the PPP protocol in order to use it, and setting up a PPP connection is easy. You can configure the PPP connections manually using the command line or graphically during an X session using Fedora's Internet Configuration Wizard. Each approach produces the same results.

PPP uses several components on your system. The first is a daemon called pppd, which controls the use of PPP. The second is a driver called the high-level data link control (HDLC), which controls the flow of information between two machines. A third component of PPP is a routine called chat that dials the other end of the connection for you when you want it to. Although PPP has many "tunable" parameters, the default settings work well for most people.

> **NOTE**
>
> You can check to see whether PPP is installed on your system by running the pppd command as root from a command line with the --help argument, like this:
>
> ```
> # pppd --help
> ```
>
> That will list the current version number and describe a few available options if PPP is installed.
>
> If PPP isn't installed on your system, use the rpm command to install the PPP package from the Fedora Core CD-ROM or use the Packages menu item from the System Settings menu. Chapter 8, "Managing Software and System Resources," covers the details of using rpm and the graphical package manager.

15

Configuring a Dial-up Connection Manually

The first step in manually configuring PPP is to log in as root in order to copy and edit the necessary files. After you're logged in, you'll use the chat command, the pppd daemon, and several files to configure PPP:

/etc/ppp/ppp-on—Used to start a PPP connection. This file contains the ISP's phone number, your username and password, as well as various options such as IP address options, the modem device, and its settings (such as baud rate) for the connection.

/etc/ppp/ppp-off—Used to terminate a PPP connection.

/etc/ppp/ppp-on-dialer—Used to perform dialing and connection with the chat command; this script contains error-handling and negotiation responses between the remote system and the chat command script.

CAUTION

Many software modems will not work with Linux because the manufacturers won't release programming information about them or provide Linux drivers. An external serial port modem or ISA bus modem will almost always work; USB and PCI modems are still problematic. It is suggested that you do a thorough Google search using your modem's name and model number to see how others have solved problems with that particular modem. Links to software modem compatibility sites appear at the end of this chapter.

Begin by copying the scripts from the /usr/share/doc/ppp*/scripts directory to the /etc/ppp directory, like so:

```
# cp -ar /usr/share/doc/ppp*/scripts/ppp-o* /etc/ppp
```

Using your favorite text editor, edit the ppp-on file (making sure to disable the line wrapping function in your editor—that varies from editor to editor—and line wrapping inserts carriage returns that cause these scripts to stop working) and change the first four entries to reflect your ISP's phone number and your username and password, like this:

```
TELEPHONE=555-1212      # The telephone number for the connection
ACCOUNT=beau            # The account name for logon
PASSWORD=pulley         # The password for this account
LOCAL_IP=0.0.0.0        # Local IP address if known. Dynamic = 0.0.0.0
```

Change the values for TELEPHONE, ACCOUNT, and PASSWORD, substituting your ISP's phone number and your username and password. Change the LOCAL_IP entry to an IP address only if your ISP provides one for use. (Dynamic IPs are typical of dial-up accounts.) Otherwise, leave the entry blank. Next, scroll through the script until you find the dialing setup, which can look like this:

```
exec /usr/sbin/pppd debug lock modem crtscts /dev/ttyS0 38400 \
     asyncmap 20A0000 escape FF kdebug 0 $LOCAL_IP:$REMOTE_IP \
     noipdefault netmask $NETMASK defaultroute connect $DIALER_SCRIPT
```

These lines (actually a single script line) contain modem options for the chat script used in the ppp-on-dialer script and will start the pppd daemon on your computer after establishing a connection. Using a text editor, change the modem device (/dev/ttyS0 in this example) to /dev/modem.

> **CAUTION**
>
> You can use /dev/modem only if Fedora Core's kudzu utility has recognized and configured the computer's modem. (If /dev/modem does not exist, use the ln command to create the file as a symbolic link pointing to the correct serial port.) To create the symlink (from /dev/ttyS2, for example):
>
> `# ln -s /dev/ttyS2 /dev/modem`
>
> If your modem was not automatically detected and the /dev/modem link configured, it is possible that you have a software modem, also known as a WinModem or HSF modem (see earlier note).

Set the baud rate (38400 in the default case) to the desired connection speed—most likely 115200 or 57600. When finished, save the file.

Next, use the chmod command to make these scripts executable, like this:

 # chmod +x /etc/ppp/ppp-o*

To debug or check the progress of your modem connection, dialing, and connection to your ISP, monitor the syslog messages by using the tail command with its -f "loop forever" option, like this:

 # /sbin/tail -f /var/log/messages

To connect to your ISP, run the ppp- script:

 # /etc/ppp/ppp-on

Use the ppp-off script to stop the PPP connection like so:

 # /etc/ppp/ppp-off

You can also move the ppp-on and ppp-off scripts to a recognized $PATH, such as /usr/local/bin. Enabling use of these scripts by normal users will entail changing permissions of the serial port and other files (which can be a security problem because unauthorized users can access it).

> **TIP**
>
> If your modem is installed and working, you can access it using a terminal program such as minicom, which usually isn't installed by default. After you install it from the .rpm file or from source code, start it the very first time with the -s argument to configure it:
>
> ```
> $ minicom -s
> ```
>
> Set the serial port to that of your modem, and then save the configuration. You can then use minicom to communicate with your modem using the AT command set and see its responses.
>
> If you don't want to go to that trouble, you can use the echo command to send commands to the modem, but the modem won't be capable of responding to you. For example, the AT&W command can be sent as follows:
>
> ```
> # echo "AT&W" > /dev/modem
> ```

Using the Fedora Core Internet Configuration Wizard

The Fedora Core Internet Configuration Wizard can be used to set up the many kinds of network connection types that exist. Fedora Core provides wizards for the following connections:

CIPE (VPN) connection (Virtual Private Network using Crypto IP Encapsulation)

Ethernet connection

ISDN connection

Modem connection

Token Ring connection

Wireless connection

xDSL connection

The example provided here uses the Wizard to configure a modem connection, the most commonly encountered home network connection. The other types are configured in essentially the same manner.

From the System Tools menu, select the Internet Configuration Wizard to configure a new Internet connection. Highlight your selection and click Forward. The Select Modem screen, shown in Figure 15.1, is then displayed.

Select "Modem connection" in the Device Type list, and then click the Forward button. You'll then be asked to select a provider, designate a name for the service, enter your ISP's phone number, and enter your username and password on the remote system, as shown in Figure 15.2. A dialing prefix (to disable call-waiting, for example) can be added in the Prefix field. Additional special settings are also included for PPP users in various countries with different ISPs, as shown by the country flags on the left.

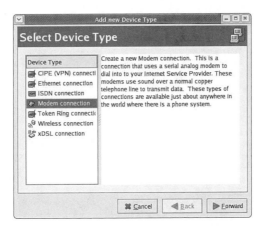

FIGURE 15.1 The Internet Connection Wizard can be used to quickly and easily configure many different kinds of Internet connections.

FIGURE 15.2 Enter a name for your ISP's service, along with the telephone number, username, and password for the service.

Enter the telephone number of your ISP's remote computer's modem. Enter a country code if needed, along with an area code and telephone number. Note that some areas require a 10-digit number for local telephone service. When finished, click the Forward button. You'll then be able to confirm the settings. Click the Finish button to create the interface. When you're done, you'll see a new ppp0 entry in the Network Configuration window, as shown in Figure 15.3.

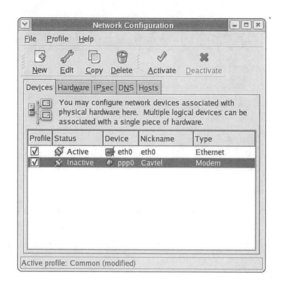

FIGURE 15.3   Your new PPP dial-up connection appears in the Network Configuration dialog, which also shows the status of the connection.

To edit the new connection identified as ppp0, select the interface, and then click the Edit button. A configuration dialog will appear as shown in Figure 15.4. Each tab presents an easy-to-use interface for setting dial-up options.

FIGURE 15.4   Here, you can edit the dial-up configuration if necessary to set IP addresses and other custom values; the defaults work for most people.

This window can be reached later from the System Settings menu as the Network menu item. Fedora Core also provides a simple control interface via the System Tools menu as the Network Device Control menu item, as shown in Figure 15.5.

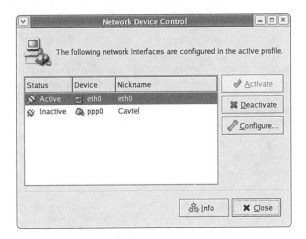

FIGURE 15.5 The Network Device Control allows you to start and stop a network interface.

Launch a PPP connection by selecting the ppp0 interface and then clicking the Activate button.

You can also use the ifup command manually (only as root) to bring up the connection like this:

```
# /sbin/ifup ppp0
```

To close the connection manually, use ifdown:

```
# /sbin/ifdown ppp0
```

If you named the dial-up connection something other than ppp0, use that name instead. Because we named ours *Cavtel*, we can bring it up manually with

```
# /sbin/ifup Cavtel
```

Configuring Digital Subscriber Line Access

Fedora Core Linux also supports the use of a Digital Subscriber Line (DSL) service. Although it refers to the different types of DSL available as xDSL, that name includes ADSL, IDSL, SDSL, and other flavors of DSL service; they can all be configured using the Internet Connection Wizard. DSL service generally provides 128Kbps to 1.0Mbps transfer speeds and transmits data over copper telephone lines from a central office to individual subscriber sites (such as your home). Many DSL services provide asymmetric speeds with download speed greater than upload speeds.

> **NOTE**
>
> DSL service is an "always on" type of Internet service, although you can turn off the connection under Fedora Core Linux using the Network Device Control. An always on connection exposes your computer to malicious abuse from crackers who trawl the Internet attempting to gain access to other computer systems. In addition to the capability to turn off such connections, Fedora Core provides a firewall to keep crackers out; you configured a simple firewall during the original installation. The firewall can also be configured from the Security Level Configuration tool found in the System Settings menu selection as Security Level.

A DSL connection requires that you have an Ethernet network interface card (sometimes a USB interface that is not easily supported in Linux) in your computer or notebook. Many users also configure a gateway, firewall, or other computer with at least two network interface cards in order to share a connection with a LAN. Chapter 13 discusses the hardware and protocol issues in detail. Advanced configuration of a firewall or router, other than what was addressed during your initial installation of Fedora Core, is beyond the scope of this book.

Understanding Point-to-Point Protocol over Ethernet

Establishing a DSL connection with an ISP providing a static IP address is easy. Unfortunately, many DSL providers use a type of PPP protocol named PPPOE (Point-to-Point Protocol over Ethernet) that provides dynamic IP address assignment and authentication by encapsulating PPP information inside Ethernet frames. Roaring Penguin's rp-pppoe clients are included with Fedora Core Linux, and these clients make the difficult-to-configure PPPOE connection much easier to deal with. You can download and install newer versions (see the Roaring Penguin link in the "Reference" section at the end of this chapter).

Configuring a PPPOE Connection Manually

The basic steps involved in manually setting up a DSL connection using Fedora Core Linux involve connecting the proper hardware, and then running a simple configuration script if you use rp-pppoe from Roaring Penguin.

First, connect your DSL modem to your telephone line, and then plug in your Ethernet cable from the modem to your computer's network interface card. If you plan to share your DSL connection with the rest of your LAN, you'll need at least two network cards—designated eth0 (for your LAN) and eth1 (for the DSL connection).

The following example assumes that you have more than one computer and will share your DSL connection on a LAN.

First, log in as `root`, and ensure that your first `eth0` device is enabled and up (perhaps using the `ifconfig` command). Next, bring up the other interface, but assign a null IP address like this:

```
# /sbin/ifconfig eth1 0.0.0.0 up
```

Now use the `adsl-setup` command to set up your system. Type the command like this:

```
# /sbin/adsl-setup
```

You'll be presented with a text script and be asked to enter your username and the Ethernet interface used for the connection (such as `eth1`). You'll then be asked to use "on demand" service or have the connection stay up all the time (until brought down by the root operator). You can also set a timeout in seconds, if desired. You'll then be asked to enter the IP addresses of your ISP's DNS servers if you haven't configured the system's `/etc/resolv.conf` file.

After that, you'll be prompted to enter your password two times, and will then have to choose the type of firewall and IP masquerading to use. (You learned about IP masquerading in the section "Using IP Masquerading in Fedora Core Linux," in Chapter 13.) The actual configuration is done automatically. Using a firewall is essential nowadays, so you should choose this option unless you intend to craft your own set of firewall rules—a discussion of which is beyond the scope of this book. After you have chosen your firewall and IP masquerading setup, you'll be asked to confirm, save, and implement your settings. You are also given a choice to allow users to manage the connection, a handy option for home users.

Changes will be made to your system's `/etc/sysconfig/network-scripts/ifcfg-ppp0`, `/etc/resolv.conf`, `/etc/ppp/pap-secrets`, and `/etc/ppp/chap-secrets` files.

After configuration has finished, use the `adsl-start` command to start a connection and DSL session, like this:

```
# /sbin/adsl-start
```

The DSL connection should be nearly instantaneous, but if problems occur, check to make sure that your DSL modem is communicating with the phone company's central office by examining the status LEDs on the modem. Because this varies from modem to modem, consult your modem user's manual.

Check to make certain that all cables are properly attached, that your interfaces are properly configured, and that you have entered the correct information to the setup script.

If IP masquerading is enabled, other computers on your LAN on the same subnet address (such as 192.168.1.*XXX*) can use the Internet, but must have the same `/etc/resolv.conf` nameserver entries and a routing entry with the DSL-connected computer as a gateway. For example, if the host computer with the DSL connection has an IP address of

192.168.1.1, and other computers on your LAN use addresses in the 192.168.1.*XXX* range, use the `route` command on each computer like this:

```
# /sbin/route add default gw 192.168.1.1
```

Note that you can also use a hostname instead if each computer has an /etc/hosts file with hostname and IP address entries for your LAN. To stop your connection, use the adsl-stop command like this:

```
# /sbin/adsl-stop
```

Troubleshooting Connection Problems

The Internet Configuration Wizard doesn't offer any Help dialogs, but the Linux Documentation Project at http://www.tldp.org/ offers many in-depth resources for configuring and troubleshooting these connections. The Internet search engine Google is also an invaluable tool for dealing with specific questions about these connections. For many other useful references, see the "Reference" section at the end of this chapter.

Here are a few troubleshooting tips culled from many years of experience:

- If your modem connects and then hangs up, you're probably using the wrong password or dialing the wrong number. If the password and phone number are correct, it's likely an authentication protocol problem.

- If you get connected but can't reach Web sites, it's likely a domain name resolver problem, meaning that DNS isn't working. If it worked yesterday and you haven't "adjusted" the associated files, it's probably a problem at the ISP's end. Call and ask.

- Always make certain that everything is plugged in. Check again—and again.

- If the modem works in Windows, but not in Linux no matter what you do, it's probably a software modem no matter what it said on the box.

- If everything just stops working (and you don't see smoke), it's probably a glitch at the ISP or the telephone company. Take a break and give them some time to fix it.

- Never configure a network connection when you have had too little sleep or too much caffeine; you'll just have to redo it tomorrow.

Configuring a Dial-in PPP Server

If you want to access your high-speed Internet connection when you're away from home, a simple dial-up PPP service can be quickly configured on your Fedora Core Linux system by configuring Linux to answer a call from a remote modem and start PPP. This is handy if you have high-speed access at home and need to use it while you're on the road. For example, our DSL connection is made through the telephone lines to our home. While at our winter vacation home, that DSL connection is not available. With a dial-in server, we use the modem in our laptop to dial home and the dial-up server connects us to the Internet (as well as our home LAN); it's like a private ISP. Not everyone will want to configure a dial-in PPP server to do this, but it does illustrate the kind of power that Linux offers a user.

You'll need a second phone line (for convenience, it's not really necessary), a serial port, and an attached modem. The modem must be set to answer incoming calls using the AT commands specific to the modem you are using (consult its manual), and with the configuration saved using the AT&W modem command. A line-monitoring application such as agetty, getty, or mgetty is then used to watch the serial port by editing an entry in the system's initialization table, /etc/inittab. You then create a special user account and script to configure Fedora Core Linux to automatically start the pppd daemon and PPP service after a user logs in.

Many modems can use a modem string such as ATE1Q0V1&C1&S0S0=1&W to auto answer calls, but this varies by modem manufacturer. Some terminal monitors, such as uugetty, have configuration files that automatically set up the modem for a particular serial port and use an entry in /etc/inittab that looks like this:

```
3:2345:respawn:/sbin/uugetty ttyS1 38400 vt100
```

This entry assumes that a modem is attached to /dev/ttyS1.

Other commands, such as agetty, can directly configure a modem port and might use an /etc/inittab entry like this:

```
3:2345:respawn:/usr/local/bin/agetty -w -I 'ATE0Q1&D2&C1S0=1\015' \
115200 ttyS1 vt100
```

If you'd prefer to use the mgetty command, which is included with Fedora Core Linux, use an entry like this:

```
3:2345:respawn:/sbin/mgetty -a -n 1 -D ttyS1
```

You will also need to edit the file /etc/mgetty+sendfax/mgetty.config to set connection speeds and whether data, fax, or data-only or fax-only connections are to be allowed.

LINUX VOICE MODEM SUPPORT

If you're the fortunate owner of a vgetty-supported voice modem, such as the Elsa MicroLink 56K Internet modem, you can download, install, and use the vgetty command to monitor the modem and have your system provide voice, data, and fax services. Edit the file /etc/mgetty+sendfax/voice.conf, create your answering voice messages in /var/spool/voice/messages, and then use a vgetty /etc/inittab entry such as

```
S0:345:respawn:/sbin/vgetty ttyS2
```

15

In order to host voice messages, you'll need to use the `wavtopvf` and `pvfspeed` commands to convert your voice sound files into a format used by the modem, like this:

```
# wavtopvf mymessage.wav mymessage.pvf
# pvfspeed -s 7200 mymessage.pvf ¦ pvftormd Elsa 4 > mymessage.rmd
```

To play your outgoing message (which should be stored in `/var/spool/voice/messages` with the name `standard.rmd`), use the following command line (needed to convert sound formats so we can play it):

```
# rmdtopvf mymessage.rmd ¦ pvfspeed -s 8000 ¦ pvftobasic >/dev/audio
```

This technique can be used to listen to any messages left by callers (which end up in the `/var/spool/voice/incoming` directory).

Browse to `http://alpha.greenie.net/vgetty/` to download `vgetty` and its documentation. Also, look at the Linux Answering machine HOWTO at `http://linuxindia.virtualave.net/lamhowto.html`.

The next step is to create a user named ppp and then to assign a password to it. Although it is possible to allow remote users to log in and start `pppd` from the command line (assuming that you've set `pppd` to SUID root), the `pppd` daemon can be started automatically by creating a short shell script and then assigning the shell script to the user for the default shell in the user's `/etc/passwd` entry, like this:

```
ppp:x:500:500::/home/ppp:/usr/local/bin/dopppdoppp
```

Made executable with `chmod +x`, it would contain the following:

```
exec /usr/sbin/pppd -detach
```

Using this approach, `pppd` will start automatically after the ppp dial-in user connects and logs in (perhaps using the `ppp-on` scripts or other clients on the remote computer). The file options under the `/etc/ppp` directory should include general dial-in options for PPP service on your system, and specific options files (such as `options.ttyS1` for this example) should be created for each enabled dial-in port. For example, `/etc/ppp/options` could contain

```
asyncmap 0
netmask 255.255.255.0
proxyarp
lock
crtscts
modem
```

There are many approaches to providing your own PPP service. IP addresses can be assigned dynamically, or a static IP address can be doled out for a user. For example, `/etc/ppp/options.ttyS1` could contain

```
IPofPPPserver:assignedIPofdialinuser
```

In this example, the first IP address is for the host computer, whereas the second IP address will be assigned to the remote user. For details about configuring PPP for Linux, read the pppd manual page or documentation under the /usr/share/doc/pppd* directory. If you're a Linux developer, browse the source code files ppp_async.c, ppp_deflate.c, ppp_generic.c, and ppp_synctty.c under the /usr/src/linux-2.6/drivers/net directory.

Saving Even More Bandwidth

If you elect to use a dial-in server, one of the problems you face when using it is that you're using a connection with narrower bandwidth. Wouldn't it be nice if you could strip out all the advertising images and compress the HTML pages before sending them over the modem? Here's how it can be done:

One approach is to use the Fedora Core–supplied privoxy proxy server or squid proxy server to filter ads and the Ziproxy (http://ziproxy.sourceforge.net/) server to convert the images to smaller, low-quality images and compress the HTML pages before sending them on to the dial-in user. A Red Hat 9 version is available at http://www.ai.mit.edu/people/wang/ziproxy-1.2.rh9.tgz, as well as a statically compiled version (requires no additional files) at http://aleron.dl.sourceforge.net/sourceforge/ziproxy/ziproxy-1.2b-static.i586.tar.bz2. Ziproxy requires a library not provided by Red Hat or Fedora Core, libconfuse (available at http://www.nongnu.org/confuse/, where you'll find a src.rpm file to compile on your system; see Chapter 8 for information on compiling source rpm files).

Another approach is to use RabbIT (http://www.khelekore.org/rabbit/), a Java Web proxy server that handles both tasks. The site mentions that 2.9MB of original data was compressed to 1.3MB and transmitted in 17 minutes instead of 75 minutes, a considerable saving. The site offers a Getting Started link on the main page describing downloading, installing, configuring, and using the application.

Both applications require ImageMagick to be installed to use the convert function to process images into low-resolution version to save bandwidth.

Relevant Fedora Core and Linux Commands

internet-druid—Fedora Core's command-line name for its graphical Internet Connection Wizard.

mgetty—An advanced serial port monitoring tool that supports data and fax modem operations with Linux.

neat—Fedora Core's command-line name for the Network Configuration tool.

system-control-network—Red Hat's command-line name for its graphical Network Device Control tool.

system-config-network-druid—Red Hat's command-line name for its Internet Connection Wizard.

system-config-network—Red Hat's command-line name for its graphical Network Configuration tool. It offers a graphical interface and a command-line interface (when used as system-config-network-tui.

Reference

`http://www.tldp.org/HOWTO/Modem-HOWTO.html`—The Linux Modem HOWTO provides a wealth of information. For example, Chapter 8 deals with locating your modem; Chapters 12 and 13 deal with dial-in use; Chapter 17 offers troubleshooting advice.

`http://www.roaringpenguin.com/pppoe/`—Home page for the fabulous rp-pppoe software package that enables DSL users to connect to the Internet using Linux. This is a "must-have" software package for Fedora Core and DSL users. You might want to grab a source RPM and rebuild it; their download page gives directions on how to do that.

`http://axion.physics.ubc.ca/ppp-linux.html`—W.G. Unruh's extensive Web page describing how to use PPP and Linux to connect to an ISP, figuring out their connection protocol, and testing the connection.

`http://www.tldp.org/HOWTO/PPP-HOWTO/`—A great place to start reading about PPP and Linux; includes directions on configuring various clients, linking LANs, and setting up a PPP server.

`http://www.tldp.org/HOWTO/DSL-HOWTO`—Information about using DSL and Linux, with details about DSL hardware, setting up a network, using USB modems, DSL use and security, and other helpful tips. Highly recommended reading for any Fedora Core Linux user contemplating use of DSL service.

`http://www.knowplace.org/ppp.html`—The 5-minute Linux PPP HOWTO. A wonderful no-frills guide to setting up PPP manually.

`http://www.tldp.org/FAQ/Linux-FAQ/index.html`—Linux Frequently Asked Questions with Answers. Section 11, "How Do Configure Dial-up PPP?" is very useful. Section 17 has answers to common general problems.

`http://www.tldp.org/HOWTO/Serial-HOWTO.html`—The Serial HOWTO covers all aspects of the serial ports used by modems.

`http://www.tldp.org/HOWTO/PCMCIA-HOWTO.html`—The Linux PCMCIA HOWTO covers PCMCIA modems used in laptop computers.

`http://www.tldp.org/HOWTO/PPP-HOWTO/index.html`—The Linux PPP HOWTO is the canonical reference for PPP.

`http://www.tldp.org/FAQ/PPP-FAQ.html`—The FAQ supplements the HOWTO and delves into troubleshooting modems in detail.

`http://walbran.org/sean/linux/linmodem-howto.html`—The Linmodem HOWTO helps you with your software modem with tips on identification, modules compiling, and a good FAQ.

`http://www.pcquest.com/content/linux/handson/102082101.asp`—Winmodems and Linux: An overview of software modems with a list of manufacturers and links to their drivers.

`http://www.linmodems.org/`—The "official" software modem site for Linux.

`http://linmodems.technion.ac.il/pctel-linux/`—The unofficial PCTEL modem site for Linux.

`http://pctelcompdb.sourceforge.net/`—An unofficial database for PCTEL modems.

`http://linmodems.technion.ac.il/`—A Linmodem support page.

`http://www-124.ibm.com/acpmodem/`—The ACP modem driver for Linux.

`http://www.swcp.com/~jgentry/pers.html`—The Linux Dialin Server Setup Guide, a step-by-step guide to configuring a dial-in server.

`https://www.redhat.com/docs/manuals/linux/RHL-9-Manual/security-guide/s1-vpn-cipe.html`—The Red Hat Guide to using Crypto IP Encapsulation (CIPE) over a Virtual Private Network (VPN) to establish a secure Ethernet connection between any two hosts.

15

## CHAPTER 16

Apache Web Server Management

IN THIS CHAPTER

- About the Apache Web Server
- Installing the Apache Server
- Starting and Stopping Apache
- Runtime Server Configuration Settings
- File System Authentication and Access Control
- Apache Modules
- Virtual Hosting
- Logging
- Dynamic Content
- Graphic Interface Configuration of Apache
- Other Web Servers for Use with Fedora
- Reference

This chapter covers the configuration and management of the Apache Web server. The chapter includes an overview of some of the major components of the server and discussions of text-based and graphical configuration of the server. You'll see how to start, stop, and restart Apache using the command line and Red Hat utilities included with Fedora. The chapter begins with some introductory information about this popular server, and then shows you how to install, configure, and start using Apache.

About the Apache Web Server

Apache is the most widely used Web server on the Internet today, according to a NetCraft survey of active Web sites in August 2004, which is shown in Table 16.1.

What's more revealing is the growth rate in the use of the Apache server versus the other server platforms in use by developers and Web sites, according to NetCraft, which has been tracking server usage since 1995. Between March 2002 and September 2003, Apache gained 7.6% of the total market share, whereas Microsoft server deployment and use declined 8.38%. More than two million Web sites abandoned Microsoft deployments in a single year, and Apache is clearly the Web server of choice on the Internet. Note that these statistics do not reflect Apache's use on internal networks, known as *intranets*.

The name *Apache* appeared during the early development of the software because it was "a patchy" server, made out of patches for the freely available source code of the NCSA HTTPd Web server. For a while after the NCSA HTTPd project was discontinued, a number of people wrote a variety of patches for the code, either to fix bugs or to add features that they wanted. A lot of this code was floating around and people were freely sharing it, but it was completely unmanaged.

TABLE 16.1   NetCraft Survey Results (August 2004)

Web Server	Number	Percentage*
Apache	36,112,220	67.70%
Microsoft**	11,115,660	21.32%
SunONE	1,656,671	3.18%
Zeus	754,721	1.45%
*Of 43,144,374 sites surveyed		
**All Web server products		

After a while, Bob Behlendorf and Cliff Skolnick set up a centralized repository of these patches, and the Apache project was born. The project is still composed of a rather small core group of programmers, but anyone is welcome to submit patches to the group for possible inclusion in the code.

There's been a surge of interest in the Apache project over the past several years, partially buoyed by a new interest in Open Source on the part of enterprise-level information services. It's also due in part to crippling security flaws found in Microsoft's IIS (Internet Information Server), the existence of malicious Web task exploits, and operating system and networking vulnerabilities to the now-infamous Code Red, Blaster, and Nimda worms. IBM made an early commitment to support and use Apache as the basis for its Web offerings, and has dedicated substantial resources to the project because it made more sense to use an established, proven Web server.

In mid-1999, The Apache Software Foundation was incorporated as a not-for-profit company. A board of directors, who are elected on an annual basis by the ASF members, oversees the company. This company provides a foundation for several different Open Source software development projects, including the Apache Web Server project.

The best places to find out about Apache are the Apache Group's Web site, `http://www.apache.org/`, and the Apache Week Web site, `http://www.apacheweek.com/`, where you can subscribe to receive Apache Week by email to keep up on the latest developments in the project, keep abreast of security advisories, and research bug fixes.

TIP

You'll find an overview of Apache in its Frequently Asked Questions (FAQ) at `http://httpd.apache.org/docs-2.0/faq/`. In addition to extensive online documentation, you'll also find the complete documentation for Apache in the HTML directory of your Apache server. You can access this documentation by looking at `http://localhost/manual/index.html` on your new Fedora system with one of the Web browsers included on your system. You'll need to have Apache running on your system!

Fedora ships with Apache 2.0, and the server, named httpd, is included on this book's CD-ROMs. You can obtain the latest version of Apache as an RPM (RPM Package Manager) installation file from a Fedora FTP server, upgrade using up2date, yum, or apt-get, or you can get the source code from the Apache Web site and, in true Linux tradition, build it for yourself.

To determine the version of Apache included with your system, use the Web server's -V command-line option like this:

```
$ /usr/sbin/httpd -V
Server version: Apache/2.0.50
Server built:   Jun 29 2004 11:11:55
Server's Module Magic Number: 20020903:8
Architecture:   32-bit
Server compiled with....
```

The output will display the version number, build date and time, platform, and various options used during the build. You can use the -v option to see more terse version information.

Installing the Apache Server

You can install Apache from RPMs or build it yourself from source code. The Apache source builds on just about any UNIX-like operating system and on Win32. If you elect to install the Web Server group of files when first installing Fedora, Apache and related software and documentation in 17 different packages will be installed automatically.

If you're about to install a new version of Apache, it's probably a good idea to shut down the old server. Even if it's unlikely that the old server will interfere with the installation procedure, shutting it down ensures that there will be no problems. If you don't know how to stop Apache, look at the "Starting and Stopping Apache" section later in this chapter.

Installing from the RPM

You can find the Apache RPM either on the Fedora Core installation media, on the Fedora FTP server, or one of its many mirror sites. You'll want to check the fedora.redhat.com site as often as possible to download updates as they become available. Updated RPM files usually contain important bug and security fixes. When an updated version comes out, install it as quickly as possible in order to be secure.

> **NOTE**
>
> Check the Apache HTTPD SERVER PROJECT page for security reports. Browse to http://
> httpd.apache.org/security_report.html for links to security vulnerabilities for Apache 1.3 and
> 2.0. Subscribe to a support list or browse through up-to-date archives of all Apache mailing lists

16

at `http://httpd.apache.org/mail/` (for various articles) or `http://httpd.apache.org/lists.html` (for comprehensive and organized archives).

If you want the most recent, experimental version of Apache for testing, check Red Hat's Rawhide distribution, which is also available on Red Hat's FTP server (`ftp://ftp.redhat.com/pub/redhat/linux/rawhide/`). This distribution is experimental and always contains the latest versions of all RPMs. However, note that the Apache package (`httpd`) might depend on new functionality available in other RPMs. Therefore, you might need to install many new RPMs to be able to use packages from Rawhide. If you still want to use an Apache version from the Rawhide distribution for testing, a better option might be to download the source code RPM (SRPM) and compile it yourself. That way, you will avoid dependencies on other new packages. (Refer to the "Working with Source RPM Files" section in Chapter 8, "Managing Software and System Resources," for information about building and installing packages from SRPM files.)

> **CAUTION**
>
> You should be wary of installing experimental packages, and never on *production* servers (that is, servers used in "real life"). Very carefully test the packages beforehand on a host that isn't connected to a network!

After you've obtained an Apache RPM, you can install it with the command-line `rpm` tool by typing the following:

```
rpm -Uvh latest_apache.rpm
```

where `latest_apache.rpm` is the name of the latest Apache RPM. For more information on installing packages with RPM, refer to Chapter 8.

The Apache RPM installs files in the following directories:

- `/etc/httpd/conf`—This directory contains the Apache configuration file, `httpd.conf`. See the section on configuring Apache later in this chapter for more information.

- `/etc/rc.d/`—The tree under this directory contains the system startup scripts. The Apache RPM installs a startup script named `httpd` for the Web server under the `/etc/rc.d/init.d` directory. This script, which you can use to start and stop the server from the command line, also automatically starts and stops the server when the computer is halted, started, or rebooted.

- `/var/www`—The RPM installs the default server icons, Common Gateway Interface (CGI) programs, and HTML files in this location. If you want to keep Web content elsewhere, you can do so by making the appropriate changes in the server configuration files.

- `/var/www/ manual/`—If you've installed the `apache-manual` RPM, you'll find a copy of the Apache documentation in HTML format here. You can access it with a Web browser by going to `http://localhost/manual/`.

- `/usr/share/man`—Fedora's Apache RPM also contains manual pages, which are placed underneath this directory. For example, the `httpd` man page is in section 8 of the man directory.

- `/usr/sbin`—The executable programs are placed in this directory. This includes the server executable itself, as well as various utilities.

- `/usr/bin`—Some of the utilities from the Apache package are placed here—for example, the `htpasswd` program, which is used for generating authentication password files.

- `/var/log/httpd`—The server log files are placed in this directory. By default, there are two important log files (among several others)—`access_log` and `error_log`—but you can define any number of custom logs containing a variety of information. See the section on logging later in this chapter for more detail.

- `/usr/src/redhat/SOURCES/`—This directory might contain a `tar` archive containing the source code for Apache and, in some cases, patches for the source. You must have installed the Apache SRPM for these files to be created.

When Apache is being run, it also creates the file `httpd.pid`, containing the process ID of Apache's parent process in the `/var/run/` directory.

16

> **NOTE**
>
> If you're upgrading to a newer version of Apache, RPM doesn't write over your current configuration files. RPM moves your current files and appends the extension `.rpmnew` to them. For example, `srm.conf` becomes `srm.conf.rpmnew`.

Building the Source Yourself

There are several ways to obtain the source code for Apache. The Fedora Project provides SRPMs containing the source of Apache, which includes patches to make it work better with the Fedora Core distribution. The most up-to-date, stable binary version for Fedora can be installed via RPM packages using the `up2date` command, or by installing a source RPM from Fedora's source repository (browse to `http:://fedora.redhat.com`, and then click on the Download link). When you install one of these SRPMs, a `tar` archive containing the Apache source is created in `/usr/src/redhat/SOURCES/`.

You can also download the source directly from `http://www.apache.org/`. The latest version at the time of this writing (2.0.50) is a 6.0MB compressed tape archive, and the latest pre-2.0 version of Apache is 1.3.31. Although many sites continue to use the older version (for script and other compatibility reasons), many new sites are migrating to or starting out using the latest stable version.

After you have the tar file, you must unroll it in a temporary directory somewhere nice, such as /tmp. Unrolling this tar file creates a directory called apache_version_number, where version_number is the version that you've downloaded (for example, apache_1.3.21).

There are two ways to compile the source—the old, familiar way (at least, to those of us who have been using Apache for many years) by editing Makefile templates, and the new, easy way using a configure script. You'll first see how to build Apache from source the easy way. The configure script offers a way to have the source software automatically configured according to your system. However, manually editing the configuration files before building and installing Apache provides more control over where the software is installed and what capabilities or features are built into Apache.

TIP

As with many software packages distributed in source code form for Linux and other UNIX-like operating systems, extracting the source code results in a directory that contains a README and an INSTALL file. Be sure to peruse the INSTALL file before attempting to build and install the software.

Using ./configure to Build Apache

To build Apache the easy way, run the ./configure script in the directory just created. You can provide it with a −prefix argument to install in a directory other than the default, which is /usr/local/apache/.

```
# ./configure —prefix=/preferred/directory/
```

This generates the Makefile that's used to compile the server code.

Next, type **make** to compile the server code. After the compilation is complete, type **make install** as root to install the server. You can now configure the server via the configuration files. See the "Runtime Server Configuration Settings" section for more information.

TIP

A safer way to install a new version of Apache from source is to use the ln command to create symbolic links of the existing file locations (listed in the "Installing from the RPM" section earlier in this chapter) to the new locations of the files. This method is safer because the default install locations are different from those used when the RPM installs the files. Failure to use this installation method could result in your Web server process not being started automatically at system startup.

Another safe way to install a new version of Apache is to first back up any important configuration directories and files (such as /etc/httpd) and then use the rpm command to remove the server. You can then install and test your new version, and if needed, easily restore your original server and settings.

It's strongly recommended that you stick with Fedora's RPM version of Apache until you really know what happens at system startup. No "uninstall" option is available when installing Apache from source!

Apache File Locations After a Build and Install

Files are placed in various subdirectories of /usr/local/apache (or whatever directory you specified with the −prefix parameter) if you build the server from source. Before version 1.3.4, files were placed in /usr/local/etc/httpd.

The following is a list of the directories used by Apache, as well as brief comments on their usage:

- /usr/local/apache/conf—This contains several subdirectories and the Apache configuration file, httpd.conf. See the section about configuration files later in this chapter.

- /usr/local/apache—The cgi-bin, icons, and htdocs subdirectories contain the CGI programs, standard icons, and default HTML documents, respectively.

- /usr/local/apache/bin—The executable programs are placed in this directory.

- /usr/local/apache/logs—The server log files are placed in this directory. By default, there are two log files—access_log and error_log—but you can define any number of custom logs containing a variety of information (see the "Logging" section later in this chapter). The default location for Apache's logs as installed by Fedora is /var/log/httpd.

A Quick Guide to Getting Started with Apache

Setting up, testing a Web page, and starting Apache using Fedora can be accomplished in just a few steps. First, make sure that Apache is installed on your system. Either select it during installation or install the server and related RPM files (refer to Chapter 8 if you need to install the server software).

Next, set up a home page for your system by editing (as root) the file named index.html under the /var/http/www/html directory on your system. Make a backup copy of the original page or www directory before you begin so that you can restore your Web server to its default state if necessary.

Start Apache (again, as root) by using the service command with the keywords httpd and start, like this:

```
# service httpd start
```

You can also use the httpd script under the /etc/rc.d/init.d/ directory, like this:

```
# /etc/rc.d/init.d/httpd start
```

You can then check your home page by running a favorite browser and using `localhost`, your system's hostname, or its Internet Protocol (IP) address in the uniform resource locator (URL). For example, with the `links` text browser, use a command line like this:

```
# links http://localhost/
```

For security reasons, you shouldn't start and run Apache as `root` if your host is connected to the Internet or a company intranet. Fortunately, Apache is set to run as the user and group `apache` no matter how it's started (by the `User` and `Group` settings in `/etc/httpd/httpd.conf`). Despite this safe default, Apache should be started and managed by the user named apache, defined in `/etc/passwd` as

```
apache:x:48:48:Apache:/var/www:/sbin/nologin
```

After you're satisfied with your Web site, use the `setup` (select Services) or `ntsysv` (select `httpd`) commands to ensure that Apache is started properly.

Starting and Stopping Apache

At this point, you've installed your Apache server with its default configuration. Fedora provides a default home page named `index.html` as a test under the `/var/www/html/usage` directory. The proper way to run Apache is to set system initialization to have the server run after booting, network configuration, and any firewall configuration. See Chapter 7, "Managing Services," for more information about how Fedora boots.

It's time to start it up for the first time. The following sections show how to either start and stop Apache or configure Fedora to start or not start Apache when booting.

Starting the Apache Server Manually

You can start Apache from the command line of a text-based console or X terminal window, and you must have root permission to do so. The server daemon, `httpd`, recognizes several command-line options you can use to set some defaults, such as specifying where `httpd` reads its configuration directives. The Apache `httpd` executable also understands other options that enable you to selectively use parts of its configuration file, specify a different location of the actual server and supporting files, use a different configuration file (perhaps for testing), and save startup errors to a specific log. The `-v` option causes Apache to print its development version and quit. The `-V` option shows all the settings that were in effect when the server was compiled.

The `-h` option prints the following usage information for the server (assuming that you're running the command as root):

```
# httpd -h
Usage: httpd [-D name] [-d directory] [-f file]
             [-C "directive"] [-c "directive"]
             [-k start¦restart¦graceful¦stop]
             [-v] [-V] [-h] [-l] [-L] [-t]
Options:
  -D name            : define a name for use in <IfDefine name> directives
  -d directory       : specify an alternate initial ServerRoot
  -f file            : specify an alternate ServerConfigFile
  -C "directive"     : process directive before reading config files
  -c "directive"     : process directive after reading config files
  -e level           : show startup errors of level (see LogLevel)
  -E file            : log startup errors to file
  -v                 : show version number
  -V                 : show compile settings
  -h                 : list available command line options (this page)
  -l                 : list compiled in modules
  -L                 : list available configuration directives
  -t -D DUMP_VHOSTS  : show parsed settings (currently only vhost settings)
  -t                 : run syntax check for config files
```

Other options include listing Apache's *static modules*, or special, built-in independent parts of the server, along with options that can be used with the modules. These options are called *configuration directives*, and are commands that control how a static module works. Note that Apache also includes nearly 50 *dynamic modules*, or software portions of the server that can be optionally loaded and used while the server is running.

The -t option is used to check your configuration files. It's a good idea to run this check before restarting your server, especially if you've made changes to your configuration files. Such tests are important because a configuration file error can result in your server shutting down when you try to restart it.

NOTE

When you build and install Apache from source and don't use Fedora's Apache RPM files, start the server manually from the command line as root (such as when testing). You do this for two reasons:

- The standalone server uses the default HTTP port (port 80), and only the superuser can bind to Internet ports that are lower than 1024.
- Only processes owned by root can change their UID and GID as specified by Apache's User and Group directives. If you start the server under another UID, it runs with the permissions of the user starting the process.

Note that although some of the following examples show how to start the server as root, you should do so only for testing after building and installing Apache. Fedora is set up to run Web service as the apache user if you install Apache using Fedora RPM files.

16

Using `/etc/rc.d/init.d/httpd`

Fedora uses the scripts in the `/etc/rc.d/init.d` directory to control the startup and shutdown of various services, including the Apache Web server. The main script installed for the Apache Web server is `/etc/rc.d/init.d/httpd`, although the actual work is done by the `apachectl` shell script included with Apache.

> **NOTE**
>
> `/etc/rc.d/init.d/httpd` is a shell script and isn't the same as the Apache server located in `/usr/sbin`. That is, `/usr/sbin/httpd` is the program executable file (the server), and `/etc/rc.d/init.d/httpd` is a shell script that uses another shell script, `apachectl`, to control the server. See Chapter 7, for a description of some service scripts under `/etc/rc.d/init.d` and how the scripts are used to manage services such as `httpd`.

You can use the `/etc/rc.d/init.d/httpd` script and the following options to control the Web server:

- `start`—The system uses this option to start the Web server during boot up. You, as `root`, can also use this script to start the server.

- `stop`—The system uses this option to stop the server gracefully. You should use this script, rather than the `kill` command, to stop the server.

- `reload`—You can use this option to send the HUP signal to the `httpd` server to have it reread the configuration files after modification.

- `restart`—This option is a convenient way to stop and then immediately start the Web server. If the `httpd` server isn't running, it will be started.

- `condrestart`—The same as the `restart` parameter, except that it restarts the `httpd` server only if it's actually running.

- `status`—This option indicates whether the server is running; if it is, it provides the various PIDs for each instance of the server.

For example, to check on the current status of your server, use the command

```
# /etc/rc.d/init.d/httpd status
```

which prints the following for me:

```
httpd (pid 15997 1791 1790 1789 1788 1787 1786 1785 1784 1781) is running...
```

This indicates that the Web server is running; in fact, there are 10 instances of the server currently running in this configuration.

In addition to the previous options, the `httpd` script also offers these additional features:

- `help`—Prints a list of valid options to the `httpd` script (which are passed onto the server as if called from the command line).

- `configtest`—A simple test of the server's configuration, which reports `Status OK` if the setup is correct. You can also use `httpd`'s `-t` option to perform the same test like this:

```
# httpd -t
```

- `fullstatus`—Displays a verbose status report.

- `graceful`—The same as the `restart` parameter, except that the `configtest` option is first used and open connections are not aborted.

> **TIP**
>
> Use the `reload` option if you're making many changes to the various server configuration files. This saves time when you're stopping and starting the server by having the system simply reread the configuration files.

Controlling Apache with Red Hat's `service` Command

Instead of directly calling the `/etc/rc.d/init.d/httpd` script, you can use Red Hat's `service` command (actually a shell script) to start, stop, and restart Apache. The `service` command is used with the name of a service (listed under `/etc/rc.d/init.d`) and an optional keyword:

```
# service <name_of_script> <option>
```

For example, you can use `service` with `httpd` and any option discussed in the previous section, like so:

```
# service httpd restart
```

This restarts Apache if it's running, or starts the server if it isn't running.

Controlling Apache with Red Hat's `chkconfig` Command

The `chkconfig` command provides a command-line–based interface to Fedora's service scripts. The command can be used to list and control what software services will be started, restarted, and stopped for a specific system state (such as when booting up, restarting, or shutting down) and run level (such as single-user mode, networking with multitasking, or graphical login with X).

16

For example, to view your system's current settings, take a look at Fedora's default run level as defined in the system initialization table /etc/inittab using the grep command:

```
# grep id: /etc/inittab
id:3:initdefault:
```

This example shows that this Fedora system will boot to a text-based login without running X11. You can then use the chkconfig command to look at the behavior of Apache for that runlevel:

```
# chkconfig --list ¦ grep httpd
httpd            0:off   1:off   2:off   3:off   4:off   5:off   6:off
```

Here you can see that Apache is turned off for run levels 3 and 5 (the only two practical run levels in a default Fedora system, although you could create a custom run level 4 for Apache). Use −level, httpd, and the control keyword on to set Apache to automatically start when booting to run level 3:

```
# chkconfig --level 3 httpd on
```

You can then again use chkconfig to verify this setting:

```
# chkconfig --list ¦ grep httpd
httpd            0:off   1:off   2:off   3:on    4:off   5:off   6:off
```

To have Apache also start when your system is booted to a graphical login using X, again use level, httpd, and the control keyword on, but this time, specify run level 5 like so:

```
# chkconfig --level 5 httpd on
```

Again, to verify your system settings

```
# chkconfig --list ¦ grep httpd
httpd            0:off   1:off   2:off   3:on    4:off   5:on    6:off
```

Use the off keyword to stop Apache from starting at a particular run level.

Controlling Apache with Red Hat's system-config-services Client

You can also use a graphical version of the chkconfig command named system-config-services during an X session to set when Apache is started or stopped and at what run level. To start system-config-services, choose the Services menu item on the Server Settings menu from your desktop panel's System Settings menu, or type the command in a terminal window like so:

```
$ system-config-services &
```

After you press Enter, you'll be prompted for the root password (as you shouldn't be running X as root).

This client is a graphical run level editor. To have Apache start when using run level 3, first use the Edit Runlevel menu to select run level 3, and then scroll through the list of services to find httpd. If you click the httpd check box as shown in Figure 16.1, and then click the toolbar's Save button, Apache will be started at that run level the next time the system starts or reboots.

You can also use the Service Configuration client to instantly control a service. Use the Edit Runlevel menu to select the current runlevel in use, highlight httpd, and then click the Start, Stop, or Restart toolbar button.

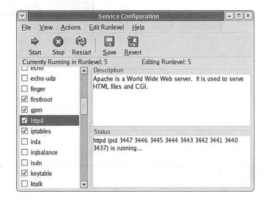

FIGURE 16.1 Use the system-config-services client to set when Apache is started or stopped on your Fedora system.

Runtime Server Configuration Settings

At this point, the Apache server will run, but perhaps you want to change a behavior, such as the default location of your Web site's files. This section talks about the basics of configuring the server to work the way you want it to work.

Runtime configurations are stored in just one file—httpd.conf, which is found under the /etc/httpd/conf directory. This configuration file can be used to control the default behavior of Apache, such as the Web server's base configuration directory (/etc/httpd), the name of the server's <u>process identification</u> (PID) file (/etc/httpd/run/httpd.pid), or response timeout (300 seconds). Apache reads the data from the configuration file when started (or restarted). You can also cause Apache to reload configuration information with the command /etc/rc.d/init.d/httpd reload, which is necessary after making changes to its configuration file. (You learn how to accomplish this in the later section, "Starting and Stopping Apache.")

Runtime Configuration Directives

You perform runtime configuration of your server with configuration directives, which are commands that set options for the httpd daemon. The directives are used to tell the server about various options that you want to enable, such as the location of files important to the server configuration and operation. Apache supports nearly 300 configuration directives using the following syntax:

```
directive option option...
```

Each directive is specified on a single line. See the following sections for some sample directives and how to use them. Some directives only set a value such as a filename, whereas others enable you to specify various options. Some special directives, called sections, look like HTML tags. Section directives are surrounded by angle brackets, such as <directive>. Sections usually enclose a group of directives that apply only to the directory specified in the section:

```
<Directory somedir/in/your/tree>
  directive option option
  directive option option
</Directory>
```

All sections are closed with a matching section tag that looks like this: </directive>. Note that section tags, like any other directives, are specified one per line.

> **TIP**
>
> After installing and starting Apache, you'll find an index of directives at http://localhost/
> _manual/mod/directives.html.

Editing httpd.conf

Most of the default settings in the config file are okay to keep, particularly if you've installed the server in a default location and aren't doing anything unusual on your server. In general, if you don't understand what a particular directive is for, you should leave it set to the default value.

The following sections describe some of the configuration file settings that you *might* want to change concerning operation of your server.

ServerRoot

The `ServerRoot` directive sets the absolute path to your server directory. This directive tells the server where to find all the resources and configuration files. Many of these resources are specified in the configuration files relative to the `ServerRoot` directory.

Your `ServerRoot` directive should be set to `/etc/httpd` if you installed the RPM or `/usr/local/apache` (or whatever directory you chose when you compiled Apache) if you installed from the source.

Listen

The `Listen` directive indicates which port you want your server to run on. By default, this is set to 80, which is the standard HTTP port number. You might want to run your server on another port—for example, when running a test server that you don't want people to find by accident. Don't confuse this with real security! See the "File System Authentication and Access Control" section for more information about how to secure parts of your Web server.

User **and** Group

The `User` and `Group` directives should be set to the UID and group ID (GID) that the server will use to process requests.

In Fedora, set these configurations to a user with few or no privileges. In this case, they're set to user apache and group apache—a user defined specifically to run Apache. If you want to use a different UID or GID, be aware that the server will run with the permissions of the user and group set here. That means in the event of a security breach, whether on the server or (more likely) in your own CGI programs, those programs will run with the assigned UID. If the server runs as `root` or some other privileged user, someone can exploit the security holes and do nasty things to your site. Always think in terms of the specified user running a command such as `rm -rf /` because that would wipe all files from your system. That should convince you that leaving apache as a user with no privileges is probably a good thing.

Instead of specifying the `User` and `Group` directives using names, you can specify them using the UID and GID numbers. If you use numbers, be sure that the numbers you specify correspond to the user and group you want and that they're preceded by the pound (#) symbol.

Here's how these directives look if specified by name:

```
User apache
Group apache
```

Here's the same specification by UID and GID:

```
User #48
Group #48
```

> **TIP**
>
> If you find a user on your system (other than root) with a UID and GID of 0, your system has been cracked.

ServerAdmin

The `ServerAdmin` directive should be set to the address of the Webmaster managing the server. This address should be a valid email address or alias, such as `webmaster@gnulix.org`, because this address will be returned to a visitor when a problem occurs on the server.

ServerName

The `ServerName` directive sets the hostname the server will return. Set it to a <u>fully qualified domain name</u> (FQDN). For example, set it to `www.your.domain` rather than simply `www`. This is particularly important if this machine will be accessible from the Internet rather than just on your local network.

You don't need to set this unless you want a different name returned than the machine's canonical name. If this value isn't set, the server will figure out the name by itself and set it to its canonical name. However, you might want the server to return a friendlier address, such as `www.your.domain`. Whatever you do, `ServerName` should be a real <u>domain name system</u> (DNS) name for your network. If you're administering your own DNS, remember to add an alias for your host. If someone else manages the DNS for you, ask that person to set this name for you.

DocumentRoot

Set this directive to the absolute path of your document tree, which is the top directory from which Apache will serve files. By default, it's set to `/var/www/html/usage`. If you built the source code yourself, `DocumentRoot` is set to `/usr/local/apache/htdocs` (if you didn't choose another directory when you compiled Apache). Prior to version 1.3.4, this directive appears in `srm.conf`.

UserDir

The `UserDir` directive disables or enables and defines the directory (relative to a local user's home directory) where that user can put public HTML documents. It's relative because each user has her own HTML directory. This setting is disabled by default, but can be enabled to store user Web content under any directory.

The default setting for this directive, if enabled, is `public_html`. Each user will be able to create a directory called `public_html` under her home directory, and HTML documents placed in that directory will be available as `http://servername/~username`, where *username* is the username of the particular user. Prior to version Apache version 1.3.4, this directive appears in `srm.conf`.

`DirectoryIndex`
The `DirectoryIndex` directive indicates which file should be served as the index for a directory, such as which file should be served if the URL `http://servername/` `_SomeDirectory/` is requested.

It's often useful to put a list of files here so that in the event `index.html` (the default value) isn't found, another file can be served instead. The most useful application of this is to have a CGI program run as the default action in a directory. If you have users who make their Web pages on Windows, you might want to add `index.htm` as well. In that case, the directive would look like `DirectoryIndex index.html index.cgi index.htm`. Prior to version 1.3.4, this directive appears in `srm.conf`.

Apache Multi-Processing Modules

Apache version 2.0 and greater now uses a new internal architecture supporting multi-processing modules (MPMs). These modules are used by the server for a variety of tasks, such as network and process management, and are compiled into Apache. MPMs enable Apache to work much better on a wider variety of computer platforms, and can help improve server stability, compatibility, and scalability.

Apache can only use one MPM at any time. These modules are different from the base set included with Apache (see the "Apache Modules" section later in this chapter), but are used to implement settings, limits, or other server actions. Each module in turn supports numerous additional settings, called *directives*, which further refine server operation.

The internal MPM modules relevant for Linux include

- `mpm_common`—A set of 20 directives common to all MPM modules

- `prefork`—A "nonthreaded, preforking" Web server that works similar to earlier (1.3) versions of Apache

- `worker`—Provides a "hybrid multiprocess multithreaded server"

MPM enables Apache to be used on equipment with fewer resources, yet still handle massive numbers of hits and provide stable service. The `worker` module provides directives to control how many simultaneous connections your server can handle.

> **NOTE**
>
> There are other MPMs for Apache related to other platforms, such as `mpm_netware` for NetWare hosts, and `mpm_winnt` for NT platforms. An MPM named `perchild`, which will provide user ID assignment to selected daemon processes, is under development. For more information, browse to the Apache Software Foundation's home page at `http://www.apache.org`.

16

Using .htaccess **Configuration Files**

Apache also supports special configuration files, known as .htaccess files. Almost any directive that appears in httpd.conf can appear in an .htaccess file. This file, specified in the AccessFileName directive in httpd.conf (or srm.conf prior to version 1.3.4) sets configurations on a per-directory (usually in a user directory) basis. As the system administrator, you can specify both the name of this file and which of the server configurations may be overridden by the contents of this file. This is especially useful for sites in which there are multiple content providers and you want to control what these people can do with their space.

To limit what server configurations the .htaccess files can override, use the AllowOverride directive. AllowOverride can be set globally or per directory. For example, in your httpd.conf file, you could use the following:

```
# Each directory to which Apache has access can be configured with respect
# to which services and features are allowed and/or disabled in that
# directory (and its subdirectories).
#
# First, we configure the "default" to be a very restrictive set of
# permissions.
#
<Directory />
    Options FollowSymLinks
    AllowOverride None
</Directory>
```

Options **Directives**

To configure which configuration options are available to Apache by default, you must use the Options directive. Options can be None, All, or any combination of Indexes, Includes, FollowSymLinks, ExecCGI, or MultiViews. MultiViews isn't included in All and must be specified explicitly. These options are explained in Table 16.2.

TABLE 16.2   Switches Used by the Options Directive

Switch	Description
None	None of the available options are enabled for this directory.
All	All the available options, except for MultiViews, are enabled for this directory.
Indexes	In the absence of an index.html file or another DirectoryIndex file, a listing of the files in the directory will be generated as an HTML page for display to the user.
Includes	Server-side includes (SSIs) are permitted in this directory. This can also be written as IncludesNoExec if you want to allow includes, but don't want to allow the exec option in them. For security reasons, this is usually a good idea in directories over which you don't have complete control, such as UserDir directories.

TABLE 16.2 Continued

Switch	Description
FollowSymLinks	Allows access to directories that are symbolically linked to a document directory. Setting this is a bad idea; you should never set this globally for the whole server and only rarely for individual directories. This option is a potential security risk because it allows Web users to escape from the document directory, and it could potentially allow them access to portions of your file system where you really don't want people poking around.
ExecCGI	CGI programs are permitted in this directory, even if it isn't a directory defined in the `ScriptAlias` directive.
MultiViews	This is part of the `mod_negotiation` module. When a client requests a document that can't be found, the server tries to figure out which document best suits the client's requirements. See `http://localhost/manuals/mod/_mod_negotiation.html` for your local copy of the Apache documentation.

> **NOTE**
>
> These directives also affect all subdirectories of the specified directory.

AllowOverrides **Directives**

The `AllowOverrides` directives specify which configuration options .htaccess files can override. You can set this directive individually for each directory. For example, you can have different standards about what can be overridden in the main document root and in UserDir directories.

This capability is particularly useful for user directories, where the user doesn't have access to the main server configuration files.

`AllowOverrides` can be set to `All` or any combination of `Options`, `FileInfo`, `AuthConfig`, and `Limit`. These options are explained in Table 16.3.

TABLE 16.3 Switches Used by the `AllowOverrides` Directive

Switch	Description
Options	The .htaccess file can add options not listed in the `Options` directive for this directory.
FileInfo	The .htaccess file can include directives for modifying document type information.
AuthConfig	The .htaccess file might contain authorization directives.
Limit	The .htaccess file might contain `allow`, `deny`, and `order` directives.

16

File System Authentication and Access Control

You're likely to include material on your Web site that isn't supposed to be available to the public. You must be able to lock out this material from public access and provide designated users with the means to unlock the material. Apache provides two methods for accomplishing this type of access: authentication and authorization. You can use different criteria to control access to sections of your Web site, including checking the client's IP address or hostname, or requiring a username and password. This section briefly covers some of these methods.

> **CAUTION**
>
> Allowing individual users to put Web content on your server poses several important security risks. If you're operating a Web server on the Internet rather than on a private network, you should read the WWW Security FAQ at `http://www.w3.org/Security/Faq/` `www-security-faq.html`.

Restricting Access with `allow` and `deny`

One of the simplest ways to limit access to Web site material is to restrict access to a specific group of users, based on IP addresses or hostnames. Apache uses the `allow` and `deny` directives to accomplish this.

Both directives take an address expression as a parameter. The following list provides the possible values and use of the address expression:

- `all` can be used to affect all hosts.

- A hostname or domain name, which can either be a partially or a fully qualified domain name; for example, `test.gnulix.org` or `gnulix.org`.

- An IP address, which can be either full or partial; for example, `212.85.67` or `212.85.67.66`.

- A network/netmask pair, such as `212.85.67.0/255.255.255.0`.

- A network address specified in classless inter-domain routing (CIDR) format; for example, `212.85.67.0/24`. This is the CIDR notation for the same network and netmask that were used in the previous example.

If you have the choice, it's preferable to base your access control on IP addresses rather than hostnames. Doing so results in faster performance because no name lookup is necessary—the IP address of the client is included with each request.

You also can use `allow` and `deny` to provide or deny access to Web site material based on the presence or absence of a specific environment variable. For example, the following statement will deny access to a request with a context that contains an environment variable named NOACCESS:

```
deny from env=NOACCESS
```

The default behavior of Apache is to apply all the deny directives first and then check the allow directives. If you want to change this order, you can use the order statement. Apache might interpret this statement in three different ways:

- Order deny,allow—The deny directives are evaluated before the allow directives. If a host isn't specifically denied access, it will be allowed to access the resource. This is the default ordering if nothing else is specified.

- Order allow,deny—All allow directives are evaluated before deny directives. If a host isn't specifically allowed access, it will be denied access to the resource.

- Order mutual-failure—Only hosts that are specified in an allow directive and at the same time do not appear in a deny directive will be allowed access. If a host doesn't appear in either directive, it will not be granted access.

Consider this example. Suppose that you want to allow only persons from within your own domain to access the server-status resource on your Web. If your domain were named gnulix.org, you could add these lines to your configuration file:

```
<Location /server-status>
    SetHandler server-status
    Order deny,allow
    Deny from all
    Allow from gnulix.org
</Location>
```

Authentication

Authentication is the process of ensuring that visitors really are who they claim to be. You can configure Apache to allow access to specific areas of Web content only to clients that can authenticate their identity. There are several methods of authentication in Apache; Basic Authentication is the most common (and the method discussed in this chapter).

Under Basic Authentication, Apache requires a user to supply a username and a password to access the protected resources. Apache then verifies that the user is allowed to access the resource in question. If the username is acceptable, Apache verifies the password. If the password also checks out, the user is authorized and Apache serves the request.

HTTP is a stateless protocol, as each request sent to the server and response is handled individually, and not in an intelligent fashion; therefore, the authentication information must be included with each request. That means each request to a password-protected area

16

will be larger and therefore somewhat slower. To avoid unnecessary system use and delays, protect only those areas of your Web site that absolutely need protection.

To use Basic Authentication, you need a file that lists which users are allowed to access the resources. This file is composed of a plain text list containing name and password pairs. It looks very much like the /etc/passwd user file of your Linux system.

CAUTION

Don't use /etc/passwd as a user list for authentication. When you're using Basic Authentication, passwords and usernames are sent as base64-encoded text from the client to the server—which is just as readable as plain text. The username and password are included in each request that is sent to the server. So, anyone who might be snooping on Net traffic would be able to get this information!

To create a user file for Apache, use the htpasswd command. This is included with the Apache package. If you installed using the RPMs, it's in /usr/bin. Running htpasswd without any options will produce the following output:

```
Usage:
        htpasswd [-cmdps] passwordfile username
        htpasswd -b[cmdps] passwordfile username password

        htpasswd -n[mdps] username
        htpasswd -nb[mdps] username password
 -c  Create a new file.
 -n  Don't update file; display results on stdout.
 -m  Force MD5 encryption of the password.
 -d  Force CRYPT encryption of the password (default).
 -p  Do not encrypt the password (plaintext).
 -s  Force SHA encryption of the password.
 -b  Use the password from the command line rather than prompting for it.
 -D  Delete the specified user.
On Windows, TPF and NetWare systems the '-m' flag is used by default.
On all other systems, the '-p' flag will probably not work.
```

As you can see, it isn't a very difficult command to use. For example, to create a new user file named gnulixusers with a user named wsb, you need do something like this:

```
# htpasswd -c gnulixusers wsb
```

You would then be prompted for a password for the user. To add more users, you would repeat the same procedure, only omitting the -c flag.

You can also create user group files. The format of these files is similar to that of /etc/groups. On each line, enter the group name, followed by a colon, and then list all users, with each user separated by spaces. For example, an entry in a user group file might look like this:

```
gnulixusers: wsb pgj jp ajje nadia rkr hak
```

Now that you know how to create a user file, it's time to look at how Apache might use this to protect Web resources.

To point Apache to the user file, use the AuthUserFile directive. AuthUserFile takes the file path to the user file as its parameter. If the file path isn't absolute—that is, beginning with a /—it's assumed that the path is relative to the ServerRoot. Using the AuthGroupFile directive, you can specify a group file in the same manner.

Next, use the AuthType directive to set the type of authentication to be used for this resource. Here, the type is set to Basic.

Now you need to decide which realm the resource will belong to. Realms are used to group different resources that will share the same users for authorization. A realm can consist of just about any string. The realm will be shown in the Authentication dialog box on the user's Web browser. Therefore, it's best to set the realm string to something informative. The realm is defined with the AuthName directive.

Finally, state what type of user is authorized to use the resource. You do this with the require directive. The three ways to use this directive are as follows:

- If you specify valid-user as an option, any user in the user file will be allowed to access the resource (that is, provided she also enters the correct password).

- You can specify a list of users who are allowed access with the users option.

- You can specify a list of groups with the group option. Entries in the group list, as well as the user list, are separated by a space.

Returning to the server-status example you saw earlier, instead of letting users access the server-status resource based on hostname, you can require the users to be authenticated in order to access the resource. You can do so with the following entry in the configuration file:

```
<Location /server-status>
    SetHandler server-status
    AuthType Basic
    AuthName "Server status"
    AuthUserFile "gnulixusers"
    Require valid-user
</Location>
```

16

Final Words on Access Control

If you have host-based as well as user-based access protection on a resource, the default behavior of Apache is to require the requester to satisfy both controls. But assume that you want to mix host-based and user-based protection and allow access to a resource if either method succeeds. You can do so using the satisfy directive. You can set the satisfy directive to All (this is the default) or Any. When set to All, all access control methods must be satisfied before the resource is served. If satisfy is set to Any, the resource is served if any access condition is met.

Here's another access control example, again using the previous server-status example. This time, combine access methods so that all users from the Gnulix domain are allowed access and those from outside the domain must identify themselves before gaining access. You can do so with the following:

```
<Location /server-status>
    SetHandler server-status
    Order deny,allow
    Deny from all
    Allow from gnulix.org
    AuthType Basic
    AuthName "Server status"
    AuthUserFile "gnulixusers"
    Require valid-user
    Satisfy Any
</Location>
```

There are more ways to protect material on your Web server, but the methods discussed here should get you started and will probably be more than adequate for most circumstances. Look to Apache's online documentation for more examples of how to secure areas of your site.

Apache Modules

The Apache core does relatively little; Apache gains its functionality from modules. Each module solves a well-defined problem by adding necessary features. By adding or removing modules to supply the functionality you want Apache to have, you can tailor Apache server to suit your exact needs.

Nearly 50 core modules are included with the basic Apache server. Many more are available from other developers. The Apache Module Registry is a repository for add-on modules for Apache, and it can be found at http://modules.apache.org/. The modules are listed in the modules directory under /etc/httpd/, but this directory is a link to the /usr/lib/httpd/modules directory where the modules reside (your list may look somewhat different):

mod_access.so	mod_cern_meta.so	mod_log_config.so	mod_setenvif.so
mod_actions.so	mod_cgi.so	mod_mime_magic.so	mod_speling.so
mod_alias.so	mod_dav_fs.so	mod_mime.so	mod_ssl.so
mod_asis.so	mod_dav.so	mod_negotiation.so	mod_status.so
mod_auth_anon.so	mod_dir.so	mod_perl.so	mod_suexec.so
mod_auth_dbm.so	mod_env.so	mod_proxy_connect.so	mod_unique_id.so
mod_auth_digest.so	mod_expires.so	mod_proxy_ftp.so	mod_userdir.so
mod_auth_mysql.so	mod_headers.so	mod_proxy_http.so	mod_usertrack.so
mod_auth_pgsql.so	mod_imap.so	mod_proxy.so	mod_vhost_alias.so
mod_auth.so	mod_include.so	mod_python.so	mod_autoindex.so
mod_info.so	mod_rewrite.so		

Each module adds new directives that can be used in your configuration files. As you might guess, there are far too many extra commands, switches, and options to describe them all in this chapter. The following sections briefly describe a subset of those modules available with Fedora's Apache installation.

mod_access

mod_access controls access to areas on your Web server based on IP addresses, hostnames, or environment variables. For example, you might want to allow anyone from within your own domain to access certain areas of your Web. Refer to the "File System Authentication and Access Control" section for more information.

mod_alias

mod_alias manipulates the URLs of incoming HTTP requests, such as redirecting a client request to another URL. It also can map a part of the file system into your Web hierarchy. For example,

```
Alias /images/ /home/wsb/graphics/
```

would fetch contents from the /home/wsb/graphics directory for any URL that starts with /images/. This is done without the client knowing anything about it. If you use a redirection, the client will be instructed to go to another URL to find the requested content. More advanced URL manipulation can be accomplished with mod_rewrite.

mod_asis

mod_asis is used to specify, in fine detail, all information to be included in a response. This will completely bypass any headers that Apache might have otherwise added to the response. All files with an .asis extension will be sent straight to the client without any changes.

As a short example of the use of `mod_asis`, assume that you've moved content from one location to another on your site. Now you must inform people who try to access this resource that it has moved, as well as redirect them to the new location automatically. To provide this information and redirection, you can add the following code to a file with an `.asis` extension:

```
Status: 301 No more old stuff!
Location: http://gnulix.org/newstuff/
Content-type: text/html

<HTML>
 <HEAD>
  <TITLE>We've moved...</TITLE>
 </HEAD>
 <BODY>
   <P>We've moved the old stuff and now you'll find it at:</P>
   <A HREF="http://gnulix.org/newstuff/">New stuff</A>!.
 </BODY>
</HTML>
```

mod_auth

`mod_auth` uses a simple user authentication scheme, referred to as Basic authentication, which is based on storing usernames and encrypted passwords in a text file. This file looks very much like UNIX's `/etc/passwd` file, and is created with the `htpasswd` command. Refer to the "File System Authentication and Access Control" section earlier in this chapter for more information about this subject.

mod_auth_anon

The `mod_auth_anon` module provides anonymous authentication similar to that of anonymous FTP. The module enables you to define user IDs of those who are to be handled as guest users. When such a user tries to log on, she will be prompted for her email address as her password. It's possible to have Apache check the password to ensure that it's a (more or less) proper email address. Basically, it ensures that there is an `@` character and at least one `.` character in the password.

mod_auth_dbm

`mod_auth_dbm` uses Berkeley DB files instead of text for user authentication files.

mod_auth_digest

An extension of the basic `mod_auth` module; instead of sending the user information in plain text, it will be sent via the MD5 Digest Authentication process. This authentication scheme is defined in RFC 2617. Compared to using Basic authentication, this is a much more secure way of sending user data over the Internet. Unfortunately, not all Web browsers support this authentication scheme.

To create password files for use with mod_auth_dbm, you must use the htdigest utility. It has more or less the same functionality as the htpasswd utility. See the man page of htdigest for further information.

mod_autoindex

The mod_autoindex module dynamically creates a file list for directory indexing. The list will be rendered in a user-friendly manner similar to those lists provided by ftp's built-in ls command.

mod_cgi

mod_cgi allows execution of CGI programs on your server. CGI programs are executable files residing in the /var/www/cgi-bin directory, and are used to dynamically generate data (usually HTML) for the remote browser when requested.

mod_dir **and** mod_env

The mod_dir module is used to determine which files are returned automatically when a user tries to access a directory. The default is index.html. If you have users who create Web pages on Windows systems, you'll probably want to also include index.htm like this:

```
DirectoryIndex index.html index.htm
```

mod_env controls how environment variables are passed to CGI and SSI scripts.

mod_expires

mod_expires is used to add an expiration date to content on your site by adding an Expires header to the HTTP response. Web browsers or cache servers won't cache expired content.

mod_headers

mod_headers is used to manipulate the HTTP headers of your server's responses. You can replace, add, merge, or delete headers as you see fit. The module supplies a Header directive for this. Ordering of the Header directive is important. A set followed by an unset for the same HTTP header will remove the header altogether. You can place Header directives almost anywhere within your configuration files. These directives are processed in the following order:

1. Core server

2. Virtual host

3. `<Directory>` and `.htaccess` files

4. `<Location>`

5. `<Files>`

mod_imap

The `mod_imap` module provides for server-side handling of imagemap files. Clickable regions are defined in a `.map` file. Six directives are available for use in the `.map` file. The directives are used to describe the layout of the clickable regions as well as the URLs they lead to.

mod_include

`mod_include` enables the use of server-side includes on your server. See the "Dynamic Content" section later in the chapter for more information about how to use SSI.

mod_info **and** mod_log_config

`mod_info` provides comprehensive information about your server's configuration. For example, it will display all the installed modules, as well as all the directives used in its configuration files.

`mod_log_config` defines how your log files should look. See the "Logging" section for further information about this subject.

mod_mime **and** mod_mime_magic

The `mod_mime` module tries to determine the MIME type of files from their extensions.

The `mod_mime_magic` module tries to determine the MIME type of files by examining portions of their content.

mod_negotiation

Using the `mod_negotiation` module, it's possible to select one of several document versions that best suits the client's capabilities. There are several options to select which criteria to use in the negotiation process. You can, for example, choose among different languages, graphics file formats, and compression methods.

mod_proxy

`mod_proxy` implements proxy and caching capabilities for an Apache server. It can proxy and cache FTP, CONNECT, HTTP/0.9, and HTTP/1.0 requests. This isn't an ideal solution for sites that have a large number of users and therefore have very high proxy and cache requirements. However, it's more than adequate for a small number of users.

mod_rewrite

mod_rewrite is the Swiss Army Knife of URL manipulation. It enables you to perform any imaginable manipulation of URLs using powerful regular expressions. It provides rewrites, redirection, proxying, and so on. There's very little that you can't accomplish using this module.

> **TIP**
>
> See http://localhost/manual/misc/rewriteguide.html for a cookbook that will give you an in-depth explanation of what the .mod_rewrite module is capable of.

mod_setenvif

mod_setenvif allows manipulation of environment variables. Using regular expressions, it's possible to conditionally change the content of environment variables. The order in which SetEnvIf directives appear in the configuration files is important. It's possible that each SetEnvIf directive might reset an earlier SetEnvIf directive when used on the same environment variable. Be sure to keep that in mind when using the directives from this module.

mod_speling

mod_speling is used to enable correction of minor typos in URLs. If no file matches the requested URL, this module will build a list of the files in the requested directory and extract those files that are the closest matches. It will try to correct only one spelling mistake.

mod_status

You can use mod_status to create a Web page containing a plethora of information about a running Apache server. The page will contain information about the internal status as well as statistics about the running Apache processes. This can be a great aid when you're trying to configure your server for maximum performance. It's also a good indicator of when something's amiss with your Apache server.

mod_ssl

mod_ssl provides secure socket layer (versions 2 and 3) and transport layer security (version 1) support for Apache. There are at least 30 directives dealing with options for encryption and client authorization that may be used with this module.

mod_unique_id

mod_unique_id generates a unique request identifier for every incoming request. This ID will be put into the UNIQUE_ID environment variable.

mod_userdir

The `mod_userdir` module enables mapping of a subdirectory in each user's home directory into your Web tree. The module provides several different ways to accomplish this.

mod_usertrack

`mod_usertrack` is used to generate a cookie for each user session. This can be used to track the user's click stream within your Web tree. You must enable a custom log that logs this cookie in to a log file.

mod_vhost_alias

`mod_vhost_alias` supports dynamically configured mass virtual hosting, which is useful for Internet service providers with many virtual hosts. However, for the average user, Apache's ordinary virtual hosting support should be more than sufficient.

There are two ways to host virtual hosts on an Apache server. You can either have one IP address with multiple CNAMEs, or you can have multiple IP addresses with one name per address. Apache has different sets of directives to handle each of these options. (You learn more about virtual hosting in Apache in the next section of this chapter.)

Again, the available options and features for Apache modules are too numerous to describe completely in this chapter. You can find complete information about the Apache modules in the online documentation for the server included with Fedora or at the Apache Group's Web site.

Virtual Hosting

One of the more popular services to provide with a Web server is to host a virtual domain. Also known as a *virtual host*, a virtual domain is a complete Web site with its own domain name, as if it were a standalone machine, but it's hosted on the same machine as other Web sites. Apache implements this capability in a simple way with directives in the `httpd.conf` configuration file.

Apache now can dynamically host virtual servers by using the `mod_vhost_alias` module you read about in the preceding section of the chapter. The module is primarily intended for ISPs and similar large sites that host a large number of virtual sites. This module is for more advanced users, and as such it goes outside the scope of this introductory chapter. Instead, this section concentrates on the traditional ways of hosting virtual servers.

Address-based Virtual Hosts

After you've configured your Linux machine with multiple IP addresses, setting up Apache to serve them as different Web sites is quite simple. You need only put a `VirtualHost` directive in your `httpd.conf` file for each of the addresses that you want to make an independent Web site:

```
<VirtualHost 212.85.67.67>
ServerName gnulix.org
DocumentRoot /home/virtual/gnulix/public_html
TransferLog /home/virtual/gnulix/logs/access_log
ErrorLog /home/virtual/gnulix/logs/error_log
</VirtualHost>
```

Use the IP address, rather than the hostname, in the VirtualHost tag.

You can specify any configuration directives within the <VirtualHost> tags. For example, you might want to set AllowOverrides directives differently for virtual hosts than you do for your main server. Any directives that aren't specified default to the settings for the main server.

Name-based Virtual Hosts

Name-based virtual hosts enable you to run more than one host on the same IP address. You must add the additional names to your DNS as CNAMEs of the machine in question. When an HTTP client (Web browser) requests a document from your server, it sends with the request a variable indicating the server name from which it's requesting the document. Based on this variable, the server determines which of the virtual hosts it should serve content from.

> **NOTE**
>
> Some older browsers are unable to see name-based virtual hosts because this is a feature of HTTP 1.1, and the older browsers are strictly HTTP 1.0–compliant. However, many other older browsers are partially HTTP 1.1–compliant, and this is one of the parts of HTTP 1.1 that most browsers have supported for a while.

Name-based virtual hosts require just one step more than IP address-based virtual hosts. You must first indicate which IP address has the multiple DNS names on it. This is done with the NameVirtualHost directive:

```
NameVirtualHost 212.85.67.67
```

You must then have a section for each name on that address, setting the configuration for that name. As with IP-based virtual hosts, you need to set only those configurations that must be different for the host. You must set the ServerName directive because it's the only thing that distinguishes one host from another:

```
<VirtualHost 212.85.67.67>
ServerName bugserver.gnulix.org
ServerAlias bugserver
DocumentRoot /home/bugserver/htdocs
```

16

```
ScriptAlias /home/bugserver/cgi-bin
TransferLog /home/bugserver/logs/access_log
</VirtualHost>

<VirtualHost 212.85.67.67>
ServerName pts.gnulix.org
ServerAlias pts
DocumentRoot /home/pts/htdocs
ScriptAlias /home/pts/cgi-bin
TransferLog /home/pts/logs/access_log
ErrorLog /home/pts/logs/error_log
</VirtualHost>
```

> **TIP**
>
> If you're hosting Web sites on an intranet or internal network, there's a good chance that users will use the shortened name of the machine rather than the fully qualified domain name. For example, users might type `http://bugserver/index.html` in their browser location field rather than `http://bugserver.gnulix.org/index.html`. In that case, Apache will not recognize that those two addresses should go to the same virtual host. You could get around this by setting up `VirtualHost` directives for both `bugserver` and `bugserver.gnulix.org`, but the easy way around it is to use the `ServerAlias` directive, which lists all valid aliases for the machine:
>
> `ServerAlias bugserver`

For more information about `VirtualHost`, refer to the help system on `http://localhost/_manual`.

Logging

Apache provides for logging just about any Web access information you might be interested in. Logging can help with

- System resource management, by tracking usage
- Intrusion detection, by documenting bad HTTP requests
- Diagnostics, by recording errors in processing requests

Two standard log files are generated when you run your Apache server: `access_log` and `error_log`. They'll be found under the `/var/log/httpd` directory. (Others include the SSL logs `ssl_access_log`, `ssl_error_log`, and `ssl_request_log`.) All logs except for the `error_log` (by default, this is just the `access_log`) are generated in a format specified by the `CustomLog` and `LogFormat` directives. These directives appear in your `httpd.conf` file.

A new log format can be defined with the `LogFormat` directive:

```
LogFormat "%h %l %u %t \"%r\" %>s %b" common
```

The common log format is a good starting place for creating your own custom log formats. Note that most of the available log analysis tools assume that you're using the common log format or the combined log format—both of which are defined in the default configuration files.

The following variables are available for LogFormat statements:

%a	Remote IP address.
%A	Local IP address.
%b	Bytes sent, excluding HTTP headers. This is shown in Apache's Combined Log Format (CLF). For a request without any data content, a - will be shown instead of 0.
%B	Bytes sent, excluding HTTP headers.
%{VARIABLE}e	The contents of the environment variable VARIABLE.
%f	Filename of the output log.
%h	Remote host.
%H	Request protocol.
%{HEADER}i	The contents of HEADER; header line(s) in the request sent to the server.
%l	Remote log name (from identd, if supplied).
%m	Request method.
%{NOTE}n	The contents of note NOTE from another module.
%{HEADER}o	The contents of HEADER; header line(s) in the reply.
%p	The canonical port of the server serving the request.
%P	The process ID of the child that serviced the request.
%q	The contents of the query string, prepended with a ? character. If there's no query string, this will evaluate to an empty string.
%r	First line of request.
%s	Status. For requests that were internally redirected, this is the status of the original request—%>s for the last.
%t	Time, in common log time format.
%{format}t	The time, in the form given by format, which should be in strftime(3) format. See the section "Basic SSI Directives" later in this chapter for a complete list of available formatting options.
%T	The seconds taken to serve the request.

16

%u	Remote user from auth; might be bogus if return status (%s) is 401.
%U	The URL path requested.
%V	The server name according to the UseCanonicalName directive.
%v	The canonical ServerName of the server serving the request.

You can put a conditional in front of each variable to determine whether the variable is displayed. If the variable isn't displayed, - will be displayed instead. These conditionals are in the form of a list of numerical return values. For example, %!401u will display the value of REMOTE_USER unless the return code is 401.

You can then specify the location and format of a log file using the CustomLog directive:

```
CustomLog logs/access_log common
```

If it isn't specified as an absolute path, the location of the log file is assumed to be relative to the ServerRoot.

Dynamic Content

The most common way to provide dynamic content on Web sites is with CGI programs. CGI is a specification of communication between server processes (such as programs that generate dynamic documents) and the server itself. SSIs allow output from CGI programs, or other programs, to be inserted into existing HTML pages.

Another way to add dynamic content to your Web site is to use PHP (PHP Hypertext Preprocessor [the name is recursive]). PHP is an HTML-embedded scripting language designed specifically for Web usage. The PHP module for Apache is one of the most popular third-party modules available.

CGI

By default, you can put any CGI program on your server in the directory defined by the ScriptAlias directive.

CGI programs can be written in any language. The most popular languages for CGI programming are Perl and C. Chapter 23, "Using Perl," provides more information about using the Perl scripting language.

These programs must be executable by the default Apache user, which means that you must change the mode of the files to 555 so that the user Apache can execute them. By default, Apache runs in Fedora as a user named apache.

```
chmod 555 program.cgi
```

To execute CGI programs outside of the ScriptAlias directory, you must enable the ExecCGI option for that directory. This is done either in your httpd.conf file or in an .htaccess file in the directory.

To test whether you've CGI configured correctly, try the CGI program in Listing 16.1. This program is written in Perl and displays the values of the HTTP environment variables.

LISTING 16.1   environment.pl

```perl
#!/usr/bin/perl -w

print <<EOF;
"Content-type: text/html"

<HTML>
 <HEAD>
  <TITLE>Simple CGI program</TITLE>
 </HEAD>
 <BODY>
EOF
for (keys %ENV)    {
    print "  $_ = $ENV{$_}<BR>\n";
}
print <<EOF;
 </BODY>
</HTML>
EOF
```

If you're going to write CGI programs in Perl, take some time to study the CGI modules that come bundled with Perl. An extensive Perl module library, which contains many modules that are designed to be used when writing CGIs, is accessible at http://www.cpan.org.

If you're using many CGIs written in Perl, examine the mod_perl module. It embeds a Perl interpreter within the Apache server. Using this module will result in faster execution times for your CGIs because there will be no need to start a new Perl interpreter for each request. You'll find information about using mod_perl under the /usr/share/doc/_mod_perl-1.99_12/docs/ directory if you install it from this book's CD-ROMs.

> **NOTE**
>
> Always check for security updates and bug fixes if you use CGIs developed by other users or outside developers. Poorly updated and improperly implemented or written CGIs can pose significant security threats in your system.

16

SSI

Server-side includes are directives written directly into an HTML page, which the server parses when the page is served to the Web client. SSIs can be used to include other files, the output from programs, or environment variables.

You can enable SSI with the XBitHack directive. XBitHack can be set to a value of on or off, and can be set in either your configuration file or in .htaccess files. If the XBitHack directive is on, it indicates that all files with the user execute bit set should be parsed for SSI directives. This has two main advantages. One is that you don't need to rename a file, and change all links to that file, simply because you want to add a little dynamic content to it. The other reason is more cosmetic: Users looking at your Web content can't tell by looking at the filename that you're generating a page dynamically, so your wizardry is just a tiny bit more impressive.

Another positive side effect of using XBitHack is that it enables you to control how clients should cache your page. Pages containing SSI statements will not usually contain a Last-modified HTTP header. Therefore, they won't be cached by proxies or Web browsers. If you enable XBitHack, the group-execute bit for files will control whether a Last-modified header should be generated. It will be set to the same value as the last modified time of the file. Be sure to use this only on files that really are supposed to be cached.

Another way to enable SSI is to indicate that files with a certain filename extension (typically .shtml) are to be parsed by the server when they're served. This is accomplished with the following lines in your httpd.conf file:

```
# To use server-parsed HTML files
#
#AddType text/html .shtml
#AddHandler server-parsed .shtml
```

If you uncomment the AddType and AddHandler lines, you will tell the server to parse all .shtml files for SSI directives.

In addition to these directives, the following directive must be specified for directories in which you want to permit SSI:

```
Options Includes
```

This can be set in the server configuration file or in an .htaccess file.

Basic SSI Directives

SSI directives look rather like HTML comment tags. The syntax is as follows:

```
<!--#element attribute=value attribute=value ... -->
```

The `element` can be one of several directives, including

- `config`

- `echo`

- `exec`

- `fsize`

- `flastmod`

- `include`

- `printenv`

- `set`

The following sections describe each of these directives and their use.

config

The `config` directive enables you to set various configuration options to determine how the document parsing is handled. Because the page is parsed from top to bottom, `config` directives should appear at the top of the HTML document. Three configurations can be set with this command:

- `errmsg`—Sets the error message that's returned to the client if something goes wrong while parsing the document. The default message is [`an error occurred while processing this directive`], but you can set the message to any text with this directive. For example,

  ```
  <!--#config errmsg="[It's broken, dude]" -->
  ```

- `sizefmt`—Sets the format used to display file sizes. You can set the value to `bytes` to display the exact file size in bytes, or `abbrev` to display the size in KB or MB. For example,

  ```
  <!--#config sizefmt="bytes" -->
  ```

- `timefmtU`—Sets the format used to display times. The format of the value is the same as that of the `strftime` function used by C (and Perl) to display dates, as shown in the following list:

  %% PERCENT

  %a Day of the week abbreviation

  %A Day of the week

  %b Month abbreviation

  %B Month

%c ctime format: Sat Nov 19 21:05:57 1994

%d Numeric day of the month

%e DD

%D MM/DD/YY

%h Month abbreviation

%H Hour, 24-hour clock, leading zeroes

%I Hour, 12-hour clock, leading zeroes

%j Day of the year

%k Hour

%l Hour, 12-hour clock

%m Month number, starting with 1

%M Minute, leading zeroes

%n NEWLINE

%o Ordinal day of month—1st, 2nd, 25th, and so on

%p AM or PM

%r Time format: 09:05:57 PM

%R Time format: 21:05

%S Seconds, leading zeroes

%t Tab

%T Time format: 21:05:57

%U Week number; Sunday as first day of week

%w Day of the week, numerically; Sunday = 0

%W Week number; Monday as first day of week

%x Date format: 11/19/94

%X Time format: 21:05:57

%y Year (two digits)

%Y Year (four digits)

%Z Time zone in ASCII, such as PST

echo

The `echo` directive displays any one of the include variables in the following list. Times are displayed in the time format specified by `timefmt`. Use the `var` attribute to indicate the variable to be displayed.

- `DATE_GMT`—The current date in Greenwich mean time.

- `DATE_LOCAL`—The current date in the local time zone.

- `DOCUMENT_NAME`—The filename (excluding directories) of the document requested by the user.

- `DOCUMENT_URI`—The (%-decoded) URL path of the document requested by the user. Note that in the case of nested include files, this isn't the URL for the current document.

- `LAST_MODIFIED`—The last modification date of the document requested by the user.

exec

The `exec` directive executes a shell command or a CGI program, depending on the parameters you provide. Valid attributes are `cgi` and `cmd`.

- `cgi`—The URL of a CGI program to be executed. The URL must be a local CGI, not one located on another machine. The CGI program is passed the `QUERY_STRING` and `PATH_INFO` that were originally passed to the requested document, so the URL specified cannot contain this information. You should use `include virtual` instead of this directive.

- `cmd`—A shell command to be executed. The results will be displayed on the HTML page.

fsize

The `fsize` directive displays the size of a file specified by either the `file` or `virtual` attribute. Size is displayed as specified with the `sizefmt` directive.

- `file`—The path (file system path) to a file, either relative to the root if the value starts with / or relative to the current directory if it doesn't.

- `virtual`—The relative URL path to a file.

flastmod

Displays the last modified date of a file. The desired file is specified as with the `fsize` directive.

16

include

The `include` directive includes the contents of a file. The file is specified with the `file` and `virtual` attributes, as with `fsize` and `flastmod`.

If the file specified is a CGI program and `IncludesNOEXEC` isn't set, the program will be executed and the results displayed. This is to be used in preference to the `exec` directive. You can pass a `QUERY_STRING` with this directive—something you can't do with the `exec` directive.

printenv

Displays all existing variables. There are no attributes. For example,

```
<!--#printenv -->
```

set

Sets the value of a variable. Attributes are `var` and `value`. For example,

```
<!--#set var="animal" value="cow" -->
```

> **NOTE**
>
> All defined CGI environment variables are also allowed as `include` variables.

> **NOTE**
>
> In your configuration files (or in `.htaccess`), you can specify `Options IncludesNOEXEC` to disallow the `exec` directive because this is the least secure of the SSI directives. Be especially cautious when Web users are able to create content (such as a guest book or discussion board) and these options are enabled!

The variables whose attributes have been set by `var` and `value` can also be used elsewhere with some of the following directives.

Flow Control

Using the variables set with the `set` directive and the various environment and include variables, a limited flow control syntax can be used to generate a certain amount of dynamic content on server-parsed pages.

The syntax of the `if/else` functions is as follows:

```
<!--#if expr="test_condition" -->
<!--#elif expr="test_condition" -->
<!--#else -->
<!--#endif -->
```

expr can be a string, which is considered true if nonempty, or a variety of comparisons between two strings. Available comparison operators are =, !=, <, <=, >, and >=. If the second string has the format /string/, the strings are compared with regular expressions. Multiple comparisons can be strung together with && (AND) and ¦¦ (OR). Any text appearing between the if/elif/else directives will be displayed on the resulting page. An example of such a flow structure follows:

```
<!--#set var="agent" value="$HTTP_USER_AGENT" -->
<!--#if expr="$agent = /Mozilla/" -->
Mozilla!
<!--#else -->
Something else!
<!--#endif -->
```

This code will display Mozilla! if you're using a browser that passes Mozilla as part of its USER_AGENT string, and Something else! otherwise.

Graphic Interface Configuration of Apache

Some of Apache's basic behavior can be configured using Red Hat's system-config-httpd, a GUI tool for the X Window System. This can provide an easy way to configure settings such as Apache's username and group name, location of PID and process locks files, or performance settings (such as the maximum number of connections), without manually editing configuration files.

> **CAUTION**
>
> If you use system-config-httpd, you shouldn't try to manually edit the httpd.conf file. Manual changes will be overwritten by the GUI client if you again use system-config-httpd!

Launch this client by using your X desktop panel's Server Settings' HTTP Server menu item, or from the command line of an X terminal window, like this

```
$ system-config-httpd &
```

After you press Enter, you'll be asked to type the root password. You'll then see the main client window shown in Figure 16.2.

In the Main tab, you can set the server name, indicate where to send email addressed to the Webmaster, and set the port that Apache will use. If you want, you can also configure specific virtual hosts to listen on different ports.

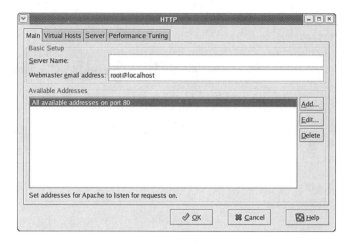

FIGURE 16.2   The `system-config-httpd` main dialog provides access to basic configuration of the Apache Web server.

Configuring Virtual Host Properties

In the Virtual Hosts tab, you can configure the properties of each virtual host. The Name list box contains a list of all virtual hosts operating in Apache. Edit a virtual host by opening the Virtual Hosts Properties dialog, shown in Figure 16.3. You do this by highlighting the name of a virtual host in the Name list box of the Virtual Hosts tab and clicking the Edit button at the right of the tab. Use the General Options item in the Virtual Hosts Properties dialog to configure basic virtual host settings.

Click the Site Configuration listing in the General Options list of this dialog to set defaults such as which files are loaded by default when no files are specified (the default is `index.*`) in the URL.

The SSL listing in the General Options pane gives you access to settings used to enable or disable SSL, specify certificate settings, and define the SSL log filename and location. Choose the Logging listing to access options for configuring where the error messages are logged, as well as where the transfer log file is kept and how much information is put in it.

Use the Environment Variables options to configure settings for the env_mod module, used to pass environment directives to CGI programs.

The Directories section configures the directory options (such as whether CGI programs are allowed to run) as well as the order entries mentioned in the `httpd.conf` section.

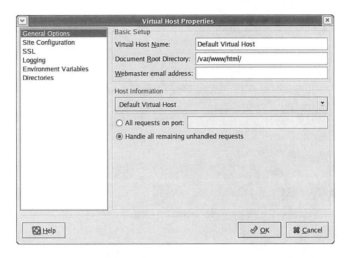

FIGURE 16.3   `system-config-httpd`'s Virtual Host Properties dialog gives you access to numerous options for configuring the properties of an Apache virtual host.

Configuring the Server

The Server tab, shown in Figure 16.4, enables you to configure things such as where the lock file and the PID file are.

In both cases, it's best to use the defaults. You can also configure the directory where any potential core dumps will be placed.

Finally, you can set which user and group Apache is to run as. As mentioned in a previous note, for security reasons, it's best to run Apache as the user named apache and as a member of the group apache.

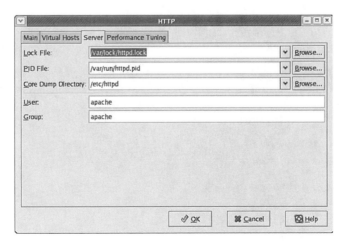

FIGURE 16.4   `system-config-httpd`'s Server configuration tab.

16

Configuring Apache for Peak Performance

Use the options in the Performance Tuning tab to configure Apache to provide peak performance in your system. Options in this tab set the maximum number of connections, connection timeouts, and number of requests per connection. When setting this number, keep in mind that for each connection to your server, another instance of the httpd program may be run, depending on how Apache is built. Each instance takes resources such as CPU time and memory. You can also configure details about each connection such as how long, in seconds, before a connection times out and how many requests each connection can make to the server.

Other Web Servers for Use with Fedora

Of course, other Web servers can be used with Fedora. Apache is by far the most popular, but this doesn't rule out the others.

To determine the best Web server for your use, consider the needs of the Web site you manage. Does it need heavy security (for e-commerce), multimedia (music, video, and pictures), or the capability to download files easily? How much are you willing to spend for the software? Do you need software that's easy to maintain and troubleshoot or includes tech support? The answers to these questions might steer you to something other than Apache.

The following sections list some of the more popular alternatives to using Apache as your Web server.

thttpd

It isn't entirely clear what the *t* in thttpd stands for. Meanings alternate between *tiny*, *turbo*, and *throttling*, depending on who you ask. Whatever meaning you opt for, it's clear that thttpd is *not* big and slow.

Throttling, in the context of thttpd, is a process in which incoming URL calls are kept under control for a certain page or collection of pages on the Web site. If traffic to these pages hits a defined limit, the requesters for the page are sent a `try again` code until the traffic returns to a more manageable level.

thttpd is, on the surface, a simple little HTTP server that can handle a fair amount of traffic with little strain. Although not as robust as Apache, it does feature a throttling control—something that isn't readily available for Apache.

thttpd is available as freeware from the thttpd Web site (`http://www.acme.com/software/thttpd`).

Sun ONE Web Server

Despite the NetCraft numbers shown in Table 16.1, there's evidence that the Sun Java System Web Server (formerly known as the iPlanet Web Server, and subsequently Sun ONE Web Server) might be even more popular than Apache in strictly corporate arenas. Netcraft has rated Sun Java System Web Server number one in market share among Fortune 100 Web sites.

The server got its start as the Netscape Enterprise Server—one of the first powerful Web servers ever to hit the market. Sun ONE Web Server comes in many different flavors, and all of them are big. In addition to the enterprise-level Web server that can be run on Red Hat, the software features application, messaging, calendar, and directory servers...just to name a few.

Sun ONE Web Server is great for handling big Web needs, and it comes with an appropriately big price tag: $1,495 (U.S.) per CPU. It's definitely not something to run the school Web site—unless your school happens to be a major state university with several regional campuses. For more information on Sun Java System Web Server, you can visit its Web site (`http://wwws.sun.com/software/products/web_srvr/home_web_srvr.html`).

Stronghold

If you're looking for something a little more secure than Apache, but still don't want to lose the Apache functionality, you can purchase Stronghold from Red Hat Software.

Although not a Web server per se, Stronghold is a server add-on that provides 128-bit cryptography and security certificates to the Apache Web server (which is included in your purchase of Stronghold).

Stronghold supports SSL and TLS security standards, as well as many of the certificate standards on the market today.

The price for this kind of security isn't particularly light. The software, which can be previewed at `http://www.redhat.com/software/stronghold/`, was advertised in 2004 at $995 (U.S.) per year.

Zope

Zope is another Open Source Web server. Although it's still relatively young and might not have as much flexibility as Apache, it's making strong inroads in the Web server market.

What makes Zope different from Apache is the fact that it's managed through a completely Web-based graphic interface. This has broad appeal for those who aren't enthused about a command-line–only interface.

Zope is a product of the Zope Corporation (formerly Digital Creations), the same firm that made the Python programming language. And, like all things open source, it's free.

Information on Zope can be found at both `http://www.zope.com` (for the commercial version) and `http://www.zope.org` (for the open-source version).

Zeus Web Server

Fedora sites can also use the Zeus Web Server from Zeus Technology. This server offers a scalable SSL implementation, security settings across multiple Web sites, and an online administration server. The current price is $1,700 for a host platform with up to two CPUs, but load balancing via the Zeus Load Balancer will cost $12,000 for each pair of load-balancing computers.

You can get more information about the Zeus Web Server at `http://www.zeus.com/products/zws/`.

TWiki

TWiki is a Web-based collaboration tool. In use, it provides pages that resemble a regular Web site, but logged-in users can add content or make other modifications using a Web browser. Content is generated while maintaining a log of all changes. TWiki is a collection of Perl scripts that can extend and complement Apache's capabilities. TWiki is available at no cost under the GPL from `http://www.TWiki.org`. You learn more about this tool in "Collaborating with TWiki," in Chapter 20, "News and Other Collaborative Communication."

Related Fedora and Linux Commands

You will use these commands when managing your Apache Web Server in Fedora:

`apachectl`—Server control shell script included with Apache

`system-config-httpd`—Red Hat's graphical Web server configuration tool

`epiphany`—A Web browser for GNOME

`httpd`—The Apache Web server

`konqueror`—KDE's graphical Web browser

`elinks`—A text-based, graphical menu Web browser

`mozilla`—The premiere Open Source Web browser

Reference

There's a plethora of Apache documentation online. For more information about Apache and the subjects discussed in this chapter, look at some of the following resources:

- `http://news.netcraft.com/archives/web_server_survey.html`—A statistical graph of Web server usage by 53,341,867 servers (as of August 2004). The research points out that Apache is by far the most widely used server for Internet sites.

- `http://www.apache.org/`—Extensive documentation and information about Apache are available at The Apache Project Web site.

- `http://www.apacheweek.com/`—You can obtain breaking news about Apache and great technical articles at the Apache Week site.

- `http://apachetoday.com/`—Another good Apache site, with original content as well as links to Apache-related stories on other sites can be found at Apache Today's site.

- `http://www.hwg.org/`—HTML, CGI, and related subjects are available at The HTML Writers Guild site.

- `http://modules.apache.org/`—Available add-on modules for Apache can be found at The Apache Module Registry Web site.

There are several good books about Apache. For example, *Apache Server Unleashed* (Sams Publishing), ISBN 0-672-31808-3.

For more information on Zope, see *The Zope Book* (New Riders Publishing), ISBN 0-7357-11372.

16

## CHAPTER 17

Administering Database Services

IN THIS CHAPTER

- A Brief Review of Database Basics

- Choosing a Database: MySQL Versus PostgreSQL

- Installing and Configuring MySQL

- Installing and Configuring PostgreSQL

- Database Clients

- Reference

This chapter is an introduction to MySQL and PostgreSQL, two database systems that are included with Fedora. You'll learn what these systems do, how the two programs compare, and how to consider their advantages and disadvantages. This information can help you choose which one to use for your organization's database needs. Finally, you'll learn how to install, initialize, and configure these popular client/server database programs and how to administer those databases to maintain tight security and full integrity of the data.

The database administrator (DBA) for an organization has several responsibilities, which vary according to the size and operations of the organization, supporting staff, and so on. Depending on the particular organization's structure, if you are the organization's DBA, your responsibilities might include the following:

- Installing and maintaining database *servers*—You might need to install and maintain the database server software. Maintenance can involve such tasks as installing patches that fix bugs and security issues as well as upgrading the software at the appropriate times. As DBA, you might need to have root access to your system and perhaps know how to manage software (see Chapter 8, "Managing Software and System Resources"). You also need to be aware of kernel, filesystem, and other security issues.

- Installing and maintaining database *clients*—The database client is the program that users use to access the database (you'll learn more on that later in this chapter, in the section "Database Clients"), either locally or remotely over a network. Your responsibilities might include installing and maintaining these client programs on users' systems. This chapter discusses how to install and work with the clients from both the Linux command line and through its graphical interface database tools.

- Managing accounts and users—Account and user management includes adding and deleting users from the database, assigning and administering passwords, and so on. In this chapter, you'll learn how to grant and revoke user privileges and passwords for MySQL and PostgreSQL while using Fedora.

- Ensuring database security—To ensure database security, you need to be concerned with things such as access control, which ensures that only authorized people can access the database, and permissions, which ensures that people who can access the database cannot do things they shouldn't do. In this chapter, you'll learn how to manage Secure Shell (SSH), Web, and local GUI client access to the database. Planning and overseeing the regular backup of an organization's database and restoring data from those backups is another critical component of securing the database.

- Ensuring data integrity—Of all the information stored on a server's hard disk storage, chances are the information in the database is the most critical. Ensuring data integrity involves planning for multiple-user access and ensuring that changes are not lost or duplicated when more than one user is making changes to the database at the same time.

A Brief Review of Database Basics

Database services under Linux that use the software discussed in this chapter are based on a *client/server* model. Database clients are often used to input data and to query or display query results from the server. You can use the command line or a graphical client to access a running server. Databases generally come in two forms: flat file and relational. A *flat file* database can be as simple as a text file with a space, tab, or some other character delimiting different parts of the information. One example of a simple flat file database is the Fedora /etc/passwd file. Another example could be a simple address book that might look something like this:

```
Doe~John~505 Some Street~Anytown~NY~12345~555-555-1212
```

You can use standard UNIX tools such as grep, awk, and perl to search for and extract information from this primitive database. Although this might work fine for a small database such as an address book that only one person uses, flat file databases of this sort have several limitations:

- They don't scale well. Flat file databases cannot perform random access on data. They can only perform sequential access. This means that they have to scan each line in the file, one by one, to look for specific information. As the size of the database grows, access time increases and performance decreases.

- Flat file databases are unsuitable for multiuser environments. Depending on how the database is set up, it either enables only one user to access it at a time, or it allows two users to make changes simultaneously, and the changes could end up overwriting each other and cause data loss.

These limitations obviously make the flat file database unsuitable for any kind of serious work in even a small business—much less in an enterprise environment. Relational databases, referred to as RDBMSs, are very good at finding the relationships between individual pieces of data. An RDBMS stores data in tables with fields much like those in spreadsheets, making the data searchable and sortable. RDBMSs are the focus of this chapter.

Oracle, DB2, Microsoft SQL Server, and the freely available PostgreSQL and MySQL are all examples of RDBMSs. The following sections discuss how relational databases work and provide a closer look at some of the basic processes involved in administering and using databases. You'll also learn about SQL, the standard language that is used to store, retrieve, and manipulate database data.

How Relational Databases Work

In order to effectively set up and administer an RDBMS, you need to know a little bit about how relational databases store information and how users can access and work with that data. This section doesn't offer a detailed lesson in relational database theory and management, but it does provide a good overview of the essential concepts and processes.

An RDBMS stores data in tables, which you can visualize as spreadsheets. Each column in the table is a field; for example, a column might contain a name or an address. Each row in the table is an individual record. The table itself has a name you use to refer to that table when you want to get data out of it or put data into it. Figure 17.1 shows an example of a simple relational database that stores name and address information.

last_name	first_name	address	city	state	zip	phone
Doe	John	501 Somestreet	Anytown	NY	55011	555-555-1212
Doe	Jane	501 Somestreet	Anytown	NY	55011	555-555-1212
Palmer	John	205 Anystreet	Sometown	NY	55055	123-456-7890
Johnson	Robert	100 Easystreet	Easytown	CT	12345	111-222-3333

FIGURE 17.1   In this visualization of how an RDBMS stores data, the database stores four records (rows) that include name and address information, divided into seven fields (columns) of data.

In the example shown in Figure 17.1, the database contains only a single table. Most RDBMS setups are much more complex than this, with a single database containing multiple tables. Figure 17.2 shows an example of a database named sample_database that contains two tables.

sample_database

phonebook

last_name	first_name	phone
Doe	John	555-555-1212
Doe	Jane	555-555-1212
Palmer	John	123-456-7890
Johnson	Richard	111-222-3333

serengeti_mammal

common_name	order	family	genus	species	sub-species
African Lion	Carnivora	Felidae	Panthera	leo	
African Elephant	Proboscidea	Elephantidae	Loxodonta	africana	
Meercat	Carnivora	Viverridae	Suricata	suricatta	
Hyena	Carnivora	Hyaenidae	Crocuta	croucuta	
Reticulated Giraffe	Artiodactyla	Giraffidae	Giraffa	cameloparalis	retciculata
Grant's Zebra	Perissodactyla	Equidae	Equus	burchelli	bohmi
Cheetah	Carnivora	Felidae	Acinonyx	jubatus	
Thompson's Gazelle	Artiodactyla	Bovidae	Gazella	thomsoni	
Hippopotamus	Artiodactyla	Hippopotamidae	Hippopotamus	amphibius	

FIGURE 17.2   A single database can contain two tables—in this case, phonebook and serengeti_mammal.

In the sample_database example, the phonebook table contains four records (rows), and each record hold three fields (columns) of data. The serengeti_mammal table holds nine records, divided into six fields of data.

If you are thinking that there is absolutely no logical relationship between the phonebook table and the serengeti_mammal table in the sample_database example, you are absolutely correct. In a relational database, users can store multiple tables of data in a single database—even if the data in one table is unrelated to the data in others.

For example, suppose you run a small company that sells widgets, and you have a computerized database of customers. In addition to storing each customer's name, address, and phone number, you want to be able to look up outstanding order and invoice information for any of your customers. You could use three related tables in an RDBMS to store and organize customer data for just those purposes. Figure 17.3 shows an example of such a database.

In the example in Figure 17.3, we have added a customer ID field to each customer record. This field holds a customer ID number that is the unique piece of information that can be used to link all other information for each customer, to track orders and invoices. Each customer is given an ID unique to that customer; two customers might have the same data in their name fields, but their ID field values will never be the same. The Customer ID field data in the Orders and Overdue tables replaces the Last Name, First Name, and

Shipping Address field information from the Customers table. Now, when you want to run a search for any customer's order and invoice data, you can search based on one key rather than multiple keys. You get more accurate results in faster, easier-to-conduct data searches.

customers

cid	last_name	first_name	shipping_address
1	Doe	John	505 Somestreet
2	Doe	Jane	505 Somestreet
3	Palmer	John	200 Anystreet
4	Johnson	Richard	1000 Another Street

orders

cid	order_num	stock_num	priority	shipped	date
1	1002	100,252,342	3	Y	8/31/01
1	1221	200,352	1	N	10/2/01
3	1223	200,121	2	Y	10/2/01
2	1225	221,152	1	N	10/3/01

overdue

cid	order_num	days_overdue	action
1	1002	32	sent letter

FIGURE 17.3 You can use three related tables to track customers, orders, and outstanding invoices.

Now that you have an idea of how data is stored in an RDBMS and how the RDBMS structure enables you to work with that data, you're ready to learn how to input and output data from the database. This is where SQL comes in.

Understanding SQL Basics

SQL (pronounced either "S-Q-L," or "se-quel") is a database query language understood by virtually all RDMBSs available today. You use SQL statements to get data into and retrieve data from a database. As with statements in any language, SQL statements have a defined structure that determines their meaning and function.

In most settings, SQL is programmed into front-end or middleweear applications that end users don't directly manipulate. Thus, most end users are unaware of SQL and its role, and they have little reason to be concerned about the structure of SQL statements.

However, as a DBA, you should understand the basics of SQL, even if you won't be doing any of the actual programming yourself. Fortunately, SQL is very similar to standard English, and learning the basics is very simple.

17

Creating Tables

As mentioned previously, an RDBMS stores data in tables that look similar to spreadsheets.
Of course, before you can store any data in a database, you need to create the necessary
tables and columns to store the data. You do this by using the CREATE statement.

For example, the serengeti_mammal table from Figure 17.2 has six columns, or fields:
common_name, order, family, genus, species, and sub_species.

SQL provides several different column types for data that define what kind of data will be
stored in the column. Some of the available types are INT, FLOAT, CHAR, and VARCHAR. (The
difference between CHAR and VARCHAR is that CHAR holds a fixed-length string, whereas
VARCHAR holds a variable-length string.)

There are also special column types, such as DATE, that take only data in a date format,
and ENUM (enumerated), which can be used to specify that only certain values are allowed.
(If, for example, you wanted to record the sex of an animal in a database, you could use
an ENUM column that accepted only the values M and F. You'll learn more about ENUM later
in this chapter.)

Looking at the serengeti_mammal table, you can see that all the columns hold character
string data. In addition, these character strings are of variable length. Based on this information, you can discern that the best type to use for all the columns is type VARCHAR. You
should notice something else about the serengeti_mammal table. All the columns in the
table, with the exception of the last one (sub_species), require a value. Not all the
animals in the table have a subspecies classification, so the last column can be left empty.
These two facts will be important when you set up the table.

You are now ready to create a table. As mentioned before, you do this by using the CREATE
statement, which uses the following syntax:

```
CREATE TABLE table_name (column_name column_type(parameters) options, ...);
```

You should know the following about the CREATE statement:

- SQL commands are not case sensitive. For example, CREATE TABLE, create table,
  and Create Table are all valid. It's a good idea to get in the habit of using all uppercase for commands because later on, when you start writing front ends to your databases in C, Perl, and so on, using all uppercase will make it easier to pick out the
  SQL code. (Keywords in C, Perl, and so on are almost always in lowercase.)

- Whitespace is generally ignored. You'll see an example of this a little later on when you create a table for the serengeti_mammal database.

The following example shows how to create the table for the serengeti_mammal database:

```
CREATE TABLE serengeti_mammal
(
 commonname VARCHAR(25) NOT NULL,
 torder VARCHAR(20) NOT NULL,
 family VARCHAR(20) NOT NULL,
 genus VARCHAR(20) NOT NULL,
 species VARCHAR(20) NOT NULL,
subspecies VARCHAR(20) NULL
);
```

Notice that the statement terminates with a semicolon. This is how SQL knows that you are finished with all the entries in the statement. (In some cases, the semicolon can be omitted. This chapter points out these cases when they arise.)

> **TIP**
>
> Notice that you use torder instead of just order for the column containing the Order information. Because order is a reserved keyword in PostgreSQL that cannot be used as a column name, you can simply put a t (or any other letter) on the front to make it a valid column name. (order isn't reserved in MySQL, and works as a column name.)

Inserting Data into Tables

After you create the tables, you can put data into them. You can insert data manually with the INSERT statement, which uses the following syntax:

```
INSERT INTO table_name VALUES('value1', 'value2', 'value3', ...);
```

This statement inserts *value1, value2,* and so on into the table *table_name*. The values that are inserted constitute one row, or record, in the database. Unless specified otherwise, values are inserted in the order in which the columns are listed in the database table. If for some reason you want to insert values in a different order (or if you want to insert only a few values and they aren't in sequential order), you can specify which columns you want the data to go in by using the following syntax:

```
INSERT INTO table_name (column1,column4) VALUES('value1', 'value2');
```

You can also fill multiple rows with a single INSERT statement, using syntax such as the following:

```
INSERT INTO table_name VALUES('value1', 'value2'),('value3', 'value4');
```

In this statement, *value1* and *value2* are inserted into the first row, and *value3* and *value4* are inserted into the second row.

The following example shows how you would insert the `African lion` entry into the `serengeti_mammal` database:

```
INSERT INTO serengeti_mammal VALUES('African Lion', 'Carnivora', 'Felidae',
¬ 'Panthera', 'leo', NULL);
```

MySQL requires the `NULL` value for the last column (`sub_species`) if you do not want to include a subspecies. PostgreSQL, on the other hand, lets you get away with just omitting the last column. Of course, if you had columns in the middle that were null, you would need to explicitly state `NULL` in the `INSERT` statement.

Normally, `INSERT` statements are coded into a front-end program so that users adding data to the database don't have to worry about the SQL statements involved.

Retrieving Data from a Database

Of course, the main reason for storing data in a database is so that you can later look up, sort, and generate reports on that data. Basic data retrieval is done with the `SELECT` statement, which has the following syntax:

```
SELECT column(s) FROM table_name WHERE search_criteria;
```

The first two parts of the statement—the `SELECT` and `FROM` parts—are required. The `WHERE` portion of the statement is optional. If it is omitted, all rows in the table *table_name* are returned.

columns(s) indicates the name of the columns that you want to see. If you want to see multiple columns, you can list them, separated by commas. If you want to see all columns, you can also use the wildcard * to show all the columns that match the search criteria. For example, the following statement would display all columns from the records that match the search criteria:

```
SELECT * FROM serengeti_mammal;
```

If you wanted to see only the common names of all the animals in the database, you could use a statement such as the following:

```
SELECT common_name FROM serengeti_mammal;
```

To select the genus and species of an animal, you could use the following:

```
SELECT genus,species FROM serengeti_mammal;
```

However, this would not produce output in the format you prefer. When stating the scientific name of an animal, the genus and species are always listed together. They make up the full species name. Both MySQL and PostgreSQL provide string concatenation functions to handle problems such as this. However, the syntax is different in the two systems.

In MySQL, you can use the CONCAT function to combine the columns genus and species into one output column. The following statement is an example:

```
SELECT CONCAT(genus," ",species) AS Scientific_Name FROM serengeti_mammal;
```

This statement lists both the genus and species under one column that has the label Scientific_Name. The blank quoted space between genus and species inserts a space between the genus and species names. Without it, the two would be run together, which isn't what you want.

In PostgreSQL, the string concatenation function is simply a double pipe (¦¦). The following command is the PostgreSQL equivalent of the preceding MySQL command:

```
SELECT (genus¦¦' '¦¦species) AS Scientific_Name FROM serengeti_mammal;
```

Note that the parentheses are optional, but they make the statement easier to read. Once again, the single quotes in the middle (note the space between the quotes) are used to insert a space between the genus and the species names. Without them, the two values would be run together as one word, and that isn't what you want.

Of course, more often than not, you don't want a list of every single row in the database. Rather, you only want to find rows that match certain characteristics. For this, you add the WHERE statement to the SELECT statement. For example, suppose that you want to find all the animals in the serengeti_mammal table that are carnivores. You could use a statement like the following:

```
SELECT * FROM serengeti_mammal WHERE torder="Carnivora";
```

Using the table from Figure 17.2, you can see that this query would return the rows for the African lion, the meerkat, the hyena, and the cheetah. This is a very simple query, and SQL is capable of handling queries much more complex than this. Complex queries can be written using logical AND and logical OR statements. For example, suppose you want to refine the query so that it lists only those carnivores that don't belong to the family Hyaenidae. You could use a query like the following:

```
SELECT * FROM serengeti_mammal WHERE torder="Carnivora" AND family!="Hyaenidae";
```

In computer programming, != means "is not equal to." So once again, looking at the table from Figure 17.2, you can see that this query will return the rows for the African lion, the meerkat, and the cheetah, but it won't return the row for the hyena because the hyena belongs to the family Hyaenidae.

So what if you want to list all the carnivores and all the artiodactyls except for those animals that belong to the families Hyaenidae and Hippopotamidae? This time, you combine logical AND and logical OR statements:

```
SELECT * FROM serengeti_mammal WHERE torder="Carnivora" OR
¬torder="Artiodactyla" AND family!="Hyaenidae" AND family!="Hippopotamidae";
```

This query would return entries for the African lion, the meerkat, the cheetah, the reticulated giraffe, and Thompson's gazelle. However, it wouldn't return entries for the hyena or the hippopotamus.

> **TIP**
>
> One of the most common errors among new database programmers is confusing logical AND and logical OR. For example, in everyday speech, you might say "Find me all records with genus Panthera and Acinonyx." At first glance, you might think that if you fed this statement to the database in SQL format, it would return the rows for the African lion and the cheetah. In fact, it would return no rows at all. This is because the database interprets the statement as "Find all rows in which the animal belongs to both the genus Panthera and the genus Acinonyx." It is, of course, impossible for an animal to belong to more than one genus, so this statement would never return any rows, no matter how many animals were stored in the table. The correct way to form this statement is with an OR statement instead of an AND statement.

Of course, SQL is capable of far more than is demonstrated here. But as mentioned before, this section isn't intended to teach you all there is to know about SQL programming; rather, it teaches you the basics so that you can be a more effective DBA.

Choosing a Database: MySQL Versus PostgreSQL

If you're just starting out and learning about using a database with Linux, the first logical step is to research which database will best serve your needs. Many different database software packages are available for Linux; some are free, and others cost hundreds of thousands of dollars. Expensive commercial databases, such as Oracle, are beyond the scope of this book. Instead, this chapter focuses on two freely available databases (RDBMSs): MySQL and PostgreSQL.

Both of these high-quality SQL databases are included on this book's CD-ROMs. But just because MySQL and PostgreSQL are free doesn't mean that they lack power. Both of these databases (PostgreSQL in particular) can handle very complex projects. They are used in commercial organizations, government agencies (for example, NASA uses MySQL), research institutions, and educational institutions.

Both of these databases are quite capable, and either one could probably serve your needs. However, each database has a unique set of features and capabilities that might serve your needs better or make developing database applications easier for you. The following sections look at some of the key features of any database and discuss how those features are implemented in MySQL and PostgreSQL. You should use the information in these sections to compare the two databases so that you can choose the one that's right for your project.

Speed

Until recently, the speed choice was quite simple: If the speed of performing queries was paramount to your application, you used MySQL. MySQL has a reputation for being an extremely fast database. Until recently, PostgreSQL was quite slow by comparison.

Newer versions of PostgreSQL have improved in terms of speed (when it comes to disk access, sorting, and so on). In certain situations, such as periods of heavy simultaneous access, PostgreSQL can be significantly faster than MySQL, as you'll see in the next section. However, MySQL is still extremely fast when compared to many other databases.

Data Locking

In order to prevent data corruption, a database needs to put a lock on data while it is being accessed. As long as the lock is on, no other process can access the data until the first process has released the lock. This means that any other processes trying to access the data have to wait until the current process completes. The next process in line then locks the data until it is finished, and the remaining processes have to wait their turn, and so on.

Of course, operations on a database generally complete quite quickly, so in environments with a small number of users simultaneously accessing the database, the locks are usually of such short duration that they don't cause any significant delays. However, in environments in which a lot of people are accessing the database simultaneously, locking can begin to create performance problems as different people wait their turn to access the database.

MySQL uses a data-locking method that is fundamentally different from the data-locking method used by PostgreSQL.

Older versions of MySQL lock data at the table level, which can be considered a bottleneck for updates during periods of heavy access. This means that when someone writes a row of data in the table, the entire table is locked so that no one else can enter data. If your table has 500,000 rows (or records) in it, all 500,000 rows are locked any time a row is accessed. Once again, in environments with a relatively small number of simultaneous users, this doesn't cause serious performance problems because most operations complete so quickly that the lock time is extremely short. However in environments in which a lot of people are accessing the data simultaneously, MySQL's table-level locking can be a significant performance bottleneck.

PostgreSQL, on the other hand, locks data at the row level. In PostgreSQL, only the row that is currently being accessed is locked. The rest of the table can be accessed by other users. This row-level locking significantly reduces the performance impact of locking in environments that have a large number of simultaneous users. Therefore, as a general rule, PostgreSQL is better suited for high-load environments than MySQL.

17

NOTE

MySQL's data locking methods are discussed in more depth at `http://www.mysql.com/doc/en/Internal_locking.html`. Fedora includes MySQL version 3.23, but the newer version, 4.0 (available at the time of this writing), provides row-level locking.

You can find more information on PostgreSQL's locking at `http://www.postgresql.org/idocs/index.php?locking-tables.html`.

ACID Compliance in Transaction Processing to Protect Data Integrity

Another way MySQL and PostgreSQL differ is in the amount of protection they provide for keeping data from becoming corrupted. The acronym ACID is commonly used to describe several aspects of data protection:

- *Atomicity* is a term derived from the word *atom*, which, as you might know, means "indivisible." In the database world, this means that several database operations will be treated as an atomic unit, often called a *transaction*. In a transaction, either all unit operations are carried out or none of them are. In other words, if any operation in the atomic unit fails, the entire atomic unit is canceled.

  If you have a power failure or server crash after an original record has been deleted, for example, but before the updated one has been added, you don't lose the record because atomic transactions ensure that the original record isn't deleted if the update portion of the atomic unit fails.

- *Consistency* ensures that no transaction can cause the database to be left in an inconsistent state. Inconsistent states can be caused by database client crashes, network failures, and similar situations. Consistency ensures that, in such a situation, any transaction or partially completed transaction that would cause the database to be left in an inconsistent state is *rolled back*, or undone. This prevents, for example, the deletion of one critical field of a database record when all other fields for that record remain (referred to as "orphaned" data). Incomplete transactions are rolled back to maintain consistency.

- *Isolation* ensures that multiple transactions operating on the same data are completely isolated from each other. This prevents data corruption if two different users try to write to the same record at the same time. The way isolation is handled can generally be configured by the database programmer. One way that isolation can be handled is through locking, as discussed previously.

- *Durability* ensures that after a transaction has been committed to the database, it cannot be lost in the event of a system crash, network failure, or other problem. This is usually accomplished through transaction logs. Durability means, for example, that if the server crashes, the database can examine the logs when it comes back up, and it can commit any transactions that were not yet complete into the database.

PostgreSQL is ACID compliant, but MySQL is rapidly catching up in features. For example, the latest version (which you can download from the Fedora Project or from the PostgreSQL home page at `http://www.postgresql.org`) supports transactions, which means that you are less likely to lose data in MySQL if you have a server crash or network failure than you are in PostgreSQL. However, many database designers feel that PostgreSQL is probably better suited for environments with a lot of users or a large amount of information being added and changed on a regular basis.

> **NOTE**
>
> MySQL AB, the company that distributes MySQL Server, advises that you always back up your databases. Safer features are also being implemented in newer versions; for example, MySQL version 4.0 has many ACID improvements, such as automated crash recovery. See `http://www.mysql.com` for more information.

SQL Subqueries

Subqueries allow you to combine several operations into one atomic unit, and they enable those operations to access each other's data. By using SQL subqueries, you can perform some extremely complex operations on a database. In addition, using SQL subqueries eliminates the potential problem of data changing between two operations as a result of another user performing some operation on the same set of data. PostgreSQL has support for subqueries. MySQL doesn't, although some workarounds are available in MySQL to simulate subqueries.

> **Importing Text Files into Tables**
>
> In MySQL and PostgreSQL, the SQL statements used to create a database table can be entered directly into the command-line clients (as you will learn later in this chapter). However, doing so introduces a lot of opportunity for error; if you make a mistake, you have to type the entire table over again from the beginning. Fortunately, both MySQL and PostgreSQL can read a list of SQL statements from a plain-text file. You could also enter SQL statements into a text editor and save the file with the filename extension `.sql`. (The `.sql` extension is helpful because it would be easy to see that this file contains SQL statements when doing a directory listing.)
>
> Statements that are saved in a text file can be imported into the database with the following commands in MySQL and PostgreSQL, respectively, where `mammal.sql` is the name of the saved text file:
>
> ```
> $ mysql database_name < mammal.sql
> $ psql database_name < mammal.sql
> ```
>
> Of course, in order for this to work, `mysql` or `psql` must be invoked by a user who has permission to create tables in the database represented by `database_name`. For more information, see the sections "Granting and Revoking Privileges in MySQL" and "Creating Database Users in MySQL," later in this chapter.

17

Procedural Languages and Triggers

A *procedural language* is an external programming language that can be used to write functions and procedures. This allows you to do things that aren't supported by simple SQL. A *trigger* allows you to define an event that will invoke the external function or procedure that you have written. For example, a trigger can be used to cause an exception if an INSERT statement containing an unexpected or out-of-range value for a column is given.

For example, in the animal tracking database, you could use a trigger to cause an exception if a user entered a coordinate data that didn't make sense. PostgreSQL has a procedural language called PL/pgSQL. Although MySQL has support for a limited number of built-in procedures and triggers, it doesn't have any procedural language. This means that you cannot create custom procedures or triggers in MySQL, although the same effects can often be achieved through creative client-side programming.

Available Applications

At this point, you might be getting the impression that there is no reason to even consider using MySQL because PostgreSQL has so many more features. Actually, there is one primary reason to consider MySQL: the number of premade applications that are available for it. For example, if you want to create an online discussion forum, you can use a program called Phorum that uses MySQL. This saves you the work of having to do all the SQL programming yourself.

> **NOTE**
>
> Although many of the previously mentioned features aren't available in the standard version of MySQL, they are available in a product called MySQL-Max, which should be suitable for a production environment in which the system has been updated to the latest version of the Linux kernel. For more information about this product, see http://www.mysql.com/downloads/.

> **Getting Started with Databases and Fedora**
>
> A number of steps are required before database services can be used with Fedora. The first step is to make sure that the database server has been properly started (usually at boot time). The root operator needs to make sure that Fedora starts the server during any anticipated system runlevel (see Chapter 7, "Managing Services," for more information). A root database user must then be created, and the database server needs to be initialized (for example, by using mysql_install_db for MySQL; see the section "Initializing the Data Directory" for more information). A root database user password is then created, along with one or more databases. The root database user can then grant authorized users various levels of access to each database.

Installing and Configuring MySQL

A free and stable version of MySQL is included with Fedora. MySQL is also available from the Web site http://www.mysql.com. The software is available in source code, binary, and

RPM format for Linux. You can elect to have MySQL installed when you install Fedora, or later on, use the redhat-config-packages client to add the software to your system. See Chapter 8 for the details on adding (or removing) software.

This section only covers a basic introduction to installing the binary and source form, and then discusses MySQL version 3.2.

> **TIP**
>
> It is a lot easier to install and use MySQL by using the RPMS included with Fedora. All system startup scripts, groups, users, and documentation will be installed automatically. Installing the binary version or from source code will require much more work, but allows you to create custom configurations.

The binary distribution is contained in a 14MB archive. Directions for installing the binary distribution are contained in a file named INSTALL-BINARY, found in the resulting directory after unpacking. You'll get step-by-step instructions for a basic install, which consists of a series of commands to create the mysql group and mysql user, unpack the binary into the /usr/local directory, run an install script, and set ownership and group ownerships on the new directory.

Get started by uncompressing the binary package (a compressed tarball) like so:

```
# tar xvzf mysql-3.23.58-pc-linux-i686.tar.gz
```

The source code form of MySQL is distributed in a 12MB archive, either in a source RPM (SRPM) or compressed tape archive format (.tgz). Download, then uncompress the archive either using the rpm or tar command. Directions for building and then installing the MySQL distribution are contained in a file named INSTALL-SOURCE, found in the resulting directory after unpacking. You'll get step-by-step instructions for a 'Quick Standard' installation similar to that required for the binary distribution.

After installing from binary or source, properly setting up the MySQL directories according to directions included in the binary and source package INSTALL file, and performing any required post-installation configuration, you can start the server from the /usr/local/ mysql directory. You do so by using a shell script named mysql_safe (found in the /usr/local/mysql/bin directory) like this:

```
# bin/mysqld_safe —user=mysql &
```

If you install from the RPM, the necessary users and groups for MySQL are created automatically. Otherwise, you should follow the source or binary instructions to create a user and group for which MySQL can run. The group and the user should both be named mysql. These accounts should be configured so that they cannot be logged in to because their only purpose is to run the MySQL server daemon. See Chapter 9, "Managing Users," for more information on how to create accounts.

17

Initializing the Data Directory in MySQL

After you have MySQL installed, you need to initialize the *grant tables*, or permissions to access any or all databases and tables and column data within a database. You can do this by issuing the `mysql_install_db` command from the `scripts` directory of the same directory in which MySQL is installed. If you install MySQL from the CDs included with this book, the directory is `/usr/bin`. This command initializes the grant tables and creates a MySQL root user. If you install MySQL from source, the default directory is `/usr/local/mysql`.

> **CAUTION**
>
> The MySQL data directory needs to be owned by the user as which MySQL will run (changing ownership using the `chown` command). In addition, only this user should have any permissions on this directory. (In other words, the permissions should be set to `700` by using `chmod`.) Setting up the data directory any other way creates a security hole.

For example, you should run the `mysql_install_db` command as root, like so:

```
# mysql_install_db
Preparing db table
Preparing host table
Preparing user table
Preparing func table
Preparing tables_priv table
Preparing columns_priv table
Installing all prepared tables
020916 17:39:05 /usr/libexec/mysqld: Shutdown Complete
...
```

The command prepares MySQL for use on the system, and it reports helpful information. The next step is to set the password for the MySQL root user, which is discussed in the following section.

> **CAUTION**
>
> By default, the MySQL root user is created with no password. This is one of the first things you must change because the MySQL root user has access to all aspects of the database. The following section explains how to change the password of the user.

Setting a Password for the MySQL Root User

To set a password for the root MySQL user, you need to connect to the MySQL server as the root MySQL user; you can use the command `mysql -u root` to do so. This command connects you to the server with the MySQL client (which is discussed later in this chapter, in the section "The MySQL Command-Line Client"). When you have the MySQL command prompt, issue a command like the following to set a password for the root user:

```
mysql> SET PASSWORD FOR root = PASSWORD("secretword");
```

secretword should be replaced by whatever you want to be the password for the root user. You can use this same command with other usernames to set or change passwords for other database users.

After you enter a password, you can exit the MySQL client by typing **exit** at the command prompt.

Creating a Database in MySQL

In MySQL you create a database by using the CREATE DATABASE statement. To create a database, you connect to the server by typing mysql -u root -p and pressing Enter. After you do so, you are connected to the database as the MySQL root user and prompted for a password. After you enter the password, you are placed at the MySQL command prompt. Then you use the CREATE DATABASE command. For example, the following commands create a database called animals:

```
# mysql -u root -p
Enter password:
Welcome to the MySQL monitor. Commands end with ; or \g.
Your MySQL connection id is 1 to server version: 3.23.58

Type 'help;' or '\h' for help. Type '\c' to clear the buffer.

mysql> CREATE DATABASE animals;
Query OK, 1 row affected (0.00 sec)
mysql>
```

Another way to create a database is to use the mysqladmin command, as the root user, with the create keyword and the name of a new database. For example, to create a new database named reptiles, you use a command line like this:

```
# mysqladmin -u root -p create reptiles
```

Granting and Revoking Privileges in MySQL

You probably want to grant yourself some privileges, and eventually you'll probably want to grant privileges to other users. Privileges, also known as *rights*, are granted and revoked on four levels:

- *Global-level* rights allow access to any database on a server.

- *Database-level* rights allow access to all tables in a database.

17

- *Table-level* rights allow access to all columns within a table in a database.

- *Column-level* rights allow access to a single column within a database's table.

> **NOTE**
>
> Listing all the available privileges is beyond the scope of this chapter. See the MySQL documentation for more information.

To add a user account, you connect to the database by typing `mysql -u root -p` and pressing Enter. You are then connected as the root user and prompted for a password. (You did set a password for the root user, as instructed in the last section, right?) After you enter the root password, you are placed at the MySQL command prompt.

To grant privileges to a user, you use the GRANT statement, which has the following syntax:

```
grant what_to_grant ON where_to_grant TO user_name IDENTIFIED BY 'password';
```

The first option, *what_to_grant*, is the privileges you are granting to the user. These privileges are specified with keywords. For example, the ALL keyword is used to grant global-, database-, table-, and column-level rights for a specified user.

The second option, *where_to_grant*, is the resources on which the privileges should be granted. The third option, *user_name*, is the username to which you want to grant the privileges. Finally, the fourth option, *password*, is a password that should be assigned to this user. If this is an existing user who already has a password and you are modifying permissions, you can omit the IDENTIFIED BY portion of the statement.

For example, to grant all privileges on a database named `sampledata` to a user named `foobar`, you could use the following command:

```
GRANT ALL ON animals.* TO foobar IDENTIFIED BY 'secretword';
```

The user `foobar` can now connect to the database `sampledata` by using the password secretword, and `foobar` has all privileges on the database, including the ability to create and destroy tables. For example, the user `foobar` can now log in to the server (by using the current hostname—shuttle2, in this example), and access the database like so:

```
$ mysql -h shuttle2 -u foobar -p animals
Enter password:
Welcome to the MySQL monitor. Commands end with ; or \g.
Your MySQL connection id is 43 to server version: 3.23.58

Type 'help;' or '\h' for help. Type '\c' to clear the buffer.

mysql>
```

> **NOTE**
>
> See the section "The MySQL Command-Line Client," later in this chapter, for additional command-line options.

Later on, if you need to revoke privileges from `foobar`, you can use the `REVOKE` statement. For example, the following statement revokes all privileges from the user `foobar`:

```
REVOKE ALL ON animals FROM foobar;
```

Advanced database administration, privileges, and security are very complex topics that are beyond the scope of this book. See the section "Reference" at the end of this chapter for links to online documentation. You can also check out Luke Welling's and Laura Thompson's book, *PHP and MySQL Development* from Sams Publishing.

Installing and Configuring PostgreSQL

The latest PostgreSQL binary files and source are available at `http://www.postgresql.org`. The PostgreSQL RPMs are distributed as several files. At a minimum, you probably want the `postgresql`, `postgresql-server`, and `postgresql-libs` RPMs. You should see the `README.rpm-dist` file in the FTP directory `ftp://ftp.postgresql.org/pub/` to determine whether you need any other packages.

If you are installing from the Fedora RPM files, a necessary `postgres` user account (that is, an account with the name of the user running the server on your system) is created for you automatically:

```
$ fgrep postgres /etc/passwd
postgres:x:26:26:PostgreSQL Server:/var/lib/pgsql:/bin/bash
```

Otherwise, you need to create a user called `postgres` during the installation. This user shouldn't have login privileges because only root should be able to use su to become this user, and no one will ever log in directly as the user. (See Chapter 9 for more information on how to add users to a Fedora system.) After you have added the user, you can install each of the PostgreSQL RPMs that you downloaded, using the standard `rpm -i` command for a default installation.

Initializing the Data Directory in PostgreSQL

After the RPMs have been installed, you need to initialize the data directory. To do so, you must first create the data directory, and you must be the root user to do so. The following example assumes that the data directory is `/usr/local/pgsql/data`.

Create the `/usr/local/pgsql/data` directory (using `mkdir`) and change the ownerships of the directory (using `chown` and `chgrp`) so that it is owned by the user `postgres`. Then use su, and as the user `postgres`, issue the following commands:

```
# mkdir /usr/local/pgsql
# chown postgres /usr/local/pgsql
# chgrp postgres /usr/local/pgsql
# su - postgres
-bash-2.05b$ initdb -D /usr/local/pgsql/data
The files belonging to this database system will be owned by user "postgres".
This user must also own the server process.

The database cluster will be initialized with locale en_US.UTF-8.
This locale setting will prevent the use of indexes for pattern matching
operations.  If that is a concern, rerun initdb with the collation order
set to "C".  For more information see the Administrator's Guide.

creating directory /usr/local/pgsql/data... ok
creating directory /usr/local/pgsql/data/base... ok
creating directory /usr/local/pgsql/data/global... ok
creating directory /usr/local/pgsql/data/pg_xlog... ok
creating directory /usr/local/pgsql/data/pg_clog... ok
creating template1 database in /usr/local/pgsql/data/base/1... ok
creating configuration files... ok
initializing pg_shadow... ok
enabling unlimited row size for system tables... ok
initializing pg_depend... ok
creating system views... ok
loading pg_description... ok
creating conversions... ok
setting privileges on built-in objects... ok
vacuuming database template1... ok
copying template1 to template0... ok

Success. You can now start the database server using:

 /usr/bin/postmaster -D /usr/local/pgsql/data
or
 /usr/bin/pg_ctl -D /usr/local/pgsql/data -l logfile start
```

This initializes the database and sets the permissions on the data directory to their correct
values.

> **CAUTION**
>
> The `initdb` program sets the permissions on the data directory to 700. You should not change
> these permissions to anything else to avoid creating a security hole.

You can start the `postmaster` program with the following command (make sure that you are still the user `postgres`):

```
$ postmaster -D /usr/local/pgsql/data &
```

If you have decided to use a directory other than `/usr/local/pgsql/data` as the data directory, you should replace the directory in the `postmaster` command line with whatever directory you are using.

> **TIP**
>
> By default, Fedora makes the PostgreSQL data directory `/var/lib/pgsql/data`. This isn't a very good place to store the data, however, because most people do not have the necessary space in the `/var` partition for any kind of serious data storage. Note that if you do change the data directory to something else (such as `/usr/local/pgsql/data`, as in the examples in this section), you need to edit the PostgreSQL startup file (named `postgres`) located in `/etc/rc.d/init.d` to reflect the change.

Creating a Database in PostgreSQL

Creating a database in PostgreSQL is very straightforward, but it must be performed by a user who has permissions to create databases in PostgresSQL—for example, initially the user named `postgres`. You can then simply issue the following command from the shell prompt (not the PSQL client prompt, but a normal shell prompt):

```
# su - postgres
-bash-2.05b$ createdb database
```

where *database* is the name of the database that you want to create.

The `createdb` program is actually a wrapper that makes it easier to create databases without having to log in and use `psql`. However, you can also create databases from within `psql` with the `CREATE DATABASE` statement. Here's an example:

```
CREATE DATABASE database;
```

You need to create at least one database before you can start the `pgsql` client program. You should create this database while you're logged in as the user `postgres`. To log in as this user, you need to use su to become root, and then use su to become the user `postgres`. To connect to the new database, you start the `psql` client program with the name of the new database as a command-line argument, like so:

```
$ psql sampledata
```

If you don't specify the name of a database when you invoke `psql`, the command attempts to connect to a database that has the same name as the user as which you invoke `psql` (that is, the default database).

17

Creating Database Users in PostgreSQL

To create a database user, you use su to become the user `postgres` from the Linux root account. You can then use the PostgreSQL `createuser` command to quickly create a user who is allowed to access databases or create new database users, like this:

```
$ createuser bball
Shall the new user be allowed to create databases? (y/n) y
Shall the new user be allowed to create more new users? (y/n) y
CREATE USER
```

In this example, the new user named `bball` is created and allowed to create new databases and database users (you should carefully consider who is allowed to create new databases or additional users).

You can also use the PostgreSQL command-line client to create a new user by typing `psql` along with name of the database and then use the `CREATE USER` command to create a new user. Here is an example:

```
CREATE USER foobar ;
```

> **CAUTION**
>
> PostgreSQL allows you to omit the `WITH PASSWORD` portion of the statement. However, doing so causes the user to be created with no password. This is a security hole, so you should always use the `WITH PASSWORD` option when creating users.

> **NOTE**
>
> When you are finished working in the `psql` command-line client, you can type `\q` to get out of it and return to the shell prompt.

Deleting Database Users in PostgreSQL

To delete a database user, you use the `dropuser` command, along with the user's name, and the user's access is removed from the default database, like this:

```
$ dropuser msmith
DROP USER
```

You can also log in to your database by using `psql` and then use the `DROP USER` commands. Here's an example:

```
$ psql demodb
Welcome to psql, the PostgreSQL interactive terminal.

Type: \copyright for distribution terms
```

```
\h for help with SQL commands
\? for help on internal slash commands
\g or terminate with semicolon to execute query
\q to quit

demodb=# DROP USER msmith ;
DROP USER
demodb=# \q
$
```

Granting and Revoking Privileges in PostgreSQL

As in MySQL, granting and revoking privileges in PostgreSQL is done with the GRANT and REVOKE statements. The syntax is the same as in MySQL except that PostgreSQL doesn't use the IDENTIFIED BY portion of the statement because with PostgreSQL, passwords are assigned when you create the user with the CREATE USER statement, as discussed previously. Here is the syntax of the GRANT statement:

```
GRANT what_to_grant ON where_to_grant TO user_name;
```

The following command, for example, grants all privileges to the user foobar on the database sampledata:

```
GRANT ALL ON sampledata TO foobar;
```

To revoke privileges, you use the REVOKE statement. Here's an example:

```
REVOKE ALL ON sampledata FROM foobar;
```

This command removes all privileges from the user foobar on the database sampledata.

Advanced administration and user configuration are complex topics. This section cannot begin to cover all the aspects of PostgreSQL administration or of privileges and users. For more information on administering PostgreSQL, see the PostgreSQL documentation or consult a book on PostgreSQL such as *PostgreSQL* (Sams Publishing).

Database Clients

Both MySQL and PostgreSQL use a client/server system for accessing databases. In the simplest terms, the database server handles the requests that come into the database, and the database client handles getting the requests to the server as well as getting the output from the server to the user.

Users never interact directly with the database server even if it happens to be located on the same machine that they are using. All requests to the database server are handled by a database client, which might or might not be running on the same machine as the database server.

Both MySQL and PostgreSQL have command-line clients. A command-line client is a very primitive way of interfacing with a database and generally isn't used by end users. As a DBA, however, you use the command-line client to test new queries interactively without having to write front-end programs for that purpose. In later sections of this chapter, you'll learn a bit about the MySQL graphical client and the Web-based database administration interfaces that are available for both MySQL and PostgreSQL.

The following sections examine two common methods of accessing a remote database, a method of local access to a database server, and the concept of Web access to a database.

> **NOTE**
>
> You should consider access and permission issues when setting up a database. Should users be able to create and destroy databases? Or should they only be able to use existing databases? Will users be able to add records to the database and modify existing records? Or should users be limited to read-only access to the database? And what about the rest of the world? Will the general public need to have any kind of access to your database through the Internet? As DBA, you must determine the answers to these questions.

SSH Access to a Database

Two types of remote database access scenarios are briefly discussed in this section. In the first scenario, the user directly logs in to the database server through SSH (to take advantage of the security benefits of encrypted sessions) and then starts a program on the server to access the database. In this case, shown in Figure 17.4, the database client is running on the database server itself.

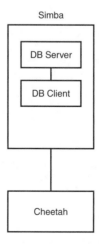

FIGURE 17.4   The user logs in to the database server located on host `simba` from the workstation (host `cheetah`). The database client is running on `simba`.

In the other scenario, shown in Figure 17.5, the user logs in to a remote host through SSH and starts a program on it to access the database, but the database is actually running on a different system. Three systems are now involved—the user's workstation, the remote host running the database client, and the remote host running the database server.

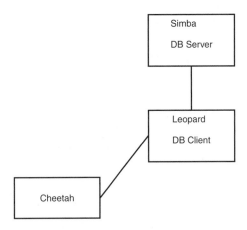

FIGURE 17.5   The user logs in to the remote host `leopard` from the workstation (host `cheetah`) and starts a database client on `leopard`. The client on `leopard` then connects to the database server running on host `simba`. The database client is running on `leopard`.

The important thing to note in Figure 17.5 is the middleman system `leopard`. Although the client is no longer running on the database server itself, it isn't running on the user's local workstation, either.

Local GUI Client Access to a Database

A user can log in to the database server by using a graphical client (which could be running on Windows, Macintosh, or a UNIX workstation). The graphical client then connects to the database server. In this case, the client is running on the user's workstation. Figure 17.6 shows an example.

Web Access to a Database

In this section, we look at two basic examples of Web access to the database server. In the first example, a user accesses the database through a form located on the World Wide Web. At first glance, it might appear that the client is running on the user's workstation. In fact, though, it isn't; the client is actually running on the Web server. The Web browser on the user's workstation simply provides a way for the user to enter the data that he wants to send to the database and a way for the results sent from the database to be displayed to the user. The software that actually handles sending the request to the database is running on the Web server in the form of a CGI script, a Java servlet, or embedded scripting such as the Hypertext Preprocessor (PHP) or Sun Microsystems, Inc.'s JavaServer Pages (JSP).

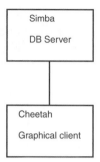

FIGURE 17.6   The user starts a GUI database program on his workstation (hostname cheetah). This program, which is the database client, then connects to the database server running on the host lion.

Often, the terms *client* and *front end* are interchangeable when speaking of database structures. However, Figure 17.7 shows an example of a form of access in which the client and the front end aren't the same thing at all. In this example, the front end is the form displayed in the user's Web browser. In such cases, the client is referred to as *middlewear*.

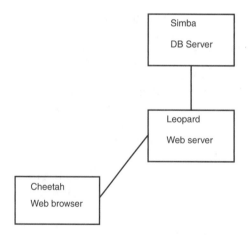

FIGURE 17.7   The user accesses the database through the World Wide Web. The front end is the user's Web browser, the client is running on *leopard*, and the server is running on *simba*.

In another possible Web access scenario, it could be said that the client is a two-piece application in which part of it is running on the user's workstation, and the other part is running on the Web server. For example, the database programmer can use JavaScript in the Web form to make sure that the user has entered a valid query. In this case, the user's query is partially processed on her own workstation and partially on the Web server. (Error checking is done on the user's own workstation. This helps reduce the load on the server and also helps reduce network traffic because the query is checked for errors before being sent across the network to the server.)

The MySQL Command-Line Client

The MySQL command-line client is `mysql`, and it has the following syntax:

```
mysql [options] [database]
```

Some of the available options for `mysql` are discussed in Table 17.1. *database* is optional, and if given, it should be the name of the database that you want to connect to.

TABLE 17.1 Command-Line Options to Use When Invoking `mysql`

Option	Action
-h *hostname*	Connects to the remote host *hostname* (if the database server isn't located on the local system).
-u *username*	Connects to the database as the user *username*.
-p	Prompts for a password. This option is required if the user you are connecting as needs a password to access the database. Note that this is a lowercase p.
-P *n*	Specifies *n* as the number of the port that the client should connect to. Note that this is an uppercase P.
-?	Displays a help message.

More options are available than are listed in Table 17.1, but these are the most common options. See the man page for `mysql` for more information on the available options.

> **CAUTION**
>
> Although `mysql` allows you to specify the password on the command line after the `-p` option, and thus allows you to avoid having to type the password at the prompt, you should never invoke the client this way. Doing so causes your password to display in the process list, and the process list can be accessed by any user on the system. This is a major security hole, so you should never give your password on the `mysql` command line.

You can access the MySQL server without specifying a database to use. After you log in, you use the `help` command to get a list of available commands, like this:

```
mysql> help

MySQL commands:
Note that all text commands must be first on line and end with ';'
help (\h) Display this help.
? (\?) Synonym for `help'.
clear (\c) Clear command.
connect (\r) Reconnect to the server. Optional arguments are db and host.
edit (\e) Edit command with $EDITOR.
ego (\G) Send command to mysql server, display result vertically.
exit (\q) Exit mysql. Same as quit.
```

17

```
go (\g) Send command to mysql server.
nopager (\n) Disable pager, print to stdout.
notee (\t) Don't write into outfile.
pager (\P) Set PAGER [to_pager]. Print the query results via PAGER.
print (\p) Print current command.
quit (\q) Quit mysql.
rehash (\#) Rebuild completion hash.
source (\.) Execute a SQL script file. Takes a file name as an argument.
status (\s) Get status information from the server.
tee (\T) Set outfile [to_outfile]. Append everything into given outfile.
use (\u) Use another database. Takes database name as argument.
```

You can then access a database by using the use command and the name of a database that has been created (such as animals) and that you are authorized to connect to, like this:

```
mysql> use animals
Database changed
mysql>
```

The PostgreSQL Command-Line Client

You invoke the PostgreSQL command-line client with the command psql. Like mysql, psql can be invoked with the name of the database to which you would like to connect. Also like mysql, psql can take several options. These options are listed in Table 17.2.

TABLE 17.2   Command-Line Options to Use When Invoking psql

Option	Action
-h hostname	Connects to the remote host hostname (if the database server isn't located on the local system).
-p n	Specifies n as the number of the port that the client should connect to. Note that this is a lowercase p.
-U username	Connects to the database as the user username.
-W	Prompts for a password after connecting to the database. In PostgreSQL 7 and later, password prompting is automatic if the server requests a password after a connection has been established.
-?	Displays a help message.

Several more options are available in addition to those listed in Table 17.2. See the psql's man page for details on all the available options.

Graphical Clients

If you'd rather interact with a database by using a graphical database client than with the command-line clients discussed in the previous section, you're in luck because a few options are available.

MySQL has an official graphical client, called MySQLGUI. MySQLGUI is available in both source and binary formats from the MySQL Web site at http://www.mysql.com.

Web-based administration interfaces are also available for MySQL and PostgreSQL. phpMyAdmin and phpPgAdmin are two such products. Both of these products are based on the PHP-embedded scripting language and therefore require you to have PHP installed. Of course, you also need to have a Web server installed.

Related Fedora and Database Commands

The following commands are useful for creating and manipulating databases in Fedora:

createdb—Creates a new PostgreSQL database

createuser—Creates a new PostgreSQL user account

dropdb—Deletes a PostgreSQL database

dropuser—Deletes a PostgreSQL user account

mysql—Interactively queries the mysqld server

mysqladmin—Administers the mysqld server

mysqldump—Dumps or backs up MySQL data or tables

pgaccess—Accesses a PostgreSQL database server

pg_ctl—Controls a PostgreSQL server or queries its status

psql—Accesses PostgreSQL via an interactive terminal

17

Reference

The following are references for the databases mentioned in this chapter:

http://www.mysql.com—This is the official Web site of the MySQL database server. Here you can find the latest versions as well as up-to-date information and online documentation for MySQL. You can also purchase support contracts here. You might want to look into this if you will be using MySQL in a corporate setting. (Many corporations balk at the idea of using software for which the company has no support contract in place.)

http://www.postgresql.org—This is the official Web site of the PostgreSQL database server. You are asked to select a mirror when you arrive at this site. After you select a mirror, you are taken to the main site. From there, you can find information on the latest versions of PostgreSQL and read the online documentation.

`http://www.postgresql.org/idocs/index.php?tutorial-start.html`—This interactive HTML documentation tree is a great place to get started with learning how to use PostgreSQL.

`http://www.pgsql.com`—This is a commercial company that provides fee-based support contracts for the PostgreSQL database.

CHAPTER **18**

Secure File Transfer Protocol Service

IN THIS CHAPTER

- Using FTP Clients
- FTP Servers
- Installing FTP Software
- The FTP User
- xinetd Configuration for wu-ftpd
- Configuring the Very Secure FTP Server
- Configuring the Wu-FTPd Server
- Using Commands in the ftpaccess File to Configure wu-ftpd
- Configure FTP Server File-Conversion Actions
- Using Commands in the ftphosts File to Allow or Deny FTP Server Connection
- Server Administration
- Reference

File Transfer Protocol (FTP) was once considered the primary method used to transfer files over a network from computer to computer. FTP is still heavily used today, although many graphical FTP clients now supplement the original text-based interface command. As computers have evolved, so has FTP, and Fedora Core includes many ways with which to use a graphical user interface, or GUI, to transfer files using the FTP protocol.

This chapter contains an overview of the available FTP software included with Fedora, along with some details concerning initial setup, configuration, and use of FTP-specific clients. Fedora also includes an FTP server software package named vsftpd, the Very Secure FTP Daemon, and a number of associated programs you can use to serve and transfer files with the FTP protocol.

The following sections provide an overview of how to use FTP clients, then how to install and configure the vsftpd FTP server.

Using FTP Clients

FTP is a client/server used to connect to the server. Nearly all FTP clients enable remote file transfers and display of remote directories. If enabled, clients also can allow users to create, delete, or modify remote directories and files.

Note however, that using FTP can pose a security risk: Usernames and passwords are transmitted in clear text across a LAN or the Internet. For this reason, many sites only enable anonymous FTP login and file retrieval. Many Linux users have turned to more secure alternatives, such as sshd and sftp or scp, included with OpenSSH (the free derivative of

Secure Shell). The following sections discuss the different types of newer and traditional interfaces to FTP and their usage.

Using `sftp` for Secure File Transfers

Use the Secure File Transfer `sftp` command, a client component of the OpenSSH distribution, to bypass the use of an FTP server and enable secure network file transfers. The `sftp` client uses the `sftp-server` server, which is not set up or configured as an FTP server, but is part of the `sshd` daemon. Using `sftp` provides the benefit of username and password encryption when logging in—your username and password will not be transmitted in clear text across a network. Although `sftp` does not have all the directory listing features of the text-based `ftp` command (such as wildcard expressions), it does have a representative subset of `ftp`'s built-in commands with many similar and matching capabilities.

The `sftp` command offers several different ways to transfer files. Most users will use `sftp` in its interactive mode—in which the IP address or remote hostname is specified on the command line in order to access the remote server, like so:

```
$ sftp 192.168.2.67
$ sftp portfolios.acme.edu
```

By default, you will access the remote server with your current username. However, you can use `sftp` to access a remote host with a different username by using an address form on the command line. For example,

```
$ sftp rnerette@portfolios.acme.edu
```

Most Linux hosts running `sshd` configure the service using port 22. However, some remote hosts can be configured to use a different port number. You can specify a specific port on the `sftp` command line by using its `-o` option, like so:

```
$ sftp -oPort=2221 rnerette@portfolios.acme.edu
```

In this example, you connect to a remote server via port 2221 with the username `rnerette`. After connecting, you will see a command prompt. You can then type a question mark (?) or the keyword `help` to see `sftp`'s built-in commands. Use commands such as `ls`, `get`, `put`, or `quit` to list, retrieve, upload, or quit the session.

You can also specify one or more files to retrieve on the command line by specifying a filename or wildcard match, like this:

```
$ sftp rnerette@portfolios.acme.edu:exam*
```

In this example, you will be prompted for the password for the user named `rnerette`. Then, all files with (or beginning with) the name `exam` will be retrieved from `rnerette`'s home directory on the remote host. If you have authentication keys set up on the local and remote server, you can transfer files without the need to enter a password.

You can use sftp to access a server if OpenSSH (which consists of the openssh-askpass, openssh-server, openssh-clients, and openssh- RPM packages) is installed and the ssh daemon is started. Secure FTP access is on by default, but can be controlled by editing the subsystem-sftp entry in /etc/ssh/sshd_config and restarting sshd (see Chapter 7, "Managing Services," to see how to start, stop, or restart services).

A companion command named scp can also be used to securely transfer files, but requires username and password access to the remote host, along with prior knowledge of the remote computer's file system and a specific pathname on the command line. For example, rnerette can transfer all files in the current directory from a PC at home to a specified directory in the home directory on a remote workstation at work using scp like so:

```
$ scp *.doc rnerette@portfolios.acme.edu:work
```

In this example, all files ending in .doc will be copied into the directory named work under the /home/rnerette directory (assuming users resides under /home on the host) on the remote workstation.

Data transfer rates will take a hit because of the overhead of encryption, but use of a secure session might be more important, especially if you're transferring files over an insecure network, such as the Internet or a wireless LAN.

The FTP Client Interface

Fedora provides FTP clients that support a graphical or a text-based FTP interface. No matter which type you choose, you can improve your understanding and use of FTP if you learn how to use the FTP client at the command line.

Using the text-based interface helps you understand what each action in a graphical FTP session does. This understanding can be handy when, for example, the graphic client doesn't automatically detect the file type being transferred. In this situation, a binary file is transferred as an ASCII file and is therefore useless. Conversely, an ASCII file transferred as a binary prints the ^M control character at the end of each line. This error typically occurs when transferring files from older Microsoft Windows operating systems to Linux, as the Windows FTP client defaulted to ASCII, not binary transfers.

The following sections describe how to use the text-based FTP client interface. After this explanation, you learn how to use the many graphical FTP clients available for Fedora.

Using the Text-based FTP Client Interface

Some of the following common commands may be used in a typical FTP session:

- ascii—Sets an ASCII file transfer type for the FTP session. You use this command before file transfers when sending or receiving text files.

- bin—Sets a binary file-type transfer for the FTP session. Use it before file transfers to send or receive binary files such as graphics images or compressed archives.

- bye—Use this command to close the FTP connection and quit the `ftp` command.

- close—Closes a connection to a remote server during an FTP session. Use this command instead of `quit` or `bye` to return to the `ftp` command prompt.

- get—Initiates a transfer of a single file from the FTP server to the user's local machine. Use this command to retrieve a single file (such as `get cartoon.jpg`).

- hash—Sets use of a hash mark (#) during file transfer. Use this command to get a visual indication of the progress of a transfer.

- mget—Initiates a transfer of multiple files from the FTP server to the user's local machine. Use this command to download (receive) multiple files with a single command (such as `mget *.jpg`).

- mput—Initiates a transfer of multiple files from the user's local machine to the FTP server. Use this command to upload (send) multiple files with a single command (such as `mput *.jpg`)/\.

- open—Opens a connection to a remote server using an IP address or hostname. Use this command when working at the `ftp` command prompt (such as `open ftp.redhat.com`).

- prompt—Is an interactive command that asks the user for input on whether to get a specific file when the `mput` or `mget` command is issued. If the user initiates an `mget *`, with prompting on, the FTP client will prompt the user to transfer each file that the * wildcard matches. This can be particularly useful when several files in a directory need to be transferred, with one or two files that are unwanted. By default, prompting is turned on.

- put—Initiates the transfer of a single file from the user's local machine to the FTP server. Use this command to upload (send) a single file (such as `put inventory.doc`).

- send—The same command as put.

- quit—The same command as bye.

> **TIP**
>
> Although this section of the chapter discusses the use of the standard FTP client, other text-based FTP clients are available for Linux. Nc-FTP, which is included on the Fedora Core CD-ROM or available from www.ncftp.com, gives users extra functionality, such as the ability to get multiple directories at one time (without performing recursive `mget`s) and reconstructing the directory structure on their local machines. The Web site for this product has a list of all features this client offers to the user—in addition to the standard set of actions described in the example.

These are just some of the commands available during an FTP session. By typing **help**, the user can see a full list of valid commands. Typing help command-name displays a brief description of what that command does. Listing 18.1 shows the help output.

LISTING 18.1   The Commands Listed by help in an FTP Session

```
Commands may be abbreviated.  Commands are:

!               cr              mdir            proxy           send
$               delete          mget            sendport        site
account         debug           mkdir           put             size
append          dir             mls             pwd             status
ascii           disconnect      mode            quit            struct
bell            form            modtime         quote           system
binary          get             mput            recv            sunique
bye             glob            newer           reget           tenex
case            hash            nmap            rstatus         trace
ccc             help            nlist           rhelp           type
cd              idle            ntrans          rename          user
cdup            image           open            reset           umask
chmod           lcd             passive         restart         verbose
clear           ls              private         rmdir           ?
close           macdef          prompt          runique
cprotect        mdelete         protect         safe
```

A Typical FTP Session Using the ftp Command

Connecting to a remote FTP server can require a username and password, but many servers also provide anonymous access. A properly configured remote FTP server responds quickly to FTP requests, and will display shared directories and files. This section shows a sample FTP session with a typical server found at many Internet sites (in this case, running the wu-ftpd server).

You connect to a remote FTP server by using the ftp command along with either the IP address or hostname of the remote computer, like so:

```
$ ftp pheniox
Connected to pheniox.
220 pheniox FTP server (Version wu-2.6.1-18) ready.
Name (pheniox:tdc): anonymous
331 Guest login ok, send your complete e-mail address as password.
Password:
230 Guest login ok, access restrictions apply.
Remote system type is UNIX.
Using binary mode to transfer files.
ftp>
```

18

In this example, `ftp` is used to connect and then login using anonymous access. This is done by entering the word anonymous at the Name prompt. After pressing Enter, a password prompt is displayed. When using anonymous access, it is considered "good form" to enter your email address as a courtesy. There is no validation of the address entered, but many FTP servers are configured to only accept a valid email address form (that is, `user@somewhere`) if any text is typed at the prompt.

> **TIP**
>
> Many FTP servers will accept a simple press of the Enter key at the password prompt if accessed anonymously.

Now that a connection has been established and authenticated to the server, you can then set up your FTP session to work the way you'd like by using internal client commands. As mentioned in the previous section, the `ftp` command has many different built-in commands, which you can view by typing a question mark at the `ftp>` prompt. These commands can affect the session display, set the type of file transfer, or obtain information about the remote server.

```
ftp> hash
Hash mark printing on (1024 bytes/hash mark).
ftp> prompt
Interactive mode off.
ftp> bin
200 Type set to I.
```

In this example, you have told `ftp` to print a hash (#) character for every 1,024 bytes that are transferred, turn off prompting, and set the transfer type to binary (which should be on by default). The hash character display provides a visual indicator of the progress of your download. Turning off prompting will allow you to retrieve multiple files without the need to confirm each transfer. Setting the transfer type to binary will ensure that binary files are transferred in the proper format instead of text.

Next, you ask the server to show a listing of what directories and files are available on the server.

```
ftp> ls
200 PORT command successful.
150 Opening ASCII mode data connection for directory listing.
total 32
d--x--x--x   2 root     root         4096 Aug 31 07:15 bin
d--x--x--x   2 root     root         4096 Aug 31 07:15 etc
d--x--x--x   2 root     root         4096 Aug 31 04:44 lib
d--x-x---x   2 root     50           4096 Sep  3 07:34 pub
226 Transfer complete.
```

If directory permissions in the FTP repository are set correctly, the pub directory should be the only directory that shows any files under it. To verify this, change directories to etc and list the contents.

```
ftp> cd etc
250 CWD command successful.
ftp> ls
200 PORT command successful.
150 Opening ASCII mode data connection for directory listing.
total 0
226 Transfer complete.
```

By setting the permissions to execute only on the directories bin, lib, and etc, a system administrator can restrict users from seeing any files in that directory. Good security dictates that remote users be denied information about a system, as any information could aid in hacking attempts.

Now that you see the server is relatively secure, change directories to pub and list the contents of that directory.

```
ftp> cd pub
250-Please read the file README
250-  it was last modified on Sun Sep  2 19:25:47 2001 - 1 day ago
250 CWD command successful.
ftp> ls
200 PORT command successful.
150 Opening ASCII mode data connection for directory listing.
total 552
-rw-r--r--   1 root      50              100 Sep  2 19:25 README
-rw-r--r--   1 root      50                8 Sep  3 07:33 configuration
-rw-r--r--   1 root      50                8 Sep  3 07:33 temp.txt
-rw-r--r--   1 root      50            15798 Sep  3 10:29 tftp-0.17-14.i386.rpm
-rw-r--r--   1 root      50            26011 Sep  3 10:30 tftp-
server-0.17-14.i386.rpm
-rw-r--r--   1 root      50           219332 Sep  3 10:29 wu-ftpd-
2.6.1-18.i386.rpm226 Transfer complete.
```

To transfer all the RPM files to your local machine, issue the mget *.rpm command.

```
ftp> mget *.rpm
local: tftp-0.17-14.i386.rpm remote: tftp-0.17-14.i386.rpm
200 PORT command successful.
150 Opening BINARY mode data connection for tftp-0.17-14.i386.rpm
(15798 bytes).###############
226 Transfer complete.
```

18

```
15798 bytes received in 0.974 secs (16 Kbytes/sec)
local: tftp-server-0.17-14.i386.rpm remote: tftp-server-0.17-
14.i386.rpm
200 PORT command successful.
150 Opening BINARY mode data connection for tftp-server-0.17-
14.i386.rpm (26011 bytes).
########################
226 Transfer complete.
26011 bytes received in 2.5 secs (10 Kbytes/sec)
local: wu-ftpd-2.6.1-18.i386.rpm remote: wu-ftpd-2.6.1-
18.i386.rpm
200 PORT command successful.
150 Opening BINARY mode data connection for wu-ftpd-2.6.1-
18.i386.rpm (219332 bytes).
##############################################################
##############################################################
##############################################################
##################
226 Transfer complete.
219332 bytes received in 50.3 secs (4.3 Kbytes/sec)
```

As described before, the mget command transferred all files with the .rpm extension to our local machine. The ftp client printed a # for each 1024 bytes transferred to our machine. This is helpful when transferring over a slow connection to ensure that the connection hasn't timed out.

> **TIP**
>
> After every action, the FTP server will return a status code and brief message showing the result of the command you issued. You can find a listing of all status codes and their corresponding messages in Request For Comment 959; you can access a copy of this listing at http://www.ietf.org/rfc/rfc959.txt.

Now you are finished with this session; you can issue the command quit or bye to end the session. Additionally, the FTP server will inform you of how many bytes your session transfers, how many files, and the total transferred data (in bytes) between your local machine and the server.

```
ftp> bye
221-You have transferred 503818 bytes in 5 files.
221-Total traffic for this session was 506422 bytes in 7 transfers.
221 Thank you for using the FTP service on pheniox.
```

This is a simple example, but average FTP sessions are similarly trivial. Several other commands are available during an FTP session, but they're rarely used. FTP has the capability to take scripted input and define macros that allow for a much more complicated session.

> **TIP**
>
> The FTP info pages are much like the man (manual) pages shipped with almost every command in Linux. More detailed information may be found in the command's source code package.

Using the `lftp` Command for File Transfers

The `lftp` command can be used for file transfers using FTP, HTTP, and various secure protocols such as HTTPS and HFTP if a remote proxy is enabled. Two great features of this command are the ability to restart a stalled download in the middle of a file transfer, as well as to start and run multiple downloads in a single session (with job control).

For example, here is a simple session showing an HTTP retrieval from a remote computer running the Apache Web server:

```
$ lftp http://192.168.2.37
cd ok, cwd=/
lftp 192.168.2.37:/> ls
-rw-r--r--   --  manual/mod/core.html
-rw-r--r--   --  manual/index.html
-rw-r--r--   --  icons/apache_pb.gif
-rw-r--r--   --  poweredby.png
lftp 192.168.2.37:/> get poweredby.png
1154 bytes transferred
lftp 192.168.2.37:/> bye
```

The `lftp` command can also be used as a "traditional" FTP client, but with some interesting features:

```
$ lftp 192.168.2.67 -u bball
Password:
lftp bball@192.168.2.67:~> cd /d2/isos/redhat/limbo
cd ok, cwd=/d2/isos/redhat/limbo
lftp bball@192.168.2.67:/d2/isos/redhat/limbo> mget disc1 &
[0] mget *disc1* &
lftp bball@192.168.2.67:/d2/isos/redhat/limbo> jobs
[0] mget *disc1*
        `limbo-i386-disc1.iso' at 56436448 (8%) 1.08M/s eta:9m [Receiving data]
lftp bball@192.168.2.67:/d2/isos/redhat/limbo> bye
[1843] Moving to background to complete transfers...
$ ps aux ¦ fgrep lftp
bball    1843  7.6  1.0  5456 2404 ?         S    19:09   0:02 lftp 192.168.2.67
```

18

A username (and password) can be passed on the command line using the -u option. You can use this feature to reduce the amount of interactive typing required when retrieving remote files, as an aid when using lftp in shell scripts, and when retrieving files with lftp as a background process.

By using an ampersand (&), the retrieval is conducted in the background, as shown in the preceding example. The jobs command is then used to show current transfers. If one logs out of the session (using the bye command), the file transfer continues as a background process if it has not completed. (This is verified by using the ps command.)

The lftp client has many additional features that can make the job of transferring files easier than using other FTP clients.

NOTE

Another handy text-based file transfer utility included with Fedora is curl, which supports HTTP for file retrieval.

Using the wget Command for File Transfers

The wget command is used for file transfers using FTP, HTTP, and various secure protocols such as HTTPS and HFTP if a remote proxy is enabled. However, wget only supports non-interactive transfers, unlike other FTP clients. This is actually a feature, as wget can be used to download files as a background process and to recursively replicate remote file directories. The command also supports download completion of partially downloaded files, which can save a lot of time during periods of intermittent connectivity or broken connections.

For example, here is a simple invocation showing FTP retrieval from a remote computer using wget and an FTP URL:

```
$ wget ftp://bball:mypasswd@stinky/mp3/*
--13:13:28--  ftp://bball:*password*@stinky/mp3/*
           => `.listing'
Resolving stinky... done.
Connecting to stinky[192.168.2.33]:21... connected.
Logging in as bball ... Logged in!
==> SYST ... done.    ==> PWD ... done.
==> TYPE I ... done.  ==> CWD /home/bball/mp3 ... done.
==> PORT ... done.    ==> LIST ... done.

   [ <=>                                  ] 648        632.81K/s

13:13:28 (632.81 KB/s) - `.listing' saved [648]


Removed `.listing'.
--13:13:28--  ftp://bball:*password*@stinky/mp3/C31821-01A.mp3
```

```
        => `C31821-01A.mp3'
==> CWD not required.
==> PORT ... done.     ==> RETR C31821-01A.mp3 ... done.
Length: 5,172,089

60% [=====================>                ] 3,123,680    264.80K/s    ETA 00:07
```

In this example, the user retrieves all files in a directory named mp3 (under /home/bball) on the remote host named stinky. The wget command will first retrieve a directory listing, then proceed to download the specified files (all marked with '*' in this example). Note that you can specify a username and password (mypasswd in the example) on the command. This generally isn't a good idea. A better, but still not really secure, approach is to save the password in a file named .wgetrc in your home directory. See the wget man page for more information.

> **TIP**
>
> Complete documentation for wget is available on a single Web page at: http://www.gnu.org/software/wget/manual/wget-1.8.1/html_mono/wget.html.

Using Graphical FTP Clients

Many graphical FTP clients are available for Linux. Fedora includes the graphical gFTP client and network-aware browsers included with GNOME and KDE. These browsers feature built-in drag-and-drop capability, thus ensuring FTP functionality. Other graphical interface clients that can be used for FTP include the Mozilla Web browser, KDE's konqueror, GNOME's epiphany, and the Nautilus file manager.

Using the gFTP Interface

The GNOME gFTP client provides all the typical features of FTP, including the ability to save profiles of common connections. Figure 18.1 shows a typical gFTP session in action. On the left panel is the local host, and on the right panel is the remote server. A connection is initiated by typing the address of the host into the host field, a specific port if not the standard FTP port (21), a valid username for the server, and a password. After the information has been entered, clicking the icon that looks like a monitor will start the connection to the server. The bottom panel displays session information, such as changing directories, as seen in Figure 18.1.

gFTP sets the file type as binary by default, which can be changed by clicking on ASCII in the FTP drop-down menu. To upload a file to the server, the user clicks on a filename in the left panel and clicks on the right arrow icon. The file is then transferred to the server, and the right panel will be updated to reflect this new file being added to the server. Similarly, to download a file from the server, the user selects the correct file type from the drop-down menu, selects the file to be downloaded, and clicks the left arrow icon. The left

18

panel will then be updated to show the result of the transfer, with logging information shown in the bottom panel.

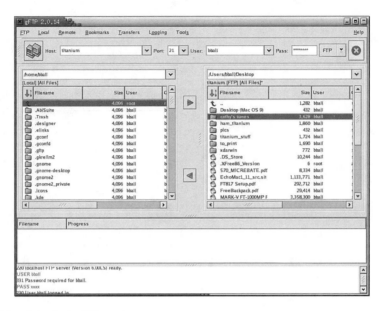

FIGURE 18.1   A typical gFTP session.

After all files are uploaded or downloaded, you must close the session. Do this by clicking the red button on the top right of the application window to issue the quit command. gFTP displays the session summary information in the log panel at the bottom of the application.

Although using a graphical interface, you still need to understand the basic functionality of FTP to use gFTP. Not knowing the file type that needs to be set can result in wasted time downloading a binary file in ASCII format, thus rendering the file unusable. gFTP defaults to a binary file type, but detects the file type during the transfer. gFTP is a robust application, providing all the necessary actions typical of an FTP session, in a pretty, easy-to-use format.

FTP Sessions with Konqueror and Nautilus

Both the K Desktop Environment (KDE) and the GNU Network Object Model Environment (GNOME) graphical browsers have integrated FTP functionality built in to window management. You can also use FTP with the Nautilus or Konqueror file browsers. Use an `ftp://` URL followed by a server name or IP address to start an anonymous FTP session. The drag-and-drop feature of KDE and the GNOME window manager allow users to select remote files and drag them to the desktop.

KDE's Konqueror Web browser is capable of handling a number of networking and file transfer protocols, including FTP. You can configure various settings for this browser, such as the appearance of the browser's toolbar, but one of Konqueror's best features is its flexibility for file transfers.

Start the browser by clicking its icon on the KDE's kicker desktop panel or by typing the following at the command line:

```
$ konqueror &
```

After launching the client, you can use the ftp:// URL form to access remote servers, as shown in Figure 18.2.

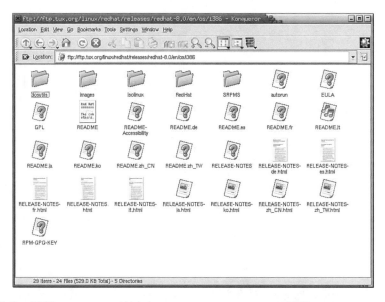

FIGURE 18.2   KDE's konqueror Web browser can access remote FTP servers.

If your window manager does not support drag and drop, you can use konqueror's copy files feature to easily retrieve a file. First, type in an FTP URL (such as ftp://ftp.tux.org). Next, navigate to a desired directory and click to select a desired file. You then click the Edit menu's Copy Files menu item (or press F7). A Save dialog will appear, and you can subsequently select your home directory to save the file. After you press Enter, a file download progress dialog will be displayed while the file is being retrieved.

You can also use the Nautilus browser to retrieve files from a remote server. Start Nautilus from the command line like this:

```
$ nautilus &
```

18

Figure 18.3 shows an anonymous login to a remote FTP server using Nautilus. Browse to a remote FTP server using an FTP URL, then simply click to select a file, select Copy from the Edit menu (or press Ctrl+C), click to go to your home directory (using the icon in the Nautilus toolbar), and then click Paste (or press Ctrl+V) to retrieve and save the file.

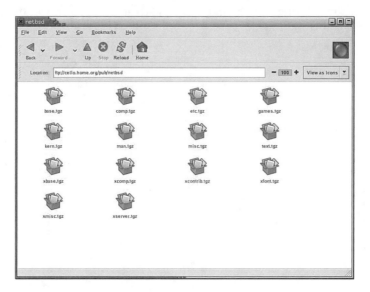

FIGURE 18.3   The Nautilus file browser can be used for FTP sessions.

These types of intuitive features can shield users from needing to know the details of how FTP works or memorizing various commands.

FTP Servers

FTP uses a client/server model. As a client, FTP accesses a server, and as a server, FTP provides access to files or storage. Just about every computer platform available has software written to enable a computer to act as an FTP server, but Fedora provides the average user the ability to do this without paying hefty licensing fees and without regard for client usage limitations.

There are two types of FTP servers and access: anonymous and standard. A *standard* FTP server requires an account name and password from anyone trying to access the server. *Anonymous* servers allow anyone to connect to the server to retrieve files. Anonymous servers provide the most flexibility, but they can also present a security risk. Fortunately, as you'll read in this chapter, Fedora is set up to use proper file and directory permissions and commonsense default configuration, such as disallowing root to perform an FTP login.

> **NOTE**
>
> Many Linux users now use OpenSSH and its suite of clients, such as the `sftp` command, for a more secure solution when transferring files. The OpenSSH suite provides the `sshd` daemon and enables encrypted remote logins. See the section "Using `sftp` for Secure File Transfers" in this chapter for information about how to use encryption in your file transfers.

Choosing an Authenticated or Anonymous Server

When you are preparing to set up your FTP server, you must first make the decision to install either the authenticated or anonymous service. *Authenticated* service requires the entry of a valid username and password for access. As previously mentioned, *anonymous* service allows the use of the username anonymous and an email address as a password for access. (Note that even if the mail address is bogus, many FTP sites will accept the anonymous login.)

Authenticated FTP servers are used to provide some measure of secure data transfer for remote users, but will require maintenance of user accounts as usernames and passwords are used. Anonymous FTP servers are used when user authentication isn't needed or necessary, and can be helpful in providing an easily accessible platform for customer support or public distribution of documents, software, or other data.

If you use an anonymous FTP server in your home or business Linux system, it's vital that you properly install and configure it to retain a relatively secure environment. Generally, sites that host anonymous FTP servers place them outside of the firewall on a dedicated machine. The dedicated machine contains only the FTP server and should not contain data that cannot be restored quickly. This dedicated-machine setup prevents malicious users who compromise the server from obtaining critical or sensitive data. For an additional, but by no means a more secure setup, the FTP portion of the file system can be mounted read-only from a separate hard drive partition or volume, or mounted from read-only media, such as CD-ROM, DVD, or other optical storage.

Fedora Core Linux includes an FTP server package with its distribution, but other FTP packages also work with Fedora Linux. The following sections discuss FTP servers in both categories.

Fedora FTP Server Packages

The Very Secure `vsftpd` server, like `wu-ftpd` also discussed in this chapter, is licensed under the GNU GPL. The server can be used for personal or business purposes. Other FTP servers are available for Fedora, but only `vsftpd` comes bundled with this book's CD-ROMs. The `wu-ftpd` and `vsftpd` servers will be covered in the remainder of this chapter.

Other FTP Servers

One alternative server is NcFTPd, available from `http://www.ncftp.com`. This server operates independently of `xinetd` (typically used to enable and start the `wu-ftp` server) and provides its own optimized daemon. Additionally, NcFTPd has the capability to cache directory listings of the FTP server in memory, thereby increasing the speed at which users can obtain a list of available files and directories. Although NcFTPd has many advantages over wu-ftpd, NcFTPd isn't GPL licensed software, and its licensing fees vary according to the maximum number of simultaneous server connections ($199 for 51 or more concurrent users and $129 for up to 50 concurrent users, but free to education institutions with a compliant domain name). Because of this licensing NcFTPd is not packaged with Fedora—you won't find it on this book's CD-ROMs.

> **NOTE**
>
> Do not confuse the ncftp client with ncftpd. The ncftp-3.1.7-4 package included with Fedora is the client software, a replacement for ftp-0.17-22, and includes the ncftpget and ncftpput commands for transferring files via the command line or by using a remote file uniform resource locator (URL) address. ncftpd is the FTP server, which can be downloaded from www.ncftpd.com.

Another FTP server package for Linux is ProFTPD, licensed under the GNU GPL. This server works well with most Linux distributions and has been used by a number of Linux sites, including ftp.kernel.org and ftp.sourceforge.net. ProFTPD is actively maintained and updated for bug fixes and security enhancements. Its developers recommend that you use the latest release (1.2.9 at the time of this writing) to avoid exposure to exploits and vulnerabilities. Browse to http://www.proftpd.org to download a copy.

Yet another FTP server package is Bsdftpd-ssl, which is based on the BSD ftpd (and distributed under the BSD license). Bsdftpd-ssl offers simultaneous standard and secure access using security extensions; secure access requires a special client. For more details, browse to http://bsdftpd-ssl.sc.ru/.

Finally, another alternative is to use Apache (and the HTTP protocol) for serving files. Using a Web server to provide data downloads can reduce the need to monitor and maintain a separate software service (or directories) on your server. This approach to serving files also reduces system resource requirements and gives remote users a bit more flexibility when downloading (such as enabling them to download multiple files at once). See Chapter 16, "Apache Web Server Management," for more information about using Apache.

Installing FTP Software

As part of the Workstation installation, the client software for FTP is already installed. You can verify that FTP-related software is installed on your system by using the RPM (Red Hat Package Manager), grep, and sort commands in this query:

```
$ rpm -qa | grep ftp | sort
```

The example results might differ, depending on what software packages are installed. In your Fedora file system, you'll find the file /usr/bin/pftp symbolically linked to

/usr/bin/ftp as well as the vsftpd server under the /usr/sbin directory. The base anonymous FTP directory structure is located under the /var/ftp directory. Other installed packages include additional text-based and graphical FTP clients.

> **NOTE**
>
> If you host an FTP server connected to the Internet, make it a habit to always check the Fedora site, http://fedora.redhat.com for up-to-date system errata, and security and bug fixes for your server software.

> **TIP**
>
> The Computer Emergency Response Team (http://www.cert.org) provides security advisories about current attacks and vulnerabilities on multiple platforms. Checking this site regularly for updates is a must for any site administrator. As a Fedora administrator (or user), you should also subscribe to Red Hat's announcement lists (see Appendix A, "Fedora Internet Resources").

Because the anonftp and wu-ftpd RPM packages are not included with Fedora, you must download and install them if you wish to use the wu-ftpd server. Retrieve the most recent packages for Linux from http://www.wu-ftpd.org/ to build from the latest source code, or obtain RPM packages from a reputable mirror.

Refer to Chapter 8, "Managing Software and System Resources," for information on how to use RPM packages, and Chapter 21, "C/C++ Programming Tools for Fedora," on how to build software packages from source code archives.

The FTP User

After installing Fedora, an FTP user will be created. This user is not a normal user per se, but a name for anonymous FTP users. The FTP user entry in /etc/passwd looks like

```
ftp:x:14:50:FTP User:/var/ftp:/sbin/nologin
```

> **NOTE**
>
> The FTP user, as discussed here, applies to anonymous FTP configurations and server setup.
>
> Also, note that other Linux distributions might use a different default directory, such as /usr/local/ftp, for FTP files and anonymous users.

This entry follows the standard /etc/passwd entry: username, password, User ID, Group ID, comment field, home directory, and shell.

To learn more about /etc/password, see the section "The Password File" in Chapter 9, "Managing Users."

18

Each of the items in this entry is separated by colons. In the preceding example, you can see that the Fedora system hosting the server uses shadowed password because an x is present in the traditional password field. The shadow password system is important because it adds an additional level of security to Fedora; the shadow password system is normally installed during the Fedora installation.

The FTP server software uses this user account to assign permissions to users connecting to the server. By using a default shell of /sbin/nologin for anonymous FTP users versus /bin/bash or some other standard, interactive shell, an anonymous FTP user, will be unable to log in as a regular user. /sbin/nologin isn't a shell, but a program usually assigned to an account that has been locked. As root inspection of the /etc/shadow file shows (see Listing 18.2), it isn't possible to log in to this account, denoted by the * as the password.

LISTING 18.2   Shadow Password File FTP User Entry

```
# cat /etc/shadow
bin:*:11899:0:99999:7:::
daemon:*:11899:0:99999:7:::
adm:*:11899:0:99999:7:::
lp:*:11899:0:99999:7:::
...
ftp:*:12276:0:99999:7:::
...
```

The shadow file (only a portion of which is shown in Listing 18.2) contains additional information not found in the standard /etc/passwd file, such as account expiration, password expiration, whether the account is locked, and the encrypted password. The * in the password field indicates that the account isn't a standard login account; thus, it doesn't have a password.

Although shadow passwords are in use on the system, passwords aren't transmitted in a secure manner when using FTP. Because FTP was written before the necessity of encryption and security, it doesn't provide the mechanics necessary to send encrypted passwords. Account information is sent in plain text on FTP servers; anyone with enough technical knowledge and a network sniffer can find the password for the account you connect to on the server. Many sites use an anonymous-only FTP server specifically to prevent normal account passwords from being transmitted over the Internet.

Figure 18.4 shows a portion of an ethereal capture of an FTP session for the user named *cathy* and her password ("ilikecatz"). The ethereal client is a graphical browser used to display network traffic in real time, and it can be used to watch packet data, such as an FTP login on a LAN.

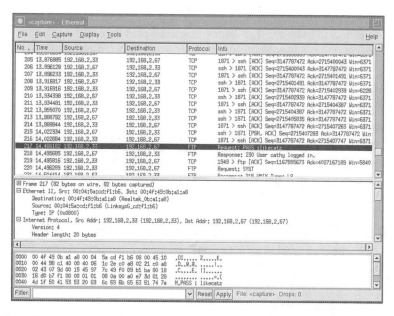

FIGURE 18.4   The `ethereal` client can filter and sniff FTP sessions to capture usernames and passwords.

Quick and Dirty FTP Service

Conscientious Linux administrators will take the time to carefully install, set up, and configure a production FTP server before offering public service or opening up for business on the Internet. However, you can set up a server very quickly on a secure LAN by following a few simple steps:

1. Ensure that the FTP server RPM package is installed, networking is enabled, and firewall rules on the server allow FTP access. See Chapter 13, "Network Connectivity," to see how to use Red Hat's `system-config-securitylevel` client for firewalling.

2. If anonymous access to server files is desired, populate the `/var/ftp/pub` directory. Do this by mounting or copying your content, such as directories and files under this directory.

3. Edit, and then save the appropriate configuration file (such as `vsftpd.conf` for `vsftpd`) to enable access.

4. If you are using `wu-ftpd`, you must then start or restart `xinetd` like so: `/etc/rc.d/init.d/xinetd restart`. If you are using `vsftpd`, you must then start or restart the server like so: `service vsftpd start`.

---

xinetd **Configuration for** wu-ftpd

`xinetd` (pronounced "zy-net-d") is the extended Internet services daemon, and handles incoming connections for network services. `xinetd` is the preferred replacement for a similar tool (used with other Linux distributions and older Red Hat releases) called inetd. However, in addition to several other improvements over inetd, xinetd allows you to apply individual access policies to different network connection requests, such as FTP.

This daemon controls a number of services on your system according to settings in configuration files under the /etc/xinetd.d directory. This section shows you how to edit the appropriate files to enable the use of the wu-ftpd FTP server.

Configuring xinetd for the wu-ftp Server

When installing wu-ftp using RPM, the RPM package may contain an xinetd configuration file, /etc/xinetd.d/wu-ftpd, as seen in Listing 18.3. You need to edit the file because its default settings disable incoming FTP requests.

> **NOTE**
>
> Don't be confused by the first line of the wu-ftpd file's text. Even though it reads default: on, FTP service is off unless you specifically configure its use. The line is a comment because it begins with a pound sign (#) and is ignored by xinetd. Whether FTP service is on is determined by the text line disable = yes.

LISTING 18.3   xinetd Configuration File for wu-ftpd

```
# default: on
# description: The wu-ftpd FTP server serves FTP connections. It uses \
#        normal, unencrypted usernames and passwords for authentication.
service ftp
{
disable = yes
        socket_type             = stream
        wait                    = no
        user                    = root
        server                  = /usr/sbin/in.ftpd
        server_args             = -l -a
        log_on_success          += DURATION
        nice                    = 10

}
```

Using an editor, change the disable = yes line to disable = no. Save the file and exit the editor. You then must restart xinetd because configuration files are only parsed at startup. To restart xinetd as root, issue the command **/etc/rc.d/init.d/xinetd restart**. This makes a call to the same shell script that is called at any runlevel to start or stop the xinetd daemon (and thus start up or shut down the system). xinetd should report its status as

```
# /etc/rc.d/init.d/xinetd restart
Stopping xinetd:                                    [  OK  ]
Starting xinetd:                                    [  OK  ]
```

Once restarted, the FTP server is accessible to all incoming requests.

Starting the Very Secure FTP Server (vsftpd) Package

Previous versions of Red Hat's Linux distributions required you to edit a file named vsftp under the /etc/xinetd.d directory in order to enable and start the Very Secure FTP server, vsftpd. However, with Fedora you can now simply use the system-config-services client or service command to start vsftpd. For example, start the server using the service command like this:

```
# service vsftpd start
Starting vsftpd for vsftpd:                         [  OK  ]
```

Use the system-config-services client or service command to start, stop, or restart the vsftpd server. Do not run two FTP servers on your system at the same time!

> **TIP**
>
> You can also use the shell script named vsftpd under the /etc/rc.d/init.d directory to start, stop, restart, and query the vsftpd server. You must have root permission to use the vsftpd script to control the server, but any user can query the server (in order to see if it is running and to see its Process ID number) using the status keyword like this:
>
> ```
> $ /etc/rc.d/init.d/vsftpd status
> ```

Configuring the Very Secure FTP Server

The vsftpd server, although not as popular as Wu-FTPd, is used by Red Hat, Inc. for its FTP server operations. (The vsftpd server home page is located at http://vsftpd. beasts.org/.) The server offers features such as simplicity, security, and speed. It has been used by a number of sites, such as ftp.debian.org, ftp.gnu.org, rpmfind.net, and ftp.gimp.org. Note that despite its name, the Very Secure FTP server does *not* enable use of encrypted usernames or passwords.

Its main configuration file is vsftpd.conf, which resides under the /etc/vsftpd directory. The server has a number of features and default policies, but these can be overridden by changing the installed configuration file.

By default, anonymous logins are enabled, but users are not allowed to upload files, create new directories, or delete or rename files. The configuration file installed by Fedora allows local users (that is, users with a login and shell account) to log in and then access their home directory. This configuration presents potential security risks because usernames and passwords are passed without encryption over a network. The best policy is to deny your users access to the server from their user accounts. The standard `vsftpd` configuration disables this feature.

Controlling Anonymous Access

Toggling anonymous access features for your FTP server is done by editing the `vsftpd.conf` file and changing related entries to YES or NO in the file. Settings to control how the server works for anonymous logins include

> `anonymous_enable`—Enabled by default; use a setting of NO, and then restart the server to turn off anonymous access.
>
> `anon_mkdir_write_enable`—Allows or disallows creating of new directories.
>
> `anon_other_write_enable`—Allows or disallows deleting or renaming of files and directories.
>
> `anon_upload_enable`—Controls whether anonymous users can upload files (also depends on the global `write_enable` setting); this is a potential security and liability hazard and should rarely be used; if enabled, consistently monitor any designated upload directory.
>
> `anon_world_readable_only`—Only allows anonymous users to download files with world-readable (444) permission.

After making any changes to your server configuration file, make sure to restart the server; this forces `vsftpd` to reread its settings.

Other `vsftpd` Server Configuration Files

You can edit `vsftpd.conf` to enable, disable, and configure many features and settings of the `vsftpd` server, such as user access, filtering of bogus passwords, and access logging. Some features might require the creation and configuration of other files, such as

> `/etc/vsftpd.user_list`—Used by the `userlist_enable` and/or the `userlist_deny` options; the file contains a list of usernames to be denied access to the server.
>
> `/etc/vsftpd.chroot_list`—Used by the `chroot_list_enable` and/or `chroot_local_user` options, this file contains a list of users who are either allowed or denied access to a home directory. An alternate file can be specified using the `chroot_list_file` option.
>
> `/etc/vsftpd.banned_emails`—A list of anonymous password entries used to deny access if the `deny_email_enable` setting is enabled. An alternate file can be specified using the `banned_email` option.
>
> `/var/log/vsftpd.log`—Data transfer information is captured to this file if logging is enabled using the `xferlog_enable` setting.

Default `vsftpd` Behaviors

The contents of a file named `.message` (if it exists in the current directory) are displayed when a user enters the directory. This feature is enabled in the installed configuration file, but disabled by the daemon. FTP users are also not allowed to perform recursive directory listings, which can help reduce bandwidth use.

The PASV data connection method is enabled to let external users know the IP address of the FTP server. This is a common problem when using FTP from behind a firewall/gateway using IP masquerading or when incoming data connections are disabled. For example, here is a connection to an FTP server (running ProFTPD), an attempt to view a directory listing, and the resulting need to use ftp's internal passive command:

```
$ ftp ftp.tux.org
Connected to gwyn.tux.org.
220 ProFTPD 1.2.5rc1 Server (ProFTPD on ftp.tux.org) [gwyn.tux.org]
500 AUTH not understood.
KERBEROS_V4 rejected as an authentication type
Name (ftp.tux.org:gbush): gbush
331 Password required for gbush.
Password:
230 User gbush logged in.
Remote system type is UNIX.
Using binary mode to transfer files.
ftp> cd public_html
250 CWD command successful.
ftp> ls
500 Illegal PORT command.
ftp: bind: Address already in use
ftp>
ftp> pass
Passive mode on.
ftp> ls
227 Entering Passive Mode (204,86,112,12,187,89).
150 Opening ASCII mode data connection for file list
-rw-r--r--   1 gbush    gbush        8470 Jan 10  2000 LinuxUnleashed.gif
-rw-r--r--   1 gbush    gbush        4407 Oct  4  2001 RHU72ed.gif
-rw-r--r--   1 gbush    gbush        6732 May 18  2000 SuSEUnleashed.jpg
-rw-r--r--   1 gbush    gbush        6175 Jan 10  2000 TYSUSE.gif
-rw-r--r--   1 gbush    gbush        3135 Jan 10  2000 TZones.gif
...
```

18

> **NOTE**
>
> Browse to http://slacksite.com/other/ftp.html for a detailed discussion regarding active and passive FTP modes and the effect of firewall blocking of service ports on FTP server and client connections.

Other default settings are that specific user login controls are not set, but you can configure the controls to deny access to one or more users.

The data transfer rate for anonymous client access is unlimited, but a maximum rate (in bytes per second) can be set using the anon_max_rate setting in vsftpd.conf. This can be useful for throttling bandwidth use during periods of heavy access. Another default is that remote clients will be logged out after five minutes of idle activity or a stalled data transfer. You can set idle and transfer timeouts (stalled connections) separately.

Other settings that might be important for managing your system's resources (networking bandwidth or memory) when offering FTP access include

> dirlist_enable—Toggles directory listings on or off.
>
> dirmessage_enable—Toggles display of a message when user enters a directory; a related setting is ls_recurse_enable, which can be used to disallow recursive directory listings.
>
> download_enable—Toggles downloading on or off.
>
> max_clients—Sets a limit on the maximum number of connections.
>
> max_per_ip—Sets a limit on the number of connections from the same IP address.

TIP

A number of techniques, such as adjusting TCP socket buffers based on bandwidth characteristics, have been researched in an effort to speed up FTP file transfers. Many factors can slow FTP server performance. Disk I/O, system resources such as RAM, and network speeds are just some of these factors. Directories containing large numbers of files can cause bottlenecks. Even the underlying file system can slow file transfers. Tuning your system's disk I/O, interrupt priorities, network interfaces, and use of TCP are only a few approaches for improving transfer speeds. For additional ideas and a list of links to other system tuning information, browse to http:// linuxperf.nl.linux.org/.

Configuring the Wu-FTPd Server

Wu-FTP uses a number of configuration files to control how it operates, including the following:

- ftpaccess—Contains the majority of server configuration settings
- ftpconversions—Contains definitions of file conversions during transfers
- ftphosts—Settings to control user access from specific hosts

These files may be created in the /etc directory during RPM installation, or may be created by a system administrator. The following sections describe each of these files and how to use the commands they contain to configure the Wu-FTP server is accessible to all incoming requests.

CAUTION

When configuring an anonymous FTP server, it is extremely important to ensure that all security precautions are taken to prevent malicious users from gaining privileged level access to the server. Although this chapter shows you how to configure your FTP server for secure use, all machines connected to the Internet are potential targets for malicious attacks. Vulnerable systems can be a source of potential liability, especially if anyone accesses and uses them to store illegal copies of proprietary software—even temporarily. There is little value in configuring a secure FTP server if the rest of the system is still vulnerable to attack. Use Red Hat's `lokkit` or `system-config-securitylevel` client to implement a firewall on your system.

TIP

Whenever editing the FTP server files, make a backup file first. Also, it's always a good idea to comment out (using a pound sign at the beginning of a line) what is changed instead of deleting or overwriting entries. Follow these comments with a brief description why the change was made. This leaves a nice audit trail of what was done, by whom, when, and why. If you have any problems with the configuration, these comments and details will help you troubleshoot and return to valid entries if necessary. You can use the `rpm` command or other Linux tools (such as `mc`) to extract a fresh copy of a configuration file from the software's RPM archive. Be aware, however, that the extracted version will replace the current version and overwrite your configuration changes.

NOTE

Back up the FTP server configuration files to another machine, should any of the working copies become corrupt. There might be a need to replicate server configurations across multiple hosts or revert back to an original copy of the defaults at some point in time. By making regular backups before changing a file, you guarantee that the changes can be undone and a working server restored with minimal down time.

18

Using Commands in the `ftpaccess` File to Configure `wu-ftpd`

The `ftpaccess` file contains most of the server configuration details. Each line contains a definition or parameter that is passed to the server to specify how the server is to operate. The directives can be broken down into the following categories, including

- Access Control—Settings that determine who can access the FTP server and how it is accessed

- Information—Settings that determine what information is provided by the server or displayed to a user

- Logging—Settings that determine if logging is enabled and what information is logged

- Permission Control—Settings that control the behavior of users when accessing the server; in other words, what actions users are allowed to perform, such as create a directory, upload a file, delete a file or directory, and so on

---

TIP

Many more options can be specified for the wu-ftpd FTP server in its ftpaccess file. The most common commands have been covered here. A full list of configuration options can be found in the ftpaccess man page after you install the server.

You can edit the ftpaccess file at the command line to make configuration changes in any of these categories. The following sections describe some configuration changes and how to edit these files to accomplish them.

Configure Access Control

Controlling which users can access the FTP server and how they can access it is a critical part of system security. Use the following entries in the ftpaccess file to specify to which group the user accessing the server is assigned.

Limit Access for Anonymous Users

This command imposes increased security on the anonymous user:

```
autogroup <group name> <class> [<class>]
```

If the anonymous user is a member of a group, he will only be allowed access to files and directories owned by him or his group. The group must be a valid group from /etc/groups or /var/ftp/etc/groups.

Define User Classes

This command defines a class of users by the address to which the user is connected.

```
class <class> <typelist> <addrglob> [<addrglob>]
```

There might be multiple members for a class of users, and multiple classes might apply to individual members. When multiple classes apply to one user, the first class that applies will be used.

The typelist field is a comma-separated list of the keywords anonymous, guest, and real. anonymous applies to the anonymous user, and guest applies to the guest access account, as specified in the guestgroup directive. real defines those users who have a valid entry in the /etc/passwd file.

The `addrglob` field is a regular expression that specifics addresses to which the class is to be applied. The (*) entry specifies all hosts.

Block a Host's Access to the Server

Sometimes it is necessary to block access to the server to entire hosts. This can be useful in order to protect the system from individual hosts or entire blocks of IP addresses, or to force the use of other servers. Use this command to do so:

```
deny <addrglob> <message_file>
```

deny will always deny access to hosts that match a given address.

addr_glob is a regular expression field that contains a list of addresses, either numeric or a DNS name. This field can also be a file reference, which contains a listing of addresses. If the address is a file reference, it must be an absolute file reference; that is, starting with a /. To ensure that IP addresses can be mapped to a valid domain name, use the !nameserver parameter.

A sample deny line resembles the following:

```
deny *.exodous.net /home/ftp/.message_exodous_deny
```

This entry will deny access to the FTP server from all users who are coming from the exodous.net domain, and will display the message contained in the file `.message_exoduous_deny` in the `/home/ftp` directory.

> **`ftpusers` File Purpose Now Implemented in `ftpaccess`**
>
> Certain accounts are created during the installation of Linux that are for the system to segment and separate tasks with specific permissions. The `ftpusers` file (located in `/etc/ftpusers`) is where accounts for system purposes are listed. It is possible that the version of `wu-ftp` you'll use with Fedora has depreciated the usage of this file, and instead implements the specific functionality of this file in the `ftpaccess` file with the commands of `deny-uid`/`deny-gid`.

Restrict Permissions Based on Group IDs

The `guestgroup` line assigns a given group name or group names to behave exactly like the anonymous user. Here is the command:

```
guestgroup <group name> [<group name>]
```

This command confines the user to a specific directory structure in the same way anonymous users are confined to `/var/ftp`. This command also limits these users to access files for which their assigned group has permissions.

The group name parameter can be the name of a group or that group's corresponding GID (Group ID). If you use a GID as the group name parameter, put a percentage symbol (%) in front of it. You can use this command to assign permissions to a range of group IDs, as in this example:

```
guestgroup %500-550
```

This entry would restrict all users with the group IDs 500–550 to be treated as a guest group, rather than individual users. In order for `guestgroup` to work, you must set up the user's home directories with the correct permissions, exactly like the anonymous FTP user.

Limit Permissions Based on Individual ID

The `guestuser` line works exactly like the `guestgroup` command you just read about, except it specifies a User ID (UID) instead of a group ID. Here's the command:

```
guestuser <username> [<username>]
```

This command limits the guest user to files for which the user has privileges. Generally, a user has more privileges than a group, so this type of assignment can be less restrictive than the `guestgroup` line.

Restrict the Number of Users in a Class

`limit` restricts the number of users in a class during given times. Here is the command, which contains fields for specifying a class, a number of users, a time range, and the name of a text file that contains an appropriate message:

```
limit <class> <n> <times> <message_file>
```

If the specified number of users from the listed class is exceeded during the given time period, the user sees the contents of the file given in the `message_file` parameter.

The `times` parameter is somewhat terse. The format for this is a comma-delimited string in the form of days, hours. Valid day strings are Su, Mo, Tu, We, Th, Fr, Sa, and Any. The hours are formatted in a 24-hour format. An example is as follows:

```
limit anonymous 10 MoTuWeThFr,Sa0000-2300 /home/ftp/.message_limit_anon_class
```

This line will limit the anonymous class to 10 concurrent connections on Monday through Friday, and on Saturday from midnight to 11:00 p.m. If the number of concurrent connections is exceeded or at 11:00 p.m. on Saturday, the users will see the contents of the file /home/ftp/.message_limit_anon_class.

Syntax for finer control over limiting user connections can be found in the `ftpaccess` man page.

Limit the Number of Invalid Password Entries

This line allows control over how many times a user can enter an invalid password before the FTP server terminates the session:

```
loginfails <number>
```

The default for `loginfails` is set to 5. This command prevents users without valid passwords from experimenting until they "get it right."

Configure User Information

Providing users with information about the server and its use is a good practice for any administrator of a public FTP server. Adequate user information can help prevent user problems and eliminate tech support calls. You also can use this information to inform users of restrictions governing the use of your FTP server. User information gives you an excellent way to document how your FTP server should be used.

You can use the commands detailed in the following sections to display messages to users as they log in to the server or as they perform specific actions. The following commands enable messages to be displayed to users when logging in to the server or when an action is performed.

Display a Prelogin Banner

This command is a reference to a file that is displayed before the user receives a login prompt from the FTP server:

```
banner <path>
```

Generally, this file contains information to identify the server. The path is an absolute pathname, relative to the system root (/), not the base of the anonymous FTP user's home. The entry might look like this:

```
banner /etc/rh8ftp.banner
```

This example uses the file named `rh8ftp.banner` under the `/etc` directory. The file can contain one or more lines of text, such as

```
Welcome to Widget, Inc.'s Red Hat Linux FTP server.
This server is only for use of authorized users.
Third-party developers should use a mirror site.
```

When an FTP user attempts to log in, the banner will be displayed like so:

```
$ ftp shuttle2
Connected to shuttle2.home.org.
220-Welcome to Widget, Inc.'s Red Hat Linux FTP server.
220-This server is only for use of authorized users.
220-Third-party developers should use a mirror site.
220-
220-
220 shuttle2 FTP server (Version wu-2.6.2-8) ready.
504 AUTH GSSAPI not supported.
504 AUTH KERBEROS_V4 not supported.
```

18

```
KERBEROS_V4 rejected as an authentication type
Name (shuttle2:bball):
```

Note that the banner does not replace the greeting text, which, by default, displays the host-name and server information, such as

```
220 shuttle2 FTP server (Version wu-2.6.2-8) ready.
```

To hide version information, use the `greeting` command in `ftpaccess` with a keyword, such as `terse`, like so:

```
greeting terse
```

FTP users will then see a short messages like this as part of the login text:

```
220 FTP server ready.
```

Also, not all FTP clients can handle multiline responses from the FTP server. The `banner<path>` command is how the banner line passes the file contents to the client. If a client cannot interrupt multiline responses, the FTP server will be useless to them. You should also edit the default banner to remove identity and version information.

Display a File

This line specifies a text file to be displayed to the user during login and when the user issues the `cd` command:

```
message <path> {<when> {<class> ...}}
```

The optional `when` clause can be `LOGIN` or `CWD=(dir)`, where `dir` is the name of a directory that is current. The optional `class` parameter enables messages to be shown only to a given class or classes of users.

Using messages is a good way to give information about where things are on your site as well as information that is system dependent, such as alternative sites, general policies regarding available data, server availability times, and so on.

You can use *magic cookies* to breathe life into your displayed messages. Magic cookies are symbolic constants that are replaced by system information. Table 18.1 lists valid magic cookies for the message command and their representation.

TABLE 18.1   Magic Cookies and Their Descriptions

Cookie	Description
%T	Local time (form Thu Nov 15 17:12:42 1990)
%F	Free space in partition of CWD (kbytes)
	[Not supported on all systems]

TABLE 18.1   Continued

Cookie	Description
%C	Current working directory
%E	The maintainer's email address as defined in `ftpaccess`
%R	Remote hostname
%L	Local hostname
%u	Username as determined via RFC931 authentication
%U	Username given at login time
%M	Maximum allowed number of users in this class
%N	Current number of users in this class
%B	Absolute limit on disk blocks allocated
%b	Preferred limit on disk blocks
%Q	Current block count
%I	Maximum number of allocated inodes (+1)
%i	Preferred inode limit
%q	Current number of allocated inodes
%H	Time limit for excessive disk use
%h	Time limit for excessive files
Ratios	
%xu	Uploaded bytes
%xd	Downloaded bytes
%xR	Upload/Download ratio (1:n)
%xc	Credit bytes
%xT	Time limit (minutes)
%xE	Elapsed time since login (minutes)
%xL	Time left
%xU	Upload limit
%xD	Download limit

To understand how this command works, imagine that you want to display a welcome message to everyone who logs in to the FTP server. An entry of

```
message /home/ftp/welcome.msg   login
message /welcome.msg            login
```

shows the contents of the `welcome.msg` file to all real users who log in to the server. The second entry shows the same message to the anonymous user.

The `welcome.msg` file isn't created with the installation of the RPM, but you can create it using a text editor. Type the following:

```
Welcome to the anonymous ftp service on %L!

There are %N out of %M users logged in.
```

```
Current system time is %T

Please send email to %E if there are
any problems with this service.

Your current working directory is %C
```

Save this file as `/var/ftp/welcome.msg`. Verify that it works by connecting to the FTP server:

```
220 FTP server ready.
504 AUTH GSSAPI not supported.
504 AUTH KERBEROS_V4 not supported.
KERBEROS_V4 rejected as an authentication type
Name (shuttle:bball): anonymous
331 Guest login ok, send your complete e-mail address as password.
Password:
230-Welcome to the anonymous ftp service on shuttle.home.org!
230-
230-There are 1 out of unlimited users logged in.
230-
230-Current system time is Mon Nov  3 10:57:06 2003
230-
230-Please send email to root@localhost if there are
230-any problems with this service.
230-Your current working directory is /
```

Display Administrator's Email Address

This line sets the email address for the FTP administrator:

```
email <name>
```

This string is printed whenever the %E magic cookie is specified. This magic cookie is used in the messages line or in the shutdown file. You should display this string to users in the login banner message so that they know how to contact you (the administrator) in case of problems with the FTP server.

> **CAUTION**
>
> Don't use your live email address in the display banner; you want others to be able to access user emails as necessary. Instead, use an alias address that routes the messages to the appropriate IT department or other address.

Notify User of Last Modification Date

The `readme` line tells the server if a notification should be displayed to the user when a specific file was last modified. Here's the command:

```
readme <path> {<when {<class>}}
```

The `path` parameter is any valid path for the user. The optional `when` parameter is exactly as seen in the message line. `class` can be one or more classes as defined in the class file. The `path` is absolute for real users. For the anonymous user, the `path` is relative to the anonymous home directory, which is `/var/ftp` by default.

Configure System Logging

Part of any system administration involves reviewing log files for what the server is doing, who accessed it, what files were transferred, and other pieces of important information. You can use a number of commands within `/etc/ftpacess` to control your FTP server logging actions.

Redirect Logging Records

This line allows the administrator to redirect where logging information from the FTP server will be recorded:

```
log <syslog>{+<xferlog>}
```

By default, the information for commands is stored in `/var/log/messages`, although the man pages packaged in some RPMs state that this information will be written to `/var/log/xferlog`. Check your server's settings for information regarding the location of your file transfer logs.

Log All User-Issued Commands

This line enables logging for all commands issued by the user:

```
log commands [<typelist>]
```

`typelist` is a comma-separated list of anonymous, guest, and real. If no `typelist` is given, commands are logged for all users. Some `wu-ftpd` RPMs set the logging of all file transfers to `/var/log/xferlog` (see the next section). However, you can add the `log` command to `ftpaccess` with the commands keyword to capture user actions. Logging will then be turned on and user actions captured in `/var/log/messages`. Here is an example of a sample log file:

```
Oct  6 12:21:42 shuttle2 ftpd[5229]: USER anonymous
Oct  6 12:21:51 shuttle2 ftpd[5229]: PASS bball@widget.com
Oct  6 12:21:51 shuttle2 ftpd[5229]: ANONYMOUS FTP LOGIN FROM 192.168.2.31
Â[192.168.2.31], bball@widget.com
Oct  6 12:21:51 shuttle2 ftpd[5229]: SYST
```

18

```
Oct  6 12:21:54 shuttle2 ftpd[5229]: CWD pub
Oct  6 12:21:57 shuttle2 ftpd[5229]: PASV
Oct  6 12:21:57 shuttle2 ftpd[5229]: LIST
Oct  6 12:21:59 shuttle2 ftpd[5229]: QUIT
Oct  6 12:21:59 shuttle2 ftpd[5229]: FTP session closed
```

The example log shows the username and password entries for an anonymous login. The CWD entry shows that a cd command is used to navigate to the pub directory. Note that the commands shown don't necessarily reflect the syntax the user typed in, but instead list corresponding system calls the FTP server received. For example, the LIST entry is actually the ls command.

Log Security Violations and File Transfers

Two other logging commands are useful in the /etc/ftpaccess configuration file. This line enables the logging of security violations:

```
log security [<typelist>]
```

Violations are logged for anonymous, guest, and real users, as specified in the typelist—the same as other log commands. If you don't specify a typelist, security violations for all users will be logged.

This line writes a log of all files transferred to and from the server:

```
log transfers [<typelist> [<directions>]]
```

typelist is the same as seen in log commands and log security lines. directions is a comma-separated list of the keywords inbound for uploaded files and outbound for downloaded files. If no directions are given, both uploaded and downloaded files will be logged. Inbound and outbound logging is turned on by default.

Configure Permission Control

Controlling user activity is an important component of securing your system's server. The ftpaccess file includes a number of commands that enable you to determine what users can and cannot execute during an FTP session. You can use these permission controls to allow users to change file permissions, delete or overwrite files, rename files, and to create new files with default permissions. You learn how to use all these ftpaccess file command lines in the following sections.

> **NOTE**
>
> By default, all the ftpaccess file command lines prohibit anonymous users from executing actions and enable authorized users to do so.

Allow Users to Change File Permissions

The chmod line determines if a user has the ability to change a file's permissions. Here is the command line:

```
chmod <yes¦no> <typelist>
```

This command acts the same as the standard chmod command.

The yes¦no parameter designates whether the command can be executed. typelist is a comma-delimited string of the keywords anonymous, guest, and real. If you don't specify a typelist string, the command will be applied to all users. An exhaustive description of its purpose and parameters can be found in the man page.

Assign Users File-Delete Permission

The delete line determines whether the user can delete files with the rm command. Here's the command line:

```
delete<yes¦no> <typelist>
```

The yes¦no parameter is used to turn this permission on or off, and typelist is the same as the chmod command.

Assign Users File-Overwrite Permission

This command line of the ftpaccess file allows or denies users the ability to overwrite an existing file. Here's the command line:

```
overwrite <yes¦no> <typelist>
```

The FTP client determines whether users can overwrite files on their own local machines; this line specifically controls overwrite permissions for uploads to the server. The yes¦no parameter toggles the permission on or off, and typelist is the same as seen in the chmod line.

Allow Users to Rename Files

You can enable or prevent a user from renaming files using this command line:

```
rename <yes¦no> <typelist>
```

The yes¦no parameter toggles the permission on or off, and typelist is the same comma-delimited string as seen in chmod.

Allow Users to Compress Files

This line determines whether the user will be able to use the compress command on files:

```
compress <yes¦no> [<classglob>]
```

18

The yes¦no parameter toggles the permission on or off, and classglob is a regular express string that specifies one or more defined classes of users. The conversions that result from the use of this command are specified in the ftpconversions file, which contains directions on what compression or extraction command is to be used on a file with a specific extension, such as .Z for the compress command, .gz for the gunzip command, and so on. See the section "Configure FTP Server File-Conversion Actions" later in this chapter.

Assign or Deny Permission to Use tar

This line determines whether the user will be able to use the tar (tape archive) command on files:

```
tar <yes¦no> [<classglob> ...]
```

The yes¦no parameter toggles the permission on or off, and classglob is a regular express string that specifies one or more defined classes of users. Again, the conversions that result from the use of this command are specified in the ftpconversions file.

Determine What Permissions Can Apply to User-Created Upload Files

This line is a bit different from the other commands in the permission control section. The umask command determines with what permissions a user can create new files; here it is.

```
umask <yes¦no> <typelist>
```

The yes¦no parameter toggles based on whether a user is allowed to create a file with his default permissions when uploading a file. Like the overwrite command you read about earlier in this section, this command line is specific to uploaded files because the client machine determines how new files are created from a download.

Configure Commands Directed Toward the cdpath

This alias command allows the administrator to provide another name for a directory other than its standard name:

```
alias <string> <dir>
```

The alias line only applies to the cd command. This line is particularly useful if a popular directory is buried deep within the anonymous FTP user's directory tree. A sample entry is the following:

```
alias linux-386 /pub/redhat/7.3/en/i386/
```

This line would allow the user to type cd linux-386 and be automatically taken to the /pub/redhat/7.3/en/i386 directory.

The `cdpath <dir>` line specifies in what order the `cd` command will look for a given string the user enters. The search path is done in the order in which the `cdpath` lines are entered in the *ftpacess* file.

For example, if the following `cdpath` entries are in the `ftpaccess` file,

```
cdpath /pub/redhat/
cdpath /pub/linux/
```

And the user types `cd i386`, the server will search for an entry in any defined aliases first in the `/pub/redhat` directory and then in the `/pub/linux` directory. If a large number of aliases are defined, it is recommended that symbolic links to the directories be created instead of aliases. This will reduce the amount of work on the FTP server and decrease wait time for the user.

Structure of the `shutdown` File

The `shutdown` command tells the server where to look for the `shutdown` message generated by the `ftpshut` command or by the user. The `shutdown` command is used with a pathname to a shutdown file, such as

```
shudown /etc/rh8ftpshutdown
```

If this file exists, the server will check the file to see when the server should shut down. The syntax of this file is as follows:

```
<year> <month> <day> <hour> <minute> <deny_offset> <disc_offset> <text>
```

`year` can be any year after 1970 (called the epoch), `month` is from 0–11, `hour` is 0–23, `minute` is 0–59, `deny_offset` is a number in minutes before shutdown in which the server will disable new connections, `disc_offset` is the number of minutes before connected users will be disconnected, and `text` is a message that will be displayed to the users at login. In addition to valid magic cookies defined in the messages section, those listed in Table 18.2 are also available.

TABLE 18.2   Magic Cookies for the Shutdown File

Cookie	Description
%s	The time the system will be shut down
%r	The time new connections will be denied
%d	The time current connections will be dropped

Configure FTP Server File-Conversion Actions

The FTP server can convert files during transfer to compress and uncompress files automatically. Suppose that the user is transferring a file to his Microsoft Windows machine that was TARed and GZIPed on a Linux machine. If the user doesn't have an archive utility installed to uncompress these files, he cannot access or use the files.

As the FTP server administrator, you can configure the FTP server to automatically unarchive these files before download, should the site support users who might not have unarchive capabilities. Additionally, you can configure an upload area for the users, and then configure the FTP server to automatically compress any files transferred to the server.

> **CAUTION**
>
> Allowing users to upload files to the FTP server is highly dangerous unless restricted to authorized local users. Anonymous upload areas have often been the breeding ground for viruses, unlicensed software, and cracking software used by system crackers for malicious usage. Should an anonymous upload area be allowed, be sure to check it regularly.

The structure of the format of the `ftpconversions` file is

```
1:2:3:4:5:6:7:8
```

where 1 is the strip prefix, 2 is the strip postfix, 3 is the add-on prefix, 4 is the add-on postfix, 5 is the external command, 6 is the types, 7 is the options, and 8 is the description.

Strip Prefix

The *strip prefix* is one or more characters at the beginning of a filename that should be automatically removed by the server when the file is requested. By specifying a given prefix to strip in a conversions rule, such as `devel_`, the user can request the file `devel_procman.tar.gz` by the command `get procman.tar.gz`, and the FTP server will perform any other rules that apply to that file and retrieve it from the server. Although this feature is documented, as of version 2.6.2, it has yet to be implemented.

Strip Postfix

The *strip postfix* works much the same as strip prefix, except one or more characters are taken from the end of the filename. Typically, this feature is used to strip the `.gz` extension from files that have been TARed and GZIPed when the server is performing automatic decompression before sending the file to the client.

Add-On Prefix

The *add-on prefix* conversion instructs the server to insert one or more characters to a filename before it is transferred to the server or client. For example, a user requests the file `procman.tar.gz`. The server has a conversion rule to add a prefix of `gnome_` to all `.tar.gz` files; thus the server would append this string to the file before sending it to the client. The user would receive a file called `gnome_procman.tar.gz`. Keywords such as `uppercase` and `lowercase` can be used in this function to change the case of the filename for those operating systems in which case makes a difference. Similar to the strip prefix conversion, this feature is not yet implemented in version 2.6.2.

Add-On Postfix

An *add-on postfix* instructs the server to append one or more characters to the end of a filename during the transfer or reception of a file. A server can contain TARed packages of applications that are uncompressed. If an add-on postfix conversion was configured on the server, the server could compress the file, append a .gz extension after the file was compressed, and then send that file to the client. The server could also do the same action for uncompressed files sent to the server. This would have the effect of conserving disk space on the server.

External Command

The *external command* entries in the ftpconversions file contain the bulk of the FTP server conversion rules. The external command entry tells the server what should be done with a file after it is transferred to the server. The specified conversion utility can be any command on the server, although generally it is a compression utility. As the file is sent, the server passes the file through the external command. If the file is being uploaded to the server, the command needs to send the result to standard in, whereas a download will send the command to standard out. For example, here is an entry specifying the tar command:

```
:    : :.tar:/bin/tar -c -f - %s:T_REG¦T_DIR:O_TAR:TAR
```

The following sections describe the fields in a conversion entry.

Types

You must use the types field of the ftpconversions file to tell the server what types of files the conversion rules apply to. Separate the file type entries with the (¦) character, and give each type a value of T_REG, T_ASCII, and T_DIR.

T_REG signifies a regular file, T_ASCII an ASCII file, and T_DIR a directory. A typical entry is T_REG ¦ T_ASCII, which signifies a regular ASCII file.

Options

The options field informs the server what action is being done to the file. Similar to the types file, options are separated by the (¦) character. Here are the valid ranges you can assign to items in the options field:

- O_COMPRESS to compress the file
- O_UNCOMPRESS to uncompress the file
- O_TAR to tar the file

An example of this field would be O_COMPRESS ¦ O_TAR, where files are both compressed and TARed.

Description

The description field allows an administrator to quickly understand what the rule is doing. This field does not have any syntax restriction, although it is usually a one word entry—such as TAR, TAR+COMPRESS, or UNCOMPRESS—which is enough to get the concept across.

An Example of Conversions in Action

Crafting complex conversion entries is a task perhaps best left to the Linux/UNIX expert, but the sample ftpconversions file included with wu-ftpd provides more than enough examples for the average Red Hat administrator. Building your own simple conversion entry is not really too difficult, so let's examine and decode an example:

```
:.Z:  :  :/bin/compress -d -c %s:T_REG¦T_ASCII:O_UNCOMPRESS:UNCOMPRESS
```

In this example, the strip prefix (field 1) is null because it isn't yet implemented, so this rule doesn't apply to prefixes. The second field of this rule contains the .Z postfix; thus it deals with files that have been compressed with the compress utility. The rule doesn't address the add-on prefix or postfix, so fields 3 and 4 are null. Field 5, the external command field, tells the server to run the compress utility to decompress all files that have the .Z extension, as the -d parameter signifies. The -c option tells compress to write the output of the compress utility to the standard out, which is the server in this case. The %s is the name of the file that the rule was applied against. Field 6 specifies that this file is a regular file in ASCII format. Field 7, the options field, tells the server that this command uncompresses the file. Finally, the last field is a comment that gives the administrator a quick decode of what the conversion rule is doing, that is, uncompressing the file.

> **EXAMPLES**
>
> Several conversion rules may be specified in wu-ftpd's default ftpconversions file. Additional examples, such as for Sun's Solaris operating system, might also be available in additional wu-ftpd documentation.

Using Commands in the ftphosts File to Allow or Deny FTP Server Connection

The purpose of the ftphosts file is to allow or deny specific users or addresses from connecting to the FTP server. The format of the file is the word allow or deny optionally followed by a username, followed by an IP or a DNS address.

```
allow username address
deny username address
```

Listing 18.4 shows a sample configuration of this file.

LISTING 18.4   ftphosts Configuration File for Allowing or Denying Users

```
# Example host access file
#
# Everything after a '#' is treated as comment,
# empty lines are ignored
allow tdc 128.0.0.1
allow tdc 192.168.101.*
allow tdc insanepenguin.net
allow tdc *.exodous.net
deny anonymous 201.*
deny anonymous *.pilot.net
```

The * is a wildcard that will match any combination of that address. For example, allow tdc *.exodous.net will allow the user tdc to log in to the FTP server from any address that contains the domain name exodous.net. Similarly, the anonymous user will not be allowed to access the FTP if he is coming from a 201 public class C IP address.

Changes made to your system's FTP server configuration files only become active after you restart xinetd because configuration files are only parsed at startup. To restart xinetd as root, issue the command /etc/rc.d/init.d/xinetd restart. This makes a call to the same shell script that is called at system startup and shutdown for any runlevel to start or stop the xinet daemon. xinetd should report its status as

```
# /etc/rc.d/init.d/xinetd restart
Stopping xinetd:                         [  OK  ]
Starting xinetd:                         [  OK  ]
```

Once restarted, the FTP server is accessible to all incoming requests.

Server Administration

Wu-FTP provides a few commands to aid in the administration of the server. These commands are

- ftpwho—Displays information about current FTP server users
- ftpcount—Displays information about current server users by class
- ftpshut—Provides automated server shutdown and user notification
- ftprestart—Provides automated server restart and shutdown message removal

Each of these commands must be executed with superuser privileges because they reference the ftpaccess configuration file to obtain information about the FTP server.

Display Information About Connected Users

This command provides information about users who are currently connected to the FTP server. Here's the command line:

```
/usr/bin/ftpwho
```

Table 18.3 shows the format of the output ftpwho displays.

TABLE 18.3   ftpwho Fields

Name	Description
Process ID	The process ID of the FTP server process.
TTY	The terminal ID of the process. This will always be a ? because the FTP daemon isn't an interactive login.
Status	Status of the FTP process. The values are
	S: sleeping
	Z: zombie, indicating a crash
	R: running
	N: normal process
Time	The elapsed processor time the process has used in minutes and seconds.
Details	Tells what host the process is connecting from, the user who connected, and the current command that is executing.

Listing 18.5 shows a typical output of this command. It lists the process ID for the ftp daemon handling requests, the class that the particular user belongs to, the total time connected, what username the user is connected as, and the status of his session.

In addition to the information given about each connected user, ftpwho will also display the total number of users connected out of any maximum that might have been set in the ftpaccess file. This information can be used to monitor the use of your FTP server.

You can pass one parameter to ftpwho. (You can find the parameter by using the *ftpwho – help* command.) The single parameter you can pass to ftpwho is -v. This parameter prints out version and licensing information for wu-ftp, as shown here:

```
# ftpwho
Service class all:
10447 ?         SN     0:00 ftpd: localhost: anonymous/winky@disney.com: IDLE
1 users (no maximum)
```

The output of ftpwho, using the -V option, which shows version information, is shown in Listing 18.5.

LISTING 18.5 ftpwho -V Command Output

Version wu-2.6.2-8

Count the Number of Connections

/usr/bin/ftpcount counts the number of connected users to the FTP server and the maximum number of users allowed. This same information is found at the end of the output for the ftpwho command. This command only takes one parameter, -V, which displays the same output as the previous ftpwho example.

```
# ftpcount
Service class all              -   4 users (no maximum)
```

Use /usr/sbin/ftpshut to Schedule FTP Server Downtime

As with any public server administration, it is always good practice to let users of the FTP server know about upcoming outages, when the server will be updated, and other relevant site information. The ftpshut command allows the administrator to let the FTP server do much of this automatically.

The ftpshut command allows the administrator to take the FTP server down at a specific time based on some parameters passed to it. The format of the command is as follows and is documented in the ftpshut man page:

18

```
ftpshut  [ -V ] [ -l min] [ -d min] time [ warning-message ... ]
```

The -V parameter displays the version information of the command. The time parameter is the time when the ftpshut command will stop the FTP servers. This parameter will take either a + number for the number of minutes from the current time, or a specific hour and minute in 24-hour clock format with the syntax of *HH:MM*.

The -l parameter allows the FTP server administrator to specify how long, in minutes, before shutdown the server will disable new connections. The default for this is 10 minutes. If the time given to shut down the servers is less than 10 minutes, new connections will be disabled immediately.

The -d parameter is similar to the -l parameter, but controls when the FTP server will terminate the current connections. By default this will occur 5 minutes before the server shuts down. If the shutdown time is less than 5 minutes, the server will terminate the connections immediately.

When you execute this command, the FTP server creates a file containing the shutdown information in the location specified in the ftpaccess file under the shutdown section. The default configuration for this file is /etc/shutmsg. If you execute the ftpshut command with warning messages, the messages are displayed when the user logs in to the server.

```
Name (pheniox:tdc): anonymous
331 Guest login ok, send your complete e-mail address as password.
Password:
230-system doing down at Mon Sep  3 06:23:00 2001
230-0 users of unlimited on pheniox.
230 Guest login ok, access restrictions apply.
Remote system type is UNIX.
Using binary mode to transfer files.
```

Here is a sample ftpshut command:

```
ftpshut -l 5 -d 5 +10 "system going down at %s %N users of %M on %R"
```

This command tells the FTP server to disconnect new connections in 5 minutes, drop all current connections in 5 minutes, shut down the server in 10 minutes, and display a warning message to the users at login. The message can be a mixture of text and magic cookies, defined in Table 18.4. It is important to keep in mind that the message can only be 75 characters in length. Additionally, it isn't important to know how many characters the magic cookies will take because the system knows this information and will truncate the message at 75 characters.

TABLE 18.4   Magic Cookies for the `ftpshut` Command

Cookie	Description
%s	Time the system will be shut down
%r	Time new connections will be denied
%d	Time the current connections will be dropped
%C	Current working directory
%E	Server administrators email address as specified in the `ftpaccess` file
%F	Available free space in the current working directories partition in kilobytes
%L	Local host time
%M	Maximum number of allowed connections in this user class
%N	Current number of connections for this user class
%R	Remote hostname
%T	Local time, in the form of Fri Aug 31 21:04:00 2001
%U	Username given at login

When `ftpshut` is issued to the system, it creates a file that stores the necessary information. The `ftprestart` command removes this file for all servers, either canceling the
impending shutdown or removing the shutdown file and restarting the FTP server. The
`ftprestart` only has one optional argument, `-V`, to show version information.

Use `/var/log/xferlog` to View a Log of Server Transactions

The `xferlog` file gives a log of what transactions have occurred with the FTP server.
Depending on the settings in the `/etc/ftpaccess` file, the contents of this file can contain
the files sent or received by who with a date stamp. Table 18.5 lists the fields of this file.
The same information can also be found in the corresponding man page included in the
`wu-ftp` RPM.

TABLE 18.5   `/var/log/xferlog` Fields

Field	Description
current-time	Current local time in the form of *DDD MMM dd hh:mm:ss YYYY,* where *DDD* is the day of the week, *MMM* is the month, *dd* is the day of the month, *hh* is the hour, *mm* is the minutes, *ss* is the seconds, and *YYYY* is the year.
transfer-time	Total time in seconds for the transfer.
remote-host	Remote hostname.
file-size	Size of the transferred file in bytes.
filename	Name of the file.

transfer-type	A single character indicating the transfer type. The types are
	   a for ascii transfers.
	   b for binary transfers.

special-action-flag	One or more character flags indicating any special action taken by the server.

18

TABLE 18.5   Continued

Field	Description
	The values are
	C for compressed files.
	U for uncompressed files.
	T for TARed files.
	- for no special action taken.
direction	Indicates whether the file was sent from or received by the server.
access-mode	The way in which the user logged in to the server. The values are
	a anonymous guest user.
	g guest user, corresponding to the guestgroup command in the /etc/
	ftpaccess file.
	r real user on the local machine.
username	If logged in as a real user, the username.
	If the access mode was guest, the password is given.
service-name	The name of the service used, usually FTP.
authentication-method	Type of authentication used. The values are
	0: none.
	1: RFC931 Authentication (a properly formed email address).
authenticated-user-id	This is the user ID returned to the server based on the authentication method used to access the server. An * is used when an authenticated user ID cannot be found.
completion-status	A single character field indicating the status of the transfer. The values are
	c: completed transfer.
	i: incomplete transfer.

An example of this file is seen in Listing 18.6.

LISTING 18.6   Sample /var/log/xferlog File with Inbound and Outbound Logging

```
Mon Sep  3 07:13:05 2001 1 localhost.localdomain 100
 /var/ftp/pub/README b  o a testing@test.com ftp 0 * c
Mon Sep  3 02:35:35 2001 1 helios 8 /var/ftp/pub/configuration a
_ o a testing@test.com ftp 0 * c
Mon Sep  3 02:35:35 2001 1 helios 8 /var/ftp/pub/temp.txt a  o a
testing@test.com ftp 0 * c
Mon Sep  3 02:35:35 2001 1 helios 8 /var/ftp/pub/tftp-server-
0.17-14.i386.rpm a  o a testing@test.com ftp 0 * c
Mon Sep  3 02:35:35 2001 1 helios 8 /var/ftp/pub/wu-ftpd-2.6.1-
18.i386.rpm a  o a testing@test.com ftp 0 * c
```

Related Fedora and Linux Commands

You'll use these commands to install, configure, and manage FTP services in Fedora Core:

`epiphany`—A graphical GNOME browser supporting FTP

`ftp`—A text-based interactive FTP command

`ftpcopy`—Copy directories and files from an FTP server

`ftpcp`—Retrieve data from remote FTP server, but do not overwrite existing local files

`gftp`—A graphical FTP client for GNOME

`konqueror`—KDE's graphical Web browser

`lftp`—An advanced text-based FTP program

`nautilus`—Red Hat's graphical file explorer and browser

`ncftp`—A sophisticated, text-based FTP program

`sftp`—Secure file transfer program

`smbclient`—Samba FTP client to access SMB/CIFS resources on servers

`system-config-services`—Red Hat's system service GUI admin utility

`vsftpd`—The Very Secure FTP daemon

`webcam`—A Webcam-oriented FTP client included with xawtv

Reference

`http://www.wu-ftpd.org/`—WU-FTP Official Web site.

`http://fedora.redhat.com/`—Red Hat's Official Fedora Core Web site.

`http://www.cert.org/`—Computer Emergency Response Team.

`http://www.openssh.com/`—The OpenSSH home page and source for the latest version of OpenSSH and its component clients, such as `sftp`.

`http://www.cert.org/tech_tips/anonymous_ftp_config.html`—CERT Anonymous FTP Configuration Guidelines.

`http://vsftpd.beasts.org/`—Home page for the `vsftd` FTP server.

`ftp://vsftpd.beasts.org/users/cevans/`—Download site for the latest releases of the `vsftpd` server.

18

CHAPTER **19**

Handling Electronic Mail

In This Chapter

- How Email Is Sent and Received

- The Mail Transport Agent

- Choosing a Mail Client (MUA)

- Attachments—Sending Binary Files As Text

- Basic Sendmail Configuration and Operation

- Using Fetchmail to Retrieve Mail

- Choosing a Mail Delivery Agent (MDA)

- Mail Daemons

- Alternatives to Microsoft Exchange Server

- Reference

Communication by electronic mail—commonly referred to as *email*—is easily the most popular activity on the Internet and intranets. Email is fast, free (apparently), and easy to use. Hidden behind that seeming ease, however, is a complex infrastructure that can be accessed and controlled with the power of Fedora Core Linux.

In this chapter, you learn how to configure Fedora Core to act as an email server. You also take a close look at the various email clients that Fedora Core makes available for your use, and you learn some techniques for working with them. Although you might not ever need to administer a mail server, understanding how they work can make you a better mail user.

A Brief Introduction to Email Terms

The email world is filled with acronyms and technical terms. The first of these covered here describes the components of the email system. Some applications combine features from among these three groups.

The Mail User Agent (MUA), mail client, or mail reader allows the user to read and compose her email. This is the application most users are familiar with; it presents a text or graphical interface to the user. Examples would be Evolution, Balsa, mutt, Mozilla Mail, or KMail. All are provided by Fedora Core.

The mail transfer agent (MTA) works behind the scenes to send and receive email between computers. Examples would be Sendmail, Postfix, Fetchmail, Exim, or Qmail. All but the last two are provided by Fedora Core. The Mail Delivery Agent (MDA) is similar to an MTA, but does not handle deliveries between systems and does not provide an interface to the user like an MUA. Examples would be Procmail or Spamassassin; both provide filtering services to the MTA, and the latter is provided by Fedora Core.

The protocols used for email are a hotbed of acronyms; these are covered next.

RFC—The Request For Comments is as close to an Internet rulebook as one can get. See the "Reference" section at the end of this chapter for links to specific RFCs. By changing the number in the link, you can look at any particular RFC. If you have Fetchmail installed, author Eric S. Raymond has included a list of RFCs (with descriptions) that are relevant to email in the file /usr/share/doc/fetchmail/NOTES.

POP—Defined by RFC-1939, the Post Office Protocol is a mail server for delivering mail to clients. (It isn't used for sending mail to servers; that's SMTP, later.) POP3 is very useful when you have one mail client on one computer, such as a typical home user. POP3 is designed for local access to mail; it downloads all mail from a central server to the local client, and then deletes the files on the server. Most ISPs offer POP3 mail access.

IMAP—It is the Internet Mail Access Protocol, which allows a user to access his email stored on a remote server rather than a local disk. This means that email can be accessed from anywhere if the user is employing a mail client with IMAP support. IMAP is a good solution to providing mail for a LAN. The version supplied with Fedora Core is the University of Washington IMAP server, found at `http://www.washington.edu/imap/`.

SMTP—Defined by RFC-821, it is the Simple Mail Transport Protocol used for sending mail from one network to another. It is a sever-to-server protocol, so some other method must be used to deliver messages to a client application to be read by a user. Extensions to the protocol add authentication and error messages to the basic protocol.

MIME—Defined by RFC-1341, 1521, 1522, 1523, 1820, and many others, Multipurpose Internet Mail Extensions address the formatting of email messages to include non-ASCII text, encoded binary images, and multimedia content.

Certainly, this is not an exhaustive list, nor is it intended to be. You might find the Jargoogle search page useful to decipher other unfamiliar terms you encounter. It's at `http://www.tuxedo.org/~esr/jargon/jargoogle.html`.

NOTE

The amazing deluge of spam and Internet scams using forged headers has spurred interest in a "better mousetrap." One such project is AMTP at `http://amtp.bw.org/`, an enhancement for SMTP. This specification calls for mail servers needing a signed security certificate and using TLS (Transport Layer Security, RFC2246). An AMTP mail server will not relay mail from an "untrusted source"—in other words, a mail server lacking the proper authentication. Although not eradicating SPAM, AMTP does provide a mechanism to identify the source.

How Email Is Sent and Received

Email is sent as plain text across networks using SMTP. SMTP is used for sending mail from one network to another. Extensions to the protocol add authentication and error messages to the basic protocol. The mail transfer agent (MTA) works behind the scenes to send and receive email between computers. Some MTAs are Sendmail, Postfix, Fetchmail, Exim, or Qmail.

SMTP helps each computer along the way figure out how to get all the mail delivered to its destination. It's a remarkable system when you think about how complex a task it is asked to accomplish.

Here's a simplified example of how email is successfully processed and sent to its destination:

1. `user1@lion.org` composes and sends an email message to `user2@cheetah.org`.

2. The MTA at `lion.org` receives `user1`'s email message and queues it for delivery behind any other messages that are also waiting to go out.

3. The MTA at `lion.org` contacts the MTA at `cheetah.org` on port 25. After `cheetah.org` acknowledges the connection, the MTA at `lion.org` sends the mail message. After `cheetah.org` accepts and acknowledges receipt of the message, the connection is closed.

4. The MTA at `cheetah.org` places the mail message into `user2`'s incoming mailbox; `user2` is notified that she has new mail the next time she logs on.

Of course, several things can go wrong during this process. Here are a few examples:

What if `user2` doesn't exist at `cheetah.org`? In this case, the MTA at `cheetah.org` will reject the email and notify the MTA at `lion.org` of what the problem is. The MTA at `lion.org` will then generate an email message and send it to `user1@lion.org`, informing her that no `user2` exists at `cheetah.org` (or perhaps just silently discard the message and give the sender no indication of the problem, depending on how the email server is configured).

What happens if `cheetah.org` doesn't respond to `lion.org`'s connection attempts? (Perhaps the server is down for maintenance.) The MTA at `lion.org` notifies the sender that the initial delivery attempt has failed. Further attempts will be made at intervals decided by the server administrator until the deadline is reached, and the sender will be notified that the mail is undeliverable.

The Mail Transport Agent

Working behind the scenes to move mail between computers on different networks, several different MTAs are available for Fedora Core—each with its own strengths and weaknesses. Some are extremely powerful, but very difficult to configure and somewhat slow; others are very fast and easy to configure, but do not contain as many features. The following sections provide more details about some of the more common MTAs available for use with Fedora Core Linux.

Sendmail

The vast majority of email traffic on the Internet is handled by an MTA called Sendmail, the default MTA shipped with Fedora Core Linux (and a number of other UNIX distributions). Sendmail has the advantage of being installed and well-supported in your Fedora Core Linux system. The commercial version (not included with Fedora Core) sports a GUI configuration utility, as well.

Sendmail is one of the oldest and most powerful MTAs in existence, but it has a few disadvantages. It is somewhat slow; in a high load environment, other MTAs, including Postfix and Qmail, typically can handle a much greater volume of messages per second. Sendmail is also notoriously convoluted; configuration files are extremely cryptic. (The best-selling book on Sendmail is more than 1,000 pages in length.)

Fortunately, the default configuration of Sendmail as provided by Fedora Core works fine for most basic installations, and only minor changes are needed to configure it for a basic email server installation. However, because of the complexity of advanced Sendmail configuration, many administrators choose to replace it with one of the alternative MTAs. (You learn the basics of configuring and using Sendmail in "Basic Sendmail Configuration and Operation," later in this chapter).

Postfix

Postfix (originally released in 1998 as the IBM Secure Mailer) is a popular Sendmail alternative; it's fast, secure, and easy to administer. Postfix is a drop-in replacement for Sendmail (meaning that other applications that expect to use Sendmail won't notice that Postfix has replaced it and will continue to work correctly), and migrating a Sendmail installation to Postfix is relatively simple. To make all this magic work, Postfix uses a Sendmail wrapper (an interface for making other programs think that it is Sendmail) so that MUAs and such can communicate with it just as if they were communicating with Sendmail.

> **CAUTION**
>
> Fedora Core provides Postfix version 2, which uses a slightly different configuration than the earlier version. If you are upgrading Postfix from an earlier Red Hat version, check your configuration files.
>
> Fedora also now compiles Postfix and Sendmail against version 2 of the Cyrus SASL library (an authentication library). The Release Notes contain detailed information on file location and option changes that will affect you if you use these libraries.

For enhanced security, many Postfix processes used to use the `chroot` facility (which restricts access to only specific parts of the file system) for improved security, and there are no `setuid` components in Postfix. With the current release of Fedora, a `chroot` configuration *is no longer used* and is, in fact, discouraged by the Postfix author. You can manually reconfigure Postfix to a `chroot` configuration, but that is no longer supported by Fedora.

If you are starting from scratch, Postfix is considered a better choice than Sendmail.

Qmail and Exim

Qmail is a direct competitor to Postfix but is not provided with Fedora Core. Postfix is designed to be easier to use than Sendmail, as well as faster and more secure. However, Qmail isn't a drop-in replacement for Sendmail, so migrating an existing Sendmail installation to Qmail isn't quite as simple as migrating from Sendmail to Postfix. Qmail is relatively easy to administer, and it integrates with a number of software add-ons, including Web mail systems and POP3 servers. Qmail is available from `http://www.qmail.org/`.

Exim is yet another MTA, and it is available at `http://www.exim.org/`. Exim is considered faster and more secure that Sendmail or Postfix, but is much different to configure that either of those. Exim and Qmail use the `maildir` format rather than `mbox`, so both are considered "NFS safe" (see the following sidebar).

MDIR Versus Mailbox

Qmail also introduced `maildir`, which is an alternative to the standard UNIX method of storing incoming mail. `maildir` is a more versatile system of handling incoming email, but it requires your email clients to be reconfigured, and it isn't compatible with the traditional UNIX way of storing incoming mail. You'll need to use mail programs that recognize the `maildir` format. (The modern programs do.)

The traditional `mbox` format keeps all mail assigned to a folder concatenated as a single file and maintains an index of individual emails. With `maildir`, each mail folder has three subfolders: `/cur`, `/new`, and `/tmp`. Each email is kept in a separate, unique file. If you are running a mail server for a large number of people, you should select a file system that can efficiently handle a large number of small files.

`mbox` does offer one major disadvantage. While you are accessing the monolithic `mbox` file that contains all your email, suppose that some type of corruption occurs, either to the file itself or to the index. Recovery from this problem can be difficult. The mbox files are especially prone to problems if the files are being accessed over a network and can result in file corruption; one should avoid accessing `mbox` mail mounted over NFS, the Network File System because file corruption can occur.

Depending on how you access your mail, `maildir` does permit the simultaneous access of `maildir` files by multiple applications; `mbox` does not.

The choice of an MUA also affects your choice of mail directory format. For example, the `pine` program does not cache any directory information and must reread the mail directory any time it accesses it. If you are using `pine`, `maildir` would be a poor choice. More advanced MUAs perform caching, so `maildir` might be a good choice, although the MUA cache can get out of synchronization. It seems that there is no perfect choice.

Fedora Core Linux provides you with mail alternatives that have both strong and weak points. Be aware of the differences among the alternatives and frequently reevaluate your selection to make certain that it is the best one for your circumstances.

Choosing an MTA

Other MTAs are available for use with Fedora Core, but those discussed in the preceding sections are the most popular. Which one should you choose? That depends on what you need to do. Sendmail's main strengths are that it is considered the standard and it can do things that many other MTAs cannot. However, if ease of use or speed is a concern to you, you might want to consider replacing Sendmail with Postfix, Exim, or Qmail. Because Sendmail is the default MTA included with Fedora Core, it is covered in more detail in the following section.

The Mail Delivery Agent

SMTP is a server-to-server protocol that was designed to deliver mail to systems that are always connected to the Internet. Dial-up systems only connect at the user's command; they connect for specific operations, and are frequently disconnected. To accommodate this difference, many mail systems also include a mail delivery agent, or MDA. The MDA transfers mail to systems without permanent Internet connections. The MDA is similar to an MTA (see the following note), but does not handle deliveries between systems and does not provide an interface to the user.

> **NOTE**
>
> Procmail or Spamassassin are examples of MTAs; both provide filtering services to the MTA while they store messages locally and then make them available to the MUA or email client for reading by the user.

The MDA uses the POP3 or IMAP protocols for this process. In a manner similar to a post office box at the post office, POP3 and IMAP implement a "store and forward" process that alleviates the need to maintain a local mail server if all you want to do is read your mail. For example, dial-up Internet users can intermittently connect to their ISP's mail server to retrieve mail using Fetchmail—the MDA provided by Fedora Core (see the section "Using Fetchmail to Retrieve Mail," later in this chapter).

The Mail User Agent

The mail user agent, or MUA, is another necessary part of the email system. The MUA is a mail client, or mail reader, that allows the user to read and compose email and provides the user interface. (It's the email application itself that most users are familiar with as "email.") Some popular UNIX command-line MUAs are elm, pine, and mutt. Fedora Core also provides modern GUI MUAs: Mozilla Mail, Balsa, Evolution, Sylpheed, and KMail. For comparison, common non-UNIX MUAs are Microsoft Outlook, Outlook Express, Pegasus, Eudora, or Netscape Messenger.

The Microsoft Windows and Macintosh MUAs often include some MTA functionality; UNIX does not. For example, Microsoft Outlook can connect to your Internet provider's mail server to send messages. On the other hand, UNIX MUAs generally rely on an external MTA such as Sendmail. This might seem like a needlessly complicated way to do things, and it is if used to connect a single user to her ISP. For any other situation, however, using an external MTA allows you much greater flexibility because you can use any number of external programs to handle and process your email functions and customize the service. Having the process handled by different applications gives you very great control over how you provide email service to users on your network, as well as to individual and SOHO users.

For example, you could

- Use Evolution to read and compose mail.

- Use Sendmail to send your mail.

- Use xbiff to notify you when you have new mail.

- Use Fetchmail to retrieve your mail from a remote mail server.

- Use Procmail to automatically sort your incoming mail based on sender, subject, or many other variables.

- Use Spamassassin to eliminate the unwanted messages before you read them.

Choosing a Mail Client (MUA)

You will use a mail client to read your mail. One console mail client, mutt, is provided by Fedora Core; others like elm or pine can be obtained from the usual sources (repositories such as Freshmeat or RPMfind) or from the my site or the application's home page. When choosing an MUA, you can choose from a number of highly configurable command-line clients and easy-to-use menu driven clients. The following sections discuss a few of these clients, along with the GUI mail client programs. GUIs are the MUAs most often chosen by new users. Many people find the console-based text MUAs useful once they try them, however, so don't cheat yourself and overlook them.

The graphical MUA you choose will most likely bear some resemblance to the Microsoft Outlook or Outlook Express mail clients. Those applications are in widespread use and familiar to many users. The modern crop of Linux GUI mail clients builds on that familiarity while providing enhancements, functionality, and configurability that are the hallmarks of the UNIX environment. The Evolution client is established as the default MUA for Fedora Core, and it closely resembles MS Outlook.

The mail Application

A UNIX utility named mail is included with all UNIX and Linux distributions. Because it has a very Spartan interface, it isn't commonly used interactively. However, mail is still an extremely useful program to use in shell scripting because it can take all the information it needs to send mail from the command line. No user interaction is required. mail is also useful for sending quick notes because it starts up quickly and doesn't require going through menus to send a message.

19

Using mail

To begin sending a message in mail, simply type **mail** at the shell prompt, followed by the email address that you want to send mail to:

```
$ mail john@cheetah.org
```

mail will then prompt you for the subject of the message. Enter the subject and press Enter. The cursor will then move down to the next blank line. You can now start entering the body of your message. When you have finished, press Ctrl+D on a blank line to exit the mail program and send the message. (You might be prompted for Cc:. If you do not want to send carbon copies to anyone, simply press Enter here.) The message will be handed off to the MTA, and your shell prompt will return. To abandon a message you are currently writing, press Ctrl+C.

If you want to retrieve your email using the mail program, simply type **mail** at the shell prompt. The system will respond with something similar to the following:

```
Mail  Type ? for help.
"/var/mail/user1": 1 message 1 unread
>U  1 user2@cheetah.org   Tue Sep 23 07:15  18/551   "Meeting tomorrow"
>N  2 spam@lamer.com      Tue Sep 23 08:25  18/542
"A large and obnoxious spam message"
>N  3 user2@cheetah.org   Tue Sep 23 09:21  17/524   "Meeting scheduled"
>N  4 user5@lion.org      Tue Sep 23 09:24  17/528   "Issues"
&
```

The & prompt is mail's way of prompting you for input.

The first column in the list of messages is a flag that indicates the status of the message. For example, U means that the message is unread. N means that the message is new. The rest of the columns are self-explanatory.

To read one of these messages, simply type the message number and press Enter.

For example,

```
& 4
Message 4

From user5@lion.org  Tue Sep 23 09:24:35 2003
Date: Tue, 23 Sep 2003 09:24:34 -0500
From: user5@lion.org
To: user1@lion.org
Subject: Issues

Hey guy,
```

```
The software build of the project appears to be broken.
It is blowing up with all kinds of errors. Any ideas?

Thanks

&
```

If you want to respond to this message, you can type **respond** and press Enter. You can also simply type **r** and press Enter. By default, the command will be applied to the currently active message, which is indicated in the message list by a > (and will be the last message that you read). If you want to have the command applied to a different message, you can simply specify the message number after the command. For example, typing **r 2** will respond to message number 2.

A complete list of commands is available within mail by typing **?** at the prompt. Note that you can abbreviate all commands to the shortest abbreviation that isn't ambiguous.

Shell Scripting with mail

As mentioned previously, `mail`'s most useful application is its use in shell scripting. The complete instruction to create and send a message can be done from the command line. For example, suppose that we have a shell script that generates a report and stores it as a text file. Now we want to email that text file to a user at the end of the script. With `mail`, we could use a command such as the following:

```
$ mail user1@lion.org -s "Report from shell script" < report.txt
```

The `-s` specifies a subject line on the command line, and then we use simple shell redirection to use the file `report.txt` as the body for the message (see Chapter 22, "Shell Scripting"). It's simple, clean, and requires no user interaction to send the message.

For other options available on the `mail` command line, see the `man` page for `mail`.

> **NOTE**
>
> The venerable pine email client is no longer provided by Fedora Core, not because it isn't a good application; it just uses a license that is incompatible with distribution by Fedora Core and Red Hat.

19

Mutt

Mutt is a relatively new command-line mail client that is rapidly becoming popular with users. The client is called mutt because it is known as "the mongrel of email clients" in that it attempts to combine the best features of several other clients such as elm and pine. Mutt is an extremely feature-rich email client, although it isn't as easy to use as pine. It is however, more secure than pine. Figure 19.1 shows the mutt interface.

To check the version and see the compile time options, use mutt -v like this:

```
$ mutt -v
Mutt 1.4.1i (2003-03-19)
Copyright (C) 1996-2002 Michael R. Elkins and others.
Mutt comes with ABSOLUTELY NO WARRANTY; for details type `mutt -vv'.
Mutt is free software, and you are welcome to redistribute it
under certain conditions; type `mutt -vv' for details.
System: Linux 2.6.5-1.358 (i686) [using ncurses 5.4]
Compile options:
-DOMAIN
-DEBUG
-HOMESPOOL   -USE_SETGID   -USE_DOTLOCK   -DL_STANDALONE
+USE_FCNTL   -USE_FLOCK
+USE_POP  +USE_IMAP  +USE_GSS  +USE_SSL  +USE_SASL
+HAVE_REGCOMP   -USE_GNU_REGEX
+HAVE_COLOR  +HAVE_START_COLOR  +HAVE_TYPEAHEAD  +HAVE_BKGDSET
+HAVE_CURS_SET  +HAVE_META  +HAVE_RESIZETERM
+HAVE_PGP  -BUFFY_SIZE -EXACT_ADDRESS  -SUN_ATTACHMENT
+ENABLE_NLS  -LOCALES_HACK  +HAVE_WC_FUNCS  +HAVE_LANGINFO_CODESET
Â+HAVE_LANGINFO_YESEXPR
+HAVE_ICONV  -ICONV_NONTRANS  +HAVE_GETSID  +HAVE_GETADDRINFO
ISPELL="/usr/bin/ispell"
SENDMAIL="/usr/sbin/sendmail"
MAILPATH="/var/mail"
PKGDATADIR="/usr/share/mutt"
SYSCONFDIR="/etc"
EXECSHELL="/bin/sh"
-MIXMASTER
To contact the developers, please mail to <mutt-dev@mutt.org>.
To report a bug, please use the flea(1) utility.
```

If you want to change the options (such as any paths) you will need to recompile mutt from the source code.

The latest versions of mutt, as well as news and information about it, are available at http://www.mutt.org. Mutt is proud to be a bug-free program, but its authors believe it might have a few "fleas"—thankfully, these are few.

The systemwide configuration file is kept at /etc/Muttrc, and each user can have his own ~/.muttrc files. Mutt configuration is often an evolving process, as each user attempts to configure this feature-rich mail client.

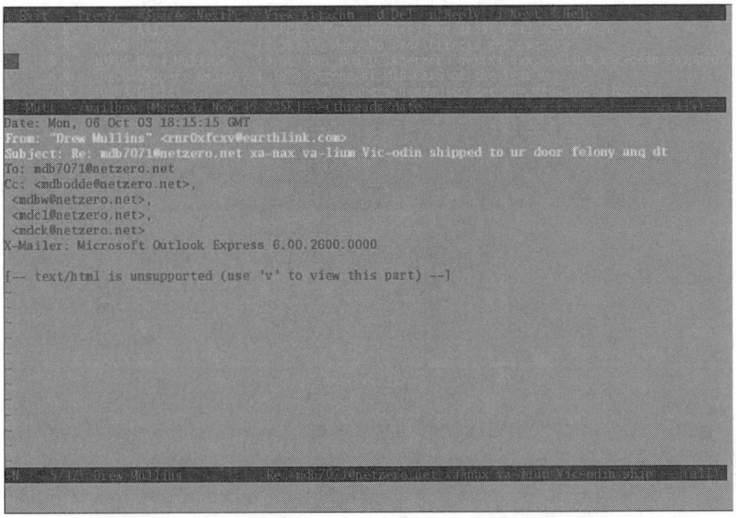

FIGURE 19.1   Mutt combines the best features of elm and pine (aside from ugly default screen colors). Fedora Core defaults the editor to *vi*, but you can choose any other editor.

Before you can use mutt, you need to configure a .muttrc file for each user's home directory. A sample file is found in /usr/share/doc/mutt-*/sample.muttrc, just copy it (or the systemwide file) to .muttrc in the appropriate home directory. There, edit it to reflect how you have your mail system configured and set your preferences; you'll find mutt highly customizable, awkward to configure, and simple to use.

Sending and receiving messages using mutt is very easy; the colorful display provides a subset of common commands, and F1 brings up the online help documents.

Evolution

The default graphical email client provided by Fedora Core is Ximian's Evolution. If you have experience with Microsoft's Outlook mail client, you'll see the resemblance. Like MS Outlook, Evolution provides integrated functions: calendar, scheduling, and the ability to receive news and information from Internet sites.

> **NOTE**
>
> Ximian (now a part of Novell) intends for Evolution to eventually act as a replacement for MS Outlook. Ximian is also working on a non-free replacement for Microsoft Exchange server so that businesses will have a choice and Linux can be used to replace the functionality of the non-UNIX product. As you'll see later, Balsa and KMail are targeted toward the MS Outlook Express user.

Start Evolution from the Internet menu; it is listed only as "Email." The first time you start Evolution, the Evolution Setup assistant presents you with a brief and simple configuration dialog, as shown in Figure 19.2.

19

FIGURE 19.2   You can launch and configure Evolution with just a few simple commands. The Identity screen, the first of several screens, asks you to enter your information. Click Forward to proceed.

The next screen permits you to configure Evolution to use your MTA. You can choose POP, IMAP, the local spools found in /var/mail in either mbox or maildir format, a local MTA, or "none" if you simply want to use the other features of Evolution. As seen in Figure 19.3, you can also set your password.

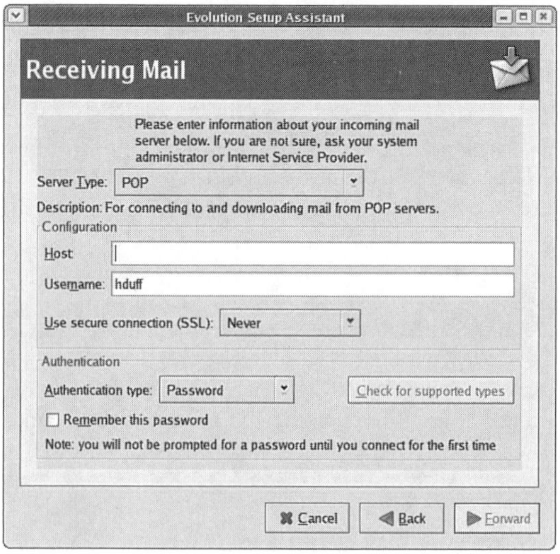

FIGURE 19.3   The Receiving Mail screen requires information from your ISP or your system administrator.

You must also choose between SMTP or Sendmail for sending your mail; enter your email address, and choose a time zone (very important for your calendar). Finally, you will see the opening Evolution Summary window in Figure 19.4.

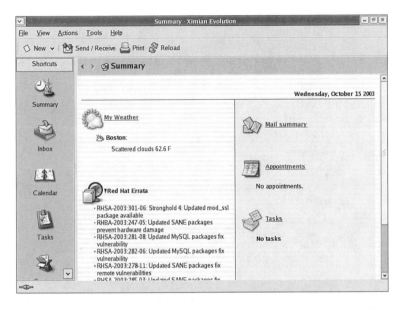

FIGURE 19.4   In the Evolution Summary window, you can receive a local weather report, check your mail, appointments, and calendar, as well as keep up-to-date on the news.

Each icon in the left-hand pane of the Evolution Summary window opens a different window when selected. Each view has options that can be configured to suit your needs; just click on the Evolution Summary window's Tools menu item, for example, to open the Tools screen, shown in Figure 19.5.

Balsa

Balsa is an email client that was designed to work with GNOME. Configuring Balsa is similar to configuring Evolution, although most of the configuration is done from the Preferences menu item, and the basic functionality is similar. Figure 19.6 shows a screenshot of the Balsa interface.

KMail

If you are using the KDE Desktop Environment rather than the Fedora Core default GNOME desktop, you will also have KMail installed. As with Balsa, it won't take users of Outlook Express or Mozilla Mail very long to get used to the Kmail interface. Some useful features found in KMail are the choice of mbox or maildir formats, improved filter creation, the ability to sort mail into threads, and the ability to apply filters at the MTA.

19

Figure 19.7 shows the KMail email program. KMail offers IMAP access, extensive filtering, `mbox` and `maildir` formats, and the ability to easily integrate MTAs such as Procmail, Spamassassin, or custom processing scripts.

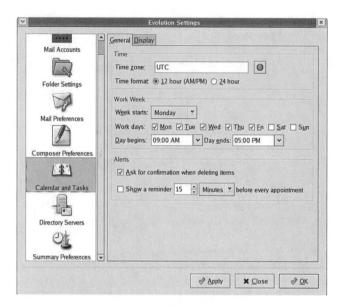

FIGURE 19.5   The calendar application Tools screen where the information can be shared with others. Here, the times and dates can be configured.

Mozilla Mail

Mozilla is more than a browser: It is an Internet Relay Chat client and a mail and newsgroup reader. The Mail and News setup wizard and preferences can be found under the Edit menu item. When you select Mail & Newsgroup Account Setup and then click on New Account, the wizard dialog will appear, as shown in Figure 19.8.

Configuration via the wizard is easy: Mozilla prompts you for the necessary information. The Mail interface (shown in Figure 19.9) is familiar to many users. If you use Mozilla for Web browsing, using it for email is a natural extension. Mozilla is, after all, the default browser for Fedora Core, and Mozilla Mail is a good choice for those who don't need all the features offered in the Evolution mail client.

Other Mail Clients

The mail clients included by Fedora Core are only a few of those available. Sylpheed-claws (not included) is very popular because it offers spell check while typing and is well-suited for use in large network environments in which network overhead and RAM usage are important considerations. You can find other mail clients and applications suitable for use with Fedora Core Linux by searching `http://freshmeat.net/`.

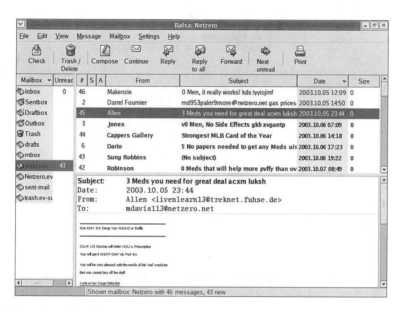

FIGURE 19.6   The Balsa email client. It shouldn't take long for users of Outlook Express or Mozilla Mail to get comfortable with the interface.

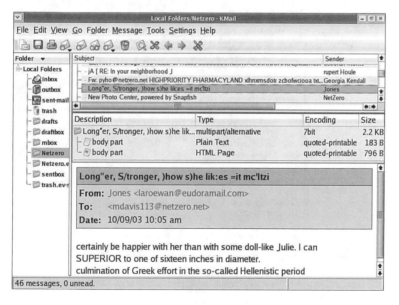

FIGURE 19.7   The KMail email client, part of the KDE Desktop Environment.

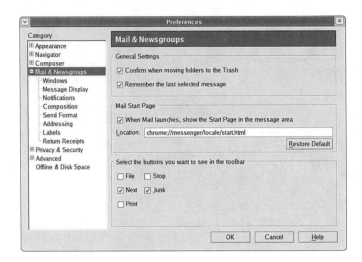

FIGURE 19.8 This is where your email and newsgroup configurations are set. Mozilla provides many choices to accommodate your individual needs.

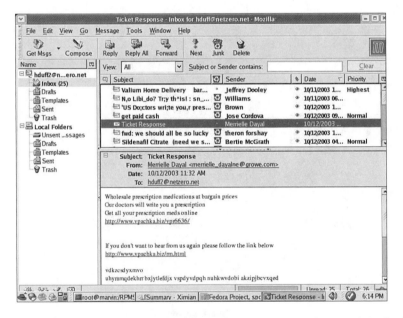

FIGURE 19.9 The interface to Mozilla Mail is familiar to many, similar to MS Outlook Express, KMail, and Balsa and is easy to use.

Attachments—Sending Binary Files As Text

The SMTP protocol can only transfer plain text, so to send images and binary files through email, you must encode the binary data as text. You then can include the encoded data in ordinary email; the recipient converts the text back to a binary format. The penalty for using this method is that the text file sizes are much larger than the binary files they replace.

The Macintosh operating system uses a program named BinHex; UNIX has traditionally used uuencoding and more recently, MIME encodings. A new player in the field is yenc encoding, which claims to be faster and compress to smaller sizes.

When encoding and decoding files manually, they all work in a similar manner to the venerable uuencode, so we have provided a detailed example of how to use that one.

NOTE

Unfortunately, Microsoft uses an attachment protocol not readily accepted by default attachment settings in a Fedora Core Linux (and other Linux) default installation. If you receive attachments from users of MS Outlook, you will receive these attachments.

The attachment type you might have trouble with is named TNEF, known as the Transport Neutral Encapsulation Format. To get around this problem, use the tnef filter; the included documentation describes its integration to your MUA. If you'd prefer to use a separate graphical decoding client, you can download and install the fentun X client.

The tnef filter is available from http://sourceforge.net/projects/tnef/.

The fentun application is available from http://www.fentun.com/.

BinHex

Apple Macintosh users encode binary files in the BinHex 4.0 format for attachment to email messages. Recipients need a decoder to view the attachment. None are included with Fedora Core Linux, but uudeview is available at http://www.fpx.de/fp/Software/UUDeview/; it codes and decodes Base64, yenc, BinHex, uuencode, and the obscure xxencode. With Tcl/Tk installed, a graphical interface is available. See RFC-1741 for details about BinHex encoding.

yenc

Jürgen Helbing, the author of yenc (the name is a munging of "My Encoder"), makes this encoder available with no copyright restrictions. Although now mostly used for Usenet messages, yenc also can be used for mail. (Support for yenc is included in the pan newsreader; see Chapter 20, "News and Other Collaborative Communication.") The site http://www.yenc.org/linux.htm hosts a page of links for yenc tools for Linux.

uuencode **and** uudecode

Fedora Core does include a program called uuencode that encodes a binary file as plain text so that it can be transferred across email with SMTP. At the destination, a companion program called uudecode decodes the text file back into its original binary form. Many times, the uuencoding and uudecoding of binary files are handled automatically by the email client, but sometimes they aren't.

If you receive a uuencoded file and your email program doesn't recognize it, you will receive something that appears to be several hundred or even a thousand lines of garbage text at first glance. However, the block of text will begin with a special line. Here is an example of what the first few lines of an uuencoded file might look like:

```
begin 644 penguin_in_tree.jpg
M_]C_X``02D9)1@`!`0$`8`!@``#_X0!.17AI9@``24DJ``@````"`#$!`@`'````
M````````````````````````````````````````````$``0``$````!`````
M`0````$``$``@`````````$``@`````````$```$``@`````````$```$``@``
M+V5F````$``0``$````$``$``$``$```$``$``$``$``$``$``$``$``$``$``
```

The first line of the block gives the permissions that the file should have when it is decoded (644) and the name of the file that should be created when the file is decoded. So how do you decode this file? Simply save the email message as a text file (for example, penguin_in_tree.txt). Next, use the uudecode program to decode it:

```
$ uudecode penguin_in_tree.txt
```

This will create a new file, which in this case would be called penguin_in_tree.jpg.

If you have a binary file that you want to encode so that you can email it to someone, you can do so with the uuencode program. uuencode uses the following syntax:

```
$ uuencode local_file remote_file
```

local_file is the name of the binary file stored on your hard disk. *remote_file* is the name that you want the file to decode later when you or someone else uses uudecode on it. Normally, you will probably want to use the same name for the local_file as the remote_file.

By default, this will send output to STDOUT, which is normally the screen. However, this isn't normally very useful, so you'll use redirection with the uuencode command. Here is an example:

```
$ uuencode penguin_in_tree.jpg penguin_in_tree.jpg > penguin_in_tree.txt
```

This command line will encode the file penguin_in_tree.jpg into a plain text file that will decode as a file with the same name (penguin_in_tree.jpg) and store the encoded file in the file penguin_in_tree.txt. This text file is suitable for emailing.

Of course, you can also use pipes to pipe the output of uuencode to another application. For example, you could pipe the results to the standard mail program and have it mailed directly to another user. For example,

```
$ uuencode penguin_in_tree.jpg penguin_in_tree.jpg ¦
Âmail -s "Penguin photograph" user1@lion.org
```

> **Hidden Messages**
>
> One of the by-products of uuencoding binary data is the need to pad each line to a specific number of characters if the data won't fill it up because the lines are always a fixed length. Normally these extra characters are random and are always ignored when decoding, but you can deliberately place information there instead of the random ASCII text. Placing information in the "holes" of other data files is known as *steganography*. Programs are available to encode and decode information this way (typically in pictures), as well as programs to scan images for hidden stenographic information. Search http://freshmeat.net/ for "steg" for a listing of interesting applications. Steganography is not limited to uuencode either.

Basic Sendmail Configuration and Operation

Because Sendmail is the Fedora Core Linux default client (and the mostly widely used client), the following sections provide a brief explanation and examples for configuring and operating your email system. As mentioned earlier, however, Sendmail is an extremely complex program with a very convoluted configuration. As such, this chapter only covers some of the basics. For more information on Sendmail, as well as other MTAs, see the "Reference" section at the end of this chapter.

Sendmail configuration is handled by files in the /etc/mail directory with much of the configuration being handled by the file sendmail.cf. The actual syntax of the configuration file, sendmail.cf, is cryptic (see the following example). In an attempt to make it easier to configure Sendmail, the sendmail.mc file was created. The following example belies that goal, however. The sendmail.mc file must be processed with the m4 macro processor to create the sendmail.cf file; the needs of that processor account for the unusual syntax of the file. You will learn how to use it later, and we will look at a Perl script that automates and simplifies the entire process. First, let's examine some basic configuration you might want to do with Sendmail.

> **NOTE**
>
> sendmail.cf has some strange syntax because of the requirements of the m4 macro processor. You needn't understand the details of m4 here, but note the quoting system. The starting quote is a backtick (`` ` ``), and the ending quote is simply a single quote ('). Also, the dnl sequence means to "delete to new line" and causes anything from the sequence up to and including the newline character to be deleted in the output.
>
> Here's a look at an excerpt from the sendmail.cf file:

19

```
CP.
# "Smart" relay host (may be null)
DS
# operators that cannot be in local usernames (i.e., network indicators)
CO @ % !
# a class with just dot (for identifying canonical names)
C..
# a class with just a left bracket (for identifying domain literals)
C[[
# access_db acceptance class
C{Accept}OK RELAY
C{ResOk}OKR
# Hosts for which relaying is permitted ($=R)
FR-o /etc/mail/relay-domains
```

And here's a quote from the sendmail.mc file for comparison:

```
dnl define(`SMART_HOST',`smtp.your.provider')
define(`confDEF_USER_ID',``8:12'')dnl
undefine(`UUCP_RELAY')dnl
undefine(`BITNET_RELAY')dnl
dnl define(`confAUTO_REBUILD')dnl
define(`confTO_CONNECT', `1m')dnl
define(`confTRY_NULL_MX_LIST',true)dnl
```

You can see why the file is described as "cryptic."

Rather than involve you in a detailed description of hand editing a file known to be among the most difficult to edit with success, we'll examine a Perl script developed by Donncha O'Caoimh. The script automates the configuration of Sendmail by prompting you for information and then doing all the heavy work by modifying the Sendmail configuration file itself. The script sets up a network mail server on a home computer running Fedora Core Linux. To use the script, you'll need to know your email address, the login names and passwords of all mail users, your mail server addresses, and the network's IP address. When you're done, Sendmail and Fetchmail will be configured. Running the script not only prompts you for all the necessary information, but it even provides some explanation and help along the way.

You should have Sendmail and Fetchmail installed on your system before you begin. The script is available for download at http://cork.linux.ie/projects/install-sendmail/. Simply uncompress the archive:

```
$ tar -zxvf install-sendmail-5.5.tar.gz
```

Now use the cd command to change to the newly created directory.

You can read a great description of this script and its use in the previously mentioned site's README, FAQ, and INSTALL files. You should read these files before you proceed with the installation; they are well-written and will answer all the questions you have. If you're interested in the power of programming with Perl, see Chapter 23, "Using Perl."

Of course, you can always configure Sendmail by hand, especially if you need any advanced options. The following five sections address some commonly used advanced options.

Configuring Masquerading

Sometimes you might want to have Sendmail masquerade as a host other than the actual hostname of your system. Such a situation could occur if you have a dial-up connection to the Internet and your ISP handles all your mail for you. In this case, you will want Sendmail to masquerade as the domain name of your ISP. For example,

```
MASQUERADE_AS(`samplenet.org')dnl
```

Using Smart Hosts

If you don't have a full-time connection to the Internet, you will probably want to have Sendmail send your messages to your ISP's mail server and let it handle delivery for you. Without a full-time Internet connection, you could find it difficult to deliver messages to some locations (such as some underdeveloped areas of the world where email services are unreliable and sporadic). In those situations, you can configure Sendmail to function as a smart host by passing email on to another sender rather than attempting to deliver the email directly. You can use a line such as the following in the sendmail.mc file to enable a smart host:

```
define(`SMART_HOST', `smtp.samplenet.org')
```

This line causes Sendmail to pass any mail it receives to the server smtp.samplenet.org rather than attempt to deliver it directly. Smart hosting won't work for you if your ISP, like many others, blocks mail relaying. Some ISPs block relaying because it's frequently used to disseminate spam.

Setting Message Delivery Intervals

As mentioned earlier, Sendmail typically attempts to deliver messages as soon as it receives them, and again at regular intervals after that. If you have only periodic connections to the Internet, as with a dial-up connection, you likely would prefer that Sendmail hold all messages in the queue and attempt to deliver them at specific time intervals or at your prompt. You can configure Sendmail to do so by adding the following line to sendmail.mc:

```
define(`confDELIVERY_MODE', `d')dnl
```

19

This line will cause Sendmail to only attempt mail delivery at regularly scheduled queue processing intervals (by default, somewhere between 20 and 30 minutes).

However, this delay time might not be sufficient if you're offline for longer periods of time. In those situations, you can invoke Sendmail with no queue processing time. For example, by default, Sendmail might start with the following command:

```
# sendmail -bd -q30m
```

This tells Sendmail that it should process the mail queue (and attempt message delivery) every 30 minutes. You can change 30 to any other number to change the delivery interval. If you want Sendmail to wait for a specific prompt before processing the queue, you can invoke Sendmail with no queue time, like this:

```
# sendmail -bd -q
```

This command tells Sendmail to process the queue once when it is started, and again only when you manually direct it to do so. To manually tell Sendmail to process the queue, you can use a command like the following:

```
# sendmail -q
```

> **TIP**
>
> If you use networking over a modem, there is a configuration file for pppd called ppp.linkup, which is located in /etc/ppp. Any commands in this file will automatically be run each time the PPP daemon is started. You can add the line sendmail -q to this file to have your mail queue automatically processed each time you dial up your Internet connection.

Building the sendmail.cf File

Books are available to explore the depths of Sendmail configuration, but the Sendmail Installation and Operation Guide is the canonical reference. Configuration guidance can also be found through a Google search; many people use Sendmail in many different configurations. Fortunately, Fedora Core has provided a default Sendmail configuration that will work "out-of-the-box" for a home user as long as your networking is correctly configured and you don't require an ISP-like Sendmail configuration.

After you have made all your changes to sendmail.mc, you need to rebuild the sendmail.cf file. First, back up your old file:

```
# cp /etc/mail/sendmail.cf /etc/mail/sendmail.cf.old
```

You must run sendmail.mc through the m4 macro processor in order to generate a usable configuration file. A command, such as the following, is used to do this:

```
# m4 /etc/mail/sendmail.mc > /etc/mail/sendmail.cf
```

This command loads the `cf.m4` macro file from `/usr/share/sendmail-cf/m4/cf.m4` and then uses it to process the `sendmail.mc` file. The output, normally sent to `STDOUT`, is then redirected to the file `sendmail.cf`, and your new configuration file is ready. You will need to restart Sendmail before the changes will take effect.

TIP

Fedora Core also provides an alternative to using `awk` to rebuild the Sendmail configuration. As root, execute

```
# make -C /etc/mail
```

Mail Relaying

By default, Sendmail won't relay mail that didn't originate from the local domain. This means that if a Sendmail installation running at `lion.org` receives mail intended for `cheetah.org`, and that mail didn't originate from `lion.org`, the mail will be rejected and won't be relayed. If you want to allow selected domains to relay through you, add an entry for the domain to the file `/etc/mail/relay-domains`. If the file doesn't exist, simply create it in your favorite text editor and add a line containing the name of the domain that you want to allow to relay through you. Sendmail will need to be restarted for this change to take effect.

CAUTION

You need a very good reason to relay mail; otherwise, don't do it. Allowing all domains to relay through you will make you a magnet for spammers who will use your mail server to send spam. This can lead to your site being blacklisted by many other sites, which then won't accept any mail from you or your site's users—even if the mail is legitimate!

Forwarding Email with Aliases

Aliases allow you to have an infinite number of valid recipient addresses on your system, without having to worry about creating accounts or other support files for each address. For example, most systems have "postmaster" defined as a valid recipient, yet don't have an actual login account named "postmaster." Aliases are configured in the file `/etc/aliases`. Here is an example of an alias entry:

```
postmaster: root
```

This entry will forward any mail received for "postmaster" to the root user. By default, almost all the aliases listed in the `/etc/aliases` file forward to root.

19

> **CAUTION**
>
> Reading email as `root` is a security hazard; a malicious email message can exploit an email client and cause it to execute arbitrary code as the user running the client. To avoid this danger, you can forward all of `root`'s mail to another account and read it from there. You can choose one of two ways for doing this.
>
> You can add an entry to the `/etc/mail/aliases` file that sends `root`'s mail to a different account. For example, `root: foobar` would forward all mail intended for `root` to the account `foobar`.
>
> The other way is to create a file named `.forward` in `root`'s home directory that contains the address that the mail should forward to.

Anytime you make a change to the `/etc/mail/aliases` file, you will need to rebuild the aliases database before that change will take effect. This is done with

```
# newaliases
```

Rejecting Email from Specified Sites

You read earlier in this chapter that you must be careful with mail relaying to avoid becoming a spam magnet. But what do you do if you are having problems with a certain site sending you spam? You can use the `/etc/mail/access` file to automatically reject mail from certain sites.

You can use several rules in the access file. Table 19.1 gives a list of these rules.

TABLE 19.1   The Various Possible Options for Access Rules

Option	Action
OK	Accepts mail from this site, overriding any rules that would reject mail from this site.
RELAY	Allows this domain to relay through the server.
REJECT	Rejects mail from this site and sends a canned error message.
DISCARD	Simply discards any message received from the site.
ERROR: "n message"	Where n is an RFC821-compliant error code number and message can be any message that you would like to send back to the originating server.

The following is an example of three rules used to control access to a Sendmail account. The first rejects messages from spam.com. The second rejects messages from lamer.com and displays an error message to that site. The third allows mail from the specific host user5.lamer.com, even though there is a rule that rejects mail from the site lamer.com. (For a more personal example of why you would bother to do this, I find that I get a lot of spam from the Hotmail domain, so I would just as soon reject it all. However, my wife uses a Hotmail account for her mail. If I did not allow her mail through, that would be a problem for me.)

```
spam.com          REJECT
lamer.com         ERROR:"550 Mail from spammers is not accepted at this site."
user5.lamer.com   OK
```

Open the /etc/access file, enter the rules of your choice, and then restart Sendmail so that your changes to the access file take effect. That can be done with

```
# /sbin/service sendmail restart
```

or any of the other ways we discussed in Chapter 7, "Managing Services."

Using Fetchmail to Retrieve Mail

SMTP is designed to work with systems that have a full-time connection to the Internet. What if you are on a dial-up account? What if you have another system store your email for you and then you log in to pick it up once in awhile? (Most users who aren't setting up servers will be in this situation.) In this case, you cannot easily receive email using SMTP, and you need to use a protocol, such as POP3 or IMAP, instead.

> **NOTE**
>
> Remember when we said that some mail clients can include some MTA functionality? MS Outlook and Outlook Express can be configured to use SMTP and, if you use a dial-up connection, will offer to start the connection and then use SMTP to send your mail, so a type of MTA functionality is included in those mail clients.

Unfortunately, many MUAs don't know anything about POP3 or IMAP. To eliminate that problem, you can use a program called Fetchmail to contact mail servers using POP3 or IMAP, download mail off the servers, and then inject those messages into the local MTA just as if they had come from a standard SMTP server. The following sections explain how to install, configure, and use the Fetchmail program.

Installing Fetchmail

Similar to other .rpm files, Fetchmail can be installed with the rpm -i command. This command will install all files to their default locations. If, for whatever reason, you need to perform a custom installation, see Chapter 8, "Managing Software and System Resources," for more information on changing the default options for rpm.

You can get the latest version of Fetchmail at http://tuxedo.org/~esr/fetchmail. It is available in both source and RPM binary formats. The version of Fedora Core Linux on the CDs accompanying this book provides a reasonably current version of Fetchmail and installs useful Fetchmail documentation in the /usr/share/doc/fetchmail directory. That directory includes an FAQ, features list, and Install documentation.

19

Configuring Fetchmail

After you've installed Fetchmail, you must create the file .fetchmailrc in your home directory, which provides the configuration for the Fetchmail program.

There are two ways to create the .fetchmailrc file. The first is by simply creating and editing the file by hand with any text editor. The second is by using the graphical fetchmailconf program. The configuration file is straightforward and quite easy to create; the following sections explain the manual method for creating and editing the file. The information presented in the following sections doesn't discuss all the options available in the .fetchmailrc file, but covers the most common ones needed to get a basic Fetchmail installation up and running. You'll need to use a text editor to create the file to include entries like the ones shown as examples—modified for your personal information, of course. For advanced configuration, see the man page for Fetchmail. The man page is well written and documents all the configuration options in detail.

> **CAUTION**
>
> The .fetchmailrc file is divided into three different sections: global options, mail server options, and user options. It is very important that these sections appear in the order listed. Do not add options to the wrong section. Putting options in the wrong place is one of the most common problems that new users make with Fetchmail configuration files.

Configuring Global Options

The first section of .fetchmailrc contains the global options. These options affect all the mail servers and user accounts that you list later in the configuration file. Some of these global options can be overridden with local configuration options, as you learn later in this section. Here is an example of the options that might appear in the global section of the .fetchmailrc file:

```
set daemon 600
set postmaster foobar
set logfile ./.fetchmail.log
```

The first line in this example tells Fetchmail that it should start in daemon mode and check the mail servers for new mail every 600 seconds, or 10 minutes. Daemon mode means that after Fetchmail starts, it will move itself into the background and continue running. Without this line, Fetchmail would check for mail once when it started and would then terminate and never check again.

The second option tells Fetchmail to use the local account foobar as a last resort address. In other words, any email that it receives and cannot deliver to a specified account should be sent to foobar.

The third line tells Fetchmail to log its activity to the file ./.fetchmail.log. Alternatively, you can use the line set syslog—in which case, Fetchmail will log through the syslog facility.

Configuring Mail Server Options

The second section of the .fetchmailrc file contains information on each of the mail servers that should be checked for new mail. Here is an example of what the mail section might look like:

```
poll mail.samplenet.org
proto pop3
no dns
```

The first line tells Fetchmail that it should check the mail server mail.samplenet.org at each poll interval that was set in the global options section (which was 600 seconds in our example). Alternatively, the first line can begin with skip. If a mail server line begins with skip, it will not be polled as the poll interval, but will only be polled when it is specifically specified on the Fetchmail command line.

The second line specifies the protocol that should be used when contacting the mail server. In this case, we are using the POP3 protocol. Other legal options are IMAP, APOP, and KPOP. You can also use AUTO here—in which case, Fetchmail will attempt to automatically determine the correct protocol to use with the mail server.

The third line tells Fetchmail that it shouldn't attempt to do a DNS lookup. You will probably want to include this option if you are running over a dial-up connection.

Configuring User Accounts

The third and final section of .fetchmailrc contains information about the user account on the server specified in the previous section. Here is an example:

```
user foobar
pass secretword
fetchall
flush
```

The first line, of course, simply specifies the username that is used to log in to the email server, and the second line specifies the password for that user. Many security conscious people cringe at the thought of putting clear-text passwords in a configuration file, and they should if it is group or world-readable. The only protection for this information is to make certain that the file is readable only by the owner; that is, with file permissions of 600.

The third line tells Fetchmail that it should fetch all messages from the server, even if they have already been read.

The fourth line tells Fetchmail that it should delete the messages from the mail server after it has completed downloading them. This is the default, so we wouldn't really have to specify this option. If you wanted to leave the messages on the server after downloading them, use the option no flush.

The configuration options you just inserted configured the entire `.fetchmailrc` file to look like this:

```
set daemon 600
set postmaster foobar
set logfile ./.fetchmail.log

poll mail.samplenet.org
proto pop3
no dns

user foobar
pass secretword
fetchall
flush
```

What this file tells Fetchmail to do is

- Check the POP3 server `mail.samplenet.org` for new mail every 600 seconds.
- Log in using the username `foobar` and the password `secretword`.
- Download all messages off the server.
- Delete the messages from the server after it has finished downloading them.
- Send any mail it receives that cannot be delivered to a local user to the account `foobar`.

TIP

You could use the graphical `fetchmailconf` client to configure, test, and use your Fetchmail settings. . If you choose to install it, start the client from the command line of an X terminal window like this:

```
# fetchmailconf &
```

As mentioned before, many more options can be included in the `.fetchmailrc` file than are listed here. However, these options will get you up and running with a basic configuration.

For additional flexibility, you can define multiple `.fetchmailrc` files in order to retrieve mail from different remote mail servers while using the same Linux user account. For example, you can define settings for your most often used account and save them in the default `.fetchmailrc` file. Mail can then quickly be retrieved like so:

```
$ fetchmail -a
```

```
1 message for bball at mail.myserver.com (1108 octets).
reading message 1 of 1 (1108 octets) . flushed
```

By using Fetchmail's -f option, you can specify an alternative resource file and then easily retrieve mail from another server like this:

```
$ fetchmail -f .myothermailrc
2 messages for bball at othermail.otherserver.org (5407 octets).
reading message 1 of 2 (3440 octets) ... flushed
reading message 2 of 2 (1967 octets) . flushed
You have new mail in /var/spool/mail/bball
```

By using the -d option, along with a time interval (in seconds), you can use Fetchmail in its daemon, or background mode. The command will launch as a background process and retrieve mail from a designated remote server at a specified interval. For more advanced options, see the Fetchmail man page, which is very well-written and documents all options in detail.

CAUTION

Because the .fetchmailrc file contains your mail server password, it should be readable only by you. This means that it should be owned by you and should have permissions no greater than 600. Fetchmail will complain and refuse to start if the .fetchmailrc file has permissions greater than this.

Choosing a Mail Delivery Agent (MDA)

Because of the modular nature of mail handling, it is possible to use multiple applications to process mail and accomplish more than simply deliver it. Getting mail from the storage area and displaying it to the user is the purpose of the mail delivery agent (MDA). MDA functionality can be found in some of the mail clients (MUAs), which can cause some confusion to those still unfamiliar with the concept of UNIX mail. As an example, the Procmail MDA provide filtering based on rulesets; KMail and Evolution, both MUAs, provide filtering, but the MUAs pine, mutt, and Balsa do not. Some MDAs perform simple sorting, and other MDAs are designed to eliminate unwanted emails, such as spam and viruses.

You would choose an MDA based on what you want to do with your mail. We'll look at five MDAs that offer functions you might find useful in your particular situation. If you have simple needs (just organizing mail by rules), one of the MUAs that offers filtering might be better for your needs. Fedora Core provides the Evolution MUA as the default selection (and it contains some MDA functionality as previously noted), so try that first and see if it meets your needs. If not, investigate one of the following MDAs provided by Fedora Core.

Unless otherwise noted, all the MDA software is provided with the Fedora Core discs. Chapter 8 details the general installation of any software.

Procmail

As a tool for advanced users, the Procmail application acts as a filter for email as it is retrieved from a mail server. It uses rulesets (known as recipes) as it reads each email message. No default configuration is provided; you must manually create a ~/.procmail file for each user, or each user can create her own.

There is no systemwide default configuration file. The creation of the rulesets is not trivial and requires an understanding of the use of regular expressions that is beyond the scope of this chapter. Fedora Core does provide three examples of the files in /usr/share/doc/procmail/examples, as well as a fully commented example in the /usr/share/doc/procmail directory, which also contains a README and FAQ. Details for the rulesets can be found in the man page for Procmail as well as the man pages for procmailrc, procmailsc, and procmailex, which contain examples of Procmail recipes.

Spamassassin

If you've used email for any length of time, you've likely been subjected to spam—unwanted email that is sent to thousands of people at the same time. Fedora Core provides an MDA named Spamassassin to assist you in reducing and eliminating unwanted emails. Easily integrated with Procmail and Sendmail, it can be configured for both systemwide and individual use. It employs a combination of rulesets and blacklists (Internet domains known to mail spam).

Enabling Spamassassin is simple. You must first have installed and configured Procmail. The README file found in /usr/share/doc/spamassasin provides details on configuring the .procmail file to process mail through Spamassassin. It will tag probable spam with a unique header; you can then have Procmail filter the mail in any manner you choose. One interesting use of Spamassassin is to use it to tag email received at special email accounts established solely for the purpose of attracting spam. This information is then shared with the Spamassassin site where these "spam trap" generated hits help the authors fine-tune the rulesets.

Squirrelmail

Perhaps you don't want to read your mail in an MUA. If you use your Web browser often, it might make sense to read and send your mail via a Web interface, such as the one used by Hotmail or Yahoo! mail. Fedora Core provides Squirrelmail for just that purpose. Squirrelmail is written in the PHP 4 language and supports IMAP and SMTP with all pages rendering in HTML 4.0 without using Java. It supports MIME attachments, as well as an address book and folders for segregating email.

You must configure your Web server to work with PHP 4. Detailed installation instructions can be found in /usr/share/doc/squirrelmail/INSTALL. Once configured, point your Web browser to http://www.yourdomain.com/squirellmail/ to read and send email.

Virus Scanners

Although the currently held belief is that Linux is immune to email viruses targeted at Microsoft Outlook users, it certainly makes no sense for UNIX mail servers to permit infected email to be sent through them. Although Fedora Core does not provide a virus scanner, one of the more popular of many such scanners is MailScanner, available from http://www.sng.ecs.soton.ac.uk/mailscanner/; a Fedora Core RPM package is available as well as the source code. It supports Sendmail and Exim, but not Postfix or Qmail. Searching on the terms "virus" and "email" at Freshmeat.net will turn up a surprising list of GPLed virus scanners that might serve your needs.

Special Mail Delivery Agents

If you already use Hotmail or another Web-based email account, the currently available MUAs will not be useful to you; formal POP3 access to a Hotmail account is not available free of charge. However, Microsoft Outlook Express can access Hotmail at no charge using a special protocol called HTTPMail. How that's done is covered in RFC-2518 as "WebDAV extensions to HTTP/1.1." No specific solution is provided by Fedora Core Linux, but the basic tools it provides are adequate when supplemented by some clever Perl programming.

Hotwayd is available from http://sourceforge.net/projects/hotwayd/ and implements this functionality, allowing you to use your favorite mail client to read mail from Hotmail.

A newer Hotmail access tool is Gotmail from http://sourceforge.net/projects/gotmail. It's a Perl script that is easy to configure. There are brief tutorials on configuring it for use with KMail and Evolution at http://www.madpenguin.org/cms/?m=show&id=437.

A similar tool exists for Yahoo! mail. FetchYahoo is available from http://fetchyahoo.twizzler.org/.

Once implemented, you can use a regular MUA, or mail client, to access your Web-based mail. None of them, however, enable you to send mail through Hotmail or Yahoo! mail.

Mail Daemons

Fedora Core provides an imap package that will install IMAP and POP daemons (servers) for your system. These servers facilitate receiving mail from a remote site. Once installed, the documentation will be found in /usr/share/doc/imap and the README is brief; Fedora Core has already done the configuration for you: You only need to start the services (see Chapter 7).

Biff and its KDE cousin KOrn are small daemons that monitor your mail folder and notify you when a message has been placed there. It is common to include biff y in the .login or .profile files to automatically start it upon user login if you want to use Biff. KOrn can be started by adding the applet to the KDE taskbar.

> **NOTE**
>
> Autoresponders automatically generate replies to received messages; they're commonly used to notify others that the recipient is out of the office. Mercifully, Fedora Core does not include one, but you can find and install an autoresponder at Freshmeat.net. If you are subscribed to a mailing list, be aware that automatic responses from your account can be very annoying to others on the list. Please unsubscribe from mail lists before you leave the office with your autoresponder activated.

Alternatives to Microsoft Exchange Server

One of the last areas in which a Microsoft product has yet to be usurped by Open Source software is a replacement for MS Exchange Server. Many businesses use MS Outlook and MS Exchange Server to access email, as well as to provide calendaring, notes, file sharing, and other collaborative functions. General industry complaints about Exchange Server center around scalability, administration (backup and restore in particular), and licensing fees.

A "drop-in" alternative needs to have compatibility with MS Outlook because it's intended to replace Exchange Server in an environment in which there are Microsoft desktops in existence using Outlook. A "work-alike" alternative provides similar features to Exchange Server, but does not offer compatibility with the MS Outlook client itself; the latter is typical of many of the open-source alternatives.

There are several "drop-in" alternatives, none of which are fully open source because some type of proprietary connector is needed to provide the services to MS Outlook clients (or provide Exchange services to the Linux Evolution client). For Outlook compatibility, the key seems to be the realization of a full, open implementation of MAPI, Microsoft's Messaging Application Program Interface. That goal is going to be difficult to achieve because MAPI is a poorly documented Microsoft protocol. For Linux-only solutions, the missing ingredient for many alternatives is a usable group calendaring/scheduling system similar in function to that provided by Exchange Server/Outlook.

Of course, independent applications for these functions abound in the open-source world, but one characteristic of "groupware" is its central administration; another is that all components can share information.

The following sections examine several of the available servers, beginning with MS Exchange Server itself and moving toward those applications that have increasing incompatibility with it. None of these servers are provided by Fedora Core.

Microsoft Exchange Server/Outlook Client

Exchange Server and Outlook seem to be the industry benchmark because of their wide-spread deployment. They offer a proprietary server providing email, contacts, scheduling, public folders, task lists, journaling, and notes using MS Outlook as the client and MAPI as the API. If you consider what MS Exchange offers as the "full" set of features, no other replacement offers 100% of the features exactly as provided by MS Exchange Server—even those considered "drop-in" replacements. The home page for the Microsoft Exchange server is `http://www.microsoft.com/exchange/`.

CommuniGate Pro

CommuniGate Pro is a proprietary, drop-in alternative to MS Exchange Server, providing, email, webmail, LDAP directories, a Web server, file server, contacts, calendaring (third-party), and a list server. The CommuniGate Pro MAPI Connector provides access to the server from MS Outlook and other MAPI-enabled clients. The home page for this server is `http://www.stalker.com/`.

Samsung Contact (Formerly Known As HP OpenMail)

This is a proprietary, drop-in alternative to MS Exchange Server (and is also used by many Fortune 500 companies). The Samsung Contact server provides what is almost a full replacement for MS Exchange Server and will (once ITEF finishes the open "calendar spec") work with all the more common Linux email clients and Web browsers. The home page is `http://www.samsungcontact.com/en/`.

Bynari

Bynari provides a proprietary group of servers to act as a drop-in replacement for MS Exchange Server for email, calendaring, public folders, scheduling, address book, webmail, and contacts. Although it runs on Linux, it offers no Linux clients and the Connector provides services to MS Outlook only. The home page is `http://www.bynari.net/`.

SuSE OpenExchange

The SuSE Linux OpenExchange message server is based on Cyrus-imap and Postfix. Most of the server's groupware features are provided by a proprietary Web-based groupware server (ComFire). SuSE OpenExchange also uses Apache, OpenLDAP, Samba, and SuSE Linux Enterprise Server 8 to provide public directories, notes, webmail, scheduler, tasks, project management, document management, forums, and bookmarks. Some compatibility with MS Outlook is provided. The home page is `http://www.suse.com/en/business/products/openexchange/`.

Kroupware

The Kroupware project was begun to provide groupware functions such as email, group calendaring, notes, and tasks, but Kroupware was not designed to be a total replacement for MS Exchange Server and Outlook. The result is composed of the Kolab Server and the KDE Kolab Client. The Kolab Server is based on the existing Open Source components of OpenLDAP, Cyrus-imapd, Postfix, and Apache. The KDE Kolab Client uses special versions of KMail, KOrganizer, KAddressBook, and KPilot that can communicate with the Kolab Server. It is necessary to use the Bynari Insight Connector to enable Outlook to communicate with the Kolab Server. The home page is `http://www.kroupware.org/`.

OpenGroupware (Formerly SKYRiX 4.1)

OpenGroupware (not affiliated with OpenOffice.org) focuses on groupware and collaboration (and does not provide its own mail server). It can replace Comfire in SuSE OpenExchange to save on the licensing cost or be used with a Cyrus-imap mail server and PostgreSQL and FrontBase (no MySQL) for the database. For connectivity to Outlook, OpenGroupware uses the ZideLook MAPI Storage Provider (proprietary, it maps MAPI to WebDAV) and the Open Source WebDAV middleware server ZideStore. ZideStore translates WebDAV requests to calls to OpenGroupware as well as clients such as Evolution and Mozilla. The home page is `http://www.opengroupware.org/en/`.

phpgroupware

phpgroupware is an open-source application written in PHP (and used with MySql or postgresql plus a Web server and an IMAP mail server). Phpgroupware provides a Web-based calendar, task list, address book, email, news headlines, and a file manager. Version 1.0 is expected to be released in 2004. The home page is `http://www.phpgroupware.org/`.

PHProjekt

PHProjekt is open-source software written in PHP (used with MySql, postgresql, Oracle, Informix, or MS-sql). PHProjekt provides calendaring, contact manager, time card system, project management, online chat, threaded discussion forum, trouble ticket system, email, public files, notes, bookmarks, voting system, task lists, reminders, site-search, and integration with the PostNuke news site application. It provides no Exchange/Outlook compatibility whatsoever. The home page is `http://www.PHProjekt.com/`.

IMP/Horde

IMP/Horde is a PHP-based application framework. When combined with an HTTP server (Apache, Microsoft IIS, Netscape) and MySql database, IMP/Horde offers modules that provide webmail, contact manager, calendar, CVS viewer, file manager, time tracking, email filter rules manager, notes, tasks, chat, newsgroups, forms, bug tracking, FAQ repository, and presentations. The home page is `http://www.horde.org/`.

Conclusion

There are no open source–only alternatives that can provide full Exchange-like services to MS Outlook clients. If you don't have Outlook clients to worry about, OpenGroupware, IMP/Horde, and PHProjekt look promising. None of them is provided with Fedora Core.

Relevant Fedora Core and Linux Commands

You'll use the following commands to manage electronic mail in Fedora Core Linux:

`balsa`—A GNOME mail user agent for X.

`biff`—A console-based mail notification utility.

`evolution`—A comprehensive and capable Ximian GNOME mail PIM for X.

`fetchmail`—A console-based and daemon-mode mail retrieval command for Linux.

`fetchmailconf`—A graphical `fetchmail` configuration client for X.

`kmail`—A graphical mail user client for KDE and X.

`korn`—A `biff` applet for KDE and X.

`mail`—A console-based mail user agent.

`mutt`—A console-based mail user agent.

`sendmail`—A comprehensive mail transport agent for UNIX and Linux.

`xbiff`—A mail notification X client.

Reference

The following references are recommended reading for email configuration. Of course, not all references will apply to you. Select the ones that apply to the email server that you are using.

Web Resources

`http://www.instinct.org/elm/`—A comprehensive information site about the elm mail program.

`http://www.washington.edu/pine/`—Home page for the Program for Internet News & Email (pine) mail program.

`http://www.sendmail.org/`—This is the Sendmail home page. Here you will find configuration information and FAQs regarding the Sendmail MTA.

`http://www.postfix.org/`—This is the Postfix home page. If you are using the Postfix MTA, documentation and sample configurations can be found at this site.

`http://www.qmail.org/`—This is the home page for the Qmail MTA. It contains documentation and links to other resources on Qmail.

`http://www.linuxgazette.com/issue35/jao.html`—IMAP on Linux: A Practical Guide. The Internet Mail Access Protocol allows a user to access his email stored on a remote server rather than a local disk.

`http://www.imap.org/about/whatisIMAP.html`—A page describing what IMAP is.

`http://www.rfc-editor.org/`—A repository of RFCs—Request for Comments—that define the technical "rules" of modern computer usage.

`http://www.procmail.org/`—The Procmail homepage.

`http://www.moongroup.com/docs/procmail/`—The Procmail FAQ, which includes suggestions for troubleshooting problems. The page also references a page of links that, in turn, reference other link collections as well as tidbits from the Procmail mail list.

`http://www.ibiblio.org/pub/Linux/docs/HOWTO/other-formats/html_single/ Qmail-VMailMgr-Courier-imap-HOWTO.html`—If you want some help configuring a mail system based on the lesser-used applications, this HOWTO will help.

Books

Sendmail from O'Reilly Publishing. This is the de facto standard guide for everything Sendmail. It is loaded with more than 1,000 pages, which gives you an idea of how complicated Sendmail really is.

Postfix from Sams Publishing. An excellent book from Sams Publishing that covers the Postfix MTA.

Running Qmail from Sams Publishing. This is similar to the Postfix book from Sams Publishing except that it covers the Qmail MTA.

CHAPTER 20

News and Other Collaborative Communication

IN THIS CHAPTER

• An Overview of Network News

• Selecting a Newsreader

• Collaborating with TWiki

• Internet Relay Chat

• Internet Messaging with GAIM

• Video Conferencing with GnomeMeeting

• Mail List Configuration and Management with Mailman

• Configuring a Local News Server

• Reference

From multinational corporations to community groups, it is increasingly less common for everyone in a workgroup to be physically located in a single place. Getting everyone together for a meeting has become impractical, if not impossible. By using the tools that Fedora Core provides with Linux (and some other well-chosen applications), it is possible to effectively collaborate with people you might never meet in person.

Next to email, one of the oldest collaborative applications on the Internet is the Usenet network news system. Usenet started out as a network of hosts connected via modems, allowing users to share information on a wide range of topics.

The Usenet newsgroups are still a popular medium people use to exchange ideas, but their use has been declining in the face of competition from Internet relay chat (IRC), Internet, or instant messaging (IM), and email mailing lists (also called mail lists). Those methods typically don't leave an easily accessible public archive, however. One of the interesting alternatives to news is a Web-based application known as TWiki, which is an interactive collaborative Web page.

Fedora Core provides software that grants you access to video conferencing over the Internet (you must supply the appropriate hardware, of course). Even the old standby of email gets a new use in Fedora Core Linux through the implementation of organized private mail lists.

This chapter describes the software included with Fedora Core Linux that can be used to configure a Linux news server to act as a standalone local or intranet news server for other news clients. It also describes how to set up a TWiki Web page, how to use IRC and IM, and how to configure Mailman for use in managing mail lists.

An Overview of Network News

The concept of newsgroups revolutionized the way information was exchanged between people across a network. The Usenet network news system created a method for people to electronically communicate with large groups of people with similar interests.

The following sections describe the Usenet network newsgroup format and how newsgroup information is transmitted between hosts. As you'll see, many of the concepts of Usenet news are embodied in other forms of collaborative communication.

Newsgroups

Usenet newsgroups act as a form of public bulletin board system. Any user can subscribe to individual newsgroups and send (or post) messages (called articles) to the newsgroup so that all the other subscribers of the newsgroup can read them. Some newsgroups include an administrator, who must approve each message before it is posted. These are called moderated newsgroups. Other newsgroups are open, allowing any subscribed member to post a message. When an article is posted to the newsgroup, it is transferred to all the other hosts in the news network.

Usenet newsgroups are divided into a hierarchy to make it easier to find individual newsgroups. The hierarchy levels are based on topics, such as computers, science, recreation, and social issues. Each newsgroup is named as a subset of the higher-level topic. For example, the newsgroup `comp` relates to all computer topics. The newsgroup `comp.laptops` relates to laptop computer issues. Often the hierarchy goes several layers deep. For example, the newsgroup `comp.databases.oracle.server` relates to Oracle server database issues.

> **NOTE**
>
> The format of newsgroup articles follows the strict guidelines defined in the Internet standards document Request for Comments (RFC) 1036. Each article must contain two distinct parts: header lines and a message body.
>
> The header lines identify information about when and from whom the article was posted. The body of the message should contain only standard ASCII text characters. No binary characters or files should be posted within news articles. To get around this restriction, binary files are converted to text data by using either the standard UNIX uuencode program or the newer Multipurpose Internet Mail Extensions (MIME) protocol. The resulting text file is then posted to the newsgroup. Newsgroup readers can then decode the posted text file back into its original binary form.

A collection of articles posted in response to a common topic is called a thread. A thread can contain many different articles as users post messages in response to other posted messages. Some newsreader programs allow the user to track articles based on the threads they belong to. This helps simplify the organization of articles in the newsgroup.

> **TIP**
>
> The free news server news.gmane.org makes the Red Hat and Fedora Core mail lists available via newsgroups. The beta list is available as gmane.linux.redhat.rhl.beta. It's a handy way to read threaded discussions and easier than using the Fedora Core mail list archives.

The protocol used to transfer newsgroup articles from one host to another is Network News Transfer Protocol (NNTP), defined in RFC 977. (You can search RFCs at ftp://metalab.unc.edu/pub/docs/rfc/;look at the file rfc-index.txt.) NNTP was designed as a simple client/server protocol that enables two hosts to exchange newsgroup articles in an efficient manner.

Selecting a Newsreader

Whether your Fedora Core server is or is not set up as a news server, you can use a newsreader program to read newsgroup articles. The newsreader programs just require a connection to a news server. It doesn't matter if the news server is on the same machine or is a remote news server on the other side of the world.

Several programs are available for UNIX systems to connect to news servers to read and post articles in newsgroups. The following sections describe the newsreaders that are available with the Fedora Core Linux distribution.

The slrn News Client

The slrn program is a text-based newsreader program included with the Fedora Core distribution. It uses the ncurses package to paint text-based windows on the terminal screen. slrn can be used to both read and post articles to newsgroups on a configured news server. If you want to use the same newsreader on different platforms, slrn runs on Linux, Mac, OS2, BeOS, Windows, and VMX. It now provides true offline reading capabilities.

The slrn program is included in the slrn RPM package; you install it by using the rpm command. After you have installed slrn, you need to create a local configuration file. Begin by setting an environmental variable:

```
$ export NNTSERVER=news.maximumhoyt.com
```

Of course, you'll use your own news server's domain name.

Then create you local configuration file with

```
$ slrn -f .jnewsrc -- create
```

and launch slrn. The configuration file, located at /etc/slrn.rc, is a well-commented file that's easy to modify and customize.

When slrn starts, it displays a list of the groups that are available on the news server. You select the group you want to read articles from, and then select the individual articles. Figure 20.1 shows a slrn screen example.

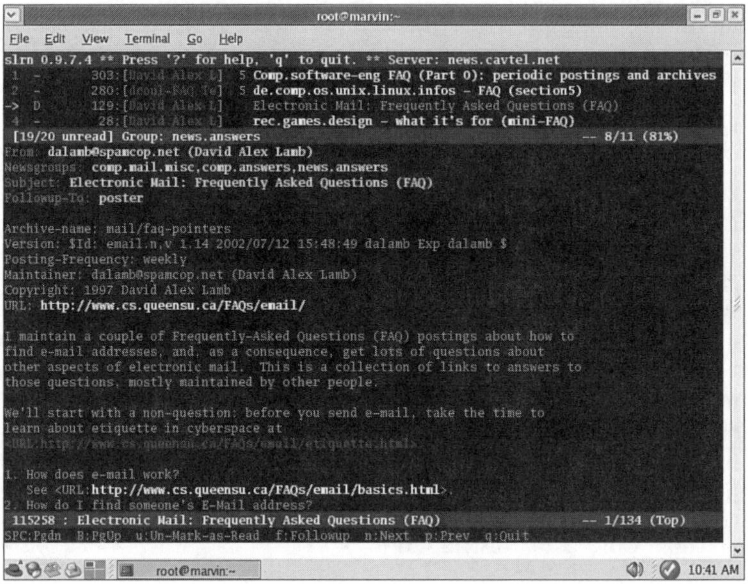

FIGURE 20.1 A slrn article display example showing a posted message about a FAQ for Internet mail.

The Pan News Client

Pan is a graphical newsreader client that works with GNOME and is the default newsreader for Fedora Core. If you have the GNOME libraries installed (and they usually are installed by default), you can also use Pan with the K Desktop Environment (KDE). Pan has the capability to download and display all the newsgroups and display posted news articles. You can launch it by using the GNOME or KDE desktop panel or from the command line of an X terminal window with the command pan &. Pan supports combining multipart messages and the yenc encoding/decoding protocol. Figure 20.2 shows a sample Pan display. Unlike the slrn program, Pan does not require a systemwide default or user-defined NNTPSERVER environment variable to define the news server address, but you do need to configure Pan.

The first time you run Pan, a configuration wizard appears and prompts you for your name, the SMTP server name, the NNTP server name, and the name you want to use to identify the connection (in the example shown in Figure 20.3, we use `Cavtel`). After the wizard is finished, you'll be prompted to download a list of the newsgroups the server provides; this may take a while. If you need to change the news server or add an additional server, you can access the Preferences item under the Edit menu to bring up the list of servers. Then, you highlight the appropriate one and click Edit to change it or just click the New button to add a new news server.

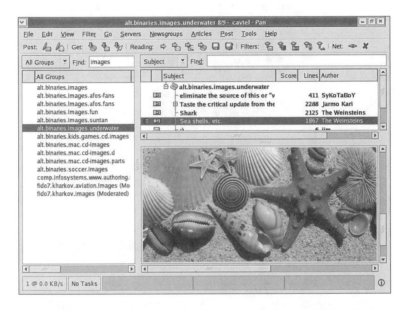

FIGURE 20.2   The Pan graphical newsreader is one of the nicest available for Linux, shown here displaying an image attached to a news article.

The KNode News Client

The KNode program is part of the `kdenetwork` RPM package—the KDE network package included in Fedora Core. KNode is usually installed by default if you select the KDE windows manager option in the Fedora Core installation.

The KNode program is an excellent graphical program (similar to MS Outlook Express) that allows you to connect to news servers (either a local or remote server) and select newsgroups where you can read and post articles. Before you can begin, though, you must configure the address of your news server in KNode. You do this from the Settings menu item on the main KNode window; select the Configure KNode item, and the KNode configuration window appears. Under the Accounts item, select the News item. A list of configured news servers appears in the window. To add a new news server, click the New button. Figure 20.4 shows the KNode New Account window, where you can enter the new news server information.

FIGURE 20.3   The Pan news server configuration window.

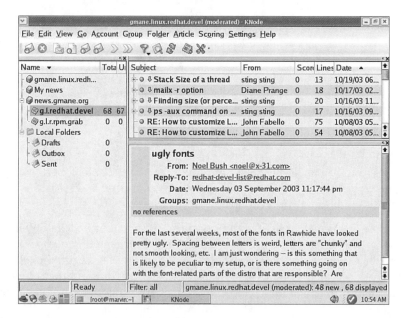

FIGURE 20.4   The KNode newsreader; setup is quick and easy. It's a great newsreader for text-only newsgroups.

The Mozilla News Client

The Mozilla Web browser supports graphical Usenet newsreading as well as Web browsing. Having numerous newsreading clients installed on a Fedora Core system offers users a wealth of choice and opportunities for developing favorites. In some cases, however, it can complicate the administrator's task of tracking and fixing client security liabilities. Using Mozilla can help simplify this task by offering an all-in-one client that provides Web browsing, email, file transfer, and newsreading capabilities. For these reasons, you might choose to use Mozilla as a browser, email client, and news client. Mozilla is the default browser for Fedora Core.

To begin newsreading with Mozilla, you launch Mozilla and select Window, Mail and Newsgroups; the window shown in Figure 20.5 appears. The menu Edit, Mail & Newsgroups Account Settings is where you configure Mozilla for your news and mail server settings. Many people prefer to use Mozilla for all their Web browsing, mail, news, and IRC.

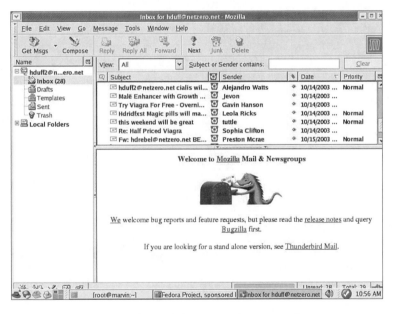

FIGURE 20.5   Mozilla is a handy, all-around integrated Internet client.

To add accounts, under Edit, Mail & Newsgroups Account Settings, click the Add Account button and select either a mail or news account to add. The Account Settings dialog is shown in Figure 20.6.

When you finish entering this information, click OK, and you arrive at the newsreader window. Click the news server name in the left pane and then select Subscribe to Newsgroups in the right pane to begin downloading a list of newsgroups from your news

20

server. At any time, you can update the list of newsgroups by clicking the Refresh button in that window.

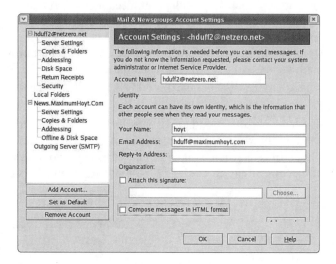

FIGURE 20.6   Here is where your configuration information is accessed. Note that we had to deliberately deselect the Compose Messages in HTML Format option, fixing a poorly chosen default.

Collaborating with TWiki

Although Usenet is a useful interactive and collaboration tool, in some cases a Web-based tool is better suited to your needs. TWiki (`http://TWiki.org/`) is a Web-based interactive collaboration tool that can also be used as a bulletin board, a knowledge base, a bug tracker, and a software archive.

> **TIP**
>
> You can examine the TWiki Success Stories on the company's home page for any encouragement you need to explore TWiki. You can also explore this Linux-related public TWiki site:
>
> `http://TWiki.org/cgi-bin/view/Wikilearn/WebHome/`

TWiki is not available from Fedora Core, and you must download it from the TWiki Web site after completing a brief registration. You then receive email instructions explaining how to download a `.zip` file from the site. (You use `unzip` to extract the files.) The program is licensed under the GPL.

You might want to first read the installation instructions located at `http://TWiki.org/cgi-bin/view/TWiki/TWikiDocumentation`. The documentation has been improved over the past year and now includes directions for installing TWiki as the non-root user. Many details are provided on file ownership and file permissions. There is also an automatic installer—the O'Wiki Installer—referenced at `http://TWiki.org/cgi-bin/view/Codev/TWikiUnixInstaller`. This might be a good approach to use if you are skilled at Apache configuration, but the install script does not set the appropriate file ownership and permissions for Fedora as mentioned later.

Here's a short list of advice for moving smoothly through the installation process on a Fedora Core Linux system (this list assumes that you are performing an installation as the `root` user and are reading the TWiki installation instructions from the TWiki Web site):

- You need to create the directory `/home/httpd/twiki`; unzip TWiki into this directory.

- The installation instructions mention the file `/etc/httpd/httpd.conf`. For Fedora Core, this file is found at `/etc/httpd/conf/httpd.conf`. You simply copy and paste the entries shown in the example supplied by the downloaded instructions.

- The path to Perl for Fedora Core is `/usr/bin/perl`.

- Fedora Core runs CGI scripts as the user `apache`, not the user `nobody`, as assumed in the default TWiki installation. You can browse to `http://localhost/twiki/bin/testenv` and read the warnings that are displayed onscreen. This is a special script run on your local machine to help you diagnose any problems with your installation. The messages should be specific to your installation, and any warning should be accompanied by a suggestion about how to fix the problem.

The TWiki installation directions suggest setting permissions and changing ownership. For Fedora Core, the permissions are set correctly, but the ownerships are wrong. To change the ownerships, implement the following steps (after each step, you should reload the `http://localhost/twiki/bin/testenv` page to check your progress):

1. Change the group ownership of everything to `apache`, but change the group ownership of `/httpd/twiki/templates` back to `root`:

```
# chgrp -r apache /home/httpd
# chgrp -r root /home/httpd/twiki/templates
```

2. Remember to edit `/home/httpd/twiki/lib/TWiki.cfg` to reflect your own domain name instead of `http://your.domain.com`.

3. Change the ownership of the RCS repository files to the user `apache`:

```
# cd /home/httpd/twiki/data
# perl -pi -e 's/nobody:/apache:/' */*,v
```

After you complete the installation, you should have a "virgin" TWiki installation that you can view at `http://localhost/twiki/bin/view`. As with any application, you need to further configure this file so that it suits your needs. The TWiki documentation explains the many configuration options and processes available to you. This documentation is included in the TWiki installation you just completed.

Internet Relay Chat

As documented in RC 2812 and RFC 2813, the IRC protocol is used for text conferencing. Like mail and news, IRC uses a client/server model. Although it is rare for an individual to establish an IRC server, it can be done. Most people use public IRC servers and access them with IRC clients.

Fedora Core provides a number of graphical IRC clients, including X-Chat, licq-kde, and Mozilla-chat, but there is no default chat client for Fedora Core. Fedora Core Linux also provides the console clients epic and licq for those who eschew X. If you don't already have a favorite, you should try them all.

CAUTION

You should never use an IRC client while you are the root user. It is better to create a special user just for IRC because of potential security problems. To use X-Chat in this manner, you open a terminal window, use su to change to your IRC user, and start the xchat client.

X-Chat is a popular IRC client, and it is the client that is used in this chapter's example. The HTML documents for X-Chat are available in /usr/share/docs/xchat. It is a good idea to read them before you begin because they include an introduction to and cover some of the basics of IRC. To launch the X-Chat client, select the IRC Client item from the Internet menu found under the Extras menu, or you can launch it from the command line, like this

```
$ xchat &
```

The X-Chat application allows you to assign yourself up to three nicknames. You can also specify your real name and your username. Because many people choose not to use their real names in IRC chat, you are free to enter any names you desire in any of the spaces provided. You can select multiple nicknames; you might be banned from an IRC channel under one name, and you could then rejoin using another. If this seems slightly juvenile to you, you are beginning to get an idea of the type of behavior on many IRC channels.

When you open the main X-Chat screen, a list of IRC servers appears, as shown in Figure 20.7. After you choose a server by double-clicking it, you can view a list of channels available on that server by choosing Window, List Window. The X-Chat Channel List window appears. In that window, you can choose to join channels featuring topics that interest you. To join a channel, you double-click it.

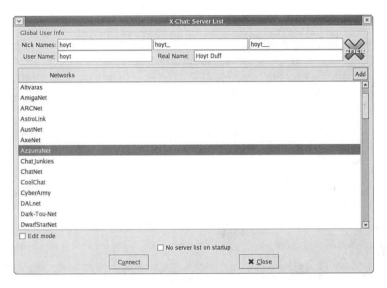

FIGURE 20.7 The main X-Chat screen presents a list of available public servers from which to select.

The Wild Side of IRC

Don't be surprised at the number of lewd topics and the use of crude language on public IRC servers. For a humorous look at the topic of IRC cursing, see http://www.irc.org/fun_docs/nocuss.html. This site also offers some tips for maintaining IRC etiquette, which is essential if you don't want to be the object of any of that profanity! Here are some of the most important IRC etiquette rules:

- Do not use colored text, all-capitalized text, blinking text, or "bells" (beeps caused by sending ^G to a terminal).
- Show respect for others.
- Ignore people who act inappropriately.

After you have selected a channel, you can join in the conversation, which appear as onscreen text. The messages scroll down the screen as new messages appear.

TIP

You can establish your own IRC server even though Fedora Core does not provide one. Setting up a server is not a task for anyone who is not well versed in Linux or IRC.

A popular server is IRCd, which you can obtain from ftp://ftp.irc.org/irc/server/. Before you download IRCd, you should look at the README file to determine what files you need to download and read the information at http://www.irchelp.org/irchelp/ircd/.

Internet Messaging with GAIM

IM has been popularized by America Online (AOL) as a way for AOL users to chat directly with each other rather than speak in chat rooms. As long as the IM clients for everyone involved in the conversation are running, they alert you to any incoming messages. The clients also announce to the server that you are active and listening for messages, so your friends can be made aware via "Buddy Lists" that you are available to chat with them.

You can use IM in place of IRC for interoffice collaboration. Fedora Core provides the GAIM IM client, for your use. To use them, you need to be communicating with a group of "buddies" who are active IM users as well.

GAIM is a GNOME (GTK-based) IM client that supports a wide range of protocols such as TOC, AIN/ICQ, Yahoo!, IRC, Jabber, Napster, Zephyr, and Gadu-Gadu. GAIM is a feature-rich message client, and it has support for plug-ins that extend the functionality of the application.

> **NOTE**
>
> GAIM supports Jabber, an open XML-based IM protocol that can be used to set up a corporate IM server. Jabber is not supplied with Fedora Core, but you can obtain additional information about it from the Jabber home page, at `http://www.jabber.com/`. You can obtain the Jabber server, Jabberd, from `http://jabberd.jabberstudio.org/`. If you want to use GAIM locally for collaboration, Jabber would be an excellent choice for a private local server.

Video Conferencing with GnomeMeeting

GnomeMeeting is an Internet videoconferencing application that provides two-way voice and pictures over the Internet by using the H.323 protocol for IP telephony (also known as Voice over IP [VoIP]). It is an application similar to Microsoft NetMeeting and is provided with Fedora Core as the default video conferencing client.

Before you can take full advantage of the phone and videoconferencing capabilities of GnomeMeeting, you must configure a full-duplex–capable sound card and video device (see Chapter 26, "Multimedia Applications") as well as a camera.

GnomeMeeting is found in the Internet menu as Video Conferencing; you click on the icon to launch it. When you start the GnomeMeeting application for the first time, a configuration wizard (called a "druid") runs and you are greeted by the first of four configuration screens. You simply enter your name, email address, and location and select your connection type. The settings for your audio and video devices are automatically detected; you can view them by selecting the Preferences item from the Edit menu.

Figure 20.8 shows GnomeMeeting in action, looking at a list of users listed with the server who are currently online.

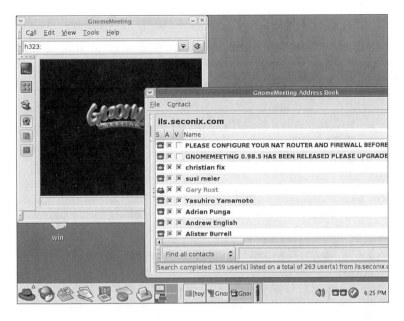

FIGURE 20.8   GnomeMeeting is surprisingly simple to use. A video source is not necessary; a static picture can be used as well.

When you have GnomeMeeting running, you must register (from within GnomeMeeting) with the server at `http://ils.seconix.com/` to enable conferencing; GnomeMeeting does this automatically for you if you have told it to do so during the initial configuration. GnomeMeeting is capable of communicating with Microsoft NetMeeting; you should ask NetMeeting users to register at `http://ils.seconix.com/` so that you can see them because NetMeeting can see only other NetMeeting users.

You can find an informative FAQ at the GnomeMeeting home page at `http://www.gnomemeeting.org/` that you should read in full before using GnomeMeeting. Also, an excellent article about VoIP is at `http://freshmeat.net/articles/view/430/`.

> **NOTE**
>
> If you frequently use VoIP applications such as GnomeMeeting, you'll tire of repetitively typing in long IP address to make connections. To avoid this hassle, you can use a "gatekeeper"—similar in purpose to a DNS server—to translate names into IP addresses. OpenH323 Gatekeeper is one such popular gatekeeper application. It is not provided with Fedora Core, but you can obtain it from `http://www.gnugk.org/`.

20

Mail List Configuration and Management with Mailman

Using a mail list is an increasingly common way for individuals in disparate geographic locations to collaborate. A mail list is a group discussion that takes place via email. However, instead of you sending a separate message to everyone who is interested in participating, you send a single message to the automated mail list server, and it sends messages to each subscribed user. When you receive mail from the list and you reply to an individual message, that message is sent to the Mailman mail list manager, and the message is then resent to everyone on the list. Red Hat maintains numerous mail lists and uses the GNU mailing list manager Mailman to do it. Fedora Core provides the Mailman mail list manager.

Mailman keeps track of who is subscribed and who does not have working email addresses. The mail list manager handles all new subscriptions and unsubscriptions through a Web interface and can even generate an archive of all the messages on the list.

For each mail list, a person is designated as the mail list administrator. The administrator has password-protected access to a special administration Web page. He can manually add and delete members from the list and remove emails determined to be offensive. It is also possible to configure the mail list to be moderated—in which case, a moderator reads all messages before they are passed on to Mailman for distribution to the subscribers. The list can also be configured to allow nonmembers to post, but that option is rarely used because most administrators want to keep unauthorized posts off the list.

Some lists, known as "high traffic" lists, have a large number of messages posted daily. "Low traffic" lists have few, if any, messages posted daily. One configuration option is to have all messages consolidated into a digest, so only one message is sent for a preestablished number of messages that are received by Mailman. The maximum message size can also be established, and attachments to messages can be prohibited.

> **NOTE**
>
> Part of the beta testing and development for Fedora Core took place on a mail list. You can view the archives at `http://www.redhat.com/archives/fedora-test-list/` if you are curious. Anyone can participate in Fedora's beta testing.

In order to collaborate with a mail list, you need to install and configure Mailman. Before you use Mailman to manage a mail list, you must first have Sendmail (or other MTA) installed and configured (see Chapter 19, "Handling Electronic Mail").

After installing the RPM package, you can look at the installed documentation in `/usr/share/doc/mailman-R   *`, paying particular attention to the simple installation instructions in the `INSTALL.REDHAT` file.

Here are some suggestions for installing and configuring Mailman:

- Set your password to something that is not easily guessed but not so difficult that it will be forgotten.

  # **/var/mailman/bin/mmsitepass** password

- The default values found in the file /var/mailman/Mailman/mm_cfg.py are fine as they are, but you should customize DEFAULT_URL_HOST and DEFAULT_EMAIL_HOST to your hostname; you can change this value later. Be sure to read the comments in the file in order to get the domain name syntax correct. Most of the Mailman defaults are in /var/mailman/Mailman/Defaults.py and don't need to be changed. If they do, read the instructions because you should not edit the Defaults.py directly.

- The default values found in the file /etc/sysconfig/sendmail are fine as they are and don't need to be changed.

- The file /etc/httpd/conf.d/mailman.conf needs to be edited to include your domain. (localhost will work in a pinch if you just want to experiment.) Restart the Web server:

  # service httpd restart

- Create a "site-wide" mail list for administration

  $ /var/mailman/newlist mailman

  and follow the prompts. The list owner's name should be in the form of an email address.

- Start the mailman service manually,

  # service mailman start

  remembering to use the chkconfig command to set it to start it automatically upon reboots.

If you experience any problems with the Mailman installation and setup, you can look for additional configuration and troubleshooting tips in the INSTALL, README.SENDMAIL, and FAQ files. The README.POSTFIX and README.EXIM files are provided by Mailman to provide configuration information for those who use the Postfix or Exim program instead of Sendmail. The errors might also have been recorded in /var/log/mailman.

All the Mailman commands are kept in /var/mailman. Although they are owned by root, they are in the mailman group.

You can administer mailman through its Web interface at http://localhost/admin, or you can do it manually.

20

To manually run the Mailman commands, you change directories to `/var/mailman/bin` and run them from there. You'll need to precede all Mailman commands with `./` because they are not in your path (on purpose, for security reasons), so the dot before the slash tells the shell to start looking for the command in the current directory rather than in the default path.

To manually create a new mail list, use the `newlist` command, like this:

```
# ./newlist
```

After you run the command, you are prompted for the name of the new mail list and for the list administrator's email address and the initial password; the `newlist` command then sends an email message to the administrator, with instructions telling the administrator that the list is active. The message also provides a URL for administration of the list and a password. Although administration on the mail list can be done manually from the `/var/mailman` directory if you are `root`, the easiest and recommended way to manage the list is through its Web interface.

If you're the list manager and didn't see that notification message, you can point your browser to `http://localhost/mailman/admin`, select the appropriate list, and enter the password. You are then directed to the options page for that list. You scroll down in this screen to read and modify the options. Beside the description of every item that you can modify is a link named (Details); you click that link to display a context-sensitive help screen.

If you would like to see how Mailman works, browse to `http://mail.python.org/` and look at its mail list shown in Figure 20.9.

Anyone who wants to subscribe to your mail list can browse to the page displayed at `http://your.domain.name/mailman/`, fill in his name and email address, and then pick a password. The person will receive an email notification of membership when he is approved.

> **NOTE**
>
> Christopher Kolar has assembled "User Documentation," a "Quick Reference Guide," and a "Manager's Guide" for managing mail lists; these guides are available free at `http://staff.imsa.edu/~ckolar/mailman/`. They are expertly written and are indispensable resources. "Site Administrator Documentation" is available at `http://www.list.org/docs.html`. This is where you find out how to use the scripts in `/var/mailman/bin` that are of most use in scripts you would write to automate many administrative tasks; it's another can't-live-without-it resource.

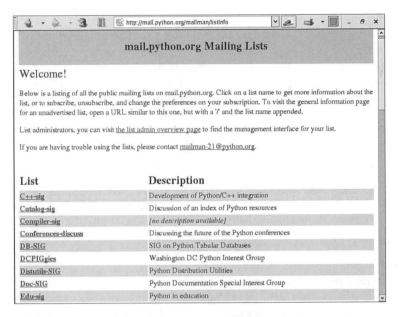

FIGURE 20.9   The `mailman` administration page at `http://mail.python.org`.

Configuring a Local News Server

The InterNetNews (INN) package is the most popular news server software used on UNIX servers. The Internet Software Consortium (ISC) currently maintains it, along with the INN Web site (`http://www.isc.org/products/INN/`). The Fedora Core Linux distribution includes the INN package as a standard RPM file.

The following sections describe how the INN package works, how to install it, and how to configure it as a local news server. Because some users consider news servers to offer the greatest server-configuration challenges, these sections are quite detailed. The information you'll learn here will help you avoid some of the common pitfalls while configuring your local news server.

Types of News Servers

Unless you are an Internet service provider (ISP) or are planning to provide news services to a large group of people, you will likely not be setting up or administering a news server for your own use. If you will be doing this, you can skip to the section "Configuring a Local News Server" at the end of the chapter.

You can use a number of different methods to implement a news server on a network, and the way you intend to use the news server determines how you must configure it. The following sections describe three of the most popular types of news servers on local networks: full newsfeed servers, leaf node servers, and local news servers.

Full Newsfeed Servers

A full newsfeed news server receives all the available Usenet newsgroup postings from an upstream news server (a large, commercial server). Because it receives all the newsgroups, it can serve as an upstream news server for other sites and provide newsfeeds to other servers. The other servers themselves might or might not subscribe to all the newsgroups. Besides providing newsfeeds for other sites, the full newsfeed news server can also support newsreader clients that connect to the news server to read and post articles to newsgroups.

Each news server receives newsfeeds and forwards postings to one or more remote news servers. The full newsfeed server must have enough storage capacity to maintain the newsfeeds for all the newsgroups it services. If the remote news servers don't connect to download their newsfeeds on a daily basis, the newsfeed server must be capable of maintaining all the newsfeeds for the intervening days. This can require a very large amount of data storage capacity beyond the capabilities of systems that are common among home users and many businesses.

Leaf Node Servers

A leaf node news server receives newsfeeds only from upstream news servers: It doesn't feed other news servers. This is the most common configuration for corporate news servers. Because the leaf node server doesn't have to feed other news servers, it doesn't have to retrieve all the newsgroups from its upstream newsfeed. You can pick and choose which newsgroups the news server retrieves from the newsfeed. The main role of the leaf node news server is to provide news service to newsreader clients.

The leaf node does, however, have to maintain a system for users to connect to the news server to read and post messages. This is often done by using UNIX, Microsoft Windows, or Apple Macintosh workstation software. Each client must connect to the leaf node to download articles from specific newsgroups, and it must upload postings made to the newsgroups. The leaf node must be capable of forwarding new postings to the newsfeed server.

Local News Servers

An organization that doesn't want to participate in the worldwide Usenet newsgroups still might want to use Usenet software to create its own news server to handle internal communications within the organization. Usually these communications need to remain private to the organization and don't need to be sent to all the Usenet newsfeed hosts around the world. This is likely the most common use of a news server you might be asked to configure.

Two methods are used to implement a local news server. An organization might create a standalone news server that doesn't receive any newsfeeds from Usenet servers. The server contains only local newsgroups that are used for internal corporate communications. Alternatively, you can create on a Usenet news server local newsgroups that aren't forwarded through any newsfeeds in the Usenet system. This enables organizations to create their own local newsgroups that their employees can participate in without sharing their information with the rest of the world.

Thus, local newsgroups can be created on news servers that either aren't connected to the Usenet network or that are connected to the Usenet network but do not forward the local groups to their upstream newsfeeds. Any postings to the local newsgroups appear only on the local news server. The Usenet news servers enable clients to post articles to both the local and Usenet newsgroups. However, only the articles posted to Usenet newsgroups are forwarded to the upstream news server. The local articles remain on only the local news server.

The INN Package and Configuration Files

The INN package (which is formed around the innd daemon) contains many different executable programs and configuration files that enable the Fedora Core Linux server to work as a network news server. The standard INN RPM package contains all the files necessary for the installation. Table 20.1 describes some of the INN programs included in the distribution, in the order in which you'll find them in the file.

TABLE 20.1   INN Package Program Files

Program File	Description
ctlinnd	Allows the user to manually send control messages to the innd program.
getlist	Obtains a list of newsgroups from a news server.
grephistory	Queries the history database files for a specific message ID value and returns the record information.
inncheck	Examines INN configuration files and databases.
innconfval	Prints the values of parameters that are specified in the innd command line.
innd	Handles all incoming newsfeeds and spawns INN programs as needed.
inndstart	Starts the innd daemon from the news user ID.
innreport	Summarizes INN log files into readable reports.
innstat	Prints a snapshot of the current status of the INN system.
innwatch	Monitors the running INN system and, if necessary, throttles the newsfeeds to help reduce the load on the news server.
mailpost	Manually sends a mail message into a specified newsgroup.
makedbz	Creates binary indexed database files from the history file.
makehistory	Creates a text history file of message IDs seen by the news server.
news.daily	Runs as a cron job to perform daily maintenance of the news server.
nnrpd	Communicates with newsreaders via the innd daemon.
nntpget	Connects to a remote news server and retrieves articles that are specified on the standard input.
nntpsend	Connects to a remote news server and posts articles to newsgroups.
ovdb_recover	Attempts to repair a damaged INN database file.
ovdb_upgrade	Attempts to upgrade an existing INN database file.
prunehistory	Removes specific filenames from the history file.
pullnews	Retrieves newsgroup articles from one news server and forwards them to another news server.

TABLE 20.1   Continued

Program File	Description
rnews	Receives newsgroup articles from a news server by using a UUCP connection.
scanlogs	Summarizes information in the INN log files and performs general cleaning and rotating of the log files.
sm	Provides a command-line interface to the article storage manager.

As you can see in Table 20.1, a number of the INN programs are used to help facilitate the news process on the server. The INN package also contains a number of configuration files that define how articles are handled. Table 20.2 lists and describes these files.

TABLE 20.2   INN Package Configuration Files

Configuration File	Description
control.ctl	Specifies how control messages are handled.
expire.ctl	Specifies how articles are expired.
incoming.conf	Specifies addresses and authentication information for servers that send newsfeeds to your news server.
inn.conf	Acts as the primary general configuration file for the innd program.
innfeed.conf	Specifies parameters for the incoming newsfeed handler.
innwatch.ctl	Determines how the innwatch program monitors the INN system.
moderators	Specifies email addresses for moderators of moderated newsgroups.
motd.news	Specifies what information is posted to newsreaders when a list motd command is sent.
newsfeeds	Specifies which newsgroups are fed to other news servers from this news server.
nnrpd.track	Specifies newsreaders or servers that should have their activity recorded during an NNTP session.
nntpsend.ctl	Specifies remote news servers that your news server will feed articles to in batch mode.
passwd.nntp	Specifies passwords used to connect to remote news servers.
readers.conf	Specifies authorized remote newsreader addresses and newsgroup permissions.
sasl.conf	Specifies file locations for the encryption keys used for the SASL configuration.
storage.conf	Specifies the storage method used for specific newsgroup articles.
subscriptions	Specifies a list of newsgroups that newsreaders can subscribe to.

Don't let the long list of configuration files in Table 20.2 worry you; most of the parameters defined in the configuration files work fine with their default settings. Typically, you need to make only a few changes to configure the INN news server to work in your particular network news environment.

Installing the INN Package

There to work in your particular network news environment, Fedora Core Linux distribution uses two separate RPM files to install the INN package. The first package, simply called `inn`, installs the necessary configuration and application files needed for the INN package to work on the system. The second package, called `inn-devel`, is used to install INN header files that some external newsreader programs use to work with `innd`. You don't have to install the `inn-devel` package for INN, but if you are using other newsreader packages on the server, you should install it. The default INN installation also installs the `inews` and `cleanfeed` packages, which are used to forward articles to the server and filter out spam.

Configuring the `innd` Package

After all the INN files are installed, you must begin the task of setting the proper parameters in the configuration files (installed in `/etc/news`) before you attempt to start the `innd` program. When you modify the INN configuration files, you must ensure that you are logged in as the news user or use the `su` command to become the news user (note that there is no password for the news user). If the ownership or permissions of any of the INN configuration files change, the `innd` package won't start.

Although there are many configuration files, only a handful of files need to be modified for a simple news server. The following sections describe common changes that must be made to the configuration files to get the news server operational.

The `inn.conf` File

The `/etc/news/inn.conf` file is the heart of the `innd` configuration. It defines the core features of the news server operation. Each parameter is listed on a separate line, using the following format:

```
parameter: value
```

A lot of parameters are defined in the `inn.conf` file, but fortunately most of them work just fine with their default values. Table 20.3 shows the parameters that should be changed in the `innd.conf` file to represent your news server environment.

TABLE 20.3   innd.conf Configuration Parameters

Parameter	Description
mta	The command used to invoke the system MTA mailer. The %s variable is included to replace the recipient address in the command line. If you have installed the default Fedora Core Sendmail package, mta should be set correctly.
organization	A text description of your organization. This value is used in the article header lines for all articles posted from your site, so be careful to enter accurate information.

TABLE 20.3   Continued

Parameter	Description
ovmethod	The storage method used for the article indexes. The default, tradindexed, is usually fine for small sites, but might not be fast enough for large sites.
pathhost	The name of the host to place in the Path: article header line. This should represent your news server hostname. In the default file, it is shown as localhost and is commented out.
pathnews	The path to the news binaries, which is already set for your Fedora Core system.
domain	The complete domain name of your Internet domain. This parameter is blank until you fill it.
mailcmd	The command that innd uses to send mail messages. Usually this should be the innmail program.
server	The name of a default NNTP server.
maxconnections	The maximum number of incoming NNTP connections your news server will support, based on your network's available bandwidth.
fromhost	The domain that the INN system uses to construct email addresses. It should be set to your local system address.
moderatormailer	The email address to which messages posted to moderated newsgroups are sent if there is no corresponding entry in the moderator's file.
status	How frequently (in seconds) innd should create a status report. A value of 0 disables this feature. (A value of 0 is not recommended if you want to receive status reports, but it's the default Fedora Core setting. Set whatever you feel comfortable with.)
timer	How frequently (in seconds) innd should report performance statistics to the logfiles. A value of 0 disables this feature. (A value of 0 is not recommended, but it's the default Fedora Core setting. Set whatever you feel comfortable with.)

The inn.conf file is a text file that you can modify by using any standard text editor. At a minimum, you should ensure that the organization, domain, mailcmd, mta, server, and fromhost parameters are specified. Listing 20.1 shows sample inn.conf file entries for a test server.

LISTING 20.1   Sample inn.conf Configuration File Entries

```
mta:             /usr/sbin/sendmail -oi -oem %s
organization:    Hoyt's MaximumNews
ovmethod:        tradindexed
domain:          maximumhoyt.com
mailcmd:         /usr/bin/innmail
status:          3600
timer:            3600
```

The sample configuration shown uses the standard Sendmail MTA for the mailer and the traditional indexed method for overview databases, and it creates new status reports every hour.

The `incoming.conf` File

The `/etc/news/incoming.conf` file is used to define the source from which the news server receives its newsfeeds. If you are building a standalone news server that doesn't receive newsfeeds, this file is still important because it also specifies the local address of the news server.

The `incoming.conf` file contains three types of data:

- Peer news server definitions

- Groups of news server definitions

- Parameter value definitions

Parameters can be defined globally, within peer definitions, and within group definitions. As you would expect, parameters that are defined globally apply to all peers and groups defined in the configuration file. Parameters that are defined within group definitions apply to all peers within the group definition and override any global definitions of the same parameter. Finally, parameters defined within peer definitions apply only to the peer, and they override any group or global definitions of the same parameter.

Ten parameters can be used to define the connection with a remote news server. In the case of a local news server only, you would not be accessing any incoming feeds, so the `incoming.conf` file can remain unmodified.

In addition, the `innfeed.conf` file that defines communication with peer news servers can remain unmodified, as can the `incoming.conf` file because no newsfeeds will be received.

The `storage.conf` File

Another important configuration file used by `innd` is the `/etc/news/storage.conf` file. This file tells the `innd` program how to store newsgroup articles on the news server. Fedora Core suggests two different methods for storing articles on the news server:

- Time hashed spool—The time hashed spool method (`timehash`) stores articles on the news server by creating directories based on the arrival time of the articles. This creates more directories with fewer articles in each directory. Using `timehash` requires additional overhead for reading articles, however, because it is more difficult for the news server to find an individual article stored in this method.

- Cyclic buffer spool—The cyclic spool (`cnfs`) method speeds up the process of storing articles by using a preconfigured file buffer. As articles are received, they are placed in a preconfigured file of a set size. This greatly speeds up processing because no new files are created as articles are received.

20

Using `cnfs` does have a drawback, however. The buffer files are created at a set size, so when the articles fill up a buffer file, the file is overwritten, starting from the beginning. This method, therefore, forces an automatic expiration of articles on the news server. Although using a set buffer file size prevents the server from running out of disk space, it can cause premature article expiration, depending on the size of the buffer file. Most news administrators who use this method learn by trial and error the buffer file size necessary to handle the standard news traffic load at their sites.

> **CAUTION**
>
> If a newsgroup isn't covered by a specific storage method, INN doesn't store the articles received for that newsgroup, and it produces an error message for each article. This can have a devastating effect on the news server. For a simple news server, it is best to select a single method of storage and configure the `storage.conf` file to use that method for all the newsgroups.

By default, the Fedora Core `/etc/news/storage.conf` file doesn't define any default storage method, but it is fully configured and commented out. You must define at least one method to use in order for INN to work properly; to do so, you can simply uncomment the desired section.

The `readers.conf` File

You use the `/etc/news/readers.conf` configuration file to define permissions for newsreaders that use your news server. If you are allowing your local users to connect to your news server to read articles, you must configure the `readers.conf` file to support them.

The `readers.conf` file consists of the following three types of data:

- An authentication definition
- An access definition
- Parameters and values

The authentication definition defines categories of users who will be accessing your news server. You can create several different categories of users, based on various factors, such as remote address, newsgroups accessed, and type of authentication method used. The syntax of the authentication section is as follows:

```
auth name {
         hosts: hostlist
         auth: auth-program
         res: res-program
         default: defuser
         default-domain: defdomain
}
```

The name value is used as a label to uniquely identify the authentication definition. The authentication definition uses parameters and values to identify its actions. The hosts parameter uses the hostlist value to identify individual remote hosts that are covered by the authentication definition. These can be listed by using either hostnames or numeric IP addresses, along with matching wildcard characters.

You can use the res parameter to specify an authentication program that is used to authenticate the connection based on its network information. Alternatively, you can use the auth parameter to specify an authentication program that can authenticate the connection by using a user ID/password pair. If you are interested in authenticating remote news servers, you should consult the INN documentation because it is a somewhat complicated process.

The access definition defines categories of access restrictions and permissions for groups of newsreaders. The syntax of the access definition is as follows:

```
access name {
          users: identity-wildcat
          newsgroups: group-wildcat
          access: permissions
}
```

The name value must match a corresponding authentication definition. The parameters defined in the access definition apply only to the hosts defined in the corresponding authentication definition. The users parameter limits the access rules to the specific set of users listed in the value. If the users parameter isn't present, the access rules apply to all users. The newsgroups parameter defines which newsgroups the group has access to, and the access parameter defines what access privileges the group has. The privileges are defined as follows:

- R—Read-only access is allowed.

- P—Posting articles is allowed.

- A—Posting approved articles is allowed (using a moderator).

- N—The NEWNEWS command is allowed.

- L—The group is allowed to post to newsgroups that are set to disallow local posting.

Here is a sample readers.conf file that allows all local newsreaders to read and post articles to all newsgroups:

```
# readers.conf
auth "localhost"
    hosts: "localhost, 127.0.0.1, 192.168.1.100, stdin"
    default: "<localhost>"
```

20

```
    }

access "localhost" {
    users: "<localhost>"
    newsgroups: "*"
    access: RPA
}
auth "localnet" {
        hosts: "192.168.*"
        default: "<user>"
        default-domain: "isp.net"
        }

access "localnet" {
        users: "*@isp.net"
        newsgroups: "*"
        access: "RP
}
```

The sample readers.conf file shown here defines two separate groups of users. The first group, called localhost, enables the local host, address 127.0.0.1, address 192.168.1.100 (the local host's network address), and any connection using the standard input to connect to the news server. The unmodified readers.conf file provided by Fedora Core allows only access from users on the local host.

The second group defines any client located on the 192.168. network; it allows both reading and posting of all newsgroups to any client on the network. You can adjust these addresses as necessary for your network.

The active and newsgroups Files

The active and newsgroups files, although not specifically identified as configuration files, are crucial to the operation of the news server. These files control what newsgroups your news server can handle. Each newsgroup handled by the news server must have an entry in both the active and newsgroups files. Both of these files are located in the /var/lib/news directory when they are installed by using the Fedora Core RPM package.

The syntax of the active file is as follows:

```
newsgroup    first    last    post
```

Each newsgroup handled by the news server is defined on a separate line in the active file. The default Fedora Core Linux INN configuration supplies a skeleton active file that defines several special newsgroups:

```
control 0000000000 0000000001 n
control.cancel 0000000000 0000000001 n
```

```
control.checkgroups 0000000000 0000000001 n
control.newgroup 0000000000 0000000001 n
control.rmgroup 0000000000 0000000001 n
junk 0000000000 0000000001 n
```

This default file is fine if you are running a standalone news server. The first field of this file defines the newsgroup name. The second and third fields define the first and last article sequence numbers. The final field defines whether posting is allowed for the newsgroup on the news server. The default newsgroups are set to n to prevent posting.

The control and control.cancel newsgroups are used to receive NNTP control articles for performing maintenance on the news server. As remote sites create new newsgroups and delete old ones, control articles are sent to the news servers to perform these tasks. The control series of newsgroups handles these articles. Also, the junk newsgroup is created to handle articles that have not been posted correctly and have no place to go.

The newsgroups file is parallel with the active file; it must contain the same newsgroup definitions as the active file.

The history Files

Also in the /var/lib/news directory are the INN history files. These files are used to keep a running index of each article posted to each newsgroup. It is crucial that these files not be tampered with because if they get out of sync with the actual newsgroup articles, the news server has problems retrieving articles.

There are two separate parts to the history files: a text history file and a set of binary index files that are created by using a database program such as the common Berkeley db package. You must create both sets of files before you can start the innd daemon.

You use the /var/lib/news/bin/makehistory command to create the text history file based on the current newsgroup articles on the server (which should be none). Fedora Core provides a blank history file.

After you create the text history file, you create the binary index files. You use the /usr/lin/news/bin/makedbz program to convert the text history file into the binary index files. The makedbz -i command creates the following three separate binary files:

- history.n.dir
- history.n.index
- history.n.hash

You should rename these files to the standard history filenames (history.dir, history.index, and history.pag) so that the innd program can recognize them. After the history files have been created, you are finally ready to start the news server.

Running innd

Using the /var/lib/news/bin/inndstart program is the best way to start the innd
daemon, which in turn starts other INN package programs. The inndstart program must
be run from the news user ID. It starts the innd program as well as the controlchan
program in background mode.

The innd program listens for newsfeeds and newsreader requests on the NNTP TCP port. If
a remote newsreader establishes a connection, the innd program spawns the active
program to authenticate the remote connection and handle the newsreader requests. If the
incoming articles are control articles, they are passed to the controlchan program for
processing.

Fedora Core has thoughtfully configured the SystemV files that are necessary for starting
the news server; you can use (in an appropriate way) chkconfig, nytsysv, service, or
system-config-services to start the server. (See Chapter 7, "Managing Services," for
details.) Here's an example:

```
# /sbin/service inn start
```

When the innd program is running, you can control it by using the ctlinnd program,
with the following syntax:

```
ctlinnd [ -h ] [ -s ] [ -t timeout ] command [ argument...]
```

The -s option suppresses any output from the ctlinnd command. This option is often
used in batch programs. The -t option specifies how long to wait for a response from the
server (in seconds). If you are connecting to a server across a slow link or you are connecting to a slow server, you can increase the value of timeout.

The command parameters define what actions the ctlinnd program should take with the
innd news server. The -h option prints a summary of all the available command parameters that can be used with ctlinnd. For now, you can use the newgroup command to create
a new local newsgroup that newsreaders can use to read and messages:

```
$ ctlinnd newgroup local.linux.group y hoyt@maximumhoyt.com
```

The newgroup command uses three parameters:

- The name of the new newsgroup

- A flag to define what type of newsgroup to create (y stands for a regular open group
  and m stands for a moderated group)

- An email address for the maintainer of the new newsgroup

The ctlinnd program should be run from the news user ID. If the command is successful,
it returns a simple OK message. You can use the ctlinnd command to check whether the
new newsgroup has been added to the news server.

Filtering Spam with the `cleanfeed` Package

One problem that has plagued the Usenet newsgroup system is the proliferation of spam Usenet messages. Spam providers often attempt to post their messages to newsgroups to force messages to a large captive audience. One of the most effective methods for blocking spam messages from being posted to a newsgroup is to use the `cleanfeed` package. The `cleanfeed` package is a Perl script that filters out spam before it hits your news server. You can configure this software by editing its configuration file, `cleanfeed.conf`, under the `/etc/news` directory.

The newsgroup example offered in this chapter is designed for a closed system and doesn't need to filter spam. But you can learn more about `cleanfeed` in the FAQ found at `http://www.exit109.com/~jeremy/news/cleanfeed/`.

Relevant Fedora Core Linux Commands

You can use the following commands to manage newsgroups and other collaborative communication processes in Fedora Core Linux:

`emacs`—The premiere editing environment that can also be used to read Usenet news

`innd`—The INN daemon and its plethora of associated commands

`knode`—KDE's graphical Usenet newsreading client

`mozilla`—The mail and newsgroups component of the open-source Mozilla browser

`pan`—An easy-to-use Usenet newsreader for GNOME

`pine`—A text-based mail client that can also read Usenet news

`slrn`—A text-based graphical Usenet newsreader

Reference

`http://www.faqs.org/rfcs/rfc977.html`—RFC 977—The NNTP protocol.

`http://www.faqs.org/rfcs/rfc1036.html`—RFC 1036—The format of news messages.

`http://www.isc.org/products/INN/`—The INN package.

`http://slrn.sourceforge.net/`—The `slrn` newsreader program.

`http://www.washington.edu/pine/`—The Pine program.

`http://apps.kde.com/`—The KNode program.

`http://pan.rebelbase.com/`—The Pan program.

`http://TWiki.org/`—The TWiki home page.

`http://www.ibiblio.org/pub/Linux/docs/HOWTO/other-formats/html_single/IRC.html`—The Linux IRC HOWTO.

20

`http://www.irc.org/techie.html`—Links to RFCs as well as documents specific to the ircd server.

`http://www.irc.org/links.html`—A links page with an extensive list of IRC-related links.

`http://www.irchelp.org/`—A site devoted to providing help for IRC users.

`http://www.licq.org/`—Home page for the LICQ Instant message application; local documentation is at `/usr/share/doc/licq-1.2.0a`.

`http://xchat.org/`—Home page for X-Chat; local documentation is at `/usr/share/doc/xchat`.

`http://gaim.sourceforge.net`—The GAIM homepage; local documentation is at `/usr/share/doc/gaim`.

`http://www.linuxcarcam.com/gaim/`—A source for GAIM plug-ins to extend the functionality of GAIM in amusing ways.

`http://www.gnomemeeting.org/`—The GnomeMeeting home page.

`http://freshmeat.net/articles/view/430/`—An excellent article covering VoIP and related Linux telephony issues.

`http://www.list.org/`—The home page for the Mailman mailing list manager.

C/C++ Programming Tools for Fedora

IN THIS CHAPTER

- Programming in C with Linux
- Elements of the C/C++ Language
- Using the C Programming Project Management Tools Provided with Fedora Core Linux
- Using the GNU C Compiler
- A Simple C Program
- Graphical Development Tools
- Additional Resources
- Reference

For many Linux users, coding means scripting. And why not? Most Linux distributions include Perl, Python, the Tool Control Language (TCL), and the bash, ksh, tcsh, and zsh shells—all of which support a wide range of commands that can be combined, in the form of scripts, into reusable programs. Command scripts for shell programs (and utilities such as GNU's gawk) can be all the programming that many users need in order to customize their computing environments. (You can learn more about scripting in Chapter 22, "Shell Scripting," and Chapter 23, "Using Perl.")

However, many programs that process scripts (such as the various Linux shells, the gawk command, and the Perl interpreter) are written in the C and C++ languages.

Learning how to fully use a computer language such as C or C++ can be more complex and difficult than learning shell scripting. You must learn to think in terms of machine resources and the way actions are accomplished within the computer, taking into account the operating system, language syntax, and assorted development tools, rather than think in terms of user-oriented commands.

The effort to learn how to use C or C++ can reap benefits. Linux and nearly all its related software is open source. So if a program doesn't work the way you want it to, you can change it! You can also find a lot of "hidden" documentation in programmer comments inside the source to nearly all Linux programs.

Fedora Core comes with an incredibly diverse toolbox of program development software. There are C and C++ compilers, debuggers (used during the development process to find and diagnose errors), project organizing clients, graphical prototyping environments, and code management software. If you perform a full installation of Fedora from this book's CD-ROMs, you'll also be able to write Fortran 77, Java, and assembler (CPU level) language programs.

This chapter focuses on C- and C++-related tools for Linux, such as the Gnu C compiler (gcc) system, and prototyping environments for GNOME and the K Desktop Environment (KDE). The information presented here introduces some of the commands used to compile C and C++ programs, along with information about related programming tools.

Programming in C with Linux

C is the programming language most frequently associated with UNIX, and today, UNIX-like operating systems such as Linux or BSD. Since the 1970s, the bulk of the UNIX operating system and its applications have been written in C. Because the C language doesn't directly rely on any specific hardware architecture, UNIX was one of the first portable operating systems. In other words, the majority of the code that makes up UNIX doesn't know and doesn't care which computer it is actually running on. Machine-specific features are isolated in a few modules within the UNIX kernel, which makes it easy for you to modify them when you are porting to different hardware architectures.

> **NOTE**
>
> In 1983, the American National Standards Institute (ANSI) established a committee to standardize the definition of C. The resulting standard is known as ANSI C, and it is the recognized standard for the language, the grammar, and a core set of libraries. The syntax is slightly different from that of the original C language, which is frequently called K&R, for Kernighan and Ritchie. There is also an International Standards Organization (ISO) C standard that is very similar to the ANSI C standard.

C is a programming language you can use to create programs for Linux. The C language is used in text files called *source code* files. The source code files are read by programs included with the GNU gcc compiler suite during the process of building a new Linux program. C is a *compiled* language, which means that C code is first analyzed by the *preprocessor* and then translated into assembler language first and then into machine instructions that are appropriate to the target CPU. An assembler then creates a binary, or *object*, file from the machine instructions. Finally, the object file is linked to any required external software support by the *linker*. A C program is stored in a text file that ends with a .c extension and always contains at least one routine, or function, such as main(), unless the file is an *include* file (with a .h extension, also known as a *header* file) containing shared variable definitions or other data or declarations. *Functions* are the commands that perform each step of the task that the C program was written to accomplish.

> **NOTE**
>
> The Linux kernel is mostly written in C, a programming language that can be used to create programs that build and run on many different platforms. This portability is one of the reasons that Linux works with so many different central processing units (CPUs). To learn more about building the Linux kernel from source using installed Linux software development tools, see Chapter 24, "Kernel and Module Management."

Programming in C++

C++ is an object-oriented extension to C. Because C++ is a superset of C, C++ compilers compile C programs correctly, and it is possible to write non–object-oriented code in C++.

The distinction between an object-oriented language such as C++ and a procedural one such as C can be subtle and hard to grasp, especially with regard to C++, which retains all of C's characteristics and concepts. One way to describe the difference is to say that when programmers code in C, they specify actions that process the data; when they write code in C++, they create data objects that can be requested to perform actions on or with regard to themselves.

Thus, a C function receives one or more values as input, transforms or acts on them in some way, and returns a result. If the values that are passed include pointers, the contents of data variables can be modified by the function. It is likely that the code that is calling a function does not know, and does not need to know, what steps the function takes when it is invoked.

Functions, the procedures that take place in a computer program, are associated with C++ objects as well. But the actions performed when an object's function is invoked can automatically differ, perhaps substantially, depending on the specific type of the data structure with which it is associated. This is known as *overloading* function names. Overloading is related to a second characteristic of C++: the fact that functions can be defined as belonging to C++ data structures, an aspect of the wider language feature known as *encapsulation*.

In addition to overloading and encapsulation, object-oriented languages allow programmers to define new abstract data types (including associated functions) and then derive subsequent data types from them. The notion of a new class of data objects, in addition to the built-in classes such as integer, floating-point number, and character, goes beyond the familiar capability to define complex data objects in C.

C++ extends the capabilities of C by providing the necessary features for object-oriented design and code. C++ compilers such as gcc correctly compile ANSI C code. C++ also provides some features, such as the capability to associate functions with data structures, that do not require the use of full, class-based, object-oriented techniques. For these reasons, the C++ language enables existing UNIX programs to migrate toward the adoption of object orientation over time.

Support for C++ programming using Fedora is provided by gcc, which you run with the name g++ when you're compiling C++ code. KDE includes some intermediate C++ tools, such as moc (the Meta Object Compiler) for use when building KDE applications.

> **NOTE**
>
> You can read the C++ Programming HOWTO, available at http://www.tldp.org, for more information on programming using C++ and Linux.

Getting Started with Linux C/C++ Programming

Linux is popular with C and C++ programmers because of gcc and its suite of related software-development tools, such as gdb, autoconf, and make. Complex C programs might have dozens or hundreds of separate object files that are created during the build process. One, more, or all these (compiled) steps can be carried out automatically by the gcc compiler system, which is run by the make utility according to project rules contained in a makefile. After a program is compiled, it can be executed over and over without recompilation.

Writing C programs for Linux requires that you understand C syntax, have some understanding of how to interface with the Linux kernel (by using one or more of 1,100 different C functions, known as *system calls*), and know how to use Linux programming tools such as gcc and make. You'll learn about each of these concepts and processes in this chapter.

To get started, you need to make sure that you have installed all the necessary software development packages (perhaps by using the system-config-packages client; see Chapter 8, "Managing Software and System Resources") to support your project. Installation of basic development software requires more than 50 different software packages and 110MB of hard drive space. If you plan to build programs for the Linux kernel, you need the Kernel development packages and an additional 180MB of storage space (not counting temporary disk space required when building a new kernel).

Developing programs for the X Window System requires installation of 20 software packages and about 40MB of software libraries, programming support files, and documentation. If you want to build GNOME clients, you need more than 60MB of additional space for nearly 50 software packages. And if you intend to develop programs for KDE, you should plan on reserving 220MB or so of your hard drive to store KDE's development software, contained in 20 different packages. Don't forget that you will also need lots of space for temporary files when you're building programs, as many intermediate files will be created during your programming sessions.

You should also become familiar with a good text editor. Although GNU purists use the emacs editing environment to write, edit, and compile programs, many other developers do just fine with an editor such as vi or nano for editing source and then use the command line to run development tools.

When programming for GNOME or KDE, you might find it most convenient to use a graphical development project manager, such as GNOME's Glade (the GTK+ User Interface Builder, glade-2), Trolltech's Qt Designer (designer), or KDE's KDevelop (the KDE development environment, kdevelop). These clients allow you to prototype an application with graphical drawing tools, which frees you to concentrate on your client's interface. You can use either to automatically generate all necessary project and source code files for skeletal applications. See the section "Graphical Development Tools," later in this chapter, for more information.

C Documentation

You'll learn some of the basics of working in C in this chapter, and you also have a wealth of other information about C available to you on your Fedora Core system. You can use the man command to read online manual pages for the gcc C compiler and installed programming tools. You can use the info command to read the online GNU info files. You can get a general overview of how to use gcc by using the man command like this:

```
$ man gcc
```

For detailed information about using gcc, you can use the info command like this:

```
$ info gcc
```

Linux kernel and system calls are documented in manual pages in section 2, and manual pages for general Linux programming and helpful C routines (known as *library routines*) are found in section 3, known as the *Linux Programmer's Manual.* Linux programs use a number of support libraries, but the main routines are documented in the manual pages. For example, to see how to use the printf() function, you could use the man command like this:

```
$ man 3 printf
```

You can also gain additional insight into Linux programming by reading *Linux Programmer's Guide,* which is somewhat dated, but still useful, and is available at http://www.tldp.org/LDP/lpg/index.html. Or you can examine the source code for Linux programs. Later in this chapter you'll be introduced to the basics of using command-line development software and graphical program development tools for Linux.

The Process of Programming

Writing and building C programs when using Fedora Core Linux can be as easy as following a few simple steps, using several software tools. The basic steps are

1. Run a text editor, such as vi or a graphical programmer's editor, such as KDE's kate.

2. Type in C source code.

3. Save the changes.

4. Compile the program using the gcc compiler.

5. Run and test (debug) the program.

6. Edit the source code to implement new features or fix problems.

On the other hand, building a large and complex application can involve the efforts of many programmers, and require installing, configuring, and maintaining a source code control system (such as CVS, discussed later in this chapter), tracking program changes, developing software manuals, and using more complex software tools in the development process (such as autoconf or the gdb debugger).

Many Linux C programmers start by writing a program that solves an immediate need, such as a simple command-line program to download or upload phone numbers or other data to a cellular phone or handheld computer. Many beginners get started by becoming proficient in using a Linux text editor, researching any required software routines and reading documentation, browsing available Linux source code, learning how to run a compiler (such as gcc, discussed later in this chapter), and then launching into the iterative process of editing, compiling, executing, and testing.

The following sections in this chapter discuss some of the required or helpful software tools included with Fedora Core. You also see how to create, compile, and run a simple C program. You'll also see how to use several graphical prototyping tools (such as Glade, Designer, or KDevelop) to shorten the process of developing a user interface for graphical programs; these tools can free up time and effort on those tasks, allowing you to concentrate on the core functions of your new program.

Elements of the C/C++ Language

If C is the language that is most associated with UNIX, C++ is the language that underlies most graphical user interfaces available today, including KDE.

The C programming language has its own *syntax*—a specific form in which all commands and code must be written in order to be understood and processed by the computer system. The syntax you should understand when beginning to program in C includes the following:

- Comments—Comments are statements that document code and describe the program. A comment begins and ends with special characters, such as /* and */, that tell the compiler to ignore all content between those characters.

- Identifiers—You need to know how to properly name values, variables, and subroutines, such as &a, *p, and my_func().

- Keywords—Keywords are words that have special meaning to C and are therefore reserved for commands or parameters. The keywords int, char, and struct, for example, are used to declare variables, arrays, structures, and so on.

- Constants—You need to know how to use constants such as integers, floating points, characters, and character strings, such as 10, a, and "hello", and you need to know how to define symbolic constants, such as #define NULL 0.

- Syntax notation—You need to know how to use operators in expressions, which are used for calculations, retrieval, or assignment of values, such as for (;;) and line[n++] = a;.

You should also learn more about the software tools you'll use for programming and the idiosyncrasies and features of the tools, such as GNU's gcc compiler system. (See the section "Using the GNU C Compiler," later in this chapter, for an overview of gcc.)

Using the C Programming Project Management Tools Provided with Fedora Core Linux

Fedora Core is replete with tools that make your life as a C/C++ programmer easier. There are tools to create programs (editors), compile programs (gcc), create libraries (ar), control the source (Revision Control System [RCS] and the Concurrent Versions System [CVS]), build code (make), debug programs (gdb and ddd), and determine where inefficiencies lie (gprof).

The following sections introduce some of the programming and project management tools included with Fedora. This book's CD-ROMs contain many of these tools, which you can use to help automate software development projects. If you have some previous UNIX experience, you will be familiar with most of these programs because they are traditional complements to a programmer's suite of software.

Building Programs with make

You use the make command to automatically build and install a C program. The make command's roots stem from an early version of System V UNIX. The version of make that is included with Fedora Core is part of the GNU utilities distribution.

Using Makefiles

The make command automatically builds and updates applications by using a *makefile*. A makefile is a text file that can contain instructions about which options to pass on to the compiler preprocessor, the compiler, the assembler, and the linker. The makefile also specifies, among other things, which source code files need to be compiled (and the compiler command line) for a particular code module and which code modules are needed to build the program—a mechanism called *dependency checking*.

The beauty of the make command is its flexibility. You can use make with a simple makefile, or you can write complex makefiles that contain numerous macros, rules, or commands that work in a single directory or traverse your file system recursively to build programs, update your system, and even function as document management systems. The make command works with nearly any program, including text processing systems such as TeX.

You could use make to compile, build, and install a software package using a simple incantation like this:

```
# make install
```

You can use the default makefile, or you can use make's -f option to specify any makefile, such as MyMakeFile, like this:

```
# make -f MyMakeFile
```

Other options might be available, depending on the contents of your makefile.

Using Macros and Makefile Targets

Using make with macros can make a program portable. Macros allow users of other operating systems to easily configure a program build by specifying local values, such as the names and locations, or *pathnames*, of any required software tools. In the following example, macros define the name of the compiler (CC), the installer program (INS), where the program should be installed (INSDIR), where the linker should look for required libraries (LIBDIR), the names of required libraries (LIBS), a source code file (SRC), the intermediate object code file (OBS), and the name of the final program (PROG):

```
# a sample makefile for a skeleton program
CC= gcc
INS= install
INSDIR = /usr/local/bin
LIBDIR= -L/usr/X11R6/lib
LIBS= -lXm -lSM -lICE -lXt -lX11
SRC= skel.c
OBJS= skel.o
PROG= skel

skel: ${OBJS}
        ${CC} -o ${PROG} ${SRC} ${LIBDIR} ${LIBS}


install: ${PROG}
        ${INS} -g root -o root ${PROG} ${INSDIR}
```

> **NOTE**
>
> The indented lines in the previous example are indented with tabs, not spaces. This is very important to remember! It is difficult for a person to see the difference, but make can tell. If make reports confusing errors when you first start building programs under Linux, you should check your project's makefile for the use of tabs and other proper formatting.

Using makefile as in the preceding example, you can build a program like this:

```
# make
```

To build a specified component of a makefile, you can use a target definition on the command line. To build just the program, you use make with the skel target, like this:

```
# make skel
```

If you make any changes to any element of a target object, such as a source code file, make rebuilds the target automatically. This feature is part of the convenience of using make to manage a development project. To build and install a program in one step, you can specify the target of install like this:

```
# make install
```

Larger software projects might have a number of traditional targets in the makefile, such as the following:

- test—To run specific tests on the final software

- man—To process an include a troff document with the -man macros

- clean—To delete any remaining object files

- archive—To clean up, archive, and compress the entire source code tree

- bugreport—To automatically collect and then mail a copy of the build or error logs

Large applications can require hundreds of source code files. Compiling and linking these applications can be a complex and error-prone task. The make utility helps you organize the process of building the executable form of a complex application from many source files.

Using the autoconf Utility to Configure Code

The make command is only one of several programming automation utilities included with Fedora Core Linux. There are others, such as pmake (which causes a parallel make), imake (which is a dependency-driven makefile generator that is used for building X11 clients), automake, and one of the newer tools, autoconf, which builds shell scripts that can be used to configure program source code packages.

Building many software packages for Linux that are distributed in source form requires the use of GNU's autoconf utility. This program builds an executable shell script named configure that, when executed, automatically examines and tailors a client's build from source according to software resources, or *dependencies* (such as programming tools, libraries, and associated utilities), that are installed on the target host (your Linux system). The idea is to increase software project portability and ease the task of the programmer who is faced with a software project expected to run on many compatible, yet potentially disparate, software platforms.

Many Linux commands and graphical clients for X downloaded in source code form include `configure` scripts. To configure the source package, build the software, and then install the new program, the `root` operator might use the script like this (after uncompressing the source and navigating into the resulting build directory):

```
# ./configure ; make ; make install
```

The `autoconf` program uses a file named `configure.in` that contains a basic *ruleset*, or set of macros. The `configure.in` file is created with the `autoscan` command. Building a properly executing `configure` script also requires a template for the makefile, named `Makefile.in`. Although creating the dependency-checking `configure` script can be done manually, you can easily overcome any complex dependencies by using a graphical project development tool such as KDE's KDevelop or GNOME's Glade. (See the section "Graphical Development Tools," later in this chapter, for more information.)

Managing Software Projects with RCS and CVS

Although `make` can be used to manage a software project, larger software projects require document management, source code controls, security, and revision tracking as the source code goes through a series of changes during its development. RCS and CVS provide source code version control utilities for this kind of large software project management. You can find both of these utilities in RPM packages on your Fedora Core Linux CD-ROMs.

The RCS and CVS systems are used to track changes to multiple versions of files, and they can be used to backtrack or branch off versions of documents inside the scope of a project. They can also be used to prevent or resolve conflicting entries or changes made to source code files by multiple developers.

Although RCS and CVS provide similar features, RCS uses a locking and unlocking scheme to control access for making revisions; CVS, on the other hand, provides a modification and merging approach to working on older, current, or new versions of software. RCS uses different programs to check in or out of a revision under a directory; CVS uses a number of administrative files in a software repository of source code modules to merge and resolve change conflicts.

> **NOTE**
>
> Numerous changes to a source tree (directory of source code files) can also be accomplished using the `patch` command. Although `patch` does not offer the source control features of RCS and CVS, it is very handy if there is a need to rapidly apply a "fix" to one or more files. You can use the `diff` command to create a patch, which is a text file that contains line-by-line differences between two files or directories of files. See "Patching the Kernel" in Chapter 24 for information on how to use `patch` to apply updates to the Linux kernel source tree.

RCS uses at least the following eight separate programs to track source code revisions:

- `ci`—Checks in revisions
- `co`—Checks out revisions
- `ident`—Starts the keyword utility for source files
- `rcs`—Changes file attributes
- `rcsclean`—Cleans up working files
- `rcsdiff`—Starts the revision comparison utility
- `rcsmerge`—Merges revisions
- `rlog`—Activates the logging and information utility

Source code control with CVS requires the use of at least the following six command options on the `cvs` command line:

- `checkout`—Checks out revisions
- `update`—Updates your sources with changes made by other developers
- `add`—Adds new files in `cvs` records
- `import`—Adds new sources to the repository
- `remove`—Eliminates files from the repository
- `commit`—Publishes changes to other repository developers

Note that some of these commands require you to use additional fields, such as the names of files.

RCS and CVS can be used for more than software development projects. These tools can be used for document preparation and workgroup editing of documents, and they can work with any text files. Both systems use registration and control files to accomplish revision management. Both systems also offer the opportunity to revisit any step or branch in a revision history and to restore previous versions of a project. This mechanism is extremely important in cross-platform development and for software maintenance.

Tracking information is usually contained in separate control files; each document within a project might contain information that is automatically updated with each change to a project. A process called *keyword substitution* is used to perform these automatic updates. CVS and RCS use similar keywords, which are usually included inside C comment strings (/* */) near the top of a document. The following are some of the available keywords:

- `$Author$`—The username of the person who performed the last check-in
- `$Date$`—The date and time of the last check-in

- $Header$—The pathname of the document's RCS file, with the revision number, date and time, author, and state inserted

- Id—Same as $Header$, but without a full pathname

- $Name$—A symbolic name (see the co man page)

- $Revision$—The assigned revision number (such as 1.1)

- $Source$—The RCS file's full pathname

- $State$—The state of the document, such as Exp for experimental, Rel for released, or Stab for stable

You can also use these keywords to insert version information into compiled programs by using character strings in program source code. For example, given an extremely short C program named foo.c, you could use the following to assign version info to a variable (rsrcid in the example), which will then be embedded in the binary program:

```
/* $Header$ */
#include <stdio.h>
static char rsrcid[] = "$Header$";
main() {
    printf("Hello, Linus!\n");
}
```

The resulting $Header$ keyword might expand to this in an RCS document:

```
$Header: /home/bball/sw/RCS/foo.c,v 1.1 1999/04/20 15:01:07 root Exp Root $
```

Getting started with RCS is as simple as creating a project directory and an RCS directory under the project directory and then creating or copying initial source files in the project directory. You can then use the ci command to check in documents. Getting started with CVS requires that you initialize a repository by first setting the $CVSROOT environment variable with the full pathname of the repository and then using the init command option with the cvs command, like this:

```
# cvs init
```

You can find documentation for RCS and CVS in various man pages, under the /usr/share/doc directories for each of them, and in GNU information documents.

TIP

Even though they're free, CVS and RCS are powerful software project management tools. Many organizations use CVS and RCS to manage the source for their projects. Commercial code-management tools (also called *version-control programs*) also exist that include fancy interfaces, homogenous platform support, and greater flexibility than RCS and CVS. But those tools require dedicated administrators and might have significant licensing costs—both of which are major disadvantages.

Making Libraries with ar

C and C++ project management tools can help ease the process of building large applications; the ar command is an example of such a tool. If several different programs use the same functions, they can be combined into a single library archive. You use the ar command to build such a library. When you include the library on the compile line, the archive is searched to resolve any external symbols. Listing 21.1 shows an example of building and using a library.

LISTING 21.1   Building and Using a Library

```
$ gcc -c sine.c
$ gcc -c cosine.c
$ gcc -c tangent.c
$ ar c libtrig.a sine.o cosine.o tangent.o

$ gcc -c mainprog.c
$ gcc -o mainprog mainprog.o libtrig.a
```

Remember that gcc is the command that you use to invoke the GNU C compiler. (The section "Using the GNU C Compiler," later in this chapter, explains what -c and -o mean.)

Debugging Tools

Debugging is both a science and an art. Sometimes, the simplest tool—the code listing—is the best debugging tool. At other times, however, you need to use other debugging tools. Three of these tools are splint, gprof, and gdb.

Using splint to Check for Source Code

The splint command is similar to the traditional UNIX lint command; it examines source code for possible problems, and it also has many additional features. Even if your C code meets the standards for C and compiles cleanly, it might still contain errors. splint performs many different types of checks and can provide extensive error information. For example, this simple program might compile cleanly and even run:

```
$ gcc -o tux tux.c
$ ./tux
```

But the splint command might point out some serious problems with the source:

```
$ splint tux.c
Splint 3.1.1 --- 17 Feb 2004

tux.c: (in function main)
tux.c:2:19: Return value (type int) ignored: putchar(t[++j] -...
  Result returned by function call is not used. If this is intended, can cast
  result to (void) to eliminate message. (Use -retvalint to inhibit warning)
Finished checking --- 1 code warning
```

You can use the splint command's -strict option, like this, to get a more verbose report:

```
$ splint -strict tux.c
```

The GNU C compiler also supports diagnostics through the use of extensive warnings (through the -Wall and -pedantic options):

```
$ gcc -Wall tux.c
tux.c:1: warning: return type defaults to `int'
tux.c: In function `main':
tux.c:2: warning: implicit declaration of function `putchar'
```

> **NOTE**
>
> If you would like to explore various C syntax-checking programs, navigate to http://www.ibiblio.org/pub/Linux/devel/lang/c/. The splint program is derived from lclint, which you can find in the lclint-2.2a-src.tar.gz file at the Web site.

Using gprof to Track Function Time

You use the gprof (profile) command to study how a program is spending its time. If a program is compiled and linked with -p as a flag, a mon.out file is created when it executes, with data on how often each function is called and how much time is spent in each function. gprof parses and displays this data. An analysis of the output generated by gprof helps you determine where performance bottlenecks occur. Using an optimizing compiler can speed up a program, but taking the time to use gprof's analysis and revising bottleneck functions significantly improves program performance.

Doing Symbolic Debugging with gdb

The gdb tool is a symbolic debugger. When a program is compiled with the -g flag, the symbol tables are retained, and a symbolic debugger can be used to track program bugs. The basic technique is to invoke gdb after a core dump (a file containing a snapshot of the memory used by a program that has crashed) and get a stack trace. The stack trace indicates the source line where the core dump occurred and the functions that were called to reach that line. Often, this is enough to identify a problem. It isn't the limit of gdb, though.

gdb also provides an environment for debugging programs interactively. Invoking gdb with a program enables you to set breakpoints, examine the values of variables, and monitor variables. If you suspect a problem near a line of code, you can set a breakpoint at that line and run gdb. When the line is reached, execution is interrupted. You can check variable values, examine the stack trace, and observe the program's environment. You can single-step through the program to check values. You can resume execution at any point. By using breakpoints, you can discover many bugs in code.

A graphical X Window interface to gdb is called the Data Display Debugger, or ddd.

> **NOTE**
>
> If you browse to http://www.ibiblio.org/pub/Linux/devel/debuggers/, you can find at least a dozen different debuggers.

Using the GNU C Compiler

If you elected to install the development tools package when you installed Fedora Core (or perhaps later on, using RPM, or other package tools), you should have the GNU C compiler (gcc). Many different options are available for the GNU C compiler, and many of them are similar to those of the C and C++ compilers that are available on other UNIX systems. Table 21.1 shows the important switches for gcc. You can look at the man page or information file for gcc for a full list of options and descriptions.

TABLE 21.1   GNU C Compiler Switches

Switch	Description
-x *language*	Specifies the language; C, C++, Java, and assembler are valid values.
-c	Compiles and assembles only; does not link.
-S	Compiles; does not assemble or link. Generates an assembler code (.s) file.
-E	Preprocesses only; does not compile, assemble, or link.
-o *file*	Specifies the output filename. a.out is the default.
-l *library*	Specifies the libraries to use.
-I *directory*	Searches the specified directory for include files.
-w	Inhibits warning messages.
-pedantic	Requires strict ANSI compliance.
-Wall	Prints additional warning messages.
-g	Produces debugging information for use with gdb.
-ggdb	Generates native-format debugging info and gdb extensions.
-p	Produces information required by gprof.
-pg	Produces information for use by gprof.
-O	Optimizes the compilation.

> **NOTE**
>
> Fedora Core includes version 3.4.1 of gcc, but newer versions of gcc appear from time to time. You should be aware that if you use gcc to develop programs for earlier versions of Linux, your programs might not load or run because of software library incompatibilities. You can always install an older version of gcc and compatible development libraries to support building programs that work with older versions of Linux. These problems can occur because older and newer versions of software libraries might have different ideas about how standard routines are used.

When you build a C program using gcc, the compilation process takes place in several steps:

1. First, the C preprocessor parses the file. To do so, it sequentially reads the lines, includes header files, and performs macro replacement.

2. The compiler parses the modified code to determine whether the correct syntax is used. In the process, it builds a symbol table and creates an intermediate object format. Most symbols have specific memory addresses assigned, although symbols defined in other modules, such as external variables, do not.

3. The last compilation stage, linking, ties together different files and libraries and then links the files by resolving the symbols that had not previously been resolved.

> **NOTE**
>
> Most C programs compile with a C++ compiler if you follow strict ANSI rules. For example, you can compile the standard hello.c program (everyone's first program) with the GNU C++ compiler. Typically, you name the file something like hello.cc, hello.C, hello.c++, or hello.cxx. The GNU C++ compiler accepts any of these names.

A Simple C Program

This section provides a simple example of how to create an executable program for Linux by using gcc. One of the shortest programs you can write in C for Linux is the quintessential "hello, world" program (popularized by Brian W. Kernighan and Dennis M. Ritchie in their 1978 book *The C Programming Language*).

To get started, type in the following text, using your favorite Linux text editor:

```
main(){
    printf("hello, world.\n");
}
```

When you are finished, save the file as hello.c, and then compile the program by using the gcc compiler system, like this:

```
$ gcc -o hello hello.c
```

This command line creates an executable program named hello, using the file hello.c as input. You can then run the program like this:

```
$ ./hello
hello, world.
```

The C program contains only one function, named main(). The gcc command line specifies the name of the output program (using the -o option) and the input source file, hello.c. Note that in order to run the new hello command, you must specify it explicitly, using the period and forward-slash characters, as the program is not installed in a normal command directory (such as /usr/bin or /usr/local/bin).

> **NOTE**
>
> You can build large programs in C. C programs can be broken into any number of files, as long as no single function spans more than one file. To compile a program, you compile each source file into an intermediate object before you link all the objects into a single executable. The -c flag tells the compiler to stop at that stage. During the link stage, all the object files should be listed on the command line. Object files are identified by the .o suffix.

Graphical Development Tools

Fedora Core includes a number of graphical prototyping and development environments for use during X sessions. If you want to build client software for KDE or GNOME, you might find the KDevelop, QT Designer, and Glade programs extremely helpful. You can use each of these programs to build graphical frameworks for interactive windowing clients, and you can use each of them to automatically generate the necessary skeleton of code needed to support a custom interface for your program.

Using the KDevelop Client

You can launch the KDevelop client (shown in Figure 21.1) from the desktop panel's start menu's Extras, Programming menu item or from the command line of a terminal window, like this:

```
$ kdevelop &
```

After you press Enter, the KDevelop Setup Wizard runs, and you are taken through several short wizard dialogs that set up and ensure a stable build environment. You must then run kdevelop again (either from the command line or by clicking its menu item under the desktop panel's Programming menu). You will then see the main KDevelop window and can start your project by selecting KDevelop's Project menu and clicking the New menu item.

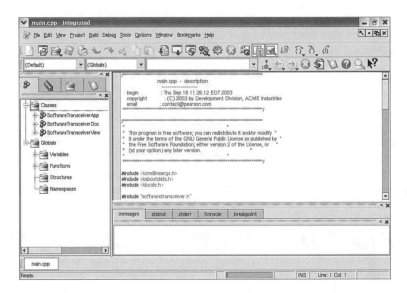

FIGURE 21.1   KDE's KDevelop is a rapid prototyping and client-building tool for use with Linux.

You can begin building your project by stepping through the wizard dialogs. When you click the Create button, KDevelop automatically generates all the files that are normally found in a KDE client source directory (including the `configure` script, which checks dependencies and builds the client's makefile). To test your client, you can either first click the Build menu's Make menu item (or press F8) or just click the Execute menu item (or press F9), and the client is built automatically. You can use KDevelop to create KDE clients, plug-ins for the `konqueror` browser, KDE `kicker` panel applets, KDE desktop themes, QT library–based clients, and even programs for GNOME.

Trolltech's QT Designer

A development environment that is related to KDevelop and is included with Fedora Core is Trolltech's QT Designer. You can use this program to build user interface "forms" for cross-platform applications. QT Designer has a complex interface that supports drawing of windows, buttons, and other client controls. You can start QT Designer from the command line of a terminal window like this:

```
$ designer &
```

You can also start the prototyping environment by clicking its menu item under the Programming menu's More Programming tools menu. The QT Designer main window (as shown in Figure 21.2) provides tools to quickly build and preview a graphical client. After first creating a directory to hold the project files, start by choosing File, New Menu to create a new project. Then, you can select a C++ project and save it with a name that ends with `.pro`.

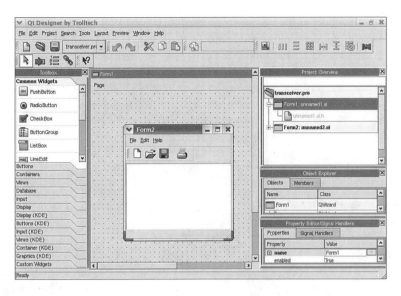

FIGURE 21.2 Trolltech's QT Designer is, like KDevelop, a capable prototyping and client-building tool for use with Linux and X.

Next, you can again use the File menu to add a file, but this time, you select a window, widget, or dialog, depending on the graphical interface you'd like to add to your project. After you design the program's GUI, you can preview your design by using the Preview menu. You can also test a build of the new client if you have added enough requisite code. You begin by navigating to your project's folder (using the cd command), and then you use the qmake and make commands, like this:

```
$ qmake -o Makefile myproject.pro
$ make
$ ./myproject
```

The Glade Client for Developing in GNOME

If you prefer to use GNOME and GNOME development tools, the Glade GTK++ GUI builder (the glade-2 client) can help you save time and effort when building a basic skeleton for a program. You launch glade-2 from the desktop panel's Programming menu or from the command line of a terminal window, like this:

```
$ glade-2 &
```

> **TIP**
>
> Click the Contents menu item from the Glade Help menu to read a step-by-step guide on building a simple client interface. You'll also find an introductory tutorial on programming with Glade by Ishan Chattopadhyaya at http://wingtk.sourceforge.net/ishan/glade.html.

When you launch Glade, a directory named Projects is created in your home directory, and you see a main window, along with two floating palette and properties windows (see Figure 21.3, which shows a basic GNOME client with a calendar widget added to its main window). You can use Glade's File menu to save the blank project and then start building your client by clicking and adding user interface elements from the Palette window. For example, you can first click the Palette window's Gnome button and then click to create your new client's main window. A window with a menu and a toolbar appears—the basic framework for a new GNOME client!

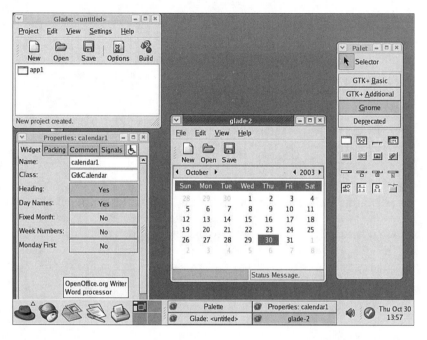

FIGURE 21.3   The GNOME Glade client can be used to build and preview a graphical interface for a custom GNOME program.

When you have finished building the client, you can select Build Source Code from the Project window's File menu, and Glade builds the necessary source code and scripts for the project. You can then build the project's configure script by executing the autogen.sh script in the project directory, like so:

```
$ ./autogen.sh
```

After you set up the project, as with KDevelop projects, you are ready to configure, build, and install your project. To begin that process, execute the following:

```
# make install
```

You'll need to add code to fill in the actions for your new KDE or GNOME client when using these rapid prototyping tools. But kdevelop, designer, and glade can help save development time and effort. Use these environments to create a working skeleton application, and then fine-tune your new client's user interface.

Related Fedora Core and Linux Commands

You'll use many of these commands when programming in C and C++ for Linux:

ar—The GNU archive development tool

as—The GNU assembler

autoconf—The GNU configuration script generator

cervisia—A KDE client that provides a graphical interface to a CVS project

cvs—A project revision control system

designer—Trolltech's graphical prototyping tool for use with QT libraries and X

gcc—The GNU C/C++ compiler system

gdb—The GNU interactive debugger

glade-2—The GNOME graphical development environment for building GTK+ clients

gprof—The GNU program profiler

kdevelop—The KDE C/C++ graphical development environment for building KDE, GNOME, or terminal clients

make—A GNU project management command

patch—Larry Wall's source patching utility

pmake—A BSD project management command

rcs—A suite of programs used to manage project documents

splint—The C source file checker

xmkmf—A shell script for X that is used to create a localized makefile for building an X client

---

Additional Resources

UNIX and Linux were built on the C language. C is a platform-independent, compiled, procedural language based on functions and on the capability to derive new, programmer-defined data structures.

NOTE

Many people consider *The C Programming Language*, by Brian W. Kernighan and Dennis M. Ritchie, to be the definitive book for those who want to learn how to program in C.

If you are interested in learning more about C and C++, you should look for the following books:

- *Sams Teach Yourself C in 21 Days*, by Peter Aitken and Bradley Jones, Sams Publishing

- *Sams Teach Yourself C++ for Linux in 21 Days*, by Jesse Liberty and David B. Horvath, Sams Publishing

- *C How to Program* and *C++ How to Program*, both by Harvey M. Deitel and Paul J. Deitel

- *The C Programming Language*, by Brian W. Kernighan and Dennis M. Ritchie

- *The Annotated C++ Reference Manual*, by Margaret A. Ellis and Bjarne Stroustrup

- *Programming in ANSI C*, by Stephen G. Kochan

Reference

`http://gcc.gnu.org/java/compile.html`—More information about egcs Java support.

`http://www.gnu.org/software/autoconf/autoconf.html`—More information about the GNU Project's autoconf utility and how to build portable software projects.

`http://sourcenav.sourceforge.net/`—Home page for Red Hat's snavigator client, a source code analysis utility.

`http://www.trolltech.com/products/qt/tools.html`—Trolltech's page for QT Designer and a number of programming automation tools (including translators) that you can use with Fedora.

`http://glade.gnome.org/`—Home page for the Glade GNOME developer's tool.

`http://www.kdevelop.org/`—Site that hosts the KDevelop Project's latest versions of the KDE graphical development environment, Kdevelop.

CHAPTER **22**

Shell Scripting

IN THIS CHAPTER

- The Shells Included with This Book
- The Shell Command Line
- The Basics of Writing, Creating, and Executing a Shell Script
- Creating and Executing a Simple Shell Program with bash
- Using Variables in Shell Scripts
- Positional Parameters
- Built-in Variables
- Special Characters
- Comparison of Expressions
- Iteration Statements
- Conditional Statements
- The break and exit Statements
- Using Functions in Shell Scripts
- Reference

Many computer users judge the quality of an operating system by the appearance and ease of use of the desktop. Various commercial Linux distributors such as Red Hat, Inc., and developer projects such as GNOME and KDE have made great strides in producing cohesive, consistent software interfaces to Linux-based operating systems. However, underneath all distributions is the Linux kernel, and perhaps with the exception of embedded device implementations, all Linux distributions offer a text-based console, or command-line interface to the kernel.

Fans of the point-and-click computer interface might not be familiar with or comfortable using a command line. The Linux command line, known as a *shell*, is an integral and essential part of the Linux operating system. In certain situations or on particular hardware, the shell might be the only way to interact with Linux (such as remotely accessing a server via dialup or over a network).

The shell is much more than a command line with sophisticated features; it has a syntax that is a programming language. Using that syntax, you can define variables, assign various values, and evaluate different results in order to create your own programs.

This chapter is an introduction to the basics of creating *shell scripts*, or executable text files written to conform to shell syntax. Shell scripts run like any other command under Linux and can contain complex logic or a simple series of Linux command-line instructions. You can also run other shell scripts from within a shell program. The features and functions for several Linux shells are discussed in this chapter after a short introduction to working from the shell command line. You learn how to write and execute a simple shell program using bash, one of the most popular Linux shells. You also get an overview of the structure of shell syntax.

The Shells Included with This Book

Fedora Core, the Linux distribution installed from the CD-ROMs that accompany this book, includes a rich assortment of capable, flexible, and powerful shells. Each shell is different, but has numerous built-in commands, configurable command-line prompts, and might include features such as command-line history, the ability to recall and use a previous command line, and command-line editing. As an example, the bash shell is so powerful that it is possible to write a minimal Web server entirely in bash's language using 114 lines of script (see the link at the end of this chapter).

Table 22.1 lists each shell, along with its description and location, in your Fedora file system.

TABLE 22.1   Shells with Fedora Core

Name	Description	Location
ash	A small shell (sh-like)	/bin/ash
ash.static	A version of ash not dependent on software libraries	/bin/ash.static
bash	The Bourne Again Shell	/bin/bash
bsh	A symbolic link to ash	/bin/bsh
csh	The C shell, a symbolic link to tcsh	/bin/csh
ksh	The Korn shell	/bin/ksh, /usr/bin/ksh
pdksh	A symbolic link to ksh	/usr/bin/pdksh
rsh	The restricted shell (for network operation)	/usr/bin/rsh
sash	A standalone shell	/sbin/sash
sh	A symbolic link to bash	/bin/sh
tcsh	A csh-compatible shell	/bin/tcsh
zsh	A compatible csh, ksh, and sh shell	/bin/zsh

> **Learning More About Your Shell**
>
> All the shells listed in Table 22.1 have accompanying man pages, along with other documentation under the /usr/share/doc directory. Some of the documentation can be quite lengthy, but it is generally much better to have too much documentation than too little! The bash shell includes more than 100 pages in its manual, and the zsh shell documentation is so extensive that it includes the zshall meta man page (use man zshall to read this overview)!

The Shell Command Line

Having a basic understanding of the capabilities of the shell command line can help you write better shell scripts. You can use the shell command line to perform a number of different tasks, including

- Searching files or directories with programs using pattern-matching, or *expressions*; these commands include the GNU gawk (linked as awk) and the grep family of commands, including egrep and fgrep.

- Getting data from and sending data to a file or command, known as *input* and *output redirection*.

- Feeding or filtering a program's output to another command (called using *pipes*).

A shell can also have built-in *job-control* commands to launch the command line as a background process, suspend a running program, selectively retrieve or kill running or suspended programs, and perform other types of process control.

Multiple commands can be run on a single command line using a semicolon to separate commands:

```
$ w ; free ; df
  6:02pm  up 4 days, 24 min,  1 user,  load average: 0.00, 0.00, 0.00
USER      TTY       FROM              LOGIN@   IDLE   JCPU   PCPU  WHAT
bball     pts/0     shuttle.home.org 1:14pm  0.00s  0.57s  0.01s  w
total         used       free     shared     buffers      cached
Mem:        190684     184420       6264         76       17620      142820
-/+ buffers/cache:      23980     166704
Swap:      1277156       2516    1274640
Filesystem           1k-blocks       Used Available Use% Mounted on
/dev/hda1            11788296    4478228   6711248  41% /
none                   95340          0     95340   0% /dev/shm
```

This example displays the output of the w, free, and df commands. Long shell command lines can be extended inside shell scripts or at the command line by using the backslash character (\). For example,

```
$ echo ""this is a long \
> command line and"" ; echo ""shows that multiple commands \
> may be strung out.""
this is a long command line and
shows that multiple commands may be strung out.
```

The first three lines of this example are a single command line. In that single line are two instances of the echo command. Note that when you use the backslash as a line-continuation character, it must be the last character on the command line (or in your shell script, as you'll see later on in this chapter).

Using the basic features of the shell command line is easy, but mastering use of all features can be difficult. Entire books have been devoted to using shells, writing shell scripts, and using pattern-matching expressions. The following sections provide an overview of some features of the shell command line relating to writing scripts.

Toward Grokking grep

If you plan to develop shell scripts to expand the capabilities of pattern-matching commands such as grep, you will benefit from learning more about using expressions. One of the definitive guides to using the pattern-matching capabilities of UNIX and Linux commands is *Mastering Regular Expressions* by Jeffrey E. F. Freidl.

Shell Pattern-Matching Support

The shell command line allows you to use strings of specially constructed character patterns for wildcard matches. This is a different, and in some ways, simpler capability than that supported by GNU utilities such as grep, which can use more complex patterns, known as *expressions*, to search through files or directories or to filter data input to or out of commands.

The shell's pattern strings can be simple or complex, but even using a small subset of the available characters in simple wildcards can yield constructive results at the command line. Some common characters used for shell pattern matching are

- *—Matches any character. For example, to find all files in the current directory ending in .txt, you could use

  $ ls *.txt

- ?—Matches a single character. For example, to find all files in the current directory ending in the extension .d?c (where ? could be 0–9, a–z, or A–Z),

  $ ls *.d?c

- [xxx] or [x-x]—Matches a range of characters. For example, to list all files in a directory with names containing numbers,

  $ ls *[0-9]*

- \x—Matches or escapes a character such as ? or a tab character. For example, to create a file with a name containing question mark,

  $ touch foo\?

Note that the shell might not interpret some characters or regular expressions in the same manner as a Linux command, and mixing wildcards and regular expressions in shell scripts can lead to problems unless you're careful. For example, finding patterns in text is best left to regular expressions used with commands such as grep; simple wildcards should be used for filtering or matching filenames on the command line. And although both Linux command expressions and shell scripts can recognize the backslash as an escape character in patterns, the dollar sign ($) will have two wildly different meanings (single-character pattern matching in expressions and variable assignment in scripts).

Redirecting Input and Output

You can create, overwrite, and append data to files at the command line, using a process called *input* and *output redirection*. The shell recognizes several special characters for this process, such as >, <, or >>.

In this example, the output of the ls command is redirected to create a file named textfiles.listing:

```
$ ls *.txt >textfiles.listing
```

Use output redirection with care because it is possible to overwrite existing files. For example, specifying a different directory but using the same output filename will over-write the existing textfiles.listing:

```
$ ls /usr/share/doc/mutt-1.4/*.txt >textfiles.listing
```

Fortunately, most shells are smart enough to recognize when you might do something foolish. Here, the bash shell warns that the command is attempting to redirect output to a directory:

```
$ mkdir foo
$ ls >foo
bash: foo: Is a directory
```

Output can be >) operator>> (append) operator>appended to a file without overwriting existing content by using the append (>>) operator. In this example, the directory listing will be appended to the end of textfiles.listing instead of overwriting its contents:

```
$ ls /usr/share/doc/mutt-1.4/*.txt >>textfiles.listing
```

You can use *input redirection* to feed data into a command by using the < like this:

```
$ cat < textfiles.listing
```

You can use the shell *here* operator to specify the end of input on the shell command line:

```
$ cat >simple_script <<DONE
> echo ""this is a simple script""
> DONE
$ cat simple_script
echo ""this is a simple script""
```

In this example, the shell will feed the cat command you're typing (input) until the pattern DONE is recognized. The output file simple_script is then saved and its contents verified. This same technique can be used in scripts to create content based on the output of various commands and define an end-of-input or delimiter.

Piping Data

Many Linux commands can be used in concert in a single, connected command line to transform data from one form to another. Stringing Linux commands together in this fashion is known as using or creating *pipes*. Pipes are created on the command line with the bar operator (¦). For example, a pipe can be used to perform a complex task from a single command line like this:

```
$ find /d2 -name '*.txt' -print ¦ xargs cat ¦ \
tr ' ' '\n' ¦  sort ¦ uniq >output.txt
```

This example takes the output of the find command to feed the cat command (via xargs) the name all text files under the /d2 command. The content of all matching files is then fed through the tr command to change each space in the data stream into a carriage return. The stream of words is then sorted, and identical adjacent lines are removed using the uniq command. The output, a raw list of words, is then saved in the file named output.txt.

> **NOTE**
>
> You'll find examples of using pipes and other shell operators throughout this book. For example, see the section "fdisk" in Chapter 10, "Managing the File System," to see how to send your system's partition table to a file or your printer. See the section "tar" in Chapter 11, "Backing Up, Restoring, and Recovery," to see how to use pipes to aid in performing incremental backups, or to save a catalog of changed files on your system.

Background Processing

The shell allows you to start a command and then launch it into the background as a process by using an ampersand (&) at the end of a command line. This technique is often used at the command line of an X terminal window to start a client and return to the command line. For example, to launch another terminal window using the xterm client,

```
$ xterm &
[3] 1437
```

The numbers echoed back show a number (3 in this example), which is a *job* number, or reference number for a shell process, and a *Process ID* number, or PID. The xterm window session can be killed by using the shell's built-in kill command, along with the job number like this:

```
$ kill %3
```

Or the process can be killed by using the kill command, along with the PID, like so:

```
$ kill 1437
```

Background processing can be used in shell scripts to start commands that take a long time, such as backups:

```
# tar -czf /backup/home.tgz /home &
```

The Basics of Writing, Creating, and Executing a Shell Script

Why should you write and use shell scripts? Shell scripts can save you time and typing, especially if you routinely use the same command lines multiple times every day. Although you could also use the history function (press the Up or Down keys while using bash or use the history command), a shell script can add flexibility with command-line argument substitution and built-in help.

Although a shell script won't execute faster than a program written in a computer language such as C, a shell program can be smaller in size than a compiled program. The shell program does not require any additional library support other than the shell or, if used, existing commands installed on your system. The process of creating and testing shell scripts is also generally simpler and faster than the development process for equivalent C language commands.

> **NOTE**
>
> Hundreds of commands included with Fedora are actually shell scripts, and many other good shell script examples are available over the Internet—a quick search will yield numerous links to online tutorials and scripting guides from fellow Linux users and developers. For example, the startx command, used to start an X Window session from the text console, is a shell script used every day by many Linux (and UNIX) users. Sending faxes can be accomplished by using the fax command, which is a shell script you can customize to include your name, phone number, and other information. To learn more about shell scripting with bash, see the Advanced Bash-Scripting Guide, listed in the "Reference" section at the end of this chapter. You'll also find *Sams Teach Yourself Shell Programming in 24 Hours* a helpful guide to learning more about using the shell to build your own commands.

When you are learning to write and execute your first shell scripts, start with scripts for simple, but useful tasks. Begin with short examples, and then expand the scripts as you build on your experience and knowledge. Make liberal use of comments (lines preceded with a pound # sign) to document each section of your script. Include an author statement and overview of the script as additional help, along with a creation date or version number. Write shell scripts using a text editor such as vi because it does not automatically wrap lines of text. Line wrapping can break script syntax and cause problems. If you use the nano editor, include its -w flag to disable line wrap.

Creating and Executing a Simple Shell Program with bash

In this section, you learn how to write a simple shell script to set up a number of *aliases* (command synonyms) whenever you log on (see "Forwarding Email with Aliases" in Chapter 19, "Handling Electronic Mail"). Instead of typing all the aliases every time you log on, you can put them in a file by using a text editor, such as vi, and then execute the file. Normally these changes are saved in systemwide shell configuration files under the /etc directory to make the changes active for all users or in your .bashrc, .cshrc (if you use tcsh), or .bash_profile files in your home directory.

Here is what is contained in myenv, a sample shell script created for this purpose (for bash):

```
#!/bin/sh
alias ll='ls -l'
alias ldir='ls -aF'
alias copy='cp'
```

This simple script creates command *aliases*, or convenient shorthand forms of commands, for the ls and cp commands. The ll alias provides a long directory listing: The ldir alias is the ls command, but prints indicators (for directories or executable files) in listings. The copy alias is the same as the cp command. You can experiment and add your own options or create aliases of other commands with options you frequently use.

You can execute myenv in a variety of ways under Linux. As shown in this example, you can make myenv executable by using the chmod command and then execute it as you would any other native Linux command:

```
$ chmod +x myenv
```

This line turns on the executable permission of myenv, which can be checked with the ls command and its -l option like this:

```
$ ls -l myenv
-rwxrwxr-x    1 winky    winky        11 Aug 26 17:38 myenv
```

Running the New Shell Program

You can run your new shell program in several ways. Each method will produce the same results, which is a testament to the flexibility of using the shell with Linux. One way to run your shell program is to execute the file myenv from the command line as if it were a Linux command:

```
$ ./myenv
```

A second way to execute myenv under a particular shell, such as pdksh, is as follows:

```
$ pdksh myenv
```

This invokes a new `pdksh` shell and passes the filename `myenv` as a parameter to execute the file. A third way will require you to create a directory named `bin` in your home directory, and to then copy the new shell program into this directory. You can then run the program without the need to specify a location or to use a shell. You do this like so:

```
$ mkdir bin
$ mv myenv bin
$ myenv
```

This works because Fedora is set up by default to include the executable path `$HOME/bin` in your shell's environment. You can view this environment variable, named `PATH`, by piping the output of the `env` command through `fgrep` like so:

```
$ env ¦ fgrep PATH
/usr/kerberos/bin:/usr/local/bin:/bin:/usr/bin: \
/usr/X11R6/bin:/sbin:/home/bball/bin
```

As you can see, the user (`bball` in this example) can use the new `bin` directory to hold executable files. Another way to quickly view an environment variable is to use the `echo` command along with the variable name (in this case, `$PATH`):

```
$ echo $PATH
/usr/kerberos/bin:/usr/local/bin:/usr/bin:/bin:/usr/X11R6/bin:/home/bball/bin
```

The Public Domain Korn Shell

The `pdksh` shell was originally created by Eric Gisin, and, like the original Korn shell by David Korn, is in the public domain. In Fedora, `pdksh` is named `ksh`. Two symbolic links, `/usr/bin/pdksh` and `/usr/bin/ksh`, point to the `pdksh` shell, named `/bin/ksh`. For more information about `pdksh`, see the `/usr/share/doc/pdksh` directory or read the `ksh` man page. You can download the latest copy of `pdksh` (in source-code form) by browsing to `ftp://ftp.cs.mun.ca/pub/pdksh/`.

On March 1, 2000, AT&T released the official version of the `korn` shell, named KornShell 93, as open source. If you're interested in trying the original `korn` shell by David Korn, download a copy from the KornShell Web page at `http://www.kornshell.com/`.

CAUTION

Never put `.` in your `$PATH` in order to execute files or a command in the current directory—this presents a serious security risk, especially for the root operator, and even more so if `.` is first in your `$PATH` search order. Trojan scripts placed by crackers in directories such as `/tmp` can be used for malicious purposes, and will be executed immediately if the current working directory is part of your `$PATH`.

Storing Shell Scripts for Systemwide Access

After you execute the command myenv, you should be able to use ldir from the command line to get a list of files under the current directory and ll to get a list of files with attributes displayed. However, the best way to use the new commands in myenv is to put them into your shell's login or profile file. For Fedora, and nearly all Linux users, the default shell is bash, so you can make these commands available for everyone on your system by putting them in the /etc/bashrc file. Systemwide aliases for tcsh are contained in files with the extension .csh under the /etc/profile.d directory. The pdksh shell can use these command aliases as well.

> **NOTE**
>
> To use a shell other than bash after logging in, use the chsh command from the command line or the system-config-users client during an X session. You'll be asked for your password (or the root password if using system-config-users), as well as the location and name of the new shell (refer to Table 22.1). The new shell will become your default shell, but only if its name is in the list of acceptable system shells in /etc/shells. See Chapter 5, "First Steps with Fedora," for details on changing your shell.

Interpreting Shell Scripts Through Specific Shells

The majority of shell scripts use a *bang line* (#!) at the beginning to control the type of shell used to run the script; this bang line calls for an sh-incantation of bash:

```
#!/bin/sh
```

A bang line tells the Linux kernel that a specific command (a shell, or in the case of other scripts, perhaps awk or Perl) is to be used to interpret the contents of the file. Using a bang line is common practice for all shell scripting. For example, if you write a shell script using bash, but want the script to execute as if run by the Bourne shell, sh, the first line of your script will contain #!/bin/sh, which is a link to the bash shell. Running bash as sh will cause bash to act as a Bourne shell. This is the reason for the symbolic link sh, which points to bash.

> **The Bang Line**
>
> The *bang line* (#!) is also colloquially known as a hash-bang or she-bang. The bang line is also a magic number, as defined in /usr/share/magic—a text database of magic numbers for the Linux file command. Magic numbers are used by many different Linux commands to quickly identify a type of file, and the database format is documented in the section five manual page named magic (read by using man 5 magic). For example, magic numbers can be used by the Linux file command to display the identity of a script (no matter what filename is used) as a shell script using a specific shell or other interpreter such as awk or Perl.

You might also find different or new environment variables available to your scripts by using different shells. For example, if you launch csh from the bash command line, you'll find several new variables or variables with slightly different definitions, such as

```
$ env
...
VENDOR=intel
MACHTYPE=i386
HOSTTYPE=i386-linux
HOST=thinkpad.home.org
```

On the other hand, bash might provide these variables or variables of the same name with a slightly different definition, such as

```
$ env
...
HOSTTYPE=i386
HOSTNAME=thinkpad.home.org
```

Although the behavior of a bang line isn't defined by POSIX, variations of its use can be helpful when you're writing shell scripts. For example, as described in the wish man page, you can use a shell to help execute programs called within a shell script without needing to hard-code pathnames of programs. The wish command is a windowing Tool Control Language (tcl) interpreter that can be used to write graphical clients. Avoiding the use of specific pathnames to programs increases shell script portability because not every UNIX or Linux system has programs in the same location.

For example, if you want to use the wish command, your first inclination might be to write

```
#!/usr/local/bin/wish
```

Although this will work on many other operating systems, the script will fail under Linux because wish is located under the /usr/bin directory. However, if you write the command line this way,

```
#!/bin/sh
exec wish "$@"
```

You can use the wish command (as a binary or a shell script itself) wish command; your first inclination might be to write in Linux.

Using Variables in Shell Scripts

This section of the book continues with discussions of using shell variables. This information will help you define, assign, and use variables in your shell scripts. The section

"Positional Parameters" will show how to access and use variables that hold arguments from the command line. Linux shells support a full-fledged programming language and, as such, use variables.

When writing shell scripts for Linux, you work with three types of variables:

- *Environment variables* are part of the system environment, and you can use them in your shell program. New variables can be defined, and some of them, such as PATH, can also be modified within a shell program.

- *Built-in variables*, such as options used on the command (interpreted by the shell as a *positional argument*) are provided by Linux. Unlike environment variables, you cannot modify them.

- *User variables* are defined by you when you write a shell script. You can use and modify them at will within the shell program.

A major difference between shell programming and other programming languages is that in shell programming, variables are not *typed*—that is, you do not have to specify whether a variable is a number or a string, and so on.

Assigning a Value to a Variable

Say that you want to use a variable called lcount to count the number of iterations in a loop within a shell program. You can declare and initialize this variable as follows:

Command	Environment
lcount=0	pdksh and bash
set lcount=0	tcsh

> **NOTE**
>
> Under pdksh and bash, you must ensure that the equal sign (=) does not have spaces before and after it.

To store a string in a variable, you can use the following:

Command	Environment
myname=Sanjiv	pdksh and bash
set myname=Sanjiv	tcsh

Use the preceding variable form if the string doesn't have embedded spaces. If a string has embedded spaces, you can do the assignment as follows:

Command	Environment
myname="Sanjiv Guha"	pdksh and bash
set myname="Sanjiv Guha"	tcsh

Accessing Variable Values

You can access the value of a variable by prefixing the variable name with a $ (dollar sign). That is, if the variable name is var, you can access the variable by using $var.

If you want to assign the value of var to the variable lcount, you can do so as follows:

Command	Environment
lcount=$var	pdksh and bash
set lcount=$var	tcsh

Positional Parameters

It is possible to pass options from the command line or from another shell script to your shell program.

These options are supplied to the shell program by Linux as *positional parameters*, which have special names provided by the system. The first parameter is stored in a variable called 1 (number 1) and can be accessed by using $1 within the program. The second parameter is stored in a variable called 2 and can be accessed by using $2 within the program, and so on. One or more of the higher numbered positional parameters can be omitted while you're invoking a shell program.

Understanding how to use these positional parameters and how to access and use variables retrieved from the command line is necessary when developing more advanced shell programs.

A Simple Example of a Positional Parameter

For example, if a shell program mypgm expects two parameters—such as a first name and a last name—you can invoke the shell program with only one parameter, the first name. However, you cannot invoke it with only the second parameter, the last name.

Here's a shell program called mypgm1, which takes only one parameter (a name) and displays it on the screen:

```
#!/bin/sh
#Name display program
if [ $# -eq 0 ]
then
```

```
    echo "Name not provided"
else
    echo "Your name is "$1
fi
```

If you execute mypgm1, as follows,

```
$ bash  mypgm1
```

you get the following output:

```
Name not provided
```

However, if you execute mypgm1, as follows,

```
$ bash  mypgm1 Sanjiv
```

you get the following output:

```
Your name is Sanjiv
```

The shell program mypgm1 also illustrates another aspect of shell programming: the built-in variables provided to the shell by the Linux kernel. In mypgm1, the built-in variable $# provides the number of positional parameters passed to the shell program. You learn more about working with built-in variables in the next major section of this chapter.

Using Positional Parameters to Access and Retrieve Variables from the Command Line

Using positional parameters in scripts can be really helpful if you need to use command lines with piped commands requiring complex arguments. Shell programs containing positional parameters can be even more convenient if the commands are infrequently used. For example, if you use your Fedora system with an attached voice modem as an answering machine, you can write a script to issue a command that retrieves and plays the voice messages. The following lines convert a saved sound file (in .rmd or voice-phone format) and pipe the result to your system's audio device:

```
#!/bin/sh
# play voice message in /var/spool/voice/incoming
rmdtopvf /var/spool/voice/incoming/$1 ¦ pvfspeed -s 8000 ¦ \
pvftobasic >/dev/audio
```

A voice message can then easily be played back using this script (perhaps named pmm):

```
$ pmm name_of_message
```

Shell scripts that contain positional parameters are often used for automating routine and mundane jobs, such as system log report generation, file system checks, user resource accounting, printer use accounting, and other system, network, or security administration tasks.

Using a Simple Script to Automate Tasks

You could use a simple script, for example, to examine your system log for certain keywords. If the script is run via your system's scheduling table, /etc/crontab, it can help automate security monitoring. By combining the output capabilities of existing Linux commands with the language facilities of the shell, you can quickly build a useful script to perform a task normally requiring a number of command lines. For example, you can create a short script, named greplog, like this:

```
#!/bin/sh
#     name:  greplog
#      use:  mail grep of designated log using keyword
# version:  v.01 08aug02
#
#   author: bb
#
# usage: greplog [keyword] [logpathname]
#
#   bugs: does not check for correct number of arguments

# build report name using keyword search and date
log_report=/tmp/$1.logreport.`date '+%m%d%y'`

# build report header with system type, hostname, date and time
echo "===============================================================" \
     >$log_report
echo "          S Y S T E M   M O N I T O R   L O G" >>$log_report
echo uname -a >>$log_report
echo "Log report for" `hostname -f` "on" `date '+%c'`        >>$log_report
echo "===============================================================" \
     >>$log_report ; echo "" >>$log_report

# record log search start
echo "Search for->" $1 "starting" `date '+%r'` >>$log_report
echo "" >>$log_report

# get and save grep results of keyword ($1) from logfile ($2)
grep -i $1 $2 >>$log_report
```

```
# build report footer with time
echo "" >>$log_report
echo "End of" $log_report at `date '+%r'` >>$log_report

# mail report to root
mail -s "Log Analysis for $1" root <$log_report

# clean up and remove report
rm $log_report
exit 0
```

In this example, the script creates the variable $log_report, which will be the filename of the temporary report. The keyword ($1) and first argument on the command line is used as part of the filename, along with the current date (with perhaps a better approach to use $$ instead of the date, which will append the script's PID as a file extension). Next, the report header (containing some formatted text, the output of the uname command, and the hostname and date) is added to the report. The start of the search is then recorded, and any matches of the keyword in the log are added to the report. A footer, containing the name of the report and the time, is then added. The report is mailed to root with the search term as the subject of the message, and the temporary file is deleted.

> **NOTE**
>
> By default, Fedora uses the logwatch log monitoring command (actually a Perl script) in your system's /etc/cron.daily directory to generate various reports each day at 0402 (4:02 a.m.). Configure logwatch by editing the file /etc/log.d/logwatch.conf. Other system monitoring tools are included, such as tripwire. System logging can be controlled by editing /etc/syslog.conf.

You can test the script by running it manually and feeding it a keyword and a pathname to the system log, /var/log/messages, like this:

```
# greplog FAILED /var/log/messages
```

Note that your system should be running the syslogd daemon. If any login failures have occurred on your system, the root operator might get an email message that looks like this:

```
Date: Thu, 23 Oct 2003 16:23:24 -0400
From: root <root@stinkpad.home.org>
To: root@stinkpad.home.org
Subject: FAILED
```

==

```
        S Y S T E M   M O N I T O R   L O G
Linux stinky 2.4.22-1.2088.nptl #1 Thu Oct 9 20:21:24 EDT 2003 i686 i686 i386
+GNU/Linux
Log report for stinkpad.home.org on Thu 23 Oct 2003 04:23:24 PM EDT
================================================================

Search for-> FAILED starting 04:23:24 PM


Oct 23 16:23:04 stinkpad login[1769]: FAILED LOGIN 3 FROM (null) FOR bball,
+Authentication failure

End of /tmp/FAILED.logreport.102303 at 04:23:24 PM
```

To further automate the process, you can include command lines using the script in another script to generate a series of searches and reports.

Built-in Variables

Built-in variables are special variables provided to shell by Linux that can be used to make decisions within a shell program. You cannot modify the values of these variables within the shell program.

Some of these variables are

> $#—Number of positional parameters passed to the shell program

> $?—Completion code of the last command or shell program executed within the shell program (returned value)

> $0—The name of the shell program

> $*—A single string of all arguments passed at the time of invocation of the shell program

To show these built-in variables in use, here is a sample program called mypgm2:

```
#!/bin/sh
#my test program
echo "Number of parameters is $#"
echo "Program name is $0"
echo "Parameters as a single string is $*"
```

If you execute mypgm2 from the command line in pdksh and bash as follows,

```
$ bash mypgm2 Sanjiv Guha
```

you get the following result:

```
Number of parameters is 2
Program name is mypgm2
Parameters as a single string is Sanjiv Guha
```

Special Characters

Some characters have special meaning to Linux shells; these characters represent commands, denote specific use for surrounding text, or provide search parameters. Special characters provide a sort of shorthand by incorporating these rather complex meanings into a simple character. Some special characters are shown in Table 22.2.

TABLE 22.2   Special Shell Characters

Character	Explanation
$	Indicates the beginning of a shell variable name
¦	Pipes standard output to next command
#	Starts a comment
&	Executes a process in the background
?	Matches one character
*	Matches one or more characters
>	Output redirection operator
<	Input redirection operator
`	Command substitution (the backquote or backtick—the key above the Tab key on most keyboards)
>>	Output redirection operator (to append to a file)
<<	Wait until following end-of-input string (HERE operator)
[ ]	Range of characters
[a-z]	All characters a through z
[a,z] or [az]	Characters a or z
Space	Delimiter between two words

Special characters are very useful to you when you're creating shell scripts, but if you inadvertently use a special character as part of variable names or strings, your program will behave incorrectly. As you learn in later parts of this section, you can use one of the special characters in a string if you precede it with an *escape character* (/, or backslash) to indicate that it isn't being used as a special character and shouldn't be treated as such by the program.

A few special characters deserve special note. They are the double quotes ("), the single quotes ('), the backslash (\), and the backtick (`)—all discussed in the following sections.

Use Double Quotes to Resolve Variables in Strings with Embedded Spaces

If a string contains embedded spaces, you can enclose the string in double quotes (") so that the shell interprets the whole string as one entity instead of more than one.

For example, if you assigned the value of abc def (abc followed by one space, followed by def) to a variable called x in a shell program as follows, you would get an error because the shell would try to execute def as a separate command.

Command	Environment
x=abc def	pdksh and bash
set x=abc def	tcsh

The shell will execute the string as a single command if you surround the string in double quotes:

Command	Environment
x="abc def"	pdksh and bash
set x="abc def"	tcsh

The double quotes resolve all variables within the string. Here is an example for pdksh and bash:

```
var="test string"
newvar="Value of var is $var"
echo $newvar
```

Here is the same example for tcsh:

```
set var="test string"
set newvar="Value of var is $var"
echo $newvar
```

If you execute a shell program containing the preceding three lines, you get the following result:

```
Value of var is test string
```

Using Single Quotes to Maintain Unexpanded Variables

You can surround a string with single quotes (') to stop the shell from expanding variables and interpreting special characters. When used for the latter purpose, the single quote is an *escape character*, similar to the backslash, which you learn about in the next section. Here, you learn how to use the single quote to avoid expanding a variable in a shell script. An unexpanded variable maintains its original form in the output.

In the following examples, the double quotes in the preceding examples have been changed to single quotes:

pdksh and bash:

```
var='test string'
newvar='Value of var is $var'
echo $newvar
```

tcsh:

```
set var = 'test string'
set newvar = 'Value of var is $var'
echo $newvar
```

If you execute a shell program containing these three lines, you get the following result:

```
Value of var is $var
```

As you can see, the variable var maintains its original format in the results, rather than having been expanded.

Using the Backslash As an Escape Character

As you learned earlier, the backslash (\) serves as an escape character that stops the shell from interpreting the succeeding character as a special character. Say that you want to assign a value of $test to a variable called var. If you use the following command, the shell reads the special character $ and interprets $test as the value of the variable test. No value has been assigned to test; a null value is stored in var:

Command	Environment
var=$test	pdksh and bash
set var=$test	tcsh

Unfortunately, this assignment may work for bash and pdksh, but it returns an error of "undefined variable" if you use it with tcsh. Use the following commands to correctly store $test in var:

Command	Environment
var=\$test	pdksh and bash
set var = \$test	tcsh

The backslash before the dollar sign (\$) signals the shell to interpret the $ as any other ordinary character and not to associate any special meaning to it. You could also use single quotes (') around the $test variable to get the same result.

Using the Backtick to Replace a String with Output

You can use the backtick (`` ` ``) character to signal the shell to replace a string with its output when executed. This special character can be used in shell programs when you want the result of the execution of a command to be stored in a variable. For example, if you want to count the number of lines in a file called `test.txt` in the current directory and store the result in a variable called `var`, you can use the following command:

Command	Environment
var=`` `wc -l test.txt` ``	pdksh and bash
set var = `` `wc -l test.txt` ``	tcsh

Comparison of Expressions

Comparing values or evaluating the differences between similar bits of data—such as file information, character strings, or numbers—is a task known as *comparison of expressions*. Comparison of expressions is an integral part of using logic in shell programs to accomplish tasks. The way the logical comparison of two operators (numeric or string) is done varies slightly in different shells. In pdksh and bash, a command called `test` can be used to achieve comparisons of expressions. In tcsh, you can write an expression to accomplish the same thing.

The following section covers comparison operations using the pdksh or bash shells. Later in the chapter, you learn how to compare expressions in the tcsh shell.

Comparison of Expressions in pdksh and bash

The pdksh and bash shell syntax provide a command named `test` to compare strings, numbers, and files. The syntax of the `test` command is as follows:

```
test expression
```

or

```
[ expression ]
```

Both forms of the `test` commands are processed the same way by pdksh and bash. The `test` commands support the following types of comparisons:

- String comparison
- Numeric comparison
- File operators
- Logical operators

String Comparison

The following operators can be used to compare two string expressions:

=—To compare whether two strings are equal

!=—To compare whether two strings are not equal

-n—To evaluate whether the string length is greater than zero

-z—To evaluate whether the string length is equal to zero

Next are some examples using these operators when comparing two strings, string1 and string2, in a shell program called compare1:

```
#!/bin/sh
string1="abc"
string2="abd"
if [ $string1 = $string2 ]; then
   echo "string1 equal to string2"
else
   echo "string1 not equal to string2"
fi

if [ $string2 != string1 ]; then
   echo "string2 not equal to string1"
else
   echo "string2 equal to string2"
fi

if [ $string1 ]; then
   echo "string1 is not empty"
else
   echo "string1 is empty"
fi

if [ -n $string2 ]; then
   echo "string2 has a length greater than zero"
else
   echo "string2 has length equal to zero"
fi

if [ -z $string1 ]; then
   echo "string1 has a length equal to zero"
else
  echo "string1 has a length greater than zero"
fi
```

If you execute `compare1`, you get the following result:

```
string1 not equal to string2
string2 not equal to string1
string1 is not empty
string2 has a length greater than zero
string1 has a length greater than zero
```

If two strings are not equal in size, the system pads out the shorter string with trailing spaces for comparison. That is, if the value of `string1` is abc and that of `string2` is ab, `string2` will be padded with a trailing space for comparison purposes—it will have a value of ab.

Number Comparison

The following operators can be used to compare two numbers:

-eq—To compare whether two numbers are equal

-ge—To compare whether one number is greater than or equal to the other number

-le—To compare whether one number is less than or equal to the other number

-ne—To compare whether two numbers are not equal

-gt—To compare whether one number is greater than the other number

-lt—To compare whether one number is less than the other number

The following shell program compares three numbers, `number1`, `number2`, and `number3`:

```
#!/bin/sh
number1=5
number2=10
number3=5

if [ $number1 -eq $number3 ]; then
   echo "number1 is equal to number3"
else
   echo "number1 is not equal to number3"
fi

if [ $number1 -ne $number2 ]; then
   echo "number1 is not equal to number2"
else
   echo "number1 is equal to number2"
fi
```

```
if [ $number1 -gt $number2 ]; then
    echo "number1 is greater than number2"
else
    echo "number1 is not greater than number2"
fi


if [ $number1 -ge $number3 ]; then
    echo "number1 is greater than or equal to number3"
else
    echo "number1 is not greater than or equal to number3"
fi


if [ $number1 -lt $number2 ]; then
    echo "number1 is less than number2"
else
    echo "number1 is not less than number2"
fi


if [ $number1 -le $number3 ]; then
    echo "number1 is less than or equal to number3"
else
    echo "number1 is not less than or equal to number3"
fi
```

When you execute the shell program, you get the following results:

```
number1 is equal to number3
number1 is not equal to number2
number1 is not greater than number2
number1 is greater than or equal to number3
number1 is less than number2
number1 is less than or equal to number3
```

File Operators

The following operators can be used as file comparison operators:

-   -d—To ascertain whether a file is a directory

-   -f—To ascertain whether a file is a regular file

-   -r—To ascertain whether read permission is set for a file

-   -s—To ascertain whether a file exists and has a length greater than zero

-   -w—To ascertain whether write permission is set for a file

-   -x—To ascertain whether execute permission is set for a file

Assume that a shell program called compare3 is in a directory with a file called file1 and a subdirectory dir1 under the current directory. Assume that file1 has a permission of r-x (read and execute permission) and dir1 has a permission of rwx (read, write, and execute permission). The code for the shell program would look like this:

```
#!/bin/sh
if [ -d $dir1 ]; then
   echo "dir1 is a directory"
else
   echo "dir1 is not a directory"
fi


if [ -f $dir1 ]; then
   echo "dir1 is a regular file"
else
   echo "dir1 is not a regular file"
fi


if [ -r $file1 ]; then
   echo "file1 has read permission"
else
   echo "file1 does not have read permission"
fi


if [ -w $file1 ]; then
   echo "file1 has write permission"
else
   echo "file1 does not have write permission"
fi


if [ -x $dir1 ]; then
   echo "dir1 has execute permission"
else
   echo "dir1 does not have execute permission"
fi
```

If you execute the shell program, you get the following results:

```
dir1 is a directory
file1 is a regular file
file1 has read permission
file1 does not have write permission
dir1 has execute permission
```

Logical Operators

Logical operators are used to compare expressions using Boolean logic, which compares values using characters representing NOT, AND, and OR.

!—To negate a logical expression

-a—To logically AND two logical expressions

-o—To logically OR two logical expressions

This example named `logic` uses the file and directory mentioned in the previous `compare3` example.

```
#!/bin/sh
if [ -x file1 -a -x dir1 ]; then
    echo file1 and dir1 are executable
else
    echo at least one of file1 or dir1 are not executable
fi

if [ -w file1 -o -w dir1 ]; then
    echo file1 or dir1 are writable
else
    echo neither file1 or dir1 are executable
fi

if [ ! -w file1 ]; then
    echo file1 is not writable
else
    echo file1 is writable
fi
```

If you execute `logic`, it will yield the following result:

```
file1 and dir1 are executable
file1 or dir1 are writable
file1 is not writable
```

Comparing Expressions with `tcsh`

As stated earlier, the method for comparing expressions in `tcsh` is different from the method used under `pdksh` and `bash`. The comparison of expression demonstrated in this section uses the syntax necessary for the `tcsh` shell environment.

String Comparison

The following operators can be used to compare two string expressions:

==—To compare whether two strings are equal

!=—To compare whether two strings are not equal

The following examples compare two strings, string1 and string2, in the shell program compare1:

```
#!/bin/tcsh
set string1 = "abc"
set string2 = "abd"

if  (string1 == string2)  then
   echo "string1 equal to string2"
else
   echo "string1 not equal to string2"
endif

if  (string2 != string1)  then
   echo "string2 not equal to string1"
else
   echo "string2 equal to string1"
endif
```

If you execute compare1, you get the following results:

```
string1 not equal to string2
string2 not equal to string1
```

Number Comparison

These operators can be used to compare two numbers:

>=—To compare whether one number is greater than or equal to the other number

<=—To compare whether one number is less than or equal to the other number

>—To compare whether one number is greater than the other number

<—To compare whether one number is less than the other number

The next examples compare two numbers, number1 and number2, in a shell program called compare2:

```
#!/bin/tcsh
set number1=5
```

```
set number2=10
set number3=5

if  ($number1 > $number2)  then
   echo "number1 is greater than number2"
else
   echo "number1 is not greater than number2"
endif

if  ($number1 >= $number3) then
   echo "number1 is greater than or equal to number3"
else
   echo "number1 is not greater than or equal to number3"
endif

if  ($number1 < $number2)  then
   echo "number1 is less than number2"
else
   echo "number1 is not less than number2"
endif

if  ($number1 <= $number3) then
   echo "number1 is less than or equal to number3"
else
   echo "number1 is not less than or equal to number3"
endif
```

When executing the shell program compare2, you get the following results:

```
number1 is not greater than number2
number1 is greater than or equal to number3
number1 is less than number2
number1 is less than or equal to number3
```

File Operators

These operators can be used as file comparison operators:

> -d—To ascertain whether a file is a directory
>
> -e—To ascertain whether a file exists
>
> -f—To ascertain whether a file is a regular file
>
> -o—To ascertain whether a user is the owner of a file
>
> -r—To ascertain whether read permission is set for a file

-w—To ascertain whether write permission is set for a file

-x—To ascertain whether execute permission is set for a file

-z—To ascertain whether the file size is zero

The following examples are based on a shell program called compare3, which is in a directory with a file called file1 and a subdirectory dir1 under the current directory. Assume that file1 has a permission of r-x (read and execute permission) and dir1 has a permission of rwx (read, write, and execute permission).

The following is the code for the compare3 shell program:

```tcsh
#!/bin/tcsh
if  (-d dir1) then
    echo "dir1 is a directory"
else
    echo "dir1 is not a directory"
endif

if (-f dir1)  then
    echo "file1 is a regular file"
else
    echo "file1 is not a regular file"
endif

if (-r file1) then
    echo "file1 has read permission"
else
    echo "file1 does not have read permission"
endif

if (-w file1) then
    echo "file1 has write permission"
else
    echo "file1 does not have write permission"
endif

if (-x dir1) then
    echo "dir1 has execute permission"
else
    echo "dir1 does not have execute permission"
endif

if (-z file1) then
```

```
   echo "file1 has zero length"
else
   echo "file1 has greater than zero length"
endif
```

If you execute the file `compare3`, you get the following results:

```
dir1 is a directory
file1 is a regular file
file1 has read permission
file1 does not have write permission
dir1 has execute permission
file1 has greater than zero length
```

Logical Operators

Logical operators are used with conditional statements. These operators are used to negate a logical expression or to perform logical ANDs and ORs:

> !—To negate a logical expression
>
> &&—To logically AND two logical expressions
>
> ¦¦—To logically OR two logical expressions

This example named `logic` uses the file and directory mentioned in the previous `compare3` example.

```
#!/bin/tcsh
if ( -x file1 && -x dir1 ) then
   echo file1 and dir1 are executable
else
   echo at least one of file1 or dir1 are not executable
endif

if ( -w file1 ¦¦ -w dir1 ) then
   echo file1 or dir1 are writable
else
   echo neither file1 or dir1 are executable
endif

if ( ! -w file1 ) then
   echo file1 is not writable
else
   echo file1 is writable
endif
```

If you execute `logic`, it will yield the following result:

```
file1 and dir1 are executable
file1 or dir1 are writable
file1 is not writable
```

Iteration Statements

Iteration statements are used to repeat a series of commands contained within the iteration statement. The following sections discuss some of these commands and show examples of their use.

The `for` Statement

The `for` statement is used to execute a set of commands once each time a specified condition is true. The `for` statement has a number of formats. The first format used by `pdksh` and `bash` is as follows:

```
for curvar in list
do
    statements
done
```

This form should be used if you want to execute `statements` once for each value in `list`. For each iteration, the current value of the list is assigned to `vcurvar`. `list` can be a variable containing a number of items or a list of values separated by spaces. The second format is as follows:

```
for curvar
do
    statements
done
```

In this form, the `statements` are executed once for each of the positional parameters passed to the shell program. For each iteration, the current value of the positional parameter is assigned to the variable `curvar`.

This form can also be written as follows:

```
for curvar in $@
do
    statements
done
```

Remember that `$@` gives you a list of positional parameters passed to the shell program, quoted in a manner consistent with the way the user originally invoked the command.

Under `tcsh`, the `for` statement is called `foreach`. The format is as follows:

```
foreach curvar (list)
    statements
end
```

In this form, `statements` are executed once for each value in `list`, and, for each iteration, the current value of `list` is assigned to `curvar`.

Suppose that you want to create a backup version of each file in a directory to a subdirectory called `backup`. You can do the following in `pdksh` and `bash`:

```
#!/bin/sh
for filename in *
do
    cp $filename backup/$filename
    if [ $? -ne 0 ]; then
        echo "copy for $filename failed"
    fi
done
```

In the preceding example, a backup copy of each file is created. If the copy fails, a message is generated.

The same example in `tcsh` is as follows:

```
#!/bin/tcsh
foreach filename (`/bin/ls`)
    cp $filename backup/$filename
    if ($? != 0) then
        echo "copy for $filename failed"
    endif
end
```

The `while` Statement

The `while` statement can be used to execute a series of commands while a specified condition is true. The loop terminates as soon as the specified condition evaluates to false. It is possible that the loop will not execute at all if the specified condition initially evaluates to false. You should be careful with the `while` command because the loop will never terminate if the specified condition never evaluates to false.

Endless Loops Have Their Place in Shell Programs

Endless loops can sometimes be useful. For example, you can easily construct a simple command that constantly monitors the 802.11b link quality of a network interface by using a few lines of script:

```
#!/bin/sh
while :
 do
    /sbin/iwconfig eth0 ¦  grep Link ¦ tr '\n' '\r'
 done
```

The script outputs the search, and then the `tr` command formats the output. The result is a simple animation of a constantly updated single line of information:

```
Link Quality:92/92  Signal level:-11 dBm  Noise level:-102 dBm
```

This technique can also be used to quickly create a graphical monitoring client for X that outputs traffic information and activity about a network interface:

```
#!/bin/sh
xterm -geometry 75x2 -e \
bash -c \
"while :; do \
    /sbin/ifconfig eth0 ¦ \
    grep 'TX bytes' ¦
     tr '\n' '\r' ; \
done"
```

The simple example uses a `bash` command-line script (enabled by `-c`) to repeatedly execute a command line. The command line pipes the output of the `ifconfig` command through `grep`, which searches `ifconfig`'s output and then pipes a line containing the string `"TX bytes"` to the `tr` command. The `tr` command then removes the carriage return at the end of the line to display the information inside an `/xterm` X11 terminal window, automatically sized by the `-geometry` option:

```
RX bytes:4117594780 (3926.8 Mb)  TX bytes:452230967 (431.2 Mb)
```

Endless loops can be so useful that Linux includes a command that will repeatedly execute a given command line. For example, you can get a quick report about a system's hardware health by using the `sensors` command. But instead of using a shell script to endlessly loop the output, you can use the `watch` command to repeat the information and provide simple animation:

```
$ watch "sensors -f ¦ cut -c 1-20"
```

In `pdksh` and `bash`, the following format is used for the `while` flow control construct:

```
while expression
do
    statements
done
```

In `tcsh`, the following format is used:

```
while (expression)
    Statements
end
```

If you want to add the first five even numbers, you can use the following shell program in pdksh and bash:

```
#!/bin/bash
loopcount=0
result=0
while [ $loopcount -lt 5 ]
do
    loopcount=`expr $loopcount + 1`
    increment=`expr $loopcount \* 2`
    result=`expr $result + $increment`
done

echo "result is $result"
```

In tcsh, this program can be written as follows:

```
#!/bin/tcsh
set loopcount = 0
set result = 0
while ($loopcount < 5)
    set loopcount = `expr $loopcount + 1`
    set increment = `expr $loopcount \* 2`
    set result = `expr $result + $increment`

end

echo "result is $result"
```

The until **Statement**

The until statement can be used to execute a series of commands until a specified condition is true.

The loop terminates as soon as the specified condition evaluates to True.

In pdksh and bash, the following format is used:

```
until expression
do
    statements
done
```

As you can see, the format of the until statement is similar to that of the while statement, but the logic is different: In a while loop, you execute until an expression is False, but in an until loop, you loop until the expression is True.

If you want to add the first five even numbers, you can use the following shell program in pdksh and bash:

```
#!/bin/bash
loopcount=0
result=0
until [ $loopcount -ge 5 ]
do
    loopcount=`expr $loopcount + 1`
    increment=`expr $loopcount \* 2`
    result=`expr $result + $increment`
done

echo "result is $result"
```

The example here is identical to the example for the while statement, except that the condition being tested is just the opposite of the condition specified in the while statement.

The tcsh shell does not support the until statement.

The repeat Statement (tcsh)

The repeat statement is used to execute only one command a fixed number of times.

If you want to print a hyphen (-) 80 times with one hyphen per line on the screen, you can use the following command:

```
repeat  80 echo '-'
```

The select Statement (pdksh)

The select statement is used to generate a menu list if you are writing a shell program that expects input from the user online. The format of the select statement is as follows:

```
select  item in itemlist
do
    Statements
done
```

itemlist is optional. If it isn't provided, the system iterates through the item entries one at a time. If itemlist is provided, however, the system iterates for each entry in itemlist and the current value of itemlist is assigned to item for each iteration, which then can be used as part of the statements being executed.

If you want to write a menu that gives the user a choice of picking a Continue or a Finish, you can write the following shell program:

```
#!/bin/ksh
select  item in Continue Finish
do
    if [ $item = "Finish" ]; then
       break
    fi
done
```

When the select command is executed, the system displays a menu with numeric choices to the user—in this case, 1 for Continue and 2 for Finish. If the user chooses 1, the variable item contains a value of Continue; if the user chooses 2, the variable item contains a value of Finish. When the user chooses 2, the if statement is executed and the loop terminates.

The shift Statement

The shift statement is used to process the positional parameters, one at a time, from left to right. As you'll remember, the positional parameters are identified as $1, $2, $3, and so on. The effect of the shift command is that each positional parameter is moved one position to the left and the current $1 parameter is lost.

The shift statement is useful when you are writing shell programs in which a user can pass various options. Depending on the specified option, the parameters that follow can mean different things or might not be there at all.

The format of the shift command is as follows:

```
shift  number
```

The parameter number is the number of places to be shifted and is optional. If not specified, the default is 1; that is, the parameters are shifted one position to the left. If specified, the parameters are shifted number positions to the left.

Conditional Statements

Conditional statements are used in shell programs to decide which part of the program to execute depending on specified conditions.

The if Statement

The if statement evaluates a logical expression to make a decision. An if condition has the following format in pdksh and bash:

22

```
if [ expression ]; then
    Statements
elif [ expression ]; then
    Statements
else
    Statements
fi
```

The if conditions can be nested. That is, an if condition can contain another if condition within it. It isn't necessary for an if condition to have an elif or else part. The else part is executed if none of the expressions that are specified in the if statement and are optional in subsequent elif statements are true. The word fi is used to indicate the end of the if statements, which is very useful if you have nested if conditions. In such a case, you should be able to match fi to if to ensure that all if statements are properly coded.

In the following example for bash or pdksh, a variable var can have either of two values: Yes or No. Any other value is invalid. This can be coded as follows:

```
if [ $var = "Yes" ]; then
    echo "Value is Yes"
elif [ $var = "No" ]; then
    echo "Value is No"
else
    echo "Invalid value"
fi
```

In tcsh, the if statement has two forms. The first form, similar to the one for pdksh and bash, is as follows:

```
if (expression) then
    Statements
else if (expression) then
    Statements
else
    Statements
endif
```

The if conditions can be nested—that is, an if condition can contain another if condition within it. It isn't necessary for an if condition to have an else part. The else part is executed if none of the expressions specified in any of the if statements are true. The optional if part of the statement (else if (expression) then) is executed if the condition following it is true and the previous if statement is not true. The word endif is used to indicate the end of the if statements, which is very useful if you have nested if conditions. In such a case, you should be able to match endif to if to ensure that all if statements are properly coded.

Using the example of the variable var having only two values, Yes and No, here is how it would be coded with tcsh:

```
if ($var == "Yes") then
    echo "Value is Yes"
else if ($var == "No" ) then
    echo "Value is No"
else
    echo "Invalid value"
endif
```

The second form of the if condition for tcsh is as follows:

```
if (expression) command
```

In this format, only a single command can be executed if the expression evaluates to true.

The case Statement

The case statement is used to execute statements depending on a discrete value or a range of values matching the specified variable. In most cases, you can use a case statement instead of an if statement if you have a large number of conditions.

The format of a case statement for pdksh and bash is as follows:

```
case str in
    str1 ¦ str2)
        Statements;;
    str3¦str4)
        Statements;;
    *)
        Statements;;
esac
```

You can specify a number of discrete values—such as str1, str2, and so on—for each condition, or you can specify a value with a wildcard. The last condition should be * (asterisk) and is executed if none of the other conditions are met. For each of the specified conditions, all the associated statements until the double semicolon (;;) are executed.

You can write a script that will echo the name of the month if you provide the month number as a parameter. If you provide a number that isn't between 1 and 12, you will get an error message. The script is as follows:

```
#!/bin/sh

case $1 in
    01 ¦ 1) echo "Month is January";;
```

```
02 ¦ 2) echo "Month is February";;
03 ¦ 3) echo "Month is March";;
04 ¦ 4) echo "Month is April";;
05 ¦ 5) echo "Month is May";;
06 ¦ 6) echo "Month is June";;
07 ¦ 7) echo "Month is July";;
08 ¦ 8) echo "Month is August";;
09 ¦ 9) echo "Month is September";;
   10) echo "Month is October";;
   11) echo "Month is November";;
   12) echo "Month is December";;
   *) echo "Invalid parameter";;
esac
```

You need to end the statements under each condition with a double semicolon(;;). If you do not, the statements under the next condition will also be executed.

The format for a `case` statement for `tcsh` is as follows:

```
switch (str)
   case str1¦str2:
      Statements
      breaksw
   case str3¦str4:
      Statements
      breaksw
   default:
      Statements
      breaksw
endsw
```

You can specify a number of discrete values—such as `str1`, `str2`, and so on—for each condition, or you can specify a value with a wildcard. The last condition should be `default` and is executed if none of the other conditions are met. For each of the specified conditions, all the associated statements until `breaksw` are executed.

The example that echoes the month when a number is given, shown earlier for `pdksh` and `bash`, can be written in `tcsh` as follows:

```
#!/bin/tcsh

set month = 5
switch ( $month )
   case 1: echo "Month is January" ;  breaksw
   case 2: echo "Month is February" ;  breaksw
```

```
    case 3: echo "Month is March" ;   breaksw
    case 4: echo "Month is April" ;   breaksw
    case 5: echo "Month is May" ;  breaksw
    case 6: echo "Month is June" ;   breaksw
    case 7: echo "Month is July" ;   breaksw
    case 8: echo "Month is August"  ;   breaksw
    case 9: echo "Month is September" ;   breaksw
    case 10: echo "Month is October" ;   breaksw
    case 11: echo "Month is November" ;   breaksw
    case 12: echo "Month is December" ;   breaksw
    default: echo "Oops! Month is Octember!" ;   breaksw
endsw
```

You need to end the statements under each condition with `breaksw`. If you do not, the statements under the next condition will also be executed.

The `break` and `exit` Statements

You should be aware of two other statements: the `break` statement and the `exit` statement.

The `break` statement can be used to terminate an iteration loop, such as a `for`, `until`, or `repeat` command.

`exit` statements can be used to exit a shell program. You can optionally use a number after `exit`. If the current shell program has been called by another shell program, the calling program can check for the code (the `$?` or `$status` variable, depending on shell) and make a decision accordingly.

Using Functions in Shell Scripts

As with other programming languages, shell programs also support *functions*. A function is a piece of a shell program that performs a particular process; you can reuse the same function multiple times within the shell program. Functions help eliminate the need for duplicating code as you write shell programs.

The following is the format of a function in `pdksh` and `bash`:

```
func(){
    Statements
}
```

You can call a function as follows:

```
func param1 param2 param3
```

The parameters *param1*, *param2*, and so on are optional. You can also pass the parameters as a single string—for example, $@. A function can parse the parameters as if they were positional parameters passed to a shell program from the command line as command-line arguments, but instead use values passed inside the script. For example, the following script uses a function named Displaymonth() that displays the name of the month or an error message if you pass a month number out of the range 1 to 12. This example works with pdksh and bash:

```
#!/bin/sh
Displaymonth() {
   case $1 in
      01 | 1) echo "Month is January";;
      02 | 2) echo "Month is February";;
      03 | 3) echo "Month is March";;
      04 | 4) echo "Month is April";;
      05 | 5) echo "Month is May";;
      06 | 6) echo "Month is June";;
      07 | 7) echo "Month is July";;
      08 | 8) echo "Month is August";;
      09 | 9) echo "Month is September";;
      10) echo "Month is October";;
      11) echo "Month is November";;
      12) echo "Month is December";;
      *) echo "Invalid parameter";;
   esac
}
Displaymonth 8
```

The preceding program displays the following output:

```
Month is August
```

Related Fedora and Linux Commands

You can use these commands and tools when using the shell or writing shell scripts:

chsh—Command used to change one's login shell

kibitz—Allows two-person interaction with a single shell

mc—A visual shell named the GNU Midnight Commander

nano—An easy-to-use text editor for the console

system-config-users—A graphical user-management utility that can be used to change one or more user login shells

shar—Command used to create shell archives

vi—The vi (actually vim) text editor

22

Reference

`http://www.gnu.org/software/bash/bash.html`—The bash home page at the GNU Software Project.

`http://www.tldp.org/LDP/abs/html/`—Mendel Cooper's "Advanced Bash-Scripting Guide."

`http://www.linuxnewbie.org/nhf/intel/shells/basic.html`—Learn basic shell commands at this site.

`http://www.cs.princeton.edu/~jlk/lj/`—"The New Korn Shell—ksh93," an article by David G. Korn, Charles J. Northrup, and Jeffery Korn regarding the `korn` shell.

`http://web.cs.mun.ca/~michael/pdksh/`—The `pdksh` home page.

`http://lug.umbc.edu/~mabzug1/bash-httpd.html`—The Bash-httpd FAQ, with links to the latest version of the bash Web server, `bash-httpd-0.02`.

`http://www.tcsh.org/`—Find out more about `tcsh` here.

`http://www.zsh.org/`—Examine `zsh` in more detail here.

CHAPTER 23

Using Perl

IN THIS CHAPTER

- Using Perl with Linux
- Perl Variables and Data Structures
- Operators
- Conditional Statements: `if`/`else` and `unless`
- Looping
- Regular Expressions
- Access to the Shell
- Switches
- Modules and CPAN
- Code Examples
- Reference

Perl (Practical Extraction and Report Language) is a powerful scripting tool you can use to manage files, create reports, edit text, and perform many other tasks when using Linux. Perl is included with Fedora and could be considered an integral part of the distribution, as Fedora depends on Perl for many types of software services, logging activities, and software tools. If you do a full install from this book's CD-ROMs, you'll find nearly 150 software tools written in Perl installed under the /usr/bin and /usr/sbin directories.

Following the birth of the World Wide Web in the early 1990s, Perl took off as the language of choice for Common Gateway Interface (CGI) programming, which is used to extend features of Web sites and make the Web more than just a resource for document publishing. With the recent interest in the open-source movement, Perl has gotten almost as much press as Linux, although many experienced Linux users have been using Perl for quite some time.

Perl is perhaps not the easiest of programming languages to learn because it's designed to be so very flexible. This chapter shows how to create and use a Perl script on your system. You'll see what a Perl program looks like, how the language is structured, where you can find modules of prewritten code to help you write your own Perl scripts, and several examples of Perl used to perform a few common functions on a computer system.

This chapter also includes additional sources of information about Perl. Consult the listing of Web sites, books, and online periodicals at the end of this chapter. A quest toward becoming a Perl hacker need not be long and arduous, but you will benefit from the generous help offered by other members of the Perl developer community. Perl works quickly and efficiently on a Linux system, but learning how to create good Perl programs will take some effort.

Using Perl with Linux

If you're familiar with some other programming languages, chances are you can write functional Perl code. Perl contains the best features of C, BASIC, and a variety of other programming languages—with a hearty dollop of awk, sed, and shell scripting thrown in. Perl was created in the mid 1980s by Larry Wall to overcome file-handling limitations of the awk command. Wall, a developer already responsible for a number of important UNIX utilities, such as the patch command (used to easily update and insert changes into a program's source code), claims that Perl really stands for "Pathologically Eclectic Rubbish Lister." Although originally designed as a data extraction and report generation language, Perl appeals to many UNIX and Linux system administrators because it can be used to create new software tools that fill a gap between the capabilities of shell scripts and compiled C programs. Another advantage of Perl over other UNIX tools is that it can process and extract data from binary files (those without line terminators or that contain binary data, such as some databases or compiled programs), whereas sed and awk can't.

> **NOTE**
>
> In Perl, "there is more than one way to do it." This is the unofficial motto of Perl, and it comes up so often that it's usually abbreviated as TIMTOWTDI.

Perl interprets its language in text files known as Perl *programs* (even though some Linux users might call these programs *scripts*). Although some consider Perl an interpreter, the programs are actually compiled in memory and then run by Perl's internal interpreter. You can use Perl at your shell's command line to execute one-line Perl programs, but most often the programs (usually ending in .pl) are run as a command. These programs will generally work on any computer platform, as Perl has been ported to just about every operating system. Perl is available by default when you install Fedora, and you'll find its RPM files on the CD-ROMs included with this book.

Perl programs are used to support a number of Fedora services, such as system logging. For example, the logwatch.pl program is run every morning at 4:20 a.m. by the crond (scheduling) daemon on your system. The 690-line Perl program physically resides under the /etc/log.d/scripts/ directory, but is launched as the symbolic link named 00-logwatch under the /etc/cron.daily directory. This program (which can be configured by editing the configuration file logwatch.conf) generates and emails a short report after analyzing selected system logs.

Other Fedora services supported by Perl include

- Amanda for local and network backups
- Fax spooling with the faxrunqd program
- Printing supported by Perl document filtering programs
- Hardware sensor monitoring setup using the sensors-detect Perl program

Perl Versions

As of this writing, the current production version of Perl is 5.8.4 (which is Perl version 5 point 8, patch level 4).

You can download the code from http://www.perl.com/ and build Perl yourself from source. You will occasionally find updated versions in RPM format for Fedora, which can be installed by updating your system. See Chapter 8, "Managing Software and System Resources," to see how to quickly get a list of available updates for Fedora.

You can determine what version of Perl you installed by typing **perl -v** at a shell prompt. If you're installing the latest Fedora distribution, you should have the latest version of Perl.

A Simple Perl Program

This section introduces a very simple sample Perl program to get you started using Perl. Although trivial for experienced Perl hackers, a short example is necessary for new users who want to learn more about Perl.

> **NOTE**
>
> You'll also find a Perl program named perlcc installed with Perl. This program can be used as a compiler to build executable commands out of Perl! The program can also be used to generate experimental C source code for use by the gcc compiler system (see Chapter 21, "C/C++ Programming Tools for Fedora").

To introduce you to the absolute basics of Perl programming, Listing 23.1 illustrates a simple Perl program that prints a short message.

LISTING 23.1   A Simple Perl Program

```
#!/usr/bin/perl
print "Look at all the camels!\n";
```

That's the entire program. Type that in and save it to a file called trivial.pl. Then make the file executable using the chmod command (see the following sidebar) and run it at the command prompt.

> **Command-Line Error**
>
> If you get the message bash: trivial.pl: command not found or bash: ./trivial.pl: Permission denied, it means that you either typed the command line incorrectly or forgot to make trivial.pl executable (with the chmod command):
>
> ```
> $ chmod +x trivial.pl
> ```

You can force the command to execute in the current directory as follows:

```
$ ./trivial.pl
```

Or you can use Perl to run the program like this:

```
$ perl trivial.pl
```

The sample program in the listing is a two-line Perl program. Typing in the program and running it (using Perl or making the program executable) shows how to create your first Perl program, a process duplicated by Linux users around the world every day!

> **NOTE**
>
> #! is often pronounced *she-bang*, which is short for *sharp* (the musicians name for the # character), and *bang*, which is another name for the exclamation point. The technical name of the # character is the *octothorpe*, a word coined by Bell Labs engineer Don Macpherson in the early 1960s. Another pronunciation of #! is *pound-bang* because most people refer to the # character on a telephone keypad as pound. This notation is also used in shell scripts. See Chapter 22, "Shell Scripting," for more information about writing shell scripts.

The #! line is technically not part of the Perl code at all. The # character indicates that the rest of the screen line is a comment. The comment is a message to the shell, telling it where it should go to find the executable to run this program. The interpreter ignores the comment line. Using a comment character is standard practice in shell programming.

Exceptions to this practice include when the # character is in a quoted string and when it's being used as the delimiter in a regular expression. Comments are useful to document your scripts, like this:

```
#!/usr/bin/perl
# a simple example to print a greeting
print "hello there\n";
```

A block of code, such as what might appear inside a loop or a branch of a conditional statement, is indicated with curly braces ({}). For example, here's an infinite loop:

```
#!/usr/bin/perl
# a block of code to print a greeting forever
while (1) {
        print "hello there\n";
};
```

Perl statements are terminated with a semicolon. A Perl statement can extend over several actual screen lines because Perl isn't concerned about whitespace.

The second line of the simple program prints the text enclosed in quotation marks. \n is the escape sequence for a newline character.

TIP

Using the perldoc and man commands is an easy way to get more information about the version of Perl installed on your system. To learn how to use the perldoc command, enter the following:

```
$ perldoc perldoc
```

To get introductory information on Perl, you can use either of these commands:

```
$ perldoc perl
$ man perl
```

For an overview or table of contents of Perl's documentation, use the perldoc command like this:

```
$ perldoc perltoc
```

The documentation is extensive and well-organized. Perl includes a number of standard Linux manual pages as brief guides to its capabilities, but perhaps the best way to learn more about Perl is to read its *perlfunc* document, which lists all the available Perl functions and their usage. You can view this document by using the perldoc script and typing perldoc perlfunc at the command line. You can also find this document online at http://www.cpan.org/doc/manual/html/pod/perlfunc.html.

The next several sections provide an overview of Perl's language syntax and data handling.

Perl Variables and Data Structures

Perl is a *weakly typed* language, meaning that it doesn't require that you declare a data type, such as a type of value (data) to be stored in a particular variable. C, for example, makes you declare that a particular variable is an integer, a character, a structure, or whatever the case may be. Perl variables are whatever type they need to be, and can change type when you need them to.

Perl Variable Types

There are three variable types in Perl: *scalars*, *arrays*, and *hashes*. In an attempt to make each data type visually distinct, a different character is used to signify each variable type.

Scalar variables are indicated with the $ character, as in $penguin. Scalars can be numerical or strings, and they can change type from one to the other as needed. If you treat a number like a string, it's a string. If you treat a string like a number, it's translated into a number if it makes sense to do so; otherwise, it probably evaluates as 0.

For example, the string "76trombones" will evaluate as the number 76 if used in a numerical calculation, but the string "polar bear" will evaluate to 0.

Perl arrays are indicated with the @ character, as in @fish. An *array* is a list of values that are referenced by index number, starting with the first element numbered 0, just as in C and awk. Each element in the array is a scalar value. Because scalar values are indicated with the $ character, a single element in an array is also indicated with a $ character.

For example, $fish[2] refers to the third element in the @fish array. This tends to throw some people off, but is similar to arrays in C in which a first array element is 0.

Hashes are indicated with the % character, as in %employee. A *hash*, which used to go by the cumbersome name *associative array*, is a list of name and value pairs. Individual elements in the hash are referenced by name rather than by index (unlike an array). Again, because the values are scalars, the $ character is used for individual elements.

For example, $employee{name} gives you one value from the hash. Two rather useful functions for dealing with hashes are *keys* and *values*. The keys function returns an array containing all the keys of the hash, and values returns an array of the values of the hash. Using this approach, the Perl program in Listing 23.2 displays all the values in your environment, much like typing the bash shell's env command.

LISTING 23.2   Displaying the Contents of the env Hash

```
#!/usr/bin/perl
foreach $key (keys %ENV)  {
    print "$key = $ENV{$key}\n";
}
```

Special Variables

Perl has a wide variety of special variables. These usually look like punctuation—such as $_, $!, and $]—and are extremely useful for shorthand code. ($_ is the default variable, $! is the error message returned by the operating system, and $] is the Perl version number.)

$_ is perhaps the most useful of these, and you'll see that variable used often in this chapter. $_ is the Perl default variable, which is used when no argument is specified. For example, the following two statements are equivalent:

```
chomp;
chomp($_);
```

The following loops are equivalent:

```
for $cow (@cattle) {
        print "$cow says moo.\n";
}
for (@cattle)         {
        print "$_ says moo.\n";
}
```

For a complete listing of the special variables, you should see the `perlvar` document that comes with your Perl distribution (such as in the `perlvar` manual page), or you can go online to `http://theoryx5.uwinnipeg.ca/CPAN/perl/pod/perlvar.html`.

Operators

Perl supports a number of operators to perform various operations. There are *comparison* operators (used to compare values, as the name implies), *compound* operators (used to combine operations or multiple comparisons), *arithmetic* operators (to perform math), and special string constants.

Comparison Operators

The comparison operators used by Perl are similar to those used by C, awk, and the `csh` shells, and are used to specify and compare values (including strings). Most frequently, a comparison operator is used within an `if` statement or loop. Perl has comparison operators for numbers and strings. Table 23.1 shows the numeric comparison operators and their behavior.

TABLE 23.1   Numeric Comparison Operators in Perl

Operator	Meaning
==	Is equal to
<	Less than
>	Greater than
<=	Less than or equal to
>=	Greater than or equal to
!=	Not equal to
..	Range of >= first operand to <= second operand
<=>	Returns –1 if less than, 0 if equal, and 1 if greater than

Table 23.2 shows the string comparison operators and their behaviors.

TABLE 23.2   String Comparison Operators in Perl

Operator	Meaning
eq	Is equal to
lt	Less than
gt	Greater than
le	Less than or equal to
ge	Greater than or equal to
ne	Not equal to
cmp	Returns -1 if less than, 0 if equal, and 1 if greater than
=~	Matched by regular expression
!~	Not matched by regular expression

Compound Operators

Perl uses compound operators, similar to those used by C or awk, which can be used to combine other operations (such as comparisons or arithmetic) into more complex forms of logic. Table 23.3 shows the compound pattern operators and their behavior.

TABLE 23.3   Compound Pattern Operators in Perl

Operator	Meaning
&&	Logical AND
¦¦	Logical OR
!	Logical NOT
()	Parentheses; used to group compound statements

Arithmetic Operators

Perl supports a wide variety of math operations. Table 23.4 summarizes these operators.

TABLE 23.4   Perl Arithmetic Operators

Operator	Purpose
x**y	Raises x to the y power (same as x^y)
x%y	Calculates the remainder of x/y
x+y	Adds x to y
x-y	Subtracts y from x
x*y	Multiplies x times y
x/y	Divides x by y
-y	Negates y (switches the sign of y); also known as the *unary minus*
++y	Increments y by 1 and uses value (prefix increment)
y++	Uses value of y and then increments by 1 (postfix increment)
−y	Decrements y by 1 and uses value (prefix decrement)
y−	Uses value of y and then decrements by 1 (postfix decrement)
x=y	Assigns value of y to x. Perl also supports operator-assignment operators (+=, -=, *=, /=, %=, **=, and others)

You can also use comparison operators (such as == or <) and compound pattern operators (&&, ¦¦, and !) in arithmetic statements. They evaluate to the value 0 for false and 1 for true.

Other Operators

Perl supports a number of operators that don't fit any of the prior categories. Table 23.5 summarizes these operators.

TABLE 23.5 Other Perl Operators

Operator	Purpose
~x	Bitwise not (changes 0 bits to 1 and 1 bits to 0)
x & y	Bitwise and
x ¦ y	Bitwise or
x ^ y	Bitwise exclusive or (XOR)
x << y	Bitwise shift left (shifts x by y bits)
x >> y	Bitwise shift right (shifts x by y bits)
x . y	Concatenate y onto x
a x b	Repeats string a for b number of times
x , y	Comma operator—evaluates x and then y
x ? y : z	Conditional expression—if x is true, y is evaluated; otherwise, z is evaluated. Provides the capability of an if statement anywhere you want (in the middle of a print, for instance)

Except for the comma operator and conditional expression, these operators can also be used with the assignment operator, similar to the way addition (+) can be combined with assignment (=), giving +=.

Special String Constants

Perl supports string constants that have special meaning or cannot be entered from the keyboard.

Table 23.6 shows most of the constants supported by Perl.

TABLE 23.6 Perl Special String Constants

Expression	Meaning
\\	The means of including a backslash
\a	The alert or bell character
\b	Backspace
\cC	Control character (like holding the Ctrl key down and pressing the C character)
\e	Escape
\f	Formfeed
\n	Newline
\r	Carriage return
\t	Tab
\xNN	Indicates that NN is a hexadecimal number
\0NNN	Indicates that NNN is an octal (base 8) number

Conditional Statements: `if/else` **and** `unless`

Perl offers two conditional statements, `if` and `unless`, which function opposite one another. `if` enables you to execute a block of code only if certain conditions are met so that you can control the flow of logic through your program. Conversely, `unless` performs the statements when certain conditions are not met.

The following sections explain and demonstrate how to use these conditional statements when writing scripts for Linux.

if

The syntax of the Perl `if/else` structure is as follows:

```
if (condition) {
     statement or block of code
     }
elsif (condition) {
     statement or block of code
     }
else {
     statement or block of code
     }
```

condition can be a statement that returns a true or false value.

> **NOTE**
>
> Truth might be relative, but in 1844, the English mathematician George Boole introduced a new branch of mathematics known as *linguistic algebra*. The discipline continues to be used today in computing science as Boolean logic. His concepts of AND, NOT, and OR enable you to compare values that are in one of two mutually exclusive states and then make a decision based on the result of the comparison. Programmers refer to the states as off/on, zero/one, true/false, and so on. This logic is used to interpret 0s and 1s and is at the very foundation of computers. Perl implements Boolean logic in its conditional statements.

Truth is defined in Perl in a way that might be unfamiliar to you, so be careful. Everything in Perl is true except `0` (the digit zero), `"0"` (the string containing the number `0`), `""` (the empty string), and an undefined value. Note that even the string `"00"` is a true value because it isn't one of the four false cases.

The statement or block of code is executed if the test condition returns a true value.

For example, Listing 23.3 uses the `if/else` structure and shows conditional statements using the `eq` string comparison operator.

LISTING 23.3   `if/elsif/else`

```
if  ($favorite eq "chocolate") {
     print "I like chocolate too.\n";
} elsif ($favorite eq "spinach") {
     print "Oh, I don't like spinach.\n";
} else {
     print "Your favorite food is $favorite.\n";
}
```

> **NOTE**
>
> Perl was designed as a natural language, and it acknowledges idiomatic expressions that corre-
> spond with spoken English. The if statement is one good example. For example, you can say the
> following:
>
> ```
>     }
> ```
>
> Alternatively, you could write it as you would more likely say it:
>
> ```
> print "Hello Rich!\n" if $name eq "Rich";
> ```

unless

unless works just like `if`, only backward. `unless` performs a statement or block if a condition is false:

```
unless ($name eq "Rich")         {
     print "Go away, you're not allowed in here!\n";
}
```

> **NOTE**
>
> You can restate the preceding example in more natural language, as you did in the if example.
>
> ```
> print "Go away!\n" unless $name eq "Rich";
> ```
>
> Although it isn't a rule, you should try to put the more important part of the statement (think of
> it as a sentence) on the left so that it's easier to read.

Looping

A *loop* is a way to repeat a program action multiple times. A very simple example is a
countdown timer that performs a task (waiting for one second) 300 times before telling
you that your egg is done boiling.

Looping constructs (also known as *control structures*) can be used to iterate a block of code as long as certain conditions apply, or while the code steps through (evaluates) a list of values, perhaps using that list as arguments.

Perl has four looping constructs: `for`, `foreach`, `while`, and `until`.

for

The `for` construct performs a *statement* (block of code) for a set of conditions defined as follows:

```
for (start condition; end condition; increment function) {
    statement(s)
}
```

The start condition is set at the beginning of the loop. Each time the loop is executed, the increment function is performed until the end condition is achieved. This looks much like the traditional `for/next` loop. The following code is an example of a `for` loop:

```
for ($i=1; $i<=10; $i++) {
    print "$i\n"
}
```

foreach

The `foreach` construct performs a statement block for each element in a list or array:

```
@names = ("alpha","bravo","charlie");
foreach $name (@names) {
    print "$name sounding off!\n";
}
```

The loop variable ($name in the example) isn't merely set to the value of the array elements; it's aliased to that element. That means if you modify the loop variable, you're actually modifying the array. If no loop array is specified, the Perl default variable $_ may be used:

```
@names = ("alpha","bravo","charlie");
foreach (@names) {
    print "$_ sounding off!\n";

}
```

This syntax can be very convenient, but it can also lead to unreadable code. Give a thought to the poor person who'll be maintaining your code. (It will probably be you.)

> **NOTE**
>
> foreach is frequently abbreviated as for.

while

while performs a block of statements as long as a particular condition is true:

```
while ($x<10) {
    print "$x\n";
    $x++;
}
```

Remember that the condition can be anything that returns a true or false value. For example, it could be a function call:

```
while ( InvalidPassword($user, $password) )         {
        print "You've entered an invalid password. Please try again.\n";
        $password = GetPassword;
}
```

until

until is the exact opposite of the while statement. It performs a block of statements as long as a particular condition is false—or, rather, until it becomes true:

```
until (ValidPassword($user, $password))  {
        print "You've entered an invalid password. Please try again.\n";
        $password = GetPassword;
}
```

last **and** next

You can force Perl to end a loop early by using a last statement. last is similar to the C break command—the loop is exited. If you decide you need to skip the remaining contents of a loop without ending the loop itself, you can use next, which is similar to the C continue command. Unfortunately, these statements don't work with do ... while.

On the other hand, you can use redo to jump to a loop (marked by a label) or inside the loop where called:

```
$a = 100;
while (1) {
   print "start\n";
   TEST: {
      if (($a = $a / 2) > 2) {
```

```
        print "$a\n";
        if (−$a < 2) {
           exit;
        }
        redo TEST;
     }
   }
}
```

In this simple example, the variable $a is repeatedly manipulated and tested in an endless loop. The word "start" will only be printed once.

do ... while **and** do ... until

The while and until loops evaluate the conditional first. The behavior is changed by applying a do block before the conditional. With the do block, the condition is evaluated last, which results in the contents of the block always executing at least once (even if the condition is false). This is similar to the C language do ... while (*conditional*) statement.

Regular Expressions

Perl's greatest strength is in text and file manipulation, which is accomplished by using the regular expression (regex) library. Regexes, which are quite different from the wildcard handling and filename expansion capabilities of the shell (see Chapter 22), allow complicated pattern matching and replacement to be done efficiently and easily.

For example, the following line of code replaces every occurrence of the string bob or the string mary with fred in a line of text:

```
$string =~ s/bob¦mary/fred/gi;
```

Without going into too many of the details, Table 23.7 explains what the preceding line says.

TABLE 23.7   Explanation of $string =~ s/bob¦mary/fred/gi;

Element	Explanation
$string =~	Performs this pattern match on the text found in the variable called $string.
s	Substitute.
/	Begins the text to be matched.
bob¦mary	Matches the text bob or mary. You should remember that it's looking for the text mary, not the word mary; that is, it will also match the text mary in the word maryland.
/	Ends text to be matched; begins text to replace it.

TABLE 23.7   Continued

Element	Explanation
fred	Replaces anything that was matched with the text fred.
/	Ends replace text.
g	Does this substitution globally; that is, replaces the match text wherever in the string you match it (and any number of times).
i	The search text is not case sensitive. It matches bob, Bob, or bOB.
;	Indicates the end of the line of code.

If you're interested in the details, you can get more information using the regex (7) section of the manual.

Although replacing one string with another might seem a rather trivial task, the code required to do the same thing in another language (for example, C) is rather daunting unless supported by additional subroutines from external libraries.

Access to the Shell

Perl is useful for administrative functions because it has access to the shell. That means Perl can perform for you any process you might ordinarily perform by typing commands to the shell. To run Linux commands in your Perl programs, use the `` ` ` `` syntax. For example, the code in Listing 23.4 prints a directory listing.

LISTING 23.4   Using Backticks to Access the Shell

```
$curr_dir = `pwd`;
@listing = `ls -al`;
print "Listing for $curr_dir\n";
foreach $file (@listing) {
    print "$file";
}
```

> **NOTE**
>
> The `` ` ` `` notation uses the backtick found above the Tab key (on most keyboards), not the single quotation mark.

You can also use the Shell module to access the shell. Shell is one of the standard modules that comes with Perl; it allows creation and use of a shell-like command line. Look at the following code for an example:

```
use Shell qw(cp);
cp ("/home/httpd/logs/access.log", "/tmp/httpd.log");
```

This code almost looks like it's importing the command-line functions directly into Perl. Although that isn't really happening, you can pretend that the code is similar to a command line and use this approach in your Perl programs.

A third method of accessing the shell is via the `system` function call:

```
$rc = 0xffff & system('cp /home/httpd/logs/access.log /tmp/httpd.log');
if ($rc == 0) {
        print "system cp succeeded \n";
}
else {
        print "system cp failed $rc\n";
}
```

The call can also be used with the `or die` clause:

```
system('cp /home/httpd/logs/access.log /tmp/httpd.log') == 0
        or die "system cp failed: $?"
```

However, you can't capture the output of a command executed through the `system` function.

> **NOTE**
>
> Access to the command line is fairly common in shell scripting languages, but is less common in higher-level programming languages.

Switches

Perl has a variety of command-line options (*switches*) that can be used to change one or more aspects of Perl's behavior. Some switches will change how input data is handled (such as end-of-line characters), whereas others toggle Perl's internal behavior (such as to turn on debugging). These switches can appear on the command line or can be placed on the `#!` line at the beginning of the Perl program.

> **NOTE**
>
> Several command-line switches can be stacked together, so `-pie` is the same as `-p -i -e`.

The following list describes all available command-line switches:

> `-0[digits]`—Specifies the input record separator (`$/`) as an octal number. `$/` is usually a newline, so you get one line per record. For example, if you read a file into an array, this gives you one line per array element. The value `00` is a special case and causes Perl to read in your file one paragraph per record.

-a—Turns on Autosplit mode when used with an -n or -p. That means each line of input is automatically split into the @F array.

-C—Enables native support and system interfaces for wide characters (multibyte character sets).

-c—Tells Perl to perform syntax checking on the specified Perl program without executing it. This is invaluable, and the error messages given are informative, readable, and tell you where to begin looking for the problem, which is a rarity in error messages.

-Dflags—Sets debugging flags. See perlrun for more details.

-d—Runs the script under the Perl debugger. See perldebug for more information.

-d:foo—Runs the script under the control of a debugging or tracing module installed as Devel::foo. For example, -d:Dprof executes the script using the Devel::DProf profiler. See perldebug for additional information on the Perl debugger.

-e commandline—Indicates that what follows is Perl code. This enables you to enter Perl code directly on the command line, rather than running code contained in a file.

```
$ perl -e 'print join " ", keys %ENV;'
```

-Fpattern—Specifies the pattern to split on if -a is also in effect. This is " " by default, and -F enables you to set it to whatever works for you, such as ',' or ';'. The pattern can be surrounded by //, "", or ''.

-h—Typing perl -h lists all available command-line switches.

-Idirectory—Directories specified by -I are prepended to the search path for modules (@INC).

-i[extension]—This indicates that files are to be edited in place. If the extension is provided, the original is backed up with that extension. Otherwise, the original file is overwritten.

-l[octnum]—Enables automatic line-ending processing, which means that end-of-line characters are automatically removed from input and put back on to output. If the optional octal number is unspecified, this is just the newline character.

-m[-]module or -M[-]module—Loads the specified module before running your script. There's a subtle difference between m and M. See perlrun for more details.

-n—Causes Perl to loop around your script for each file provided to the command line. Does not print the output. The following example, from perlrun, deletes all files older than a week:

```
$ find . -mtime +7 -print | perl -nle 'unlink;'
```

-P—This causes your script to be run through the C preprocessor before compilation by Perl.

-p—This is just like -n except that that each line is printed.

-S—This searches for the script using the PATH environment variable.

-s—This performs some command-line switch parsing and puts the switch into the corresponding variable in the Perl script. For example, the following script prints '1' if run with the -fubar switch. Your Perl code might look like this:

```
#!/usr/bin/perl -s
print $fubar;
```

When you execute it, you would enter

```
$ ./myperl -fubar
```

-T—This enables *taint* checking. In this mode, Perl assumes that all user input is tainted, or insecure, until the programmer tells it otherwise. This helps protect you from people trying to exploit security holes in your code and is especially important when writing CGI programs.

-U—This enables you to do unsafe things in your Perl program, such as unlinking directories while running as superuser.

-u—An available, but obsolete switch to tell Perl to dump core after compiling a program.

-V—This prints a summary of the major Perl configuration values and the current value of @INC.

```
-V:names
```

This parameter displays the value of the names configuration variable.

-v—This prints the version and patch level of your Perl executable. For example,

```
$ perl -v
This is perl, v5.8.4 built for i386-linux-thread-multi
(with 1 registered patch, see perl -V for more detail)

Copyright 1987-2003, Larry Wall
-

Perl may be copied only under the terms of either the Artistic License or the
GNU General Public License, which may be found in the Perl 5 source kit.

Complete documentation for Perl, including FAQ lists, should be found on
this system using `man perl' or `perldoc perl'.  If you have access to the
Internet, point your browser at http://www.perl.com/, the Perl Home Page.
```

-W—This tells Perl to display all warning messages.

-w—This tells Perl to display warning messages about potential problems in the program, such as variables used only once (might be a typo), using = instead of == in a comparison, and the like. This is often used in conjunction with the -c flag to do a thorough program check.

```
$ perl -cw finalassignment.pl
```

-X—This tells Perl to disable all warning messages.

-x directory—This tells Perl that the script is embedded in something larger, such as an email message. Perl throws away everything before a line starting with #!, containing the string 'perl', and everything after _END__. If a directory is specified, Perl changes to the directory before executing the script.

> **NOTE**
>
> The Perl documentation is referred to a few times in this section. `perldebug`, `perlrun`, `perlmod`, and `perlmodlib`, for example, are documents from the Perl documentation. To see these documents, just type **perldoc perlmodlib** at the shell prompt. You can also see all the Perl documents online at `http://www.cpan.org/doc/index.html` or on any CPAN site. CPAN is the Comprehensive Perl Archive Network. See the "Modules and CPAN" section later in this chapter for more information.
>
> Perl documentation is written in POD (plain old documentation) format and can be converted into any other format, such as TeX, ASCII, or HTML, with the pod2* tools that ship with Perl. For example, to produce HTML documentation on the `Fubar` module, you would type **pod2html Fubar.pm > Fubar.html**.

23

Modules and CPAN

A great strength of the Perl community (and the Linux community) is the fact that it's an open source community. This community support is expressed for Perl via CPAN, which is a network of mirrors of a repository of Perl code.

Most of CPAN is made up of *modules*, which are reusable chunks of code that do useful things, similar to software libraries containing functions for C programmers. These modules help speed development when building Perl programs and free Perl hackers from repeatedly reinventing the wheel when building a bicycle.

There are thousands of Perl modules that do everything from sending email to maintaining your Cisco router access lists to telling you whether a name is masculine or feminine to printing the time in some fancy format. If you can think of doing something with a Perl script, chances are pretty good that a module exists to help you. If there's no module that helps, you're encouraged to write one and share it with the rest of the community.

Perl comes with a set of standard modules installed. Those modules should contain much of the functionality that you'll initially need with Perl. If you need to use a module not installed with Fedora, use the CPAN module (which is one of the standard modules) to download and install other modules onto your system. At `http://www.perl.com/CPAN/`, you'll find the CPAN Multiplex Dispatcher, which will attempt to direct you to the CPAN site closest to you.

Typing the following command will put you into an interactive shell that gives you access to CPAN. You can type **help** at the prompt to get more information on how to use the CPAN program.

```
$ perl -MCPAN -e shell
```

After you've installed a module from CPAN (or written one of your own), you can load that module into memory where you can use it with the use function:

```
use Time::CTime;
```

use looks in the directories listed in the variable @INC for the module. In this example, use looks for a directory called Time, which contains a file called CTime.pm, which in turn is assumed to contain a package called Time::CTime. The distribution of each module should contain documentation on using that module.

For a list of all the standard Perl modules (those that come with Perl when you install it), see perlmodlib in the Perl documentation. You can read this document by typing **perldoc perlmodlib** at the command prompt.

Code Examples

Over the last few years, many people have picked up the notion that Perl is a CGI language, as though it weren't good for anything else. Nothing could be further from the truth. You can use Perl in every aspect of your system administration and as a building block in whatever applications you're planning to run on your shiny new Linux system.

The following sections contain a few examples of things you might want to do with Perl.

Sending Mail

There are several ways to get Perl to send email. One method that you see frequently is opening a pipe to the sendmail command and sending data to it (shown in Listing 23.5). Another method is using the Mail::Sendmail module (available through CPAN or directly at http://www.cpan.org/authors/id/M/MI/MIVKOVIC/), which uses socket connections directly to send mail (as shown in Listing 23.6). The latter method is faster because it doesn't have to launch an external process. Note that sendmail must be running on your system in order for the Perl program in Listing 23.5 to work.

LISTING 23.5   Sending Mail Using sendmail

```perl
#!/usr/bin/perl
open (MAIL, "¦ /usr/sbin/sendmail -t"); # Use -t to protect from users
print MAIL <<EndMail;
To: dpitts\@mk.net
From: rbowen\@mk.net
Subject: Email notification

David,
 Sending email from Perl is easy!
Rich

.
EndMail
close MAIL;
```

> **NOTE**
>
> Note that the @ sign in the email addresses must be escaped so that Perl doesn't try to evaluate an array of that name.
>
> The syntax used to print the mail message is called a *here document*. The syntax is as follows:
>
> ```
> print <<EndText;
> .....
> EndText
> ```
>
> The EndText value must be identical at the beginning and at the end of the block, including any whitespace.

LISTING 23.6   Sending Mail Using the `Mail::Sendmail` Module

```perl
#!/usr/bin/perl
use Mail::Sendmail;
%mail = ('To' => 'dpitts@mk.net',
        'From' => 'rbowen@mk.net'
        'Subject' => 'Email notification',
        'Message' => 'Sending email from Perl is easy!',
        );
sendmail(%mail);
```

Perl ignores the comma after the last element in the hash. It's convenient to leave it there; if you want to add items to the hash, you don't need to add the comma. This is purely a style decision.

> **Using Perl to Install a CPAN Module**
>
> You can use Perl to interactively download and install a Perl module from the CPAN archives by using the `-M` and `-e` commands. Start the process by using a Perl like this:
>
> ```
> # perl -MCPAN -e shell
> ```
>
> After you press Enter, you'll see some introductory information and be asked to choose an initial automatic or manual configuration, which is required before any download or install takes place. Type **no** and press Enter to have Perl automatically configure for the download and install process; or, if desired, simply press Enter to manually configure for downloading and installation. If you use manual configuration, you'll be asked a series of questions regarding paths, caching, terminal settings, program locations, and so on. Settings will be saved in a directory named `.cpan` in current directory.
>
> When finished, you'll see the CPAN prompt:
>
> ```
> cpan>
> ```

To have Perl examine your system and then download and install a large number of modules, use the `install` keyword, specify `Bundle` at the prompt, and then press Enter like this:

```
cpan> install Bundle::CPAN
```

To download a desired module (using the example in Listing 23.6), use the `get` keyword like so:

```
cpan> get Mail::Sendmail
```

The source for the module will be downloaded into the `.cpan` directory. You can then build and install the module using the `install` keyword, like this:

```
cpan> install Mail::Sendmail
```

The entire process of retrieving, building, and installing a module can also be accomplished at the command line by using Perl's `-e` option like this:

```
# perl -MCPAN  -e "install Mail::Sendmail"
```

Note also that the @ sign didn't need to be escaped within single quotation marks (' '). Perl doesn't *interpolate* (evaluate variables) within single quotation marks, but does within double quotation marks and here strings (similar to << shell operations).

Purging Logs

Many programs maintain some variety of logs. Often, much of the information in the logs is redundant or just useless. The program shown in Listing 23.7 removes all lines from a file that contain a particular word or phrase, so lines that you know aren't important can be purged. For example, you might want to remove all the lines in the Apache error log that originate with your test client machine because you know those error messages were produced during testing.

LISTING 23.7   Purging Log Files

```perl
#!/usr/bin/perl
#       Be careful using this program!!
#       This will remove all lines that contain a given word
#       Usage:  remove <word> <file>
$word=@ARGV[0];
$file=@ARGV[1];
if ($file)  {
    # Open file for reading
    open (FILE, "$file") or die "Could not open file: $!";     @lines=<FILE>;
    close FILE;
    # Open file for writing
    open (FILE, ">$file") or die "Could not open file for writing: $!";
    for (@lines)  {
```

LISTING 23.7   Continued

```
        print FILE unless /$word/;
    } # End for
    close FILE;
} else {
    print "Usage:  remove <word> <file>\n";
} # End if...else
```

The code uses a few idiomatic Perl expressions to keep it brief. It reads the file into an array using the <FILE> notation; it then writes the lines back out to the file unless they match the pattern given on the command line.

The die function kills program operation and displays an error message if the open statements fail. $! in the error message, as mentioned in the section on special variables, is the error message returned by the operating system. It will likely be something like 'file not found' or 'permission denied'.

Posting to Usenet

If some portion of your job requires periodic postings to Usenet—a FAQ listing, for example—the following Perl program can automate the process for you. In the sample code, the posted text is read in from a text file, but your input can come from anywhere.

The program shown in Listing 23.8 uses the Net::NNTP module, which is a standard part of the Perl distribution. You can find more documentation on the Net::NNTP module by typing 'perldoc Net::NNTP' at the command line.

LISTING 23.8   Posting an Article to Usenet

```
#!/usr/bin/perl
open (POST, "post.file");
@post = <POST>;
close POST;
use Net::NNTP;
$NNTPhost = 'news';
$nntp = Net::NNTP->new($NNTPhost)
      or die "Cannot contact $NNTPhost: $!";
# $nntp->debug(1);
$nntp->post()
   or die "Could not post article: $!";
$nntp->datasend("Newsgroups: news.announce\n");
$nntp->datasend("Subject: FAQ - Frequently Asked Questions\n");
$nntp->datasend("From: ADMIN <root\@rcbowen.com>\n");
$nntp->datasend("\n\n");
```

LISTING 23.8   Continued

```
for (@post)      {
    $nntp->datasend($_);
} # End for
$nntp->quit;
```

One-Liners

One medium in which Perl excels is the one-liner. Folks go to great lengths to reduce tasks to one line of Perl code. Perl has the rather undeserved reputation of being unreadable. The fact is that you can write unreadable code in any language. Perl allows for more than one way to do something, and this leads rather naturally to people trying to find the most arcane way to do things.

> **TIP**
>
> Just because you can do something isn't a particularly good reason for doing it. For example, it can be more convenient to write somewhat lengthier pieces of Perl code for something that could be done in just one line, just for the sake of readability, and could save time later on. It can be irritating to go back to a piece of code reduced to one line for efficiency, but then later on have to spend 30 minutes trying to figure out what it does.
>
> Document your Perl scripts for readability. Use comments liberally because they'll help you (or your co-workers who get to maintain your code) in the future.

Named for Randal Schwartz, a *Schwartzian Transform* is a way of sorting an array by something that isn't obvious. The sort function sorts arrays alphabetically; that's pretty obvious. What if you want to sort an array of strings alphabetically by the third word? Perhaps you want something more useful, such as sorting a list of files by file size? A Schwartzian Transform creates a new list that contains the information that you want to sort by, referencing the first list. You then sort the new list and use it to figure out the order that the first list should be in. Here's a simple example that sorts a list of strings by length:

```
@sorted_by_length =
  map { $_ => [0] }            # Extract original list
  sort { $a=>[1] <=> $b=>[1] } # Sort by the transformed value
  map { [$_, length($_)] }     # Map to a list of element lengths
  @list;
```

Because each operator acts on the thing immediately to the right of it, it helps to read this from right to left (or bottom to top, the way it is written here).

The first thing that acts on the list is the map operator. It transforms the list into a hash in which the keys are the list elements and the values are the lengths of each element. This is where you put in your code that does the transformation by which you want to sort.

The next operator is the `sort` function, which sorts the list by the values.

Finally, the hash is transformed back into an array by extracting its keys. The array is now in the desired order.

Command-line Processing

Perl is great at parsing the output of various programs. This is a task for which many people use tools such as `awk` and `sed`. Perl gives you a larger vocabulary for performing these tasks. The following example is very simple, but illustrates how you might use Perl to chop up some output and do something with it. In the example, Perl is used to list only those files that are larger than 10KB:

```
$ ls -la ¦ perl -nae 'print "$F[8] is $F[4]\n" if $F[4] > 10000;'
```

The `-n` switch indicates that I want the Perl code run for each line of the output. The `-a` switch automatically splits the output into the `@F` array. The `-e` switch indicates that the Perl code is going to follow on the command line. (Refer to the "Switches" section earlier in this chapter for more information.)

> **Related Fedora and Linux Commands**
>
> You'll use these commands and tools when using Perl with Linux:
>
> a2p—A filter used to translate `awk` scripts into Perl
>
> find2perl—A utility used to create Perl code from command lines using the `find` command
>
> pcregrep—A utility used to search data using Perl-compatible regular expressions
>
> perlcc—A compiler for Perl programs
>
> perldoc—A Perl utility used to read Perl documentation
>
> s2p—A filter used to translate `sed` scripts into Perl
>
> vi—The `vi` (actually `vim`) text editor

Reference

The first place to look is in the Perl documentation and Linux man pages.

Perl, all of its documentation, and millions of lines of Perl programs are all available free on the Internet. A number of Usenet newsgroups are also devoted to Perl, as well as shelves of books and a quarterly journal.

Books

Although your local bookstore might have dozens of titles on Perl, the following are some of the more highly recommended of these. You might also look at the *Camel Critiques* (Tom Christiansen; `http://language.perl.com/critiques/index.html`) for reviews of other available Perl books.

- *Advanced Perl Programming*, by Sriram Srinivasan, O'Reilly & Associates

- *Sams Teach Yourself Perl in 21 Days, Second Edition*, by Laura Lemay, Sams Publishing

- *Sams Teach Yourself Perl in 24 Hours, Second Edition*, by Clinton Pierce, Sams Publishing

- *Learning Perl, Third Edition*, by Randal L. Schwartz, Tom Phoenix, O'Reilly & Associates

- *Programming Perl, Third Edition*, by Larry Wall, Tom Christiansen, and Jon Orwant, O'Reilly & Associates

- *Effective Perl Programming: Writing Better Programs with Perl*, by Joseph Hall, Addison-Wesley Publishing Company

- *CGI Programming with Perl, Second Edition*, by Gunther Birznieks, Scott Guelich, Shishir Gundavaram, O'Reilly & Associates

- *Mastering Regular Expressions*, by Jeffrey Friedl, O'Reilly & Associates

Usenet

Check out the following on Usenet:

- `comp.lang.perl.misc`—Discusses various aspects of the Perl programming language. Make sure that your questions are Perl specific, not generic CGI programming questions. The regulars tend to flame folks who don't know the difference.

- `comp.infosystems.www.authoring.cgi`—Discusses authoring of CGI programs, so much of the discussion is Perl specific. Make sure that your questions are related to CGI programming, not just Perl. The regulars are very particular about staying on topic.

WWW

Check these sites on the World Wide Web:

- `http://www.perl.com/`—Tom Christiansen maintains the Perl language home page. This is the place to find all sorts of information about Perl, from its history and culture to helpful tips. This is also the place to download the Perl interpreter for your system.

- `http://www.perl.com/CPAN/`—This is part of the site just mentioned, but it merits its own mention. CPAN (Comprehensive Perl Archive Network) is the place for you to find modules and programs in Perl. If you write something in Perl that you think is particularly useful, you can make it available to the Perl community here.

- `http://www.perl.com/pub/q/FAQs`—Frequently Asked Questions index of common Perl queries; this site offers a handy way to quickly search for answers about Perl.

- `http://learn.perl.org/`—One the best places to start learning Perl online. If you master Perl, go to `http://jobs.perl.org`.

- `http://www.hwg.org/`—The HTML Writers Guild is a not-for-profit organization dedicated to assisting Web developers. One of its services is a plethora of mailing lists. The `hwg-servers` mailing list and the `hwg-languages` mailing list are great places for asking Perl-related questions.

- `http://www.pm.org/`—The Perl Mongers are local Perl users groups. There might be one in your area. The Perl advocacy site is `http://www.perl.org`.

- `http://www.tpj.com/`—*The Perl Journal* is "a reader-supported monthly e-zine" devoted to the Perl programming language. *TPJ* is always full of excellent, amusing, and informative articles, and is an invaluable resource to both new and experienced Perl programmers.

- `http://www-106.ibm.com/developerworks/linux/library/l-p101/`—A short tutorial about one-line Perl scripts and code.

Other

Other valuable resources not falling into any of the preceding categories are Perl-related Internet Relay Chat channels. You can usually find several channels available on an IRC server. However, the questions, discussions, and focus of similarly named channels will vary from server to server. For example, a `#perlhelp` channel is usually for general questions about installing, using, and learning about Perl. A `#perl` channel is generally for more advanced questions, but on some servers beginner questions might be welcomed. You might also find some helpful answers on `#cgi` and `#html` channels. Browse to `http://perl-begin.berlios.de/irc/` for a list of servers.

23

CHAPTER **24**

Kernel and Module Management

IN THIS CHAPTER

- The Linux Kernel
- Managing Modules
- When to Recompile
- Kernel Versions
- Obtaining the Kernel Sources
- Patching the Kernel
- Compiling the Kernel
- Choosing a Configuration Interface
- When Something Goes Wrong
- Kernel Tuning with `sysctl`
- Reference

A kernel is a complex piece of software that manages the processes and process interactions that take place within an operating system. As a user, you rarely, if ever, interact directly with it. Instead, you work with the applications that the kernel manages.

The Linux kernel is Linux. It is the result of years of cooperative (and sometimes contentious) work by numerous people around the world. There is only one common kernel source tree, but each major Linux distribution massages and patches its version slightly to add features, performance, or options. Each Linux distribution, including Fedora Core Linux, comes with its own precompiled kernel as well as the kernel source code, providing you with absolute authority over the Linux operating system. In this chapter, we'll examine the kernel and learn what it does for us and for the operating system.

In this chapter, you also learn how to obtain the kernel sources, as well as how and when to patch the kernel. The chapter leads you through an expert's tour of the kernel architecture and teaches you essential steps in kernel configuration, how to build and install modules, and how to compile drivers in Fedora Core Linux. This chapter also teaches you important aspects of working with GRUB, the default Fedora Core Linux boot loader. Finally, the chapter's troubleshooting information will help you understand what to do when something goes wrong with your Linux kernel installation or compilation process. As disconcerting as these problems can seem, this chapter shows you some easy fixes for many kernel problems.

Most users find that the precompiled Fedora Core Linux kernel suits their needs. At some point, you might need to recompile the kernel to support a specific piece of hardware or add a new feature to the operating system. If you've heard horror stories about the difficulties of recompiling the Linux kernel, you can relax; this chapter gives you all the information you need to understand when recompiling is necessary and how to painlessly work through the process.

The Linux Kernel

The Linux kernel is the management part of the operating system that many people call "Linux." Although many think of the entire distribution as Linux, the only piece that can correctly be called Linux is the kernel. Fedora Core Linux, like many Linux distributions, includes a kernel packaged with add-on software that interacts with the kernel so that the user can interface with the system in a meaningful manner.

The system utilities and user programs enable computers to become valuable tools to a user.

The First Linux Kernel

In 1991, Linus Torvalds released version .99 of the Linux kernel as the result of his desire for a powerful, UNIX-like operating system for his Intel 80386 personal computer. Linus wrote the initial code necessary to create what is now known as the Linux kernel and combined it with Richard Stallman's GNU tools. (Because many of the Linux basic system tools come from the GNU Project, many people refer to the operating system as GNU/Linux.) Since then, Linux has benefited as thousands of contributors add their talents and time to the Linux project. Linus still maintains the kernel, deciding on what will and will not make it into the kernel as official releases, known to many as the "vanilla" or "Linus" Linux kernel.

The Linux Source Tree

The source code for the Linux kernel is kept in a group of directories called the kernel source tree. The structure of the kernel source tree is important because the process of compiling (building) the kernel is automated; it is controlled by scripts interpreted by the make application. These scripts, known as makefiles, expect to find the pieces of the kernel code in specific places or they will not work. You will learn how to compile a kernel later in this chapter.

It is not necessary for the Linux kernel source code to be installed on your system for the system to run or for you to accomplish typical tasks such as email, Web browsing, or word processing. It is necessary that the kernel sources be installed, however, if you want to compile a new kernel. In the next section, we'll show you how to install the kernel source files and how to set up the special symbolic link required. That link is /usr/src/ linux-2.6, and it's how we will refer to the directory of the kernel source tree as we examine the contents of the kernel source tree.

The /usr/src/linux-2.6 directory contains the .config and the Makefile files among others. The .config file is the configuration of your Linux kernel as it was compiled.

There is no .config file by default; you must select one from the /configs subdirectory. There, you'll find configuration files for each flavor of the kernel Fedora provides; simply copy the one appropriate for your system to the default directory and rename it .config.

We've already discussed the contents of the /configs subdirectory, so let's examine the other directories found under /usr/src/linux-2.6. The most useful for us is the Documentation directory. In it and its subdirectories, you will find almost all the documentation concerning every part of the kernel. The file 00-INDEX (each /Documentation subdirectory also contains a 00-INDEX file as well) contains a list of the files in the main directory and a brief explanation of what they are. Many files are written solely for kernel programmers and application writers, but a few are useful to the intermediate or advanced Linux user when attempting to learn about kernel and device driver issues. Some of the more interesting and useful documents are

> devices.txt—A list of all possible Linux devices that are represented in the /dev directory, giving major and minor numbers and a short description. If you have ever gotten an error message that mentions char-major-xxx, this file is where that list is kept. Devices are mentioned in Chapter 10, "Managing the File System."
>
> ide.txt—If your system uses IDE hard drives, this file discusses how the kernel interacts with them and lists the various kernel commands that can be used to solve IDE-related hardware problems, manually set data transfer modes, and otherwise manually manage your IDE drives. Most of this management is automatic, but if you want to understand how the kernel interacts with IDE devices, this file explains it.
>
> initrd.txt—Chapter 10 also discusses the initial ramdisk. This file provides much more in-depth knowledge of initial ramdisks, giving details on the loopback file system used to create and mount them and explaining how the kernel interacts with them.
>
> kernel-parameters.txt—In Chapter 7, "Managing Services," we touch briefly on kernel arguments, which are commands that can be passed to the kernel at boot time to configure kernel or hardware settings. This file is a list of most of those kernel arguments, but it doesn't appear too useful at first glance because it's just a list. However, knowing that a parameter exists and might relate to something you're looking for can assist you in tracking down more information because now you have terms to enter into an Internet search engine such as http://www.google.com/linux.
>
> sysrq.txt—If you have ever wondered what that key on your keyboard marked "SysRq" was used for, this file has the answer. Briefly, it's a key combination hardwired into the kernel that can help you recover from a system lockup. Fedora Core disables this function by default for security reasons. You can re-enable it by entering the command # echo "1" > /proc/sys/kernel/sysrq and disable it by echoing a value of 0 instead of 1.

In the other directories found in Documentation, you'll find similar text files that deal with the kernel modules for CD-ROM drivers, file system drivers, gameport and joystick drivers, video drivers (not graphics card drivers—those belong to X11R6 and not to the kernel), network drivers, and all the other drivers and systems found in the Linux operating system. Again, these documents are usually written for programmers, but they can provide useful information to the intermediate and advanced Linux user as well.

The directory named /scripts contains many of the scripts that make uses. It really doesn't contain anything of interest to anyone who isn't a programmer or a kernel developer (also known as a kernel hacker).

After a kernel is built, all the compiled files will wind up in the /arch directory and its subdirectories. Although you can manually move them to their final location, we'll show you later in this chapter how the make scripts will do it for you. In the early days of Linux, this post-compilation file relocation was all done by hand; you should be grateful for make.

> **NOTE**
>
> The make utility is a very complex program. Complete documentation on the structure of make files, as well as the arguments that it can accept, can be found at http://www.gnu.org/software/make/manual/make.html.

The remainder of the directories in /usr/src/linux-2.6 contain the source code for the kernel and the kernel drivers. When you install the kernel sources, these files are placed there automatically. When you patch kernel sources, these files are altered automatically. When you compile the kernel, these files are accessed automatically. Although you never need to touch the source code files, they can be useful. The kernel source files are nothing more than text files with special formatting, which means that we can look at them and read the programmers' comments. Sometimes, a programmer will write an application, but can't (or often won't) write the documentation. The comments he puts in the source code are often the only documentation that exists for the code.

Small testing programs are even "hidden" in the comments of some of the code, along with comments and references to other information. Because the source code is written in a language that can be read as easily—almost—as English, a non-programmer might be able to get an idea of what the application or driver is actually doing (see Chapter 21, "C/C++ Programming Tools for Fedora"). This information might be of use to an intermediate to advanced Linux user when he is confronted by kernel- and driver-related problems.

> **NOTE**
>
> The interaction and control of hardware is handled by a small piece of the kernel called a *device driver*. The driver tells the computer how to interact with a modem, a SCSI card, a keyboard, a mouse, and so on in response to a user prompt. Without the device driver, the kernel does not know how to interact with the associated device.

Types of Kernels

In the early days of Linux, Linux kernels were a single block of code containing all the instructions for the processor, the motherboard, and the other hardware. If you changed hardware, you were required to recompile the kernel code to include what you needed and discard what you did not. Including extra, unneeded code carried a penalty since the kernel became larger and occupied more memory. On older systems that had only 4MB–8MB of memory, wasting precious memory for unnecessary code was considered unacceptable. Kernel compiling was something of a "black art" as early Linux users attempted to wring the most performance from their computers. These kernels compiled as a single block of code are called *monolithic kernels*.

As the kernel code grew larger and the number of devices that could be added to a computer increased, the requirement to recompile became onerous. A new method of building the kernel was developed to make the task of compiling easier. The part of the kernel's source code that composed the code for the device drivers could be optionally compiled as a module that could be loaded and unloaded into the kernel as required. This approach to building the kernel is called *modular*. Now, all the kernel code could be compiled at once—with most of the code compiled into these modules. Only the required modules would be loaded; the kernel could be kept smaller, and adding hardware was much simpler.

The typical Fedora Core kernel has some drivers compiled as part of the kernel itself (called *in-line* drivers) and others compiled as modules. Only device drivers compiled in-line are available to the kernel during the boot process; modular drivers are only available after the system has been booted.

> **NOTE**
>
> As a common example, drivers for SCSI disk drives must be available to the kernel if you intend to boot from SCSI disks. If the kernel isn't compiled with those drivers in-line, the system won't boot because it won't be able to access the disks.
>
> A way around this problem for modular kernels is to use an initial Ram disk (initrd) discussed later in "Creating an Initial RAM Disk Image." The initrd loads a small kernel and the appropriate device driver, which then can access the device to load the actual kernel you want to run.

Some code can only be one or the other (for technical reasons unimportant to the average user), but most code can be compiled either as modular or in-line. Depending on the application, some system administrators prefer one way over the other, but with fast modern processors and abundant system memory, the performance differences are of little concern to all but the most ardent Linux hackers.

When compiling a kernel, the step in which you make the selection of modular or in-line is part of the make config step that we'll detail later in this chapter. Unless you have a specific reason to do otherwise, we suggest that you select the modular option when given a choice. The process of managing modules is addressed in the next section because you'll be managing them more frequently than you will be compiling a kernel.

Managing Modules

When using a modular kernel, special tools are required to manage the modules. Modules must be loaded and unloaded, and it would be nice if that were done as automatically as possible. We also need to be able to pass necessary parameters to modules when we load them—things such as memory addresses and interrupts. (That information varies from module to module, so you'll need to look at the documentation for your modules to determine what, if any, information needs to be passed to it.) In this section, we'll cover the tools provided to manage modules and then look at a few examples of using them.

Linux provides the following module management tools for our use. All these commands (and modprobe.conf) have man pages:

lsmod—This command lists the loaded modules. It is useful to pipe this through the less command because the listing is usually more than one page long.

insmod—This command loads the specified module into the running kernel. If a module name is given without a full path, the default location for the running kernel, /lib/modules/*/, will be searched. Several options are offered for this command—the most useful is -f, which forces the module to be loaded.

rmmod—This command unloads (removes) the specified module from the running kernel. More than one module at a time can be specified.

modprobe—A more sophisticated version of insmod and rmmod, it uses the dependency file created by depmod and automatically handles loading, or with the -r option, removing modules. There is no force option, however. A useful option to modprobe is -t. If you were unsure of what module would work for your network card, you would use this command:

```
# modprobe -t net
```

The term net is used because that is the name of the directory (/lib/modules/*/kernel/net) where all the network drivers are kept. It will try each one in turn until it loads one successfully.

modinfo—This will query a module's object file and provide a list of the module name, author, license, and any other information that is there. It often isn't very useful.

depmod—This program creates a dependency file for kernel modules. Some modules need to have other modules loaded first; that is, they "depend" on the other modules. (A lot of the kernel code is like this because it eliminates redundancy in the code base.) During the boot process, one of the startup files contains the command depmod -a and it is run every time you boot to re-create the file /lib/modules/*/modules.dep. If you make changes to the file /etc/modprobe.conf, run depmod -a manually. The depmod command, its list of dependencies, and the /etc/modprobe.conf file enable kernel modules to be automatically loaded as needed.

/etc/modprobe.conf—This is not a command, but a file that controls how `modprobe` and `depmod` behave; it contains kernel module variables. Although the command syntax can be quite complex, most actual needs are very simple. The most common use is to alias a module and then pass it some parameters. For example, in the following code, we alias a device name (from `devices.txt`) to a more descriptive word and then pass some information to an associated module. The `i2c-dev` device is used to read the CPU temperature and fan speed on our system. These lines for /etc/modprobe.conf were suggested for our use by the program's documentation. We added them with a text editor.

```
alias char-major-89 i2c-dev
options eeprom ignore=2,0x50,2,0x51,2,0x52
```

A partial listing of `lsmod` is shown here, piped through the `less` command, allowing us to view it a page at a time:

```
# lsmod ¦ less
Module            Size  Used by
parport_pc       19392  1
Module            Size  Used by
parport_pc       19392  1
lp                8236  0
parport          29640  2 parport_pc,lp
autofs4          10624  0
sunrpc          101064  1
```

The list is actually much longer, but here we see that the input module is being used by the `joydev` (joystick device) module, but the joystick module is not being used. This computer has a joystick port that was autodetected, but no joystick is connected. A scanner module is also loaded, but because the USB scanner is unplugged, the module is not being used. You would use the `lsmod` command to determine whether a module was loaded and what other modules were using it. If you examine the full list, you'd see modules for all the devices attached to your computer.

To remove a module, `joydev` in this example, use

```
# rmmod joydev
```

or

```
# modprobe -r joydev
```

A look at the output of `lsmod` would now show that it is no longer loaded. If we removed input as well, we could then use `modprobe` to load both `input` and `joydev` (one depends on the other, remember) with a simple

```
# modprobe joydev
```

24

If Fedora Core Linux were to balk at loading a module (because it had been compiled using a different kernel version from what we are currently running; for example, the nVidia graphics card module), we could force it to load like this:

```
# insmod -f nvidia
```

We would ignore the complaints (error messages) in this case if the kernel generated any. (It won't.)

In Chapter 25, "Productivity Applications," you learn about loading a scanner module; in the example there, you manually load the scanner module and pass it the vendor ID. The scanner was not included in the lookup list because it isn't supported by the GPL scanner programs; as a result, the scanner module was not automatically detected and loaded. However, the scanner will work with a closed-source application after the module is loaded. Automatic module management is nice when it works, but sometimes it's necessary to work with modules directly.

When to Recompile

Fedora Core systems use a modified version of the plain vanilla Linux kernel (a modified version is referred to as a *patched* kernel) with additional drivers and other special features compiled into it.

Fedora Core has quite an intensive testing period for all distribution kernels and regularly distributes updated versions. The supplied Fedora Core kernel is compiled with as many modules as possible to provide as much flexibility as possible. A running kernel can be further tuned with the sysctl program, which enables direct access to a running kernel and permits some kernel parameters to be changed (see "Kernel Tuning with sysctl" at the end of the chapter). As a result of this extensive testing, configurability, and modularity, the precompiled Fedora Core Linux kernel does everything most users need it to do. Most users only need to recompile the kernel to

- Accommodate an esoteric piece of new hardware.

- Conduct a system update when Fedora Core has not yet provided precompiled kernels.

- Experiment with the system capabilities.

Fedora Core supplies several precompiled versions of the kernel for Athlon and Pentium processors, for single- and multi-processor motherboards, and for Enterprise-class systems (higher security; uses 4GB of memory). These kernel versions are provided in RPM format. Installing them is as easy as

```
# rpm -Uvh new_kernel.rpm
```

The kernel (but not the source) RPM files include installation scripts that will automatically alter your boot loader configuration, making the new kernel the default. If you don't want that to happen, just manually edit the /etc/lilo.conf or /boot/grub/grub.conf files and change them back. You can obtain information on configuring both the lilo and GRUB boot loaders in Chapter 7.

> **CAUTION**
>
> You always rpm -U (upgrade), rather than rpm -i (install), a new kernel rpm to avoid overwriting the old, but still working, kernel. This is done as a safety measure. What if the new one doesn't work?

Each new kernel has an associated kernel source RPM, and it is installed with

```
# rpm -Uvh kernel-source-new_version.src.rpm
```

The source code is automatically installed to /usr/src.

Kernel Versions

The Linux kernel is in a constant state of development. As new features are added, bugs are fixed, and new technology is incorporated into the code base, it becomes necessary to provide stable releases of the kernel for use in a production environment. It's also important to have separate releases that contain the newest code for developers to test. To keep track of the kernels, version numbers are assigned to them. Programmers enjoy using sequential version numbers that have abstract meaning. Is version 8 twice as advanced as version 4 of the same application? Is version 1 of one application less developed than version 3 of another? The version numbers can't be used for this kind of qualitative or quantitative comparison. It's entirely possible that higher version numbers can have fewer features and more bugs than older versions. The numbers exist solely to differentiate and organize sequential revisions of software.

For the latest development version of the kernel at the time of writing, for example, the kernel version number is 2.6.7-1.

The kernel version can be broken down into four sections:

- major version—This is the major version number, now at 2.

- minor version—This is the minor version number, now at 6.

- sublevel number—This number indicates the current iteration of the kernel; here it is number 7.

- extraversion level—This is the number representing a collection of patches and additions made to the kernel by the Red Hat engineers to make the kernel work for them (and you). Each collection is numbered, and the number is indicated here in the kernel name. From our preceding example, it is 1.

Typing uname -r at the command prompt displays your current kernel version.

```
# uname -r
2.6.7-1
```

> **NOTE**
>
> The stock Fedora Core kernel included with this book is the 2nd major version, the 6th minor level, the 7th patch level, and an extra version level of 1. The extra version level indicates a Fedora Core specific implementation of the 2.6.7 kernel, which generally addresses some code issues in the stock kernel necessary for special applications or hardware support.
>
> The version number for Fedora Core is 2.6.7-1.

Even-numbered minor versions are stable kernels, whereas odd-numbered minor versions are development releases. Version 2.6.x is the stable production kernel, whereas version 2.5.x is the development Linux kernel. When a new version of the development kernel is started, it will be labeled 2.7.x.

For production machines, you should always use the kernels with even minor numbers. The odd minor numbers introduce new features, so you might want to use those on a test machine if you need features they provide.

Obtaining the Kernel Sources

The Linux kernel has always been freely available to anyone who wants it. If you just want to recompile the existing kernel, install the kernel-sources RPM from the CD using rpm from the command line or the Fedora Core graphical tool as described in Chapter 8, "Managing Software and System Resources." To get the very latest "vanilla" version, open an FTP connection to ftp.kernel.org using your favorite FTP client and log in as anonymous. Because you are interested in the 2.6 kernel, change directories to /pub/linux/kernel/v2.6. The latest stable kernel as of this writing is 2.6.8.

> **NOTE**
>
> ftp.kernel.org receives more than its share of requests for download. It is considered a courtesy to use a mirror site to reduce the traffic that ftp.kernel.org bears. http://www.kernel.org/mirrors/ has a list of all mirrors around the world. Find one close to your geographic location and substitute that address for ftp.kernel.org.

A number of different entries are on the FTP archive site for 2.6.6, but because you are only interested in the full kernel for 2.6.6, it is only necessary to get the full package of source code. There are two of these packages:

```
linux-2.6.6.tar.gz
linux-2.6.6.bz2
```

Although these are the same kernel packages, they're built using different compression utilities: The .gz extension is the gzip package, found on almost every Linux system available. The .bz2 extension is the newer bzip2 utility, which has slightly better compression than gzip. Both packages have the same content, so download the one compressed with the program you use.

Once downloaded, move the package to a directory other than /usr/src and unpack it. If you downloaded the .gz package, the unpacking command is tar -xzvf linux-2.6.6.tar.gz. Otherwise, the bzip2 unpack command is tar -xjvf linux-2.6.6.tar.bz2. Once unpacked, the package will create a new directory, linux-2.6.6. Copy it to /usr/src or move it there. Then, create a symbolic link of linux-2.6 to linux-2.6.6 (otherwise, some scripts won't work). Here's how to create the symbolic link:

```
# rm /usr/src/linux-2.6
# ln -s /usr/src/linux-2.6.6 /usr/src/linux-2.6
```

By creating a symbolic link to /usr/src/linux-2.6, it is possible to allow multiple kernel versions to be compiled and tailored for different functions: You'll just change the symbolic link to the kernel directory you want to work on.

> **CAUTION**
>
> The correct symbolic link is critical to the operation of make. Always have the symbolic link point to the version of the kernel sources you are working with.

Patching the Kernel

It is possible to patch a kernel to the newest Linux kernel version as opposed to downloading the entire source code. This choice can be beneficial for those who aren't using a high-speed broadband connection. (A typical compressed kernel source file is nearly 30MB for a download time of about 10 minutes on a 512Kb DSL connection; adjust accordingly for your connection.) Whether you are patching existing sources or downloading the full source, the end results will be identical.

Patching the kernel isn't a mindless task. It requires the user to retrieve all patches from her current version to the version she wants to upgrade to. For example, if you are currently running 2.6.1 (and have those sources) and want to upgrade to 2.6.8, you must retrieve the 2.6.2, and 2.6.3 patch sets, and so on. Once downloaded, these patches must be applied in succession to upgrade to 2.6.8. This is more tedious than downloading the entire source, but useful for those who keep up with kernel hacking and want to perform incremental upgrades to keep their Linux kernel as up-to-date as possible.

To patch up to several versions in a single operation, you can use the patch-kernel script located in the kernel source directory for the kernel version you currently use. This script applies all necessary version patches to bring your kernel up to the latest version.

The format for using the patch-kernel script looks like this:

```
patch-kernel source_dir patch_dir stopversion
```

The source directory defaults to /usr/src/linux if none is given, and the patch_dir defaults to the current working directory if one isn't supplied.

For example, assume that you have a 2.6.6 kernel code tree that needs to be patched to the 2.6.8 version. The 2.6.7 and 2.6.8 patch files have been downloaded from ftp.kernel.org and are placed in the /patch directory in the source tree. You issue the following command in the /usr/src/linux-2.6 directory:

```
# scripts/patch-kernel /usr/src/linux-2.6.6 /usr/src/linux-2.6.6/patch
```

Each successive patch file is applied, eventually creating a 2.6.8 code tree. If any errors occur during this operation, files named xxx# or xxx.rej are created, where xxx is the version of patch that failed. You will have to resolve these failed patches manually by examining the errors and looking at the source code and the patch. An inexperienced person will not have any success with this because you need to understand C programming and kernel programming to know what is broken and how to fix it. Because this was a stock 2.6.6 code tree, the patches were all successfully applied without errors. If you are attempting to apply a nonstandard third-party patch, the patch might likely fail.

When you have successfully patched the kernel, you are ready to begin compiling this code tree as if we started with a fresh, stock 2.6.8 kernel tree.

Using the patch Command

If you have a special, nonstandard patch to apply—such as a third-party patch for a commercial product, for example—you can use the patch command rather than the special patch-kernel script that is normally used for kernel source updates. Here are some quick steps and an alternative method of creating patched code and leaving the original code alone.

1. Create a directory in your home directory and name it something meaningful, like mylinux.

2. Copy the pristine Linux source code there with

   ```
   cp -ravd /usr/src/linux-2.6/* ~/mylinux
   ```

3. Copy the patch file to that same directory with

   ```
   cp patch_filename ~/mylinux
   ```

4. Change to the ~/mylinux directory with

   ```
   cd ~/mylinux
   ```

5. Apply the patch with

   ```
   patch -p1 < patch_filename  > mypatch.log 2>&1
   ```

(This last bit of code saves the message output to a file so that you can look at it later.)

6. If the patch applies successfully, you are done and haven't endangered any of the pristine source code. In case the newly patched code doesn't work, you won't have to reinstall the original, pristine source code.

7. Copy your new code to /usr/src and make that special symbolic link described elsewhere in the chapter.

Compiling the Kernel

If you want to update the kernel from new source code you have downloaded, or you have applied a patch to add new functionality or hardware support, you'll need to compile and install a new kernel to actually use that new functionality. Compiling the kernel involves translating the kernel's contents from human-readable code to binary form. Installing the kernel involves putting all the compiled files where they belong in /boot and /lib and making changes to the boot loader.

The process of compiling the kernel is almost completely automated by the make utility as is the process of installing. By providing the necessary arguments and following the steps covered next, you can recompile and install a custom kernel for your use.

Here's a checklist of steps to compile and configure the kernel:

1. Verify a working boot disk for the old kernel to be able to reboot your system in case something goes wrong with the new kernel.

> **CAUTION**
>
> Before making any changes to your current, working kernel, make sure that you have a backup copy on a floppy disk. This will allow you to boot into your system with a known working kernel in case something goes wrong during configuration. The command to do this is as follows:
>
> ```
> # mkbootdisk —device /dev/fd0 `uname -r`
> ```
>
> This assumes that your floppy drive is /dev/fd0. (Here's a good shell script tip: the ` character tells the shell to execute what is within ` first and then returns that output as part of the input of the mkbootdisk command.) On this machine, the result is
>
> ```
> # mkbootdisk —device /dev/fd0 2.6.7-1
> ```
>
> This command won't be echoed to your screen, but it is what the system will execute.

2. Apply all patches, if any, so that you have the features you desire. See the previous section for details.

3. Back up the .config file, if it exists, so that you can recover from the inevitable mistake. Use the following cp command:

```
# cp .config .config.bak
```

> **NOTE**
>
> If you are recompiling the Fedora Core default kernel, the `/usr/src/linux-2.6/configs` directory contains several versions of configuration files for different purposes.
>
> Fedora Core provides a full set of `.config` files in the subdirectory configs, all named for the type of system they were compiled for. (For example, `kernel-2.6.7-i686-smp.config` is a configuration file for a multiprocessor Pentium-class computer.) If you want to use one of these default configurations as the basis for a custom kernel, simply copy the appropriate file to `/usr/src/linux-2.6` and rename it `.config`.

4. Run the `make mrproper` directive to prepare the kernel source tree, cleaning out any old files or binaries.

5. Restore the `.config` file that the command `make mrproper` deleted, and edit the Makefile to change the `EXTRAVERSION` number.

> **NOTE**
>
> If you want to keep any current version of the kernel that was compiled with the same code tree, manually edit the `Makefile` with your favorite text editor and add some unique string to the `EXTRAVERSION` variable.
>
> You can use any description you prefer, however.

6. Modify the kernel configuration file using `make config`, `make menuconfig`, or `make xconfig`—we recommend the latter, but read the "Choosing a Configuration Interface" section for details.

7. Run `make dep` to create the code dependencies used later in the compilation process.

> **TIP**
>
> If you have a multiprocessor machine, you can use both processors to speed the make process by inserting `-jx` after the `make` command, where as a rule of thumb, x is one more than the number of processors you have. You might try a larger number and even try this on a single processor machine (we have used `-j8` successfully on an SMP machine); it will only load up your CPU. For example,
>
> `# make -j3 bzImage`
>
> All the make processes except `make dep` will work well with this method of parallel compiling.

8. Run `make clean` to prepare the sources for the actual compilation of the kernel.

9. Run `make bzImage` to create a binary image of the kernel.

> **NOTE**
>
> Several choices of directives exist, although the most common ones are as follows:
>
> zImage—This directive compiles the kernel, creating an uncompressed file called zImage.
>
> bzImage—This directive creates a compressed kernel image necessary for some systems that require the kernel image to be under a certain size for the BIOS to be able to parse them; otherwise, the new kernel won't boot. It's the most commonly used choice. However, the Fedora kernel compiled with bzImage is still too large to fit on a floppy, so a smaller version with some modules and features removed is used for the boot floppies. Fedora recommends that you boot from the rescue CD-ROM.
>
> bzDisk—This directive does the same thing as bzImage, but it copies the new kernel image to a floppy disk for testing purposes. This is helpful for testing new kernels without writing kernel files to your hard drive. Make sure that you have a floppy disk in the drive because you will not be prompted for one.

10. Run `make modules` to compile any modules your new kernel needs.

11. Run `make modules_install` to install the modules in `/lib/modules` and create dependency files.

12. Run `make install` to automatically copy the kernel to `/boot`, create any other files it needs, and modify the boot loader to boot the new kernel by default.

13. Using your favorite text editor, verify the changes made to `/etc/lilo.conf` or `/boot/grub/grub.conf`; fix if necessary and rerun `/sbin/lilo` if needed.

14. Reboot and test the new kernel.

15. Repeat the process if necessary.

Choosing a Configuration Interface

Over time, the process for configuring the Linux kernel has changed. Originally, you configured the kernel by responding to a series of prompts for each configuration parameter (this is the `make config` utility described shortly). Although you can still configure Linux this way, most users find this type of configuration confusing and inconvenient; moving back through the prompts to correct errors, for instance, is impossible.

The `make config` utility is a command-line tool. The utility presents a question regarding kernel configuration options. The user responds with a Y, N, M, or ?. (It's not case sensitive.) Choosing M configures the option to be compiled as a module. A response of ? displays context help for that specific option, if available. (If you choose ? and no help is available, you can turn to the vast Internet resources to find information.) We recommend that you avoid the `make config` utility, shown in Figure 24.1.

24

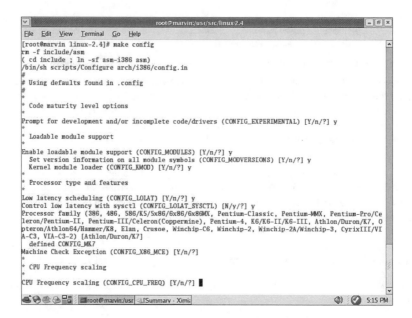

FIGURE 24.1   The make config utility in all its Spartan glory.

If you prefer to use a command-line interface, you can use make menuconfig to configure the Linux kernel. menuconfig provides a graphical wrapper around a text interface. Although it isn't as raw as make config, menuconfig isn't a fancy graphical interface either; you can't use a mouse, but must navigate through it using keyboard commands. The same information presented in make config is presented by make menuconfig, but as you can see in Figure 24.2, it looks a little nicer. Now at least, you can move back and forth in the selection process in case you change your mind or have made a mistake.

In make menuconfig, you use the arrow keys to move the selector up and down and the spacebar to toggle a selection. The Tab key moves the focus at the bottom of the screen to either Select, Exit, or Help.

If a graphical desktop is not available, menuconfig is the best you can do. However, both menuconfig and xconfig (see below) offer an improvement over editing the config file directly. If you want to configure the kernel through a true graphical interface—with mouse support and clickable buttons—make xconfig is the best configuration utility option. To use this utility, you must have the X Window System running. The application xconfig is really nothing but a Tcl/Tk graphics *widget set* (providing borders, menus, dialog boxes, and the like) interface used to wrap around data files that are parsed at execution time. Figure 24.3 shows the main menu of xconfig for the 2.6.7 kernel.

After loading this utility, you use it by clicking on each of the buttons that list the configuration options. Each button you click opens another window that has the detail configuration options for that subsection. Three buttons are at the bottom of each window: Main

Menu, Next, and Prev(ious). Clicking the Main Menu button closes the current window and displays the main window. Clicking Next takes you to the next configuration section. When configuring a kernel from scratch, click the button labeled Code Maturity Level Options, and then continue to click the Next button in each subsection window to proceed through all the kernel configuration choices. When you have selected all options, the main menu is again displayed. The buttons on the lower right of the main menu are for saving and loading configurations. Their functions are self-explanatory. If you just want to have a look, go exploring! Nothing will be changed if you elect not to save it.

FIGURE 24.2   The `make menuconfig` utility, a small improvement over `make config`.

If you are upgrading kernels from a previous release, it isn't necessary to go though the entire configuration from scratch. Instead, you can use the directive `make oldconfig`; it uses the same text interface that `make config` uses, and it is noninteractive. It will just prompt for changes for any new code.

Using `xconfig` to Configure the Kernel

For simplicity's sake, during this brisk walk-through, we will assume that you are using `make xconfig`. Prior to this point, we also assume that you will have completed the first five steps in our kernel compilation checklist shown previously.

As you learned in the preceding section, you configure the kernel using `make xconfig` by making choices in several configuration subsection windows. Each subsection window contains specific kernel options. With hundreds of choices, the kernel is daunting to configure. We can't really offer you detailed descriptions of which options to choose because your configuration will not match your own system and setup.

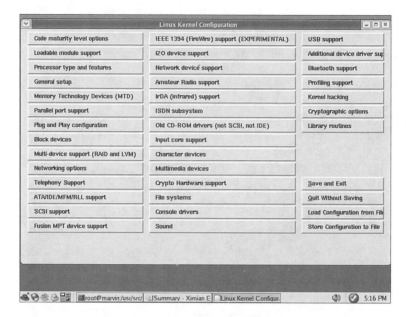

FIGURE 24.3   The much nicer `make xconfig` GUI interface. We recommend that you use this interface.

Table 24.1 provides a brief description of each subsection's options so that you can get an idea of what you might encounter. We recommend that you copy your kernel's `.config` file to `/usr/src/linux-2.6` and run `make xconfig` from there. Explore all the options. As long as you don't save the file, absolutely nothing will be changed on your system.

TABLE 24.1   Kernel Subsections for Configuration

Name	Description
Code maturity level options	Enables development code to be compiled into the kernel even if it has been marked as obsolete or as testing code only. This option should only be used by kernel developers or testers because of the possible unusable state of the code during development.
General setup	This section contains several different options covering how the kernel talks to the BIOS, whether it should support PCI or PCMCIA, whether it should use APM or ACPI, and what kind of Linux binary formats will be supported. Contains several options for supporting kernel structures necessary to run binaries compiled for other systems directly without recompiling the program.

TABLE 24.1   Continued

Name	Description
Loadable module support	Determines whether the kernel enables drivers and other nonessential code to be compiled as loadable modules that can be loaded and unloaded at runtime. This option keeps the basic kernel small so that it can run and respond more quickly; in that regard, choosing this option is generally a good idea.
Processor type and features	Several options dealing with the architecture that will be running the kernel.
Power management options	Options dealing with ACPI and APM power management features.
Bus options	Configuration options for the PCMCIA bus found in laptops and PCI hotplug devices.
Memory technology devices (MTD)	Options for supporting flash memory devices, such as EEPROMS. Generally, these devices are used in embedded systems.
Parallel port support	Several options for configuring how the kernel will support parallel port communications.
Plug and Play configuration	Options for supporting Plug and Play PCI, ISA, and plug-and-play BIOS support. Generally, it is a good idea to support plug-and-play for PCI and ISA devices.
Block devices	Section dealing with devices that communicate with the kernel in blocks of characters instead of streams. This includes IDE and ATAPI devices connected via parallel ports, as well as enabling network devices to communicate as block devices.
ATA/IDE/MFM/RLL support	Large collection of options to configure the kernel to communicate using different types of data communication protocols to talk to mass storage devices, such as hard drives. Note that this section doesn't cover SCSI.
SCSI device support	Options for configuring the kernel to support Small Computer Systems Interface. This subsection covers drivers for specific cards, chipsets, and tunable parameters for the SCSI protocol.
Old CD-ROM drivers	Configuration options to support obscure, older CD-ROM devices that don't conform to the SCSI or IDE standards. These are typically older CD-ROM drivers that are usually a proprietary type of SCSI (not SCSI, not IDE).
Multidevice support (RAID and LVM)	Options for enabling the kernel to support RAID devices in software emulation and the different levels of RAID. Also contains options for support of a logical volume manager.

24

TABLE 24.1   Continued

Name	Description
Fusion MPT device support	Configures support for LSI's Logic Fusion Message Passing Technology. This technology is for high performance SCSI and local area network interfaces.
IEEE1394 (FireWire) support	Experimental support for FireWire devices.
I20 device support	Options for supporting the Intelligent Input/Output architecture. This architecture enables the hardware driver to be split from the operating system driver, thus enabling a multitude of hardware devices to be compatible with an operating system in one implementation.
Networking support	Several options for the configuration of networking in the kernel. The options are for the types of supported protocols and configurable options of those protocols.
Amateur radio support	Options for configuring support of devices that support the AX25 protocol.
IrDA (infrared) support	Options for configuring support of the infrared Data Association suite of protocols and devices that use these protocols.
Bluetooth support	Support for the Bluetooth wireless protocol. Includes options to support the Bluetooth protocols and hardware devices.
ISDN subsystem	Options to support Integrated Services Digital Networks protocols and devices. ISDN is a method of connection to a large area network digitally over conditioned telephone lines, largely found to connect users to ISPs.
Telephony support	Support for devices that enable the use of regular telephone lines to support VOIP applications. This section doesn't handle the configuration of modems.
Input device support	Options for configuring Universal Serial Bus (USB) Human Interface Devices (HID). These include keyboards, mice, and joysticks.
Character devices	Configuration options for devices that communicate to the server in sequential characters. This is a large subsection containing the drivers for several motherboard chipsets.
Multimedia devices	Drivers for hardware implementations of video and sound devices such as video capture boards, TV cards, and AM/FM radio adapter cards.
Graphics support	Configures VGA text console, video mode selection, and support for frame buffer cards.
Sound	Large subsection to configure supported sound card drivers and chipset support for the kernel.

TABLE 24.1   Continued

Name	Description
USB support	Universal Serial Bus configuration options. Includes configuration for USB devices, as well as vendor-specific versions of USB.
File system	Configuration options for supported file system types. See Chapter 10 for a description of the file systems supported by the kernel.
Additional device driver support	A section for third-party patches.
Profiling support	Profiling kernel behavior to aid in debugging and development.
Kernel hacking	This section determines whether the kernel will contain advanced debugging options. Most users won't want to include this option in their production kernels because it increases the kernel size and slows performance by adding extra routines.
Security options	Determines whether NSA Security Enhanced Linux (SELinux) is enabled.
Cryptographic options	Support for cryptography hardware (Fedora patches not found in the "vanilla" kernel sources).
Library routines	Contains zlib compression support.

After you select all the options you want, you can save the configuration file and continue with step 7 in the kernel compiling checklist shown earlier.

Creating an Initial RAM Disk Image

If you require special device drivers to be loaded in order to mount the root file system (for SCSI drives, network cards or exotic file systems, for example), you must create an initial RAM disk image named /boot/initrd.img. For most users, it isn't necessary to create this file, but if you're not certain, it really doesn't hurt. We covered the initrd.img in Chapter 10. To create an initrd.img file, use the shell script /sbin/mkinitrd.

The format for the command is the following:

```
/sbin/mkinitrd file_name kernel_version
```

Where *file_name* is the name of the image file you want created.

mkinitrd looks at /etc/fstab, /etc/modprobe.conf, and /etc/ raidtab to obtain the information it needs to determine which modules should be loaded during boot. For our system, we use

```
# mkinitrd initrd-2.6.7-1.img 2.6.7-1
```

When Something Goes Wrong

Several things might go wrong during a kernel compile and installation, and several clues will point to the true problem. You will see error messages printed to the screen, and some error messages will be printed to the file /var/log/messages, which can be examined with a text editor. If you have followed our directions for patching the kernel, you will need to examine a special error log as well. Don't worry about errors because many problems are easily fixed with some research on your part. Some errors may be unfixable, however, depending on your skill level and the availability of technical information.

Errors During Compile

Although it's rare that the kernel will not compile, there's always a chance that something has slipped through the regression testing. Let's take a look at an example of problem that might crop up during the compile.

It is possible that the kernel compile will crash and not complete successfully, especially if you attempt to use experimental patches, add untested features, or build newer and perhaps unstable modules on an older system. For example, the kernel compile will fail on an older stock Red Hat 7.2 installation using the 2.4.9 kernel when selecting the NTFS file system, either as a loadable module or inline, as shown here:

```
gcc -D__KERNEL__ -I/usr/src/linux-2.4.9/include -Wall -Wstrict-prototypes
-Wno-trigraphs -O2 -fomit-frame-pointer -fno-strict-aliasing -fno-common
-pipe -mpreferred-stack-boundary=2 -march=athlon  -DMODULE -DMODVERSIONS
-include /usr/src/linux-2.4.9/include/linux/modversions.h
Â-DNTFS_VERSION=\"1.1.16\" Â\
   -c -o unistr.o unistr.c
unistr.c: In function `ntfs_collate_names':
unistr.c:99: warning: implicit declaration of function `min'
unistr.c:99: parse error before `unsigned'
unistr.c:99: parse error before `)'
unistr.c:97: warning: `c1' might be used uninitialized in this function
unistr.c: At top level:
unistr.c:118: parse error before `if'
unistr.c:123: warning: type defaults to `int' in declaration of `c1'
unistr.c:123: `name1' undeclared here (not in a function)
unistr.c:123: warning: data definition has no type or storage class
unistr.c:124: parse error before `if'
make[2]: *** [unistr.o] Error 1
make[2]: Leaving directory `/usr/src/linux-2.4.9/fs/ntfs'
make[1]: *** [_modsubdir_ntfs] Error 2
make[1]: Leaving directory `/usr/src/linux-2.4.9/fs'
make: *** [_mod_fs] Error 2
```

At this juncture, you have two options:

- Fix the errors and recompile.

- Remove the offending module or option and wait for the errors to be fixed by the kernel team.

Most users will be unable to fix some errors because of the complexity of the kernel code, although you should not rule out this option. It is possible that someone else discovered the same error during testing of the kernel and developed a patch for the problem: check the Linux kernel mailing list archive. If the problem is not mentioned there, a search on Google might turn up something.

The second option, removing the code, is the easiest and is what most people do in cases in which the offending code is not required. In the case of the NTFS module failing, it is almost expected because NTFS support is still considered experimental and subject to errors. This is primarily because the code for the file system is reverse-engineered instead of implemented via documented standards. Read-only support has gotten better in recent kernels; write support is still experimental.

Finally, should you want to take on the task of trying to fix the problem yourself, this is a great opportunity to get involved with the Linux kernel and make a contribution that could help many others.

If you are knowledgeable about coding and kernel matters, you might want to look in the MAINTAINERS file in the /usr/src/linux-2.6/ directory of the kernel source and find the maintainer of the code. The recommended course of action is to contact the maintainer and see if he is aware of the problems you are having. If nothing has been documented for the specific error, submitting the error to the kernel mailing list is an option. The guidelines for doing this are in the README file in the base directory of the kernel source under the section "If Something Goes Wrong."

Runtime Errors, Boot Loader Problems, and Kernel Oops

Runtime errors occur as the kernel is loading. Error messages are displayed on the screen or written to the /var/log/messages file. Boot loader problems display messages to the screen; no log file is produced. *Kernel oops* are errors in a running kernel, and error messages are written to the /var/log/messages file.

Excellent documentation on the Internet exists for troubleshooting just about every type of error that LILO, GRUB, or the kernel could give during boot. The best way to find this documentation is to go to your favorite search engine and type in the keywords of the error you received. You'll need to adjust the keywords you use as you focus your search.

In this category, the most common problems deal with LILO configuration issues. Diagnosis and solutions to these problems can be found in the LILO mini-HOWTO found on the Linux Documentation project's Web site at http://www.ibiblio.org/pub/Linux/docs/HOWTO/other-formats/html_single/LILO.html.

24

If you have GRUB problems, the GRUB manual is online at `http://www.gnu.org/software/grub/manual/`.

TIP

For best results, go to `http://www.google.com/linux` to find all things Linux on the Internet. Google has specifically created a Linux area of its database, which should allow faster access to information on Linux than any other search engine.

The usenet newsgroup postings are searchable at `http://www.google.com/grphp`.

Mail list discussions can be searched in the Mailing listARChives (MARC) at `http://marc.theaimsgroup.com/`.

Kernel Tuning with `sysctl`

As the Linux kernel developed over time, developers sought a way to fine-tune some of the kernel parameters. Before `sysctl`, those parameters had to be changed in the kernel configuration and then the kernel had to be recompiled.

The `sysctl` command can change some parameters of a running kernel. It does this through the `/proc` file system, which is a "virtual window" into the running kernel. Although it might appear that a group of directories and files exist under `/proc`, that is only a representation of parts of the kernel. We can read values from and write values to those "files," referred to as variables. We can display a list of the variables as shown in the following. (An annotated list is presented because roughly 250 items [or more] exist in the full list.)

```
# sysctl -A
net.ipv4.tcp_max_syn_backlog = 1024
net.ipv4.tcp_rfc1337 = 0
net.ipv4.tcp_stdurg = 0
net.ipv4.tcp_abort_on_overflow = 0
net.ipv4.tcp_tw_recycle = 0
net.ipv4.tcp_syncookies = 0
net.ipv4.tcp_fin_timeout = 60
net.ipv4.tcp_retries2 = 15
net.ipv4.tcp_retries1 = 3
net.ipv4.tcp_keepalive_intvl = 75
net.ipv4.tcp_keepalive_probes = 9
net.ipv4.tcp_keepalive_time = 7200
net.ipv4.ipfrag_time = 30
```

The items shown are networking parameters, and actually tweaking these values is beyond the scope of this book. If we wanted to change a value, however, the -w command is used:

```
# sysctl -w net.ipv4.tcp_retries 2=20
```

This increases the value of that particular kernel parameter.

> **NOTE**
>
> Fedora Core provides a graphical interface to the `sysctl` command in `system-config-proc`. It's still a beta-quality application, and it must be launched from the command line. The interface itself is unremarkable, and it does not provide a means to manipulate all the possible values, but it does offer useful help for the kernel variables it addresses.

If you find that a particular setting is useful, you can enter it into the `/etc/sysctl.conf` file. The format is as follows, using the earlier example:

```
net.ipv4.tcp_retries 2=20
```

Of more interest to kernel hackers than regular users, `sysctl` is a potentially powerful tool that continues to be developed and documented.

> **Relevant Fedora Core and Linux Commands**
>
> You'll use the following commands when managing the kernel and its modules in Fedora Core Linux:
>
> `gcc`—The GNU compiler system
>
> `make`—GNU project and file management command
>
> `mkbootdisk`—Fedora Core's boot disk creation tool
>
> `sysctl`—The interface to manipulating kernel variables at runtime
>
> `mkinitrd`—Create a RAM-disk file system for bootloading support

Reference

`http://www.kernel.org/`—Linux Kernel Archives. The source of all development discussion for the Linux kernel.

`http://www.kerneltraffic.org/kernel-traffic/index.html`—Linux Kernel Traffic. Summarized version and commentary of the Linux Kernel mailing list produced weekly.

`http://www.gnu.org/`—Free Software Foundation. Source of manuals and software for programs used throughout the kernel compilation process. Tools such as `make` and `gcc` have their official documentation here.

`http://slashdot.org/article.pl?sid=01/08/22/1453228&mode=thread`—The famous AC Patches from Alan Cox, for whom they are named.

`http://www.tldp.org/LDP/tlki/`—The Linux Kernel. Online book about the 2.4 Linux kernel describing the internals of the Linux kernel.

http://www.digitalhermit.com/linux/Kernel-Build-HOWTO.html—The Linux Kernel Rebuild Guide; configuration, compilation, and troubleshooting.

http://www.ibiblio.org/pub/Linux/docs/HOWTO/other-formats/html_single/ KernelAnalysis-HOWTO.html—KernelAnalysis HOWTO. Describes the mysterious inner workings of the kernel.

http://www.ibiblio.org/pub/Linux/docs/HOWTO/other-formats/html_single/ _Module-HOWTO.html—Kernel Module HOWTO. Includes a good discussion about unresolved symbols.

http://www.ibiblio.org/pub/Linux/docs/HOWTO/other-formats/html_single/ Modules.html—The Linux Kernel Modules Installation HOWTO; an older document discussing recompiling kernel modules.

http://www.tldp.org/—The Linux Documentation Project. The Mecca of all Linux documentation. Excellent source of HOWTO documentation, as well as FAQs and online books, all about Linux.

http://www.minix.org/—The unofficial minix Web site. It contains a selection of links to information about minix and a link to the actual homepage. Although minix is still copyrighted, the owner has granted unlimited rights to everyone. See for yourself the OS used to develop Linux.

http://jungla.dit.upm.es/~jmseyas/linux/kernel/hackers-docs.html—Web page with links to Linux kernel documentation, books, hacker tomes, and other helpful information for budding and experienced Linux kernel and kernel module developers. This list will also be found in the file /usr/src/linux-2.6/Documentation/kernel-docs.txt if you install the Fedora Core Linux kernel sources.

Productivity Applications

Today's modern businesses are beginning to learn what experienced Linux users have known for years: There are great cost benefits when using Linux and free productivity software. Stepping off the software licensing and upgrade treadmill immediately contributes to the bottom line. This chapter provides some details about popular office productivity software included with and available for Fedora Core Linux. Despite the nay-saying of a few tech industry pundits, Fedora Core Linux can be used to support desktop operations in business settings. You can create efficient personal computing environments by carefully choosing and installing select productivity software packages. A wealth of usable, reliable, and free software is available for Fedora Core Linux.

Productivity clients include free office suites and tools that can be used for creating documents and for scheduling, organizing, and calculating.

In this chapter, we examine the default office productivity applications that Fedora Core provides. You'll see how easy it could be to migrate your employees to Linux desktops because similar applications are available that can make use of existing Microsoft-formatted data files. You'll learn about alternative applications provided by Fedora Core Linux, as well as some applications that you can install yourself. This chapter describes how to install, configure, and launch the applications; information on using the applications is provided only to make you aware of special issues associated with the use of a given application.

Office Suites for Fedora Core Linux

Most office suites include productivity applications, such as word processors, spreadsheet programs, calculators, database programs, and drawing tools. A number of office suites have been created for use with Linux. Many of them are free, but a

IN THIS CHAPTER

- Office Suites for Fedora Core Linux

- PDA Connectivity

- Scanner Applications for Fedora Core Linux

- Web Design Tools

- Fax Client Software

- Other Office and Productivity Tools Included with Fedora Core Linux

- Productivity Applications Written for Microsoft Windows

- Reference

number of commercial products are available as well. Many of these office suites contain applications that mimic the functionality of popular Windows-based productivity applications, and many are designed to be compatible with the file formats of those applications.

Fedora Core has not developed its own office suite, but it has provided a default set of office applications that are designed to have wide appeal and provide useful functionality. The main components, OpenOffice.org and the GNOME Office suite, are included on this book's CD-ROMs. In the following sections, you'll learn about the applications included in these productivity packages and get some tips for installing and configuring them. You'll also learn about the KDE office suite (KOffice) that's included, as well as other office suites that are available for free download or by purchase for use with Linux.

Working with OpenOffice.org

If your primary need is to achieve compatibility with proprietary Microsoft file formats, the OpenOffice.org suite of applications is a front-runner for meeting that need. Microsoft file formats are the most commonly used in business settings, so compatibility with those formats is a primary concern of most businesses that are choosing office suites. OpenOffice.org contains applications that are largely compatible with Microsoft file formats, but they don't offer 100% compatibility. That level of compatibility is impossible for GNU Public License (GPL) applications because the file formats are proprietary and import/export filters must be reverse-engineered. There might be some esoteric formatting that does not import or export well—you can only judge that with a personal test on your own files—but all the basics work well.

Many home Fedora Core users prefer OpenOffice.org because its user interface is similar to (but not identical) that of the Microsoft applications they've used in the past. This interface familiarity is an important point if you are attempting to move from Microsoft Office in your home or office.

OpenOffice.org recognizes and opens nearly 120 file formats and types of documents, ranging from popular commercial office suites to various graphics file formats and is capable of exporting nearly 70 types of documents.

What's in OpenOffice.org?

OpenOffice.org contains a number of productivity applications for use in creating text documents, preparing spreadsheets, organizing presentations, managing projects, and more. The following components of the OpenOffice.org package are included with Red Hat Linux:

- **OpenWriter**—This word processing program enables you to compose, format, and organize text documents. If you are accustomed to using Microsoft Word, the functionality of OpenOffice.org Writer will be familiar to you. The presentation of these functions in the application menus is slightly different from Microsoft Word's, however, so you'll have to hunt for familiar functions. Spell checking, a thesaurus, macros, styles, and a help facility are built in to OpenOffice.org Writer and work in a manner consistent with other word processors and applications.

- **OpenCalc**—This spreadsheet program enables you to manipulate numbers in a spreadsheet format. Support for all but the most esoteric Microsoft Excel functions means that trading spreadsheets with Excel users should be successful. OpenCalc offers some limited compatibility with Excel macros, but those macros will generally have to be rewritten. OpenCalc also supports data exchange formats such as the Data Interchange Format and dBASE format.

- **Impress**—This presentation program is similar to Microsoft PowerPoint and enables you to create slide show presentations that include graphs, diagrams, and other graphics. Impress also works well with PowerPoint files. When it is opened, OpenOffice.org Impress starts with a wizard that steps you through the creation of a new presentation, lets you use an existing template (although none are provided), or allows you to open an existing presentation.

- **Math**—This math formula editor enables you to write mathematical formulas with a number of math fonts and symbols for inclusion in a word processing document. Such symbols are highly specialized and not easily included in the basic functionality of a word processor. It is of interest primarily to math and science writers, but Math can be useful to anyone who needs to include a complex formula in their text.

- **Open Database Connectivity (ODBC)**—You must configure the provided database front end to use MySQL or PostgreSQL (as described in the following sidebar). After you do so, ODBC functions as a database organizer similar to Microsoft Access. (See Chapter 17, "Administering Database Services," for more information on MySQL and PostgreSQL.)

Enabling a Database for OpenOffice.org

OpenOffice.org's cousin, StarOffice, comes with a closed-source database name Adabas. Of course, it can't be included in OO.org, but all the MS Access-like interfaces are already there in OO.org. All it takes to make them useful is installing ODBC for Linux and editing the configuration files to have OO.org use MySQL (or `PostgreSQL`, if you prefer).

A very useful PDF document is available at `http://www.unixodbc.org/doc/OOoMySQL9.pdf`, written by John McCreesh. It provides not only step-by-step instructions with tests to perform along the way, but also provides examples on how to use the newfound database functionality. The document is Red Hat 9–specific (it also provides some information for users of Red Hat 7.3 and 8.0), although nothing appears to have changed in the current Fedora Core that would affect the general instructions.

The directions are summarized as follows:

1. Install, start and test MySQL.
2. Install `MyODBC-2.50.*.i386.rpm` from the Fedora Core CD.
3. Create and edit the `/etc/odbcinst.ini` and `/etc/odbc.ini` files (examples are provided in the PDF document); you need to verify that the links to the libraries described in the example are present on your system and adjust accordingly, then test ODBC per the examples.
4. Step through the examples to explore the new database tool you have installed.

- **OpenDraw**—This graphics application allows you to create images for inclusion in the documents produced with OpenOffice.org. It saves files only in OpenOffice.org format, but it can import most common image formats. It is not meant as a replacement for more general graphics applications, but it has enough features to meet most needs.

- **Dia**—This technical drawing editor from the GNOME Office suite enables you to create measured drawings, such as those used by architects and engineers. Its functionality is similar to that of Microsoft Visio.

- **Planner**—You can use this project management application for project planning, scheduling, and tracking; this application is similar to, but not compatible with, Microsoft Project. It's found in the Office menu as the Project Management item.

A Brief History of OpenOffice.Org

The OpenOffice.org office suite has its roots in an application known as StarOffice. Originally developed by a German company, StarOffice was purchased by Sun Microsystems in the United States. One of the biggest complaints about the old StarOffice was that all the component applications were integrated under a StarOffice "desktop" that looked very much like a Microsoft Windows desktop, including a Start button and menus. This meant that in order to edit a simple document, unneeded applications had to be loaded, making the office suite slow to load, slow to run, and quite demanding on system resources.

After the purchase of StarOffice, Sun Microsystems released a large part of the StarOffice code under the GPL, and development began on what has become OpenOffice.org, which is freely available under the GPL. Sun continued development on StarOffice and released a commercial version as StarOffice 6.0. The significant differences between the free and commercial versions of the software are that StarOffice provides more fonts and more import/export file filters than OpenOffice.org (these filters can't be provided in the GPL version because of licensing restrictions) and StarOffice provides its own relational database, Software AG's Adabas D database. (If you are seeking a free alternative to the StarOffice database, see Chapter 17).

Installing and Configuring OpenOffice.org

Fedora Core Linux provides an RPM package for OpenOffice.org. If you don't install the RPM package during your initial Fedora Core Linux installation, you can install it later, using the Add/remove Applications tool or by using `# rpm -ivh` from the command line.

TIP

OpenOffice.org is constantly improving its productivity applications. You can check the OpenOffice.org Web site (`http://www.openoffice.org/`) for the latest version. The Web site provides a link to download the source or a pre-compiled version of the most current working installation files. A more current version might offer file format support that you need.

The initial Fedora Core installation of OpenOffice.org is done on a systemwide basis, but no individual users are configured. To install local files and use OpenOffice.org, a user can simply click any OpenOffice.org icon on her desktop, and her files are installed by the installation wizard. This initial installation takes some time, and OpenOffice.org unfortunately does not display a dialog about what is going on in the background. During the delay, some users might assume that the application has not started, but that is not the case.

After the automatic file installation, the user sees the first installation screen, as shown in Figure 25.1. This is the only configuration screen she sees, and after the appropriate address book is selected or the dialog is closed, the application is ready for use. This initial configuration screen will not be seen again.

Also shown in Figure 25.1 are icons on the left of the desktop panel that represent the different components of OpenOffice.org as well as other applications. From left to right, beginning with the Fedora Core icon that opens the main menu, the icons represent the Mozilla Web browser, Evolution email, and the Print Manager. The icons displayed on your desktop might vary from those shown here. If you click the Fedora Core icon, the main menu opens, and all the OpenOffice.org applications can be accessed from the Office menu.

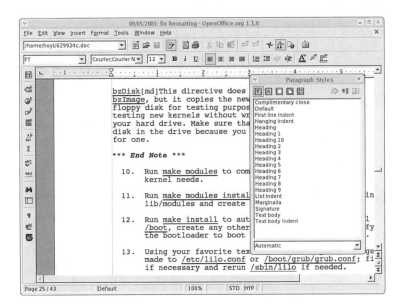

FIGURE 25.1   The OpenOffice.org suite provided by Fedora Core is simple to configure and use. After you configure the address book, the application is ready to go to work.

As with many Linux applications, in OpenOffice.org you can be overwhelmed with configuration options. The dialog to configure those many options is well organized in the OpenOffice.org suite. From the Tools menu (which you open by selecting Tools from the menu bar in any OpenOffice.org application), you select Options to launch the Options dialog, as shown in Figure 25.2. All the settings for the entire suite of applications can be configured from this dialog, and each application provides access to this same dialog. For example, the default work path is set to your home directory, but you can change that default work path. To do so, select Tools, Options to open the dialog. Then click the Paths list item and click and edit the My Documents setting, as shown in Figure 25.2.

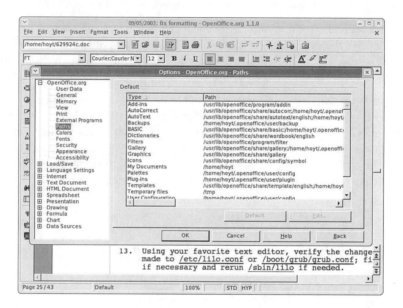

FIGURE 25.2   You can edit the OpenOffice.org path settings to change default locations of files and directories. This configuration dialog sets options for all the OpenOffice.org applications.

TIP

Two Web sites provide additional information on the functionality of OpenOffice.org:

`http://lingucomponent.openoffice.org/download_dictionary.html`—This site provides instructions and files for installing spelling and hyphenation dictionaries, which are not included with OpenOffice.org.

`http://sourceforge.net/projects/ooextras/`—This site provides templates, macros, and clip art, which are not provided with OpenOffice.org.

OpenOffice.org is a work in progress, but the current release is on a par with the Sun version of StarOffice 6.0. You can browse to the OpenOffice.org Web site to get documentation and answers to frequently asked questions and to offer feedback.

Working with GNOME Office

Rather than developing an integrated suite of applications from scratch, the GNOME project has brought together an offering of GTK-based applications from different developers to meet general office needs (see sidebar). Because Sun plans to integrate StarOffice/OpenOffice.org with GNOME, continued support and development for some of the GNOME Office components might be in doubt.

The GTK Widget Set

In order to make it easier to program GUI applications, small pieces of code are prewritten to describe some graphical functions of the graphical interface; these functions include drop-down lists, radio buttons, Save As dialogs, window buttons, and the like. Such functions are referred to as widgets, and the collection of widgets is referred to as a tool kit or a widget set. Rather than write the code for all these functions from scratch, programmers need only reference the widgets. This makes writing GUI applications easier. Whereas Windows and Mac programmers only have one set of widgets to work with, UNIX and Linux programmers have many sets; unfortunately, these sets are incompatible with one another. The KDE desktop uses the QT widget set, Netscape uses the Motif widget set, and GNOME applications use the GTK widget set.

GTK is an acronym for Gimp Tool Kit. The GIMP (The GNU Image Manipulation Program) is a graphics application very similar to Adobe Photoshop. By using the GTK-based jargon, we save ourselves several hundred words of typing and help move along our discussion of GNOME Office. You might also see similar references to QT and Motif, as well as other widget sets, in these chapters.

Here are some of the primary components of the GNOME Office suite that are available in Fedora Core Linux:

- **AbiWord**—This word processing program enables you to compose, format, and organize text documents and has some compatibility with the Microsoft Word file format. It uses plug-ins (programs that add functionality such as language translation) to enhance its functionality.

- **Gnumeric**—This spreadsheet program enables you to manipulate numbers in a spreadsheet format. Support for all but the most esoteric Microsoft Excel functions means that users should have little trouble trading spreadsheets with Excel users.

- **The GIMP**—This graphics application allows you to create images for general use. It can import and export all common graphics file formats. The GIMP is analogous to Adobe's Photoshop application and is described in Chapter 26, "Multimedia Applications."

- **Evolution**—Evolution is a mail client with an interface similar to Microsoft Outlook, providing email, scheduling, and calendaring. It is described in Chapter 19, "Handling Electronic Mail."

25

- **Balsa**—This lightweight mail client is in the mold of Microsoft Outlook Express. It is described in Chapter 19.

The loose association of applications known as GNOME Office includes several additional applications that duplicate the functionality of applications already provided by Fedora Core. Those extra GNOME applications are not included in a default installation of Fedora Core to eliminate redundancy. They are all available from the GNOME Office Web site, at `http://www.gnome.org/projects/ooo/` and some are on the installation CDs.

Fedora Core provides the AbiWord editor, shown in Figure 25.3. AbiWord can import XML, Microsoft Word, RTF, UTF8, plain text, WordPerfect, Kword, and a few other formats. AbiWord is notable for its use of plug-ins, or integrated helper applications, that extend its capabilities. These plug-ins add language translation, HTML editing, a thesaurus, a Linux command shell, and an online dictionary, among other functions and features. If you just need a lightweight but powerful word processing application, you should examine AbiWord.

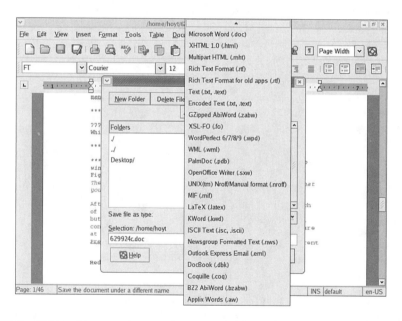

FIGURE 25.3   AbiWord is a word processing program for Fedora Core Linux, GNOME, and X11. It handles some formats that OpenOffice.org cannot, but does not yet do well with MS Word formats.

The AbiWord application icon is found in the More Office Applications menu, under the Office menu (along with Gnumeric and the KOffice applications we'll discuss later in this section) as the Word Processor item. Simply click on the icon to launch the application, or you can launch it from the command line, like this:

```
$ abiword &
```

If you are familiar with Microsoft Works, the AbiWord interface will be familiar to you because its designers used it as their model.

You can use the Gnumeric spreadsheet application to perform financial calculations and to graph data, as shown in Figure 25.4. It can import comma- or tab-separated files, text, or files in the Gnumeric XML format, saving files only as XML or text. To launch Gnumeric from the menu, choose Office, More Office Applications, and then Gnumeric Spreadsheet. You can also launch the spreadsheet editor from the command line, like this:

```
$ gnumeric &
```

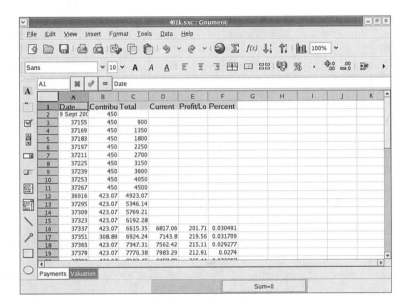

FIGURE 25.4 GNOME's Gnumeric is a capable financial data editor—here being used to track a 401K retirement account. OpenOffice.org also provides a spreadsheet application as does KOffice.

After you press Enter, the main Gnumeric window appears. You enter data in the spreadsheet by clicking a cell and then typing in the text box. To create a graph, you click and drag over the spreadsheet cells to highlight the desired data, and then you click the Graph Wizard icon in Gnumeric's toolbar. Gnumeric's graphing component launches, and you're guided through a series of dialogs to create a graph. When you're finished, you can click and drag a blank area of your spreadsheet, and the graph appears.

The Planner application is useful for tracking the progress of projects, much like its Win32 counterpart Microsoft Project. When the main window is displayed, you can start a new project or import an existing project. The application provides three views: Resources, Gantt Chart, and Tasks.

> **NOTE**
>
> Some productivity applications fall into the category of "groupware"; these include shared calendars, files, notes, email, and the like. These applications are covered in detail in Chapter 19.

Working with KOffice

The K Desktop Environment, known as KDE, is not the default desktop environment for Fedora Core. KDE comes with its own set of libraries, widgets, and a system of inter-application communication (drag-and-drop) that is incompatible with the default Gnome desktop environment. This doesn't mean that the KDE applications are not usable if you choose a GNOME desktop (or vice versa). Although KDE duplicates a lot of the functionality of the Gnome offerings, the KDE applications often present a unique approach to solving familiar problems and might be just what you are looking for.

The KDE office suite KOffice was developed to provide tight integration with the KDE desktop. Integration enables objects in one application to be inserted in other applications via drag-and-drop, and all the applications can communicate with each other, so a change in an object is instantly communicated to other applications. The application integration provided by KDE is a significant enhancement to productivity. (Some GNOME desktop applications share a similar communication facility with each other.) If you use the KDE desktop instead of the default GNOME desktop, you can enjoy the benefits of this integration, along with the Konqueror Web and file browser.

The word processor for KOffice is KWord. KWord is a frames-based word processor, meaning that document pages can be formatted in framesets that hold text, graphics, and objects in enclosed areas. Framesets can be used to format text on a page that includes columnar text and images that the text needs to flow around, making KWord an excellent choice for creating documents other than standard business letters, such as newsletters and brochures.

KWord and other components of KOffice are still under development and lack all the polished features of OpenOffice.org and AbiWord, as well as the necessary Microsoft file format support. If Microsoft compatibility is unimportant to you and you and your associates use the KDE desktop environment rather than GNOME, KOffice is worth considering. The next version of KOffice will include the Kolab groupware applications referred to in Chapter 19; GNOME lacks similar groupware functionality at present.

You can access the KOffice components from the More Office Applications submenu under the Office menu. You can also access them from the KOffice shell, which can be launched from the command line, like this:

```
$ koshell &
```

After you press Enter, you see the main window of KOffice shell, as shown in Figure 25.5. On the left are icons representing all the KOffice applications available to you. Clicking on one starts a dialog to open an existing file or begin work in a new file.

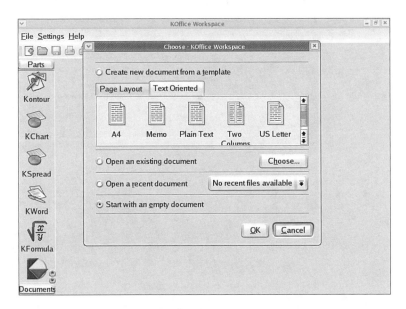

FIGURE 25.5   KDE's KOffice provides a workspace office suite environment. Here is the Open File dialog.

You can click on icons on the left side of the main window to launch the KWord word processing client, the KSpread spreadsheet program, and other components. You can also launch individual clients from the command line without using the KOffice workspace. For example, to use KWord, enter the following:

```
$ kword &
```

KWord then asks you to select a document for your session. The KWord client, shown in Figure 25.6, offers sophisticated editing capabilities, including desktop publishing.

The KOffice KSpread client is a functional spreadsheet program that offers graphing capabilities. Like KWord, KSpread can also be launched from the command line. After you use a command like this, you are asked to choose a type of document (new or previous document):

```
$ kspread &
```

KSpread is still in development and (at the time of this writing) had difficulty importing the Gnumeric spreadsheet used in an earlier example in Gnumeric format. When developed, a strength of KSpread will be its ability to share data with other KOffice applications.

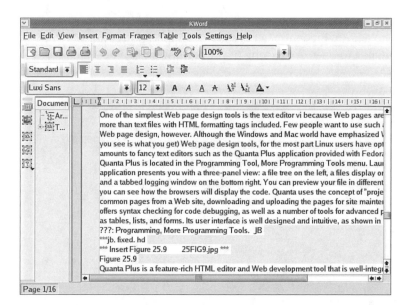

FIGURE 25.6 The KOffice KWord word processing component is a sophisticated frames-based WYSIWYG editor that is suitable for light desktop publishing, supporting several formats, including WordPerfect.

KDE includes other productivity clients in its collection of KOffice and related applications. These clients include an address book, time tracker, calculator, notepad, and scheduler. One popular client is KOrganizer, which provides daily, weekly, work week, and monthly views of tasks, to-do lists, and scheduled appointments with background alarms. A journal, or diary, function is also supported within it, and you can synchronize information with your Palm Pilot by using KPilot (discussed later in the section "GUI PDA Client Software"). You can launch this client from the KDE desktop panel's menu or from the command line, like this:

```
$ korganizer &
```

A typical KOrganizer window is shown in Figure 25.7.

Commercial Office Suites for Linux

Several commercial office suites are available for Linux in addition to StarOffice, already mentioned. None of these commercial suites are provided with Fedora Core. Of note is Hancom Office. Using the same QT widget set found in the KDE desktop, Hancom Office scores well on Microsoft file format compatibility. The suite includes a word processor, a spreadsheet presentation tool, and a graphics application. Corel produced a version of its WordPerfect Office 2000 for Linux before it discontinued the release of any new Linux products. It still offers a support page, but the software is no longer available, nor is the excellent—but whiskered—WordPerfect8 for Linux.

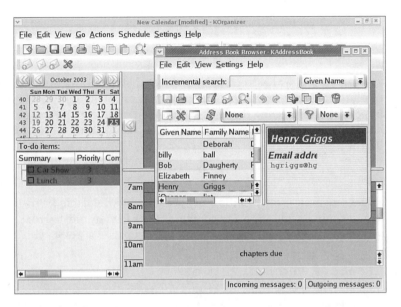

FIGURE 25.7 KDE's KOrganizer client supports editing of tasks and schedules that you can sync with your PDA. Shown here is the address book as well.

PDA Connectivity

Fedora Core Linux provides programs and clients for use with Palm-type personal digital assistants (PDAs). You can use these programs to transfer information to and from a PDA, send and retrieve email, manage and sync your calendaring programs, and more.

Command-Line PDA Software for Fedora Core Linux

The most popular PDA-related software suite is the collection of utilities included with the `pilot-link` package. You can use this application from the command line to perform a variety of tasks with your Palm, Handspring, Handera, TRGPro, or Sony PDA, including the following:

- Extracting and uploading addresses
- Installing date book information
- Transferring text memos to and from the PDA
- Managing PDA to-do lists
- Managing user settings
- Sending and retrieving email documents
- Installing new PDA programs

- Backing up, syncing, and restoring the contents of a PDA

- Acquiring expense database account information

You use `pilot-xfer` without a GUI to perform many of these tasks; the suite of commands includes 31 separate programs. After configuring the software, determining the proper serial (or USB) port, and connecting the PDA to a desktop or notebook PC that is running Fedora Core Linux, you can back up the contents of the PDA with the `pilot-xfer` command, like this:

```
$ pilot-xfer -p /dev/ttyS1 -b backupdirectory
```

This command automatically creates a directory according to the name following the `-b` option and then downloads and saves the contents of the PDA in the designated directory. The full set of pilot-link commands is explored in the `man` page for `pilot-link`.

GUI PDA Client Software

Fedora Core provides the GNOME `gpilot` graphical interface to these commands, which is not included as an item in the menu system. Fedora does provide a Gnome panel applet that can be configured by starting it from the command line as

```
$ gpilotd-control-applet &
```

which leads you through a setup wizard that does little more than allow you to configure the port and sync the PDA.

Another graphical PDA client, shown in Figure 25.8, is the comprehensive J-Pilot application. It will manage, retrieve, install, back up, and sync any information for your Palm-related PDA. You can click on the Date Book, To-Do List, Address Book, and Memo Pad buttons to perform related tasks. You use the Sync and Backup buttons to update or preserve a copy of a PDA's data. Open this client by choosing J-Pilot from the Accessories, More Accessories menu.

> **NOTE**
>
> Fedora Core provides several mail clients for your use—with Evolution (a Microsoft Outlook work-alike) being provided as the default. All the mail clients are covered in detail in Chapter 19. Graphics applications, including The GIMP, are discussed in Chapter 26.

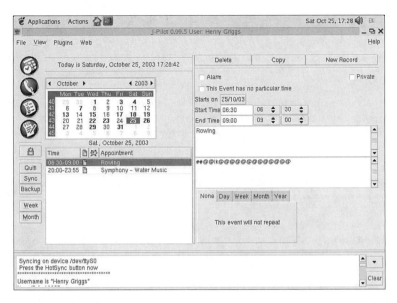

FIGURE 25.8   The J-Pilot PDA client supports PalmOS devices, shown here syncing with one.

Scanner Applications for Fedora Core Linux

The use of a scanner provides a wealth of options to enhance productivity. You can manipulate scanned images in graphics applications such as The GIMP, OpenDraw, and Kontour and then print, fax, or embed them in a word processing document. You can scan paper documents for archival purposes, or you can process them with optical character recognition (OCR) software to translate images into words that can be edited in a text editor or word processor. Fedora Core provides the Xsane and Kooka applications to assist you with scanning.

Scanner support is provided by Scanner Access Now Easy (SANE). If your scanner is supported, it is listed on the SANE support page at `http://www.sane-project.org/`.

NOTE

The development version of SANE supports scanners that aren't supported in the regular version. If your scanner is supported only in the development version, you need to download and compile the CVS version of SANE. That's a complex operation suitable for advanced Linux users only, and it is beyond the scope of this chapter. For information on that process, see the CVS-RCS HOWTO Document for Linu (Source Code Control System) at `http://www.tldp.org/HOWTO/_CVS-RCS-HOWTO.html`.

The VueScan Scanner Application

If your scanner doesn't support SANE, you might consider the excellent VueScan scanner application. VueScan, available from `http://www.hamrick.com/`, supports more scanners than SANE. It is designed for photography professionals but is easy to use. A full list of VueScan's supported scanners can be found at `http://www.hamrick.com/vuescan/vuescan.htm#supported`.

You can download VueScan for evaluation. The program is unrestricted but places a watermark on any scan until you purchase a serial number (current cost: U.S. $60; U.S. $80 for upgrades past 12 months). The site offers some of the best documentation and support concerning scanner usage we have seen.

VueScan provides features in addition to scanning commands that allow you to crop, rotate, and color correct images. A detailed tutorial on using VueScan can be found at `http://homepage.mac.com/onelucent/VS/vsm.html`.

The Xsane application, as shown in Figure 25.9, is a graphical front end to SANE. It allows you to acquire and manipulate scanned images. It can be run as a plug-in from The GIMP. (The GIMP is discussed in more detail in Chapter 26.)

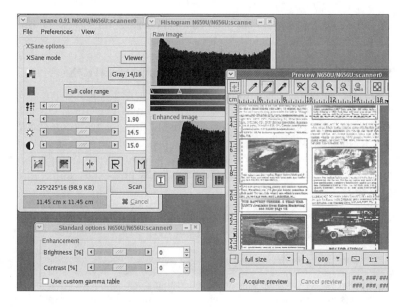

FIGURE 25.9   Upon starting, Xsane presents several related screens on your desktop: a control interface, a histogram, a preview screen, and an options dialog.

Kooka is a KDE application that provides similar functionality to Xsane, but it provides OCR capabilities as well as an image gallery function. Because Kooka is a KDE application, it can provide scanning services to other KDE applications (such as KOffice and KView) if they are written to use it. Kooka uses gocr (`http://jocr.sourceforge.net/`) as an application for character recognition, but support for Clara OCR (`http://www.claraocr.org/`) is planned for the future.

The configuration of scanner devices is covered in detail in Chapter 26.

Web Design Tools

One of the simplest Web page design tools is the text editor `vi` because Web pages are really nothing more than text files with HTML formatting tags included. Few people want to use such a simple tool for Web page design, however. Although the Windows and Mac world have emphasized WYSIWYG (what you see is what you get) Web page design tools, for the most part Linux users have opted for what amounts to fancy text editors such as the Quanta Plus application provided with Fedora Core.

Quanta Plus is located in the Programming Tool, More Programming Tools menu. Launching the application presents you with a three-panel view: a file tree on the left, a files display on the upper right, and a tabbed logging window on the bottom right. You can preview your file in different browsers so that you can see how the browsers will display the code. Quanta uses the concept of "projects" to manage common pages from a Web site, downloading and uploading the pages for site maintenance. Quanta offers syntax checking for code debugging, as well as a number of tools for advanced page elements such as tables, lists, and forms. Its user interface is well designed and intuitive, as shown in Figure 25.10.

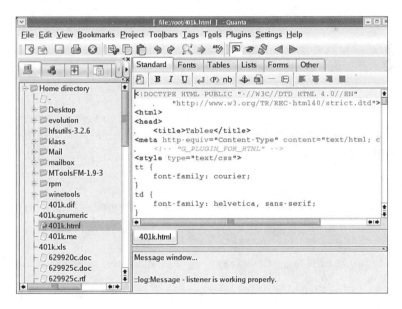

FIGURE 25.10   Quanta Plus is a feature-rich HTML editor and Web development tool that is well-integrated into KDE.

The following are some of the many Web development tools that are not provided with Fedora Core:

- **Bluefish**—Found at `http://bluefish.openoffice.nl/`, Bluefish is a GTK-based HTML editor similar in function to Quanta Plus. It supports anti-aliased fonts and UTF8 encoding, so it is compatible with Fedora Core Linux.

- **IBM WebSphere Studio Homepage Builder**—A commercial application, available at `http://www-3.ibm.com/software/awdtools/hpbuilder/`, is a WYSIWYG editor from Big Blue.

- **Coffee Cup**—A free commercial editor available at `http://www.coffeecup.com/linux/`, Coffee Cup provides a number of preconfigured templates and Java code examples.

OpenOffice.org (included with Fedora Core Linux) can also be used as an effective HTML editor. From the File:Autopilot menu in OpenOffice.org Writer, you select the Web Page Wizard to create HTML pages.

> **NOTE**
>
> Fedora Core Linux includes a wealth of other tools you can use to create Web pages or intranet content. See Chapter 16, "Apache Web Server Management," for information on how to set up, start, and run Apache, the Web server for Fedora Core Linux.

Fax Client Software

Fedora Core Linux provides several clients that handle different aspects of composing, viewing, and sending faxes. Two graphical clients are available: The KFax application is used to view faxes, and the KdeprintFax application is used to send faxes and comment a cover sheet for them. The XSane application can also be used to fax scanned images. The actual sending and receiving of faxes is handled by the Efax application, a command line application (see Figure 25.11).

You can use any text editor to create the document you will be faxing. If you want something fancy, you can select the OpenOffice.org Fax Wizard from the File:Autopilot menu and it will step you through the creation of an elaborate fax document. You can also choose to simply select a plain-text document with KdeprintFax, edit the cover page, and send it.

You access KdeprintFax through the Accessories, More Accessories menu. To use it, you add the file you want to fax by using the Add File dialog. You can view the file by clicking the View File button. The application provides an address book for your use. Note the "Efax" field in the bottom right of the screen, which confirms that Efax will be used to actually send the fax.; KdeprintFax simply collects the information and uses Efax to actually do the sending.

FIGURE 25.11 KdeprintFax allows you to send faxes from your Linux desktop. It's a GUI front end to Efax, a command-line application.

> **NOTE**
>
> Using multiple fax applications might seem unnecessarily complicated to fax users who are used to sending and receiving their faxes on their own machine through a modem connected to that machine. The Linux (and UNIX) approach is more complicated because it is network focused. A single computer can be set up to send and receive faxes for the entire network of hundreds of computers. None of the individual computers has a need for Efax or a fax modem; they just need a fax reader/viewer and a convenient way to send them a fax document to the central fax server.

The `/usr/bin/fax` script provides a simple command-line interface to Efax that allows you to send, receive, view, or print faxes without a GUI. You can view the commands available for faxing by entering **fax help** at the command line. You can use the **fax make** command to turn a text file into a fax file. Fedora Core also provides the `efix` command-line application to convert files formats from `fax`, `text`, `bitmap`, and `grayscale` formats, if necessary. All these applications can be called from scripts to automate the process of converting fax messages, so the end user never has to bother with it.

> **TIP**
>
> You can find more information on the workings of `fax` and Efax in the `man` pages and at the Efax home page at `http://www.cce.com/efax/documentation/`.

Efax is really designed for a single user; there are other fax applications mentioned here that can handle entire offices. If you have more that one fax user, Efax is likely to be too simple for your needs.

HylaFax is a fax management application that can utilize fax modems distributed around a network and service a large number of users because of its client/server architecture. A FAQ is maintained at the HylaFax Web site at `http://www.hylafax.org/HylaFAQ/index.html`. RPM packages for Red Hat are available from the HylaFax FTP site at `ftp://ftp.hylafax.org/binary/linux/redhat/RPMS/i386/`, as are a HOWTO, setup information, and a FAQ.

The traditional Linux way to handle faxes has been with `mgetty+sendfax`. The `mgetty+sendfax` application involves `mgetty`, a modem-aware `getty`. (`getty` is an application that interacts with a terminal, known as a "tty," from its Teletype heritage.). Unfortunately, the configuration of `mgetty+sendfax` is complex and beyond the scope of this chapter. You can find complete documentation for the installed version of `mgetty+sendfax` from the CD-ROMs that accompany this book, under the `/usr/share/doc/mgetty-1.1.30` directory. The files also include a directory of instructions on how to set up voice mail by using the `vgetty` command (`vgetty` is included in the `mgetty+sendfax` package), which is discussed in more detail in Chapter 15, "Internet Connectivity." The documentation for `mgetty` can be found at `http://alpha.greenie.net/mgetty/`, which includes a HOWTO and a FAQ and the `vgetty` documentation is at `http://alpha.greenie.net/vgetty/`.

Other Office and Productivity Tools Included with Fedora Core Linux

Fedora Core Linux is distributed with a number of other useful productivity tools. Under the Accessories menu choice, you can find a calculator, a Web-based dictionary to access the MIT dictionary server (see Figure 25.12), and a lightweight text editor. You can also open the Graphics menu to access a PDF document viewer. (OpenOffice.org can create PDF documents for you.)

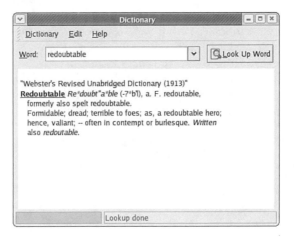

FIGURE 25.12   The Web-enabled Dictionary, found under the Accessories menu, can also be conveniently called from a KDE panel applet.

Under the More Accessories menu, there are a multitude of useful small applications, including these:

- The KHexEdit application, an editor for hexadecimal code files

- The Kjots note taking application

- The KTimer, an application to time the execution time of other applications

The "More" menus also include items for other programming environments, graphics viewers, and dozens of other applications, including games. You should take some time to search through the "More" menus and experiment with some of the productivity (and non–productivity) tools you find there.

A Look at an Open-Source Office

Mark Davis, the director of Information Systems at Lake Taylor Transitional Care Hospital (LTH) in Norfolk, Virginia (http://www.laketaylor.org), has recently transitioned the facility from the use of SCO UNIX to Linux and has enhanced office productivity.

Because LTH uses a thin-client topology and all applications are served from a central location to X terminals located throughout the facility, special attention to network bandwidth issues was necessary. Although it was recognized that commercial applications would be used when no viable open-source alternative was available, applications that emphasized nonproprietary, open standards were given the highest consideration. Using open-source applications allowed Davis to edit the source code and customize the applications for use at LTH, permitting the easy integration of applications into the overall system.

A common modification was to remove functionality that represented potential security compromises (such as access to command prompts or unneeded functions) and to reduce network bandwidth (such as removing animated icons and splash screens).

With the new Linux system in place, the LTH staff enjoys a work environment that presents all the productivity applications necessary in a modern business. The total cost of ownership (TCO) is significantly reduced, and the system is as stable as or more stable than when LTH used the commercial SCO UNIX.

Among others, the open-source applications used at LTH are: Mozilla, Dillo, HylaFax, OpenOffice, Seyon, Sylpheed-claws, IceWM, The GIMP, Apache, Postfix, Gnumeric, Ghostscript, J-Pilot, Quanta, WebCal, Dia, gdict, and VNC. LTH uses a number of commercial applications, including Recital, Netscape, WordPerfect, FoxBASE, Merge, Applixware, Gerimenu, Context Codelink, Monette Ultracare, Kronos Time Keeper Central, and AIS Xess. Because one vendor (that could not be replaced) would not provide a UNIX version of its application, a single computer running Microsoft Windows (modified to limit security problems) is now used along with VNC to run the application.

Productivity Applications Written for Microsoft Windows

Microsoft Windows is fundamentally different from Linux except you can install and run some Microsoft Windows applications in Linux by using an application named Wine. Wine enables you to use Microsoft Windows and DOS programs on UNIX-based systems. Wine includes a program loader that you can use to execute a Windows binary, along with a `.dll` library that implements Windows command calls, translating them to the equivalent UNIX and X11 command calls. Because of frequent updates to the Wine codebase, Wine is not included with Fedora Core. Download a current version of Wine from `http://www.winehq.org/`.

To see if your favorite application is supported by Wine, you can look at the Wine application database at `http://appdb.winehq.org/appbrowse.php`.

As well, there are other solutions to using Microsoft productivity applications, primarily Codweaver's Crossover and Transgaming's implementations of Wine.

Relevant Fedora Core Linux Commands

The following commands give you access to productivity applications, tools, and processes in Fedora Core Linux:

`fax`—A script that acts as a front end to the Efax application

`gimp`—A graphical image editor for X

`koshell`—KDE's KOffice office suite shell

`kspread`—KDE's KSpread spreadsheet

`oowriter`—The word processor in OpenOffice.org

`gnumeric`—A spreadsheet editor for GNOME

`planner`—A project management client for GNOME

`abiword`—A graphical word processor for GNOME

`pilot-xfer`—A comprehensive command-line tool for PalmOS PDA users

Reference

`http://www.openoffice.org`—The home page for the OpenOffice.org office suite.

`http://www.pclinuxonline.com/modules.php?name=News&file=article&sid=3199`—A set of links to tips, tricks, and enhancements for OpenOffice.org. One link at the site is to a PDF file that explains how to use OpenOffice.org as a database front end for MySQL.

`http://www.gnome.org/projects/ooo/`—The GNOME Office site.

`http://www.koffice.org`—The home page for the KOffice suite.

`http://en.hancom.com/`—The home page for the Hancom Office suite.

`http://www.sun.com/software/star/staroffice/6.0/`—The StarOffice 6.0 site.

`ftp://ftp.corel.com/pub/linux/Office2000/updates/installscript`—A download site for an improved installer script that enables a less error-prone installation of Corel's WordPerfect Office 2000 suite under Red HatFedora Core Linux and other distributions.

`http://bulldog.tzo.org/webcal/webcal.html`—The home page of the excellent WebCal Web-based calendar and scheduling program.

`http://quanta.sourceforge.net`—The Quanta Plus Web development tool for KDE.

`http://www.kronos.com/products/TKC.htm`—A Linux-based timekeeping system that supports open standards and is more affordable that the competition.

`http://www.hgriggs.com/palm.html`—Tutorial and exposition on getting a Palm Pilot device working with Linux as well as several useful applications.

25

Multimedia Applications

IN THIS CHAPTER

- Burning CDs and DVDs in Fedora Core Linux

- Sound and Music

- Viewing TV and Video

- Using Still Cameras with Fedora Core Linux

- Using Scanners in Fedora Core Linux

- Graphics Manipulation

- Linux Gaming

- Reference

Movies, music, animation, live video conferencing, and other multimedia functions have become essential capabilities for many home and business computing environments. Without question, multimedia has driven the growth of the Internet and the advances in computer hardware as much as the traditional services of mail, news, and other Internet-related services.

Fedora Core Linux includes several different programs you can use to perform feats of magic that include graphics, video, and audio formats used on other, less capable operating systems.

This chapter provides an overview of some of the basic multimedia tools included with Fedora Core Linux. You'll see how to create your own CDs, watch TV, rip audio CDs into the open source OGG audio format for playback, scan and manipulate graphics images, and perform other productive and enjoyable tasks.

> **NOTE**
>
> Continuing a move begun with the release of Red Hat 9, Fedora maintains a philosophy that has been controversial with many longtime users. Because of concerns of potential liability arising from copyright and patent issues in the United States, Red Hat and Fedora have voluntarily removed any functionality that could violate the intellectual property rights of others or subject Red Hat to any penalties. That doesn't mean individual users would be violating those same rights, so we have provided resources to the reader as to how some of that functionality can be restored; the choice is yours.
>
> By installing and using APT or YUM as described in Chapter 8, "Managing Software and System Resources," you can easily restore full multimedia functionality to Fedora.

Because Fedora Core uses UTF-8 language encoding, some non-Fedora applications will have display problems if they are not UTF-8 compliant. You can fix this by placing the following line in /etc/bashrc:

```
export LANG=en_US SUPPORTED="en_US"
LC_MESSAGES=C LC_ALL=C
```

Burning CDs and DVDs in Fedora Core Linux

Burning (or creating) your own CDs is a fundamental skill for Linux multimedia enthusiasts. The CD and DVD (Digital Video Disc) have become the standard media for multimedia content because of the increasingly larger size of typical media files. (Individual songs, even in compressed audio format, usually require several megabytes of storage space.) You can use CDs to

- Record and store multimedia data, such as backup files, graphic images, and music, on a CD.

- Rip audio tracks from a music CD (ripping refers to extracting music tracks from a music CD) and compile your own music CD for your personal use.

Linux audio clients and programs support the creation and use of many different types of audio formats. Later sections of this chapter discuss sound formats, sound cards, music players, and much more. Because CD burning is used for many other purposes in Fedora Core Linux, we cover the essentials of that process first in this chapter. To record multimedia data on a CD, you must have installed a drive with CD-write capabilities on your system. Chapter 4, "Post-Installation Issues," explains the rudiments of getting a CD writer configured and working properly. The hardware should have been set up properly during the initial Fedora installation or configured properly when detected by Kudzu. To make certain that your CD writer is working, use cdrecord -scanbus to get the information for using the CD drive under SCSI (small computer system interface) emulation:

```
# cdrecord -scanbus
Cdrecord-Clone 2.01a32-dvd (i686-pc-linux-gnu) Copyright (C) 1995-2001 Jörg
Schilling
Linux sg driver version: 3.5.27
Using libscg version 'schily-0.8'
scsibus0:
        0,0,0     0) 'HL-DT-ST' 'RW/DVD GCC-4120B' '2.01' Removable CD-ROM
        0,1,0     1) *
        0,2,0     2) *
        0,3,0     3) *
        0,4,0     4) *
        0,5,0     5) *
```

```
0,6,0    6) *
0,7,0    7) *
```

Here, we see that the CD writer (in this example, a CD writer/DVD reader) is present and is known by the system as device `0,0,0`. The numbers represent the scsibus/target/lun (logical unit number) of the device. You'll need to know this device number when you burn the CD, so write it down or remember it.

TIP

An IDE drive used to create CDs and DVDs needs to be emulated as a SCSI drive. Fedora does this automatically when you first install it, but in case you need to do it manually, here are the few items you need to configure (assuming that the CD drive is at `/dev/hdd`):

- Add the following line to the `/etc/modules.conf` file:

  ```
  probeall ide-scsi
  ```

- Edit the `/boot/grub/menu.1st` file to add the following to the kernel commands:

  ```
  hdd=ide-scsi
  ```

- Reboot your computer.

These items will load the appropriate modules and provide SCSI emulation. You would no longer refer to the CD drive as `/dev/hdd`, but as `/dev/scd0`. Check the symbolic for `/dev/cdrom` to make certain that it points to `/dev/scd0`.

When the 2.6 kernel is used, SCSI emulation will not be needed.

Creating CDs from the Command Line

In Linux, creating a CD is a two-step process. You first create the `iso9660`-formatted image, and you then burn or write the image onto the CD. The `iso9660`, as you learned in Chapter 10, is the default file system for CD-ROMs.

Use the `mkisofs` command to create the ISO image. The `mkisofs` command has many options (see the man page for a full listing), but use the following for quick burns:

```
$ mkisofs -r -v -J -l -o /tmp/our_special_cd.iso /source_directory
```

The options used in this example are as follows:

- `-r`—Sets the permission of the files to more useful values. UID and GID (individual and group user ID requirements) are set to zero, all files are globally readable and searchable, and all files are set as executable (for Windows systems).

- `-v`—Displays verbose messages (rather than terse messages) so that you can see what is occurring during the process; these messages can help you resolve problems if they occur.

-J—Uses the Joliet extensions to ISO9660 so that our Windows-using buddies can more easily read the CD. The Joliet (for Windows), Rock Ridge (for UNIX), and HSF (for Mac) extensions to the iso9660 standard are used to accommodate long filenames rather than the eight-character DOS filenames that the iso9660 standard supports.

-l—Allows 31 character filenames; DOS won't like it, but everyone else does.

-o—Defines the directory where the image will be written (that is, the output) and its name. The /tmp directory is convenient for this purpose, but the image could go anywhere you have write permissions.

/source_directory—Indicates the path to the source directory; that is, the directory containing the files we want to include. There are ways to append additional paths and exclude directories (and files) under the specified path—it's all explained in the man page if you need that level of complexity. Our simple solution is to construct a new directory tree and populate it with the files we want to copy, and then make the image using that directory as the source.

Many more options are available, including options to make the CD bootable.

After you've created the ISO image, you can write it to the CD with the cdrecord command:

```
$ cdrecord -eject -v speed=12 dev=0,0,0 /tmp/our_special_cd.iso
```

The options used in this example are as follows:

-eject—Ejects the CD when the write operation is finished.

-v—Displays verbose messages.

speed=—Sets the speed; the rate depends on the individual drive's capabilities. If the drive or the recordable medium is poor, you can use lower speeds to get a good burn.

dev=—Specifies the device number of the CD writer (the number I told you to write down earlier).

NOTE

You can also use the blank= option with the cdrecord command to erase CD-RW disks. The cdrecord command has fewer options than does mkisofs, but it offers the -multi option, which enables you to make multi-session CDs. A multi-session CD enables you to write a data track, quit, and then add more data to the CD later. A single session CD can be written to only once; any leftover CD capacity is wasted. Read about other options in the cdrecord man page.

Current capacity for CD media is 700MB of data or 80 minutes of music. (There are 800MB/90 minuted CDs, but they are rare.) Some CDs can be over burned; that is, recorded to a capacity in excess of the standard. The cdrecord command is capable of overburning if your CD-RW drive supports it. You can learn more about overburning CDs at http://www.cdmediaworld.com/hardware/cdrom/cd_oversize.shtml/.

Creating DVDs from the Command Line

There are several competing formats for DVD (Digital Versatile Disk), and with prices rapidly falling, it is more likely that DVD-writing drives will become commonplace. The formats are as follows:

DVD+R

DVD-R

DVD+RW

DVD-RW

Differences in the + and − formats have mostly to do with how the data is modulated onto the DVD itself with the + format having an edge in buffer underrun recovery. How this is achieved impacts the playability of the newly created DVD on any DVD player. The DVD+ format also has some advantages in recording on scratched or dirty media. Most drives support the DVD+ format. As with any relatively new technology, Your Mileage May Vary.

We will focus on the DVD+RW drives because most drives sold support that standard. The software supplied with Fedora Core has support for writing to DVD-R/W (re-writable) media as well. It will be useful for you to review the DVD+RW/+R/-R[W] for Linux HOWTO at `http://fy.chalmers.se/~appro/linux/DVD+RW/` before attempting to use the `dvd+rw-tools` you'll need to install to enable DVD creation (also known as "mastering") as well as the `cdrtools` package. You can ignore the discussion in the HOWTO about kernel patches, compiling the tools.

> **TIP**
>
> The 4.7GB size of DVD media is measured as 1000 Megabytes per Gigabyte, instead of the more commonly used 1024 Megabytes per Gigabyte, so don't be surprised when the actual formatted capacity, about 4.4GB, is less than you anticipated. The `dvd+rw-tools` will not allow you to exceed the capacity of the disk.

You need to have the `dvd+rw-tools` package installed (as well as the `cdrtools` package). The `dvd+rw-tools` package contains the `growisofs` application (that acts as a front end to `mkisofs`) as well as the DVD formatting utility.

You can use DVD media to record data in two ways. The first way is much the same as that used to record CDs in a "session," and the second way is to record the data as a true file system using packet writing.

Session Writing

To record data in a session, you use a two-phase process:

- Format the disk with `dvd+rw-format /dev/scd0` (only necessary the first time you use a disk).

26

- Write your data to the disk with growisofs -Z /dev/scd0 -R -J /your_files

The growisofs command simply streams the data to the disk. For subsequent sessions, use the -M argument instead of –Z. The -Z argument is used only for the initial session recording; if you use the -Z argument on an already used disk, it simply erases the existing files.

TIP

Writing a first session of at least 1Gb helps maintain compatibility of your recorded data with other optical drives. This is because the DVD players calibrate themselves by attempting to read from specific locations on the disk; you need data there for the drive to read it and calibrate itself.

Also, because of limitations to the ISO9660 file system in Linux, do not start new sessions of a multi-session DVD that would create a directory past the 4GB boundary. If you do so, it will cause the offsets used to point to the files to "wrap around" and point to the wrong files.

Packet Writing

Packet writing treats the DVD disk like a hard drive in which you create a file system (like ext3) and "format" the disk, and then write to it randomly like a conventional hard drive. This method, although commonly available on MS Windows computers, is still experimental for Linux and is not yet covered in detail here.

TIP

DVD+RW media are capable of only about 1,000 writes, so it is very useful to mount them with the noatime option to eliminate any writing to update their inodes or simply mount them read-only when it's not necessary to write to them.

It is possible to pipe data to the growisofs command:

```
# your_application ¦ growisofs -Z /dev/scd0=/dev/fd/0
```

It's also possible to burn from an existing image (or file, named pipe, or device):

```
# growisofs -Z /dev/scd0=image
```

The dvd+rw-tools documentation, found at /usr/share/doc/dvd+rw-tools-*/index.html, is required reading before your first use of the program. We also suggest that you experiment with DVD-RW (re-writable) media first, as DVD-R (record once) media is not yet as inexpensive as CD-R media.

Currently, there are no GUI clients for DVD creation, so all your DVD work will be done at the command line. We suggest that you practice with a re-writable DVD because of the expense of DVD disks.

Creating CDs with Fedora Core Linux Graphical Clients

Although adequate for quick burns and use in shell scripting, the command-line technique for burning CDs is an awkward choice for many people until they become proficient at it and learn all the arcane commands. Fortunately, Fedora provides several graphical clients.

With Fedora, enhanced functionality has been included in the default file browser Nautilus. Under the Places menu item is a CD Creator selection. To use it, insert a blank CD into your CD-RW drive. You will need to have two Nautilus windows open: one showing the files you want to save to the CD, and a second one that is opened to the burn:/// location. Click on the Write CD button as shown in Figure 26.1 to bring up the Write dialog; click on the Write files to CD button to actually create the CD. It's that simple, or it should be. There are some reports of difficulty with Nautilus being able to burn CDs.

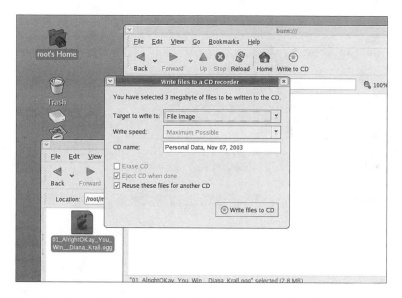

FIGURE 26.1   Creating a CD using the Nautilus browser is made easy with the drag-and-drop features it provides.

The following sections describe X-CD-Roast, as well as a number of other graphical clients for burning audio and data CDs.

TIP

An excellent Internet site for CD-related information is `http://www.cdmediaworld.com/`.

Also, the Gracenote CDDB Music Recognition Service licenses a database service to software developers so that they can include additional functionality in their application by accessing the database and having their application display information about the music CD, including the artist and song title, the CD's track list, and so on. The database server at `cddb.cddb.org` will, when contacted by the appropriate software, identify the appropriate CD and send the information to be displayed locally. Many CD player applications provide this functionality. The service is interactive: If you have a CD that isn't in the CDDB database, the Web site tells you how you can add the information to the database.

Each GUI application for burning CDs has different strengths and weaknesses. You should experiment with all the different graphical tools as well as try your hand at command-line burning and you'll have a significantly richer multimedia experience with Fedora Core Linux.

X-CD-Roast

X-CD-Roast, shown in Figure 26.2, is the default standalone CD creator provided with Fedora Core Linux. It can be found in the System Tools menu as the CD Writer menu item, or it can be launched from the command line, like this:

```
$ xcdroast &
```

When you first start it, X-CD-Roast is deceptively plain, giving little indication of the true power of this application. The very first time it's run, it begins with a dialog warning you to enter the Setup dialog, which will be the only button presented to you in the next screen other than Exit. The application autodetects your CD drive, but you must tell it which drive (if you have more than one) is the CD-RW drive and select the users who are allowed to use the application. The dialogs for setting this information are straightforward and easy to follow. Make certain that you choose a default directory for temporary image storage that offers enough room to store several images.

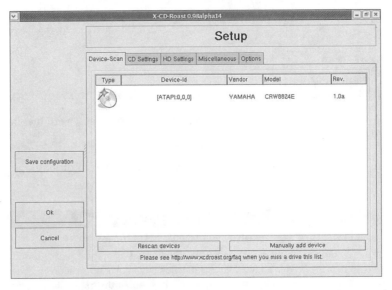

FIGURE 26.2   X-CD-Roast is the default CD creation client for Fedora, and it must be configured from the Setup dialog.

The main X-CD-Roast menu offers you the choice to duplicate or create CDs. The latter operation is shown in Figure 26.3.

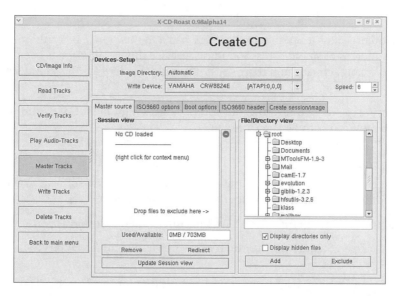

FIGURE 26.3   The X-CD-Roast Create CD window allows access to the full range of options, including creating music CDs.

Other Graphical CD Clients
Fedora provides the GNOME Grip client to advance ripping to a fine art. Working as both a player and a ripper, it uses `cdparanoia` and `cdda2wav` to rip music tracks and access Internet databases for retrieving track information from disc database servers. To launch Grip, click on its icon in the Sound & Video menu found in the More Sound & Video Applications menu. Use the options in the Grip dialog box tabs to choose, configure, and rip tracks. Also provided is the similar Sound Juicer application.

Sound and Music

Linux has a reputation of lacking good support for sound and multimedia applications in general. Certainly, there is less sound card support than that found in Microsoft Windows. (However, Microsoft no longer supports the Microsoft Sound Card, but Linux users still enjoy support for it, no doubt just to tweak the folks in Redmond.) However, UNIX has always had good multimedia support as David Taylor, UNIX author and guru, points out:

> "The original graphics work for computers was done by Evans & Sutherland on UNIX systems.
> The innovations at MIT's Media Lab were done on UNIX workstations. In 1985, we at HP Labs
> were creating sophisticated multimedia immersive work environments on UNIX workstations,

> so maybe UNIX is more multimedia than suggested. Limitations in Linux support doesn't mean UNIX had the same limitations. I think it was more a matter of logistics, with hundreds of sound cards and thousands of different possible PC configurations."

That last sentence sums it up quite well. UNIX had a limited range of hardware to support; Linux has hundreds of sound cards. Sound card device driver support has been long lacking from manufacturers, and there's still no single standard for the sound subsystem in Linux.

In the following section, you learn about sound cards, sound file formats, and the sound applications provided with Fedora Core Linux.

Sound Cards

Fedora Core Linux supports a wide variety of sound hardware and software. Two models of sound card drivers compete for prominence in today's market:

- ALSA, the Advanced Linux Sound Architecture, which is entirely open source.

- OSS, the Open Sound System, which offers free and commercial drivers.

Fedora uses ALSA because ALSA is the sound architecture for the 2.6 series kernels.

ALSA supports a long list of sound cards. You can review the list at `http://www.alsa-project.org/alsa-doc/`. If your sound card isn't supported, it might be supported in the commercial version of OSS. You can download a trial version of commercial software and test your sound card at `http://www.opensound.com/download.cgi`.

TIP

You can check the directory `/usr/src/linux-2.6/` for documentation for each sound module. Be aware, however, that the documentation is likely to be out-of-date. Although even this out-of-date documentation can be useful, you should research any new sound card you might purchase to ascertain its level of support in Linux. Use `http:/www.google.com/linux` to search Linux Web sites and Linux newsgroups for mention of any sound card you're using.

Fedora Core Linux detects most sound cards during the original installation. If you add or replace a sound card after the initial install, the Kudzu "new hardware configuration" utility will automatically detect and configure it at the next reboot. To configure the sound card at any other time, use the `system-config-soundcard` graphical tool. The graphical tool can be found under the System Settings menu as the Soundcard Detection menu item. For additional details about configuring your sound card, refer to Chapter 4.

Recording Sound

Fedora Core Linux provides a number of tools that enable you to control volume, mix, and other sound recording functions. The Kmix sound mixer acts as a virtual mixing board, taking sound inputs from different sources, enabling you to adjust their individual volumes, mute them, and listen to them through your sound card.

If you need to control sound from command line, use the alsamixer command, which can be used to adjust balance or volume in text mode using the left and right cursor keys to select a channel and the up and down keys to adjust the volume.

```
$ alsamixer
```

The Sound Recorder, shown in Figure 26.4, along with the Volume Control application, is provided to enable you to play and record .wav files. You can use the SoX utility (covered later in this chapter) to convert the recorded sound if necessary.

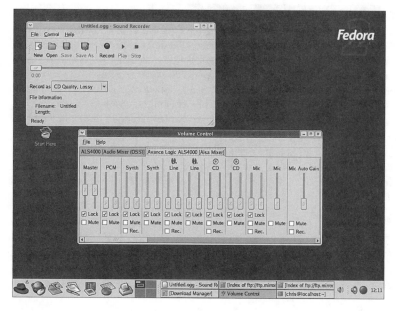

FIGURE 26.4   Simplicity in design and layout make the Sound Recorder and Volume Control applications easy to use.

Sound Formats

A number of formats exist for storing sound recordings. Some of these formats are associated with specific technologies, and others are used strictly for proprietary reasons. Fedora Core Linux supports several of the most popular sound formats, including

- raw (.raw)—More properly known as headerless format, audio files using this format contain an amorphous variety of specific settings and encodings. All other sound files contain a short section of code at the beginning—a header—that identifies the format type.

- MP3 (.mp3)—A popular, but commercially licensed, format for the digital encoding used by many Linux and Windows applications. MP3 isn't supported by any software included with Fedora (which advises you to use the open source Ogg-Vorbis format instead).

- WAV (.wav)—The popular uncompressed Windows audio-visual sound format. It's often used as an intermediate file format when encoding audio.

- Ogg-Vorbis (.ogg)—Fedora preferred audio encoding format. You'll enjoy better compression, audio playback, and freedom from lawsuits by using this open source encoding format for your audio files.

NOTE

Because of patent and licensing issues, Fedora has removed support for the MPEG, MPEG2, and MPEG3 (MP3) file formats in Fedora Core Linux. Although we can't offer any legal advice, it appears that individuals using MP3 software are okay; it's just that Fedora can't distribute the code because it sells its distribution. It seems—at this point—perfectly all right for you to obtain an MP3-capable version of Xmms (for example), which is a Winamp clone that plays MPEG1/2/3 files. (You learn more about Xmms in the "Music Players" section later in this chapter.) You can get Xmms directly from http://www.xmms.org/ because that group has permission to distribute the MP3 code.

Another alternative is to use the Ogg-Vorbis format; it's completely free of restrictions. A free-but-not-GPL Ogg-Vorbis ripper for CD music is available from http://www.thekompany.com/projects/tkcoggripper/ and an MP3-to-Ogg converter is available from http://faceprint.com/code/. Or, you could download and install the non-crippled versions of multi-media applications from FreshRPMs at http://www.freshrpms.net/.

Fedora includes software (such as the sox command used to convert between sound formats) so that you can more easily listen to audio files provided in a wide variety of formats, such as AU (from NeXT and Sun), AIFF (from Apple and SGI), IFF (originally from Commodore's Amiga), RA (from Real Audio), and VOC (from Creative Labs).

TIP

To learn more about the technical details of audio formats, read Chris Bagwell's Audio Format FAQ at http://www.cnpbagwell.com/audio.html.

Fedora Core Linux also offers utilities for converting sound files from one format to another. Conversion utilities come in handy when you want to use a sound in a format not accepted by your current application of choice. A repository of conversion utilities resides at http://ibiblio.org/pub/linux/apps/sound/convert/!INDEX.html and includes MP3 and music CD–oriented utilities not found in Fedora. You'll have to know how to compile and install from source, however. If you see something useful, have a look at http://www.rpmfind.net/ to locate a binary RPM if you don't feel up to the task.

Fedora does provide sox, a self-described sound translator that will convert music between the AIFF, AU, VAR, DAT, OGG, and WAV formats, among others. It also can be used to change many other parameters of the sound files.

Timidity is a MIDI to WAV converter and player. If you're interested in MIDI and musical instruments, Timidity is a handy application; it handles karaoke files as well, displaying the words to accompany your efforts at singing.

Music Players

Fedora provides music players. One of the most popular is Xmms, a Winamp clone, which in the full version can play not only music, but MPEG1/2/3 video as well. Xmms supports a number of plug-ins that can add dancing, lighted oscilloscope-like displays, redirect its output to other devices, support unusual file formats, sync animations to the music, and otherwise increase its geek appeal exponentially. You can find Xmms as the Media Player item in the Sound & Video menu.

The default music player is Rhythmbox, which is designed to play music files from playlists and Internet radio stations much like Xmms. It is found in the Sound & Video menu as the Music Player menu item.

Kmid, found in the More Sound & Video Applications submenu, is a karaoke and MIDI mapper; it supports external synthesizers. MIDI mappers enable you to map MIDI channels to the synthesizer instruments you want them to control. If you enjoy karaoke, Kmid will also enable you to change the tempo of songs without changing the pitch, and permits the organization of your songs into collections with a selectable play order.

Gnome-CD is the CD Player menu item found in the Sound & Video menu. As the default CD player application, it provides a basic GUI interface for playing CDs in your CD-ROM drive.

Other music and sound-related applications can be found in the Sound & Video menu, and, of course, you are free to install your own selection of applications as well. You might have a problem adding them to the menu, however, so we provide the following tip to enable menu editing in Fedora Core.

26

TIP

Menu editing is available in the GNOME/metacity desktop provided as the default Fedora Core desktop, but it is inexplicably disabled. To enable it, working as root perform the following steps:

```
# cd /etc/gnome-vfs-2.0/modules
# mv default-modules.conf default-modules.conf.without-menu-editing
# cp default-modules.conf.with-menu-editing  default-modules.conf
```

Upon restarting GNOME, you can edit the menu by right-clicking on the menu item or by using the URL applications:/// in Nautilus.

Streaming Audio

Streaming audio is for playing games, listening to Internet radio, and other online audio content. Streaming audio is designed to produce an uninterrupted sound output, but it requires the system to perform a content "juggling act." Essentially, the system's audio buffer is continually filled with audio information, which is fed to the buffer through the system's Internet connection. Because of server and connection capabilities, the rate of input might vary. Because audio is used at a constant rate, the trick to managing streaming audio is to always keep the buffer full, although you might not be able to fill it at a constant rate.

Streaming audio is handled in Fedora Core Linux in the `.m3u` format. The MPEG formats are also used for streaming audio. Although Xmms supports streaming audio, another popular application is the Real Player, available from `http://www.real.com/linux/`. An excellent resource for music and sound in Linux is `http://linux-sound.org/`. The Network Audio section of that Web site contains an extensive list of streaming audio applications.

The Icecast application, not provided with Fedora Core Linux, is a popular streaming audio server. You can use Icecast to serve your MP3 music collection over your home LAN. You can learn more about Icecast at `http://www.icecast.org/`. A nice tutorial on Icecast is available at `http://www.linuxnetmag.com/en/issue4/m4icecast1.html`.

> **TIP**
>
> You can also read Chapter 13, "Network Connectivity," to see how to use the Network File System (NFS) to mount a remote directory of music files over your network.

Viewing TV and Video

You can use Fedora Core Linux tools and applications to view movies and other video presentations on your PC. This section presents some TV and motion picture video software tools included with the Fedora Core Linux distribution you received with this book.

In addition to the information you read here, you should review Chapter 3, "Installing Fedora," and Chapter 6, "The X Window System," to learn more about installing and configuring your video graphics card.

TV and Video Hardware

To watch TV and video content on your PC, you must install a supported TV card or have a video/TV combo card installed. A complete list of TV and video cards supported by Fedora Core Linux is at `http://www.exploits.org/v4l/`. See the Gatos Project at `http://gatos.sourceforge.net` for information on ATI video combo cards.

Freely available Linux support for TV display from video cards that have a TV-out jack is poor. That support must come from the X11 driver, not from a video device that

Video4Linux supports with a device driver. Some of the combo TV-tuner/video display cards have support, including the Matrox Marvel, the Matrox Rainbow Runner G-Series, and the RivaTV cards. Many other combo cards lack support, although an independent developer might have hacked something together to support his own card. Your best course of action is to perform a thorough Internet search using Google.

Many of the TV-only PCI cards are supported. In Linux, however, they are supported by the video chipset they use, and not by the name some manufacturer has slapped on a generic board (the same board is typically sold by different manufacturers under different names). The most common chipset is the Brooktree Bt*** series of chips; they're supported by the bttv device driver.

If you have a supported card in your computer, it should be detected during installation. If you add it later, the Kudzu hardware detection utility should detect it and configure it. You can always configure it by hand.

To determine what chipset your card has, use the lspci command to list the PCI device information, find the TV card listing, and look for the chipset that the card uses. For example, the lspci output for our computer shows

```
# lspci
00:00.0 Host bridge: Advanced Micro Devices [AMD] AMD-760 [IGD4-1P]
➡System Controller (rev 13)
00:01.0 PCI bridge: Advanced Micro Devices [AMD] AMD-760 [IGD4-1P]
➡ AGP Bridge
00:07.0 ISA bridge: VIA Technologies, Inc. VT82C686 [Apollo Super South]
➡ (rev 40)
00:07.1 IDE interface: VIA Technologies, Inc. VT82C586B PIPC Bus Master IDE
➡ (rev 06)
00:07.2 USB Controller: VIA Technologies, Inc. USB (rev 1a)
00:07.3 USB Controller: VIA Technologies, Inc. USB (rev 1a)
00:07.4 SMBus: VIA Technologies, Inc. VT82C686 [Apollo Super ACPI]
➡ (rev 40)
00:09.0 Multimedia audio controller: Ensoniq 5880 AudioPCI (rev 02)
00:0b.0 Multimedia video controller: Brooktree Corporation Bt878 Video Capture
➡ (rev 02)
00:0b.1 Multimedia controller: Brooktree Corporation Bt878 Audio Capture
➡ (rev 02)
00:0d.0 Ethernet controller: Realtek Semiconductor Co., Ltd. RTL-8029(AS)
00:0f.0 FireWire (IEEE 1394): Texas Instruments TSB12LV23 IEEE-1394
➡ Controller
00:11.0 Network controller: Standard Microsystems Corp [SMC]
➡ SMC2602W EZConnect
01:05.0 VGA compatible controller: nVidia Corporation NV15 [GeForce2 Ti]
➡ (rev a4)
```

26

Here, the lines listing the multimedia video controller and multimedia controller say that our TV board uses a Brooktree Bt878 Video Capture chip and a Brooktree Bt878 Audio Capture chip. This card uses the Bt878 chipset. Your results will be different, depending on what card and chipset your computer has. This card happened to be an ATI All-in-Wonder VE (also known as ATI TV-Wonder). (The VE means Value Edition; hence, there's no TV-out connector and no radio chip on the card; what a value!) The name of the chipset tells us that the card uses the bttv driver.

The documentation for the bt878 kernel sound module used for recording sound is found in /usr/src/linux-2.6/Documentation/sound/ossbtaudio. The documentation for the video driver is found under /usr/src/linux-2.6/Documentation/video4linux/bttv.

In the documentation directory, we find a file named CARDLIST, and in that file is the following entry, among others:

```
card=64 - ATI TV-Wonder VE
```

There are 105 cards listed as well as 41 radio cards, including:

```
card=0 -  *** UNKNOWN/GENERIC ***
```

which is what we would have used had we not known the manufacturer's name for our card.

The file named Modules.conf, located in the same directory, gives us the following example of information to place in our /etc/modules.conf file:

```
# i2c
alias char-major-89    i2c-dev
options i2c-core       i2c_debug=1
options i2c-algo-bit   bit_test=1

# bttv
alias char-major-81    videodev
alias char-major-81-0  bttv
options bttv           card=2 radio=1
options tuner          debug=1
```

All we need do is enter this information into /etc/modules.conf and change the value for card=2 to card=64 to match our hardware. We can delete the reference to the radio card (radio=2) because we don't have one and leave the other values alone. Then we must execute

```
# depmod -a
```

to rebuild the modules dependency list so that all our modules are loaded automatically.

When finished, all we need do is execute

```
# modprobe bttv
```

and our TV card should be fully functional. All the correct modules will be automatically loaded every time we reboot. Fedora Core is clever enough to detect and configure a supported TV card that is present during installation.

> **TIP**
>
> Other useful documentation can be found in `/usr/src/linux-2.6/Documentation/` `_video4linux`. After you've identified a driver for a device, it won't hurt to look at the source code for it because so little formal documentation exists for many drivers; much of it is in the source code comments.

The development of support for TV cards in Linux has coalesced under the Video4Linux project. The Video4Linux software provides support for video capture, radio, and Teletext devices in Fedora Core Linux.

Video Formats

Fedora Core Linux recognizes a variety of video formats. The formats created by the MPEG group, Apple, and Microsoft predominate, however. At the heart of video formats are the *codecs*—the encoders and decoders of the video and audio information. These codecs are typically proprietary, but free codecs do exist. Here is a list of the most common video formats and their associated file extensions:

- `.mpeg`—The MPEG video format; also known as `.mpg`
- `.qt`—The QuickTime video format from Apple
- `.mov`—Another QuickTime video format
- `.avi`—The Windows audio visual format

> **TIP**
>
> An RPM that provides a DivX codec for Linux can be found at `http://www.freshrpms.net/`. DivX is a patented MPEG-4 video codec that is the most widely used codec of its type. It allows for compression of MPEG-2 video by a factor of 8. See `http://www.divx.com/` for more information.
>
> The GetCodecs application is a Python script with a GUI interface that will download, install, and configure your Fedora Core system with multimedia codecs not provided by Fedora Core, such as MP3, DivX and DVD codecs. The script can be obtained from `http://sourceforge.net/` `projects/getcodecs/`.

26

If you need to convert video from one format to another, you use encoder applications called *grabbers*. These applications take raw video data from a video device such as a camera or TV card, and convert it to one of the standard MPEG formats or to a still image format, such as JPEG or GIF. Fedora Core Linux doesn't supply any encoder applications (other than ppmtompeg which encodes MPEG-1 video), but you can find them at http://www.freshrpms.net/ or another online source (see the "Reference" section at the end of this chapter).

Viewing Video in Linux

Because of the patent and licensing issues mentioned earlier, the ability to play video files has been removed from Fedora. This functionality can be restored if you install the full version of the applications described in this section from FreshRPMs at http://www.freshrpms.net/. There, you will find multimedia applications such as Ogle, Xine, AlsaPlayer, Gstreamer, Grip, Mplayer, VCDImager, VideoLAN-client, Xmms, and Zapping.

You can use Linux software to watch TV, save individual images (take snapshots) from a televised broadcast, save a series of snapshots to build animation sequences, or capture video, audio, or both. The following sections describe some of the ways in which you can put Linux multimedia software to work for you.

The noatun viewer is provided with Fedora Core Linux to use as an embedded viewer in the Konqueror browser. noatun is set up as the default association for the video files formats it plays. Open a video file in Konqueror or Nautilus, and the video will be shown in the viewer if it's supported. The viewer provides basic Start, Stop, and Fast-Forward VCR-type functions.

You can watch MPEG and DVD video with Xine. Xine is a versatile and popular media player that is not included with Fedora Core Linux. Xine is used to watch AVI, QuickTime, OGG, and MP3 files (the latter disabled in Fedora Core).

Macromedia Flash

The Macromedia Flash plug-in for the Mozilla browser is a commercial multimedia application that isn't provided with Fedora, but many people find it useful. Macromedia Flash enables you to view Flash content at Web sites that support it. The Mozilla plug-in can be obtained from http://macromedia.mplug.org/. Both .rpm and .tar.gz files are provided.

Download the file for Linux and, if using the .tar.gz file, uncompress it with

```
# tar zxvf install_flash_player_6_linux.tar.gz
```

This produces a directory named flashplayer_installer. Install the plug-in with

```
# ./install_flash_player_6_linux/flashplayer-installer
```

and follow the screen prompts to install it and make it available to the Mozilla browser.

Having trouble with the Macromedia Flash plugin for Mozilla? Just manually copy the files `flashplayer.xpt` and `libflashplayer.so` to `/usr/lib/mozilla/plugins`. An `.rpm` file for Flash that should install without problems is available from `http://macromedia.mplug.org/`.

Another interesting video viewer application is MPlayer (not provided by Fedora), a movie player for Linux. MPlayer can use Win32 codecs and it supports a wider range of video formats than Xine, including DivX and some RealMedia files. MPlayer also uses some special display drivers that support Matrox, 3Dfx, and Radeon cards and can make use of some hardware MPEG decoder boards for better MPEG decoding. Look for Fedora packages at `http://www.MPlayerHQ.hu/homepage/`; a Win32 codec package is also available, as well as other codec packages and a GUI interface.

Viewing Television with Linux

You can configure a number of video input sources to feed television images to your computer. You can use any supported TV device as described previously to connect cable TV, an Xbox, Sega Dreamcast, PS/2, or even an external television antenna to your computer and view the images on your video display.

Fedora provides the `tvtime` TV viewing application to enable you to watch *South Park* without leaving your computer.

> **NOTE**
>
> The kdetv application (formerly known as QtVision) is steadily growing in terms of both popularity and features and is worth a look. It can be downloaded from `http://www.kdetv.org/`.

Start `tvtime` from the command line:

```
$ tvtime &
```

Right-clicking on it will toggle the display of the Options menu. Adjust the settings to suit your hardware.

```
$ scantv
```

The `tvtime` configuration file details are contained in the `man` page for `tvtime`.

An alternative TV-viewing application available at FreshRPMs.Net is Zapping, a GNOME viewer that supports Vide4Linux, Vide4Linux2, and Xvideo and is extensible in functionality through plug-ins. The home page is `http://zapping.sourceforge.net/`.

Personal Video Recorders

The best reason to attach a television antenna to your computer, however, is to use the video card and the computer as a personal video recorder.

The commercial personal video recorder, TiVo, uses Linux running on a PowerPC processor to record television programming with a variety of customizations. TiVo has a clever interface and wonderful features, including a record/playback buffer, programmed recording and pause, slow motion, and reverse effects. Fedora Core Linux doesn't provide any of the many applications that attempt to mimic the TiVo functionality on a desktop PC running Linux. However, several such applications, including DVR, The Linux TV Project, and OpenPVR, are listed at `http://www.exploits.org/v4l/`. These projects are in development and don't provide `.rpm` files, so you'll need to know how to download from CVS and compile your own binaries. For something a little easier, check out MythTV at `http://www.mythtv.org/`; a Fedora `.rpm` file should be available from FreshRPMs.Net.

Linux, the TiVo, and PVRs

Some TiVo users say that using this Linux-based device has changed their lives. Indeed, the convenience of using a personal video recorder (PVR) can make life a lot easier for inveterate channel surfers; I own two of them. Although PVR applications aren't included with Fedora Core Linux, open-source developers are working on newer and better versions of easy-to-install and easy-to-use PVR software for Linux. For more information about TiVo, which requires a monthly charge and a phone line (or broadband connection with a newer TiVo2), browse to `http://www.tivo.com/`. Unrepentant Linux hardware hackers aiming to disembowel or upgrade a TiVo can browse to `http://www.9thtee.com/tivoupgrades.htm` or read the TiVo Hack FAQ at `http://www.tivofaq.com/hack/faq.html`. (Such an enhanced TiVo is used by me.) A PVR makes viewing television a lot more fun!

A number of Linux sites are devoted to PVR software development. Browse to the DVR project page at `http://dvr.sourceforge.net/`.

DVD and Video Players

You can now easily play DVDs using Fedora Core Linux as long as you install the appropriate software. (Fedora doesn't provide any.) Browse to `http://www.videolan.org/`, and then download, build, and install the `vlc` client.

You'll need a CPU of at least 450MHz and a working sound card to use a DVD player. The default Fedora Core Linux kernel supports the DVD CD-ROM file system. As mentioned earlier, Xine and MPlayer do a great job of playing DVD files.

NOTE

The VideoLAN HOWTO found at `http://videolan.org/` discusses the construction of a network for streaming video. Although you might not want to do that, a great deal of useful information about the software and hardware involved in the enterprise can be generalized for use elsewhere, so it's worth a look. The site also contains a link to a HOWTO about cross-compiling on Linux to produce a Windows binary.

Using Still Cameras with Fedora Core Linux

Most still cameras used in connection with Fedora Core Linux fall into one of two categories: Webcams (small, low-resolution cameras connected to the computer's interface) or handheld digital cameras that record image data on disks or memory cards for downloading and viewing on a PC. Fedora Core Linux supports both types. Other types of cameras, such as surveillance cameras that connect directly to a network via wire or wireless connections, need no special support (other than a network connection and viewing software) to be used with a Linux computer.

Fedora Core Linux supports hundreds of different digital cameras, from early parallel-port (CPiA chipset-based) cameras to today's newer USB-based cameras. You can even use Intel's QX3 USB microscope with Fedora. If you prefer a standalone network-based Webcam, explore the capabilities of Linux-based cameras from Axis (at `http://www.axis.com/ products/video/camera/productguide.htm`). The following sections describe some of the more commonly used still camera hardware and software supported by Fedora Core Linux.

Webcams

Webcams are typically small, low-resolution cameras connected to your computer via a parallel port or USB port. The camera can act in two modes: streaming (for a series of images of a moving object) and grabbing (for a single still image). The most common uses for Web cams include video conferencing and Web voyeurism. The latter isn't as lurid as it might sound, although some Web cam sites are notorious for their pornographic content. Web cams can be used to send almost-live images to an online correspondent; many people include screen grabs of themselves at their computer workstations just because they can.

26

> **Coffee Pot Cam**
>
> One of the more interesting uses of a Webcam was the legendary "Internet coffee pot" cam (started in 1991, but turned off on August 22, 2001—a day that will live in infamy). A Webcam was trained on a coffee maker, and the sysadmin could see whether fresh coffee was available without leaving his cubicle. Some Webcams take grabs of intersections in various cities. You'll likely find some similar worthwhile use for your Webcam.

You can use any of the video applications that can access a video4linux device to view Web cam or still camera images in Fedora Core Linux. You also can use GnomeMeeting (discussed in Chapter 20, "News and Other Collaborative Communication") as a viewer for your Webcam.

Not all Web cams are supported in Linux and the drivers are based on the chipset used, rather than the model or manufacturer. Some of the files in `/usr/src/linux-2.6/ Documentation/usb` contain information about USB Web cams and drivers supported by Fedora Core Linux, including:

- `ibmcam.txt`

- `ov511.txt`

- `phillips.txt`

- `se401.txt`

- `stv0608.txt`

Documentation on parallel port cameras, including the CQ cam (`Cqcam.txt`) and CPiA camera (`README.cpia`), is found in `/usr/src/linux-2.6/Documentation/video4linux/` if you have installed the kernel documentation on your computer.

> **TIP**
>
> Unfortunately, most of the documentation provided for Web cams is abysmal, and it's difficult to associate the Web cam you just purchased with a related driver. If you're interested in a particular USB Web cam, but aren't sure whether it's supported by Linux, browse to `http://www.qbik.ch/usb/devices/showdevcat.php?id=9`.

Handheld Digital Cameras

Handheld cameras have been a hit with consumers since they were introduced, especially digital cameras. You can capture your photographs to a disk or memory card, view and print photos on your computer screen, and store and edit the images on a CD. Unfortunately, the instant gratification afforded by digital cameras is often overcome with frustration when users try to link those devices to a Linux workstation. Most software provided by digital camera manufacturers is designed for use with Microsoft's operating system.

Fedora Core does provide some useful camera applications, but you must use them with a supported device. Most USB cameras, when connected to a computer as SCSI storage devices, are detected during the initial Fedora Core Linux or after reboot. To see whether your camera is detected when connected, look at the output of

```
# cat /proc/bus/usb/devices
```

or

```
# lsusb
```

Your camera will likely be detected as `/dev/sda1`, the first SCSI data device.

Fedora Core Linux also includes the GNOME `gtkam` digital camera support client, listed as Digital Camera Tool in the Graphics menu selection. When you first launch `gtkam` by clicking on the menu icon, you're asked to select the type of camera and connection port it uses. The Select Camera drop-down menu demonstrates that an extensive list of digital cameras is supported.

After saving your configuration, you can download selected images from your camera or download an index of thumbnail views. You can retrieve images in batches from your camera by clicking on individual thumbnail images. The images will then be displayed in individual windows, which you can access in full view by choosing them from gtkam's main window with your mouse.

The GIMP graphics program, included with Fedora Core Linux, also can import images from cameras. You can use The GIMP's extensive options to edit images by adjusting the contrast, brightness, and color. You also can use the GIMP to edit out content and alter images with special effects.

Using Scanners in Fedora Core Linux

You can also use many types of image scanners with The GIMP. In the recent past, the most capable scanners required a SCSI port. Today, however, many scanners work through a USB port. You must have scanner-support enabled for Linux (usually through a loaded kernel module, scanner.o) before using a scanner with The GIMP.

Although some scanners can work via the command line, you'll enjoy more productive scanning sessions using a graphical interface because image manipulation tasks, such as previewing and cropping, can save time before actually scanning an image. Most scanners in use with Linux use the Scanner Access Now Easy (SANE) package that supports and enables graphical scanning sessions.

SANE consists of two software components. A low-level driver enables the hardware support and is specific to each scanner. Next, a graphical scanner interface X client known as xsane is used as a plug-in, or ancillary program (or script) that adds features to The GIMP.

26

> **NOTE**
>
> Although xsane is commonly used as a GIMP plug-in, it can also be used as a standalone program. Another useful program is Joerg Schulenburg's gocr client, used for optical character recognition (OCR). Although not a standalone application, it is included in the Kooka scanning application. This program works best with 300 dots per inch (dpi) scans in several different graphics formats. OCR is a resource-intensive task and can require hundreds of megabytes of disk storage!

A list of currently supported scanners can be found at http://www.sane-project.org/sane-supported-devices.html. Unfortunately, if your scanner doesn't appear on the list, you shouldn't expect it to work with the SANE software. There is also a list on that same page for drivers not yet included, but you must be able to compile the application from source to use them.

Supported USB scanners are automatically detected and the appropriate driver is loaded automatically. The USB devices "tell" the USB system several pieces of information when they're connected—the most important of which is the vendor ID and the device ID. This identification is used to look up the device in a table and load the appropriate driver.

Many scanners are supported in Linux. If yours isn't, it still might be possible to use it. The Kooka and Xsane scanner applications are included with Fedora Core Linux, and are covered in detail in Chapter 25, "Productivity Applications." They can be found in the Graphics menu as the Scanning and Scan & OCR Program menu items.

USB Scanner Success Is Elusive

Because a failure is sometimes more educational than a success, for previous editions of this book, we attempted to configure a USB scanner that wasn't supported: the Canon N650U. With the release of the version of SANE included with Fedora Core, the scanner is now supported, and it is automatically detected!

However, here are the manual steps we used for detecting and configuring this scanner in Linux when it did not work properly:

First, connect the scanner. For this USB scanner, look at the output of:

```
# cat /proc/bus/usb/devices/
```

(We've truncated the output here to show only the scanner. You can also use the `lsusb` command.)

```
T:  Bus=01 Lev=01 Prnt=01 Port=00 Cnt=01 Dev#=  2 Spd=12  MxCh= 
D:  Ver= 1.00 Cls=00(>ifc ) Sub=00 Prot=00 MxPS= 8 #Cfgs=  1
P:  Vendor=04a9 ProdID=2206 Rev= 1.00
S:  Manufacturer=Canon
S:  Product=CanoScan
C:* #Ifs= 1 Cfg#= 1 Atr=80 MxPwr=500mA
I:  If#= 0 Alt= 0 #EPs= 3 Cls=ff(vend.) Sub=00 Prot=ff Driver=(none)
E:  Ad=81(I) Atr=03(Int.) MxPS=   1 Ivl=16ms
E:  Ad=82(I) Atr=02(Bulk) MxPS=  64 Ivl=0ms
E:  Ad=03(O) Atr=02(Bulk) MxPS=  64 Ivl=0ms
```

`Driver=(none)` at the end of the seventh line tells us that the device wasn't found in the lookup table. Because we now have the "magic" vendor ID and device ID, we can attempt to load the driver manually with

```
# /sbin/modprobe scanner vendor=0x04a9 product=0x2206
```

Now the output of the `catlsusb` command from before tells us that the scanner device driver is associated with our scanner:

```
I:  If#= 0 Alt= 0 #EPs= 3 Cls=ff(vend.) Sub=00 Prot=ff Driver=usbscanner
```

and the Kooka and Xsane applications now recognize the scanner.

Graphics Manipulation

If you've ever wanted to change a photograph slightly—red eyes returned to their normal color, dark areas lightened, funny Uncle Bert removed—and longed for a way to accomplish that task, you've been granted your wish. Now, you can accomplish all of these tasks with the tools provided with Fedora Core Linux (and a digital image from a digital camera or from a scanner).

This section of the chapter discusses The GIMP, a powerful graphics manipulation tool. (You learned about the other graphics tools that Fedora provides in Chapter 25.) In this section of the chapter, you also learn about graphic file formats supported by Fedora Core Linux, as well as some tools you can use to convert them if the application you want to use requires a different format.

The GNU Image Manipulation Program

One of the best graphics clients is the GIMP. The GIMP is a free, GPLed image editor with sophisticated capabilities that can import and export more than 30 different graphics formats, including files created with Adobe Photoshop. It's often compared with Photoshop, and the GIMP represents one of the GNU Projects' first significant successes. You'll see many images in Linux that have been prepared with the GIMP.

The GIMP can be started by clicking a desktop panel menu item or by using the command line, like this:

```
$ gimp &
```

You'll see an installation dialog box when the GIMP is started for the first time, and then a series of dialog boxes that display information regarding the creation and contents of a local GIMP directory. This directory can contain personal settings, preferences, external application resource files, temporary files, and symbolic links to external software tools used by the editor.

> **What Does Photoshop Have That Isn't in The GIMP?**
>
> Although the GIMP is powerful, it does lack two features Adobe Photoshop offers that are important to some graphics professionals.
>
> The first of these is the ability to generate color separations for commercial press printers (CMYK for the cyan, magenta, yellow, key [or black] colors). The GIMP uses RGB (red, green, and blue) which is great for video display, not so great for printing presses. The second feature GIMP lacks is the use of Pantone colors (a patented color specification) to ensure accurate color matching.
>
> If these features are unimportant to you, the GIMP is an excellent tool. If you must use Adobe Photoshop, the current version of Codeweaver's Crossover Office will run Photoshop in Linux.
>
> These deficiencies might not last long. A CMYK plugin is in the works, and the Pantone issues will likely be addressed in the near future as well.

26

After the initial configuration has finished, The GIMP's main windows and toolboxes appear. The GIMP's main window contains tools used for selection, drawing, movement, view enlargement or reduction, airbrushing, painting, smudging, copying, filling, and color selection. Depending on the version installed on your system, the toolbox can host more than 25 different tools.

The toolbox's File, Xtns, and Help menus are used for file operations (including the ability to send the current image by electronic mail), image acquisition or manipulation, and documentation, respectively. If you right-click an open image window, you'll see the wealth of The GIMP's menus, as shown in Figure 26.5.

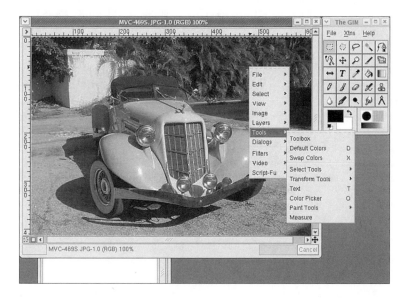

FIGURE 26.5   Right-click on an image window to access the GIMP's cascading menus.

Working with Graphics Formats

Image file formats are developed to serve a specific technical purpose (lossless compression, for example, where the file size is reduced without sacrificing image quality) or to meet a need for a proprietary format for competitive reasons. Many file formats are covered by one or more patents. For example, the GIF format has fallen into disfavor with the open-source crowd because the patent holder has only recently decided to begin enforcing his patent rights.

If you want to view or manipulate an image, you need to identify the file format in order to choose the right tool for working with the image. The file's extension is your first indicator of the file's format. The graphics image formats supported by the applications included with Red Hat include

- .bmp—Bitmapped graphics, commonly used in Microsoft Windows

- .cgm—Computer graphics metafile

- .g3—CCITT Group 3 FAX image

- .gif—CompuServe Graphics Interchange Format

- .ico—Microsoft Windows icon image

- .jpg—Joint Photographic Experts Group

- .mng—Multiple-image Network Graphic image

- .pbm—Portable Bitmap File Format

- .pcx—IBM Paintbrush

- .pgm—Portable Graymap File Format

- .png—Portable Network Graphics

- .pnm—Portable Anymap

- .ppm—Portable Pixmap File Format

- .rgb—Raw red, green, and blue samples

- .rs—Sun raster image

- .svg—Scalable Vector Graphics

- .tif—Tagged Image File Format

- .xbm—X bitmap image

- .xpm—X Pixmap image, commonly used for Linux icons images

An extensive list of image file extensions can be found in the man page for ImageMagick, an excellent application included with Fedora, which you learn more about in upcoming sections of this chapter.

> **TIP**
>
> Fedora Core Linux includes dozens of graphics conversion programs, and there are few, if any, graphics file formats that can't be manipulated when using Linux. These commands can be used in Perl scripts, shell scripts, or command-line pipes to support many types of complex format conversion and image manipulation tasks. See the manual pages for the ppm, pbm, pnm, and pgm families of commands. Also see the man page for the convert command, which is part of a suite of extremely capable programs included with the ImageMagick suite.

Often, a file you want to manipulate in some way is in a format that can't be used by either your graphics application or the final application. The solution is to convert the image file—sometimes through several formats. The convert utility from ImageMagick is useful as are the netpbm family of utilities. If it isn't already installed, ImageMagick can be installed with the Add Remove Software GUI found in the System Settings menu; the netpbm tools are always installed by default.

The convert utility converts between image formats recognized by ImageMagick. Color depth and size also can be manipulated during the conversion process. You can use ImageMagick to append images, surround them with borders, labels, rotate and shade them, and perform other manipulations well-suited to scripting. Commands associated with ImageMagick include display, animate, identify, and import. The application supports more than 130 different image formats—(all listed in the man page for ImageMagick).

Fun with ImageMagick's identify

You can use ImageMagick's identify command to identify details about image files. The welcoming splash image used for the GRUB bootloader is located in /boot/grub and is a gzipped .xpm image. If you run identify on the image, you'll discover that it's a 640x480 xpm image with 16-bit color depth. That's all you need to know to construct a replacement image of your own. Using The GIMP or another graphics tool, crop or resize your chosen image to 640x480 and change the color depth to 16 bits. Save the image as splash.xpm and then gzip the resulting file. Replace the original Red Hat file, and you now have a custom boot image. The use of identify helped you duplicate the parameters of the original image to comply with the requirements of GRUB.

The identify command is useful to identify unknown image files and to determine whether they're corrupt.

The netpbm tools are installed by default because they compose the underpinnings of graphics format manipulation. The man page for each image format lists related conversion utilities; the number of those utilities gives you some indication of the way that format is used and shows how one is built on another:

- The man page for ppm, the portable pixmap file format, lists 47 conversion utilities related to ppm. This makes sense because ppm, or portable pixmap, is considered the lowest common denominator for color image files. Because of this, it's often used as an intermediate format.

- The man page for pgm, the portable graymap file format, lists 22 conversion utilities. This makes sense because pgm is the lowest common denominator for grayscale image files.

- The man page for pnm, the portable anymap file format, lists 31 conversion utilities related to it. However, there is no format associated with PNM because it operates in concert with ppm, pgm, and pbm.

- An examination of the man page for pbm, the portable bitmap file format, reveals no conversion utilities. It's a monochrome format and serves as the foundation of the other related formats.

Capturing Screen Images

You can use graphics manipulation tools to capture images that are displayed on your computer screen. Although this technique was used for the production of this book, it has broader uses; there's truth to the cliché that a picture is worth a thousand words. Sometimes, it's easier to show an example than it is to describe it.

A captured screen image (also called a screen grab or a screenshot) can be used to illustrate an error in the display of an application (a font problem, for example) or an error dialog that's too complex to copy down by hand. You might just want to share an image of your beautifully crafted custom desktop configuration with your friends or illustrate your written documents. In this section, you learn how to capture screen images for these and other purposes.

When using the GNOME desktop, you can take advantage of the built-in screenshot mechanism (gnome-panel-screenshot). Access this tool by pressing the Print Screen key. (Alt+Print Screen takes a screenshot of only the window that has "focus" on a desktop.). Captured images are saved in .png format.

You also can capture screen images from a remote computer using tools supported by Red Hat Linux. The import command (one of ImageMagick's commands) was used to take the screenshots for this book, for example, using a local computer and a remote computer on a LAN.

First, we ran $ xhost + on the remote computer to allow another computer access to the X server on the remote machine; the command to take the screenshot is run on our local machine like this:

```
$ import -window root -display 192.168.168.4:0 26fig07.jpg
```

This utility made a difficult task easy because the publisher required the screenshots be done from an 800 × 600 screen (too small to comfortably work in) to accommodate its printing and production equipment.

We could also have used the classic UNIX tool xwd to take screenshots. The command would have looked similar to that of import:

```
$ xwd -root -display 192.168.168.4:0 -out 26fig07.jpg
```

Although the screenshots could have been taken with the GIMP and saved in the appropriate format, we would have had to be running the GIMP on that computer and navigating the menus every time we captured an image—the remote option of import was very convenient.

We didn't use Ksnapshot (not included in the menus, but available from the command line) because it doesn't support the `.pcx` format the publisher used to use and it must be run locally, but it can take screenshots easily and is our preferred tool for use on a single machine.

Linux Gaming

Red Hat Linux has three sources of games: the GNOME games, the KDE games, and the X games. All are free and fun to play. Our favorite is Shisen-Sho, shown in Figure 26.6. A more complete list is found at the end of this chapter, but part of the fun of playing these games is discovering them yourself.

Many arcade-style and action games are available for use with Red Hat Linux. In addition, there are traditional card games such as solitaire and traditional board games such as chess. More sophisticated commercial games are also available for Linux, and Fedora Core Linux—with a little outside help—can be used to play these games as well.

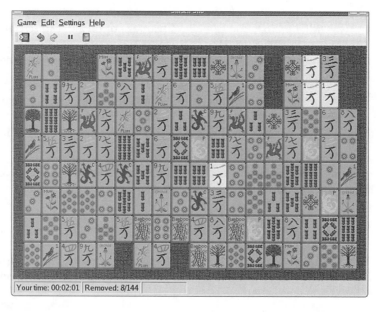

FIGURE 26.6   Matching tiles with no more than three straight lines connecting them is more of a challenge than you might imagine.

Because of their popularity, we'll examine the process of installing proprietary drivers for an nVidia graphics display card and install the freely available demo of Unreal Tournament 2003 from Epic Games.

Installing nVidia Video Drivers

Fedora doesn't provide the official nVidia display drivers because they're closed source. The latest drivers can be downloaded from `http://www.nvidia.com/object/linux.html`. The linux 2.6 kernel series does not actually support the nVidia graphics drivers out of the box because of a kernel "feature" that limits the stack size to 4KB in size. The nVidia driver requires the older 8KB stack size, which has now been completely removed from the kernel.

The only workaround for this is, unfortunately, to get a kernel with a larger stack size. A modified 2.6.7 kernel that is known to work with the nVidia drivers can be found at `http://www.linuxant.com/driverloader/wlan/full/downloads-fc2-kernel-i686.php`.

Installing Unreal Tournament 2003

The free demo can be downloaded from the home page at `http://www.unrealtournament.com/` or from any other source on the Internet; it's a 96MB download, however. After it has been downloaded, the game can be installed with

```
# sh ./ut2003demo-lnx*.sh.bin
```

It will install in `/usr/local/games/ut2003_demo` by default. The game can be launched with

```
$ /usr/local/games/ut2003_demo/ut2003_demo &
```

A nice feature is the online update available through the Loki Installer. (Thanks, Loki, for all those great games you folks ported to Linux!) Simply `cd` to the `./updater` directory in which you installed UT2003, and run

```
# ./loki_update /usr/local/games/ut2003_demo/
```

This command also updates your game for you.

Installing Wolfenstein—Enemy Territory

While the earlier Return to Castle Wolfenstein was both single- and multiplayer, the freely available Wolfenstein—Enemy Territory is multiplayer only. Available in Win32 and Linux native versions, it can be downloaded through `http://www.SplashDamage.com/`. After you download the 260MB file named `et-linux-2.55.x86.run`, install the game with

```
# sh et-linux-2.55.x86.run
```

and accept the defaults. There will be a symlink in `/usr/local/bin` to the script that loads the game. When using the KDE desktop, we had difficulty with sound due to because of a conflict with the KDE sound daemon `artsd`. The fix was prepending a line to the `et` script that read `killall artsd`.

Wolfenstein—Enemy Territory, as seen in Figure 26.7, does not require an nVidia graphics card to play the game, unlike UT2003. We found the game playable on a 16MB Voodoo 3-3000 AGP video card.

FIGURE 26.7   Teamwork is the key to victory in this lush-but-hostile graphical environment.

Find more Linux games at `http://www.garagegames.com/` and at `http://www.linuxgames.com/`. An interesting and little-known snowboarding game can be found at `http://soulride.com/products/jay_peak.html`.

TIP

The key to successful gaming in Linux is to always read the documentation thoroughly, always investigate the Internet resources thoroughly, and always understand your system well. Installing games is a great way to learn about your system because the reward of success is so much fun.

Enabling Java

Some multimedia content relies on Sun's Java and Java Web browser plug-ins.

Getting the Java plug-in to work correctly with the Mozilla browser can be a challenge. Download the latest version (versions prior to 1.4.1 will not work) from `http://java.sun.com/`. (You can find a modified `.rpm` version of the files at `http://dag.wieers.com/packages/j2re/`.) As root, make the downloaded file executable with `chmod +x` and unpack it with `./j2re-1_4_2_05linux-i586-rpm.bin`; install the resulting `rpm` file with

`# rpm ivh j2re-1_4_2_05 -linux-i586.rpm`

To make the Java plug-in work with Mozilla, you need to link it correctly:

```
# ln -s /usr/java/j2re1.4.2_05/plugin/i386/ns610-gcc32/libjavaplugin_oji.so
 /usr/lib/mozilla/plugins/
```

You might also need to link the Java binary into /usr/bin:

```
# ln -s /usr/java/j2re1.4.2_05/bin/java /usr/bin/java
```

Java can be difficult to install properly because of PATH problems. Here's a way to do it correctly:

Edit your /etc/profile file to add the following lines. This will inform the system where the Java executable is found.

```
JAVA_HOME=/usr/java/j2re1.4.2_05
PATH=/usr/java/j2re1.4.2_05/bin:$PATH
```

You can also find numerous multimedia goodies at http://freshrpms.net/ and at http://www.cs.trinity.edu/ftp/pub/FC2-Software-Additions//. The multimedia applications that used to be part of Fedora before its merger with Red Hat are now housed at http://rpm.livna.org. To add this repository to YUM, add to /etc/yum.conf the lines

```
[livna-stable]
name=Livna.org Fedora Compatible Packages (stable)
baseurl=
  http://rpm.livna.org/fedora/$releasever/$basearch/yum/stable
gpgcheck=1
```

and for APT, add this line to /etc/apt/sources:

```
rpm http://rpm.livna.org/ fedora/1/i386 stable
```

and for Up2date,

```
yum livna-stable
http://rpm.livna.org/fedora/1/i386/yum/stable
```

Add the GPG key as detailed on the Livna home page. See Chapter 8 for details on using these package management tools.

Relevant Fedora Core Linux Commands

You'll use these commands when working with multimedia applications for Fedora Core Linux:

CD/DVD Disks

cdda2wav—Copies WAV files from CDs; used by other applications

cdlabelgen—Creates labels for CD jewel cases; used in scripts

cdp—A text-mode CD player

cdparanoia—A CD ripper

cdrecord—A command-line tool to record CDs

dvd+rw-tools—A command-line tool to create DVDs

grip—A CD music ripper

mkisofs—Creates ISO files

xcdroast—A CD recorder

Sound and Music

alsamixer—A console audio mixer

kmid—A MIDI player

mikmod—A MOD music player

rhythmbox—The default music player; it can play from playlists or Internet radio stations

sox—A sound conversion tool

sound-juicer—A CD ripping tool

system-config-soundcard—Default sound card configuration utility

vorbis-tools—The OGG Vorbis codecs

xmms—An MP3 player

Video

kaboodle—A KDE media player

noatun—KDE media player

tvtime—A television viewer

xine—A video player

xmms—An MPEG1/2/3 player

Cameras

gtkam—A front end for gPhoto2

kamera—The KDE digital camera utility

dvgrab—A video camera capture utility using a Firewire connection

Scanners

kooka—The KDE scanner application

xsane—A scanner application

Graphics

eog—Eye of Gnome image viewer

ImageMagick—An image manipulation application

gimp—The GNU Image Manipulation Program

gqview—GNOME image viewer

kcoloredit—KDE palette editor

kiconedit—KDE icon editor

kpaint—A graphics application

kuickshow—KDE image-viewing application

kview—KDE embedded image viewer.

ntpbm-progs—Tools for manipulating netpbm-formatted graphics

xfig—A vector graphic application

Games

maelstrom—Space combat

chromium—Space shooter

fortune-mod—Displays your fortune

freeciv—The FreeCiv multiplayer game

joystick—Configures a joystick for the games

tuxracer—A 3D penguin slalom (inadvertently omitted from the Fedora Core CD, but available from the Fedora Project site)

xboard—Chess

Reference

http://www.cdcopyworld.com/—A resource for technical information about CD media and CD writers.

http://hardware.redhat.com/hcl/—A database of supported hardware.

http://www.opensound.com/download.cgi—The commercial OSS sound driver trial version download.

http:/www.xmms.org/—Home to the Xmms audio player.

http://www.thekompany.com/projects/tkcoggripper/—A free (but not GPL) OGG CD ripper.

http://faceprint.com/code/—An MP3 to OGG converter named mp32ogg.

http://www.ibiblio.org/pub/linux/apps/sound/convert/!INDEX.html—Home to several sound conversion utilities.

http://linux-sound.org/—An excellent resource for Linux music and sound.

http://www.cnpbagwell.com/audio.html—The Audio Format FAQ.

http://www.icecast.org/—A streaming audio server.

http://www.linuxnetmag.com/en/issue4/m4icecast1.html—An Icecast tutorial.

http://linuxselfhelp.com/HOWTO/MP3-HOWTO-7.html—The MP3 HOWTO contains brief descriptions of many audio applications and, although it focuses on the MP3 format, the information is easily generalized to other music formats.

http://www.exploits.org/v4l/—Video for Linux resources.

26

http://fame.sourceforge.net/—Video encoding tools.

http://teletext.mb21.co.uk/faq.shtml—The Teletext FAQ.

http://xine.sourceforge.net/—Home of the Xine DVD/video player.

http://www.MPlayerHQ.hu/homepage/—Home to the MPlayer video player.

http://www.videolan.org/—A VideoLAN project with good documentation.

http://www.nvidia.com/object/linux.html—A resource for scanners.

http://www.nvidia.com/object/linux_display_archive.html—Download page for nVidia drivers.

http://www.ati.com/support/driver.html—Download the Linux graphics drivers for ATI graphics cards.

http://fy.chalmers.se/~appro/linux/DVD+RW/—The DVD+RW/+R/-R[W] for Linux, a HOWTO for creating DVDs under Linux.

PART IV

Appendix

IN THIS PART

APPENDIX A   Fedora Internet Resources   873

Fedora Internet Resources

Linux enjoys a wealth of Internet support in the form of Web sites with technical information, specific program documentation, targeted whitepapers, bug fixes, user experiences, third-party commercial technical support, and even free versions of specialized, fine-tuned clone distributions.

This appendix lists many of the supporting Web sites, FTP repositories, Usenet newsgroups, and electronic mailing lists that you can use to get more information and help with your copy of Fedora Core.

If You Need Help 24/7

If you're a small business, corporate, or enterprise-level Red Hat Linux user, don't forget that you can always turn to the source, Red Hat, Inc., or third-party companies, such as Levanta (http://www.levanta.com/) for commercial technical support on a 24/7 onsite basis, by phone, by electronic mail, or even on a per-incident basis. Red Hat, Inc. offers a spectrum of support options for its software products. You can read more about support options when you purchase Red Hat software at http://www.redhat.com/software/rhel/purchase/.

The appendix is divided into the following sections:

- Web sites with Linux information arranged by category
- Usenet newsgroups pertaining to Linux
- Mailing lists providing Linux user and developer discussions
- Internet Relay Chat groups for Linux information

This appendix also lists Web sites that might be of general interest when using Fedora or specific components such as XFree86. Every effort has been made to ensure the accuracy of the URLs, but keep in mind that the Internet is always in flux!

Keep Up-to-Date with up2date **or** yum

Keeping informed about bug fixes, security updates, and other errata is critical to the success and health of a Red Hat Linux or Fedora system. To keep abreast of the most important developments when using a commercial Red Hat Linux distro, make sure to register with Red Hat's network, subscribe to Red Hat announcements, or regularly browse http://www.redhat.com/security/. You can also use the up2date client to maintain your workstation or server—but you'll need to subscribe to Red Hat's commercial support.

Fedora users can use the yum command (as root) to keep up with bug fixes, new software packages, or security updates.

Web Sites and Search Engines

Literally thousands of Web sites exist with information about Linux and Red Hat Linux. The key to getting the answers you need right away involves using the best search engines and techniques. Knowing how to search can mean the difference between frustration and success when troubleshooting problems. This section provides some Internet search tips and lists Red Hat, Fedora, and Linux-related sites sorted by various topics. The lists aren't comprehensive, but have been checked and were available at the time of this writing.

Web Search Tips

Troubleshooting problems with Linux by searching the Web can be an efficient and productive way to get answers to vexing problems. One of the most basic rules for conducting productive searches is to use specific search terms to find specific answers. For example, if you simply search for "Red Hat Linux," you'll end up with too many links and too much information. But if you search for "Fedora Core sound," you're more likely to find the information you need. If you've received an error message, use it; otherwise, use the Linux kernel diagnostic message as your search criterion.

Other effective techniques include

- Using symbols in the search string, such as the plus sign (+) to force matches of Web pages containing both strings (if such features are supported by the search engine used by Web search site)

- Searching within returned results

- Sorting results (usually by date to get the latest information)

- Searching for related information

- Stemming searches; for example, specifying returns for not only "link" but also "linking" and "linked"

Invest some time and experiment with your favorite search engine's features—the result will be more productive searches. In addition to sharpening your search skills, also take the time to choose the best search engine for your needs.

Google Is Your Friend

Some of the fastest and most comprehensive search engines on the Web are powered by Linux, so it makes sense to use the best available resources. Out of the myriad number of Web sites with search engines, `http://google.com` stands out from the crowd with 10 million or more users per month. The site uses advanced hardware and software to bring speed and efficiency to your searches. If you're looking for specific Linux answers, take advantage of Google's Linux page at `http://google.com/linux`.

Why is Google (named after a math number) so powerful? You can find get a quick idea from the Google folks at `http://www.google.com/technology/index.html`. Part of its success is because of great algorithms, good programming, and simple interface design, but most users really seem to appreciate Google's uncanny capability to provide links to what you're looking for in the first page of a search return. Google's early success was also assured because the site ran its search engine on clusters of thousands of PCs running Red Hat Linux!

Google has the largest database size of any search engine on the Web, with more than a billion Web pages and a petabyte (1024TB) of storage. The database size is important because empty search results are useless to online users, and the capability to return hits on esoteric subjects can make the difference between success and failure or satisfaction and frustration. Some of Google's features include a GoogleScout link to return similar pages on the results page, the capability to see the exact version of a Web page as returned to a search engine (known as a "cached" feature), advanced searches, and more recently, a link to an active Usenet news feed!

To get a better idea of what Google can offer you, browse to `http://www.google.com/options/`. You'll find links to more than two dozen different services and tools covering specialized searches, databases, information links, translators, and other helpful browsing tools.

Red Hat Package Listings

You can quickly and easily view a list of the installed RPM packages installed on your Red Hat Linux or Fedora Core system, along with a short description of each package, by using the `rpm` command:

```
$ rpm -qai ¦ less
```

Fedora Core users can also use the yum command to view package names and information about not only installed packages, but any available updated packages, like this:

```
$ yum info ¦ less
```

If you use Fedora and only want to see info about your installed packages, use the yum command's installed list option like so:

```
$ yum info installed ¦ less
```

However, the Fedora Project conveniently provides a list and description of each package in each Fedora release at http://fedora.redhat.com/projects/package-list/. A list of packages included with the last free Linux distribution from Red Hat, Inc., Red Hat Linux 9, can be found at http://www.fedora.us/pkglists/fedora-9-stable.html l.

Certification

Linux certification courses are part of the rapidly growing information technology training industry. Hundreds of different vendors now offer courses about and testing of Linux skillsets. However, because Linux is open-source software, there are no formal rules or mandates concerning what knowledge or level of expertise is required for certification. If you are interested in certification using Red Hat Linux and would like to pursue a career or obtain employment with a company using Red Hat Linux, you really should seek training from the one best and most-qualified company: Red Hat, Inc.

That said, the following Web sites might be of interest if you'd like to pursue a certification track for Red Hat or other Linux distributions:

- http://www.lpi.org—The Linux Professional Institute, with Linux vendor- and distribution-neutral programs

- http://www.redhat.com/training/—Entry page to Red Hat, Inc.'s Global Learning Services and information about the Red Hat Certified Engineer program

Commercial Support

Commercial support for Linux and Red Hat Linux is an essential ingredient to the success of Linux in the corporate and business community. Although hundreds, if not thousands, of consultants well versed in Linux and Unix are available on call for a fee, here's a short list of the best-known Linux support providers:

- http://www.redhat.com/apps/support/—Red Hat, Inc.'s main support page with links to its various support programs.

- http://www.levanta.com—Home page for Levanta (formerly known as Linuxcare), providing local and remote technical support for many types of installations and customers.

- http://www.ibm.com/linux/—Linux services offered by IBM include e-business solutions, open-source consulting, database migration, clustering, servers, and support. In addition to service-oriented support companies, nearly every commercial distributor of Linux has some form of easily purchased commercial support. There are various ways in which to take advantage of support services (such as remote management, onsite consulting, device driver development, and so on), but needs will vary according to customer circumstances and installations.

The Benefits of Joining a Linux User Group

Join a local Linux Users Group (LUG)! Joining and participating in a local LUG has many benefits. You'll be able to get help, trade information, and learn many new and wonderful things about Linux. Most LUGs don't have membership dues, and many often sponsor regular lectures and discussions from leading Linux, GNU, and open-source experts. For one great place to start, browse to http://www.tux.org/luglist.html.

Documentation

Nearly all Linux distributions include thousands of pages of documentation in the form of manual pages, HOWTO documents (in various formats, such as text and HTML), mini-HOWTO documents, or software package documentation (usually found under the /usr/share/doc/ directory). However, the definitive site for reading the latest versions of these documents is the Linux Documentation Project, found at http://www.tldp.org.

Linux Guides

If you're looking for more extensive and detailed information concerning a Linux subject, try reading one of the many Linux guides. These guides, available for a number of subjects, dwell on technical topics in more detail and at a more leisurely pace than a HOWTO. You find copies of

- "Advanced Bash-Scripting Guide," by Mendel Cooper; a guide to shell scripting using bash

- "LDP Author Guide," by Mark F. Komarinski; how to write LDP documentation

- "Linux Administration Made Easy," by Steve Frampton

- "Linux Administrator's Security Guide," by Kurt Seifried

- "Linux Consultants Guide," by Joshua Drake; a worldwide listing of commercial Linux consultants

- "Linux from Scratch," by Gerard Beekmans; creating a Linux distribution from software

A

- "Linux Kernel 2.4 Internals," by Tigran Aivazian; a guide to the 2.4 kernel

- "Linux Kernel Module Programming Guide," by Ori Pomerantz; a somewhat dated guide to building 2.0 and 2.2 series modules

- "Securing and Optimizing Linux," by Gerhard Mourani; specific to Red Hat Linux

- Linux certification

- "The Linux Network Administrator's Guide, Second Edition," by Olaf Kirch and Terry Dawson; a comprehensive Net admin guide

The Fedora Project

- `http://fedora.redhat.com`—Home page for the Fedora Project, Red Hat, Inc.'s community-based free Linux distribution. Fedora Core is the main release of this Linux distribution, and includes thousands of software packages that form the core of an up-to-date, cutting-edge Linux-based desktop.

- `http://www.fedora.us/`—Home page for the original Fedora Linux Project, hosted by the University of Hawaii ICS Department. The original project aimed at producing contributor packages for Red Hat Linux, similar to those available for the Debian Project (`http://www.debian.org`). On September 22, 2003, the Red Hat Linux Project merged with the Fedora Linux Project to become the Fedora Project.

Red Hat Linux

- `http://www.redhat.com`—Home page for Red Hat, Inc.'s distribution of Red Hat Linux for the Alpha CPU, Intel-based hardware, and the new Itanium processor. Support is also provided for older, but now discontinued, versions of the SPARC.

- `http://www.redhat.com/apps/support/documentation.html`—Specific Web page with links to current official Red Hat manuals and guides, FAQs, HOWTOs, white-papers, free books, mailing list archives, hardware compatibility lists, and other documentation.

Mini-CD Linux Distributions

Mini-CD Linux distributions are used for many different purposes. Some distributions are used to boot to a read-only firewall configuration; others are used to provide as complete a rescue environment as possible; whereas others are used to either install or help jumpstart an install of a full distribution. Mini-CDs are available in a wide variety of sizes, such as 3" CD-Rs (or CD-RW) with sizes ranging from 185MB to 210MB. You can also download an `.iso` image and create a Linux bootable business card, typically fitting on a 40MB or 50MB credit card–sized CD-R (consider using a mini–CD-RW, especially if you want to upgrade your distribution often). Here are some links to these distributions:

- `http://www.lnx-bbc.org`—Home page for the Linux BBC, a 40MB image hosting a rather complete live Linux session with X, a Web browser, and a host of networking tools.

- `http://crux.nu/`—Home page of the CRUX i686–optimized Linux distribution.

- `http://www.trustix.net/`—Home page for the free version of the Trustix Secure Linux distribution, which currently uses the latest 2.4 kernel. Trustix is RPM based.

- `http://www.smoothwall.org/community/home/`—The 22MB SmoothWall distribution, which easily fits on a bootable business card and is used to install a Web-administered firewall, router, or gateway with SSH, HTTP, and other services.

- `http://www.phy.olemiss.edu/debian-cd/`—A 185MB Debian 3.0 (Woody) distribution with enough software to bring up a working Debian system. X isn't included, so you must download and install other packages to expand the system.

Floppy-Based Linux Distributions

- `http://www.linuxrouter.org`—Home page for the Linux Router Project

- `http://floppix.ccai.com/index.html`—A Debian-based floppy

- `http://www.toms.net/rb/`—Tom's root and boot disk distribution

- `http://www.coyotelinux.com/`—Secure routing and embedded Linux disk distributions

- `http://trinux.sourceforge.net`—An ultra-secure Linux distribution on floppy

- `http://PenguinBackup.sourceforge.net/`—A unique, floppy-based distribution that allows quick backup of your Palm-type PDA

Various Intel-Based Linux Distributions

Choosing a Linux distribution (distro) for an Intel-based PC is generally a matter of personal preference or need. Many Linux users prefer Red Hat's distro because of its excellent support, commercial support options, and widespread use around the world. However, many different Linux distributions are available for download. One of the best places to start looking for a new distro or new version of your favorite distro is `http://www.distrowatch.com`:

- `http://www.xandros.net`—New home of the original and improved version of Corel's Debian-based Linux

- `http://www.debian.org`—The Debian Linux distribution, consisting only of software distributed under the GNU GPL license

- `http://www.independence.seul.org`—A newer Red Hat–based Linux distribution

- `http://www.libranet.com`—A Linux distribution based on Debian

- `http://www.slackware.com`—Home page for download of the newest version of one of the oldest Linux distributions, Slackware

- `http://www.suse.com`—Home page for SuSE Linux, also available for the PowerPC

- `http://www.linux-mandrake.com`—A Pentium-optimized, RPM-based distribution, originally based on Red Hat's Linux distribution

PowerPC-Based Linux Distributions

- `http://penguinppc.org/`—Home page for the PowerPC GNU/Linux distribution

- `http://www.suse.com`—SuSE PPC Linux; moving to UnitedLinux

- `http://www.yellowdoglinux.com`—Home page for Terra Soft Solutions' Yellow Dog Linux for the PowerPC, which is based on Red Hat

Linux on Laptops and PDAs

One of the definitive sites for getting information about running Linux on your laptop is Kenneth Harker's Linux Laptop site. Although not as actively updated as in the past, this site (`http://www.linux-laptop.net`) still contains the world's largest collection of Linux and laptop information, with links to user experiences and details concerning specific laptop models.

Another site to check is Werner Heuser's Tuxmobil-Mobile Unix Web site at `http://www.tuxmobil.org`. You'll find links to information such as IrDA, Linux PDAs, and cell phones. Linux Zaurus PDA users can browse to `http://www.openzaurus.org` to download a complete open-source replacement operating system for the Zaurus 5000 and 5500 models.

The X Window System

Although much technical information is available on the Internet regarding the X Window System, finding answers to specific questions when troubleshooting can be problematic. If you're having a problem using X, first try to determine whether the problem is software or hardware related. When searching or asking for help (such as on Usenet's `comp.os.linux.x` newsgroup, which you can access through Google's Groups link; see the next section for other helpful Linux newsgroups), try to be as specific as possible. Some critical factors or information needed to adequately assess a problem include the Linux distribution in use; the kernel version used; the version of X used; the brand, name, and model of your video card; the names, brands, and models of your monitor and other related hardware.

This section lists just some of the basic resources for Linux XFree86 users. Definitive technical information regarding X is available from `http://www.X.org`:

- `http://www.lesstif.org/`—Home page for the GPL'd OSF/Motif clone, LessTif

- `http://www.motifzone.net`—Site for download of the open source version of Motif for Linux, Open Motif

- `http://www.rahul.net/kenton/index.shtml`—Ken Lee's X and Motif Web site with numerous links to tutorial, development, and other information about X

- `http://www.xfree86.org`—Home page for The XFree86 Project, Inc., developers of XFree86, used with Red Hat Linux

- `http://www.xig.com/`—Home page for a commercial version of X for Linux (along with other software products)

Usenet Newsgroups

Linux-related Usenet newsgroups are another good source of information if you're having trouble using Linux. (Refer to Chapter 20, "News Servers and Other Collaborative Communication," for more information about using newsgroups.) If your ISP doesn't offer a comprehensive selection of Linux newsgroups, you can browse to `http://groups.google.com/`.

The primary Linux and Linux-related newsgroups are

- `alt.os.linux.caldera`—All about Caldera's OpenLinux

- `alt.os.linux.corel`—All about Corel's Linux

- `alt.os.linux.dial-up`—Using PPP for dial-up

- `alt.os.linux.mandrake`—All about Mandrake Linux

- `alt.os.linux.redhat`—Alternative discussions about Red Hat Linux

- `alt.os.linux.slackware`—Using Slackware Linux

- `alt.os.linux.suse`—Using SuSE Linux

- `comp.os.linux.admin`—Administering Linux

- `comp.os.linux.advocacy`—Heated discussions about Linux and other related issues

- `comp.os.linux.alpha`—Using Linux on the Alpha CPU

- `comp.os.linux.announce`—General Linux announcements

- `comp.os.linux.answers`—Releases of new Linux FAQs and other information

- `comp.os.linux.development.apps`—Using Linux development tools

A

- `comp.os.linux.development.system`—Building the Linux kernel
- `comp.os.linux.embedded`—Linux embedded device development
- `comp.os.linux.hardware`—Configuring Linux for various hardware devices
- `comp.os.linux.help`—Help with Linux
- `comp.os.linux.m68k`—Linux on Motorola's 68K-family CPUs
- `comp.os.linux.misc`—Miscellaneous Linux topics
- `comp.os.linux.networking`—Networking and Linux
- `comp.os.linux.portable`—Using Linux on laptops
- `comp.os.linux.powerpc`—Using PPC Linux
- `comp.os.linux.questions`—Questions about Linux
- `comp.os.linux.redhat`—All about Red Hat Linux
- `comp.os.linux.security`—Linux security issues
- `comp.os.linux.setup`—Linux installation topics
- `comp.os.linux.x`—Linux and the X Window System
- `comp.windows.x.apps`—Using X-based clients
- `comp.windows.x.i386unix`—X for Unix PCs
- `comp.windows.x.intrinsics`—X Toolkit library topics
- `comp.windows.x.kde`—Using KDE and X discussions
- `comp.windows.x.motif`—All about Motif programming
- `comp.windows.x`—Discussions about X
- `linux.admin.*`—Two newsgroups for Linux administrators
- `linux.debian.*`—30 newsgroups about Debian
- `linux.dev.*`—25 or more Linux development newsgroups
- `linux.help`—Get help with Linux
- `linux.kernel`—The Linux kernel
- `linux.redhat.*`—Red Hat-based discussions: `linux.redhat.announce`, `linux.redhat.list`, `linux.redhat.applixware`, `linux.redhat.misc`, `linux.redhat.devel`, `linux.redhat.pam`, `linux.redhat.development`, `linux.redhat.ppp`, `linux.redhat.digest`, `linux.redhat.rpm`, `linux.redhat.install`, `linux.redhat.sparc`, `linux.redhat.axp`

Mailing Lists

Mailing lists are interactive or digest-form electronic discussions about nearly any topic. To use a mailing list, you must generally send an email request to be subscribed to the list, and then verify the subscription with a return message from the master list mailer. After subscribing to an interactive form of list, each message sent to the list will appear in your email inbox. However, many lists provide a digest form of subscription in which a single- or half-day's traffic is condensed in a single message. The digest form is generally preferred unless you've set up electronic mail filtering (Chapter 20 also discusses the use of mailing lists in Fedora Core).

The main Fedora Project mailing lists are detailed here, but there are quite a few Linux-related lists. Red Hat's offerings are also provided here. You can search for nearly all online mailing lists by using a typical mailing list search Web page, such as the one at `http://www.lsoft.com/lists/list_q.html`.

GNOME and KDE Mailing Lists

GNOME users and developers should know that more than two-dozen mailing lists are available through `http://mail.gnome.org/`. KDE users will also benefit by perusing the KDE-related mailing lists at `http://www.kde.org/mailinglists.html`.

Fedora Project Mailing Lists

The Fedora Project is still in its infancy at the time of this writing. You'll find many other knowledgeable users with answers to your questions by participating in one of Fedora's mailing lists. The lists are focused on using, testing, and developing and participating in Fedora Core's development:

- `fedora-devel-list@redhat.com`—Developer information exchanges

- `fedora-docs-list@redhat.com`—For Fedora users working on project documentation

- `fedora-list@redhat.com`—Discussions among users of Fedora Core releases

- `fedora-test-list@redhat.com`—Queries and reports from testers of Fedora Core test releases

Red Hat Mailing Lists

Red Hat, Inc., provides a comprehensive archive and mailing list management Web page at `http://www.redhat.com/mailman/listinfo` /. You can use this page to subscribe to one of more than 40 mailing lists related to Red Hat Linux. Some of the more pertinent lists are

- `redhat-announce-list`—General announcements about Red Hat Linux
- `redhat-devel-list`—Information for developers using Red Hat Linux
- `redhat-install-list`—Installation issues about Red Hat Linux
- `redhat-list`—A general Red Hat Linux discussion list
- `redhat-ppp-list`—Issues regarding PPP and dial-up under Red Hat Linux
- `redhat-secure-server`—Using Red Hat, Inc.'s secure server
- `redhat-watch-list`—Announcements of bug fixes, updates for Red Hat Linux
- `rpm-list`—Using the Red Hat Package Manager
- `under-the-brim`—Red Hat's helpful electronic newsletter

Internet Relay Chat

Internet Relay Chat (IRC) is a popular form and forum of communication for many Red Hat Linux developers and users because it allows an interactive, real-time exchange of information and ideas. To use IRC, you must have an IRC client and the address of a network and server hosting the desired chat channel for your discussions.

You can use the `irc.freenode.net` IRC server, or one listed at `http://www.freenode.net/` to chat with other Fedora Project users. Two current channels are

- #fedora channel—General chat about Fedora
- #fedora-devel—Hangout for a number of Fedora Project developers

One comprehensive list of active Linux-related IRC channels can be found at `http://www.helsinki.fi/~rvaranka/Computer/Linux/IRC.shtml`. To get help with getting started with IRC, browse to `http://www.irchelp.org/`. Some of the channels of interest might be

- #linux—General discussions about Linux
- #linuxhelp—A help chat discussion for new users

Most IRC networks provide one or more Linux channels, although some providers require sign-up and registration before you can access any chat channel.

Index

Symbols & Numerics

& (ampersand), 720

@ (at) character, 762

\ (backslash), 734

` (backtick), 735, 771

#! (bang line, hash-bang, or she-bang), 724-725, 760

| (bar) operator, 720

$ (dollar) character, 761

|| (double pipe), 557

" (double quotes), 733

... (ellipse), 719

/ (escape character), 732-734

% (percent) character, 762

(pound) sign, 721

; (semicolon), 760

$PATH (shell environment variable), 140

' (single quote), 733

10BASE-T networks, 382

100BASE-T networks, 383

802.11 standard, 422

A

AbiWord word processing program, 817-818

ac command, 247

access control
 Apache Web server
  allow and deny directives, 520-521
  overview of, 520, 524
 database clients
  GUI, 573
  SSH, 572-573
  Web and, 573-574
 ftpaccess file and, 604-607
 Sendmail, configuring for, 650-651
access control lists (ACLs), 266, 474
accessing
 shell with Perl, 771-772
 value of variables, 727
 variable data files, /var directory and, 128
 variables using positional parameters, 728
Accessories menu, 830
account management for databases, 550
ACLs (access control lists), 266, 474
active file (INN package), 688
ad blocking with caching nameserver, 453
Add a New Print Queue configuration dialog
 box, 356
Add Partition dialog box, 68
add-on postfixes, 617
add-on prefixes, 616
Add/Remove Software, 215-216
adding users, 245-247
address-based virtual hosts, 530
addressing and TCP/IP, 376-378
administrative tools for controlling services at
 boot
 chkconfig, 199-200
 system-config-services tool, 202
administrator email addresses, displaying, 610
Adobe Photoshop, 859
adsl-setup command, 493

adsl-start command, 493
adsl-stop command, 494
Advanced Linux Sound Architecture (ALSA), 95,
 844
Advanced Power Management (APM), 101-102
afio tool, 329
agetty command, 495
aliases, 649-650, 722
all-in-one devices, troubleshooting, 373
allow directive, 520-521
AllowOverrides directive (.htaccess files), 519
ALSA (Advanced Linux Sound Architecture), 95,
 844
alsactl command, 95
alsamixer command, 95, 845
always on Internet connection, 492
Amanda backup application, 321, 328-329
America Online (AOL) service, 481
American National Standards Institute (ANSI),
 694
American Registry for Internet Numbers, 376
ampersand (&), 720
Anaconda (installer), 18, 62
AND statement (SQL), 557-558
anonymous access to FTP servers, controlling,
 600
anonymous FTP servers, 592-593
anonymous users, limiting access of, 604
ANSI (American National Standards Institute),
 694
AOL (America Online) service, 481
Apache Software Foundation, 502
Apache Web server
 dynamic content and
  CGI, 534-535
  flow control, 540
  SSI, 536-540

file system authentication and access control

  allow and deny directives, 520-521

  authentication, 521-523

  overview of, 520, 524

FTP and, 594

graphic interface configuration of

  overview of, 541

  Performance tab, 544

  Server tab, 543

  virtual host properties, 542

installing

  building source code for, 505-506

  file locations after build and install, 507

  from RPM, 503-505

logging, 532-534

modules

  mod.access, 525

  mod.alias, 525

  mod.asis, 525

  mod.auth, 526

  mod.auth.anon, 526

  mod.auth.dbm, 526

  mod.auth.digest, 526

  mod.autoindex, 527

  mod.cgi, 527

  mod.dir, 527

  mod.env, 527

  mod.expires, 527

  mod.headers, 527

  mod.imap, 528

  mod.include, 528

  mod.info, 528

  mod.log.config, 528

  mod.mime, 528

  mod.mime.magic, 528

  mod.negotiation, 528

  mod.proxy, 528

  mod.rewrite, 529

  mod.setenvif, 529

  mod.speling, 529

  mod.ssl, 529

  mod.status, 529

  mod.unique.id, 529

  mod.userdir, 530

  mod.usertrack, 530

  mod.vhost.alias, 530

  overview of, 524

overview of, 501-503, 508

quick start guide, 507-508

runtime configuration settings

  configuration directives, 514

  editing httpd.conf file, 514-517

  .htaccess files, 518-519

  multiprocessing modules (MPMs), 517

  overview of, 513

starting manually, 508-509

starting or stopping

  chkconfig command, using, 511-512

  /etc/rc.d/init.d/httpd, using, 510

  service command, using, 511

  system-config-services client, using, 512-513

virtual hosting

  address-based, 530

  name-based, 531

APM (Advanced Power Management), 101-102

apm command, 102

apmsleep command, 102

applications. *See* **software**

apropos command, 135, 142

APT, installing and configuring, 218-219

apt-get (Debian Project), 17

ar command, 705

archives, restoring files from

with cpio, 324

with tar, 323

arithmetic operators (Perl), 764

ark archiving tool (KDE), 326-327

arrays (Perl), 761

assessing backup needs and resources, 313

assigning

permissions, 149-150

priorities to processes, 229-231

usernames, 134

value to variables, 726

asterisk in password field, 248

at (@) character, 762

AT Attachment Packet Interface (ATAPI), 108

AT command, 488

atomicity in transaction processing, 560

attachments to email, sending binary files as text

BinHex, 643

uuencode and uudecode, 644-645

yenc, 643

audio

commands for, 868

DAO (Disk-At-Once) audio, creating, 113

formats, 845-847

music players, 847

recording, 844

streaming audio, 848

AUS-CERT advisory AL-1999.004, 477

authenticated FTP servers, 593

authentication

overview of, 521-523

Pluggable Authentication Modules (PAMs), 250-251

autoconf utility, 701-702

autofs, 287

automated installation method, 48-51

Automatically Partition button, 66

automating tasks, 729-731

automount daemon (amd), 287

autoresponders, 658

Axis network-based Webcams, 855

B

background processing, 720

backing up

assessing needs and resources for, 313

before changing configuration file, 205

before editing configuration file, 154

before partitioning drive, 46

data loss, reasons for, 312-313

frequency of, determining, 314

FTP server files, 603

full backup, strategies for

with incremental backup, 317

on periodic basis, 316

hardware and media for, choosing, 318

kernel, 797

Master Boot Record, 340

mirroring data or RAID arrays, 317

network storage, 320

practices for, 314

principles of, 314

removable storage media

CD-RW and DVD+RW/-RW drives, 319

FireWire drives, 319

USB and solid-state drives, 319

Zip drives, 318

sample strategies for, 315-316

software for

afio tool, 329

Amanda backup application, 328-329

cdbackup tool, 329

cpio, 323-324

dd command, 327

flexbackup tool, 329

free, 329

GNOME File Roller, 325

KDE ark and kdat tools, 326-327

tar, 321-323

strategy for, choosing, 311, 318

tape drives, 320

xorg.conf file, 95

backslash (\), 734

backtick (`), 735, 771

backup levels, 316

badblocks command, 303

Balsa email client, 639, 818

bandwidth, saving, 497

bang line (#!), 724-725, 760

bar (|) operator, 720

bash (Bourne Again SHell)

comparison of expressions

file operators, 738-739

logical operators, 740

numbers, 737-738

overview of, 735

strings, 736-737

overview of, 138, 716

shell scripts and

interpreting through specific shells, 724-725

running new program, 722-723

storing for systemwide access, 724

Basic Authentication (Apache), 521-523

Basic Input Output System

autodetect feature, 289

description of, 190

entering, 44

tuning disk using, 299

Berkeley Internet Name Domain (BIND)

overview of, 434

providing DNS with

logging, 462

named.conf file, 457-461

overview of, 454-456

resolver configuration, 463

rndc.conf file, 456

running named (nameserver daemon), 464

beta releases, testing, 24

Biff mail daemon, 657

/bin directory, 121

binary files, sending as text

BinHex, 643

uuencode and uudecode, 644-645

yenc, 643

BIND (Berkeley Internet Name Domain)

overview of, 434

providing DNS with

logging, 462

named.conf file, 457-461

overview of, 454-456

resolver configuration, 463

rndc.conf file, 456

running named (nameserver daemon), 464

BIND configuration tool, 471

BinHex 4.0 format, 643

BIOS (Basic Input Output System)

autodetect feature, 289

description of, 190

entering, 44

tuning disk using, 299

block devices, managing files for

mknod command, 305

naming conventions, 305

overview of, 303-304

How can we make this index more useful? Email us at indexes@samspublishing.com

blocking host access to servers, 605

blocks, 265-266

Bluecurve, 160

Bluefish—Found HTML editor, 828

Boolean logic, 766

/boot directory, 122

boot loaders

    choosing, configuring, and installing, 69-70

    in boot process, 190-191

    LILO, 190

    overview of, 56-57

    troubleshooting, 807

    See also GRUB

boot process

    boot loader and, 190-191

    init scripts and, 197-198

    loading Linux kernel, 191-192

    overview of, 189-190

boot prompt, installation options for, 61

boot time, activating DHCP at, 400

bootdisk, creating, 46, 75

booting

    from generic boot floppy, 342

    from GRUB boot floppy, 342

    into default runlevel, 194-196

    into non-default runlevel with GRUB, 196-197

    See also boot loaders; boot process

booting system and installation, 56-57

BootMagic, 191

Bootp (protocol), 397

break statement, 754

bridges (network), 385

broadcast addressing, 381

Bsdftpd-ssl server, 594

BugTraq Web site, 429, 473

built-in variables, 726, 731

burning CDs and DVDs

    from command line

        overview of, 837-839

        packet writing, 840

        session writing, 839-840

    with GUI client

        GNOME Grip, 843

        overview of, 841-842

        X-CD-Roast, 842-843

    overview of, 836-837

business

    features related to, 20-21

    operating system

        choosing for, 28

        considerations for, 29-30

BusyBox program, 344

button assignment, 130

Bynari, 659

bzDisk directive, 799

bzImage directive, 799

C

c

    overview of, 694

    simple program example, 708-709

C++, 695-696

cables (network)

    fiber optic, 385

    unshielded twisted pair (UTP), 384

caching nameserver, 452-453

cameras

    handheld digital, 856-857

    Webcams, 855-856

capturing screen images, 863

Card Services software, 106-108

cardctl command, 108

case sensitivity of SQL commands, 554

case statement, 752-753

cat command, 126

cd command, 142

CD drives

configuring

checking drive assignment, 108

overview of, 108-110

initializing IEEE-1394 drives, 110-113

CD-ROM

burning

from command line, 837-838

with GUI client, 841-843

overview of, 836-837

installing from, 55-58

performing media check of, 62

preparing to install from, 44

software, installing all included on, 54

CD-ROM filesystems, 274

CD-ROM media, testing, 18

CD-RW drives

configuring

checking drive assignment, 108

overview of, 108-110

overview of, 319

cdbackup tool, 329

cdda2wav command, 113

cdparanoia command, 113

cdpath commands, configuring, 614

cdrdao command, 113

cdrecord command, 58, 111, 838

cdrecord -scanbus command, 836

cdrtools package, 839

cellular networking, 421

certification courses, 876

CGI (Common Gateway Interface) programming

Apache Web server and, 534-535

Perl and, 757

change command, 261

changing

default window managers, 176-177

file permissions, 151, 240

passwords in batch, 252

resolution on-the-fly, 167

runlevels, 203

user information, 134

character devices, managing files for

mknod command, 305

naming conventions, 305

overview of, 303-304

checking drive assignment, 108

CheckInstall program, 225

checklists

hardware inventory, 40-43

predeployment planning, 30-31

chfn command, 134, 152

chgrp command, 240

chipsets, 849

chkconfig command, 93, 511-512

chkconfig tool, 199-200

chmod command, 151, 240

chown command, 240

chpasswd command, 252

chroot feature (UNIX), 473

chsh command, 138, 245

classes and TCP/IP addressing, 377

cleanfeed package, 691

client interface (FTP), 581

client/server model, 550, 592

clients

database, installing and maintaining, 549

X Window System and, 159

How can we make this index more useful? Email us at indexes@samspublishing.com

Coda network filesystem, 267

codecs, 851

Coffee Cup editor, 828

coffee pot cams, 855

column types (SQL), 554

column-level rights (MySQL), 566

command line

Perl and, 781

system administration and, 118

using, 117-118

command-line clients

description of, 572

email (mutt), 635-637

mysql, 575

psql, 576

commands

ac, 247

for accessing productivity tools, 832

adsl-setup, 493

adsl-start, 493

adsl-stop, 494

agetty, 495

alsactl, 95

alsamixer, 95, 845

apm, 102

apmsleep, 102

apropos, 135, 142

ar, 705

AT, 488

badblocks, 303

/bin and /sbin directories, 121

for cameras, 868

for CD/DVD discs, 867

cardctl, 108

cat, 126

cd, 142

cdda2wav, 113

cdparanoia, 113

cdpath, 614

cdrdao, 113

cdrecord, 58, 111, 838

cdrecord -scanbus, 836

change, 261

for changing permissions, 240

chfn (change finger information), 134, 152

chgrp, 240

chkconfig, 93, 511-512

chmod, 151, 240

chown, 240

chpasswd, 252

chsh, 138, 245

for compressing and decompressing files, 143

for configuring X Window System, 185

console Internet and network, 157

cp, 312, 331-332

for creating filesystems, 279

date, 104

dd, 78, 292, 327

depmod, 790

dump, 325

e2fsck, 302

echo, 127

for emacs editor, 147

for email management, 661

env, 139

exit, 133

fax, 721

fax help, 829

fax make, 829

fdisk, 78

fgrep, 96

file, 225

for file management, 142, 157

find, suid and sgid permissions, 153

finding documentation on, 136

finger, 134

ftp, 583-586

for FTP access, 602

for FTP service management, 625

for FTP session, 581-583

ftphosts file, 618-619

ftpshut, 621-623

for games, 869

for getting information, 157

GNU Project, 136

gpasswd, 242

gprof, 706

for graphics, 868

grep, output of chkconfig and, 199

groupadd, 242

groupdel, 242

groupmod, 242

groups, 261

growisofs, 840

grpck, 242

hdparm, 300-301

htpasswd, 522

hwclock, 72, 104

ifconfig, 140, 376, 389-391

init, 192

insmod, 113, 790

internet-druid, 113, 497

iwconfig, 420

iwlist, 420

iwpriv, 420

iwspy, 420

job-control, 717

keyboard-related for Linux and X, 86

kill, 228

last, 247

lastb, 247

less, 23, 136

lftp, 587-588

links, 137

linux rescue, 343

ln, 506

loadkeys, 87, 131

locate, 142

logname, 261

logout, 133

logwatch, 730

lokkit, 424-426

losetup, 292

lp, 367

lpc, 367

lpg, 367

lprm, 367

lpstat, 367

ls, 119, 238

lsmod, 89, 790-791

lspci, 849

make, 699-701

man, 23, 136

for management

    of filesystems, 306-307

    of network connectivity, 430

    of newsgroups, 691

    of running programs, 157

mget, 585

mgetty, 497

mkbootdisk, 56

mkdir, 150

mkdosfs, 282

mke2fs, 280, 302

mkfs.ext3, 280-281

mkisofs, 837

mknod, 305

mkpasswd, 134

mkreiserfs, 281

modinfo, 790

modprobe, 387-388, 790

mount, 283-284, 303

mouseconfig, 131

mysql_install_db, 564

neat, 497

netstat, 393

newusers, 252

nice, 229

nmap, 365

nohup, 131

ntsysv, 92, 513

parted, 279

passwd, 152, 155, 245

patch, 702, 796-797

perldoc, 761

print-related, 353

printenv, 139

for printing, 367-368, 374

for programming, 713

ps, 226-227

restore, 325

rm, 154

rmmod, 790

route, 391-393

rpm

    command-line options, 209-211

    freshen option, 213

    overview of, 144, 207, 875

    query options, 212

    rebuilddb option, 213

    software installation and, 211

    update options, 212

rpmbuild, 211

rsync, copying files with, 335-337

for scanners, 868

scp, 333-335, 581

sendmail and Perl, 776

sensors, 114

for server administration, 619

service, starting or stopping Apache server
    using, 511

setfonts, 131

setserial, 98

setup, 205

sftp, 335, 580

shutdown, 78, 156-157, 615

smbclient, 414

smbstatus, 413

sndconfig, 88

for sound and music, 868

sox, 846-847

splint, 705

SQL and case sensitivity, 554

startx, 174-175, 721

statserial, 97

su, 154, 252-254

sudo, 154, 254-257

sync, 301

sysctl, 808-809

tar, 144

telinit, 203

telnet, 133

testparm and Samba, 413

time, 229

top, 230-231

touch, 148

tree, 119

tune2fs, 297, 302

umask, 148

umount, 284

up2date, 505

uptime, 231

for user and group management, 157

useradd, 155, 242-245

useradd -G, 244

userdel, 156, 245

userinfo, 261

usermod, 242, 245

userpasswd, 261

for using Perl, 781

for vi editor, 146

for video, 868

vimtutor, 147

w, 247

wget, 588-589

whatis, 142

whereis, 136, 142

which, 138

for writing shell scripts, 755

yum, 874-876

for YUM, 220

zless, 23

comment character, 760

comments, 698, 721

commercial support providers, 876

Common Gateway Interface (CGI) programming

    Apache Web server and, 534-535

    Perl and, 757

common log formats, 533

Common UNIX Printing System (CUPS)

    database of defined printers, 350

    overview of, 349-351

    printer entry, creating, 369-370

    using, 369

CommuniGate Pro, 659

comp.protocols.tcp-ip.domains FAQ Web site, 468

comparison of expressions

    overview of, 735

    pdksh and bash

        file operators, 738-739

        logical operators, 740

        number comparison, 737-738

        overview of, 735

        string comparison, 736-737

    tcsh

        file operators, 742-744

        logical operators, 744

        numbers, 741-742

        overview of, 740

        strings, 741

comparison operators (Perl), 763

compatibility with proprietary Microsoft file formats, 812

compiled languages, 694

compiling

    kernel, 797-798, 806-807

    software from source

        RPM files, 222-224

        src.rpm files, 221-222

        tar files, 224-225

compound operators (Perl), 764

Comprehensive Perl Archive Network (CPAN), 775-777

compressing files

    allowing users to, 613

    with shell, 143-144

Computer Emergency Response Team, 595

CONCAT function (MySQL), 557

concatenation function, 557

conditional statements

    case, 752-753

    if, 750-752

Perl

if/else, 766

unless, 767

config directives (SSI), 537-538

configuration files, backing up, 312

Configure Keyboard dialog box, 85

Configure Mouse dialog box, 90

./configure script, using to build Apache server code, 506

configuring

anonymous FTP servers, 603

Apache Web servers

configuration directives, 514

editing httpd.conf file, 514-517

graphic interface configuration, 541

.htaccess files, 518-519

multiprocessing modules (MPMs), 517

Performance tab, 544

runtime configuration settings, 513

Server tab, 543

virtual host properties, 542

APT, 218

boot loader, 69-70

caching nameserver, 452-453

CD, DVD, and CD-RW drives

checking drive assignment, 108

initializing IEEE-1394 CD drives, 110-113

overview of, 108-110

console-based printers, 366

DHCP, 401-402

dial-in PPP servers, 494-497

dial-up Internet access

Internet Configuration Wizard, 488-491

manual configuration, 486-487

overview of, 485

disk quotas manually, 260

display graphics, 93-95

DNS for clients

DHCP and, 437

/etc/host.conf file, 435

/etc/hosts file, 436-437

/etc/nsswitch.conf file, 435-436

/etc/resolv.conf file, 437

overview of, 434-435

DSL access

overview of, 491-492

PPPOE and, 492-493

Fetchmail

global options, 652

mail server options, 653

user accounts, 653-655

FTP servers, file-conversion actions, 615-618

gdm, 172

INN package

active and newsgroups files, 688

history files, 689

incoming.conf file, 685

inn.conf file, 683-684

readers.conf file, 686-688

storage.conf file, 685-686

kdm, 172-174

kernel

initial RAM disk image, creating, 805

overview of, 799-801

xconfig and, 801-805

keyboards with Linux, 84-87

loopback interface manually, 484

LPRng, 361

mail list with Mailman, 676-678

modems

controllerless, 100

fax type, 99

minicom script and, 100

serial-port, 96-99

mouse, 125

MySQL

    initializing data directory, 564

    overview of, 562-563

    password, setting for root user, 564

network hosts with DHCP, 402-404

network interface cards, 376

network services with BIND configuration tool, 471

network-attached printing, 364-365

networks

    command-line tools, 389-393

    /etc/host.conf file, 396

    /etc/hosts file, 394

    /etc/nsswitch file, 395

    /etc/resolv.conf file, 395

    /etc/services file, 394

    /etc/sysconfig/network file, 396

    graphical tools, 396-397

    network configuration files, 393

    overview of, 388

    /sbin/ifconfig, 389-391

    /sbin/netstat, 393

    /sbin/route, 391-393

new hardware devices and kudzu service, 82-83

NFS clients, 408

NFS servers, 406-407

non-supported scanners, 858

OpenOffice.org, 815-816

pointing devices, 88-92

PostgreSQL, 567-568

power management, 101-102

print services

    console-based printers, 353

    GUI-based printers, 352-353

    overview of, 351

printers

    editing printer settings, 359-360

    overview of, 356

    print queue, creating, 356-358

    print queues, multiple, creating, 359

resolver software for BIND, 463

Samba with /etc/samba/smb.conf

    [global] section, 411

    [homes] section, 411-412

    overview of, 410-411

    [printers] section, 412

Samba with Samba Web Administration Tool (SWAT), 415-419

Sendmail

    forwarding email with aliases, 649-650

    mail relaying, 649

    masquerading, 647

    message delivery intervals, 647-648

    overview of, 645-646

    rejecting email from specified sites, 650-651

    sendmail.cf file, building, 648

    smart hosts, 647

sound cards, 844

sound devices, 95-96

system for dual-booting, 46

Tripwire, 427-428

vsftpd server, 599

Wu-FTPd server

    access control, 604-607

    cdpath commands, 614

    ftpaccess file, 603

    overview of, 602

    permission control, 612-614

    shutdown file, 615

    system logging, 611-612

    user information, 607-611

How can we make this index more useful? Email us at indexes@samspublishing.com

X Window System

   commands for, 185

   overview of, 167

   with system-config-display client, 168-170

   with xorg.conf file, 171

   xdm, 174

   xinetd for wu-ftpd, 597-598

   YUM, 219

connecting

   to Internet, 22, 492

   Samba with smbclient command, 414

   See also Internet connectivity

connections, counting number of, 621

consistency in transaction processing, 560

console print control, 366

console-based printers, configuring, 353

console-based sessions, keyboard and mouse techniques for, 130-131

constants, 699

Control Center dialog box (kdm), 173

controllerless modems, configuring, 100

controlling processes, 227

converting

   ext2 filesystem to ext3

      floppy image files, examining, 299

      initial ramdisk, examining, 298

      initial ramdisk, making, 297-298

      overview of, 296

   graphics formats, 861-862

   sound files, 846

copying

   files

      with cp, 331-332

      with cpio, 332

      with mc, 332

      overview of, 82, 330

      with rsync, 335-337

      with scp, 333-335

      with sftp, 335

      with tar, 330-331

   text, 130

counting number of connections, 621

coerce code files, 694

cp command

   backing up configuration files before editing with, 312

   copying files with, 331-332

CPAN (Comprehensive Perl Archive Network), 775-777

CPiA camera, 856

cpio tool

   archives, creating and restoring files from, 324

   copying files with, 332

   overview of, 323

CPU problems during installation, preparing for, 38

CQ cam, 856

CREATE DATABASE statement

   MySQL, 565

   PostgreSQL, 569

CREATE statement (SQL), 554

CREATE USER statement (PostgreSQL), 570

createdb program, 569

crond daemon, 758

ctlinnd program, 690

Ctrl+Alt+Del, 130

CUPS (Common UNIX Printing System)

   database of defined printers, 350

   overview of, 349-351

   printer entry, creating, 369-370

   using, 369

cupsd, 351

curl utility, 588

custom installation option, 18, 35

CVS system, 702-704

cyclic spool method, 685

D

DAO (Disk-At-Once) audio, creating, 113

Data Display Debugger (ddd), 707

data locking, 559

data loss, reasons for, 312-313

database administrators (DBAs), responsibilities of, 549-550

database clients

　GUI access and, 573

　overview of, 571

　SSH access and, 572-573

　Web access and, 573-574

database systems

　client/server model, 550

　comparing

　　ACID compliance and, 560-561

　　available applications, 562

　　data locking and, 559

　　importing text files into tables, 561

　　overview of, 558

　　procedural language, 562

　　speed and, 559

　　subqueries and, 561

　getting started with, 562

　overview of, 549

　relational (RDBMS), 551-553

　See also MySQL; PostgreSQL

database-level rights (MySQL), 565

databases

　enabling for OpenOffice.org, 813

　querying with rpm command, 212

SQL

　overview of, 553

　retrieving data from databases, 556-558

　tables, creating, 554-555

　tables, inserting data into, 555-556

　See also MySQL; PostgreSQL

date, resetting, 104-106

date command, 104

DBAs (database administrators), responsibilities of, 549-550

dd command, 78, 292, 327

ddd (Data Display Debugger), 707

Debian (The Debian Project), 33

debugfs program, 296

debugging tools

　gdb, 706-707

　gprof command, 706

　splint command, 705

decompressing files with shell, 143-144

defining user classes, 604

defragmenting and ext3 filesystem, 270

delegation problems with DNS, 469

deleting users, 156, 570

Denial Of Service (DOS) attack, 127

deny directive, 520-521

dependency checking, 699

dependency errors, 122

deployment, planning

　business considerations, 28

　checklist for, 30-31

　factors in successful installation, 31

　overview of, 28

　system considerations, 29-30

　user considerations, 30

depmod command, 790

description field (ftpconversions file), 618

desktop environment

GNOME, 182-183

overview of, 160, 176, 182

themes, 180-182

virtual desktops, 175-176

See also KDE

detecting modems, 96

/dev directory, 122

devfs (Device Filesystem), 306

device drivers, 788

device labels, 286

Device section (xorg.conf file), 166

devices

all-in-one, troubleshooting, 373

block, character, and special, managing files for

mknod command, 305

naming conventions, 305

overview of, 303-304

Ethernet, configuring, 71

new hardware and kudzu service, 82-83

PCI, 102

pointing, configuring, 88-92

security of, 428

sound, configuring, 95-96

USB, 37, 90

viewing stored, 122

See also multimedia

devices.txt, 787

dhclient, 401-402

DHCP (Dynamic Host Configuration Protocol)

activating at installation and boot time, 400

broadcast addressing and, 381

configuring network hosts with, 402-404

DNS and, 437

overview of, 399

securing, 429

software installation and configuration, 401-402

troubleshooting, 404

uses for, 405

DHCP servers, 402

dhcpd file, 401

dhcpd.conf file, 403-404

Dia technical drawing editor, 814

dial-in PPP servers, configuring, 494-497

dial-up Internet access, configuring

Internet Configuration Wizard, 488-491

manually, 486-487

overview of, 485

dial-up login, text-based, 131

dictionary, Web-enabled, 830

dig (Domain Information Groper) tool, 448-449

digital images, managing, 22

Digital Subscriber Line (DSL) access

overview of, 491-492

PPPOE and, 492-493

directory permissions, 150-152

directory structure

basic Linux directories, 121

/bin and /sbin directories, 121

/boot and /dev directories, 122

/etc directory, 123-125

/home directory, 126

/proc directory, 126-127

/tmp directory, 128

universal layout of, 118-119

/usr directory, 127

/var directory, 128

DirectoryIndex directive (httpd.conf file), 517

Disk Druid, 66, 279

disk filesystems, 267-268

Disk Partitioning Setup screen, 66

disk quotas

implementing, 259

manually configuring, 260

overview of, 232, 259

disk tuning

BIOS and kernel, using, 299

hdparm command, 300-301

Disk-At-Once (DAO) audio, creating, 113

display graphics, configuring, 93-95

display managers

configuring

gdm, 172

kdm, 172-174

xdm, 174

description of, 171-172

Display Power Management Signaling (DPMS), 102

Display Settings main screen (system-config-display client), 169

displaying

administrator email address, 610

environment variables, 139

files at login, 608-609

free and used memory, 231

information about connected users, 620

prelogin banners, 607-608

distributed processing, 160

distribution version numbers, 17

DivX codec, 851

dmesg output, 81

DNS

caching nameserver, configuring, 452-453

configuring for clients

DHCP and, 437

/etc/host.conf file, 435

/etc/hosts file, 436-437

/etc/nsswtich.conf file, 435-436

/etc/resolv.conf file, 437

overview of, 434-435

name resolution in practice, 440-444

name servers and, 439

name service information and, 439-440

overview of, 434, 438-439

providing

forward zone, 465-467

overview of, 464

registering domain, 468

reverse zone, 467-468

providing with BIND

logging, 462

named.conf file, 457-461

overview of, 454-456

resolver configuration, 463

rndc.conf file, 456

running named (nameserver daemon), 464

resolver, information learned by, 447

reverse resolution, 444-447

security issues

ACLs, defining, 474

DNSSEC, using, 477-478

named, alerting to potential problem hosts, 476-477

overview of, 472-474

queries, controlling, 475

split DNS, using, 478

zone transfers, controlling, 476

third-party, 453

tools

dig (Domain Information Groper), 448-449

host, 449

nslookup, 450

overview of, 448

whois, 450-452

troubleshooting

    delegation problems, 469

    overview of, 468

    reverse lookup problems, 469

    serial number accuracy, 470

    tools for, 471

    zone file problems, 470

DNS Security Extensions (DNSSEC), 477-478

DNSRD Tricks and Tips Web site, 468

DNSSEC (DNS Security Extensions), 477-478

dnswalk tool, 469-471

do, until statement and looping (Perl), 770

do, while statement and looping (Perl), 770

documentation

    getting most of, 22-24

    man command, 136

    on software packages, 136-137

    overview of, 135, 877

    writing, 25

    See also HOWTO documents

Documentation directory, 787

DocumentRoot directive (httpd.conf file), 516

dollar ($) character, 761

Domain Information Groper (dig) tool, 448-449

Domain Name Service. *See* **DNS**

domain names and third-party DNS, 453

domains, registering, 468. *See also* **DNS**

DOS (Denial Of Service) attack, 127

DOS filesystems, 273, 282

DOS session, booting from, 56

double pipe (||), 557

double quotes ("), 733

downtime for FTP servers, scheduling, 621-623

DPMS (Display Power Management Signaling), 102

drive geometry, 275

drives

    checking drive assignment, 108

    configuring CD, DVD, and CD-RW, 108-113

    DVD+RW/-RW, 319

    FireWire, 319

    IDE, 837

    in-line, 789

    installing new, 288-289

    tape, 320

    USB and solid-state, 319

    Zip, 318

    See also hard drives

DROP USER statement (PostgreSQL), 570

DSL access, configuring

    overview of, 491-492

    PPPOE and, 492-493

dual-boot configuration, creating, 46

dumb gateways, 385

dummy interface, 484

dump command, 325

dumpe2fs program, 294-295

durability in transaction processing, 560

DVD drives, configuring, 108-110

DVD players, 854

dvd+rw-tools package, 839-840

DVD+RW/-RW drives, 319

DVDs, burning

    from command line

        packet writing, 840

        session writing, 839-840

    overview of, 836-837

DVR application, 854

dynamic content and Apache Web servers

    CGI, 534-535

    flow control, 540

    SSI, 536-540

Dynamic DNS, 400

Dynamic Host Configuration Protocol (DHCP)

    activating at installation and boot time, 400

    broadcast addressing and, 381

    configuring network hosts with, 402-404

    DNS and, 437

    overview of, 399

    security, 429

    software installation and configuration, 401-402

    troubleshooting, 404

    uses for, 405

E

e2fsck command, 302

echo command, 127

echo directive (SSI), 539

Edit a Print Queue dialog box, 359

editing

    /etc directory files, 123-125

    /etc/modprobe.conf file, 387

    FTP server files, 603

    httpd.conf file

        DirectoryIndex directive, 517

        DocumentRoot directive, 516

        Listen directive, 515

        overview of, 514

        ServerAdmin directive, 516

        ServerName directive, 516

        ServerRoot directive, 515

        User and Group directives, 515

        UserDir directive, 516

    printer settings, 359-360

    vsftpd.conf file, 600-602

    See also text editors

Efax application, 828-829

efix application, 829

802.11 Standard, 422

electronic mail. *See* email

elevation of privileges, 238

emacs text editor, 147, 696

email

    attachments, sending binary files as text

        BinHex, 643

        uuencode and uudecode, 644-645

        yenc, 643

    autoresponders, 658

    command-line clients (mutt), 635-637

    commands for managing, 661

    forwarding with aliases, 649-650

    graphical clients

        Balsa, 639, 818

        Evolution, 637-639, 817

        KMail, 639

        Mozilla Mail, 640

        Sylpheed-claws, 640

    mail daemons, 657

    process of sending and receiving, 628-629

    protocols, 628

    rejecting from specified sites, 650-651

    sending with Perl, 776-778

    See also Fetchmail; Sendmail

enabling

    Java, 866-867

    network printing on LAN, 361-363

    scrolling with mouse, 92

encapsulation, 695

endless loops, 746-747

entering BIOS, 44

Enterprise Linux (Red Hat, Inc.)

    overview of, 13

    release cycle, 17

    uses of, 20-21

How can we make this index more useful? Email us at indexes@samspublishing.com

env command, 139

environment variables, 726

environment variables of shell, 139-141

error messages

   dependency errors, 122

   troubleshooting, 81

escape character (/), 732-734

/etc directory, 83, 123-125

/etc/cups directory, 350

/etc/dhcpd.conf file, 403-404

/etc/exports file, 406-407

/etc/fstab file, 284-286, 408

/etc/group file, 241

/etc/host.conf file, 396, 435

/etc/hosts file

   DNS and, 436-437

   hosts, adding, 394

/etc/modprobe.conf file

   editing, 387

   overview of, 791

/etc/named.conf file

   overview of, 457-458

   zone section

      NS and PTR records, 461

      overview of, 459-460

      SOA record, 460-461

/etc/nsswitch file, 395

/etc/nsswitch.conf file and DNS, 435-436

/etc/passwd file

   authentication and, 522

   overview of, 248

   user account information and, 237

/etc/printcap, 350-352

/etc/rc.d/init.d/httpd, starting or stopping
Apache server using, 510

/etc/resolv.conf file

   DNS and, 437

   overview of, 395

/etc/rndc.conf file, 456

/etc/samba/smb.conf file

   [global] section, 411

   [homes] section, 411-412

   overview of, 410-411

   [printers] section, 412

/etc/services file

   configuring networks, 394

   ports and, 379-380

/etc/shadow file, 249-250

/etc/skel file, 244

/etc/sysconfig/network file, 396

ethereal tool, 233

Ethernet devices, configuring during installation, 71

etiquette of IRC, 673

Evolution email client (Ximian), 637-639, 817

examining

   floppy image files, 299

   initrd image files, 298

   structure of filesystems with dumpe2fs, 294-295

exec directive (SSI), 539

Exim, 631

exit command, 133

exit statement, 754

experimental packages, installing, 504

expressions

   description of, 143, 717-718

   resources on, 718

   See also comparison of expressions

ext2 filesystem (ext2fs)

   overview of, 268

   undeletion process, 337-338

ext3 filesystem

alternatives to, 272

converting ext2 filesystem to

floppy image files, examining, 299

initial ramdisk, making and examining, 297-298

overview of, 296

journaling options, 270-271

overview of, 19, 268-269

structure of, 269-270

verifying integrity in, 271-272

extended partitions, 276

external commands, 617

F

failsafe window managers, 178

FAT (File Allocation Table), 268, 273

fault tolerance, 81

fax client software, 828-830

fax command, 721

fax help command, 829

fax make command, 829

fax modems, configuring, 99

FDDI (Fiber Distributed Data Interface) networks, 383

fdisk command, 78

fdisk utility

cautions for using, 277

IDE partitions and, 276

manually restoring partition table using, 341

Microsoft version of, 274

overview of, 276-278

Fedora Core

assisting with, 24

business-related features, 20-21

components of, 16

description of, 13-15

distribution of, 15

documentation, 22-24

filesystem features, 19

home-related features, 22

installing, 18

Red Hat software tools included with, 16

upgrades to, 17

Fedora Core Installer Firewall Configuration dialog box, 71

Fedora Project

description of, 13

mailing lists, 883

Web sites, 878

Fedora Project (APT provider), 218

Fetchmail

configuring

global options, 652

mail server options, 653

user accounts, 653-655

installing, 651

overview of, 651

FetchYahoo MDA, 657

fgrep command, 96

FHS (Filesystem Hierarchy Standard), 118

Fiber Distributed Data Interface (FDDI) networks, 383

fiber optic cable, 385

fiber optics, 383

File Allocation Table (FAT), 268, 273

file attributes, 265

file command, 225

file formats, Microsoft, compatibility with, 812

file operators

pdksh and bash, 738-739

tcsh, 742-744

file ownership, traditional UNIX form of, 238

file permissions. *See* **permissions**

File Roller application, 221

file system. *See* **filesystems**

File Transfer Protocol. *See* **FTP**

file-conversion actions

configuring, 615-617

example of, 618

files

accessing variable data files using /var directory, 128

compressing and decompressing, 143-144, 613

copying

with cp, 331-332

with cpio, 332

with mc, 332

overview of, 82, 330

with rsync, 335-337

with scp, 333-335

with sftp, 335

with tar, 330-331

displaying at login, 608-609

/etc/modprobe.conf, 791

extracting from RPM package, 214

HTML, browsing, 137

locations of after Apache build and install, 507

managing for character devices, block devices, and special devices

mknod command, 305

naming conventions for, 305

overview of, 303-304

managing with shell, 142-143

network configuration

/etc/host.conf, 396

/etc/hosts, 394

/etc/nsswitch, 395

/etc/resolv.conf, 395

/etc/services, 394

/etc/sysconfig/network, 396

overview of, 393

permissions for, changing, 151

restoring from archives

with cpio, 324

with tar, 323

rename, allowing users to, 613

restoring from backup, 82

undeleting

reformatting with –S option, 338

with ext2fs, 337-338

with mc, 338-339

uploading to FTP servers, 616

See also permissions

Files section (xorg.conf file), 163

Filesystem Hierarchy Standard (FHS), 118

filesystems

authentication with Apache Web server

Basic Authentication, 521-523

overview of, 520

/bin and /sbin directories, 121

blocks, 266

/boot and /dev directories, 122

CD-ROM

iso9660, 274

Universal Disk Format (UDF), 274

converting ext2 to ext3

floppy image files, examining, 299

initial ramdisk, examining, 298

initial ramdisk, making, 297-298

overview of, 296

creating disk as storage device, 275

disk tuning

BIOS and kernel, using, 299

hdparm command, 300-301

DOS, 273, 282

/etc directory, 123-125

examining structure of with dumpe2fs, 294-295

ext3

alternatives to, 272

journaling options, 270-271

structure of, 269-270

verifying integrity in, 271-272

features of, 19

/home directory, 126

hosting parts of on separate partitions, 47

inodes and file attributes, 265

JFS and XFS, 273

journaling, 268, 272

kernel modules for supported, 264

loopback, creating for testing

blank image file, making, 292

filesystem, making, 292

filesystem, mounting, 293

managing, commands for, 306-307

mkdosfs command, 282

mke2fs command, 280

mkfs.ext3 command, 280-281

mkreiserfs command, 281

mounting

automatically with /etc/fstab, 284-286

GUI tools for, 286-287

mount command, 283-284

overview of, 282-283

partitions as read-only on running systems, 296

network and disk, 267-268

overview of, 118-119, 263, 274, 279

partition tables, creating

fdisk and, 276-278

overview of, 275

parted command, 279

partitions, 266

physical structure of, 265

/proc directory, 126-127

Reiser, creating, 281

relocating

creating partition table and formatting disk, 290

installing new drive, 288-289

mounting partition and populating with files, 290-291

synchronizing, 301

/tmp directory, 128

tuning

badblocks command, 303

e2fsck command, 302

mke2fs command, 302

noatime option for mount command, 303

overview of, 301

tune2fs command, 302

unmounting with umount command, 284

/usr directory, 127

/var directory, 128

viewing, 119-121, 268-269

find command, suid and sgid permissions, 153

finger command, 134

Finish and Create New Print Queue dialog box, 358

firewalls

configuration, installation process and, 71-72

hosts as, 378

lokkit and system-config-securitylevel for, 424-426

firewire drives, 319

flastmod directive (SSI), 539

flat file databases, 550

flexbackup tool, 329

Floppy Formatter (KDE), 287

How can we make this index more useful? Email us at indexes@sampublishing.com

floppy image files, examining, 299

floppy-based Linux distributions Web sites, 879

flow control and Apache Web servers, 540

focus policy, 176

for loop (Perl), 768

for statement, 745-746

foreach loop (Perl), 768

formats

   graphics

      converting, 861-862

      overview of, 860-861

   high-level, 279

   HTML and PostScript, reading, 24

   sound, 845-847

   video, 851

formatting hard drives, 290

forwarding email with aliases, 649-650

free utility, 231

frequency of backups, determining, 314

FreshRPMs (APT provider), 218

fsck utility

   ext3 filesystem and, 271-272

   journaling filesystems and, 270

fsize directive (SSI), 539

fstab file, 123

FTP (File Transfer Protocol)

   client interface, 581

   client/server model, 592

   graphical client interface

      gFTP, 589-590

      Konqueror, 590-591

      Nautilus browser, 591-592

   installing software, 594

   security issues, 579

   servers

      anonymous access, controlling, 600

      Apache, 594

      authenticated versus anonymous, 593

      Bsdftpd-ssl, 594

      file-conversion actions, configuring, 615-618

      ftphosts file commands, 618-619

      NcFTPd, 593

      ProFTPD, 594

      quick LAN setup, 597

      Very Secure (vsftpd), 593, 599

      vsftpd.conf file, 600-602

   sftp command, 580-581

   speed of file transfers, 602

   text-based client interface

      ftp command, 583-586

      lftp command, 587-588

      overview of, 581-583

      wget command, 588-589

   users, 595-596

   wu-ftp server administration

      counting number of connections, 621

      displaying information about users, 620

      overview of, 619

      scheduling downtime, 621-623

      viewing transaction log, 623-624

   Wu-FTPd server

      access control, configuring, 604-607

      cdpath commands, configuring, 614

      configuring, 602

      ftpaccess file, configuring with, 603

      permission control, configuring, 612-614

      shutdown file, 615

      system logging, configuring, 611-612

      user information, configuring, 607-611

      xinetd configuration for, 597-598

ftp command, 583-586

FTP sites

   AUS-CERT advisory AL-1999.004, 477

   ftp.kernel.org, 794

ftpaccess file, configuring Wu-FTPd server with

access control, 604-607

cdpath commands, 614

overview of, 603

permission control, 612-614

shutdown file, 615

system logging, 611-612

user information, 607-611

ftpconversions file

description field, 618

external commands in, 617

options field, 617

structure of format of, 616

types field, 617

ftphosts file commands, 618-619

ftpshut command, 621-623

ftpusers file, 605

ftpwho fields, 620

full backups, 316-317

full newsfeed servers, 680

fully qualified domain name (FQDN), 439

function keys and installation process, 61

functionality of multimedia applications and intellectual property rights, 835

functions

C and, 694

C++ and, 695

shell scripts and, 754-755

G

GAIM IM client, 674

gaming software, installing

nVidia video drivers, 865

overview of, 864

Unreal Tournament 2003, 865

Wolfenstein-Enemy Territory, 865-866

gatekeepers, 675

gbd tool, 706-707

gcc (GNU C compiler)

compilation process, 708

man and info commands and, 697

overview of, 695, 707

gdm, configuring, 172

GDM Setup window, 172

GECOS field (/etc/passwd file), 248

General Purpose Mouse (gpm) drivers, 92

General Purpose Mouse (gpm) servers, 130-131

generic boot floppy, booting from, 342

GetCodecs application, 851

gFTP interface, 589-590

Ghostscript interpreter, 350, 354-355

GIDs (Group IDs), 239

Gigabit Ethernet, 383

GIMP (GNU Image Manipulation Program)

Adobe Photoshop compared to, 859

cameras and, 857

menus, 860

overview of, 817, 859

Gimp Tool Kit (GTK) widget set, 817

Glade client, 711-713

global-level rights (MySQL), 565

GNOME desktop environment, 182-183

GNOME ethereal client, 376

GNOME File Roller, 325

Gnome gtkam digital camera support client, 856

Gnome mailing list, 883

GNOME Office, 817-820

Gnome-CD, 847

gnome-panel-screenshot tool, 863

gnome-system-monitor tool, 233

How can we make this index more useful? Email us at indexes@samspublishing.com

GNOME/metacity desktop, 847

GnomeMeeting, 674-675, 855

GNU C compiler (gcc)

compilation process, 708

man and info commands and, 697

overview of, 695, 707

GNU Image Manipulation Program (GIMP)

Adobe Photoshop compared to, 859

cameras and, 857

menus, 860

overview of, 817, 859

GNU Privacy Guard (GPG) signatures, 208

GNU Project commands, 136

GNU Public License (GPL) applications, 812

Gnumeric spreadsheet program, 817-819

GNUparted, 279

Google search engine

overview of, 875

troubleshooting error messages and, 82

Gotmail MDA, 657

gpasswd command, 242

GPG (GNU Privacy Guard) signatures, 208

gphoto2 client, 22

gpilot graphical interface, 824

GPL (GNU Public License) applications, 812

gpm (General Purpose Mouse) drivers, 92

gpm (General Purpose Mouse) servers, 130-131

gprof command, 706

grabbers, 852

Gracenote CDDB Music Recognition Service, 841

GRand Unified Bootloader. *See* GRUB

GRANT statement

MySQL, 566

PostgreSQL, 571

grant tables (MySQL), 564

Graph view (System Monitor), 234

graphical client interface (FTP)

gFTP, 589-590

Konqueror, 590-591

Nautilus browser, 591-592

graphical clients (MySQL), 577

graphical development tools

Glade client, 711-713

KDevelop client, 709-710

overview of, 84, 697, 709

QT Designer (Trolltech), 710-711

graphical email clients

Balsa, 639, 818

Evolution, 637-639, 817

KMail, 639

Mozilla Mail, 640

Sylpheed-claws, 640

graphical process and system management tools, 232-233

graphics formats

converting, 861-862

overview of, 860-861

graphics manipulation

GIMP image editor, 859-860

screen images, capturing, 863

greeting text, 608

grep command and output of chkconfig, 199

Grip client, 843

Group directive (httpd.conf file), 515

Group IDs (GIDs), 239, 605

groupadd command, 242

groupdel command, 242

groupmod command, 242

groups

managing

command-line tools for, 242-243

overview of, 240-241

permissions and, 150

groups command, 261

growisofs command, 840

grpck command, 242

GRUB (GRand Unified Bootloader)

boot floppy, booting from, 342

booting into non-default runlevel with, 196-197

description of, 46, 56, 191

installing and configuring, 69

troubleshooting, 807

gs client, 350, 354-355

GTK (Gimp Tool Kit) widget set, 817

GUI and database access, 573

GUI Network Configuration tool, 437

GUI-based printers, configuring, 352-353

guides, 877

gv client, 355

H

Hancom Office, 822

handheld digital cameras, 856-857

hard disks as storage devices, 275

hard drives

formatting, 290

partitioning

before and during installation, 45-46

during installation, 66-69

hosting parts of filesystem on separate partitions, 47

scheme, choosing, 47

strategy, planning, 55

space consumed by full installation of X, 161

storage, planning for, 34-35

hardware

adding or replacing and kudzu service, 82-83

for backups

network storage, 320

removable storage media, 318-319

software and, 321

tape drives, 320

BIOS, boot process, and, 190

compatibility issues, 30, 35-36

inventory, preparing and using, 40-43

for networking

bridges, 385

cables, 384-385

hubs, 385

initializing, 386-388

network interface cards, 382-383

overview of, 381

routers, 386

health monitoring, 102

keyboard, video, and mouse (KVM), 93-94

specifications, researching, 53

workarounds, specifying, 18

hardware requirements

compatibility issues, 30, 35-36

hard drive storage, planning for, 34-35

legacy hardware, 33

minimum, meeting, 32

overview of, 32

problems, preparing for

controllerless modems, 37

CPU, symmetric multiprocessing, and memory problems, 38-40

motherboard-based hardware, 38

Universal Serial Bus devices, 37

Hardware settings (system-config-display client), 169

hash-bang (#!), 724-725, 760

hashes (Perl), 761

hdparm command, 300-301

header files, 694

heatsink for CPU, attaching, 39

high-level format, 279

history files (INN package), 689

/home directory, 47, 126

home users, backup strategy for, 315

home-related features, 22

host utility, 449

hostnames, 433

hosts

    configuring with DHCP, 402-404

    limiting access of, 605

Hotwayd MDA, 657

HOWTO documents

    C++ Programming, 696

    chroot-BIND, 473

    description of, 23, 136

    DVD+RW/+R/-R[W], 839

    Keyboard and Console, 130

    LILO, 807

    Linux Answering machine, 496

    Linux Hardware, 36

    Logical Volume Management, 291

    Network Boot and Exotic Root, 426

    PPP, 382

    Quota mini, 261

    SMP, 39

    VideoLan, 854

    virtual consoles, 94

    Xinerama, 170

.htaccess files and Apache servers

    AllowOverrides directive, 519

    Options directive, 518-519

HTML editors, 827-828

HTML files, browsing, 137

HTML format, reading, 24

htpasswd command, 522

HTTP (Hypertext Transfer Protocol), installing using, 59

httpd script, starting or stopping Apache server using, 510

httpd server and Apache 2.0, 503

httpd.conf file

    editing

        DirectoryIndex directive, 517

        DocumentRoot directive, 516

        Listen directive, 515

        overview of, 514

        ServerAdmin directive, 516

        ServerName directive, 516

        ServerRoot directive, 515

        User and Group directives, 515

        UserDir directive, 516

    runtime configurations and, 513

hubs (network), 385

hwclock command, 72, 104

HylaFax application, 830

Hypertext Transfer Protocol (HTTP), installing using, 59

I

IBM JFS, 19

Icecast application, 848

IDE drives, emulating as SCSI drives, 837

ide.txt, 787

identifiers, 698

Identity screen (Evolution), 637

IEEE-1394 CD drives, initializing, 110-113

if statement, 750-752

if/else statement (Perl), 766

ifconfig command, 140, 376, 389-391

IM (Internet messaging), 674

im sensors software package, 102

ImageMagick application

convert utility, 861

file extensions list, 861

identify command, 862

import command, 863

IMAP (Internet Mail Access Protocol)

description of, 628

MDA and, 632

immutable, making file, 265

IMP/Horde, 660

Impress presentation program, 813

in-line drivers, 789

include directive (SSI), 540

incoming.conf file, 685

incremental backups, 317

individual IDs, restricting permissions based on, 606

init command, 192

init process, 191

init scripts, 197-198

initdb program, 568

initial RAM disk image, creating, 805

initializing

data directory

MySQL, 564

PostgreSQL, 567-568

network hardware

/etc/modprobe.conf file, editing, 387

modprobe command, 387-388

overview of, 386-387

initrd image files, creating and examining, 297-298

initrd.txt, 787

inittab file, 123, 130

INN (InterNetNews) package

configuration files, 682

configuring

active and newsgroups files, 688

history files, 689

incoming.conf file, 685

inn.conf file, 683-684

readers.conf file, 686-688

storage.conf file, 685-686

innd, running, 690

installing, 683

overview of, 679

program files, 681-682

inn.conf file, configuring, 683-684

innd, running, 690

inodes, 265

input redirection, 717-719

InputDevice section (xorg.conf file), 164

INSERT statement (SQL), 555-556

inserting data into tables, 555-556

insmod command, 113, 790

installation disk, using recovery facility from, 343-344

installing

Apache Web server

building source code for, 505-506

file locations after build and install, 507

from RPM, 503-505

APT, 218

boot loader and, 56-57, 69-70

bootdisk, creating, 75

from CD-ROM, 55, 58

CPAN modules with Perl, 777

deployment, planning

   business considerations, 28

   checklist for, 30-31

   system considerations, 29-30

   user considerations, 30

DHCP, activating when, 400

DHCP software

   dhclient, 401-402

   server, 402

experimental packages, 504

factors in successful installation, 31

Fetchmail, 651

finishing process of, 77

firewall and security configuration and, 71-72

FTP software, 594

hardware inventory, preparing and using, 40-43

hardware problems, preparing for

   controllerless modems, 37

   CPU, symmetric multiprocessing, and memory problems, 38-40

   motherboard-based hardware, 38

   Universal Serial Bus devices, 37

hardware requirements

   compatibility issues, 30, 35-36

   hard drive storage, planning for, 34-35

   legacy hardware, 33

   minimum, meeting, 32

INN package, 683

kickstart method of, 48-51

Mailman, 676

methods for, 43, 57

MySQL, 562-563

network configuration and, 70-71

network, using, 58-59

new drives, 288-289

NFS, 405

nVidia video drivers, 865

OpenOffice.org, 814

overview of, 18

partition strategy, planning, 55

partitioning drive, 66-69

Personal Desktop, 22

PostgreSQL, 567

preinstallation plans, 27

preparing for

   from CD-ROM, 44

   hosting parts of filesystem on separate partitions, 47

   overview of, 43-44

   partitioning hard drive, 45-46

   partitioning scheme, choosing, 47

researching hardware specifications, 53

root password and user accounts, creating, 73-74

Samba, 409

software

   installation software, selecting, 74-75

   options, choosing, 54

   rpm command and, 211

starting process, 60-65

step-by-step guidelines for, 60

stopping process, 62

time zone, setting, 72

TWiki, 671

type of installation, choosing, 54

Unreal Tournament 2003, 865

Wolfenstein-Enemy Territory, 865-866

YUM, 219

integrity of data

   ACID compliance and, 560-561

   database administrators and, 550

Intel-based Linux distributions Web sites, 879

intellectual property rights, 835

interacting with kernel, /proc directory and, 126-127

InterMezzo network filesystem, 267

Internet Configuration Wizard, 488-491

Internet connectivity

    checking availability of, 483

    common configuration information, 482

    configuring manually, 483-484

    dial-in PPP servers, configuring, 494-497

    dial-up

        configuring, 485

        configuring manually, 486-487

        Internet Configuration Wizard, 488-491

    DSL

        configuring, 491-492

        PPPOE and, 492-493

    overview of, 22

    troubleshooting, 494

Internet Mail Access Protocol (IMAP)

    description of, 628

    MDA and, 632

Internet messaging (IM), 674

Internet Printing Protocol (IPP), 349

Internet Relay Chat (IRC), 253, 672-673, 884

Internet service providers (ISPs), 482-483

Internet Software Consortium Web site, 402

internet-druid command, 113, 497

InterNetNews (INN) package

    configuration files, 682

    configuring

        active and newsgroups files, 688

        history files, 689

        incoming.conf file, 685

        inn.conf file, 683-684

        readers.conf file, 686-688

        storage.conf file, 685-686

    innd, running, 690

    installing, 683

    overview of, 679

    program files, 681-682

interpreting shell scripts through specific shells, 724-725

IP addressing

    hostnames and, 433

    static versus dynamic, 482-483

IP masquerading, 378

IPP (Internet Printing Protocol), 349

iptables, 425

IPv4 (IP version 4), 376

IPv6 (IP version 6), 378

IRC (Internet Relay Chat), 253, 672-673, 884

ISO image, creating, 837

isolation in transaction processing, 560

iso9660 filesystem, 274

ISPs (Internet service providers), 482-483

iteration statements

    for, 745-746

    overview of, 745

    repeat, 749

    select, 749-750

    shift, 750

    until, 748-749

    while, 746-748

iwconfig command, 420

iwlist command, 420

iwpriv command, 420

iwspy command, 420

J

J-Pilot program, 824

Jabber IM protocol, 674

Jargoogle search page, 628

Java, enabling, 866-867

JetDirect adapter (HP), 364-365

JFS (IBM), 19

JFS (journaled file system), 268, 273

job-control commands, 717

journal mode (ext3 filesystem), 271

journaled file system (JFS), 268, 273

journaling filesystems

    description of, 19, 268

    ext3, 270-271

    Reiser, 272

joysticks, support for, 88

jumper settings, 288

K

KDE (K Desktop Environment)

    ark archiving tool, 326-327

    disk- and filesystem-related utilities, 286

    mailing list, 883

    overview of, 184

    process and system monitoring tools, 234

KdeprintFax application, 828

kdetv application, 853

KDevelop client, 709-710

kdf tool, 234

KDiskFree (KDE), 286

kdm, configuring, 172-174

kernel

    built-in protection in, 424

    C and, 695

    compiling, 797-798

    configuring

        initial RAM disk image, creating, 805

        overview of, 799-801

        xconfig and, 801-805

    interacting with using /proc directory, 126-127

    loading during boot process, 191-192

    managing modules, 790-792

    numbering system for, 17

    obtaining sources, 794-795

    overview of, 785-786

    patching, 795-796

    recompiling, 785, 792-793

    security issues and, 29

    source tree, 786-788

    troubleshooting compile and installation, 806-807

    tuning disk using, 299

    tuning with sysctl command, 808-809

    types of, 789

    versions of, 793-794

kernel modules, manually loading, 387-388

kernel oops, 807

Kernel Tuning utility, 300

kernel-parameters.txt, 787

Keyboard dialog box, 86

keyboard, video, and mouse (KVM) hardware, 93-94

keyboards

    configuring with Linux, 84-87

    console-based techniques for, 130-131

    selecting for installation process, 64

    support for, 84

keys function, 762

keyword substitutions, 703

keywords, 698

KFax application, 828

KHexEdit application, 831

Kickstart Configuratior dialog box, 49

kickstart installation method, 48-51

kill command, 228

Kjots application, 831

KMail email client, 639

Kmid, 847

KNode news client, 667

KOffice, 820-821

Konqueror interface (KDE), 590-591

Kooka application, 826, 858

KOrganizer, 822

KOrn mail daemon, 657

kppp client (KDE), 97

Kroupware, 659

KSane application, 828

Ksnapshot, 864

KSpread spreadsheet program, 821

ksysguard tool, 234

KTimer application, 831

kudzu service, 82-83, 125

KVM (keyboard, video, and mouse) hardware, 93-94

KwikDisk (KDE), 286

KWord word processing program, 820

L

Lake Taylor Transitional Care Hospital, 831

lame delegation, 469

LANG (shell environment variable), 139

languages

compiled, 694

for installation, selecting, 63

for keyboards, selecting, 85

object-oriented, 695

See also Perl; programming languages

LANs (local area networks)

enabling network printing on, 361-363

quick FTP server setup on, 597

security issues, 379

laptop Web site, 880

laptops

connecting and using external monitors with, 94

controllerless modems for, configuring, 100

hardware compatibility issues and, 36

partitioning hard drive and, 47

PCMCIA and, 106-108

large enterprises, backup strategy for, 315

last command, 247

last modification date, notifying users of, 611

last statement and looping (Perl), 769

lastb command, 247

LBA (Logical Block Addressing), 289

LD_LIBRARY_PATH (shell environment variable), 139

leaf node servers, 680

legacy hardware and installation, 33

legacy printers, troubleshooting, 373

less command, 23, 136

lftp command, 587-588

libraries, making, 705

library routines, 697

LILO, 191

linguistic algebra, 766

linkers, 694

links command, 137

Linux

basic directories, 121

configuring keyboards with, 84-87

console-based session, keyboard and mouse techniques for, 130-131

logging in to

  from remote computer, 132-133

  text-based console login, 128

  virtual consoles, 129

logging out of, 132

manual pages, 23

projects, efforts, and partnerships of, 14

success of, 14

users, types of, 118

See also Enterprise Linux; Fedora Core

Linux Documentation Project, 494, 877

linux rescue command, 343

Linux TV Project application, 854

Linux Users Groups, 877

Listen directive (httpd.conf file), 515

listings

backticks to access shell, 771

displaying contents of env Hash, 762

environment.pl, 535

FTP session, commands listed by help in, 583

ftphosts configuration file, 619

ftpwho -V command output, 620

if/elsif/else, 766

inn.conf configuration file entries, 684

library, building and using, 705

Perl, simple program, 759

posting article to Usenet, 779

purging log files, 778

sending mail using sendmail, 776

sendmail module, 777

shadow password file ftp user entry, 596

/var/log/xferlog file with logging, 624

xinetd configuration file for wu-ftpd, 598

ln command, 506

loading modules, 792

loadkeys command, 87, 131

LOADLIN program, 56, 78

local area networks (LANs)

enabling network printing on, 361-363

quick FTP server setup on, 597

security issues, 379

local news servers, 680

localhost interface, 483-484

locate command, 142

locking users out of accounts, 245

LogFormat statements, 533

logging

Apache Web server and, 532-534

security violations and file transfers, 612

user-issued commands, 611

logging in

after installation process, 78

changing login shell, 138

to Linux

  from remote computer, 132-133

  overview of, 128

  text-based console login, 128

  virtual consoles, 129

process for users, 257-259

logging options for DNS, 462

logging out of Linux session, 132

Logical Block Addressing (LBA), 289

logical operators

pdksh and bash, 740

tcsh, 744

Logical Volume Management (LVM), 19, 291

logname command, 261

logout command, 133

logs, purging with Perl, 778-779

logwatch command, 730

logwatch.pl program, 758

lokkit command, 424-426

loopback addressing, 377

loopback filesystems, 292-293

loopback interface

  checking availability of, 483

  configuring manually, 484

looping constructs (Perl)

  do, while and do, until, 770

  for, 768

  foreach, 768

  last and next, 769

  overview of, 767

  until, 769

  while, 769

losetup utility, 292

loss of data, reasons for, 312-313

lp command, 367

lpc command, 367

lpg command, 367

lprm command, 367

LPRng, configuring, 361

lpstat command, 367

ls command, 119, 238

lsmod command, 89, 790-791

lspci command, 849

LVM (Logical Volume Management), 19, 291

M

MAC (Media Access Control) address, 382

MACHINE (shell environment variable), 139

Macromedia Flash plug-in, 852

macros, 700-701

magic cookies

  descriptions for, 608-609

  ftpshut command, 622

magic numbers, 724

mail daemons, 657

Mail Delivery Agent (MDA)

  choosing, 655

  overview of, 627

  Procmail, 656

  SMTP, 632

  Spamassassin, 656

  special, 657

  Squirrelmail, 656

  virus scanners, 657

mail list, configuring with Mailman, 676-678

mail relaying, 649

mail transfer agent (MTA)

  choosing, 631

  Exim, 631

  overview of, 627-629

  Postfix, 630

  Qmail, 631

  See also Sendmail

Mail User Agent (MUA), 627, 632-633

mail utility

  overview of, 633

  sending and reading messages using, 634-635

  shell scripting and, 635

maildir format, 631

mailing lists

  Fedora Project, 883

  overview of, 25, 883

  Red Hat, 884

Mailman, 676-678

major number, 304

make command, 699-701

make config utility, 799

make menuconfig utility, 800

make utility, 788

make xconfig utility, 800-805

makefile targets, 700-701

makefiles, 699, 786

man command, 23, 136

man pages

Linux, 23

for shells, 716

managing

digital images, 22

disk space, 259-260

email, commands for, 661

files for character devices, block devices, and special devices, 303-305

files with shell, 142-143

filesystems, commands for, 306-307

groups

command-line tools for, 242-243

commands for, 157

overview of, 240-241

modular kernels, 790-792

network connectivity, commands for, 430

newsgroups, commands for, 691

passwords

changing in batch, 252

/etc/passwd file, 248

overview of, 247

policy for, 248

security of, 251

shadow passwords, 249-250

print jobs, 367-368

print services, 353-355

resources, 207

running programs, commands for, 157

users

adding new, 245-247

command-line tools for, 244-245

commands for, 157

monitoring activity on system, 247

overview of, 243

See also software management

manual pages

Linux, 23

for shells, 716

Manually Partition with Disk Druid button, 66

masquerading by Sendmail, 647

Master Boot Record (MBR), 190, 275, 340

Math (math formula editor), 813

Maximum Transmission Unit (MTU), 391

mbox format, 631

mc (Midnight Commander)

copying files with, 332

overview of, 214

undeleting files with, 338-339

MDA (Mail Delivery Agent)

choosing, 655

overview of, 627

Procmail, 656

SMTP, 632

Spamassassin, 656

special, 657

Squirrelmail, 656

virus scanners, 657

Media Access Control (MAC) address, 382

meminfo file, 126

memory

adding to legacy hardware, 33

displaying free and used, 231

problems with during installation, preparing for, 39-40

testing, 18

menu editing, 847

message delivery intervals, setting, 647-648

metacity window manager, 181

mget command, 585

mgetty command, 497

mgetty+sendfax application, 830

Microsoft

   compatibility with proprietary file formats of, 812

   Exchange Server, alternatives to

      Bynari, 659

      CommuniGate Pro, 659

      IMP/Horde, 660

      Kroupware, 659

      OpenGroupware, 660

      overview of, 658-659

      phpgroupware, 660

      PHProjekt, 660

      Samsung Contact, 659

      SuSE OpenExchange, 659

   fdisk utility, 274

   file formats, compatibility with, 812

   IIS (Internet Information Server), 502

   Outlook, 659

   Windows, productivity software written for, 832

Microsoft Tape Format (MTF), 322

Midnight Commander (mc)

   copying files with, 332

   overview of, 214

   undeleting files with, 338-339

migration to new operating system, 28

MIME (Multipurpose Internet Mail Extensions), 628

mini-CD Linux distributions Web sites, 878

minicom program, 488

minicom script for modems, 100

mirroring data, 317

mkbootdisk command, 56

mkdir command, 150

mkdosfs command, 282

mke2fs command, 280, 302

mkfs.ext3 command, 280-281

mkinitrd utility, 297

mkisofs command, 837

mknod command, 305

mkpasswd command, 134

mkreiserfs command, 281

modems

   controllerless, 37

   detecting and configuring

      controllerless modems, 100

      fax modems, 99

      minicom script and, 100

      serial-port modems, 96-99

   networking over, 648

modinfo command, 790

modprobe command, 387-388, 790

modprobe.conf file, 123

modular kernels, 789-792

Module section (xorg.conf file), 164

modules

   Apache Web server

      mod.access, 525

      mod.alias, 525

      mod.asis, 525

      mod.auth, 526

      mod.auth.anon, 526

      mod.auth.dbm, 526

      mod.auth.digest, 526

      mod.autoindex, 527

      mod.cgi, 527

      mod.dir, 527

      mod.env, 527

      mod.expires, 527

      mod.headers, 527

      mod.imap, 528

mod.include, 528

mod.info, 528

mod.log.config, 528

mod.mime, 528

mod.mime.magic, 528

mod.negotiation, 528

mod.proxy, 528

mod.rewrite, 529

mod.setenvif, 529

mod.speling, 529

mod.ssl, 529

mod.status, 529

mod.unique.id, 529

mod.userdir, 530

mod.usertrack, 530

mod.vhost.alias, 530

overview of, 524

Perl and, 775

Monitor section (xorg.conf file), 165

monitoring

system, tools for

console-based, 226-228

disk quotas, 232

free utility, 231

graphical process and management, 232-233

KDE, 234

kill command, 228

overview of, 226

priority scheduling and control, 229-231

vmstat utility, 231

user activity on system, 247

monitors

configuring, 169

connecting and using external with notebooks, 94

installation process and, 60, 64

monolithic kernels, 789

More Accessories menu, 831

motherboard-based hardware, 38

Motif Window Manager (mwm), 179

mount command, 283-284, 303

mounting

description of, 267

filesystems

automatically with /etc/fstab, 284-286

GUI tools for, 286-287

mount command, 283-284

overview of, 282-283

new partitions, 290-291

partitions as read-only on running systems, 296

Samba shares, 414

mouse

configuring, 125

console-based techniques for, 130-131

three-button, 90, 131

mouseconfig command, 131

mouseconfig tool, 84

Mozilla browser, Macromedia Flash plug-in for, 852

Mozilla Mail, 640

Mozilla news client, 669

MP3 format, 846

MPEG format, 846

MPlayer, 853-854

MPMs (multiprocessing modules) for Apache server, 517

MTA (mail transfer agent)

choosing, 631

Exim, 631

overview of, 627-629

Postfix, 630

Qmail, 631

See also Sendmail

MTF (Microsoft Tape Format), 322

.m3u format, 848

MTU (Maximum Transmission Unit), 391

MUA (Mail User Agent), 627, 632-633

multiprocessing modules (MPMs) for Apache server, 517

multicast addressing, 381

multicasting mode (NICs), 390

multimedia

    cameras

        handheld digital, 856-857

        Webcams, 855-856

    DVD and video players, 854

    gaming

        nVidia video drivers, installing, 865

        overview of, 864

        Unreal Tournament 2003, installing, 865

        Wolfenstein-Enemy Territory, installing, 865-866

    Java, enabling, 866-867

    music players, 847

    overview of, 843

    personal video recorders, 853

    recording sound, 844

    scanners, 857-858

    sound cards, 844

    sound formats, 845-847

    streaming audio, 848

    TV and video

        formats, 851

        hardware for, 848-851

        viewing, 848, 852-853

    See also graphics manipulation

multimedia applications

    burning CDs and DVDs

        from command line, 837-843

        overview of, 836-837

    intellectual property rights and, 835

Multipurpose Internet Mail Extensions (MIME), 628

music players, 847

mutt email client, 635-637

mwm (Motif Window Manager), 179

myenv sample shell script, 722

MySQL

    ACID compliance and, 560-561

    available applications, 562

    CONCAT function, 557

    data locking and, 559

    database client, 571

    databases, creating, 565

    granting and revoking privileges, 565-567

    graphical clients, 577

    importing text files into tables, 561

    initializing data directory, 564

    installing and configuring, 562-563

    mysql command-line client, 575

    password, setting for root user, 564

    PostgreSQL compared to, 558

    procedural language, 562

    speed and, 559

    subqueries and, 561

MySQL-Max, 562

mysql_install_db command, 564

MythTV application, 854

N

name resolution in practice, 440-444

name servers and DNS, 439

name service information and DNS, 439-440

name-based virtual hosts, 531

named (nameserver daemon)

alerting to potential problem hosts, 476-477

running, 464

security issues with, 473-474

named-checkconf tool, 471

named-checkzone tool, 471

named.conf file

logging section, 462

overview of, 457-458

zone section

NS and PTR records, 461

overview of, 459-460

SOA record, 460-461

naming conventions for block and character devices, 305

nano text editor, 696, 721

NAT (Network Address Translation), 378

Nautilus browser (GNOME), 591-592, 841

Nautilus shell, 183

navigating

installation screens, 65

with shell, 142

Nc-FTP client, 582

NcFTPd server, 593

NCP network filesystem, 267

neat client, 97

neat command, 497

netmasks, 377, 380-381

netpbm tools, 861-862

netstat command, 393

Network Address Translation (NAT), 378

Network Configuration dialog box, 489

Network Device Control, 491

Network File System (NFS)

client configuration, 408

installing, starting, or stopping, 405

installing, using, 59

overview of, 59, 267, 405

security, 429

server configuration, 406-407

network filesystems, 267

network interface cards (NICs)

10BASE-T, 382

100BASE-T, 383

configuring, 376

description of, 382

fiber optic and Gigabit Ethernet, 383

token-ring, 382

troubleshooting, 387

wireless, 383

network news system

newsgroups, 664

newsreaders

KNode, 667

Mozilla, 669

Pan, 666-667

slrn, 665

overview of, 664

spam messages, 691

Network News Transfer Protocol (NNTP), 665

network printers

creating on LAN, 361-363

network-attached printer configuration and printing, 364-365

Session Message Block printing, 363-364

network services, configuring with BIND configuration tool, 471

network storage, 320

networking

cellular, 421

over modems, 648

security issues

devices, 428

DHCP, 429

firewalling, 424-426

keeping up-to-date on, 429

NFS, 429

overview of, 423

passwords and physical security, 426

patches and upgrades, 430

Samba, 429

TCP/IP, 427

Tripwire, configuring and using, 427-428

with TCP/IP

    addressing, 376-378

    IP Masquerading, 378

    overview of, 375-376

    ports, 379-380

wireless

    advantages of, 421

    overview of, 383, 419

    protocol, choosing, 422

    security issues, 423

    support for, 419-420

    telnet command and, 133

networks

broadcast, unicast, and multicast addressing, 381

configuring

    command-line tools, 389-393

    /etc/host.conf file, 396

    /etc/hosts file, 394

    /etc/nsswitch.conf file, 395

    /etc/resolv.conf file, 395

    /etc/services file, 394

    /etc/sysconfig/network file, 396

    graphical tools, 396-397

    installation process and, 70-71

    network configuration files, 393

    overview, 388

/sbin/ifconfig, 389-391

/sbin/netstat, 393

/sbin/route, 391-393

dual-host no-NIC, 382

hardware for

    bridges, 385

    cables, 384-385

    hubs, 385

    initializing, 386-388

    network interface cards, 382-383

    overview of, 381

    routers, 386

installing using, 58-59

organization of, 380

subnet masks, 380-381

subnetting, 380

troubleshooting, 385

See also networking

news servers, 679-680

newsgroup file (INN package), 688

newsgroups, 664

newsreaders

KNode, 667

Mozilla, 669

Pan, 666-667

slrn, 665

newusers command, 252

next statement and looping (Perl), 769

NFS (Network File System)

client configuration, 408

installing, starting, or stopping, 405

installing, using, 59

overview of, 59, 267, 405

securing, 429

server configuration, 406-407

nice command, 229

NICs (network interface cards)

10BASE-T, 382

100BASE-T, 383

configuring, 376

description of, 382

fiber optic and Gigabit Ethernet, 383

token-ring, 382

troubleshooting, 387

wireless, 383

nmap command, 365

nmapfe tool, 233

NNTP (Network News Transfer Protocol), 665

noatun viewer, 852

nohup command, 131

notebooks. *See* laptops

notifying users of last modification date, 611

nslint tool, 471

nslookup tool, 450

ntpd time daemon, 105

ntsysv command, 92, 513

ntsysv utility, 200

number comparison

pdksh and bash, 737-738

tcsh, 741-742

numbering system for kernels, 17

numeric comparison operators

Perl, 763

nVidia video drivers, installing, 865

O

object-oriented languages, 695

obtaining kernel sources, 794-795

ODBC (Open Database Connectivity), 813

office suites

commercial, 822

GNOME Office, 817-820

KOffice, 820-821

OpenOffice.org

components of, 812-814

enabling database for, 813

history of, 814

installing and configuring, 814-816

overview of, 811

Ogg-Vorbis format, 846

one-liners (Perl), 780-781

Open Database Connectivity (ODBC), 813

Open File dialog box (KOffice), 821

Open Sound System (OSS), 844

open-source business development model, 14

OpenCalc spreadsheet program, 813

OpenDraw graphics program, 814

OpenGroupware, 660

OpenH323 Gatekeeper, 675

OpenOffice.org

components of, 812-814

enabling database for, 813

Fax Wizard, 828

history of, 814

HTML editor, 828

installing and configuring, 814-816

OpenPVR application, 854

OpenSSH, 593

OpenWriter word processing program, 812

operating system

choosing for business, 28

considerations for, 29-30

operators (Perl)

arithmetic, 764

comparison, 763

compound, 764

other, 764-765

/opt directory and partitioning, 48

Options directives (.htaccess files), 518-519

options field (ftpconversions file), 617

OR statement (SQL), 557-558

ordered mode (ext3 filesystem), 271

OSS (Open Sound System), 844

output redirection, 717-719

overclocking, 39

overloading function names, 695

P

Package Group Selection dialog box, 74

package management, 215-216

package organization with RPM, 214

packet writing, 840

packet-based data, 375

PAMs (Pluggable Authentication Modules), 250-251

Pan news client, 666-667

parallel port cameras, 856

parted command, 279

partition tables

creating

fdisk and, 276-278

overview of, 275, 290

parted command, 279

restoring manually, 341

partition types, 266

partitioning hard drive

before and during installation, 45-46

during installation, 66-69

hosting parts of filesystem on separate partitions, 47

scheme, choosing, 47

strategy, planning, 55

partitions

mounting as read-only on running systems, 296

mounting new and populating with files, 290-291

See also partition tables

passwd command

initial password for user, creating, 155

overview of, 245

suid permissions and, 152

passwd file, 123

passwords

for boot loader, assigning, 70

creating, 134

forgetting, 74

for GRUB, 196

mail server, 655

managing

changing in batch, 252

/etc/passwd file, 248

overview of, 247

policy for, 248

security of, 251

shadow passwords, 249-250

network and, 426

restricting number of invalid entries, 606

root

installation process and, 73-74

overview of, 154

setting for MySQL, 564

shadow password system, 596

pasting text, 130

patch command, 702, 796-797

patched kernels, 792

patching kernels, 795-796

PATH (shell environment variable), 139

pathnames, 700

pattern matching, 718

PCI (Peripheral Control Interface) devices and power management, 102

PCI cards, TV-only, 849

PCMCIA, 106-108

PDA connectivity

    GNOME gpilot graphical interface, 824

    J-Pilot program, 824

    pilot-link package, 823-824

PDA Web sites, 880

PDF documents, reading, 24

pdksh (public domain Korn shell)

    comparison of expressions

        file operators, 738-739

        logical operators, 740

        numbers, 737-738

        overview of, 735

        strings, 736-737

    description of, 723

Penggy page, 482

percent (%) character, 762

performance

    ext3 filesystem and, 269

    FTP file transfers, 602

Peripheral Control Interface (PCI) devices and power management, 102

Perl

    code examples

        command-line processing, 781

        installing CPAN modules, 777

        one-liners, 780-781

        overview of, 776

        posting to Usenet, 779

        purging logs, 778-779

        sending mail, 776-778

conditional statements

    if/else, 766

    unless, 767

documentation, 775

looping constructs

    do, while and do, until, 770

    for, 768

    foreach, 768

    last and next, 769

    overview of, 767

    until, 769

    while, 769

modules and CPAN, 775

operators

    arithmetic, 764

    comparison, 763

    compound, 764

    other, 764-765

overview of, 757-758

programs, 535, 758

regular expressions, 770-771

shell access and, 771-772

simple program example, 759-761

special string constants, 765

special variables, 762

switches, 772-774

variable types, 761

versions of, 759

perlcc program, 759

perldoc command, 761

permission control, configuring, 612-614

permissions

    allowing users to change, 613

    assigning to users

        file-delete, 613

        file-overwrite, 613

        overview of, 149-150

tar command usage, 614

   for upload files, 614

categories of, 239-240

directory permissions, 150-152

file ownership and, 238

groups and, 240

overview of, 148-149

restricting

   based on group IDs, 605

   based on individual IDs, 606

SUID and SGID, 152-153

of system administrator, granting to regular users

   restricted shells and, 257

   su command, 252-254

   sudo command, 254-257

See also root user

Personal Desktop, 18, 22, 34

personal video recorders, 853

Photoshop (Adobe), 859

PHP (PHP Hypertext Preprocessor), 534

phpgroupware, 660

PHProjekt, 660

physical security of network, 426

PID (process ID), 191

pilot-link package, 823-824

pine email client, 635

piping data, 720

plain text files, reading, 23

Planner project management program, 814, 819

platters, 275

Pluggable Authentication Modules (PAMs), 250-251

Point-to-Point Protocol (PPP), 485

Point-to-Point Protocol over Ethernet (PPPoE), 492-493

pointing devices, configuring, 88-92

poisoning, 472

POP (Post Office Protocol), 628, 632

Portable Document Format (PDF) documents, 24

ports and TCP/IP, 379-380

positional parameters

   accessing and retrieving variables from command line, 728

   automating tasks with simple scripts, 729-731

   example of, 727-728

Post Office Protocol (POP), 628, 632

post-installation configuration problems

   troubleshooting, 81-82

Postfix, 630

PostgreSQL

   || (double pipe), 557

   ACID compliance and, 560-561

   available applications, 562

   data locking and, 559

   database client, 571

   databases, 569-570

   granting and revoking privileges, 571

   importing text files into tables, 561

   initializing data directory, 567-568

   installing and configuring, 567

   MySQL compared to, 558

   procedural language, 562

   psql command-line client, 576

   speed and, 559

   subqueries and, 561

posting to Usenet and Perl, 779

PostScript documents, viewing, 355

PostScript format, reading, 24

pound (#) sign, 721

power management, configuring, 101-102

PowerPC-based Linux distributions Web sites, 880

ppmtompeg, 852

PPP (Point-to-Point Protocol), 485

ppp.linkup file, 648

pppd, 485

PPPoE (Point-to-Point Protocol over Ethernet), 492-493

prefdm shell script, 172

prelogin banners, displaying, 607-608

preparing for installation

from CD-ROM, 44

hosting parts of filesystem on separate partitions, 47

overview of, 43-44

partitioning hard drive, 45-46

partitioning scheme, choosing, 47

preprocessors, 694

print queues

creating, 356-358

multiple, creating, 359

printcap file, 123

printenv command, 139

printenv directive (SSI), 540

Printer model dialog box, 357

printers

adding to system, 350

console print control, configuring, 366

creating and configuring

editing printer settings, 359-360

print queue, creating, 356-359

network, creating

on LAN, 361-363

network-attached printer configuration and printing, 364-365

Session Message Block printing, 363-364

See also printing

printers.conf file, 350

printing

commands for, 367-368, 374

configuring

GUI-based printers, 352

managing print services and, 351

print services, 353

managing

print jobs, 367-368

print services, 353-355

overview of, 350-351

troubleshooting, 373

priorities, assigning to processes, 229-231

pristine sources, 207

privileges, granting and revoking

MySQL, 565-567

PostgreSQL, 571

/proc directory, 126-127

procedural language, 562

process ID (PID), 191

Process Listing view (System Monitor), 233

process reporting, 226

processes

assigning priorities to, 229-231

stopping running, 228

Procmail MTA, 632, 656

productivity software

commands for accessing, 832

example of implementation of, 831

for Microsoft Windows, 832

office suites

commercial, 822

GNOME Office, 817-820

KOffice, 820-821

OpenOffice.org, 812-816

overview of, 811

other, 830

overview of, 811

ProFTPD server, 594

programming

    commands for, 713

    debugging tools

        gdb, 706-707

        gprof command, 706

        splint command, 705

    gcc, 707-708

    graphical development tools

        Glade client, 711-713

        KDevelop client, 709-710

        QT Designer (Trolltech), 710-711

    project management tools

        ar, 705

        autoconf utility, 701-702

        make, 699-701

        RCS and CVS, 702-704

    steps for, 697-698

programming languages

    C

        overview of, 694

        simple program example, 708-709

    C++, 695-696

    elements of, 698

    getting started with, 696

    weakly typed, 761

    See also Perl

programs. *See* software

promiscuous mode (NICs), 390

protecting contents of user directories, 126

protocols

    email, 628

    wireless, choosing, 422

    See also specific protocols

ps command, 226-227

PS101 print server adapter (NETGEAR), 364

psql client program, 569-570

purging logs, Perl and, 778-779

PWD (shell environment variable), 139

Q

q key, 24

Qmail, 631

QT Designer (Trolltech), 710-711

Quanta Plus HTML editor, 827

queries, controlling, 475

query language. *See* SQL

querying database with rpm command, 212

Queue type dialog box, 357

quitting document, 24

qv client, reading document with, 24

R

RabbIT proxy server, 497

RAID arrays, 19, 317

RAM. *See* memory

RARP (Reverse Address Resolution Protocol), 381

raw format, 845

RAWRITE utility, 78

rc.sysinit script, 191

RCS system, 702-704

RDBMSs (relational databases), 551-553

readers.conf file, 686-688

reading

    compressed version of file, 23

    HTML format, 24

    PDF document, 24

plain text files, 23

PostScript format, 24

Real Player, 848

rebooting system, 157, 342

Receiving Mail screen (Evolution), 639

recompiling kernel, 785, 792-793

recording sound, 844

Recovery Facility from installation disk, 343-344

Red Hat Linux

mailing lists, 884

Web sites, 878

Red Hat Network (RHN), 217

Red Hat Package Manager. *See* **RPM**

Red Hat, Inc.

desktop, 160

Enterprise Linux

overview of, 13

release cycle, 17

uses of, 20-21

overview of, 14

See also Linux

redhat-config-keyboard utility, 125

redhat-config-mouse tool, 125

redirecting input and output, 719

redundant filesystem descriptors, 265

registering domains, 468

regular expressions (Perl), 770-771

Reiser filesystem, 272, 281

rejecting email from specified sites, 650-651

relational databases (RDBMSs), 551-553

relocating filesystems

creating partition table and formatting disk, 290

installing new drive, 288-289

mounting partition and populating with files, 290-291

remote client use, support for, 160

remote computers, logging in and out from, 132-133

removable storage media

CD-RW and DVD+RW/-RW drives, 319

firewire drives, 319

USB and solid-state drives, 319

zip drives, 318

removing modules, 791

renaming files, allowing users to, 613

repeat statement, 749

replacing hardware and kudzu service, 82-83

reporting

media mount point information, 127

problems, 24

request for comments (RFC), 628

rescue disk

rebooting from, 342

using, 340

rescue mode, 343-344

rescuing system, 18

researching hardware specifications, 53

resetting date and time, 104-106

resolution, changing on-the-fly, 167

resolver software

configuring for BIND, 463

description of, 433, 439

information learned by, 447

resource management, importance of, 207

resource records, 438

resources

for backup, assessing, 313

description of, 161

Internet Relay Chat (IRC), 884

mailing lists, 883-884

Usenet newsgroups, 881-882

See also FTP sites; HOWTO documents; man pages; Web sites

restore command, 325

restoring

from backup, 82

Master Boot Record, 340

partition table manually, 341

restricted shells, 257

restricting

number of invalid password entries, 606

number of users in classes, 606

permissions

based on group IDs, 605

based on individual IDs, 606

retrieving data from databases, 556-558

Reverse Address Resolution Protocol (RARP), 381

reverse lookup problems with DNS, 469

reverse resolution, 444-447

REVOKE statement

MySQL, 567

PostgreSQL, 571

RFC (request for comments), 628

RFC 1912 Web site, 468

RHN (Red Hat Network), 217

Rhythmbox, 847

rights. See privileges

rm command, 154

rmmod command, 790

rndc.conf file, 456

root accounts, creating, 74

root name servers, 441

root user

description of, 16, 118

elevation of privileges, 238

IRC (Internet Relay Chat) client as, 253, 672

privileges of, granting to regular users

restricted shells and, 257

su command, 252-254

sudo command, 254-257

reading email as, 650

rebooting system, 157

setting password for in MySQL, 564

shutting down system, 156

sysadmin duties and, 239

user accounts and, 238

users, creating and deleting, 155-156

working as, 153-154

route command, 391-393

routers (network), 386

RPM (Red Hat Package Manager)

administering from command-line, 211-213

command-line and graphical clients, 209-211

extracting file from package, 214

files, working with, 222-224

installing Apache Web server from, 503-505

overview of, 207-208

package organization with, 214

upgrading and, 17

rpm command, 144, 875

.rpm packages, 208

RPM packages, viewing list of installed, 875

rpmbuild command, 211

rsync command, 335-337

rulesets, 425

runlevels

booting

into default, 194-196

into non-default with GRUB, 196-197

changing, 203

definitions for, 192-193

description of, 171

ntsysv tool and, 200

overview of, 189, 192

How can we make this index more useful? Email us at indexes@samspublishing.com

running

innd, 690

named (nameserver daemon), 464

new shell program, 722-723

runtime errors, troubleshooting, 807

S

-S argument, reformatting with when experiencing unrecoverable filesystem errors, 338

Samba

configuring with /etc/samba/smb.conf

[global] section, 411

[homes] section, 411-412

overview of, 410-411

[printers] section, 412

configuring with Samba Web Administration Tool (SWAT), 415-419

connecting with smbclient command, 414

installing, 409

mounting shares, 414

overview of, 363, 408-409

securing, 429

smbstatus command, 413

starting with smbd, 413

testing with testparm command, 413

unmounting shares, 415

Samba Web Administration Tool (SWAT), 409, 415-419

Samsung Contact, 659

SANE (Scanner Access Now Easy), 825, 857

saving bandwidth, 497

sawfish window manager, 179-180

/sbin directory, 121

/sbin/ifconfig, 389-391

/sbin/netstat, 393

/sbin/route, 391-393

scalars (Perl), 761

Scanner Access Now Easy (SANE), 825, 857

scanner applications, 825-826

scanners, 857-858

scheduling FTP server downtime, 621-623

Schwartzian Transform, 780

scp command, 333-335, 581

screen images, capturing, 863

Screen section (xorg.conf file), 167

ScriptAlias directive, 534

Scripts directory, 788

scrolling with mouse, enabling, 92

SCSI disk drivers, 789

SCSI disks, 276

SCSI drives, emulating IDE drive as, 837

searching

with shell, 142

Web with Google search engine, 874-875

Secure File Transfer (sftp) command, 580-581

Secure Shell (ssh) client

logging in to remote computer using, 132

ports and, 379

security issues

anonymous FTP servers, 603

Apache Web servers, 503

Computer Emergency Response Team, 595

databases, 550

DNS

ACLs, defining, 474

DNSSEC, using, 477-478

named, alerting to potential problem hosts, 476-477

overview of, 472-474

queries, controlling, 475

split DNS, using, 478

zone transfers, controlling, 476

DSL service, 492

firewall and security configuration during installation process, 71-72

FTP and, 579

keeping up-to-date on, 429

Microsoft IIS (Internet Information Server), 502

networks

    devices, 428

    DHCP, 429

    firewalling, 424-426

    NFS, 429

    overview of, 379, 423

    passwords and physical security, 426

    patches and upgrades, 430

    Samba, 429

    TCP/IP, 427

    Tripwire, configuring and using, 427-428

overview of, 29

passwords, 251

reading email as root, 650

shadow passwords, 249-250

SUID and SGID permissions, 153

Trojan scripts, 723

UNIX, 473-474

wireless network, 423

select statement, 749-750

SELECT statement (SQL), 556-557

semicolon (;), 760

Sender Policy Framework (SPF), 461-462

sending mail and Perl, 776-778

Sendmail

configuring

    forwarding email with aliases, 649-650

    mail relaying, 649

    masquerading, 647

    message delivery intervals, 647-648

    overview of, 645-646

    rejecting email from specified sites, 650-651

    sendmail.cf file, building, 648

    smart hosts, 647

overview of, 630

sendmail command and Perl, 776

sendmail.cf file

building, 648

syntax, 645

sendmail.mc file, syntax, 646

sensors command, 114

serial number accuracy and DNS, 470

serial-port modems, configuring, 96-99

server administration (wu-ftp)

counting number of connections, 621

displaying information about users, 620

overview of, 619

scheduling downtime, 621-623

viewing transaction log, 623-624

server installation option, 18, 34

server layout, 162

Server Message Block (SMB) protocol, 267

server-side includes (SSI) and Apache Web servers

config directives, 537-538

directives, 536

echo directive, 539

exec directive, 539

flastmod directive, 539

fsize directive, 539

include directive, 540

overview of, 536

printenv directive, 540

set directive, 540

ServerAdmin directive (httpd.conf file), 516

ServerLayout section (xorg.conf file), 163

How can we make this index more useful? Email us at indexes@sampspublishing.com

ServerName directive (httpd.conf file), 516

ServerRoot directive (httpd.conf file), 515

servers

    database, installing and maintaining, 549

    FTP

        anonymous access, controlling, 600

        Apache, 594

        authenticated versus anonymous, 593

        Bsdftdp-ssl, 594

        file-conversion actions, configuring, 615-618

        ftphosts file commands, 618-619

        NcFTPd, 593

        ProFTPD, 594

        quick LAN setup, 597

        Very Secure (vsftpd), 593, 599

        vsftpd.conf file, 600-602

    IRC, 673

    news, 679-680

    Wu-FTPd

        access control, configuring, 604-607

        cdpath commands, configuring, 614

        configuring, 602

        ftpaccess file, configuring with, 603

        permission control, configuring, 612-614

        shutdown fil, 615

        system logging, configuring, 611-612

        user information, configuring, 607-611

    See also Apache Web server; Web servers

service command, starting or stopping Apache server using, 511

Service Configuration tool, 202

Services dialog box, 92

session management, 176

Session Message Block (SMB) printing, 363-364

Session Message Block (SMB) protocol and Samba, 408

session writing, 839-840

sessions, 129

set directive (SSI), 540

set group ID (SGID) permissions, 152-153

set user ID (SUID) permissions, 152-153

setfont command, 131

setserial command, 98

setup command, 205

sftp command, 335, 580-581

SGID (set group ID) permissions, 152-153

shadow passwords, 249-250, 596

shared data, working with using /usr directory, 127

sharing, enabling for network printing, 362

she-bang (#!), 724-725, 760

shell

    changing login, 138

    compressing and decompressing files with, 143-144

    description of, 137, 715

    environment variables, 139-141

    with Fedora Core, 716

    managing files with, 142-143

    Nautilus, 183

    navigating and searching with, 142

    restricted, 257

    selecting, 138

    See also shell command line; shell scripts

SHELL (shell environment variable), 139

shell access with Perl, 771-772

shell accounts, 131

shell command line

    background processing, 720

    input and output redirection, 719

    overview of, 716-717

    pattern-matching support, 718

    piping data, 720

shell programming and comment character, 760

shell scripts

bash

interpreting through specific shells, 724-725

running new program, 722-723

storing for systemwide access, 724

break and exit statements, 754

built-in variables, 731

comparison of expressions

pdksh and bash, 735-740

tcsh, 740-744

conditional statements

case, 752-753

if, 750-752

description of, 137, 715

endless loops in, 746-747

functions, 754-755

iteration statements

for, 745-746

repeat, 749

select, 749-750

shift, 750

until, 748-749

while, 746-748

mail utility and, 635

overview of, 721

positional parameters

accessing and retrieving variables from command line, 728

automating tasks, 729-731

example of, 727-728

prefdm, 172

special characters

backslash (\), 734

backtick (`), 735

double quotes ("), 733

overview of, 732

single quote ('), 733

variables

accessing value of, 727

assigning value to, 726

using in, 725

shells file, 123

shift statement, 750

Shisen-Sho game, 864

shutdown command, 78, 156-157

shutdown file, 615

shutting down

computer, 78

system, 156

Simple Mail Transport Protocol (SMTP)

description of, 628, 632

mail servers, 628

ports and, 379

single quote ('), 733

skript kiddies, 423

slrn news client, 665

small enterprises, backup strategy for, 315

Small Office Home Office (SOHO)

backup strategy for, 315

users in, 22

smart gateways, 386

SMB (Server Message Block) protocol, 267, 408

SMB (Session Message Block) printing, 363-364

smb.conf file

[global] section, 411

[homes] section, 411-412

overview of, 410-411

[printers] section, 412

smbclient command, 414

smbd daemon, starting Samba with, 413

smbstatus command, 413

SMP (Symmetric Multi-Processing) problems during installation, preparing for, 39

SMTP (Simple Mail Transport Protocol)

description of, 628, 632

mail servers, 628

ports and, 379

sndconfig command, 88

software

for backups

afio tool, 329

Amanda backup application, 328-329

cdbackup tool, 329

cpio, 323-324

dd command, 327

flexbackup tool, 329

free, 329

GNOME File Roller, 325

hardware and, 321

KDE ark and kdat tools, 326-327

tar, 321-323

Card Services, 106-108

compiling from source

RPM files, 222-224

src.rpm files, 221-222

tar files, 224-225

fax client, 828-830

finding and reading documentation on, 136-137

installation options, choosing, 54

installing all on CD-ROM, 54

multimedia

burning CDs and DVDs, 836-843

intellectual property rights and, 835

MySQL compared to PostgreSQL, 562

passing on for minimalist system, 35

PDA connectivity

GNOME gpilot graphical interface, 824

J-Pilot program, 824

pilot-link package, 823-824

productivity

commands for accessing, 832

commercial, 822

example of implementation of, 831

GNOME Office, 817-820

KOffice, 820-821

for Microsoft Windows, 832

OpenOffice.org, 812-816

other, 830

overview of, 811

programming and, 696

resolver

configuring for BIND, 463

description of, 433, 439

information learned by, 447

Samba, 363

scanner, 825-826

selecting and installing during installation process, 74-75

Web design tools, 827-828

software management

Add/Remove Software, 215-216

APT, 218-219

CheckInstall program, 225

Red Hat Network (RHN), alternatives to, 217-218

RPM and

administering from command-line, 211-213

command-line and graphical clients, 209-211

extracting file from package, 214

overview of, 207-208

package organization, 214

YUM, 219

software modems, 486

solid-state drives, 319

sound

commands for, 868

DAO (Disk-At-Once) audio, creating, 113

formats, 845-847

music players, 847

recording, 844

streaming audio, 848

sound cards, 844

sound devices, configuring, 95-96

Sound Recorder application, 845

source code for installing Apache Web server

./configure, using to build, 506

obtaining, 505

source trees, 702

sox command, 846-847

spam Usenet messages, 691

Spamassassin MTA, 632, 656

.spec file (RPM), 223

special devices, managing files for

mknod command, 305

naming conventions, 305

overview of, 303-304

special shell characters

backslash (\), 734

backtick (`), 735

double quotes ("), 733

overview of, 732

single quote ('), 733

special string constants (Perl), 765

special variables (Perl), 762

speed

of database applications, 559

FTP file transfers, 602

SPF (Sender Policy Framework), 461-462

splint command, 705

split DNS, 478

spoofing, 473

SQL

overview of, 553

retrieving data from databases, 556-558

subqueries, 561

tables

creating, 554-555

inserting data into, 555-556

Squirrelmail, 656

src.rpm files, building RPMS from, 221-222

SSH (Secure Shell) client

database access and, 572-573

logging in to remote computer using, 132

ports and, 379

sshd daemon, 580-581

SSI (server-side includes) and Apache Web servers

config directives, 537-538

directives, 536

echo directive, 539

exec directive, 539

flastmod directive, 539

fsize directive, 539

include directive, 540

overview of, 536

printenv directive, 540

set directive, 540

standard FTP servers, 592

StarOffice, 814

starting

Apache Web server

chkconfig command, using, 511-512

/etc/rc.d/init.d/httpd, using, 510

manually, 508-509

service command, using, 511

system-config-services client, using, 512-513

Evolution email client, 637

GIMP editor, 859

install process, 60-65

MySQL, 563

NFS, 405

postmaster program, 569

Samba with smbd, 413

system services

manually, 202-203

methods for, 192

vsftpd server, 599

X Window System

from console with startx command, 174-175

overview of, 171

startx command, 174-175, 721

statserial command, 97

steganography, 645

stopping

Apache Web server

chkconfig command, using, 511-512

/etc/rc.d/init.d/httpd, using, 510

service command, using, 511

system-config-services client, using, 512-513

install process, 62

NFS, 405

running processes, 228

system services

manually, 202-203

methods for, 192

storage

devices for, disks as, 275

on hard drive, planning for, 34-35

temporary, in /tmp directory, 128

See also removable storage media

storage.conf file, 685-686

storing

booted kernel, 122

shell scripts for systemwide access, 724

streaming audio, 848

Strict RFC1179 Compliance option for printing, 363

string comparison

pdksh and bash, 736-737

tcsh, 741

string comparison operators (Perl), 763

strip postfixes, 616

strip prefixes, 616

Stronghold Web server, 545

su command, 154, 252-254

subnet masks, 380-381

subnetting, 380

subqueries (SQL), 561

sudo command, 154, 254-257

SUID (set user ID) permissions, 152-153

Summary window (Evolution), 639

Sun Microsystems, 814

Sun ONE Web server, 545

superblocks, 265

SuperRescue CD, 344

superuser (root user)

description of, 16, 118

elevation of privileges, 238

IRC (Internet Relay Chat) client as, 253

privileges of, granting to regular users

restricted shells and, 257

su command, 252-254

sudo command, 254-257

rebooting system, 157

shutting down system, 156

sysadmin duties and, 239

user accounts and, 238

users, creating and deleting, 155-156

working as, 153-154

SuSE OpenExchange, 659

swap partition, 68

SWAT (Samba Web Administration Tool), 415-419

switchdesk utility, 176-177

switches (Perl), 772-774

Sylpheed-claws email client, 640

symbolic links, 197, 795

Symmetric Multi-Processing problems during installation, preparing for, 39

SYN flooding attack, 127

Synaptic graphical interface (APT), 219

sync command, 301

synchronizing filesystems, 301

syntax notation, 699

sysadmin. *See* system administrators

sysconfig directory, 123

sysctl command, tuning kernel with, 808-809

sysrq.txt, 787

system administrators

    backups and, 314

    command line and, 118

    duties as root user, 239

    evaluating previous backup strategy, 316

    stereotypes of, 240

    See also superuser

system calls, 696

system logging, configuring, 611-612

System Monitor menu, 233

system monitoring tools

    console-based, 226-228

    disk quotas, 232

    free utility, 231

    graphical process and management, 232-233

    KDE, 234

    kill command, 228

    priority scheduling and control, 229-231

    vmstat utility, 231

system rescue

    backing up and restoring Master Boot Record, 340

    booting

        from generic boot floppy, 342

        from GRUB boot floppy, 342

    manually restoring partition table, 341

    overview of, 339

    rebooting from rescue disk, 342

    recovery facility from installation disk, using, 343-344

    rescue disk, 340

system services

    controlling at boot

        chkconfig, 199-200

        system-config-services tool, 202

    running through xinetd, 198

    starting and stopping

        manually, 202-203

        methods for, 192

    troubleshooting, 204-205

System Settings menu, Users and Groups item, 243

system states

    booting

        into default, 194-196

        into non-default with GRUB, 196-197

    changing, 203

    definitions for, 192-193

    description of, 171

    ntsysv tool and, 200

    overview of, 189, 192

system users, 239

System V method, 192

system-config-bind tool, 471

system-config-date tool, 104-106

system-config-display tool, 94, 162, 168-170

system-config-httpd tool

overview of, 541

Performance tab, 544

Server tab, 543

Virtual Hosts tab, 542

system-config-keyboard tool, 84-85, 88

system-config-mouse tool, 84

system-config-network tool, 97, 396-397

system-config-nfs tool, 407

system-config-packages tool, 17, 215-216

system-config-printer tool

editing printer settings, 359-360

JetDirect option, 365

launching, 356

overview of, 350

print queue, creating, 356-359

system-config-printer-gui, 352

system-config-printer-tui program, 352-353, 366

system-config-securitylevel tool, 424-426

system-config-services tool, 202, 512-513

system-config-soundcard tool, 96, 844

T

Tab key, installation process and, 63

Tab Window Manager (twm), 178

table-level rights (MySQL), 566

tables, database

creating, 554-555

importing text files into, 561

inserting data into, 555-556

tape drives, 320

tar command, 144

tar files, compiling software from, 224-225

tar tool

compressing, encrypting, and sending tar streams, 331

copying files with, 330-331

full and incremental backups, creating with, 322-323

overview of, 321-322

restoring files from archive with, 323

TCP (Transport Control Protocol), 376

TCP/IP

addressing, 376-378

IP Masquerading, 378

networking with, 375-376

ports, 379-380

security issues, 427

tcsh, comparison of expressions

file operators, 742-744

logical operators, 744

numbers, 741-742

overview of, 740

strings, 741

technical support, 873

telinit command, 203

telnet command, 133

TERM (shell environment variable), 139

terminal clients, 162

testing

beta releases, 24

creating filesystems for

blank image file, making, 292

filesystem, making and mounting, 292-293

installer and, 18

Samba with testparm command, 413

testparm command and Samba, 413

text, copying and pasting, 130

text editors

    emacs, 147

    nano, 721

    overview of, 144-145, 696

    vi, 146, 721, 827

text files, importing into database tables, 561

text-based client interface (FTP)

    ftp command, 583-586

    lftp command, 587-588

    overview of, 581-583

    wget command, 588-589

text-based console login, 128

text-based interface, installing using, 60

themes

    metacity window manager and, 182

    sawfish window manager and, 180

third-party DNS, 453

thttpd Web server, 544

time

    Linux system, 103

    resetting, 104-106

time command, 229

time hashed spool method, 685

Time To Live (TTL), 459-461

Time Zone Selection dialog box, 72

time zone, setting, 72

timewarp, 247

Timidity, 847

TiVo, 854

/tmp directory, 48, 128

TNEF (Transport Neutral Encapsulation Format), 643

token ring networking, 382

tools

    for creating, examining, and modifying partition tables

        fdisk, 276-278

        overview of, 275

        parted command, 279

    group management, 242-243

    for mounting filesystems, 286-287

    user management, 244-245

    See also specific tools

top command, 230-231

Torvalds, Linus, 786

touch command, 148

touchpads, support for, 88

trackballs, support for, 88

transaction logs, viewing, 623-624

transaction processing, 560

transition cost, 28

Transport Control Protocol (TCP), 376

Transport Control Protocol/Internet Protocol (TCP/IP)

    addressing, 376-378

    IP Masquerading, 378

    networking with, 375-376

    ports, 379-380

    security issues, 427

Transport Neutral Encapsulation Format (TNEF), 643

tree command, 119

Tripwire, configuring and using, 427-428

Trojan scripts, 723

Trolltech QT Designer, 710-711

troubleshooting

    dependency errors, 122

    DHCP server, 404

DNS
  delegation problems, 469
  overview of, 468
  reverse lookup problems, 469
  serial number accuracy, 470
  tools for, 471
  zone file problems, 470
Internet connection, 494
kernel compile and installation
  errors during compile, 806-807
  runtime errors, 807
network connections, 385
NICs, 387
PCMCIA, 107
Perl, 759
post-installation configuration problems, 81-82
printing, 373
service management and, 204-205
sound card configuration, 95
USB devices, 90
X11 configuration, 95
TTL (Time To Live), 459-461
tune2fs command, 297, 302
tuning filesystems
  badblocks command, 303
  e2fsck command, 302
  mke2fs command, 302
  noatime option for mount command, 303
  overview of, 301
  tune2fs command, 302
tuning kernel with sysctl command, 808-809
TV
  hardware for, 848-851
  video formats, 851
  viewing, 848, 853
tvtime application, 853

Tweedie, Stephen C., 19
TWiki tool, 670-671
TWiki Web server, 546
twm (Tab Window Manager), 178
TXT records and SPF, 461-462
type of installation, selecting, 65
types field (ftpconversions file), 617

U

UDF (Universal Disk Format) filesystem, 274
UDP (User Datagram Protocol), 376
UIDs (user IDs), 239
umask command, 148
umount command, 284
uname command, viewing date Linux kernel was compiled using, 17
uncompressing tar file, 224
undeleting files
  with ext2fs, 337-338
  with mc, 338-339
  overview of, 337
  reformatting with –S option, 338
unicast addressing, 381
Universal Disk Format (UDF) filesystem, 274
Universal Serial Bus (USB) devices, 37, 90
UNIX
  backup levels, 316
  Linux compared to, 14
  security issues, 473-474
unless statement (Perl), 767
unmounting
  filesystems with umount command, 284
  Samba shares, 415
Unreal Tournament 2003, installing, 865
unshielded twisted pair (UTP) cable, 382-384

until loop (Perl), 769

until statement, 748-749

up2date client, 17, 874

up2date command, 505

updating installer, 18

UPG (User Private Group), 241

upgrade installation option, 18

upgrading and release cycles, 17

uplink ports, 385

uptime command, 231

USB devices, 37, 90

USB drives, 319

USB printers, troubleshooting, 373

Usenet network news system

    newsgroups, 664

    posting to with Perl, 779

    spam messages, 691

Usenet newsgroups, Linux-related, 881-882

USER (shell environment variable), 139

user accounts

    adding in MySQL, 566

    Fetchmail, configuring, 653-655

    installation process and, 73-74

    overview of, 237

user considerations for preinstallation planning, 30

User Datagram Protocol (UDP), 376

User directive (httpd.conf file), 515

user IDs (UIDs), 239

user information, changing, 134

user management and databases, 550

User Manager interface, adding account using, 246

User Mount Tool (KDE), 287

User Private Group (UPG), 241

user variables, 726

useradd -G command, 242-244

useradd command, 155, 244-245

userdel command, 156, 245

UserDir directive (httpd.conf file), 516

userinfo command, 261

usermod -G command, 242

usermod command, 245

usermount graphical filesystem management client, 286

usernames, 134, 247

userpasswd command, 261

users

    allowing to change file permissions, 613

    anonymous, limiting access of, 604

    assigning permissions to

        file-delete, 613

        file-overwrite, 613

        tar command usage, 614

        for upload files, 614

    compressing files, 613

    creating, 155, 570

    defining classes of, 604

    deleting, 156, 570

    displaying information about connected, 620

    file permissions, 239-240

    FTP, 595-596

    ftpaccess file and, 607-611

    locking out of accounts, 245

    login process for, 257-259

    managing

        adding new, 245-247

        command-line tools for, 244-245

        monitoring activity on system, 247

        overview of, 243

    regular, 238

    renaming files, 613

    restricting number in classes, 606

    stereotypes of, 240

How can we make this index more useful? Email us at indexes@samspublishing.com

system administrator privileges, granting to
   restricted shells and, 257
   su command, 252-254
   sudo command, 254-257
  types of, 118, 237
  uploading files to FTP servers, 616
  user IDs and group IDs, 239
  See also root user

Users and Groups item (System Settings menu), 243

/usr directory, 48, 127

/usr/bin/fax script, 829

/usr/src/linux-2.6 directory, 786-788

/usr/src/linux-2.6/configs directory, 798

/usr/X11R6 directory, 162

UTF-8 language encoding, 836

UTP (unshielded twisted pair) cable, 382-384

uudecode, 644-645

uuencode, 644-645

V

values function, 762

/var directory, 48, 128

/var/log/messages file, 81

/var/log/wtmp file, 247

variables
  accessing and retrieving from command line using positional parameters, 728
  built-in, 731
  Perl, 761
  shell scripts and
   accessing value of, 727
   assigning value to, 726
   overview of, 725

vendors, choosing, 32

verifying integrity in ext3 filesystem, 271-272

version numbers, 17

version-control programs, 704

Very Secure FTP server (vsftpd), 593, 599

vi text editor
  commands, 146
  overview of, 146, 696
  shell scripts and, 721
  as Web page design tool, 827

video
  formats, 851
  hardware for, 848-851
  viewing, 848, 852-853

Video Card dialog box (system-config-display client), 169

video cards, 169, 848

video conferencing, 674-675

video drivers, installing, 865

video players, 854

Video4Linux project, 851

viewing
  filesystems, 119-121, 268-269
  FTP server transaction logs, 623-624
  list of installed RPM packages, 875
  Postscript documents, 355
  stored devices, 122
  TV and video
   formats, 851
   hardware for, 848-851
   overview of, 848, 852-853

vimtutor command, 147

virtual consoles, 94, 129

virtual desktops, 175-176

virtual filesystem, 126

virtual hosting and Apache Web server
  address-based virtual hosts, 530
  name-based virtual hosts, 531

virtual resolution, 167

virus scanners, 657

vlc client, 854

vmstat utility, 231

vncviewer tool, 232

voice modem support, 495

Voice over IP (VoIP), 674

Volume Control application, 845

vsftpd (Very Secure FTP) server, 593, 599

vsftpd.conf file, editing, 600-602

VueScan application, 826

W

w command, 247

war driving, 423

WAV format, 846

Web access to databases, 573-574

Web design tools, 827-828

Web servers

    Stronghold, 545

    Sun ONE, 545

    thttpd, 544

    TWiki, 546

    Zeus, 546

    Zope, 545

    See also Apache Web server

Web sites

    Access Control Lists (ACLs), 266

    alt.sysadmin.recovery FAQ, 240

    American Registry for Internet Numbers, 376

    AMTP mail servers, 628

    Apache Group, 502

    Apache Web server, 503

    APT providers, 218

    audio formats, 846

    Axis network-based Webcams, 855

    Bsdftpd-ssl server, 594

    BugTraq, 429, 473

    CD-related information, 841

    certification courses, 876

    CheckInstall program, 226

    commercial support providers, 876

    Computer Emergency Response Team, 595

    Debian Project, 33

    DNS troubleshooting, 468

    documentation, 22, 877

    Dynamic DNS, 400

    Fedora, 13, 135

    Fedora Project, 878

    Fetchmail, 651

    floppy-based Linux distributions, 879

    for technical support, 873

    games, 866

    GNOME Office, 818

    Google, 82

    GPG encryption key, 211

    GRUB manual, 807

    hardware compatibility issues, 35

    IBM JFS, 19

    Intel-based Linux distributions, 879

    Internet Software Consortium, 402

    IP addressing, 378

    Jargoogle search page, 628

    KornShell, 723

    laptops and PDAs, 880

    Linux Documentation Project, 494

    Linux Ethercard Status, Diagnostic and Setup Utilities page, 387

    Linux Network Administrator's Guide, 381

    Linux USB Project, 376

    mini-CD Linux distributions, 878

    MySQL, 561

How can we make this index more useful? Email us at indexes@samspublishing.com

NcFTPd server, 593

OpenOffice.org, 814

overview of, 874

Penggy, 482

PostgreSQL, 561

PowerPC-based Linux distributions, 880

ProFTPD server, 594

Red Hat Linux, 28, 878

rejecting email from specified, 650-651

Request For Comment 959, 586

Scanner Access Now Easy (SANE), 825

SPF, 462

user issues, 30

vendors, 32

window managers, 176

wu-ftpd server, 595

X Window System, 880-881

XFree86 3.3.6, 34

Ximian Desktop, 183

See also HOWTO documents

Webcams, 855-856

WebSphere Studio Homepage Builder, 828

welcome.msg file, 609

wget command, 588-589

whatis command, 142

whereis command, 136, 142

which command, 138

while loop (Perl), 769

while statement, 746-748

whitespace in SQL commands, 555

whois utility, 450-452

wildcards, 143

window managers

    changing default, 176-177

    metacity, 181

    mwm (Motif Window Manager), 179

    overview of, 162, 175-176

    sawfish, 179-180

    twm (Tab Window Manager), 178

Wine application, 832

wireless networking

    advantages of, 421

    overview of, 383, 419

    protocol, choosing, 422

    security issues, 423

    support for, 419-420

    telnet command and, 133

Wolfenstein-Enemy Territory, installing, 865-866

working with shared data, 127

workstation installation option, 19, 34

writeback mode (ext3 filesystem), 271

writing

    documentation, 25

    init scripts, 198

wu-ftp, server administration

    counting number of connections, 621

    displaying information about users, 620

    overview of, 619

    scheduling downtime, 621-623

    viewing transaction log, 623-624

Wu-FTPd server

    configuring

        access control, 604-607

        cdpath commands, 614

        ftpaccess file, 603

        overview of, 602

        permission control, 612-614

        shutdown file, 615

        system logging, 611-612

        user information, 607-611

    overview of, 595

    xinetd configuration for, 597-598

X

X protocol, 160

X server, 161

X Window System

    configuring

        commands for, 185

        overview of, 167

        with system-config-display client, 168-170

        with xorg.conf file, 171

    desktop environment

        GNOME, 182-183

        KDE, 184, 234, 286, 326-327, 883

    display managers, configuring

        gdm, 172

        kdm, 172-174

        overview of, 171-172

        xdm, 174

    features of, 161

    overview of, 94, 159

    server, 161

    starting

        from console with startx command, 174-175

        overview of, 171

    text editors for, 145

    /usr/X11R6 directory, 162

    window managers

        changing default, 176-177

        metacity, 181

        mwm (Motif Window Manager), 179

        overview of, 175-176

        sawfish, 179-180

        twm (Tab Window Manager), 178

    X protocol and, 160

xorg.conf file

    Device section, 166

    Files section, 163

    InputDevice section, 164

    Module section, 164

    Monitor section, 165

    overview of, 162-163

    Screen section, 167

    ServerLayout section, 163

    See also X11

X Window System Web sites, 880-881

XBitHack directive, 536

X-CD-Roast, 842-843

X-Chat, 672

xconfig utility, configuring kernel with, 800-805

xcpustate client, 232

xdm, configuring, 174

X11

    configuration, troubleshooting, 95

    keyboards, 86

xferlog file, 623-624

XFree86 3.3.6, 34

XFree86 server, video chipset support, 166

xfs (font server), 164

XFS filesystem, 268, 273

Ximian Desktop 2 (Novell, Inc.), 182

Ximian Evolution, 637-639

Xine media player, 852-854

Xinerama, 169

xinetd configuration for wu-ftp, 597-598

xinetd daemon, 198

xminicom script for modems, 100

Xmms, 846-847

X.Org Foundation, 159

xorg.conf file

    configuring X with, 171

    Device section, 166

How can we make this index more useful? Email us at indexes@samspublishing.com

Files section, 163

InputDevice section, 164

Module section, 164

Monitor section, 165

overview of, 94-95, 162-163

Screen section, 167

ServerLayout section, 163

xosview client, 232

xpdf client, reading document with, 24

Xsane application, 826

Xsane client, 857

xwd tool, 863

Y

YellowDog Updater Modified (YUM), 17, 217-219

yenc, 643

yum command, 874-876

Z

Zapping application, 853

Zeus Web server, 546

zImage directive, 799

zip disks, 276

zip drives, 318

Ziproxy server, 497

zless command, 23

zone file problems with DNS, 470

zone section (named.config file)

NS and PTR records, 461

overview of, 459-460

SOA record, 460-461

zone transfers, controlling, 476

Zope Web server, 545

License Agreement

By opening this package, you are agreeing to be bound by the following agreement:

Individual programs and other items on the CD-ROM/DVD-ROM are copyrighted or are under an Open Source license by their various authors or other copyright holders.

This software is sold as-is without warranty of any kind, either expressed or implied, including but not limited to the implied warranties of merchantability and fitness for a particular purpose. Neither the publisher nor its dealers or distributors assumes any liability for any alleged or actual damages arising from the use of this program. (Some states do not allow for the exclusion of implied warranties, so the exclusion may not apply to you.)

This book includes Fedora Core 3 and a special 2 CD set of the Publisher's Edition of Fedora™ Core 3, which you may use in accordance with the license agreement found at http://fedora.redhat.com/licenses. Red Hat does not provide support services for Fedora Core. You may purchase Red Hat® Enterprise Linux® and technical support from Red Hat through its Web site (www.redhat.com) or its toll-free number 1.888.2REDHAT.

Installation

You may need to change your BIOS settings to boot directly from a CD-ROM or DVD-ROM drive. If you are not sure if you can boot from a CD-ROM or DVD-ROM, then you should start or reboot your computer and go into the computer's BIOS setup utility. Hitting the DEL (Delete) or the F2 key usually accesses this utility while the computer is starting up. Once in the BIOS setup utility, look for a boot priority option. If your computer is capable of booting from a CD-ROM or DVD-ROM, your CD-ROM or DVD-ROM drive will be listed. Make sure the CD-ROM or DVD-ROM drive has a higher boot priority than your hard drive(s) to enable booting from a CD-ROM or DVD-ROM.

Once you have determined that you can boot from the CD-ROM or DVD-ROM, start or reboot your machine with the Installation Disc (Disc 1 if booting from CD-ROM) or the DVD-ROM in your CD or DVD drive. After a few moments, you should see the Fedora Core Linux installation routine. Follow the onscreen prompts to finish the installation.

If your computer cannot start the Fedora Core Linux installation program from the CD-ROM or DVD-ROM, you will need to create boot disks to launch the installation program. You will find instructions for how to do this on the first CD-ROM or the DVD-ROM in a file called README in the images directory.

NOTE: The setup program requires your system to have 128 or more megabytes of memory to launch in a full screen graphics mode. If you have less than 128 megabytes of memory, the setup program will go to a text-only mode which is functionally identical to, but visually different from, the graphical install.

What's On the DVD

The book's DVD includes the binary version of Fedora Core 3—the equivalent of four CDs.

NOTE: If you do not have a DVD drive available, or if you simply don't have an immediate need for all the extras that are available on the DVD, the two CDs that are also included provide a quick, but still very complete, installation of the Fedora Core 3 Linux distribution.

DESKTOPS

- X.Org 6.8.1-12
- GNOME 2.8.0-3
- K Desktop Environment 3.3.0-8

APPLICATIONS

Editors

- Joe's Own Editor (JOE) 3.1-6
- Emacs 21.3.17
- Vi IMproved (VIM) 6.3.030-3
- NEdit 5.4-3
- Vi IMproved for X11 6.3.030-3
- XEmacs 21.4.15-9

Engineering and Scientific

- Parallel Virtual Machine (PVM) 3.4.4-21
- Gnuplot Version 4.0.0-4
- Octave 2.1.57-7
- Linear Algebra PACKage (LAPACK) 3.0-25
- Local Area Multicomputer (LAM) 7.0.6-3
- units 1.80-10
- Basic Linear Algebra Subprograms (BLAS) 3.0-25

Graphical Internet

- X-Chat 2.4.0-3
- FireFox 1.0PR1.20
- Mozilla 1.7.3-17
- Epiphany 1.4.4-4
- Balsa 2.2.4-1
- Konqueror 3.3.0-8
- Ximian Evolution 2.0.2-3
- Gaim 1.0.1-3
- Pan 0.14.2-8
- GnomeMeeting 1.0.2-8

Text-based Internet

- Slang Read News (slrn) 1.4.9-6
- NcFTP 3.1.8-2

Text-based Internet
(continued)

- Mutt 1.4.1-10
- ELinks 0.9.2-2
- fetchmail 6.2.5-6
- Lynx 2.8.5-18
- EPIC 1.0.1-18

Office/Productivity

- KDE-PIM 3.3.0-2
- Gnumeric 1.2.13-6
- MagicPoint 1.11b-1
- GnuCash 1.8.9-2
- KOffice 1.3.3-1
- GPdf 2.8.0-5
- GGV 2.8.0-1
- Xpdf 3.00-10
- OpenOffice.org 1.1.2-10
- TeTeX-xdvi 2.0.2-21
- AbiWord 2.0.12-3

Sound and Video

- SoX 12.17.5-3
- aumix 2.8-9
- MikMod 3.1.6-30
- Kdemultimedia 3.3.0-2
- Sound Juicer 0.5.14-1
- Cdparanoia alpha9.8-24
- XMMS (and skins) 1.2.10-9
- Cdrecord 2.01.1-5
- Grip 3.2.0-3
- dvgrab 1.6-1
- dvd+rw-tools 5.21.4.10.8-2
- cdda2wav 2.01.1-5
- X-CD-Roast 0.98a15-6
- Vorbis Tools 1.0.1-4
- cdlabelgen 3.0.0-1

Authoring and Publishing

- Docbook styles and utilities
- Linux Documentation Tools 0.9.20-14
- xmlto 0.0.18-4
- XHTML DTDs 1.0-7
- TeTeX 2.0.2-21

Graphics

- ImageMagick 6.0.7.1-4
- GIMP Print plugin 4.2.7-2
- netpbm-progs 10.25-2
- libsane-hpoj 0.91-9
- Xfig 3.2.4-5
- XSane GIMP plugin 0.92-13
- GIMP 2.0.5-5
- SANE Frontends 1.0.12-4
- GIMP Data Extras 1.2.0-12
- XSane 0.92-13
- Kdegraphics 3.3.0-3
- Dia 0.94-5

Games and Entertainment

- Maelstrom 3.0.6-6
- Tux Racer 0.61-28
- GNOME games 2.8.0-4
- Freeciv 1.14.2-1
- KDE games 3.3.0-2
- KDE edutainment 3.3.0-1
- BZFlag 1.10.6-2
- XBoard 4.2.7-6
- joystick 1.2.15-18

SERVERS AND NETWORKING

Server Configuration Tools

- Red Hat's server configuration tools

Web

- Apache HTTPD Server 2.0.52-3
- mod_ssl 2.0.52-3
- php-odbc 4.3.9-3
- mod_auth_mysql 20030510-5
- php-pgsql 4.3.9-3
- mod_auth_pgsql 2.0.1-6
- Squid 2.5.STABLE6-3
- php-ldap 4.3.9-3
- mod_perl 1.99_16-3
- Tux 3.2.18-2
- cryptoutils 2.1-4

Web
(continued)

- PHP 4.3.9-3
- PHP-MySQL 4.3.9-3
- httpd-manual 2.0.52-3
- Webalizer 2.01_10-25
- mod_python 3.1.3-5
- php-imap 4.3.9-3

Mail

- Sendmail 8.13.1-2
- SquirrelMail 1.4.3a-5
- SpamAssassin 3.0.0-3
- Mailman 2.1.5-26
- Dovecot 0.99.11-1
- Postfix 2.1.5-2.2

Windows Files Server

- SAMBA 3.0.8-0pre1.3 client/server

DNS/Name

- BIND 9.2.4-2
- CachingNameServer 7.3-3

FTP

- Very Secure FTP Daemon (vsftpd) 2.0.1-5

SQL Databases

- TOra 1.3.14.1-2
- PostgreSQL server 7.4.6-1
- MySQL server 3.23.58-13
- perl-DBD-Pg 1.31-6
- unixODBC 2.2.9-1

News

- INN 2.3.5-11

Networking

- Telnet 0.17-30
- Finger 0.17-26
- FreeRADIUS 1.0.1-1
- Remote WHO (rwho) 0.17-22
- Remote Shell (rsh) 0.17-23
- Virtual Network Computing (VNC) 4.0-8